LET'S GO  Y0-CZD-577

California

"This guide is useful to almost any budget traveler, not just students. And the hip, critical attitude is often right on the mark."
—*Travel Books World-Wide*
on Let's Go: California

"Lighthearted and sophisticated, informative and fun to read. *[Let's Go]* helps the novice traveler navigate like a knowledgeable old hand."
—*Atlanta Journal-Constitution*

"The guides are aimed not only at young budget travelers but at the independent traveler, a sort of streetwise cookbook for traveling alone."
—*The New York Times*

Let's Go writers travel on your budget.

"Retains the spirit of the student-written publication it is: candid, opinionated, resourceful, amusing info for the traveler of limited means but broad curiosity."
—*Mademoiselle*

"The writers seem to have experienced every rooster-packed bus and lunar-surfaced mattress about which they write."
—*The New York Times*

"All the dirt, dirt cheap."
—*People*

Great for independent travelers.

"A world-wise traveling companion—always ready with friendly advice and helpful hints, all sprinkled with a bit of wit."
—*The Philadelphia Inquirer*

"Lots of valuable information for any independent traveler."
—*The Chicago Tribune*

Let's Go is completely revised each year.

"Unbeatable: good sight-seeing advice; up-to-date info on restaurants, hotels, and inns; a commitment to money-saving travel; and a wry style that brightens nearly every page."
—*The Washington Post*

"Its yearly revision by a new crop of Harvard students makes it as valuable as ever."
—*The New York Times*

All the important information you need.

"Enough information to satisfy even the most demanding of budget travelers...*Let's Go* follows the creed that you don't have to toss your life's savings to the wind to travel—unless you want to."
—*The Salt Lake Tribune*

"Value-packed, unbeatable, accurate, and comprehensive."
—*The Los Angeles Times*

Let's Go Publications

Let's Go: Alaska & the Pacific Northwest 1998
Let's Go: Australia 1998 **New title!**
Let's Go: Austria & Switzerland 1998
Let's Go: Britain & Ireland 1998
Let's Go: California 1998
Let's Go: Central America 1998
Let's Go: Eastern Europe 1998
Let's Go: Ecuador & the Galápagos Islands 1998
Let's Go: Europe 1998
Let's Go: France 1998
Let's Go: Germany 1998
Let's Go: Greece & Turkey 1998
Let's Go: India & Nepal 1998
Let's Go: Ireland 1998
Let's Go: Israel & Egypt 1998
Let's Go: Italy 1998
Let's Go: London 1998
Let's Go: Mexico 1998
Let's Go: New York City 1998
Let's Go: New Zealand 1998 **New title!**
Let's Go: Paris 1998
Let's Go: Rome 1998
Let's Go: Southeast Asia 1998
Let's Go: Spain & Portugal 1998
Let's Go: USA 1998
Let's Go: Washington, D.C. 1998

Let's Go Map Guides

Berlin	New Orleans
Boston	New York City
Chicago	Paris
London	Rome
Los Angeles	San Francisco
Madrid	Washington, D.C.

Coming Soon: Amsterdam, Florence

**Let's Go
Publications**

LET'S GO

California

1998

Anna C. Portnoy
Editor

Jessica Niles
Associate Editor

St. Martin's Press ✿ New York

HELPING LET'S GO

If you want to share your discoveries, suggestions, or corrections, please drop us a line. We read every piece of correspondence, whether a postcard, a 10-page email, or a coconut. Please note that mail received after May 1998 may be too late for the 1999 book, but will be kept for future editions. **Address mail to:**

**Let's Go: California
67 Mt. Auburn Street
Cambridge, MA 02138
USA**

Visit Let's Go at **http://www.letsgo.com,** or send email to:

**fanmail@letsgo.com
Subject: "Let's Go: California"**

In addition to the invaluable travel advice our readers share with us, many are kind enough to offer their services as researchers or editors. Unfortunately, our charter enables us to employ only currently enrolled Harvard-Radcliffe students.

ADVERTISING DISCLAIMER

About Let's Go

Back in 1960, a few students at Harvard University banded together to produce a 20-page pamphlet offering a collection of tips on budget travel in Europe. This modest, mimeographed packet, offered as an extra to passengers on student charter flights to Europe, met with instant popularity. The following year, students traveling to Europe researched the first, full-fledged edition of *Let's Go: Europe,* a pocket-sized book featuring honest, irreverent writing and a decidedly youthful outlook on the world. Throughout the 60s, our guides reflected the times; the 1969 guide to America led off by inviting travelers to "dig the scene" at San Francisco's Haight-Ashbury. During the 70s and 80s, we gradually added regional guides and expanded coverage into the Middle East and Central America. With the addition of our in-depth city guides, handy map guides, and extensive coverage of Asia and Australia, the 90s are also proving to be a time of explosive growth for Let's Go, and there's certainly no end in sight. The first editions of *Let's Go: Australia* and *Let's Go: New Zealand* hit the shelves this year, expanding our coverage to six continents, and research for next year's series has already begun.

We've seen a lot in 38 years. *Let's Go: Europe* is now the world's bestselling international guide, translated into seven languages. And our new guides bring Let's Go's total number of titles, with their spirit of adventure and their reputation for honesty, accuracy, and editorial integrity, to 40. But some things never change: our guides are still researched, written, and produced entirely by students who know first-hand how to see the world on the cheap.

HOW WE DO IT

Each guide is completely revised and thoroughly updated every year by a well-traveled set of over 200 students. Every winter, we recruit over 140 researchers and 60 editors to write the books anew. After several months of training, Researcher-Writers hit the road for seven weeks of exploration, from Anchorage to Adelaide, Estonia to El Salvador, Iceland to Indonesia. Hired for their rare combination of budget travel sense, writing ability, stamina, and courage, these adventurous travelers know that train strikes, stolen luggage, food poisoning, and marriage proposals are all part of a day's work. Back at our offices, editors work from spring to fall, massaging copy written on Himalayan bus rides into witty yet informative prose. A student staff of typesetters, cartographers, publicists, and managers keeps our lively team together. In September, the collected efforts of the summer are delivered to our printer, who turns them into books in record time, so that you have the most up-to-date information available for your vacation. And even as you read this, work on next year's editions is well underway.

WHY WE DO IT

We don't think of budget travel as the last recourse of the destitute; we believe that it's the only way to travel. Living cheaply and simply brings you closer to the people and places you've been saving up to visit. Our books will ease your anxieties and answer your questions about the basics—so you can get off the beaten track and explore. Once you learn the ropes, we encourage you to put *Let's Go* down now and then to strike out on your own. As any seasoned traveler will tell you, the best discoveries are often those you make yourself. When you find something worth sharing, drop us a line. We're Let's Go Publications, 67 Mount Auburn St., Cambridge, MA 02138, USA (email: fanmail@letsgo.com).

HAPPY TRAVELS!

BANANA BUNGALOW HOSTELS USA!

•Santa Barbara
1-(800) 3-HOSTEL

•New York
1-(800) 6-HOSTEL

•Hollywood
1-(800) 4-HOSTEL

•San Diego Beach
1-(800) 5-HOSTEL

•Miami Beach
1-(800) 7-HOSTEL

Contents

HAWAII 436

APPENDIX 508
INDEX 515

Maps

Acknowledgments

A weary and wild congrats to Jessica, who shares my appreciation for intensity. Thanks for Poe-etics, creative synergy, delirious fits of laughter, and lists. Many thanks to Katie and her fortuitous flights to L.A. and Cambridge: I'm not sure what we would have done without her. Thanks to Melissa for support and a refined red pen. Thanks to: 'da Domestics, especially Kate who lent a cool head to the frontier; Dave and Melanie who answered my facile questions with consistent cheer; a super team of MEs; Jake who made me smile; and Derek McKee for his fine example. Through it all, I learned that doubts double as dreams—thanks to Sarah for helping me tap in to the well of dreams, and then sharing them with me (so much awaits). To Mom who continues to ground me. To Sharon, who is my sunny California. And most of all, to David, who gave me more than he knows. Thanks also to: 1902 Mass Ave., apartment by day and club by night; 3rd and 4th floor office friends; the girls of Trowbridge Place; Dad, Nick, and co. **-ACP**

If Let's Go is the flagship, we in the Domestic Room are a separate crew. Who could forget such memorable characters as Frank "Squash King" Beidler, Canadian ambassador Rob MacDougal, and those wacky night shift folk, Scott Brown and Jace Clayton, who were always willing to share their power bars. Sharing my pain and my late-night Pringles jokes was the incomparable Anna Portnoy, who never once complained. Always willing to rush out for a late-night coffee-and-scone break, Anna was what an editor should be. Others who deserve thanks are Melissa, who did all the crap we didn't want to, and Katie, who saved us from certain ruin. Thanks also to everyone who facilitated my extended absence from real life; Jennifer and Sarah, who gave me girl talk; David, who took care of my interlibrary loans; and all the office-mates, who never said anything about the suspicious similarity of my day-to-day outfits (it'll be different after this, guys, I promise). Thanks to the Kids for reminding me what Cali is all about (especially Schuyler Ellers, for his inside scoop on Nevada City). And last of all, thanks to my encouraging mom and my hilarious dad, both of whom had summers almost as frantic as mine. Time for a nap. **-JAN**

Editor	Anna C. Portnoy
Associate Editor	Jessica Niles
Managing Editor	Melissa M. Reyen
Publishing Director	John R. Brooks
Production Manager	Melanie Quintana Kansil
Associate Production Manager	David Collins
Cartography Manager	Sara K. Smith
Editorial Manager	Melissa M. Reyen
Editorial Manager	Emily J. Stebbins
Financial Manager	Krzysztof Owerkowicz
Personnel Manager	Andrew E. Nieland
Publicity Manager	Nicholas Corman
Publicity Manager	Kate Galbraith
New Media Manager	Daniel O. Williams
Associate Cartographer	Joseph E. Reagan
Associate Cartographer	Luke Z. Fenchel
Office Coordinators	Emily Bowen, Charles Kapelke
	Laurie Santos
Director of Advertising Sales	Todd L. Glaskin
Senior Sales Executives	Matthew R. Hillery, Joseph W. Lind
	Peter J. Zakowich, Jr.
President	Amit Tiwari
General Manager	Richard Olken
Assistant General Manager	Anne E. Chisholm

Researcher-Writers

Brian Algra   *Las Vegas, the Desert, Sierra Nevada, San Diego, Rosarito*
The original desert misanthrope, Brian plunged into the shrieking void that is the
Mojave with an intellectual vigor strong enough to defeat the heat—though the Mint
Oreo Blizzards certainly helped. After his shocking discovery that Pringles could melt
and later regain their trademark shape, he moved on to the cooler climes of the
Sierra, where he brought his wilderness wisdom to bear on the national parks. After
playing *Knight Rider* on canyon highways, he raced to San Diego to meet romance.
Covering nearly half of California, Brian proved himself a true Western hero.

Katherine Brown   *San Francisco Bay Area,*
                              Santa Cruz, Monterey, Carmel, Big Sur
Klub Kid Katherine leapt into the city with indefatigable enthusiasm, immediately
revamping the orientation section before moving on to bigger and badder things.
After a hard day of pounding the pavement, Katherine partied till the wee hours in
the name of research. Working her way through a quagmire of romance, she found
time to hustle down to Big Sur, where her literary allusions, in true Beat style, displayed an impeccably postmodern cynicism. Though the pace was hectic, through it
all she remained hipper than North Beach and more dynamic than the Mission.

Katrina Lundberg   *Lake Tahoe, Reno, Wine Country,*
                          North Coast, Northern Interior
A die-hard demi-goddess of dirt roads and descriptive prose, Katrina biked, canoed,
spelunked, and hiked her way through Northern California. Although she was constantly pursued by TV cameras and marriage-minded poets, Katrina gave us the inside
scoop on the Sierra scene, and her snow-capped sensitivity revolutionized our coverage of Tahoe's winter wonderland. Always researching to the beat of her own drum
(literally), Katrina proved to NorCal that she was the best thing since the gold rush.

Kimble Poon   *Hawaii*
Pumped to the max and ready for relaxation, Kimble well-deserved a Hawaiian
reward after last summer's Germanic explorations. Skipping across the isles with true
Southern grace, he managed to wiggle his way into almost everything for free. From
the Big Island to the island of the lepers, Kimble sent us so many coconuts, *leis,* and
Italian porn that even Cambridge felt like a tropical vacation. Whether battling weird
hostel owners, renting cars from mafia bosses, or doing a little nude bathing, everybody's favorite R-W remained the cutest thing on two legs. Go, Kimbo!

Katie Unterman   *L.A., Southern L.A. County, Central Coast*
Two-time *Let's Go* veteran Katie jumped onto the Team Cali lovebus just in time to
save it from careening over an unexpected cliff. After taking on the world, L.A. was a
cinch. Katie put her Valley Girl wits to a workout to create a new shopping section
that even Alicia Silverstone wouldn't mess with. And after all this, she arrived in Cambridge just in time to lock herself in the office with us. She's a goddess!

Gina Paik   *Downtown L.A., Orange County, East of L.A.*
Gina tackled her hometown nitty-gritty and sweated SoCal's most touristed spots
before heading into the hills. Her sharp eye made for detailed, insightful copy.

Hillary Stevens   *Grand Canyon*
Abigail Mnookin   *Ashland & Brookings*
Ana Lara   *Tijuana & Ensenada*
Sonesh Chaihani   *Mexicali*

Let's Go Picks

Here is where we bag our objective pose and say it straight. Though we have many favorites from our forays, these are the picks among the picks. For more extensive listings, see the pages that follow. All Let's Go Picks are indexed.

Best Places to Stop and Smell the Flowers: Berkeley Rose Garden, Berkeley (see p. 299). Roses traipse on one terrace after another. **Huntington Botanical Gardens,** near Pasadena (see p. 106). Blooming beauties from all over the world.

Best Places to Commune With Nature: James Irvine Trail, Redwood National Forest (see p. 351). Prehistoric redwoods give a glimpse of the past. **Moro Rock,** Sequoia National Park (see p. 415). A stunning panoramic of the southern sierra. **The Pacific Crest Trail,** wherever you cross its path (see p. 49). **Rubicon Trail,** Lake Tahoe (see p. 389). Five-mile hike along emerald water dazzles. **Horseshoe Lake,** Lassen National Park (see p. 369). Where the deer and the wildflowers play.

Best Place to Lose Your Money: Circus Circus, Reno (see p. 398), or in Las Vegas (see p. 201). Slot machines suck up nickels more than they cough out coins, and with carnivals and arcades, the whole family can lose money here.

Best Place to Strike it Rich: Gold Country, (see p. 354). We'll show you how.

Best Campgrounds: Bear Harbor Campground, Lost Coast (see p. 342). So beautiful it looks like Japanese gardens on turbo growth. **D.L. Bliss State Park,** Lake Tahoe (see p. 387). Lives up to its name with sites in secluded forest nooks.

Best Hostels: Ojai Farm Hostel, Ojai (see p. 211). Fresh O.J. on the table in the most eco-conscious of hostels. **Banana Bungalow,** San Diego (see p. 148). Where the European elite meet on the beach. **The Kauai International Hostel,** Kauai (see p. 491). Camaraderie like no other. **Arnott's Lodge,** near Hilo, HI (see p. 476). One of the state's best hostels near lava-rock beach. **Sanborn Park Hostel,** San Jose (see p. 311). Log cabin nestled in the redwoods—a perfect escape.

Best Acronym: Fresno Area Regional Transit, Fresno (see p. 433). Excuse me.

Best Scenic Drives: Marin Headlands, Marin County (see p. 323). Ghostly, misty drive just west of the Golden Gate Bridge. **Tioga Road,** into Yosemite National Park (see p. 402). The highest strip of road in the country winds through the park, looking over plunging granite slopes and canyons.

Best Free Samples: Wine and Produce Visitors Center, Monterey (see p. 234). Hot spiced mead. Wow. **Sebastiani,** Sonoma Valley (see p. 331). Grapes for the heavy weights.

Best Celebrity Worship: Hello Gorgeous!, San Francisco (see p. 266). Learning to love Babs has never been so easy. **L. Ron Hubbard Exhibition,** Hollywood (see p. 82). **Liberace Museum,** Las Vegas (see p. 200). Audacious displays of fur, velvet, and rhinestones worn by the legend himself.

Best Theme Restaurants: Stinking Rose, North Beach (see p. 277). Garlic galore! **Chocolate Cow,** Sonoma Valley (see p. 330). Udderly decadent!

Best Bookstores: Earthling Bookshop, Santa Barbara (see p. 217). Browse to your biblophilic delight. **Moe's,** Berkeley (see p. 301). An eclectic selection, Berkeley style. **A Clean Well-Lighted Place for Books,** San Francisco (see p. 283). Lives up to its moniker. **A Different Light Bookstore,** in L.A. (see p. 110) and San Francisco (see p. 282). Largest queer bookseller in America has all the camp you could ever want, and then some.

Best Specialty Cafes: Legal Grind, Santa Monica (see p. 114). Where you can get your daily dose of free legal advice. **Law Dogs,** San Fernando Valley (see p. 102). Chew on more free legal advice as well as chili-smothered "judge dogs."

Best Place to Be Scared: Skull Ice Cave, Lava Beds National Park (see p. 376). Climb down into darkness until the floor is so cold it freezes to ice. Yikes!

Best Places to Encounter a Ghost: Drum Barracks Civil War Museum, Wilmington (see p. 125). Ten million Elvis fans and *Unsolved Mysteries* can't be wrong. **The Whaley House,** San Diego (see p. 153). One of only two "official haunted houses" in California. Seriously.

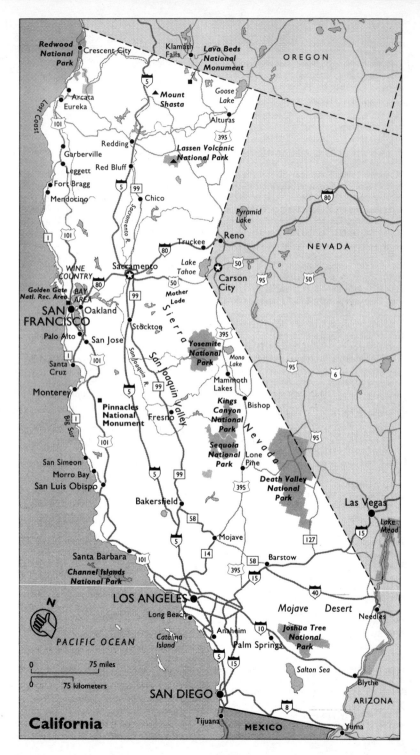

California

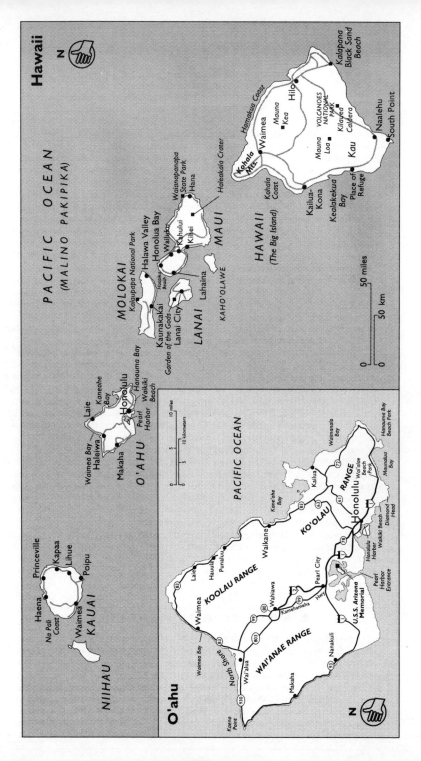

Hawaii

N

PACIFIC OCEAN
(MALINO PAKIPIKA)

Kauai
Haena
Na Pali Coast
Princeville
Kapaa
Lihue
Waimea
Poipu

NIIHAU

O'AHU
Laie
Kaneohe Bay
Haleiwa
Waimea Bay
Makaha
Honolulu
Pearl Harbor
Waikiki Beach
Hanauma Bay

MOLOKAI
Kalaupapa National Park
Halawa Valley
Kaunakakai
Garden of the Gods
Lanai City

LANAI

KAHO'OLAWE

Honolua Bay
Wailuku
Kahului
Kihei
Lahaina

MAUI
Waianapanapa State Park
Hana
Haleakala Crater

Hamakua Coast

Waimea
Mauna Kea
Hilo
Kohala MTS.
Kohala Coast
Kailua-Kona
Kealakekua Bay
Place of Refuge
Mauna Loa
VOLCANOES NATIONAL PARK
Kilauea Caldera

HAWAII
(The Big Island)

Kau
Naalehu
South Point
Kalapana Black Sand Beach

50 miles
50 km
0

O'ahu

N

Koolau Range
Ko'olau
Wai'anae Range
Koolau Range

PACIFIC OCEAN

Koene Point
Waimea Bay
North Shore
Wai'alua
Waimea
Laie
Haula'a
Punalu'u
Waikane
Wahiawa
Kamehameha
Hwy
Pearl City
Kane'ohe Bay
Kailua
Wai'olee Beach Park
Waimanalo Bay
Hanauma Bay Beach Park
Maunalua Bay

Makaha
Nanakuli
Honolulu
U.S.S. Arizona Memorial
Pearl Harbor Entrance
Honolulu Harbor
Waikiki Beach
Diamond Head

930
81
83
803
99
80
78
76
61
63
65
72

10 miles
10 kilometers
5
0

How to Use This Book

This book is not a toy. In the hands of the right person, it can be the source of much joy, happiness, and power. In the wrong hands, this book can become a powerful obstacle to overcome. The most important thing to realize is that though it takes planning to keep a trip together, it also takes an adventuresome spirit to break off the beaten path. The guide we provide is just that, a guide. What we have between the covers is what we know to be fun, exciting, and even enlightening…at least to us.

That said, the guide is organized in what appears to us a logical order. The beginning **Essentials** section is chock-full of information on trip planning, how to come and go from the grand old U.S. of A., and how to get around while you're there. Read it *before* you venture out and then relax in informed bliss while on the road.

Practicalities out the of the way, we move on to the state of California itself. We believe a little introduction is in order here—thus the **California** section, brimming with info about the people, events, and movies that have made the state golden. The actual journey starts in the hub of the state, that sprawling megalopolis we love to hate, **Los Angeles.** In **Around L.A.,** we cover all of the cities and suburbs of greater Los Angeles, including South Bay and Orange County to the south, and the wilderness to the east and north. From there, we head southward to the pastel paradise of **San Diego** and its ignominious extension in Baja California. Next we strap on our sand goggles, fill up on water and gas, and head into the **Desert;** split into the Low Desert (Palm Springs, Joshua Tree, Anza Borrego, and Needles), and the High Desert (Barstow, the eastern Mojave, Death Valley, and the decadent debauchery of Las Vegas). Wiping the sweat from our brow and bemoaning our lost chips, we scurry on to the **Central Coast,** blasting along the Pacific Coast Highway until we drift into the fog and incense of San Francisco. Surviving the steep hills, we stroll through the **Bay Area,** getting into the groove with eco-yuppies and pseudo-intellectual coffeehouses, and into the booze with Wine Country. Nursing a wicked hangover, we then meander up the **North Coast,** dangerously close to the edge. So, we plunge back into the **Interior,** starting with the state house in Sacramento, chiseling our way through Gold Country, climbing the Cascades, and even crossing the Oregon border. Finally, we hit the **Sierra Nevada** at its northern end, taking a breather in the alpine Tahoe resort area before taking on the national parks of Yosemite, Sequoia, and Kings Canyon and their eastern Sierra counterparts. And after the desolate, oven-hot towns of the San Joaquin Valley, we whisk ourselves away for a fun-filled frolic through each of the islands in **Hawaii** (Oahu, Maui, the Big Island, Kauai, Molokai, and Lanai). Calling it a day, we go out and get *leid.* Repeatedly.

At this point, we will have exhausted our limits, but you might want to put on your new training pants and seek another world to explore. You could try *Let's Go: Alaska and the Pacific Northwest, Let's Go: USA including Canada, Let's Go: Mexico,* or *Let's Go: Central America.* But do what you want to. After all, you are your own dog.

A NOTE TO OUR READERS

The information for this book is gathered by *Let's Go's* researchers from late May through August. Each listing is derived from the assigned researcher's opinion based upon his or her visit at a particular time. The opinions are expressed in a candid and forthright manner. Other travelers might disagree. Those traveling at a different time may have different experiences since prices, dates, hours, and conditions are always subject to change. You are urged to check beforehand to avoid inconvenience and surprises. Travel always involves a certain degree of risk, especially in low-cost areas. When traveling, especially on a budget, always take particular care to ensure your safety.

ESSENTIALS

ESSENTIALS

How you travel is as much a matter of personal style as what you wear or how you speak. Some might like to blow through all seven Hawaiian islands in as many days, others may prefer to linger in Death Valley until the Grim Reaper comes a-knockin'. At the very least, setting priorities and having a game plan for your trip can prevent you from being stuck in Chico without the cash for a Greyhound ticket home. This Essentials section and the Practical Information listings in state and city introductions provide the addresses and phone numbers of informational services.

PLANNING YOUR TRIP

■ When to Go

Whenever you want. You can show up in California or Hawaii just about anytime and be assured that there will be ample opportunities for snorkeling, snowshoeing, or just lying around in the sun. Visitors flock to California and Hawaii year-round; between December and April, in particular, the warmer shores of these two states are packed with cold-weather refugees.

Many seasonal attractions in California have lower rates during the off season, which varies depending on location. Contrary to popular opinion, the weather is not perfect. Winter can produce nasty rains in the north and thick fog in the Bay Area, while summer heat can be a serious problem in the valleys. May and September lie midway between the established "seasons," and often bring lower prices, smaller crowds, and perfect temperatures. In Hawaii the weather is more consistently dazzling, and tourist attractions are open year-round. As a consequence, more visitors from less hospitable climes travel to Hawaii in the winter.

In both states, official holidays may mean extended hours at some tourist attractions, but many banks, offices, shops, and services will close for the day. The dates of U.S. national holidays, as well as regional festivals, for 1998 are listed in the appendix (see p. 509).

■ Useful Information

TOURIST BUREAUS AND OFFICES

Contact the tourist bureau (often called the "visitors center" in the U.S.) in any city you plan to visit for more than a few days. Ask them anything. They can provide invaluable last-minute advice about special deals on accommodations, tours, or newly opened establishments, and some might even make reservations for you. Don't hesitate—you aren't the first tourist they've met. Addresses for local tourist offices throughout California and Hawaii are in the Practical Information section for each town or region. The U.S. **consulate** nearest you handles all promotional tourism needs outside the United States.

TRAVEL ORGANIZATIONS

American Automobile Association (AAA) Travel Services, 1000 AAA Dr. (mail stop 100), Heathrow, FL 32746-5080 (407-444-8411; fax 444-7380). Free road maps and travel guides for members. Offers emergency road services (800-222-4357), travel services, and auto insurance (free for members, small fee for non-members). To become a member, call 800-222-4357.

1

International Student Travel Confederation, Herengracht 479, 1017 BS Amsterdam, The Netherlands (tel. (031) 20 421 2800; fax 20 421 2810; http://www.istc.org; email istcinfo@istc.org). The ISTC is a nonprofit confederation of student travel organizations who work to facilitate travel among young people. Member organizations include International Student Surface Travel Association (ISSA), Student Air Travel Association (SATA), IASIS Travel Insurance, the International Association for Educational and Work Exchange Programs (IAEWEP), and the International Student Identity Card Association (ISIC).

Council on International Educational Exchange (CIEE), 205 East 42nd St., New York, NY 10017-5706 (888-COUNCIL/268-6245; fax 212-822-2699; http://www.ciee.org). A private, nonprofit organization, CIEE administers work, volunteer, academic, internship, and professional programs around the world. They also offer identity cards (including the ISIC and the GO25) and a range of publications such as the free *Student Travels*. Call or write for further info.

Federation of International Youth Travel Organizations (FIYTO), Bredgade 25H, DK-1260 Copenhagen K, Denmark (tel. (045) 33 33 96 00; fax 33 93 96 76; email mailbox@fiyto.org; http://www.fiyto.org), is an international organization promoting educational, cultural, and social travel for young people. Member organizations include language schools, educational travel companies, national tourist boards, accommodation centers, and other suppliers of travel services to youth and students. FIYTO sponsors the GO25 Card (http://www.go25.org).

USEFUL PUBLICATIONS

Adventurous Traveler Bookstore, P.O. Box 1468, Williston, VT 05495 (801-282-3963; fax 677-1821; email books@atbook.com; http://www.AdventurousTraveler.com). Free 40-page catalogue upon request. Specializes in outdoor adventure travel books and maps. Their web site offers extensive browsing capabilities.

Blue Guides, published in Britain by A&C Black Limited, 35 Bedford Row, London WC1R 4JH; in the U.S. by W.W. Norton & Co., Inc., 500 Fifth Ave., New York, NY 10110; and in Canada by Penguin Books Canada Ltd., 10 Alcorn Ave., #300, Toronto, Ontario N4V 3B2. Provides unmatched historical and cultural info as well as sight-seeing routes, maps, tourist info, and listings of pricey hotels.

Bon Voyage!, 2069 W. Bullard Ave., Fresno, CA 93711-1200 (800-995-9716, outside U.S. 209-447-8441; fax 266-6460; email 70754.3511@compuserve.com). Annual mail order catalogue offers books, travel accessories, luggage, electrical converters, maps, and videos. All merchandise may be returned for exchange or refund within 30 days of purchase, and prices are guaranteed (lower advertised prices will be matched and merchandise shipped free).

Michelin Travel Publications, Michelin North America, P.O. Box 19008, Greenville, SC 29602-9008 (800-223-0987; fax 378-7471; http://www.michelin-travel.com). Publishes 4 major lines of travel-related material: *Green Guides,* for sight-seeing, maps, and driving; *Red Guides,* hotel and restaurant ratings; *In-Your-Pocket Guides,* which are perfect travel-size; and detailed, reliable road maps and atlases. All are available at bookstores and distributors throughout the world.

Rand McNally, 150 S. Wacker Dr., Chicago, IL 60606 (800-333-0136; http://www.randmcnally.com), publishes one of the most comprehensive road atlases of North America ($10). Headquarters located at 8255 N. Central Park Ave., Skokie, IL 60076. Phone orders are available.

Specialty Travel Index, 305 San Anselmo Ave., #313, San Anselmo, CA 94960 (415-459-4900; fax 459-4974; email spectrav@ix.netcom.com; http://www.spec-trav.com). Published twice yearly with extensive listings of "off the beaten track" and specialty travel opportunities. One copy $6, 2 copies $10.

Ten Speed Press, P.O. Box 7123, Berkeley, CA 94707 (800-841-2665; fax 510-559-1629; email order@tenspeed.com). *The Packing Book* ($9) provides various checklists and suggested wardrobes, addresses safety concerns, and imparts packing techniques. Other products include several travel journals ($9-10) and the *Traveler's Weather Guide* ($9), a book about global weather patterns.

U.S. Customs Service, P.O. Box 7407, Washington, D.C., 20044 (202-927-6724; http://www.customs.ustreas.gov). Publishes 35 books, leaflets, and flyers on various aspects of customs. *Know Before You Go (KYBG)* lists everything the international traveler needs to know about customs requirements (*Pocket Hints* is the condensed version of *KYBG*).

■ Internet Resources

Along with everything else in the 90s, budget travel is moving rapidly into the information age, with the **Internet** as a leading travel resource. Today, the 'net allows people to make their own airline, hotel, hostel, or car rental reservations and connect personally with others abroad, becoming their own budget travel planners. **NetTravel: How Travelers Use the Internet,** by Michael Shapiro, is a thorough and informative guide to this process ($25).

There are a number of ways to access the Internet. Most popular are commercial Internet services, such as **America Online** (800-827-6364), and **Compuserve** (800-433-0389). Many employers and schools also offer gateways to the Internet, often at no cost (unlike the corporate gateways above). The form of the Internet most useful to 'net-surfing budget travelers is the World Wide Web.

THE WORLD WIDE WEB

Increasingly the Internet forum of choice, the **World Wide Web** provides its users with text, graphics, and sound. This and the huge proliferation of web pages (individual sites within the World Wide Web) have made the Web the most active and exciting destination on the Internet. Unfortunately, the Web's lack of hierarchy makes it difficult to distinguish between good info, bad info, and marketing. **Search engines** (services that search for web pages under specific subjects) can significantly aid the search process. **Yahoo!** is a well-organized search engine; check out its travel links at http://www.yahoo.com/Recreation/Travel. The search engine for **WIRED Magazine** is also useful; find it at www.hotbot.com. Another good way to explore is to find a good site and start "surfing" from there, through links from one web page to another. *Let's Go* lists relevant web sites throughout different sections of the Essentials chapter. Check out Let's Go's own page (http://www.letsgo.com) for a current list of links, or try some of our favorites directly:

Great Outdoor Recreation Pages (Gorp), has pages about outdoor destinations in both California (http://www.gorp.com/location/ca/ca.htm), and Hawaii (http://www.gorp.com/location/hi/hi.htm).

Rent-A-Wreck's Travel Links (http://www.rent-a-wreck.com/raw/travlist.htm), is a very complete list of excellent links.

Big World Magazine (http://www.paonline.com/bigworld), a budget travel e-zine, has a web page with a great collection of links to travel pages.

The CIA World Factbook (http://www.odci.gov/cia/publications/nsolo/wfb-all.htm), has tons of vital statistics.

Shoestring Travel (http://www.stratpub.com), is a budget travel e-zine, with feature articles, links, user exchange, and accommodations info.

The Student and Budget Travel Guide (http://asa.ugl.lib.umich.edu/chdocs/travel/travel-guide.html), has info on accommodations, transport, and packing.

TravelHUB (http://www.travelhub.com), is a great site for cheap travel deals.

Let's Go may be reached by email at "fanmail@letsgo.com."

■ Documents and Formalities

In preparing for a trip to California or Hawaii from another country, be sure to file all document applications several weeks or months in advance of your planned departure date. Most offices suggest you apply in the off-season (Aug.-Dec.) for speedier service. When you travel, *always carry on your person two or more forms of identification, including at least one photo ID*. With the recent acts of terrorism in Oklahoma City (federal building bombing) and Atlanta (Olympic stadium bombing), airplanes now require passengers to carry a photo ID on board. A passport combined with a driver's license or birth certificate usually serves as adequate proof of your identity and citizenship. Many establishments, especially banks, require several IDs before cashing traveler's checks. Never carry your passport, travel ticket, identification documents, money, traveler's checks, insurance, and credit cards all together; you run the risk of being left entirely without ID or funds in the case of theft or loss. Carry several extra passport-size photos that you can attach to the sundry IDs or passes you may eventually acquire.

ENTRANCE REQUIREMENTS

Foreign visitors to the United States are required to have a **passport** and **visa/proof of intent to leave.** To visit the country, you must be healthy and law-abiding, and demonstrate the ability to **support yourself financially** during your stay.

U.S. Embassies and Consulates

Contact your nearest embassy or consulate to obtain info regarding visas and passports to the United States. The U.S. **State Department** publishes *Key Officers of Foreign Service Posts,* listing detailed info on every overseas mission ($3.75); write to the Superintendent of Documents, U.S. Government Printing Office, Washington, D.C. 20402 (202-512-1800; fax 512-2168), to order a copy, or consult the free Internet version at http://www.state.gov/www/about_state/contacts/index.html.

U.S. Embassies In **Australia,** Moonah Pl., Canberra, ACT 2600 (tel. (02) 6270 5000; fax 270-5970); in **Canada**, 100 Wellington St., Ottawa, ON, K1P 5T1 (613-238-5335 or 238-4470; fax 238-5720); in **Ireland,** 42 Elgin Rd., Ballsbridge, Dublin 4 (tel. (016) 68 7122); in **New Zealand,** 29 Fitzherbert Terr., Thorndon, Wellington (tel. (04) 472 2068; fax 472 3537); in the **U.K.,** 24/31 Grosvenor Sq., London W1A 1AE (tel. (0171) 499 9000; fax 409 1637); in **South Africa,** 877 Pretorius St., Arcadio 0083; P.O. Box 9536, Pretoria 0001 (tel. (012) 342 1048; fax 342 2244).

U.S. Consulates In **Australia,** MLC Centre, 19-29 Martin Place, 59th fl., Sydney NSW 2000 (tel. (02) 9373 9200; fax 373 9125); 553 St. Kilda Rd, P.O. Box 6722, Melbourne, VIC 3004 (tel. (03) 9526 5900; fax 9510 4646); 16 St. George Terr., 13th floor, Perth, WA 6000 (tel. (08) 9231 9400; fax 231 9444); in **Canada,** P.O. Box 65, Postal Station Desjardins, Montréal, QP, H5B 1G1 (514-398-9695; fax 398-0973); 2 Place Terrasse Dufferin, CP939, Québec City, QP, G1R 4T9 (418-692-2095; fax 692-4640); 360 University Ave., Toronto, ON, M5G 1S4 (416-595-1700; fax 595-0051); 1095 W. Pender St., Vancouver, BC V6E 2M6 (604-685-4311); in **New Zealand,** 4th fl., Yorkshire General Bldg., corner of Shortland and O'Connell St., Auckland (tel. (09) 303 2724; fax 342 2244); in the **United Kingdom,** Queen's House, 14 Queen St., Belfast, N. Ireland, BT1 6EQ (tel. (0123) 232 8239); 3 Regent Terr., Edinburgh, Scotland EH7 5BW (tel. (0131) 556 8315; fax 557 6023); in **South Africa,** Broadway Industries Centre, Heerengracht, Foreshore, Capetown (tel. (021) 214 280; fax 254 151); Kim Centre, 11th Fl., P.O. Box 2155, Johannesburg (tel. (021) 331 1327; fax 838 3920).

PASSPORTS

If you lose your passport, immediately notify the local police and the nearest embassy or consulate of your home government (for locations in California, see **Embassies and Consulates,** p. 37). Any visas stamped in your old passport will be irretrievably lost. In an emergency, ask for immediate temporary traveling papers that will permit you to re-enter your home country. A replacement may take weeks to process, and it may be valid only for a limited time, although some consulates can issue new passports within 24 hours if you have proof of citizenship. To expedite the process, know all info previously recorded and show ID and proof of citizenship. Before you leave home, photocopy the page of your passport that contains your photograph, passport number, and other identifying info. Carry one photocopy in a safe place apart from your passport, and leave another copy at home. Consulates also recommend that you carry an expired passport or an official copy of your birth certificate in your baggage separate from other documents. If you are planning an extended stay, register your passport with an embassy or consulate.

Your passport is a public document belonging to your nation's government. You may have to surrender it to a U.S. government official, but if you don't get it back in a reasonable amount of time, inform the nearest mission of your home country.

Australia Adult passports cost AUS$126 (for a 32-page passport) or AUS$188 (64-page); children's passports cost AUS$63 or AUS$94. For more info, call toll-free (in Australia) 13 12 32.

Canada Citizens may apply in person at any of 28 regional Passport Offices across Canada; travel agents can direct applicants to the nearest location. Passports cost CDN$60. For additional info, contact the Canadian Passport Office, Dept. of Foreign Affairs and International Trade, Ottawa, ON, K1A 0G3 (613-994-3500; http://www.dfait-maeci.gc.ca/passport). Travelers may also call 800-567-6868 (24hr.); in Toronto 416-973-3251; in Vancouver 604-775-6250; in Montréal 514-283-2152.

Ireland Citizens may apply for a passport by mail to either the Department of Foreign Affairs, Passport Office, Setanta Centre, Molesworth St., Dublin 2 (tel. (01) 671 1633), or the Passport Office, Irish Life Building, 1A South Mall, Cork (tel. (021) 272 525). Passports cost IR£45; citizens under 18 or over 65 may request a 3-year passport that costs IR£10.

New Zealand Applicants should contact the Passport Office, P.O. Box 10526, Wellington, New Zealand. Passports cost NZ$80 (adult), and NZ$40 (child). An urgent passport service is also available for an extra NZ$80.

South Africa Citizens may apply for a passport at any Home Affairs Office or South African Mission. Tourist passports, valid for 10 years, cost SAR80. Children under 16 must be issued their own passports, valid for 5 years, which cost SAR60. For further info, contact the nearest Department of Home Affairs Office.

United Kingdom Citizens may apply in person or by mail to one of the passport offices located in London, Liverpool, Newport, Peterborough, Glasgow, or Belfast. Passports cost UK£18. The London office offers same-day, walk-in service; arrive early. For more info, contact the U.K. Passport Agency (tel. (0990) 21 04 10; http://www.open.gov.uk/ukpass).

VISAS

A visa, stamped into a traveler's passport by the government of a host country, allows the bearer to stay in that country for a specified purpose and period of time. The **Center for International Business and Travel (CIBT)**, 25 W. 43rd St., #1420, New York, NY 10036 (212-575-2811 or 800-925-2428), secures travel visas to and from all possible countries for a variable service charge. To obtain a U.S. visa, contact the nearest embassy or consulate. According to U.S. law, **HIV-positive persons** are not permitted to enter the U.S. However, HIV testing is conducted only for those planning to immigrate permanently. Travelers from areas with particularly high concentrations of HIV-positive persons or persons with AIDS might be required to provide more info when applying for a visa.

Travelers from certain nations may enter the U.S. without a visa through the **Visa Waiver Pilot Program.** Visitors qualify as long as they are traveling for business or pleasure, are staying for 90 days or less, have proof of intent to leave (e.g., a returning plane ticket), have a completed I-94W form (arrival/departure certificate attached to your visa upon arrival), and enter aboard particular air or sea carriers. Participating countries include Australia, France, Germany, Ireland, Italy, Japan, New Zealand, and the U.K. Contact a U.S. consulate for more info; countries are added frequently.

Most visitors obtain a **B-2,** or "pleasure tourist" visa at the nearest U.S. consulate or embassy, which normally costs $20 and is usually valid for six months. For general visa inquiries, consult the Bureau of Consular Affairs (http://travel.state.gov/visa_services.html). Don't lose your visa, as it is irreplaceable. If you lose your I-94W form (see above), you can replace it at the nearest **U.S. Immigration and Naturalization Service (INS)** office (800-755-0777 or 202-307-1501; http://

ESSENTIALS

www.ins.usdoj.gov), though it's very unlikely that the form will be replaced within the time of your stay. **Extensions** for visas are sometimes obtainable with a completed I-539 form; call the forms request line (800-870-3676).

CUSTOMS: ENTERING

Upon entering the U.S., you must declare certain items from abroad and pay a **duty** on the value of any articles that exceed the allowance established by that country's customs service. Make a list, including serial numbers, of any valuables that you carry with you from home; if you register this list with customs before your departure and have an official stamp it, you will avoid import duty charges and ensure an easy passage upon your return. Be sure to document items manufactured abroad.

Passing customs should be routine, but take it seriously; don't joke around with customs officials or airport security personnel. The U.S. restricts the importation of firearms, explosives, ammunition, fireworks, controlled substances, most plants and animals, lottery tickets, obscene literature and films, and articles made from the skins and furs of certain animals. To avoid problems when you transport prescription drugs, ensure that the bottles are clearly marked, and carry a copy of the prescription to show the customs officer. You can bring any amount of currency, but if you carry over $10,000 in cash, you'll need to report it. For a detailed description of the relevant codes, contact the **Animal and Plant Health Inspection Service (APHIS),** 4700 River Rd., Riverdale, MD 20737 (http://www.aphis.usda.gov/oa/travel.html). The **U.S. Customs Service,** 1301 Constitution Ave., Washington, D.C. 20229 (202-927-5580; http://www.customs.ustreas.gov), publishes the helpful brochure *Customs Guidelines for Visitors to the United States*. It details everything the international traveler needs to know about customs requirements.

CUSTOMS: GOING HOME

Upon returning home, you must declare all articles you acquired abroad and pay a **duty** on the value of those articles that exceed the allowance established by your country's customs service. Goods and gifts purchased at **duty-free** shops abroad are not exempt from duty or sales tax at your point of return; you must declare these items as well. "Duty-free" merely means that you need not pay a tax in the country of purchase. Keeping receipts for purchases made abroad will help establish values when you return. Contact your country's customs service for more information.

YOUTH, STUDENT, & TEACHER IDENTIFICATION

The **International Student Identity Card (ISIC)** is the most widely accepted form of student identification. Present the card wherever you go to get discounts. It also provides insurance benefits (see **Insurance,** p. 15). In addition, cardholders have access to a toll-free 24-hour ISIC helpline whose multilingual staff can provide assistance in medical, legal, and financial emergencies.

Many student travel agencies around the world issue ISICs, including STA Travel in Australia and New Zealand; Travel CUTS in Canada; USIT in Ireland and Northern Ireland; SASTS in South Africa; Campus Travel and STA Travel in the U.K.; Council Travel, Let's Go Travel, and STA Travel in the U.S.; and any of the other organizations under the auspices of the International Student Travel Confederation (ISTC). When you apply for the card, request a copy of the *International Student Identity Card Handbook,* which lists by country some of the available discounts. The card costs $19 or CDN$15. Applicants must be at least 12 years old and degree-seeking students of a secondary or post-secondary school. Because of the proliferation of phony ISICs, many airlines and some other services require other proof of student identity, such as a signed letter from the registrar, or your school ID card. The $20 **International Teacher Identity Card (ITIC)** offers the same insurance coverage, and more limited discounts. For more info on these cards, consult the organization's web site (http:\\www.istc.org; email isicinfo@istc.org).

The Federation of International Youth Travel Organizations (FIYTO) issues a discount card to travelers who are under 26 but not students. Known as the **GO25 Card,** this one-year card offers many of the same benefits as the ISIC, and most organizations that sell the ISIC also sell the GO25 Card. A brochure that lists discounts is free when you purchase the card. Applicants must provide a passport, valid driver's license or birth certificate, and a passport-sized photo with your name printed on the back. The fee is $19, CDN$15, or UK£5. Info is available on FIYTO's web site (http://www.fiyto.org), and GO25's web site (http://www.go25.org).

DRIVING PERMITS AND CAR INSURANCE

The U.S. recognizes all foreign driving permits; however, some visitors may choose to get an international driver's permit from their home automobile associations.

Most credit cards cover standard insurance. If you rent, lease, or borrow a car, you will need a green card, or **International Insurance Certificate,** to prove that you have liability insurance. Obtain it through the car rental agency; most include coverage in their prices. If you lease a car, you can obtain a green card from the dealer; some travel agents also offer the card. Verify whether your auto insurance applies outside of your home country, but even if it does, you will still need a green card to certify this to officials. If you have a collision outside of your home country, the accident will show up on your records if you report it to your insurance company.

■ Money

If you stay in hostels and prepare your own food, expect to spend anywhere from $20-60 per person per day, depending on the local cost of living and your needs. Transportation will increase these figures. Don't sacrifice your health or safety for a cheaper tab—both California and Hawaii are expensive travel destinations, and no trip is fun if you're always hungry or tired. Carrying cash around with you, even in a money belt, is risky but necessary; personal checks from home will probably not be acceptable no matter how many forms of identification you have, and even traveler's checks may not be acceptable in some locations.

CURRENCY AND EXCHANGE

It is cheaper to buy domestic currency than to buy foreign, so you should convert most of your money *after* arriving in the U.S. However, converting some money before you go will allow you to zip through the airport while others languish in exchange lines. Bring enough American currency to last for the first few days of a trip, to avoid getting stuck with no money after banking hours or on a holiday.

Watch out for commission rates and check newspapers to get the standard rate of exchange. Banks generally have the best rates, but this is by no means a hard and fast rule. A good rule of thumb is to go to places which have only a 5% margin between their buy and sell prices. (Be sure that both prices are listed.) Since you lose money with every transaction, convert in large sums (unless the currency is depreciating rapidly), but don't convert more than you need, because it may be difficult to change it back to your home currency, or to a new one. If you are using traveler's checks or bills, be sure to carry some in small denominations ($50 or less), especially for times when you are forced to exchange money at disadvantageous rates. The exchange rates listed below should give you a rough idea of what to expect:

CDN$1 = US$.73
AUS$1 = US$0.76
IR£1 = US$1.51
NZ$1 = US$0.69
UK£1 = US$1.63

US$1= CDN$1.39
US$1 = AUS$1.32
US$1 = IR£0.66
US$1 = NZ$1.45
US$1 = UK£061

ESSENTIALS

The main unit of currency in the U.S. is the dollar, which is divided into 100 cents. Paper money is green in the U.S.; bills come in denominations of $1, $5, $10, $20, $50, and $100. Coins are 1¢ (penny), 5¢ (nickel), 10¢ (dime), and 25¢ (quarter).

TRAVELER'S CHECKS

Traveler's checks are one of the safest and least troublesome means of carrying funds, as they can be refunded if stolen. Several agencies and many banks sell them, usually for face value plus a small percentage commission. (Members of AAA, and some banks, can get American Express checks commission-free; see **Travel Organizations,** p. 1.) Keep in mind that in small towns, traveler's checks are less readily accepted than in cities with large tourist industries. If you're ordering your own checks, do so well in advance, especially if requesting large sums.

Each agency provides refunds for **lost or stolen checks.** (Note that you may need a police report verifying the loss or theft.) Inquire about refund hotlines, emergency services, and stolen credit card assistance when you purchase traveler's checks. You should expect a fair amount of red tape and delay in the event of theft or loss of traveler's checks. To expedite the refund process, keep your check receipts separate from your checks and store them in a safe place or with a traveling companion. It is also a good idea to record check numbers when you cash them and to leave a list of check numbers with someone at home. Keep a separate supply of cash or traveler's checks for emergencies. Never countersign your checks until you cash them, and always bring your passport with you when you plan to use the checks.

American Express: In Australia, call (800) 25 19 02; in New Zealand (0800) 44 10 68; in the U.K. (0800) 52 13 13; in the U.S. and Canada 800-221-7282. Elsewhere, call U.S. collect 801-964-6665. American Express traveler's checks are the most widely recognized worldwide and the easiest to replace if lost or stolen. Checks can be purchased for a 1-4% commission at American Express Travel Service Offices, banks, and American Automobile Association offices (AAA members can buy the checks commission-free). Cardmembers can also purchase checks at American Express Dispensers at Travel Service Offices at airports or by ordering them via phone (800-ORDER-TC/673-3782). American Express offices cash their checks commission-free, although they often offer slightly steeper rates than banks. You can also buy *Cheques for Two* which can be signed by either of two people traveling together. Visit their online travel offices (http://www.aexp.com).

Citicorp: Call 800-645-6556 in the U.S. and Canada; in Europe, the Middle East, or Africa (44) 171 508 7007; from elsewhere call U.S. collect 813-623-1709. Sells both Citicorp and Citicorp Visa traveler's checks for a 1-2% commission. Checkholders are automatically enrolled for 45 days in the Travel Assist Program (hotline 800-250-4377 or collect 202-296-8728), which provides travelers with doctor, lawyer, and interpreter referrals as well as check refund assistance and general travel info. Citicorp's World Courier Service guarantees hand-delivery of traveler's checks when a refund location is not convenient. Call 24hr.

Thomas Cook MasterCard: Call 800-223-9920 in the U.S. and Canada; from the U.K. call (0800) 622 101 free or (1733) 318 950 collect; elsewhere call U.S. collect 609-987-7300. Offers 24hr. cashing and refund assistance. Commission 1-2% for purchases. Thomas Cook offices may sell checks for lower commissions and will cash checks commission-free. Thomas Cook MasterCard Traveler's Checks are also available from **Capital Foreign Exchange,** in the eastern U.S. (toll-free 888-842-0880; fax 202-842-8008), or **International Currency Express,** on the West Coast (toll-free 888-278-6628; fax 310-278-6410). They will mail the checks overnight ($12) or second-day ($10) at competitive exchange rates.

Visa: Call 800-227-6811 in the U.S.; in the U.K. (0800) 895 492; from elsewhere call collect (01733) 318 949. Call for the location of their nearest office, to report lost Visa traveler's checks, and for general assistance.

CREDIT CARDS

Credit cards are a very handy thing to have in California and Hawaii. Most places accept them—*Let's Go* notes exceptions. **MasterCard** and **Visa** are accepted at **ATMs** (automatic teller machines) throughout California and Hawaii. **American Express** cards also work in some ATMs, as well as at AmEx offices and major airports. All such machines require a **Personal Identification Number (PIN).** You must ask American Express, MasterCard, or Visa to assign you one before you leave home; without this PIN, you will be unable to withdraw cash with your credit card. Credit card companies get the wholesale exchange rate, which is generally 5% better than the retail rate used by banks. However, you will be charged ruinous interest rates if you don't pay off the bill quickly, so be careful when using this service.

Credit cards are invaluable in an **emergency**—an unexpected hospital bill, ticket home, or loss of traveler's checks—which may leave you temporarily without other resources. Furthermore, credit cards offer an array of other services, from insurance to emergency assistance; these depend completely on the issuer.

American Express (800-843-2273), has a hefty annual fee ($55), but offers a number of services. AmEx cardholders can cash personal checks at AmEx offices outside the U.S. In addition, U.S. Assist, a 24hr. hotline offering medical and legal assistance in emergencies, is also available (800-554-2639 in U.S. and Canada; from abroad call U.S. collect 301-214-8228). Cardholders can take advantage of the American Express Travel Service; benefits include assistance in changing airline, hotel, and car rental reservations, baggage loss and flight insurance, sending mailgrams and international cables, and holding your mail at one of the more than 1700 AmEx offices around the world.

MasterCard (800-999-0454), and **Visa** (800-336-8472), are issued in cooperation with individual banks and some other organizations. Ask the issuer about services which go along with the cards.

CASH CARDS AND ATM MACHINES

Cash cards—popularly called **ATM** cards—are all over California and Hawaii. Depending on the system that your bank at home uses, you will probably be able to access your own personal bank account whenever you're in need of funds. (Be careful, however, and keep all receipts–even if an ATM won't give you your cash, it may register a withdrawal on your next statement.) Happily, ATMs get the same wholesale exchange rate as credit cards. Despite these perks, do some research before relying too heavily on automation. There is often a limit on the amount of money you can withdraw per day, and computer network failures are not uncommon. If your PIN is longer than four digits, be sure to ask your bank whether the first four digits will work, or whether you need a new number. Be cautious around poorly lit ATMs in urban areas: robbers prey on unsuspecting tourists in these places, especially in urban centers. The two major international money networks are **Cirrus** (800-4-CIRRUS/424-7787), and **PLUS** (800-843-7587).

GETTING MONEY FROM HOME

One of the easiest ways to get money from home is to bring an **American Express** card. AmEx allows green-card holders to draw cash from their checking accounts at any of its major offices and many of its representatives' offices, up to $1000 every 21 days (no service charge, no interest). AmEx also offers Express Cash, with over 100,000 ATMs located in airports, hotels, banks, office complexes, and shopping areas all over California and Hawaii. Express Cash withdrawals are automatically debited from the Cardmember's checking account. Green card holders may withdraw up to $1000 in a seven-day period. There is a 2% transaction fee for each cash withdrawal, with a $2.50 minimum and $20 maximum. To enroll in Express Cash, Cardmembers may call 800-CASH-NOW/227-4669. Outside the U.S. call collect 904-

565-7875. Unless using the AmEx service, avoid cashing checks in foreign currencies—they usually take weeks and a $30 fee to clear.

Money can also be wired abroad through international money transfer services operated by **Western Union** (800-325-6000). In the U.S., call Western Union any time at 800-CALL-CASH/225-5227, to cable money with your Visa, Discover, or MasterCard within the domestic United States and the U.K. The rates for sending cash are generally $10 cheaper than with a credit card, and the money is usually available in the country you're sending it to within an hour, although this may vary.

Some people also choose to send money in cash via **Federal Express** to avoid transmission fees and taxes. FedEx is reasonably reliable; however, this method may be illegal, it involves an element of risk, and it requires that you remain at a legitimate address for a day or two to wait for the money's arrival. In general, it may be safer to swallow the cost of wire transmission and preserve your peace of mind.

TIPPING AND BARGAINING

Sales tax is the U.S. equivalent of Europe's Value Added Tax. The sales tax in California varies slightly from region to region (8.25-8.5%). In Hawaii, the tax is a uniform 4%; in Nevada, 7%. In addition, a **tip** of 12-18% is expected by restaurant servers, taxi drivers, bartenders, hairdressers…usually anyone who pays attention to you. Don't even try to **bargain** in the U.S.—the capitalist populace will laugh in your face.

■ Safety and Security

PERSONAL SAFETY

Tourists are particularly vulnerable to crime because they often carry large amounts of cash and they lack local street savvy. To avoid unwanted attention, try to **blend in** as much as possible. Look over your map before setting out so that you can act as if you know where you are going.

When **walking at night,** you should turn daytime guidelines into mandates. Stick to busy well-lit streets and avoid dark alleyways or parks. Whenever possible, *Let's Go* warns of unsafe neighborhoods, but only your eyes can tell you for sure if you've wandered into one. Buildings in disrepair, vacant lots, and general desertedness are all bad signs. City districts in California can change character drastically in the course of a single block, but the flow of people can reveal a great deal about an area; look for children playing, women walking in the open, and other signs of an active community. Find out about unsafe areas from visitors centers, from the manager of your hotel or hostel, or from a local whom you trust. If traveling alone, be sure that someone knows your itinerary. Never say that you're traveling alone, and memorize the emergency number of the city or area. In California and Hawaii, dialing 911 will get you a number of emergency services.

If you are **traveling by car,** learn local driving signals. Wearing a **seatbelt** is the law in California. Children under 40 lb. must ride in a specially-designed **carseat,** which can be obtained for a small fee from most car rental agencies. In California, and in Los Angeles in particular, keep your doors locked at all times; **car-jacking** still occurs. If you plan on spending a lot of time on the road, you may want to bring spare parts. Study route maps carefully; some roads have poor (or nonexistent) shoulders and few gas stations. In many regions, most notably mountainous areas, road conditions necessitate driving especially slowly and cautiously. *Let's Go* does not recommend **hitchhiking,** particularly for women—see **By Thumb** (p. 35) for more. **Sleeping in your car** is one of the most dangerous (and often illegal) ways to get your rest. If your car breaks down, wait for the police to assist you. If you must sleep in your car, do so as close to a police station or a 24-hour service station as possible. Sleeping out in the open can be even more dangerous—camping is recommended only in official, supervised campsites or in wilderness backcountry.

Exercise extreme caution when using pools or **beaches** without lifeguards. Hidden rocks and shallow depths may cause serious injury or even death. Heed warning signs about dangerous undertows. If you rent scuba diving equipment, make sure that it is up to par before taking the plunge.

There is no sure-fire set of precautions that will protect you from all of the situations you might encounter when you travel. A good self-defense course will give you more concrete ways to react to different types of aggression, but it often carries a steep price tag. **Impact, Prepare,** and **Model Mugging** courses cost $50-400 (800-345-KICK/5425). Women's and men's courses are offered. Community colleges frequently offer inexpensive self-defense courses.

For official **United States Department of State** travel advisories, call their 24-hour hotline at 202-647-5225 or check their web site (http://travel.state.gov), which provides travel information and publications.

FINANCIAL SECURITY

Don't put money in a wallet in your back pocket. A **money belt** is the best way to carry cash—buy one at most camping supply stores or through the Forsyth Travel Library (see **Useful Publications,** p. 2). The best combination of convenience and invulnerability is the nylon, zippered belt pouch that sits inside a waistband. Avoid keeping anything precious in a fanny-pack (even if it's worn on your stomach). It assures that your valuables will be highly visible and easy to steal, and is tantamount to wearing a sign that says "Naïve Tourist—Rob Me!" In city crowds, pick-pockets are amazingly deft at their craft. Making **photocopies** of important documents will allow you to recover them in case they are lost or filched (see **Passports,** p. 4).

If you take a **car** on your travels, do not leave valuable possessions such as radios or luggage in it while you're off rambling. If your tape deck or radio is removable, hide it in the trunk or take it with you. If it isn't, conceal it under a lot of junk. Similarly, hide baggage in the trunk. Most insurance companies offer emergency hotlines and assistance to travelers (see **Insurance,** p. 15).

DRUGS AND ALCOHOL

In California and Hawaii, as in the rest of the United States, the **drinking age** is a strictly enforced 21 years of age. The U.S. takes **drunk driving** seriously (as it should). If your driving suggests possible intoxication to police, you will be pulled over and asked to take the **field sobriety test.** Your ability to perform simple motor functions will determine whether your blood-alcohol level (the percentage, by weight, of alcohol in your blood) is tested. If you are found to exceed the limit, criminal charges will be pressed against you. Beyond the legal problems, drunk driving can also be extremely dangerous to yourself and others. If you are carrying **prescription drugs,** have a copy of the prescription. Traveling with **illicit drugs** is a remarkably bad idea. The U.S. takes a hard line toward drugs, and penalties for possession are stiff. Remember that you are subject to the laws of the country in which you travel, not to those of your home country, and it is your responsibility to know these laws before arriving.

■ Health

California and Hawaii are relatively healthy places to travel around. Nevertheless, you should always be aware of the health risks. Common sense is the simplest prescription for good health while you travel: eat well, drink enough water, get enough sleep, and don't overexert yourself. Travelers complain most often about their feet and their gut, so take precautionary measures. Drinking lots of fluids can prevent **dehydration** and **constipation,** and wearing sturdy shoes and clean socks can help keep your feet comfortable. To minimize the effects of jet lag, "reset" your body's clock by adopting the time of your destination immediately upon arrival. Most travelers feel acclimatized to a new time zone after two or three days.

BEFORE YOU GO

Though no amount of planning can guarantee an accident-free trip, preparation can help minimize the likelihood of contracting a disease and maximize the chances of receiving effective health-care in the event of an emergency.

For minor health problems on the road, a compact **first-aid kit** should suffice. Some hardware stores carry ready-made kits, but it's easy to assemble your own. Include bandages, aspirin, acetaminophen or ibuprofen, antiseptic soap or antibiotic cream, a thermometer in a sturdy case, a Swiss Army knife with tweezers, moleskin, a decongestant, a motion sickness remedy, medicine for diarrhea and stomach problems, sunscreen, insect repellent, burn ointment, and an elastic bandage.

In your passport, write the names of any people you wish to be contacted in case of a medical **emergency,** and also list any allergies or medical conditions you would want doctors to be aware of. If you wear **glasses** or **contact lenses,** carry extras or arrange to have your doctor or a family member send a replacement pair in an emergency. **Allergy** sufferers should find out if their conditions are likely to be aggravated in the regions they plan to visit, and obtain a full supply of any necessary medication before the trip, since matching a prescription to a foreign equivalent is not always easy, safe, or possible. Carry up-to-date, legible prescriptions or a statement from your doctor, especially if you use insulin, a syringe, or a narcotic. While traveling, be sure to keep all medication with you in carry-on luggage.

Travelers over two years old should check with a doctor to be sure that the following **vaccines** are up to date: Measles, Mumps, and Rubella (MMR); Diptheria, Tetanus, and Pertussis (DTP or DTap); and Hepatitis B (HBV).

For general health info, contact the **American Red Cross (ARC).** The ARC publishes a *First-Aid and Safety Handbook* ($15), available for purchase by calling or writing the American Red Cross, 285 Columbus Ave., Boston, MA 02116-5114 (800-564-1234). The American Red Cross also offers many inexpensive first-aid and CPR courses. Be aware that HIV-positive travelers are not legally allowed into the U.S., but testing is only required of those intending to stay in the country permanently.

Those with **medical conditions** (e.g., diabetes, allergies to antibiotics, epilepsy, heart conditions) may want to obtain a stainless steel **Medic Alert** identification tag ($35 first year, each additional year $15), which identifies the disease and gives a 24-hour info number. Contact Medic Alert at 800-825-3785, or write to Medic Alert Foundation, 2323 Colorado Ave., Turlock, CA 95382. Diabetics can contact the **American Diabetes Association,** 1660 Duke St., Alexandria, VA 22314 (800-232-3472), to receive copies of the article "Travel and Diabetes" and a diabetic ID card.

If you are concerned about being able to access medical support while traveling, contact **Global Emergency Medical Services (GEMS),** 2001 Westside Drive, #120, Alpharetta, GA 30201 (800-860-1111; fax 770-475-0058). They offer products called *MedPasses,* which provide 24-hour international medical assistance through registered nurses who have on-line access to your medical info, your primary physician, and a worldwide network of doctors and hospitals. Subscribers also receive a personal medical record that contains vital info in case of emergencies.

FOOD- AND WATER-BORNE DISEASES

Parasites (tapeworms, etc.) hide in unsafe water and food. *Giardia,* for example, is acquired by drinking untreated water from streams or lakes all over the world, including the U.S. It can stay with you for years. Symptoms of parasitic infections include swollen glands or lymph nodes, fever, rashes or itchiness, digestive problems, eye problems, and anemia.

Hepatitis B is a viral infection of the liver transmitted by sharing needles, having unprotected sex, or coming into direct contact with an infected person's lesioned skin. If you think you may be sexually active while traveling or if you are working or living in rural areas, you are typically advised to get the vaccination for Hepatitis B (see **Before You Go,** p. 12). Vaccination should begin six months before traveling.

Hepatitis C is like Hepatitis B, but it is transmitted more directly through blood-to-blood contact. Doctors are unsure about the level of risk in sexual contact.

ANIMAL- AND INSECT-BIORNE DISEASES

Taking precautionary measures will minimize the chances of contracting a disease while traveling. Avoid animals with open wounds, and beware around dogs which may not have been given **rabies** shots. If you are bitten, be sure to clean your wound thoroughly and seek medical help immediately.

Many diseases are transmitted by insects—mainly mosquitoes, fleas, ticks, and lice. **Mosquitoes** are most active around dusk and dawn. Use **insect repellents;** DEET, which comes in spray or liquid form, should be used sparingly, especially on children. Soak or spray your gear with permethrin, which is licensed in the U.S. for use on clothing. Calamine lotion or topical cortisones (like Cortaid) may stop insect bites from itching, as can a bath with a half-cup of baking soda or oatmeal.

Ticks carry the infamous **Lyme disease,** a bacterial infection marked by a circular bull's-eye rash of two inches or more that appears around the bite. Other symptoms include fever, headache, tiredness, aches, and pains. Antibiotics are effective if administered early. Left untreated, Lyme disease can cause problems in joints, the heart, and the nervous system. Avoid tick bites by wearing long pants, tucked into your socks, and long sleeves (if possible) while hiking, and by using a bednet for camping. Brush off ticks periodically when walking, using a fine-toothed comb on your neck and scalp (they are flat, dark bugs with short legs). If you do find a tick attached to your skin, grasp the tick's head parts with tweezers as close to your skin as possible and apply slow, steady traction. If you remove a tick before it has been attached for more than 24 hours, you greatly reduce your risk of infection. The risk of Lyme is greatest when hiking through the forests of Northern California.

FIRST AID

While you travel, pay attention to the signals of pain and discomfort that your body may send you. Check with the publications and organizations listed above for more complete information or obtain the American Red Cross's *First-Aid and Safety Handbook* ($15) by writing to the **American Red Cross,** 285 Columbus Ave., Boston, MA 02116 (800-564-1234). If you plan to romp in the **forest,** try to learn of any regional hazards. Know that any three-leaved plant might be poison ivy, poison oak, or poison sumac—itchy, pernicious plants. (Remember: "Leaves of three, let it be.")

HOT AND COLD

Common sense goes a long way toward preventing **heat exhaustion:** take it easy in hot weather, drink lots of non-alcoholic fluids, and lie down indoors if you don't feel well. Continuous heat stress can eventually lead to **heatstroke,** characterized by rising body temperature, severe headaches, and cessation of sweating. To avoid heatstroke, wear a hat, sunglasses, and a lightweight longsleeve shirt. Victims should be cooled off with wet towels and taken to a doctor as soon as possible. Always drink enough liquids to keep your urine clear. Alcoholic beverages are dehydrating, as are coffee, strong tea, and caffeinated sodas. If you'll be sweating a lot, be sure to eat enough salty food to prevent electrolyte depletion, which causes severe headaches. Less debilitating, but still dangerous, are **sunburns.** If you're prone to sunburn, bring sunscreen with you, and apply it liberally and frequently. If you get sunburned, drink more fluids than usual.

Extreme cold is just as dangerous as heat—overexposure to cold brings the risk of **hypothermia.** Warning signs are easy to detect: body temperature drops rapidly, resulting in the failure to produce body heat. You may suffer from shivering, poor coordination, slurred speech, exhaustion, hallucinations, or amnesia. *Do not let hypothermia victims fall asleep* if they are in the advanced stages—their body temperature will drop more and if they lose consciousness they may die. Seek medical help as soon as possible. To avoid hypothermia, keep dry and stay out of the wind.

ESSENTIALS

In wet weather, wool and most synthetics will keep you warm while most other fabric, especially cotton, will make you colder. Dress in layers, and watch for **frostbite** when the temperature is below freezing. Look for skin that has turned white, waxy, and cold, and if you find frostbite *do not rub the skin*. Drink warm beverages, get dry, and warm the area *very slowly* with dry fabric or steady body contact.

Travelers to **high altitudes** must allow their bodies a couple of days to adjust to lower oxygen levels in the air before exerting themselves. Also be careful about alcohol; at high altitudes the air has less oxygen and booze will do you in quickly.

WOMEN'S HEALTH

Women traveling in unsanitary conditions are vulnerable to **urinary tract and bladder infections,** common and uncomfortable bacterial diseases which cause a burning sensation and painful, frequent urination. If infected, drink vitamin-C-rich juice and water, and urinate often, especially after intercourse. If symptoms persist, see a doctor; these infections can have serious effects if untreated. Refer to the *Handbook for Women Travellers,* by Maggie and Gemma Moss (published by Piatkus Books) or to the women's health guide *Our Bodies, Our Selves* (published by the Boston Women's Health Collective). For more info, see **Women Travelers,** p. 18.

BIRTH CONTROL

In California and Hawaii, as in most of the U.S., **condoms** can be purchased from nearly all drugstores and pharmacies. Women on the pill should bring enough to allow for possible loss or extended stays, and also their prescription.

Abortion is legal in the U.S. For info about abortions in California or Hawaii, contact the **National Abortion Federation hotline,** 1436 U St. NW, Washington, DC 20009 (800-772-9100; Mon.-Fri. 9:30am-12:30pm and 1:30-5:30pm). For info on contraception, condoms, and abortion worldwide, contact the **International Planned Parenthood Federation,** European Regional Office, Regent's College Inner Circle, Regent's Park, London NW1 4NS (tel. (0171) 487 7900; fax 487 7950).

AIDS, HIV, STDS

Acquired Immune Deficiency Syndrome (AIDS) is a growing problem around the world. The World Health Organization estimates that there are around 13 million people infected with the HIV virus, and California has the second highest caseload in the U.S. The easiest mode of HIV transmission is through direct blood to blood contact with an HIV-positive person; *never* share intravenous drug, tattooing, or other needles. The most common mode of transmission is sexual intercourse. Health professionals recommend the use of latex condoms. Casual contact (like sharing glasses or utensils with an infected person) is not believed to pose a risk.

For more information on AIDS, call the **U.S. Center for Disease Control** (24hr. hotline 800-342-2437). In Europe, write to the **World Health Organization,** attn: Global Program on AIDS, 20 Avenue Appia, 1211 Geneva 27, Switzerland (tel. (022) 791-2111), for statistical material on AIDS internationally. Or write to the **Bureau of Consular Affairs,** #6831, Department of State, Washington, D.C. 20520 (http://travel.state.gov). Council's brochure, *Travel Safe: AIDS and International Travel,* is available at all Council Travel offices.

Sexually transmitted diseases (STDs) such as gonorrhea, chlamydia, genital warts, syphilis, and herpes are a lot easier to catch than HIV, and can be as deadly. Warning signs for STDs include: swelling, itching, redness, sores, bumps, or blisters on sex organs, rectum, or mouth; pain during urination and bowel movements; swelling or redness in the throat, flu-like symptoms with fever, chills, and aches. If symptoms develop, see a doctor immediately. During intercourse, condoms may protect you from some STDs, but oral or tactile contact can lead to transmission.

■ Insurance

Beware of buying unnecessary travel coverage—your regular insurance policies may well extend to many travel-related accidents. **Medical insurance** (especially university policies) often covers costs incurred abroad; check with your provider. Canadians are protected by their home province's health insurance plan for up to 90 days after leaving the country; check with the provincial Ministry of Health or Health Plan Headquarters for details. Australia has Reciprocal Health Care Agreements (RHCAs) with several countries; when traveling in these nations Australians are entitled to many of the services that they would receive at home. The Commonwealth Department of Human Services and Health can provide more info. Your **homeowners' insurance** (or family's coverage) often covers theft during travel. Homeowners are generally covered against loss of travel documents up to $500.

ISIC and **ITIC** provide basic insurance benefits, including $100 per day of in-hospital sickness for a maximum of 60 days, and $3000 of accident-related medical reimbursement (see **Youth, Student, and Teacher Identification,** p. 6). Cardholders have access to a toll-free 24-hour helpline whose multilingual staff can provide assistance in medical, legal, and financial emergencies (800-626-2427 in the U.S. and Canada; elsewhere call the U.S. collect 713-267-2525). **Council** and **STA** offer a range of plans to supplement basic insurance coverage, with options covering medical treatment and hospitalization, accidents, and baggage loss. Most **American Express** cardholders receive automatic car rental (collision and theft, but not liability) insurance and travel accident coverage ($100,000 in life insurance) on flight purchases made with the card; contact customer service (800-528-4800) for details.

Remember that insurance companies usually require a copy of the police report for thefts, or evidence of having paid medical expenses (doctor's statements, receipts) before they will honor a claim and may have time limits on filing for reimbursement. Always carry policy numbers and proof of insurance. Check with each insurance carrier for specific restrictions and policies.

Access America, 6600 West Broad St., P.O. Box 11188, Richmond, VA 23230 (800-284-8300; fax 804-673-1491). Covers trip cancellation, on-the-spot hospital admittance costs, emergency medical evacuation, sickness, and baggage loss. 24hr. hotline (if outside the U.S., call the hotline collect at 804-673-1159 or 800-654-1908).

Avi International, 90 Rue de la Victoire, 75009 Paris, France (tel. (01) 44 63 51 07; fax 40 82 90 35). Caters to the international youth traveler, covering emergency travel expenses, medical/accident, dental, and baggage loss. 24hr. hotline.

The Berkely Group/Carefree Travel Insurance, 100 Garden City Plaza, P.O. Box 9366, Garden City, NY 11530-9366 (800-323-3149). "Visitors from Abroad" program offers accident and medical coverage for foreign nationals visiting the U.S. for a period less than 12 months.

Globalcare Travel Insurance, 220 Broadway, #201, Lynnfield, MA 01940-2376 (800-821-2488; fax 617-592-7720; email global@nebc.mv.com; http://www.nebc.mv.com/globalcare). "Visit USA—Healthcare" covers medical expenses incurred by non-U.S. citizens traveling in the U.S.

Travel Assistance U.S.A., by Worldwide Assistance Services, Inc., 1133 15th St. NW, #400, Washington, D.C. 20005-2710 (800-821-2828 or 202-828-5894; fax 828-5896; email wassist@aol.com). Provides medical coverage for foreign visitors to the U.S. Offers 24hr. free hotline, and medical, travel, and communication assistance.

■ Alternatives to Tourism

STUDY

In order to live the life of a **real American college student,** you might want to consider a visiting student program lasting either a semester or a full year. Contact colleges and universities in your home country to see what kind of exchanges they administer with those in California or Hawaii. A more complicated option is to enroll full-time in an American institution. California is home to a number of outstanding private institutions, such as Stanford and CalTech. The three-tiered state system is among the finest in the country: the **University of California** has nine campuses, **California State University** has 22, and there are numerous community colleges. Unfortunately for non-Californians, these state schools have rather high out-of-state tuition and are extremely popular with residents, who receive priority consideration. The free booklet *Introducing the University of California* gives a quick rundown of the system and individual UC campuses. To order, write to Communication Services, University of California, Office of the President, 300 Lakeside Dr., 17th fl., Oakland, CA 94612-3550 (510-987-9716).

Specializing in marine sciences, tropical agriculture, and Pacific Asian studies, the **University of Hawaii at Manoa** is the principal campus in Hawaii's ten-campus state university system. Write University of Hawaii, Office of Admissions and Records, 2600 Campus Rd., Room 1, Honolulu, HI 96822 (808-956-8975).

Foreign students who wish to study in the United States must apply for either a M-1 visa (vocational studies) or an F-1 visa (for full-time students enrolled in an academic or language program). If English is not your native language, you will probably be required to take the **Test of English as a Foreign Language (TOEFL),** which is administered in many countries. The international students office at the institution you will be attending can give you more specifics. Contact the **TOEFL/TSE Publications,** P.O. Box 6152, Princeton, NJ 08541-6152 (609-771-7100; http://www.toefl.org).

If you want more general information on schools in California and Hawaii, check out your local bookstore for college guides. The *Fiske Guide to Colleges*, by Edward Fiske (NY Times Books, $16), and *Barron's Profiles of American Colleges* ($19) are very useful. If you still can't get enough, try the Internet study abroad website (http://www.studyabroad.com/liteimage.html). Investigate one of the following for specific programs they might have with any university in California or Hawaii:

Council on International Education Exchange, 205 E. 42nd St., New York, NY 10017 (888-COUNCIL/268-6245; fax 212-822-2699; email info@ciee.org; http://www.ciee.org). Sponsors over 40 study abroad programs throughout the world.

Institute of International Education (IIE), 809 United Nations Plaza, New York, NY 10017-3580 (212-984-5413; fax 984-5358). For book orders: IIE Books, Institute of International Education, P.O. Box 371, Annapolis Junction, MD 20701 (800-445-0443; fax 301-206-9789; email iiebooks@pmds.com). A nonprofit international and cultural exchange agency. Publishes *Academic Year Abroad* ($43, $5 postage) and *Vacation Study Abroad* ($37, $5 postage).

International Association for the Exchange of Students for Technical Experience (IAESTE), 10400 Little Patuxent Pkwy., #250, Columbia, MD 21044-3510 (410-997-3068; fax 997-5186; email iaeste@aipt.org; http://www.aipt.org). Operates 8- to 12-week programs in over 50 countries for college students who have completed 2 years of study in a technical field. Non-refundable $50 application fee; apply by Dec. 10 for summer placement.

Peterson's Guides, P.O. Box 2123, Princeton, NJ 08543-2123 (800-338-3282; fax 609-243-9150; http://www.petersons.com). Their comprehensive *Study Abroad* ($30) annual guide lists programs all over the world and provides essential info on study abroad. Their new *Learning Adventures Around the World* ($25) annual guide lists volunteer, museum-hopping, study, and travel programs all over the world. Purchase a copy at your local bookstore or call their toll-free number in the U.S.

WORK

There's no better way to immerse yourself in a foreign culture than to become part of its economy. It's easy to find a **temporary job,** but it will rarely be glamorous and may not even pay for your plane fare, let alone your accommodation. If you are not a U.S. citizen but hope to work there, there are numerous rules which you must be aware of. The place to start getting specific info on visa categories and requirements is your nearest U.S. embassy or consulate (see **Longer Stays**, p. 41). The Council on International Exchange offers a Work and Travel Program and an Internship U.S.A. program for **non-U.S. citizens** wishing to work in the United States. Contact Council for more info (see **Study**, p. 15).

Useful Publications

Vacation Work Publications, 9 Park End St., Oxford OX1 1HJ, U.K. (tel. (01865) 24 19 78; fax 79 08 85). Publishes a wide variety of guides and directories with job listings and info for the working traveler, including *Work Your Way Around the World* (UK£11), and *The Au Pair and Nanny's Guide to Working Abroad* (UK£9). Opportunities for summer or full-time work in numerous countries. Write for a catalogue of their publications.

Uniworld Business Publications, Inc., 257 Central Park West, 10A, New York, NY 10024-4110 (212-496-2448; fax 769-0413; email uniworld@aol.com; http://www.uniworldbp.com). Check your local library for their *Directory of Foreign Firms Operating in the United States* (1995; $200). They also publish regional and country editions of their Directories ($29 and up).

VOLUNTEERING

Volunteer jobs are available throughout California and Hawaii. Some jobs provide room and board in exchange for labor. Listings in Vacation Work Publications's *International Directory of Voluntary Work* (UK£10) can be helpful (see above).

The Archaeological Institute of America, 656 Beacon St., Boston, MA 02215-2010 (617-353-9361; fax 353-6550; email aia@bu.edu; http://csa.brynmawr.edu/web2/aia.html), puts out the Archaeological Fieldwork Opportunities Bulletin (nonmembers $11) which lists over 300 field sites throughout the world. Purchase through Kendall/Hunt Publishing, 4050 Westmark Dr., Dubuque, Iowa 52002 (800-228-0810).

Council on International Education Exchange has a Voluntary Services Dept., 205 E. 42nd St., New York, NY 10017 (888-COUNCIL/268-6245; fax 212-822-2699; email info@ciee.org; http://www.ciee.org), offering 2- to 4-week environmental or community service projects in over 30 countries. Participants must be at least 18 years old. Minimum $295 placement fee; additional fees may also apply.

Volunteers for Peace, 43 Tiffany Rd., Belmont, VT 05730 (802-259-2759; fax 259-2922; email vfp@vfp.org; http://www.vfp.org). A nonprofit organization that arranges speedy placement in 2-3 week work groups of 10-15 people. VFP offers over 1000 programs in 70 countries. The annual *International Workcamp Directory* ($15) is a complete listing. Registration fee $200. Some work camps are open to 16 and 17 year olds for $225. Free newsletter.

Willing Workers on Organic Farms (WWOOF), Postfach 59, CH-8124, Maur, Switzerland (email wwoof@dataway.ch), and 50 Hans Crescent, London SW1X ONA, England (tel. (0171) 823-9937). Provides a list of names of organic farmers who offer room and board in exchange for help on the farm. Include 2 international postal reply coupons with your request or contact them by email.

Service Civil International Voluntary Service (SCI-VS), 5474 Walnut Level Rd., Crozet, VA 22932 (804-823-1826; fax 823-5027; email sciivsusa@igc.apc.org). Arranges work in North America (ages 16-18). Local organizations sponsor groups for physical or social work. Registration $50-250.

USDA Forest Service, Southwest Region, Human Resources, 630 Sansome St., San Francisco, CA 94111 (415-705-1032). If you're into fresh air and sublime scenery, consider working for the **National Forest Service.** Positions differ depending on location.

ESSENTIALS

■ Specific Concerns

TRAVELING ALONE

There are many benefits to traveling alone, among them greater independence and challenge. As a lone traveler, you have better opportunity to meet and interact with natives. On the other hand, you may also be a more visible target for robbery and harassment. Lone travelers need to be well-organized and look confident at all times. Try not to stand out as a tourist, and if questioned, never admit that you are traveling alone. Maintain regular contact with someone at home who knows your itinerary. If the drawbacks sound too daunting, the following publications may be helpful:

Connecting: News for Solo Travelers, P.O. Box 29088, 1996 W. Broadway, Vancouver, BC V6J 5C2, Canada (604-737-7791 or 800-557-1757). Bi-monthly newsletter has feature articles and listings of singles looking for travel companions. Annual directory lists tours and lodgings with reduced or no single supplement; subscription $25.

A Foxy Old Woman's Guide to Traveling Alone, by Jay Ben-Lesser, encompasses a wide range of specific concerns and offers anecdotes and tips concerning solitary adventure. Available in bookstores and from Crossing Press in Freedom, CA (800-777-1048). $11.

Roadrunner Hostelling Treks, 6762 A Centinela Ave., Culver City, CA 90230 (310-390-7495 or 800-873-5872). Inexpensive guided trips (maximum 13 travelers). Hostelling International accommodations.

The Single Traveler Newsletter, P.O. Box 682, Ross, CA 94957 (415-389-0227). Bi-monthly newsletter with good tips on avoiding single-supplement fees. Subscription $29.

Travel Companions, P.O. Box 833, Amityville, NY 11701 (516-454-0880). Monthly newsletter with listings and helpful tips. Subscription $48.

Traveling On Your Own, by Eleanor Berman ($13). Lists info resources for "singles" (old and young) and single parents. Crown Publishers, Inc., 201 East 50th St., New York, NY 10022

Travelin' Woman, 855 Moraga Dr., #14, Los Angeles, CA 90049 (310-472-6318 or 800-871-6409). Monthly newsletter with news and tips. Subscription $48.

WOMEN TRAVELERS

Women exploring on their own inevitably face additional safety concerns. Trust your instincts—if you'd feel better somewhere else, move on. Always carry extra money for a phone call, bus, or taxi. You might consider staying in hostels which offer single rooms that lock from the inside or in religious organizations that offer rooms for women only. Communal showers in some hostels are safer than others; check them before settling in. Stick to centrally located lodgings and avoid solitary late-night treks or metro rides. Women should never **hitchhike** alone; even a group of women can be in danger. Choose train compartments occupied by other women or couples. When in a foreign country, the less you look like a tourist, the better. Look as if you know where you're going (even when you don't) and consider approaching women or couples for directions if you're lost or feel uncomfortable.

If you spend time in cities, you may be harassed no matter how you're dressed. Your best answer to harassment is no answer at all. Feigning deafness, sitting motionless, and staring at the ground will do more good than having a loud and assertive reaction. The extremely persistent can sometimes be dissuaded by a firm, loud, and very public "Go away!"

Don't hesitate to seek out a police officer or a passerby if you are being harassed. *Let's Go* lists emergency numbers (including rape crisis lines) in the **Practical Information** listings of most cities. In an **emergency,** call **911 toll-free** from anywhere in the U.S. Carry a **whistle** or an airhorn on your keychain, and don't hesitate to use it in an emergency. A **Model Mugging** course will not only prepare you for a potential mugging, but will also raise your awareness of your surroundings as well as your confidence (see **Safety and Security,** p. 10). Women also face additional health concerns when traveling (see **Women's Health,** p. 14).

For general information, contact the **National Organization for Women (NOW),** which has branches across the country that can refer women travelers to rape crisis centers and counseling services, and provide lists of feminist events. Main offices include 22 W. 21st St., 7th fl., **New York,** NY 10010 (212-260-4422); 1000 16th St. NW, 7th fl., **Washington, D.C.** 20004 (202-331-0066); and 3543 18th St., **San Francisco,** CA 94110 (415-861-8960; fax 861-8969; email sfnow@sirius.com; http://www.sirius.com/~sfnow/now.html).

Handbook For Women Travellers, by Maggie and Gemma Moss (UK£9). Encyclopedic and well-written. Available from Piatkus Books, 5 Windmill St., London W1P 1HF (tel. (0171) 631 07 10).

A Journey of One's Own, by Thalia Zepatos, ($17). Interesting and full of good advice, with a bibliography of books and resources. **Adventures in Good Company,** on group travel by the same author, costs $17. Available from The Eighth Mountain Press, 624 Southeast 29th Ave., Portland, OR 97214 (503-233-3936; fax 233-0774; email eightmt@aol.com).

Women's Travel in Your Pocket, Ferrari Guides, P.O. Box 37887, Phoenix, AZ 85069 (602-863-2408), an annual guide for women (especially lesbians) traveling in the U.S., Canada, the Caribbean, and Mexico ($14, plus shipping).

Women Going Places is a women's travel and resource guide geared towards lesbians which emphasizes women-owned enterprises. Advice appropriate for all women. $15 from Inland Book Company, 1436 W. Randolph St. Chicago, IL 60607 (800-243-0138; fax 800-334-3892), or a local bookstore.

A Foxy Old Woman's Guide to Traveling Alone, by Jay Ben-Lesser. See **Traveling Alone,** p. 18.

TRAVELERS WITH CHILDREN

California and Hawaii offer many activities tailored to **kids,** from Disneyland and Raging Waters Park to gentle hiking trails and wave-free beaches. Be careful when you're organizing a trip, though—family vacations are recipes for disaster, unless you slow your pace and plan ahead a bit. When deciding where to stay, remember the special needs of young children; if you pick a B&B, call ahead and make sure it's child-friendly. If you rent a car, make sure the rental company provides a car seat for younger children. Consult local newspapers or travel bureaus to find out about events that might be of special interest for young children. Be sure that your child carries some sort of ID in case of an emergency or if he or she gets lost, and arrange a reunion spot in case of separation when sight-seeing.

Restaurants often have children's menus and discounts. Virtually all museums and tourist attractions also have a children's rate. Children under two generally fly for 10% of the adult airfare on international flights (this does not necessarily include a seat). International fares are usually discounted 25% for children ages 2-11.

Some of the following publications offer tips for adults traveling with children or fun traveling distractions for the kids themselves. You can also contact the publishers to see if they have other related publications that you might find useful.

Backpacking with Babies and Small Children ($10). Published by Wilderness Press, 2440 Bancroft Way, Berkeley, CA 94704 (800-443-7227 or 510-843-8080; fax 548-1355; email wpress@ix.netcom.com).

Kidding Around books ($8, postage under $5). Illustrated books for children about cities across the U.S. Educational (and distracting) books that could prove invaluable for keeping little ones happy on long trips. Published by John Muir Publications, P.O. Box 613, Santa Fe, NM 87504 (800-285-4078; fax 505-988-1680; contact Kathleen Chambers).

Travel with Children, by Maureen Wheeler ($12, postage $1.50). Published by Lonely Planet Publications, Embarcadero West, 155 Filbert St., #251, Oakland, CA

ESSENTIALS

94607 (800-275-8555 or 510-893-8555; fax 893-8563; email info@lonely-planet.com; http://www.lonelyplanet.com). Also at P.O. Box 617, Hawthorn, Victoria 3122, Australia.

BISEXUAL, GAY, AND LESBIAN TRAVELERS

Prejudice against gays and lesbians is still very much a reality in many areas of California and Hawaii, as evidenced by the recent legal battles over same-sex marriage (though it is now officially legal in Hawaii, the case is under appeal). Public display of affection between same-sex couples is illegal in Nevada. And although neither California nor Hawaii have laws against homosexuality per se, homophobia may be a problem for the openly gay or lesbian traveler, particularly in rural areas. However, many cities (most notably San Francisco and L.A.) have large and active queer communities. Wherever possible, *Let's Go* lists local gay and lesbian info lines and community centers. The following organizations and publishing houses also offer info and resources for the gay and lesbian traveler.

Damron Travel Guides, P.O. Box 422458, San Francisco, CA 94142 (415-255-0404 or 800-462-6654; fax 415-703-9049; email damronco@ud.com; http://www.damron.co). Publishes queer-oriented travel guides such as the *Damron Road Atlas* ($16), which contains color maps of 56 major North American and European cities and gay and lesbian resorts and listings of bars and accommodations. Mail order is available for an extra $5 shipping.

Ferrari Guides, P.O. Box 37887, Phoenix, AZ 85069 (602-863-2408; fax 439-3952; email ferrari@q-net.com; http://www.q-net.com). Gay and lesbian travel guides like *Ferrari Guides' Gay Travel A to Z* ($16). Available in bookstores or by mail order (postage/handling $4.50 for the first item, each additional item $1 within the U.S. Overseas, call or write for shipping cost).

Gayellow Pages, P.O. Box 533, Village Station, New York, NY 10014 (212-674-0120; fax 420-1126; email gayellow_pages@juno.com; http://gayellow-pages.com). An annually updated listing of accommodations, resorts, hotlines, and other items of interest to the gay traveler. U.S./Canada edition $16.

Giovanni's Room, 345 S. 12th St., Philadelphia, PA 19107 (215-923-2960; fax 923-0813; email giolphilp@netaxs.com). An international feminist, lesbian, and gay bookstore with mail-order service; carries many of the publications listed here.

International Gay and Lesbian Travel Association, P.O. Box 4974, Key West, FL 33041 (800-448-8550; fax 305-296-6633; email IGTA@aol.com; http://www.rainbow-mall.com/igta). Organization of over 1300 companies serving gay and lesbian travelers worldwide. Call for travel agents, accommodations, and events.

Spartacus International Gay Guides ($33), published by Bruno Gmunder, Postfach 61 01 04, D-10921 Berlin, Germany (tel. (30) 615 00 3-42; fax (30) 615 91 34). Lists bars, restaurants, hotels, and bookstores around the world catering to gay people. Also lists hotlines and homosexuality laws for various countries. Available in bookstores and in the U.S. by mail from Lambda Rising, 1625 Connecticut Ave. NW, Washington D.C., 20009-1013 (202-462-6969).

Women Going Places (Inland Books, $14). See **Women Travelers,** p. 18.

MINORITY TRAVELERS

Both California and Hawaii are extremely diverse states, and unfortunately not totally harmonious. Though "minority" groups are quickly becoming the majority in California, the state as a whole has a strong anti-immigrant feeling, aimed at Mexican people in particular (or anyone who looks as if they could be Mexican). The best advice for the traveler in either state is to simply be aware of the racial tensions which do exist, and to try to avoid confrontations.

OLDER TRAVELERS

The U.S. is a great place for senior citizens to travel in. Senior citizens are eligible for many discounts; if you don't see a senior citizen price listed, ask and you may be delightfully surprised. Proof of age is usually required (see **Parks and Forests,** p. 47, for info on free park entry).

Walking the World, P.O. Box 1186, Fort Collins, CO 80522 (970-225-0500; fax 225-9100; email walktworld@aol.com). Arranges group travel in North America.

American Association of Retired Persons (AARP), 601 E. St. NW, Washington, D.C. 20049 (202-434-2277). Members 50 and over receive benefits and services including the AARP Motoring Plan from AMOCO (800-334-3300), and discounts on lodging, car rental, cruises, and sight-seeing. Annual fee $8 per couple; 3yr. $20; lifetime membership $75.

Elderhostel, 75 Federal St., 3rd fl., Boston, MA 02110-1941 (617-426-7788; fax 426-8351; email Cadyg@elderhostel.org; http://www.elderhostel.org). For those 55 or over (spouse of any age). Programs at colleges, universities, and other learning centers in over 70 countries on varied subjects lasting 1-4 weeks.

National Council of Senior Citizens, 8403 Colesville Rd., Silver Spring, MD 20910-31200 (301-578-8800; fax 578-8999). Memberships cost $13 per year, $33 for 3 years, or $175 for a lifetime. Individuals or couples can receive hotel and auto rental discounts, a senior citizen newspaper, and use of a discount travel agency.

No Problem! Worldwise Tips for Mature Adventurers, by Janice Kenyon. Advice and info on insurance, finances, security, health, and packing. Useful appendices. $16 from Orca Book Publishers, P.O. Box 468, Custer, WA 98240-0468.

Unbelievably Good Deals and Great Adventures That You Absolutely Can't Get Unless You're Over 50, by Joan Rattner Heilman. After you finish reading the title page, check inside for some great tips on senior discounts. $10 from Contemporary Books.

DISABLED TRAVELERS

Planning a trip presents extra challenges to individuals with disabilities, but the difficulties are by no means insurmountable. Fortunately, California and Hawaii are two of the most disabled-friendly places in the world: many places even provide discounts to people with disabilities. National law in the U.S. mandates that hotels and restaurants be wheelchair-accessible; *Let's Go* notes exceptions.

If you research areas ahead of time, your trip will go more smoothly. Call ahead to restaurants, hotels, parks, and other facilities to find out about the existence of ramps, the widths of doors, the dimensions of elevators, etc. For info on transportation in individual U.S. cities, contact the local chapter of the Easter Seals Society; state or local tourist offices may also have info for handicapped travelers.

Hertz, Avis, and National **car rental agencies** have hand-controlled vehicles at some locations; be sure to give them sufficient notice. In the U.S., both **Amtrak** and major airlines will accommodate disabled passengers if notified at least 72 hours in advance. Hearing-impaired travelers may contact Amtrak using teletype printers (800-872-7245, in PA. 800-322-9537). **Greyhound** buses will provide free travel for a companion; if you are without a fellow traveler, call Greyhound (800-752-4841), at least 48 hours, but no more than one week, before you plan to leave and they will make arrangements to assist you. See **Parks and Forests,** p. 47, for discounts on park entry.

The following organizations provide useful info or publications:

American Foundation for the Blind, 11 Penn Plaza, #300, New York, NY 10011 (212-502-7600). Provides information and services for the visually impaired (open Mon.-Fri. 8:30am-4:30pm). For a catalogue of products, contact Lighthouse Enterprises, 36-20 Northern Boulevard, Long Island City, NY 10011 (800-829-0500).

Facts on File, 11 Penn Plaza, 15th fl., New York, NY 10001 (212-967-8800). Publishers of *Disability Resource,* a reference guide for travelers with disabilities ($45 plus shipping). Available at bookstores or by mail order.

Mobility International, USA (MIUSA), P.O. Box 10767, Eugene, OR 97440 (514-343-1284 voice and TDD; fax 343-6812; email info@miusa.org; http://miusa.org). International Headquarters in Brussels, Rue de Manchester 25 Brussels, Belgium,

B-1070 (tel. (322) 410-6297, fax 410-6874). Contacts in 30 countries. Info on travel programs, international work camps, accommodations, access guides, and organized tours for disabled travelers. Membership $30 per year. Sells the 3rd Edition of *A World of Options: A Guide to International Educational Exchange, Community Service, and Travel for Persons with Disabilities* ($30, nonmembers $35; organizations $40).

Society for the Advancement of Travel for the Handicapped (SATH), 347 Fifth Ave., #610, New York, NY 10016 (212-447-1928; fax 725-8253; email sath-travel@aol.com; http://www.sath.org). Publishes the quarterly color travel magazine *OPEN WORLD* (free for members, or by subscription $13 for nonmembers). Also publishes a wide range of info sheets on disability travel facilitation and accessible destinations. Annual membership $45, students and seniors $30.

Twin Peaks Press, P.O. Box 129, Vancouver, WA 98666-0129 (360-694-2462, MasterCard and Visa orders 800-637-2256; fax 696-3210; email 73743.2634@compuserve.com; http://netm.com/mall/infoprod/twinpeak/helen.htm). Publishers of *Travel for the Disabled,* which provides travel tips, lists of accessible tourist attractions, and advice on other resources for disabled travelers ($20). Also publishes *Directory for Travel Agencies of the Disabled* ($20), *Wheelchair Vagabond* ($15), and *Directory of Accessible Van Rentals* ($10). Postage $3.50 for first book, each additional book $1.50.

The following organizations arrange tours or trips for disabled travelers:

Flying Wheels Travel Service, 143 W. Bridge St., Owatonne, MN 55060 (800-535-6790; fax 451-1685). Arranges trips for groups and individuals in wheelchairs or with other sorts of limited mobility.

The Guided Tour Inc., Elkins Park House, 114B, 7900 Old York Rd., Elkins Park, PA 19027-2339 (800-783-5841 or 215-782-1370; fax 635-2637). Organizes travel programs for persons with developmental and physical challenges and those requiring renal dialysis. Call, fax, or write for a free brochure.

DIETARY CONCERNS

No matter what kind of dietary restrictions you observe, you should be able to find sustenance in California and Hawaii, two of the most diverse and liberal states in the U.S. **Vegetarians** in particular should have no problem finding suitable cuisine; most restaurants have vegetarian selections on their menus, and some cater specifically to herbivores. **Vegans** will find fewer hassles traveling in California than elsewhere. Services in many college towns offer meat- and dairy-free entrees in restaurants as well as "cruelty-free" products in shops.

Travelers who keep **kosher** should contact synagogues in larger cities for info on kosher restaurants; your own synagogue or college Hillel should have access to lists of Jewish institutions. If you are strict in your observance, consider preparing your own food on the road. **The Jewish Travel Guide** lists synagogues, kosher restaurants, and Jewish institutions worldwide. Available from Ballantine-Mitchell Publishers, Newbury House 890-900, Eastern Ave., Newbury Park, Ilford, Essex, U.K. IG2 7HH (tel. (0181) 599 88 66; fax 599 09 84), or in the U.S. from Sepher-Hermon Press, 1265 46th St., Brooklyn, NY 11219 (718-972-9010; $15 plus $2.50 shipping).

Contact the following organizations for more info:

North American Vegetarian Society, P.O. Box 72, Dolgeville, NY 13329 (518-568-7970), publishes *Transformative Adventures,* a guide to vacations and retreats ($15), and the *Vegetarian Journal's Guide to Natural Food Restaurants in the U.S. and Canada* ($12). Membership $20; family membership $26. Members receive a 10% discount on all publications.

The International Vegetarian Travel Guide (UK£2), was last published in 1991. Order back copies from the Vegetarian Society of the U.K. (VSUK), Parkdale, Dunham Rd., Altringham, Cheshire WA14 4QG (tel. (0161) 928 0793). VSUK also publishes other titles; call or send a self-addressed, stamped envelope for a listing.

■ Packing

If you want to get away from it all, don't take it all with you.

The more you know, the less you need, so plan your packing according to the type of travel (multi-city backpacking tour, week-long stay in one place, etc.), and the high and low temperatures in the area you will be visiting (see climate charts in the **appendix,** p. 509). The more things you have, the more you have to lose, and the larger your pack, the more cumbersome it is to store and carry. Before you leave, pack your bag, strap it on, and imagine yourself walking uphill on hot asphalt for the next three hours. **A good general rule is to lay out only what you absolutely need, then take half the clothes and twice the money.**

LUGGAGE

Backpack: If you plan to cover most of your itinerary by foot, a sturdy backpack is unbeatable. See **Camping and Hiking Equipment,** p. 45, for more info.

Suitcase or trunk: Fine if you plan to live in 1 or 2 cities and explore from there, but a bad idea if you're going to be moving around a lot. Make sure it has wheels and consider how much it weighs even when empty. Hard-sided luggage is more durable but heavier; soft-sided luggage should be durably built and lined.

Daypack, rucksack, or courier bag: Bringing a smaller bag in addition to your pack or suitcase allows you to leave your big bag behind while you go sight-seeing. It can also be used as an airplane carry-on to keep essentials with you.

Moneybelt or neck pouch: Guard your money, passport, railpass, and other important articles in either one of these, available at any good camping store, and keep it with you *at all times.* The moneybelt should tuck inside the waist of your pants or skirt. See **Safety and Security,** p. 11, for more info on protecting valuables.

CLOTHING AND FOOTWEAR

Clothing: When choosing your travel wardrobe, aim for versatility and comfort, and avoid fabrics that wrinkle easily. Solid colors match and mix best. Always bring a jacket or wool sweater, as even California and Hawaii get chilly in the mountains and along windy beaches.

Walking shoes: Well-cushioned **sneakers** are good for walking, though you may want to consider a good water-proofed pair of **hiking boots.** Bring a pair of flip-flops for protection in the shower. Talcum powder in your shoes and on your feet can prevent sores, and moleskin is great for blisters.

Rain gear: A waterproof jacket and a backpack cover will cover you and your stuff at a moment's notice. Gore-Tex® is a miracle fabric, both waterproof and breathable.

For more info on outdoor clothing, see **Camping and Hiking Equipment,** p. 45.

MISCELLANEOUS

Sleepsacks: If you plan to stay in **youth hostels,** don't pay the linen charge—make the requisite sleepsack yourself. Fold a full-size sheet in half the long way, then sew it closed along the open long side and one of the short sides. Sleepsacks can also be bought at any HI outlet store.

Contact lenses: Machines which heat-disinfect contact lenses will require a small converter (about $20) if you are visiting the U.S. from an area with a different current. Consider switching temporarily to a chemical disinfection system if it's safe for your lenses. Bring a backup pair of glasses in addition.

Washing clothes: *Let's Go* attempts to provide info on laundromats in the **Practical Information** listings for each city, but sometimes it may be easiest to use a sink. Bring a small bar or tube of detergent soap, a rubber squash ball to stop up the sink, and a travel clothes line.

Electric current: In most European countries, electricity is 220 volts AC, not compatible with the 110V North American current. Visit a hardware store for an adapter (which changes the shape of the plug) and a converter (which changes the voltage). Don't make the mistake of using only an adapter (unless appliance instructions explicitly state otherwise), or you'll melt your radio.

Film: It's expensive just about everywhere. If you're not a serious photographer, you might want to consider bringing a **disposable camera** or two rather than an expensive permanent one. Despite disclaimers, airport security X-rays *can* fog film, so either buy a lead-lined pouch, sold at camera stores, or ask the security to hand inspect it. Always pack it in your carry-on luggage, since higher-intensity X-rays are used on checked luggage.

Other useful items: First-aid kit; umbrella; sealable plastic bags (for damp clothes, soap, food, shampoo, and other spillables); alarm clock; waterproof matches; sun hat; moleskin (for blisters); needle and thread; safety pins; sunglasses; a personal stereo (Walkman) with headphones; pocketknife; plastic water bottle; compass; string (makeshift clothesline and lashing material); towel; padlock; whistle; rubber bands; toilet paper; flashlight; cold-water soap; earplugs; insect repellant; electrical tape (for patching tears); clothespins; maps and guidebooks; tweezers; garbage bags; sunscreen; vitamins.

GETTING THERE AND GETTING AROUND

■ Budget Travel Agencies

Students and people under 26 ("youth") with proper ID qualify for reduced airfares. These are rarely available from airlines or travel agents, but instead from student travel agencies which negotiate special reduced-rate bulk purchase with the airlines, then resell them to the youth market. Return-date change fees also tend to be low (around $35 per segment through Council or Let's Go Travel). Most flights are on major airlines, though in peak season some agencies may sell seats on less reliable chartered aircraft. Student travel agencies can also help non-students and people over 26, but probably won't be able to get the same low fares.

Council Travel (http://www.ciee.org/travel/index.htm), the travel division of Council on International Education Exchange, is a full-service travel agency specializing in youth and budget travel. They offer discount airfares on scheduled airlines, railpasses, hosteling cards, low-cost accommodations, guidebooks, budget tours, travel gear, and international student (ISIC), youth (GO25), and teacher (ITIC) identity cards. U.S. offices include: Emory Village, 1561 N. Decatur Rd., **Atlanta,** GA 30307 (404-377-9997); 2000 Guadalupe, **Austin,** TX 78705 (512-472-4931); 273 Newbury St., **Boston,** MA 02116 (617-266-1926); 1138 13th St., **Boulder,** CO 80302 (303-447-8101); 1153 N. Dearborn, **Chicago,** IL 60610 (312-951-0585); 10904 Lindbrook Dr., **Los Angeles,** CA 90024 (310-208-3551); 1501 University Ave. SE, #300, **Minneapolis,** MN 55414 (612-379-2323); 205 E. 42nd St., **New York,** NY 10017 (212-822-2700); 953 Garnet Ave., **San Diego,** CA 92109 (619-270-6401); 530 Bush St., **San Francisco,** CA 94108 (415-421-3473); 1314 NE 43rd St., #210, **Seattle,** WA 98105 (206-632-2448); 3300 M St. NW, **Washington, D.C.** 20007 (202-337-6464). For **U.S. cities not listed,** call 800-2-COUNCIL/226-8624. Also at 28A Poland St. (Oxford Circus), **London,** W1V 3DB (tel. (0171) 287 3337), **Paris** (146 55 55 65), and **Munich** (089 39 50 22).

STA Travel, 6560 Scottsdale Rd., #F100, Scottsdale, AZ 85253 (800-777-0112; fax 602-922-0793; http://sta-travel.com). A student and youth travel organization offering discount airfares, railpasses, accommodations, tours, insurance, and ISICs. Offices in the U.S. include: 297 Newbury Street, **Boston,** MA 02115 (617-266-6014); 429 S. Dearborn St., **Chicago,** IL 60605 (312-786-9050); 7202 Melrose Ave., **Los Angeles,** CA 90046 (213-934-8722); 10 Downing St., Room G, **New York,** NY 10003 (212-627-3111); 4341 University Way NE, **Seattle,** WA 98105 (206-633-5000); 2401 Pennsylvania Ave., **Washington, D.C.** 20037 (202-887-0912); 51 Grant Ave., **San Francisco,** CA 94108 (415-391-8407); and in **Miami** (305-461-3444). In the U.K., 6 Wrights Ln., **London** W8 6TA (tel. (0171) 938 47

11). In New Zealand, 10 High St., **Auckland** (tel. (09) 309 97 23). In Australia, 222 Faraday St., **Melbourne** VIC 3050 (tel. (03) 9349 69 11).

Let's Go Travel, Harvard Student Agencies, 17 Holyoke St., Cambridge, MA 02138 (617-495-9649; fax 495-7956; email travel@hsa.net; http://hsa.net/travel). Railpasses, HI-AYH memberships, ISICs, ITICs, FIYTO cards, guidebooks (including *Let's Go*), maps, bargain flights, and a complete line of budget travel gear. All items available by mail; call or write for a catalogue (or see the catalogue in center of this publication).

Campus Travel, 52 Grosvenor Gardens, London SW1W 0AG (http://www.campustravel.co.uk). Forty-six branches in the U.K. Student and youth fares on plane, train, boat, and bus travel. Skytrekker, flexible airline tickets. Discount and ID cards for students and youths, travel insurance for students and those under 35, maps, and guides. Puts out travel suggestion booklets. Telephone booking service: in Europe (0171) 730 34 02; in North America (0171) 730 21 01; worldwide (0171) 730 81 11; in Manchester (0161) 273 17 21; in Scotland (0131) 668 33 03.

Journeys International, Inc., 4011 Jackson Rd., Ann Arbor, MI 48103 (800-255-8735; fax 313-665-2945; email info@journeys-intl.com; http://www.journeys-intl.com). Offers small-group, guided explorations. Call or email to obtain their free 74-page color catalogue, *The Global Expedition Catalogue.*

Travel CUTS (Canadian Universities Travel Services Limited), 187 College St., Toronto, ON, M5T 1P7 (416-979-2406; fax 979-8167; email mail@travelcuts). Canada's national student travel bureau is the equivalent of Council, with 40 offices across Canada. Also in the U.K., 295-A Regent St., **London** W1R 7YA (tel. (0171) 637 31 61). Discounted airfares open to all; special student fares to all destinations with valid ISIC. Issues ISIC, FIYTO, GO25, and HI-AYH hostel cards, as well as railpasses. Offers free *Student Traveller* magazine and info on the Student Work Abroad Program (SWAP).

Usit Youth and Student Travel, 19-21 Aston Quay, O'Connell Bridge, Dublin 2 (tel. (01) 677-8117; fax 679-8833). In the U.S.: New York Student Center, 895 Amsterdam Ave., New York, NY 10025 (212-663-5435; email usitny@aol.com). Additional offices in Cork, Galway, Limerick, Waterford, Maynooth, Coleraine, Derry, Athlone, Jordanstown, Belfast, and Greece. Specializes in youth and student travel. Offers low-cost tickets and flexible travel arrangements all over the world. Supplies ISIC and FIYTO-GO25 cards in Ireland only.

■ By Plane

The **airline industry** attempts to squeeze every dollar from customers; finding a cheap airfare will be easier if you understand the system. Call every toll-free number and don't be afraid to ask about discounts; if you don't ask, it's unlikely they'll be volunteered. Have knowledgeable **travel agents** guide you; better yet, have an agent who specializes in your destination guide you. Travel agents may not want to spend time finding the cheapest fares (for which they receive the lowest commissions), but if you travel often, you should definitely find an agent who will cater to your needs, and track down deals in exchange for your frequent business.

Students and others under 26 should never need to pay full price for a ticket. **Seniors** can also get great deals: many airlines offer senior traveler clubs or airline passes with few restrictions and discounts for their companions as well. Sunday newspapers often have travel sections that list bargain fares from the local airport. Outsmart airline reps with the phone-book-sized *Official Airline Guide* (check your local library; at $359 per year (with fares, $479), the tome costs as much as some flights), a monthly guide listing nearly every scheduled flight in the world, and toll-free phone numbers for all the airlines which allow you to call in reservations directly. More accessible is Michael McColl's *The Worldwide Guide to Cheap Airfare* ($15), an incredibly useful guide for finding cheap airfares.

There is also a steadily increasing amount of travel info to be found on the **Internet.** The *Official Airline Guide* has a website (http://www.oag.com), which allows access to flight schedules. (One-time hookup fee $25 and user's fee of $17-47 per min.). The **Air Traveler's Handbook** (http://www.cis.ohio-state.edu/hypertext/

ESSENTIALS

faq/usenet/travel/air/handbook/top.html), is an excellent source of general info on air travel. Marc-David Seidel's **Airlines of the Web** (http://www.itn.net/airlines), provides links to pages for most of the world's airlines.

Most airfares peak between mid-June and early September. Midweek (Mon.-Thurs. morning) round-trip flights run about $40-50 cheaper than on weekends; weekend flights, however, are generally less crowded. Traveling from hub to hub (for example, Los Angeles to Sydney) will win a more competitive fare than from smaller cities. Return-date flexibility is usually not an option for the budget traveler; traveling with an "open return" ticket can be pricier than fixing a return date and paying to change it. Whenever flying internationally, pick up your ticket well in advance of the departure date, have the flight confirmed within 72 hours of departure, and arrive at the airport at least three hours before your flight.

COMMERCIAL AIRLINES

When dealing with any commercial airline, buying in advance is best. Periodic **price wars** may lower prices in spring and early summer months, but they are unpredictable; don't delay your purchase in hopes of catching one. To obtain the cheapest fare, buy a round-trip ticket, stay over at least one Saturday, and travel on off-peak days (Mon.-Thurs. morning) and off-peak hours (overnight **"red-eye"** flights can be cheaper and faster than primetime). Chances of receiving discount fares increase on competitive routes. Fees for changing flight dates range from $25 (for some domestic flights) to $150 (for many international flights). Most airlines allow children under two to fly free (on the lap of an adult).

Since travel peaks June to August and around holidays, reserve a seat several months in advance for these times. Call the airline the day before your departure to confirm your flight reservation, and get to the airport early to ensure you have a seat; airlines often overbook. (Of course, being "bumped" from a flight doesn't spell doom if your travel plans are flexible—you will probably leave on the next flight

and receive a free ticket or cash bonus. If you would like to be bumped to win a free ticket, check in early and let the airline officials know.)

The following programs, services, and fares may be helpful for planning a reasonably-priced airtrip, but always be wary of deals that seem too good to be true:

APEX (Advance Purchase Excursion Fare): The commercial carriers' lowest regular offer; specials advertised in newspapers may be cheaper, but have more restrictions and fewer seats. APEX fares provide you with confirmed reservations and often allow "open-jaw" tickets (landing and returning from different cities). Generally, reservations must be made seven to 21 days in advance, with seven- to 14-day minimum and up to 90-day maximum stay limits, and hefty cancellation and change penalties (fees rise in summer). Look into flights to less-popular destinations or on smaller carriers. For the adventurous or the bargain-hungry, there are other, perhaps more inconvenient or time-consuming options, but before shopping around it is a good idea to find out the average commercial price in order to measure just how great a "bargain" you are being offered.

Frequent-flyer tickets: It is not wise to buy frequent-flyer tickets from other people, as most airlines now check photo ID before boarding. If you have a frequent-flyer account, make sure you're getting credit when you check in.

Air Passes: Many major U.S. airlines offer special **Visit USA** air passes and fares to international travelers. You must purchase these passes outside of North America, paying one price for a certain number of flight vouchers. Each voucher is good for one flight on an airline's domestic system; typically, all travel must be completed within 30-60 days. The point of departure and destination for each coupon must be specified at the time of purchase, and once in the U.S., changes carry a $50-$75 fee. Dates of travel may be changed once travel has begun, usually at no extra charge. **US Airways** offers on-line packages (anywhere that US Airways travels) from $309. **United, Continental, Delta,** and **TWA** sell vouchers as well. TWA's **Youth Travel Pak** offers a similar deal to students ages 14-24, including North Americans. Available only to travelers who are not citizens in any North American country, **Canadian Regional Airlines** and its affiliate **Horizon Air** (England office 1737-55 53 00; fax 1737-55 53 00; email airpass@aol.com), offer 1-, 2-, and 3-week unlimited flight air passes for the Western U.S. (1-week AirPass UK£139, 2-week UK£175, 3-week UK£259).

Days of the Week

While round-trip tickets may be cheaper during the week than on weekends, they also mean crowded flights, which in turn means competition for frequent-flier upgrades. Scheduling weekend flights is more expensive, but less crowded, and proves the best bet for using frequent-flier upgrades. Most business travelers travel on Thursdays, which makes stiff competition for upgrade hunters. Saturdays and Sundays present the best opportunities for frequent fliers.

TICKET CONSOLIDATORS

Ticket consolidators sell unbooked commercial and charter airline seats for very low prices, but deals include some risks. Tickets are sold on a space-available basis which does not guarantee you a seat; the earlier you arrive at the airport the better. Consolidators tend to be more reliable on domestic flights, both in getting you on the flight and in getting you exactly where you want to go. This may be a good route to take if you are traveling: on short notice (you bypass advance purchase requirements, since you aren't tangled in airline bureaucracy); on a high-priced trip; to an offbeat destination; or in the peak season, when published fares are jacked way up. Before committing, contact the local Better Business Bureau to find out your company's track record. Get the company's policy in writing: insist on a receipt that gives full details about the tickets, refunds, and restrictions, and record who you talked to and when. Kelly Monaghan's **Consolidators: Air Travel's Bargain Basement** ($7 plus $2 shipping) from the Intrepid Traveler, P.O. Box 438, New York,

NY 10034 (email intreptrav@aol.com), is an invaluable source for more info and lists of consolidators by location and destination.

Cheap Tickets, 6151 West Century Blvd., #100, Los Angeles, CA 90045 (800-377-1000 or 310-645-5054). Additional offices in San Francisco (415-588-3700), Honolulu (808-947-3717), New York City (212-570-1179), Fullerton, CA (714-229-0131), and Seattle (206-467-7979).

Mr. Cheap's Travel, 9123 SE St. Helen's St., #280, Clackamas, OR 97015 (800-672-4327 or 503-557-9101; fax 800-896-8868; http://www.mrcheaps.com). Additional office in San Diego, CA (800-636-3273 or 619-291-1292).

NOW Voyager, 74 Varick St., #307, New York, NY 10013 (212-431-1616; fax 334-5243; email info@nowvoyagertravel.com; http://www.nowvoyagertravel.com), acts as a consolidator with reliability rivaling that of most charter companies (97% of customers get on flights the first time) and prices which are considerably lower. Also arranges courier flights.

STAND-BY FLIGHTS

Stand-by flights will add a certain thrill to the prospect of when you will leave and where exactly you will end up. Complete flexibility on both ends of the trip is necessary: you buy not a ticket, but the promise that you will get to a destination near where you're intending to go within a window of time (usually 5 days) from a location in a region you've specified. You call in before your date-range to hear all of your flight options for the next few days and your probability of boarding. You then decide which flights you want to try to make and present a voucher at the airport which grants you the right to board a flight on a space-available basis. This procedure must be followed again for the return trip. Be aware that you may only receive a monetary refund if all available flights which departed within your date-range from the specified region are full, but future travel credit is always available. As with consolidator companies, be sure to read all the fine print.

Airhitch, 2641 Broadway, 3rd fl., New York, NY 10025 (800-326-2009 or 212-864-2000; fax 864-5489), and Los Angeles, CA (310-726-5000). There are several offices in Europe; the main one is in Paris (tel. (01) 47 00 16 30). The "USAhitch" program connects the northeastern United States with the West (Boston to San Francisco $129).

Air-Tech, Ltd., 588 Broadway, #204, New York, NY 10012 (212-219-7000; fax 219-0066). Rate from Europe to the West coast is $239. Domestic travelers must give a 3-day travel window; flights primarily from NYC (Boston departures possible). West Coast to Hawaii $129 each way with a 5-day window. Air-Tech also arranges courier flights and regular confirmed-reserved flights at discount rates.

Better Safe than Sorry

Everyone who flies should be concerned with airline safety. The type and age of the aircraft used often indicate the airline's safety level—aircraft not produced by one of the major manufacturers sometimes fall below acceptable standards, and aircraft over 20 years old require increased levels of maintenance. Travel agencies can tell you the type and age of aircraft on a particular route, as can the *Official Airline Guide* (http://www.oag.com). The **International Airline Passengers Association** (972-404-9980), publishes a survey of accident rates on airlines outside the U.S. and provides safety information on carriers worldwide. The **Federal Aviation Administration** (http://www.faa.gov), reviews the airline authorities for countries whose airlines enter the U.S. and divides the countries into three categories: stick with carriers in category 1. Call the **U.S. State Department** (202-647-5225; http://travel.state.gov/travel_warnings.html), to check for posted travel advisories which sometimes involve foreign carriers.

CHARTER FLIGHTS

Charters are flights a tour operator contracts with an airline (usually one specializing in charters) to fly extra loads of passengers to peak-season destinations. Charters are often cheaper than flights on scheduled airlines, especially during peak seasons, and restrictions on minimum advance-purchase and minimum stay are more lenient. However, charter flights fly less frequently than major airlines, make refunds particularly difficult, and are almost always fully booked. Schedules and itineraries may also change or be cancelled at the last moment (as late as 48 hours before the trip, and without a full refund), and check-in, boarding, and baggage claim are often much slower. As always, pay with a credit card if you can; consider traveler's insurance against trip interruption.

Try **Interworld** (305-443-4929; fax 443-0351), **Travac** (800-872-8800; fax 212-714-9063; email mail@travac.com; http://www.travac.com), or **Rebel,** with locations in Valencia, CA (800-227-3235; fax 805-294-0981; http://rebeltours.com; email travel@rebeltours.com), and Orlando, FL (800-732-3588). Don't be afraid to call every number and hunt for the best deal.

COURIER COMPANIES AND FREIGHTERS

Courier travel works like this: you are a traveler seeking an inexpensive ticket to a particular location, and the courier service is a company seeking to transport merchandise to a particular location. If your destinations and schedules coincide, the courier service will sell you a cheap ticket in exchange for use of the luggage space which accompanies it. Courier services offer some great prices, but with restrictions: their schedules may be confining, and luggage is limited to carry-on bags only. You must be over 21 (18 in some cases), have a valid passport, and procure your own visa (if necessary). Most flights are round-trip only with short fixed-length stays (usually one week), and only single tickets are issued. **Most courier services do not fly to California or Hawaii;** however, to check all your options, get more info through the following organizations. For an annual fee of $45, the **International Association of Air Travel Couriers,** 8 South J St., P.O. Box 1349, Lake Worth, FL 33460 (561-582-8320), informs travelers (via computer, fax, and mailings) of courier opportunities worldwide. Steve Lantos publishes a monthly update of courier options in **Travel Unlimited,** and general info on budget travel (write P.O. Box 1058A, Allston, MA 02134 for a free sample newsletter; subscription $25 per yr.).

■ By Boat

If you really have travel time to spare, **Ford's Travel Guides,** 19448 Londelius St., Northridge, CA 91324 (818-701-7414; fax 701-7415), lists **freighter companies** that will take passengers worldwide. Ask for their *Freighter Travel Guide and Waterways of the World* ($16, plus $2.50 postage if mailed outside the U.S.).

■ By Train

Locomotion is still one of the cheapest ways to tour the U.S., but keep in mind that discounted air travel, particularly on longer trips, may be cheaper than train travel. As with airlines, you can save money by purchasing your tickets as far in advance as possible, so plan ahead and make reservations early. It is essential to travel light on trains; not all stations will check your baggage.

Amtrak (800-USA-RAIL/872-7245; http://www.amtrak.com), is the only provider of inter-city passenger train service in the U.S. Most cities have Amtrak offices which directly sell tickets, but in some small towns tickets must be bought through an agent. The informative web page lists up-to-date schedules, fares, arrival and departure info, and allows reservations. **Discounts** on full rail fares include: senior citizens (15% off); students (15% off with a Student Advantage Card; call 800-96-AMTRAK/962-6872 to purchase a card for $20); travelers with disabilities (15% off); children under 15 accompanied by a parent (50% off); children under age two (free); current members of the U.S. armed forces, active-duty veterans, and their dependents (25% off). Circle trips and holiday packages can also save money. Call for up-to-date info and reservations. Amtrak also offers some **special packages:**

All-Aboard America: This fare divides the Continental U.S. into three regions—Eastern, Central, and Western. During the peak season (June 20-Aug. 17 and Dec. 19-Jan. 4), rates are $228 for travel within one region, $318 within and between two regions, and $378 among all three (rates for the remainder of the year are $198, $258, and $318). The price includes travel with up to three stopovers within a 45-day period. The route may not be changed once travel has begun, though the times may be changed at no cost. Fares are subject to availability; make reservations for summer travel well in advance.

Air-Rail Travel Plan: Amtrak and United Airlines allow you to travel in one direction by train and return by plane, or to fly to a distant point and return home by train. The train portion of the journey can last up to 30 days and include up to 3 stopovers. The transcontinental plan, which allows coast-to-coast travel originating on either coast, sells for $517. The West Coast plan, which allows travel roughly as far east as Tucson, AZ, including cities from Las Vegas to Seattle, sells for $259/$223. Contact **Amtrak Vacations** (see below) for details.

USA Rail Pass: A discount option available only to those who aren't citizens of North America; allows unlimited travel and stops over a period of either 15 or 30 days. A 30-day nationwide travel pass sells for $480 during peak season (June 20-Aug. 17 and Dec. 19-Jan. 4) and $350 during the off-season; a 15-day nationwide pass is $375/$260. A 30-day pass limited to travel in the western region (as far east as the Mississippi River) is $350/250; the 15-day pass for the west is $280/$195. A 30-day pass for the far West (as far east as Denver) costs $285/$230; the 15-day option is $230/$180. A 30-day pass limited to the coast is $265/$215.

City Escapades: Tours of major American cities. Tickets and departures from Amtrak stations; contact **Amtrak Vacations** (see below) for details.

Amtrak Vacations, 2211 Butterfield Rd. Downers Grove, IL 60515 (800-321-8684). An Amtrak-affiliated travel agency which offers packages in conjunction with airlines and hotel chains and, occasionally, discounts not to be found anywhere else. Programs vary throughout the year.

▓ By Bus

Buses generally offer the most frequent and complete service between the cities and towns of the U.S. Often a bus is the only way to reach smaller locales without a car. In rural areas and across open spaces, however, bus lines tend to be sparse. *Russell's Official National Motor Coach Guide* ($14.45 including postage) is an indispensable tool for constructing an itinerary. Updated each month, *Russell's Guide* contains schedules of every bus route (including Greyhound) between every town in the U.S. and Canada. Russell's also publishes two semi-annual *Supplements,* one which includes a *Directory of Bus Lines and Bus Stations* ($6), and one which offers a series of *Route Maps* ($6.45). To order any of the above, write Russell's Guides, Inc., P.O. Box 278, Cedar Rapids, IA 52406 (319-364-6138; fax 364-4853).

Greyhound

Greyhound (800-231-2222; http://www.greyhound.com), operates the largest number of routes in the U.S., though local bus companies may provide more extensive services within specific regions. Schedule info is available at any Greyhound terminal, on their web page, or by calling the 800 number. Reserve with a credit card over the phone at least 10 days in advance, and the ticket can be mailed anywhere in the U.S. Otherwise, reservations are available only up to 24 hours in advance. You can buy your ticket at the terminal, but arrive early. If **boarding at a remote "flag stop,"** be sure you know exactly where the bus stops. It's a good idea to call the nearest agency and let them know you'll be waiting and at what time. Catch the driver's attention by standing on the side of the road and flailing your arms wildly—

better to be embarrassed than stranded. If a bus passes (usually because of over-crowding), a later, less-crowded bus should stop. Whatever you stow in compartments underneath the bus should be clearly marked; be sure to get a claim check for it, and watch to make sure your luggage is on the same bus as you.

Advance purchase fares: Reserving space far ahead of time ensures a lower fare, although discounts are smaller during the busy summer months (June 5-Sept. 15). For tickets purchased more than 21 days in advance, the one-way fare anywhere in the US will not exceed $79, while the round-trip price is capped at $158 (from June to September, the one-way cap is $99 and the round-trip $198). Fares are also reduced for 14 day advance purchases on many popular routes; call the 800 number for updated pricing, or consult the user-friendly web page.

Discounts on full fares: Senior citizens (10% off); children ages 2-11 (50% off); travelers with disabilities and special needs ride with their companions for the price of one. Active and retired U.S. military personnel and National Guard Reserves (10% off with valid ID), and their spouses and dependents, may take a round-trip between any two points in the U.S. for $169. With a ticket purchased 3 or more days in advance, a friend can travel along for free; during the summer months, if purchased 7 days in advance, the freeloadin' friend gets half off.

Ameripass: Allows adults unlimited travel for 7 days ($189), 15 days ($299), 30 days ($409), or 60 days ($599). Prices for students and senior citizens are slightly less: 7 days ($169), 15 days ($269), 30 days ($369), or 60 days ($539). Children's passes are half the price of adults. The pass takes effect the first day used. Before purchasing an Ameripass, total up the separate bus fares between towns to make sure that the pass is really more economical, or at least worth the unlimited flexibility it provides. **TNMO Coaches, Vermont Transit,** and **Continental Panhandle Line** are Greyhound subsidiaries, and as such will honor Ameripasses; most bus companies in the U.S. will do so, but check for specifics.

International Ameripass: For travelers from outside North America. A 4-day pass, which cannot be used during a weekend, is $109; 5-day pass $129; 7-day pass $159; 15-day pass $239; 30-day pass $319; 60-day pass $499. Call 888-GLI-PASS/454-7277 for schedule info. Primarily peddled in foreign countries by Greyhound-affiliated agencies; telephone numbers vary by country and are listed on the web page. **Australia** (02) 4934 2088. **New Zealand** (09) 479 6555. **South Africa** 0113312911. **United Kingdom** 01342-317317. Orders can also be made over email (send request to Dialcorp!jetpo01!Greyhound@jetsave.mail.att.net), or purchased in Greyhound's International Office, 625 Eighth Ave., New York, NY 10018 (800-246-8572 or 212-971-0492; fax 402-330-0919; email international@greyhound.com).

Green Tortoise

Green Tortoise, 494 Broadway, San Francisco, CA 94133 (415-956-7500 or 800-867-8647; http://www.greentortoise.com), has "hostels on wheels" in remodeled diesel buses done up for living and eating on the road. Meals are prepared communally. Prices include transportation, sleeping space on the bus, and tours of the regions through which you pass. Deposits (around $100) are generally required since space is tight. Trips run from June to October. Trips from Hartford, Boston, or New York to San Francisco take 10 to 14 days ($299-380 plus $81-91 for food). There are also round-trip vacation loops that start and finish in San Francisco, winding through Yosemite National Park, Northern California, Baja California, the Grand Canyon, or Alaska along the way. Prepare for an earthy trip—the buses have no toilets and little privacy. It is a good idea to reserve one to two months in advance, but some trips have space available at departure.

■ By Car

Whether you're in California or Hawaii, knowing the highway system is key—some of your trip will almost certainly be by car. The best way to figure out the highway system is to grab a map and study it *before* you take off; the freeways are hard enough to understand without having to fight traffic while trying to decipher them. *Let's Go* lists U.S. highways thus: "I" (as in "I-90") refers to Interstate highways, "U.S." (as in "U.S. 1") to United States highways, and "Rte." (as in "Rte. 7") to state and local highways.

HOW TO NAVIGATE THE INTERSTATES

A number of major interstates and highways crisscross California. Travelers moving north-south have the choice of three major routes. If you're looking for speed, hop on **I-5**, which runs north-south from the Mexican border through San Diego, Los Angeles, the San Joaquin Valley, and Sacramento on its way to Oregon. I-5 is direct and the fastest route from L.A. to San Francisco (8 hr.), but it's also deadly boring, affording at best a view of agricultural flatlands and odiferous cow pastures. **U.S. 101** winds north-south from Los Angeles, closer to the coast than I-5, through Santa Barbara, San Luis Obispo, San Francisco, Santa Rosa, and Eureka. It's slower than I-5, but considerably more scenic and pleasant a drive. The third option is **Rte. 1** (called **Hwy. 1** in this book), the Pacific Coast Highway, which follows the California coast (9½ hr.). Hwy. 1 is very slow, and often traffic-congested, but the scenery is some of the most spectacular in the West, particularly on the breathtaking, cliff-hanging turns of Jack Kerouac's Big Sur.

In the 1950s, President Eisenhower envisioned the current **interstate system,** an easily comprehensible, consistent system for numbering interstates. Even-numbered interstates run east-west and odd ones run north-south, decreasing in number toward the south and the west. Three-digit numbers signify branches of other interstates (e.g., I-285 is a branch of I-85), which are often bypasses skirting a large city.

ON THE ROAD

Tune up the car before you leave, make sure the tires are full and in good repair, and get good maps. **Rand McNally'sa Road Atlas,** covering all of the U.S. and Canada, is one of the best ($10, available at bookstores and gas stations). A **compass** and a **car**

manual can also be very useful. You should always carry a **spare tire** and **jack, jumper cables, extra oil** and **gas, flares,** a **flashlight,** and **blankets** (in case you break down at night or in the winter). When traveling in the summer or in the desert bring five gallons of **water** for drinking and for the radiator. In extremely hot weather, use the air conditioner with restraint; if you see the car's temperature gauge climbing, turn it off. Turning the heater on full blast will help cool the engine. If radiator fluid is steaming, turn off the car for half an hour. *Never pour water over the engine to cool it, and never lift a searing hot hood.* In remote areas, remember to bring emergency food and water.

Sleeping in a car or van parked in the city is extremely dangerous—even the most dedicated budget traveler should not consider it an option. Be sure to **buckle up**—seat belts are required by law in California. The **speed limit** in the U.S. varies considerably from region to region. Most urban highways retain a limit of 55 mph (63 kph), while rural routes range from 65 mph (104 kph) to 80 mph (128 kph). Heed the limit; not only does it save gas, but most local police forces and state troopers make frequent use of radar to catch speed demons. **Gas** in the U.S. costs about $1.65 per gallon.

AUTOMOBILE CLUBS

American Automobile Association (AAA), 1050 Hingham St., Rocklin, MA 02370 (800-AAA-HELP/222-4357; http://www.aaa.com). Offers free trip-planning services, roadmaps and guidebooks, emergency road service anywhere in the U.S., free towing, and commission-free traveler's checks from American Express with over 1000 offices scattered across the country. Discounts on Hertz car rental (5%-20%), Amtrak tickets (10%), various motel chains, and theme parks. AAA has reciprocal agreements with the auto associations of many other countries, which often provide full benefits while traveling. AAA has two types of memberships, basic and plus, but the 2 services do not differ greatly. Basic membership fees are $55 for the first year with $39 annual renewal; each additional family member $23 per year. Call 800-JOIN-AAA/800-564-6222 to sign up.

AMOCO Motor Club, P.O. Box 9049, Des Moines, IA 50368 (800-334-3300). Services include trip planning and travel info, 24hr. towing (free for 5mi. or back to the tower's garage), and emergency road service. Two memberships available: AARP gives discounts at Avis, Hertz, and National (one person $40, two $48, family $68); AMOCO gives discounts at Alamo, Avis, and Hertz (couple $60, family $85). Premier membership ($68-$110) gives 50mi. free towing.

RENTING

Although the cost of renting a car can be prohibitive for long distances, local renting may be reasonable. **Auto rental agencies** fall into two categories: national companies with hundreds of branches, and local agencies serving one city or region.

National chains usually allow cars to be picked up in one city and dropped off in another (for a hefty charge, sometimes in excess of $1000). Occasional promotions linked to coastal inventory imbalances may cut the fee dramatically. By calling a toll-free number you can reserve a reliable car anywhere in the country. Drawbacks include steep prices (a compact rents for about $45-80 a day) and high minimum ages for rentals (usually 25). Most branches rent to ages 21-24 with an additional fee, but policies and prices vary from agency to agency. If you're 21 or older and have a major credit card in your name, you may be able to rent where the minimum age would otherwise rule you out.

Most rental packages offer unlimited mileage, although some allow you a certain number of miles free before the usual charge of 25-40¢ per mile takes effect. Most quoted rates do not include gas or tax, so ask for the total cost before handing over the credit card—many large firms have added airport surcharges not covered by the designated fare. Return the car with a full tank unless you sign up for a fuel option plan that stipulates otherwise. When dealing with any car rental company, be sure to ask whether the price includes insurance against theft and collision. There may be an additional charge, the collision and damage waiver (CDW), which usually comes to about $12-15 per day. If you use **American Express** to rent the car, they automatically cover the CDW; call AmEx (800-338-1670), for more info.

Alamo (800-327-9633; http://www.goalamo.com), rents to ages 21-24 with a major credit card for a surcharge of $20 per day.

Avis (800-331-1212; http://www.avis.com). Some branches are willing to rent to ages 21-24 with a credit card.

Budget (800-527-0700), rarely rents to ages 21-24 with a credit card.

Hertz (800-654-3131; http://www.hertz.com), enforces a minimum age of 25, unless the renter has a corporate account.

Dollar (800-800-4000). Some branches rent to ages 21-24; $20 per day surcharge.

Thrifty (800-367-2277; http://www.thrifty.com). Some branches rent to ages 21-24 for a surcharge of about $20 per day.

Rent-A-Wreck (800-421-7253; http://www.rent-a-wreck.com), specializes in supplying vehicles that are past their prime for lower-than-average prices; a barebones compact less than 8 years old rents for around $20.

BUYING

Adventures on Wheels, 42 Hwy. 36, Middletown, NJ 07748 (800-WHEELS-9/943-3579 or 732-583-8714; fax 583-8932), will sell domestic and international travelers a motorhome, camper, or station wagon, organize its registration and provide insurance, and guarantee that they will buy it back from you after you have finished your travels. Buy a camper for $6000-9000, use it for 5-6 months, and sell it back for $3000-5000. The main office is in New York/New Jersey; there are other offices in Los Angeles, San Francisco, and Miami. Vehicles can be picked up at one office and dropped off at another.

AUTO TRANSPORT COMPANIES

These services match drivers with car owners who need cars moved from one city to another. The only expenses are gas, tolls, and living expenses. Some companies insure their cars; with others, your security deposit covers any breakdowns or damage. You must be at least 21, have a valid license, and agree to drive about 400 mi. per day on a fairly direct route. Companies regularly inspect current and past job references, take your fingerprints, and require a cash bond. Cars are available between most points, although it's easiest to find cars for coast to coast travel; New York and Los Angeles are popular transfer points. If offered a car, look it over first. Think twice about accepting a gas guzzler since you'll be paying for the gas. With the company's approval, you may be able to share the cost with several companions.

Auto Driveaway, 310 S. Michigan Ave., Chicago, IL 60604 (800-346-2277; fax 312-341-9100; http://www.autodriveaway.com).

A. Anthony's Driveaway, 4391 NW 19th Ave., Pompano Beach, FL 33064 (954-970-7384; fax 970-3881).

Across America Driveaway, 3626 Calumet Ave., Hammond, IN 46320 (800-619-7707 or 219-852-0134; fax 800-334-6931; http://www.schultz-international.com). Other offices in L.A. (800-964-7874 or 310-798-3377), and Dallas (214-745-8892).

■ By Bicycle

Before you rush onto the byways of America pedaling your banana-seat Huffy Desperado, remember that safe and secure cycling requires a quality helmet and lock. A good **helmet** costs about $40—much cheaper than critical head surgery. U-shaped Kryptonite or Citadel **locks** run about $30 and carry insurance against theft for one or two years if your bike is registered with the police. Bike Nashbar, 4111 Simon Rd., Youngstown, OH 44512 (800-627-4227; fax 456-1223), will beat any nationally advertised in-stock price by five cents, and will ship anywhere in the U.S. and Canada. They also have a techline (330-788-6464; open Mon.-Fri. 8am-midnight, Sat.-Sun. 8am-4pm), to answer questions about repairs and maintenance.

There are a ton of **publications** that will help you get the most out of your bicycle. *Bicycle Gearing: A Practical Guide* ($9), available from The Mountaineers Books, 1001 SW Klickitat Way, #201, Seattle, WA 98134 (800-553-4453; fax 206-223-6306; email mbooks@mountaineers.org), discusses in lay terms how bicycle gears work, covering everything you need to know in order to shift properly and get the maximum propulsion from the minimum exertion. *Cuthbertson's All-in-One Bike Repair Manual* ($12 plus $3.50 shipping) available from Ten Speed Press, Box 7123, Berkeley, CA 94707 (800-841-2665; fax 510-559-1629), provides vital info on repair and maintenance during long-term bike sojourns. Rodale Press, 33 E. Minor St., Emmaus, PA 18098-0099 (610-967-5171 or 800-848-4735), publishes a number of books for the intrepid would-be cyclist, including *Cycling for Women* ($9 plus $3.50 shipping), *Mountain Biking Skills* ($18 plus shipping), and the popular *Bicycle Maintenance and Repair* ($20 plus shipping).

Adventure Cycling Association, P.O. Box 8308-P, Missoula, MT 59807 (406-721-1776; fax 721-8754; email acabike@aol.com; http://www.adv-cycling.org). A national, nonprofit organization that researches and maps long-distance routes and organizes bike tours for members. Membership $28 in the U.S., $35 in Canada and Mexico.

Backroads, 801 Cedar St., Berkeley, CA 94710-1800 (800-462-2848; fax 510-527-1444; http://www.backroads.com), offers tours in both California and Hawaii. Travelers cycle from campsite to campsite. All prices include meals, guide services, maps, directions, and van support. Trips range from a weekend excursion ($299) to a 9-day extravaganza ($1098).

▓ By Motorcycle

It may be cheaper than car travel, but it takes a tenacious soul to endure a motorcycle tour. If you must carry a load, keep it low and forward where it won't distort the cycle's center of gravity. Fasten it either to the seat or over the rear axle in saddle or tank bags. Those considering a long journey should contact the **American Motorcyclist Association,** 33 Collegeview Rd., Westerville, OH 43801 (614-891-2425 in Canada or 800-AMA-JOIN/262-5646; fax 891-5012; email ama@ama-cycle.org; http://ama-cycle.org), the linchpin of U.S. biker culture. A full membership ($29 per year) includes a subscription to the extremely informative *American Motorcyclist* magazine, discounts on insurance, rentals, and hotels, and a kick-ass patch for your riding jacket. For an additional $25, members benefit from emergency roadside assistance, including pick up and delivery to a service shop.

Of course, **safety** should be your primary concern. Motorcycles are incredibly vulnerable to crosswinds, drunk drivers, and the blind spots of cars and trucks. Always ride defensively, especially at night. **Helmets** are required by law in California; wear the best one you can find. Americans should ask their State's Department of Motor Vehicles for a motorcycle operator's manual; the AMA web page (see above) lists relevant laws and regulations for all 50 states.

▓ By Thumb

No, no, no. While this may be comparatively safe in some areas of Alaska, Europe, and Australia, it is generally a bad idea in California and in L.A. in particular. We do NOT recommend it. We strongly urge you to find other means of transportation and to avoid situations where hitching is the only option.

If you feel you have no other alternative, there are many precautions that must be taken. First, assess the risks and chances of getting a ride. A woman and a man is perhaps the best compromise between safety and utility; women should never hitch-

hike alone, and men have a hard time getting rides. Next, don't take any chances with drivers. Don't get in the car if you don't know where the driver is going. Don't put yourself where you can't exit the car quickly. Never get into the back seat of a two-door car, or into a car whose passenger door doesn't open from the inside. Beware of cars with driver-controlled locks that can keep you in against your will. Never hesitate to refuse a ride if you will feel at all uncomfortable with the driver. Experienced hitchers talk with the driver—even idle chatter informs hitchers about their drivers—but never divulge any information that they would not want a stranger to know.

Road Rules

It's hard for us to tell you hitching in California is a bad idea, especially when the entertainment industry has glamorized it as such a sexy way to travel. Creedence Clearwater Revival's tune *Sweet Hitchhiker* portrays hitchers as sensuous, buxom vixens. In Aerosmith's video *Amazing,* Alicia Silverstone merely has to stick her thumb out and hike her skirt up to get a safe ride. And what were the producers of the hitchers-from-hell flick *Kalifornia* thinking when they cast Juliette Lewis and babe-a-licious Brad Pitt as the hitchers? No driver would ever refuse those cute faces a ride. So these entertainment industry examples are misleading, but can help us to modify our advice a little. Hitching in California is detrimental to your health, except on certain movie sets in Hollywood.

ONCE THERE

■ Embassies and Consulates

Most foreign embassies in the U.S. are located in Washington, D.C., but there are consulates in California which could be helpful in an emergency. For a more extensive list of embassies and consulates in the U.S., consult the website http://www.embassy.org.

> **Consulates in California: Australia,** 611 N. Larchmont Blvd., Los Angeles, CA 90004 (213-469-4300), and 1 Bush St., #700 (415-362-6160), at Market, San Francisco, CA 94101; **Canada,** 550 S, Hope St., 9th fl., Los Angeles, CA 90071 (213-346-2711); **Ireland,** 44 Montgomery St., #3830, San Francisco, CA 94101 (415-392-4214); **New Zealand,** 12400 Wilshire Blvd., #1150, Los Angeles, CA 90025 (310-207-1605); **South Africa,** 50 N. La Cienega Blvd., # 300, Beverly Hills, CA 90211 (310-657-9200); **United Kingdom,** 11766 Wilshire Blvd., #400, Los Angeles, CA 90025 (213-385-7381), and 1 Sansome St., #850 (981-3030), at Market, San Francisco, CA 94104.

■ Accommodations

California and Hawaii have a variety of inexpensive alternatives to hotels and motels. Before you set out, try to locate places to stay along your route and make reservations, especially if you plan to travel during peak tourist seasons. Even if you find yourself in dire straits, don't spend the night under the stars; it's often uncomfortable and unsafe, and it's usually illegal, except in some national park and forest areas. If you don't have the money for lodgings, the local crisis center hotline may have a list of persons or groups who will house you.

HOTELS AND MOTELS

Many visitors centers have hotel coupons that can save you a bundle; if you don't see any, ask. Budget motels are usually clustered off the highway several miles out-

side of town, but the carless (and the light of wallet) may do better to try the hostels, YMCAs, YWCAs, and dorms downtown. The annually updated *National Directory of Budget Motels* ($6 plus $2 shipping), from **Pilot Books,** 103 Copper St., Babylon, NY 11702 (516-477-1095; fax 516-422-2227), covers over 2200 low-cost chain motels in the U.S. Pilot Books also publishes *The Hotel/Motel Special Program and Discount Guide* ($6 plus shipping), which lists hotels and motels offering special discounts. Also look for the comprehensive *State by State Guide to Budget Motels* ($13), from Marlor Press, Inc., 4304 Brigadoon Dr., St. Paul, MN 55126 (800-669-4908 or 612-484-4600; fax 612-490-1182; email marlor@ix.netcom.com).

Chains usually adhere to a level of cleanliness and comfort more consistent than locally operated budget competitors. The cellar-level price of a single is about $30. Some budget chains are **Motel 6** (800-466-8356), **Super 8 Motels** (800-800-8000; fax 605-229-8907; http://www.super8motels.com/super8.html), **Choice Hotels International** (800-453-4511), and **Best Western International** (800-528-1234 or 602-957-4200; fax 602-957-5505; inquire about discounts for seniors, families, frequent travelers, groups, or government personnel).

HOSTELS

A Hosteler's Bill of Rights

There are certain standard features that we do not include in our hostel listings. Unless we state otherwise, you can expect that every hostel has: no lockout, no curfew, a kitchen, free hot showers, secure luggage storage, and no key deposit.

For tight budgets and those lonesome traveling blues, hostels can't be beat. Generally dorm-style accommodations, hostels often have large single-sex rooms with bunk beds; some hostels offer private rooms for families and couples. They often have kitchens and utensils for your use, bike or moped rentals, storage areas, and laundry facilities. There can be drawbacks; some hostels close during certain daytime "lock-out" hours, have a curfew, impose a maximum stay or, less frequently, require that you do chores. Fees range from $5-25 per night, and hostels associated with one of the large hostel associations often have lower rates for members. *The Hostel Handbook for the U.S.A. & Canada* ($4, $6 outside the U.S.; available from Department IGH, 722 Saint Nicholas Ave., New York, NY 10031; email InfoHostel@aol.com; http://www.hostels.com/handbook), lists over 500 hostels. If you have Internet access, check out the **Internet Guide to Hostelling** (http://hostels.com). If you plan to stay in hostels, consider joining an organization like **Hostelling International-American Youth Hostels (HI-AYH),** 733 15th St. NW, Suite 840, Washington, D.C. 20005 (202-783-6161; fax 783-6171; email hiayhserv@hiayh.org; http://www.hiayh.org). HI maintains 35 offices and over 150 hostels in the U.S. Memberships can be purchased at many travel agencies (see p. 24) or the national office in Washington, D.C. (1yr. membership $25, under 18 $10, over 54 $15, family cards $35; includes *Hostelling North America: The Official Guide to Hostels in Canada and the United States*). Reserve by letter, phone, fax, or through the **International Booking Network (IBN;** 202-783-6161), a computerized reservation system which lets you book HI-AYH hostel accommodations up to 6 months in advance for a nominal fee. Basic HI-AYH rules are: check-in 5-8pm, check-out 9:30am (although most urban hostels have 24hr. access), maximum stay 3 days, no pets or alcohol allowed on the premises. Fees are $5-22 per night.

BED AND BREAKFASTS

B&Bs (residential houses with rooms available to travelers) offer a cozy, if potentially less amenity-packed alternative to impersonal hotel rooms. They cover a wide range quality- and service-wise; hosts can be very accommodating, but some B&Bs do not provide phones, TVs, or private bathrooms.

Several travel guides and reservation services specialize in B&Bs. *The Complete Guide to Bed and Breakfasts, Inns and Guesthouses in the U.S., Canada, and Worldwide* ($17), list over 11,000 B&Bs and inns (available through Lanier Publications, P.O. Box D, Petaluma, CA 94953; 707-763-0271; fax 763-5762; email lanier@travelguides.com; http://www.travelguides.com).

Bed and Breakfast: The National Network (TNN) of Reservation Services, P.O. Box 4616, Springfield, MA 01101 (800-884-4288; fax 401-847-7309; email annas@wsii.com; http://www.tnn4bnb.com), can book reservations at over 7000 B&Bs throughout the U.S. A travel kit will be mailed upon request.

Bed and Breakfast California, P.O. Box 282910, San Francisco, CA 94128-2910 (800-872-4500 or 415-696-1690; fax 696-1699). Established in 1978, B&BC is the oldest B&B reservation service in the U.S. Lodging is available in private home B&Bs, small inns, and houseboats in California and Nevada. 2-night min. stay. Rates range from $60-150 per night; occasional discounts for singles, families with children, and stays over 1 week.

YMCA AND YWCAS

Not all **Young Men's Christian Association (YMCA)** locations offer lodging; those that do are often located in urban downtowns, which can be convenient but a little gritty. YMCA rates are usually lower than a hotel's but higher than a hostel's, and may include use of libraries, pools, air conditioning, and other facilities. Many YMCAs accept women and families (group rates often available), and some (as in Los Angeles) will not lodge people under 18 without parental permission. All reservations must be made and paid for in advance, with a traveler's check, U.S. money order, certified check, or credit card. Call the local YMCA for fee information. For info or reservations (reservation fee $3, overseas $6), contact **Y's Way International,** 224 E. 47th St., New York, NY 10017 (212-308-2899; fax 212-308-3161; http://www.ymca.int for links to branches worldwide). For Y's in **Canada,** contact the Montréal YMCA at 1450 Stanley St., Montréal, QP, H3A 2W6 (514-849-8393; fax 849-8017), or the YMCA of Greater Toronto, 42 Charles St., Toronto, ON, M4Y 1T4 (416-928-9622 or 800-223-8024; fax 416-928-2030).

Most **Young Women's Christian Associations (YWCAs)** accommodate only women or, sometimes, couples. Nonmembers are often required to join when lodging. For more info or a world-wide directory ($10), write **YWCA-USA,** 726 Broadway, New York, NY 10003 (212-614-2700).

■ Longer Stays

If you decide to stay in the U.S. permanently, there are many details and documents you will need to arrange. Most importantly, you will need to find work and housing, and the info below should help you to get started. Food shopping and the other details of living should not be difficult to arrange; *Let's Go* attempts to list the most significant markets and supermarkets in the Food sections.

EMPLOYMENT

To work in the U.S., you will need a **work permit** or "green card" (see **Entrance Requirements,** p. 4). Your employer must obtain this document, usually by demonstrating that you have skills that locals lack—not the easiest of tasks. There are, however, ways to make it easier. Friends in your destination country can help expedite work permits or arrange work-for-accommodations swaps. Students can check with their universities' foreign language departments, which may have connections to job openings. The rigmarole of obtaining a worker's visa may seem complex, but it's critical that you go through the proper channels, particularly in California, where sentiment against undocumented workers is virulent. Above all, do not try to fool your consular officer. Working or studying in the U.S. with only a B-2 visa is grounds for deportation. If the U.S. consulate suspects that you may be trying to enter the

country as a worker under the aegis of a pleasure trip, you will be denied a visa altogether. For more info, contact the U.S. embassy or consulate in your home country (see **U.S. Embassies and Consulates,** p. 4).

In general, when looking for a **job,** it's likely you'll have better luck in cities. Council's work program will help with job-placement and housing (see **Work,** p. 16) as well as the visa, residency, and taxation regulations which could easily thwart your best-laid plans.

ACCOMMODATIONS

Once you have a source of funds, **housing** will probably be your most pressing concern. Real estate agencies may be able to arrange rentals or leases, or you may want to rent a room instead of a whole house or apartment. Check the larger city papers for employment and apartment listings. Also check college campus noticeboards.

Home exchange and rentals

Home exchange offers travelers the opportunity to live like a native and to dramatically cut down on accommodation fees—usually only an administration fee is paid to the matching service. Once the introductions are made, the choice is left to the two hopeful partners. Most companies have pictures of member's homes and info about the owners. Many exchange companies are listed on the web at http://www.aitec.edu.au/~bwechner/Documents/Travel/Lists/HomeExchange-Clubs.html. Renting a home may also be a good deal for some, depending on the length of stay and the desired level of services.

fair tours, Postbox 615, CH-9001 St. Gallen, Switzerland (email fairtours@gn.apc.org; http://www.gn.apc.org/fairtours), is a home exchange program for environmentally conscious travelers, which provides the opportunity to avoid large-scale commercial tourism. Personal matching service. Send 2 international reply coupons for further info, or visit the web page.

The Invented City: International Home Exchange, 41 Sutter St., #1090, San Francisco, CA 94104 (800-788-CITY/2489 in the U.S. or 415-252-1141 elsewhere; fax 415-252-1171; email invented@aol.com). Lists 1700 homes worldwide. For $50, get your offer listed and receive 3 catalogues. Details of the swap are worked out between members.

Dorms

Many **colleges and universities** open their residence halls to travelers when school isn't in session, and some do so even during term-time. The dorms are usually clean, close to student areas, and good sources for info on entertainment, lodging, and transportation. No single policy covers all these institutions. Getting a room may be difficult, but rates tend to be low, and many offer free local calls. *Let's Go* lists colleges which rent dorm rooms among the accommodations for appropriate cities.

■ Camping and the Outdoors

USEFUL PUBLICATIONS

California and Hawaii present a variety of camping alternatives; few areas in the world are as accessible to the traveler or as naturally beautiful. For excellent topographical maps of the U.S. ($4), write the **U.S. Geological Survey,** Branch of Information Services, P.O. Box 25286, DFC, Denver, CO 80225 (800-435-7627; fax 303-202-4693). All maps are less than $15. For info on camping, hiking, and biking, contact the publishers listed below to receive a free catalogue.

Sierra Club Bookstore, 85 Second St., 2nd fl., San Francisco, CA 94109 (800-935-1056 or 415-977-5600; fax 923-5500). Books on national parks and different

regions of the U.S., as well as *Learning to Rock Climb* ($14), *The Sierra Club Family Outdoors Guide* ($12), and *Wildwater* ($12).

Wilderness Press, 2440 Bancroft Way, Berkeley, CA 94704-1676 (800-443-7227 or 510-843-8080; fax 548-1355; email wpress@ix.netcom.com). Publishes over 100 hiking guides and maps for the western U.S., including *Backpacking Basics* ($$11), and *Backpacking with Babies and Small Children* ($11).

Recreational Equipment, Inc. (REI), P.O. Box 1700, Sumner, WA 98352–0001 (800-426-4840), publishes *The U.S. Outdoor Atlas* ($17), an annually updated catalogue of American campsites. Few of their books are offered via mail-order, so check their retail stores.

Woodall Publications Corporation, P.O. Box 5000, 13975 W. Polo Trail Dr., Lake Forest, IL 60045 (847-362-6700 or 800-323-9076; fax 362-8776; http://www.woodalls.com). Covers all of North America, publishing the ever-popular and annually updated *Woodall's Campground Directory* ($20), and *Woodall's Plan-it, Pack-it, Go!: Great Places to Tent, Fun Things To Do* ($13), which are generally available in American bookstores.

CAMPING AND HIKING EQUIPMENT

Purchase equipment before you leave so you know exactly what you have and how much it weighs. Whether buying or renting, finding sturdy, light, and inexpensive equipment is a must.

Sleeping bags: Most good **sleeping bags** are rated by "season," or the lowest outdoor temperature at which they will keep you warm ("summer" means 30-40°F, "three-season" means 20°F, and "four-season" or "winter" means below 0°F). Sleeping bags are made either of down (warmer and lighter, but more expensive, and miserable when wet) or of synthetic material (heavier, more durable, and warmer when wet). Prices vary, but range from $65-100 for a summer synthetic to $250-550 for a down winter bag. **Sleeping bag pads,** including foam pads ($15 and up) and air mattresses ($25-50) cushion the back and neck and provide insulation from the ground. Another good alternative is the **Therm-A-Rest,** which is part foam and part air-mattress and inflates to full padding when unrolled.

Tents: The best **tents** are free-standing, with their own frames and suspension systems—they set up quickly and require no staking (except in high winds). Low-profile dome tents are the best all-around. When pitched, their internal space is almost entirely usable, which means little unnecessary bulk. Tent sizes can be somewhat misleading: 2 people *can* fit in a 2-person tent, but will find life more pleasant in a 4-person. Still, if you're hiking, stick with a smaller tent that weighs no more than 3-4 lbs. Good 2-person tents start at $150, 4-person tents at $400, but last year's model is usually half the price. Tent seams should be sealed with waterproofer, and a rain fly is necessary.

Backpacks: Hikers should definitely have a frame backpack. **Internal-frame packs** mold better to the back, keep a lower center of gravity, and can flex adequately to allow strenuous hiking that requires a lot of bending and maneuvering. **External-frame packs** are more comfortable for long hikes over even terrain, since they keep the weight higher and distribute it more evenly. All packs should have a strong, padded hip belt, which transfers weight from the shoulders to the legs. Any serious backpacking requires a pack of at least 4000 cubic inches. A sleeping bag will take up an additional 500 cubic inches in internal-frame packs. Sturdy backpacks cost $125-500.

Boots: Hiking boots should have good **ankle support** and be appropriate for the terrain. Your boots should fit snugly and comfortably over one or two wool socks and a thin liner sock. Be sure that the boots are broken in before your trip—a bad blister will ruin your hiking for days.

Other necessities: Rain gear should come in two pieces, a top and pants, rather than a poncho. **Synthetics,** like polypropylene tops, socks, and long underwear, along with a pile jacket, will keep you warm even when wet. When camping in autumn, winter, or spring, bring along a **"space blanket,"** which helps you to retain your body heat and doubles as a groundcloth ($5-15). Plastic **canteens** or water bottles keep water cooler than metal ones do, and are virtually leak-proof. Large, collapsible **water sacks** will significantly improve your lot in primitive campgrounds, and weigh practically nothing when empty, though they can get bulky. Bring **water-purification tablets** for when you can't boil water. Though most campgrounds provide campfire sites, you may want to bring a small **metal grate** or **grill** of your own. For those places that forbid fires or the gathering of firewood, you'll need a **camp stove**. The classic Coleman starts at about $30. A **first aid kit, swiss army knife, insect repellent, calamine lotion,** and **waterproof matches** or a **lighter** are essential camping items. Other items include: a **battery-operated lantern,** a **plastic groundcloth,** a **nylon tarp,** a **waterproof backpack cover** (although you can also store your belongings in plastic bags inside your backpack), and a **"stuff sack"** or plastic bag to keep your sleeping bag dry.

The mail-order firms listed below offer lower prices than those you'll find in many stores, but shop around locally first in order to determine what items actually look like and weigh.

Campmor, P.O. Box 700, Saddle River, NJ 07458-0700 (outside the U.S. 201-825-8300, within the U.S. 800-CAMPMOR/526-4784; email customer-service@campmor.com; http://www.campmor.com), has wide selection of name-brand equipment at low prices. One-year guarantee on unused or defective merchandise.

Recreational Equipment, Inc. (REI), 1700 45th St. E., Sumner, WA 98390 (800-426-4840; http://www.rei.com), stocks a wide range of the latest in camping gear and holds great seasonal sales. Many items are guaranteed for life (excluding normal wear and tear).

L.L. Bean, Freeport, ME 04033-0001 (800-441-5713 in Canada or the U.S.; (0800) 962 954 in the U.K.; 207-552-6878 elsewhere; fax 207-552-3080; http://www.llbean.com). Monolithic equipment and outdoor clothing supplier offers high quality and loads of info. Call or write for their free catalogue. The customer is guaranteed 100 percent satisfaction on all purchases; if it doesn't meet your expectations, they'll replace or refund it. Open 24hr.

Sierra Designs, 1255 Powell St., Emeryville, CA 94608 (510-450-9555; fax 654-0705), carries all seasons and types of especially small and lightweight tents.

WILDERNESS AND SAFETY CONCERNS

Stay warm, stay dry, and **stay hydrated.** The vast majority of life-threatening wilderness problems stem from a failure to follow this advice. On any hike, however brief, you should pack enough equipment to keep you alive should disaster befall. This includes **rain gear, hat** and **mittens,** a **first-aid kit, high energy food,** and **water.** See **Camping and Hiking Equipment,** p. 45, for more info.

Check **weather forecasts** and pay attention to the skies when hiking. Whenever possible, let someone know when and where you're going, either a friend, your hostel, a park ranger, or a local hiking organization. Do not attempt a hike beyond your ability—you may be endangering your life. See **Health,** p. 11, for info about outdoor ailments as well as basic medical concerns and first-aid. A good guide to outdoor survival is *How to Stay Alive in the Woods,* by Bradford Angier (Macmillan, $8).

ENVIRONMENTALLY RESPONSIBLE TOURISM

While protecting yourself from the elements, also consider protecting the wilderness from you. At the very least, a responsible traveler practices **"minimum impact camping"** techniques. Leave no trace of your presence when you leave a site. Make sure your campsite is at least 150 feet from water supplies or bodies of water. If there are no toilet facilities, bury human waste (but not paper) at least four inches deep and above the high-water line, 150 ft. or more from any water supplies and campsites. Above all, responsible tourism means being aware of your impact on the places you visit, and taking responsibility for your own actions. For more info on ecotourism or responsible travel in a particular region, contact the **Center for Responsible Tourism,** P.O. Box 827, San Anselmo, CA 94979 (415-258-6594).

BEAR IN MIND

Think you won't run into bears in California? Think again. Despite our continuing encroachment into the natural environment that was once theirs, bears are still here. If you do come across one, we know, they're irresistibly cute, but don't be fooled—they're wild and dangerous animals who are simply not intimidated by humans. A basic rule of thumb to follow is that if you're close enough for a bear to be observing you, you're too close.

When you sleep, don't even think about leaving food or other scented items (trash, toiletries, clothes that you cooked in) near your tent. The best way to keep your toothpaste from becoming a condiment is to **bear-bag.** This amounts to hanging your delectables from a tree, out of reach of hungry paws; ask a salesperson at a wilderness store to show you how.

If you see a bear at a distance, calmly walk (don't run) in the other direction. If it seems interested, back away slowly while speaking to the bear in firm, low tones and head for a safe area, ideally up a tree. Always shine a flashlight when walking at night: the bears will clear out before you arrive if given sufficient warning. If you stumble upon a sweet-looking bear cub, leave immediately, lest its over-protective mother stumble upon you. If you are attacked by a bear, get in a fetal position to protect yourself, put your arms over the back of your neck, and play dead. If you find this unsuccessful, defend yourself as best you can. In all situations, remain calm; loud noise and sudden movement can trigger an attack.

ORGANIZED ADVENTURE

Organized adventure tours offer another way of exploring the wild. Activities include hiking, biking, skiing, canoeing, kayaking, rafting, climbing, photo safaris, and archaeological digs, and go *everywhere.* Begin by consulting tourism bureaus, which can suggest parks, trails, and outfitters as well as answer more general questions. The **Specialty Travel Index,** 305 San Anselmo Ave., San Anselmo, CA 94960 (415-459-4900; fax 459-4974; http://www.specialtytravel.com), is a directory listing hundreds of tour operators worldwide. The **Sierra Club,** 85 Second St., 2nd fl., San Francisco, CA 94105-3441 (415-977-5630; fax 977-5795; email national.outings@sierraclub.org; http://www.sierraclub.org/outings), plans many adventure outings, both through its San Francisco headquarters and its local branches throughout Canada and the U.S. **Footloose** (http://www.footloose.com), is an outfit run by TrekAmerica which plans more sedate adventures for a somewhat older clientele. **Roadrunner International,** 6762A Centinela Avenue, Culver City, CA 90230 (800-TREKUSA/873-5782 in North America, (01892) 51 27 00 in Europe and the U.K.), offers hostel tour packages. **Incredible Adventures** (800-777-8464 or 415-759-7071; email info@incadventures.com; http://www.incadventures.com), based in San Francisco, specializes in backcountry hikes through Yosemite, the Central Coast, and the Sierra Nevada. The informative guides lead one- to seven-day hiking tours.

PARKS AND FORESTS

National Parks protect some of the most spectacular scenery in California and Hawaii. Though their primary purpose is preservation, the parks also host recreational activities like ranger talks, guided hikes, skiing, and snowshoe expeditions. Generally, internal roads allow you to reach the interior and major sights even if you are not a hiker. For info pertaining to the national park system, contact the **National Park Service,** Office of Public Inquiries, P.O. Box 37127, Room 1013, Washington, D.C. 20013-7127 (202-208-4747). The slick web page (http://www.nps.gov) lists info on all the parks, including detailed maps and fee and reservation data. The **National Park Foundation**, 1101 17th St. NW, #1102 Washington, D.C. 20036 (202-785-4500), distributes *The Complete Guide to America's National Parks* by mail-order ($16, plus $3 shipping).

National park entrance fees vary. The larger and more popular parks charge a $5-20 entry fee for cars and sometimes a $1-5 fee for pedestrians and cyclists. The

Golden Eagle Passport ($50), available at park entrances, allows the passport-holder's party entry into all national parks for one year. U.S. citizens or residents 62 and over qualify for the lifetime **Golden Age Passport** ($10 one-time fee), which entitles the holder's party to free park entry, a 50% discount on camping, and 50% reductions on various recreational fees for the passport holder. Persons eligible for federal benefits due to disabilities can enjoy the same privileges with the **Golden Access Passport** (free). Golden Age and Access Passports must be purchased at a park entrance with proof of age or federal eligibility, respectively; Golden Eagle Passports can also be bought by writing to ATTN: Golden Eagle Passport, 1100 Ohio Dr., SW, Room 138, Washington, D.C. 20242. All passports are also valid at National Monuments, Forests, Wildlife Preserves, and other national recreation sites.

Most national parks have both backcountry and developed tent **camping;** some welcome RVs, and a few offer grand lodges. At the more popular parks, reservations are essential, available through **DESTINET** (800-365-2267 in U.S., 619-452-8787 outside the U.S.; fax 619-546-1709; http://www.destinet.com/nps/nps1.html), no more than five months in advance. Lodges and indoor accommodations should be reserved months in advance. Campgrounds often observe first-come, first-camped policies. Arrive early—many campgrounds fill up by late morning. Some limit your stay and/or the number of people in a group. Fortunately for **bikers,** California state law requires that no bicyclist be turned away from a state campground, no matter how crowded the site—and they only have to pay $3 per night.

Often less accessible and less crowded, U.S. **National Forests** (http://www.fs.fed.us), provide a purist's alternative to parks. While some have recreation facilities, most are equipped only for primitive camping—pit toilets and no water are the norm. Entrance fees, when charged, are $10-20, but camping is generally less than $3-4. Backpackers can take advantage of specially designated wilderness areas, which have regulations barring all vehicles—the necessary wilderness permits can be obtained at the U.S. Forest Service field office in the area. If you are interested in exploring a National Forest, call or write for a copy of *A Guide to Your National Forests* (publication FS #418), ATTN: PAO, Public Publications, USDA, Forest Service, 201 14th St. SW, Auditors Building, Washington, D.C. 20250 (202-205-0957; fax 205-0885). This booklet includes a list of all national forest addresses. Request maps and other info directly from the forest you plan to visit. Reservations, with a one-time $16.50 service fee, are available for most forests, but are usually unnecessary except during high season at the more popular sites. Write or call up to one year in advance (National Recreation Reservation Center, P.O. Box 900, Cumberland, MD 21501-0900; 800-280-2267; fax 301-722-9802).

Many states have parks of their own, which offer some of the best camping around—handsome surroundings, elaborate facilities, and plenty of space. In contrast to national parks, the primary function of **state parks** is recreation. Prices for camping at public sites are almost always better than those at private campgrounds. Seniors receive a $2 discount at most state parks. Write the **California Department of Parks and Recreation,** Attn.: Publications, P.O. Box 942896, California State Parks Store, Sacramento, CA 94296 (916-653-4000). They offer state parks brochures, a map titled *Guide to California State Parks* ($2), and the book *Visitor's Guide to California State Parks* ($15). For Hawaii, write the **Department of Land and Natural Resources,** Division of State Parks, P.O. Box 621, Honolulu, HI 96809. For reservations and info, including the pamphlet *Guide to Hawaii's State Parks,* contact 808-587-0300 (fax 808-587-0311).

Adventurers who plan to explore some real wilderness should check in at a Forest Service field office or ranger station before heading out. Write ahead to order detailed and accurate maps ($4-8). Always try the **Pacific Southwest Region,** U.S. Forest Service, 630 Sansome St., San Francisco, CA 94111 (415-705-2874), as they are more helpful and less busy than the central office.

HIKING

Hiking is the only way to reach some of the most beautiful areas in California and Hawaii. *Let's Go* describes many daytrips and longer hikes; ask fellow travelers, locals, travel offices, park ranger stations, and outdoor equipment shops for other treks. Before setting off, it's a good idea to take a mile-long, pre-trip practice hike to test your shoes and pack weight. If you get lost, your chances for emerging safely will increase if you conserve your energy. Don't wander around until you're exhausted. Instead, wait for others to find you.

California's **Pacific Crest Trail,** stretching from the Mexican border into Canada, is particularly attractive for one- or two-week hiking trips along shorter segments. The San Bernardino National Forest, in the San Gorgonio Wilderness Area, has a beautiful stretch of trail in southern California. In central California, Desolation Wilderness and the John Muir Wilderness are particularly scenic. Although all of the trail's scenery in northern California is awe-inspiring, the Trinity Alps, Castle Crags, and Russian Wilderness (in the Shasta-Trinity National Forest), as well as the Lassen National Forest—a volcanic park—are especially recommended. For the USDA Forest Service's informational packet on the trail, write them at the address listed above under **Parks and Forests.** A word of warning: when hiking, be wary of unstable rock formations, ledges, and cliffs. For more information, see **From Crest to Crest: the Trail of the West** on p. 409.

Hawaii also has excellent hiking, on trails winding from steamy tropics to stark volcanoes. The best destinations for hikers are the **Na Pali Coast** on the lush island of Kauai, and Hawaii's two national parks, **Haleakala** on Maui and **Hawaii Volcanoes** on the Big Island. In Hawaii, take particular care to clean your boots before moving between islands to prevent the spread of plant diseases.

■ Keeping in Touch

U.S. MAIL

Offices of the **U.S. Postal Service** are usually open Monday to Friday from 9am to 5pm, and sometimes on Saturday until about noon; branches in many larger cities open earlier and close later. All are closed on national holidays. If you don't want to make the trip to the post office, most **hotels** and **hostel owners** will mail stamped postcards or letters for you if you ask. Postal rates in the U.S. are, **within the U.S.,** postcards 20¢, letters 32¢. Because of recent mail bomb scares, the U.S. Postal Service now requires that **overseas** letters over 1 lb. be mailed directly from the post office and be accompanied by a customs form. **Overseas rates** are: postcards 50¢, ½oz. 60¢, 1oz. $1, 40¢ per additional ounce. **Aerogrammes,** sheets that fold into envelopes and travel via air mail, are available at post offices for 50¢. Domestic mail generally takes 3-5 days; overseas mail, 7-14 days. Write **"AIR MAIL"** on the front of the envelope for speediest delivery.

If people want to get in touch with you, mail can be sent **General Delivery** to a city's main post office. You should bring a passport or other ID to pick up General Delivery mail. Always write "Hold for 30 Days" in a conspicuous spot on the envelope. Family and friends can send letters to you labeled like this:

Michael J. <u>FOX</u> (underline last name for accurate filing)
c/o General Delivery
Post Office Street Address
Sitcomsville, GA 30605
USA (if from another country)

In both the U.S. and Canada, **American Express** offices will act as a mail service for cardholders if contacted in advance. Under this free **"Client Letter Service,"** they will hold mail for 30 days, forward upon request, and accept telegrams. A complete list is available free from AmEx (800-528-4800), in the booklet *Traveler's Companion* or online at http://www.americanexpress.com/shared/cgi-bin/tsos-erve.cgi?travel/index.

If regular airmail is too slow, there are a few faster, more expensive, options. **Federal Express** (800-463-3339), is a reliable private courier service that guarantees overnight delivery anywhere in the continental U.S., for a price (a letter under ½ lb. sets you back $13.26). The cheaper but more sluggish U.S. Postal Service **Express Mail** will deliver a ½ lb. parcel in two days for $10.75 from any post office.

TELEPHONES

Telephone numbers in the U.S. and Canada consist of a three-digit area code, a three-digit exchange, and a four-digit number, written as 123–456-7890. Numbers with an **800** area code are toll-free numbers. A quick guide:

Local calls: Dial the last 7 digits.
Long-distance calls within the U.S.: 1 + area code + 7-digit number. Same area code calls are not always local; for long-distance calls within an area code: 1 + 7-digit number. For toll-free 800 numbers: 1 + 800 + 7-digit number.
International calls: Dial the universal international access code (011) followed by the country code, the city code, and the local number. Country codes and city codes may sometimes be listed with a zero in front (e.g., 033 for France), but when using 011, drop successive zeros (e.g., 011-33). In some areas you will need to give the number to the operator, who will then place the call for you. See **appendix** (p. 509) for some country codes.

Evening rates are considerably less than weekday rates (generally Sun.-Fri. 5-11pm), and **night and weekend rates** are even cheaper than evening rates (generally Mon.-Fri. 11pm-8am, all day Sat., and all day Sun. except 5-11pm).

Dialing **"0"** will get you the **operator,** who is omnipotent in all matters remotely connected with phones. To obtain local phone numbers for a specific place or to find area codes for other cities, call **directory assistance** at **411** or look in the local **white pages** telephone directory; for **long-distance directory assistance,** dial 1-(area code)-555-1212.

Pay phones are plentiful, most often stationed on street corners and in public areas. Put your coins (10-25¢ for a local call depending on the region) into the slot before dialing. If there is no answer or if you get a busy signal, you will get your money back after hanging up, but if you connect with an answering machine the phone will gobble your coins. If you're at a pay phone and don't have change, you can dial "0" for the operator and ask to place one of the following types of calls:

Collect call: If whoever picks up the phone call accepts the charges, he or she will be billed for the call. The cheapest is MCI's 800-COLLECT/205-5328 service, which is 20-44% less expensive than other collect rates. AT&T's collect service, 800-CALL-ATT, guarantees AT&T lines and rates for the call.
Person-to-person collect call: A little more expensive than a normal collect call, but a charge appears only if the person you wish to speak to is there (for example, if you want to speak to Michelle but not her parents).
Third-party billing: Bills the call to a third party. Have the number of the place you want to call and the number of the place you want to foot the bill (e.g., home).

A **calling card** is probably your best and cheapest bet; your local long-distance service provider will have a number for you to dial while traveling (either toll-free or charged as a local call) to connect instantly to an operator in your home country. The calls (plus a small surcharge) are then billed either collect or to the calling card. For more information, call **AT&T** about its **USADirect** and **World Connect** services (888-288-4685, or from abroad 810-262-6644 collect), **Sprint** (800-877-4646, or from abroad 913-624-5335 collect), or **MCI WorldPhone** and **World Reach** (800-444-4141, or from abroad dial the country's MCI access number). In Canada, contact Bell Canada **Canada Direct** (800-565-4708); in the U.K., British Telecom **BT Direct** (800 34 51 44); in Ireland, Telecom Éireann **Ireland Direct** (800 250 250); in Australia, Telstra **Australia Direct** (13 22 00); in New Zealand, **Telecom New Zealand** (123); and in South Africa, **Telkom South Africa** (09 03). Travelers with British Telecom, Telecom Eireann, New Zealand Telecom, Telkom South Africa, or Telecom Australia accounts at home can use special **access numbers** to place calls from the U.S. through their home systems. All companies except Telkom South Africa have different access numbers depending on whether their cooperative partner in the U.S. is AT&T, MCI, or Sprint. Access numbers are: British Telecom (800-445-5667 AT&T, 800-444-2162 MCI, 800-800-0008 Sprint); Telecom Australia (800-682-2878 AT&T, 800-937-6822 MCI, 800-676-0061 Sprint); Telkom South Africa (800-949-7027).

Some enterprising companies have created "callback" phone services. Under these plans, you call a specified number, ring once, and hang up. The company's computer calls back and gives you a dial tone. You can then make as many calls as you want, at rates about 20-60% lower than you'd pay using credit cards or pay phones. This option is most economical for loquacious travelers, as services may include a $10-25 minimum billing per month. For information, call **America Tele-Fone** (800-321-5817), **Globaltel** (770-449-1295), **International Telephone** (800-638-5558), and **Telegroup** (800-338-0225).

Remember **time differences** when you call. Britain, for example, is eight hours ahead of California, and 11 ahead of Hawaii.

OTHER COMMUNICATION

Domestic and international **telegrams** offer an option slower than phone but faster than post. Fill out a form at any post or telephone office, and cables arrive in one or two days. Telegrams can be quite expensive—**Western Union,** (800-325-6000), for example, adds a surcharge to the per-word rate depending on the country. You may wish to consider **faxes** for more immediate, personal, and cheaper communication. Major cities have bureaus where you can pay to send and receive faxes, or you can simply go to the nearest photocopying center.

If you're spending a year abroad and want to keep in touch with friends or colleagues in a college or research institution, **electronic mail (email)** is an attractive option. With minimal computer knowledge and a little planning, you can beam messages anywhere for no per-message charge. **Traveltales.com** (http://traveltales.com), provides free, web-based email for travelers and maintains a list of cybercafes, travel links, and a travelers' chat room. Other free, web-based email providers include **Hotmail** (http://www.hotmail.com), **RocketMail** (http://www.rocketmail.com), **Juno** (www.juno.com), and **USANET** (http://www.usa.net).

Travelers who have the luxury of a laptop with them can use a **modem** to call an internet service provider. Long-distance phone cards specifically intended for such calls can defray normally high phone charges. Check with your long-distance phone provider to see if they offer this option; otherwise, try a **C.COM Internet Phone-Card** (888-464-2266), which offers Internet connection calls for 15¢ per minute, with a minimum initial purchase of $5.

CALIFORNIA

California is all about attitude, but just which attitude you want to cop is up to you. You'll have plenty of choices: the average perception of California is so skewed and distorted by the funhouse mirror of media culture that no one can truly characterize the Golden State. Is it the place of dreams? A battleground of gang warfare? The ultra-chic home of pop culture and glamor? An urban nightmare? A natural wonderland? All of it, baby, and more. No other state (and few other countries) can claim such a divergent blend of cultural influences.

The Golden State is the third-largest in the nation, bigger than the entire country of Italy. All of this land leaves plenty of room for diversity. The glare of spotlights, the clang of a trolley, and the bustle of the *barrio* are all California. The soft vanilla scent of Jeffery pines, the auburn sunset over an alpine lake, and the ghostly shimmer of the desert floor are all California. The breezy liberalism of the Bay Area, the chic styl-ization of L.A., and the trendy traditionalism of San Diego are all California. It is not without conflict that these visions collide. The anti-war movements of the 60s and 70s, the political tensions of the 80s, and the resurgent racial issues of the 90s are tes-tament to the delicate balance which exists in the state, and to the strength of the people and ideas that bring it together.

For hundreds of years, settlers have come to California in search of the elusive and the unattainable. The Spanish conquistadors came for the mythical land of El Dorado, the '49ers hunted for the Mother Lode, and the naïve and beautiful still search for star-dom. The movie and music industries in Southern California, and the hip intelligen-tsia in San Francisco, lure the world's beautiful people to this image-obsessed state. And image *is* everything—California is far ahead of its time in trendiness and taboo-breaking, setting the tone for the rest of the nation through the glittering images which remain the state's main export and commodity. Leave it to the rest of the world to uphold tradition, but California makes its own rules.

PRACTICAL INFORMATION

Postal Abbreviation: CA.
Capital: Sacramento.
Visitor Information: California Office of Tourism, 801 K St., #1600, Sacramento 95814 (call 800-862-2543 for tourism materials).
National Park Information: (415-556-0560).
Time Zone: Pacific (1hr. behind Mountain, 2hr. behind Central, 3hr. behind Eastern, 3hr. ahead of Hawaii, 8hr. behind GMT, 15hr. behind much of Asia).
Area: 158,693 sq. mi., third largest state in the U.S.A., and larger than Italy.
Population: 33,000,000.

IMPRACTICAL INFORMATION

Nickname: The Golden State.
Motto: *Eureka* (I have found it).
State Animal: Grizzly Bear.
State Song: "I Love You, California."
Unofficial State Song: "California Über Alles."
State Flower: Golden Poppy.
State Tree: Redwood.

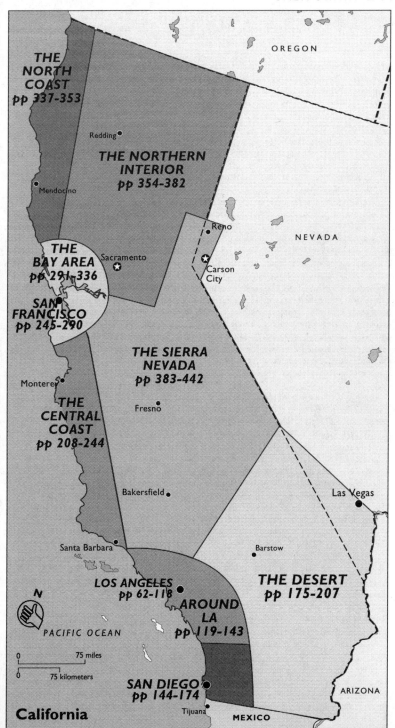

THE
NORTH
COAST
pp 337–353

OREGON

Redding

THE NORTHERN
INTERIOR
pp 354–382

Mendocino

Reno

NEVADA

THE
BAY AREA
pp 291–336

Sacramento

Carson
City

SAN
FRANCISCO
pp 245–290

THE SIERRA
NEVADA
pp 383–442

Monterey

THE
CENTRAL
COAST
pp 208–244

Fresno

Bakersfield

Las Vegas

Santa Barbara

Barstow

THE DESERT
pp 175–207

N

LOS ANGELES
pp 62–118

AROUND
LA
pp 119–143

PACIFIC OCEAN

0   75 miles

0   75 kilometers

SAN DIEGO
pp 144–174

Tijuana

ARIZONA

MEXICO

California

■ The California Story

The Early Years And Exploration

Before California was California, it was **Mexico.** And before it was Mexico, it was home to more than 100 **Native American** cultures, descendents of the original Paleo-Siberian immigrants, each with their own political system, social customs, and language. California's tribes made up the densest population north of Mesoamerica.

In 1542, **Spain** made the first European contact with California tribes when explorers Bartolome Ferrelo and Juan Rodríguez de Cabrillo (actually a Portuguese conquistador) sailed into San Diego. Finders keepers, after all, and the Spanish influence in the area remains strong even to this day, in everything from architecture to language. The Spanish named the region *California* after the mythical land full of gold, jewels, and tall, bronze Amazons in the romance *Las Sergas de Esplandian* (1510). The California girl was born.

The **English,** not to be outdone, followed the Spanish lead; sea dog Sir Francis Drake encountered the Miwoks, one of the largest of the California tribes, near present-day San Francisco in 1578. As it turned out, it was not English or Spanish aggression, but rather the European **diseases** they brought along which proved to be the tribes' main enemy: between 25 to 50% of California's native population died from smallpox, tuberculosis, and measles.

The area began to be settled en masse from 1769, when King Charles ordered colonization in order to prevent other countries from encroaching into the area. Coastal cities like San Francisco (founded 1776) and Los Angeles (founded 1787) cropped up alongside Catholic **missions,** which were introduced by **Father Junípero Serra** (see below). Many of the state's Native American residents were denied their own religion, Christianized, and coerced into working at the missions. Relegated to a serf-like status in the Spanish feudal order, the cultures which had thrived here for thousands of years were about to come to an end.

A Man with a Mission

Along with the new governor and the fleets of Spanish soldiers that arrived in California in 1769 came Father Junípero Serra, a Franciscan priest with a proselytizing fervor like the Native Americans had never seen. Over the next 54 years, he and his successor founded 21 missions up and down the California coast along a path called El Camino Reál (The Royal Road), which roughly corresponds to the modern U.S. 101. Despite a shortage of materials and labor, Serra pushed for new missions with such zealousness that the Spanish governor swore it was "nothing less than the temptation of the evil one." Serra's obsession with his missions has been passed down in the hearts of many Californians, who take a fierce pride in the fact that such structures can be found nowhere else in the United States. When the edifices began to fall into ruin in the early 20th century, mission-loving citizens banded together to campaign for restoration funds. Over the next 50 years, nearly all the buildings (save the churches) were stripped to the ground and painstakingly rebuilt in perfect adobe replicas of the originals. Today, every fourth grader in California faithfully follows in the footsteps of these philanthropists and builds a miniature model of one of Father Serra's missions out of milk cartons and popsicle sticks. For a list of all the missions, see p. 460 of the index.

The Nineteenth Century: Statehood

Beginning in the early 19th century, the Spanish met with competition in the form of a Russian fur trading post at Fort Ross (occupied 1812-1841), just north of San Francisco (see p. 337). Fortunately for the newly independent republic of **Mexico** (declared in 1824), Russian occupation was short-lived, but Mexico now had a more determined and formidable enemy: the USA.

With the mission system dissolved by 1833, the lands were divided up among privileged Mexicans called **rancheros** who dominated vast parcels of land. At the same time, a slow, steady trickle of American settlers headed west to the mythical land fancifully described as "edenic" in national newspapers. Unhappy with the Mexican government and driven by nationalistic fervor, the settlers staged the Bear Flag Revolt in 1846 and proclaimed California's **independence.** The nation of California turned out to be fleeting however, as the U.S. soon declared war on Mexico in an effort to control the area.

The campaign for California was the last frontier of **Manifest Destiny,** a popular concept of the necessity for Western expansion. Fueled by a desire for land, the region's plentiful resources, and undisguised racism, would-be Californians decided that this land was their birthright. America's "noble mission," according to an article published in the 1847 edition of the *Congressional Globe,* was to force the Mexicans and natives to "yield to a superior population…out-living, out-trading, exterminating the weaker blood." The **acquisition** of California was supported not only by politicians (including President Polk), but also by popular opinion. Even the poet Walt Whitman joined in the rally, writing in the *Brooklyn Eagle,* "Mexico must be thoroughly chastised!…Let our arms now be carried with a spirit which shall teach the world that…America knows how to crush, as well as how to expand!"

Under such severe pressure, Mexico eventually surrendered. In the 1848 Treaty of Guadalupe Hidalgo, Mexico ceded half of its territory, including California, to the USA. For the U.S., the timing was golden. While the cession became official, James Marshall discovered the precious metal at Sutter's Mill, and the rush was on. The feverish search for **gold** by a motley torrent of fortune seekers—known collectively as the 49ers—deluged the region in 1849, and the non-native population proliferated sixfold within four years. The miners' demands for food and supplies created an economic boom, galvanizing San Francisco's development into an international port. A savvy retailer named Levi-Strauss capitalized on demand for sturdy pants by making denim jeans the clothing of choice for miners (and generations since).

> A savvy retailer named Levi-Strauss capitalized on demand for sturdy pants by making denim jeans the clothing of choice for miners.

Realizing they were sitting on a veritable goldmine, the Californians quickly wrote their own constitution and inaugurated John C. Fremont as their first governor a full year before they were granted **statehood** by the U.S. Congress. The profitable new territory was made a free (non-slave) state in a political deal to pass the Fugitive Slave Act in 1850; California's now-famous liberalism was starting to grow. Unfortunately, Californians were less concerned with the rights of Native Americans than those of African-Americans, and the 1850s were marked by the Mariposa and Modoc Wars, of which several sites can still be seen (see Captain Jack's Stronghold, p. 376).

The completion of the **Transcontinental Railroad** in 1869 made travel to California a viable option for fortune-seekers everywhere, and the state has been an American Dream ever since.

The 20th Century: All That Glitters

Rapid growth continued into the 20th century as the state's population doubled between the two World Wars. Due in large part to its new status as movie capital of the world, the area around Los Angeles grew in tandem with the automobile, and innovations such as center dividing lines on highways and automatic traffic signals got their start. **Studios** and **stars** cropped up around the City of Angels, and a quiet little company run by Walt Disney drew up plans for world domination. By 1939, products such as **oranges** made California the leading agricultural state in the nation. The grape industry grew a bunch following the repeal of Prohibition, and by 1940 California supplied 90% of the nation's **wine,** table grapes, and raisins.

After the war production boom of the 40s, post-war projects such as the irrigation canals and freeways of Southern California promoted even swifter expansion. In 1964, California redefined the power centers of America by overtaking New York as the nation's most populous state. During the early 60s, the **surf culture** of Frankie and Annette, longboards, and the Beach Boys created a carefree image of California which persists to this day. In the later 60s, the beach party ended and nationwide waves of upheaval began to shake the college campuses and ghettoes of California. In 1967, San Francisco's Haight-Ashbury neighborhood declared a **"Summer of Love,"** and young people voiced their disgust with the Establishment by—in Timothy Leary's words—"turning on, tuning in, and dropping out." At the same time, UCLA film school student **Jim Morrison** (a classmate of Francis Ford Coppola and Oliver Stone) decided to start a band whose name he lifted from Aldous Huxley's *The Doors of Perception*. But even as this radical subculture flourished, California managed to thrust **Richard Nixon** and **Ronald Reagan** into the political limelight.

In the 70s, water and fuel shortages and the unbearable L.A. smog forced Californians to alter their once-inviolable ways of life. Governor Jerry "Moonbeam" Brown romanced Linda Ronstadt while Proposition 13, a popular initiative limiting state taxes, captured nationwide attention. The enthusiasm died out, however, when state services were stripped to the bone, and Californians discovered that starving government wasn't the panacea they had hoped. New problems arrived in the 80s as cellular phones jammed airways and Beemers jammed freeways. From the San Fernando Valley sprung the **Valley Girl,** changing the face of mall culture, like, forever. **Pollution** and gross industrialization continued to cloud the state's utopian vision. Illegal Mexican immigrants streamed across the border in greater numbers, initiating new debates on issues of freedom and human rights. In 1992, the Los Angeles riots signalled that the U.S. has yet to solve what W.E.B. DuBois prophetically called "the problem of the 20th century"—the issue of **race.** The passage of Proposition 187 explicitly, and the O.J. Simpson trial implicitly, renew questions of ethnicity and tolerance quietly swept under the carpet with the original conquest of California in the 19th century. Once hailed as a haven of acceptance, California is finding it hard to ignore the prejudice and class division which tarnish the state's golden reputation.

Recent News

In a state as diverse as California, there are bound to be some conflicts, but the 90s have brought an unprecedented amount of racial turmoil and violence to the area. Most recently, public outcry has been great over the passage of **Proposition 209,** which outlaws any "preferential treatment" (affirmative action or quotas) in state programs (like public education) and employment. While the proposition, strongly supported by Governor Pete Wilson, has been implemented to some degree, court injunction brought things to a screeching halt after a coalition of civil rights groups filed a complaint. The debate continues, as Wilson argues that judgment should be based purely on merit, and civil rights activists insist that accepted measures of merit (e.g. standardized tests) discriminate implicitly against minorities. On a related note, the University of California system has called a halt to all **affirmative action** programs and has subsequently reported an alarming drop in minority student admissions and enrollment.

The "Trial Lasting a Century" finally drew to a close in February 1997 when a civil jury demanded that **O.J. Simpson** pay $25 million in punitive damages to the families of murder victims Nicole Brown Simpson and Ronald Goldman. This verdict came, paradoxically, after Simpson had been declared "not guilty" by a criminal jury. Nobody ever said L.A. made sense.

In December of 1996 the Oakland school board announced that it would begin using English as a Second Language (ESL) tools to aid African-American inner-city students, many of whom speak the "black English" dialect dubbed **Ebonics,** in learning standard English. This sparked waves of controversy all over the country, as President Clinton refused to allow federal ESL funds to be used in this way and many African-American activists argued that the measure would only alienate black students. The school board has since modified its policy.

While the state of California was embroiled in these political debates, 39 people quietly committed ritual suicide in a wealthy San Diego suburb in March of 1997. Members of the **Heaven's Gate cult,** they subscribed to a millennialist belief system which incorporated elements of Christianity and science fiction. The group, led by the charismatic Marshall Applewhite, viewed the passing of the Hale-Bopp comet as a sign from the Next Level, and hoped to board the spaceship which they believed to be hovering behind the comet.

■ The Arts

FILM AND TELEVISION

Hollywood has no counterpart. It is a strictly West Coast phenomenon, sometimes evoking disdain from its Eastern counterparts as nothing more than a glitzy, obnoxious proxy for "the legitimate theater." As the English actor Sir Cedric Hardwicke once said, "I believe that God felt sorry for actors so he created Hollywood to give them a place in the sun and a swimming pool." Today, this "place in the sun" exerts an increasingly influential hold over global pop culture.

Hollywood's emergence as movie capital of the U.S. had modest beginnings. Before 1910, independent New York filmmakers were being continually harassed by a movie trust seeking to drive out competition. The independents moved west and set up shop in sunny Hollywood, then a sleepy sheep-raising town. From there, a quick dash across the Mexican border could foil attempts to confiscate cameras and film. Moreover, they could take advantage of California's sun to light shots—artificial lighting had not yet been perfected.

As the balance of movie power began to shift west, the Hollywood studios instituted the **"star system."** For the first time, actors themselves were advertised and used to attract adoring fans to movie after movie. One of the first film divas was Mary Pickford, also known as "America's Sweetheart." Charlie Chaplin, Buster Keaton, Douglas Fairbanks, and that lover of lovers, Rudolph Valentino, soon attained legendary status by virtue of their appearances on the silver screen.

The 1920s witnessed two major developments: sound and scandal. "Talkies," films with sound, were introduced with Al Jolson's *The Jazz Singer* in 1927. Scandals were ushered in when Fatty Arbuckle went on trial for the death of starlet Virginia Rappe. A suspicion that Hollywood was becoming a moral cesspool led to the appointment of Postmaster General Will Hays as "movie czar." His puritanical edicts established a model which "would have suited the strictest of convent nuns."

Gone With the Wind was the first large-scale extravaganza, pioneering exorbitant budgets, flamboyant costumes, and casts of thousands. The media hype that accompanied a nationwide search for an actress to play Scarlett O'Hara and the ensuing opening of the movie in Atlanta helped give cinema a permanent place in American popular culture. A less extravagant but equally important film event occurred in 1941, when Orson Welles unveiled his masterpiece, **Citizen Kane,** a work whose innovations expanded contemporary ideas about the potential of film.

> "God felt sorry for actors so he created Hollywood to give them a place in the sun and a swimming pool."

The increasing accessibility of television during the 50s magnified the scope and impact of Hollywood's image industry. In the 60s and 70s, shows like *Star Trek* and *All in the Family* gave Americans a common currency. The 80s and 90s have seen the mass-production of television go global; patriarchal adolescent fantasy *Baywatch,* a.k.a. "Babewatch," reigns as the world's most popular television show—the fourth of the Seven Signs of the Apocalypse. Shows like *Beverly Hills 90210, Melrose Place,* and MTV's *Real World* series (filmed in both San Francisco and L.A.) reinforce the popular idea of California as a ditzy blond place.

Let's Go often notes filming sites of well-known movies. For a sliver of real and unreal life in Cali, watch:

Bill & Ted's Excellent Adventure: (1989) An earlier, male version of **Clueless;** Keanu Reeves stars as a seminal slacker in this quintessential teenage-male flick.

The Big Sleep: (1946) Classic detective story, starring Lauren Bacall and Humphrey Bogart, who plays Raymond Chandler's hard-boiled Philip Marlowe.

Bird Man of Alcatraz: (1962) Based on the true story of convicted killer Robert Stroud, played by bird-friendly Burt Lancaster. Stroud, who was sentenced to death for killing a prison guard, wrote two books on bird diseases after being pardoned by President Wilson.

Boyz n the Hood: (1991) A hard-hitting portrayal of life in the poverty-stricken neighborhoods of South Central L.A. Director John Singleton's debut film.

Chinatown: (1974) Jack Nicholson sleuths through a creepy nighttime Los Angeles. Hold your breath for the famous last line.

Clueless: (1995) Alicia Silverstone stars in this fluffy flick about the lives, fashions, and annoying inflections of three valley high school girls. The plot's similarities to Jane Austen's *Emma* prove that this flick isn't as clueless at it seems.

Dirty Harry: (1971) Housewife fave Clint Eastwood plays a dangerous San Francisco cop. Directed by Don Siegel.

Devil in a Blue Dress: (1995) An African-American detective classic. Denzel Washington plays Walter Mosely's "Easy" Rawlins.

Earthquake: (1974) Los Angeles, predictably, crumbles; Charlton Heston stars.

The Graduate: (1967) Dustin Hoffman plays a recent college grad in a bizarre love triangle, set to the tune of Simon and Garfunkel's "Mrs. Robinson." Watch for the shot of the Bay Bridge, and notice our hero is driving the wrong way.

L.A. Story: (1991) Steve Martin's love song to the City of Angels. He even gets to rollerblade in the Museum of Contemporary Art!

Pulp Fiction: (1994) Much-hyped, *fin de siecle* vision of California cool. The soundtrack alone makes it worth watching.

Rebel Without a Cause: (1955) Teen icon James Dean in the quintessential story of disaffected youth. Shot at Hollywood High.

Short Cuts: (1993) Vignettes based on the short stories of Raymond Carver are linked through their L.A. suburbiana. The fruit fly spraying is no joke.

Speed: (1994) All right, we'll let you watch Keanu Reeves one more time. And no, the L.A. bus system never moves that fast.

Vertigo: (1958) Arguably Hitchcock's best thriller, starring Kim Novak and the breathtaking backdrop of San Francisco.

Who Framed Roger Rabbit: (1988) A hilarious melange of animation and real live actors. Wannabe detective story pokes fun at Raymond Chandler's stories of the seamy Southern California underside.

LITERATURE

California is second only to New York City as a shelter and inspiration for literary American minds. The state has been rooted in imagination since its earliest beginnings—even the name California comes from the fictional story of Queen Calafia. In later days, explorers and settlers praised this nouveau paradise in verse and in legend, and the literary flow began in earnest with the influx of the gold rush. The siren song of precious metal attracted more than a flood of scruffy miners; the 49er contingent included several authors whose writing introduced the world to the state's natural splendor and the rough-and-tumble culture of mining towns. Vestiges of the early California that appeared in the writing of **Bret Harte** and **Mark Twain** can still be seen in the relatively unspoiled hills and ghost towns of Gold Country. Even **Jack London,** Oakland's literary native son, spent some time panning for gold and writing pastoral short stories on the side. His "The Valley of the Moon" provides an evocative portrait of the Sonoma and San Joaquin Valleys before they were largely consumed by wineries and agribusiness. Poet and lover **Robinson Jeffers** composed his paeans in and around the Big Sur coast of Monterey County. **John Steinbeck** won the Nobel Prize for his stark representations of life in Depression-era California. His *Cannery Row* was based on the district of the same name in the city of Monterey, though the heavily commercialized present-day version hardly resembles Steinbeck's gritty evocation. During the 50s, **Jack Kerouac** and **Allen Ginsberg** combined candid autobiography with visionary rapture to become the gurus of

> Jack Kerouac and Allen Ginsberg combined autobiography with visionary rapture to become gurus of the Beat Generation.

the **Beat Generation;** they appropriated San Francisco's North Beach as their spiritual homeland. In the 70s, Hunter Thompson took the Beatniks' road trip motif in a new direction with his narcotic-laden tour through Southern California's barren Mojave Desert and into the City of Sin. Nineties Americana owes one of its most pervasive catch-phrases to the lonely ennui of Palm Springs's overripe resort culture, which spawned **Douglas Coupland's** seminal *Generation X.*

MUSIC

The California music scene past and present is as diverse as its topography. Sure, it never reached the true musical eminence of Britain—who saved the world with the influential likes of **Madness** and **Wham**—but California has nonetheless made its mark. Some of the world's best and worse music originated in the sunny West, mainly in the urban centers of Los Angeles and San Francisco.

Punk bands flourish in the Bay Area, and clubs host both local and big-name acts. Hometown boys include adolescent faves **Green Day** and **Offspring,** and the **Dead Kennedys** are such a big presence here that lead singer **Jello Biafra** reputedly once ran for mayor. **Surf-punk** bands like **NOFX** have broken the beach/brawl barrier, while purists prefer the **happy harmonies** of the **Beach Boys** and **Dick Dale and the Del-tones.** In the mainstream **"alternative"** scene, **No Doubt, Concrete Blonde** and **Oingo Boingo** have won the public's heart, while the noisier **Faith No More** (residing in the where-are-they-now file) was a little shorter-lived. **Jane's Addiction**-*cum*-**Porno for Pyros, Pavement, Rage Against the Machine, Guns 'n'** Posers (oops, Roses), **Metallica, Red Hot Chili Peppers,** and the **Stone Temple Pilots** have catered to many a teenaged boys' mosh pit fantasies.

Pop exports include **Paula Abdul,** the **Bangles** (apparently not an Eternal Flame), **Sheila E.,** disco kings **Earth, Wind and Fire,** the **Go-Go's, Huey Lewis and the** (Old) **News, Chris Isaak, Journey,** one-hit wonder **Quiet Riot, Tiffany** (could've been so beautiful), and **Toto.** Some of California's musicians are just famous for being **tacky;** this category includes **Cher** (Wait, does it count as music?) and love-child-*cum*-politician **Sonny Bono, Ricky Nelson** and his bleached offspring **Nelson, Linda Ronstadt, Santana, Sly and the Family Stone,** and **Van Halen.**

The "Summer of Love" has had long-lasting repercussions in this most liberal of states; **trippy** bands like **the Doobie Brothers, the Grateful Dead, Iron Butterfly, Jefferson Airplane** (post-identity crisis, just Starship), **the Mamas and the Papas, Frank Zappa,** and the Lizard Kings of them all, **the Doors,** are ever-popular here. Some, like **Creedence Clearwater Revival, the Eagles ,** and tree-hugger **Don Henley,** just won't go away.

The words "L.A. Music Scene" probably conjure up the (thankfully) brief **80s glam rock** phenomenon (see **Hair Today, Gone Tomorrow,** p. 117) but these days the city is more noted for rap artists like **2Pac, Coolio, Cypress Hill, Dr. Dre, Eazy E, Ice Cube, NWA, Snoop Doggy Dogg,** and **Warren G.** The recent death of rapper **Tupac** in a drive-by shooting has stirred up controversy over the violent content of hard-core rap.

VISUAL ARTS

Californians really do patronize their local artists. The local art festival is an institution, gently stroking the resident "artistes" who display their efforts. Much of the art is of the sea- or landscape genre and may remind you of the decor in your Motel 6 room. Some Golden State natives, however, have played a significant role in the development of American art. **Clyfford Still's** jagged abstract Expressionist canvases and **Richard Diebenkorn's** landscapes of the Santa Monica seashore (the *Ocean Park* series) are found in many California museums. **Wayne Thiebaud** captured San Francisco in the 70s with hyperbolic perspective and strikingly rich color. The brilliant hues and geometrical perspectives of **David Hockney's** paintings of California people and places attracted attention during the 80s, and he has since explored new media such as photography and stage design.

Much of Californian artists' best works are in the region's museums. The **Oakland Museum** (p. 305), for example, exclusively exhibits works of the state's residents. **Los Angeles** houses the eclectic Armand Hammer Museum of Art (p. 90), the Museum of Contemporary Art (p. 98), and the newly relocated Getty Center (p. 91), which holds some of the gems of Western painting. San Francisco is home to both the M. H. De Young Memorial Museum (p. 270), which exhibits the largest collection of Asian art outside of Asia, and the world-class SFMOMA (p. 262), probably the best museum in the state. Many of the state's smaller cities have regional museums or art galleries, and in the larger cities you may find museums dedicated to science, natural history, or cultural history.

Maybe it's something about the light here, or the variety of the scenery, but California has been infested with photographers since the medium was invented. The state has been home to some of this century's best professionals. In the 30s, **Dorothea Lange's** photos of the working and living conditions of migrant workers helped to convince the federal government to build public housing projects. Her 1936 photo *Migrant Mother* became a national symbol of the suffering caused by the Great Depression. In a different vein, **Ansel Adams'** photographs of Yosemite National Park and the Sierra have graced calendar pages everywhere and become among the most recognized photos in the U.S.

Until the late 19th century, Californian **architecture** generally consisted of simple, practical structures or emulations of eastern Victorian and Queen Anne styles. It came into its own when history blended with local materials, forming a unique new style. The "missionary revival" architecture of the 1890s, inspired by the Mexican ranch-style, first incorporated native materials and local design traditions. In the 1910s and 20s, architects like **Charles** and **Henry Greene** developed the shingle-style of California's redwood bungalows, particularly evident in the hills of the Bay Area.

> **The M. H. De Young Memorial Museum exhibits the largest collection of Asian art outside of Asia.**

In the 30s, **Julia Morgan** designed over 600 homes, among them the famous Hearst castle (see p. 226). **Frank Lloyd Wright,** one of the 20th century's most experimental architects, designed 25 buildings in the state, including the Barnsdale House in Hollywood and the Marin Civic Center. In recent years, **Frank Gehry** has attracted attention by building houses with angular surfaces and unorthodox materials, such as sheet metal and raw plywood. The California jumble of materials and methods was evident as early as 1930, when **Nathanael West** observed that L.A.'s canyons were lined with "Mexican ranch houses, Samoan huts, Mediterranean villas, Egyptian and Japanese temples, Swiss chalets, Tudor cottages, and every possible combination of these styles."

■ Outdoor Recreation

Where else but California could you go snowboarding and boogieboarding in a single day? Besides the sand-and-surf pastimes which have made the state famous, California offers climbing and hiking in the Sierra Nevada and the desolate Mojave Desert, kayaking and rafting in the rivers and lakes, and skiing and snowboarding at a number of resorts. Best of all, the state has the kind of weather which allows you to be outdoors all year long—though that may be outdoors in the snow. Check the visitor centers at the various national parks for details on the activities in that area. The best source is The Sierra Club, 85 Second St., San Francisco, CA 94105 (415-977-5630; fax 415-977-5797; e-mail information@sierraclub.org; http://www.sierraclub.org/outings), which has information on year-round outings.

SPECTATOR SPORTS

For those who'd rather watch than participate, this place is heaven—California is home to more professional sports teams than any other state. The five **Major League Baseball** representatives include the **Oakland Athletics** (or **A's**); the **L.A. Dodgers,** home to five out of the last six NL Rookies of the Year; the **Anaheim Angels;** the **San Diego Padres;** and the **San Francisco Giants.** Three **NFL football** teams call the state home: the **Oakland Raiders;** the **San Francisco '49ers,** '95 Superbowl victors; and the **San Diego Chargers,** '95 Superbowl runners-up. Four **NBA basketball** teams play here: the **L.A. Lakers** and their $124 million mercenary center/rap "singer"/ movie "star" Shaquille O'Neal; the rapidly improving **Golden State Warriors** (who play in the Bay Area); and two teams near the bottom of the league, the **Sacramento Kings** and the **L.A. Clippers.** Two **WNBA** (women's basketball) teams also call the state home: the **Sacramento Monarchs** and the **Los Angeles Sparks,** with the league's most popular player, Lisa Leslie.

In the land of surf and sun, three **NHL ice hockey** teams have melted their audience's hearts: the **L.A. Kings,** the **Anaheim Mighty Ducks,** and the **San Jose Sharks,** whose biting logo is the second most popular in American pro sports after the Chicago Bulls'. The fledgling **Major League Soccer (MLS)** league has two Californian representatives: the **L.A. Galaxy** and the **San Jose Clash.**

The **college sports** scene is dominated by USC, UCLA, Stanford, and UC Berkeley, all of whom boast powerhouse NCAA Division I programs in a variety of sports from swimming and tennis to fencing.

■ Land of Milk and Honey

California's gastronomic libido is matched by its sumptuous produce and innovative cuisine. Kitchens across the state turn out mouth-watering concoctions running the gamut from local favorites such as sourdough bread and Dungeness crab to Basque specialties. The Bay Area is home to the best Chinese food in North America, while L.A.'s Vietnamese and Mexican chow are unmatched outside their native countries. California leads the country in agricultural production, with fruits, vegetables, and nuts pouring forth in a 365-days-per-year growing season. This agricultural bounty, among other things, helped give the state the nickname "Land of Fruits and Nuts."

The state was also the inventor of a number of national food fads, including the 1950s-revival diner (Johnny Rockets, being the best) and drive-thru fast food (see **Feeding the Good, the Bad, and the Ugly,** p. 79). The California **wine** industry has successfully overcome obstacles from Prohibition to pesticides, and today, four of every five bottles sold in the U.S. are corked in Cali. Sorority girls everywhere owe their favorite social lubricant to the Wine Country, birthplace of the wine cooler.

Cuisinart

Don't go to California expecting to see the natives munching on granola and wheat germ; that stuff is for the crunchy folk up in Oregon and Washington. The hip food in the Golden State today is known by the broad generic "California Cuisine." Born, according to legend, at San Francisco's Chez Panisse, it's not a tradition nor even a movement—it's a *concept,* where the culinary and the aesthetic blend to create a total eating experience. The uninitiated may have trouble recognizing this trendy genre upon first contact. Telltale signs include cheeseless and/or sauceless pizza, angel hair pasta, and anything cooked on an oakwood grill. Look for combinations of radicchio, fontinella, cilantro, gorgonzola, sun-dried tomatoes, and shiitake mushrooms. And if you find yourself at an outdoor blond-wood table and the entree you ordered looks much smaller and involves much more mango than you had expected, fear not. Just nod approvingly and ask for a half-caf. All is cool.

CALIFORNIA

Los Angeles

Myth and anti-myth stand comfortably opposed in Los Angeles. Some see in its sweeping beaches and dazzling sun an extravagant demi-paradise, a bountiful land of opportunity where the most opulent dreams can be realized. Others point to its congestion, smog, and crime, and declare Los Angeles a sham—a converted wasteland where TV-numbed masses go to wither in the sun.

The popularity of L.A.-bashing has increased dramatically in recent years. With so many targets, is it any wonder? Of late, California's largest city has been plagued with a litany of crises: race riots, devastating earthquakes, floods, and rising homelessness. But alongside these disasters, millions of denizens defiantly call the city home. What might explain the fierce loyalty of Angelenos in the face of such catastrophes? Perhaps it's the persistence of L.A.'s peculiar mystique, the implacable veneer of a city whose most celebrated industry is the production and dissemination of images. The glitter of the studios, the mammoth billboards on Sunset Strip, and the glamour of Rodeo Drive all attest to the resilience of L.A.'s fixation.

Here is a wholly American urban phenomenon, one that developed not in the image and shadow of Europe, but contemporaneously with America's international ascendancy. It is this autonomy which gives L.A. its peculiar sense of pastlessness. In a city where nothing seems more than 30 years old, the latest trends curry more respect than the venerably ancient. Many come to this historical vacuum to make (or re-make) themselves. And what better place? Without the tiresome duty of kowtowing to the gods of an established high culture, Angelenos are free to indulge not in what they must, but in what they choose. The resulting atmosphere is deliciously rife with potential. Some savor L.A.'s image-bound culture, others may be appalled by the shallowness of its unabashed excess, but either way it's a hell of a show.

■ Practical Information

Visitor Information:

Los Angeles Convention and Visitor Bureau, 685 S. Figueroa St. (213-689-8822), between Wilshire and 7th in the Financial District. Hundreds of brochures. Staff speaks English, French, German, Spanish, Japanese, and Tagalog. Maps of L.A., sights, and buses, each about $2. Maps of celebrity sights and California roads $4. Distributes *Destination: Los Angeles,* a free booklet including tourist and lodging info. Open Mon. 8am-5pm, Sat. 8:30am-5pm.

National Park Service, 30401 Agoura Rd. (818-597-9192), in Agoura Hills in the Conejo Valley. Info on the Santa Monica Mountains, including outdoor activities and special events. Open Mon.-Fri. 8am-5pm., Sat.-Sun. 9am-5pm.

Sierra Club, 3345 Wilshire Blvd. #508 (213-387-4287). Hiking, biking, and backpacking information. Ask about group outings. Three-month schedule of events $7.50. Open Mon.-Fri. 10am-6pm.

Budget Travel:

Council Travel, 10904 Lindbrook Ave. (310-208-3551; fax 310-208-4407), in Westwood Village. Cheap flights, HI-AYH memberships, ISICs. Limited selection of backpacks, travel guides, and hostel sheets. Open Mon.-Tues. and Thurs.-Fri. 9am-5pm, Wed. 11am-6pm, Sat. 11am-3pm. Walk-in clients only. **STA Travel,** 7202 Melrose Ave. (213-934-8722), has similar services, although they do not offer travel accessories. Two other offices, in Westwood and on Melrose. Open Mon.-Fri. 10am-6pm.

Los Angeles HI-AYH: 1434 2nd St. (310-393-3413), Santa Monica. Info and supplies for travelers. Guidebooks, backpacks, moneybelts, low-cost flights, rail passes, and ISICs. Open Mon.-Thurs. 9am-7pm, Fri.-Sat. 9am-5pm.

Consulates: Australia, 2049 Century Park E., 19th fl. (310-229-4800). Open Mon.-Fri. 8am-5pm; visa desk open Mon.-Fri. 10am-4pm. **France,** 10990 Wilshire Blvd. (310-235-3200), at Veteran. Open Mon.-Fri. 9am-noon and 2:30-5pm. **Germany,** 6222 Wilshire Blvd. (213-930-2703). Open Mon.-Fri. 8am-4pm for calls, 8-11am for

Southern California

visas. **Japan,** California Plaza I, 350 S. Grand Ave., 17th fl. (213-617-6700). Open Mon.-Fri. 9:30-11:30am and 1-4pm for calls, 1-4pm only for visas. **South Africa,** 50 N. La Cienega Blvd. (310-657-9200). Open Mon.-Fri. 9am-4pm, visa desk open 9am-noon. **U.K.,** 11766 Wilshire Blvd. #400 (310-477-3322). Open 6:30am-4pm for calls, 9am-noon for visas. For visas, arrive at the consulate between 8 and 9am or else face a long line.

Currency Exchange: Available at most LAX terminals (see **Getting There,** p. 69), but rates are exorbitant. **American Express** offices have better rates and don't charge fees to change currency ($3 fee for non-AmEx traveler's checks). AmEx **downtown,** 901 W. 7th St. (627-4800). Open Mon.-Fri. 8am-6pm. Also in **Beverly Hills,** 327 N. Beverly Hills Dr. (310-274-8277). Open Mon.-Fri. 10am-6pm, Sat. 6am-5pm. Other locations in **Pasadena, Torrance,** and **Costa Mesa. World Banknotes Exchange,** 406B W. 6th St., at Hill, doesn't charge to change currency, but 2% fee for traveler's checks. Open Mon.-Fri. 8am-5:30pm, Sat. 8am-3pm.

Airport: Los Angeles International Airport (LAX) (310-646-5252), in Westchester 15mi. southwest of downtown. Metro buses, car rental companies, cabs, and airport shuttles offer rides from here to requested destinations (see **Getting There,** p. 69).

Buses: Greyhound-Trailways Information Center, 1716 E. 7th St. (800-231-2222), at Alameda, downtown. Call for fares, schedules, and local ticket info. See neighborhood listings for other stations, and **Getting There** 69, for info on the main downtown terminal.

Public Transportation: MTA Bus Information Line, (213-626-4455 or 800-COM-MUTE/266-6883). Open Mon.-Fri. 6am-8:30pm, Sat.-Sun. 8am-6pm. You may be put on hold long enough to walk to your destination. **MTA Customer Service Center,** 5301 Wilshire Blvd., is open Mon.-Fri. 8:30am-5:30pm.

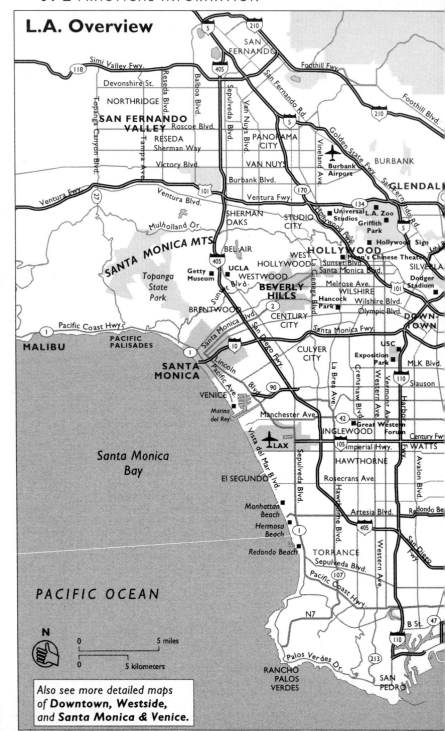

L.A. Overview

Also see more detailed maps
of **Downtown**, **Westside**,
and **Santa Monica & Venice**.

Taxis: Checker Cab (482-3456), **Independent** (385-8294), **United Independent** (653-5050). If you need a cab, it's best to call. Approximate fare from LAX to downtown is $24-$33.

Automobile Club: Automobile Club of Southern California, 2601 S. Figueroa St. (213-741-3111), at Adams. Lots of maps and info. Club privileges free for AAA members, $2-3 fee for nonmembers. Their *Westways* magazine is a good source for daytrips or vacations. Open Mon.-Fri. 9am-5pm. Numerous other offices in greater L.A.; call for locations.

Library: Central Public Library, 630 W. 5th St. (213-612-3200), between Grand and Flower. Present ID with current address to get a library card; reading room open to all. First floor's East Wing houses foreign-language books, weekly exhibits, and activities including readings, films, and workshops. Docent tours Mon.-Fri. 12:30pm, Sat. 11am and 2pm, Sun. 2pm. Library open Mon. and Thurs.-Sat. 10am-5:30pm, Tues.-Wed. noon-8pm, Sun. 1-5pm.

Cultural, Community, and Religious Centers:

African-American Community Unity Center, 944 W. 53rd St. (213-789-7300). Youth services, cultural workshops, and educational outreach programs. Call for activities listings. Open Mon.-Fri. 9am-5pm.

Chinese Chamber of Commerce, 977 N. Broadway (213-617-0396). Educational and recreational activities. Open Mon.-Fri. 10am-5pm; call ahead.

Gay and Lesbian Community Services Center, 1625 Schrader Blvd. (213-993-7400), 1 block from Hollywood Blvd. in Hollywood. Youth and senior groups, counseling, housing, educational, legal, and medical services. Building open Mon.-Sat. 9am-10pm, Sun. 9am-6pm, but most offices close around 5pm.

Japanese-American Cultural and Community Center, 244 S. San Pedro St., #505 (213-628-2725). Houses a garden, live theater, and the Doizaki Gallery. Library available by appointment only. Hours depend on current displays; in general, open Mon.-Fri. 9am-6pm.

Jewish Community Center, 5870 W. Olympic Blvd. (213-938-2531), 3 blocks east of Fairfax. Recreational facilities, senior services, day care, and health club. Open to people of all faiths. Olympic-size pool and gym open until 10pm, all other facilities open 9am-3pm. One-day guest pass $10.

Korean Cultural Center, 5505 Wilshire Blvd. (213-936-7141). Cultural activities, language workshops, and monthly film presentations. Houses a library, museum, and art gallery. Open Mon.-Fri. 9am-5pm, Sat. 10am-1pm.

Senior Recreation Center, 1450 Ocean Ave. (310-458-8644), in Palisades Park, Santa Monica. Lively international crowd partakes in outings, dance classes, and cultural activities. Hot lunches "like Mom used to make" Mon.-Fri. Open Mon.-Fri. 9am-4pm, Sat.-Sun. 11am-4pm.

Los Angeles County Commission on Disabilities, 500 W. Temple St. (213-974-1053). Info on transportation, equipment, and recreational facilities for people with disabilities. Open Mon.-Fri. 8am-5pm.

California Relay Service for the Hearing Impaired (800-735-2929/TTD/TTY). Lines are open 24hr.

Ticket Agency: Ticketmaster (213-381-2000), charges substantial surcharges. A better bet is to contact the box office directly.

Copies: Kinko's, 835 Wilshire Blvd. (213-892-1700), at Figueroa. Über copy shop offers photocopies, UPS, stamps, phone cards, and fax. Open 24hr. Call 800-2-KIN-KOS/254-6567 for other locations.

Surf Conditions: (310-457-9701) for recorded info on Malibu, Santa Monica, and South Bay. Surf-specific info (900-844-WAVE/9283). Urges callers to check it out, dude. Most FM radio stations have a surf report at noon.

Weather Conditions: (213-554-1212). Detailed region-by-region report.

Highway Conditions: (800-427-7623). May help you stave off an afternoon parked on the freeway. KFWB 980 AM has reports every 10min. if you're already stuck.

Crisis Lines: AIDS Hotline (800-922-2437), or national hotline (800-342-5971). 24hr. **Rape Crisis** (213-295-4673). 24hr.

24-Hour Pharmacy: Sav-On, 3010 S. Sepulveda Blvd. (310-478-9821), near downtown in West L.A. Call (800) 627-2866 for other 24hr. locations.

Medical Services:

Hospitals: Cedar-Sinai Medical Center, 8700 Beverly Blvd. (310-855-5000, emergency 855-6517). **Good Samaritan,** 616 S. Witmer St. (977-2121). **UCLA Medical Center,** 10833 Le Conte Ave. (310-825-9111, emergency 825-2111).

Planned Parenthood, 1057 Kingston St. (213-226-0800), near downtown. Birth control, prenatal care, STD treatment, abortions, and counseling. Call for appointments (1 week in advance) or other locations. Fees based on sliding scale. Hours vary.

Free Clinics: Hollywood-Sunset Free Clinic, 3324 W. Sunset Blvd. (213-660-7959). Provides general medicine, family planning, and psychiatric care. No mandatory fees at this state-funded clinic, but donations requested. Appointments only; call Mon., Wed., Fri. 10am-noon to schedule. **Valley Free Clinic,** 5648 Vineland Ave. (818-763-8836), 1 block north of Burbank, N. Hollywood. Women's health, birth control, medical counseling, drug diversion services, and free HIV testing. Appointments only; call Mon.-Sat. 10am-4pm to schedule.

Emergency: 911.

Internet Access: Many L.A. coffeehouses have **CaféNet** computers, which allow you to surf the 'net, but do not provide access to email. The following locations have both Internet access and Telnet. **Cyber Java,** 1029 Abbot Kinney Blvd. (310-581-1300), Venice. Internet access $9 per hr. Cyber Java special: 10hr. of access for $45. Open daily 7am-11pm. **Media Lab,** 1335 N. La Brea, #1 (213-874-7492), Hollywood. Internet access $10 per hr., $15 per 2hr. Open Mon.-Fri. 10am-9pm, Sat. 10am-6pm. **Dolphin House,** 1732 Abbot Kinney Blvd. (310-822-1237), Venice. Proceeds go to a children's charity. Internet access $5 per hr. or 10¢ per min. Open Tues. and Thurs.-Fri. 8am-3pm, Wed. 8am-10:30pm, Sat.-Sun. 9am-3pm.

Post Office: Centrally located branch at 900 N. Alameda St. (310-431-6546), at 9th. Open Mon.-Fri. 9am-5pm, Sat. 9am-noon. **ZIP Code:** 90086.

Area Codes: Downtown Los Angeles, Hollywood, Huntington Park, Vernon, and Montebello **213.** Malibu, Pacific Coast Highway, Westside, southern and eastern Los Angeles County **310.** Burbank, Glendale, and Pasadena **626.** San Fernando, Van Nuys, and La Cañada **818.** Orange County **714.** San Diego County **619.** Eastern border of Los Angeles County **909.** Ventura County **805.**

HOLLYWOOD

Visitor Information: Bureau located in **The Janes House,** 6541 Hollywood Blvd. (213-689-8822), in Janes House Square. Formerly the "Schoolhouse to the Stars": Cecil B. DeMille's kid went here, among others. Stocks a plethora of free L.A. and Hollywood visitor guides including *Discover Hollywood,* a comprehensive (if sometimes out-of-date) guide to the arts. Pick up *L.A. Weekly* and *New Times* for weekly info. Open Mon.-Sat. 9am-1pm and 2-5pm.

Currency Exchange: Cash It Here, 6565 Hollywood Blvd. at Whitley. No commission. Open 24hr., closed Sun. 5pm-Mon. 8am.

Buses: Greyhound, 1409 N. Vine St. (213-466-1249), 1 block south of Sunset. To: Santa Barbara (5 per day, $11, round-trip $19); San Diego (11 per day, $11, round-trip $22); San Francisco (6 per day, $32, round-trip $63). Terminal open daily 6:30am-9pm. Lockers available 24hr. for passengers ($2).

Public Transportation: MTA Customer Service Center, 6249 Hollywood Blvd. (213-922-6000). Free info, maps, and timetables. Open Mon.-Fri. 10am-2pm and 3-6pm. **Important buses:** #1 along Hollywood Blvd., #2 and 3 along Sunset Blvd., #4 along Santa Monica Blvd., #10 along Melrose Ave. Janes House has schedules and helpful advice; the MTA itself may be less than helpful. Fare $1.35, transfers 25¢. One-month pass $42, ½-month $21.

Parking: Public lot north of Hollywood Blvd. at Cherokee (marked by rubber shoes impaled on steel rods outside). First 2hr. free, each additional hr. $1, max. $3.

Hospital: Queen of Angels Hollywood Presbyterian Medical Center, 1300 N. Vermont Ave. (213-413-3000). Emergency room open 24hr.

Police: 1358 N. Wilcox Ave. (213-485-4302).

Post Office: 1615 Wilcox Ave. (213-464-2194). Open Mon.-Fri. 8am-5pm, Sat. 8am-1pm. **ZIP Code:** 90028.

Area Code: 213.

SANTA MONICA

Visitor Information: Santa Monica Visitors Center, 1400 Ocean Ave. (310-393-7593), in Palisades Park. Sparse selection of local maps and brochures, but the free *Official Visitors Guide* and maps offer a good overview of the area. The helpful staff at this walk-up kiosk can also provide info on attractions and events. Open daily 10am-5pm in summer, 10am-4pm in winter.

ATM: Bank of America and **Wells Fargo Bank,** at 4th and Arizona, across from the AmEx office. **Sanwa Bank,** at Colorado and 4th. **Home Savings of America,** at Santa Monica and 4th.

Currency Exchange: Western Union, 1454 4th St. (310-394-7211), at Broadway. No commission. Open Mon.-Fri. 9am-6pm, Sat. 9am-4pm.

American Express: 1250 4th St. (310-395-9588), at Arizona. Foreign exchange at decent rates. AmEx traveler's checks cashed for no extra fee; $3 charge for non-AmEx checks. Open Mon.-Fri. 9am-5pm, Sat. 10am-1pm.

Buses: Greyhound stop on 4th between Colorado and Broadway. Tickets can be purchased from the driver.

Public Transportation: Santa Monica Municipal Bus Lines (310-451-5444). With over 1000 stops in Santa Monica, L.A., and Culver City, the "Big Blue Bus" is faster and cheaper than the MTA (as featured in *Speed*). Fare for most routes 50¢ and transfer tickets for MTA buses 25¢; transfers to other Big Blue buses free. **Important buses:** #1 and 2 connect Santa Monica and Venice; #10 provides express service from downtown Santa Monica (at 7th and Grand) to downtown L.A. **The Tide Shuttle:** Downtown shuttle. 25¢. Signs with route info litter the downtown area. Runs every 15min. Mon.-Fri. noon-10pm.

Parking: Six lots flank the 3rd St. Promenade; 3 are accessible from 4th St. and 3 from 2nd St. First 2hr. free, each additional ½hr. 75¢. Santa Monica Place Mall has free parking for up to 3hr.; others are metered (50¢ per hr.). Downtown streets have meters as well (also 50¢ per hr.). All-day beachside parking $5-10.

Library: L.A. Public Library branch on 6th St. (310-458-8600), at the corner of Santa Monica. Open Mon.-Thurs. 10am-9pm, Fri.-Sat. 10am-5:30pm, Sun. 1-5pm.

Laundromat: Easywash Laundromat, 1306 Wilshire Blvd. (310-451-0046).

Medical Services: Santa Monica/UCLA Medical Center, 1250 16th St. (310-319-4765). Emergency room open 24hr.

Police: 1685 Main St. (310-395-9931 or 458-8491).

Post Office: 1248 5th St. (576-2626), at Arizona. Open Mon.-Fri. 9am-6pm, Sat. 9am-1pm. **ZIP Code:** 90401.

Area Code: 310.

■ Publications

The free *L.A. Weekly,* which comes out on Thursdays, is the definitive source of **entertainment** listings. Copies available at shops, restaurants, and newsstands all over the city. L.A. has a number of "industry" (e.g. **movie**) papers, with the best-known being *Variety* and *The Hollywood Reporter*. The *Los Angeles Times* (newsstand 25¢, weekends $1.50) defeats all rival **dailies** with top reporting, an excellent sports section, and a challenging crossword. The *Times* "Calendar" section has accurate and up-to-date dope on the L.A. scene. *The Los Angeles Sentinel* is L.A.'s largest **African-American** paper. **UCLA's** student paper, *The Daily Bruin,* is published during the school year. The two most popular **gay** magazines are *The Frontiers* and *Edge*.

L.A. also has numerous foreign-language publications. The **Spanish** *La Opinión* is the largest, but two **Korean** papers *(The Korean Central Daily* and *The Korean Times)* have circulations approaching 50,000 each. The *International Daily News* and the *Chinese Daily News* serve the **Chinese**-speaking community. International travelers craving news from home should keep an eye peeled for L.A.'s gargantuan newsstands, which offer not only copious copies of muscle, car, sports, fashion, and skin mags, but also many foreign-language publications. **World Wide,** 1101 Westwood Blvd. at Kinross, is a fine example (open daily 7am-midnight).

■ Orientation

Located 127 mi. north of San Diego and 403 mi. south of San Francisco, the City of Angels spreads its wings across the flatland basin between the coast of Southern California and the inland mountains. You can still be "in" L.A. even if you're 50 mi. from downtown. Greater L.A. encompasses the urbanized areas of Orange, Riverside, San Bernardino, and Ventura counties.

GETTING THERE

By Plane
Los Angeles International Airport (LAX) is located in **Westchester,** about 15 mi. southwest of downtown, 10 mi. southeast of Santa Monica, and one mile east of the coast. The airport complex is divided into two levels: the upper serves departures and the lower serves arrivals. The Tom Bradley International Terminal and terminals 2, 5, and 6 harbor international flights. LAX can be a confusing airport, but there are plenty of electronic information kiosks both inside and out with Chinese, English, French, German, Japanese, Korean, and Spanish options. **LAX information** is 310-646-5252. **Airport security** (24hr.) can be contacted at 310-646-4268. **Traveler's Aid** (446-2270), an information and referral service for major transit emergencies, is available in all terminals (open daily 7am-10pm). **Currency Exchange** is available at **L.A. Currency Agencies** (310-417-0366), in terminals 2 and 5 and in the Tom Bradley International Terminal (7am-11pm), but the American Express offices often offer more attractive rates.

Do *not* accept an offer of free transportation to an unknown hostel from the airport—chances are good you'll end up being charged $30 a night to stay in someone's garage. Airport solicitation is illegal and is a good indicator that a potential hostel is operating illegally as well. Do not compromise your safety in exchange for a ready ride and an empty promise. *Let's Go* lists a number of established hostels, many of which *will* provide transportation assistance if you call from the airport or bus station (see **Accommodations,** p. 75).

Aside from renting a car, there are several other **transit** options. Before hopping into any of the vehicles below, check with the place at which you plan to stay; many of them offer complimentary or reduced-rate transportation from the airport.

Metropolitan Transit Authority (MTA) Buses: Orange signs highlight the traffic island where shuttle "C" transports bus-bound passengers to the **transfer terminal** at Sepulveda and 96th St. To: **Westwood/UCLA,** bus #561 (Mon.-Fri. 6am-midnight, Sat.-Sun. 8am-midnight); **downtown,** bus #42 (Mon.-Sat. 5am-11pm, Sun. 7am-11pm); **Long Beach,** bus #232 (Mon.-Fri. 5am-11pm, Sat.-Sun. 6am-11pm); **West Hollywood** and **Beverly Hills,** bus #220 (Mon.-Fri. 6:30am-7:30pm, Sat.-Sun. 7:30am-7:30pm); **Hollywood,** from West Hollywood, bus #1 (along Hollywood Blvd.; Mon.-Sat. 4am-midnight, Sun. 5am-midnight), bus #2 (along Sunset Blvd.; Mon.-Fri. 5am-1am, Sat. 6am-1am, Sun. 6:30am-11pm), or bus #4 (along Santa Monica Blvd.; 24hr.). For specific info regarding MTA buses, cabs, and shuttles, ask at the **information kiosks** located on the sidewalks directly in front of the terminals or look for a **courtesy phone.**
Taxis: Cabs are costly; fare to downtown and Hollywood $28; to Disneyland, a goofy $80. (For more info, see **Practical Information,** p. 66.)
Shuttle vans: Vans offer door-to-door service from the terminals to different parts of L.A. for a flat rate. Compare rates at the information booth; prices vary widely. Typical rates are $15 to downtown, $16 to Santa Monica, $35 to San Fernando Valley. Ask one of the airport employees just outside the baggage claim area to find you a shuttle.

By Train and Bus
Amtrak rolls into **Union Station,** 800 N. Alameda St. (213-624-0171 or 800-USA-RAIL/872-7245), an architectural melange of Art Deco, southwestern, and Moorish

details, at the northwestern edge of downtown Los Angeles. Opened in May 1939, Union Station brought together the Santa Fe, Union Pacific, and Southern Pacific railroads. Like everywhere else in L.A., the station has been featured in a number of films, including *Bugsy, The Way We Were,* and *House Party II.* Trains run to San Francisco along the coast (1 per day, 11hr., $42-77, round-trip $84-154) and more frequently, through Bakersfield (4 per day, 9hr., $42, round-trip $84); and to San Diego (9 per day, 3hr., $20, round-trip $40). To Santa Monica, take bus #33; to West Hollywood, take bus #68.

The **Greyhound** station at 1716 E. 7th St. (800-231-2222), at Alameda, is in an *extremely* rough neighborhood. Greyhound also stops in Hollywood, Santa Monica, Pasadena, and other parts of the metropolitan area (see **Practical Information,** p. 63). Going on to other area stations is far safer than disembarking downtown, especially after dark. If you must get off downtown, be very careful near 7th and Alameda, one block southwest of the station, where you can catch MTA bus #60 traveling north to the Gateway Transit Plaza at Union Station. Greyhound buses go to: San Diego (28 per day, 2-3hr., $11); Santa Barbara (11 per day, 2-3½hr., $11); San Francisco (17 per day, 7-11hr., $32). Lockers are $1 per day.

Green Tortoise (800-TORTOIS/867-8647), has northbound hostel-mobiles leaving L.A. every Sunday night, with stops in Venice, Hollywood, and downtown ($35) as well as 3-day trips to San Francisco ($119). Call for reservations and exact departure location and times. (For more info, see **Essentials: By Bus,** p. 30.)

By Car

From San Francisco, L.A. is a six-hour drive down I-5, an eight-hour drive via U.S. 101, and a ten-hour jaunt down Hwy. 1, which winds along the dramatic coastline. The main arteries pumping traffic to Greater L.A. are **I-5** from the south, **Hwy. 1, U.S. 101,** or **I-5** from the north, and **I-10** or **I-15** from the east. The city is crisscrossed by over a dozen freeways, and traffic can be horrible.

Life will degrade quickly into a series of wrong turns and missed interchanges without the aid of a good **map.** L.A., a city with 6500 miles of streets and 40,000 intersections, remains untamed, unknown, and unseen otherwise. Locals swear by the *Thomas Guide: Los Angeles County Street Guide & Directory* ($16 for L.A. county, $26 for L.A. and Orange County). Travelers should pick up regional maps to boot. L.A. is a city of distinctive boulevards; its shopping areas and business centers are distributed along these 4- and 6-lane behemoths. Streets are designated east, west, north, and south from First and Main St. at the center of **downtown.**

L.A. COMMUNITIES

A legitimate **downtown** Los Angeles exists, but it won't help orient you to the rest of the city. The numbered streets (1st, 2nd…) running east-west downtown are a one-way labyrinth. The heart of downtown, full of earthquake-proof skyscrapers, is reasonably safe on weekdays, but avoid walking there after dark and on weekends.

The predominately Latino section of the city is **East L.A.,** immortalized in song and film by the decidedly mortal Cheech and Chong, begins east of downtown's Western Ave. with **Boyle Heights, Montebello,** and **El Monte.** North of East L.A., **Monterey Park** is the only city in the U.S. with a predominately Asian-American population. Asian restaurants and stores line Atlantic Blvd., the main drag.

The **University of Southern California (USC), Exposition Park,** and the predominantly African-American districts of **Inglewood, Watts, Huntington Park,** and **Compton** stretch south of downtown. **South Central,** the name by which this area is collectively known, suffered the brunt of the 1992 fires and looting. South Central, as Coolio fans know, is considered crime-ridden and attracts few tourists. If you're hellbent on visiting, go during daylight and don't leave valuables in the car.

Glittering **Hollywood** lies northwest of downtown. Its main east-west drags (from south to north) are Beverly, Melrose, Sunset, and Hollywood. Melrose Ave. links a chain of quasi-trendy cafes and boutiques. Sunset Blvd., which runs from the ocean to downtown, presents a cross-section of virtually everything L.A. has to offer: beach communities, lavish wealth, famous nightclubs, and sleazy motels. Hollywood Blvd., home of the Walk of Fame and a seedy string of tourist shops, runs just beneath the star-studded **Hollywood Hills.**

The region known as the **Westside** encompasses the prestigious West Hollywood, Westwood, Century City, Culver City, Bel Air, Brentwood, and **Beverly Hills,** home to Kelly, Donna, and some of the highest tax brackets in the state. Aside from the fancy residential estates, Westside's attractions include the **University of California at Los Angeles (UCLA),** in Westwood, and fashionable Melrose Ave. hangouts in West Hollywood. The area west of downtown is known as the **Wilshire District,** after its main boulevard. **Hancock Park,** an affluent residential area, covers the northeast portion of the district (the 5900 area) and harbors the Los Angeles County Museum of Art. It also intersects **Fairfax,** a large Jewish community.

The **Valley Region** sprawls north of the Hollywood Hills and the Santa Monica Mountains. For most people, the valley is, like, the **San Fernando Valley,** where almost two million people wander among malls and TV studios. The valley's most notable city is **Pasadena,** home of the worst air quality and best Rose Parade in the state. The basin is bounded to the north and west by the Santa Susanna Mountains and the Ronald Reagan Freeway (Rte. 118), to the south by the Ventura Freeway (Rte. 134), and to the east by the Golden State Freeway (I-5).

Eighty miles of beaches line L.A.'s **Coastal Region. Zuma,** the inspiration for the 1975 Neil Young album of the same name, is northernmost, followed by **Malibu,** which lies 15 mi. up the coast from **Santa Monica.** A bit farther south is the funky beach community of **Venice.** The beach towns south of Santa Monica include **Manhattan, Hermosa,** and **Redondo Beaches.** South across the hob-nobby **Palos Verdes Peninsula** is **Long Beach,** a port city of a half-million people and home to a large gay population. Farthest south are the **Orange County** beach cities: **Seal Beach, Sunset Beach, Huntington Beach, Newport Beach,** and **Laguna Beach.**

Confused yet? Everyone is. Invest in good maps.

PUBLIC TRANSPORTATION

Nowhere is the great god Automobile held in greater reverence than in L.A. In the 1930s and '40s, General Motors, Firestone, and Standard Oil conspired to buy up the streetcar companies and run them into the ground, later ripping up the rails. This increased dependence on buses and, later, on cars. In 1949 G.M. was convicted in federal court of criminal conspiracy—but it didn't bring back the trolleys.

By MTA Bus

Nary an Angeleno will suggest moving about L.A. in anything but a car, and the sprawling metropolis does not facilitate efficient public transit, but L.A.'s buses are not altogether useless. The **Metropolitan Transit Authority (MTA)** used to be known as the RTD (Rapid Transit District) and some of its older buses may still be labeled as such. Apparently, the name was changed because, even though the bus in *Speed* couldn't go under 55 mph, most L.A. buses cannot be called "rapid," by any definition of the word. With over 200 routes and with several independent municipal transit systems connecting to the MTA, its no easy task to study the timetables.

Using the MTA to sightsee in L.A. can be frustrating simply because attractions tend to be spread out. Those determined to see *everything* in L.A. should get behind the wheel of a car. If this is not possible, base yourself in downtown or in Hollywood (where there are plenty of bus connections), make daytrips, and have plenty of change for the bus. Bus service is dismal in the outer reaches of the city and two-hour journeys are not unusual. Transferring often involves interminable waits and L.A. traffic congestion is enough to make you cry.

To familiarize yourself with the MTA, write for "sector maps," MTA, P.O. Box 194, Los Angeles 90053, or stop by one of the 10 **customer-service centers.** There are three downtown: Gateway Transit Center, Union Station (open Mon.-Fri. 6am-6:30pm); Arco Plaza, 505 S. Flower St., Level C (open daily 7:30am-3:30pm); and 5301 Wilshire (open daily 8:30am-5pm). If you don't have time to map your route in advance, call 800-COMMUTE/266-6883 (TDD 800-252-9040; open daily 5:30am-11:30pm) for transit info and schedules. Ninety percent of MTA routes offer **wheelchair-accessible buses** (call 1hr. in advance, 800-621-7828 daily 6am-10pm). Appropriate bus stops are marked with the international symbol for disabled access.

MTA's basic fare is $1.35, seniors and disabled 45¢; transfers 25¢, seniors and disabled 10¢; exact change required. Transfers can be made between MTA lines or to other transit authorities. **Unless otherwise noted, all route numbers are MTA.**

Bus service is best downtown and along the major thoroughfares west of downtown. (There is 24hr. service, for instance, on Wilshire Blvd. and Santa Monica Blvd.) The downtown **DASH shuttle** costs only 25¢ and serves major tourist destinations including Chinatown, Union Station, Gateway Transit Center, and Olvera St. Given the hellish downtown traffic, the scope of the shuttle routes make them an attractive option. DASH also operates a shuttle on Sunset Blvd. in Hollywood, as well as in Pacific Palisades, Watts, Fairfax, Midtown, Crenshaw, Van Nuys/Studio City, Warner Center, and Southeast L.A. (Downtown DASH operates Mon.-Fri. 6:30am-6:30pm, Sat. 10am-5pm. Pacific Palisades shuttles do not run on Sat. Venice DASH operates every 10min. on summer weekends 11am-6pm. Parking costs $2.50, but this is much cheaper than at the beach. Call 213-485-7201 for pickup points. Schedule info: 800-2LA-RIDE/252-7433.)

By Subway

L.A. continues work on a system of light-rail connections which is still far from complete. The existing rails reach a select few areas. The **Blue Line** serves the southern L.A. communities and Long Beach. The **Green Line** goes along I-105 from Norwalk to El Segundo. The **Red Line** will one day reach Hollywood and the Valley, but for now is known as the "bagel bus," as its clientele consists primarily of office workers rushing off to downtown lunch dates. A one-way trip costs $1.35, with transfers to bus and rail $1.60; seniors and disabled 45¢, with transfers 55¢. All lines run daily 5am to 11pm. Call 800-2LA-RIDE/252-7433 for more info on stops.

By Metrolink Train

Metrolinks trains serve Orange County, San Bernardino, Riverside, Oxnard, and Lancaster. A one-way pass costs $3-9. You can only buy them from machines in the station three hours before you plan to travel. Beware—trains come and go up to five minutes ahead of schedule. Call 808-LINK/5465 (no area code required from anywhere in the L.A. area) for info.

NON-PUBLIC TRANSPORTATION

Freeways

The freeway is perhaps the most enduring image of L.A. No matter what may separate Angelenos—race, creed, or class—the one thing that unites everyone is the freeway system, a maze of 10- and 12-lane concrete roadways. "Traffic bogged down," is the all-purpose excuse for tardiness, guaranteed to garner knowing nods and smiles of consolation from co-workers and acquaintances. Needless to say, the term "rush hour" is wrong on all counts—there's no way anyone can rush anywhere amid the frequent commuter congestion. When planning your route, be mindful of heavy traffic moving towards downtown from 7 to 10am on weekdays and streaming outbound from 4 to 7pm. Expect major interchanges to be a madcap do-si-do frenzy as cars merge every which way. When in doubt, remember the only solution: Patience. No matter how crowded the freeway is, it's almost always quicker and safer than taking surface streets to your destination. A good rule of thumb is that surface streets will take five times longer than the freeway.

Uncongested freeways offer the ultimate in speed and convenience; the trip from downtown to Santa Monica can take as little as 20 minutes. A nighttime cruise along the Harbor Freeway (I-110) past downtown, whizzing through the tangle of interchanges and on- and off-ramps, the lights of L.A.'s skyscrapers providing a futuristic backdrop, can be exhilarating, especially if you've been stuck in traffic all day.

Angelenos refer to their highways by names not numbers. These names are little more than hints of a freeway's route, hints at best harmless, at worst misleading. For freeway info, call **CalTrans** (213-897-3693), and refer to the **L.A. Overview map**.

L.A.'s family of freeways welcomed a new member three years ago. Route **I-105**, the $2 billion **Glen Anderson Freeway**, runs east from LAX and the San Diego Freeway to the San Gabriel Riverbed, which parallels Rte. 605. It was named in honor of a policeman who drove off a collapsed freeway in the '95 Northridge earthquake while rushing into town to help those in need. Its newness makes it less well-known than other routes; as a result, it is often less crowded.

Fruity!

Forget race riots, water shortages, or Divine Brown—one of the biggest nuisances Angelenos have recently faced is a pesky bug called the Medfly (Mediterranean fruit fly). One of the world's most destructive pests, the Medfly breeds by laying its eggs in healthy fruit. If it became established in California, it would decimate this agricultural breadbasket and result in nearly $1 billion of damages per year. Fears of an epidemic in the late '80s led the city to hire helicopters to fly overhead by night to dump insecticides. Unfortunately, the sprayings, depicted in the movie *Short Cuts*, maimed more pets than fruit flies and incited residents to sue the city for ruining their beloved cars' paint jobs. Signs denoting the boundaries of quarantine areas still exist on some freeways. The danger is less severe now, but Angelenos, ever mindful of disaster, have distributed cautionary pamphlets everywhere, warning of the next big plague.

Cars

L.A. may be the most difficult city in the U.S. to get around in without a car. Unfortunately, it may also be the most difficult city in which to **rent** a car, especially for younger travelers. Most places will not rent to people under 21 and the ones that do are likely to impose a surcharge that only movie stars can afford to pay (nearly double the standard rate). Drivers under 25 will incur a lesser surcharge.

Nationally known agencies are reputed to have more dependable cars, but the demand for rental cars assures that even small local companies can survive and many have far lower rates than the big guys. Some of them are even willing to bargain. Those planning long-distance road trips should consider a national chain—in the event of a breakdown, such franchises will often exchange your immobile two tons of steel for a working automobile within hours, making your travels considerably less painful. Comparison shopping and searching for weekly rates will help you save. Be warned: local rental companies may quote a very low daily rate, but once you rent a car from them, they may add extra fees when you return the car. Read the fine print and ask questions. Remember that the Collision and Damage Waiver (CDW) is optional, but be sure that you have sufficient insurance coverage if you want to waive it. The prices quoted below are intended to give a rough idea of what to expect, but prices can vary widely. Ask about airline-related discounts.

Avis (310-914-7700), on Santa Monica Blvd. between Barrington Ave. and Bundy. Economy cars $34 per day or $169 per week with unlimited mileage. CDW $9 per day. Must have major credit card. Open Mon.-Sat. 7:30am-6pm, Sun. 8am-5pm.

Avon, 8459 Sunset Blvd. (213-650-2631; fax 654-4979). Rent economy-size cars for as low as $25 per day with 100 free mi.; 25¢ per mi. thereafter. $150 per week with 700 miles free. CDW $9 per day. Ages 18-20 must pay $15 per day surcharge; ages 21-24 pay $5 per day; $250 deposit required. Open Mon.-Fri. 7:30am-8:30pm, Sat.-Sun. 9:30am-4:30pm.

Thrifty (800-367-2277), at LAX. As low as $35 per day, unlimited mileage within CA, NV, and AZ. $180 per week. CDW $9 per day. Must be 21 with credit card. Under 25 pay $20 per day surcharge. Open 24hr.

Alamo (800-327-9633), at LAX. Prices vary with availability; around $30 per day, $200 per week, unlimited mileage. CDW $9 per day. Must be 21 with major credit card. Under 25 pay $20 per day surcharge. Open 24hr.

Capri, 8620 Airport Blvd. (310-641-2323). Free transport to and from LAX. $25 per day with 150 free mi.; students $19.95. CDW $9 per day. Must be 25 with a major credit card. $300 refundable deposit required. Open daily 8am-8pm.

Dollar, 5630 Arbor Vitae Ave. (310-645-9333). Free transport to and from LAX. Changeable rates. Unlimited miles in CA, AZ, OR, and NV. Must be 21 with credit card. $300 refundable deposit required. Open 24hr.

Park your car in a paid lot (about $3) or a secure motel lot rather than on the street; not only for safety reasons, but because a quarter will buy a measly 7½ minutes of street parking time. Generously dispensed parking violations are some of L.A.'s less beloved souvenirs.

Bicycles

Unless you have legs and lungs of steel, a bicycle in L.A. is useful only for recreational purposes. Air quality is poor, distances are long, and drivers aren't used to looking out for cyclists. Always wear a helmet, unless you enjoy paying hefty fines; it's illegal to bike on roads without one.

The most popular route is the **South Bay Bicycle Path,** one of the best of the beach routes. It runs from Santa Monica to Torrance (19mi.), winding over the sandy beaches of the South Bay past sunbathers, boardwalks, and pesky spandex-clad in-line skaters. The path continues all the way to San Diego. Other bike paths include **San Gabriel River Trail,** 37 mi. along the river, with views of the San Gabriel Valley; **Upper Rio Hondo** and **Lario Trails,** 9 and 22 mi., both free from traffic; **Kenneth Newell Bikeway,** 10 mi. through residential Pasadena; **Sepulveda Basin Bikeway,** 7 mi. around the Sepulveda Dam Recreation Area, a large loop of some major San Fernando Valley streets; **Griffith Park Bikeway,** 4½ mi. past the L.A. Zoo and Travel Town train park; **Bolsa Chica Bike Path,** 10 mi. along Huntington Beach; **Santa Ana River Bike Trail,** 22 mi. along the Santa Ana River; and the **Santa Ana Canyon Bikeway,** 7 mi. of both street and canyon terrain. Recently, there has been some violence and gang-related activity on bike trails (e.g. South Bay Bicycle Path, San Gabriel River Trail, Lario Trails, and Santa Ana River Bike Trail). It should be alright to ride during the day, but avoid night biking.

Most rental shops stand near the piers of the various beaches, with an especially high concentration on Washington Blvd. in Venice/Marina del Rey. (Specific shops for this area are listed individually under **Venice: Sights,** p. 95.)

Walking and Hitchhiking

L.A. pedestrians are a lonely breed. The largely deserted streets of commercial centers will seem eerie to the first-time visitor. Unless you're running in the L.A. Marathon, moving from one part of the city to another on foot is a ludicrous idea—distances are just too great. Nevertheless, some colorful areas such as Melrose, Westwood, the Santa Monica Promenade, Hollywood, and Old Pasadena are best explored by foot. For lovers of coastal culture, Venice Beach is one of the most enjoyable (and popular) places to walk, with sights and shopping areas relatively close to one another. *Destination: Los Angeles,* the publication of the Convention and Visitor Bureau, has an excellent list of walking tours (see **Practical Information: Publications,** p. 62). Since some of the best tour companies are one-person operations, schedules and prices are not written in stone. Look for theme tours (i.e., graveyard, O.J. Simpson) geared to your interests (or obsessions). The **Los Angeles Conservancy** (213-623-2489), offers 10 different tours of the downtown area. Tours cost $5 and advance reservations are required. Call **Tree People** (818-753-4600), for information on Sunday walking tours of Coldwater Canyon Park.

Once the sun sets, those on **foot,** especially outside West L.A. and off well-lit main drags, should exercise caution, especially when alone. When exploring, plan your route carefully, and remember—it is worth a detour to avoid passing through particularly crime-ridden areas. **If you hitchhike you will probably die.** It is uncommon and exceptionally dangerous in L.A. and anyone who picks up a hitchhiker probably has ulterior motives. It is also illegal on freeways and many streets. So there.

■ Accommodations

As in any large city, cheap accommodations in Los Angeles are often unsafe as well. It can be difficult to gauge quality from the exterior, so ask to see a room before you plunk down any cash. Be suspicious of rates below $35; they're probably not the kind of hotels most travelers would feel secure in. For those willing to share a room and a bathroom, hostels (see below) are a saving grace. Americans should be aware that some hostels accept international travelers only. These hostels require an international passport, but well-traveled Americans who can prove that they are traveling (passports, out-of-state identification, or plane tickets often do the trick) may be welcomed with open arms. It never hurts to ask for off-season or student discounts, and occasionally managers will lower prices to snare a hesitant customer.

In choosing where to stay, the first consideration should be car accessibility. If you don't have wheels, you would be wise to decide what element of L.A. appeals to you the most. Those visiting for the beaches would do well to choose lodgings in Venice or Santa Monica. Avid sightseers will probably be better off in Hollywood or the more expensive (but cleaner and nicer) Westside. Downtown has numerous public transportation connections but is unsafe after dark. Even those with cars should choose accommodations proximate to their interests to keep car-bound time to a minimum. **Listed prices do not include L.A.'s 14% hotel tax.**

HOLLYWOOD

Although Tinseltown has worked up quite a bit of tarnish in recent years, its location, sights, and nightlife keep the tourists coming. Exercise caution if scouting out one of the many budget hotels on Hollywood or Sunset Blvd.—especially east of the main strips, the area can be dangerous, particularly at night. The hostels here are generally excellent, and as a whole, a much better value than anything else in L.A.

Banana Bungalow Hollywood, 2775 Cahuenga Blvd. (213-851-1129 or 800-4-HOSTEL/446-7835; fax 851-1569; email HWres@bananabungalow.com), just north of the Hollywood Bowl. The Bungalow's efficient staff and robust backpacker clientele make for a summer-camp atmosphere that is relentlessly wacky, especially in the restaurant/party area—not for the retiring traveler. Free shuttle from the airport, and $2 transit to area beaches and attractions (including Disneyland, Magic Mountain, and Universal Studios). Free nightly movies, arcade, and frequent dances in restaurant area. Pool, hoops, weight room, Internet access ($5 per hr.), and "snack shack." Free continental breakfast, free linens. Check-in 24hr. Check-out 10:30am. Co-ed dorms (6-10 beds) with bathroom and TV. Dorms $18; doubles $36-45. Meal charge $4.50. Free parking. **Passport and international airline ticket required** for dorms, but Americans can stay in the private rooms.

Student Inn International Hostel, 7038½ Hollywood Blvd. (213-469-6781 or 800-557-7038). Look no further. Free tickets to Disneyland, Universal Studios, and Magic Mountain. Free city tours. No strings attached. This is not a misprint. This friendly hostel has a small kitchen, free breakfast, free linens, and free pickup from LAX, Union Station, and Greyhound. 4-bed dorms with private bath $13.50, off-season $15; doubles $30. Those low on cash can crash on floor mattresses ($10) or work at the reception in exchange for a free night's stay. Free parking. Call far in advance for credit card reservations. **International passport required.**

Orange Drive Manor, 1764 N. Orange Dr. (213-850-0350). Spiffy, restored craftsman-style home in a low-key residential neighborhood just around the corner from Mann's Chinese Theater. Kitchen, cable TV lounge, lockers, and free linens. Spacious dorms have 2-4 beds and sport antique furniture (some private baths). Check-out noon. No curfew. Dorms $15; private rooms $25. Parking $5 per night. Reservations recommended during the summer. No credit cards.

Hollywood International Hostel, 6820 Hollywood Blvd. (213-463-0797 or 800-750-6561). Sparkling clean budget nirvana. Capacious lounge with TV, a video game, free pool and foosball, nightly movies, laundry, email, and fax. Free pickup from LAX, Greyhound, and Amtrak. Tours and BBQs ($4). Single-sex dorms have 2-4 beds and common bath. Reception open 24hr. Dorms $13.25, off-season $12; private rooms $32. Weekly: $92, $224. Parking $3 per night. Reserve ahead with credit card, but no on-site credit card charges. **International passport required.**

Liberty Hotel, 1770 Orchid Ave. (213-962-1788), 1 block north of Mann's Chinese Theater. Brand-new, and it shows in the glistening modern rooms and amenities. Residential street is cleaner and calmer, but still near Hollywood Blvd. TV, laundry, free coffee. Free pickup from LAX, Greyhound, and Amtrak. Singles $40; doubles $45, with microwave and fridge $50. Free parking.

Hollywood Hills Hostel, 6772 Hawthorn (213-462-3777 or 800-524-6783; fax 213-462-3228), off Highland Ave. between Hollywood and Sunset Blvd. Building shows its age, but rooms are well maintained. Free pickup from LAX, Greyhound, and Amtrak. Organizes tours. Kitchen, outdoor patio, free breakfast, free linens. Co-ed dorms have 6-8 beds and private bath. Dorms $16; private rooms $38. Weekly: $96, $228. Free parking. **Passport or proof of travel required.**

SANTA MONICA, VENICE, AND MARINA DEL REY

Venice Beach hostels beckon all the young budget travelers, especially foreign students, who are lured by the area's blend of indulgent beach culture and lively nightlife. Most of the cheap accommodations that pepper the coast cater to raucous party kids, but there are some quiet gems in the mix. Parking in Venice (especially near the beach) is expensive—travelers with cars should look for an accommodation with parking or consider staying off the beach. If you do decide to venture into L.A.'s depths, the city center connects to Santa Monica's Big Blue Bus or the MTA.

Los Angeles/Santa Monica (HI-AYH), 1436 2nd St., (310-393-9913; fax 393-1769), Santa Monica, 2 blocks from the beach and across from the Third St. promenade. Take MTA #33 from downtown (Union Station) to 2nd and Broadway, Blue Bus #3 from LAX to 4th and Broadway, or Blue Bus #10 from downtown (Greyhound station). Located next door to the associated Santa Monica Travelers Center (393-3413), which offers budget travel services. Modern and meticulous, it looks more like a swank office complex than an inexpensive hostel. Extremely tight security; lobby manned 24hr. Colossal kitchen and laundry, 2 nightly movies, library, central courtyard, bi-weekly BBQs ($5), and hot breakfast daily (75¢-$2.75). 28-night max. stay. Guests get discounts at many restaurants and shops. Dorms (4-10 beds) $17-19, nonmembers $20-22; private doubles $48, nonmembers $51. Safe deposit boxes and lockers available. No parking, pay garages nearby.

Cadillac Hotel, 8 Dudley Ave. (310-399-8876; fax 399-4536), Venice. An ab-fab art-deco landmark directly on the beach. International crowd and helpful staff. Tour desk, well-equipped gym, laundry, sauna, rooftop sundeck. Lounge has cable TV, pool table, Venetian gondola, and a piece of the Berlin wall. 4-bunk dorm rooms have private bath and lockers. Dorms $20; private suites $60 and up. LAX shuttle $5. Free parking. No reservations for bunks—show up at 11am and hope.

Share-Tel Apartments, 20 Brooks Ave. (310-392-0325), ½ block from the beach. This fun-loving hostel offers free breakfasts, dinners, and keg parties (Mon.-Fri. only). Social lounge with TV and board games. Free airport pickup and city tour planning. Dorm rooms have 8 beds, private baths, kitchenettes, and fridges. No curfew. Dorms $17; private rooms $22-25. Weekly: dorms $110, off-season $100. Lockers $1. Key and linen deposit $20. Parking $10 per night, off-season $5. No reservations. No credit cards. **International passport required.**

Venice Marina Hostel, 2915 Yale Ave. (310-301-3983), off Washington Blvd. in Marina del Rey. The quiet residential street offers a respite from the manic pace closer to the shore. Low-key atmosphere calls to mind *Dazed and Confused.* TV room, laundry, big common bathrooms, and kitchen. Free shuttle from LAX. No curfew. Check-in 24hr. Free breakfast and linen. Keg parties on Thurs. ($3). Dorms

(10 beds) $14, weekly $91. U.S. travelers admitted with out-of-state I.D. Cash or traveler's checks only. Two lucky folks get to crash in the van o' lovin'.

Jim's at The Beach, 17 Brooks Ave. (310-399-4018; fax 399-4216), Venice. Outstanding location ½ block off the boardwalk. Run by Jim of *Backpacker's Bible* fame. Up to 6 beds per clean and sunny room. Kitchen, laundry, free breakfast and dinner, frequent BBQs. No curfew. Dorms $19; weekly $130. Key and linen deposit $1. Parking $5 per night. **Passport required,** but Americans welcome.

Venice Beach Cotel, 25 Windward Ave. (310-399-7649; fax 399-1930), Venice, 1 block from the boardwalk. From LAX, take Blue Bus #3 to Lincoln Ave., then MTA #33 to Venice Beach Post Office; walk 1 block west. LAX shuttle $5. Small but amazingly pristine rooms, some with ocean views. Lively BYOB bar area has cozy, colorful tables. No kitchen or laundry. Free tea and coffee, linen, use of tennis rackets, paddle tennis, and boogieboards ($20 deposit). Free margarita at check-in. Reception open 24hr.; excellent security. Dorms (3-4 beds) $13, with private bath $15; doubles $33-44, some with private bath and TV; triples $49. Parking $10 per night, off-season $3. **Passport required,** but Americans welcome.

Hostel California, 2221 Lincoln Blvd. (310-305-0250; fax 305-8590), Venice, off Venice Blvd. Take MTA #33 from downtown, free airport pickup. Festive place where many nationalities bump elbows in a Mexican restaurant-like setting. Bike and skate rental ($7 per day), pool table, big-screen TV. Co-ed and single-sex dorms, kitchen, and laundry room. You can check-out any time you like (though they prefer 10:30am), but you can never leave. Check-in 24hr. Dorms (6 beds) $15, weekly $90; 25-person barrack (bunk $12); doubles $36. Linen included. Free parking. No credit cards. **Passport required,** but Americans with proof of travel welcome.

Venice Beach Hostel, 701 Washington Blvd. (310-306-5180), above Celebrity Cleaners on a fairly noisy street. Not to be confused with the Venice Beach Hostel on Pacific (no affiliation). Blue Bus #3 stops at Lincoln Ave. up the road. Free shuttle bus from LAX. Very lived-in rooms. Frequent field trips to local bars. Rooftop deck, full kitchen, lockers, Thurs. keg parties ($3), weekend BBQ, and cable TV lounge. Reception open 24hr. No curfew. Dorms $13, weekly $84. No credit cards. **Passport or proof of out-of-state residence required.**

Planet Venice's Venice Beach Hostel, 1515 Pacific Ave. (310-452-3052), Venice, 1 block from the boardwalk. In a historic building with colorful murals that almost hide the cracks. Lounge, kitchen, and laundry room. Free weekday breakfast, free Internet access. Check-in 24hr. No curfew. Dorms $17, off-season $11, weekly $110; rooms with kitchen $41. Reservations accepted. No credit cards.

WESTSIDE: BEVERLY HILLS, WESTWOOD, WILSHIRE

The snazzy and relatively safe Westside has excellent public transportation to the beaches. The area's affluence, however, means less bang for your buck, and there are no hostel-type accommodations. Those planning to stay at least one month in summer or six months during the school year can contact the **UCLA Off-Campus Housing Office,** 350 Deneve Dr. (310-825-4491; http://www.housing.ucla.edu/housing/cho.html), where a "roommate share board" lists students who have a spare room.

Bevonshire Lodge Motel, 7575 Beverly Blvd. (213-936-6154; fax 934-6640), near Farmer's Market. Looks like *Melrose Place* with a color-blind set designer. Pool in the central courtyard is open year-round. Spacious rooms have sparkling, newly-renovated bathrooms that make all the shower scenes fun, and beds big enough for Amanda to bring all her conquests home. Singles $39; doubles $43; rooms with kitchen $49. Free parking. 10% ISIC discount.

The Little Inn, 10604 Santa Monica Blvd. (310-475-4422; fax 475-3236), West L.A. Found on "Little Santa Monica," the smaller road paralleling the divided boulevard to the south. Take one step into the courtyard and reach budget-travel bliss. Though the lack of style in the sparsely decorated rooms is *so* un-L.A., the rooms are sizable and clean. A/C, cable TV, and fridges. Check-in 24hr. Check-out 11am. Singles $50-55; doubles $65; rooms with kitchens $75. Free parking.

LOS ANGELES

Stars Inn, 10269 Santa Monica Blvd. (310-556-3076; fax 310-277-6202). Several blocks east of the Little Inn, the Stars is managed by the same group, and delivers a similarly high level of quality—spacious, clean rooms, sparkling bathrooms, A/C, fridges, and cable TV. Cool location across from the Century City Shopping Center. Check-out 11am. Singles $55; doubles $65; triples $75. Off-season: $45, $55, $65. Weekly rates for $5 less per night. Free parking.

Crest Motel, 7701 Beverly Blvd. (213-931-8108), near Hollywood, across the street from the CBS studios. Though it could use a facelift, Crest is clean and rooms are equipped with TVs, fridges, and A/C. Outdoor pool open year-round. Check-in 24hr. Check-out 11am. Singles $40; doubles $45. Free parking.

Claremont Hotel, 1044 Tiverton Ave. (310-208-5957 or 800-266-5957; fax 310-208-2386), Westwood Village, near UCLA. Clean rooms (maid service daily) have antique dressers, ceiling fans, private baths, and phones. Microwave and free coffee in lobby. Check-in 24hr. Check-out noon. Singles $40; doubles $48; triples $54. Weekly rates available. Reservations recommended, especially around June.

Westwood Inn Motel, 10820 Wilshire Blvd. (310-474-3118; fax 474-3213), in Westwood down the street from the AVCO Cinema. Many rooms recently renovated, but all are immaculate and come with cable TV, A/C, and comfy couches or chairs. Free local calls. Some rooms with fridges at no extra cost. Singles $48; doubles $54; suites $82. Free parking. Reservations recommended.

Hotel del Flores, 409 N. Crescent Dr. (310-274-5115), across from the 90210 post office in Beverly Hills. Built in 1926, this building has relaxing garden patio seats. Clean rooms (after all, this *is* Beverly Hills) with TV, phones, and ceiling fans. Fridges or microwaves upon request. Lounge with TV, magazines, and fridge. Street parking only. Check-in 24hr. Check-out noon. Singles with shared bath $65, doubles with private bath $72 and up. Weekly rates, ISIC discount available.

Wilshire Orange Hotel, 6060 W. 8th St. (213-931-9533), near Wilshire and Fairfax in West L.A. MTA buses #20, 21, and 22 serve Wilshire from downtown. One of L.A.'s better-located budget accommodations, but not the cheapest. Near major sights in a residential section. All rooms have fridges and TV. Long-term stays encouraged; many semi-permanent residents. Street parking only. Singles $44 and up; doubles $54 and up. Weekly rates available. Reservations recommended 2 weeks in advance.

DOWNTOWN L.A.

Though busy and relatively safe by day, the downtown area empties and becomes dangerous after 6pm and on weekends. Both men and women should travel in groups after dark, especially in the area between Broadway and Main. Some decent lodgings can be found in the area, however—don't be afraid to haggle, especially during the off-season. Cheaper weekly rates are sometimes available.

Hotel Stillwell, 838 S. Grand Ave. (213-627-1151 or 800-553-4774; fax 622-8940). Recently refurbished, this ultra-clean hotel is one of the most sensible downtown options. Rooms are bright and have A/C and cable TV. Parking area next door ($3 per day). Singles $39, $175 per week; doubles $49, $225.

Milner Hotel, 813 S. Flower St. (213-627-6981 or 800-827-0411; fax 623-9751). Central location makes up for slightly worn decor. Pub, grill, and flag-bedecked lounge in lobby. Free breakfast and rides to LAX, Union, and Greyhound station. Rooms have A/C and cable TV. Parking $4. Singles $50; doubles $60.

Park Plaza Hotel, 607 S. Park View St. (213-384-5281), on the west corner of 6th across from green but unsafe MacArthur Park. Built in 1927, this grandiose Art Deco giant has a 3-story marble-floored lobby and a monumental staircase. All of the clean but small rooms have TV, some have A/C. Pool and weight room. Singles $57; doubles $63.

Metro Plaza Hotel, 711 N. Main St. (213-680-0200; fax 620-0200), on the corner of Cesar Chavez. Near Chinatown, Olvera St., and Union Station. Clean rooms have TVs and refrigerators. Free parking. Singles $59; doubles $69.

■ Camping

Los Angeles has no **campgrounds** convenient to public transportation. Even motorists face at least a 40-minute commute from the nearest campsites to downtown. One relatively pleasant L.A. County campground that is vaguely nearby is at **Leo Carrillo State Beach** (310-457-1324), PCH (Hwy. 1), 20 mi. north of Malibu at the Ventura County line: it has 135 developed sites ($14-16, showers, flush toilets). Nearby **Pt. Mugu** has 57 sites at Sycamore Canyon ($14-16, showers, flush toilets) and 75 primitive sites at the Thornhill Broome area ($7-9, cold outdoor showers, chemical toilets). **Malibu Creek State Park,** off Las Virgenes Rd. in Santa Monica Mountains, has 62 developed sites ($14, flush toilets, showers). Call (800-444-7275) to make mandatory summer reservations for any sites. •

■ Eating in L.A.

Eating in Los Angeles, the city of the health-conscious, is more than just a gustatory experience. Thin figures and fat wallets are a powerful combination—L.A. lavishes in the most heavenly *and* healthy recipes around. Of course, there are also restaurants where the main objective is to be seen, and the food is secondary, as well as those where the food itself seems too beautiful to be eaten—it was here, after all, that 80s *nouvelle cuisine* reached its height (see **Cuisinart,** p. 61).

Fortunately for the budget traveler, Los Angeles elevates fast-food and chain restaurants to heights virtually unknown in the rest of the country. The "mom and pop" diner is a rarity in L.A., where restaurants live by P.T. Barnum's mantra, "give the people what they want." What Angelenos want, of course, is not only quality food but also convenience—chains are a way of life here. For the optimal burger-and-fries experience, try **In 'n' Out Burger,** a beloved chain evoking a '57 Chevy. **Johnny Rocket's** revives the never really lost era of the American diner. Their milkshakes are the food of the gods. The current hot 'n' spicy craze is lard-free, cholesterol-free "healthy Mexican"—**Baja Fresh** leads the pack.

In this city of sunshine, chic refreshments are a necessity. Long before frappucinos made their way onto Starbucks' menus, Angelenos flocked to get their ice-blended mochas at **The Coffee Bean and Tea Leaf.** The ubiquitous smoothie, now a countrywide phenomenon, allows the health-conscious to indulge in a sweet blend of fruit, juice, frozen yogurt, and energy-boosting additives like spirulina and protein powder. **The Juice Club** makes the biggest and the best, with over 20 smoothie flavors, and shots of fresh-blended grass for die-hard fiberphiles. Most coffeehouses have added the smoothie to their repertoire of fancy concoctions.

Of course, food in L.A. isn't just about California cuisine. The range of culinary options is directly proportional to the city's ethnic diversity. Certain food types are

---

Feeding the Good, the Bad, and the Ugly

Los Angeles has been home to many tasteless trends, but few realize that it's also the birthplace of perhaps the world's furthest sweeping trend, one *guaranteed* to leave a curious taste in your mouth—good ol' American **fast food.** Unlikely as it sounds, this obsessively health-conscious city spawned some of the nation's greasiest, most cholesterol-packed grub. An international synonym for fast food, **McDonald's** was founded by Angeleno brothers Richard and Maurice McDonald in 1937 (serving, incidentally, hot dogs only). The oldest standing golden arches still glare proudly at 10807 Lakewood Blvd. in Downey, where it's walk-up rather than drive-thru service. Home to the original double-decker hamburger, the oldest **Bob's Big Boy,** 4211 Riverside Dr. (818-843-9334), in Burbank, still looks as sleek and streamlined as the day it opened in 1949. Check out the honest-to-goodness car-hop service (Sat.-Sun. 5-10pm). **Carl's Jr.** started off as a downtown hot dog stand at Florence and Central Ave. in 1941, and the **Denny's** and **Winchell's** chains also got their start in the Los Angeles basin.

concentrated in specific areas. Jewish and Eastern European food is most prevalent in Fairfax; Mexican in East L.A.; Japanese, Chinese, Vietnamese, and Thai around Little Tokyo, Chinatown, and Monterey Park, and seafood along the coast. Vietnamese, Italian, Indian, and Ethiopian restaurants are scattered throughout the city.

L.A. restaurants tend to shut down early. Angelenos eat out between 7 and 10pm, and restaurants are closed by 11pm. Fast-food chains are rarely open past midnight. For restaurant listings, see the different neighborhoods of Los Angeles below. To find listings on **late-night** restaurants and cafes, see **Entertainment** (p.106). Recently, Los Angeles became the first city in the U.S. to ban smoking in all restaurants, excluding bars and clubs (though it is still legal in many outdoor areas).

Markets

L.A.'s enormous public markets give the visitor a first-hand look at the variety and volume of foodstuffs available here. **Farmer's Market,** 6333 W. 3rd St. (213-933-9211), at Fairfax in the Wilshire District, has over 160 produce stalls, as well as international food booths, handicraft shops, souvenir stores, and a phenomenal juice bar. There's delectable produce, but bargains are becoming increasingly rare (open Mon.-Sat. 9am-7pm, Sun. 10am-6pm). A less touristy and less expensive source of produce is the **Grand Central Public Market,** 317 S. Broadway (213-624-2378), a large baby-blue building downtown, between 3rd and 4th. The main market in the Hispanic shopping district was 80-years-old in 1997. Grand Central has more than 50 stands selling not only produce, but also clothing, housewares, costume jewelry, vitamins, and fast food. This vast space is always riotously busy and entertaining (open daily 9am-9pm). **Trader Joe's** is a super-cool chain specializing in budget gourmet food. They save by doing their own packaging and, as a result, you get amazing deals like $4 bottles of choice Napa wines. There are 84 locations (most of which are in the trendier areas); call 800-SHOPTJS/746-7857 to find the one nearest you (all open daily 9am-9pm).

▓ Food and Sights

HOLLYWOOD

Modern Hollywood is no longer the upscale home of movie stars and production studios. In fact, all the major studios, save Paramount, have moved to the roomier San Fernando Valley. Left behind are those things that could not be taken: historic theaters and museums, a crowd of souvenir shops, several famous boulevards, and an American fascination. With the exception of the never-ending string of movie premieres, the only star-studded part of Hollywood is the sidewalk, where prostitutes and panhandlers, tattoo parlors and porn shops abound. At 110 years, Hollywood has changed dramatically since it first housed the nascent motion picture industry; yet its glorious past assures it will be larger than life for decades to come.

Food

Screenwriters and starlets still comprise much of Hollywood's population. Most are single, hungry, and nearly broke after paying the rent on their bungalows. As a result, Hollywood offers the best budget dining in L.A. As an added bonus, if you're in the right place at the right time, you can catch stars chowing down on the same lunch special as you, but don't bother them. **Hollywood** and **Sunset Blvd.** have excellent international cuisine, while **Fairfax** hosts Mediterranean-style restaurants and Kosher delis. **Melrose** is full of chic cafes, many with outdoor people-watching patios. As Hollywood is the heart of L.A.'s pounding nightlife, many of its best restaurants are open 'round-the-clock (see **Late-Night Restaurants,** p. 113).

> **Toi on Sunset,** 7505½ Sunset Blvd. (213-874-8062), in Hollywood. Decor is a way-trendy melange of posters, funky lamps, leopard-skin armchairs, and psychedelic murals. Clientele is as hip as the interior decorating. Tarantino is a regular. *Pad thai* $6.95. Lunch specials $4.95. Open daily 11am-4am. $10 min. for credit cards.

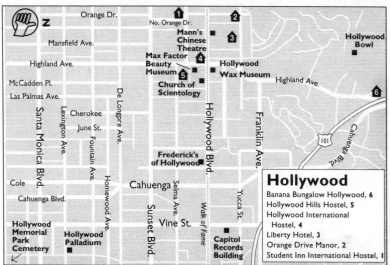

Map labels:
Orange Dr.
No. Orange Dr.
Mansfield Ave.
Mann's Chinese Theatre
Hollywood Bowl
Highland Ave.
Max Factor Beauty Museum
Hollywood Wax Museum
Highland Ave.
McCadden Pl.
Las Palmas Ave.
Church of Scientology
De Longpre Ave.
Cherokee
June St.
Lexington Ave.
Santa Monica Blvd.
Fountain Ave.
Hollywood Blvd.
Franklin Ave.
Frederick's of Hollywood
Cole
Cahuenga Blvd.
Cahuenga
Homewood Ave.
Selma Ave.
Sunset Blvd.
Vine St.
Walk of Fame
Yucca St.
Hollywood Memorial Park Cemetery
Hollywood Palladium
Capitol Records Building

Hollywood
Banana Bungalow Hollywood, 6
Hollywood Hills Hostel, 5
Hollywood International Hostel, 4
Liberty Hotel, 3
Orange Drive Manor, 2
Student Inn International Hostel, 1

Swingers Hollywood Diner, 8020 Beverly Blvd. (213-653-5858), at Laurel in the rump of the Beverly Laurel Hotel. Where the hippest L.A. club kids (and lonely L.A. *Swingers* Mikey and Trent) come to snack on olives, spinach and tofu burritos ($5.25), and 5 flavors of "smart drinks" that organically stimulate the brain ($5.50-6.50). Warhol-inspired walls with pink cows and plaid vinyl booths. This place is *so* money! Open Sun.-Thurs. 8am-2am, Fri.-Sun. 8am-4am.

Chin Chin, 8618 Sunset Blvd. (310-652-1818), in West Hollywood. Other locations in Brentwood, Studio City, Marina del Rey, and Encino. Immensely popular with the lunchtime set for its handmade "*dim sum* and then sum" ($5). Shredded chicken salad ($6.50) is California-ized Chinese cuisine. Outdoor seating and take-out. Special lite menu. Open Sun.-Thurs. 11am-11pm, Fri.-Sat. 11am-midnight.

Duke's Coffee Shop, 8909 Sunset Blvd. (310-652-3100), at San Vicente in West Hollywood. Best place in L.A. to see hungover rock stars. The walls are a kaleidoscope of posters and autographed album covers. Perfect for brunch. Try the "Revenge"—eggs scrambled with avocado, sour cream, onions, tomatoes, and peppers ($6.75). Entrees $5-8. Open Mon.-Fri. 7:30am-9pm, Sat.-Sun. 8am-3:45pm. No credit cards.

Pink's Famous Chili Dogs, 711 N. La Brea Ave. (213-931-4223), Hollywood. More of an institution than a hot dog stand, Pink's has been serving up chili-slathered doggies to locals and celebs since 1939. Mouth-watering chili dogs ($2.10) and chili fries ($1.85). Bruce Willis proposed to Demi here all those films ago. Open Sun.-Thurs. 9:30am-2am, Fri.-Sat. 9:30am-3am. No credit cards.

El Coyote, 7312 Beverly Blvd. (213-939-2255), at Poinsettia in Hollywood. Some of the best-tasting Mexican-ish food in L.A. Enormous combo plates come with corn tortillas and all the chips and salsa you could ever want ($5.60). Frothy margaritas $3. Parking $1.50 after 4pm. Open Sun.-Thurs. 11am-10pm, Fri.-Sat. 11am-11pm.

Sights

The **Hollywood sign**—those 50-foot-high, slightly erratic letters perched on Mt. Cahuenga north of Hollywood—stands with New York's Statue of Liberty and Paris's Eiffel Tower as a universally recognized symbol of its city. The original 1923 sign, which read HOLLYWOODLAND, was an advertisement for a new subdivision in the Hollywood Hills (a caretaker lived behind one of the "L"s). Over the years, people came to think of it as a civic monument, and the city, having acquired the sign by 1978, reconstructed the crumbling letters, and left off the last syllable. The sign has been a target of college pranksters who have made it read everything from "Hollyweird" to "Ollywood" (after the infamous Lt. Col. Oliver North). You can't go frolic on the sign like Robert Downey. Jr. did in *Chaplin,* or take a leap from it like all the faded 1920s starlets—there is a $500 fine if you're caught (which is likely). You can snap a great picture by driving north on Vine, turning right on Franklin, left on Beachwood, and left on Belden into the Beachwood Supermarket parking lot. To get a close-up of the sign in all its monumental glory, continue up Beachwood, turn left on Ledgewood, and drive all the way up to Mulholland Hwy. Resting beneath the Hollywood sign, at 6342 Mulholland Hwy. (to the left, at the corner of Canyon Lake Dr.), is the eyesore known as **Castillo del Lago.** Once the gambling den of gangster Bugsy Siegel, the red and beige striped house also belonged to **Madonna,** but she recently sold it after an obsessed fan stalked her there.

Hollywood Boulevard itself, lined with souvenir shops, clubs, and theaters, is busy day and night, especially around the intersection of Highland and Hollywood and then west down Hollywood. To the east, things turn even seedier. For a star-studded stroll, head to the **Walk of Fame,** along Hollywood and Vine, where the sidewalk is embedded with over 2500 bronze-inlaid stars, inscribed with the names of the famous, the infamous, and the downright obscure. Stars are awarded for achievements in one of five categories—movies, radio, TV, recording, and live performance; only Gene Autry has all five stars. To catch a glimpse of today's (or yesterday's) stars in person, call the Chamber of Commerce (213-469-8311) for info on star-unveiling ceremonies.

The **Mann's Chinese Theater** (formerly Grauman's), 6925 Hollywood Blvd. (213-464-8111), between Highland and La Brea, is a garish rendition of a Chinese temple, and the hottest spot for a Hollywood movie premiere. The exterior columns, which once supported a Ming Dynasty temple, are strangely authentic for Hollywood. Tourists crowd the courtyard to pay photographic homage to the impressions made by many a movie star in the cement, including Whoopi Goldberg's dreds, Betty Grable's legs, R2D2's wheels, Jimmy Durante's nose, and George Burns's cigar. Just across the street from Mann's is the **El Capitan Theatre,** 6838 Hollywood Blvd. (213-467-9545), where the 1941 Hollywood premiere of *Citizen Kane* was held. This restored cinema house features ornate faux-exotic 1920's interior decoration and high prices (a symptom of the Disney disease).

Two blocks east of Mann's is the **Hollywood Wax Museum,** 6767 Hollywood Blvd. (213-462-8860), where you'll meet 200 figures, from Jesus to Elvis, who may wish you had some matches. Not surprisingly, the sculpture of Michael Jackson is one of the few that a chisel and putty have recreated nearly perfectly (open daily 10am-midnight; admission $9, children $7). Across the street from the Wax Museum you'll find a few touristy "Odd-itoriums." The lingerie museum in **Frederick's of Hollywood,** 6608 Hollywood Blvd. (213-466-8506), displays bras worn by everyone from Marilyn Monroe to Milton Berle (open Mon.-Sat. 10am-6pm, Sun. noon-5pm; free). The **Guinness World of Records,** 6764 Hollywood Blvd. (213-463-6433), has the tallest, shortest, heaviest, most tattooed, and other curious superlatives on display (open daily 10am-midnight; admission $9, children $7; with Wax Museum ticket $4, children $2). Similar, but wackier, **Ripley's Believe It or Not!,** 6780 Hollywood Blvd. (213-466-6335), has a side-show mentality strangely in keeping with the rest of Hollywood (open Mon.-Fri. 10am-11pm, Sat.-Sun. 10am-midnight; admission $9, children $6).

Music is another industry that, like film, finds a center in Los Angeles. The pre-eminent monument of the modern record industry is the 1954 **Capitol Records Tower,** 1750 Vine St., just north of Hollywood. The cylindrical building, which was designed to look like a stack of records, has fins sticking out at each floor (the "records") and a needle on top, which blinks H-O-L-L-Y-W-O-O-D in morse code.

At the corner of Hollywood and McCappen sits the massive inner sanctum of **Scientology**—the faith of the stars. The billboard on the side notes the number of copies of *Dianetics* sold to date. The **L. Ron Hubbard Life Exhibition,** 6331 Hollywood Blvd. (213-960-3511), has an array of E-meters, the "prime religious artifact of the Scientology religion," and a display outlining Ron's Way to Happiness with passages from his "non-religious moral code," which is strangely similar to the Ten Commandments (open daily 10am-10pm with 1½hr. required tour; free). Tom Cruise, Nicole

Kidman, John Travolta, Kirstie Alley, and Lisa Marie Presley are just a few of the members who flock to the Scientology Celebrity Center to be purified.

Music fans of all types might make a strike at **Hollywood Bowl** if there's a rehearsal or concert in session, but it serves up sights as well as sounds. All sparkly after its recent facelift, the **Hollywood Bowl Museum** (213-850-2058), has several exhibits as well as listening stations where you can swoon to Stravinsky, Aron Copeland, and the Beatles, all of whom played the Bowl in the same week during the 60s (open Tues.-Sat. 9:30am-8:30pm; free). Honoring television history is the **Hollywood Entertainment Museum,** 7021 Holly wood Blvd. (213-465-7900), which has original sets from *Cheers* and *Star Trek* (open Tues.-Sat. 10am-6pm; tours every 30min.; admission $7.50, students $4.50, seniors $4.50, children $4; parking $2).

The **Hollywood Studio Museum,** 2100 N. Highland Ave. (213-874-2276), across from the Bowl, provides a glimpse into early Hollywood filmmaking. In 1913, famed director Cecil B. DeMille rented this former barn as studio space for Hollywood's first feature film, *The Squaw Man.* Antique cameras, costumes worn by Douglas Fairbanks and Rudolph Valentino, props, vintage film clips, and other memorabilia fill the museum (open Sat. 10am-4pm, Sun. noon-4pm, weekdays by appointment only; admission $4, students $3, seniors $3, ages 6-12 $2; ample free parking).

Barnsdall Art Park, 4808 Hollywood Blvd., contains the **Hollyhock House** (213-662-7272), commanding a 360° view of L.A. and the mountains. Completed in 1922 for eccentric oil heiress Aline Barnsdall, the house was one of **Frank Lloyd Wright's** initial attempts to develop a distinct Southern Californian style of architecture and his first work to reflect the influence of Mayan temples. The house is named for Barnsdall's favorite flower, which Wright reproduced (begrudgingly and abstractly) all over the house. (Tours on the hr. Wed.-Sun. noon-3pm. Tickets $2, seniors $1.50, under 12 free. Buy tickets at the Municipal Art Gallery, 213-485-4581.)

If you still haven't had enough showbiz glitz of years gone by, visit the **Hollywood Memorial Park,** 6000 Santa Monica Blvd. (213-469-1181), between Vine and Western, a decaying cemetery that feels almost haunted. Here rest deceased stars such as Rudolph Valentino, Jayne Mansfield, Douglas Fairbanks Sr., Cecil B. De Mille, and many forgotten ones (open Mon.-Fri. 8am-5pm; mausoleums close at 4:30pm).

If I Were a Groupie

Long gone are the days when groupies could reach out and touch their favorite musicians by just telephoning backstage or hanging around after the show. It may have worked for Pamela Des Barres in the 70s, but today's groupie has to have skills which would put FBI agents to shame. It's a full-time occupation requiring insightful thinking, careful planning, and well-honed "people skills." *Let's Go* cannot give you the well-trained eyes and ears necessary for success, but we can point you in the right direction. The first thing you need to know is that stars tend to stay in the same hotels. Armed with this knowledge, you can narrow your search. The **Rock 'n' Roll Hyatt,** on the Sunset Strip, was the site of Led Zeppelin's orgies and Jim Morrison's antics and is now the preferred haunt of bands like Live and Smashing Pumpkins. Almost directly across the street is **St. James Club,** a pricier and more refined spot which caters to older bands such as Duran Duran. By the base of the famous billboards on Sunset is the **Chateau Marmont,** where Keanu Reeves and Dustin Hoffman have made extended stays. Farther up the Strip on Alta Loma is the **Sunset Marquis.** This extremely expensive hotel houses the biggest musical acts (Rolling Stones, Peter Gabriel, George Michael). Hiding on a residential street near the corner of Melrose and La Cienega is **Le Parc,** which caters to a mixture of the bigger bands who want peace and quiet (Morrissey) and most newer British acts (Blur, Elastica). Finally, as any savvy groupie knows, all bands register under fake names these days, so you'll have to rely on your big, bountiful, buxom wits—and charm.

WILSHIRE DISTRICT AND HANCOCK PARK

L.A.'s culture vultures convene in the Wilshire District to peruse the latest in Hancock Park, which lies along the Miracle Mile, enclosed by Wilshire Blvd. and 6th St.

Food

The Wilshire District's eateries are sadly out of step with its world-class museums. Inexpensive (and often kosher) restaurants dot Fairfax and Pico Blvd., but health nuts should stay away—there's no keeping the cholesterol down in these parts.

The Apple Pan, 10801 W. Pico (310-475-3585), 1 block east of Westwood, across from the Westside pavillion. Suburban legend has it that *Beverly Hills 90210*'s Peach Pit was modeled after The Apple Pan. Paper-plated burgers $3-6, pie $2.40. Open Sun. and Tues.-Thurs. 11am-midnight, Fri.-Sat. 11am-1am. No credit cards.

Cassell's Hamburgers, 3266 W. 6th St. (213-480-8668). Some say these burgers are the finest in the city. They're juicy, enormous, and come with as much potato salad and cottage cheese as you can fit on your sizable plate. Basic burger $4.60, turkey burger $4.60, chicken breast $5. Open Mon.-Sat. 10am-4pm. No credit cards.

Shalom Pizza, 8715 W. Pico Blvd. (213-271-2255). Kosher (i.e. vegetarian) pizza in a quiet Jewish business district. Large cheese $11, slice $1.60. Some may take issue with the kosher status of their tuna melt ($2.50). Open Sun.-Thurs. 11am-9pm, Fri. 11am-sundown, Sat. sundown-2am. No credit cards.

Sights

The **Los Angeles County Museum of Art (LACMA),** 5905 Wilshire Blvd. (213-857-6000; http://www.lacma.org), at the west end of Hancock Park, has a distinguished collection which rebuts those who say that L.A.'s only culture is in its yogurt. Opened in 1965, the LACMA is the largest museum in the West, with five major buildings clustered around the **Times-Mirror Central Court.** The **Steve Martin Gallery,** in the Anderson Building, houses the famed benefactor's collection of Dada and Surrealist works, including Rene Magritte's *Treachery of Images.* (This explains how Steve was able to roller skate through LACMA's halls in *L.A. Story.*) The museum sponsors free jazz (Fri. 5:30-8:30pm), chamber music (Sun. 4-5pm), film classics and documentaries (tickets $6, seniors $2, children $1), and a variety of free daily tours. The info desk in the Central Court (ticket office 213-857-6010), and the Docent Council (213-857-6108), provide schedules. (Open Mon.-Tues., Thurs. noon-8pm, Fri. noon-9pm, Sat.-Sun. 11am-8pm. Admission $6, students $4, seniors $4, under 18 $1; free 2nd Tues. of each month. Parking $5, free after 6pm. Wheelchair accessible.

Next door, in Hancock Park, an acrid petroleum stench pervades the vicinity of the **La Brea Tar Pits,** which enticed thirsty mammals of bygone geological ages. These unsuspecting creatures drank enthusiastically from pools of water only to find themselves stuck in the tar that lurked below. Most of the one million recovered bones are housed in the **George C. Page Museum of La Brea Discoveries,** 5801 Wilshire Blvd. (213-934-PAGE/7243 or 857-6311), at Curson. On display are reconstructed Ice Agers, murals of prehistoric L.A. The only human unearthed in the pits stands out in holographic horror—the **La Brea woman** was presumably thrown into the tar after having holes drilled into her skull to Alleve her headache. Archaeologists continue their digging in **Pit 91** behind the adjacent art museum. The museum has a lot to offer, so stay around—just don't get stuck. (Open Tues.-Sun. 10am-5pm, July-Sept. daily 10am-5pm. Admission $6, students $3.50, seniors $3.50, ages 5-10 $2; free 1st Tues. of each month. Parking $5. Museum tours Wed.-Sun. 2pm, tours of grounds 1pm. Wilshire buses stop in front of the museum.)

Across the street is the acclaimed **Petersen Automotive Museum,** 6060 Wilshire Blvd. (930-CARS/2277), which showcases L.A.'s most recognizable symbol—the automobile. With 300,000 square feet, it is the world's largest car museum and the nation's second largest history museum (the Smithsonian is the first largest). Full-day parking ($4) is convenient to LACMA. (Open Tues.-Sun. 10am-6pm. Admission $7, students $5, seniors $5, kids $3.)

WEST HOLLYWOOD

Once considered a no-man's land between Beverly Hills and Hollywood, West Hollywood has more recently formed an identity for itself with a thriving **gay community,** and some of L.A.'s best nightlife (see **Nightlife,** p. 112). The section of Santa Monica Blvd. around San Vincente is the city's oldest and most assertive homosexual district, and the city was one of the country's first to be governed by openly gay officials. The proximity of Hollywood and West Hollywood causes the borders to blend together. It can be difficult to tell where the district (Hollywood) ends and the city (West Hollywood) begins. In the years before its 1985 incorporation, lax zoning laws gave rise to **Sunset Strip,** originally lined with posh nightclubs frequented by stars—these have now been supplanted by pseudo-grungy rock clubs (also frequented by stars). The area's music scene is among the country's most fertile, and many world-famous bands from The Doors to Guns 'n' Roses got their start here. Weekend nights attract tremendous club crowds and traffic jams. The Strip's famous **billboards** are, on some blocks, as massive and creative as those in New York's Times Square. At 8218 Sunset Blvd., 15-foot-high plaster effigies of **Rocky and Bullwinkle** commemorate the duo's creator, Jay Ward. The courtyard is inscribed à la the Mann's Chinese Theater with the signature of June Foray (the voice of Rocky *and* Natasha) and the elbowprints of the cartoon's writers. The former offices of Jay Ward Productions now houses the **Dudley Doo-right Emporium,** 8200 Sunset Blvd. (see **Shopping,** p. 110).

Melrose Avenue, running from the southern part of West Hollywood to Hollywood, is lined with chi-chi restaurants, art galleries, and shops catering to all levels of the counter-culture spectrum, from ravers to skaters. The choicest stretch is between La Brea and Fairfax. While much that is sold here is pre-owned (vintage), none of it is really cheap. **Aardvark's,** 7579 Melrose Ave. (213-655-6769), is the pick of the litter among Melrose's vintage clothing stores (see **Shopping,** p. 110). **Retail Slut,** 7308 Melrose Ave. (213-462-7588), is a mecca for punks, goths, and sluts of all ilks. It's the place to find the fetish gear you've been searching for, or just a cool spot to browse a huge selection of ear- and body-rings. The rest of the evening's needed equipment can be found at **Condom Mania,** 7306 Melrose Ave. (213-933-7865).

North of the Beverly Center, at Melrose and San Vicente, is the **Pacific Design Center,** 8687 Melrose Ave. (310-657-0800), a sea-green glass complex, nicknamed the **Blue Whale,** and constructed in the shape of a rippin' wave. In addition to design showrooms, the PDC houses a public plaza and 350-seat amphitheater, used to stage free summer concerts (Sun. 6-7:30pm). It also hosts an awesome **Gay Pride Weekend Celebration** in late June.

BEVERLY HILLS

The very name Beverly Hills evokes images of palm-lined boulevards, tanned and taut skin, and million-dollar homes with guitar-shaped pools. While that may have been true in Hollywood's glamor days of the 40s and 50s, reality has set in. The reason why all the maps to stars' homes only seem to show dead stars is that while the privileged may still *shop* here, most no longer *live* here. The area still houses many a multi-millionaire and lives up to the well-manicured ideal that visitors expect, but the real fame and money has long since moved away from the hype to areas which afford privacy (see **Bel Air, Brentwood,** and **Pacific Palisades,** p. 90). Take advantage of all the public parking lots offering the first one or two hours free and browse to your heart's content. Shopkeepers can no longer tell who's got the cash and who hasn't (though it's a good idea to leave the shorts and t-shirts in the closet), so you'll probably find them more tolerable than Julia Roberts did in *Pretty Woman.*

Food

Yes, there is budget dining in Beverly Hills; it just takes a little looking.

World Wrapps, 168 S. Beverly Dr. (310-859-9010). Cashing in on the hottest new trend, it takes "healthy Mexican" to new, international, Cali-gourmet heights.

Mostly take-out, but colorful interior and outdoor seating invite eat-ins. Thai chicken wrapps (small $3.50, regular $5) and Samurai salmon wrapps ($4.25, $6.50) are available in spinach and tomato tortillas. Open daily 8am-10pm.

Nancy's Health Kitchen, 225 S. Beverly Dr. (310-385-8530). Calorie and fat contents are kept to a minimum in this cheery cafe. Mexican baked potato with turkey or vegetarian chili, low-fat cheddar, tomatoes, "no oil" corn chips, and salsa $5.50. Salads $5-6. Air-baked fries $1.85. Open Mon.-Fri. 10am-9pm, Sat.-Sun. noon-9pm.

Finney's in the Alley, 8840 Olympic Blvd. (310-888-8787). Heading east on Olympic, turn right on Clark, and immediately right into the alley; look for a yellow awning. The manager refuses to advertise for fear that "the secret will get out." This walk-up lunch counter really is one of Beverly Hills' best-kept secrets. Finney's most expensive offering is a Philly steak sandwich ($4.20). Open Mon.-Sat. 11am-6pm.

Ed Debevic's, 134 N. La Cienega Blvd. (310-659-1952), Beverly Hills. This site of many a Sweet Sixteen party has big and yummy food served by a 50s-attired waitstaff with attitude à la *Pulp Fiction*. Entrees $6-8. Full bar. Open Mon.-Thurs. 11:30am-3pm and 5:30-10pm, Fri.-Sat. 11:30am-midnight, Sun. 11:30am-10pm.

The Original California Pizza Kitchen, 207 S. Beverly Dr. (310-275-1101). Though it now has locations nationwide, CPK began right here on Beverly in 1985. Menu features creative wood-fired pizza, pastas, and stars the Original Barbeque Chicken Pizza ($9). Try it on honey wheat crust. Free refills on soda and on their well-loved lemonade. Open Sun.-Thurs. 11:30am-10pm, Fri.-Sat. 11:30am-11pm. Other locations all over L.A. After all, it's an institution.

Sights

Get ready to gawk. Extravagant displays of opulence sometimes border on the vulgar, as Beverly Hills' residents try their hardest to make sure everyone knows just how much money they have. Admire (or admonish) the mansions on the palm-lined 700-900 blocks of **Beverly Dr.,** where each and every manicured estate begs for attention. The heart of the city is in the **Golden Triangle,** a wedge formed by Beverly Dr., Wilshire Blvd., and Santa Monica Blvd., centering on **Rodeo Drive,** known for its flashy clothing boutiques and jewelry shops. Built like an old English manorhouse, Polo Ralph Lauren (444 N. Rodeo) stands out from the white marble of the other stores. The divine triple-whammy of adjacent Cartier (370 N. Rodeo), Gucci (347 N. Rodeo), and Chanel (400 N. Rodeo) sits on some of the area's prime real estate, where rents are as high as $40,000 per month. The all-pedestrian shopping complex of **2 Rodeo Dr.** contains Dior, Tiffany's, and the Salon of Jose Eber, stylist to the stars and TV make-over king. Though it fakes European antiquity, the entire promenade—cobblestone street, lamp posts, and all—was constructed in the last decade. Across the way is the venerable **Beverly Wilshire Hotel** (310-275-5200), whose old and new wings are connected by **El Camino Real** and its Louis XIV gates. The **Beverly Hills City Hall,** 455 N. Rexford Dr. (310-285-1000), just below Santa Monica Blvd., would look out of place anywhere but here. This Spanish Renaissance building was erected during the heart of the Great Depression, and is now engulfed by Beverly Hills's new white phoenix of a **Civic Center,** which took nine years to build at a cost of $120 million. The **Beverly Hills Library,** 444 N. Rexford Dr. (213-228-2220), is a case study in the city's overriding concerns—the interior is adorned with marble imported from Thailand, but contains only an average collection of books. As always, though, Beverly Hills coordinates well: the library's tiling matches the colors on City Hall's dome.

Fans of *Beverly Hills 90210* should come to grips with the fact that West Beverly High is, alas, only a television construct (filmed, incidentally, at the less-glamorous Torrance High School). Still, the *real* **Beverly Hills High,** 241 Moreno (310-201-0661), between Olympic and Spalding, is not without interest. The indoor swimming pool is open in the summer (open Mon.-Thurs. 1-5pm, Fri. 2-4pm), and has a sliding floor cover that converts the pool into a basketball court. It's where Jimmy Stewart and Donna Reed danced the aquatic Charleston in *It's a Wonderful Life.*

Moving farther north, the **Beverly Hills Hotel,** 9641 Sunset Blvd. (310-276-2251), is a pink, palm-treed collection of poolside cottages. Howard Hughes established his infamous germ-free apartment here, while Marilyn Monroe reportedly had affairs

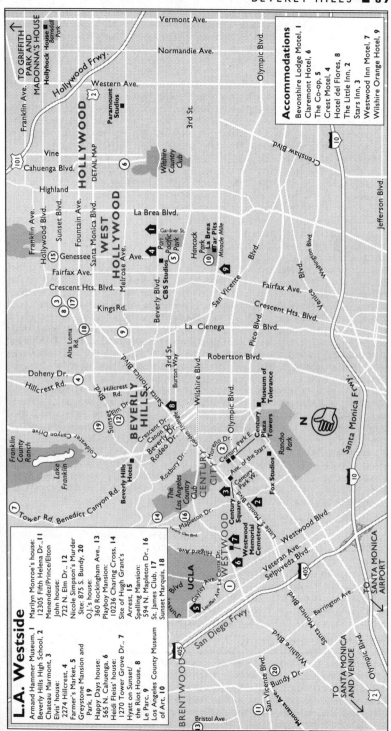

with both JFK and RFK in other bungalows. It is also home to the **Polo Lounge,** where countless media industry deals have gone down. The Sultan of Brunei paid $185 million for it in 1987, but ten years later you can get a room for a mere $275.

The Celebrity Tour

A conspicuous way to tour the city is in the 1914 trolley car replica operated by the Beverly Hills Chamber of Commerce (310-271-8126). The 40-minute **tour of the city and stars' homes** costs $5 and leaves from the corner of Rodeo and Dayton (on the hr. June-Sept. Tues.-Sat. 1-5pm). If you prefer a cooler approach, go solo with a star map ($5-7.50), sold along Sunset Blvd. but not within Beverly Hills, or take the following *Let's Go* abbreviated tour (consult the L.A. Westside map for reference).

Elvis had two homes in L.A. He purchased the first, at 1174 Hillcrest, shortly after his marriage to Priscilla in 1967, but quickly relocated to 144 Monovale because it offered more privacy. Today, Priscilla still resides near those old memories at 1167 Summit Dr. The 55-room **Greystone Mansion** at nearby 905 Loma Vista Dr. (310-550-4654), just off Doheny, was the most expensive home in Beverly Hills in the 1920s. The mansion was built by oil mogul **Doheny** for his son Edward, who was found dead with his male secretary only a few weeks after moving in, giving rise to unconfirmed rumors that the two were lovers. Now owned and operated by the city, the Tudor and Jacobean revival house with its two gatehouses and glorious gardens is now used extensively as a filming location, most notably in *The Witches of Eastwick, Ghostbusters,* and *The Bodyguard* (open daily 10am-6pm; gardens free). Head back to Sunset, make a right, and then make a left on Elm Dr. The estate at 722 N. Elm has been owned by **Elton John, The Artist Formerly Known as Prince,** and was most recently the site of the **Menendez** murders. **Frank Sinatra** owns the house at nearby 915 Foothill Rd., one street west of Elm. Head back to Sunset again, make a left, and another left onto Roxbury Dr. Nice-guy actor/poet **Jimmy Stewart** resided at 918 Foothill Rd. If you dig serious power, have a glance at the walls of the massive **David Geffen** mansion, 1801 Angelo Dr. Follow Roxbury north as it turns into Hartford, make a left onto Benedict Canyon, and another left on Angelo Dr. to the Geffen mansion. Now, turn back to Benedict Canyon, make a left, then a right onto Tower. **Jay Leno,** at 1151 Tower Rd., lives just around the corner from the home of **Heidi Fleiss,** at 1270 Tower Grove Dr. Head back down Benedict Canyon toward Sunset, make a right, and then another right onto Carolwood. **Barbra Streisand** lives at 301 Carolwood, and the house at 355 is where **Walt Disney** lived until his death. Turn back to Sunset and head towards Westwood, making a left on the tiny and windy Charing Cross. The estate at 10236 is **The Playboy Mansion.** Charing Cross becomes N. Mapleton, site of the largest and most extravagant residence in Beverly Hills: producer **Aaron Spelling's** mansion, 594 N. Mapleton, is larger than the Taj Mahal. Wife Candy Spelling's closets reportedly take up an entire wing.

South of Beverly Hills

Just south of Beverly Hills is the sobering **Beit HaShoa Museum of Tolerance,** 9786 W. Pico Blvd. (310-553-8043), at Roxbury. This hands-on, high-tech museum, which opened in 1992, has interactive exhibits designed to help visitors explore their own prejudices, and offers displays on the Holocaust, the Croatian genocide, the L.A. Riots, and the U.S. civil rights movement. Upstairs is the **Simon Weisenthal Center** for Holocaust research and artifacts from concentration camps. (2½-4hr. tours Mon.-Thurs. 10am-4pm, Fri. 10am-3pm, and Sun. 10:30am-5pm. Admission $8, seniors $6, students $5, ages 3-11 $3. Free parking. Wheelchair accessible.)

WESTWOOD AND UCLA

Bordering Bel Air, Westwood is an exclusive neighborhood on par with Brentwood and Pacific Palisades, while also being home to the mammoth University of California at Los Angeles (UCLA), and the Westwood Village shopping area. Myriad movie theaters, trendy boutiques, upscale bistros, and coffeehouses fill Westwood Village, but they don't reflect the diversity and dynamism of the nearby student community. For

LOS ANGELES

the most part, the town is safe, and generally overrun by high-schoolers. Friday and Saturday nights hum with caffeinated activity.

Food

Westwood is home to tens of thousands of students, meaning that despite the surrounding high rent, this is budget traveler paradise. What do students want? Cheap food and beer. Consequently, both can be found in abundance. Find the cheapest beer in town at **Tacos Tacos,** 1084 Glendon Ave., where Bud, the budget beer of choice, goes for 99¢ per pint, $2 per pitcher (open Mon.-Fri. 3-7pm).

Gypsy Cafe, 940 Broxton Ave. (310-824-2119). All the comforts of home (if home is Bohemia)—red velvet walls and drapes strewn from the ceiling. Its most defining atmospheric quality: smoking is not only permitted (except 8-10pm), it's encouraged (cigars $3-7). Mix 'n' match 5 pastas and 20 sauces ($7). Sandwiches $4.25, espresso $1.50. Open Sun.-Thurs. 8am-midnight, Fri.-Sat. 8am-1am.

José Bernstein's, 935 Broxton Ave. (310-208-4992). Standard deli-diner with Mexican tendencies. Breakfast special of 2 eggs, bacon or sausage, and potatoes $2.30. The Tacominator is 2 soft tacos, rice, beans, chips, and a drink ($3.25). Open Mon.-Wed. 7am-1am, Thurs.-Sat. 10am-2:30am, Sun. 1pm-1am. No credit cards.

Don Antonio's, 1136 Westwood Blvd. (310-209-1422). Relax in the outdoor seating while waiting for your custom-designed pizza ($5.50). Sinatra, red-checkered tablecloths, and wood-paneled walls. Lunch special (Mon.-Fri. 11am-3pm): large slice of pizza, salad, and all-you-can-drink ($3.50). Open daily 11am-3am. No credit cards.

Captgo Coffee and Tea Company, 923 Broxton Ave. (310-824-2277). More a place to chat and chill than to chow, Captgo is one of the biggest off-campus hangouts for students, always wide awake—perhaps due to the espresso ($1.85). You may be hard-pressed to find a seat in the evening. Smoothies $3, sandwiches $4. Open Mon.-Fri. 6:30am-midnight, Sat. 8am-1am, Sun. 8am-midnight.

Subbie's Roll-Inn, 972 Gayley Ave. (310-208-2354). If you're down to your last 3 bucks, roll-inn to the hut with the yellow and white striped awning. With $1.50, an 8-inch sub will roll your way, while $2 pays for a whole foot. A cheap way to get parking validation, if necessary. Open daily 10am-3am. No credit cards.

Headliner's Diner and Press Club, 10922 Kinross Ave. (310-208-2424), at Gayley. Headlines don the walls of this 50s-style diner, but the only press here is the occasional full court one, when the UCLA Bruins come to devour the low priced hefty portions. Subscriptions Special for a heap 'o breakfast ($2.77). Open Mon.-Thurs. 7am-midnight, Fri. 7am-1am, Sat. 9am-1am, Sun. 9am-midnight. No credit cards.

Sights

Get a feel for UC-style mass academia at the **University of California at Los Angeles (UCLA),** which sprawls over 400 acres in the foothills of the Santa Monica Mountains. A prototypical Californian university, UCLA sports an abundance of grassy open spaces, bike and walking paths, dazzling sunshine, and pristine buildings in a hodgepodge of architectural styles. Voted #1 jock school in the country by *Sports Illustrated* for its rip-roarin' success on the courts and in the fields (UCLA has won more NCAA titles than any other school), excellent athletic facilities, and high participation rates, UCLA also boasts an illustrious film school whose graduates include James Dean, Jim Morrison, Oliver Stone, Francis Ford Coppola, and Tim Robbins. The school is directly north of Westwood Village and west of Beverly Hills. To reach the campus by car, take the San Diego Fwy. (I-405) north to the Wilshire Blvd./Westwood Exit, heading east into Westwood. Take Westwood Blvd. north off Wilshire, heading straight through the center of the village and directly into the campus. By bus, take MTA route #2 along Sunset Blvd., #21 along Wilshire Blvd., #320 from Santa Monica, or #561 from the San Fernando Valley, or Santa Monica Blue Bus #1, 2, 3, 8, or 12. Shell out the $5 to get a parking pass from campus information stands at all entrances—parking ticket cops *live* to ticket unsuspecting visitors here.

The **Murphy Sculpture Garden,** which contains over 70 pieces scattered through five acres, lies directly in front of the Art Center. The collection includes works by such major artists as Rodin, Matisse, and Miró. Opposite the sculpture garden is

MacGowen Hall, which contains the **Tower of Masks.** UCLA's **inverted fountain** is located between Knudsen Hall and Schoenberg Hall, directly south of Dickson Plaza. An innovation in the field of fountain design, water spouts from its perimeter and rushes down into the gaping hole in the middle, like a giant toilet bowl.

The **Fowler Museum of Cultural History** (310-825-4361), in Haines Hall, displays artifacts from contemporary, historic, and prehistoric cultures (open Wed. and Fri.-Sun. noon-5pm, Thurs. noon-8pm; admission $5, students $3, seniors $3, under 17 free; Thurs. free). The museum is presently a source of controversy since it preserves Native American bodies here for their archaeological value, despite laws protecting Native Americans' rights to sacred burial.

UCLA's arts departments have loads of events, exhibitions, and performances year-round; call the **UCLA Arts Line** (310-UCLA-ART/825-2278) for details. The Center for the Performing Arts (310-825-2101), presents weekly concerts and dance recitals, with reserved seating (tickets $20-40; ask about student discounts). The Department of Art and Architecture (310-825-3281), hosts free lectures at the Graduate Studio, 8535 Warner Dr., in Culver City. The renowned **School of Film and Television** (310-206-FILM/3456), sponsors various film festivals, often with foreign films and profiles on groundbreaking filmmakers (double features $6, students $4, select films free).

Ackerman Union, 308 Westwood Plaza (310-206-0833), a campus information bank and the hub of student social activity, stands downhill from the quadrangle on Bruin Walk. A calendar lists the lengthy line-up of movies (first-runs often free), lectures, and campus activities. The huge **Associated Student Store** swallows up most of the ground floor with a bevy of UCLA paraphernalia (open in summer Mon.-Fri. 8:30am-6pm, Sat. 10am-5pm, Sun. noon-5pm; school-year daily 7:45am-7:30pm). Upstairs, there's good grub at the Cooperage, and unlimited video gaming at the XCape for $6. (Union open daily 8am-11pm.)

The **Armand Hammer Museum of Art and Cultural Center,** 10899 Wilshire Blvd. (310-443-7000), houses a small, but impressive collection of European and American works from the 16th century to the present day. Something of a "Who's Who" of European painters, Hammer's collection includes works by Rembrandt, Chagall, and Cézanne, but its real gem is Van Gogh's *Hospital at Saint Rémy*. The museum holds the world's largest collection of works by acerbic French lithographer Honoré Daumier. Oil and baking soda tycoon Armand Hammer purportedly wanted to donate his collections to the L.A. County Museum of Art, but demanded that the works be exhibited together in a separate wing. The museum refused, telling Hammer to build his own place—and he did just that. The gallery hosts free summer concerts (Fri. 6-8pm) and seasonal cultural programs. (Open Tues.-Wed. and Fri.-Sat. 11am-7pm, Thurs. 11am-9pm, Sun. 11am-5pm. Admission $4.50, students $3, seniors $3, under 7 free; Thurs. free after 6pm and free between seasonal exhibits. Free tours daily at 1pm. 3hr. parking $2.75. Wheelchair accessible.)

BEL AIR, BRENTWOOD, AND PACIFIC PALISADES

Most of today's stars live in these three affluent communities, not in Beverly Hills farther downhill and to the east. Next to UCLA is the well-guarded community of **Bel Air,** where **Ronald Reagan** has retired to become the new Fresh Prince. His estate is at 668 St. Cloud, adjacent to the *Beverly Hillbillies* mansion (750 Bel Air Rd.) and a few blocks up from the former home of **Sonny and Cher** (364 St. Cloud). **Elizabeth Taylor** is literally around the (windy) corner (700 Nimes). Back in the golden days, Bel Air was the area *de rigeur* for the glamorous celebs, including **Judy Garland** (924 Bel Air Rd.), **Alfred Hitchcock** (10957 Bel Air Rd.), and **Lauren Bacall** and **Humphrey Bogart** (232 Mapleton Dr.) during their spat at marital bliss.

Farther west on Sunset Blvd. is **Brentwood,** home to many young actors and **O.J. Simpson.** Actually, O.J. no longer lives here; his estate (360 Rockingham, if you didn't know) was repossessed and auctioned off for a meager $2.63 million (guess there were some bloodstains). On August 4, 1962, **Marilyn Monroe** was found dead at her home (12305 Fifth Helena Dr.). The celeb-city of Brentwood also includes the homes of Michelle Pfeiffer, Harrison Ford, Meryl Streep, and Rob Reiner.

The considerably more secluded **Pacific Palisades** is the place to live these days. Many streets are entirely closed to anyone but residents and their guests, but you can try to catch a glimpse of **Tom Cruise** and **Nicole Kidman** outside 1525 Sorrento, or **Steven Spielberg** at 1515 Amalfi (this home, incidentally, belonged to David O. Selznick when he was producing *Gone with the Wind*). **Arnold Schwarzenegger** and Maria Shriver practice family fitness at 14209 Sunset Blvd., **Tom Hanks** lives at 321 S. Anita Ave., and **Michael Keaton** resides at 826 Napoli Dr. Billy Crystal, Chevy Chase, and John Travolta also own homes in the area. The cliffs give way to the ocean at the popular **Will Rogers State Beach,** on the 16000 block of Pacific Coast Highway (PCH). At 1501 Will Rogers State Park Rd., you can hike around **Will Rogers State Historical Park** (310-454-8212), take in the panoramic views of the city and distant Pacific, visit the famous humorist's home, or eat a picnic brunch while watching a Saturday afternoon polo match (matches Sat. 2-5pm and Sun. 10am-noon). Follow Chatauqua Blvd. inland from PCH to Sunset Blvd., or take MTA #2, which runs along Sunset. (Park is open daily 8am-8pm; Rogers's house is open daily 10:30am-5pm, with tours on the ½hr.)

Off the Map: The Celebrity Tour Continued

Above Pacific Palisades, Brentwood, and Bel Air, **Mulholland Drive** is one street blessed with much sought-after seclusion and the best views in L.A. It stretches from the west end of the valley to the Hollywood Freeway, skirting the dividing line between the City and the Valley, gleaning the best of both worlds without really belonging to either. The narrow, winding road offers a detached, yet privileged, bird's eye view of the City of Sin, making it an ideal location for the most aloof celebrity enclaves. From the street, you won't be able to see most of these places, but you just might get lucky and smash into one of their owners and gain instant celebrity status yourself, like the lucky woman who accidently hit Tom Cruise's car two years ago and was soon conducting exclusive interviews everywhere. Across from the Mulholland Estates at 14111 is the home of **Don Henley. Warren Beatty** and **Annette Bening** live at 13671, while **Bruce and Demi** are one block up at 13511. The elusive **Jack Nicholson** lives at 12850, next door to the even more elusive **Marlon Brando** at 12900. Wrap up your drive in style with a visit to the original Super Freak **Rick James,** at 8115 Mulholland Terrace. **Julian Lennon, Shaun Cassidy, Richard Grieco,** and **Rob Lowe** also live on Mulholland Drive, but, because they would surely be inundated with admiring minions and become prisoners in their own homes, we cannot print their addresses.

In the Santa Monica Mountains above Bel Air is the new **J. Paul Getty Museum and Getty Center,** 1200 Getty Center Dr. (310-440-7330). Formerly located in Malibu, the new center (scheduled to open Dec. 16, 1997) unites L.A.'s beloved Getty museums with its institutes on one site, designed by renowned architect Richard Meier. (The Malibu Villa will reopen in 2001 as an antiquities center.) The museum itself is housed in five pavilions around the three-acre Central Garden, designed by Robert Irwin, a living work of art that changes with the seasons. The museum includes the permanent Getty collection, which includes Van Gogh's *Irises,* Impressionist paintings, Renaissance drawings, and one of the nation's best Rembrandt collections. The new galleries have twice as much exhibit space as the old facilities; many rooms are illuminated by natural light, and some are designed in the style of 17th- and 18th- century interiors. The Getty hosts a number of programs open to the public, including gallery talks by local artists, lectures, films, a concert series, and studio demonstrations. "Friday Nights at the Getty" feature plays, films, and readings (call 310-440-7330 for info). To reach the Getty Center, take the San Diego Fwy. (I-405) to Getty Center Dr.; parking costs $5 and requires advance reservations (310-440-7300). MTA #561 stops at the museums' front entrance on Sepulveda Blvd. (Open Tues.-Wed. 11am-7pm, Thurs.-Fri. 11am-9pm, Sat.-Sun. 10am-6pm. Free.)

SANTA MONICA

Santa Monica, the Bay City of Raymond Chandler's novels, was once known as the "Gold Coast" because of the fabulously wealthy stars who called it home. Today, the area is less pretentious, hosting a hep and more low-key affluent set. The liberal community is known for its philanthropy toward the city's homeless population. The **Third Street Promenade** is now the city's most popular spot to shop by day and schmooze by night, and the nearby beaches are jam-packed. Despite the resultant hassles (parking, prices, lines), Santa Monica has an unbeatable assemblage of diversions, and is safer than most L.A. communities. It takes about a half–hour (with no traffic) to reach Santa Monica on MTA #33 or 333 or on the Santa Monica Fwy. (I-10) from downtown. Santa Monica's efficient Big Blue Bus system connects to other L.A. bus routes. The **Visitors Information Office,** 1400 Ocean Ave., (310-393-7593), in Palisades Park, gives free maps of the bus system (open daily 10am-5pm).

Food

Santa Monica's restaurants fall unmistakably into the "see and be seen" category, especially along the Third St. Promenade. Prices are elevated accordingly, but so is the quality of the food. Organic and vegetarian fare is just as prevalent as the trendy beauties that feed on it.

Babalu, 1002 Montana Ave. (310-395-2500). Cuban specialties that would make Ricky proud, and "cross pollinated island cuisine" that would please his friends Lunch $7-8. Coconut shrimp $9, Cuban beefsteak with beans, rice, *plantanos* $12.25. Open Tues.-Thurs. 8am-10pm. Fri.-Sat. 8am-11pm, Sun. 8am-9:30pm.

Real Food Daily, 514 Santa Monica Blvd. (310-451-7544). Charming and sunny organic cafe. All food is animal-, dairy-, egg-, cholesterol-, and sugar-free, but surprisingly tasty (though not free of charge). International selection of daily specials ($10). Cajun wrap sandwich $8. Miso soup $3.75. Open daily 11:30am-10pm.

El Cholo, 1025 Wilshire Blvd. (310-899-1106). Like the Cancun cantinas it mimics, this is *the* spot to be seen, at least for the moment. Cheese enchilada, beans, rice, and choice of a taco, *chile relleno,* or tamale $7.75. "L.A. Lemonade" margarita is a pricey $6.25, but was ranked the city's best by *L.A. Magazine.* Bar with couches, big-screen TV. Open Sun.-Thurs. 11am-10pm, Fri.-Sat. 11am-11pm.

Topper Restaurant and Cantina, 1111 2nd St. (310-393-8080), topping the Radisson Huntley Hotel. The budget-minded probably can't afford the entrees here, but the scoop on Happy Hour (daily 4:30-7:30pm) is spreading fast: buy one drink (sodas $1.50, beer $2.75 and up), and get all-you-can-eat free food from the bountiful buffet. Open daily 6am-midnight.

Ye Olde King's Head, 116 Santa Monica Blvd. (310-451-1402), Santa Monica. An authentic British pub owned by a Birmingham expatriate. Ploughman's Plate of cheeses, chutneys, and bread is $7. And it wouldn't be Brit if it didn't have a broad assortment of English beers and ales ($3.75 a pint). Perhaps the only place in town to catch rugby, cricket, and football games among all the Commonwealth member countries. Royal Afternoon Tea Mon.-Fri. 3-5pm. Open daily 11am-1:30am.

Shambala Cafe, 607 Colorado Ave. (310-395-2160). Cozy cafe with healthy, low-priced dishes—no small feat in Santa Monica. Recipes from around the globe, with a heavy emphasis on veggies, tofu, and soy meat (some chicken and tuna selections as well). Sandwiches $4-6. Samosas $1.50-2.40. Asian noodle selection changes daily. Open Mon.-Sat. 11:30am-8:30pm, Sun. noon-8pm. No credit cards.

Sights

Santa Monica is the place that put the "Bay" in *Baywatch.* While there are cleaner waters with better waves on the beaches to the north and south, SaMo (as it's called by the locals) is known more for its shoreside scene than its shore. As the closest beach to the city, Santa Monica's sands are packed year-round with sunbathers sporting skimpy bikinis and buff, bronzed beach volleyball players, as well as families and people-watchers who have come for the view. (Note: As this is real life, not all beachgoers are as beautiful as those on *Baywatch.* Sorry.)

TO MALIBU

Montana Ave.
Idaho Ave.
Washington Ave.
California Ave.

Lincoln Park
Wilshire Blvd.

Douglas
Park

Santa
Monica
State
Beach

PO

Greyhound
Depot

Arizona Ave.

Santa Monica Blvd.

Broadway

Big Blue
Bus Depot

Colorado Ave.

Memorial
Park

Santa
Monica
Pier

Ocean
Park

SANTA MONICA

Pico Blvd.

Santa
Monica
Bay

Olympic Blvd.

TO
HOLLYWOOD

Jocelyn
Park

Los
Amigos
Park

OCEAN
PARK

Ocean Park Blvd.

Ashland Ave.

Santa Monica Fwy.

N

Rose Ave.

Penmar
Golf Course

Dewey St.

Santa Monica
Airport

VENICE

Venice
Beach

Pearl St.

Palms Blvd.

Venice
Pier

Venice Blvd.

Washington St.

Venice
Beach

Washington Blvd.

Palawan Way

Admiralty Way

Burton
Chase Park

Mindanao Ave.

Fiji Way

MARINA
DEL REY

Via Marina

Culver Blvd.

Jefferson Blvd.

Pershing Dr.

Manchester Ave.

TO L.A. INT'L
AIRPORT

Loyola
Marymount
University

The paved bicycle path stretching south to the Venice Beach boardwalk, 2.8 mi. away, is popular for walking, in-line skating, and cycling. The path continues along the coastline for 18.4 mi. to Torrance Beach. Rent equipment from **Perry's Beach Rentals** in those eye-catching blue buildings, north of the pier at 930, 1100, and 1200 PCH, and south of the pier at 2400 and 2600 Promenade. (In-line skates and bikes $6 per hr., $15 per day; tandem bikes $10 per hr., $30 per day; boogieboards $2 per hr., $10 per day. Open Mon.-Fri. 9:15am-7:30pm, Sat.-Sun. 9:15am-8pm.)

Renovated in 1996, the **Santa Monica Pier** has the feel of an old-fashioned boardwalk, complete with the aroma of popcorn, a few pizza joints, an arcade, and tons of tacky souvenirs. During the summer, the pier hosts a Twilight Dance Series on Thursdays at 7:30pm. The gem of the pier is the restored 1922 carousel, which was featured in *The Sting*. Together with a few miniature roller coasters and a ferris wheel, it makes up the diminutive Pacific Park, which resembles a county fair more than a modern amusement park (open daily 10am-10pm; tickets $1, rides cost up to 3 tickets). An ATM is located in the Playland arcade. The harbor patrol at the end of the pier has info on **grunion runs,** which usually occur during the three nights after a new of full moon. These small silvery fish deliberately strand themselves on the beach to lay their eggs, and hordes of (unlicensed) kids scoop the fish up (illegally) in their hands.

On the scenic bluff overlooking the pier, **Palisades Park** boasts the **Stairpath,** the fearful 189-step outdoor Stairmaster. Located at 4th and Adelaide, it leads *down* to the beach. The **Camera Obscura,** at the Senior Recreation Center, 1450 Ocean Ave., catches an unusual (or even obscure) view of the beach. This Aristotelian contraption uses convex lenses to project a 360° bird's-eye view of the beach onto a screen in a dark room (open Mon.-Fri. 9am-4pm, Sat.-Sun. 11am-4pm; free).

A mere three blocks from the beach, the ultra-popular **Third Street Promenade** is a major walking, shopping, people-watching, and movie-viewing thoroughfare. Before its present incarnation of fashionable boutiques and yuppie cafes, Third St. was known as one of L.A.'s artsier areas, and is still home of the city's better book and music stores (see **Shopping,** p. 110). The area truly comes to life at night, when street artists come out and the ivy-lined mesh dinosaur sculptures light up. Kids with clipboards often sign people on for **free movie passes.** This is, after all, the film screening capital of the world. Nearby **Main St.** is an equally chic, but less crowded area for the consummate shopper and snacker. **Schatzi on Main,** 3110 Main St. (310-399-4800), is owned by **Arnold Schwarzenegger** and Maria Shriver.

Away from the main drag, the **Museum of Flying,** 2772 28th St. (310-392-8822), on the airstrip of Santa Monica Airport, is a small hangar museum featuring the *'24 New Orleans,* which flew around the world, and a theater that shows aviation films (open Wed.-Sun. 10am-5pm; admission $7, seniors $5, children $2).

VENICE

You think you've been to a beach town before? Think again. Think liberal politics Berkeley could only dream of. Think diversity any college admissions board would boast—if this unorthodox crowd were ever accepted anywhere. Think electric guitars, dredlocks, tie dye, rollerblades—all sported on the same person. Think bikinis, bodybuilders, and beach volleyball. Think nude sand sculptures and graffiti masterpieces. Venice is tattoos, corn dogs, and a million wild-eyed visionaries. Venice is the safest psychedelic trip you'll ever take. Venice could only happen in California.

Food

Venetian cuisine runs the gamut from greasy to ultra-healthy, as befits its beachy-hippie crowd. The boardwalk offers cheap grub in fast-food fashion—pay more than $1 for a pizza slice, hot dog, or serving of fries, and you're getting ripped off.

Van Go's Ear 24 Hour Restaurant and Gallery, 796 Main St. (310-314-0022). Quintessential Venice with a psychedelic mural of the cafe's namesake complete with neon earring. Ridiculously large portions of tasty chow. All entrees named for second-rate celebs, such as the Kato Kaelin Salad ($3). "Tightwad menu" has 8 breakfast combos under $2 (served weekdays 6-11am). The *Fruit Fuck* is a smoothie potion concocted with oranges, apples, pears, kiwi, and bee pollen ($3.75). Some part of the 2-story mega-shack is always open. No credit cards.

Sidewalk Cafe, 1401 Ocean Front Walk (310-399-5547). *The* most popular spot on the boardwalk. It's big (i.e. not a dinky boardwalk food hut), and it sports a dazzling view of the beach. Entrees are named after writers, keeping in step with the adjacent bookstore. Omelettes $5.50-7, sandwiches $5-9. Big bar in back (pints $3). Open Sun.-Thurs. 8am-11pm, Fri.-Sat. 8am-midnight.

Rose Cafe, 220 Rose Ave. (310-399-0711), at Main St. The sunlight streaming in *so* complements the airy interior, *dahling*. Roses-on-steroids murals remind you what street you're on. Deli specials (sandwiches $5, salads $4) are a steal. Live jazz Fri.-Sat. 8-11pm. Open Mon.-Fri. 7am-10pm, Sat. 8am-10pm, Sun. 8am-5pm.

Figtrees Cafe, 429 Ocean Front Walk (310-392-4937). Finished festooning on the ocean front and fostering a feeling known to forerunners as "a farthing famished"? Festinate to Figtrees for fab food and first-rate fun. It would be a fathomless felony to fester inside when a fantastic, festive patio is to be found. Only a fingerling of fat in these fabled foods full of finesse. Don't forget to finagle for the "flavorful, faultless" latkes ($7.50). They are filling. No fooling. Functioning daily 9am-9pm.

On The Waterfront Cafe, 205 Ocean Front Walk (310-392-0322). This charming bar/cafe, with pool table and boardwalk seating, is a favorite among international (read: German) crowd. Erdlinger Weißbräu on tap. Salads, bratwurst sandwiches, and pasta to suit any palate. Best mussels on the beach ($12, serves 2). Beer half-price Mon.-Fri. 6-8pm. Open Mon.-Fri. 11am-midnight, Sat.-Sun. 9am-midnight.

Windward Farms Market, 105 Windward Ave. (310-392-3566). Organic supermarket with whole grain breads and fresh fruit. Sells deli sandwiches ($2.50-4), salads ($4 per lb.), and fresh juices ($2.50). Perfect picnic fare. Open daily 8am-7:30pm.

Sights

At the turn of this century, Abbot Kinney envisioned a touch of Old World charm, moustached gondoliers, and the social elite strolling on an oceanside promenade. Instead, he ended up with a huge dose of New World neuroses. **Ocean Front Walk,** Venice's main beachfront drag, is a seaside three-ring circus of fringe culture. Street people converge on shaded clusters of benches, evangelists drown out off-color comedians, and bodybuilders of both sexes pump iron in skimpy spandex outfits at the original **Muscle Beach,** 1800 Ocean Front Walk, closest to 18th and Pacific. Fire-juggling cyclists, joggers, master sand sculptors, groovy elders (such as the **"skateboard grandma"**), and bards in Birkenstocks make up the balance of this playground population. Vendors of jewelry, snacks, and beach paraphernalia overwhelm the boardwalk. Collect your wits and people-watch at one of the cafes or juice bars, or check out life in the fast lane on the bike path stretching from Santa Monica. **Patrick's Venice Rollerworks,** 7 Westminster Ave. (310-450-0669), off the 1200 block of Ocean Front Walk, rents in-line skates for $5 per day. A bicycle rental shop can be found on the 500 block of Ocean Front Walk ($5 per hr., $15 per day). Or leap into a game of hoops at the popular basketball court at 17th and Ocean Front, featured in the movie *White Men Can't Jump.* The area is full of L.A.P.D. cops—a sign that it is hugely dangerous or totally safe, depending on your perspective. During the day, things are relatively safe, but when the sun begins to fall, it's time to go.

Kinney's dream of another San Marco failed, and so did his vision of gondola-laden canals. High-society types like Mary Pickford took boat rides when the **canals** were first built, but when the water became dirty and oily, most of canals were filled in and forgotten. Skateboarders still use some of the others. One of the few surviving canals is at Strong's Dr., off Washington Street. Ducks are its lively inhabitants.

Venice's anything-goes attitude attracts some of L.A.'s most innovative artists (and not just the guy who makes sand sculptures of Jesus). The Chiat Day offices at 340 Main St. were designed by Frank Gehry to look like a pair of **enormous binoculars—**architecture as a pop-art sculpture at its best. Venice's **street murals** are another free show. Don't miss the graffiti-disfigured, but still brilliant homage to Botticelli's *Birth of Venus* on the beach pavilion at the end of Windward Ave.—a woman of ostensibly divine beauty sporting short shorts, a band-aid top, and roller skates boogies out of her seashell. The post office's mural sums up Venice's cluttered history in an appropriately jumbled way—with oil derricks perched on Kinney's shoulders. For roof-topped art, stop by the **L.A. Louver,** 45 N. Venice Blvd. (310-822-4955), a free gallery showing the work of some L.A. artists (open Tues.-Sat. noon-5pm).

To get to Venice from downtown L.A., take MTA #33 or 333 (or 436 during rush hour). From downtown Santa Monica, take Santa Monica Blue Bus #1 or 2. Avoid hourly meter-feedings by parking in the $5-per-day lot at Pacific and Venice.

MARINA DEL REY

Venice's immediate neighbor to the south, Marina del Rey, is older, more expensive, and considerably more sedate. Built in 1965 as a yacht harbor, Marina del Rey is the **largest man-made marina in the world,** home to 6000 private yachts and 3000 boats in dry storage. If you're not in the market for a new yacht, the only real reason to come here is for **Aunt Kizzy's Back Porch,** 4325 Glencoe Ave. (310-578-1005), serving the **best soul food** in L.A. (according to *L.A. Magazine*). Daily lunch specials ($9) like chicken and dumplings or smothered pork chops crowd the plate with corn-bread, rice, gravy, and veggies. Aunt Kizzy is no soul sister with her SoCal strip mall location, but she kicks back for live blues on Friday and Saturday nights. (open Sun.-Thurs. 11am-10pm, Fri.-Sat. 11am-11pm, Sun. brunch buffet 11am-3pm).

MALIBU

The celebrity-*cum*-surfer colony of Malibu stretches along the low 20000 blocks of PCH. With their multi-million-dollar homes and famous neighbors, Malibu residents can afford to be (and often are) hostile to outsiders. Mel Gibson, Janet Jackson, Diana Ross, Sting, and Cher are just a handful of Malibu's more illustrious residents.

The public beaches here are cleaner and less crowded than any others in L.A. County, and as a whole offer better surfing. Surf's up at **Surfrider Beach,** a section of Malibu Laguna State Beach located north of the pier at 23000 PCH. You can walk onto the beach via the **Zonker Harris** access way (named after the beach-obsessed Doonesbury character), at 22700 PCH. **Malibu Ocean Sports,** 22935 PCH (310-456-6302), across from the pier, rents surfboards ($10 per hr., $25 per day), kayaks (single $15 per hr., $35 per day; double $20 per hr., $50 per day), boogieboards ($12 per day), and wet suits ($10 per day), and offers surfing lessons ($74 for 2hr.) and tours (open daily 8am-7pm). Refuel downstairs at **Malibu Chicken** (310-456-0365), with sandwiches, pasta, ribs, and other standards (bean and cheese burrito $2; Da Grind Special with chicken, veggies, and teriyaki $4.75; open daily 11:30am-9pm).

Corral State Beach, a remote windsurfing, swimming, and scuba-diving haven, lies on the 26000 block of PCH, followed by the clothing-optional **Point Dume State Beach,** which is small and generally uncrowded, except for those looking for a really killer tan. Along the 30000 block of PCH, lies **Zuma,** L.A. County's northernmost, largest, and most user-friendly county-owned sandbox. Restrooms, lifeguards, and food stands guarantee that Zuma regularly draws a diverse crowd. Proximity to parking lot drop-off spots makes sections six to eight a big draw for swarms of local kids, while relative distance from bathrooms make sections nine to eleven less populous. Swimmers should only dive near manned lifeguard stations; because of the killer **riptide,** rescue counts are high. The free street parking is highly coveted, so expect to park in the beach lot ($6, off-peak hr. $2). Though it's disguised as a modest deli, **Malibu Ranch Market,** 29575 PCH, in the Zuma Beach Plaza at the southern end of the beach, rents boogieboards (small $10 per day, large $20 per day), and sells sandwiches, amino acid supplements, and alcohol (open Sun.-Thurs. 7am-11pm, Fri.-Sat. 7am-midnight). There are fewer footprints at **Westward Beach,** just southeast of Zuma, where cliffs shelter the beach from the highway.

DOWNTOWN L.A.

Mayor Richard Riordan and his band of merry civil servants strive valiantly to project downtown as the font of L.A.'s diversity and culture. We hate to break it to you Dick, but money can't buy credibility. The only "diversity" here is the stark contrast between the towering glass business cages and the cardboard hovels in their shadows. An uneasy truce prevails between the bustling financiers and the substantial street population, but visitors should be cautious—the area is especially unsafe after business hours and on weekends. Park in a secure lot, rather than on the streets. Parking is costly; try to arrive before 8am to take advantage of early-bird specials, or park in one of the guarded lots around 9th and Figueroa, which charge $2-3 per day, to avoid a $20 tab come 6pm.

Food

Financial District eateries vie for the coveted businessperson's lunchtime dollar. Their secret weapon is the lunch special, but finding a reasonably priced dinner can be a challenge—you probably shouldn't hang out here that late anyway.

Philippe's, The Original, 1001 N. Alameda St. (213-628-3781), 2 blocks north of Union Station. The best place in L.A. to feel like Raymond Chandler. Philippe's claims to have originated the French-dipped sandwich (don't argue); varieties include beef, ham, turkey, or lamb ($3-4). Top it off with a large slice of pie ($1.90) and a glass of iced tea (40¢) or a cup of coffee (90¢), and you've got a colossal lunch at this L.A. institution. Open daily 6am-10pm.

The Pantry, 877 S. Figueroa St. (213-972-9279). Open since the 20s, it hasn't closed once since—not for the earthquakes, not for the riots (when it served as a National Guard outpost), and not even when a taxicab drove through the front wall. Known for its large portions, free cole slaw, and fresh sourdough bread. Be prepared to wait for the giant breakfast specials ($6), especially on weekends. Coincidentally owned by nobody's favorite mayor. Open 24hr. No credit cards.

It's a Wrap!, 818 W. 7th St. (213-553-9395). Downtown's answer to McDonald's offers "healthy gourmet fast food," including special low-fat dishes. As the name suggests, wrap sandwiches like the BBQ Chicken wrap are the house specialty ($4-6). Open daily 6:30am-5pm. No credit cards.

Mon Kee Restaurant, 679 N. Spring St. (213-628-6717), Chinatown. Somewhat on the expensive side, but widely acclaimed as one of L.A.'s best Chinese restaurants. The menu is vast, and the seafood excellent. Dinner entrees from $8. Open Sun.-Thurs. 11:30am-9:45pm, Fri.-Sat. 11:30am-10:15pm.

Sights

Say "downtown" to almost any Angeleno and they'll wince—either because they don't know what you're referring to, they know but don't go there, or they work there and hate the thought. It is L.A.'s netherland—the place over there. It does, however, have some impressive buildings. The **Los Angeles Conservancy** (213-623-2489), offers Saturday tours of downtown's historic spots for $5 (make reservations one week in advance). Those who prefer to travel solo should take **DASH Shuttles** (fare 25¢; for more info, see **Public Transportation,** p. 71). Sight-seeing on foot is unsafe and impractical, and taking a car means paying for parking.

The **financial district** is a typical urban fusion of glass and steel, where gigantic offices crowd the busy downtown center (an area bounded roughly by 3rd, 6th, Figueroa, and Grand). Unless you want to reshape your portfolio or dabble in mortgage-based derivatives, there is little for a tourist to do but gaze upwards at the architectural behemoths. The **First Interstate World Center,** 633 W. 5th St., is the tallest building in L.A. at 1017 ft., and the **Westin Bonaventure Hotel,** 4045 Figueroa St., has appeared in *Rain Man, In the Line of Fire,* and that perennial classic, *Spinal Tap.* The easily amused can spend hours in the **high-speed elevators.** Don't scoff—the view from the 32nd floor is better than the view from most helicopters. Just a bit southeast of the Bonaventure is the historic **Biltmore,** 506 S. Grand Ave., a $10 million, 1000-room hotel designed by Schultze and Weaver (best known for the Waldorf-

Astoria in New York). It has served as a filming location for *Dave, Independence Day, Ghostbusters,* and *The Sting,* which featured scenes in the hotel's Crystal Ballroom.

To the north of the financial district is L.A.'s **Music Center,** 135 N. Grand Ave., comprised of the **Dorothy Chandler Pavillion** (213-972-7211), site of the Oscars, the **Mark Taper Forum** (213-972-0700), and the **Ahmanson Theatre** (213-972-7200), home to the Los Angeles Philharmonic Orchestra and the Joffrey Ballet.

The **Civic Center,** a solid wall of bureaucratic architecture bounded by the Hollywood Fwy. (U.S. 101), Grand, 1st, and San Pedro, runs east from the Music Center. It ends at **City Hall,** 200 N. Spring St. Another of the best-known buildings in the Southland, the hall "has starred in more movies than most actors." Perhaps the most ironic of its numerous appearances was as the Vatican in *The Thorn Birds.*

Historic L.A.

The historic birthplace of L.A. lies farther north, bounded by Spring, Arcadia, and Macy. In the place where the original city center once stood, **El Pueblo de Los Angeles State Historic Park** (213-6228-1274), preserves a number of historically important buildings from the Spanish and Mexican eras (open daily 9am-9pm; free). The **visitors center,** 622 N. Main St. (213-628-1274), in the Sepulveda House, offers free walking tours (every hr. Tues.-Sat. 10am-1pm). Tours start at the **Old Plaza,** with its century-old Moreton Bay fig trees and huge bandstand, and wind their way past the **Avila Adobe,** 10 E. Olvera St., the "oldest" house in the city (the original adobe was built in 1818, and true to L.A. style, has been replaced with concrete in order to meet earthquake regulations). The tour then moves on to **Pico House,** 500 N. Main St., once L.A.'s most luxurious hotel. Farther down, the **Plaza Church,** at 535 N. Main St., established in 1818, has an incongruously soft, rose adobe facade. The visitors center also screens the film *Pueblo of Promise,* an 18-minute history of Los Angeles, on request. **Olvera Street,** one of L.A.'s original roads, is packed with touristy little stands selling Mexican handicrafts and food. The street is the sight of the *Cinco de Mayo* celebrations of L.A.'s Chicano population (see **Seasonal Events,** p. 117). Across Alameda St. from El Pueblo is the grand old **Union Station,** famous for its appearance in *Blade Runner.*

Chinatown (DASH shuttle B) lies north of this area, roughly bordered by Yale, Spring, Ord, and Bernard St. **Little Tokyo,** centered on 2nd and San Pedro St. on the eastern edge of downtown, is decidedly more upscale. The **Japanese Village Plaza** (213-620-8861), in the 300 block of E. 2nd St., is the center of the district and is a florid fusion of an American shopping mall and Japanese design. The **Japanese-American National Museum** (see p. 66) is housed in a refurbished Buddhist temple designed by Isamu Noguchi, who crafted a monumental sculpture for the courtyard. This community-oriented museum features interactive computers with access to World War II relocation camp records.

Broadway, south of 1st, is a predominantly Mexican-American community. Bargain hounds can haggle to their heart's delight in the **garment district,** which is farther down Broadway bordered by 6th and 9th. The **Cooper Building,** 860 S. Los Angeles St., is a good first stop. The equally well-stocked **Grand Central Public Market** (see **Eating in L.A.,** p. 79) has its own stars in the sidewalk out front, each bearing the name of a Chicano celebrity—a *rambla de fama* to complement Hollywood's. Across the street, the **Bradbury Building,** 304 S. Broadway, stands as a relic of L.A.'s Victorian past. Uninspiring from the street, this 1893 office building is mostly lobby, but what a beautiful lobby it is. Ornate staircases and elevators are bathed in the sunlight pouring through the glass roof. No wonder this served as Harrison Ford's home in *Blade Runner* (open Mon.-Fri. 9am-5pm, Sat. 9am-4pm).

The most striking museum in the area is the **Museum of Contemporary Art (MOCA),** which showcases art from 1940 to the present. The main museum is located at California Plaza, 250 S. Grand Ave. (213-626-6222 or 621-1732; http://www.moca-la.org), and is a sleek and geometric architectural marvel. Its exhibits often focus on L.A. artists, but the collection includes some impressive abstract expressionist works. (Free tours led by local artists at noon, 1, and 2pm; also at 6pm

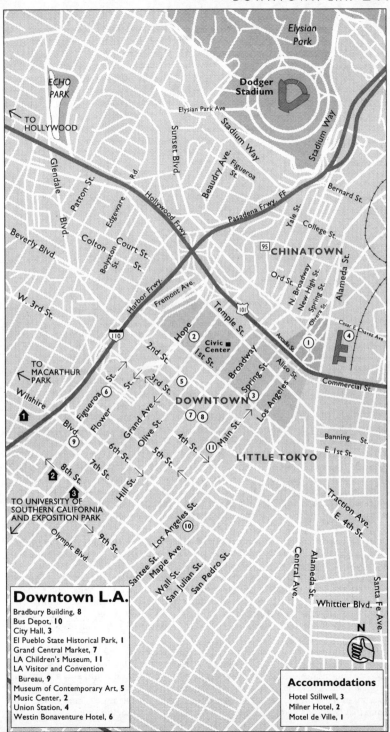

LOS ANGELES

Downtown L.A.

Bradbury Building, 8
Bus Depot, 10
City Hall, 3
El Pueblo State Historical Park, 1
Grand Central Market, 7
LA Children's Museum, 11
LA Visitor and Convention
  Bureau, 9
Museum of Contemporary Art, 5
Music Center, 2
Union Station, 4
Westin Bonaventure Hotel, 6

Accommodations

Hotel Stillwell, 3
Milner Hotel, 2
Motel de Ville, 1

Thurs. only.) The second MOCA facility is the **Geffen Contemporary,** 152 N. Central Ave. (213-621-1727), in Little Tokyo. Parking here ($2.50-3) is cheaper than at the main building, which is accessible by DASH. (Main MOCA open Tues.-Wed. and Fri.-Sun. 11am-5pm, Thurs. 11am-8pm. Admission to both buildings $6, students and seniors $4, under 12 free. Free Thurs. 5-8pm. Wheelchair accessible.)

Across from City Hall, between the Santa Ana Fwy. (I-5) and Temple in the L.A. Mall, is the **L.A. Children's Museum,** 310 N. Main St. (213-687-8800), where everything can be (and has been) touched. (Open year-round Sat.-Sun. 10am-5pm, and June 23-Sept. 5 Mon.-Fri. 11:30am-5pm. Large groups should call 213-687-8825.)

Near Downtown: Exposition Park

At the turn of the century, this area was an upscale suburb of downtown. The area then entered a period of decline, plummeting to its lowest point in the 20s. This deterioration was counteracted with the Olympic Games first came to town in 1932. This neighborhood was revitalized yet again for the 1984 Olympics, which introduced a simple concept in civic planning that seems to bewilder most of L.A., that of *clustered* attractions. Today, the entire area could use another Olympic-class revitalization. The museums of Exposition Park are generally safe and well-visited, but visitors should exercise caution outside the park, especially at night. The park is southwest of downtown, just off the Harbor Fwy. (I-110), and is bounded by Exposition, Figueroa, Vermont, and Santa Barbara. From downtown, take DASH shuttle C, or MTA #40 or 42 (from Broadway between 5th and 6th) to the park's southern edge. From Hollywood, take #204 or 354 down Vermont. From Santa Monica, take #20, 22, 320, or 322 on Wilshire, and transfer to #204 at Vermont. Park at the lot at the intersection of Figueroa and Exposition ($5, with IMAX validation $4).

The park is dominated by several major museums, including the **California Museum of Science and Industry (MSI),** 700 State Dr. (213-744-7400). The interactive exhibits on physics and math in Technology Hall make science come alive. A display on California's faultlines has a jarring rendition of an 8.3 earthquake. Ironically, McDonald's sponsors a display on nutrition. The **Aerospace Building,** as big as a hangar, exhibits $8 million worth of aircrafts, including the Gemini 11 space capsule. (Museum open daily 10am-5pm. Free.) The five-story, 70 ft. wide **IMAX Theater** (213-744-2014), shows 45-minute features on nature, space, and special effects (shows every hr. daily 11am-9pm; admission $6.25, students $4.25, seniors $4.25, ages 4-12 $3.75). Evening shows often sell out; call 213-744-2019 to reserve tickets.

The expansive, formal **rose garden** in front of the MSI is the last remnant of the days when all of Exposition Park was an exposition of horticulture. More than 19,000 specimens of 200 varieties of roses surround walking paths, green lawns, gazebos, fountains, and a lily pond. In the same complex is the **California African-American Museum,** 600 State Dr. (213-744-7432), with a collection of indigenous African art, paintings from the Harlem Renaissance in the 20s, and contemporary mixed-media works (open Tues.-Sun. 10am-5pm; free).

Another of the park's attractions is the **Natural History Museum,** 900 Exposition Blvd. (213-744-3414). The museum has exhibits about pre-Columbian cultures and American history until 1914, and as their main attraction features "habitat halls" with North American and African mammals and dinosaur skeletons. The hands-on **Discovery Center** allows visitors to dig for fossils, meet live fish and reptiles, and explore the insect zoo. Tours run daily at 1pm during summer, on weekends only during winter. (Open July-Aug. daily 10am-5pm; closed Mon. the rest of the year; free the first Tues. of the month, but no tours. Admission $6, students $3.50, students $3.50, ages 5-12 $2, under 5 free.)

Exposition Park also includes the **Los Angeles Memorial Coliseum,** 3939 S. Figueroa St., home of the **USC Trojans** football team, and the **Sports Arena,** 2601 S. Figueroa St., home of the **Los Angeles Clippers** basketball team, and a common venue for rock concerts. The colossal Coliseum, which seats over 100,000, is the only stadium in the world to garner the honor of hosting the Olympic Games twice. The torch that held the Olympic flame still towers atop the Coliseum's roof.

The **University of Southern California (USC)** (213-740-6605), campus sits opposite Exposition Park on Exposition Blvd. It's beautiful and generally safe, but take care after dark. (Walking tours of campus are available on the hr. Mon.-Fri. 10am-3pm.) The **Fisher Gallery** (213-740-4561), has a collection of post-17th-century works by lesser-known Europeans (open Tues.-Fri. noon-5pm, Sat. 11am-3pm; free).

The very rough city of **Inglewood,** southwest of Exposition Park, is home to most of the sporting events in L.A. At the corner of Manchester and Prairie is the **Great Western Forum** (310-673-1300), home of the **Los Angeles Kings** hockey team, as well as the **Los Angeles Lakers** basketball team. Tickets for these games are in high demand (season runs Nov.-June). Kings tickets start at $11, while Lakers tickets start at $21; call the Forum box office (Kings tickets 310-419-3160; Lakers tickets 310-419-3182; open daily 10am-6pm), or Ticketmaster (213-480-3232).

Elysian Park

Elysian Park, located about 3 mi. northeast of downtown, curves around the northern portion of Chavez Ravine, home of **Dodger Stadium** (213-224-1400), and the perennially popular **Los Angeles Dodgers** baseball team. Tickets ($6-12) are a hot commodity during the April to October season when the Dodgers are playing well or when Hideo Nomo is pitching. Call 213-224-1448 to purchase tickets in advance.

GRIFFITH PARK

One of few recreational parks in L.A., Griffith Park is the site of many outdoor diversions ranging from golf and tennis to hiking. The L.A. Zoo, Griffith Observatory and Planetarium, Travel Town, a bird sanctuary, and 52 mi. of hiking trails decorate the dry hills (open daily 5am-10pm). The park stretches for 4107 acres from the hills above North Hollywood to the intersection of the Ventura (Rte. 134) and Golden State Fwy. (I-5), making it five times the size of New York's Central Park. Several of the mountain roads through the park (especially the aptly named **Vista Del Valle Dr.**) offer panoramic views of downtown L.A., Hollywood, and the Westside. Unfortunately, heavy rains have made them unsafe for cars, but foot traffic is allowed on most. The 5 mi. hike to the top of **Mt. Hollywood,** the highest peak in the park, is quite popular. For information, stop by the **Visitors Center and Ranger Headquarters,** 4730 Crystal Spring Dr. (213-665-5188; open daily 5am-10pm).

The white stucco and copper domes of the Art Deco **Observatory and Planetarium** (213-664-1181, recording 664-1191) are visible from around the park. You might remember the planetarium from the climactic denouement of the James Dean film *Rebel Without A Cause.* But even without Dean, the astronomy exhibits are a show of their own. A telescope with a 12-inch lens is open to the public every clear night (open for viewing daily dusk-9:45pm; winter Tues.-Sun. 7-9:45pm; call 213-663-8171 for a sky report). The planetarium presents popular **Laserium** light shows (818-901-9405), a psychotronic romp through the strawberry fields of your consciousness. (Observatory open daily 12:30-10pm; winter Tues.-Fri. 2-10pm, Sat.-Sun. 12:30-10pm. Planetarium shows Mon.-Fri. at 1:30, 3, and 7:30pm, Sat.-Sun. also 4:30pm; in winter Tues.-Fri. 3 and 7:30pm, Sat.-Sun. also 1:30 and 4:30pm. Admission $4, seniors $3, under 12 $1, under 5 not admitted. Children under 12 only admitted to the 1:30pm show. Laser shows blaze daily at 6 and 8:45pm, Tues.-Sat. also 9:45pm. Admission $7-8, children $6-7.) To get to the observatory, take MTA #203 from Hollywood.

A large **bird sanctuary** sits at the bottom of the observatory hill, but if you crave a wider assortment of fauna, try the **L.A. Zoo,** 333 Zoo Dr. (213-666-4090), at the park's northern end. The zoo's 113 acres accommodate 2000 animals, and the facility is consistently ranked among the nation's best (open daily 10am-5pm; admission $8, seniors $5.25, ages 2-12 $3.25). **Travel Town** (213-662-5874), is an outdoor museum showcasing period vehicles, emphasizing trains (open Mon.-Fri. 10am-5pm, Sat.-Sun. 10am-6pm; free). To reach the zoo and Travel Town, take MTA #96 from downtown. There is no bus service between north and south Griffith Park.

Those hankerin' to relive those wild days of yore will enjoy the **Autry Museum of Western Heritage,** 4700 Western Heritage Way (213-667-2000), across from the zoo. This museum covers the fact and fiction of the Old West, with exhibits on pioneer life, outlaws, and the legacy of the Westerns, including relic costumes of Robert Redford and Clint Eastwood, the Lone Ranger mask, and a Gary Cooper toupee (open Tues.-Sun. 10am-5pm; admission $7.50, students $5, seniors $5, children ($3).

On the lighter side, **Forest Lawn Cemetery,** 1712 Glendale Ave. (818-241-4151), in Glendale, includes reproductions of many Michelangelo pieces, as well as the "largest religious painting on earth" (a 195 ft. version of the *Crucifixion*), among their works of "art." The trippy music piped across the gardens makes the typical graveyard experience even creepier. Among the illustrious names on the headstones are Clark Gable, George Burns, Gracie Allen, Sammy Davis Jr., and Errol Flynn. Stop at the entrance for a map of the cemetery's sights and pick up a guide to the paintings and sculpture at the administration building nearby. (Grounds open daily 8am-6pm, mausoleum 9am-4:30pm.) From downtown, take MTA #90 or 91 and get off just after the bus leaves San Fernando Rd. to turn onto Glendale Ave. By car, take Los Feliz Blvd. from the Golden State Fwy. (I-5) or Glendale Fwy. (Rte. 2).

SAN FERNANDO VALLEY

All the San Fernando Valley wants is a little respect. After all, nearly every one of L.A.'s **movie studios** and a third of its residents reside here—more than the entire population of Montana. Yet it can't seem to shake the infamy it gained (largely as a result of a certain Frank Zappa song) as breeding grounds for the **Valley Girl,** who started a worldwide trend in the 80s with her neon mini-skirts, huge hair, and like, totally far-out diction. Today, the Valley gets dissed on *Clueless* and *Beverly Hills, 90210,* and often overlooked in City Hall's affairs. It's no wonder the Valley is threatening to secede from the rest of Los Angeles. Maybe it isn't as glamorous as the city, but the Valley is more than just a satellite of L.A.—with its cookie-cutter houses and strip malls, it is suburban ritual elevated to its highest form. **Ventura Blvd.** marks the Valley's spiritual center—it's, like, where you go shopping.

Food

Ventura Blvd. is lined with eateries. Stars often dine outside the studios in **Studio City,** but because of an unwritten law—you can stare all you want, but don't bother them and *don't ask for autographs.*

Dalt's Grill, 3500 W. Olive Ave. (818-953-7752), at Riverside in Burbank. Classic, yet classy American grill across from Warner Studios. Frequented by the DJs and music guests from the radio station upstairs, KROQ. Large selection of burgers and sandwiches $5-8. Chicken fajita caesar salad $7.69. Small oak-lacquered bar. Open Mon.-Thurs. 11am-11pm, Fri.-Sat. 11am-1am (bar open until 2am), Sun. 9am-11pm.

Miceli's, 3655 W. Cahuenga Blvd. (818-851-3444), across from Universal Studios in Universal City. Would-be actors serenade dinner guests. Don't worry about losing your appetite during the Broadway, cabaret, and opera numbers—waiters are required to have vocal auditions. Pasta, pizza, or lasagna $10. Wine $3.50. Open Sun.-Thurs. 11:30am-11pm, Fri. 11:30am-midnight, Sat. 4pm-midnight.

Poquito Más, 3701 Cahuenga Blvd. (818-760-8226), across from Universal Studios in Universal City. Wildly popular Mexican take-out spot known for its fish tacos ($3.25-5 for two). Skimps on atmosphere, but so what? A fabulous *carnita* is only $1.85. Open Sun.-Thurs. 10am-midnight, Fri.-Sat. 10am-1am. No credit cards.

The Nerve Lounge, 13718 Ventura Blvd. (818-990-0051), Sherman Oaks. Where chess-masters meet teenagers who haven't yet decided what they're rebelling against. House special is Blended Nightmare ($3.50), with 4 shots of espresso. Sandwiches ($4), with chips or potato salad. Live music nightly, ranging from jazz to Israeli folk. Open Mon.-Fri. 7am-1am, Sat.-Sun. 8am-2am. No credit cards.

Law Dogs 14114 Sherman Way (818-989-2220), at Hazeltine in Van Nuys. Just your average hot dog stand with **free legal advice.** The attorney is available Wed. 7-9pm. "Judge dog" with mustard, onions, and chili ($1.55) Open Mon.-Tues. and Thurs. 10am-5pm, Wed. and Fri. 10am-9pm, Sat 10am-8pm. No credit cards.

Sights

Movie studios have replaced the Valley Girl as the Valley's defining feature. As the Ventura Fwy. (Rte. 134) passes Burbank, you can see what are today the Valley's trademarks: the **NBC peacock,** the **Warner Bros. water tower,** and the carefully-designed **Disney dwarves.** Urban legend has it that the runoff water pipes are orchestrated such that the seven dwarves appear to be pissing on daddy Disney when it rains. Most of the studios have **free TV show tapings** (see **Entertainment,** p.106).

The most popular spot in today's Tinseltown is the movie-themed amusement park, **Universal Studios** (818-622-3801). Visit the Bates Hotel from *Psycho,* escape the raptors of *Jurassic Park* and a shark attack by *Jaws,* ride the de Lorean from *Back to the Future,* survive an 8.3 earthquake, and don't miss the *Waterworld* stage show. Expect long waits—after all, it is the largest film and television studio in the world. (Open daily 9am-6:30pm; July-Aug. 8am-10pm. Last tram leaves at 5:15pm. Tours in Spanish daily. Admission $36, seniors $29, ages 3-11 $26. Parking $6.) Take MTA #420 west from downtown or east from the valley.

If you still haven't gotten your Hollywood fix after Universal Studios, head to the adjacent **Universal City Walk.** The mammoth green guitar outside the Hard Rock Cafe and colossal 18-screen Cineplex Odeon movie theater set the precedent for this larger-than-life window-shopping extravaganza, where each store is bigger and brighter than the one before. Most of the knick-knack and movie memorabilia shops (see **Shopping,** p. 110) are open until 10pm on weekdays, 11pm on Friday and Saturday. The jewel in City Walk's technicolor crown is **B.B. King's Blues Club** (818-622-5464), where the thrill is long from gone—just check out the big name blues, deep-fried southern food (howlin' hot wings $7), and cigar bar. (Open Mon.-Thurs. 7pm-1am, Fri.-Sun. 5pm-2am; dinner 7-9pm. Cover $5-12, $3 for dinner guests. Must be 21 after 10pm.) City Walk parking costs $6, but you get a full refund if you buy two movie tickets before 6pm, $2 refund after 6pm.

Down in the residential area of Studio City lurks the epicenter of American 70s culture: the **Brady Bunch house.** Clearly, they did not live in the one-story house at 11222 Dilling St. (just north of Ventura Blvd. off Tujunga Ave.); everyone knows the Brady's had that huge staircase up to the *second floor* from which Bobby threw down his ball and broke the vase. Continuing back up Ventura farther into the valley, make a left onto Hayvenhurst in Encino to see the house where **Michael Jackson** resided for much of his life. His parents still live at 4641, so don't disturb.

One of the few L.A. sights with any history is the **Mission San Fernando Ray De España,** 15101 San Fernando Mission Blvd. (818-361-0186), in Mission Hills. The mission was founded in 1797 by Padre Fermin Lasuen but, unfortunately, no structures remain from this period. An amazing recreation, teeming with Pope-abilia stands today (open daily 9am-4:30pm; admission $4, seniors $3, children $3; mass Sun.-Tues. and Thurs.-Sat. 7:25am).

North of the Valley: Magic Mountain

At the opposite end of the Valley, 40 minutes north of L.A. on the I-5 Exit at Magic Mountain Pkwy. in Valencia is **Six Flags Magic Mountain** (818-367-5965), also known as *National Lampoon's* Wally World. Not for novices, Magic Mountain has the hairiest roller coasters in Southern California. Highlights of the park include the Revolution, a smooth metal coaster with mind-blowing loops; the Colossus, the world's largest wooden roller coaster; the Viper (as seen in *True Romance*), whose speed (110mph) is said to approach the limits of coaster technology; the Tidal Wave (stand on the bridge for an impromptu shower); and the park's newest attractions, the Suspended Batman and the 100 mph Superman (meaning 6½ seconds of weightlessness). Despite a Looney Tunes playland for the kiddies, under 48-inchers are often turned away. Temperatures here frequently soar above 100°F in the summer, so bring plenty of bottled water. (Open Sun.-Thurs. 10am-10pm, Fri.-Sat. 10am-midnight; mid-Sept. to Memorial Day Sat.-Sun. 10am-6pm only. Admission $35, seniors $20, kids under 48" $17, under 3 free. Parking $6.) Next door, Six Flags' waterpark, **Hurricane Harbor,** features the world's tallest enclosed speed slide and an intriguing "adult activity pool" (open Mon.-Thurs. 10am-7pm, Fri.-Sun. 10am-8pm; admission $18, seniors $11, kids under 48" $11, under 3 free).

PASADENA

Every New Year's Day, millions of hungover viewers with wayward snowplows blocking their driveways park in front of the TV and jealously dream as the blessed in Pasadena march down the sunny street with roses in tow to a football game on real grass. With its world-class museums, graceful architecture, lively shopping district, and idyllic weather, Pasadena is a welcome change from its noisy downtown neighbor. Old Town Pasadena sequesters intriguing historic sights and an up-and-coming entertainment scene. The **Pasadena Fwy.** (Rte. 110), built as a WPA project between 1934 and 1941, is one of the nation's oldest. The WPA engineers did not anticipate the needs of the modern motorist—50 years later, drivers at a dead stop are required to merge almost instantaneously with 55+ mph traffic, so be more careful than usual. A good first stop in Pasadena is the **Convention and Visitors Bureau,** 171 S. Los Robles Ave. (626-795-9311; fax 795-7656), which has numerous promotional materials and guides to regional art events (open Mon.-Fri. 8am-5pm, Sat. 10am-4pm).

Food

Eateries of all ilk cluster around **Colorado Blvd.** from Los Robles to Orange Grove in Old Town, it is Pasadena's answer to Santa Monica's Third St. Promenade.

Goldstein's Bagel Bakery, 86 W. Colorado Blvd. (626-792-2435). Manhattan fare with a California twist, the New Yorker bagel sandwich (with smoked salmon, cream cheese, tomato, onions $4.40) rivals the L.A. Nosh (with tuna, avocado, swiss cheese, tomato, sprouts $4.15). Variety of 18 bagels include your old faves (50¢ each) and your soon-to-be new ones (peanut butter chocolate chip bagel 75¢). Open Sun.-Thurs. 6am-9pm, Fri.-Sat. 6am-11:30pm.

Pita! Pita!, 37 S. Fair Oaks (626-356-0106). Tasty and innovative Middle Eastern cuisine—just wait 'til you see what they can do with an eggplant. Big, bright, plant-filled interior makes it pleasant to lounge. Chicken kabob $6; fresh pita with hummus or tabouli $3. Open Sun.-Thurs. 11am-10pm, Fri.-Sat. 11am-11pm.

Yoshiz, 34 E. Holly St. (626-577-7925), between Raymond and Fair Oaks, 2 blocks north of Colorado. This Japanese hole-in-the-wall is a local addiction. California rolls $3, other yummies under $5. Open Mon.-Fri. 10am-5pm, Sat. 11am-3pm.

Santorini Deli, 62 W. Union St. (626-564-4204), in the One Colorado Plaza between Delancey and Fair Oaks. This cozy cafe specializes in creative sandwiches with fresh Mediterranean ingredients. Murano grilled veggies on rosemary bread $5.50; Moroccan spiced lamb $6.50. Open Sun.-Thurs. 7am-8pm, Fri.-Sat. 7am-10pm.

Mi Piace, 25 E. Colorado Blvd. (626-795-3131). The name is Italian for "I like it," and apparently the critics do, as many have named it the best of Old Town's plethora of upscale cafes. Interior decorator has mastered the art of minimalist chic, but chefs don't skimp on the large portions of California-style pizza and pasta ($7-10). Power people-watching lunch spot with multi-course specials (Mon.-Fri. until 3pm). Full bar. Open Sun.-Thurs. 11:30am-11:30pm, Fri.-Sat. 11:30am-1am.

Ernie Jr.'s Taco House, 126 W. Colorado (626-792-9951). While the facade may not look like much compared to most of Old Town's sleek exteriors, locals drool over Ernie's tacos ($2-2.50) and burritos ($4.50). Specials come with rice and beans ($5-7.50). Corona (22oz.) $3.75. Open Mon.-Fri. 11am-10pm, Sat.-Sun. 11:30am-11pm.

Crown City Brewery, 300 S. Raymond Ave. (626-577-5548), at Del Mar, 3 blocks south of Colorado. Brick and brass microbrewery for the international traveler who considers beer food. Homebrew $3 per pint. Tasty pizza $7.75. Kids' menu $4. Open Sun.-Thurs. 11am-10pm, Fri.-Sat. 11am-12:30am; bar open 2hr. later.

Sights

The city provides **free shuttles** which loop between Old Town and the downtown area around Lake Ave. Each of the seven buses has a theme (i.e., performing arts, Arroyo Seco desert, multiculturalism) reflected in the decor. Buses run Mon.-Thurs.

11am-7pm, Fri. 11am-10pm, Sat. noon-8pm. The buses uptown run Mon.-Fri. 7am-6pm, Sat.-Sun. noon-5pm. Call 626-405-4055 for more info.

At the western end of Old Town lies the sleek and modern **Norton Simon Museum of Art,** 411 W. Colorado Blvd. (626-449-6840), at Orange Grove Blvd., featuring a world-class collection, chronicling Western art from Italian gothic to 20th-century abstract. The Impressionist and Post-Impressionist hall is particularly impressive, and the collection of Southeast Asian art is one of the world's best. Well-written informational plaques inform the least knowledgable admirer. The museum is small enough not to be daunting, and Simon's eclectic, slightly idiosyncratic taste gives it flair. Don't miss the sculpture garden and newly-constructed tea house. Some parts of the museum may be closed for renovations, so call ahead (open Thurs.-Sun. noon-6pm; admission $4, students $2, seniors $2, under 12 free; wheelchair accessible). Take MTA #180 west on Colorado between Lake and N. Orange or south on Lake between Washington and Colorado. Alternatively, take #181 west on Colorado between Lake and N. Orange.

The 1905 **Fenyes Estate,** 470 W. Walnut St. (626-577-1660), a couple of blocks east off Orange Grove, is the residence of the **Pasadena Historical Society and Museum,** the Pasadena city archives, and an eclectic collection of Renaissance furniture, Egyptian sculpture, and local art amassed by Eva Scott Fenyes. (Admission $4, students $3, seniors $3. Tours of museum Thurs.-Sun. 1-4pm. Closed Aug.).

The **Gamble House,** 4 Westmoreland Pl. (626-793-3334), just north of Orange Grove at Walnut, was designed in 1908 by the Greene brothers as a retirement residence for the heirs to the Proctor and Gamble fortune. Everything in this bungalow-style masterpiece—trim, paneling, carpets, and all—was custom-designed by the Greenes to complement the Gambles' family art pieces, many of which were actually crafted in their Pasadena workshop (1hr. tours Thurs.-Sun. noon-3pm; admission $5, seniors $4, students $3, children free). A map detailing other renowned neighborhood buildings are available in the Gamble House Bookstore for $1.

In the gorge that forms the city's western boundary stands Pasadena's most famous landmark, the **Rose Bowl,** 991 Rosemont Blvd. (626-577-3106). Home to the "grand-daddy" of the college-football bowl games, the annual confrontation between the champions of the Big Ten and Pac 10 conferences, the Rose Bowl is the regular-season venue for **UCLA Bruins** football, the championship soccer team **The Galaxy,** and the **world's largest swap meet** (213-560-7469; held the 2nd Sun. of each month 9am-4:30pm; spectators $5, bargain hunters admitted at 7:30am for $12, 6am for $15).

Besides spectator sports, Pasadena's main draw is **Old Town,** the vibrant shopping and dining mecca for the been-there-done-that-what's-next? crowd. The **Pasadena Civic Auditorium,** 300 E. Green St. (626-449-7360), north of Colorado, is the centerpiece of the city's Spanish-influenced architecture. City Hall is a beautiful example of this style, complete with open courtyard, lush gardens, and a fountain. This is where the red carpet is rolled out each year for television's **Emmy Awards.** Just east of the Civic Center is the **Pacific Asia Museum,** 46 N. Los Robles Ave. (626-449-2742), between Colorado and Union, which features a small collection of Tibetan buddha, Southeast Asian ceramics, and a *koi* pond (open Wed.-Sun. 10am-5pm; admission $4, students $2, seniors $2; call ahead to book a free tour). The **Pasadena Playhouse,** 39 S. El Molino Ave. (626-356-7529), between Colorado and Green, was founded in 1917 and nurtured the careers of William Holden and Gene Hackman, among others. Restored in 1986, it now offers some of the city's finest theater (see **Theater,** p.109).

Some of the world's greatest scientific minds do their work at the **California Institute of Technology (Cal Tech),** 1201 E. California Blvd. (626-356-6811), about 2½ mi. southeast of Old Town. Founded in 1891, Cal Tech has amassed a faculty that includes several Nobel laureates (Albert Einstein once taught here) and a student body that prides itself both on its staggering collective intellect and its often ingenious practical jokes. These range from the simple (unscrewing all the chairs in a lecture hall and bolting them in backwards) to the more elaborate (altering the Rose Bowl scoreboard during the game with the aid of computers). **NASA's Jet Propul-**

LOS ANGELES

sion Laboratory, 4800 Oak Grove Dr. (626-354-4321), about 5 mi. north of Old Town, executed the journey of the Mars Pathfinder. Call ahead to schedule a free weekday tour of the facilities, and ask to see pictures of the face on Mars.

Near Pasadena: Museums

A half-mile south of Cal Tech lies the complex of **Huntington Library, Art Gallery,** and **Botanical Gardens,** 1151 Oxford Rd. (626-405-2100, ticket info 626-405-2275), in San Marino. The conglomeration was built in 1910 as the home of businessman Henry Huntington, "the Carnegie of the West," who made his money in railroads and Southern California real estate. The stunning botanical gardens are home to 207 acres of plants, many of them rare. (No picnicking or sunbathing allowed.) The library houses one of the world's most important collections of rare books and English and American manuscripts, including a Gütenberg Bible, Benjamin Franklin's handwritten autobiography, a 1410 manuscript of Chaucer's *Canterbury Tales,* and a number of Shakespeare's first folios. The art gallery is known for its 18th- and 19th-century British paintings. Sentimental favorites on exhibit include Thomas Gainsborough's *Blue Boy* and Sir Thomas Lawrence's *Pinkie.* American art is on view in the **Virginia Steele Scott Gallery.** The Annabella Huntington Memorial Collection features Renaissance paintings and 18th-century French decorative arts (open in summer Tues.-Sun. 10am-4:30pm; in winter Tues.-Fri. noon-4:30pm, Sat.-Sun. 10:30am-4:30pm; admission $7.50, students $4, seniors $6,under 12 free; first Thurs. of the month free). Tea is served in the Rose Garden daily (call 626-683-8161 for reservations). The Huntington Museum sits between Huntington Dr. and California Blvd. in San Marino, south of Pasadena, about 2 mi. south of the Allen Ave. Exit of I-210. From downtown L.A., bus #79 leaves from Union Station goes straight to the library (45min.).

Recent remodeling and a spate of innovative exhibits may earn the **Southwest Museum,** 234 Museum Dr. (213-221-2164), in Highland Park, the attention it deserves. The slightly misnamed palatial Hispano-Moorish building houses artifacts including a Sioux teepee and a Tlinglit totem pole. Take bus #83 along Broadway to Museum Dr. and trek uphill. Take the Pasadena Fwy. (I-110) to Ave. 43 and follow the signs. (Open Tues.-Sun. 11am-5pm. Admission $5, students $3, seniors $3, ages 7-18 $2. Library open Wed.-Sat. 11am-5pm.) **Griffith Park** (see p. 101) is also nearby.

Not near Pasadena: San Dimas

Missing Bill and Ted's home town of San Dimas and **Raging Waters** water park, 111 Raging Waters Dr. (909-592-6453 for recorded message and directions), would be an egregious miscalculation, especially in summer. Beat the heat with 44 acres of slides, pools, whitewater rafts, inner tubes, fake waves, and a fake island. Hurl yourself over the seven-story waterslide "Drop Out" (if you dare) or slide through a tropical rain forest. (Open Mon.-Fri. 10am-9pm, Sat. 9:30am-10pm, Sun. 9:30am-9pm until early Sept. During winter open daily 9am-9pm. Admission $22, under 48in. $13, under 3 free. Senior and evening discounts. Parking $5.) And San Dimas really does have a **Circle K,** 301 E. Walnut (909-592-5085), at Bonita. "San Dimas High School Football Rules!"

■ Entertainment

Without entertainment, there would be no L.A. There are numerous ways to indulge in the glitz, the glamor, the glory that the entertainment capital of the world hold so dear. **Shopping,** for example, is a major form of entertainment in L.A., one that has been crafted into what some might call an art (see p. 110). For off-hours fun, see **Nightlife,** p. 112. For the ultimate in contrived, pre-packaged entertainment, see the listings for the theme parks Disneyland (p. 130), Knott's Berry Farm (p. 131), Magic Mountain (p. 103), and Universal Studios (p. 102). For the classic L.A. form of entertainment, that of the film and recording industries, read on.

FILM AND TELEVISION STUDIOS

Many tourists feel a visit to the world's entertainment capital is not complete without some exposure to the actual business of making a movie or TV show. Fortunately, most production companies oblige. **Paramount** (213-956-5000), **NBC** (818-840-3537), and **Warner Bros.** (818-954-1744) offer two-hour guided walking tours, but as they are *made* for tourists, they tend to be crowded and overpriced. The best way to get a feel for the industry is to land yourself some tickets to a TV taping. All tickets are free, but most studios tend to overbook, so holding a ticket does not always guarantee that you'll get into the taping. Show up early and you'll have a chance of seeing your fave stars up close in an operating studio backlot.

NBC, 3000 W. Alameda Ave. (recording 818-840-3537), at W. Olive Ave. in Burbank, is your best spur-of-the-moment bet. Show up at the ticket office on a weekday at 8am for passes to Jay Leno's **Tonight Show,** filmed at 5pm the same evening. Studio tours run on the hour (Mon.-Fri. 9am-3pm, Sat. 10am-2pm; admission $7, children $3.75). Many of NBC's "Must See TV" shows are taped at **Paramount Pictures,** 5555 Melrose Ave. (213-956-1777), in Hollywood. Sitcoms like *Ellen* and *Frasier* are taped September through May; call the studio five working days in advance to secure tickets. NBC's most popular shows, *Seinfeld* and *Friends,* are filmed before a private audience, so unless you know Jerry himself or you are a friend of a Friend, you're out of luck—begging won't help. As it is one of just a few major studios still in Hollywood, Paramount's tours are very popular (on the hr. Mon.-Fri. 9am-2pm; admission $15).

A **CBS box office,** 7800 Beverly Blvd. (213-852-2458), next to the Farmer's Market in West Hollywood, hands out free tickets to *The Price is Right* up to one week in advance (open Mon.-Fri. 9am-6pm). Audience members must be over 18. You can request up to 10 tickets on a specific date by sending a self-addressed stamped envelope to The Price is Right Tickets, 7800 Beverly Blvd., Los Angeles, CA 90036, about four weeks in advance.

If all else fails, **Hollywood Group Services,** 1918 Magnolia Blvd., #203, Burbank, CA 91506 (818-556-1516), and **Audiences Unlimited, Inc.,** 100 Universal City Plaza, Universal City, CA 91608 (818-506-0067), offer guaranteed seating, but charge $10 to no-shows. To find out what shows are available during your visit, send a SASE to either address. Hollywood Group Services will fax a list of all available shows within 24 hours of a call-in request. At **Universal Studios,** the filming is done on the backlot, and you won't see a thing from the tour. To them, it's a studio, but to us non-industry folk, it's an amusement park. To see an **on-location movie shoot,** stop by in person to the City/County Film Office, 7083 Hollywood Blvd., 5th floor (213-957-1000), for a "shoot sheet," which lists current filming locations, but be aware that film crews may not share your enthusiasm about audience participation.

CINEMA

Countless theaters show films the way they were meant to be seen: in a big space, on a big screen, with top-quality sound. Angelenos are often amazed at the "primitive" sound at theaters they go to in the rest of the country. It would be a cinematic crime not to take advantage of the incredible experience that is movie-going in L.A.

The gargantuan theaters at **Universal City** or **Century City,** as well as those in **Westwood Village** near UCLA are incredibly popular, especially on weekends. You *will* wait in line at all the best theaters, especially for new releases, but lively crowds, state-of-the-art sound, and large screens more than justify the wait. In **Santa Monica,** a remarkable 22 theaters rest between Santa Monica Pl. and the Third St. Promenade alone.

Devotees of second-run, foreign-language, and experimental films are rewarded by the Santa Monica theaters away from the Promenade. Foreign films play consistently at the eight **Laemmle Theaters** in Beverly Hills (213-274-6869 and 213-848-3500), West L.A. (310-477-5581), Santa Monica (310-394-9741), Pasadena (626-796-9704 and 818-793-6149), Encino (818-981-9811), and downtown (213-617-0268).

So You Wanna Be an Extra

Honey! Baby! Sweetheart! You don't have to be beautiful and proportionally perfect to grace celluloid these days—just look at Tom Arnold or Juliette Lewis. The quickest way to get noticed is to land yourself a job as an extra—no experience necessary. One day's work will land $40-130 in your pocket and two meals in your tummy. Step One is to stop calling yourself an extra—you're an "atmosphere actor" now (it's better for your ego and your resume). Step Two is to contact a *reputable* casting service. **Cenex** (1700 W. Burbank Blvd. 2nd fl., Burbank, CA 91506; 818-562-2888, ext. 3219), is the biggest, and a good place to start. You must be at least 18 and a U.S. citizen or Green Card holder. Step Three is to show up on time; you'll need the clout of DeNiro before you can waltz in after call. Don't forget to bring $20 in cash to cover the "photo fee." Step Four is to dress the part: don't wear red or white, which bleed on film and render you unusable. Finally, after you collect three SAG (Screen Actors Guild; 5757 Wilshire Blvd., Los Angeles, CA 90036; 213-937-3441) vouchers, you'll be eligible to pay the $1050 to join showbiz society. See you in the movies!

L.A.'s giant movie industry does not, surprisingly, include world-class film festivals like Cannes or Sundance. On the other hand, the city hosts a number of smaller, less expensive, and more accessible film showcases, including the **Annual L.A. International Gay and Lesbian Film Festival** (213-951-1247; each film $8-10), in July, and the **Asian Pacific Film and Video Festival** (310-206-8013; each film $6, seniors $4, students $4), in August. The largest in the area is the October **Annual AFI L.A. International Film Festival,** which shows 150 shorts, documentaries, and features from around the world (213-856-7707 or 856-7709 from outside the U.S.; each film $7).

If you'd like to stand outside and ogle the stars as they walk the red carpet into the theater for a **premiere,** call the four premiere-hounds: Mann's Chinese (about 2 per month), El Capitan (Disney films only), the Village, and Fox in Westwood. For info on what's playing in L.A., call 213-777-FILM/3456, or pick up the daily Calendar section of the *Los Angeles Times.* Tickets at all theaters listed below are $8, seniors $5, children $5; discounts where noted.

Cineplex Odeon Universal City Cinemas (818-508-0588), atop the hill at Universal City Walk. Opened in 1987 as the world's largest cinema complex, its 18 widescreen theaters and 2 *Parisienne*-style cafes put all others to shame. Tickets $4.75 before 6pm. Parking free with validation, $4 after 6pm.

Pacific Cinerama Dome, 6360 Sunset Blvd. (213-466-3401), near Vine. The ultimate movie screen wraps itself 180° around the theater, like the surround-sound.

Mann's Chinese Theater, 6925 Hollywood Blvd. (213-464-8111). Hype to the hilt. For details, see **Hollywood Sights,** p. 80. Student tickets $5.25; tickets for first 2 shows before 6pm $4.75, weekends and holidays $5. Parking ($6.50) is more than the movie.

El Capitan, 6838 Hollywood Blvd. (213-467-7674 or 808-559-6247), across from Mann's Chinese in Hollywood. Disney glitz straight out of *Fantasia,* with live stage shows and exhibitions in the gallery downstairs. The theater's standard prices can soar to $20 (seniors and children $15) for new releases. Parking $6.50.

Village Theatre, 961 Broxton Ave. (310-208-5576), Westwood. No multiplex nonsense here. One auditorium, one big screen, one great THX sound system, a balcony, and Art Deco design. Watch the back rows and balcony for late-arriving celebrities. Student tickets $5.50, matinee tickets $4.75, Sat.-Sun. $5.

Revival Theaters

Nuart Theatre, 11272 Santa Monica Blvd. (310-478-6379), just west of the San Diego Fwy. (I-405) in West L.A. Perhaps the best-known revival house. The playbill changes nightly. Classics, documentaries, and modern films. The *Rocky Horror Picture Show* screens Sat. at midnight. Discount card (5 movie tickets, $25).

New Beverly Cinema, 7165 Beverly Blvd. (213-938-4038), in the Wilshire District. Shows foreign films and old faves from as recently as last year. Schedule changes every 2-3 days. Tickets $5, students $4, children $4.

UCLA's James Bridges Theater (310-825-2345), near Sunset and Hilgard on the northeastern corner of campus. Eclectic film festivals. Student films (free) at the end of each semester, archived foreign films, and previews of Universal films. All shows 7:30pm. Tickets $5, UCLA students free.

LACMA's Bing Theater, 5905 Wilshire Blvd. (213-857-6010), at the L.A. County Museum of Art in the Wilshire District. Classic films on the big screen for less than a video rental. Shows Tues. at 1pm only. Tickets $2, seniors $1.

THEATER

In spite of the growing number of shows about L.A., very few Broadway/West End-style productions come out of this city. On the other hand, 115 "equity waiver theaters" (under 100 seats) offer a dizzying choice for theater-goers, who can also take in small productions in museums, art galleries, universities, parks, and even garages. For the digs on what's hot, browse the listings in the *L.A. Weekly*. Theater L.A. (213-614-0556), sells same-day tickets for half-price at their "Theater Times" booth in the Beverly Center, 8500 Beverly Blvd. at La Cienega, in West L.A.

James A. Doolittle Theater, 1615 N. Vine St. (213-462-6666 or 800-233-3123), Hollywood. Big names and Tony Award winners in this medium-sized venue with around 1000 seats. Tickets around $45, weekend shows $50; rush tickets (around $20) available 30min. before showtime, except last.

Geffen Playhouse (formerly the Westwood Playhouse), 10886 LeConte Ave. (310-208-5454), Westwood. Off-Broadway and Tony award-winning shows in a cozy setting. Tickets around $27-37; student rush tickets ($10) 15min. before show.

Pasadena Playhouse, 39 S. El Molino Ave. (626-356-PLAY/7529 or 800-233-3123), Pasadena. California's premier theater and historical landmark has spawned Broadway careers and productions. Tickets around $13-38, weekend shows $13-42. Call for rush tickets. Matinees Sat.-Sun.

Shubert Theatre, 2020 Ave. of the Stars (800-233-3123), Century City. Big Broadway shows and musicals in a high-glam setting. Tickets $35-65, weekend shows $45-75; rush tickets ($25) available 2hr. before showtime.

Pantages, 6233 Hollywood Blvd. (213-468-1770), Hollywood. L.A.'s other place for big Broadway spectacles and cabaret acts. Call Ticketmaster (213-480-3232) for tickets and events information. No rush tickets.

CONCERTS

L.A.'s music venues range from small clubs to massive venues. The **Wiltern Theater** (213-380-5005), shows alterna-rock/folk acts. The **Hollywood Palladium** (213-962-7600), is of comparable size with 3500 seats. Mid-size acts head for the **Universal Amphitheater** (818-777-3931), and the **Greek Theater** (213-665-1927). Huge indoor sports arenas, such as the **Forum** (310-673-1300), double as concert halls for big acts. Few dare to play at the 100,000-seat **Los Angeles Memorial Coliseum and Sports Arena**—only U2, Depeche Mode, and Guns 'n' Roses have filled the stands in recent years. Call Ticketmaster (213-480-3232) to purchase tickets for any of these venues.

Hollywood Bowl, 2301 N. Highland Ave. (213-850-2000), Hollywood. The bowl hosts a summer music festival from early July to mid-Sept. Although sitting in the back of this outdoor, 18,000-seat amphitheater makes even the L.A. Philharmonic sound like transistor radio, bargain tickets and a sweeping view of L.A. from the bowl's south rim make it worthwhile. Free open-house rehearsals by the Philharmonic and visiting performers Tues. and Thurs. Parking at the bowl is a major hassle, not to mention a major expense ($10). Better options are parking away from the bowl and walking up Highland, using MTA's Park 'n' Ride service (213-850-2000), or taking bus #420 west from downtown or east from the valley. Call Ticketmaster (213-480-3232) to purchase tickets.

Music Center, 135 N. Grand Ave. (213-972-7211), downtown at the corner of 1st in the heart of the city (see **Downtown,** p. 97). Includes the **Mark Taper Forum,** the **Dorothy Chandler Pavilion,** and the **Ahmanson Theatre.** Performance spaces host the L.A. Opera, Broadway and experimental theater, and dance. Some performances, like the American Ballet Theater, offer student rush tickets ($10; call in advance and arrive 1hr. early). Parking $7 after 6pm.

■ Shopping

In Los Angeles, shopping isn't just a practical necessity; it's a way of life. Popular shopping areas like **Santa Monica's Third Street Promenade** and **Pasadena's Old Town** are lined with identical chain boutiques with the latest fashions. Tucked away from the shuffle, though, are a number of cool speciality shops with more one-of-a-kind items. Remember, dahling, when the going gets tough, the tough go shopping.

BOOKSTORES

L.A. might not seem like the most literary of cities. After all, while subway commuters in other cities immerse themselves in the newspaper, Angelenos listen to news radio while caught in an early-morning traffic jam. Hollywood bios and tell-alls line the front shelves of most L.A. bookstores. But fear not, voracious reader, you don't have to resort to the ubiquitous Barnes and Noble megastores just yet.

Book Soup, 8818 and 8820 Santa Monica Blvd. (310-854-0770), **West Hollywood.** A maze of new books in every category imaginable, with especially strong film, architecture, poetry, and mystery sections. The comprehensive newsstand wrapping around the building includes industry mags and international newspapers. A new annex next door carries sale items, including an "under $3" table and lots of hardcover art, photo, and design books at reduced prices. Open daily noon-8pm.

Samuel French Bookshop, 7623 Sunset Blvd. (213-876-0570), **Hollywood;** and 11963 Ventura Blvd. (818-762-0535), **Studio City.** Pure L.A. Get prepped for your audition at this haven for all things thespian: acting directories, TV and film reference books, trade papers, and a vast selection of plays and screenplays. Lists local theaters that are currently casting. Occasional script signings by local playwrights. Hollywood location open Mon.-Fri. 10am-6pm, Sat. 10am-5pm; Studio City location open Mon.-Fri. 10am-9pm, Sat. 10am-6pm, Sun. noon-5pm.

Vagabond's, 11706 San Vicente Blvd. (310-475-2700), **Brentwood.** *Harper's Magazine* called it L.A.'s best used bookstore, though they prefer to call themselves an "out-of-print" specialist. If someone's read it, it's here. Open Mon.-Sat. 11am-6pm.

A Different Light, 8853 Santa Monica Blvd. (310-343-4002; http://www.adl-books.com/~adl), **West Hollywood.** The nation's largest gay and lesbian bookseller has a diverse selection: gay fiction and classics, self-help, law, queer theory. Videos, music, gift items, readings, and book signings. Open daily 10am-midnight.

Beyond Baroque, 681 Venice Ave. (310-822-3006), **Venice.** For the artsier set, this bookstore is a second home. Sells small press books, self-published titles, and 'zines. Free poetry and fiction workshops. Readings Fri. and Sat. at 8:30pm ($7-8). Open Sun.-Tues. and Thurs. 2-6pm, Wed. 2-10pm, Fri.-Sat. 2-6pm and 8:30-10pm.

MUSIC STORES

Used music stores are a dime a dozen, especially in **Westwood** and along **Melrose Ave.** Many buy old CDs and tapes or trade them for store credit, which unfortunately makes for selections of "rejections." Here are some gems in the mix, those that offer the best selections or cater to less mainstream tastes.

Moby Disc, in **Santa Monica,** 2114 Wilshire Blvd. (310-828-2887); **Encino,** 14622 Ventura Blvd. (818-990-2970); and **Pasadena,** 28 E. Colorado Blvd. (626-449-9975). The blue whale of used CD stores in Los Angeles, the odds for good finds are in your favor. Fairly non-discriminating in buying used CDs (for cash or store credit). Smaller new CD and used cassette sections. Open daily 10am-11pm.

Vinyl Fetish, 7305 Melrose Ave. (213-935-1300), **West Hollywood.** The LP collection you can only *wish* you owned, suckah. Top-rate rock, funk, industrial, ska, punk, new wave, and disco. Records $5-20, depending on condition and rarity. CDs, tapes, books, t-shirts, and accessories to die for. Open daily 11am-10pm.

Aron's, 1150 N. Highland Ave. (213-469-4700), between Sunset and Santa Monica Blvd. in **Hollywood.** Well-loved for its massive new and used CD collection, which ranges from soul to ska to showtunes. If you can't find it here, the only place left is the nearby **Virgin Megastore,** at 8000 Sunset Blvd. (213-650-8666). Virgin's got everything, but Aron's won't suck your wallet dry. Aron's open Sun.-Thurs. 10am-10pm, Fri.-Sat. 10am-midnight. Virgin Megastore open Mon. 9am-12:30am, Tues., Thurs., and Sun. 9am-midnight, Wed. 10am-midnight, Fri.-Sat. 9am-1am.

Rhino Records, 1720 Westwood Blvd. (310-474-2525), **West L.A.** Specializes in the obscure, the alternative, and those never-played promotional albums that couldn't find a home. Strong blues, jazz, exotica, and dance sections. Definitive collection of titles on the Rhino label. Open Sun.-Thurs. 10am-11pm, Fri.-Sat. 10am-midnight.

Mayhem, 1411 3r St. Promenade (310-451-7600), **Santa Monica** and 10967 Weyburn Ave. (310-824-7600), **Westwood Village.** Planning to rebel against the mainstream? Come here to find moral support and all the counterculture music and accessories you'll need. Punk, ska, techno, gothic. New, used. Posters, t-shirts, patches, stickers, body jewelry, smoking paraphernalia, chains, and hair dyes. Run amok—it's mayhem. Open Sun.-Thurs. 10am-midnight, Fri.-Sat. 10am-1am.

CLOTHING STORES

It's a fashion war out there, so you've got to look your best. Unfortunately, with so many overpriced boutiques in L.A., that's not always easy for someone on a budget. **Melrose Ave.** has an abundance of used clothing stores—and they're chic too. Some stores even carry studio clothes perfumed by your favorite actress, so with luck you can find designer labels for a fraction of the original price.

Aardvark's, 7579 Melrose Ave. (213-655-6769), **West Hollywood;** and 85 Market St. (310-392-2996), **Venice.** Used gear galore from practical (used Levi's $10-20) to fabulous (pink faux-leather miniskirts $15). Lots of hats, leather jackets, and wigs. Dresses for any decade. Open Mon.-Sat. 11am-7pm, Sun. 11am-9pm.

It's A Wrap, 3315 W. Magnolia Blvd. (818-567-7366), **Burbank.** Keep up with the trends by dressing like your favorite *Melrose Place* characters—*just* like them. Sells studio wardrobes from TV shows like *Roseanne, Mad About You, Seinfeld,* and *All My Children. Baywatch* bathing suits $10. Hot labels at 50% the retail cost, *and* they've been sweated in by stars. But don't worry, it's all been dry-cleaned. Open Mon.-Fri. 11am-8pm, Sat.-Sun. 11am-6pm.

Star Wares, 2817 Main St. (310-399-0224), **Santa Monica.** It's A Wrap's big screen equivalent (though there's no relation), with used movie wardrobes and props. Some, like Brandon Lee's *Crow* outfit (though not the one he was shot in) go for up to $20,000, but the stars' personal clothes still cost less than in the boutiques where they bought them. Open Mon.-Sat. 10:30am-6pm, Sun. 11am-4pm.

Hidden Treasures, 154 Topanga Canyon Rd. (310-455-2998), 4mi. up from PCH in **Malibu.** There's a sizable selection of surprisingly wearable used clothes, and better yet, an eclectic sea-themed decor, and better yet still, a mountaintop teepee. Sit around the campfire, beat the drums, smoke a peace pipe. You don't even need to buy anything. Open daily 10am-6pm.

NOVELTY STORES

L.A. has its share of eccentrics, and they need to shop somewhere too. Novelty stores sells kitsch that just screams L.A.

Skeletons in the Closet, 1104 Mission Rd. (213-343-0760), **downtown.** It's actually the L.A. Coroner's gift shop, and yes, it's as terrifically tasteless as it sounds. Sells personalized toe tags and beach towels with body outlines among other morbid memorabilia. All profits go to drunk driving programs. Open Mon.-Fri. 8am-5pm.

Dudley Doo-Right Emporium, 8200 Sunset Blvd. (213-656-6550), **West Holly-wood.** Cartoonist Jay Ward's old production office now teems with memorabilia based on his characters, Rocky and Bullwinkle, George of the Jungle, and Dudley Doo-Right. T-shirts ($16-20), stuffed animals ($17-30), and original showscripts. Open daily 11am-5pm. No credit cards.

Baby Jane of Hollywood, 7985 Santa Monica Blvd. (213-848-7080), **West Holly-wood.** Popular with gay men and lonely women, Baby Jane carries more than just your typical melange of old movie posters, classic records, vintage tabloids, and autographed glossies ($35-75). It's also got shots of your fave celebs in, shall we say, revealing poses, as well as priceless collectibles like Adam West's phone bill (though they price it at $150). Open daily noon-8pm.

Psychic Eye Book Shop, 218 Main St. (310-396-0110), **Venice;** and 13435 Ventura Blvd. (818-906-8263), the Valley in **Sherman Oaks.** Traveling can be rough on the aura. Fortunately for those in need, there's a place to pick up karma-enhancing astrology charts, hookahs, candelabras, gargoyles, statues of your fave goddesses, and all things gothic. Psychic readings $20 for 20min., $50 per hr., as well as tarot classes, hypnosis sessions, and Tibetan massage. Open Mon.-Sat. 10am-10pm, Sun. 11am-8pm.

Sparky's, on Universal City Walk (818-622-29215), **Universal City.** "Really swell" new and vintage toys from the days when Barbie was the queen of the prom. Trace the evolution of the board game from a 1956 Yahtzee ($40) to modern monopoly sets ($20). Pieces of classic Americana like Cracker Jack and Coca-Cola memora-bilia. Open Sun.-Thurs. 9am-10pm, Fri.-Sat. 9am-11pm.

MALLS

Going to the mall is a full-day activity—you need a few hours to see, be seen, and see all there is to see. Many shopping complexes are open-air, making the stroll down a sunny, tree-lined walkway half the experience. The **Century City Shopping Complex,** 10250 Santa Monica Blvd. (310-277-3898), just southwest of Beverly Hills in **West L.A.,** offers 200 upper-class stores, boutiques, and cafes, but few come just for the shops. Its well-manicured, labyrinthine walkways are a good place to spot celeb-rities, though nothing is guaranteed. It also features the 14-screen AMC Century 14 theaters (310-289-4AMC/4262) and Steven Spielberg's yellow submarine-themed res-taurant, **The Dive!** (310-788-DIVE/3483), naturally specializing in submarine sand-wiches ($8-12; open Sun.-Thurs. 11:30am-10pm, Fri.-Sat. 11:30am-11pm).

Malls are everywhere, but like many things in L.A., the ones here are bigger and posher. A prime example is the **Beverly Center,** 8500 Beverly Blvd. (310-854-0070), at La Cienega in **West L.A.** This monstrous neon megalith sits smack dab in the mid-dle of the city, complete with voyeuristic escalators going up the building's glass sid-ing. Though it's the same old mix of mall stores, the display windows are more showy. Attached to the Beverly Center is the nation's first (and the world's second) **Hard Rock Cafe** (310-276-7605), with a pink Cadillac doing a Thelma and Louise out of the roof (open Sun.-Thurs. 11:30am-11pm, Fri.-Sat. 11:30am-midnight).

Shopaholics head to the mother of all malls, the **South Coast Plaza,** 3333 Bristol St. (714-435-2000 or 800-782-8888), in Orange County's **Costa Mesa.** With 500 stores and a 1.6-acre garden path, the novice L.A. shopper will appreciate the free maps and inter-plaza shuttles. **Don't forget the plastic, and shop 'til you drop, babe!** (Open Mon.-Fri. 10am-9pm, Sat. 10am-7pm, Sun. 11am-6:30pm.)

■ Nightlife

L.A.'s nightlife is second only New York's. Clubs last longer and get busted less often in L.A. They range from teenie danceterias and ephemeral warehouse raves to more exclusive lounge-type clubs catering to the showbiz elite. In between, there is some-thing for everyone else.

LATE-NIGHT RESTAURANTS

As clubs are hit or miss depending on the night of the week, and cafes often open and shut their doors in the same month, late-night restaurants have become *the thing*. As the mainstay of L.A. nightlife, they're the best place to giggle at the painfully trendy underage club kids trolling among the celebs.

Jerry's Deli, has multiple locations, including **West Hollywood,** 8701 Beverly Blvd. (310-289-1811); **Westwood,** 10923 Weyburn Ave. (310-208-3354); and **Studio City,** 12655 Ventura Blvd. (818-980-4245). The menu is longer than Methuselah's beard. Matzoh ball soup $3.75, sandwiches $5-9. Open 24hr.

The Rainbow Grill, 9015 Sunset Blvd. (310-278-4232), **West Hollywood,** beside the Roxy on the Sunset Strip. Dark red vinyl booths cradle just about every famous butt in L.A. Marilyn Monroe met future husband Joe DiMaggio on a blind date here. Yummy pizza ($7) and calamari. The $10 you shell out to get in goes towards your tab. Open Mon.-Fri. 11am-2am, Sat.-Sun. 5pm-2am—so it closes when the clubs do.

Canter's, 419 N. Fairfax Ave. (213-651-2030), **Fairfax.** An L.A. institution, this delicatessen has been the heart and soul of the historically Jewish Fairfax community since 1931. Incredible pastrami. Giant sandwiches $6-8. The music crowd invades the Kibbitz Room every night to hear live rock, blues, jazz, and cabaret-pop stylists (from 9:30pm). Cheap beer ($1.50) served until 2am. Open 24hr.

Barney's Beanery, 8447 Santa Monica Blvd. (213-654-2287), **Hollywood.** L.A. at its best, but minus the pretension. Over 600 items on the menu, 250 bottled beers, and 200 on tap—if they don't have it, you don't need it. Janis Joplin and Jim Morrison were regulars, and it hasn't changed much since then. Strange mix of glam clubbers, international kids, and local pool sharks (billiards 50¢). Happy Hour Mon.-Fri. 10am-6pm. Open daily 10am-2am. Free valet parking.

Tommy's Original Hamburgers, 2575 W. Beverly Blvd. (213-389-9060), **Wilshire District.** Ignore the multitude of Tommy's knock-offs and head to the winner of the sloppiest chili dog contest—the paper towel dispensers every 2ft. along the counters aren't there for looks. Whatever you eat, bring breath mints. Chili dog $1.60, burgers $1.45, double cheeseburger $2.25. Open 24hr. No credit cards.

Izzy's Deli, 1433 Wilshire Blvd. (310-394-1131), **Santa Monica.** Despite its low glitz factor, Izzy's proclaims itself the "deli of the stars" (though few under 40 will recognize many of the silver-haired celebs and 2 ex-presidents on the wall of fame). Staff kibitzes in fluent NY Yiddish-speak. Delicious "overstuffed" sandwiches $5-7.75, matzoh ball soup $3. Open 24hr.

COFFEEHOUSES

In this city where no one eats very much for fear of rounding out that bony figure, espresso, coffee, and air are the only options. This is where you'll find the hip, younger crowd who don't earn enough to hit the restaurants. Bring a book (preferably in a foreign language) and hide behind it while scoping out everyone else.

Highland Grounds, 742 N. Highland Ave. (213-466-1507), **Hollywood.** Nightly live shows (6pm) cover all grounds with folk singers, performance artists, and empowerment speakers. Outdoor patio with blazing fire—ah, ambience. Full menu. Beer and wine. Lattes $1.50 before noon. Cover $2 after 8pm. Open Mon. 9am-6pm, Tues.-Thurs. 9am-12:30am, Fri.-Sat. 9am-1am, Sun. 10am-9pm.

Wednesday's House, 2409 Main St. (310-452-4486), **downtown.** The Partridge Family on espresso. Self-consciously hip Gen-X crowd swaps sex stories and yoga tips. Should you feel out of place, grab some "vintage" threads from clothing racks beside the coffee. Rethink those hot pants, lest you stick to the plastic slipcovered couches. Open mike every other Wed. Open 8am-2am. No credit cards.

Nova Express, 426 N. Fairfax Ave. (213-658-7533), **Fairfax.** A psychedelic version of the *Star Wars* cantina. Wacky space-art created by the owner. Sci-fi books and comics adorn shelves. Espresso $1.75. Pizza $1.85 per slice, or $13 for the "Spiral Galaxy." Live rock Fri., acoustic Sat. Delivers until closing. Open daily 9am-4am.

Bourgeois Pig, 5931 Franklin Ave. (213-962-6366), **Hollywood.** Revel in the bourgeois goth—ionic columns, antique chandeliers, and surprisingly, throbbing techno. Everything black except for the red felt pool table. "Death Drinks" ($2.25). Open daily 9am-2am. No credit cards.

Weho Lounge, 8861 Santa Monica Blvd. (310-659-6180), **West Hollywood.** The first-ever coffeehouse/AIDS info center. Plush sofas and lots of books. Many gay men, but all types chat it up in the outdoor patio. **Free HIV testing** Tues. and Sat. 6-10pm. Bring 10 condom wrappers and get a free coffee. Open daily 2pm-2am.

Anastasia's Asylum, 1028 Wilshire Blvd. (310-394-7113), **Santa Monica.** Casual and intimate, with the candles to inspire a seance and art to inspire a breakdown. Two levels of comfortably worn furniture, board games, and a full vegetarian menu. 3 bands per night, mostly folk or jazz; first show at 8-9pm. Open Mon.-Thurs. 6:30am-1am, Fri. 6:30am-2am, Sat. 8am-2am, Sun. 8am-1am.

Equator, 22 Mills Alley (626-564-8656), off Colorado in **Pasadena.** Hollywood's cafe of choice attracts the self-consciously artsy. Earthy decor was a set for *Clueless, Party of Five, 90210,* and *The Cable Guy.* Art gallery and Internet access. Specialty coffees $2.50-3.25, smoothies $3. 15% off with ISIC. Open Mon.-Thurs. 7:30am-11:30pm, Fri. 7:30am-12:30am, Sat. 9am-12:30am, Sun. 9am-11:30pm.

Stir Crazy, 6917 Melrose Ave. (213-934-4656), **Hollywood.** A cozy purist's paradise. Cappuccinos ($2) and lime rickeys ($2) served to the sounds of Glenn Miller and Artie Shaw. Scads of people on laptops pretending to work on their screenplays. Open daily 9am-12:30am. No credit cards.

Legal Grind, 2640 Lincoln Blvd. (310-452-8160), **Santa Monica.** Get **free legal advice** from the attorney *du jour* as you sip the coffee of the day ($1.15). Wed. 3-5pm is the big draw—entertainment law, copyrights, and contracts. Mini law library. Sandwiches $2-4. Open Mon.-Sat. 7am-7pm, Sun. 8am-3pm.

BARS

Smoky cocktail lounges are all the rage in L.A. these days, but even if martinis and stogies aren't your style, there are still plenty of no-nonsense watering holes around.

Dublin's, 8240 Sunset Blvd. (213-656-0100), **Hollywood.** Bigger than most clubs, Dublin packs in everyone from young starlets to 60-year-old pool sharks. Pool tables, foosball, darts, and loud music, though there are some quieter nooks and crannies. Swanky upstairs dining room serves lunch, and dinner until 11pm. Open daily 11am-2am. Must be 21.

Liquid Kitty, 11780 W. Pico (310-473-3707), **West L.A.** No one can show the gin to the vermouth quite like the bartenders here. Martini in one hand, cigar in the other, L.A.'s hippest come for the cutting-edge DJs that spin techno, trance, and hip hop on Tues. and Thurs., and live blues, swing, and jazz on Sun. Martinis $6. Open Mon.-Fri. 6pm-2am, Sat.-Sun. 8pm-2am. Must be 21.

Jones, 7205 Santa Monica Blvd. (213-850-1727), **Hollywood.** Though it aims for a "down-home" feel with its red checkered tablecloths, Jack Daniels displays, and bandana-print couches, a hip young Hollywood set brings the glam factor way up. Full dinner menu. Open Mon.-Fri. noon-2am, Sat.-Sun. 7pm-2am. Must be 21.

Alligator Lounge, 3321 Pico Blvd. (310-449-1844), **Santa Monica.** Lounge-y atmosphere verging on clubdom with live bands every night, from ska to rockabilly. Avant-jazz on Mon. Open nightly 8pm-1:30am. Cover $5, free Tues. All ages.

Formosa Cafe, 7156 Santa Monica Blvd. (213-850-4050), **Hollywood.** Come for the ambiance—Chinese lanterns, background jazz, and L.A.'s most beautiful people. Mellow and smoky atmosphere. Full Chinese dinner menu. Open Mon.-Fri. 11am-2am, Sat.-Sun. 6pm-2am. Must be 21.

The Coach and Horses, 7617 Sunset Blvd. (213-876-6900), **Hollywood.** Former speakeasy turned pub dive. Young hipsters come here to drown their post-audition sorrows. Beers $2, wells $3.50. Pool 76¢ a pop. Open Mon.-Fri. 11am-2am, Sat. noon-2am, Sun. 5pm-2am. No credit cards.

COMEDY CLUBS

The talent may be imported from New York, but that doesn't change the fact that L.A.'s comedy clubs are the **best in the world** (unless you happen to chance upon an amateur night, which is generally a painful, painful experience). Though prices are steep, it's worth the setback to catch the newest and wackiest comedians, guffaw as famous veterans hone new material, or preside over the latest trends in stand-up comedy competitions. Call ahead to check age restrictions. Weekday cover charges are cheaper, when the clubs are less crowded, but just as drunk.

Comedy Store, 8433 Sunset Blvd. (213-656-6225), **West Hollywood.** The shopping mall of comedy clubs, with 3 different rooms, each featuring a different type of comedy (and another cover charge). The Main Room has the big names and the big prices ($10-15). The Original Room features mid-range comics for $5-8 (free Mon.). The Belly Room has the real grab-bag material (under $5); every Sat. is Gay and Lesbian Comedy Night. 2-drink min., with drinks starting at $4.50 (ouch!). Open nightly until 2am. Reserve up to a week in advance. Must be 21.

The Improvisation, 8162 Melrose Ave. (213-651-2583), **West Hollywood.** Offers L.A.'s best talent—Robin Williams and Jerry Seinfeld have made their appearances. Restaurant serves Italian fare (entrees $6 and up). Shows Sun.-Thurs. at 8pm, Fri.-Sat. at 8:30 and 10:30pm. Bar open nightly until 1:30am. Cover $8-11. 2-drink minimum. Reservations recommended. Must be 16.

Groundling Theater, 7307 Melrose Ave. (213-934-9700), **Hollywood.** The best improv "forum" in town—alums include PeeWee Herman and many *Saturday Night Live* regulars. Polished skits and light refreshments. Shows Thurs. at 8pm, Fri.-Sat. at 8 and 10pm, Sun. at 7:30pm. Cover $10-17.50. No age limit.

The Laugh Factory, 8001 Sunset Blvd. (213-656-1336), **West Hollywood.** Comedy for the 90s with young, scene-breaking talent—you can say you saw them first. Tues. is open-mic night for the first 20 people in line at 6pm. Nightly showcases at 8 and 10pm. Cover $8-10, 2-drink minimum. Must be 21.

The Ice House, 24 N. Mentor Ave. (626-577-1894), **Pasadena.** The 30-year-old granddaddy of clubs, its alums pop in for the occasional visit. Seats 200. Multiple nightly shows. Cover $8.50-12.50, 2-drink minimum. Reservations recommended.

HBO Workspace, 733 N. Seward St. (213-993-6099), **Hollywood.** Experimental workspace for cutting-edge comedians, especially female acts. It's a risk, but it's also free. Shows at 7:30pm; call for dates. Reservations recommended.

CLUBS

L.A. is famous, perhaps infamous, for its club scene. With the highest number of bands per capita in the world, most clubs are able to book top-notch acts night after night. The distinction between music and dance clubs is a bit sketchy in L.A.—most music clubs have DJs a few times a week, and vice versa. Many clubs are simply host spaces for managements that change nightly; these clubs can be L.A.'s hottest thing one month, and disappear the next. Before their club listings, the *L.A. Weekly* prints, "Due to the erratic lives of L.A. musicians and the capricious personalities of booking agents, all of the following are subject to change for no apparent reason."

L.A. clubs are often expensive, but many are still feasible for budgeters. Coupons in *L.A. Weekly* (see **Publications,** p. 68), and handed out in bushels inside the clubs, can save you a bundle. To enter the club scene, it's best to be at least 21—the next-best option is to be a beautiful woman. Nevertheless, if you're over 18, you can still find a space to dance, but it may mean a hefty cover charge in a less desirable venue.

The Derby, 4500 Los Feliz Blvd. (213-663-8979), **Silverlake.** The kings of swing reign once again in this swanky velvet joint. Ladies, grab your snoods—many dress the 40s part. Free swing lessons Tues.-Thurs. and Sun. 8pm. The menu is from Louise's Trattoria (choice Italian fare) next door. Full bar. Happy Hour daily 4-7pm. Big band music nightly (Big Bad Voodoo Daddies play Wed). Open Mon. 4pm-2am, Tues.-Sun. noon-2am. Cover $5-7, Mon. free. Must be 21.

Luna Park, 665 N. Robertson Blvd. (310-652-0611), **West Hollywood.** Home to many a record/CD release party and an eclectic, ultra-hip crowd. Live funk, jazz, and rock nightly; club DJ Thurs. Supper club, full bar, outdoor patio, trancy dance floor. Open nightly until 2am. Cover $3-10, big-name acts $20. Must be 21.

Billboard Live, 9039 Sunset Blvd. (310-274-5800), **West Hollywood.** A colossal, crowded multimedia experience complete with black lights, neon galore, and TV screens showcasing the frenetic dance floor. Stage show extravaganzas. Live acts and DJ productions, depending on the night. Visit the tequila library on the first floor. Open nightly 8pm-2am. Cover $20. Occasional 18-and-over shows.

Martini Lounge, 5657 Melrose Ave. (213-467-4068), **Hollywood.** The crowds may wear retro, but the space-age decor and nightly bands couldn't be more in the moment. Usually more mingling than dancing. Cigars $10. Music ranges from R&B to indie. Cover $5. Shows at 9pm. Open nightly until 2am. Must be 21.

Arena, 6655 Santa Monica Blvd. (213-462-0714), **Santa Monica.** 22,000 sq. ft. floor lends itself to frenzied techno, house, and Latin beats. Fun-filled theme night, killer drag shows on Sat. Dance! Dance! Dance! Open Thurs. 9pm-2:30am, Fri. 9pm-4am, Sat. 9pm-3am, Sun. 8pm-2am. Cover $6-10. Must be 18 Sun.-Fri.; must be 21 Sat.

Roxy, 9009 Sunset Blvd. (310-276-2222), **Sunset Strip.** Known as the "Sizzling Showcase," it's one of the best-known Sunset Strip clubs. Live rock, blues, alternative, and occasionally hip-hop. Many big tour acts. Cover up to $15; Tues. free. Opens at 7pm. All ages. Buy tickets at the door or call Ticketmaster (213-480-3232).

The Palace, 1734 N. Vine St. (213-462-3000), **Hollywood.** This legendary Hollywood club has featured Rudy Vallee and the madcap Rolling Stones. Today, it spins hip-hop, house, and old school. Dance floor, patio, VIP lounge, and balcony. Full bar and menu. Lots of discounts. Open nightly 10pm-2am. Cover $10-20. Must be 18.

Whisky A Go-Go, 8901 Sunset Blvd. (310-652-4205), **West Hollywood.** The great prophet of L.A.'s music history. Whisky hosted many progressive bands in the late 70s and early 80s, and was big into the punk explosion. No dancy techno here, only live bands, 5-6 groups playing nightly from 8pm. Hard rock to alternative. Two full bars. Cover Mon.-Fri. $10, Sat.-Sun. $12-15. All ages.

Dragonfly, 6510 Santa Monica Blvd. (213-466-6111), **Hollywood.** The young, multi-pierced crowd isn't afraid to dance to the groove, hard funk, and rock played nightly—if there's enough room to boom. Lounge, patio, and "trance garden" offer space to breathe. Fri. and Sat. are official "dance nights," but hell, every night's a dance night. Cover $7-10. Open nightly 9pm-2am. Must be 21.

The Viper Room, 8852 Sunset Blvd. (310-358-1880), **West Hollywood.** For those on a River Phoenix pilgrimage, this Johnny Depp-owned nightspot is a must-see. For everyone else, the crowd of aging hipsters and retired frat boys make this one of the Strip's less interesting spots. If you must go, hide in the neo-rummage chic lounge downstairs or indulge in the live music upstairs. DJ on Sat. Cover $15. Open nightly until 2am. Must be 21.

Kingston 12, 814 Broadway (310-451-4423), **Santa Monica.** L.A.'s only full-time reggae club presents local and foreign acts. Dredlocks flow freely. Jamaican food, dance floor, 2 bars. Rasta! Cover varies. Open Thurs.-Sun. 9pm-2am. All ages.

GAY AND LESBIAN NIGHTLIFE

Many ostensibly "straight" clubs have gay nights. Check the *L.A. Weekly* for more listings or contact the Gay and Lesbian Community Services Center (see **Practical Information,** p. 66). Free weekly magazine *fab!* lists happenings in the gay and lesbian community. Nightlife centers around **Santa Monica Blvd.** in West Hollywood.

Axis, 652 N. La Peer Dr. (310-659-0471), **West Hollywood.** With 2 clubs, 2 bars, faux leopard skin carpet, red pool tables, and great music, Axis is the hub of West Hollywood's gay and lesbian scene. Wed. Latin night, Fri. Girl Bar, Sat. house music. Open nightly 9pm-2am. Cover $5-10. Must be 21; Thurs. must be 18.

The Abbey, 692 Robertson Blvd. (310-289-8410), **West Hollywood.** This Spanish-revival coffeehouse buzzes into the night. Psychic readings, Internet access, free pool. Huge double latte $3. Open Sun.-Thurs. 7:30am-2am, Fri.-Sat. 7:30am-3am.

Love Lounge, 657 N. Robertson Blvd. (310-659-0472), **West Hollywood.** This off-shoot of Axis aims to please all. Tues. drag shows, Wed. 80s flashback, Thurs. Bud-

Hair Today, Gone Tomorrow

I mean, if all you're singing about is partying and getting laid, how memorable is that?

—Dokken Bassist Jeff Pilson

In the 80s, burgeoning developments in the fields of spandex, leather, and hair gel brought on the ultimately forgettable genre of **Hair Metal.** L.A., and especially Sunset Strip were on the cutting edge of this musical trend, with innovators like **RATT, Warrant,** and **LA Guns** leading the charge. Today, however, the groupie chicks are gone and *Cherry Pie* is in the Bargain Bin at Tower. Where did they go?

Well, after 7 million albums sold, Warrant lost the major-label contract, went broke, and had their singer and guitarist quit (though singer Jani Lane later returned). Their latest album, *Ultraphobic,* is currently languishing. The LA Guns, stifled under the shadow of mega-act Guns 'n' Roses, didn't have quite as far to fall. Frontman Phil Lewis went on to side projects like Filthy Lucre, but always came back to the Guns. Their latest album, *Vicious Circle,* has a self-described "soulful sound," and Lewis has been working on a screenplay about **Hank Williams.** No one really knows what happened to RATT, but some people think that they were once popular and released some albums. Rumors about their wandering through the desert like bedouins are just that. Warrant and the LA Guns are still playing club shows, so you still may be able to catch them in action...if you're still ready to rock.

dha lounge (with Asian male strippers), Fri. new wave, Sat. lesbian night. The dancing gets frenetic, and the lights aren't the only thing that's throbbing. Full bar, pool tables. Open Tues.-Sun. 10pm-2am. Cover $5-10. Must be 21.

Micky's, 8857 Santa Monica Blvd. (657-1176), **West Hollywood.** Large, popular wetspot filled with delectable men of all ages. On Thurs. at 8pm, male porno stars come to "hang around" and "dispense autographs." Weekend Beer Bust 4-9pm. Cover $3-20. Open daily noon-2am. Must be 21.

7969, 7969 Santa Monica Blvd. (213-654-0280), **West Hollywood.** Sometimes a strip club, sometimes a drag or S&M show. Dancing, fetish gear, and rubber anything— not for the faint-of-heart. Thurs. hip-hop/burlesque night is popular. Mixed gay and lesbian crowd. Open nightly 10pm-2am. Cover $6-10. Must be 21.

The Palms, 8572 Santa Monica Blvd. (310-652-6188), **West Hollywood's** oldest women's bar. Pool room and full bar with lots of drink specials. DJ Wed.-Sun., music ranges from house to disco to salsa. Men are welcome, but may feel very alone. Wed. $1 drinks 5-9pm. Sun. Beer Bust and BBQ $5. Open daily until 2am.

Firehouse, 696 N. Robertson Blvd. (310-289-1353), **West Hollywood.** Hotter than hell, and not just because the dance floor's crammed with sweaty, gyrating bodies. DJ normally spins funk; Thurs. more of an underground scene; Fri. trance and jungle. Mostly gay men, but anyone who doesn't mind a packed house is welcome. Open Tues.-Sun. until 2am. Cover $5, Fri.-Sat. $7. Must be 21.

Rage, 8911 Santa Monica Blvd. (310-652-7055), **West Hollywood.** Its glory days may have passed, but this enormous institution still rages on with nightly DJs, drag nights, male strippers, and disco 'til you drop. Mostly gay men. Open daily noon-2am. No cover except Fri. ($5, includes a drink). Must be 21.

■ Seasonal Events

Tournament of Roses Parade and Rose Bowl (626-449-7673), Jan. 1, Pasadena. New Year's Day is always a perfect day in Southern California. Some of the wildest New Year's Eve parties happen along Colorado Blvd., the parade route. If you miss the parade, which runs 8-10am, you can still see the floats up close on display that afternoon and on Jan. 2 at the intersection of Paloma and Sierra Madre ($1). The champions of the Pac 10 and Big 10 football conferences meet that afternoon for the rowdy Rose Bowl Game. Only a few end zone tickets are available to the public; call 626-449-4100 after Nov. 1.

Chinese New Year (213-617-0396), late Feb., Chinatown. Fireworks and dragon processions.

Whale-watching is best Dec.-March, as the Pacific Grays migrate south. For the past 2 years, 90% of the world's blue whale population has summered off the Channel Islands (see **Channel Islands,** p. 211). Boats depart from Ventura, Long Beach, and San Pedro to witness the migration. Call any of the state beaches.

Grunion runs occur throughout spring and summer. This late-night pastime appeals to those who want to watch slippery, silver fish squirm onto the beaches (especially San Pedro) to mate. The fish can be caught by hand, but a license is required for those over 16. Obtain licenses from the Fish and Game Department, 330 Golden Shore (562-590-5132), in Long Beach, for $15.75; they're valid until Dec. 31 each year. One-day license $6.6o. Grunion fishing prohibited May-June. Free programs on the Grunion run given March-July at the Cabrillo Marine Museum in San Pedro (310-548-7562).

Renaissance Pleasure Faire (800-52-FAIRE/523-2473), from the daffodil's first blossom to the day of the shortest night (weekends, late April to mid-June) in the Glen Helen Regional Park in San Bernardino. The name is quite arousing, but save for the occasional kissing bridge, it's a pretty tame scene. From the haven angelic (L.A.), gallop apace on fiery-footed steeds (drive) to Phoebus' lodging (east) along I-10 to I-15 north and look for signs as you draw near the site of happy reveling (city of Devore). Garbed in their best Elizabethan finery, San Bernardino teens are versed in the bard's phrases before working. Open daily 10am-6pm. $17.50, seniors and students $13.50, children $7.50.

Cinco de Mayo (213-625-5045), May 5, especially downtown at Olvera St. Huge celebrations mark the day the Mexicans kicked the French out of Mexico.

UCLA Mardi Gras (310-825-8001), mid-May, at the athletic field. Billed as the world's largest collegiate activity (a terrifying thought). Festivities run from 7pm-2am. Proceeds benefit charity.

UCLA Jazz and Reggae Festival (310-825-6564), Memorial Day weekend in late May, at the intramural field. Free concerts of these musical genres, as well as a cultural marketplace and food.

Summer Nights at the California Plaza (213-621-1741), Thurs. nights from June-September, California Plaza, 250 Grand Ave., downtown. Concert festival features dance, music, theatre, circuses, and gallery showing in the Museum of Contemporary Art. Free admission. Beer and wine sold. Parking $4.40 after 5pm.

Playboy Jazz Festival (310-449-4070), June 13-14, Hollywood Bowl. 2 days of entertainment by top-name jazz musicians of all varieties, from traditional to fusion. Call Ticketmaster (213-381-2000) for prices.

Gay Pride Weekend (213-860-0701), June 27-28, Pacific Design Center, 8687 Melrose Ave., West Hollywood. L.A.'s lesbian and gay communities celebrate in full effect. Art, politics, dances, and a big parade. Tickets $10.

Shakespeare Festival/LA (213-489-1121), July-Aug., Wed.-Sun.; Hollywood, downtown, Palos Verdes, and Pasadena. This theater company aims to make Shakespeare accessible to all. Canned food donation accepted in lieu of admission at performances within the city of L.A.; $12.50 otherwise.

Celebration USA (626-577-3100), July 4, Rose Bowl, Pasadena. Fireworks and fun. Call for prices, many different levels of seating available.

Pasadena Doo Dah Parade, (626-449-3689), Nov. Pasadena's other parade—known for its own wackiness, like the Briefcase Brigade.

Los Posados (213-485-9777), Dec. 16-24, along Olvera St., downtown. This celebration includes a candlelight procession and the breaking of a piñata.

Around Los Angeles

There's no rhyme or reason to the hodge-podge of land surrounding Los Angeles, except that it's more the stuff of poetry than the big city itself. The beaches of the South Bay are cleaner, quieter, and better for surfing than those close to downtown. Angelenos get a breath of fresh air and bond with Mother Nature in the western Angeles National Forest, the northern Santa Monica Recreation Area, and the popular hiking and snorkeling getaway of Catalina Island. And if the verdant rolling hills in yuppified Orange County don't cause you to burst out in song, the legendary merriment of Disneyland (for better or worse) just might do the trick.

SOUTHERN L.A. COUNTY

Head to L.A. County's southern communities for the most precious of Southern Californian souvenirs—a tan. Easily accessible by public transportation, or just a half-hour hop down I-405, these stereotypically beachy towns are more casual and less congested than the massive metropolis looming to the north. South Bay provides a haven for surfers, beach volleyball players, and sun worshippers, and the sandy campsites and snorkeling spots off Catalina Island are the closest it gets to a local tropical paradise. Though Long Beach's urban sprawl overshadows its stretch of shoreline, the city fosters a growing nightlife and shopping scene underneath the industrial facade.

■ South Bay

South Bay life is beach life. All activity revolves around the sand, and a cloudy sky is reason enough not to get up in the morning. **Hermosa Beach** wins both bathing suit and congeniality competitions. Its slammin' volleyball scene, gnarly waves, and killer boardwalk, make this the überbeach. The mellower **Manhattan Beach** exudes a yuppified charm, while **Redondo Beach** is by far the most commercially suburban. Richie Rich-esque **Rancho Palos Verdes** is a coast of a different breed. From early morning to late evening, these famed sandboxes are overrun by gaggles of eager skaters, bladers, volleyball players, surfers, and sunbathers. At night, the crowds move off the beach and toward Manhattan and Hermosa Ave. for an affordable nighlife scene.

PRACTICAL INFORMATION

Visitor Information: Manhattan Beach Chamber of Commerce, 425 15th St. (545-5315). Open Mon.-Fri. 9am-5pm. **Hermosa Beach Chamber of Commerce and Visitor Information Center,** 1007 Hermosa Ave. (376-0951). Open Mon.-Thurs. 9am-5pm, Fri. 9am-4pm. **Redondo Beach Chamber of Commerce,** 200 N. Pacific Coast Hwy. (376-6911). Open Mon.-Fri. 8:30am-5pm. **San Pedro Chamber of Commerce,** 390 W. 7th St. (832-7272). Open Mon.-Fri. 9am-5pm. **South Bay Community Pages** (http://www.commpages.com), has links to each city's home page with events and entertainment.

ATM: Citibank, at the corner of Pier and Hermosa in Hermosa Beach.

Public Transportation: MTA (800-266-6883). Bus #443 leaves L.A. Union Station for N. Torrance, Redondo Beach, and Palos Verdes. #444 leaves Union Station as well, and serves W. Torrance, Rolling Hills Estates, and Rancho Palos Verdes.

Car Rental: Robin Hood, 1209 N. Sepulveda Blvd. (318-9955), Manhattan Beach. Steals from the rich. Promises to beat other rental companies by 15%. Credit card required. Gives to the poor. Prices start at $27 for unlimited mi. within L.A. County, $40 out of county. Ages 18-21 must have proof of liability insurance, under 25 pay $10 per day surcharge. Open Mon.-Fri 7am-6pm, Sat 8am-5pm.

Equipment Rental: Each community has at least a few stores that rent bikes ($5-7 per hr.), in-line skates ($5-6 per hr.), and surfboards ($6-7 per hr.). Some also rent volleyballs, boogieboards, umbrellas, and beach chairs. **Paradise Surf and Sport,** 920 Manhattan Ave. (374-7577), Manhattan Beach (open daily 10am-8pm); **Jeffers Rentals,** 39 14th St. (372-9492), Hermosa Beach (open daily 10am-6:30pm); **Marina Rentals,** 505 N. Harbor Dr. (318-BIKE/2453), Redondo Beach.

Weather and Surf Conditions: (379-8471).

Medical Services: South Bay Free Clinic, 1807 Manhattan Beach Blvd. (318-2521, appointment desk 376-9474), Manhattan Beach. Hours vary. **South Bay Medical Center,** 514 N. Prospect Ave. (376-9474), Redondo Beach.

Emergency: 911.

Police: Redondo Beach, 401 Diamond St. (379-2477); **San Pedro,** 2175 Gibson Blvd. (548-7605).

Internet Access: Javaconnection, 528 Pacific Coast Hwy. (376-1144). $8 per hr., students $6 per hr. Open Mon.-Thurs. 6am-10pm, Fri. 6am-midnight, Sat. 8am-midnight, Sun. 8am-10pm.

Post Offices: Redondo Beach, 1201 N. Catalina Ave. (800-275-8777). Open Mon.-Fri. 8:30am-5pm, Sat. 8:30am-12:30pm. **ZIP Code:** 90277. **San Pedro,** 839 S. Beacon St. (800-275-8777). Open Mon.-Fri. 8:30am-5pm, Sat. 9am-noon. **ZIP Code:** 90731.

Area Code: 310.

ACCOMMODATIONS

South Bay harbors two of L.A.'s finest hostels. The one in Hermosa Beach has a bitchin' social scene, while the one in San Pedro may make you want to take up *tai chi*. There are no campsites near this area.

Los Angeles Surf City Hostel, 26 Pier Ave. (798-2323; fax 798-0343), ½ block from the beach, in **Hermosa Beach.** Free airport pick-up, $5 drop-off. Take bus #439 to 11th and Hermosa, walk 2 blocks north, and make a left on Pier. Adorned with hand-painted murals—paint one and stay free. Young, international crowd. Free linens, bodyboards, and breakfast. Discount car rentals, hall showers, laundry, kitchen, and TV lounge, but no parking. Weekly keg bashes. 28-night max. stay. 4-6 bunk dorms $15, off-season $12; private rooms $35. Key deposit $10. Reservations recommended. **Passport or proof of out-of-state residence required.**

Los Angeles South Bay (HI-AYH), 3601 S. Gaffey St., Bldg. #613 (831-8109; fax 831-4635), in Angels Gate Park (entrance by 36th) in **San Pedro.** Bus #446 runs from here to downtown and Union Station during rush hours. From LAX transfer terminal, take the Metro green line to Harbor Fwy., where you can catch #446. The Korean Friendship Bell dominates the nighttime sky, lending an almost mystic feel to the place. Bus schedules, travel books, some food available at desk. Kitchen, laundry, TV room, volleyball courts, free parking. Mixed, slightly older clientele. 7-night max. stay. Reception open 7am-midnight, closed 11am-4pm in winter. 3-6 bed dorms $12; dorm doubles $13.50; private rooms $29.50. Non-members add $3. Linens $2 (no sleeping bags allowed).

Moon Lite Inn, 625 S. Pacific Coast Hwy. (540-4058), **Redondo Beach,** 2 blocks from the ocean. Newly-renovated rooms with all the amenities: HBO, A/C, fridge, microwave, and phone. Free parking. Singles $40; doubles $45.

FOOD AND NIGHTLIFE

Most South Bay communities are slightly upscale versions of die-hard beach towns. Prices are a bit elevated, but so is quality. Look for combination bar/restaurants or one of the many new coffeehouses. Keep in mind that there are over 50 bars around the **Hermosa Beach Pier,** particularly along Hermosa Ave.

Good Stuff, 1286 The Strand (374-2334), at 13th St. in **Hermosa Beach.** The name is an understatement. The fresh, healthy food is great, and the view of the ocean is drop-dead phenomenal. Burgers $4.75-7, salads $5-7.25. Open daily 7am-9pm.

The Spot, 110 2nd St. (376-2355), **Hermosa Beach.** L.A.'s oldest vegetarian restaurant, still a fave of the resident New Age population. Tempting tempeh, tofu, and tahini. "Inflation buster" combos are under $6. Open daily 11am-10pm.

Cafe Boogaloo, 1238 Hermosa Ave. (310-318-2324), **Hermosa Beach.** Blues, R&B, and California cuisine with Louisiana soul. Full bar with 27 microwbrews on tap ($3). Dinner 5-11pm ($10 and up). Nightly shows begin around 8pm, weekends 9pm. Cover Thurs.-Sat. $5-15. Open Mon.-Fri. 4pm-1:30am, Sat.-Sun. 1pm-1:30am.

Yesterday's Coffeehouse and Bookstore, 126 N. Catalina Ave. (318-2499), **Redondo Beach.** The only place in South Bay where the people aren't bronzed. Hard-core (indoor) lounging spot with couches, chessboards, and books to browse (or buy). Coffee $1.50-2.50, teas $2, and a few baked goods. Open daily 6am-10pm.

Lighthouse Cafe, 30 Pier Ave. (372-6111), **Hermosa Beach.** Frequented by local volleyball players, this cool dance club features nightly music ranging from dance to blues. Reasonably priced munchies. Happy Hour pizza $1.75. Opens Mon.-Thurs. 6pm-2am, Fri. 4pm-2am, Sat. 11am-2am, Sun. 9am-2am. Sun. jazz brunch.

The Kettle, 1138 N. Highland Ave. (545-8511), **Manhattan Beach.** Come nightfall, the families move out of this leafy diner and the surfers move in. After all, it's the only 24hr. spot around. Sandwiches and salads $7. "Hangover" omelette $6.75. Beer and wine served until 2am. Open 24hr.

Sacred Grounds Coffeehouse and Art Gallery, 399 W. 6th St. (514-0800), **San Pedro.** Eclectic furniture, coffee, and nifty bottled sodas. Poetry Mon., open mic Wed., blues and jazz Thurs.-Sun. Cover $2-5; Sun. free. Open Mon.-Thurs. 7am-midnight, Fri. 7am-1am, Sat. 8am-1am, Sun. 9am-10pm. No credit cards.

La Villa, 1141 Manhattan Ave. (546-4163), **Manhattan Beach.** Mexican combos with sides of rice and beans or tortillas and homefries $4-6. Tacos start at $1.55. Huge, fresh tostadas are piled high. Beer and wine $2. Open daily 11am-11pm.

SIGHTS

About 20 mi. south of downtown L.A., the **Pacific Coast Highway** (Hwy. 1) swings by the sand at **Manhattan Beach** and continues through **Hermosa Beach,** which tops the list of urban beaches in L.A. County. The sort of community spirit found in Venice prevails, though in a more upscale version. Manhattan Beach's main drag, **Manhattan Ave.,** is lined with charming but overpriced cafes and shops. At the end of the Manhattan Beach Pier, the **Roundhouse Marine Studies Lab** (379-8117), has a shark aquarium and tide pool touch tanks (open Mon.-Fri. 3pm-sunset, Sat.-Sun. 10am-sunset; free). Manhattan is the place for a serious game of **beach volleyball,** which was born on these sands in the late 1970s. The courts at **Marine Ave.** (along with those at the state beach in Pacific Palisades) are the elite training grounds for young players. The **Manhattan Beach Open** (late July), is the oldest professional beach volleyball tournament in the world, while the **Hermosa Beach Open** (end of Aug.) awards the most prize money. Call the Hermosa Beach Chamber of Commerce (see **Practical Information,** p. 119) for schedules. Numerous public courts line Hermosa Beach, and the neighborhood around **Pier St.** is abuzz with South Bay's best bars, cafes, surfer boutiques, and people-watching. The **Either/Or Bookstore,** 124 Pier St. (374-2060), epitomizes Hermosa, with both a water sports section and a "Metaphysics Room" with shelves on zen, the occult, and UFOs (open daily 10am-11pm). **The Strand** is a boardwalk/bike path that runs along Manhattan Ave. south through Hermosa, where it becomes a blur of bikers and skaters. (Pedestrians are well advised to watch from the side.) Parking meters are closely monitored (25¢ per 30min.; 3hr. limit). Surfers converge at the sight of water. In August, the **International Surf Festival** (305-9546), takes over Manhattan Beach with lifeguarding contests and sand castle competitions. Anyone can enter the competitions for a fee.

Redondo Beach is the next town down the coast, and its main attractions are the pier, boardwalk, and marina complex. The adjacent **King Harbor** shelters thousands of pleasure boats and hosts some excellent sport fishing. The **Monstad Pier**

supports a small assortment of restaurants, bars, clubs, and the local fishing community. While the view from the pier is picturesque at night, it is best not seen alone.

For a concentrated dose of Southern California's floral paradise, head to **South Coast Botanic Gardens,** 26300 Crenshaw Blvd. (544-6815), in Rancho Palos Verdes. This former county landfill has metamorphosed into an 87-acre garden, where over 75% of the plants are drought-resistant—practical but also pretty. On weekends, there's a tram ($1.50) to cart you around. (Romp in the roses daily 9am-5pm. Admission $5, students $3, seniors $3, ages 5-12 $1; free 3rd Tues. of each month.)

Whale watch for free (Dec.-April) from the gardens of the **Point Vicente Interpretive Center,** 31501 S. Palos Verdes Dr. (377-5370), a small museum with neat exhibits on gray whales (open daily 10am-7pm, off-season 10am-5pm; admission $2, seniors and disabled $1, children $1; free tours). The Point Vicente **lighthouse,** which is open to visitors for free, supposedly houses the ghost of a woman whose lover died in a shipwreck here. Two miles down the road at 5755 S. Palos Verdes Dr. stands the all-glass **Wayfarer's Chapel** (377-1650). Often passed off as a creation of Frank Lloyd Wright, it was actually designed by his son, **Lloyd Wright.** Like his father, Wright Jr. combines architecture with the nature surrounding it, with stunning results (open daily 9am-5pm, but chapel closes for weddings and services).

Still water and tide pools draw many families to **Cabrillo Beach** farther south in **San Pedro.** The **Cabrillo Marine Museum,** 3720 Stephen White Dr. (548-7562), presents touch tanks, marine history exhibits, and a rather disturbing view of pickled squid and whale skeletons (open Tues.-Fri. noon-5pm, Sat.-Sun. 10am-5pm; free). Call 548-7562 for more info on their evening **grunion runs** ($1 per person) in the early summer. (Beach parking $6.50; free parking in surrounding neighborhood.)

Cafes and antique shops line **6th St.,** which runs into Berth 84 at the water's edge, and the **Los Angeles Maritime Museum** (548-7618), which celebrates Southern California's nautical history (open Tues.-Sun. 10am-5pm; $1 donation requested; parking free). The **Fort MacArthur Military Museum,** 3601 Gaffey St. (548-7705), is a nearly intact coastal fortification (open Sat.-Sun. noon-5pm; free). At the end of Gaffey St. is the otherworldly beauty of the **Korean Friendship Bell,** contained within **Angels Gate Park,** a nice daytime picnic spot, but *not* the place for a stroll come dusk.

▓ Long Beach

Long Beach, as its chamber of commerce proudly proclaims, is "the #1 container shipping port in the world"—hardly the most glamorous distinction for a city to hold. There's something to be said for the 5½ mi. of pristine beaches and thriving entertainment district in this city (pop. 430,000), but any place with inescapable views of 10-story loading cranes, diesel trucks, and container barges will never quite be a hotspot. One word of caution: the inland areas of Long Beach are best avoided—to understand why, just listen to any of Snoop Doggy Dogg's lyrics.

PRACTICAL INFORMATION AND ORIENTATION

Visitor Information: Long Beach Convention and Visitors Bureau, 1 World Trade Center, #300 (436-3645 or 800-452-2829), at Ocean and the Long Beach Fwy. (I-710). Tons of free brochures. Open Mon.-Fri. 8:30am-5pm.

ATM: Farmer's and Merchants Bank, at Pine and 3rd.

Airport: Long Beach Municipal Airport (570-2600), about 10mi. north of downtown. Take LBT bus #111 from downtown.

Buses: Greyhound, 464 W. 3rd St. (432-1842 or 800-231-2222), at Magnolia. To: L.A. ($8), San Diego ($12), San Francisco ($32). Open daily 5:30am-8pm.

Public Transportation: Long Beach Transit (LBT), 1963 E. Anaheim St. (591-2301), runs 37 bus routes. Most buses stop downtown at the **Transit Mall,** on 1st St. between Pacific Ave. and Long Beach Blvd. High-tech bus shelters have route maps and video screens with bus info. Fare 90¢, students 75¢, seniors 45¢, transfers 10-35¢. **Long Beach Runabout,** 1963 E. Anaheim St. (591-2301), is a separate division of the LBT, with service along Ocean Blvd. and Pine Ave., as well as to the Queen Mary (free). One route runs from downtown to Belmont Shores (90¢).

Car Rental: Budget, at Long Beach Airport (421-0143), and at 249 E. Ocean Blvd. (491-5319). Economy cars $36 (unlimited mi.). Must be 21 with major credit card. Open Mon.-Fri. 7:30am-6pm, Sat.-Sun. 8am-4pm; airport location open later.

Bike Rental: Bikestation, at 1st and the Promenade (436-BIKE/2453), downtown. Bikes $5 per hr., $25 per day. Open Mon.-Fri. 6am-7pm, Sat.-Sun. 9am-6pm.

Equipment Rental: Long Beach Windsurf Center, 3850 E. Ocean Blvd. (433-1014). In-line skates ($8 per hr., $20 per day), as well as kayaks, sailboards, and wetsuits. Open Mon.-Sat. 10am-6pm, Sun. 10am-5pm.

Auto Repair: AAA Road Service, 4800 Airport Plaza Dr. (800-668-9231). Open Mon.-Fri. 9am-5pm.

Laundromat: Super Suds, 250 Alamitos Ave. (436-1859). The Disneyland of laundromats. Wash $1, 15min. dry 25¢. Open daily 7am-10pm (last wash at 9pm).

Weather Conditions: (714-675-0503). **Beach/Surf Conditions:** (451-8761).

Emergency: 911.

Police station: 400 W. Broadway (435-6711).

Post Office: 300 N. Long Beach Blvd. (800-275-8777). Open Mon.-Fri. 8:30am-5pm, Sat. 9am-2pm. **ZIP Code:** 90801.

Area Code: 562.

Long Beach is located 24 mi. south of downtown L.A. and just down the coast from South Bay. To reach Long Beach from downtown L.A. by public transit, take the MetroRail Blue Line or the Green Line from LAX. Bus #232 runs from LAX to Long Beach ($1.35). By car, take the Harbor Fwy. (I-110) south to the San Diego Fwy. (I-405). Exit at the Long Beach Fwy. (I-710), which runs directly south to Long Beach.

ACCOMMODATIONS

Daytrips to Long Beach from L.A. are cheap and easy, and an overnight trip doesn't need to be any different. There is a string of reasonably priced surf motels along Ocean Blvd. between Belmont Shores and downtown.

Belmont Shore Inn, 3946 E. Ocean Blvd. (434-6236), within walking distance from the beach. Clean rooms sleep 4 and come with color TV and fridge. Rooms $35, with kitchenette $40. Weekly: $175. Free parking. Reservations recommended.

Surf Motel, 2010 E. Ocean Blvd. (437-0771; fax 437-0900). Immaculate shoreside rooms with a mint-green motif. Cable TV, fridges. Pool, private access to beach. Doubles $55, off-season $49. Rooms with ocean view and kitchenette $75, off-season $55. Weekly rates. Free parking. Reservations recommended.

City Center Motel, 255 Atlantic Ave. (435-2483). Plain Jane motor inn brightened up by pastel decor and the fact that it is *smack* in the middle of city center. TVs, fridges, phones. Outdoor pool. Singles $35; doubles $40. Free parking.

FOOD

Downtown area restaurants may delight your palette as well as your wallet. Many eateries lining Pine St. between 1st and 3rd aren't as expensive as the valets out front might lead you to believe. Exercise caution at night. Buy cheap produce at the **open air market** (Fri. 10am-4pm) on Promenade St.

Bonadonna's Shorehouse Cafe, 5271 E. 2nd St. (433-2266). Comfy diner setting that is very surfer-friendly and reasonably veggie-friendly. Omelettes made from your choice of 30 tasty fillings ($4.25 and up). Huge burgers $4-7. Open 24hr.

Taco Surf, 211 Pine Ave. (983-1337), and 5316 E. 2nd S. (434-8646), in Belmont Shores. Dude, this place is so chill that even the beer hangs in a hammock. Fresh and festive feel. Combo meals with rice and beans $6.50. Happy Hour Mon.-Fri. 2-5pm. Open Sun.-Thurs. 11am-11pm, Fri.-Sat. 11am-midnight.

Alegria, 115 Pine Ave. (436-3388). Tapas bar with bakery next door. Painfully hip Miró-inspired interior. Tasty tapas $4-8, entrees $8-13. Weekly Latin jazz and flamenco dancers. Entertainment begins at 8pm. No cover; 1-drink minimum. Open Mon.-Wed. 11:30am-11pm, Thurs.-Fri. 11:30am-midnight, Sat.-Sun.5pm-2am.

Pasta Presto, 200 Pine Ave. (436-7200). Ultra-cheesy decor, but a great deal nonetheless. **Dinner and a movie pass** $9.50, students $8.50, seniors $8.50. Use the pass (good for a year) at the AMC 16-screen megaplex across the street. Pasta combos, pizzas, sandwiches. Open Sun.-Thurs. 11am-9pm, Fri.-Sat. 11am-11pm.

SIGHTS

Long Beach's central preoccupation is shipping; tourism is clearly an afterthought. To get a hold on the city's cargo, cross the majestic **Vincent Thomas Bridge** to central San Pedro (50¢, free from the other direction). The **Queen Mary,** moored at the end of Queensway Dr. (435-3511), is a 1934 Cunard luxury liner that's now a swank hotel with art exhibits, historical displays, and upscale bars. There are still remnants of the days when she was used as a troopship during WWII (Hitler offered the highest honors to anyone who could sink her). **Swing dance** with the seniors to a live band Tues. noon-2pm, or watch **fireworks** every Sat. at 9pm. (Open daily 10am-6pm. Admission $10, seniors $8, children $6; tours $6, children $3. Parking $5.) The huge, white dome next door used to be the roost of the Spruce Goose, but now functions as a massive soundstage. On the other side is the **tallest free-standing bungee crane in North America.** To take the plunge, call **Megabungee** (435-1880; leaps Wed.-Sun. 10am-6pm; $85 per jump, students Wed.-Fri. $68, Sat.-Sun. $77). Back along Ocean Blvd., the cylindrical **Long Beach Arena** is the canvas for the world's largest mural—another of **Wyland's Whaling Walls.**

The downtown area east of Long Beach Blvd. is boutique-orama. **Meow,** 2210 E. 4th St. (438-8990), is where the *Seinfeld* costumers buy **Kramer's shirts** (open Tues.-Sat. noon-6pm, Sun.-Mon. noon-5pm). **Acres of Books,** 240 Long Beach Blvd. (437-6980), is 6½ mi. (a lot of acres) of used books and a favorite of Ray Bradbury (open Tues.-Sat. 9:15am-5pm). **Broadway Blvd.,** east of downtown, has yet more chic boutiques. **Pine Ave.,** off Ocean, is the area's hotspot; be careful after dark.

East of the Convention Center, along the waterfront, is the **Long Beach Museum of Art,** 2300 Ocean Ave. (439-2119), built by famed Pasadena architects Greene and Greene at the turn of the century. The museum features a single rotating exhibit as well as videos by its grant recipients. (Open Wed.-Sun. 10am-5pm, Fri. 10am-8pm. Admission $2, students $1. Summer garden concerts Wed. 7-10pm. Tickets $11.)

The scenic **Shoreline Bike Path** follows the coast from downtown to **Belmont Shores,** Long Beach's upscale, uptown neighborhood. The family-oriented, glamor-free beach here is reputed to be the city's best. Park at the meters near the intersection of Ocean and La Verne (25¢ for 15min., 10hr. max.). **Second St.,** between Santa Ana and Park in Belmont Shores, is Long Beach's main drag.

It's a Matter of Distinction

Though Long Beach can not stretch its sands to world-class distances (after all, its Long Beach, not Longest Beach), it certainly stretches its imagination to wedge its way into the world of superlatives. The **world's largest mural,** entitled *Planet Ocean,* is painted on the side of Long Beach Arena. It took environmental artist Wyland 3000 gallons of paint to create the 10-story masterpiece, which is often mistaken for a giant glass aquarium. The **nation's narrowest house,** at 708 Gladys Ave., is a tight squeeze at 10 ft. by 50 ft. The Yard House in Shoreline Village pleases dipsomaniacs with the **world's largest number of beers on tap**—more than 450 brewed beauties. And the Megabungee in the Queen Mary Seaport is the **tallest free-standing bungee jump in North America,** a 220 ft. rush with a 21-story plunge. With neighboring Los Angeles holding onto the dubious distinctions of most malls and facelifts per capita, Long Beach has much to be proud of. Long Beach *is* long, though not the longest. But in terms of distances, it has gone great lengths, if not the greatest lengths, to distinguish itself.

Just past Belmont Shores is **Naples Island,** which, like Venice Beach, was planned around a series of canals. Unlike Venice Beach, the canals here still exist, and the Rivo Alto canal even has gondoliers. (Call 433-9595 for info on moonlight cruises; 1hr. dinner cruise for 2 $55.) It also harbors **Alamitos Bay,** from whence the *S.S. Minnow* set sail on its infamous three-hour tour from the opening sequence of *Gilligan's Island.*

The **Long Beach Yacht Club,** 6201 Appian Way (310-598-9401), holds races throughout the year. The **Long Beach Grand Prix** revs along downtown streets in mid-April (436-9953). Summer sounds jazz up downtown at **Jazz Fest** in mid-August (436-7794), and the **Day of Music** jazz and blues extravaganza in mid-September (435-2525). For more on seasonal events, contact the Convention and Visitors Council (see **Practical Information,** p. 122).

Near Long Beach: Civil War Museum

In nearby Wilmington, the **Drum Barracks Civil War Museum,** 31052 Banning Blvd. (310-548-7509), is the last tangible reminder of the Civil War in the L.A. area. Fearing that L.A. would turn Confederate, the Union established Camp Drum in 1861 (completed 1863). The only remaining building is the Junior Officers Quarters, which houses an excellent collection of period weapons, a Civil War research library, and several **ghosts** (ask about Colonel Curtis). The museum is open for tours only (Tues.-Thurs. 10, 11am, and noon; Sat. 12:30, 1:30, and 2:30pm; $2.50 donation requested).

ENTERTAINMENT

Long Beach supports a quiet gay community and a vibrant blues and jazz scene (try the **Blue Cafe** on any given night). A popular coffeehouse is **Portfolio,** 2300 E. 4th St. (434-2486), with live soul and blues on weekends (open Sun.-Tues. 6am-midnight, Wed.-Sat. 6am-3am). Most gay and lesbian nightspots cluster around East Broadway and Falcon. Bars around 2nd and Pine soak up much of L.A.'s mainstream.

Jillian's Billiards Cafe, 110 Pine Ave. (310-628-8866). This artfully-restored turn-of-the-century bank building has billiards, live jazz, and a full menu. **The Vault** is its underground nightclub (shows Fri.-Sat. 10pm; cover $6-10; must be 21). Happy Hour Mon.-Fri. 4-7pm. Open 11:30am-2am.

Bayshore, 5335 E. 2nd St. (433-9150), one of the liveliest of 2nd St.'s many night spots. Home of "shoot-the-root," a delectable drink invented here in 1986 which contains a shot of root beer schnapps in a cup of beer ($3). Pool table for those sober enough to rack 'em up. Happy Hour(s) daily 11am-7pm ($1 drafts, $2 wells). Free food Mon.-Fri. 4-7pm. Open Tues.-Fri. 10am-1am, Sat. 4pm-2am.

The Library, 3418 E. Broadway (433-2393). Fab bohemian joint frequented heavily (though not exclusively) by gays. Walls are lined with thousands of books, and the rooms are festooned with lots of luxurious couches. Cup of damn fine joe $1.35. Jazz shows Sun., Wed., and Fri. at 8pm. Open Mon.-Thurs. 6am-midnight, Fri. 6am-1am, Sat. 7am-1am, Sun. 7am-midnight.

■ Catalina Island

Once the exclusive refuge of the wealthy, Catalina Island finds itself in the precarious position of being an island paradise located a mere 22 mi. and $30 away from the largest metropolitan area in the U.S. The potential for profit has not been lost upon the hotel owners and merchants found in the island's only city, Avalon. Tourists leaving the boat are deluged by offers of tram tours ($10-80), boat trips ($25-100), and rental "opportunities." This rampant commercialism is mitigated by two facts: 86% of the island is owned by a non-profit group dedicated to conservation, and the tours *do* take you to some of the most beautiful and unspoiled land in the L.A. area. The non-profit group goes to great lengths to ensure that the land remains natural—bike permits ($50) effectively prevent biking and tours are limited to the main roads. If you have the inclination and the constitution, hiking is free and snorkeling is cheap (rentals around $5 per hr.). The extra $1 for fish food is well-spent, as otherwise you'll be looking at the bottom of the ocean the whole time. The island's best sights are outside of Avalon, so be sure to get inland or on the water.

PRACTICAL INFORMATION

Visitor Information: Chamber of Commerce and Visitor Bureau, P.O. Box 217, Avalon, CA 90704 (510-1520; fax 510-7606), on the left side of Avalon's Pleasure Pier. Open Mon. and Wed.-Sun. 8am-5pm, Tues. 8am-4:30pm. **Catalina Island Conservancy,** 125 Claressa Ave., P.O. Box 2739, Avalon 90704 (510-2595). This non-profit group (see above) owns 86% of Catalina. Hiking permits (free), trail advice (free), and maps (25¢) available here. Open daily 8:30am-5pm. **Biking permits** ($50, families $75) are required outside of Avalon. They can be obtained at the Conservancy, as well as the Catalina airport, and the Two Harbors Visitors Center (510-2880).

ATM: Bank of Southern California, at Crescent and Catalina. Also in the **Vons Market** (see below).

Public Transportation: A **bus** travels between Avalon and Catalina's other "town" of Two Harbors, stopping at a few of the campgrounds along the way (full one-way trip takes just over 1hr.; fare $18). **Catalina Express** (310-519-1212 or 800-464-4228) runs a **water shuttle** between the towns June-Sept. (one-way $13).

Bike Rental: Brown's Bikes, 360ft. from the boat dock (510-0986). Single-speed bikes $5 per hr., $12 per day; 6-speed bikes $6 per hr., $15 per day; 21-speed mountain bikes $9 per hr., $20 per day.

Market: Vons, 121 Metropole St. (510-0280). Open daily 7am-11pm. ATM inside.

Laundromat: California Coin Laundry, in the Hotel Metropole shopping arcade by Vons. Wash $1.50, 15min. dry 25¢. Save water!

Showers: Public facilities located on Casino Way across from the Tuna Club. Entrance $1, each additional 5min. $1. Assorted preening implements $1 each. Open daily 7am-8pm, off-season 7-11am and 3-5pm.

Emergency: 911.

Post Office: In the Arcade Bldg. between Sumner and Metropole. **ZIP Code:** 90704.

Area Code: 310.

GETTING THERE

If you don't have your own yacht, the best (and cheapest) way to get to Catalina is via **Catalina Cruises** (800-CATALINA/228-2546), which departs from Long Beach and San Pedro to Avalon or two Harbors (round-trip $25, ages 2-11 $20, under 2 $2; 2hr; up to 29 departures daily). A faster, more expensive way is the sleek **Catalina Express** (310-519-1212 or 800-464-4228), which departs from Long Beach and San Pedro to Avalon or Two Harbors (round-trip $36, seniors $32.50, ages 2-11 $27, under 2 $2; up to 25 departures daily). The catamaran-hulled **Catalina Flyer** (714-673-5245), leaves from Newport Beach at 9am for Avalon and returns at 4:30pm daily (round-trip $36, under 12 $20).

CAMPING AND ACCOMMODATIONS

The island's only budget accommodation is **Hostel La Vista,** 145 Marilla (510-0603), 100 yards from the Avalon harbor. The historic hotel, built in 1920, recently metamorphosed into hostel-style lodging, with a common fridge (but no kitchen), and free towels and linens. The name is appropriate considering its spectacular ocean views (4-person dorm $15; doubles $25, with private bath $60-80; open June-Oct.).

While **no wilderness camping** is permitted, the five campgrounds on Catalina each offer distinct camping experiences. **Hermit Gulch** (510-0025), a 1½ mi. walk from the boat landing, is populated by carousing campers and rich folks who missed the boat on one of many "no vacancy" nights. It has hot showers, flush toilets, a coin microwave, BBQs, and a vending machine ($7.50 per person; June-Sept. $8.50), and a limited number of stoves and lanterns ($5). No gear? No worries—they rent tee-pees ($20), tents ($10-15), and sleeping bags ($6). You can get closer to nature at the other four campgrounds, all run by Two Harbors Management (510-2800). To get to any of these sites from Avalon, take the shuttle bus; you may have to hike 1½ mi. from the nearest stop. Eleven large, secluded pine forest sites ($7.50 per person) comprise **Blackjack.** It has cold showers, running water, and fire rings, but be prepared for large herds of buffalo to amble through. Only ¼ mi. from Two Harbors, **Little Fisherman's Cove** has the most popular beach camping, with 54 campsites, cold showers, chemical toilets, and rental gear (tents $10-25, sleeping bags $7.50). **Little Harbor's** incredible 16 beach sites offer a secluded cove for surfing and body-surfing, a ranger station, potable water, picnic tables, and chemical toilets ($8.50 per person). Head to **Parson's Landing,** on the west tip of the island, if you want to be alone. The six sunny sites come with 2½ gallons of purified water and a bundle of firewood. You must check in at Two Harbor Visitors Center (510-2800) to get the key (basic rate $16.50, each additional person $6.50).

FOOD, SIGHTS, AND ENTERTAINMENT

Avalon, centered on **Crescent Ave.**, is the only spot where there is any action. Land a fresh catch of the day combo for about $5 at **Lloyd's of Avalon** (510-1579), at Summer and Crescent (open daily 6am-10pm, off-season 6am-6pm). A brief trek up Arroyo Canyon Rd. away from the tourist- and yacht-infested harbor leads to **Sand Trap** (510-1349), at Brook Park. Relax over massive Mexican combos ($4.25-6) or veggie burgers ($5) on the outdoor patio (open daily 7:30am-5:30pm; cash only).

At the end of Arroyo Canyon Rd. (2mi. outside Avalon), you can pick up the hilly **Hermit Gulch Trail,** a 3½ mi. loop past canyons, secluded coast, the **Wrigley Memorial** (a monolithic remembrance of the gum magnate, who once owned the island), and the 38-acre **Botanic Gardens** (510-2288; open daily 8am-5pm; $1 donation). Bison and wild boars inhabit the area along the 4mi. **Black Jack-Cape Reservoir Loop.** Two or three hundred buffalo are the descendents of the 25 originally ferried over for the filming of Zane Grey's *The Vanishing American* in 1924. The rigorous 8 mi. **Black Jack Trail** leads to Little Harbor. Pick up either of the last trails at the Black Jack Junction, accessible by the **airport shuttle** (round-trip $14.50).

Some of the best sights in Catalina lie under ever-clear water, so strap on mask and snorkel or hop on a tour boat to get a taste. Rather than take the **Glass Bottom Boat Trips** (40min.; fare $8, seniors $7, ages 2-11 $4.25; additional 50¢ at night), the budget adventurer should gather dive gear at **Catalina Diver's Supply** (800-353-0330), on the left-hand side of Pleasure Pier (mask/snorkel/fin package or wetsuit $5 per hr., $10 per day). **Lover's Cove** is the most convenient spot to snorkel, but gets way crowded with tourists and boat traffic. The best place to snorkel is among the garibaldi in the kelp forests off **Casino Point.** Rocks along the coast can graze unprotected skin, so wear a wetsuit.

The **Casino Building** (510-7400), on the end of Crescent Ave., was never a gambling den; William Wrigley Jr. built it as a ballroom dancing hall in 1929 (casino means "gathering place" in Italian). The best way to visit the building itself is to bypass the $8 architectural tour and go to the movies! Take in the elegant Art Deco murals and catch a film for $7; weekend showings (7 and 9:30pm) include a free concert on the antique page organ. The Casino hosts occasional **jazz concerts** and a **New Year's Eve bash** which resembles the Catalina of the 1930s and 1940s, when it was a palace for the sultans of swing. Ask about the **Silent Film Festival** (June; for tickets call 800-866-8729). Tucked beneath the Casino is the **Catalina Island Museum** (510-2414), which has exhibitions on island history, Native American inhabitants, and filmmaker Zane Grey (open daily 10:30am-4pm; donation requested). **Zane Grey's Avalon pueblo** is now the hotel overlooking the Casino.

ORANGE COUNTY

Directly south of L.A. County is Orange County, or "O.C." as locals call it. This place embodies popular stereotypes of Southern California: beautiful beaches, bronzed surfer dudes, strip malls, Walt Disney's playground, and traffic snarls frustrating enough to make the most jaded Angeleno weep.

Recently, many have called the county's typically Californian reputation into question, as the county's homogeneously white population contrasts starkly with the vibrant heterogeneousness of L.A. County. Orange County is one of only two staunchly Republican counties in California, although this, too, is changing.

The area around Anaheim is ironically depressing, but Disneyland—for all its joy joy silliness—is worth seeing. Visit the coast not only for the breathtaking beaches, but also for the calm beauty of the sparsely covered rolling hills around San Juan Capistrano. Traveling through this largely undeveloped region, one can understand the attraction this desolate but elegant land held for the first solemn *padres* and the last dreary suburbanites. O.C. residents still refuse to believe they are a part of the L.A. sprawl—they click their heels three times and say, "We're not the suburbs of Los Angeles, we're not the suburbs of Los Angeles ..." Whatever.

PRACTICAL INFORMATION

Visitor Information: Anaheim Area Visitors and Convention Bureau, 800 W. Katella Ave. (999-8999), in the Anaheim Convention Center. Lodging and dining guides. Open Mon.-Fri. 8:30am-5pm. **Huntington Beach Conference and Visitors Bureau,** 101 Main St., #2A (969-3492 or 800-SAY-OCEAN/729-62326 outside of area code). Open Mon.-Fri. 8:30am-noon and 1-5pm. If the helpful staff doesn't know something, they'll find someone who does. A plethora of good maps and brochures. **Newport Harbor Area Chamber of Commerce,** 1470 Jamboree Rd. (729-4400; email info@newportbeach.com), Newport Beach. Offers free maps, info, and shiny Republican smiles. Open Mon.-Fri. 8:30am-5pm. **Newport Visitors Bureau,** 3300 West Coast Hwy. (644-3309 or 800-94-COAST/942-6278 outside of area code), Newport Beach. Free maps and brochures, including a self-guided walking tour of Balboa Island.

Airport: John Wayne Orange County (252-5006), on Campus Dr. 20min. from Anaheim. Newer, cleaner, and easier to get around than LAX; domestic only.

Trains: Amtrak (800-872-7245 for reservations). Stops (from north to south): **Fullerton,** 120 E. Santa Fe Ave. (992-0530); **Anaheim,** 2150 E. Katella Blvd. (385-1448); **Santa Ana,** 1000 E. Santa Ana St. (547-8389); **Irvine,** 15215 Barranca Ave. (753-9713); **San Juan Capistrano,** Santa Fe Depot, 26701 Verdugo St. (240-2972); **San Clemente,** at the pier.

Buses: Greyhound has 3 stations in the area: **Anaheim,** 100 W. Winston St. (999-1256), 3 blocks south of Disneyland (open daily 6:30am-8pm); **Santa Ana,** 1000 E. Santa Ana Blvd. (542-2215; open daily 7am-8pm); **San Clemente,** 510 Avenida de la Estrella (492-1187; open Mon.-Thurs. 7:45am-6:30pm, Fri. 7:45am-8pm).

Public Transportation: Orange County Transportation Authority (OCTA), 550 S. Main St. (636-RIDE/7433), Garden Grove. Thorough service is useful for getting from Santa Ana and Fullerton Amtrak stations to Disneyland, and for beach-hopping along the coast. Long Beach, in L.A. County, serves as the terminus for several OCTA lines. Bus #1 travels the coast from Long Beach down to San Clemente (hourly until 8pm). #394 links San Juan Capistrano and Doheny; #397 covers San Clemente. Fare $1, transfers free. Info center open Mon.-Fri. 6am-8pm, Sat.-Sun. 8am-5pm. **MTA Info** (626-4455). Lines open daily 5am-10:45pm. MTA buses run from L.A. to Disneyland and Knott's Berry Farm.

Auto Repairs: AAA Emergency Road Service, in Huntington Beach (848-2227), and Anaheim Hills (921-2850). Open Mon.-Fri. 9am-5pm, Sat. 9am-1pm.

Bi-Gay-Lesbian Organizations: Gay-Lesbian Community Center, 12832 Garden Grove Blvd. (534-0862), in Garden Grove. Open Mon.-Fri. 10am-10pm.

Surf and Weather Conditions: (213-554-1212).

Crisis Lines: Poison Control Center (800-777-6476). 24hr. **Rape Crisis Hotline** (831-9110). 24hr. **O.C. Sexual Assault Network** runs an info line (534-0862), and hotline (894-4242).
Medical Services: St. Jude Medical Center, 101 E. Valencia Mesa (871-3280), Fullerton. **Lestonnac Free Clinic,** 1215 E. Chapman Ave. (633-4600).
Emergency: 911.
Police: Anaheim, 425 S. Harbor Blvd. (254-1900). **Huntington Beach** (960-8811).
Post Office: 701 N. Loara (520-2601), Anaheim, 1 block north of Anaheim Plaza. Open Mon.-Fri. 8:30am-5pm, Sat. 8:30am-2pm. **ZIP Code:** 92803.
Area Code: 714; in Seal Beach 310.

■ Anaheim

Anaheim, which means "home by the river" in German, may still have a weekly polka show on the radio (Saturday mornings on FM 89.3), but that is as far as its German roots dig these days. As the home of the strip mall and the ultimate amusement park, Anaheim (pop. 350,000) is quintessential suburban America. In the late 50s, it was the city of the future, and aspiring Californians flocked to Orange County's capital, but the days of booming business, astroturf patios, and tract homes were not to last. With a shrinking economy and rising crime, the only fantasyland here today is in Disneyland. Not content to leave it at that, Disney recently submitted a proposal to buy 40% of Anaheim and turn it into a theme park entitled "The California Adventure," the latest step in their plan to make this small world a small *Disney* world.

ACCOMMODATIONS

The Magic Kingdom is the sun around which the Anaheim universe revolves, so budget motels and garden variety "clean comfortable rooms" flank it on all sides. Keep watch for family and group rates posted on marquees, and seek out establishments offering the "3 for 2" passport (3 days of Disney for the price of 2) if you can stand three days of Mickey and Donald.

Fullerton (HI-AYH), 1700 N. Harbor Blvd. (738-3721; fax 738-7925), in Fullerton 15min. north of Disneyland. Shuttle from LAX $18. OCTA bus #43 runs along Harbor Blvd. to Disneyland. Enthusiastic staff invites questions but frowns on drinking. Offers services including ISICs. Kitchen, communal bathrooms, and single-sex and co-ed dorms. 7-night max. stay. Check-in 8-11am and 4-11pm. No curfew. Dorms $14, nonmembers $17. Linens $1. Laundry free. Reservations encouraged.
Golden Forest Inn, 1050 W. Katella Ave. (776-7910), within walking distance of Disneyland in Anaheim. Pool, laundry room, and nighttime security. Spacious rooms have A/C, couch, refrigerator, cable TV, and microwave. Singles $45, off-season $29; each additional person (up to 5) $7.
Magic Carpet Motel, 1016 W. Katella Ave. (772-9450), and the **Magic Lamp Motel,** 1030 W. Katella Ave. (772-7242), Anaheim. The rugs can't show you a whole new world, but these twin establishments do have a great location across the street from Disneyland. Both have pools, laundry, TV, and A/C. Rooms $34, with kitchenette $36; deluxe suite (up to 7) $65; each additional person (up to 6) $2. Reservations recommended (800-422-1556; fax 772-5461).
Skyview Motel, 1126 W. Katella Ave. (533-4505), at the southwest corner of Disneyland. Clean rooms with HBO and A/C. Balconies offer a good view of Disney's nightly fireworks. Some rooms have vibrating beds, but most have been broken. Heh, heh. Small pool, many kids. Singles $30. Reservations recommended.

FOOD

Anaheim is more mini-mall than city. There are countless fast-food restaurants to choose from, but hold out for one of the various inexpensive ethnic restaurants tucked into the strip malls that line Anaheim's streets. Many specialize in take-out or will deliver chow right to your motel room.

Angelo & Vicini's Cafe Ristorante, 550 N. Harbor Blvd. (879-4022), Fullerton. The word "cheesy" describes both the food (artery-clogging) and the decor (Christmas lights, cheese wheels, and the Mona Lisa) at this *ristorante,* perhaps the only restaurant in O.C. with a walking tour. Lunch special (huge slice of pizza, pasta, and salad) $2.50. Open Sun.-Thurs. 11am-9:45pm, Fri.-Sat. 11am-11:45pm.

El Pollo Inka, 400 S. Euclid Blvd. (772-2263). Locals congregate under a black-light mural of Machu Picchu to devour Anaheim's best Peruvian food. The *arroz con pollo* (rice and chicken, $6) is a filling treat. If you still have room, the *mazzomorra morada* ($1.50), a purple corn pudding, makes for an excellent dessert. Open Mon.-Thurs. 11:30am-9pm, Fri.-Sat. 11:30am-10pm.

Normandy's Heavenly Juice and Java, 1788 Euclid Blvd. (533-8205; email java-jeb@ix.netcom.com). Behind the *Wienerschnitzel* exterior lurks a chummy, jumpin' coffee house for young hipsters. Poetry readings, live music, and a lending library. Bagel and coffee $2. Smoothies are the house specialty ($3, extra charge for the aphrodisiac bee pollen). Open daily 7:30am-10pm.

SIGHTS

Disneyland

Disneyland calls itself the "happiest place on earth," and if happiness is measured in line lengths this must certainly be the case, at least on weekends. By normal definitions, however, weekday visitors will undoubtedly be the happiest. *Disneyland Today!* lists parade and show times, so while the kids crane to catch a glimpse of the floats, take advantage of the shorter lines and jump on as many rides as you can. Remember: the park was designed for youngsters, so only those visitors who are in touch with their inner child will truly enjoy themselves.

Main Street, USA, a sugar-coated recreation of small-town America, has most of the park's shopping, but the prices prove that the Disney execs know the advantage of a captive market. Although these shops stay open an hour after the park itself closes, don't be fooled into thinking you'll get your souvenirs on the way out—everyone else has the same idea. Disney and his designers skewed the perspective on Main Street so that the street seemed longer upon entering and shorter upon exiting, thereby creating visitor anticipation and making the walk to the car less daunting after a long day. How thoughtful.

To the left of the Main Street is **Adventureland,** home to the new **Indiana Jones Adventure.** Pass the time in line with a few chapters of *War and Peace,* or decode the inscriptions inside the Temple of Maya (hint: the ride is sponsored by AT&T). In order to ensure repeat riders, the designers created three different paths on which riders are randomly sent. As a more subtle lure for the female contingent, the ride is punctuated by an animatronic Harrison Ford suggestively saying, "You were good in there…very good." The **Jungle Cruise** next door has a new landing with a swing band to entertain the poor souls languishing in the notoriously long line.

Next door is **New Orleans Square,** home to the best shops and dining in the park. Find New Orleans cuisine at the **French Market** (dinner $7) or the **Blue Bayou** (dinner much more expensive) where there seems to be a surcharge for atmosphere. Among the low-key but entertaining rides are the charmingly faux-creepy **Haunted Mansion,** and Michael Jackson's personal fave, the campy **Pirates of the Caribbean.**

Those with a Wild West fetish will find amusement galore in **Frontierland,** especially on **Big Thunder Railroad.** Replace the lunch you just lost at **Big Thunder Ranch,** right behind the ride. From here, the Mark Twain **riverboat** departs for a tour around **Tom Sawyer's Island,** which looks suspiciously like a clever way to isolate children on an island away from everyone else.

Most of the park's cute things lurk around **Critter Country.** The main attraction here is **Splash Mountain,** a wet log ride past singing rodents and down a thrilling vertical drop. Its host, **Brer Rabbit,** originated in the humor-filled stories about racism in the post-Civil War South. The deep message of this ride is "Everybody's got a laughin' place," and you'll certainly find yours when you see the snapshot of your terror-frozen face on the way down.

Fantasyland is the geographical and spiritual center of the park. It contains the trademark castle as well as the scintillating **Matterhorn Bobsleds,** and numerous kiddie rides like the trippy **It's A Small World,** which will fiendishly burn its happy, happy song into your brain. This area is best enjoyed when the rides light up at night, the kidlets go home, and the couples emerge.

Mickey's Toontown lies at the rear of the park, providing the key source of fun for the 10-and-under crowd. Mickey and Co. can often be found strolling about, followed by a stampede of kids in hot pursuit. To the right of Main Street is **Tomorrowland,** recently remodeled after Disney executives recognized that its supposed imagination of the future was sadly stuck in the 60s. This area of the park is due to reopen in the spring of 1998. The **Astro-orbiter**—rockets that circle around moving planets—will join some of the park's best rides, such as newly-refurbished **Space Mountain** and **Star Tours.** Lines here tend to move more quickly than those in the rest of the park.

The **unlimited use passport** ($34, seniors $30, under 12 $26) allows repeated single-day entrance into the park, as does the parking pass ($6 per day). The park's main entrance on Harbor, and a smaller one on Katella, may be approached by car via I-5 to Katella. From L.A., MTA bus #460 travels from 4th and Flower (about 1½hr.) to the Disneyland Hotel (service to the hotel begins at 4:53am, service back to L.A. until 1:20am). **Free shuttles** link the hotel to Disneyland's portals, as does the **Disneyland monorail.** The park is also served by Airport Service, OCTA, Long Beach Transit, and Gray Line (see **Practical Information,** p. 128). Parking in the morning is painless, but leaving in the evening is not. Park hours vary (call 999-4565 for exact info), but are approximately Sun.-Thurs. 9am-10pm, Fri.-Sat. 9-1am.

Knott Disneyland

Buena Park offers a cavalcade of non-Disney diversions, some of which are better than others. The first theme park in America, **Knott's Berry Farm,** 8039 Beach Blvd. (714-220-5200 for recorded info), is at La Palma Ave. in Buena Park just 5 mi. northeast of Disneyland. (Bus #460 stops here on its way to Disneyland.) Back in 1932, Walter Knott combined a red raspberry, a blackberry, and a loganberry and, lo and behold, he had invented the boysenberry. His popular roadside stand quickly grew into a restaurant and, when he imported the Old Trails Hotel (from Prescott, Arizona) and the last narrow gauge railroad in the country to form "Ghost Town," the seed of the amusement park was born. After the opening of "the other place" in Anaheim in 1955, Knott's Farm added other theme sections such as Fiesta Village and myriad rides. The park's highlights include roller coasters like **Montezuma's Revenge, Boomerang,** and the **Windjammer.** The Doolittle-ish **Birdcage Theater** is where Steve Martin got his start (admit it, Steve!), and the **Kit Kat Klub** offers free dance lessons the second weekend of each month. At Halloween, the park is rechristened Knott's Scary Farm and, at Christmas, Knott's Merry Farm. The food inside is what you'd expect; the best deal, **Mrs. Knott's Chicken Dinner Restaurant** (220-5080), is outside the park. Soup, salad, corn, biscuits, chicken, and dessert (the specialty is—surprise—boysenberry pie) cost only $10. (Park hours vary, but are approximately Sun.-Thurs. 9am-11pm, Fri.-Sat. 9am-midnight. Admission $32, seniors $24, ages 3-11 $24.)

Movieland Wax Museum, 7711 Beach Blvd. (522-1155), offers a huge collection of celebrity facsimiles, including the entire original *Star Trek* crew (open daily 9am-7pm; admission $13, seniors $11, ages 4-11 $7). Across the way are the Eurocentric "oddity" exhibits at **Ripley's Believe It or Not! Museum,** 7850 Beach Blvd. (522-1152), likely to be the only place shameless enough to advertise a *Last Supper* fashioned from 280 pieces of toast. (Open daily 10am-7pm, box office closes at 6pm. Combo admission to both attractions $17.) Amusement parks of the wetter variety can be found at **Wild Rivers Waterpark,** 8770 Irvine Center Dr. (768-9453), in Irvine, off I-405 South. With over 40 waterslide rides and two wave pools, this is almost as good as a cold shower (call for hours; admission $20, seniors $10, ages 3-9 $16).

Farther inland is the highly uncritical monument to Tricky Dick, the **Richard Nixon Library and Birthplace,** 18001 Yorba Linda Blvd. (993-5075), Yorba Linda. The first native-born Californian president was born in this house, which has now become an extensive museum of the American presidency. Rotating exhibits cover such topics as "Rock and Roll and the White House." Skeptics can investigate the Watergate Room, where the tiny, dimly lit text is written white on black—conveniently making it impossible to read. Coincidence? We think not. (Open Mon.-Sat. 10am-5pm, Sun. 11am-5pm. Admission $6, seniors $4, ages 8-11 $2.)

For more evidence of Disney's world domination, catch a sports game; they own both of Anaheim's teams. The major league **Anaheim Angels** (634-2000 or 800-6-ANGELS/626-4357), play from early April to October (general tickets $7). Hockey action takes place at the **Pond,** 2695 E. Katella Ave. (704-2500), one block east of Rte. 57. This arena is the home of the NHL's **Mighty Ducks.** It's just like the movie, except there are no kids and Emilio Estevez isn't coaching.

The **Crystal Cathedral,** 12141 Lewis St. (971-4000), in Garden Grove, hosts Dr. Robert H. Schuller's weekly TV show, *Hour of Power.* Opinions are split on this shining all-glass structure; some find it inspiring, others garish (tours Mon.-Sat. 9am-3:30pm; English services Sun. at 9:30 and 11am; Spanish service at 12:45pm; free).

■ Orange County Beach Communities

Taking town planning to the extreme, O.C.'s various beach communities have cleaner sand, better surf, and less vitality than their L.A. county counterparts. Sights are scarce along the entire 35 mi. between Huntington Beach and San Clemente, featuring only the quaint Mission San Juan Capistrano and the chi-chi South Coast Plaza (the largest mall in this mall-obsessed state). If you're into touring suburbia-by-the-sea or catching a few waves, you might want to make O.C. a daytrip from L.A. Otherwise, it's a nice place to live, but you wouldn't want to visit.

ACCOMMODATIONS

O.C.'s prime coastline and pricey real estate mean a dearth of bargain rates. Those without multi-million-dollar summer homes in the area can try their luck along the Pacific Coast or Newport Blvd. in Newport Beach. *Accommodations, camp-grounds, food, nightlife, and sights are listed from north to south.*

Huntington Beach Colonial Inn Youth Hostel, 421 8th St. (536-3315; fax 536-9485), 4 blocks inland at Pecan in Huntington Beach. Take OCTA #29 (which also goes to Disneyland and Knott's) or #50. Familial staff and international crowd inhabit a large yellow wooden house. Common showers and bathroom, large kitchen, reading/TV room, coin-op laundry, deck, and surfboard shed. Free breakfast. Check-in 7am-11pm. No lockout. Dorms $14; dorm doubles $15. Key deposit $20. Must have picture ID. Reserve 2 days in advance for summer weekends.

HI San Clemente Beach (HI-AYH), 233 Avenida Granada (492-2848; fax 492-2848; email HIAYHSD1@aol.com), 2 blocks west of El Camino in San Clemente. This airy hostel is so laid-back it's almost comatose, perfect for those weary of the urban scene. Near the beach and shopping. Patio, comfy couches, and entertainment center. The lack of nightlife in San Clemente makes the 11pm curfew easy to meet. Single-sex dorms $11, nonmembers $14. Private rooms available for 2-5 people. Lockers. Cash or traveler's checks only. Open May-Oct.

CAMPING

O.C.'s state beaches have **campgrounds** that aren't the stuff of dreams, but this doesn't crimp their *extreme* popularity. Reservations are required for all sites (reservation fee $6.75), can be made through DESTINET (800-444-7275), a maximum of seven months in advance, and should be made as soon as possible in the summer.

Doheny, 25300 Dana Point Harbor Dr., (496-6172), Hwy. 1 at the south end of Dana Point. With the only beachside locations in the area, Doheny is the most popular O.C. campground. Beachfront sites $22, others $17.

San Clemente, 3030 Del Presidente (492-3156), off I-5 in San Clemente. Ocean bluffs and hot showers (coin-operated) draw families and surfers alike. Hookups at 72 of the 160 sites. Self-guided nature trail. Sites $17-18, with hookup $23-24.

San Onofre (492-4872), off I-5 3mi. south of San Clemente. About 90 of these 221 sites are suitable for tents; others are for RVs only. All are crammed onto 10ft. strips of dirt between the parking area and the coastal bluff. The waves of nearby highway traffic drown out those of the distant surf. Trails lead to a lovely beach. Sites $17, weekends $18. Dogs $1 per day.

FOOD

O.C.'s restaurants tend toward typical California cuisine (see **Cuisinart,** p. 61), especially light, seafood-oriented fare. The prevalence of outdoor seating allows diners to pursue two favorite local pastimes at the same time: tanning and people-watching.

Sugar Shack, 213½ Main St. (536-0355), Huntington Beach. Tanned surfer-types favor this friendly hangout. Their self-declared "best all-natural fruit smoothies in H.B." may be the *only* smoothies in town, but they are good. Lunch specials Mon.-Fri. ($3.50-4.75). Open Sun.-Thurs. 7am-3:30pm, Fri.-Sat. 6:30am-9pm.

Newport Beach Brewing Company, 2920 Newport Blvd. (675-8449), Newport Beach. Seared tuna salad ($9) and mediterranean pasta ($7.29) are wonderful. Appetizers half-price during Happy Hour (Mon.-Fri. 3-6:30pm). All beers brewed on the premises. Open Sun.-Thurs. 11:30am-11:30pm, Fri.-Sat. 11:30am-1am.

Wahoo's Fish Tacos, 1133 S. Coast Hwy. (497-0033), 1mi. south of Main Beach in Laguna Beach. Also located at 120 Main St. in Huntington Beach. Delectable tacos ($1.75) and burritos ($3.50) filled with meat, veggies, or the fish of the day. Informal atmosphere perfect for those shirtless beach days. Open Mon.-Sat. 11am-10pm, Sun. 11am-9pm. Cash only.

Laguna Village Cafe, 577 S. Coast Hwy. (494-6344), Laguna Beach. Off the main drag, this old-style joint maintains its local color. Lovely beachside tables provide the perfect atmosphere for noshing some seafood or the house specialty, chicken curry dumplings ($7.75). Open daily 8:30am-dusk.

BREW

Midnite Expresso, 201D Main St. (969-7336), Huntington Beach. Favorite local hangout for surfers and sophisticates. Decor reminiscent of "Friends," but pleasant nonetheless. Live music Fri.-Sun. nights. Single espresso $1.35, double $1.95. Midnite Frosty ice-blended drinks ($2.75) are godsends on summer days. Open Sun.-Thurs. 5:30am-midnight, Fri.-Sat. 5:30am-1am.

Blender's, 424 Pacific Coast Hwy. (494-6663). One of the original smoothie shops in the area, Blender's focuses on nutrition: calorie and fat content of all drinks is listed. The hardest part is choosing what to have, but the Strawberry Sunrise ($3.25) and Peach Toadie ($2.95) are particularly luscious. Open daily 6am-8pm.

The Boom-Boom Room, 1401 S. Coast Hwy. (494-7588), at Mountain St. in the Coast Inn, Laguna Beach. Lively gay hangout has pool tables, live DJs, and American fare. Boom-Boom specials include Sun. evening "Beer Busts" (4-10pm) with $1 drafts and an occasional bartender bare bust. Open daily noon-2am.

BrewBakers, 412 Walnut Ave. (374-BEER/2337), is a beer lover's delight. The inventive can create their own brew for $110, and the lazier (and poorer) can buy it pre-brewed for $2.50 per bottle. Eight different breads ($3-5) ensure that nobody drinks on an empty stomach. Open Wed.-Mon. 11am-9pm.

SIGHTS

Apart from pre-fabricated amusement park joy, fun in the sun O.C.-style revolves around the Pacific—along the Pacific Coast Highway (PCH), in particular. On the average, the **beaches** are cleaner, less crowded, and more charming than those in

L.A. County. Nevertheless, visitors should not be lulled off-guard by the swishing coastal waters and magical inland attractions. As in any city, pedestrians should take extreme care after dusk. Beachside camping outside official campgrounds is both illegal and unsafe.

Huntington Beach (H.B.)

Most of the danger in Huntington Beach is in the water. Named the "safest large city in the country" three years in a row by the FBI, H.B. hosts more wave-shredding than shoplifting. This town's activity of choice is surfing, and the proof is in the **Surfing Walk of Fame** (the sidewalk along PCH at Main) and the **International Surfing Museum,** at 411 Olive (960-3483; open daily noon-5pm, Wed.-Sun. only in winter; admission $2, students $1). The pier is the best place to watch the continuing cavalcade of surfing contests, but will be under construction until spring of 1998. By night, H.B.'s bars and microbreweries become a beach party brew-ha-ha.

Newport Beach and the Balboa Peninsula

Newport Beach is divided into wealthy and immaculate residential neighborhoods and dingier tourist areas. Multi-million dollar summer homes are jam-packed along **Newport Harbor,** the largest leisure-craft harbor in the world, while the beach is crowded with young, frequently rowdy hedonists cloaked in neon.

The sands of Newport Beach run south onto the **Balboa Peninsula,** separated from the mainland by Newport Bay. The peninsula itself is only two to four blocks wide and can be reached from the Pacific Coast Hwy. (PCH). **Ocean Front Walk,** which extends the length of the peninsula, is the best place to stroll along the beach. At the end of the peninsula, **The Wedge,** seasonally pounded by storm-generated waves up to 20 ft. tall, is a **bodysurfing** mecca.

On the opposite side of the peninsula, at the end of Main St., is the ornate **Balboa Pavilion.** Once a sounding ground for Big Band great **Benny Goodman,** the pavilion is now a hub for harbor tours and winter whale-watching. The bi-level *Pavilion Queen* and smaller *Pavilion Paddy* offer 45 minute (fare $6, children $2) and one hour (fare $8, children $2) cruises of the harbor. The *Catalina Flyer* (round-trip $36, ages 3-12 $20, under 3 $2) leaves for Catalina Island at 9am and returns at 4:30pm. Call 673-5245 for reservations. The harborside melee, **Funzone,** stretches its ferris wheels and bumper cars northwest of the Pavilion. From this area is visible upscale **Balboa Island,** a haven for chic eateries, boutiques, and bikini shops. A vintage **ferryboat** (673-1070) travels there from the peninsula. (Ferry runs every 5min., Sun.-Thurs. 6:30am-midnight, Fri.-Sat. 6:30am-2am. Car and driver $1, each additional passenger 35¢, children 15¢.) The island is also accessible from the Pacific Coast Hwy. via the Jamboree Rd. bridge.

Most of the crowds navigate Newport Beach and the Balboa Peninsula by **bicycle** or **in-line skates.** Ubiquitous stands rent just about anything the aspiring beach bum might crave. (Bike rentals $5-7 per hr., $15 per day. Skates $3-6 per hr., $15 per day. Boogieboards $5-6 per day.) Bikers should pick up *Bikeways,* a map of trails in Newport Beach, at the visitors center.

Laguna Beach

Laguna Beach, 4 mi. south of Newport, is a much sleepier burg. Back in the day, the 8½ mi. coastal area was known as the "Artist Colony by the Sea," but no properly starving artists can afford to live here now, although surviving galleries add a unique twist to the standard SoCal beach culture thriving on Laguna's sands. Punctuated by rocky cliffs, coves, and lush hillside vegetation, the town's character is decidedly Mediterranean. **Ocean Ave.** at Pacific Coast Hwy. and **Main Beach** are the prime parading areas. **Westry Beach,** which spreads south of Laguna just below **Aliso Beach Park,** and **Camel Point,** between Westry and Aliso, is the hub of the local **gay** crowd. For beach access, park on residential streets to the east and look for Public Access signs between private properties.

The latest incarnation of the original 1914 Laguna Beach art association is the **Laguna Beach Museum of Art,** 307 Cliff Dr. (494-8971). The collection showcases local and California art, including some excellent early 20th-century Impressionist works. (Open Tues.-Sun. 11am-5pm. Admission $5, students and seniors $4, children under 12 free. Docent tours daily at 2pm.)

San Juan Capistrano

The mission of San Juan Capistrano (248-2048) is a half-hour south of Anaheim on I-5. Established by Father Junípero Serra in 1776, this is considered the "jewel of the missions." Though most of the original structure collapsed in the earthquake of 1812, this is the only standing site where Serra himself is known to have said mass, and the oldest building still in use in the state. The crumbling ivy-covered walls of the beautiful **Serra Chapel** are warmed by a 17th-century Spanish cherrywood altar and Native American designs painted on the walls and ceiling. The last Sunday of each month is **Living History Day,** when costumed folk demonstrate leather tooling and the ever-popular adobe making—visitors get to sling mud on sacred ground! (Open daily 8:30am-5pm. Admission $5, seniors $4, ages 3-12 $4. Tours available in Italian, Spanish, and German; call ahead.) The mission is best known as a home to the swallows who return here annually to nest in mid-March. The **San Juan Capistrano Historical Society** is in the **O'Neil Museum,** 31831 Los Rios St. (493-8444), and offers architectural and garden walking tours of the historic adobes lining Los Rios St. (Museum open Tues.-Fri. 9am-noon and 1-4pm, Sun. noon-3pm.)

A brief trip down **Camino Capistrano** leads to **Dana Point,** whose spectacular bluffs were popularized in namesake Richard Henry Dana's *Two Years Before the Mast.* Its rocky shore is great for **tidepooling.** Farther south is **San Onofre State Beach** and its famous "Trestles" area, a prime surf zone. The south end of the beach is frequented by **nudists.** (Drive down as far as you can go, and walk left on the trail for ¼-½mi. There are gay and straight areas.) **Nude bathing** is illegal; you'll be fined if you're caught with your pants down.

SEASONAL EVENTS

Strawberry Festival (638-0981), Memorial Day weekend, in downtown Garden Grove on the village green. Garden Grove is the U.S.'s leading producer of strawberries, and the festival includes some arduous strawberry-pie-eating contests.

Festival of Arts and **The Pageant of the Masters** (800-487-3378), July-Aug., take place together in the Irvine Bowl, 650 Laguna Canyon Rd. in Laguna Beach. Life literally imitates art in the pageant as residents who have rehearsed for months don the makeup and costumes of figures in famous paintings and pose for 90-second tableaux, astonishingly similar to the original artwork. Admission $2, seniors $1. Art show open daily 10am-4pm. Tickets $12-30. For reservations, contact the Festival of Arts, P.O. Box 1659, Laguna Beach, 92652.

Sawdust Festival (494-3030), July-Aug., across the street from The Pageant of the Masters. Arts, crafts, and children's activities a-plenty.

Christmas Boat Parade of Lights (729-4400), the week before Christmas, in Newport Harbor. Over 200 boats and zillions of lights create a dazzling display.

EAST OF L.A.

L.A.'s huddled masses who yearn to be free—and breathe free—oft pack up their kids, cell phones, and cares, and head for the hills. Granite mountains, scenic hiking trails, campgrounds, and scented pine forests repose a mere 45-minute drive above and beyond the inversion layer (the altitude at which the smog ends).

In the mountains, outdoor activities flourish year-round, but winter is definitely the high season. While the Sierra Nevada resorts that cluster around Lake Tahoe and Mammoth Lake are the destination of choice for serious Californian skiers, daytrips to the smaller resorts of the San Bernardino mountains have become increasingly

AROUND LOS ANGELES

popular. Temperatures typically allow ski resorts to operate from November through April. Always call ahead to check conditions and bring tire chains. But even when the snow melts, the coastal mountains are an ideal getaway. The Angeles and San Bernardino National Forests sprawl across majestic mountains, and have many campgrounds, hiking trails, and mountain villages. The driving in these mountains is breathtaking, both in terms of scenery and fear induced by cliffside roads.

■ Angeles National Forest

National forest land covers about a quarter of Los Angeles County, north of Pasadena and east of Valencia. Cradling the northern edge of the L.A. Basin and San Gabriel Valley are the San Gabriel Mountains. The highest peak, **Mt. San Antonio,** or "Old Baldy," tops out at 10,064 snow-capped feet. This area is popular year-round and attracts, in season, mountain bikers, anglers, bird watchers, and hikers. Harsh weather and frequent brush fires often rearrange the place, but ranger-given directions are always helpful. Skiers will probably find Big Bear more worthwhile than the closer resorts at **Mt. Baldy** (818-887-3311) and **Mt. High West** (619-249-5477).

RANGER STATIONS

All ranger stations listed are open Monday through Friday from 8am to 4:30pm (exceptions noted). Three visitors centers offer info about activities and rentals: **Chilao** (818-796-5541) is located on the Angeles Crest Hwy. (Rte. 2), 26 mi. from La Cañada; **Grassy Hollow** is also on Rte. 2, 50 mi. from Wrightwood; **Mt. Baldy** is north of Ontario on Mt. Baldy Rd. In an **emergency,** contact the Angeles National Forest Dispatcher (818-447-8991).

Angeles National Forest Headquarters, Supervisor's Office, 701 N. Santa Anita Ave., Arcadia 91006 (818-574-1613; fax 818-574-5207). Comprehensive forest maps ($4.33), as well as a wide selection of other literature about the area.
Arroyo Seco Ranger District, Oak Grove Park, Flintridge 91011 (818-790-1151). This is the south-central area of the forest, just north of Pasadena. Gateway to the Angeles National Forest via Rte. 2. There are 20 campgrounds in this district.
Mt. Baldy Ranger District, 110 N. Wabash Ave., Glendora 91740 (818-335-1251). The southeastern district of the forest includes several 8000ft. peaks, hiking trails, the cascading San Antonio Falls, and scenic Glendora Ridge Rd.
Saugus Ranger District, 30800 Bouquet Canyon Rd., Saugus 91350 (805-296-9710). Northwest of the main forest. Pyramid, Elizabeth, and Castaic Lakes have boating and fishing facilities. Many campgrounds available.
Tujunga Ranger District, 12371 N. Little Tujunga Canyon Rd., San Fernando 91342 (818-899-1900). Covers the west end of the San Gabriel Mountains. Hiking and horseback-riding trails, and 5 overnight campgrounds. Closed Wed.
Valyermo Ranger District, P.O. Box 15, 29835 Valyermo Rd., Valyermo 93553 (805-944-2187). This district sprawls across the northeastern sector of the San Gabriels. Many campgrounds along Big Pines Hwy., which runs southeast from Pear Blossom into the northeast corner of the forest. Big Pines is the first stop on the earthquake fault tour, a self-guided route passing scars left by major tremors. Closed Wed.

CAMPING

The Forest Service maintains an impressive array of well-groomed hiking trails and camping facilities. Be forewarned that many of the 526 mi. of trails cross each other, so maps are vital. Campsites are a scant $5-12 per night (payment is by the honor system). Sites are first-come, first-camped (14-night max. stay). The National Forest Adventure Pass allows visitors to park near the trails (see p. 130).

Chilao, 25mi. northeast of La Cañada Flintridge off Rte. 2, has broad, flat mountaintop camping. Visitors center and forest amphitheater offer nature walks, talks, and children's activities. All 110 sites have fire rings, tables, water, and toilets, but no hookups. Sites $12.

Buckhorn, 26mi. southwest of Wrightwood on Rte. 2, has 35 sites surrounded by lush ferns and towering redwoods. All have fire rings, tables, water, and toilets, but no hookups. Sites $12. Open April-Nov.

Glen Camp, located at the end of the **West Fork National Bike Trail** (16mi. round-trip), off Rte. 39 north. There is no piped water for the 7 sites. Free.

HIKING

Many of the area's trailheads are at campgrounds. The **West Fork National Bike Trail** (16mi. round-trip), ends at Glen Camp campground off Rte. 39 north. The trail from Buckhorn campground to **Cooper Canyon** (4½mi. round-trip) is one of the prettiest hikes in the forest. A number of longer trails connect to Cooper Canyon, such as the one to **Mt. Waterman** (7mi. round-trip from Buckhorn)— watch for bighorn sheep. The **Chilao to Devil's Canyon Trail** (7mi. round-trip) is accessible from Chilao campground and passes through dense forest on its way to Devil's Canyon. Only experienced hikers should continue beyond the canyon. The 4½ mi. **Rattlesnake Trail** to **Mt. Wilson** departs from the West Fork campground. It has fantastic views of Mt. Wilson, Mt. Baldy, the Channel Islands, and the L.A. Basin, and no, there are no more snakes here than anywhere else. To get there, take Rte. 2 and turn south on Rincon-Red Box Rd. from the Red Box Ranger Station. The beautiful 9 mi. **Vincent Gap to Prairie Fork Trail** departs 53 mi. out of La Cañada Flintridge on Rte. 2, and passes the creepy **Bighorn Mine.**

Longer hikes make **trail camping** necessary. Fortunately, it is free and legal, but fire permits are required (available at ranger stations) and camping is not allowed within 200 ft. of any stream. The three-day, 53 mi. **Gabrielino Trail** connects Oak Grove Park and the north end of Windsor Ave. in La Cañada Flintridge.

Descanso Gardens, 4118 Descanso Dr. (818-952-4400), is in nearby La Cañada, by the intersection of Rte. 2 and 210. The garden includes the world's largest camellia forest, a historic rose collection, and man-made waterfalls (open daily 9am-4:30pm; admission $5, students $3, seniors $3, ages 5-12 $1).

■ Big Bear

Hibernating in the San Bernardino Mountains, the town of **Big Bear Lake** entertains hordes of visitors with winter skiing and summer hiking, biking, and boating. The consistent winds, no doubt made up of the sighs of relaxing Angelenos, make the lake one of the best for sailing in the state.

PRACTICAL INFORMATION AND ORIENTATION

The **Big Bear Chamber of Commerce,** 630 Bartlett Rd., P.O. Box 2860, Big Bear Lake 92315 (909-866-4608; fax 866-5412) dispenses glossy brochures and arranges lodgings and ski packages (open Mon.-Fri. 8am-5pm, Sat.-Sun. 9am-5pm). The **Big Bear Hotline** (866-7000) has info on lodging, local events, and ski and road conditions (open Mon.-Fri. 8am-5pm, Sat.-Sun. 9am-5pm). The **area code** is 909.

To reach Big Bear Lake, take the **San Bernardino Fwy. (I-10)** to the junction of Rte. 30 and 330. Follow **Rte. 330,** also known as Mountain Rd., to **Rte. 18,** a *very* long and winding uphill road. About halfway up the mountain, Rte. 18 becomes Big Bear Blvd., the main route encircling the lake. A less-congested route is via I-10 to Redlands and then **Rte. 38** to Big Bear Lake. Driving time from L.A. is about 2½ hr., barring serious weekend traffic or road closures. The loneliest route to Big Bear Lake curls across the high desert along **Rte. 18** through the Lucerne Valley. Weekend day skiers should wait until after 6pm to head home, thereby avoiding the 4pm rush. **Mountain Area Rapid Transit Authority (MARTA)** (584-1111) runs three buses per day between Big Bear and San Bernardino (2 per day on Sat.). The bus picks up at the Greyhound station in San Bernardino (fare $3.75, seniors and disabled $2.50).

AROUND LOS ANGELES

Buses also run along Big Bear Blvd.; it takes one hour to get from one end to the other (fare $1, students 75¢, seniors and disabled 50¢).

ACCOMMODATIONS

Big Bear has few budget accommodations, especially in the winter. The best option for daytrippers is probably to stay in Redlands or San Bernardino, although the drive down Rte. 18 can be tough at night. **Big Bear Boulevard,** the main drag on the lake's south shore, is lined with lodging possibilities, but groups can find the best deals by sharing a cabin. **Mountain Lodging Unlimited** (800-487-3168), arranges lodging and lift packages (from $46 per person; open Mon.-Sat. 9am-5pm, Sun. 10am-2pm). The **lodging hotline** (866-7000) has up-to-date info. Reservations are always necessary.

Hillcrest Lodge, 40241 Big Bear Blvd. (866-7330, reservations 800-843-4449), is a favorite for honeymooners. Pine paneling and skylights give these cozy rooms a ritzy feel at a budget price. Jacuzzi, cable TV, and free local calls. Small rooms $35-39; 4-person units $79; deluxe suites with hearth and kitchen $57.

Cozy Hollow Lodge, 40409 Big Bear Blvd. (866-9694 or 800-882-4480). Cute gingerbread-style cabins are furnished accordingly. Complimentary breakfast, fireplace, TV, and kitchenette. Rooms $59-99. Discounts available in spring and fall.

Embers Lodge, 40229 Big Bear Blvd. (866-2371). Wood-paneled studios with kitchen, fireplace, TV, and phone sleep 2-4 people ($47-70).

CAMPING

Camping is permitted at U.S. Forest Service sites throughout the area. Several of the grounds listed below accept reservations through MISTIX (800-280-CAMP/2267). Most are open from May to November. Tent campers can avoid crowds by camping outside of designated campgrounds on U.S. Forest Service land, at least 200 ft. from streams and lakes. The new **National Forest Adventure Pass** is required for vehicles, unless there is a site fee (see below). Maps and the necessary fire permit (free) are available at the Big Bear Ranger Station (866-3437), 3 mi. east of Fawnskin on Rte. 38. In **emergencies** call 383-5651.

Pineknot (7000ft.), south of Big Bear on Summit Blvd. Amid thick woods, these 49 sites are surprisingly isolated. Flush toilets and water. Nestled at the base of Snow Summit, this spot is popular with mountain bikers. Sites $15. Wheelchair access.

Hanna Flat (7000ft.), 2mi. northwest of Fawnskin on Forest Rd. 3N14. Lush vegetation surrounds 88 roomy sites. Hiking, water, flush toilets. Sites $15.

Serrano (6800ft.), 1½mi. east of Fawnskin off Rte. 38. One of the most popular campgrounds around because of its hot showers. Within sight of the road, this is city-slicker camping. Hookups at 55 of the 130 sites. Sites $15.

Big Pine Flat (6800ft.), on Forest Rd. 3N14, 7mi. northwest of Fawnskin. Dirt-bikers and other off-roaders favor these 17 sites because of their proximity to an off-highway vehicle area. Sites $10.

Holcomb Valley (7400ft.), 4mi. north on Forest Rd. 2N09 to 3N16, east for ¾mi. For those brave enough to rough it, these 19 sites have pit toilets and no water. Located near Pacific Coast Trail. Sites $10.

FOOD AND DRINK

Food can get pricey, so those with kitchens should forage at **Vons,** 42170 Big Bear Blvd. (866-8459). Many of the cutesy village eateries offer all-you-can-eat specials.

Big Bear Prospectors, 40771 Lakeview Dr. (866-6696), offers the mother of all champagne brunches (Sundays 9am-2pm; $7, under 10 $3). Overlooks the lake. Open Mon.-Sat. 11am-9pm, Sun. 9am-9pm.

Belotti's Pizzeria, 41248 Big Bear Blvd. (866-9686). More bakery than pizzeria, Belotti's is popular among locals for its unbelievable array of pastries. Pizza $7-20, pastry $1.25-2. Open Sun.-Thurs. 7am-10pm, Fri.-Sat. 7am-midnight.

Chad's Place, 40740 Village Dr. (866-2161), has been Big Bear's main party spot since 1915. Skiers and dart board enthusiasts flock here for the 75¢ draft specials. Free pool Wed., live rock Thurs.-Sun. 8:30pm-1:30am. Open daily 11am-2am.

Queen of Siam, 40271 Big Bear Blvd. (866-2863). The best Thai food you'll find at Big Bear. Entrees $5-11. Lunch special ($5) offered Tues.-Fri. 11am-3pm (10% discount for *Let's Go* readers). Open Tues.-Thurs. 11am-9pm, Fri.-Sun. 11am-10pm.

SUMMER RECREATION

The **National Forest Adventure Pass** is required for vehicles brought into the Angeles, Cleveland, Los Padres, and San Bernardino National Forests, though not for vehicles parked at ranger stations, ski resorts, or campgrounds where a fee is charged. Passes can be purchased at ranger stations (day pass $5, one-year pass $30).

The **hiking** here is both free and priceless. Maps, trail descriptions, and the *Visitor's Guide to the San Bernardino National Forest* are available at the Big Bear Ranger Station (866-3437), on Rte. 38 (open daily 8am-4:30pm, closed Sat. in winter). The easy 1½ mi. **Woodland Trail** begins about one mile east of the ranger station and has 20 nature stops along the way. The moderately difficult 3 mi. **Pineknot Trail** begins at the Aspen Glen picnic area. The high altitudes here make slow climbing necessary. Serious hikers may want to catch a piece of the **Pacific Crest Trail,** which extends 2638 mi. from Mexico to Canada and has trail camps every 10 mi. (for more info, see **From Crest to Crest: the Trail of the West,** p. 409). The ranger station can direct hikers to any of the multiple entry points in the area.

Mountain biking is a popular activity in Big Bear when the snow melts. **Snow Summit** (866-5766), operates lifts in summer so thrill-seeking bikers can plummet downhill without the grueling uphill ride ($7 per ride, day pass $19; helmet required). **Team Big Bear** (866-4565), sponsors several organized bike races each summer. (For more info, call April-Oct. daily 9am-5pm, or write Team Big Bear, Box 2932, Big Bear Lake 92315.) Those without wheels of their own can rent them from **Big Bear Bikes,** 41810 Big Bear Blvd. (866-2224; $6 per hr., 8hr. $31). Many summer activities take place on the water. **Fishing** licenses are available at area sporting goods stores (day $10, season $27), and the **Big Bear Fishing Association** (866-6260), cheerfully dispenses info. **Holloway's Marina,** 398 Edgemor Rd. (800-448-5335), on the South Shore, rents **boats** (½ day $39-83). **Thrills Without Spills,** 1350 W. Big Bear Blvd. (585-8585) offers introductory **handgliding** lessons and simulator rides (first ride $10, each additional ride $5; open in summer daily 10am-5pm).

Live out your *Gentle Ben* fantasies at the **Moonridge Animal Park** (866-0130), south of Big Bear Blvd. at the end of Moonridge Rd. This animal care center has the only big bears in Big Bear: **grizzlies.** The little male cub is named Harley, in honor of his sponsors, the Big Bear Hell's Angels (open daily May-Oct. 10am-5pm, Nov. April 10am-4pm; admission $2, ages 3-10 $1). **Magic Mountain Recreation Area,** 800 Wild Rose Ln., west of Big Bear Lake Village, operates an **alpine slide** (one ride $3, 5 rides $12) and **waterslide park** (one ride $1, unlimited rides $10) for summer visitors (open daily 10am-9pm in the summer).

WINTER RECREATION

When conditions are favorable, ski areas sell out of lift tickets quickly. **Tickets** for the resorts listed below may be purchased over the phone through Ticketmaster (213-480-3232 or 714-740-2000). Driving the crowded mountain roads to destinations of choice can challenge both vehicle and driver. Gas stations are scarce on the way up the mountain, and signs notify drivers of tire chain requirements. Call 800-427-7623 for info on road conditions.

Bear Mountain Ski Resort (585-2519), 1½mi. southeast of downtown Big Bear Lake. Twelve lifts cover 195 acres of terrain including huge vertical drops. More expert runs than other area slopes. Lift tickets $40, midweek student (ages 13-23) tickets $30. Skis $17, snowboards $27. New skier/snowboarder packages include group lesson, lift ticket, and equipment rental (weekdays $30, weekends $40).

Snow Summit (866-5766, reservations 909-866-5841), 1mi. east of Big Bear Lake. Eleven lifts including 2 high-speed quads, over 40 runs with a well-rounded assortment of beginner runs, snowmaking, and night skiing. Lift tickets $42. Snowboards $28, skis $16; deposit required.

Snow Valley (867-2751, snow report 867-5151), near Running Springs. 13 lifts, 800 to 5000ft. runs, snowmaking, and night skiing. The most family-oriented resort in Big Bear, with a children's obstacle course and beginner trails. Lift ticket $38 (1-9pm $29), under 13 $23 (1-9pm $17). Equipment rental $14, under 13 $10.

■ San Bernardino

San Bernardino is the kingpin of the mega-county of the same name. More than twice the size of Rhode Island, the county is the largest area-wise in the U.S., but the county seat has no such dreams of grandeur. This somnolent burg is best visited as a stopover en route to Big Bear or the desert beyond.

Practical Information The **San Bernardino Convention and Visitors Bureau,** 201 North E. St., #103 (889-3980), is off the 2nd St. Exit from Rte. 215. The dearth of brochures reflects the area's level of activity, but maps and the *Inland Empire Adventure Guide!* are available (open Mon.-Fri. 8am-5pm). An **ATM** is at the **Bank of America** on North D St., near the courthouse. The **Metrolink** (800-808-LINK/5465) connects L.A. and San Bernardino with 75 trains on five routes (fare $7.50; call Mon.-Fri. 4:30am-10:30pm, Sat.-Sun. 9am-9pm). **MARTA** buses (584-1111), run to Big Bear and Arrowhead. For a taxi, call **Yellow Cab** (884-1111). **San Bernardino Community Hospital,** 1805 Medical Ctr. Drive (887-6333), provides 24hr. emergency care. In an **emergency,** call 911. The **police** are at 384-5742. The **post office** is at 390 W. 5th St. (884-3626), downtown (open Mon.-Fri. 9am-5pm). The **area code** is 909.

Accommodations, Food, and the largest single-purpose nightclub in the U.S. Out-of-towners (that's you) should stick to the north end of town, which is safer than the south. **Motel 6,** 1960 Ostrems Way (887-8191), is at the University Pkwy. Exit off Rte. 215, near the university (singles $30; doubles $34). **Stater Bros.,** 1085 Highland Ave. (886-1517) and 648 W. 4th St. (888-0048), can supply provisions for the long drive ahead (open daily 7am-11pm). **Mitla Cafe,** 602 N. Mt. Vernon Ave. (888-0460), offers cheap but tasty Mexican food. *Grande* combos ($7.50) served to the sounds of Mexican polka music (open Tues.-Thurs. 9am-2:30pm, 4:30-8pm, Fri.-Sun. 9am-9pm). Should you be stuck here for the night, swallow your pride and try line-dancing at **Midnight Rodeo,** 295 E. Caroline St. (824-5444), the largest single-purpose nightclub in the U.S. (Cover $5 Thurs.-Sat. Dance lessons nightly at 7 and 8pm. Open Wed.-Sun. 5pm-2am.)

■ Idyllwild and Nearby Mountains

More idle than wild, Idyllwild is the victim of L.A. over-hype. Like the rest of California, this area has had its share of brush fires, but the town and hiking trails remain untouched. Despite the growing number of visitors, the ornery natives, and the seemingly endless drive along the edge of a precipice, Idyllwild is worth the trouble for avid hikers and campers. Alpine novices and experienced climbers alike will find dozens of trails offering incredible views of the desert and the smoggy city below.

PRACTICAL INFORMATION AND ORIENTATION

Visitor Information:
 Idyllwild Chamber of Commerce, 54295 Village Center Dr. (659-3259; http://www.idylmtn.com/idyllwild), downstairs in the *Town Crier* building across from the Idyllwild Inn. Info and restaurant coupons. Open Mon.-Fri. 10am-5pm.

San Jacinto Ranger District, 54270 Pine Crest (659-2117). Maps of hiking trails and campgrounds ($1-4). Free mandatory wilderness permits for day hiking and overnight backpacking. Open daily 8am-4:30pm; winter Mon.-Sat. 8am-4:30pm.
Mt. San Jacinto State Park and Wilderness Headquarters, 25905 Rte. 243 (659-2607). Mandatory day hiking permits available. Open daily 8am-5pm.
Ski Conditions and Tram Info: (619-325-1391). Tram from Palm Springs to Mt. San Jacinto runs every ½hr. Round-trip fare $17, seniors $12, under 12 $11. Open Mon.-Fri. 10am-9pm, Sat.-Sun. 8am-9pm. Closes 1hr. earlier in winter.
Emergency: 911. **Riverside Mountain Rescue Unit, Inc.** (654-6200). Search and rescue missions for injured or lost hikers in the San Jacinto mountains.
Police: Riverside County Sheriff (800-950-2444); **Banning Sheriff** (849-6744). 24hr.
Post Office: 54391 Village Center Dr. (659-2349), in the Strawberry Creek shopping center. Open Mon.-Fri. 9am-5pm. **ZIP Code:** 92549.
Area Codes: 909; 619 when noted (Mt. San Jacinto marks the dividing line).

From L.A., the swiftest approach is via **I-10** and **Rte. 243** south from Banning. This route is curvy enough to make any traveler's ears pop and stomach drop. From San Diego, there are no major interstates, but there are a number of routes to Palm Springs. Drivers should fill up the gas tank before starting, as gas in Idyllwild is expensive and difficult to find. The Palm Springs Aerial Tramway offers the only **public transportation** to Mt. San Jacinto; from there the town of Idyllwild is accessible by hiking or skiing. (See **Practical Information,** above, or **Palm Springs: Sights and Activities,** p. 178, for more info on the tramway.)

ACCOMMODATIONS

Hiking and camping enthusiasts could stay here for weeks for a pittance, but those who would rather relax on the porch of a cabin will find steep prices unless they're traveling in a group of four or more. **Idyllwild Lodging Information** (659-5520), gives a rundown of the available options. The best bet for a group is **Knotty Pine Cabins,** 54340 Pine Crest Dr. (659-2933), off Rte. 243 north of town in an alpine setting. The eight cabins have wood-panelled interiors, linen, dishes, cooking utensils, and cable TV (2-person cabins $52, weekdays $45; $7 discount for stays of 2 or more weeknights). **Tahouitz Motel,** 25840 Rte. 243 (659-4554), has a pool and spa. Large, cozy rooms have TVs, kitchens, and fireplaces (doubles $45, weekends $55).

CAMPING

Area campsites are operated by the **San Bernardino National Forest, Mt. San Jacinto State Park, San Bernardino County,** and private entrepreneurs. Wilderness maps (75¢) are available at the State Park Headquarters and give a good overview of patchwork jurisdictions. Reservations are available through DESTINET (800-444-7275). U.S. Forest Service grounds tend to be the cheapest and best maintained, while State Park grounds are for hardcore nature lovers. **Dark Canyon,** 6 mi. north of town on Rte. 243, is by far the best campsite in Idyllwild. With water, vault toilets, hiking, and fishing, the 69 sites fill up fast. The other campgrounds in the area, **Fern Basin** and **Marion Mountain,** are worthy backups with comparable size and amenities. **Boulder Basin** is 15 mi. north of Idyllwild off Rte. 243, high on the Black Mountain. The 34 sites offer vault toilets, water, and splendid views of Marion Mountain and surrounding valleys, but the dirt road is difficult in spots and not made for RVs. All sites are $9 per night and are closed from November through April. Reserve through MISTIX (800-280-CAMP/2267) at least five days in advance.

FOOD

Restaurant prices rise with the altitude, so supermarkets are the cheapest option. **Fairway Supermarket** (659-2737), in the Strawberry Creek Square off Village Center Dr., has reasonable prices (open Mon.-Sat. 9am-9pm, Sun. 9am-7pm). The **Squirrel's Nest** (659-3993), on the corner of Rte. 243 and Pinecrest Ave., has sandwiches and burgers, including a $4 cheeseburger special with fries and drink (open Sun.-Thurs. 10am-7pm, Fri.-Sat. 10am-8pm). The **Village Market Deli,** 2600 Rte. 243 (659-3169), has a wide array of sandwiches ($4, daily special $2) and fresh-baked goods that are perfect for taking on long hikes (open daily 8am-10pm).

SIGHTS

Idyllwild's natural setting offers visitors far more than the town itself does. The mountains challenge rock climbers while hundreds of miles of trails lead hikers through tranquil forests. Summer comes slowly; it is customary for over 10 ft. of snow to blanket the mountain peaks above the town in May and even June. The view of the desert and surrounding mountains is amazing, especially where the Santa Rosa/San Jacinto ranges come to a screeching halt and plummet 9000 ft. in under 6 mi. The **Palms-to-Pines Hwy.,** which connects with Rte. 74, offers a driver's-eye view of the transition from desert to mountain. The highway runs 36 mi. between Mountain Center (south of Idyllwild at the junction of Rte. 74 and 243) and Palm Desert.

The **Ernie Maxwell Scenic Trail** (2½mi.), named after the original town crier and guru, makes a gentle loop through the forest for day hikers. This is the only trail that does not require a wilderness permit. More serious backpackers can travel a section of the 2600 mi. **Pacific Crest Trail** (55mi. lie in the San Jacinto District). For more info, see **From Crest to Crest: the Trail of the West,** p. 409. Pick up the trail at Rte. 74 one mile east of Rte. 371 or at Black Mountain's scenic **Fuller Ridge Trail.** Some of the most rewarding and exhausting hikes begin in the canyons owned by Native Americans on the southwest fringe of Palm Springs and climb slowly into the foothills. Routes along the **Devil's Slide Trail** are excellent, but the limited number of permits for this area are given out by the ranger station within 20 minutes of its opening on summer weekends. Those who want peak views without a strenuous hike should try the **Deer Spring Trail** to Suicide Rock (3mi.), which continues to the Palm Springs tram. **Nomad Ventures** (659-4853), gives insider hiking tips, and rangers can direct visitors to other trails including desert and high mountain routes.

Idyllwild ARTS (659-2171), at the end of Toll Gate Rd. off Rte. 243, gives frequent dance, drama, and music performances ($5-8), exhibitions, and workshops. The emphasis is on Native American arts and crafts. Call 800-886-3443 for info on the August **Jazz in the Pines** festival ($20-25).

NORTH OF L.A.

At least overcrowded L.A. had the good sense not to develop northward. Today, government legislation ensures a profusion of prime hiking and camping in this vast expanse of protected parkland. The unspoiled coastline, chaparral, and rolling hills stretch from the Santa Monica mountains up to the southern end of the Central Coast, displaying some of the most spectacular scenery California has to offer.

■ Santa Monica National Recreation Area

"Recreation area" is a suitably vague term for the massive amalgamation of private and public lands that constitutes the Santa Monica National Recreation Area. Though the park is under both state and national jurisdiction, the best place for the nature-lover to gather information is at the **National Park Service Headquarters,** 30401 Agoura Rd. (818-597-9192, ext. 201; open Mon.-Fri. 8am-5pm, Sat.-Sun. 9am-5pm), in Agoura Hills, off the Reyes Adobe Exit on U.S. 101.

The National Park Service administers only the **Happy Hollow Family Walk-In** campgrounds at the **Circle X** site. The tent-only sites ($6) are first-come, first-camped, and are usually uncrowded (chemical toilets, no wood fires). On summer weekends, though, it is wise to arrive before noon to ensure yourself a spot. For group reservations (818-597-91992, ext. 201), the fee is $2 per person per night. Take the PCH to Yerba Buena Rd., then go north about 5 mi. to the **ranger station** on the right. Nearby are three state campsites: **Leo Carrillo** and **Pt. Mugu** cost $3-16, and **Malibu Creek** (see **Accommodations,** p. 75) costs $14. Reserve through DESTINET (800-444-7275). Backcountry camping is only permitted at **Topanga State Park** ($3).

These hills sport more than 50 **hiking trails** of widely varying difficulty, so ask a ranger for advice before heading out. The excellent guide book, *Hike Los Angeles, Vol. 1* (sold in the ranger station), includes a couple of the most popular walks in the park, with relevant info about the area's ecology and history. If **Malibu Creek** looks vaguely like the set of *M*A*S*H,* that's because it was. Much of the set was dismantled after the show's shooting ended in 1982, more of it was destroyed in subsequent fires, but an easy 1½ mi. hike from the Crags Rd. trailhead leads to the remaining jeep and ambulance, and the **flat area** above the bank that was the helipad. Die-hard outdoor enthusiasts might want to taste the pain of the **Backbone Trail,** a 70 mi., five-day journey from Pt. Mugu to Sunset Blvd. in the Pacific Palisades. Not all sections of the trail have been completed, so consult a ranger first.

The National Park Service also administers the **Paramount Ranch Site,** which was used as a location for several Paramount films between 1927 and 1953. Director Cecil B. DeMille and actors Gary Cooper and Mae West all worked here at a time when filmmakers were first experimenting with turning nearby landscapes into distant locales. The ranch served as colonial Massachusetts in *The Maid of Salem,* ancient China in *The Adventures of Marco Polo,* and early San Francisco in *Wells Fargo.* After purchasing the property in 1980, the National Park Service revitalized the old movie set, and **Western Town** is now used as the set for television's *Dr. Quinn, Medicine Woman.* The set is open to visitors (and popular with *Quinn* groupies) during the filming season (Sept.-June). Call the Dr. Quinn Info Line (818-597-1992, ext. 551) for details. To reach the ranch, take U.S. 101 to Agoura Hills. Exit at Kanan, travel south ¾ mi., turn left on Cornell, and continue 2½ mi. to the entrance on the right.

AROUND LOS ANGELES

San Diego

San Diegans are fond of referring to their garden-like town as "American's Finest City." Even the stodgiest members of the East Coast establishment would find this claim difficult to dispute—San Diego has all the virtues of other California cities without their frequently-cited drawbacks. No smog fills this city's air, no sewage spoils its silverly seashores, and no civic conflict flares in its lily-white, elderly population. Its zoo is the nation's best, its food and lodging prices are fractions of their L.A. counterparts, and its city center contains a greater concentration of museums than any spot in America save Washington, D.C.

The seafaring Spanish also thought this was a pretty nifty place, when they prolonged an onshore foray in 1769 and founded the first permanent settlement in the present-day United States. Despite this early start, San Diego remained a small town throughout the California population boom of the early 20th century—it didn't even become a city proper until the 1940s. When it became the headquarters of the U.S. Pacific Fleet following the Pearl Harbor attack, however, its population exploded. Even today, San Diego is home to more sailors than anyone could possibly take on in a single night—11 naval bases dot the area, and parts of the city's skyline are composed of hulking superstructures atop aircraft carriers and cruisers.

More peaceful days have settled on San Diego, and the military no longer dominates—the Kmart standing across the street from the Chief Office of Naval Operations is just one symbol among many that other industries are starting to catch up with the military here. This is the country's sixth-largest city (pop. 2,700,000) and one of its fastest growing, as immigrants flock to its cheery climes and dilute the area's staunch conservatism.

■ Practical Information

Visitor Information: International Visitor Information Center, 11 Horton Plaza (236-1212), downtown at 1st and F St. Multilingual staff dispenses publications, brochures, and discount coupons. 3hr. parking validation. Open Mon.-Sat. 8:30am-5pm; in summer also Sun. 11am-5pm. **Old Town and State Park Info,** 4002 Wallace Ave. (220-5422), in Old Town Sq. Take the Taylor St. Exit off I-8 or bus #5. Free walking tour leaves daily at 2pm. Open daily 10am-5pm.

Budget Travel: San Diego Council of American Youth Hostels, 521 Market St. (338-9981), in the Metropolitan Hostel at 5th St. Free budget guides.

American Express: Locations at 7610 Hazard Center Dr. (297-8101), 258 Broadway (234-4455); 1020 Prospect (459-4161), in La Jolla.

Airport: San Diego International (Lindbergh Field), at the northwest edge of downtown. Bus #2 goes downtown ($1.50), and so do cabs ($7).

Trains: Amtrak Santa Fe Depot, 1050 Kettner Blvd. (239-9021 or 800-872-7245), at Broadway. To L.A. (8 per day Mon.-Fri., $20). Station has info on bus, trolley, car, and boat transportation (ticket office open 5:40am-9pm, and 10-10:20pm).

Buses: Greyhound, 120 W. Broadway (239-8082 or 800-668-9231), at 1st. To L.A. ($11). Ticket office open 24hr.

Auto Repairs: AAA Emergency Road Service (800-400-4222).

Community Centers:

   Senior Citizens Services, 202 C St. (236-6905), in the City Hall Bldg. Provides senior ID cards and plans daytrips. Open Mon.-Fri. 8am-5pm.

   The Access Center, 1295 University Ave., #10 (293-3500, TDD 293-7757), Hillcrest. Attendant referral, wheelchair repair and sales, emergency housing, motel/hotel accessibility referral. Open Mon.-Fri. 9am-5pm. **Accessible San Diego,** 2466 Bartel St. (279-0704), also has info (open daily 10am-4pm).

   Women's Center, 2467 E St. (233-8984). Offers rape and domestic violence counseling and legal services. Open Mon.-Fri. 8am-4:30pm.

   Bi-Gay-Lesbian Organizations: Lesbian and Gay Men's Center, 3916 Normal St. (692-2077), provides counseling and info. Open daily 9am-10pm. The **Gay Youth**

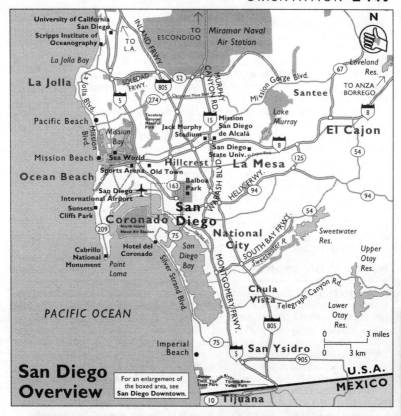

San Diego
Overview

For an enlargement of
the boxed area, see
San Diego Downtown.

SAN DIEGO

Alliance (233-9309), is a support and social group for people under 24. For a listing of queer events and establishments, check *Update* (299-0500), available at virtually all queer businesses, bookstores, and bars. The *Gay and Lesbian Times,* released Thurs., provides event, bar, and club listings.

Ticket Agency: Ticketmaster (concert info 581-1000 or 226-7866; jazz info 454-4981; tickets 220-8497). Beware of the high service charge.

Laundromat: Teri's Cleaners, 500 W. Broadway (239-0820), in the YMCA building. Wash $1, 12min. dry 25¢. Open Mon.-Fri. 7am-6pm, Sat. 8am-5pm.

Weather Conditions: Weather Report (221-8884). Updated daily, as if the weather ever changes. Daytime highs around 70, nighttime lows 60.

Crisis Lines: Crime Victims (688-9200). 24hr. **Lesbian and Gay Men's Center Crisis Line** (692-4297). Open Mon.-Sat. 6am-10pm. **Women's Center Rape Hotline** (233-3088). 24hr.

24-Hour Pharmacy: Thrifty Drugs, 535 Robinson Ave. (291-3705).

Emergency: 911.

Police: (531-2000).

Post Office: Main Branch, 2535 Midway Dr. (674-0000). Take bus #6, 9, or 35. Open Mon.-Fri. 7am-1am, Sat. 8am-4pm. **ZIP Code:** 92138.

Area Code: (619). This number can be called upside-down.

■ Getting Around

ORIENTATION

San Diego rests in the extreme southwest corner of California, 127 mi. south of L.A. and 15 mi. north of Mexico. Three major freeways link the city to its regional neighbors: **I-5** runs south from L.A. and skirts the eastern edge of downtown; **I-15** runs northeast to Nevada; and **I-8** runs east-west along downtown's northern boundary, connecting the desert with Ocean Beach. The major downtown thoroughfare, **Broadway,** also runs east-west. **Bus** and **train** stations sit on the western end of Broadway in reasonably safe areas. The downtown hotels listed below lie east and north of these stations in areas that are safer still, but exercise caution when walking downtown, as the area attracts aggressive panhandlers.

The most obvious landmark in San Diego is **Balboa Park,** home to many museums and to the justly heralded San Diego Zoo. The cosmopolitan **Hillcrest** and **University Heights** districts, both centers of the gay community, border the park to the northeast. Southeast of the park lies the city's downtown business district, where San Diegans take time out from their busy relaxation schedules to put in a few hours at the office. South of downtown, between 4th and 6th St., is the newly revitalized **Gaslamp District,** full of nightclubs, chic restaurants, and coffeehouses.

The downtown area is situated between San Diego's two major bays: **San Diego Bay,** formed by **Coronado Island,** lies just to the south, while **Mission Bay,** formed by the **Mission Beach** spit, lies to the northwest. Up the coast from Mission Beach are the communities of **Ocean Beach, Pacific Beach,** and wealthy **La Jolla.** Still further north lie the cities and sights of San Diego's **North County** (see p. 159).

PUBLIC TRANSPORTATION

Unlike its sprawling northern neighbor, San Diego has a fairly well-developed system of public transportation. Info on San Diego's buses, trains, and trolleys can best be obtained from the **Transit Store** (234-1060 or 233-3004), at 1st and Broadway, which has bus, trolley, and ferry tickets and timetables, as well as the free pamphlet *How to Ride* (open Mon.-Fri. 8am-5:30pm, Sat.-Sun. noon-4pm). The **Public Transit Information Line** (233-3004), is also a good source, though it can be difficult to get through (open Mon.-Fri. 5:30am-8:30pm, Sat.-Sun. 8am-5pm). **Buses** cost $1.50 for local routes and $1.75-2 for express buses (the route number ends with a zero). They require exact fare, but accept dollar bills (free transfer for 1½ hr.). All buses are wheelchair accessible. If getting to a bus stop presents a problem, call the door-to-bus-stop service **DART** (293-3278; applies only to certain areas). The **Coaster buses** (233-3004), glide in from Oceanside (fare $1.60-3.25).

The bright red **San Diego Trolley** (233-3004), consists of two lines leaving from downtown for El Cajon, San Ysidro, and points in between. The El Cajon line leaves from 12th and Imperial; the San Ysidro line leaves from the Old Town Transit Center and continues to the Mexican border. It is wise to buy a ticket; although there are no turnstiles, the inspector does indeed check and the fine is most definitely not within reach of the budget traveler (run daily 5am-1am; fare $1-1.75).

If you plan to use public transit extensively, buy the **Day Tripper** ($5; available on trolleys and buses), which allows unlimited rides on buses, ferries (such as the one to Coronado), and trollies for one day. The four-day pass ($15) can be purchased at the Transit Store and is good only for consecutive days.

Various tour buses and trolley-shaped vans carry tourists around San Diego. **Old Town Trolley Tours** (298-8687), allows travelers to stop and sightsee before reboarding (daily every ½hr. 9am-5pm; fare $17, ages 6-12 $8).

CARS

Southern California is the land of the automobile; renting a car will make your life easier and your trip more enjoyable. Most places will not rent to drivers under 21, but do not lose hope; a letter from your insurer, stating that you are covered for rental car crashes, should go a long way toward assuaging companies' fears.

Bargain Auto, 3860 Rosecrans St. (299-0009). A rare find which actually rents to 18-year-olds. Cars $17-29 per day, $95-185 per week; 150 free mi. per day, 500 per week. Ages 18-21 pay $8 per day surcharge, ages 21-25 pay $4 per day. Mexican insurance $10 per day. Credit card required. Open daily 8am-6pm.

Aztec, 2401 Pacific Hwy. (232-6117 or 800-231-0400). Cars $22-50 per day with 150 free mi. (in California only). Must be 21 with major credit card. With purchase of Mexican insurance ($16 per day), cars can venture as far as Ensenada, Mexico (80mi.). Open Mon.-Fri. 7am-7pm, Sat.-Sun. 8am-5pm.

Dollar, 2499 Pacific Hwy. (234-3388). Cars $28-54 per day with unlimited age. Must be 21 with major credit card; ages 21-25 pay $15 per day surcharge. Can travel as far as Mexican border. Open daily 5:30am-midnight.

BICYCLES

San Diego has an extensive system of fairly easy **bike routes.** Some are separate from the road, some are specially marked outer lanes, and some must be made up as you go along. The flat, paved route along Mission Beach and Pacific Beaches toward La Jolla affords ocean views and soothing sea breezes. But bikers beware: pedestrian traffic along the beaches rivals the automobile blockades on the boulevards.

Buses equipped with bike carriers make it possible to cart bikes almost anywhere in the city (call 233-3004 to find out which routes have carriers), and bikes are also allowed on the San Diego Trolley with a $4 permit (available at **Transit Store**). For more bike info, contact the City Bicycle Coordinator (533-3110), or **CalTrans,** 4040 Taylor St., San Diego 92110 (231-2453), in Old Town. Write to request maps and pamphlets, including the free *San Diego County Bike Route Map.*

WALKING

Downtown, Balboa Park, and Old Town are easily handled on foot, but beaches are less accessible because of the wide distances between them. **Walkabout International,** 835 5th Ave., #407 (231-7463), sponsors about 150 walks each month, ranging from downtown architectural walks to 20 mi. treks to La Jolla (open Mon.-Fri. 9:30am-2:30pm; expect an answering machine). San Diegans worship the god of the walk signal, perhaps in part because of some obedience gene, but more likely because jaywalking is actively prosecuted here.

■ Accommodations

San Diego's tourist traffic and room rates skyrocket during the summer months, particularly on weekends. Reservations can save you disappointment, and weekly rates (offered at many area residential hotels and hostels) can save you dollars. Accommodations here are still a bargain—$35 rooms in San Diego are comparable to $60 rooms in L.A. Those with cars can find bargains and bliss by camping on the beaches outside of the city (see **Camping,** p. 148), and those without can use the buses that pass most downtown hotels.

DOWNTOWN

San Diego Metropolitan (HI-AYH), 521 Market St. (525-1531), at 5th, in the heart of the Gaslamp. Quiet and impeccable hostel is near San Diego's most popular attractions and clubs. Airy common room, communal bathrooms, laundry room, and lockers (bring a lock). No curfew. Dorms (4-6 beds) $16-18; doubles $36; nonmembers $3 more. IBN reservations available. Desk open 7am-midnight

Grand Pacific Hostel, 437 5th Ave. (232-3100 or 800-GET-TO-CA/438-8622), between G and F St. in the Gaslamp. Guests relax around a central staircase. Free linens, breakfast, and shuttle to nearby sights. Coin-op laundry. Tijuana tours $10. Clean and spacious dorms $12-16; doubles $30.

J Street Inn, 222 J St. (696-6922; fax 696-1295), near San Diego's Convention Center and ritzy waterfront. All 221 fabulous studio rooms have cable TV, microwave, fridge, and bath. Gym and reading room. Singles $35; each additional person $10. Weekly and monthly rates available. Enclosed parking $5 per day, $16 per week.

Downtown Hostel at Baltic Inn, 521 6th Ave. (237-0687). Clean rooms with toilet, sink, microwave, mini-fridge, cable TV. Communal showers. No curfew, 24hr. security. Laundry. Singles $20; doubles $28. Weekly: $75-115. Key deposit $10.

Corinthian Suites Hotel, 1840 4th Ave. (236-1600; fax 231-4734), at Elm, 2 blocks from Balboa Park. Brand-new hotel near zoo and museums has laundry facilities and cable TV. Rooms with fridge, bar, sink, and microwave. Singles $35-45, weekly $150. Security deposit $15, weekly $65.

OLD TOWN

Old Town Inn, 4444 Pacific Hwy. (260-8024 or 800-225-9610; fax 296-0524), 10min. walk from Old Town, closer to the I-5 than the ocean. Some rooms have kitchenettes; continental breakfast included. For an even Older Town experience, ask to stay in the old building. Check-out 11am. Singles $40; doubles $60. Weekly rates (fall only) start at $197.

Travelodge (297-2271; fax 542-1510), beside I-8. Pool and plenty of no-nonsense rooms. Singles $55, off-season $40.

THE COAST

Banana Bungalow, 707 Reed Ave. (273-3060 or 800-5-HOSTEL/546-7835, reservations 888-2-GO-BANANAS/246-2262), just off of Mission Blvd. in Mission Beach. Take bus #34 to Mission and Reed. Popular hostel offers lots of amenities: common room with cable TV, beachside location, free breakfast, and shuttles to L.A. ($14), Mexico ($49), and Las Vegas/Grand Canyon ($190). No curfew. Check-out 10am. Dorms $14-18; doubles $45 (available in winter only). Linens included. **Must have an international passport.** Call in advance.

Ocean Beach International (OBI), 4961 Newport Ave. (223-SURF/7873 or 800-339-SAND/7263), Ocean Beach—look for high-flying international flags. One of San Diego's newest hostels, the OBI features cable TV, kitchen, and laundry, all near the beach. Free Friday night BBQ and keg parties, free pasta on Tues. Free pick-up from airport, train, and bus terminals. Dorms $16; private rooms with bath $18. **Proof of international travel required.**

HI-Elliott (HI-AYH), 3790 Udall St. (223-4778), Point Loma, 1½mi. from Ocean Beach. Take bus #35 from downtown to the first stop on Voltaire. If driving, head west on Sea World Dr. from I-5 and bear right on Sunset Cliff Blvd. Take a left on Voltaire and a right on Worden. Udall is 1 block away—look for the hostel sign painted on a blue church. Large kitchen, patio, and common room with TV. Bike rental $10 per day. Office open 8-10pm. Check-out 10:30am. No curfew. 7-night max. stay. Dorms $12, nonmembers $15. Reserve 2 days in advance.

Western Shore Motel, 4345 Mission Bay Dr. (273-1121), off Grand Ave. Exit from I-5. Take bus #30. High-ceilinged rooms with A/C and TV are 2mi. from beach, ½mi. from bay. Singles $33; doubles $34. Rates lower in winter. If paying in advance, 7th night is free. Reservations recommended.

Super 8 Mission Bay, 4540 Mission Bay Dr. (274-7888), off Grand Ave. Exit from I-5. Great location 5min. from beach. Pool, free movies, and cable TV. Free airport pick-up. Singles $49-58; doubles $54-63.

■ Camping

Camping outside of San Diego is an attractive and cheap alternative for travelers with cars. Sites fill up in summer, so reserve through DESTINET (800-444-7275).

South Carlsbad Beach State Park (438-3143), off Rte. 21 near Leucadia, in north San Diego County. Half of the 226 sites are for tents. On cliffs over the sea. Showers, laundry facilities. No hiking trails. Oceanfront sites $22, weekends $23.

San Elijo Beach State Park (753-5091), Rte. 21 south of Cardiff-by-the-Sea. 271 sites (150 for tents) in a setting similar to that at South Carlsbad to the north. Strategic landscaping gives a secluded feel. Hiker/biker campsites available, but no hiking or biking trails. Laundry and showers. Oceanfront sites $22; inland $17.

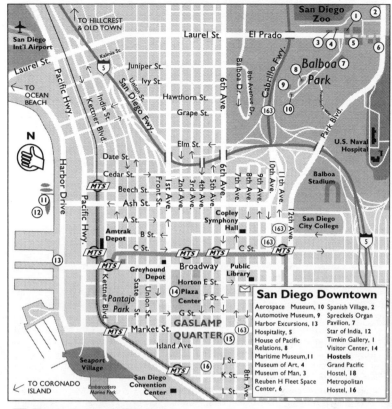

San Diego Downtown

Aerospace Museum, 10
Automotive Museum, 9
Harbor Excursions, 13
Hospitality, 5
House of Pacific
Relations, 8
Maritime Museum,11
Museum of Art, 4
Museum of Man, 3
Reuben H Fleet Space
Center, 6

Spanish Village, 2
Spreckels Organ
Pavilion, 7
Star of India, 12
Timkin Gallery, 1
Visitor Center, 14
Hostels
Grand Pacific
Hostel, 18
Metropolitan
Hostel, 16

■ Food and Sights

Although San Diego's growth as a city has been a relatively recent phenomenon, the character of its inland neighborhoods reflects its pride in its past. Lurking below San Diego's downtown skyscrapers are the pre-1910 commercial buildings of the **Gaslamp Quarter,** now being resurrected as upscale shops, restaurants, and clubs. Not far away is **Old Town,** home to many Spanish colonial buildings and the self-proclaimed "birthplace of California," and **Balboa Park,** where museums surround the San Diego Zoo. California's first city—like its own trendy Gaslamp quarter—is a place where past and future are growing into something new.

DOWNTOWN

San Diego's downtown attractions are concentrated in the corridor that includes its business, Gaslamp, and waterfront districts, all teeming testaments to San Diego's continuing renaissance. Within this center of commerce and entertainment can be found the city's skyscrapers, its ultra-modern convention center (which played host to the 1996 Republican National Convention), and its newest nexus of nightlife hot spots. Travelers should be careful outside of this corridor, however, as the immediately neighboring areas are not as safe.

Food

The demands of the lunchtime business crowd have spawned a horde of downtown eateries, almost all of which specialize in cheap, but well-made, meals. Unfortunately, as the work day dwindles, so do the area's open doors—dinner can be hard to find. The selection at **Horton's Plaza's** food court goes beyond the standard panoply of junk food. Good restaurants also cluster along C St., Broadway, and in the Gaslamp.

> **El Indio Mexican Restaurant,** 409 F St. (239-8151). Just damn good food at damn good prices. Combo plates $4, burritos $3. The $6 lunch buffet on Fri. may be enough to stave off hunger for a week. Open Mon.-Sat. 11am-8pm.
>
> **Karl Strauss' Old Columbia Brewery and Grill,** 1157 Columbia St. (234-2739). San Diego's first microbrewery and the local favorite for power lunches. BBQ ribs and linguini $10, lighter fare $6-8. Open Mon.-Thurs. 11:30am-midnight, Fri.-Sat. 11:30am-1am, Sun. 11:30am-10pm.
>
> **Sammy's California Woodfired Pizza,** 770 4th Ave. (230-8888). Upscale pizza joint offers 22 gourmet pizzas ($8-10) that have been called the best in SoCal. Huge salads ($5-10). Open Mon.-Thurs. 11:30am-10pm, Fri.-Sat. 11:30am-11pm.
>
> **Royal Thai Cuisine,** 465 5th St. (230-THAI/8424). Nouveau Thai cuisine with a "healthy dining" menu (entrees $7-8). Open Mon.-Wed. 11am-3pm and 5-10pm, Thurs. 5-10pm, Fri.-Sun. noon-3pm and 5pm-midnight.

Sights

The jewel of San Diego's redevelopment efforts is **Horton Plaza,** at Broadway and 4th. This pastel-hued urban confection is an open-air, multi-level shopping center covering seven blocks. Three blocks west of Horton Plaza lies the **Santa Fe Amtrak Depot,** 1050 Kettner Blvd., a masterpiece of Mission Revival architecture whose arches welcomed visitors to the 1915 Panama California Exposition. On weekdays, Broadway bustles with professionals and panhandlers, but when the workday ends, only the latter remain.

To the south of Horton Plaza is the historic **Gaslamp Quarter,** which is comprised of antique shops, Victorian buildings, and trendy restaurants. Formerly the city's red-light district and home to the original **Pappy's, Inc.** adult bookstore, the area's new bars and bistros have grown popular with upscale after-hours revelers (see **Nightlife,** p. 157). By day, the area's charm lies in its history. The **Gaslamp Quarter Foundation,** William Heath Davis House, 410 Island Ave. (233-4692), offers guided walking tours (Sat. 11am.; 90min.; tickets $5, students $3, seniors $3, ages 12-18 $3, under 12 free). Self-guided audio tours are narrated by "Wyatt Earp" himself, the legendary lawman whose spirit is said to stalk the halls of the luxurious **Horton Grand Hotel,** 311 Island Ave. (800-542-1886), along with the phantom of Babe Ruth.

Moored windjammers, cruise ships, and the occasional naval destroyer face the boardwalk shops and museums along the **Embarcadero** (Spanish for "dock"). The military and merchant marine vessels anchored here, as well as the distantly visible North Island Naval Air Station, the Point Loma Submarine Base, and the South Bay's mothballed fleet, serve as constant reminders of the U.S. Navy's prominent presence in San Diego. Afternoon tours of most naval crafts are free. Visitors can also tour the magnificently restored 1863 sailing vessel *Star of India,* which is docked in front of the **Maritime Museum,** 1306 N. Harbor Dr. (234-9153; http://www.sdmarine.com). The ship is open daily from 9am to 9pm (admission $5, seniors $4, ages 13-17 $4, ages 6-12 $2). Along the harbor to the south, kitschy **Seaport Village** (235-4014), houses shingled boutiques, ice cream shops, and a century-old carousel (village open daily 10am-10pm, off-season 10am-9pm; carousel rides $1).

BALBOA PARK AND THE SAN DIEGO ZOO

Balboa Park was the creation of pioneering horticulturists whose plantings transformed a once-treeless pueblo tract into a botanical montage. The park's first seedlings were planted in 1889, when San Diego was a town of about 3000. Today, the redwood trees tower over climbing roses and water lilies at the center of a teeming city. Balboa Park is known for its concerts, cultural events, lush vegetation, and most of all for the fabulous San Diego Zoo. The park is accessible by bus #7. Parking is free in museum and zoo lots; posted signs warn park-goers against scam artists who attempt to wheedle lot fees from the unsuspecting. Tuesday is the best day to visit the park, as the museums offer free admission on a rotating basis.

Food

The best food near Balboa Park is north and west in nearby Hillcrest, Mission Hills, and University Heights. These districts are so trendy that "Happy Hour" is as likely to mean cheap espresso as cheap *mai tais*. Affordable eateries line the roads and a number of restaurants offer dinner specials for two.

The Golden Dragon, 414 University Ave. (296-4119; delivery 275-7500), Hillcrest. Where Marilyn Monroe and Frank Sinatra ate when in town. Eclectic menu offers over a hundred dishes (many vegetarian) for $6-9. Open daily 4:30pm-3am.

Kansas City Barbecue, 610 W. Market St. (231-9680). No fewer than 8 signs at this popular BBQ joint proclaim that *Top Gun*'s sleazy bar scene was shot here. Giant lunches and dinners ($4-9) more than make up for the constant jukebox strains of "You've Lost that Lovin' Feeling." Open daily 11am-1am.

Corvette Diner Bar & Grill, 3946 5th Ave. (542-1476). A real Corvette and booming oldies complete the pseudo-50s decor. Old-fashioned shakes $3. Serves burgers and fries 'cause it's a diner, veggie sandwiches 'cause it's Hillcrest. Open Sun.-Thurs. 11am-11pm, Fri.-Sat. 11am-midnight.

City Delicatessen, 535 University Ave. (295-2747). New York-style deli has huge selection, pink tables, jukebox, and that sticky vinyl that gets really uncomfortable in the summer. Breakfast specials ($2-3) are served all day. Open Sun.-Thurs. 7am-midnight, Fri.-Sat. 7am-2am.

The Vegetarian Zone, 2949 5th Ave. (298-7302). The motto in this carnivore-unfriendly zone is that "the human body doesn't require any form of meat to operate optimally." Just nod your head and chow down on optimal food like the soups ($4) and flaky Greek spinach pie ($9). Open Mon.-Thurs. 11:30am-9pm, Fri. 11:30am-10pm, Sat. 8:30am-10pm.

San Diego Zoo

With over 100 acres of exquisite fenceless habitats, the **San Diego Zoo** (234-3153; http://www.sandiegozoo.org), well deserves its reputation as one of the finest in the world. Its unique "bioclimatic" exhibits group animals and plants together by habitat. For example, the **Polar Bear Plunge** contains polar bears, Siberian reindeer, and arctic foxes that fish and frolic tundra-style beside their own chilled, Olympic-size pool.

The most thorough way to tour the zoo is on foot, but those limited by time or crippled by laziness should consider the 40-minute open-air **double-decker bus tour,** which covers 80% of the park. (Tickets $4, ages 3-11 $3. Sit on the left.) Young *Homo sapiens* can watch the hatching and feeding of other animal kingdom toddlers in the **children's petting zoo** (free). The **Skyfari Aerial Tramway** rises 170 ft. above the park (one-way $1). The ride lasts about two minutes—at about 1¢ per second, it's hardly worth it. Most of the zoo is wheelchair accessible (wheelchairs can be rented), but steep hills make assistance necessary. (Entrance open daily 9am-9pm, off-season 9am-6pm. Admission $13, ages 3-11 $6, military in uniform free, of course. Group rates available. Free on Founder's Day, the second Monday in Oct.)

Balboa Park and the El Prado Museums

Though they may not be Smithsonian-quality, **Balboa Park** has the greatest concentration of museums in the U.S. outside of Washington, D.C. Most of them reside within the resplendent Spanish colonial-style buildings which line **El Prado,** a street running west to east through the Park's central **Plaza de Panama.** These ornate structures—designed for the Panama California Exposition of 1915-16 and for the International Expositions of 1935-36—were originally intended to last two years. Since many of the buildings are now going on 80, they are being renovated, this time with a more permanent construction.

While the **House of Hospitality** is being rebuilt, the **park visitors center** (239-0512) operates out of a temporary location in front of the Museum of Art. The center sells simple park maps (a well-spent $1), and the **Passport to Balboa Park,** containing coupons for a week's worth of entry to all of the park's museums ($19). Passports are also available at participating museums (center open daily 9am-4pm).

The star of the western axis of the Plaza de Panama is the California State Building, now the **Museum of Man** (239-2001). Its much-photographed tower and dome gleam with Spanish mosaic tiles, while inside human evolution is traced with exhibits on primates and early man. (Open daily 10am-4:30pm. Admission $4, ages 13-18 $2, ages 6-12 $1, military in uniform free; free 3rd Tues. of each month.)

Behind the Museum of Man is the **Old Globe Theater**, the oldest professional theater in California. Classical and contemporary plays are performed here at the adjoining **Lowell Davies Outdoor Theatre** (Tues.-Sun. evenings and weekend matinees). Tickets for both stages can be purchased at the box office (239-2255; tickets around $30). Passing jets occasionally cause the actors to freeze mid-soliloquy and wait for the engine roar to subside before resuming—alas, poor Yorick. Screaming turbines scarcely affect the action at the nearby **Spreckels Organ Pavilion** (226-0819); the racket created by its resonant resident—the world's largest outdoor musical instrument—can be heard for miles around (free performances Sun. 2pm and Mon. 8pm; in winter Sun. only).

Across the Plaza de Panama is the **San Diego Museum of Art** (232-7931), whose collection ranges from ancient Asian to contemporary Californian works. (Open Tues.-Sun. 10am-4:30pm. Admission $7, seniors $5, military with ID $4, ages 6-17 $2, under 5 free. Free 3rd Tues. of each month.) Nearby is the outdoor **Sculpture Garden Court** (696-1990), where a sensuous Henry Moore piece presides over other large abstract blocks. The **Timken Art Gallery,** 1500 El Prado (239-5548), next door, houses several superb portraits by Rubens and a collection of Russian church icons (open Oct.-Aug. Tues.-Sat. 10am-4:30pm, Sun 1:30-4:30pm; free).

Farther east along the plaza stands the **Botanical Building** (234-8901), a wooden structure filled with the scent of jasmine and the murmur of fountains (open Fri.-Wed. 10am-4pm; free). The horticulturally inclined can meet here Saturdays at 10am for a free botanist-led tour of the park (call 235-1121 for more info). The **Desert and Rose Gardens,** 2200 Park Blvd. (235-1100), offer a strange contrast between the two types of flora. What a difference a rain makes.

The **Casa de Balboa,** a recent reconstruction of the 1915 Electricity Building, contains four distinct museums. The **Museum of Photographic Arts** (239-5262), presents exhibits that rotate every two months (open daily 10am-5pm; admission $3.50, under 12 free; free 2nd Tues. of each month). The **San Diego Hall of Champions** (234-2544), is a slick sports museum complete with Astroturf carpeting. Only a glass pane (thankfully scent-proof) separates you from jerseys and shoes worn by Ted Williams and Bill Walton. (Open daily 10am-4:30pm. Admission $3, seniors $2, military with ID $2, ages 6-17 $1, under 6 free. Free 2nd Tues. of each month.) Elsewhere in the building are the **Research Archives** and the **Museum of San Diego History** (232-6203; open Wed.-Sun. 10am-4:30pm; admission $4, seniors $3, military with ID $3, children 5-12 $1.50; free 2nd Tues. of each month). Downstairs, hobbyists preside over their toys in the **San Diego Model Railroad Museum** (696-0199; open Tues.-Fri. 11am-4pm, Sat.-Sun. 11am-5pm; admission $3, seniors $2.50, military $2.50, students $2.50, under 15 free; free 1st Tues. of each month).

From the end of El Prado St. (which is closed to cars), a left onto Village Place St. will take you to **Spanish Village** (233-9050), a colony of 250 artists at work in 36 studios. Towering ominously over the village is the Moreton Bay **fig tree,** which spreads its limbs 63 ft. up and over helpless tourists below. At the east end of El Prado lies the **Natural History Museum** (232-3821), where life-size robotic dinosaurs enhance the standard fossils, and a recreated mine displays gems. (Open Fri.-Wed. 9:30am-5:30pm, Thurs. 9:30am-6:30pm. Admission $6, seniors $5, military $5, ages 6-17 $3; free 1st Tues. of each month; half-price Thurs. 4:30-6:30pm.) Across El Prado from the Natural History Museum is the **Reuben H. Fleet Space Theater and**

Science Center (238-1233; reservations 232-6860), which houses an **Omnimax** projector, 153 speakers, and a hemispheric planetarium (10-14 Omnimax shows per day; tickets $6.50, students $5.20, military $5.20, seniors $5, ages 5-15 $3.50). Your ticket to the space theater, plus an additional $1, will get you into the nearby **Science Center** (open Sun.-Wed. 9:30am-9pm, Thurs.-Sat. 9:30am-10pm; admission $2.50, ages 5-15 $1.25; free 1st Tues. of each month). The **Aerospace Museum** (234-8291), in the drum-shaped Ford Pavilion, exhibits full-scale replicas of over 70 planes (open daily 10am-4:30pm, mid-June to Labor Day daily 10:30am-5:30pm; admission $6, seniors $5, ages 6-17 $2, under 6 free, military free; free 4th Tues. of each month).

OLD TOWN

Old Town is the site of the first Spanish settlement on the West Coast. Although a colonial flavor still pervades the area, it has in modern times become less a settlement and more a tourist center.

Food

This is *the* place to eat Mexican food in California. Although fast food dominates San Diego's cuisine, many of these establishments prove that fast food is not always bad news. In the land of the speedy burrito, some restaurants have perfected the art of quick Mexican and none of them are named Taco Bell. Two of the best chains are **Roberto's Taco Shop** (3202 Mission Blvd.) and **Perkyland** (1030 Torrey Pines Rd.).

Casa de Bandini, 2754 Calhoun St. (297-8211). The charming patio and mariachi-filled interior (built in 1829) create a fabulous atmosphere for the scarfing of super-sized chimichangas ($7), mouth-watering combo plates ($8-9), and monster margaritas ($5). Repeatedly voted "San Diego's best Mexican restaurant." Open Mon.-Thurs. 11am-9:30pm, Fri.-Sat. 11am-10pm, Sun. 10am-9:30pm.

Casa de Pico, 2754 Calhoun St. (296-3267), next to Casa de Bandini. Gigantic plates overflowing with gooey cheese enchiladas ($5-8). Soup-bowl-sized margaritas are terrifically tasty. Open Sun.-Thurs. 10am-9:30pm, Fri.-Sat. 10am-10pm.

Cafe Coyote, 2461 San Diego Ave. (291-4695). Great food (burritos $5) and 90 different tequilas will make you howl. On weekend afternoons, vendors sell fresh tortillas (3 for $1). Open Sun.-Thurs. 7:30am-10pm, Fri.-Sat. 7:30am-11pm.

Great Wall Cafe, 2543 Congress St. (291-9428). Celebrated Mandarin Chinese food. Lunch combos ($5) and dinner specials ($6-8) offer vegetarian options. Open Mon.-Thurs. 11am-9:30pm, Fri.-Sat. 11am-10:30pm, Sun. 12:30-9:30pm.

Berta's, 3928 Twiggs St. (295-2343). You may have to buy a copy of *Let's Go: Latin America* to make your way through this menu. Dozens of Guatemalan, Colombian, Honduran, and Costa Rican specialities. Open daily 11am-10pm.

Sights

In 1769, a group of Spanish soldiers accompanied by Father Junípero Serra established a fort and mission in the area now known as Old Town. Today, Old Town's museums, parks, and sundry attractions commemorate the historic outpost which has given rise to the modern metropolis of San Diego.

Presidio Park is the most impressive of these historical areas, containing the **Serra Museum** (279-3258). Its stout adobe walls were raised in 1929 at the site of the original fort and mission. Inside are exhibits documenting the settlement; outside is a really, really huge flagpole marking the location of **Fort Stockton** (museum open Tues.-Sat. 10am-4:30pm, Sun. noon-4:30pm; admission $3, under 12 free).

Below Presidio Park is **Old Town State Park,** the most popular of the area's attractions. The park's early-19th-century buildings contain museums, shops, and the restaurants listed above. Walk off a hefty Mexican meal with a tour of the **Whaley House,** 2482 San Diego Ave. (298-2482), which displays an authentic Lincoln life mask and the piano used in *Gone With the Wind.* The house stands on the site of San Diego's first gallows, which may have something to do with the fact that it is one of the two **official haunted houses** recognized by the State of California. Across the street is **Heritage Park,** a group of seven 150-year-old Victorian buildings (six houses and one temple) collected from around the city. Four are open to the public.

Father Serra's soldiers were apparently a rough and unholy bunch, because in 1774 the padre moved his mission some 6 mi. away to its current location at **Mission Basilica San Diego de Alcalá** (281-8449). The mission is still an active parish church (mass held daily 7am and 5:30pm; visitors welcome), and contains a chapel, gardens, a small museum, and a reconstruction of Serra's living quarters. To get to the park, take bus #43 or I-8 east to the Mission Gorge Rd. Exit. For more info, see **A Man with a Mission** (p. 54).

If you've been wondering about the lightning bolt stickers posted all over town, head to **Qualcomm Stadium** on a fall Sunday and look closely at the helmets of the **San Diego Chargers,** the city's pro football team. The stadium, which is west of the Mission near the junction of I-8 and I-15, also hosts baseball's **San Diego Padres** (for Chargers or Padres tickets, call 280-2121 or 525-8282, respectively).

COASTAL SAN DIEGO

San Diego's western boundary is lined by miles of soft, sloping beaches crowded with surfers. When sun, sand, surf, and Sea World get dull, head inland to San Diego's beach communities, where there's plenty to explore away from the shore.

Coronado Island

Coronado is actually a peninsula—the "Silver Strand," a slender 7 mi. strip of sand, connects it to the mainland just above the Mexican border—but its pristine platinum beaches feel so remote you may think you're on some paradisiacal tropical isle. The action in Coronado takes place in two areas: residents and merchants stick to the south, while sailors and aviators populate the **North Island Naval Base.**

The graceful **Coronado Bridge,** built in 1969, guides cars to Coronado from downtown San Diego along I-5 (toll $1), and bus #901 follows the same route. Those who would rather skim the ocean than the asphalt can take the **Bay Ferry,** which leaves for Coronado on the hour from 9am to 9pm and returns on the half-hour from 9:30am to 9:30pm. Tickets ($2) are available at **San Diego Harbor Excursion,** 1050 N. Harbor Dr. (234-4111), which also runs one-hour ($15) and two-hour ($17) tours of the harbor. Once across, the **Coronado Shuttle** carries passengers from the landing to the Hotel Del Coronado and back (50¢); it leaves every hour at 20 min. past. The **Coronado Visitors Bureau,** 1047 B Ave. (437-8788 or 800-622-8300; fax 437-6006), provides info on the upscale shops and restaurants lining **Orange Ave.**

Coronado's most famed sight is its Victorian-style **Hotel del Coronado,** 1500 Orange Ave. (435-6611), one of America's largest wooden buildings. The long, white verandas and the vermilion spires of the "Del" were built in 1898. It has since become one of the world's great hotels, hosting 12 presidents and one blonde bombshell (Marilyn Monroe's 1959 classic *Some Like it Hot* was filmed here). A salmon burger ($7) from the lobby's **Del Deli** will help to power your tour of the hotel's considerable grounds and the uncrowded white beach out back. **Bikes and Beyond** (435-7180), at the ferry landing on 1st St., rents bikes ($5 per hr., mountain bikes $6 per hr.) and in-line skates ($5 per hr.; open daily 8:30am-dusk).

Point Loma

Although the U.S. government owns the outer two-thirds of this peninsula, most of it remains open to citizens and visitors. The **Cabrillo National Monument** (557-5450), at the tip of Point Loma, is dedicated to the great Portuguese explorer, João Rodrigues Cabrillo (the first European to land in California), but is best known for its views of San Diego and migrating whales. **Whale-watching** season is mid-December to February, and the monument is prime seating (whale info in winter 557-5450). From north country, take I-5 to Rosecrans Blvd. (there is no Rosecrans Exit northbound), and follow signs for Rte. 209 to the entrance, or take bus #6A. The 2 mi. harborside **Bayside Trail** teaches about native vegetation and historic military installations. Point Loma's ocean side is rife with **tide pools** (turn right off Rte. 209 onto Cabrillo Rd., and drive down to the parking lot at the bottom of the hill). At the highest point of the peninsula sits the museum at **Old Point Loma Lighthouse** (open daily 9am-5:15pm; summer hours vary; parking $4 per car, walk-ins and bikers $2).

Ocean Beach (O.B.) caters to a crowd of surfers much more low-key than the swankier set to the north. This relaxed atmosphere, along with gentle surf conditions, make O.B. a great place to learn the art of wave-riding. Those who would rather stay out of the water can angle from the longest fishing pier in the Western Hemisphere or watch the sinking sun from **Sunset Cliffs.** Most of the area's inexpensive restaurants and bars are clustered along the westernmost stretch of **Newport Ave.,** one of San Diego's trendiest drags. The **Newport Bar and Grille,** 4935 Newport Ave. (222-0168), is the local favorite; try their raspberry chicken ($7; open Mon.-Wed. 11am-midnight, Thurs.-Fri. 11am-2am, Sat. 8am-2am, Sun. 8am-midnight). **Margarita's,** 4955 Newport Ave. (224-7454), has an atmosphere as chillin' as its namesake. Great Mexican vegetarian fare (Bean L-T sandwich $4.50) and wine margaritas ($2).

Mission Beach and Pacific Beach

Much of San Diego's younger population is drawn to these communities by the respectable surf and the hopping nightlife—noisy bars and grills crowd these shores. **Kono's Surf Club,** 704 Garnet Ave. (483-1669), across from the Crystal Pier in Pacific Beach, is a surfer's shrine that serves breakfast all day ($2-3). The Egg Burrito #3 includes bacon, cheese, potatoes, and pica-sauce, all for $2.75 (open Mon.-Fri. 7am-3pm, Sat.-Sun. 7am-4pm). **Cafe Crema,** 1001 Garnet Ave. (273-3558 or 800-54-CREMA/542-7362), is a Euro-style coffeehouse stacked with pastries and bagel sandwiches ($3-5; open Sun.-Thurs. 6am-2am, Fri.-Sat. 6am-4am). **Luigi's,** 32210 Mission Blvd. (488-2818), is new in the Mission Beach area, but it has already become a local institution for its extraordinarily huge slices of pizza ($2.25). Farther inland is **World Curry,** 1423 Garnet Ave. (689-2222), small, but serving delicious curries ($5).

Across the street from Luigi's is **Belmont Park,** a combination amusement park/ shopping center which draws a youthful crowd from all over the city. Gulp down a meal at the **Mission Beach Cantina** (specialty burritos start at $6), or risk losing your last one on the bumpy **Giant Dipper** rollercoaster (rides $3, Mon.-Tues. after 5pm 75¢; free parking). The **Ocean Front Walk** through Pacific Beach toward La Jolla is always packed with joggers, walkers, cyclists, and the usual beachfront shops.

Although both beaches accommodate those who limit their physical activity to shifting on their towels, active beaching is acceptable as well. Beachside sports are very popular—competition sometimes wears the face of conflict among passionate crowds. Be sure to avoid swimming near surfers, and always don protective gear when skating. **Star Surfing Co.,** 4655 Mission Blvd. (273-7827), in Pacific Beach north of Garnet Ave., rents surfboards ($4 per hr., $17 per day) and boogieboards

SAN DIEGO

Of Cars and Constellations

After one ride on **Belmont Park's Giant Dipper,** you may find yourself beaten and bruised by the rickety rollercoaster's excessively bumpy turns and tumbles. Imagine riding the coaster nearly **3000 times** in a row. Can't? Well, three hardy San Diegans recently did it, and all for a radio promotion. The city's Star 98.7 FM chose an initial field of 22 contestants, sat them aboard the coaster, and told them that the one who stayed on the longest—short bathroom breaks and park closing hours excepted—would win a new Nissan automobile. The Dipper's rough and tumble rails claimed 19 victims with relative ease, but three stubborn souls were determined to win the prize. For weeks they battled broken ribs, bump-befuddled brains, and bubbling bile until Star and Nissan both broke down, awarding them each a car of their own. The trials of these truly amazing American heroes dominated the San Diego nightly news at the time, and their act of courage makes a powerful statement to us all about the need for a car in Southern California.

($2.50, $10) to those with a driver's license or credit card (open daily 10am-6pm). **Mike's Bikes 'n' Blades,** 756A Ventura Pl. (488-1444; open daily 8am-9pm), in Mission Beach, rents bikes (first hr. $4, each additional hr. $2, $10 per day) and blades ($12 per day). **Crown Point Water Sports,** 1710 W. Mission Bay Dr. (226-8611; open daily 9am-6pm), rents sailboats ($20 per hr., $50 per ½ day). **Windsport,** 844 Mission Bay Dr. (488-4642), rents kayaks ($10 per hr., $35 per day), bodyboards ($5 per day), surfboards ($15), and wetsuits ($15).

Sea World

Take Disneyland, subtract the rides, add a whole lot of fish, and you've got **Sea World** (226-3901; http://www.4adventure.com), a water wonderland whose signature creature isn't a pip-squeak mouse but a four-ton orca known as **Shamu.** (Actually, the original Shamu died years ago, but his immortality has been ensured by way of a fiendish ruse—giving his 10 replacements the same name.) Shamus aside, the park contains shark, penguin, and dolphin displays, as well as jet-ski and watersport shows and a virtual-reality underwater experience. The highlight of any Sea World visit may well be the always delightful **sea otters**—the only creatures sober enough to survive the Exxon Valdez disaster unscathed.

Visitors often buy a map and schedule upon entering the parking lot ($5); even the most popular events occur only a few times daily, so a quick perusal of the schedule is a good idea. The park's most popular show takes place in **Shamu Stadium,** where four orcas, including the arena's namesake, cavort with trainers in a five-million-gallon tank. Watch the performances from the upper deck if dryness is a priority—each show a substantial fraction of the tank's total volume ends up splashed on spectators seated in the first 20 rows. If it's your mind and not your water-filled pockets that needs emptying, head for the **Baywatch at Sea World** ski show, where high-speed hilarity is a way of life. The performance's plot is just as gripping as the TV show's, and part of the event is narrated by international heartthrob **David Hasselhoff.** The park's newest attraction is **Wild Arctic,** a recreated habitat zone for polar bears, beluga whales, walruses, and harbor seals. Those who feel they need a little cooling down should head to the **Anheuser-Busch Hospitality Tent,** which will give each (21 and over) guest up to **two free cups of beer.** (Park open Sun.-Thurs. 9am-10pm, Fri.-Sat. 9am-11pm. Hours shorter in off-season. Park admission $33, ages 3-11 $25.)

La Jolla

Perched on a rocky promontory, this gilded "jewel" of a city lives up to its name. La Jolla (pronounced la HOY-a; say la JOLL-a and you're exposing yourself to potentially fatal levels of ridicule) began as a hideaway for wealthy Easterners who built luxurious houses atop the ocean bluffs in the 1930s and 40s. The pink walls and Spanish mosaics of the **La Valencia Hotel,** 1132 Prospect St. (451-0772), glow with the wealth of monied tenants, but the town's character has recently taken a West Egg-ish turn—newer wealth and a younger population have taken over. To reach La Jolla, take the Ardath Exit west from I-5 or buses #30 or 34 from downtown.

Girard Avenue is the Rodeo Drive of San Diego, crammed with upscale shops and eateries. If you look hard enough, however, you can find some relatively inexpensive places to eat. **La Terraza,** 8008 Girard Ave. (459-9750), specializes in *cucina Toscana,* featuring such delicacies as pasta with eggplant and smoked mozzarella. Pizzas are $8-10 (open daily 11am-11pm). Upstairs is **Roberto's at the Cove** (454-2222), the best place for inexpensive Sunday champagne brunch ($10; open Sun.-Thurs. 11am-10pm, Fri.-Sat. 11am-11pm). **Mr. Juice,** a classic California healthnut joint, is next door to Roberto's. Drink deep from a $3 smoothie, fruit shake, or juice concoction while watching the wheat grass grow in the window. San Diego's mellow ways have even subdued the usually boisterous **Hard Rock Cafe,** 909 Prospect St. (454-5101). Nibble quietly at a $6 burger or suck softly away at a $3 milkshake—the stuff's the same, but it somehow goes down easier here (open Sun.-Thurs. 11:30am-11pm, Fri.-Sat. 11:30am-midnight). The **Living Room,** 1010 Prospect St. (459-1187), is a coffeehouse serving the usual grind, but decorated in an Alice-in-Wonderland-meets-Philippe-Stark kinda way. Try the Iced Vietnamese (a quadruple espresso, $3.50) only if you know no fear (open daily 7am-midnight).

At the foot of Girard Ave. in **La Jolla Village** is **Scripps Park,** where wanton waves shake the rocky shore, sending up great plumes of silver sea spray. Ocean lovers, or lovers of any ilk, stroll here in the evenings and loll on the carefully manicured lawns. The **San Diego Museum of Contemporary Art,** 700 Prospect St. (454-3541), houses an impressive collection of pop (particularly Andy Warhol), minimalist, and conceptualist artwork in galleries overlooking the Pacific (admission $4, students $2, seniors $2, military $2, ages 12-18 $2; open Tues.-Sat. 10am-5pm, Sun. noon-5pm). The **Animation Celection,** 1002 Prospect St. (459-4278), is a gallery featuring contemporary art of a more sugared sort, including hand-painted acetate originals of everything from *The Jungle Book* to *The Jetsons*. The **Stephen Birch Aquarium-Museum,** 2300 Expedition Way (534-FISH/3474; http://aqua.ucsd.edu), at the Scripps Institute of Oceanography, feeds Humphrey (the fat octopus) and funds his friends, oceanographic researchers (open daily 9am-5pm; admission $6.50, students $4.50, seniors $5.50, ages 3-12 $3.50).

In addition to these attractions, La Jolla claims some of the finest **beaches** in the city. The **La Jolla Cove** is popular with scuba divers, snorkelers, and brilliantly colored Garibaldi goldfish (the state saltwater fish). Surfers are especially fond of the waves at **Tourmaline Beach** and **Windansea Beach,** which can be too strong for novices. **La Jolla Shores,** next to Scripps/UCSD, has clean and gentle swells ideal for bodysurfers, boogieboarders, swimmers, and families. **Black's Beach** is not *officially* a **nude beach,** but there are more wieners and buns on display here than in a *Wienerschmitzel* supply warehouse. The north end generally attracts gay patrons.

Torrey Pines Glider Port is where hang gliders leap into the breeze and the young and unafraid cliff-dive into the high tide. (As always, Let's Go does not recommend cliff-diving.) To reach the Glider Port, take I-5 to Genesee Ave., go west and turn left on N. Torrey Pines Rd. The beach is accessible via a steep staircase just south of the glider port. A treacherous cliffside trail starts at the long parking lot north of the port.

The **University of California at San Diego (UCSD)** chills above La Jolla. Buses #30 and 34 take you to campus, but cars or bikes are invaluable for trekking among the campus's many residential and academic colleges. Kiosks on Gilman and Northview Dr. dispense maps (534-2208; open Mon.-Fri. 7am-9pm, Sat.-Sun. 6:30am-9pm). The **La Jolla Playhouse** (550-1070), presents shows at the Mandell Weiss Theatre on campus; turn onto Expedition from N. Torrey Pines Rd.

■ Nightlife

Nightlife in San Diego is not centered around a particular strip, but scattered in several distinct pockets of action. Upscale locals and trend-seeking tourists flock to the **Gaslamp,** where numerous restaurants and bars feature live music nightly. The **Hillcrest** area, next to Balboa Park, draws a young, largely gay crowd to its clubs and dining spots. Away from downtown, the **beach areas** (especially Garnet Ave. in Pacific Beach) are loaded with clubs, bars, inexpensive eateries, and college-age revelers. The city's definitive source of entertainment info is the free *San Diego Reader,* found in shops, coffeehouses, and visitors centers. Listings can also be found in the *San Diego Union Tribune*'s Thursday "Night and Day" section.

RESTAURANTS AND CLUBS

Although the restaurants below offer complete meals, they are better-known as nightspots—bars, music clubs, or dance clubs.

Pacific Beach Grill and Club Tremors, 860 Garnet Ave. (272-1242 and 277-7228, respectively), Pacific Beach. Live DJ packs the 2-level dance floor nightly with a young and slinky crowd—imagine MTV's *The Grind* in the flesh. Cover $1-5.

Open nightly 8:30pm-1:30am. Quieter upstairs bar serves cheap food (open 11am-1:30am, kitchen closes 11pm).

Dick's Last Resort, 345 4th Ave. (231-9100), Gaslamp. Buckets of Southern grub attract a wildly hedonistic bunch. Dick's stocks beers from around the globe, from Africa to Trinidad, on top of native brews like the appropriate Dixieland Blackened Voodoo Lager. No cover for the nightly rock or blues, but you'd better be buyin'. Burgers under $4, entrees $9-15. Open daily 11am-1:30am.

Cafe Lu Lu, 419 F. St. (238-0114), Gaslamp. Funky vegetarian coffeehouse was designed by local artists. See and be seen as you eat for under $5, sipping all the while a raspberry-mocha espresso ($3.50). Standing room only after midnight. Open Sun.-Thurs. 9am-2am, Fri.-Sat. 9am-4am.

CLUBS AND BARS

Lesbian and **gay clubs** cluster in University Heights and Hillcrest. Some of the more popular hangouts include: **The Flame,** 3780 Park Blvd. (295-4163), in Hillcrest, a lesbian dance club (open Sat.-Thurs. 5pm-2am, Fri. 4pm-2am); **Bourbon Street,** 4612 Park Blvd. (291-0173), in University Heights, a piano bar with a gay following (open daily 11am-1:30am); and **The Brass Rail,** 3796 5th Ave. (298-2233), in Hillcrest, featuring dancing and drag on weekends (open daily 10am-2am).

Velvet, 2812 Kettner Blvd. (692-1080), near Old Town. Live and loud, the Velvet hosts San Diego's up-and-coming rock 'n' roll acts, as well as the occasional more established band. Pool table. Alternative rock 6 nights a week. Cover Wed.-Sat. $5. Open daily 8pm-2am. 21and over.

The Comedy Store, 916 Pearl St. (454-9176), La Jolla. One of the few joints around where you can be a part of the scene—clamber onstage Mon. at 8pm for Potluck Night (call and sign up after 3pm). Better-known comedians featured other evenings. Shows Thurs. at 8pm ($7), Fri.-Sat. at 8 and 10:30pm ($10). College ID gets you 2-for-1 admission Wed.-Thurs. 2-drink minimum. Drinks $3. Must be 21.

Club Sevilla, 555 4th Ave. (233-5979). Live bands every night lead patrons in Latin dances from salsa to flamenco. *Tapas* bar upstairs with adjoining dining room; don't miss *"paella* madness" on Tues. ($11). Open daily 5pm-2am. Must be 21.

Java Joe's, 4994 Newport Ave. (523-0356). Formerly the Rumors Cafe, this coffee-house has a genuinely cozy, church-basement atmosphere with a few pool tables. Bigger venue for live music—mostly folk and blues—than most coffeehouses. Open Mon.-Fri. 7am-midnight and Sat.-Sun. 8am-midnight.

Croce's Top Hat Bar and Grille and Croce's Jazz Bar, 802 5th Ave. (233-4355), at F St. in the Gaslamp. Ingrid Croce, widow of singer Jim Croce, created this rock/blues bar and classy jazz bar side by side on the 1st floor of the historic Keating building. Live music nightly. Cover up to $7. Open daily 7:30am-2am.

Society, 1051 Garnet Ave. (272-7665), Pacific Beach. Nestled against the black interior of this slick pool hall are 15 pool tables on 2 floors. Despite the wanna-be Fast Eddie types; there are plenty of beginners around. Gas up for hustling sessions with appetizers, wine, coffee, and 70 beers. No cover. Open daily 11am-2am.

■ Seasonal Events

Gorgeous weather and a strong community spirit make the San Diego area an ideal place for local festivals. The following is by no means a comprehensive list—check the beach community weeklies for further festival information.

Penguin Day Ski Fest (276-0830), New Year's Day, De Anza Cove, Mission Bay. This unique festival requires its participants to water-ski in the ocean or to lie on a block of ice without a wet suit; those who do are honored with a "penguin patch," while those who fail get only a "chicken patch."

Ocean Beach Kite Festival, 4726 Santa Monica Ave. (531-1527), 1st Sat. in March, Ocean Beach. Kite-construction and flying competitions.

San Diego Crew Classic (488-0700), April, Mission Bay. Crews from both coasts compete at the only major collegiate regatta on the West Coast.

Summer Stargazing (594-6182), Fri.-Sat. nights from June 1-Labor Day, San Diego State University's Mount Laguna Observatory. Open to the public with free tickets available through the U.S. Forest Service (Fri. 2-6pm, Sat. 9am-5pm).

Ocean Beach Street Fair and Chili Cook-Off (224-4906), last weekend in June, Ocean Beach. Newport St. is lined with arts booths during this 2-day fest.

Sunset Cinema Film Festival (485-7373), early-to-mid-Aug. View film classics and cartoons from the beach as they are projected onto a barge's screen. Free.

Hillcrest Cityfest Street Fair (299-3330), early Aug., on 5th. Ave between Ivy Lane and University Ave., in the heart of San Diego's gay community. Arts, crafts, food, live entertainment, and beer garden.

U.S. Open Sand Castle Competition (424-6663), mid-Aug., Imperial Beach pier. Sand-sculpting demigods exercise their craft in this largest and longest-running of American sand castle events. Parades, fireworks, and children's castle contest.

SummerFest La Jolla Chamber Music Festival (459-3724), late Aug., La Jolla Museum of Contemporary Art.

La Jolla

Rough Water Swim (456-2100), early Sept. Start and finish at the La Jolla cove. Largest annual rough water swim in the U.S.

SAN DIEGO'S NORTH COUNTY

In the recent film *Demolition Man,* Sylvester Stallone plays a police officer who patrols the city of "San Angeles," a fictional future metropolis which consists of unbroken development from Los Angeles south through San Diego to the Mexican border. This fantasy is well grounded in reality—the drive along I-5 from L.A. to San Diego never really passes through an undeveloped area. Fortunately, most of these towns have beautiful beaches, the best of which belong to the coastal communities of San Diego's North Country: Del Mar, Encinitas, Leucadea, Carlsbad, and Oceanside. All five towns are easily accessible along Rte. 21—the Pacific Hwy.—by car, bike, or bus. Take North Country Transit District bus #301 from La Jolla's University Towne Centre as far as Oceanside (every ½hr. daily 6am-10pm; fare $1, free transfer). For more North Country info, call 743-6283 or 722-6283.

▓ Del Mar

Just north of La Jolla is the affluent suburb of Del Mar, home to thoroughbred racing and famous fairgrounds. Its **Chamber of Commerce,** 1104 Camino Del Mar (793-5292), has brochures and handouts (open Mon.-Tues. 10am-5pm, Wed. noon-2pm, Thurs. 10am-noon, Fri. noon-5pm). The Del Mar **Amtrak** station (481-0114), the first stop on the run from San Diego to Los Angeles, is on the beach (8 per day). Take a left onto 15th off Rte. 21 (here called Camino Del Mar).

Food Intruding on Camino Del Mar's real estate offices is the **Del Mar French Pastry Cafe,** 1140 Camino Del Mar (481-8622), where pastries and hearty sandwiches ($4) are served beneath a billowing *tricoleur* (open Mon.-Sat. 6am-6pm, Sun. 7am-6pm). One block away is **Board and Brew,** 1212 Camino del Mar (481-1021), and its California Delight ($4), which is chock full of turkey, cream cheese, and sunflower seeds (open daily 10am-7pm). **Tony's Jacal,** 621 Valley Ave. (755-2274), is a family-run establishment serving up zesty burritos ($4; open Mon.-Thurs. 11am-2pm and 5-10pm, Fri.-Sat. 11am-2pm and 5-10:30pm, Sun. 3-10pm).

Sights and Entertainment Racing season (late July to mid-Sept.) at the **Del Mar Racetrack** (755-1141), is a celeb-fest. Take I-5 to Via de la Valle, and follow your nose west to Jimmy Durante Blvd. This is one of the most beautiful racetracks in the world and has been popular with entertainers since Bing Crosby and Pat O'Brien founded it in 1937. (Gates open Mon.-Thurs. noon, Fri. 4pm, and Sat.-Sun. 11:30am. First post time 2pm. Admission $3 grandstand, $6 clubhouse.)

Torrey Pines State Park, 12000 Torrey Pines Rd. (755-2063), 4 mi. south of Del Mar on the coast, is one of only two native Torrey Pine groves on earth. (The other is on the Channel Islands; see p. 211.) To the layperson, however, Torrey Pine trees look like all the rest. The **Torrey Pines Lodge** (follow the signs to the golf course) provides info on activities and hiking trails (open daily 9am-6pm). The park trails are wonderful for runners, cyclists, and those who enjoy rules—no picnicking, no food, no smoking, no dogs (even if kept in cars), and no straying off the established trails. The 6 mi. of slightly rocky beach are popular with hang gliders (park open 9am-sunset; admission $4 per vehicle, pedestrians and bicyclists free).

More earthy than neighboring Del Mar, **Solana Beach** is also more hospitable to tourists who'd rather relax than spend. The beach is off the Loma Santa Fe Exit from I-5 (free parking). From the **Solana Beach City Park** parking lot (755-1569), a steep staircase climbs to a promontory with a spectacular view of the ocean below. The **Belly Up Tavern,** 143 S. Cedros Ave. (481-9022), once a warehouse near the train tracks, now belts blues, rock, reggae, and jazz. Patrons can shoot pool or belly up to the long bar. "Big Mama" Thorton, The Smithereens, and John Lee Hooker have all played at this kickin' joint. Charge tickets by phone (481-8140), by computer (http://www.bellyup.com/butorder.html), or at the door. (Open daily 11am-1:30am; live music daily at 9pm with occasional afternoon shows. Cover varies with artist. Happy Hour with live big band music daily at 5:30pm.)

■ Encinitas, Leucadia, and Carlsbad

North of Del Mar along eucalyptus-shaded Rte. 21 lie the towns of Encinitas and Leucadia, which betray traces of their hippie-mecca past through their hallucinogenic beauty and their tie-dyed inhabitants. Farther up the coast is the charming lagoon hideaway of Carlsbad, where Rte. 21 winds past silky sands and shingled homes adorned with wild rose bushes.

The cheapest indoor lodging near Carlsbad is **Motel 6,** 6117 Paseo del Norte (438-1242), off Palomar Airport Rd. Exit from I-5. (Singles $33; doubles $39.) Other locations are in downtown Carlsbad (434-7135), and farther south at Raintree Dr. (431-0745). Camping on the beach is allowed at **South Carlsbad State Park** (438-3143). Reservations are available through DESTINET (800-365-2267; sites $22 by the ocean, $17 inland). **Cardiff-by-the-Sea** in Encinitas has several beachfront restaurants bursting with character. **Filiberto's Mexican Food,** 101 Encinitas Blvd. (753-9590), at Brea, serves up delicious burritos and tacos ($2). With each order, they'll hand you some hot sauce, but for the love of God, be careful: this ain't no watered-down picante you're dealing with (open 24hr.). **George's Restaurant,** 641 U.S. 101 (942-9549), is a classic surf diner. The latest issue of *Surfer* is the perfect accompaniment to a pile of pancakes ($3-4; open daily 7am-2pm.) **Miracles Cafe,** 1953 San Elijo (943-7924), has banana Belgian waffles ($4) and the Supreme Scream sandwich (swiss cheese, avocado, tomato, cucumber, and sprouts; open Mon.-Sat. 6am-11pm, Sun. 7am-10pm).

The state maintains a number of undeveloped beaches, good for both sun and surf. The stone steps at **Leucadia State Beach** descend from the cliffs at South El Portal St. to over 3 mi. of public sands. **Carlsbad State Beach** is long and attractive despite the view of the mammoth Encinitas Power Plant, which occupies the coast to the south. Boards are available at **Offshore Surf Boards,** 3179 Carlsbad Blvd. (729-4934), on Rte. 21. (Boogieboards $3 per hr., $10 per day; $100 deposit or credit card required. Open daily 9am-7pm.) **Bikes** can be rented from **Carlsbad Cyclery,** 2796 Carlsbad Blvd. (434-6681), which also offers beach gear rentals. (Bikes or in-line skates $10 for 2hr., $15 per day; boogieboards $2 per hr., $8 per day; fins or beach chairs $5 per day; major credit card required; open daily 10am-5pm.) **Cardiff-by-the-Sea** is enhanced by **San Elijo Beach State Park** (753-5091) and **Cardiff**

State Beach to the south. For camping info, see **Camping,** p. 148. If you have a car, these beautiful sites are worth the drive.

■ Oceanside

Oceanside is the largest and most varied of the beach towns north of San Diego, probably because the beach at **Oceanside Harbor** (I-5 and Oceanside Harbor Dr.) is one of the world's greatest surfing beaches. The pier at Pierview Way attracts serious surfers year-round, especially during the annual West Coast Pro-Am Surf Contest (mid-July; 433-6187), PSSA Championships (mid-June), World Body Surfing Championships (mid-Aug.; 966-4536), and Longboard Championships (late Aug.; 439-5334). Beaches are patrolled by lifeguards and surfers stick to designated areas. Parking costs $3 by the harbor, and $1 by the track, but free curb spots can be found nearby. With so much surfing history made along its shores, Oceanside is the perfect place for the **California Surf Museum,** 233 Rte. 21 (721-6876; open Thurs.-Mon. 10am-4pm; free). The exceptionally enthusiastic folks at the **Oceanside Visitors Center,** 928 N. Coast Hwy. (721-1101; fax 722-8336), have info about goings-on.

   Mission San Luis Rey de Francia (757-3651), was founded in 1798, but the only original building still standing is the church (c. 1807). Follow Missions Ave. (Rte. 76) east from N. Coast Hwy. (Rte. 21), or take NCTD bus #303 at Rte. 21 and Mission. (Open Mon.-Sat. 10am-4:30pm, Sun. noon-4:30pm. Admission $3, ages 8-14 $1.)

   Amtrak (722-4622), and **Greyhound** (722-1587), share the **Oceanside Transit Center,** 235 S. Tremont and 2055 Tremont. The center's towering signs make it easy to spot from any point in town.

■ Escondido

The diverse denizens of Escondido—30 mi. due north of San Diego—range from rich celebrities to undocumented agricultural laborers. Victorian mansions, fields of wildflowers, and numerous wineries nurture this North County community.

Practical Information The **San Diego North County Convention and Visitor Bureau,** 720 N. Broadway (745-4741), dispenses info on Escondido and the beach cities to the west (open Mon.-Fri. 8:30am-5pm, Sat. 10am-4pm; 24hr. hotline 800-848-3336). **Greyhound** (745-6522), stops at 700 W. Valley Pkwy. The **North County Transit Department** can be reached at 743-NCTD/6283. In an **emergency,** call 911. The **area code** is 619.

Accommodations There are a number of budget motels clustered off of I-15. To get to the main motel strip, take Rte. 78 east to Center City Pkwy., and turn right on Washington. The **Sixpence Inn,** 509 W. Washington Blvd. (743-6669; fax 489-5937), is the cheapest in the area. It features clean rooms, pool, cable TV, and A/C (singles $28; doubles $32). The **Super 8,** 528 W. Washington Blvd. (747-3711), has gorgeous rooms and free continental breakfast, cable TV, A/C, pool, and jacuzzi (singles $38; doubles $44).

Sights An essential part of any trip to San Diego, the **San Diego Wild Animal Park** (234-6541), is dedicated to the preservation and display of endangered species. The park's main selling point is its lack of cages—its animals roam freely in extensive habitats engineered to mirror the real thing. The park's entrance has shops, restaurants, and a short trail, but most of its 800 accessible acres can be reached only by way of the open-air **Wgasa Bush Line,** a 50-minute monorail tour through the four habitat areas (tours 9:30am-6pm, Sept.-mid-June 9:30am-4pm; sit on the right if possible). Renting binoculars ($3) at the camera hut before boarding the monorail may enhance the tour. The park has recently begun to add to its visitor attractions, supplementing the monorail tour with such activities as the one-mile Heart of Africa hike, the Roar and Snore overnight camping safari (800-934-CAMP/

2267), and the open-air Photo Caravan (760-738-5022). Most of the park, including the monorail, is wheelchair accessible, but steep hills may require detours or assistance (admission $19, seniors $16, ages 3-11 $12; parking $3; open Mon.-Wed. 9am-7pm, Thurs.-Sun 9am-10pm).

Also in Escondido is the "wunnerful, wunnerful" **Welk Resort Center,** the personal barony of late champagne-music conductor Lawrence Welk. The center has three championship golf courses, a luxury hotel, and a 330-seat dinner theatre which holds small-scale Broadway productions. The **Lawrence Welk Museum,** 8860 Lawrence Welk Dr. (800-932-WELK/9355), is in the theatre's lobby; exhibits include Welk's golf cart. Anyone under the age of 60 stands out in this crowd (open Sun.-Mon. and Wed. 10am-4:15pm, Tue. and Thurs.-Sat. 10am-7pm; free).

■ North of Escondido

Although the Hale telescope at **Palomar Observatory** (742-2119), on Palomar Mountain is over 40 years old, it remains one of the world's largest and greatest astronomical tools. The observatory is accessible via San Diego County Rte. S6, the "Highway to the Stars," which winds through avocado orchards. Inside the observatory, a museum displays celestial photographs taken through Hale's 200-inch aperture. A smug notice points out that research, not education, is the observatory's mission, and touring is limited to gazing at the telescope from behind plate glass (open daily 9am-4pm; free).

The observatory and several campgrounds are contained within **Cleveland National Forest.** Rte. S6 rockets past federally run **Fry Creek** and **Observatory campgrounds,** and a left onto Rte. S7 at the mountain top touches down at **Palomar Mountain State Park** (742-3462). Camping is permitted at the park's state-run **Doane Valley campground** (742-3462). Sites are over 5000 ft. above sea level, so bring your woolies. Showers, hiking trails, and fishing are available, but no swimming is allowed (sites $15, weekends $16; hiker/biker sites $3).

West of Mt. Palomar, on Rte. 76, is one of the few operating missions in California, **Mission Asistencia San Antonio de Pala** (742-3317), on the Pala Indian Reservation. The mission was founded as an outpost of Oceanside's Mission San Luis Rey in 1816 and has since converted thousands of Native Americans to Christianity.

BAJA CALIFORNIA

Peeled away from the mainland geological ages ago by earthquakes, Baja California is a desert peninsula spanning 40,000 square miles between the Sea of Cortés on the east and the Pacific Ocean on the west. A solid stream of tourists flows from California into Baja to surf, fish, and drink to their hearts' content.

The completion of the Transpeninsular Highway has made it quicker to travel the peninsula by **car,** but be prepared to be cruising along at 60 mph and suddenly careen into a rutted curve that can only be taken at 30 mph. If you need roadside assistance, the *Ángeles Verdes* (Green Angels) pass along Hwy. 1 twice per day. Unleaded gas may be in short supply along this highway, so don't pass a PEMEX station without filling your tank. All of Baja is in the *Zona Libre* (Free Zone), so strict vehicle permits are not required. If you will be driving in Baja for more than 72 hours, you need to get a free permit at the border by showing the vehicle's title and proof of registration.

All major towns in Baja are served by **bus.** If you plan to navigate the peninsula by bus, be forewarned that you have to leave at inconvenient times, fight to procure a ticket, and then probably stand the whole way. Any way you cut it, Baja beaches and other points of interest are often inaccessible on public transportation; buses don't stop at coastal spots between Tijuana and San Quintín.

If your travels in Mexico will be limited to Tijuana and Ensenada, you will probably not need to exchange your dollars for pesos; the vast majority of shops and restaurants in these cities are more than willing to take greenbacks. If you plan to travel farther into Baja, prices will be quoted in pesos and some establishments will not accept U.S. dollars, or, if they do, will give you a bad rate. The right **exchange rate** fluctuates around 7.5 pesos per U.S. dollar, but you should check the exact rate in the local newspaper. For extended forays into Mexico we use and endorse *Let's Go: Mexico* and Gibson guitars.

■ Tijuana

Tijuana (pop. 2,000,000) is perhaps the most notorious specimen of the peculiar border subculture. Visitors clomp down Avenida Revolución, the city's wide main drag, past hawking, haggling shopkeepers into a three-ringed, duty-free extravaganza, complete with English-speaking, sleazy club promoters and every decadent way of blowing money, from a seamy, faded jai-alai palace to dark, dingy strip joints, from mega-curio shops to Las Vegas-style hotels to wet, throbbing dance clubs. And it is exactly how most of its 30 million yearly tourists want it to be.

A short distance from this gorge of gringo greenbacks, thousands of undocumented emigrants leave their tin shacks on the Mexican side of the border's invisible line to make a midnight run for the U.S. But with the fastest growth rate (13.6%) of all the world's major cities, Mexico's fourth-largest metropolis isn't going anywhere. To foreigners, though, Tijuana (a.k.a. TJ) is a parody of itself, more often gawked at as a spectacle and chuckled about knowingly than visited as a city. It's hard to say whether it's the city's skanky charm, its cheap booze, or its sprawling, unapologetic hedonism that attracts tourists to Tijuana like flies.

PRACTICAL INFORMATION

Tourist Office: Av. Revolución 711 at Calle 1 (tel. 88-05-55). English-speaking staff doles out maps and advice. Open Mon.-Sat. 9am-7pm, Sun. 10am-5pm. A booth on Revolución between Calles 3 and 4 also has maps and may be less crowded.

Customs Office: (tel. 83-13-90). At the border on the Mexican side, after crossing the San Ysidro bridge. Open Mon.-Fri. 8am-3pm.

Consulates: Canada, German Gedovius 10411 (tel. 84-04-61), in the Zona del Río. Open Mon.-Fri. 9am-1pm. **U.K.,** Blvd. Salinas 1500 (tel. 81-73-23), in Aviacón. Open Mon.-Fri. 8am-3pm. **U.S.,** Tapachula Sur 96 (tel. 81-74-00), in Col. Hipódromo, adjacent to the Agua Caliente racetrack southeast of town. In an emergency, call 28-17-62 and ask for the U.S. Duty Officer. After hours, leave a message and they'll respond shortly. Open Mon.-Fri. 8am-4:30pm.

Currency Exchange: Banks along Constitución exchange currency at the same rate. **Banamex,** Constitución at Calle 4 (tel. 88-00-21, 88-00-22, or 85-82-06). Open for exchange Mon.-Fri. 9am-5pm. *Casas de cambio* (exchange booths) all over town offer better rates, but generally do not exchange traveler's checks. **Cambio de Divisas,** located in the market directly behind the Secretario de Turismo (open Mon.-Tues. 9am-7pm, Wed.-Fri. 1-7pm, Sat. 1-5pm), offers good rates and changes traveler's checks.

Public Transportation: (tel. 21-29-83 or 21-29-84). To reach the bus station from downtown, board the blue-and-white buses marked Buena Vista or Camionera on Niños Héroes between Calles 3 and 4 (2.50 pesos), or jump in a brown-and-white **communal cab** on Madero between Calles 2 and 3 (3 pesos). **Autotransportes de Baja California** (tel. 21-29-82 through -87) runs to Mexicali (every ½hr., 3hr., 69 pesos) and Ensenada (5, 6:30, 7, 8, and 9am; every ½hr., 9am-9pm; 1½hr., 45 pesos). **Greyhound** (tel. 21-29-82), runs to Los Angeles (every hr., 5am-11:30pm, 3hr., $18), and connects from there to other locations.

Car Rental: Dollar, Blvd. Sánchez Taboada 10521 (tel. 81-84-84), in front of the VW dealership. Starting at 248 pesos per day, including insurance and 200km free. Minimum age is 25; license and credit card required. Open Mon.-Fri. 9am-6pm, Sat. 9am-2pm. **Bargain Auto Rentals,** in San Diego, 3860 Rosecrans St. (619-299-0009), is fairly priced, and you only have to be 18 to rent. Credit card required. Open daily 8am-6pm.

Market: Calimax, Calle 2 at Constitución (tel. 88-08-94). Open 24hr.
Pharmacy: Farmacia Vida, Calle 3 at Revolución (tel. 85-14-61). Some English spoken. Open 24hr. **Discount Pharmacy,** Av. Revolución 615 (tel. 88-31-31), between Calle 2 and Calle 3.
Medical Services: Centenario 10851 (tel. 84-09-22), in the Zona del Río.
Emergency: Dial 134.
Police: Constitución at Calle 8 (tel. 21-71-13 or 21-72-66).
Post Office: Negrete at Calle 11 (tel. 84-79-50). Open Mon.-Fri. 8am-7pm, Sat.-Sun. 9am-1pm. **Postal Code:** 22001.
Phone Code: 66.

ORIENTATION

From San Diego to Tijuana, take the red **Mexicoach** bus (tel. 85-14-70 or 619-428-9517 in the U.S.) from its terminal at the border (every ½hr., 9am-9pm). It passes Plaza Pueblo Amigo on the Mexican side and eventually drops you off beside the Frontón Palacio on Revolución between Calles 7 and 8. An easier way might be to grab a **trolley** to San Ysidro, at Kettner and Broadway in downtown San Diego ($1.75), and walk across the border. Transfers from airport buses are also available.

Driving across the border is fairly hassle-free, though traffic can be heavy at times. However, driving in Tijuana can be harrowing: many stoplights function merely as stop signs, and the crowded streets can leave you ready to turn around. If you're only there for a day, it's a much better idea to leave your car in a lot on the U.S. side and join the throngs of people walking across the border. Parking rates start at $3 per day and increase as you move closer to Mexico. Bring proper ID to re-enter the U.S. While a driver's license or other photo ID is acceptable, a passport ensures the speediest passage. Leave fruits, veggies, and shoulder-fired missiles behind.

If you arrive at the central **bus station,** avoid the cab drivers' high rates (80 pesos to downtown) and head for the public bus (every 5min., 5am-10pm, ½hr., 2.50 pesos). When you exit the terminal, turn left, walk to the end of the building, and hop on a bus marked *Centro Línea*. It will let you off on Calle 3 and Constitución. Other *avenidas* run parallel to **Constitución,** notably **Niños Héroes** and **Martínez** to the west and **Revolución** (the main tourist drag), **Madero, Negrete,** and **Ocampo** to the east. *Calles* run east-west; *avenidas* run north-south.

ACCOMMODATIONS

Tijuana's budget hotels cluster on Calle 1 between Revolución and Mutualismo, and they tend toward the roachy side. The area teems with people during the day and is relatively safe. Come nightfall, it becomes something of a red-light district, especially on Calle 1 between Revolución and Constitución. Women should be extra cautious when walking in this area at night; to return to your hotel, head down Calles 2 or 3, or take a taxi ($2) from anywhere on Revolución.

Hotel El Jalisciense, Calle 1 #7925 (tel. 85-34-91), between Niños Héroes and Martínez. A great deal. Clean, smallish rooms with high, resilient beds and private baths. Singles and doubles 100 pesos, each additional person 20 pesos.

Hotel Perla de Occidente, Mutualismo 758 (tel. 85-13-58), between Calles 1 and 2. A healthy hike from the bedlam of Revolución. Large, soft beds, roomy bathrooms, and fans on request. Singles 90 pesos; spacious doubles 160 pesos.

Hotel La Posada, Calle 1 #8190 (tel. 85-41-54 or 85-83-91), at Revolución. Just seconds away from all the action. Select your room carefully—the good ones have fans, comfy beds, and bathrooms your mother would approve of. Singles 50 pesos, with bath 100 pesos; doubles 105 pesos; rooms for 3 or more 120 pesos.

Motel Díaz, Revolución 650 (tel. 85-71-48 or 85-85-85), at Calle 1 smack in the middle of things. Firm beds, hot-water shower, fans, and TV complement the rooms' simplicity. Not an outstanding value, but a bright spot in a pit of lodging mediocrity; your extra pesos will be paid back in cleanliness and light. Parking lot. Singles 200 pesos and up; doubles 250 pesos.

FOOD

Tijuana's touristy eats are essentially Tex-Mex, but some cheap *típico* restaurants line Constitución and the streets leading from Revolución to Constitución. Even cheaper are the mom-and-pop mini-restaurants all over town. If you choose the ubiquitous taco stands, select carefully to protect your stomach. If you must, tourist restaurants and gringo fast-food chains (think KFC) crowd Revolución, usually with slightly higher prices than their American counterparts. Pay in pesos, even if the menu quotes prices in dollars.

Los Panchos Taco Shop, Revolución (tel. 85-72-77), at Calle 3. Orange plastic booths are packed with hungry locals munching on ultra-fresh tortillas. Steak taco $1, bean burrito $2. Open Sun.-Thurs. 8am-8pm, Fri-Sat. 8am-2am.

El Pipirín Antojitos, Constitución 630 (tel. 88-16-02), between Calles 2 and 3. Load up your tacos with a counterful of condiments. *Flautas gigantes* 12 pesos, super *quesadilla* with meat and cheese 18 pesos. Open daily 8am-8:30pm.

Hotel Nelson Restaurant (tel. 85-77-50), Revolución at Calle 1, under the hotel. Good, cheap food in a clean, fan-cooled, coffee-shop atmosphere. Gringo breakfast (eggs, hotcakes, ham) 15 pesos; 3 enchiladas 18 pesos. Open daily 7am-11pm.

Lonchería Tico-Tico, Madero 688 on the corner of Calle 1. Provides friendly and homey service. Both the cooks and the clients enjoy themselves. *Batida de platano* 8 pesos; breakfast tacos 12 pesos, 14 pesos with coffee. Open daily 6am-6pm.

Café Flor de Loto, at Calle 1 and Revolución (tel. 88-28-76). Enjoy down-home Mexican, American, or Chinese in the pleasantly kitschy surroundings. *Pollo en mole* (chicken in mole sauce) 18 pesos. Open daily 8am-2am.

SIGHTS

Fun in Tijuana has long revolved around clubs, money, and their concomitant **vices**—shopping, drinking, and gambling. Of late, numerous diversions outside the conventional bar scene have cropped up. Try **people-watching** while strolling down **Revolución;** you'll see plenty of surprising and revolting sights, like tourists having their pictures taken with donkeys painted as zebras and wearing gaudy sombreros. Walk down Calle 1 to the **artisan's market** to see *mariachis* serenading the crowds of shoppers. When you get tired, relax in the beautiful and shady **Parque Teniente Guerrero,** Calle 3 and 5 de Mayo. It's one of the safer, more pleasant parts of town, and is only a few blocks from Revolución. The **cathedral,** with its massive chandelier, is nearby at Niños Héroes and Calle 2. **Morelos State Park,** Blvd. de los Insurgentes 26000 (tel. 25-24-70), features an exotic bird exhibition and picnic area (open Tues.-Sun. 9am-5pm; admission 4 pesos, children 1.50 pesos). To get there, board the green-and-white bus on Calle 5 and Constitución.

The family-owned **L.A. Cetto Winery,** Cañón Johnson 2108 (tel. 85-30-31), just off Constitución at Calle 10, squeezes its specialty from grapes grown in the Valle de Guadalupe, northeast of Ensenada. Tours are available; just don't try to remove a bottle from the storeroom—one American woman recently did so, causing a wine avalanche that broke and spilled thirty cases of bottles (tours Mon.-Sat. every ½hr., 10am-5:30pm; admission $1, with wine-tasting $2, with wine tasting and souvenir goblet $3; reservations recommended 1hr. before the tour).

Walk off your wine buzz with a visit to one of Tijuana's museums. The **Museo de Cera** (tel. 88-24-78), on Calle 1 between Revolución and Madero, is home to a motley crew of wax figures, including such strange bedfellows as Whoopi Goldberg, the Ayatollah, and Tom Cruise (open Mon.-Fri. 10am-7pm, Sat. 10am-8pm; admission $1 or 7 pesos, under 6 free). The nearby **Mexitlán** (tel. 38-41-01), Calle 2 and Ocampo, showcases a vast field of over 200 intricate miniatures depicting famous historical, religious, and cultural monuments. Absorb Maya architecture, Mexico City's Paseo de la Reforma, and Teotihuacán, and buy a piece of Mexican folk art to take back with you (open Wed.-Sun. 9am-7pm; admission $1.25).

SPORTS

Jai-alai is played in the majestic **Frontón Palacio** (tel. 85-78-33), Revolución at Calle 7. Two to four players take to the three-sided court at once, using arm-baskets to catch and throw a Brazilian ball of rubber and yarn encased in goatskin. The ball travels at speeds reaching 180 mph; jai-alai is reputedly the world's fastest game. If you can, try to catch a doubles match—the points are longer and require more finesse. Players are treated like horses, with betting and odds. All employees are bilingual, and the gambling is carried out in greenbacks (open Mon.-Thurs. noon-4:30pm and 8pm-12:30am, afternoons only on Fri., evenings only on Sat.; admission $3-15; free admission coupons are often distributed outside).

Tijuana has two bullrings. **El Toreo de Tijuana** (tel. 80-18-08), east of Agua Caliente and Cuauhtémoc downtown, hosts *corridas* (bullfights) on chosen Sundays at 4:30pm from early May to July. The more modern **Plaza Monumental,** northwest of the city near Las Playas de Tijuana (follow Calle 2 west), employs famous *matadores* and hosts fights from August to mid-September. Tickets to both rings are sold at the gate. To get to the Plaza Monumental, catch a blue-and-white bus on Calle 3 between Constitución and Niños Héroes.

ENTERTAINMENT

If bullfighting turns your stomach, head for the **Tijuana Centro Cultural** (tel. 84-11-11), on Paseo de los Héroes at Mina (open daily 8am-9pm); it houses the **Space Theater,** an auditorium with a giant 180° screen that shows American OmniMax movies dubbed in Spanish (shows Mon.-Fri. every hr., 3-9pm; Sat.-Sun. every 2hr., 11am-9pm; tickets 20 pesos, children 10 pesos). A **performance center** *(Sala de Espectáculos)* and open-air **theater** *(Caracol al Aire Libre)* host visiting cultural attractions, including the **Ballet Folklórico.** The **Sala de Video** screens free documentaries, and the **Ciclo de Cine Extranjero** shows foreign films (Wed.-Fri. 6 and 8pm, Sat.-Sun. 4, 6, and 8pm; 10 pesos). Pick up a monthly calendar at the information booth in the Centro's art gallery.

All of this is just swell, but if you've come to party, brace yourself for a raucous good time. Strolling down Revolución after dusk, you'll be bombarded by thumping music and abrasive club promoters hawking "two-for-one" margaritas (all places listed below charge $4 for two). Most clubs check ID (must be 18), with varying criteria for what's acceptable, and many frisk for firearms. If you'd like to check out a more local scene, peek into the small clubs on Calle 6 off Revolución.

Iguanas-Ranas (tel. 88-38-85), Revolución at Calle 3. Lively on weeknights; packed on weekends. A 20ish crowd of both *norteños* and *norteamericanos* drinks and raises hell on the dance floor amid the pervasive clown motif. For a break, head to the outdoor terrace. Beer $2. Open daily 10am-4am.

Vibrations, Revolución by Calle 6. Prepare yourself for this three-tiered party palace. Miami-esque neon decor and pool tables bring in the masses. Drink down those two-dollar margaritas. Cover only on weekends (women $3, men $5).

Caves (tel. 88-06-09), Revolución and Calle 5. Flintstonian entrance leads to a dark but airy bar and disco with orange decor, stalactites, and black lights. It may seem like goth night, but hey, it's different. Drink a beer ($2) with the blond clientele. No cover. Open Sun.-Thurs. 11am-2am, Fri.-Sat. 11am-6am.

Tilly's 5th Avenue (tel. 85-90-15), Revolución and Calle 5. The tiny wooden dance floor in the center of this upscale, balloon-filled restaurant/bar resembles a boxing ring. Side tables illuminated by lovely stained-glass lamps. Tends to serve a slightly older crowd, but Tilly's is packed on weekends. Beer $2. Wed. night is "Student Night"—all drinks $2. Open Mon.-Thurs. 10:30am-2am, Fri.-Sun. 10:30am-5am.

■ Rosarito

Once a practically unpopulated playground for the rich and famous, Rosarito has expanded at breakneck speed to accommodate the throngs of sunseekers who flood its hotels, restaurants, shops, and beaches. The town is a virtual gringo colony—most visitors are from the north or are semi-permanent U.S. expats. English is ubiquitous and prices are quoted in dollars. On weekends, the sands and surf overflow with people, volleyball games, and horses—finding a place for your towel may be a struggle.

Practical Information The **tourist office** (tel. 2-02-00), on Juárez at Centro Comercio Villa Floreta, has tons of brochures. Some English is cautiously spoken (open Mon.-Fri. 9am-7pm, Sat.-Sun. 10am-5pm). **Banamex** (tel. 2-15-56/-57/-58 or 2-24-48/-49), is on Juárez at Ortiz (open Mon.-Fri. 9am-5pm). On weekends, you'll have to go to a *casa de cambio,* which charges a commission. The well-stocked **Comercial Mexicana Supermarket** (tel. 2-09-34), is at the north end of Juárez before Quinta del Mar (open daily 8am-10pm). **Lavamática Moderna** is on Juárez at Acacias (wash and dry 10 pesos; open Mon.-Sat. 8am-8pm, Sun. 8am-6pm). The **Red Cross** (tel. 132), is on Juárez and Ortiz just north of the tourist office. **Farmacia Hidalgo** (tel. 2-05-57), is on Juárez at Acacias (open Mon.-Sat. 8am-10pm, Sun. 8am-9pm). The **IMSS Hospital** (tel. 2-10-21), is on Juárez and Acacias behind the post office (open 24hr.). In an **emergency,** dial 134. The **police** (tel. 2-11-10), are next to the tourist office. The **post office** (tel. 2-13-55), is across from Oceana Plaza (open Mon.-Fri. 8am-5pm, Sat. 9am-1pm). The **postal code** is 72100. The **phone code** is 661.

Orientation Rosarito lies about 27km south of Tijuana. Virtually everything in town is on the main street, **Boulevard Juárez,** upon which street numbers are nonsequential. Most of what is listed below is near the purple Ortega's Restaurant in Oceana Plaza. To get to Rosarito from Tijuana, grab a yellow-and-white *taxi de ruta* (½hr.; 5 pesos) that leaves from Madero, between Calles 5 and 6. To return to Tijuana, flag down a *taxi de ruta* along Juárez or at its starting point in front of the Rosarito Beach Hotel. Getting to Ensenada is more of an adventure. Take a blue-and-white striped cab marked "Primo Tapia" from Festival Plaza, north of the Rosarito Beach Hotel, to the toll booth *(caseta de cobro)* on Hwy. 1 (3 pesos). There you can catch a bus to Ensenada (every ½hr. until about 9pm, 18 pesos).

Accommodations and Food Budget hotels in Rosarito are either inconvenient or cramped, with the exception of the outstanding **Hotel Palmas Quintero** (tel. 2-13-49), on Lázaro Cárdenas near the Hotel Quinta del Mar, three blocks inland from north Juárez. A friendly staff and dog welcome tourists to giant rooms with double beds and clean, private baths with hot water. Chill in the patio under the palm trees (singles $15 or 110 pesos). **Rosarito Beach Rental Cabins** (tel. 2-09-68), on Lázaro Cárdenas two blocks toward the water, are so cheap that most cabins are already occupied by permanent residents. You get what you pay for—each bug-sized cabin contains bunk beds, a toilet, and a sink (erratically open 8am-2pm and 4-7pm; singles $7, with shower $10; doubles $12, with shower $15; key deposit $5).

Fresh produce and seafood abound in the restaurants that line Juárez. For an economical seafood dinner, head to **Vince's Restaurant** (tel. 2-12-53), on Juárez next to Motel Villanueva. Enjoy a feast of soup, salad, rice, potatoes, tortillas, and an entree—*filete especial* (fillet of Halibut, 28 pesos), jumbo shrimp (40 pesos), or a veritable seafood extravaganza of fish, shrimp, octopus, and lobster (46 pesos). The casual atmosphere is enhanced by plastic plates and vacationers in swimwear (open daily 8am-10pm). **Tacos Sonora,** on Juárez 306, serves fresh fish tacos and quesadillas (7 pesos; open daily 7am-until the last customer leaves). Sit down to a staggeringly cheap breakfast at **Ortega's Ocean Plaza,** Juárez 200 (tel. 2-00-22), in a gaudy purple building. Prick your appetite with a cactus omelette ($2), or catch the all-you-can-eat Mexican buffet (open Sun.-Thurs. 8am-10pm, Fri.-Sat. 8am-11pm). If you have wheels and a hankering for lobster, you might want to drive 13km south to the tiny town of **Puerto Nuevo,** where several restaurants serve economical meals (around $8) of grilled lobster, rice, beans, tortillas, and free margaritas.

Sights and Entertainment People don't come to Rosarito to change the world; they come to swim, dance, and drink. **Rosarito Beach** boasts soft sand and gently rolling surf. Once the sun goes down, travelers live the dream at **Papas and Beer,** Calle de Coronales 400 (tel. 2-04-44), one block north of the Rosarito Beach Hotel and two blocks toward the sea. The open-air dance floor, bar, and sandy volleyball courts are packed with revelers on the weekends. Beer is 15 pesos, mixed drinks 17-25 pesos (cover $5-10 Sat. and holidays; open daily 11am-3am). Don't forget the ID; they take carding very seriously.

■ Mexicali

The highly industrialized and polluted capital of Baja California Norte, Mexicali (pop. 1,000,000) nudges the border between the namesake mainlands: California and Mexico. (Mexicali is not to be confused with Calexico on the other side of the border.) Mexicali, as its hybrid name might suggest, is an important gateway of transit to and from the U.S., and some parts of town, including the mall and surrounding plaza, wear the American facade so well that if not for the language, one could be in the States. It never quite lives up to the "cali" ideal, though, and Mexicali is not a big tourist destination.

Still, Mexicali is a good place to stock up on supplies and to check out the local Chinese cuisine before heading south. Because of turn-of-the-century immigration, thousands of Chinese still live in Mexicali; Chinese food is more ubiquitous than Mexican food, and a Chinese-influenced dialect has emerged in the city center.

PRACTICAL INFORMATION

Tourist Office: Comité de Turismo y Convenciones (tel. 57-23-76; fax 52-58-77), a white building at Mateos and Compresora facing the Vicente Guerrero monument and park, 30km from the border. Brochures, blessedly oversized maps, and English-speaking staff (open Sept.-July Mon.-Fri. 8am-6pm, Aug. 8am-4:30pm). **Tourist cards** available at the Federal Immigration office at the border.

Currency Exchange: Exchange currency at any *casa de cambio* along Madero, or try **Banamex** at Altamirano and Lerdo (tel. 54-28-00 or 54-29-29), where you can exchange traveler's checks. 24hr. **ATM**. Open Mon.-Fri. 9am-5pm.

Public Transportation: (tel. 57-24-10, 57-24-15, 57-24-22, or 57-24-55). Near the intersection of Mateos and Independencia, about 4km south of the border. A blue-and-white bus will take you to the station from the border (2 pesos). **Autotransportes de Baja California** (tel. 57-24-20, ext. 2229), sends buses to Ensenada (4 per day, 14hr., 87 pesos), and on a roller-coaster ride to Tijuana (every hr., 3½hr., 66 pesos; *plus* service 76 pesos). **Transportes del Pacífico** (tel. 57-24-61), offers service to Tijuana (*primera clase* 68 pesos, *segunda clase* 60 pesos). **Golden State** (tel. 53-61-69), sends buses to Californian cities, including Los Angeles (8am, 2:30, and 10pm, 4½hr., $28) and Palm Springs (8am, 2:30, and 10pm, 2½hr., $18).

Pharmacy: Farmacia de Dios (tel. 54-15-18), at López Mateos and Morelos. With a name like this, how can you go wrong? Some English spoken. Open Mon.-Fri. 8am-1:30am, Sat. 8-11:30pm, Sun. 8am-6pm.

Hospital: IMSS Centro de Salud (tel. 53-56-16), Lerdo at Calle F, has an English-speaking staff. **Hospital Civil** (tel. 54-11-23 or 54-11-30).

Police: (tel. 134, 54-21-32, or 52-91-98), at Calle Sur and Mateos. English spoken.

Post Office: Madero 491 (tel. 52-25-08), at Morelos. Open Mon.-Fri. 9am-5pm, Sat. 9am-1pm. **Postal Code:** 21000.

Phone Code: 65.

ORIENTATION

Though far from the ordinary route between the U.S. and Mexico, Mexicali serves as a a gateway to the south. The city lies on the California border 189km inland from Tijuana, with Calexico and the Imperial Valley immediately to the north.

Mexicali is perhaps one of the most difficult cities in Mexico to navigate. Run directly to the **tourist office** and pick up a deluxe **map.** The city is plagued with streets that zig-zag haphazardly and street numbers slightly less patterned than the digits of π. The main boulevard leading away from the border is **López Mateos,** which heads southeast, cutting through the downtown area. North-south *calles* and east-west *avenidas* both intersect Mateos, causing even more confusion. **Cristóbal Colón, Madero, Reforma, Obregón, Lerdo,** and **Zaragoza** (in that order, from the border) run east-west. From west to east, **Azueta Altamirano, Morelos, México,** and streets **A-L** run north-south, starting from where Mateos meets the border (a gigantic green canopy marks the spot). Don't try to make sense of the border area (particularly the intersection of Morelos and Obregón) from a map; guesswork and a few well-directed questions might be your best bet.

To reach the border from the bus station, take the local bus marked Centro (every 10min., 5am-11pm, 2.50 pesos), from outside the bus terminal, just across the footbridge. Ride past the Vicente Guerrero monument and the enormous new mall; get off at López Mateos and walk down until the border crossing.

ACCOMMODATIONS

Budget hotels crowd the noisy bar strip on Altamirano between Reforma and Lerdo and line Morelos south of Mateos. Hotels on Madero close to Mateos will dig deeper into your wallet but are cleaner.

Hotel México, Av. Lerdo 476 (tel. 54-06-69), at Morelos. Newly remodeled, this hotel offers rooms as clean and pink as a bouncing baby boy's butt. Rooms have color TV and A/C and overlook a central patio. Bathrooms are small but clean. The office doubles as a grocery store, and the staff is *muy simpático.* Singles 130 pesos; doubles 170 pesos.

Hotel Imperial, Madero 222 (tel. 53-63-33, 53-61-16, or 53-67-90), at Azueta. Minty-fresh rooms are stocked with rock-hard beds, desks, squeaky fans, A/C, and color TVs. Private baths with narrow showers. Purified water. Singles 160 pesos; doubles 200 pesos. Key deposit 10 pesos.

Hotel Malibu, on Morelos near Lerdo. Look out for the big sign. Although the hotel doesn't quite live up to its name, the worn rooms are clean and come with the basics. One of the cheapest joints in town—for the hard-core budget traveler. Singles 50 pesos, with bath 60 pesos, with bath and TV 70 pesos; doubles with bath 80 pesos, with bath and TV 88 pesos.

FOOD

Some of the best and cheapest food in town can be had at the food court in Mexicali's huge mall on Lopez Mateos. Here, yummy, cheap Chinese cuisine is bountiful, and places usually have plates that combine three entrees for 15 pesos, four entrees for 19 pesos. To find the best ones, follow the crowds of locals.

Restaurant Buendía, Altamirano 263 (tel. 52-69-25). Despite sharing a name with the illustrious family of Gabriel García Márquez's epic, Buendía specializes in Chinese cuisine. Try a heaping plate of beef with broccoli, fried rice, egg roll, and fried chicken (30 pesos). Three burritos are 30 pesos. Herbivores can delight in a veggie combo for only 24 pesos. Open daily 7am-9pm.

Tortas El Chavo, Reforma 414 at Altamirano, off Mateos, 3 blocks from the border. A fast-food joint with plastic booths; mirrored walls reflect the green and yellow "furniture." *Tortas,* any style, are 13 pesos; *tacos de machaca* (tacos filled with strips of beef) go for a mere 4 pesos. Open daily 8:30am-8pm.

Restaurant Hollis, Morelos and Mateos opposite Farmacia de Dios. Serves American, Chinese, and Mexican food. Lots of locals converse casually as they enjoy home-cooked meals. Chinese combo plates 12-18 pesos. Filling steak sandwiches 10 measly pesos (open daily 8am-10pm).

SIGHTS

Mexicali's **park, forest, lake,** and **zoo** (tel. 55-28-33), are located in the southwestern part of town, on Alvarado between San Marcos and Lázaro Cárdenas. Wink at the birds in the aviary, pedal a paddleboat on the lake, or admire lions and tigers from the train that circles the park and nature reserve. The grounds contain carousels, bumper cars, a pool, and a science museum (open Tues.-Sat. 9am-5pm, Sun. 9am-5pm; admission 3 pesos, children 2 pesos). To reach the park area, board a black and white *colectivo* marked "Calle 3" downtown. If you've got wheels, drive south on Azueta over the Río Nuevo (unfortunately one of the most polluted rivers in the world), where the road becomes Uxmal; turn left on Independencia, then right on Victoria.

ENTERTAINMENT

Bullfights are staged regularly in the fall at the **Plaza de Toros Calafia,** on Calafia at Independencia (tel. 56-11-96), in the *centro;* take a 10-minute ride on the blue-and-white bus (2.50 pesos) from the *centro* to the plaza, which holds up to 11,500 people (11,499 if the bull's having a good day). Wild and crazy rodeos rampage in the winter and spring at **Lienzo Charro del Cetys,** at Cetys and Ordente. Check with the tourist office for schedules. Good, clean fun awaits at **Mundo Divertido,** an amusement park at Mateos 850 (tel. 52-56-75), across from the mall (open Mon.-Fri. noon-9pm, Sat.-Sun. 11am-10pm). To get to the park, board a blue-and-white bus marked Centro Cívico at Madero and Altamirano (departs every 10min., 5am-11pm, 2.50 pesos). Mexicali's biggest diversion is the **Centro Comercial Gigante,** the mega-mall often referred to as **La Cochanillo.** Filled with cheap food stands, video arcades, and the **Cinema Gemelos,** showing flicks for 20 pesos.

■ Ensenada

The secret is out—beachless Ensenada (pop. 72,000) is becoming a weekend hot spot. The masses of Californians that arrive every Friday evening have gringo-ized the town to an incredible degree; everyone speaks some English, and store clerks resort to calculators if you try to buy something with pesos. Still, Ensenada is less brash than its insatiable cousin to the north, the infamous TJ. Cooled by sea breezes, the town is more pleasant during the week, when fewer tourist-consumers populate the city and the center of town might even be called endearing.

The ride from Tijuana to Ensenada offers continuous views of the Pacific, and its last 20 minutes are breathtaking if you take the Ensenada *cuota* (toll road), as the buses do. There are three toll gates along the way, each charging $1.62 or 13 pesos. Don't begrudge the money, though—it's well worth the view of the ocean, sand dunes, stark cliffs, and broad mesas. The less scenic *libre* (free road) is a poorly maintained two-lane highway that parallels the toll road to La Misión then cuts inland for the remaining 40km to Ensenada. If you're coming by car, drive during the day—there are no streetlights and many tight curves. Be sure to drive in the right lane; the left is for passing only. Some great rest spots can be found along the road to absorb the view, or to hike down and walk along the lonely cliffs.

Practical Information The **tourist office,** Blvd. Costero 540 (tel. 78-24-11 or 78-36-75; fax 78-85-88), at Gastelum, has maps and pamphlets in English (open Mon.-Fri. 9am-2pm and 4-7pm, Sat. 10am-3pm, Sun. 10am-2pm). The **Chamber of Commerce,** Mateos 693 at Macheros, 2nd fl. (tel. 78-37-70, 78-23-22, or 74-09-96), is closer to the center of town and provides brochures and maps (open Mon.-Fri.

8:30am-2pm and 4-6:30pm). **Banks** cluster along Juárez at Av. Ruiz. **Bancomer,** on Juárez at Av. Ruiz (tel. 78-11-08), exchanges dollars and traveler's checks (open Mon.-Fri. 9am-12:30pm). **ATMs** are along Juárez in the bank district, including one at **BanOro,** Juárez and Gastelum. There is also a 24hr. **ATM,** Calle 3 and Ruiz.

   Autotransportes de Baja California (tel. 78-66-80), runs buses to several destinations (daily 10am, noon, 7, 8, 9:30, and 11pm). To Mexicali (4hr., 101 pesos) and Tijuana (every ½hr., 1½hr., 45 pesos). **Transportes Aragón,** on Riveroll between Calles 8 and 9 (tel. 74-07-17), runs to Tijuana (every hr., 5am-9pm, 40 pesos). Local *urbano* buses (tel. 78-25-94), leave from Juárez and Calle 6, and from Calle 2 and Macheros (every 8-15min., 3 pesos).

   Hertz, Calle 2 and Riveroll (tel. (66) 8-29-82), rents cars ($45 per day with unlimited mi.; open Mon.-Fri. 8am-2pm and 4-6pm, Sat. 9am-4pm). **Supermarket Calimax,** Gastelum at Calle 4 (tel. 78-33-97), has just about everything (open daily 6am-2am). A laundromat, **Lavandería Lavadero** (tel. 78-27-37), is on Obregón between Calles 6 and 7, across from Parque Revolución (open Mon.-Sat. 8am-7pm, Sun. 8am-2pm). **Farmacia del Sol,** on Av. Ruiz 447 (tel. 74-05-26), between Calle 4 and Juarez, is open 24hr. The **Hospital General** (tel. 76-78-00 or 76-44-44), is on the Transpeninsular Highway at the 111km mark (open 24hr.). In an **emergency,** dial 134. **Police** (tel. 76-24-21), are at Calle 9 at Espinoza. The **post office** (tel. 76-10-88), is on Mateos and Club Rotario (open Mon.-Fri. 8am-7pm, Sat. 9am-1pm). The **postal code** is 22800. The **telephone code** is 61.

Orientation Ensenada is 108km south of Tijuana on Hwy. 1. If you're driving, follow signs on Hwy. 1 to the *centro.* You'll come into town on **Azueta,** which later becomes **Gastelum.** Buses from Tijuana arrive at the main terminal, at Calle 11 and Riveroll. Turn right as you come out of the station, walk 10 blocks, and you'll be at **Mateos** (also called **Primera**), the main tourist drag. **Juárez (Calle 5)** runs parallel to Mateos, while from north to south, **Avenidas Ryerson, Moctezuma, Obregón, Ruiz, Gastelum, Miramar, Riveroll, Alvarado, Blancarte,** and **Castillo** are perpendicular to it above the *arroyo,* a grassy trench crossed by small bridges. Below the *arroyo,* **Avenidas Espinoza, Floresta, Guadalupe, Hidalgo, Iturbide,** and (later) **Balboa** also run perpendicular to Mateos. **Blvd. Costero** traces the shoreline, parallel to (and west of) Mateos. Streets are numbered, avenues are named; together they form a grid. *Calles* run northwest-southeast, while most *avenidas* run northeast-southwest (Juárez and Mateos are exceptions). After sundown, avoid the area near the shoreline and the regions bounded by Av. Miramar and Macheros, and Mateos and Cuarta. Keep in mind while orienting yourself that the large residential Chapultepec Hills lie to the north, and the water to the west.

Accommodations Budget hotels line Mateos between Espinoza and Riveroll and at Miramar. Most rooms are a 25-minute stroll from the beachfront "boardwalk" and 10 minutes from the popular clubs. Although many owners quote prices in greenbacks, pay in pesos. **Motel Pancho** (tel. 78-23-44), on Alvarado at Calle 2, one block off Mateos, has big rooms and clean baths with tiny showers (singles and doubles 90 pesos). **Motel Caribe,** Av. López Mateos 627 (tel. 78-34-81), offers great rooms and a superb location, right across the street from some of Ensenada's popular dance clubs and bars. Comfortably firm beds and carpeted floors deck out the rooms (singles 120 pesos; doubles 160 pesos; higher rates on weekends). RV parks line the stretch between Tijuana and Ensenada; close to Ensenada is **Ramona RV Park** (tel. 74-60-45), on km 104 of the Transpeninsular Hwy. (full hookup $9).

Food The cheaper restaurants in town line Juárez and Espinoza. Fresh fruit, seafood, and taco stands abound, but be wary of how the food is handled. Quality food can be found at **supermarkets** along Gastelum. At the friendly **Cafetería Monique Colonial** (tel. 76-40-41), Calle 9 and Espinoza, locals sit in anxious anticipation of their breaded steak with salad and fries (25 pesos; no alcohol; open Mon.-Sat. 6am-10pm, Sun. 6am-5pm). Chefs at **Las Parrillas** (tel. 76-17-28), Espinoza at Calle 6, grill up fresh meat cutlets on the flaming pit as customers make like Pavlov's dog. Squeeze onto a counter stool in the diner-like atmosphere and scarf down burritos (18 pesos) and *súper hamburguesas* with veggies, avocado, and chili (13 pesos; open daily 7:30am-11pm). **Mary's Restaurant,** Av. Miramar 609, between Costero and Mateos, serves typical seaside fare, burritos starting at $3, and a complete breakfast (eggs, tortillas, beans, and coffee) for $2.75. Keep an eye out for the altar to the *Virgincita* woven into the nets, and similarly random photos of Bruce Lee flicks.

Sights Seeing Ensenada requires more than a quick cruise down Mateos. For a view of the entire city, climb the **Chapultepec Hills.** The steep road to the top begins at the foot of Calle 2; expect a 10- to 15-minute hike. Less taxing is a stroll down **Av. López Mateos,** where curio shops make for hours of mindless shopping.

The mild, dry climate of Northern Baja's Pacific coast has made it Mexico's prime grape-growing area. **Bodegas de Santo Tomás,** Miramar 666 (tel. 78-33-33), devilishly located in a less-visited part of town, has produced wine since 1888. Today, they distill over 500,000 cases of champagne and wine every year. Tours include free wine tasting and an assortment of breads and cheeses (11am, 1, and 3pm; $2).

In the well-manicured **Plaza Civil,** on Costero between Riveroll and Alvarado, the larger-than-life golden busts of Venustiano Carranza, Miguel Hidalgo, and Benito Juárez stare seriously onto the town's plaza. The nearby gardens of the **Centro Cívico, Social, y Cultural de Ensenada** (tel. 76-43-10 or 76-42-33), are one block from Costero (admission $1). High, flapping flags, each representing a Latin American country, sprout from flowerbeds. The centro is a shrine to Ensenada's archeological and social history. The **Instituto Nacional de Antropología e Historia,** Ryerson 99 at Virgilio Uribe (tel. 78-25-31), is the oldest building in town. Artifacts from all over Baja include a charming photograph of two elderly Cucapa men standing next to their shared young wife, whom they acquired during a robbery in a nearby town (open Mon.-Fri. 9am-4pm; free). A healthy 15-minute walk from Mateos is the **Museo de Ciencias,** Obregón 1463 (tel. 78-71-92; fax 78-63-35), at Catorce. Housed in an old wooden boat, the museum displays photographs of and information about the endangered species of Baja (open Mon.-Fri. 9am-5pm, Sat. noon-5pm; admission 5 pesos).

Entertainment Most of the popular hangouts along Mateos are members of the hybrid species known as the restaurant/bar/disco. Food and drink are served only until 8pm or so, when the eateries metamorphose into full-fledged dance-club monsters. On weekends festive-feeling American youth pack the house.

Better known than Ensenada itself is **Hussong's Cantina** (tel. 78-32-10), on Ruiz between Mateos and Calle 2. Now 105-years-old, Hussong's is the prototypical Mexican watering hole: with dark, wood-paneled walls and a sawdust on the floor, you get the true *cantina* flavor with your *Tecate.* Gulp down beer (7-9 pesos) or a margarita (12 pesos) at the long, shiny bar (open daily 10am-2am). When you tire of the continuous stream of *mariachis,* cross the street to **Papas and Beer** (tel. 74-01-45; http://www.papasandbeer.com/baja), a high-tech music emporium popular with a young crowd that swigs large margaritas (21 pesos) and spends horse-choking wads of cash. Escape the congestion and decor by stepping onto the terrace, where hockey-rink-like plexiglass boards prevent carousers from cross-checking each other off the balcony to the street below. Thursday night is theme night (birthday, pajamas, whatever) and Sunday is Ladies Night; women drink free, and men aren't let in until 10pm (cover $3-5; open Wed., Sat. 10am-3am, other days noon-3am).

If you don't drink, join the gyrating mass of teens whirling to late-80s pop hits at **Roller Ensenada** (tel. 76-11-59), a roller rink on Mateos at Hidalgo (open Tues.-Thurs. 2-10pm, Fri.-Sun.10am-10pm; admission 9 pesos—with or without skates). If you just want to zone out in front of a big screen, **Cinema Gemelos** (tel. 76-36-16 or 76-36-13), on Balboa and Mateos at the southern end of town, screens subtitled American features (shows 4-10pm; admission 20 pesos).

Whistle While You...What?

Mexicans have transformed the simple act of whistling into a language unto its own. Stepping off a curb too soon, trying to parallel park, wearing that tank top on a hot day—all these might receive a whistle carefully selected from a copious vocabulary. There is the **attention-getting, taxi-hailing, traffic-stopping** whistle: a simple burst of sound, sometimes presented in a two-tone combination, which could be your only hope of slowing down the local bus you're chasing. There is the pulsating, directional, **you-can-back-up-another-meter-ooops** whistle, frequently used for parallel parking, which sounds like the high-pitched sounds of a Mack truck backing up. Then, of course, there's the **hey-chula-please-turn-and-look-at-me-I'm-so-bored** whistle, which certainly possesses the richest repertoire of permutations, from a long, drawn out exhale to a sharp, quick, breathy whisper. If you have two X chromosomes, you'll be sure to get your share. More welcome is the **you're-not-Mexican-are-you** whistle, which varies according to the imagination and tonal range of the whistler. The delight in sitting on a stoop and messing with passersby's minds may not initially be apparent to the tired traveler. After a short time in Mexico, however, you, too, will want to indulge in melodic discourse in the dark hostel hallway or on the crowded *pesero*. Sure, it's a complicated language, but just think how far it could get you.

■ Near Ensenada

Ensenada is an excellent base from which to explore Baja's natural wonders. Unfortunately, to reach most of them, you'll need some wheels—preferably a 4WD or all-terrain vehicle. Try Hertz in Ensenada, or, better yet (if you're driving down from Cali), Bargain Auto Rentals in San Diego (see **San Diego: Cars,** p. 146).

BEACHES

Good sand to accompany your swim in the bucolic Bahía de Todos Santos can only be found outside of the city. To the north, **Playa San Miguel,** with its rocky coastlines and large waves, is great for surfers, but might not be ideal for others. To get there, drive north up Calle 10 until the toll gate, and then turn left at the sign marked Playa San Miguel; or take a bus marked San Miguel departing from Gastelum and Costero (3 pesos). Buses back must be flagged down.

Somewhat more frequented beaches lie 8km south of Ensenada off the Transpeninsular Highway. Probably the nicest beach around is **Playa Estero,** dominated by the Estero Beach Resort and by Americanization. Volleyball courts fill the beach's clean but hard and unforgiving sand. You can rent water skis, banana boats, or bicycles ($5 per hr.). The **Estero Beach Museum** (tel. 6-62-35), displays Mexican folk art (open Wed.-Mon. 9am-6pm; free). To get there, take a right at the Estero Beach sign on Hwy. 1 heading south. Free parking is available in the first lot of the hotel. Alternatively, catch a bus marked Aeropuerto, Zorrillo, Maneadero, or Chapultepec from Pl. Cívica. **Playa El Faro** (tel. 7-46-30; fax 7-46-20), is similarly rife with volleyball courts and Americans, but has slightly better sand, and offers camping on the beach (campsite, parking, and bathroom privileges $7 for 4 people; full RV hookup $12; rooms with bath $30 for 2 people). Another nearby beach is **Playa Santa María,** where you can rent a horse ($9 per hr.) and ride around the bay.

Heading onto the Punta Banda peninsula (continuing south from Ensenada, take the paved road BCN 23, which splits west off Hwy. 1 north of Maneadero), you will find lonelier beaches along the stretch known as **Baja Beach**, where rolling hills and marshes provide the backdrop. Horses are available for rent, and swimming is always free. The Baja Beach Resort also runs a pool of hot springs, located on Hwy. 1 on the left, 2km before turning off onto the Punta Banda peninsula. To get to Baja Beach, walk down a dirt road after the sign, on the right hand side. By car, bear right at the first fork in the road after turning onto the peninsula.

HIKING

The area's most beautiful spots remain essentially undiscovered by most tourists. Breathtaking hikes around the mountains of the Punta Banda peninsula approaching La Bufadora can be completed on well-kept trails of U.S. National Park quality. Bring a snack, as there are some good picnic stops. And don't forget a bathing suit—when you reach the bottom, you can relieve your sweaty body with a dip amid the rocks in the chilly Pacific.

The best spot to enter the trails is **Cerro de la Punta,** on the road to La Bufadora near the end of the Punta Banda Peninsula. Turn right up a long driveway at the Cerro de la Punta sign (parking 10 pesos). You'll see a small clearing and a large house on the cliffs; here, you can hike up among the cacti to the top of the mountains for views of the surrounding area or down beautiful trails on the oceanside.

Other stops earlier along the road to La Bufadora are equally scenic, and a few are near unique cave-like rock enclosures created when the mountain was blasted to build the road. The bus to La Bufadora (see below) will drop you off anywhere along this road, including Cerro de la Punta, but if you don't hitch, you may be waiting quite a while for the bus back (*Let's Go* does not recommend hitchhiking). **Punta Banda** itself has a roadside **grocery market** and **post office** (open Mon.-Fri. 8am-2pm; but, honestly, go to Ensenada), on the main road after the turnoff for Baja Beach. A good place to camp or park an RV in Punta Banda is **Villarino** (tel. 3-20-45 or 6-42-46; fax 3-20-44), adjacent to the plaza, which has modern shower and bathroom facilities and full hookups ($5 per person per night).

Hiking further inland offers completely different terrain, ranging from deep lagoons to cactus forests to ponderosa pine. The rugged mountain range east of Ensenada is the solitary **Sierra de Juárez,** where **Parque Nacional Constitución de 1857** is located. Be forewarned that you'll need an all-terrain vehicle or pickup truck to make the trek. If you can afford it, find a guide who can show you the correct paths to take once off the main roads—dirt roads and brush make the paths difficult to navigate. To get there, follow Rte. 3 east from Avenida Juárez in Ensenada all the way to **Ojos Negros.** At km 39, turn onto the dirt road leading into the park. Follow signs (or, better, ask a guide for help), and you will eventually find yourself at **Laguna Hanson,** a little lake surrounded by basic camping spots. If you aren't wheeled, **Ecotour** (tel. 76-44-15; fax 74-67-78), offers excursions. The owner, Francisco Detrell, also leads tours in Ensenada and other parts of Baja. Call or fax at least three days in advance in order to book a tour.

Southeast of Ensenada is the more famous **Sierra San Pedro Martir,** home to **Picacho del Diablo,** Baja's tallest peak at 3087m (10,126ft.). Getting there demands an all-terrain vehicle. Drive 127km south on Rte. 1 to **San Telmo;** from there, turn east onto a gravel road (108km) until you reach the park. For more information, call the **Ensenada Tourist Office. Ecotour** also leads tours here (call in advance).

LA BUFADORA

La Bufadora, the largest geyser on the Pacific coast, is 30km south of Ensenada. On a good day, the "Blowhole" shoots water 40m into the air out of a water-carved cave. On some days, visitors will have to be satisfied with the beautiful view from the Bufadora peak. Unfortunately, the droves of visitors, cheesy curio shops, and food vendors have made the area rather unpleasant. In spite of the garbage strewn everywhere, though, the hole itself makes the trip worthwhile. To get there, drive south on the Transpeninsular Highway (take a right onto the highway off López Mateos at the southern end of town), head straight past the exits for the airport, military base, and Playa Estero, and take a right after about 20 minutes at the sign marked La Bufadora. Continue on that road until its end. You'll know you're there after you've finished a brain-numbing series of road loops and you find yourself on a small street with multi-colored vending stalls (parking $1 or 7 pesos). Alternatively, you can take a yellow *microbús* to **Maneadero** (3 pesos), and a connecting bus to La Bufadora (2 pesos).

The Desert

Mystics and misanthropes from Native Americans to modern city slickers have long been fascinated by the austere scenery and the vast open spaces of the California desert. In winter the desert is a pleasantly warm refuge, in spring, a technicolor floral landscape, and in summer, a blistering wasteland. A barren place of overwhelming simplicity, the desert's beauty lies not so much in what it contains, but in what it lacks—the crowds, congestion, and chaos that pervade the planet today.

ORIENTATION

California's desert divides roughly into the Low and High Deserts, names which indicate differences in both altitude and latitude. The **Sonoran,** or **Low Desert,** occupies southeastern California from the Mexican border north to Needles and west to the Borrego Desert. The **Mojave,** or **High Desert,** averages elevations of 2000 ft. and spans the south central part of the state, bounded by the Sonoran Desert to the south, San Bernardino and the San Joaquin Valleys to the west, the Sierra Nevada to the north, and Death Valley to the east. Four major east-west highways cross the desert. In the Low Desert, **I-8** hugs the California-Mexico border, while **I-10** skims past Joshua Tree and through Blythe. Cutting through the heart of the Mojave is **I-15.** From Barstow, the Mojave's main pit stop, I-15 continues on to Las Vegas, while **I-40** cuts southeast through Needles and on to the Nevada desert.

DESERT SURVIVAL

Here, **water,** not bread, is the staff of life. The body loses at least a gallon of liquid per day in the desert (two gallons during strenuous activity), so keep drinking *always.* Drinking huge quantities of water after physical exertion to quench your thirst is not as effective as taking preventative measures to stay hydrated. Whether you are driving or hiking, tote **two gallons of water per person per day.** Designate at least one container as an emergency supply, and always have water at your side. In the car, keep back-up containers in a cooler. When drinking sweet beverages, dilute them with water to avoid an over-reaction to high sugar content. Avoid alcohol and coffee, which cause dehydration. For long-term stays, a high-quality beverage with potassium compounds and glucose, such as ERG (an industrial-strength Gatorade available from wilderness outfits and camping suppliers), will help keep your strength up.

Most people need a few days to adjust to the heat, especially before strenuous activity. Sunglasses with 100% UV protection, sunscreen, and a hat are essential **sun protection,** but clothing is the most effective protection. Light colors reflect the sun, and wearing a sweaty shirt, though uncomfortable, prevents dehydration more effectively than removing it. For added relief from the heat, wrap a dampened bandanna around your head. Thick-soled shoes and two pairs of socks may help to keep feet comfortable on a hike in summer, when sand temperatures reach 150-200°F.

Heat is not the desert's only climactic extreme. At high elevations, temperatures during winter nights can be well below freezing (a sweater is often necessary even in the summer). Fall and spring **flash floods** are can cause water to come down from rain-drenched higher elevations and wreak Biblical devastation upon lands below, turning dry gulches into raging rivers—choose campsites accordingly.

Hiking expeditions should be attempted only in temperatures under 90°F, and *never* alone. Almost all parks require hikers to register with the park office before hitting the trails. If you're on private or unmanaged public land, *always* notify someone of your itinerary. **Hitchhiking in the desert** is risky, if not suicidal.

Driving in the Desert

Desert conditions are just as grueling on cars as they are on bodies; only recently serviced cars in good running condition can take the heat. Bring at least five gallons of radiator water, extra coolant, and a few quarts of oil (car manuals recommend appropriate oil weights for varying temperatures). In addition to a spare tire and necessary tools for the basic mishap on the road, a board and shovel are useful for sand-stuck cars. A 4WD vehicle is recommended for unpaved roads.

Although settlements are sometimes sparse, major roads usually have enough traffic to ensure that breakdowns will be noticed. Even so, isolated areas of the parks pose a threat, especially in summer, when few tourists visit. *Stay with your vehicle if it breaks down;* it is easier to spot than a person and provides crucial shade.

Use **air conditioning** with extreme restraint. Turn it off immediately if the car's temperature gauge starts to climb. Air from open windows should be sufficiently comfortable at highway speeds. If your car overheats, pull off the road and turn the heater on full force to cool the engine. If radiator fluid is steaming or bubbling, turn off the car for about half an hour. If not, run the car in neutral at about 1500 rpms for a few minutes, allowing the coolant to circulate. Never pour water over the engine and never try to lift a searing hood. **Desert water bags** are available at hardware or automotive stores for about $5-10. When strapped onto the front of the car and filled with water, these large canvas bags prevent overheating by speeding up evaporation. Driving in the evening, night, and early morning is preferable to burning mid-day.

THE LOW DESERT

The Low Desert, home of Anza-Borrego Desert State Park and the Salton Sea, is flat, dry, and barren. Only the oases in this area can promote super-resort tourism as well. Despite its arid climate, much of this region has become agriculturally important, as water from the Colorado River irrigates the Imperial Valley and the Coachella Valley.

■ Palm Springs

Even in its very first days, when Cahuillan Indians settled here for a winter respite, Palm Springs was a rambunctious resort. Subsequent Native American inhabitants displaced the Cahuillans, European settlers displaced these newer tribes, and it was only a matter of time before this glitzy desert community elected Sonny Bono as its mayor. Today, the medicinal waters of the city's natural hot springs ensure not only the health of its opulent residents, but also its longevity as a resort town. While Palm Springs is home to gaggles of retirees, it is also a popular spring break destination for students and a winter destination for fat-cat golfers. With warm temperatures, celebrity residents, and more pink than a *Miami Vice* episode, this desert city (pop. 42,000) provides a sunny break from everyday life. Although Palm Springs may challenge the budget traveler, it offers enough affordable fun to merit a stop en route to Joshua Tree or an escapist excursion from the chaos of L.A.

PRACTICAL INFORMATION

Visitor Information: Chamber of Commerce, 190 W. Amado Rd. (325-1577). Friendly advice, maps ($2), and hotel reservations. Pick up *The Desert Guide,* a free monthly magazine outlining attractions and entertainment. Open Mon.-Fri. 8:30am-4:30pm. **Visitors Center,** 2781 N. Palm Canyon Dr. (748-8418 or 800-34-SPRINGS/347-7746). Highlights local arts and entertainment. Info on restaurants and hotels; ask about discounts. Open Mon.-Sat. 9am-5pm, Sun. 9am-4pm.

Bank: Bank of America, 588 S. Palm Canyon Dr. and 750 N. Palm Canyon Dr. (340-1867), has **ATMs** and friendly tellers to make spendin' easy. Open Mon.-Thurs. 9am-6pm, Fri. 9am-7pm, Sat. 9am-2pm.

Airport: Palm Springs Regional, 3400 S. Tahquitz-Canyon Rd. (323-8161). State and limited national service.

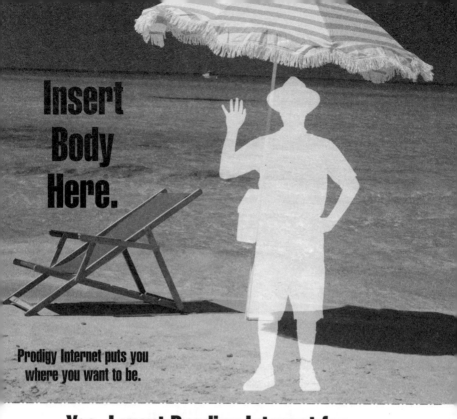

Use Prodigy Internet to plan your next vacation.

Before you go on your next vacation, use Prodigy Internet to help make your trip a lot less expensive and a lot more fun. You'll be able to plan your entire vacation online, including:

http://travel.prodigy.net

- Booking air, hotel and car reservations
- Finding money-saving cruise packages
- Accessing Internet travel guides, such as **Let's Go** (www.letsgo.com)
- Receiving low-fare alerts via email

Plus, you'll have access to **Traveling Lite** (http://travelinglite.prodigy.com), a student/budget site brought to you by Prodigy Internet.

To get your Prodigy Internet software with one FREE* month, call 1-800-PRODIGY, ext. 3302 Or simply return the attached card below.

*Limit one free trial per individual. Valid credit card required. Additional charges apply for certain features. Phone company charges not included. Supplemental access charges may apply. To avoid being charged your first monthly fee, simply cancel your membership before your free one month trial ends. For Basic 10 Plan and Unlimited Plan pricing after your one month trial, refer to the online Customer Service or Help sites. Offer subject to change without notice.

Prodigy Internet and the Prodigy Internet logo are trademarks of Prodigy Services Corporation. Other names are registered trademarks or trademarks of their respective owners. ©1997 Prodigy Services Corporation. All Rights Reserved.

NO POSTAGE
NECESSARY IF
MAILED IN THE
UNITED STATES

BUSINESS REPLY MAIL
FIRST CLASS MAIL   PERMIT NO. 10   PLYMOUTH, MA

POSTAGE WILL BE PAID BY ADDRESSEE

prodigyinternet™

PRODIGY SERVICES CORPORATION
PO BOX 1740
PLYMOUTH, MA 02362-9903

Buses: Greyhound, 311 N. Indian Canyon Dr. (800-231-2222), near downtown. To L.A. (7 per day, $14, round-trip $21). No advance purchase necessary.

Public Transportation: Sun Bus (343-3451). Local bus service connecting all Coachella Valley cities (daily 6am-6pm). Lines #21 and 23 cover the downtown area. Fare 75¢, transfers 25¢; seniors and disabled 25¢, transfers 10¢, weekends free. The *Rider's Guide,* available at information centers and in most hotel lobbies, includes schedules and a system map. **Sun Dial** (343-3451), transports disabled patrons from doorstep to destination. Fare $1 within the city, 50¢ outside the city. Reserve 4-5 days in advance. Must be over 60 or have ADA card.

Taxis: Checker Cab (325-2868). **Valley Cab Company** (340-5845). Both 24hr.

Car Rental: Rates fluctuate and are higher in winter. **Rent-A-Wreck,** 67555 Palm Canyon Dr., #A105 (324-1766), Cathedral City. Must be 21 with major credit card. **Budget** (327-1404), at Palm Springs Regional Airport. Ages 18-21 must have proof of full-coverage insurance; drivers under 25 pay $10 per day surcharge.

Bike Rental: Desert Cyclery, 70053 Rte. 111 (321-9444). Mountain bikes $7 per hr., $19 per day. Open Mon.-Sat. 9:30am-5:30pm, Sun. noon-5pm.

Laundromat: Arenas Coin-Op, 220 E. Arenas Rd. (322-7717), ½ block east of Indian Canyon. Wash $1, 10min. dry 25¢. Open daily 5am-8pm.

Road Conditions: (345-2767). **Weather Conditions:** (345-3711).

Crisis Lines: Rape Crisis Hotline (568-9071). **Regional Poison Control Center** (800-777-6476). **AIDS Hotline of Southern California** (800-922-2437).

Medical Services: Desert Hospital, 1150 N. Indian Canyon Dr. (323-6511, emergency 323-6251).

Emergency: 911.

Post Office: 333 E. Amado Rd. (325-9631). Open Mon.-Fri. 8am-5pm, Sat. 9am-1pm. **ZIP Code:** 92262.

Area Code: 760.

ORIENTATION

Palm Springs is a two to three hour drive from L.A. along I-10, depending on traffic. A longer but more scenic route is the **Palms-to-Pines Hwy. (Rte. 74),** where sparse desert cactus and sagebrush give way to lush evergreens. The major gateway to Palm Springs, however, is **I-10** East. Approaching from the north on I-15, take Rte. 215 East to Rte. 60 East to I-10 East. From I-10 East, take **Rte. 111** to the Palm Springs Exit. The visitors center is located one block beyond Tramway Rd. on the right side. To orient yourself within the town, find **Indian Canyon Dr.** and **East Palm Canyon Dr.,** the city's two main drags. East Palm Canyon Dr. winds west-northwest through town before subtly turning due north and creeping into Indian Canyon. There are two major east-west boulevards. **Tahquitz-Canyon Rd.** runs east to the airport, while **Ramon Rd.,** four blocks to the south, provides access to I-10.

ACCOMMODATIONS

Like most famous resort communities, Palm Springs caters mainly to those seeking a tax shelter, not a night's shelter. Yet affordable lodging *is* available. Motels slash their prices 20-40% in the summer; call ahead for prices and don't be shy about bargaining. Many hotels offer discounts through the visitors center. Motels in nearby communities such as Cathedral City and Desert Hot Springs are less attractive but more affordable. Prices listed don't include the county's 10% accommodation tax.

Budget Host Inn, 1277 S. Palm Canyon Dr. (325-5574 or 800-829-8099), offers large, clean rooms with refrigerators, phones, and pool/jacuzzi access. In-room movies, coffeemaker, and continental breakfast included. Rooms $79, weekends $99. Off-season: $29, $39. Laundry.

Motel 6, 660 S. Palm Canyon Dr. (327-4200), conveniently located south of city center. Other locations at 595 E. Palm Canyon Dr. (325-6129), and 63950 20th Ave. (251-1425), near the I-10 off-ramp. The cheapest rates in town (*especially* during winter). Each has a pool and A/C. Some on-the-spot rooms available. Summer: singles $35; doubles $41. Only a few bucks higher in winter.

THE DESERT

Palm Court Inn, 1983 N. Palm Canyon Dr. (416-2333), close to downtown. Water-melon-hued exterior houses 80 rooms, 2 heated pools, a spa, and a fitness center. Rooms $49, off-season $39; each additional guest (after 4) $8.

Hampton Inn, 2000 N. Palm Canyon Dr. (320-0555). The extra bit of luxury you get for your extra hit of money is what Palm Springs is all about. Features comfy rooms, complimentary continental breakfasts, a beautiful outdoor pool, and cable TV. In summer: doubles $54, weekends $64.

FOOD

The largest of the desert towns, Palm Springs has more dining options than most desert pit stops—diners and ethnic eateries are common. To cook up your own chow, head for the **Vons Supermarket,** 4733 E. Palm Canyon Dr. (324-4502).

Las Casuelas-The Original, 368 N. Palm Canyon Dr. (325-3213). Its immediate success made chainhood inevitable, but locals insist that The Original is where it's at. Authentic Mexican dishes ($6 and up), dingy lighting, and tattooed waitresses give it that slightly outlaw south-of-the-border feel. Open daily 10am-10pm.

Thai Smile, 651 N. Palm Canyon Dr. (320-5503), between Tamarisk and Alejo. Many vegetarian options. Spicy *pad thai* chicken $6.50. Lunch $5-6, dinner $7-10. Open daily 11am-10pm.

Carlo's Italian Delicatessen, 119 S. Indian Canyon Dr. (325-5571). Palm Springs' finest budget-minded deli (sandwiches $6) offers you the privilege of eating under the watchful eyes of the local personalities portrayed on the wall. Open Wed.-Fri. 10am-6pm, Sat. 10am-8pm, Sun. 10am-5pm; closed Wed. in winter.

The Wheel Inn, 50900 Seminole Dr. (909-849-7012), Cabazon Exit on I-10. Legendary joint where Pee-Wee Herman met Simone after his encounter with Large Marge (see **Let's Not Go: The Fetid Salton Sea,** p. 181). Those unfamiliar with haute cinema still come for the Cap'n's Plate ($6) or tasty pie ($1.50). The inn displays the friendly dinosaurs seen in *Pee-Wee's Big Adventure* (open 24hr).

SIGHTS AND ACTIVITIES

Most people come to Palm Springs to drink, party, and schmooze with has-been celebs, but the city also has its share of sights. **Mt. San Jacinto State Park,** Palm Springs' primary landmark, offers outdoor recreation opportunities for visitors of all fitness levels. Hiking trails are accessible year-round, and cross-country skiing is available in winter at higher elevations. If Mt. San Jacinto's 10,804 ft. escarpment is too much for your legs to take, try the world-famous **Palm Springs Aerial Tramway** (325-1391), on Tramway Rd. off Rte. 111. Rising nearly 6000 ft., the observation deck has excellent views of the Coachella Valley. (Trams run every ½hr. Mon.-Fri. 10am-8pm, Sat.-Sun. 8am-8pm. Round-trip fare $17, seniors $14, under 12 $11.)

A trip to Palm Springs would not be complete without a visit to the town's namesakes. The **Desert Hot Springs Spa,** 10805 Palm Dr. (329-6495), on the north side of I-10, features six naturally heated mineral pools of different temperatures, as well as saunas, massage professionals, and bodywraps. (Simmer daily 8am-10pm. Mon. and Wed.-Fri. $5, after 3pm $3; Tues. $3 all day; Sat.-Sun. $6, after 3pm $3.)

The remarkable **Palm Springs Desert Museum,** 101 Museum Dr. (325-0189), markets a touch of true natural beauty with its collection of Native American art, talking desert dioramas, and live animals. The museum sponsors performances in the 450-seat **Annenberg Theatre** (325-4490), as well as curator-led field trips ($3) into the canyons. (Museum open Tues.-Sun. 10am-5pm. Admission $6, seniors $5, students $3, ages 6-17 $3; free 1st Tues. of each month. Take Sun Bus #111.)

For those travelers who saw more than enough desert simply getting to Palm Springs, a tour of **celebrity homes** offers an alternative view (guided tours start at $11, students and under 16 $6). Alternatively, the budget tour costs only as much as the cheapest map of downtown; rented bikes offer a somewhat less conspicuous way of getting around. Be forewarned that these celebrities came to the desert for seclusion; your closest brush with greatness might be seeing Bob Hope's gardener weeding outside of Bob's high adobe wall.

Palm Springs has a number of public **tennis** and **golf** facilities. There are eight courts at **Ruth Hardy Park,** 700 Tamarisk Dr., at Avenida Caballeros. **Tahquitz Creek Golf Resort,** 1885 Golf Club Dr. (328-1005), managed by Arnold Palmer, claims to be one of the nation's top municipal golf courses (18 holes off-season $30, weekends $40; green fees include cart). For more info on Palm Springs' many lawns and links, call the city's **Leisure Center** (323-8272).

The **Living Desert Reserve,** 47900 Portola Ave. (346-5694), in Palm Desert 1½ mi. south of Rte. 111, houses Arabian oryces, iguanas, desert unicorns, and zebras alongside indigenous flora in the **Botanical Gardens.** The twilight reptile exhibit is a must-see. (Leer at the lizards daily Oct.-June 9am-5pm and Sept. 8am-noon. Admission $7.50, seniors $6.50, under 12 $3.50; Sept. admission $6, ages 3-12 $3.)

The four **Indian Canyons** (325-5673), 5 mi. south of the town at the end of S. Palm Canyon Dr., shelter desert animals in the world's greatest concentration of naturally occurring palm trees. The canyons also offer the city's only naturally cool water as well as remnants of Native American communities. (Open daily fall-winter 8am-5pm, spring-summer 8am-6pm. Admission $5, students $3.50, seniors $2.50, children $1.)

To hear the incongruous roar of surf among the sagebrush, visit **Oasis Water Park** (325-SURF/7873), off I-10 South on Gene Autry Trail between Ramon and E. Palm Canyon Dr. You can surf, slide, and soak in the wave pool, inner tube river, and eight waterslides. (Open mid-March to mid-Sept. daily 11am-6pm, mid-Sept.-Oct. weekends only 11am-5:30pm. Admission $18 if taller than 5ft., seniors and children 40in. or taller $11.50, under 4 free. Boogieboards and surfboards available.)

ENTERTAINMENT AND SEASONAL EVENTS

The glitzy persona of Palm Springs doesn't disappear with the setting sun—the city's nightlife is almost as heralded as its golf courses. Although a night of total indulgence here might run the budget traveler a bit deep, several bars provide nightly drink specials and lively people-watching. **La Taquería,** 125 E. Tahquitz Way (778-5391), has mystic ambience and a misty atmosphere—the mist-covered tile patio is just as inviting as the Moonlight Margaritas ($6). Another option is **Chillers,** 262 S. Palm Canyon Dr. (325-3215). The vodka and pink lemonade ($5) is one of the best offerings from the spinning wall of frozen drinks. Both bars book live music nightly. **Zelda's,** 169 North Indian Dr. (325-2375), has DJ-driven dancing every night but Sunday, when a live band takes over (open daily 8pm-2am; cover $5-7).

Village Fest (320-3781) takes over Palm Canyon Dr. downtown every Thursday night from 7 to 10pm. Over 100 vendors from surrounding communities market food, jewelry, and local crafts in a bargain bonanza while townsfolk enjoy live music. Attempting to fulfill his campaign promise to heighten Palm Springs' glamor quotient, former Mayor Bono instituted the annual **Palm Springs International Film Festival** (778-8979), in mid-January. The 49th annual **National Date Festival** (863-8247), Rte. 111 in Indo, is not a hook-up scene, but rather a bash for those looking to thwart dyspepsia (mid-Feb.). Palm Springs is also famous for its professional golf and tennis tournaments like the **Bob Hope Chrysler Classic** (341-2299), in mid-January, and the **Nabisco Dinah Shore Classic** (324-4546), in late March.

■ Near Palm Springs

Coachella Valley is the self-proclaimed "Date Capital of the World." So comb your hair, suck down a breath mint, and head to the **Shields Date Gardens,** 80653 Rte. 111 (347-0996), in nearby Indio. Tours, date shakes, and a film titled "The Sex Life of the Date" will dispel any slanderous ideas you may be harboring for the fruit that nearly poisoned the woman in *Raiders of the Lost Ark*. If Palm Springs isn't enough of a zoo for you, you can observe wildlife at the **Big Morongo Wildlife Reserve** or **Covington Park,** a wildlife sanctuary and bird-watching site (open Wed.-Sun. 7:30am-sunset; free). The visitors center can help you plan a hike through the **Thousand Palm Oasis** or the mesas in **Coachella Valley Preserve.**

■ Anza-Borrego Desert State Park

This largest California state park claims a sizable wedge of the state's southern desert, layered with both natural and human history. A popular diversion from Palm Springs or San Diego, Anza-Borrego sprouts many cactus and plant species found nowhere else in California. Barbed *cholla* cacti, bruise-blossomed indigo bush, and thirsty tamarisk all draw life from a bioregion that is covetous of water but blessed with a surplus of sunlight. Beneath these specimens lies a geologically diverse landscape full of dunes, badlands, mountains, springs, oases, and active faults. Nestled within these natural features hide the remains of forgotten Native American, Spanish, and oil pioneers' settlements. Visit in the winter or early spring when the searing sun is off the offensive. In the words of one ranger, it is "just plain stupid" to visit this area during the scorching summer months—much of the park is closed and the temperatures make travel unpleasant and dangerous.

PRACTICAL INFORMATION AND ORIENTATION

Visitor Information: Anza-Borrego Desert State Park Visitors Center, 200 Palm Canyon Dr. (767-4205), Borrego Springs. Topographical maps, books, exhibits, and slideshows. Rangers offer lifesaving backcountry and safety info; stop here before hiking or camping in the park. Open Sept.-May daily 9am-5pm, June-Aug. Sat.-Sun. 9am-5pm. For more info during summer months, call **Anza Park Headquarters** at 767-5311 (open Mon.-Fri. 8am-5pm).
Buses: Northeast Rural Bus System (765-0145), services the San Diego backcountry (info line open Mon.-Sat. 7am-noon and 2-5pm).
Auto Repair: AAA Emergency Road Service (800-458-5972).
Weather Conditions: (289-1212). **Desert Wildflower Hotline:** (767-4684).
Medical Services: Borrego Medical Center, 4343 Yaqui Pass Rd. (767-5051), on Rams Hill in Borrego Springs. Open Mon.-Fri. 8am-5pm, Sat. 8am-noon.
Emergency: 911.
Area Code: 619.

The park is accessible via **Rte. 78** or **S-22.** From the west, Rte. 79 from I-8 connects to Rte. 78 in Julian. From the east, Rte. 86 runs south from I-10 to Rte. 78 or S-22. From 78, follow the signs on S-3 to Borrego Springs.

ACCOMMODATIONS, CAMPING, AND FOOD

The small community of **Borrego Springs** provides adequate accommodations for park visitors. **Hacienda del Sol,** 610 Palm Canyon Dr. (767-5442), offers comfy old rooms (singles $34, winter $44; doubles $37, winter $47). The clashing decor at **Stanlunds,** 2771 Borrego Springs Rd. (767-5501), may hurt your eyes, but the prices won't damage your wallet (singles $30-45, winter $42-62).

Anza-Borrego permits free open **camping** anywhere in the park (reserve through DESTINET, 800-444-7275), which may be an option for hard-core desertphiles, but is not feasible in the summer. Temperatures over 100°F spoil food, hasten dehydration, and turn tents into solar-powered ovens. Backpackers in any season should carry sufficient water (2 gallons per person per day) and register their itineraries with park officials. The most hospitable of the area's primitive campsites is along S-3 in **Culp Valley.** At 3400 ft., it is the highest and coolest camp in the park. The **Borrego Palm Canyon Campground,** 3 mi. from town on S-3, features flush toilets, showers, and food lockers (sites $14). **Agua Caliente Springs Park,** on S-2 south of Vallecito Stage Station, offers restrooms, laundry facilities, a wading pool, and natural hot springs. The nearby store and gas station make it a convenient hiking base (sites $10-15).

Groceries and supplies can be purchased at **Center Market,** 590 Palm Canyon (767-3311), in Borrego Springs (open Mon.-Sat. 8:30am-6:30pm, Sun. 8:30am-5pm). Across the street is the local favorite, **Kendall's Cafe,** 528 Palm Canyon Dr. (767-3491). Dinners ($7-10) include low-fat, half-pound buffalo burgers (open daily 6am-8pm, in July Tues.-Wed. 6am-2pm).

SIGHTS

The most popular areas of exploration in Anza-Borrego are **Coyote Canyon Creek** and its network of tributaries. These creeks water the lands around them, giving life to plants unable to survive elsewhere in the park. Wildlife are also drawn to their waters, including the fascinating **bighorn sheep.** The **Southern Emigrant Trail** follows a wagon trail used by immigrants to reach California. Along the trail is a sod **stage station** built in 1852. With 4WD, **Font's Point** is accessible for a view of the spectacular Borrego Badlands. The park's chief attraction is its **wildflower season,** which turns barren wastelands into brightly-blossomed wonderlands every spring. Ask rangers about special guided activities.

Let's Not Go: The Fetid Salton Sea

This man-made "wonder" was formed in 1905-1907 when the aqueduct from the Colorado River broke and flooded the Coachella Valley. The accident resulted in a stagnant 35-by-15 mi. lake where once was desert. The lake festered for a while until the 60s, when someone thought it was a great idea to market the area as a tourist attraction. Fresh and saltwater fish were stocked in the sea, and marinas were built in ill-fated anticipation of a thriving resort and vacation industry. Hopes were cruelly dashed when decaying vegetation in the still water produced a foul odor and high salt content killed all but a few hardy species of fish. The sea is now ringed by abandoned buildings and **Salton City** is a defunct resort town withering in the desert sun. If it still sounds appealing, call the **West Shores Chamber of Commerce,** P.O. Box 5185, Salton City, CA 92705.

■ Joshua Tree National Park

When the Mormon pioneers crossed this desert area in the 19th century, they named the enigmatic desert tree they encountered after the Biblical prophet Joshua. Perhaps it was the heat, but the tree's crooked limbs seemed to them an uncanny image of the Hebrew general, who with his arms upraised, beckoned them to the promised land. Although in the Mojave the Mormons still hadn't found what they were looking for, its climes—slightly cooler and wetter than the harsh Arizona desert—must have made them feel at the time as though they'd arrived in God's country.

Even today, Joshua Tree National Park has the mystical power to inspire Biblical allusions as well as Irish rock bands. Stacks of wind-sculpted boulders flanked by seemingly-jubilant Joshua trees evoke the magnificent devastation of Jericho. The park's five oases look lushly Edenic against the desolate backdrop of the surrounding desert, and combine with the park's spectrum of high and low desert ecologies to create a vast mosaic of landscape and vegetation.

In recent years, climbers, campers, and daytrippers from Southern California have added to the mosaic. The boulder formations that punctuate the desert badlands and bullet the blue sky provide climbers with over 4000 opportunities to practice their skills. History buffs will appreciate the vestiges of human occupation—ancient rock petroglyphs, dams built in the 19th century to catch the meager rainfall for livestock, and gold mine ruins dot the landscape. But the most attractive aspect of Joshua Tree is its remoteness, its freedom from the commercial mayhem that has infested many other National Parks. Even after over 60 years in the arms of America, the natural beauty of Joshua Tree is interrupted only by a few paved roads and signs. The **park entrance fee** is $5 per person or $10 per car; valid for seven days.

PRACTICAL INFORMATION

Visitor Information: Headquarters and Oasis Visitors Center, 74485 National Park Dr. (367-7511), ¼mi. off Rte. 62 in Twentynine Palms, is the best place to familiarize yourself with the park. Friendly rangers, displays, guidebooks, maps, and water. Open daily 8am-5pm. **Cottonwood Visitors Center,** at the southern gateway of the park, 7mi. north of I-10, 25mi. east of Indio. Usually open daily 8am-4pm; call ahead. **Indian Cove Ranger Station,** 7295 Indian Cove Rd. (362-4367). Open Oct.-May daily 8am-4pm; summer hours vary. **West Entrance Information Kiosk,** Park Blvd. (366-2056), 5mi. southeast of the town of Joshua Tree. **Twentynine Palms Chamber of Commerce,** 6136 Adobe Rd. (367-3445), provides updated info on transportation options.

Car Rental: Enterprise, 55940 Twentynine Palms Hwy. (369-0525). Must be 21. Rates from $130 per week.

Equipment Rental: Cottonwood Company, 6376 Adobe Rd. (367-9505), Twentynine Palms, stocks climbing, hiking, rappelling, and backpacking gear.

Medical Services: Hi-Desert Medical Center, 6601 White Feather Rd. (366-3711), in Joshua Tree. Emergency care 24hr.

Emergency: 911. **Ranger services** (367-3523). **24hr. dispatch center** (909-383-5651). Call collect.

Post Office: Twentynine Palms Post Office, 73839 Gorgonio Dr. (367-3501). Open Mon.-Fri. 8:30am-5pm. **ZIP Code:** 92277.

Area Code: 760 (recently changed from 619).

ORIENTATION

Joshua Tree National Park covers 558,000 acres northeast of Palm Springs, about 160 mi. east of L.A. The park is ringed by three highways: **I-10** to the south, **Rte. 62 (Twentynine Palms Hwy.)** to the west and north, and **Rte. 177** to the east. The northern entrances to the park are off Rte. 62, at the towns of **Joshua Tree** and **Twentynine Palms.** The south entrance is at **Cottonwood Spring,** off I-10. Unfortunately, this is where the streets have no name; just look for the Joshua Tree sign 25 mi. east of Indio.

ACCOMMODATIONS AND CAMPING

Those who cannot stomach the thought of desert camping but want to spend more than a day at the park can find inexpensive motels next door in the marines training base of **Twentynine Palms.** The town offers some very cheap options, though some local establishments supposedly feature more fauna than the park itself. The **29 Palms Inn,** 73950 Inn Dr. (367-3505), is an attraction in and of itself. Its 14 distinctly different rooms face the Mara Oasis, which has supported life for over 20,000 years. More recently, the life here has been of the celebrity variety with guests like Michelle Pfeiffer and Nicholas Cage. Of the plants, Robert Plant gets the most attention; he composed his post-Zeppelin hit "29 Palms" in a room here. (Rooms May-Jan. $40-60, weekends $60-85; Feb.-April $5-10 more. Reservations required Feb.-April.) Reliable ol' **Motel 6,** 72562 Twentynine Palms Hwy. (367-2833), is clean and has a pool (singles $34, each additional person $4).

Camping is an enjoyable and inexpensive way to experience the beauty of the park, except perhaps in the scorching heat of summer. Pre-noon arrivals are the best way to guarantee a site since most campgrounds in the park operate on a first-come, first-camped basis and accept no reservations. Spring weekends and holidays are the busiest times. Reservations can be made for group sites only at Cottonwood, Sheep Pass, Indian Cove, and Black Rock Canyon through DESTINET (800-436-7275). Visitors who dislike the crowds of the developed campgrounds might prefer the backcountry, where unlimited camping is permitted. Ask at a ranger station for details. All campsites have tables, fireplaces, and pit toilets, and are **free** unless otherwise noted. Few sites offer water or flush toilets—those who plan any sort of extended stay should pack their own supplies and cooking utensils. Campground stays are limited to 14 days October through May and to 30 days in the summer.

Hidden Valley (4200ft.), in the center of the park, off Quail Springs Rd. Secluded alcoves are perfect for pitching tents, and enormous boulders provide shade and serve as perches from which to view the sun at dusk and dawn. Its proximity to

Wonderland of Rock and the Barker Dam Trail make this a rock climber's heaven. The 39 sites fill up quickly

Jumbo Rocks (4400ft.), located near Skull Rock Trail on the eastern edge of Queen Valley. Take Quail Springs Rd. 15mi. south of the visitors center. The highest, and therefore, the coolest campground in the park. The well-spaced sites surround (you guessed it) jumbo rocks. Front spots have best shade and protection. 125 sites, 65 in summer. Wheelchair accessible.

Indian Cove (3200ft.), on the north edge of the Wonderland of Rocks. Enter from the north. Rains create dramatic waterfalls. Popular spot for rock climbers. 107 sites, 45 in summer; 13 group sites $20-35; family sites $10.

Ryan (4300ft.). With fewer rocks than nearby Hidden Valley, there's also less privacy and shade. The 3mi. round-trip trail ascends to Ryan Mountain, which served as the headquarters and water storage location for the Lost Horse gold mine. The sunrise is spectacular from nearby Key's View. 29 sites. May be closed in summer.

White Tank (3800ft.). Excellent for RVs, despite the slightly bumpy road going in. Fewer people—but watch out for coyotes who may try to keep you company. Cowboys built up White Tank to serve as a reliable cattle watering hole. 15 sites. Often closed in summer.

Black Rock Canyon (4000ft.), at the end of Joshua Ln. off Rte. 62 near Yucca Valley. This woodland site is the inspiration for Jellystone Park, the home of Yogi Bear and friends. The animals only visit on weekends because they are busy filming during the week. 100 sites, flush toilets, and running water. Sites $10. Reservations accepted. Wheelchair accessible.

Cottonwood (3000ft.). In the midst of the arid, open Colorado Desert portion of the park. No shade. This is the first place where wildflowers appear when there's been sufficient rain. 62 sites, 30 in summer, flush toilets, and running water. Sites $8; 3 group sites for 10-70 people $25. Wheelchair accessible.

Sheep Pass (4500ft.), located in center of park near trail to Ryan Mountain. Yes, sheep pass here. 6 group sites $20-35. Reserve up to 3 months in advance.

Belle (3800ft.), is accessible from the north entrance by a 4WD-only road. Within view of the Pinto Mountains. One of the furthest spots in the park from civilization, it is an ideal place to stare at the starry heavens. 17 sites. Closed in summer.

FOOD

Though there are no food facilities within the park, Twentynine Palms offer both groceries and grub. Keep in mind, however, that to stay in business these establishments need only offer food and service superior to that in a Marine Corps mess hall—those looking for fine dining will surely be disappointed. If you are willing to do your own cooking, the **Stater Bros.** market, 71727 Twentynine Palms Hwy. (367-6535), saves you a bundle and offers a good selection (open daily 7am-10pm). Otherwise, it's fast food or its local equivalent. **The Finicky Coyote,** 73511 Twentynine Palms Hwy. (367-DELI/3354), is a cafe with sandwiches, coffee, and ice cream that will make you howl (open Mon.-Thurs. 6am-8pm, Fri. 6am-9pm, Sat. 7am-9pm, Sun. 9am-6pm). **Ramona's,** 72115 Twentynine Palms Hwy. (367-1929), serves cheap Mexican food in shiny red booths (open Mon.-Sat. 11am-8:30pm).

SIGHTS AND ACTIVITIES

Over 80% of the park is designated as wilderness area, safeguarded against development, and lacking paved roads, toilets, and campfires. Joshua Tree offers truly remote territory for backcountry desert hiking and camping. Hikers who seize the opportunity should pack plenty of water and keep alert for flash floods and changing weather conditions. The park's most temperate weather is in late fall (Oct.-Dec.) and early spring (March-April); temperatures in other months often span uncomfortable extremes (summer highs 95-115°F).

The awesome sights of the park are most scintillating at **sunrise** and **sunset,** when pink, purple, and red skies accentuate the angular arms of the Joshua trees and paint the mountains and rock piles deep crimsons and auburns. Daytrippers miss out terribly when they leave for home before dusk—the setting sun may well be the day's highlight. A self-paced **driving tour** is an easy way to explore the park and linger to a later hour. All park roads are well-marked, and signs labelled Exhibit Ahead point the way to unique floral and geological formations. One of these tours, a 34 mi. stretch across the center of the park from Twentynine Palms to the town of Joshua Tree, provides access to all the park's most outstanding sights and hikes. One leg of road that should not be missed is **Key's View** (5185ft.), 6 mi. off the park road just west of Ryan campground. On a clear day, you can see forever—or at least to Palm Springs and the Salton Sea. It's also a great spot for watching the sun rise. The longer drive through the park, from Twentynine Palms to I-10, traverses high and low desert landscapes. The **Cholla Cactus Garden,** a grove of spiny succulents resembling deadly three-dimensional asterisks, lies in the Pinto Basin just off the road.

Those with **4WD** vehicles have even more options, including the 18 mi. **Geology Tour Road,** which climbs through striking rock formations and ends in the Little San Bernardino Mountains. In the spring and fall, **bikers** can enjoy these roads, especially the unpaved and relatively unpopulated 4WD roads through **Pinkham Canyon** and past the **Black Eagle Mines,** which both begin at the Cottonwood Visitors Center (see p. 181). Bikers should check the free park guide for further information.

Despite the plethora of park roads, **hiking** is perhaps the best way to experience Joshua Tree. Only on foot can visitors tread through sand, scramble over boulders, and walk among the park's hardy namesakes. Although the **Barker Dam Trail,** next to Hidden Valley, is often packed with tourists, its painted petroglyphs and eerie tranquility make it a worthwhile hike. The **Lost Horse Mine,** near Key's View, is reached by a 1½ mi. trail and evokes the region's gold prospecting days with rusted machinery and abandoned mineshafts. From the top of **Ryan Mountain** (5461ft.), the boulder formations in the encircling valley bear an unsettling resemblance to Herculean beasts of burden slouching toward a distant destination. Bring plenty of water for the strenuous, unshaded climb to the summit. The visitors center has info on the park's many other hikes, which range from the 15-minute stroll to the **Oasis of Mara** to a three-day trek along the **California Riding and Hiking Trail** (35mi.). Ask about ranger-led weekend programs, hikes, and activities in the spring and fall. Anticipate slow progress even on short walks; the oppressive heat and the scarcity of shade can force even the hardiest of hikers to feel as though they're running to stand still.

Even if you view Joshua Tree merely as a break from the monotony of the interstate, you should still leave your car from time to time to take a look at the stunning variety of **flora** and **fauna.** Larger plants like Joshua trees, cholla, and the spidery ocotillo have adapted to the severe climate in fascinating ways, and the wildflowers that dot the desert terrain each spring (mid-March to mid-May) attract thousands of visitors. To avoid the harsh social stigma which accompanies floral ignorance, get updates on the blooming status of yucca, verbena, cottonwood, mesquite, and dozens of other wildflowers by calling the **Wildflower Hotline** (818-768-3533).

These beautiful beds of wildflowers serve as habitat for Joshua Tree's many animal species, and the trees and reeds of the Park's oases play host to ladybugs, bees, golden eagles, and bighorn sheep. Kangaroo rats and lizards run about at all times of the day, while wily coyotes and bobcats stalk their prey (including, if you're not careful, your unleashed pet) only at night. Those equipped with time and patience are more likely to see the living beauty of their surroundings revealed.

Energetic visitors with less patience are often drawn to Joshua Tree for its **rock climbing:** the world-renowned boulders at **Wonderland of Rocks** and **Hidden Valley** are especially challenging and attract thousands of climbers each year. All in all, the park contains more than 4000 climbing locations, enough to satisfy casual and expert climbers alike. Those of a more serious persuasion can contact the visitors center for info on established rope routes and on wilderness areas where the placement of new bolts is restricted. **Joshua Tree Rock Climbing** (800-890-4745), Box 29, Joshua Tree, provides instruction and equipment rental.

■ Near Joshua Tree: Yucca Valley

Yucca Valley, northwest of the park, is graced with a few unusual attractions and a genuinely helpful **Chamber of Commerce,** 56300 Twentynine Palms Hwy., Suite D, 92284 (365-6323; open Mon.-Fri. 8:30am-5pm). The **Hi-Desert Nature Museum,** 57116 Twentynine Palms Hwy. (369-7212), has gemstones, captive scorpions and snakes, and chunks of bristlecone pine, including a cone from the world's oldest living tree (open Tues.-Sun. 10am-5pm; free). For breathtaking views of Joshua Tree and the Morongo Basin, ask about the town's nature trails. **North Park Nature Trail** is just over 2 mi. and is suitable for the casual hiker.

A simply divine experience can be had with Jesus and friends at Yucca's **Desert Christ Park,** 57090 Twentynine Palms Hwy., north from the highway at the end of Mohawk Trail. Concrete figures (12-15ft.) reverently compose Biblical scenes. Ironically, the missing appendages on many of the prophets make them look more like lepers than the holy healers they are meant to be. (Open dawn-dusk and free as air.)

The town of **Landers,** north of Yucca Village, offers even more wacky fun for the whole family at **Giant Rock,** the **world's largest solitary boulder.** Seven stories high, it's the former site of George Van Tassel's famous **Interplanetary Spacecraft Convention.** Take Old Woman Springs Rd. to Landers and ask locals for guidance. Sorry, but only the 4WD-equipped will be able to make the trek.

■ Needles

Needles was named after the salient mountain peaks at the south end of the Colorado River once used as a landmark to guide pioneers to water. In the eyes of today's desert-weary travelers, the sight of these mountains conjures the same enthusiasm as experienced by those of old. Home to Snoopy's bedraggled brother Spike, this quiet desert town offers few sights, but is convenient to the Colorado, Lake Mead (see p. 202), and the local gambling digs in **Laughlin, Nevada.**

Practical Information The **Chamber of Commerce,** 100 G St. (326-2050), is located at the junction of Front and G St. (open Mon.-Fri. 10am-3pm). **Bank of America,** 1001 W. Broadway, has an **ATM** (open Mon.-Thurs. 9am-5pm, Fri. 9am-6pm). Buses run out of the **Greyhound** station, 1109 Broadway (326-5066), to: Las Vegas ($26), L.A. ($41), and Barstow ($26). For medical emergencies, **Needles Hospital,** 1401 Bailey Ave. (326-4531), is open 24 hr. The **post office,** 628 3rd St. (326-2612), is open Mon.-Fri. 9am-4:30pm. The **ZIP code** is 92363. In an **emergency,** call 911. The **area code** is 619.

THE DESERT

Accommodations, Camping, and Food The inexpensive motels of Needles present a veritable oasis for those weary travelers who are thirsting after free in-room porn. Families with corruptible children may wish to stick to well-known chain hotels, which are dirt-free in every sense of the word. The **Travelodge,** 1910 Needles Hwy. (326-3881), for example, offers squeaky clean rooms at slimmed-down prices (singles $23; doubles $25; weekends $30, $37). **The Traveler's Inn,** 1195 3rd St. Hill (326-4900 or 800-633-8300), has spiffy rooms with access to a pool and, more importantly, a McDonald's (singles $31; doubles $37). For campers looking to rough it in the robust outdoors, Needles doesn't have much to offer. However, it does have **more RV parks per capita** than any other town in the world. **Rainbo Beach,** River Rd. (326-3101), on Needles Hwy., one mile north of Needles, has sites from $18, including electricity, pools, and restrooms. Those who don't need hookups might try heading outside town to find a riverside spot.

The Hungry Bear, 1906 W. Broadway (326-2988), serves feasts to sate every appetite. The favorite is creatively entitled "Bear's Favorite Burger" ($6; open daily 5:30am-10pm.) Needles's newest restaurant, **California Pantry,** 2411 Needles Hwy. (326-5225), is a classy 24-hour coffee shop specializing in chicken fried steak ($7).

Sights and Outdoor Activities The **Colorado River** offers a variety of recreational opportunities. Visitors can break the silence and explore galore on jet ski. **Sea Doo Rentals,** 125 Needles Hwy. (326-5355), offers rentals for around $35 per hour (rates vary). If you want to enjoy the quiet, grab your rod and call the folks at the **U.S. Fish and Wildlife Commission** (326-3853), for news on what's bitin'. **Havasu National Wildlife Refuge** is a 4000-acre marshy network of ponds, bays, and channels where dove, quail, and beaver dwell (call the Fish and Wildlife Commission for info).

THE HIGH DESERT

Scorching, silent, and barren, the High Desert is a picture of desolation. John Steinbeck called it a "terrestrial hell," and in the summer months only the most sun-crazed desert rats would disagree with this description. Today, the empty spaces and scattered trailer towns of the area serve as a bleak backdrop for a rootless subculture of military itinerants. Travelers usually hurry through, anxious to reach gentler climes. It's hard to contest such instincts, but the desert offers an opportunity to banish the confusion of civilization. The Mojave conceals unlikely treasures for undaunted adventurers patient and brave enough to explore it. Genuine attractions are rare and the summer heat withers many mere mortals. However, winter is much cooler, making it temperate enough to hike across dizzying sand dunes and inspect spooky ghost towns.

▓ Barstow

Don't let the ubiquitous beauty parlors fool you—Barstow is anything but a cosmopolitan center for the coiffed and chic. Poised midway between Los Angeles and Las Vegas on I-15, Barstow is significant only for its location. A hub for hotels, restaurants, and gas stations, it is the ideal place to prepare for any type of desert foray.

Practical Information The **Barstow Chamber of Commerce,** 222 E. Main St. (256-8617), has info on hotels and restaurants as well as Southern California tourist attractions (open Mon.-Fri. 9am-5pm). The **California Desert Information Center,** 831 Barstow Rd. (255-8760), has the scoop on outdoor recreation from off-roading to hiking. A seemingly abandoned **Amtrak** station lies at 7685 N. 1st St. (800-USA-RAIL/872-7245), well beyond the bridge that crosses the railroad tracks. Buy tickets on board to travel to L.A. ($39) or Las Vegas ($49). The **Greyhound,** 681 N. 1st St. (256-8757), has buses to L.A. (10 buses per day, $22) and Las Vegas (6 per day, $25). It's a bit of a march from Main St., so be prepared to call a cab. You'll have to pay through the teeth, though: **Yellow Cab,** 831 W. Main St. (256-6868), holds a monopoly in Barstow and charges $2 per mi. **Diane's Laundromat,** 1300 E. Main St. (256-5312), charges $1.25 for a wash, 25¢ for a 12-minute dry (open 6:30am-10pm). In an **emergency** call **911;** for other concerns, call the **police** (256-2211) or the **highway patrol** (256-1617). The **post office,** 425 S. 2nd Ave. (256-8494), is open Mon.-Fri. 9am-5pm, Sat. 10am-1pm. The **ZIP Code** is 92312. The **area code** is 619.

Accommodations What Barstow lacks in charm it makes up in utility. Inexpensive motels and eateries abound. **Motel 6,** 150 N. Yucca Ave. (256-1752), is relatively close to the bus and train stations, and only a block from a 24-hour grocery and drugstore. Standard rooms have cable (singles $28; doubles $34). **Economy Inns of America,** 1590 Coolwater Lane (256-1737), lies off E. Main St. near I-40 (singles $24; doubles $33; quads $36). For campgrounds outside of Barstow, see p.187.

Food Every restaurant chain this side of the Pecos has a branch on Main St. You'll find a more inviting variety along E. Main St. than along W. Main St. The **Barstow**

Station McDonald's, 1611 E. Main St. (256-1233), made from old locomotive cars, is the busiest McDonald's in the U.S. And if you'd like a beer to complement your "Royale with Cheese," pop into the adjoining liquor store (open Sun.-Thurs. 5am-10pm, Fri.-Sat. 5:30am-midnight). **Carlo's and Toto's,** 901 W. Main. St. (256-7513), is a local favorite for saucy, cheesy, and cheap Mexican food. Choice of 21 lunches ($4.25) and almost as many margaritas ($2; open Mon.-Thurs. 11am-10pm, Fri.-Sat. 11am-11pm, Sun. 9:30am-10pm). If you'd rather make your own meals, **Vons,** 1270 E. Main St. (256-8105), stocks supermarket specialties (open daily 6am-11pm).

■ Near Barstow

The **Calico Early Man Site** (Desert Info: 255-8760), lies along I-15 at the Minneola off-ramp. This is the only New World site that "Lucy" discoverer Louis Leakey ever bothered to excavate. The 20,000-year-old stone tools unearthed here make Calico the oldest find in the Western Hemisphere. On display are artifacts and photographs from the excavations (open Wed. 1:30-3:30pm, Thurs.-Sun. 9:30-4pm; free tours every 2hr.).

Twelve miles north of Barstow along Barstow Rd. is **Owl Canyon,** a great example of badland topography, colored with jasper, agate, and turquoise. Because the area is rich in fossilized remains, rockhounding (stealing rocks) is illegal, and bears a steep penalty. Nearby, **Rainbow Basin** offers an exceptional vantage for stargazing, with almost no light pollution. Bureau of Land Management **camping** facilities at Owl Canyon are equipped with fireplaces, drinking water, and toilets (sites $4).

■ Eastern Mojave Desert

The rugged land between I-15 and I-40 is among the most isolated in California. The list of human settlements begins and ends with Barstow and Baker. Travelers who pit-stop only in these towns, however, bypass Mojave's stunning natural attractions. Dramatic geological formations rise from the seemingly infinite landscape and hardy creatures crawl along the scorched terrain. Serene as the emptiness may be, it is still empty, and most drivers press onward, praying that their cars remain faithful.

Afton Canyon Natural Area (Desert Info: 255-8760), lies 38 mi. northeast of Barstow on the way to Las Vegas. Follow I-15 to Afton Rd. The flowing water you see in this "Grand Canyon of the Mojave" is no mirage, but a rare above-ground appearance of the Mojave River. Canyon walls tower 300 ft. above the rushing water and its willow-lined shores. Golden eagle, bighorn sheep, and desert tortoise reside around the canyon. **Hikers** may enjoy exploring the **caves** and side canyons tucked along unmarked trails. Bring a flashlight. Visitors can stay in 22 developed sites with water, fire pits, tables, and restrooms ($6 per person).

Near **Kelso** is the most spectacular system of **dunes** in California. Stretching lengths of four miles and reaching heights of 700 ft., the dunes are off-limits to off-road vehicles. Hiking in the dunes is permitted. From the top, you can hear the dunes sing—the cascading sand mimics the vibration of cello strings. Kelso is about 30 mi. southeast of Baker via Kelbaker Rd. from Barstow; either take I-40 to the Kelbaker Rd. Exit 80 mi. to the east or I-15 to Baker.

Providence Mountains State Recreation Area, P.O. Box 1, Essex 92332 (928-2586), 10 mi. east of Kelso, is a popular, high-altitude (4000-5000ft.) region with six primitive campsites for $12. Unless you have 4WD, however, the direct route will be too much for your vehicle to handle. The **visitors center** is 17 mi. north of I-40 on Essex Rd. **Hiking trails** weave through lowland sage and juniper trees flanked by toothy crags, offering some good rock climbing options. Spelunkers might try the spectacular **Mitchell Caverns** (928-2586). Tours are offered through stalactite-cluttered limestone chambers. (1½hr. tours Sept.-May Mon.-Fri. at 1:30pm, Sat.-Sun. at 10am, 1:30, and 3pm; June-Aug. Sat.-Sun. 1:30pm. Tours $6, ages 6-12 $3)

The Bureau of Land Museum maintains 48 primitive but beautiful sites at the **Mid Hill** and the **Hole-in-Wall campgrounds** in the East Mojave National Scenic Area.

THE DESERT

From Essex Rd., follow Black Canyon Rd. to Mid Hill or Wild Horse Canyon Rd. to Hole-in-Wall. Both sites provide restrooms, tables, fire rings, and occasionally water. The forest-dwelling Mid Hill sites are pleasantly cool in the summer at 5600 ft. Embellished with rock formations, Hole-in-Wall (4200ft.) attracts climbers in the spring and fall. **Backcountry** camping is available at locations along hiking trails.

Dune buggies and **jeeps** are still permitted at the **Dumont Dunes,** about 25 mi. north of Baker, just off Rte. 127. Ask a local to show you exactly where they are—there is no sign. (Where's Ace of Base when you need them?) The dunes are strewn with man-made striations—those from World War II training exercises are still visible in parts of the Mojave. Tracks persist in the sands for decades, so consider what legacy you want to leave behind before plunging into the dunes.

The fabulous **Baker Bun Boy** (733-4660), is a good place to stop for coffee and conversation (bacon cheeseburger $6.75; open daily 24hr.). Even if you tried, you couldn't miss Baker's claim to fame: the **world's tallest working thermometer.**

■ Death Valley National Park

The devil owns a lot of real estate in Death Valley. Not only does he grow crops (at the **Devil's Cornfield**) and hit the links (at the **Devil's Golf Course**), but the park is also home to **Hell's Gate** itself. It's not surprising, then, that the area's astonishing variety of topographical and climactic extremes can support just about anyone's idea of the Inferno. Visitors can stare into the abyss from the appropriately named **Dante's View,** one of several panorama points approaching 11,000 ft. in elevation, or gaze wistfully into the heavens from **Badwater,** which at 282 ft. below sea level is the lowest point in the Western Hemisphere. Winter temperatures dip well below freezing, and summer readings rival even the hottest Hades. In fact, the second highest temperature ever recorded in the world (134°F in the shade) was measured at the Valley's **Furnace Creek Ranch** on July 10, 1913. Of that day, ranch caretaker Oscar Denton said, "I thought the world was going to come to an end. Swallows in full flight fell to the ground dead, and when I went out to read the thermometer with a wet towel on my head, it was dry before I returned."

Fortunately, the fatal threshold of 130°F is rarely crossed, and the region can sustain a surprisingly intricate web of life. Many threatened species, including the desert tortoise and the desert bighorn sheep, have made Death Valley home. If you see something unusual, go to the nearest visitors center and fill out a **wildlife sighting card,** but don't bring one of these animals along as evidence; most of them are endangered. The **park entrance fee** is $5 per vehicle, collected year-round at Furnace Creek Visitors Center and Oct.-May at Grapevine and Stovepipe Wells. Resist the temptation not to pay—the Park Service needs all the money it can get (besides, it will get you a nice map with pretty pictures).

History

In 1849, a group of immigrants looking for a shortcut to California's Gold Country stumbled into the valley. After weeks of searching for a western pass through the Panamint Range, and losing one of their party in the process, the group found a way out of the valley. Looking back at the scene of misery, one member exclaimed, "Good-bye, death valley!" thus naming the area for posterity. After this tragedy, few were anxious to return until 1883, when miners in the region discovered borax, a type of salt. Borax mining provided fortunes for a few and a livelihood for many in towns like Rhyolite and Skidoo. However, the rapid depletion of the borax mines transformed boom towns into ghost towns, which the area's low humidity has left well-preserved. With no promise of new industry, most folks have forsaken the valley itself, leaving it largely undisturbed. In 1933, the government set aside over three million acres of this desert wilderness as the largest national park outside Alaska, bringing a tourist influx.

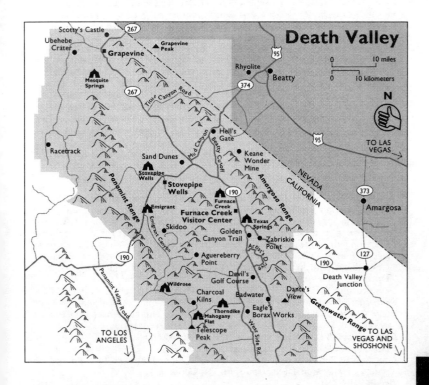

WHEN TO VISIT

Yes, Ireland is green and Death Valley is hot. Although the average high temperature in July is 116°F and the nighttime low 88°F, even summer visits can be enjoyable with wise planning. To this end, the Furnace Creek Visitors Center distributes the free pamphlet *Hot Weather Hints.* (For more info, see **Desert Survival,** p. 175.)

You can drive through and admire the valley in July and August, but to enjoy the many hiking and camping options, visit in winter, *not* summer. Winter is the coolest time (40-70°F in the valley, freezing temperatures and snow in the mountains) and also the wettest, with infrequent but violent rainstorms that can flood canyons and obliterate roads and ill-placed tract housing. Call ahead to find out which areas, if any, are washed out before exploring the park.

In March and April desert wildflowers bloom everywhere, despite the fact that they are accompanied by tempestuous winds that whip sand and dust into a blinding frenzy for hours or even days. In late October and the first two weeks of November, over 50,000 people crowd into Death Valley's facilities during the **49ers Encampment** festival (a tribute to the miners). Traffic jams, congested trails and campsites, hour-long lines for gas, and four-hour waits at Scotty's Castle plague the area on three-day winter weekends, Thanksgiving, the winter holidays, and Easter.

PRACTICAL INFORMATION

Visitor Information:
Furnace Creek Visitors Center (786-2331), on Rte. 190 in the east-central section of the valley. For info by mail, write the Superintendent, Death Valley

THE DESERT

National Park, Death Valley, CA 92328. Purchase guides and topographic maps for hiking ($2-10), get a schedule of activities and guided ranger hikes, check the latest weather forecast, and slurp from the park's only cold drinking fountain (it's hidden amongst the posters). A simple and informative **museum** dispels myths (such as the claim that all the original settlers perished here) and houses an impressive contour model of the valley. A 12min. slide show every ½hr. and a nightly lecture during the winter provide further orientation. Open summers daily 8am-5pm, off-season 8am-7pm.

Ranger Stations: Grapevine (786-2313), junction of Rte. 190 and 267 near Scotty's Castle; **Stovepipe Wells** (786-2342), on Rte. 190; and **Shoshone** (832-4308), outside the southeast border of the valley at the junction of Rte. 178 and 127. Also in **Beatty, NV** (702-553-7200), on Rte. 374. Weather report, weekly naturalist program, and park info posted at each station. Emergency help provided. Open daily 8am-5pm.

Death Valley Hikers' Association: Write for info c/o Darrell Tomer, P.O. Box 123, Arcata, CA 95521. The *Dustdevil* is the Association's stellar publication.

Gas Stations: Get tanked outside Death Valley at Olancha, Shoshone, or Beatty, NV. Otherwise, you'll pay about 20¢ more per gallon at the stations across from the Furnace Creek Visitors Center (open 7am-7pm), in Stovepipe Wells Village (open 7am-8pm), at Scotty's Castle (open 9am-5:30pm), or in Panamint Springs (open 9am-5pm). Don't play macho with the fuel gauge; fill up often. **AAA towing service, propane gas,** and **diesel fuel** are available at the Furnace Creek Chevron; **white gas** at Furnace Creek Ranch and Stovepipe Wells Village stores.

Market: Furnace Creek Ranch Store (786-2381), is well-stocked and expensive. Open daily 7am-10pm. **Stovepipe Wells Village Store** (786-2578), is smaller. Open daily 7am-9pm. Both stores sell charcoal, firewood, and ice.

Laundromat: Facilities at Furnace Creek Ranch on Roadrunner Ave. Open 24hr.

Swimming Pools and Showers: Showers and swimming at Stovepipe Wells Village (fee for non-guests $2; open daily 9am-9pm) and at Furnace Creek Ranch (swimming $2, showers $1; open daily 9am-11pm; showers close at 9pm).

Emergency: 911 or 786-2330 for 24hr. ranger dispatch.

Police: (786-2330).

Post Office: Furnace Creek Ranch (786-2223). Open June-Sept. Mon.-Fri. 8:30am-3pm; Oct.-May Mon.-Fri. 8:30am-5pm. **ZIP Code:** 92328.

Area Code: 760.

GETTING THERE AND AROUND

By Car

The drive to Death Valley is three and a half hours from Vegas, five hours from Los Angeles, seven hours from Tahoe City, and ten and a half hours from San Francisco.

Cars are the best way to get to and around Death Valley. If you're sharing gas costs, renting a car can be cheaper and far more flexible than any bus tour. The nearest agencies are in Las Vegas (p. 196), Barstow (p. 186), and Bishop (p. 425).

Conditions in Death Valley are notoriously hard on automobiles (see **Desert Survival,** p. 175). Be sure you have a reliable car that can withstand long uphill grades and intense heat, and ease off on the air-conditioning, especially on steep roads, to avoid wasting valuable gasoline and straining the engine. Radiator water (*not* for drinking) is available at critical points on Rte. 178 and 190 and NV Rte. 374. There are only three **service stations** in the park (see **Gas Stations,** p. 190), and the extreme heat, rapid increases in altitude, and air conditioning will drain your tank rapidly—keep it as full as possible at all times. Know how to make minor repairs, bring along appropriate topographic maps, leave an itinerary with the visitors center, and take a CB radio. Check ahead for road closings, and do not drive on wet and slippery backcountry roads.

Although a **4WD** vehicle will give you access to narrow roads that lead to some of Death Valley's most spectacular scenery, these roads are intended for drivers with backcountry experience and are dangerous no matter what you're driving. Fill up on gas and bring chains, extra tires, gas, oil, water (for drinking and for the radiator), and spare parts. In case of a breakdown, stay with your vehicle or find nearby shade. For more tips, see **Desert Survival** 175, and consult the visitors center.

Of the nine **park entrances,** most visitors choose Rte. 190 from the east. The road is well-maintained, the pass is less steep, and the visitors center is relatively close. But since most of the major sights adjoin the north-south road instead, the daytripping visitors with a trusty vehicle will be able to see more of the park by entering from the southeast (Rte. 178 west from Rte. 127 at Shoshone) or the north (direct to Scotty's Castle via NV Rte. 267). Unskilled mountain drivers should not attempt to enter via the smaller Titus Canyon or Emigrant Canyon Drive roads.

Not By Car

There is no regularly scheduled public transportation into Death Valley. Bus tours are monopolized by **Fred Harvey's Death Valley Tours,** which operates Oct.-May out of Furnace Creek Ranch (786-2345, ext. 222). A tour of the lower valley stops briefly at Zabriskie Point, Mushroom Rock, Devil's Golf Course, Badwater, and Artist's Drive (3½hr.; admission $20, children $12). A tour of the north explores Scotty's Castle, Ubehebe Crater, Sand Dunes, and Stovepipe Wells (5hr.; admission $32, seniors $28, children $28). The best tour is the excursion into Titus Canyon, an area of the park few casual tourists ever see because it is accessible by 4WD vehicle only (5hr.; admission $30, children $20). Excursions also available to Beatty, NV and to Amargosa. Group rates are available, and in all cases reservations must be made a day in advance. If you **hitchhike,** you will probably **die.** It's that simple.

ACCOMMODATIONS AND FOOD

In Death Valley, beds and fine meals within a budget traveler's reach are as elusive as the desert bighorn sheep. Cheaper options in surrounding towns draw many visitors outside the park at nightfall. During the winter months, camping out with a stock of groceries is a good way to save both money and driving time.

Furnace Creek Ranch Complex (786-2345, reservations 800-236-7916; fax 786-2514), is a former terminus that once housed and fed Death Valley's borax miners. Today, it is deluged with tour bus refugees who challenge the adjacent 18-hole golf course (America's lowest, at 214ft. below sea level) and relax in the 85°F spring-fed swimming pool. Older cabins with A/C and 2 double beds $85. Remodeled motel-style accommodations $105. Furnace Creek has a cafeteria (open daily 6-9am, 11am-2pm, and 5-9pm) and a few more expensive restaurants.

Stovepipe Wells Village (786-2387), comes complete with a large, heated mineral pool and that utter necessity, a beauty salon. The hotel charges $53 per night for one or two people, $11 each additional person. The pool ($2) stays open until midnight in the hot summer months. The hotel office is open year-round. RV sites available. Sites $15, includes pool use.

Panamint Springs Resort (764-2010), is only slightly cheaper than Stovepipe (doubles from $50). RV sites start at $15. Sweaty tourists line up for greasy cheeseburgers ($5.50) at the restaurant and bar (open daily 6:30am-midnight). Fill up the tank before you reach Panamint Springs; gas here costs over $2 per gallon.

CAMPING

The National Park Service maintains nine campgrounds in Death Valley, only two of which accept reservations (Texas Springs and Furnace Creek accept them Oct.-April). The visitors center (see **Practical Information,** p. 189) keeps records on site availability; be prepared to battle for a space if you come during peak periods (see **When to Visit,** p. 189). All campsites have toilets but none have showers. Water availability is not very reliable and supplies can at times be unsafe; always pack your own. Collecting wood is forbidden everywhere in the park, so pack your own firewood, and bring a stove and fuel to use where open fires are prohibited. Roadside camping is not permitted, but **backcountry camping** is free and legal, provided you check in at the visitors center and pitch tents at least 1 mi. from any road, 5 mi. from any established campsite, and ¼ mi. from any backcountry water source. The camp-grounds below are in geographic order from north to south. Stays at all sites are limited to 30 days, with the exception of **Furnace Creek,** which has a 14-day limit.

Wildrose (4100ft.), on the road to the Charcoal Kilns in Wildrose Canyon, 40mi. north of Trona, 21mi. south of Emigrant campground. An old summer residence of the Shoshone Indians, this forested, mountainside location has the most comfortable temperatures in the park. Convenient base for trips to Skidoo, Aguer-eberry Point, and Telescope Peak. You may need 4WD. Thirty sites. No water. Open fires permitted. Free. May be closed at any time due to inclement weather.

Texas Springs (sea level), in the hills above the Furnace Creek Inn, 600ft. beyond the Sunset campground on the same road. The Harmony Borax mining company's former water source is now the best place for tents near the Furnace Creek activities. Some of the 92 sites are shaded. For wind protection, stick close to the base of the hills. Generators prohibited. Water and picnic tables provided. Open fires permitted. Sites $10. Open Oct.-April.

Mesquite Springs (1800ft.), near Scotty's Castle, 2mi. south of Grapevine Ranger Station. All 50 sites are without shade. Located on the former watering hole of the prospectors. Overlooks Death Valley Wash and alluvial fans. Listen for coyote and owls. Ideal for tents. Tables provided and open fires permitted. Sites $10.

Emigrant (2100ft.), off Rte. 190, 9mi. west of Stovepipe Wells Village across from the ranger station, on the way down from Towne Pass through the Panamint Range. Offers a gorgeous view of Stovepipe Wells and the valley. The 10 sites are comfortable in summer. No fires. Free. Open April-Oct.

Thorndike (7500ft.) and **Mahogany Flat** (8200ft.), 10mi. east of Wildrose and over ½mi. higher, just beyond the Charcoal Kilns in Wildrose Canyon. Depending on conditions, a sturdy car with an able driver may make it to either site, although a 4WD vehicle is preferable. No trailers. Gets cold and dark early; the sun sets quickly in the canyon. Can be snowy even in April and Oct. Tables provided. No water. Free. Open March-Nov.

Furnace Creek (196ft. below sea level), north of the visitors center. Near the Furnace Creek Ranch facilities (pool, showers, laundry). A few of the 168 sites are shaded. Generally gets crowded first, especially with RVs. Sites $10. (Don't confuse with the $16 sites offered by the Furnace Creek Ranch.) Open year-round. Make reservations Oct.-April through MISTIX (800-365-CAMP/2267).

Stovepipe Wells (sea level). Near an airstrip, Jeep trails, and sand dunes. Reminiscent of a drive-in movie lot. Tenters will have to compete with clumps of RVs for one of 200 gravel sites. Try for a spot close to the trees for protection from spring sandstorms. Short walk to all the hotel and general store amenities. (Don't confuse it with the trailer park.) No fires. Sites $10. Open Oct.-April.

SIGHTS AND ACTIVITIES

It pays to pre-plan your approach to Death Valley. See **Getting There and Around** (p. 190), for a discussion of the various entrances. If you're doing the valley in a day, you should adopt a north-south or south-north route, rather than heading directly to the Furnace Creek Visitors Center via Rte. 190, which connects east with west. Camera-toters should keep in mind that the best photo-ops are at sunrise and sunset.

At the Visitors Center

At the **visitors center and museum** (see **Practical Information,** p. 189), rangers and handouts will detail the distances and times of recommended hikes. Ranger-led programs are generally unavailable in the summer, but many popular programs, such as the **car caravan tours** and **stargazing talks,** are available in winter and spring. If you dig astronomy, speak to a ranger; they often set up telescopes at Zabriskie Point and offer freelance stargazing shows. During **wildflower season,** rangers also offer tours of the choicest bloom sites, including **Hell's Gate, Jubilee Pass,** and **Hidden Valley.** Wildflower-watching is best after a heavy rainfall, when the parched petals of Death Valley's flowers rouse themselves in gratitude for the moisture from above.

South of the Visitors Center

The **Harmony Borax Works** and the **Borax Museum** (786-2345, ext. 215), are a short drive from the visitors center. The first successful borax operation in Death Valley, the Harmony plant is not terribly scenic, although the free museum (originally the company's bunkhouse, kitchen, and office) merits investigation, especially in summer, when the A/C is on. Highlights include a picture of Ronald Reagan holding borax bottles, in addition to a mineral display, rusty mining implements, and Native American artifacts (open Mon.-Fri. 9:30am-5pm).

Alongside the entrance to Furnace Creek Ranch are the remains of a 20-mule team wagon which starred in both the 1904 St. Louis World's Fair and President Wilson's inauguration. Old Dinah, the team's "Iron Mule" replacement, languishes nearby.

One mile east of the museum on Rte. 190 lies the turn-off for **Zabriskie Point.** Immortalized by Antonioni's film of the same name, Zabriskie Point is a marvelous place from which to view Death Valley's corrugated badlands. The view of the choppy orange rock formations is particularly stunning late in the day when the dried lake beds fill with burnt light. Before the sunset ends, scamper two mi. (and 900ft.) down Gower Gulch to colorful **Golden Canyon** (3mi. south of Furnace Creek by car), where the setting sun makes the cliffs glitter convincingly.

Perhaps the most spectacular sight in the park is the vista at **Dante's View,** reached by a 13 mi. paved road from Rte. 190. Just as the Italian poet stood with Virgil looking down on the damned, so the modern observer gazes from 5475 ft. upon the vast inferno that is Death Valley. On a clear day, you can see the Sierra Nevada, and on a *really* clear day, you can see both the highest point in the continental U.S. (Mt. Whitney, 14,494ft.) and the lowest (Badwater, 282ft. below sea level). Dante's View can be snowy in mid-winter and cold anytime but mid-summer.

Ten miles south of the visitors center on Rte. 178, **Artist's Drive** is a one-way loop which twists its way through rock formations of colors akin to those found in Crayola sets. The loop's early ochres and burnt siennas give way at **Artist's Palette** to sea green, lemon yellow, periwinkle blue, and salmon mineral deposits in the hillside. The effect is most intense in the late afternoon as the colors change rapidly with the setting sun. The dizzying 9 mi. drive turns back upon itself again and again, ending up on the main road 4 mi. north of the drive's entrance.

About 5 mi. south of this exit is **Devil's Golf Course.** But don't expect to tee off here—the "golf course" is a plane of sharp salt pinnacles made up of the precipitate from the evaporation of Lake Manly, the 90 mi. long lake that once filled the lower valley. The windswept crags are made from pure sodium chloride.

Three miles south of Devil's Golf Course lies **Badwater,** an aptly named briny pool four times saltier than the ocean. Huge in the winter, it contracts to a large puddle in the summertime. The surrounding salt flat dips to the lowest point in the Western Hemisphere—282 ft. below sea level. The pool forms the habitat for the threatened Badwater snails, whose bodies are often crushed by the trampling feet of wading tourists who are trying to cool off—this is the hottest part of the Valley.

Behind Badwater lie the **Panamint Mountains** and the 14 mi. trail up to **Telescope Peak** (11,049ft.). In the cool early morning, you can climb up to watch the light play upon the tiny landscape below—if you have the proper hiking equipment. The strenuous hike (14mi. round-trip) begins at Mahogany Flat Campground and winds 3000 ft. past charcoal kilns and bristlecone pines, providing unique views of Badwater and Mt. Whitney. Seasoned backpackers can hike this in winter, but may need an ice axe.

North of the Visitors Center

For an entertaining one-day excursion, take **Beatty Road** (turn-off 12mi. north of the visitors center) east toward the Nevada border. Five miles along you'll reach the turn-off to the **Keane Wonder Mine and Mill,** a site that died quickly, but not before yielding sacks of gold. You'll need a 4WD to reach the mine, and take care when poking around the mill's ramshackle wooden trams. A one-mile hike from the mill parking lot leads to Keane Wonder Springs and an abandoned stamp mill.

THE DESERT

Continuing along Beatty Rd., cross Hell's Gate before traversing Daylight Pass, the apex of which marks the California-Nevada border. Ten miles downhill will bring you to **Beatty,** Nevada, via **Rhyolite,** the "Queen City of Death Valley" that was once home to 10,000 people (see p. 196). The return trip to Death Valley via **Titus Canyon Road** (open Oct.-April) shows off the gorge's jagged cliffs and spectacular vistas. The 26 mi. trek down this narrow way, full of dips and switchbacks, is recommended for 4WD vehicles only. Though it is the most extensively traversed backroad trail in the park, make sure you have gas, water, and a flood-free canyon.

A grotesquely twisted stand of faulted rock monoliths lie en route to **Leadfield,** a mining boomtown that lasted less than a year. Entrepreneur Charles Julian wooed stockbuyers with luxurious meals, mine tours, and promises of a town orchestra, and was just about to build the 93-block town when the government discovered that he didn't have a state permit. Julian's plans were immediately scrapped, and the site now stands as an inspiration to anti-government militias the world over.

Ten miles north of the visitors center, **Death Valley's tallest sand dunes** stand hundreds of feet high. Although barefoot galumphing on the dunes can be sensuous when the sands are cool, be wary of tumbleweeds and mesquite spines. The most accessible dunes for day hikers lie 2.2 mi. east of Stovepipe Wells Village. Park in the sand dunes parking area and follow the 2 mi. trail. Visit in the late afternoon, when the dunes glow with a golden sheen. The dunes were favorites of Ansel Adams. If you try to emulate the master, know that sand will fool your light meter; increase exposure one F-stop to catch such details as footprints and ripples.

Scotty's Castle, in the far northern tip of the park (from Rte. 190, look for sign near mile marker 93 and take road junction to Park Rte. 5; follow Rte. 5 for 33 mi. to castle), seems remarkably out of place in the desert. The saga of the "Castle's" construction began with the friendship between Chicago insurance millionaire Albert Johnson and the infamous flim-flam man Walter Scott (a.k.a. "Death Valley Scotty"). When Johnson fell ill, his doctor persuaded him to move to a warm, dry locale, and Scotty convinced him to build this palatial hacienda in Death Valley. Scotty became Johnson's caretaker for the rest of their lives, enjoying fame as the world's most famous "permanent guest/leech" until Kato Kaelin came along. The real fascination of the castle is its imaginative exterior, complete with minaret and Arabian-style colored tile, which you can enjoy for free. The interior provides welcome relief from the heat (Humbert H. sought shelter here in *Lolita*); though the waterfall in the living room has been switched off, the remote-controlled piano and organ remain. Park service tours (1hr.) depart hourly from Oct.-April, less frequently May-Sept. Call 786-2392 for schedule info. You can purchase tickets until one hour before closing, but there are often lines (open daily 9am-5pm; tours $8, seniors and ages 6-11 $4).

Ubehebe Crater, 8 mi. west of Scotty's Castle, is a blackened volcanic blast site nearly one-mile wide and 462 ft. deep. The view is spectacular despite the gale-force winds that assault the edges of this giant hole. The twisty gravel trail leading to the floor of the crater increases appreciation for the hole's dimensions, but not nearly as much as the grueling climb back out. An unpaved road continues 23 mi. south of the crater to the vast **Racetrack Plaza,** a dried-up lake basin providing access to 4WD routes into Hidden Valley and up White Top Mountain. For an outstanding view of the Racetrack, follow the **Ubehebe Peak Trail** (6mi. round-trip) from the Grandstand parking area along a steep, twisting pathway.

West of the Visitors Center

West along Rte. 190 is **Mosaic Canyon,** a ½ mi. long corridor of collaged and eroded marble walls. To view this natural wonder, take the turn-off one mile west of Stovepipe Wells to the 2½ mi. alluvial fan, accessible by foot, horseback, or car. A simple 2 mi. trail leads from the parking lot around the canyon to some awesome vistas. Occasional bighorn sheep sightings are a trail bonus.

Winding **Emigrant Canyon Road** leads from the Emigrant Campground to Wildrose Canyon Dr. In between, there is a turn-off for the 4WD skedaddle to the ruins of **Skidoo,** another ghost town 5700 ft. up in the Panamint Range. Skidoo was the backdrop for the only full-length movie ever shot in Death Valley (*Greed*, 1923). A few miles farther along Emigrant Canyon Rd. is the turn-off for the dirt road up to **Aguereberry Point,** known for its fine morning views (may require 4WD).

A left turn at Wildrose Canyon Dr. followed by a 10 mi. drive will bring you to the 10 conical furnaces known as the **Charcoal Kilns,** huge beehive-shaped ovens which once fired 45 cords of wood to manufacture charcoal for mines.

Animal life persists in Death Valley, despite the desolate environment. Fragile pupfish inhabit tiny pools, and rare desert bighorn sheep traipse through the rocks at higher elevations. The infamous Death Valley **burros**—beasts of burden transported from their native Middle East in the 1850s and freed when the automobile made them obsolete—have unwittingly decimated the park's bighorn sheep population by wolfing down edible shrubs and fouling the water. Several years ago the park service authorized a three-year burro banishment plan to get their asses out of there with helicopters (they were sold as pets). Over 6000 have been removed, and remaining burros may be adopted for $75. Contact the California Federal Building, 2800 Cottage Way #E-2841, Sacramento, CA 95825 (916-978-4725).

■ Beyond Death Valley

West of Death Valley

Only ghost towns like **Darwin** and a few slightly more populated communities remain on U.S. 395 near the Rte. 190 turn-off. In **Olancha,** the **Ranch Motel** (764-2387), on U.S. 395 provides clean, attractive rooms in cottage-type buildings. (Singles $35; doubles $45; quads $60. Four-day "Getaway Special" Mon.-Thurs. $129, each additional person $20, if Olancha really tickles your fancy.) The truckers' rigs outside signal that the best eats in town are at the **Ranch House Cafe** (764-2363). Beneath stuffed moose heads, dine on a bacon and eggs breakfast ($4.10) that will stay in your colon for years (open daily 6am-midnight).

Southeast of Death Valley

Sick of all this natural beauty? Take time out at **Death Valley Junction** (junction of Rte. 127 and 190, 29mi. from Furnace Creek) to meet mime and ballet dancer Marta Becket, whose **Amargosa Opera House** (852-4441; fax 852-4138), is the sole outpost of desert *haute couture.* Becket fell in love with the tiny, decaying town when her car died here in 1968. She revitalized the old movie theater, which entertained employees of the Pacific Coast Borax Company during the early 20s, commissioning a mural of cupids, kings, angels, monks, and nuns, transforming it into the veritable Sistine Chapel of Death Valley. Becket incorporates classical ballet, modern dance, and **pantomime** into a one-woman show with 47 different characters for packed houses. (Performances are given Sat. Oct.-May, as well as Mon. during Nov. and Feb.-April. Doors open at 7:45pm, shows begin at 8:15pm. $10, under 12 $8.)

The town of **Shoshone** stands at the junction of Rte. 127 and 178, 56 mi. southeast of Furnace Creek. It serves as an automotive gateway to the Valley and a base for outdoor adventures—near here you can go mountain biking, frolic in the monstrous Dumont dunes, or explore the Castles of Clay caves. The **Charles Brown General Store and Service Station** (852-4242), is open daily 8am-9pm. The **Shoshone Inn** (852-4335), next door, has a natural spring swimming pool and cable TV. (Singles $39; doubles $48.) The nearby Shoshone Trailer Park (852-4569), has RV hookups, showers, a pool, and even some shade (sites $10, with full hookup $15).

Northeast of Death Valley

When approaching Death Valley from the north, consider kicking back for a brief spell in the town of **Beatty,** Nevada. Located about 90 mi. northwest of Las Vegas on Rte. 95, Beatty offers the weary traveler air conditioning and ample gambling facilities to prepare for the desolation of the valley.

According to one resident, the favorite pastimes in this country boy's Las Vegas, are "drinkin' an' gamblin'." Compared to those in Reno and Las Vegas, Beatty's casinos are unbelievably relaxed. Wager as little as $1 at blackjack and jaw with the dealers, folk who play slow and seem genuinely sorry to take your money. All casinos are theoretically open 24 hours, but by 2am the dealers start eyeing the clock. **Legal prostitution** is the other great vice of Beatty; the town is a scheduled stop on the Hell's Angels' annual "Whorehouse Run."

Information about the town can be collected at the **Beatty Visitor Information Center** (702-553-2424), on 119 E. Main St. (open 8am-4pm, days of operation vary). The **Beatty Ranger Station** (553-2200), is staffed daily from 8am to 4pm and is well-stocked with books, maps, and safety info for desert-bound drivers. Sleep in peace at the **Stagecoach Hotel** (533-2419 or 800-4-BIG-WIN/424-4946), ½ mi. north of town on Rte. 95. Amenities include a pool, jacuzzi, casino, and bar. Singles and doubles start at $35. The **Burro Inn** (553-2225), at Rte. 95 and 3rd St., serves up standard lunch counter fare (open 24hr.). Don't pass over the gas and water at the service station before heading out of town.

Just outside of town, heading toward Death Valley on Rte. 374, lurks the ghost town of **Rhyolite,** which exploded after prospector Shorty Harris's 1904 discovery of gold in the area. For several madcap years, the town pitched ahead in a frenetic rush of prospecting, building, and saloon-hopping. At its height it was home to an opera house and a stock exchange, but townsfolk fled when a 1911 financial panic struck. The jail and train depot still stand, but the most infamous relic of its wild and crazy heyday is the **Bottle House,** constructed from 51,000 liquor bottles by miner Tom "Iron Liver" Kelly.

■ Las Vegas

Only in Vegas could there be a major museum devoted to Liberace. As close as the modern world comes to Sodom and Gomorrah, Vegas has exchanged the worship of pagan idols for supplication to that 20th-century deity, *Money*—sacrifices from all major credit cards are gleefully accepted. Its muses, namely the ever-present cocktail waitresses, wear outfits combining the worst of ancient Athens with Victoria's Secret. The normal rules of societal conduct do not apply in this temple for the baser impulses of humanity. It's a gaudy fantasyland where you can get a stripper delivered faster than a pizza, or impersonate Elvis and not look out of place.

Lately, the casinos have turned to ever more extreme measures to take your money away. They have rolled out Disneyland-style mirth to satisfy the young-uns while the geezers mindlessly feed the slot machines. Each casino is a self-contained amusement park with its own theme: circus, medieval castle, Roman empire, ancient Egypt… something for every twisted imagination. As you stare at these modern-day pantheons, it is easy to forget that Vegas has witnessed much more heartache than mirth. Vegas has shattered many a dream: Nicolas Cage and Sheryl Crow both talked about *Leaving Las Vegas* for good. Vegas makes its money by taking others' money away—some say that gambling is a tax on the stupid.

But 'twas not always like this. Before L.A. gangster Bugsy Siegel invaded with the Flamingo Hotel-Casino in 1947, Vegas was a quiet Mormon mining town. Ideals in modern Las Vegas have moved from Mormon to mammon—the tables have turned and observances now call for visitors to martyr their monies to the card dealer behind them. So gamble, gorge on bland buffet chow, marry that special someone you met in the casino yesterday, or just watch the show from a distance. Vegas is entertainment in itself.

PRACTICAL INFORMATION

Visitor Information: Las Vegas Convention and Visitor Authority, 3150 Paradise Rd. (892-0711 or 892-7575; fax 226-9011), at the Convention Center, 4 blocks from the Strip by the Hilton. Up-to-date info on headliners, conventions, shows, hotel bargains, and buffets. Open Mon.-Fri. 8am-6pm, Sat.-Sun. 8am-5pm.
Drinkin' an' Gamblin' Age: 21.

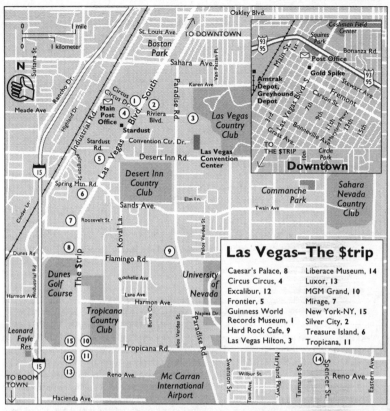

Las Vegas—The $trip

Caesar's Palace, 8	Liberace Museum, 14
Circus Circus, 4	Luxor, 13
Excalibur, 12	MGM Grand, 10
Frontier, 5	Mirage, 7
Guinness World	New York-NY, 15
Records Museum, I	Silver City, 2
Hard Rock Cafe, 9	Treasure Island, 6
Las Vegas Hilton, 3	Tropicana, 11

Tours: Gambler's special bus tours leave L.A., San Francisco, and San Diego for Las Vegas early in the morning and return at night or the next day. Ask at tourist offices in the departure cities or call casinos for info. **Gray Line,** 1550 S. Industrial Rd. (800-634-6579; fax 384-6549). Mini City Tours (1 per day, ½ day, $17.50). Bus tours from Las Vegas to: Hoover Dam/Lake Mead (2 per day, 8am and noon, 5hr., $19); Grand Canyon's South Rim (3 per week; 2 days; singles $139, doubles $111, triples and quads $99). Discounted prices with coupons from Vegas tourist publications. Reserve in advance. **Sightseeing Tours Unlimited,** 612 S. 3rd St. (471-7155). To Hoover Dam (4hr., $13); Hoover Dam/Lake Mead Cruise (8hr., $25). Pick-up 9:15-10:15am and drop-off at most hotels. Reserve in advance for the lowest fares.

Kwik Cash: ATMs located in all major casinos.

Bank: Bank of America, 101 Convention Center Dr. (654-1000), ½ block from the Strip. Open Mon.-Thurs. 9am-5pm, Fri. 9am-6pm. Phone assistance 24hr.

Airport: McCarran International (261-5743), at the southeast end of the Strip. Main terminal is on Paradise Rd. and within walking distance of University of Nevada campus. Vans to the Strip and downtown $3-5; taxi to downtown $23.

Buses: Greyhound, 200 S. Main St. (382-2292 or 800-231-2222), at Carson downtown. To L.A. (6 per day, 5hr., Mon.-Thurs. $31, Fri.-Sun. $32) and San Francisco (3 per day, 15hr., Mon.-Thurs. $38, Fri.-Sun. $40). Open daily 4:30am-1am.

Public Transportation: Citizens Area Transit (CAT) (228-7433; fax 455-5151). Bus #301 serves downtown and the Strip 24hr. Buses #108 and 109 serve the airport. Fares for routes on the Strip $1.50, for residential routes $1, seniors and ages 6-17 50¢. Most buses operate every 10-15min. daily 5:30am-1:30am. **Las Vegas Strip Trolleys** (382-1404), are not moving stripjoints. They cruise the Strip every 20 min. daily 9am-2am ($1.20 in exact change).

THE DESERT

Taxis: Yellow, Checker, and **Star Taxis** (873-2000). Initial charge $2.20, each additional mi. $1.50. 24hr. service.

Car Rental: Rebel, 5021 Swenson St. (597-0427 or 800-372-1981). Rentals start at $20 per day. Unlimited mi. within Clark County. Must be 21 with major credit card; under 25 surcharge $15 per day. Discounts in tourist publications.

Marriage: Marriage License Bureau, 200 S. 3rd St. (455-4415). Must be 18 or obtain parental consent. Licenses issued for $35, cash only. No waiting period or blood test required. Open Mon.-Thurs. 8am-midnight, Fri. 8am-Sun. midnight.

Divorce: You must be a Nevada resident for at least 6 weeks and pay a $140 service fee. Permits available at the courthouse Mon.-Fri. 8am-5pm.

Bi-Gay-Lesbian Organization: Gay and Lesbian Community Center, 912 E. Sahara Ave. (733-9800). Hours dependent on volunteer staff availability.

Road Conditions: Nevada (793-1313).

Crisis Lines: Compulsive Gamblers Hotline (800-LOST-BET/567-8238). 24hr. **Rape Crisis Center Hotline** (366-1640). 24hr. **Gamblers Anonymous** (385-7732). 24hr. **Suicide Prevention** (731-2990). 24hr.

Emergency: 911.

Police: 795-3111.

Post Office: 2300 E. Tropicana Ave. (736-5189), in Lucky's groceries. Open Mon.-Sat. 10:30am-7pm, Sun. 11am-7pm. General delivery pick-up Mon.-Fri. 10am-3pm. **ZIP Code:** 89101.

Area Code: 702.

ORIENTATION

Driving to Vegas from Los Angeles involves a straight, 300 mi. shot on I-15 (5hr.). From Arizona, take I-40 west to Kingman and then U.S. 93/95 north. Las Vegas has two major casino areas. The **downtown** area, around Fremont and 2nd St., has been converted into a foot-friendly pedestrian promenade; casinos cluster close together beneath a shimmering space-frame structure covering over five city blocks. The other main area, known as the **Strip,** is a collection of mammoth casinos on both sides of **Las Vegas Boulevard.** Parallel to the Strip and in its shadow is **Paradise Boulevard,** also strewn with casinos. As in any city where money reigns supreme, many areas of Las Vegas are unsafe. Always stay on brightly lit pathways and do not wander too far from the major casinos and hotels. The neighborhoods just north and west of downtown can be especially dangerous.

Despite all its debauchery, Las Vegas has a **curfew.** Cruisers under 18 are not allowed unaccompanied in public places from midnight to 5am, those under 14 from 10pm to 5am. On weekends, no one under 18 is allowed unaccompanied on the Strip or in other designated areas from 9pm to 5am.

ACCOMMODATIONS

Even though Vegas has over 90,000 rooms, most hotels fill up on weekend nights. Coming to town on a Friday or Saturday night without reservations is flirting with homelessness, so *make reservations as far in advance as possible.* If you get stuck call the **Room Reservations Hotline** (800-332-5333). The earlier you reserve, the better chance you have of snagging a special rate. Room rates at most hotels in Vegas fluctuate all the time. Many hotels use two rate ranges—one for weeknights, the other for weekend nights. In addition, a room that costs $20 during a promotion can cost hundreds during a convention. Check local publications such as *What's On In Las Vegas, Today in Las Vegas, Vegas Visitor, Casino Player, Tour Guide Magazine,* and *Insider Viewpoint of Las Vegas* for discounts and coupons; they are all free and available at the visitors center, hotels, and attractions.

Strip hotels are at the center of the action and within walking distance of each other, but their inexpensive rooms sell out quickly. Motels line **Fremont St.,** from downtown south. Another option, if you have a car, is to stay at one of the hotel-casinos in Jean, NV (approximately 30 mi. south on I-15, near the California border). These tend to be less crowded and cheaper than in-town hotels. Members of the same sex sharing a hotel room may have to book a room containing two twin beds, as public displays of affection by homosexual couples are illegal in Nevada.

Las Vegas International Hostel (AAIH/Rucksackers), 1208 Las Vegas Blvd. S (385-9955). Flashing blue arrows point the way to this European-flavored joint. Tidy, spartan rooms with A/C and fresh sheets every day. Ride-board in kitchen. Free lemonade, tea, coffee. TV room and basketball court. Extremely helpful staff is excellent source for advice about budget Vegas. Office open daily 7am-11pm. Check-out 7-10am. Shared bathrooms. Dorms Sun.-Thurs. $12, Fri.-Sat. $14; singles $26. Laundry. Key deposit $5. Rates lower Dec.-March.

Somerset House Motel, 294 Convention Center Dr. (738-4411; fax 369-2388). A straightforward, no-frills establishment within short walking distance of the major Strip casinos. Many rooms feature kitchens and balconies; all are sizable and impeccably clean. Dishes and cooking utensils provided upon request. Singles $32, weekends $40; doubles $40, weekends $50; each additional person $5. Rates lower for seniors.

Center Strip Inn, 3688 Las Vegas Blvd. S (739-6066; fax 736-2521). Despite its proximity to Caesar's, this inn is neither gaudy nor pricey. Video library in the lobby. Rooms come with TV, refrigerator, and safe (for those feeling especially lucky). Standard room with 2 double beds $30-69, Fri.-Sat. $69-84.

Circus Circus, 2880 Las Vegas Blvd. S (734-0410 or 800-444-CIRCUS/247287; fax 734-2268). Only hotel with its own clown shop. Rooms with TV and A/C for 1-4 people. Sun.-Thurs. $29-79, Fri.-Sat. $49-99, holidays $65-125. Roll-away bed $7. In summer, fills 2-3 months in advance for weeknights, 3-4 months for weekends.

Boomtown, 3333 Blue Diamond Rd. (263-7777 or 800-588-7711). Although its ghost town theme is ominous in the Vegas context, this slightly remote hotel-casino offers the swagger of the Strip at affordable prices. A free shuttle transports guests back to Las Vegas Blvd. Singles and doubles $49, weekends $70.

Econo Lodge Downtown, 520 S. Casino Center Blvd. (384-8211). A seasoned traveler herself, Econo Lodge proprietor Juanita Wilson fiercely defends the voyager's right to clean rooms at consistently low prices. Rooms here are spotless and come with refrigerator and coffee-maker. Walking distance to the Greyhound bus station and downtown casino area. Singles $35, weekends $45; doubles $45, weekends $55; each additional person (up to 5) $5.

Goldstrike, 1 Main St. in Jean, NV (800-634-1359; fax 874-1349), 30 mi. south of Vegas on I-15 (Exit 12). A Vegas-style casino with a variety of inexpensive restaurants (prime rib $4, dinner buffet $5). Registration open 24hr. Singles and doubles $25, weekends $48; each additional person (up to 5) $3.

CAMPING

Lake Mead National Recreation Area (293-8906), 25mi. south of town on U.S. 93/95. Sites $10, with hookup $14-18. For details, see p.202.

Circusland RV Park, 500 Circus Circus Dr. (734-0410), a part of the Circus Circus hotel on the Strip. Laundry facilities, showers, pool, jacuzzi, and convenience store. Sun.-Thurs. $13, Fri.-Sat. $17.

FOOD

Almost every hotel-casino in Vegas courts tourists with cheap all-you-can-eat invitations, but expect greasy, cafeteria-quality food and long lines at peak hours. Most casinos dole out alcoholic drinks for free to those who are gambling and for under $1 to those who aren't…yet. Vegas isn't all bland buffets—just west of the Strip, particularly along **Decatur Blvd.,** are a number of low-priced eateries that can revive your taste buds.

Restaurants

Rincon Criollo, 1145 Las Vegas Blvd. S (388-1906), across from the youth hostel. Dine on filling Cuban food beneath a wall-sized photograph of palm trees. Daily special includes steak prepared *palomillas*-style, rice, and black beans for an unbeatable $6. Hot sandwiches $3.50-4.50. Open Tues.-Sun. 11:30am-9:30pm.

THE DESERT

Hippo & the Wild Bunch Restaurant and Lounge, 4503 Paradise Rd. (731-5446), across from the Hard Rock Hotel. Munch on a famous ½ lb. "Hippoburger" ($6) against a backdrop of outlandish jungle decor. Also features pizza and pasta. Open Mon.-Thurs. 11am-3am, Fri.-Sat. 11am-5am.

Buffet Bonanza

Circus Circus, 2800 Las Vegas Blvd. S (734-0410). The cheapest buffet in town. Rows of serving stations make you feel like a circus circus animal at a feed trough. Breakfast $3 (6-11:30am), brunch $4 (noon-4pm), dinner $5 (4:30-11pm).

Bally's Big Kitchen, 3645 Las Vegas Blvd. S (739-4930). Locals say it has the best buffets on the Strip. A bit pricier, but worth it if you dig casino buffet food. Breakfast $9, lunch $10, dinner $14. Open daily 7:30am-2:30pm and 4-10pm.

Luxor's Pharaoh's Pheast, 3900 Las Vegas Blvd. S (262-4000). The Luxor's recent upgrade is reflected in its improved buffet. Breakfast $5 (6:30-11:30am), lunch $6 (11:30am-4:30pm), dinner $8 (4:30-11pm).

SIGHTS

The casinos are the main attraction, but a few non-gambling alternatives exist. Fans of classical music and kitsch will be delighted by the **Liberace Museum,** 1775 E. Tropicana Ave. (798-5595), devoted to the flamboyant late "Mr. Showmanship." Liberace's audacious uses of fur, velvet, and rhinestone boggle the rational mind (open Mon.-Sat. 10am-5pm, Sun. 1-5pm; admission $6.95, students $3.50, seniors $4.50, ages 6-12 $2). **The Guinness World Records Museum,** 2780 Las Vegas Blvd. S (792-3766), showcases displays describing the most tattooed lady and the largest pizza, among other record-breakingly wacky stuff. (Open June-Aug. daily 9am-8pm; Sept.-May daily 9am-6pm. Admission $5, students $4, seniors $4, ages 5-12 $3.)

Las Vegas offers some unconventional and relatively inexpensive sporting activities for those craving a less offensive thrill. **Flyaway Indoor Skydiving,** 200 Convention Center (731-4768), simulates a plunge from a plane (open Mon.-Fri. 11am-7pm, Sat. 10:30am-7pm, Sun. 10:30am-5pm; first flight $27, each additional flight $19). If land speed is more your forte, try the impressive four-track **Las Vegas Mini Grand Prix,** 1401 N. Rainbow Blvd. (259-7000; single ride $4, 5 rides $17.50). Look for coupons in tourist publications.

The nearby city of **Henderson** offers a quartet of free food factory tours and a break from casino craziness. All the factories have shops; most have free samples. **Kidd's Marshmallow Factory** (564-3878), is a standout. Watch huge sheets of white gooey sugary sludge become the innards of the StayPuft Marshmallow Man.

CA$INO-HOPPING AND NIGHTLIFE

Johnny Rotten proclaimed, "The only notes that matter come in a wad." Casinos have resorted to ever more extreme measures to get these notes. Where once the casinos stuck to the quintessentially Vegas themes of cheap buffets, booze, and entertainment, they now spend millions of dollars a year trying to fool guests into thinking that they are somewhere else. Hollywood, New York, Rio, and Monte Carlo can already be visited on the Strip, and Paris (replete with Eiffel Tower) is due this year. Despite these alluring amusements, however, gambling remains Vegas's biggest draw, and it is *illegal for those under 21.* If you are of age, look for casino "funbooks" which allow you to buy $50 in chips for only $15. Never bring more money than you're prepared to lose cheerfully. And always remember: *in the long run, you will almost definitely lose cash.* Keep your wallet in your front pocket, and beware of the thieves who prowl casinos to nab big winnings from unwary jubilants. Most casinos offer free gambling lessons; check out *Today* in Las Vegas for current dates and times. In addition, the more patient dealers may offer a tip or two (in exchange for one from you). Casinos, nightclubs, and wedding chapels stay open 24 hours.

New York-New York, 3790 Las Vegas Blvd. S (740-6969; http://www.nynyhotel-casino.com), the most recent addition to Strip, puts even Disneyland to shame with its fine-tuned gimmickry. Its towers mimic the Manhattan skyline and every last interior detail has its place in the New York scheme of things, creating all the glory of the Big Apple without the crime *or* the grime. Busts abound at **Caesar's Palace,** 3570 Las Vegas Blvd. S (731-7110). Some of these are plaster; the rest are barely concealed beneath the low-cut classical costumes of the cocktail waitresses who roam the casino floor. Their male counterparts strut about with false Roman noses. In the **Festival Fountain show,** statues move, talk, battle, and shout amid a laser-light show (every hr., daily 10am-11pm). Next door, the majestic confines of the **Mirage,** 3400 Las Vegas Blvd. S (262-4000), are certainly no illusion. Among its attractions are a dolphin habitat (admission $3), Siegfried and Roy's white tigers, and a volcano that erupts in fountains and flames every half hour (daily 8pm-1am).

At **Treasure Island,** 3300 Las Vegas Blvd. S (894-7111), pirates battle with cannons staged on giant wooden ships in a Strip-side "bay" on the Strip (every 1½hr., daily 4:30pm-midnight). Before the watchful eyes of the sprawling sphinx and the towering black pyramid of **Luxor,** 3900 Las Vegas Blvd. S (262-4000), a dazzling laser light show is reminiscent of imperial ancient Egypt. Boat rides stream through the "Nile" (a.k.a. the hotel lobby) every 20 min. (daily 9am-12:30am; $4). Wander into the depths of the desert at **King Tut Tomb and Museum,** which houses replicas of the artifacts uncovered at the king's grave (open daily 9am-11pm; $4). The hotel's three 3-D **holographic films,** *Search of the Obelisk, Luxor Live,* and *The Theater of Time* have dazzling special effects ($4-5 each).

Relive the glory days of Hollywood at the **MGM Grand,** 3799 Las Vegas Blvd. S (891-1111). It features the Grand Adventures Amusement Park, complete with an indoor rollercoaster, an erupting volcano, and the *Temple of Gloom.* (Park open daily 10am-10pm. Admission $17, seniors $9, ages 4-12 $10.)

Circus Circus, 2880 Las Vegas Blvd. S (734-0410), attempts to cultivate a (dys-functional) family atmosphere; while parents run to the card tables and slot machines downstairs, their children spend their quarters upstairs on the souped-up carnival midway and in the titanic video game arcade. Beware of the carnival area's "Camel Chase" game; it's far more addictive than any Vegas slot machine. Two stories above the casino floor, tightrope-walkers, fire-eaters, and acrobats perform (daily 11am-midnight). Within the hotel complex, the **Grand Slam Canyon** is a Grand Canyon theme park with a rollercoaster and other rides—all enclosed in a glass shell. (Open Sun.-Thurs. 11am-6pm, Fri.-Sat. 10am-midnight. Admission and 2 small rides $4, seniors and under 3 free. Each additional ride $2-4; unlimited rides $14, ages 3-9 $10.) **Excalibur,** 3850 Las Vegas Blvd. S (800-937-7777), has a medieval English theme which may make you nostalgic for the Black Plague. At *King Arthur's Tournament,* jousters and jesters entertain spectators while they eat a medieval banquet ($30). There are over 50 other casinos in Vegas, but they are generally less bombastic versions of the listed ones. Check with the visitors center (p.196) for details.

Extra bucks will buy you a seat at a made-in-the-USA phenomenon—the **Vegas spectacular.** These stunning casino-sponsored productions happen twice per night and feature marvels such as waterfalls, explosions, fireworks, and casts of thousands (including animals). You can also see Broadway plays and musicals, ice revues, and individual entertainers in concert. All hotels have city-wide ticket booths in their lobbies. Some "production shows" are topless; most are tasteless. For a show by one of the musical stars who haunt the city, such as Diana Ross or Wayne Newton, you may have to fork over $40 or more. "Revues" featuring imitations of (generally deceased) performers are far more reasonable. But why pay? You can't turn around in Vegas without bumping into an aspiring Elvis clone, or perhaps the real Elvis, pursuing anonymity in the brilliant disguise of an Elvis impersonator.

Nightlife in Vegas gets rolling around midnight and keeps going until everyone drops or runs out of money. At Caesar's Palace (731-7110), **Cleopatra's Barge,** a huge ship-disco, is one boat that's made for rockin' (open Tues.-Sun. 10pm-4am; cover Fri.-Sat. $5). Another popular disco, **Gipsy,** 4605 Paradise Rd. (731-1919), southeast of the Strip, may look deserted at 11pm, but by 1am the medium-sized dance floor packs in a gay, lesbian, and straight crowd (cover $4). Be forewarned that the Gipsy dancers get crazy on Topless Tuesdays. Downtown, the **Fremont Street Blues and Reggae Club** (474-7209), at Fremont and 4th, provides live music every night (open Sun.-Thurs. 7pm-3am, Fri.-Sat. 7pm-5am).

■ Near Las Vegas: Lake Mead

Appearing as a turquoise oasis as U.S. 93 approaches the Nevada desert, Lake Mead has earned the nickname "The Jewel of the Desert" from its residents. The lake extends 110 mi. behind **Hoover Dam,** the brainchild of its eponymous president, the Western Hemisphere's highest concrete damn (727 ft.), and the site of many death-defying movie stunts. Harnessing the Colorado River, Hoover Dam is a testament to Depression-era dreams of a better world achieved through engineering. The dam, made from 3.25 million cubic yards of concrete, generates enough hydroelectricity to power 500,000 homes *and* keep viewing area drinking fountains cold in the triple-digit heat. The **Hoover Dam Visitors Center** (293-8321), offers guided 30-minute tours (open daily 8:30am-5:40pm; tours $6, seniors $5, ages 6-16 $2).

Backcountry camping is permitted and free in most areas. Numerous National Park Service **campgrounds** lie within the recreation area as well (sites $10). The most popular is **Boulder Beach** (293-8990), accessible by Lakeshore Rd. off U.S. 93. The **Lake Shore Trailer Village** (293-2540), has RV sites with showers for around $15. (Reservations required Memorial Day, July 4th, and Labor Day weekends; all other times first-come, first-served.)

U.S. 93 runs right over Hoover Dam. There are several free parking lots at intervals along the highway; they tend to be crowded, but less so on the Arizona side. Shuttle bus services are available from the more remote lots. Public transportation does not serve Hoover Dam, but **Gray Line** buses and **Sightseeing Tours Unlimited** offer rides from Las Vegas (see **Las Vegas: Practical Information, p.196**).

GRAND CANYON

Even the weariest of travelers snap to attention upon first sight of the Grand Canyon (277mi. long, 10mi. wide, and over 1mi. deep). King of natural wonders and famed destination of the American family vacation, the canyon descends past looming walls of limestone, sandstone, and shale. The U.S. began designating its most daunting wild regions as national park sites for two reasons—first, to compensate with natural grandeur for the country's short cultural tradition, and second, to preserve unfarmable lands for recreation. Both breathtaking and hell on a plow, the Grand Canyon exemplifies the national park as it was originally conceived. The hike down to the gorge will assure you of this at the very least. Many TV shows and movies have depicted its largess, including *Independence Day* and the *National Lampoon's Vacation.*

The **Grand Canyon National Park** is divided into three areas. The **South Rim,** which includes Grand Canyon Village, is slightly more accessible than the higher, more heavily forested **North Rim** and draws 10 times as many visitors. The South Rim is open all year, though the North Rim only welcomes travelers mid-May to mid-October depending on the weather. The 13 mi. trail that traverses the **canyon floor** itself makes a two-day adventure for sturdy hikers, while the 214 mi. perimeter road is a good five-hour drive for those who would rather explore from above. Observe all safety precautions, use common sense, and drink lots of water. Every year several careless hikers take what locals morbidly call "the 12-second tour."

■ South Rim

In summer, everything on two legs or four wheels converges on this side of the Grand Canyon. If you plan to visit during the mobfest, make reservations for lodging, campsites, or mules well in advance—and prepare to battle the crowds. That said, it's much better than Disney World. A friendly Park Service staff, well-run facilities, and beautiful scenery help ease crowd anxiety. During winter there are fewer tourists; however, the weather is brisk and many hotels and facilities close.

PRACTICAL INFORMATION

Tourist Office: The **visitors center** (638-7888) is 6mi. north of the south entrance station. Ask for the *Trip Planner*. Free and informative, *The Guide* is available here, in case you somehow missed it at the entrance. Open daily 8am-6pm; off season 8am-5pm. Write the **Superintendent,** Grand Canyon National Park, P.O. Box 129, Grand Canyon, 86023, for info before you go.

Buses: Nava-Hopi Bus Lines (800-892-8687), leave the Flagstaff Amtrak station for the Grand Canyon daily 7:45am and 2:30pm, returning from Bright Angel Lodge 10:15am and 5pm. Fare $12.50, under 14 $6.25; round-trip $25, $12.50. Entrance fee ($10) not included. Times vary by season, so call ahead.

Local Transportation: Bright Angel Lodge Transport Info Desk (638-2631), makes reservations for mule rides, bus tours, Phantom Ranch, taxis, everything. Open daily 6am-7pm. A **free shuttle bus** rides the West Rim Loop (daily 7:30am-sunset) and the Village Loop (daily 6:30am-9pm) every 20min. A free **hiker's shuttle** runs every ½hr. between Grand Canyon village and South Kaibab Trailhead near Yalci Point. **Mule trips** from the South Rim are booked up to one year in advance (call 303-297-2757 for reservations). **Whitewater rafting** trips through the canyon last from 3 days to 2 weeks; advance reservations required. Call the transport info desk for a list of trips.

Auto Repairs: Grand Canyon Garage (638-2631), east of the visitors center on the park's main road near Maswik Lodge. Garage open daily 8am-noon and 1-5pm. 24hr. emergency service.

Equipment Rental: Babbitt's General Store (638-2854), in Mather Center, Grand Canyon Village near Yavapai Lodge and the visitors center. Rents comfortable hiking boots, socks included (first day $8, each additional day $5); sleeping bags ($7-9, $5); tents ($15-18, $9); and other camping gear. Hefty deposits required on all items. Open daily 8am-8pm.

Weather and Road Conditions: (638-7888).

Medical Services: Grand Canyon Clinic (638-2551 or 638-2469), several mi. south on Center Rd. Open Mon.-Fri. 8am-5:30pm, Sat. 9am-noon. 24hr. emergency aid.

Emergency: 911.

Post Office: (638-2512), across the street from the visitors center. Open Mon.-Fri. 9am-4:30pm, Sat.-Sun. 10am-2pm. **ZIP Code:** 86023.

Area Code: 520.

There are two entrances to the park: the main **south entrance** lies on U.S. 180 N., the eastern **Desert View** entrance lies on I-40 W. From Las Vegas, the fastest route to the Canyon is U.S. 93 S. to I-40 E., and then Rte. 64 N. From Flagstaff, I-40 E. to U.S. 89 N. is the most scenic; from there, Rte. 64 N. takes you to the Desert View entrance. Straight up U.S. 180 N. is more direct.

The Grand Canyon's **entrance fee** is $20 per car and $10 for travelers using other modes of transportation—even bus passengers must pay. The pass lasts for one week. If you're coming from Flagstaff, check noticeboards in hotels and hostels; travelers who have moved on sometimes leave their valid passes behind.

Inside the park, posted maps and signs make orienting yourself easy. Lodges and services concentrate in **Grand Canyon Village,** at the end of Park Entrance Rd. The east half of the village contains the visitors center and the general store, while most of the lodges and the **Bright Angel Trailhead** lie in the west section. The south **Kaibab Trailhead** is off East Rim Dr., to the east of the village.

ACCOMMODATIONS AND CAMPING

Compared to the six million years it took the Colorado River to carve the Grand Canyon, the 11 months it will take you to get a room on the South Rim will pass in the blink of an eye. It is almost impossible to sleep indoors anywhere near the South Rim without reservations or a wad of cash. If you arrive unprepared, check at the visitors center and the Bright Angel Transport Info Desk after 4pm for vacancies.

Most accommodations on the South Rim are very expensive. The campsites listed here usually fill early in the day. Campground overflow generally winds up in the **Kaibab National Forest,** along the south border of the park, where you can pull off a dirt road and camp for free. No camping is allowed within ¼ mi. of U.S. 64. Sleeping in cars is *not* permitted within the park, but is allowed in the Kaibab Forest. For more info, contact the **Tusayan Ranger District,** Kaibab National Forest, P.O. Box 3088, Grand Canyon 86023 (638-2443). Any overnight hiking or camping within the park requires a **Backcountry Use Permit** ($20 plus a $4 impact fee) which is available at the **Backcountry Office** (638-7875), ¼ mi. south of the visitors center (open daily 8am-noon; calls answered Mon.-Fri. 1-5pm). Permit requests are accepted by mail or in person only, up to five months in advance. The earlier you make your request, the better. Call the Backcountry Office for a list of the info you must include in a mail-in permit request. Once reserved, the permit must be picked up *no later than 9am* on the day you plan to camp, or it will be cancelled. Guests with advance reservations at Phantom Ranch Lodge do not need permits. While you're hiking, extra luggage may be checked at Bright Angel Lodge for 50¢ per day. Reservations for **Bright Angel Lodge, Maswik Lodge, Trailer Village,** and **Phantom Ranch** can be made through Grand Canyon National Park Lodges, P.O. Box 699, Grand Canyon 86023 (638-2401). All rooms should be reserved 11 months in advance for summer visits. For same-day reservations (usually not available), the Bright Angel Transport Info Desk lists last-minute cancellations; call the Grand Canyon operator (638-2631) and ask to be connected with the proper lodge.

Bright Angel Lodge (638-2401), Grand Canyon Village. Rustic cabins with plumbing but no heat. Very convenient to Bright Angel Trail and shuttle buses. Singles or doubles $56-114, depending on how much plumbing you want. "Historic" cabins for 1 or 2 people $66. Each additional person $7.

Maswik Lodge (638-2401), Grand Canyon Village. Small, clean cabins with showers. Singles or doubles $59; private room $72-107; each additional person $7-9.

Phantom Ranch (638-2401, reservations 303-297-2757), on the canyon floor, a 4hr. hike down the Kaibab Trail. Dorms $22; cabins (sleep 1-2) $56; each additional person $11. Don't go without reservations—they'll send you back up the trail.

Mather Campground (DESTINET 800-365-2267), Grand Canyon Village, 1mi. south of the visitors center. 320 shady, relatively isolated sites with no hookups. 7-day max. stay. Sept.-May $12; June-Aug. $15. For March-Nov. reserve up to 8 weeks in advance; Dec.-Feb. sites available on a first-come, first-camped basis only. Check at the office, even if the sign says the campground is full.

Camper Village (638-2887), 7mi. south of the visitors center in Tusayan. RV and tent sites $15-22. First-come, first-camped tent sites; reservations for RVs.

Cottonwood Campground (638-7888), 17mi. from the Bright Angel trailhead on the North Kaibab trail. 14 free sites. Reservations recommended. Open May-Oct.

Indian Garden (638-7888), 4½ mi. from the South Rim Bright Angel trailhead and 3100ft. below the rim. 15 free sites, toilets, and water. Reservations required.

Trailer Village (638-2401), next to Mather Campground. Clearly designed with the RV in mind. Showers and laundry nearby. 7-day max. stay. Office open daily 8am-noon and 1-5pm. 84 sites for 2 people. Sites (with hookup) $19; each additional person $1.75. Reservations required 6-9 months in advance.

Desert View Campsite (638-7888), 26mi. east of Grand Canyon Village. 50 sites with phone and restroom access, but no hookups. Sites $10. No reservations; arrive early; usually full by noon. Open mid-May to Oct.

Ten-X Campground (638-2443), in the Kaibab National Forest, 10mi. south of Grand Canyon Village off Rte. 64. Pine-shaded sites, toilets, water, no hookups. Sites $10. Available on a first-come, first-camped basis. Open May-Sept.

FOOD

Fast food hasn't sunk its greasy talons into the rim of the Canyon, but you *can* find meals for fast-food prices. **Babbitt's General Store** (638-2262), near the visitors center, has a deli counter (sandwiches $2-4) and a reasonably priced supermarket. Stock up on trail mix, water, and gear (open daily 8am-8pm; deli open 8am-7pm). **The Maswik Cafeteria,** in Maswik Lodge, puts out a variety of inexpensive grill-made options (hot entrees $5-7, sandwiches $2-4) served in a wood-paneled cafeteria atmosphere (open daily 6am-10pm). **Bright Angel Dining Room** (638-2631), in Bright Angel Lodge, serves hot sandwiches for $6-8 (open daily 6:30am-10pm). The soda fountain at Bright Angel Lodge chills 16 flavors of ice cream (1 scoop $1.60) for hot hikers emerging from trails (open daily 6:30am-8pm).

SIGHTS AND ACTIVITIES

From your first glimpse of the canyon, you will feel a compelling desire to see it from the inside, an enterprise which is much harder than it looks. Even the young at heart should remember that an easy downhill hike can become a nightmarish 50° incline on the return journey. Also keep in mind that the lower you go, the hotter it gets. Heat exhaustion, the second greatest threat after slipping, is marked by a monstrous headache and termination of sweating. It is absolutely necessary to take *two quarts of water per person.* A list of hiking safety tips can be found in *The Guide.* Don't overestimate your limits; parents should think twice about bringing children more than one mile down any trail.

The two most accessible trails into the Canyon are the **Bright Angel Trail,** originating at the Bright Angel Lodge, and **South Kaibab Trail,** from Yaki Point. Bright Angel is outfitted for the average tourist, with rest houses strategically stationed 1½ mi. and 3 mi. from the rim. **Indian Gardens,** 4½ mi. down, offers the tired hiker restrooms, picnic tables, and blessed shade; all three rest stops usually have water in the summer. Kaibab is trickier, steeper, and lacking in shade or water, but it rewards the intrepid with a better view of the canyon.

If you've made arrangements to spend the night on the canyon floor, the best route is the **South Kaibab Trail** (4-5hr., depending on conditions) and back up the Bright Angel (7-8hr.) the following day. Hikes down Bright Angel Trail to Indian Gardens and **Plateau Point,** 6 mi. out, where you can look down 1360 ft. to the river, make excellent daytrips (8-12hr.), but it's best to start early (around 7am).

If you're not up to descending into the canyon, follow the **Rim Trail** east to **Grandeur Point** and the **Yavapai Geological Museum,** or west to **Hermit's Rest,** using the shuttles. The Eastern Rim Trail swarms with sunset-watchers at dusk, and the observation deck at the Yavapai Museum, at the end of the trail, has a sweeping view of the canyon during the day. The Western Rim Trail leads to several vistas; **Hopi Point** is a favorite for sunsets, and the **Abyss** overlooks a nearly vertical cliff, leading to the **Tonto Plateau** 3000 ft. below. To watch a sunset (or sunrise), check *The Guide* for the time. Show up at your chosen spot 45 min. beforehand.

The **Grand Canyon Railway** (800-THE-TRAIN/843-8724) leaves from Williams and offers tours for the whole family. The freedom tour takes passengers to great views in the Canyon ($13, children $7). The park service rangers present a variety of free, informative talks and hikes including a free talk at 8:30pm (in winter 7:30pm) in **Mather Amphitheater,** behind the visitors center.

THE DESERT

■ North Rim

If you are coming from Utah or Nevada, or you simply want to avoid the crowds at the South Rim, the park's North Rim is a bit wilder, a bit cooler, and much more serene—all with a view as groovy as that from the South Rim. Unfortunately, because the North Rim is less frequented, it's hard to reach by public transportation.

PRACTICAL INFORMATION

Tourist Office: National Park Service Information Desk (638-7864), in the lobby of Grand Canyon Lodge (see below). Info on North Rim viewpoints, facilities, and some trails. Open daily 8am-8pm.

Public Transportation: Transcanyon, P.O. Box 348, Grand Canyon 86023 (638-2820). Buses to South Rim depart 7am (5hr.); return buses depart 1:30pm (5hr.). Fare $60, round-trip $100. Call for reservations. Open late May-Oct.

Medical Services: North Rim Clinic (638-2611, ext. 222), located in cabin #7 at Grand Canyon Lodge. Staffed by a nurse practitioner. Walk-in or appointment service. Open Fri.-Mon. 9am-noon and 3-6pm, Tues. 9am-noon and 2-5pm.

Weather Info: (638-7888).

Emergency: 911.

Post Office: (638-2611), in Grand Canyon Lodge with everything else. Open Mon.-Fri. 8am-4pm, Sat. 9am-1pm. **ZIP Code:** 86052.

Area Code: 520.

The **entrance fee** for the North Rim admits you to both rims for seven days ($20 per car, $4 per person on foot, bike, bus, or holy pilgrimage). From South Rim, take Rte. 64 east to U.S. Rte. 89 N., which runs into Alt. 89; from Alt. 89, follow Rte. 67 south to the edge. Altogether, the drive is over 200 mi. and is beautiful. Snow closes Rte. 67 from the mid-October through mid-May, and visitor facilities close in the winter.

ACCOMMODATIONS, CAMPING, AND FOOD

Since camping within the confines of the Grand Canyon National Park is limited to designated campgrounds, only a lucky minority of North Rim visitors get to spend the night "right there." Advance reservations can be made through DESTINET (800-365-2267). Otherwise, mark your territory by 10am. If you can't get in-park lodgings, visit the **Kaibab National Forest,** which runs from north of Jacob Lake to the park entrance. You can camp for free, as long as you're ½ mi. from official campgrounds and the road. The nearest low-priced motels are a one-hour drive to the north, in **Kanab, UT** and **Fredonia.** Hotel rooms in Kanab, 80 mi. north, hover around $40; the **Canyonlands International Youth Hostel (AAIH/Rucksackers)** rents dorm rooms for $9.

Grand Canyon Lodge (303-297-2757), on the edge of the rim. Front desk open 24hr. Pioneer cabins shelter 4 people for $80. Singles or doubles in frontier cabins $60. Western cabins and motel rooms $70-85. late Oct. to mid-May.

Jacob Lake Inn (643-7232), 30mi. north of the North Rim entrance at Jacob Lake. Reasonably priced dining room. Reception open daily 6:30am-9:30pm. Cabins for 2 $66-71, for 3 $76-78, for 4 $81-84. Pricier motel units available for $10-15 more.

Kaibab Camper Village (643-7804), ¼mi. south of the Inn. Over 100 sites available at this large site. Tent sites $12; RV sites (for 2) $20-22; each additional person $2. Open May to Mid-Oct.

North Rim Campground (DESTINET 800-365-2267), on Rte. 67 near the rim, the only campground in the park. You can't see into the canyon from the pine-covered site, but you know it's there. Food store nearby, laundry facilities, recreation room, and showers. 7-day max. stay. 82 sites $12. Closes Oct. 21.

DeMotte Park Campground, 5mi. north of the park entrance in the Kaibab National Forest. 23 woodsy sites $10. First-come, first-camped.

Both feeding options on the North Rim are placed strategically at the **Grand Canyon Lodge** (638-2611). The restaurant serves dinners for $13 and up (reservations only) and breakfast for $3-7. A sandwich at the **Snack Bar** costs $2.50 (open daily 7am-9pm). North Rim-ers are better off eating in Kanab or stopping at the **Jacob Lake Inn** for snacks and great milkshakes (lunch dishes about $5; open daily 6am-9pm).

SIGHTS AND ACTIVITIES

A ½ mi. paved trail takes you from the Grand Canyon Lodge to **Bright Angel Point,** which commands a seraphic view of the Canyon. **Point Imperial,** an 11 mi. drive from the lodge, overlooks **Marble Canyon** and the **Painted Desert.** The North Rim's *The Guide* lists trails in full. Only one trail, the **North Kaibab Trail,** leads into the Canyon from the North Rim; a shuttle runs to the trailhead from Grand Canyon Lodge (daily 6am-8pm; fare $5). Overnight hikers must get permits from the **Backcountry Office** in the ranger station (open daily 7:30am-noon), or write Backcountry Office, PO Box 129, Grand Canyon 86023; it may take a few days.

The North Rim offers nature walks, lectures, and evening programs at the North Rim Campground and at Grand Canyon Lodge. Check the info desk or campground bulletin boards for schedules. One-hour ($15) or half-day **mule trips** ($35) descend into the canyon from the lodge (638-9875; open daily 7am-7pm). If you'd rather tour the Canyon wet, pick up a *Grand Canyon River Trip Operators* brochure and select from among the 20 companies which offer trips.

On warm evenings, the Grand Canyon Lodge fills with an eclectic group of international travelers, U.S. families, and rugged adventurers. Thirsty hikers will find a bar and a jukebox at the **Saloon,** within the lodge complex (open daily 11am-10pm). Others look to the warm air rising from the canyon, a full moon, and the occasional shooting star for their intoxication at day's end.

THE DESERT

The Central Coast

Although the popular image of the California dream is manufactured by the media machine in Los Angeles, the image itself comes from the Central Coast. The four-hundred-mile stretch of coastline between Los Angeles and San Francisco embodies all that is purely Californian—rolling surf crashing onto secluded beaches, dramatic cliffs and mountains, self-Actualizing New Age adherents, and always a hint of the off-beat. This is the solitary magnificence of the Central Coast that inspired Robinson Jeffers' paeans, John Steinbeck's prose reminisces, and Jack Kerouac's reflective musings. Among the smog-free skies, sweeping shorelines, dense forests, and plunging cliffs, there is a point where inland farmland communities and old seafaring towns conjoin, beckoning citified residents to journey out to the quiet drama of the coast. The landmarks along the way are well worth visiting—Hearst Castle, the Monterey Bay Aquarium, Carmel, the historic missions—but the real point of the Central Coast is the journey itself.

THE PACIFIC COAST HIGHWAY

The quintessential Californian road, the **Pacific Coast Highway** (known by Angelenos as **PCH,** by Californians as **Hwy. I,** and by maps as Rte. 1), loops along the entirety of the state's coastline. Begun in 1920, the PCH required $10 million and 17 years for completion. After skirting the coastal communities of Los Angeles, the highway curves north from Ventura to genteel Santa Barbara, and then winds past vineyards, fields of wildflowers, and miles of beach on the journey northward to San Luis Obispo. William Randolf Hearst's San Simeon, north of San Luis, anchors the southern end of Big Sur, the legendary 90 mi. strip of sparsely inhabited coastline. Climbing in and out of Big Sur's mountains, Hwy. 1 inches motorists to the edge of jutting cliffs hanging precipitously over the surf. From Ventura to Santa Cruz, state parks and national forests offer peaceful campgrounds and daring recreation. The **Los Angeles** (see p. 62), **Bay Area** (see p. 291), and **North Coast** (see p. 337) sections have more on PCH's route.

■ Ventura

The coastal hamlet of Ventura is home to the mellowest of both worlds—surfers and seniors. Spring cleaning seems to be a year-round activity here and Main St.'s legion of thrift stores, used bookstores, and antique dealers aren't complaining. If your mouth waters and your eyes sparkle at the prospect of a 50s silk Hawaiian shirt, then Ventura will suit you just fine. If vintage shopping doesn't turn you on, Ventura's beaches are a great spot to relax and enjoy a sand-and-surf scene reminiscent of Southern California's best.

Practical Information Ventura Visitors Bureau, 89C S. California St. (648-2075; open Mon.-Fri. 8:30am-5pm, Sat.-Sun. 10am-4pm), has a good selection of maps and brochures, including schedules for the 25¢ **Ventura Trolley** (382-8300), which sweeps through downtown, the beach, the pier, and Harbor Village (runs Wed.-Sun., and Tues. in summer 10am-5pm, Fri.-Sat. 10am-10pm). Those interested in visiting the **Channel Islands Wildlife Preserve and National Park** should seek out the **National Park Headquarters,** 1901 Spinnaker Dr. (658-5730; open Mon.-Fri. 8am-5pm, Sat.-Sun. 8am-5:30pm). Rent bikes from **Cycles 4 Rent,** 239 W. Main St. (652-1114; $5 per hr., $21 per day; open Mon.-Fri. 10am-4pm, Sat.-Sun. 9am-6pm). Get medical assistance at **County Hospital,** 3291 Loma Vista Rd. (800-746-8885). The **police** are at 110 N. Olive St. (648-8133). In an **emergency,** call 911. The **post office** is at 675 E. Santa Clara St. (643-5457). The **ZIP Code** is 93001. The **area code** is 805.

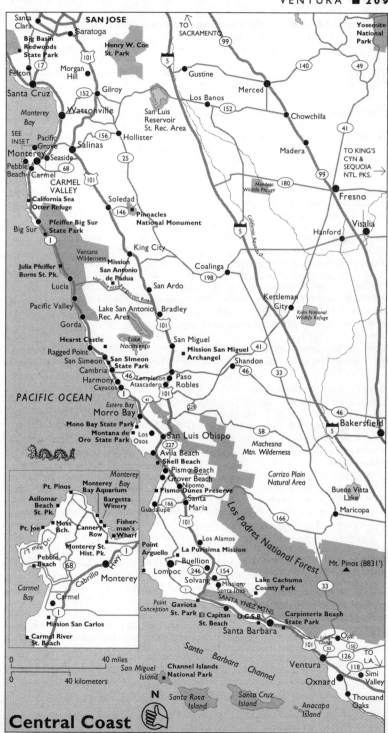

Central Coast

Accommodations and Camping A number of cheap motels line E. Thompson Ave., but most are over 40-years-old and in desperate need of renovation. The **Traveler's Beach Inn,** 929 E. Thompson Ave. (648-2557), is a standout with clean, rose-scented rooms ($50; higher in summer). The **Crystal Lodge,** 1787 E. Thompson Ave. (648-2272), has rooms with kitchens (singles $35; doubles $45). Trusty **Motel 6,** 2145 E. Harbor Blvd. (643-5100), off U.S. 101, offers singles for $36, doubles for $42.

Beach camping is in no short supply in and around Ventura, but conditions lean toward the primitive side. As always, reservations can be made through DESTINET (800-444-7275). **Emma Wood State Beach Campground** (654-4610), west of town off Main St., has limited facilities and chemical toilets, but its 61 campsites are right on the ocean (sites $12). **McGrath State Beach Campground** (654-4610), just south of town in Oxnard, is a popular spot with 174 campsites (sites $18).

Food and Entertainment You'll find cheap food and lots of civic pride along Main St. **Cafe Voltaire,** 34 N. Palm St. (641-1743), whose namesake polished off over 50 cups of java per day, has everything: coffee $1.10, stuffed sandwiches $6.95, booze, fashion bugs, live music nightly, and frustrated intellectuals. (Open Mon.-Thurs. 9am-10pm, Fri. 9am-midnight, Sat. 10am-midnight, Sun. 10am-9pm.) **Franky's,** 456 E. Main St. (648-6282), offers healthy, delectable pita pockets ($6) and turkey burgers (open Sun.-Thurs. 7am-3pm, Fri.-Sat. 7am-9pm). **Top Hat,** 299 E. Main St. (643-9696), at Palm, is a burger shack swarming with locals clutching chili cheese burgers ($1.85; open Mon.-Fri. 9am-5pm, Sat. 9am-6pm). The hip, spacious **Nicholby's Upstairs,** 404 Main St. (653-2320), has a bar, pool table, an eclectic mix of live music, and weekly swing lessons (open Mon.-Fri. 5pm-1:30am, Sat. 6pm-1:30am, Sun. 6pm-midnight; cover Fri.-Sat. $6). Ventura's attempt at a real club comes in the form of **Metro Nite Club,** 317 E. Main St. (653-CLUB/2582), where local radio DJs spin dance and alternative tunes nightly (open daily 8pm-2am).

Sights and Activities Billed as California's "Gold Coast," the beaches near Ventura are clean, uncrowded, and offer fantastic surfing. **Emma Wood State Beach,** on Main St. (State Beaches Exit off U.S. 101), and **Oxnard State Beach Park,** about 5 mi. south of Ventura, are quiet and peaceful. **San Buenaventura State Park,** at the end of San Pedro St., entertains a family-friendly crowd with its volleyball courts and nearby restaurants. **Surfer's Point,** at the end of Figueroa St., has the most bitchin' surfin' around, but novices should start at **McGrath State Beach,** about 3 mi. south of Ventura down Harbor Blvd. You can pick up on-the-sly surfing tips and wildly discounted outdoor gear at **Real Cheap Sports,** 36 W. Santa Clara St. (648-3803; open Mon.-Sat. 10am-6pm, Sun. 11am-5pm). The shoreside hotspots are **Seaward Village, Santa Clara River Mouth, Oxnard Shores,** and the pier at the end of **California St.**

Ventura's ever-burgeoning skateboarding culture is facilitated by **Skate Street,** 1990-B Knoll Dr. (650-1213). With multiple ramps and a 12,000 square foot street course, it's any skater's fantasy. Spectators watch from a second story viewing area (open Mon.-Thurs. 1-11pm, Fri.-Sat. 12:30-10:30pm; 3½hr. sessions $11).

Mission San Buenaventura, 211 E. Main St. (643-4318), still functions as a parish church, and houses a tiny museum of treasures from Father Serra's order (open Mon.-Sat. 10am-5pm, Sun. 10am-4pm; donation requested). For more info, see **A Man with a Mission** (p. 54). The tiny **Albinger Archaeology Museum,** 113 Main St. (648-5823), chronicles the story of the Native Americans, Spanish invaders, and Chinese immigrants who created the community of Ventura. (Open June-Aug. Wed.-Sun. 10am-4pm; Sept.-May Wed.-Fri. 10am-2pm, Sat.-Sun. 10am-4pm. Donation requested.) Across the street is the **Museum of History and Art** (653-0323), which has a rotating exhibit of handcrafted miniature figures from history, such as "Traitors, Tyrants and Sycophants," with effigies of Cromwell, Rasputin, and the like (open Tues.-Sun. 10am-5pm; admission $3, under 17 free).

■ Near Ventura: Channel Islands National Park

Ventura serves as the point of departure for the desolate Channel Islands, home to an ecosystem of endemic species almost as unique as the Galápagos Islands', many brown pelicans, and the ruins of a Paleolithic village. The park consists of five islands: **Anacapa** (the most visitor-friendly, with snorkeling and tide pools), **Santa Cruz** (known for its strangely dwarfed species), **Santa Rosa** (basically a huge fossil bed and full-time archaeological dig), **San Miguel** (with its eerie fossilized caliche forest and thousands of seals), and tiny **Santa Barbara** (with the rare Elephant Seal and rigorous hiking). Unfortunately, unless you're a marine biology student or happen to own your own yacht, you'll have to call **Island Packers,** 1867 Spinnaker Dr. (reservations 642-1393, 24hr. info 642-7688), in Ventura Harbor. Their virtual monopoly on island transport means rates range from a slightly obnoxious $21 to an outrageous $235, depending on which island is your destination and what diversions (camping, hiking, kayaking, or the Chumash painted sea cave, on Santa Cruz) you have in mind. Island Packers also runs whale watching tours (Dec.-March and June-Sept.). The camping is free on all islands, but you'll need a permit from park headquarters, your own water, and a high tolerance for foghorns and seagulls. The **Channel Islands National Park Visitors Center,** 1901 Spinnaker Dr. (658-5730), has all the info you'll need, and an observation tower with views of the islands (open Mon.-Fri. 8am-5pm, Sat.-Sun. 8am-5:30pm; closes 1hr. earlier in winter).

Nearby **San Nicolas Island,** a.k.a. Scott O'Dell's *Island of the Blue Dolphins,* is not part of the park, but rather a Navy base. An ordinary civilian can get to the island by volunteering for the **Nature Conservancy** (962-9111). In return for helping to piece the place back together, you get a free cot at the research station.

■ Ojai

The verdant Ojai Valley, 15 mi. north of Ventura on Rte. 33, was once the playpen of the Hollywood elite, who came to romp in the spas and natural hot springs. Then the hippies came. Though many hot springs have closed, Ojai still fosters a vibrant artistic and spiritual community. New Age enthusiasts flock to the Eastern spiritual centers at the **Krishnamurti Library,** 1130 McAndrew Rd. (646-4948; open Wed. 1-9pm, Thurs.-Sun. 1-5pm), and **Krotona Institute of Theosophy,** 2 Krotona Hill (646-2653; open Tues.-Fri. 10am-4pm, Sat.-Sun. 1-4pm). **Meditation Mount** (646-5508), Reeves Rd., has a meditation room and garden (open daily 10am-sunset; free).

The **Ojai Valley Chamber of Commerce,** 150 W. Ojai Ave. (646-8126), has maps and info on Ojai's 20 prolific art galleries. The **Ojai Center for the Arts,** 113 S. Montgomery St. (646-0117), has art, dance, and theater (open daily 11am-5pm).

The **Ojai Farm Hostel,** 913 Oso Rd. (646-0311), epitomizes the town's earthy aura—any fruit in the organic orchard is yours for the pickin'. Laid-back owner Gordon has only two rules—no smoking, and no meat in the kitchen. He also offers two TV rooms and free use of bikes. Guests stay in single-sex rooms in converted trailers or in a giant teepee ($12 per night). **International passport or plane ticket required.** Call Gordon from the bus or train station in Ventura and he'll pick you up.

Ojai is also the southernmost gateway to **Los Padres National Forest** (see p. 218). There are many impressive hikes in this area, particularly to **Rose Valley Falls** and to the **Sespe Hot Springs.** Get maps, camping info, and an Adventure Pass (required at Los Padres recreation areas; $5 per day, $30 per year) at the **Los Padres Ojai Ranger Office,** 1190 E. Ojai Ave. (646-4348; open Mon.-Fri. 8am-4:30pm).

▨ Santa Barbara

There's a reason why Santa Barbara epitomizes worry-free living and abandon of responsibility, why all memories of the past seem to melt to nothing in the endless sun. When padre Junípero Serra arrived here with his fervent proselytizing spirit and merry band of soldiers and priests, he ran into the Chumash Indians. Seemingly unappreciative of the unknown and deadly bacteria Serra brought along, the Chumash abruptly died off. Over their ashes, the Spanish, and later the Americans, built Santa Barbara.

The past may not be pretty; these days, though, the living is good. Today's Santa Barbara is an enclave of wealth and privilege, true to its soap opera image, but in a significantly less aggressive way than its Southern Californian counterparts. Spanish Revival architecture decorates the residential hills that rise gently over a lively pedestrian district centered on State St. This sanitized palm-lined promenade is filled with inexpensive cafes and thrift stores as well as glamorous boutiques and galleries—enough to engage the casual visitor for an entire day. Santa Barbara's golden beaches, museums, historic mission, and scenic drive add to what makes this a frequent weekend escape for the rich and famous and an attractive destination for surfers, artists, and hippies alike.

PRACTICAL INFORMATION

Visitor Information: Tourist Office, 1 Santa Barbara St. (965-3021), at Cabrillo near the beach. Hordes of folks clambering for maps and brochures. Only 10min. free parking, so you'd better run. Open Mon.-Sat. 9am-5pm, Sun. 10am-6pm; closes at 4pm Dec.-Jan., and at 6pm July-Aug. **Hotspots,** 36 State St. (963-4233 or 564-1637 for reservations). Espresso bar with free tourist info, hotel reservation service, and an **ATM** (open Mon.-Sat. 9am-9pm, Sun. 8am-4pm).

ATM: Sanwa Bank, 1036 State St. (564-4466), at Figueroa St.

Airport: Santa Barbara Aviation, 500 Fowler Rd. (967-7111), Goleta. Intrastate as well as limited national service, including American and United.

Trains: Amtrak, 209 State St. (963-1015; for schedule and fares 800-872-7245). Be careful around the station after dark. To L.A. ($16-21) and San Francisco ($46-73). Reserve in advance. Open daily 6:30am-9pm. Tickets sold until 8pm.

Buses: Greyhound, 34 W. Carrillo St. (962-2477), at Chapala. Storage lockers for ticketed passengers only. To L.A. ($11) and San Francisco ($29). Open Mon.-Sat. 5:30am-midnight, Sun. 7am-midnight; open until 8pm in winter. **Green Tortoise** (415-956-7500 or 800-227-4766), the "hostel on wheels," picks up from Banana Bungalow Hostel heading south on Sat. at 5:30am, north on Sun. at 11:45pm.

Public Transportation: Santa Barbara Metropolitan Transit District (MTD), 1029 Chapala St. (683-3702), at Cabrillo, behind Greyhound station. Bus schedules available at this transit center, which serves as the transfer point for most routes (open Mon.-Fri. 6am-7pm, Sat. 8am-6pm, Sun. 9am-6pm). 1 out of 3 buses on each route is wheelchair accessible. Fare 75¢, seniors and disabled 30¢, under 5 free; transfers free. The MTD runs a **downtown-waterfront shuttle** along State St. and Cabrillo Blvd. every 10min. Sun.-Thurs. 10:15am-6pm, Fri.-Sat. 10:15am-8pm. Stops designated by circular blue signs. Fare 25¢.

Taxis: Yellow Cab Company (965-5111). 24hr.

Car Rental: U-Save, 510 Anacapa St. (963-3499). Cars start at $24 per day, with 150 free mi.; $139 per week with 1050 free mi.; each additional mi. 20¢. Must be 21 with major credit card. Open Mon.-Fri. 8am-6pm, Sat. 8am-2pm.

Bike Rental: Cycles-4-Rent, 101 State St. (966-3804), 1 block from the beach. Rent a 1-speed beach cruiser for $4 per hr., $17 per day; 21-speed $7, $30. There are 2 other locations on the beach (with slightly higher prices) at 633 E. Cabrillo Blvd. and in the Radisson Hotel. All locations open daily 8am-8pm.

In-line Skate Rental: Ocean Wear Sports, 22 State St. (966-6733). Rentals $5 for first hr., each additional hr. $3. Safety gear included. Open daily 8am-9pm.

Laundromat: Mac's Laundry, 17 E. Haley St. (966-6716). Pink and purple wonder features ever-entertaining Spanish TV. Wash $1, 15min. dry 25¢. Open daily 6am-midnight; last load 10:30pm.

Library: 40 E. Anapamu St. (962-7653), across from the courthouse. Open Mon.-Thurs. 10am-9pm, Fri.-Sat. 10am-5:30pm, Sun. 1-5pm.

Bi-Gay-Lesbian Organization: Gay and Lesbian Resource Center, 126 E. Haley St., #A-17 (963-3636). Counseling for alcohol and drug abuse. AIDS hotline, testing, and social services. Open Mon.-Fri. 10am-5pm.

Pharmacy: Long's Drugs, 1109 State St. (564-3267). Open Mon.-Sat. 7am-10pm. Sun. 8am-8pm.

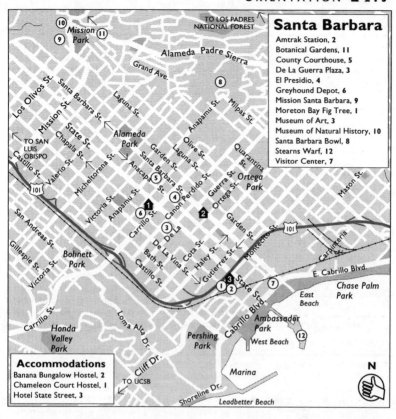

Santa Barbara

Amtrak Station, 2
Botanical Gardens, 11
County Courthouse, 5
De La Guerra Plaza, 3
El Presidio, 4
Greyhound Depot, 6
Mission Santa Barbara, 9
Moreton Bay Fig Tree, 1
Museum of Art, 3
Museum of Natural History, 10
Santa Barbara Bowl, 8
Stearns Warf, 12
Visitor Center, 7

Accommodations

Banana Bungalow Hostel, 2
Chameleon Court Hostel, 1
Hotel State Street, 3

Hospital: St. Francis Medical Center, 601 E. Micheltorena St. (962-7661), 6 blocks east of State.

Emergency: 911.

Police: 215 E. Figueroa (897-2300).

Internet Access: The eCafe, 1219 State St. (897-3335). Coffeehouse and cybercafe by day, trance and jungle haven by night (Internet $2 per 15min.). Open Mon.-Fri. 7am-9pm, Sat. 10am-8pm.

Post Office: 836 Anacapa St. (564-2266), 1 block east of State. Open Mon.-Fri. 8am-5:30pm, Sat. 10am-5pm. **ZIP Code:** 93102.

Area Code: 805.

ORIENTATION

Santa Barbara is 96 mi. northwest of L.A. and 27 mi. past Ventura on **U.S. 101.** Since the town is built along an east-west traverse of shoreline, its street grid is slightly skewed. The beach lies at the south end of the city, and **State St.,** the main drag, runs northwest from the waterfront. All streets are designated east and west from State St. The major east-west arteries are U.S. 101 and **Cabrillo Blvd.**

Driving in Santa Barbara can be bewildering; dead-ends and one-way streets abound. Many downtown lots and streets offer 90 minutes of free **parking,** including two subterranean lots at Pasco Nuevo, accessible from the 700 block of Chapala St. All parking is free on Sundays. **Biking** is a breeze, as most streets are equipped with special lanes. The **Cabrillo Bikeway** runs east-west along the beach from the Bird Refuge to the City College campus. MTD buses run throughout the city (see **Practical Information** above).

ACCOMMODATIONS

A 10-minute drive north or south on U.S. 101 rewards the bed-seeker with cheaper lodgings than those in Santa Barbara proper. Trusty **Motel 6** is always an option. In fact, Santa Barbara is where this glorious chain of budget-friendly motels originated. There are two locations: at the beach at 443 Corona del Mar Dr. (564-1392), and downtown at 3505 State St. (687-5400). Prices start at $45 in winter, $55 in summer.

Hotel State Street, 121 State St. (966-6586; fax 962-8459), 1 block from the beach. European clientele. Pristine common bathrooms. Private rooms have sinks, skylights, and cable TV. Continental breakfast. One double bed $40; 2 single beds $45; 2 double beds $55; prices $15-25 higher in summer. Reservations recommended (with credit card). Limited free parking.

Traveler's Motel, 3222 State St. (687-6009; fax 687-0419). Take bus #6 or 11 from downtown. Clean rooms with cable TV, direct-dial phones, A/C, and fridges. Singles $50, off-season $35; rooms with kitchenettes $55; each additional person (up to 4) $5. Prices higher on weekends.

Banana Bungalow Santa Barbara, 210 E. Ortega St. (963-0154), just off State, in busy area. Party-oriented hostel with lived-in feel and tropical motif. Young, international crowd. Kitchen, laundry, coin lockers, TV room, pool table, video games. Cheap equipment rentals. Co-ed and women-only dorms $17; thatched-roof bunks $15. No reservations; show up around 10:30am. Limited free parking.

Chameleon Court Hostel, 1011-B State St. (962-1054), at Carrillo St. Feels like an apartment—just one big room with 8 beds, a small bathroom, and a kitchen. Great location near the State St. bars. Exposed shower leaves little room for modesty. Free tea and coffee. Check-in by 7pm. Beds $15, ANT travelers $13. **International passport or out-of-state residence required.** Key and linen deposit $5.

CAMPING

The free *Santa Barbara Campsite Directory* lists prices, directions to sites, and reservation numbers for all campsites in the area, and is available at the visitors center. State campsites can be reserved through DESTINET (800-444-7275), up to seven months in advance. **Carpinteria Beach State Park** (684-2811), 12 mi. southeast of Santa Barbara along U.S. 101, has 262 developed tent sites with hot showers (sites $17, with hookup $22-28; weekends: $18, $23-29; off-season: $15, $20-26). There are two other state beaches within 30 mi. of Santa Barbara (sites $17, weekends $18, off-season $14; seniors $2 discount), but none are served by buses. All three are perched between the railroad tracks and U.S. 101. **El Capitán** (968-1033), has 140 well-kept sites, some with views of the Channel Islands. **Refugio** (968-1350), has 85 crowded sites just steps from the beach (wheelchair accessible). If all of these are full, you may want to try the **private campground** (685-3887), next door to El Capitán (also called El Capitán), which has a swimming pool, though sites are dusty and closely packed (sites $18, with hookup $22; each additional vehicle $6).

North of Santa Barbara are more than 100 sites in the **Los Padres National Forest.** The nearest of these are almost 20 mi. from downtown, but many are free and the others are inexpensive (sites $8). Buy a map for $3 at the **Supervisor's Office,** U.S. Forest Service, 6144 Calle Réal, Goleta 93117 (683-6711; open Mon.-Fri. 8am-4:30pm). Direct specific questions to the **Los Prietos Ranger Station,** U.S. Forest Service, Santa Barbara Ranger District, Star Route, Santa Barbara, CA 93105 (967-3481; open Mon.-Fri. 8am-5pm, Sat. 8am-noon and 1-5pm). Unlikely to be full, **Lake Cachuma County Park** (688-4658), 20 mi. north of Santa Barbara on Rte. 154, has 435 campsites (sites $14, with hookup $18) on a first-come, first-camped basis.

FOOD

State and Milpas St. both many places to eat, but State is hipper. Ice cream lovers flock to award-winning **McConnel's,** 201 W. Mission St. (569-2323; open daily 10am-midnight). There's an open-air **farmer's market** on the 400 block of State St. (Tues. 4-7:30pm), and another on Santa Barbara St. at Cota St. (Sat.

8:30am-12:30pm). **Tri-County Produce,** 335 S. Milpas (965-4558), sells fresh produce and prepared foods (open Mon.-Sat. 9am-7:30pm, Sun. 9am-6pm).

The Natural Cafe, 508 State St. (962-9494). Healthy, attractive clientele dines on healthy, attractive food. Smoothies $3.75, sandwiches $3.50-5. Herbal medicine shop next door. Open daily 11am-11pm.

Castagnola's, 205 Santa Barbara St. (962-8053). The cheapest fresh seafood in town. Retreat to the patio to escape the fast-food feel and pungent odor inside. Shrimp cocktail $4, fish and chips $5.25. Charbroiled fish of 20 types of charbroiled fish $9-11. Open Sun.-Thurs. 11am-8pm, Fri.-Sat. 11am-9pm.

Palace Express (899-9111), Center Court, Paseo Nuevo Mall at 800 block of State St. Naw'lins soul food in a jiffy. Jambalaya, etouffeés, and po' boys with 2 muffins and 2 side orders ($4.75-6.50). Live zydeco Fri. 6-8:30pm. Open Mon-Thurs. 11am-9pm, Fri.-Sat. 11am-10pm, Sun. 11am-8pm. Credit cards with $20 min.

R.G.'s Giant Hamburgers, 922 State St. (963-1654). Yellow formica joint, was voted best burgers in S.B. 7 years running. Basic burger $3. Call 10min. ahead, and it'll be waiting when you arrive. Open in summer Mon.-Sat. 7am-10pm, Sun. 7am-9pm; in winter Mon.-Thurs. 9am-9pm, Fri.-Sat. 9am-10pm, Sun. 9am-8pm.

Left at Albuquerque, 803 State St. (564-5040). Even if you made a wrong turn, you've still found Tex-Mex heaven. Green Monster enchilada $9, quesadillas $5-7. Margarita specials. Route 66 is a 66oz. pitcher with unlimited straws ($11.75). Open Sun.-Wed. 11:30am-11:30pm, Thurs.-Sat. 11:30am-12:30am; kitchen open until 11pm.

Super Cuca's Taquería, 626 W. Micheltorena St. (962-4028). Insanely delicious super-burrito with beans and rice $4.30. Open daily 9am-10pm. No credit cards.

Zeus and Company, Paseo Nuevo Mall, #17 (568-3663), on 800 block of State St. Greek cafe with "interpretations" of artists on the walls. Serves fruit nectar smoothies ($3) that are the food of the gods. Ambrosial Mediterranean wraps $4.50-5. Beer and wine served—but where's the ouzo? Open daily 10am-10pm.

SIGHTS

State St. is Santa Barbara's monument to city planning. Everything that doesn't move—mailboxes, telephones, the restrooms at the public library—has been slathered in Spanish tile. To get the full impact of the city's architectural homogeneity and a killer view of the ocean, take the elevator up to the **observation deck** of the **Santa Barbara County Courthouse,** 1100 Anacapa St. (962-6464). Compared to the more prosaic Mission Revival buildings found elsewhere in California, the courthouse is a work of genius, with its sculpted fountain, sunken gardens, historic murals, wrought-iron chandeliers, and hand-painted vaulted Gothic ceilings. (Tours Mon.-Sat. at 2pm, Fri. at 10:30am. Open daily 10am-5pm. Tower closes at 4:45pm. Free). Pick up *Santa Barbara's Red Tile Tour,* a map and walking tour guide (free at the visitors center; 25¢ at the Chamber of Commerce inside the courthouse).

At the end of Las Olivas St. (bus #22) on the northern side of town is **Mission Santa Barbara** (682-4719). Praised as the "Queen of Missions" when built in 1786, the mission assumed its present incarnation in 1820. Towers containing splayed Moorish windows stand on either side of a Greco-Roman facade, and a Moorish fountain burbles in front. The museum contains period rooms and a sampling of items from the mission archives. Visitors welcome to (respectfully) drop in on mass (Mon.-Fri. 7:30am, Sat. 4pm, Sun. 7:30am-noon). Franciscan friars and 4000 christianized Mission Indians are buried in the cemetery (open daily 9am-5pm; admission $3, under 16 free). For more info, see **A Man with a Mission** (p. 54). The ruins of a pottery shack lie across the street and a small Chumash cave painting can be found in the hills (off Camino Cielo).

Two blocks north of the mission is the **Santa Barbara Museum of Natural History,** 2559 Puesta del Sol Rd. (682-4711, observatory 682-3224). Signs lead the way. This museum includes a collection of original lithographs by Audubon and other naturalists, the largest collection of Chumash artifacts in the West, an extensive archive on the Channel Islands, and a **planetarium.** (Planetarium shows daily in summer, Wed. and Sat.-Sun. in winter. $1 plus admission. Museum open Mon.-Sat. 9am-5pm, Sun. and holidays 10am-5pm. Admission $5, seniors $4, ages 13-17 $4, under 13 $3.)

The **Santa Barbara Botanical Garden,** 1212 Mission Canyon Rd. (682-4726), is not served by bus and is a trek without a car. Five miles of hiking trails wind through 65 acres of native Californian trees, wildflowers, and cacti. The garden's water system was built by the Chumash and is one of the last vestiges of the region's heritage. (Open March-Oct. Mon.-Fri. 9am-5pm, Sat.-Sun. 9am-6pm; Nov.-Feb. closes 1hr. earlier. Tours daily 2pm, Thurs. and Sat.-Sun. also 10:30am. Admission $3, students $2, seniors $2, teens $2, ages 5-12 $1.) Nearby are several **hiking trails.** The trailhead for **Seven Falls Trail** is at the junction of Tunnel and Spyglass. From the end of Las Canoas Rd. off Tunnel Rd., you can pick up the 3½ mi. **Rattlesnake Canyon Trail,** with many waterfalls, pools, and secluded spots. The 7.3 mi. trek from the **Cold Springs Trail** to **Montecito Peak** is considerably more strenuous. (From U.S. 101 south, take a left at the Hot Springs Rd. Exit, and another left on Mountain Dr. to the creek crossing.) The Botanic Garden gift shop has maps with more trails.

Back downtown, the **Public Library,** 40E Anapamu St. (962-7653), and the **Santa Barbara Museum of Art,** 1130 State St. (963-4364), are linked by a pedestrian plaza. The museum owns an impressive collection of classical Greek, Asian, and European works spanning 3000 years. It prides itself most on its American art, Chagall's *Young Girl in Pursuit,* and Dalí's *Honey is Sweeter then Blood* (showcased in a new wing opening in Jan. 1998). Over 90% of the works in the permanent collection were gifts from Santa Barbara's wealthy residents. (Open Tues.-Wed. and Fri.-Sat. 11am-5pm, Thurs. 11am-9pm, Sun. noon-5pm. Tours Tues.-Sun. 1pm. Admission $4, students $1.50, seniors $3, ages 6-16 $1.50; free on Thurs. and 1st Sun. of each month.)

The **Arlington Center for Performing Arts,** 1317 State St. (box office 963-4408), is one of the rarest of movie theater species—a uniplex. The murals over the entrance of the Spanish-Moorish building depict scenes from California's Hispano-Mexican era. Its tower is one of the few structures in this low stucco town to rival the palm trees in height. Call the box office for info on upcoming events. (Movie tickets $7.50, seniors $4, ages 2-12 $4; 1pm matinee $5; twilight show at 3:30 or 4pm $4.)

At the corner of Montecito and Chapala St. stands the famed **Moreton Bay Fig Tree.** Brought from Australia by a sailor in 1877, the tree's gnarled branches now span 160 ft., and can provide shade for upwards of 1000 people. If you'd rather be **drinking** than standing in the shade with 999 other people, join the young snitties slurping award-winning wine at the **Santa Barbara Winery,** 202 Anacapa St. (963-3633; open for free tastings daily 10am-5pm; tours 11:30am and 3:30pm).

Nearby are the **Andree Clark Bird Refuge** and the **Santa Barbara Zoo,** 500 Niños Dr. (962-6310), off Cabrillo from U.S. 101. The zoo can be reached by bus #14 or the downtown waterfront shuttle. The delightfully leafy habitat has low fences and such an open feel that the animals seem kept in captivity only through sheer lethargy. Attractions include a miniaturized African *veldt,* where giraffes stroll, lazily silhouetted against the Pacific. A miniature train ($1) provides a park tour every 15 minutes. In the zoo's own words, "We're as wild as Santa Barbara gets." (Open daily 10am-5pm. Admission $6, seniors and ages 2-12 $4, under 2 free; free parking.)

For an extra dose of wildlife, try the **Sea Center** (962-0885) on **Stearns Wharf,** at the foot of State St., it's the oldest operating wharf on the Pacific. The center features sea-life dioramas, a touch tank of sea-lings, and a rollicking trash exhibit explaining Channel ecology (open daily 10am-5pm; admission $2, seniors $1.50, ages 3-17 $1).

The city's "Scenic Drive," clearly marked out on road signs, winds through the hillside bordering the town along **Alameda Padre Serra.** This part of town is known as the **American Riviera.** If money could talk, this area would shut up Jenny Jones fast.

The beach at **Summerland,** east of Montecito (bus #20), is frequented by the **gay** and **hippie** communities. Go here if only to eat at **The Big Yellow House,** 108 Pierpoint Ave. (969-4140), a Victorian estate turned restaurant. It is reported to be inhabited by two ghosts: Hector haunts the downstairs area, while his mistress sticks to the women's bathroom upstairs. Ask to eat in the bedroom with the secret door (open Sun.-Thurs. 8am-9pm, Fri.-Sat. 8am-10pm). **Rincon Beach,** 3 mi. southeast of Carpinteria, has some of the county's best surfing. **Gaviota State Beach,** 29 mi. west of Santa Barbara, also has good surf, and the western end is a (sometimes) **clothing-optional** beach, although nude sunbathing is illegal in Santa Barbara. You can **whale-watch** from late November to early April, as the Pacific Grays migrate.

The **University of California at Santa Barbara (UCSB)** is stuck in Goleta, a shapeless mass of suburbia, gas stations, and coffee shops that surrounds the university. Take U.S. 101 or bus #11 to the university and visit the excellent **art museum** (893-2951), which houses the Sedgwick Collection of 15th- to 17th-century European paintings (including a Bellini *Madonna and Child*) and hosts innovative contemporary exhibits (open Tues.-Sat. 10am-4pm, Sun. 1-5pm; free).

SHOPPING

State St. is a shopping mecca with two miles of mildly trendy shops and the upscale **Paseo Nuevo Mall,** at Canon Perdido St. Local craftspeople line Cabrillo Blvd. for the **Arts and Crafts Show,** where they sell their hand-crafted wared every fair-weathered Sunday and holiday from 10am to dusk.

Earthling Bookshop & Cafe, 1137 State St. (965-0926, cafe 564-6096). This bookstore is more earth (down to earth *and* worldly) than ling (small, young, or inferior)—the Earthling kicks the chain bookstores' big butts. Save the Earthling—the institution of the bookstore is in danger of going out of business (even with a Barnes & Nobles in town). S.B. bibliophiles browse bookshelves full of new and used books, and then settle down for a (long) read around a central fireplace. Bookshelves and display tables are lined with staff "picks" and short handwritten commentaries. Flip through the latest foreign newspaper under the watchful gaze of Hemingway in the Earthling Cafe (cappuccino, juice, and pastry $4; soup and salad $4.25). Pick up a schedule of events: live music nightly, Sun. author readings, Mon. open mic, Tues. film screenings, Wed. travel slide show, Thurs. opera. Open Sun.-Thurs. 9am-11pm, Fri.-Sat. 9am-midnight; cafe opens Mon.-Fri. 7:30am.

As Seen on TV, 1125 State St. (564-4100). Late-night infomercials can open new horizons of consumer cravings. Find everything "guaranteed to…" Love handle removal, perfect hair in minutes, and the clearest pores a teenager has ever known. The most popular item is the Sobakawa Buckwheat Pillow ($24.99)—Dr. Kazu Watanabe swears you'll sleep like a baby. Psychic Hotline phone cards $9.99. Open Mon.-Thurs. 10am-8pm, Fri.-Sat. 10am-9pm, Sun. 11am-7pm.

Victorian Vogue, 1224 State St. (962-8824). A time machine of *haute couture*, from flapper outfits of the 20s to squeaky-clean styles of the 50s. Ethnic fashions as well, from saris to sombreros. Accessorize with vintage jewelry and ties. Open Mon.-Wed. 11am-6pm, Thurs. 11am-8pm, Fri.-Sat. 11am-10pm, Sun. noon-7pm.

ENTERTAINMENT AND NIGHTLIFE

Every night of the week, the clubs on State St. are packed. This town is full of locals and tourists who love to eat, drink, and be mirthful. Consult the *Independent* to see who's playing on a given night.

Maikai Cafe and Bar, 217 State St. (963-9276). During the day, it has Hawaiian-themed kitschy revelry (*mahi mahi* $5.50), but come Fri. and Sat. nights, the Lava Lounge becomes **Comedy Sportz,** a competitive improv team complete with astroturf and a half-time referee. Showtime Fri. 8:30pm, Sat. 8pm, doors open ½hr. early. Tickets $8, students $6. Open daily 11am-10pm. All ages.

Madhouse, 434 State St. (962-5516). Decadent faux-dive for the jet set. Sounds of Sinatra, mambo, and Afro-Cuban music. Exotic cocktails, outdoor patio, pool

CENTRAL COAST

tables. Cardboard icon of Sean Connery beckons you into the Martini Lounge (owner Duncan does a mean Bond). Light up and smoke away! Live music and drink specials nightly (5-8pm). No cover. Open daily 5pm-2am. Must be 21.

Fathom, 423 State St. (882-2082). Gay dance club (all are welcome) that's the closest it gets to a rave in Santa Barbara. Wear something that glows for a night of hard-core house music. Pool tables, lots of drink specials. Martini happy hour 4-8pm (well drinks $2). Open nightly 4pm-2am. Cover Thurs.-Sun. $5. Must be 21.

Brickyard Ale House, 525 State St. (899-2820). Bricks and beer. And more beer. And more bricks. Live bands Sun.-Wed., DJ Thurs.-Sat. Recreation area has pool tables, darts, video games, big screen TV. 85 beers on tap. $1 pints on Thurs. No cover unless there's a big name. Open Mon.-Sat. 11sm-2am, Sun. 11am-midnight.

Yucatan, 1117 State St. (564-1889), a.k.a "The Partyn Cantina." Every frat boy's dream come true. Upstairs "Billiards Club" with 9 pool tables ($5 per hr.) and foosball! Satellite sports TV! DJ spins! Happy Hour Mon.-Fri. 3-7pm (drafts $1.50). Cover $3-5. Open daily 11am-1:30am. Must be 21 (Sun. and Wed. 18). Party on!

Joe's Cafe, 536 State St. (966-4638). Most locals start their nights of bacchanalia here. Super-strong, super-cheap drinks. Martinis $3.75, margaritas $4.75, Mocha Joe (with kahlua) $4.75. If the mounted deer head starts to move, you've had too much. Open Mon.-Thurs. 11am-midnight, Fri.-Sat. 11pm-1am, Sun. 4pm-midnight.

SEASONAL EVENTS

Hang Gliding Festival (965-3733), early Jan., Mesa Flight Park.

Santa Barbara International Film Festival (967-6331), 10 days in March. Sponsored by the Arlington Center (see p. 216). Premieres U.S. and foreign films.

Vintners' Festival (688-0881), early April. Held in a different lush setting each year, with regional wines and samples from local restaurants.

Italian Street Painting Festival (569-3873), Memorial Day weekend. Both professional and amateur chalk paintings decorate the Old Mission Courtyard.

Santa Barbara Shakespeare Festival (963-0408), throughout the summer. Also features works by Molière, Stoppard, and others. Tickets $10-16.

Summer Solstice Parade and Fair (965-3396), on the Sat. nearest the summer solstice (June 21). Pre-Bacchanal fun on State St. Come as an 18ft. dinosaur or a tidal wave and you'll fit right in.

Old Spanish Days Fiesta (962-8101), early Aug. Spirited fiesta with rodeos, carnivals, flamenco guitar, and plenty of sangria.

Music Academy of the West, 1070 Fairway Rd., (897-0300), holds a series of inexpensive concerts throughout the summer. Stop by for a brochure.

Santa Barbara International Jazz Festival (310-452-5056), early Sept.

■ Near Santa Barbara: Los Padres National Forest

Land of the Chumash and condors, the vast **Los Padres National Forest** (683-6711) stretches north of Santa Barbara into San Luis Obispo County and beyond. The area includes four mountain ranges and climatic zones that range from semiarid desert to coniferous forest to marine habitat. Los Padres is a leader in wildlife recovery programs, reintroducing many endangered plants and birds, such as the bald eagle and the falcon. The **San Rafael Wilderness** alone contains 125 mi. of trails and a sanctuary for the nearly extinct California condor. The nearby **Chumash painted cave** is only 20 minutes north of Santa Barbara. Take U.S. 101 to Rte. 154 to Painted Cave Rd., past the village, and down into the oak glen. The cave is up on the right (parking is scarce). The impressive red ochre handiwork of native shamans dates back to 1677. There are tons of hiking and camping opportunities in the area (see **Santa Barbara: Camping,** p. 214). The **Adventure Pass,** available at the **Santa Barbara Ranger District Office** (967-3481), is now needed in all recreation areas in the national forest ($5 per day or $30 per year). Take Rte. 154 for 10 mi. to Paradise Rd. and turn right. The office is 5 mi. ahead, on the left (open Mon.-Sat. 8am-4:30pm).

■ Santa Ynez Valley

To the northwest of Santa Barbara along Rte. 154 lies the lovely **Santa Ynez Valley,** home to thousands of acres of vineyards, hundreds of ostriches, and Michael Jackson's **Wonderland Ranch.** The free *Santa Barbara County Wineries Touring Map,* available at the Santa Barbara Visitors Center, gives comprehensive listings. One of the prettiest vineyards is **Gainey Vineyard,** 3950 E. Rte. 246 (688-0558), where Rte. 246 and 154 intersect (tours and $3 tastings daily at 11am, and 1, 2, and 3pm).

Expatriate Danes will shed a tear at **Solvang Village,** an overpriced Disneyesque Danish-land, a stone's throw away east down Rte. 246. Solvang is crammed with *konditoris* (bakeries)—try the **Solvang Bakery,** 460 Alisal Rd. (688-4939). Next door is the graceful **Mission Santa Ines,** 1760 Mission Dr. (688-4815). Check out the cemetery, which has 1700 Chumash graves, and look for the precious footprint of a young Chumash boy in the Chapel of the Madonnas (open daily 9am-4:30pm in winter, 9am-7pm in summer; admission $3, under 16 free). For more info, see **A Man with a Mission** (p. 54). Four miles west, at Rte. 246 and U.S. 101 is the town of **Buellton,** home to Andersen's Split Pea Soup, famed to be as thick as the fog.

Farther to the northwest, at the juncture of Hwy. 1 and Rte. 246, is the city of **Lompoc,** home to **the nation's largest producer of flower seed.** The acres upon acres of blooms, which peak near the end of June, are both a visual and an olfactory explosion. Purple sweet elysium and crimson sweet pea are just two of the many blossoms. Lompoc holds a **flower festival** at the season's peak. **La Purisma Mission State Park,** 2295 Purisma Rd. (733-7781), off Mission Rd., houses the most fully restored of Father Serra's missions and extensive hiking trails (open daily 9am-5pm; parking $5). For more info, see **A Man with a Mission** (p. 54).

Don't Keep Your Fool Head in the Sand!

When you think of weird California wildlife, what springs to mind? Condors? Elephant seals? Michael Jackson's chimpanzee Bubbles? They're boring compared to some even funkier fauna. **Ostriches** populate the desert and inland central coast regions. They're not wild, though. They've been imported by ranchers who want to market the lucrative hides of these creatures (ostrich boots are all the rage among the line-dancin' crowd). At an ostrich farm, you'll have a rare chance to observe these nine-foot fowl, but you should honor ostrich etiquette. You can approach the birds' enclosure from a distance (provided the owners don't object), but **don't pet their dinky heads** and don't and taunt these beasts. They may look like they have their heads in the sand, but they've got really bad tempers too, so stay cool. Ostrich ranches congregate along Refugio Rd., off Rte. 246 in Santa Ynez. You can sample an ostrich burger or buy your very own pet chick at **Ostrich Farm,** on Rte. 246, just west of Solvang. Enjoy!

■ San Luis Obispo

The quickest way to brand yourself a tourist is to give this city's name its correct Spanish pronunciation. To sound like a local, say "sann-LOO-eez oh-BIZ-bow," or "San Luis"—or maybe just "SLO." This area grew into a full-fledged town only after the Southern Pacific Railroad was built in here 1894. Ranchers and oil-refinery employees make up a significant percentage of today's population, but its Cal Poly State University that ranches and refines the town's charm. Along the main drags, the hippest young herbivores graze to their heart's delight and top it off with a dose of wheatgrass and bee pollen, while fashion mavens hit the stores lined with the latest arrivals from Milan. Those seeking the soothing balm of small-town life can happily cool their heels in this affable burg—its acronym isn't SLO for nothing.

PRACTICAL INFORMATION

Visitor Information: Visitors Center for the Chamber of Commerce, 1039 Chorro St., San Luis Obispo 94301 (781-2777). Watch for signs on U.S. 101. Open

Mon.-Wed. 8am-5pm, Thurs.-Fri. 8am-8pm, Sat. 10am-8pm. **State Parks Office,** 3220 S. Higuera St., #311 (549-3312). Open Mon.-Fri. 8am-5pm.

ATM: Great Western Bank, 1235 Chorro St. (595-5602), at Marsh St., downtown.

Trains: Amtrak, 1011 Railroad Ave. (541-0505 or 800-USA-RAIL/872-7245), at the foot of Santa Rosa Ave., 7 blocks south of Higuera. To L.A. ($21), San Francisco ($40-62), and Santa Barbara ($18-20). Open daily 6am-9pm.

Buses: Greyhound, 150 South St. (543-2121), ½mi. from downtown. To get to downtown, walk west on South St., then north on Higuera St. Seven buses per day to L.A. ($32) and San Francisco ($39). Luggage lockers (for ticketed passengers only). Open daily 7am-9:30pm.

Public Transportation: The **Central Coast Area Transit** (541-2228) links SLO and Morro Bay (#7; fare $1.25), Los Osos (#7; $1.50), Pismo Beach (#10; fare $1), and Paso Robles (#9; $1.75). Unlimited-use day pass $3. Buses depart from City Hall at Osos and Palm St. On the weekends, only bus #9 (north to Paso Robles) and bus #10 (south to Santa Maria) are operational. All buses wheelchair-accessible. **SLO Transit** (541-2877), runs buses throughout the city, and they go faster than the acronym would suggest. Fare 75¢, seniors 35¢; free transfers. Buses run Mon.-Fri. 6am-7pm, Sat.-Sun. 8am-6pm (on weekends, only bus #3 and 5 are operational). SLO Transit offers a free trolley service around downtown (runs Sun.-Wed. and Fri.-Sat. noon-5pm, Thurs. noon-9:30pm). Additional service to hotels along Monterey.

Car Rental: Thrifty Car Rental, 2750 Broad St. (544-3777). Cars start at $34 per day with unlimited mileage within California. Must be 21. Ages 21-25 pay additional $5 per day surcharge. Personal damage waiver $9 per day, $4 per day for passengers. Open Mon.-Fri. 7am-9pm, Sat. 8am-5pm, Sun. 9am-9pm.

Library: 995 Palm St. (781-5991). Open Mon.-Wed. 10am-8pm, Thurs. and Sat. 10am-5pm, Fri. 11am-5pm.

Laundromat: California Coin Laundry, 552 California Blvd. (544-8266). Wash $1.75, dry 50¢. Open 24hr.

Weather Conditions: (541-6666, ext. 25). **Road Conditions:** (800-427-7623).

Crisis Line: (544-6163). Counseling and referrals 24hr.

Hospital: SLO General Hospital, 2180 Johnson Ave. (781-4871).

Police: 1042 Walnut St. (781-7342).

Emergency: 911.

Internet Access: The Library, 723 Higuera St. (542-0199). Actually, it's a bar, not a real library. $3 per hr. Open Mon.-Fri. 10am-2am, Sat.-Sun. 2pm-2am.

Post Office: 893 Marsh St. (543-3062). Open Mon.-Fri. 8:30am-5:30pm, Sat. 10am-5pm. **ZIP Code:** 93405.

Area Code: 805.

ORIENTATION

San Luis Obispo is nestled deep in the bosom of the Central Coast, but it is not *on* the coast. It sits inland on **U.S. 101,** burrowed among ranch-laden mountains. This small town serves as a hub between Morro Bay, 12 mi. north on Hwy. 1, and Avila, Shell, and Pismo Beaches, about 12 mi. south on Hwy. 1.

Downtown, **Higuera St.** (north-south) and **Broad St.** (east-west), are the two main drags. Walking here is easy; driving is not. The lack of stop signs and profusion of one-way streets makes survival here a matter of luck. Ninety-minute **free parking** is available downtown at the Palm St. (at Morro) and Marsh St. (at Chorro) lots.

ACCOMMODATIONS

Asked for their rates, proprietors in San Luis Obispo frequently respond, "That depends"—on the weather, the season, the number of travelers that day, or even on the position of the waxing and waning moon. There is a little less fluctuation in nearby Pismo Beach or Morro Bay, but the average prices are the same. If you can find a $40 room in downtown SLO, grab it. And reserve *well* in advance for mid-June (Cal Poly commencement). For all prices, figure in SLO's 10% hotel tax.

San Luis Obispo (HI-AYH), 1292 Foothill Blvd. (544-4678; fax 544-3142; email esimer@slonet.org). Big green house with porch swing, piano, organic garden, dog, free bagels in the kitchen, and a brand new jacuzzi! Just clear out 10am-5pm. Reception open 7:30-9:30am and 5-10pm. Clean, airy single-sex rooms have 5-8 bunks. Dorms $14; private rooms $32. Nonmembers $16, $34. Linens $1, towels 50¢. Limited free parking. No credit cards.

Coachman Inn Motel, 1001 Olive St. (544-0400; fax 541-3079). Huge, immaculate, cheap rooms have cable TV and fridges. Singles $32-35; doubles start at $35. Off-season: $25-30, $32-35. Summer weekends prices can rise to $100.

Sunbeam Hotel, 1656 Monterey St. (543-8141; fax 787-0138). Looks like an apartment complex with rooms as sunny as the staff. Cable TV, A/C, fridges, phones, coffeemakers. Singles $30-32; doubles $38-45. Prices jump in summer.

Los Padres Motel, 1575 Monterey St. (543-5017 or 800-543-5090; fax 547-1664). Your friendly hosts Harry and Nina have renovated their pretty in pink motel and offer cable TV with HBO, direct-dial phones, and complimentary breakfast. Rooms start at $59 in summer, $39 off-season. Reservations recommended.

Vergin' on Tacky

The **Madonna Inn,** 100 Madonna Rd. (543-3000), off U.S. 101 (take the Madonna Rd. Exit) in south SLO, is probably the only hotel in the world that sells postcards of each room. Alex S. Madonna, the contractor behind the construction of much of U.S. 101 and I-5, decided in 1958 to build a Queen Anne-style hotel of 12 rooms. He put his wife, Phyllis, in charge of the design. By 1962, the vision had grown into a hot pink behemoth of 110 rooms on 2200 acres of land. The men's room features a giant laser-operated waterfall which doubles as a urinal. Every room has a theme—the Caveman Room, the Daisy Mae Room, and a room with a working waterwheel serving as a headboard. (Rooms range from $87-240. Seven to nine people in the posh 3-bedroom **Harvard Square** suite is a $240 bargain.) Even non-guests can enjoy coffee and a bun from the Madonna's own oven and the photo album of the rooms in the reception area. At night, there's swing music from 7-11pm in the lounge to keep things hoppin'.

CAMPING

All state park sites can be reserved through DESTINET (800-444-7275) up to 7 months in advance. For a list of more campsites in the area, contact State Parks Information (see **Practical Information,** p. 219). In summer, you need reservations at beach parks; especially crowded parks require reservations year-round.

Pismo Beach State Park (489-2684), on Hwy. 1, south of Pismo Beach. **North Beach** has 103 tent sites ($18, winter $14) and restrooms. **Oceano** has 40 tent sites ($18) and 42 RV hookups ($24, winter $20). Both have showers, but North Beach sites are larger and closer to the beach. Call for reservations.

Montana de Oro State Park (528-0513), on Pecho Rd., south of Los Osos, 12mi. from SLO via Los Osos Valley Rd. 50 primitive sites in a gorgeous, secluded park. Outhouses and cold running water (but bring your own drinking water). Sites $10, winter $7. Reserve in advance between Memorial Day and Labor Day.

Morro Bay State Park (772-2560), 12mi. west of SLO on Hwy. 1. Popular park between ocean and forest has 135 developed sites, 20 with hookups. Hot showers and running water. More accessible than Montana de Oro, also more likely to be full. Sites $18, winter $14; with hookups $24, winter $20. Reserve year-round.

FOOD

Higuera St. and the streets running across it are lined with restaurants and cafes. The area just south of the mission along the creek is popular with lunchtime crowds. A **farmer's market** takes over Higuera St. every Thursday from 6 to 9pm.

CENTRAL COAST

Big Sky Cafe, 1121 Broad St. (545-5401). No militias here—just lofty ceilings, an earthy atmosphere, and savory food. Sandwiches $5-7. Choice wines. Margaritas or swanky Kir Royales $3.50. Open Mon.-Sat. 7am-10pm, Sun. 8am-8pm.

Woodstock's Pizza Parlour, 1000 Higuera St. (541-4420). Popular hangout sweeps annual best pizza awards. Young crowd keeps it lively into the night. Three sizes of pizza for $4.20, $8, and $11. Toppings $.50-1. Happy Hour Mon.-Sat. 2-5pm ($3 pitchers of beer, $1 slices). Open Sun.-Thurs. 11am-1am, Fri.-Sat. 11am-2am.

Paradiso, 690 Higuera St. (544-5282). Homemade organic pastas and raviolis with lots of vegetarian sauces ($5-7). Daily special includes pasta, salad, and focaccia bread for $5. Cappuccino $1. Open daily 11am-9pm.

Tio Alberto's, 1131 Broad St. (546-4696), and 295 Santa Rosa St. (546-9646). Portions larger than the *vacas* they came from. Burritos $3-5.50, combo plates $5. Open Sun.-Thurs. 9am-11pm, Fri.-Sat. 9am-3am. No credit cards.

Mo's Smokehouse BBQ, 970 Higuera St. (544-6193). One of the few places in town that caters to carnivores only. Check out memorabilia from "Mo's journey through the BBQ Belt"—a quest for the perfect ribs. Sandwiches $5. Open Sun.-Wed. 11am-9pm, Thurs.-Sat. 11am-10pm.

Art of Sandwich Delicatessen, 717 Higuera St. (544-7775). Dagwood masterpieces (about $5) complemented by eclectic art and a pleasing palate of beers (pints $2 after 4pm with purchase of a sandwich). Open daily 10:30am-9pm.

SIGHTS AND ACTIVITIES

Once the center of town life and still in the town center, the **Mission San Luis Obispo de Tolosa** (543-6850), is easy to miss. Founded in 1772, the mission was at one time covered in white clapboards and crowned with a steeple in emulation of a New England church. In the late 1800s, however, the town made a concerted effort to revive the mission's Spanish origins; by the 1930s, it was fully restored and still serves as the Catholic parish church for SLO (open daily 9am-5pm, off-season 9am-4pm; $1 donation requested). For more info, see **A Man with a Mission** (p. 54). It faces **Mission Plaza,** where Father Serra held the area's first mass, but which houses the **SLO Historical Museum** (543-0638), with a display of Chumash pottery and over 17,000 historical photos (open Wed.-Sun. 10am-4pm; free), and the **SLO Art Center,** 1010 Broad St. (543-8562), with lectures, art classes, and multi-media exhibits by regional artists (open Tues.-Sun. 11am-5pm; free).

The nearby **Jack House,** 536 Marsh St. (781-7299), at Beach St., is a restored Victorian residence with the original 19th-century furnishing inside and a gazebo and garden outside (45min. tours May-Aug. Mon.-Thurs. 2-5pm, Sept.-April on the first Sun. of the month 2-5pm; admission $2). **San Luis Little Theater,** 888 Morro St. (786-2440), has performances by local thespians (Thurs.-Sat. 8pm, Sun. 2pm; tickets $14, students $12, seniors $12, Thurs. $10). For kiddie terror, check out the **SLO Children's Museum,** 1010 Nipomo St. (544-KIDS/5437), where there's a "creative learning station featuring communicable diseases" (open Mon.-Tues. and Thurs.-Sat. 10am-5pm, Sun. 1-5pm; limited winter hours; admission $4, under 2 free).

Hollywood flicks often show at the grand Art Deco **Freemont Theatre,** 1035 Monterey, designed in 1942 by the preeminent Southern Californian architect Charles Lee. The main theater seats 850 and maintains the original murals, but be warned—there's no air-conditioning (tickets $6.75, seniors $4.75, children $4.75; matinees before 6pm $4). The **Palm Theater,** 817 Palm St. (541-5161), screens artsy and revival films (tickets $6, seniors $3.75, children $3.75; Mon. $3).

Although the visitors center tries to deny its existence like The Man denies Roswell, **Bubble Gum Alley** is fact. You can find the 12-foot-high walls of gum graffiti at 735 Higuera St. And you thought there was nothing to do in SLO.

ENTERTAINMENT

One half of SLO's population is under the age of 24—this town can't help but party. It gets particularly wild after the **Thursday night farmer's market,** along Higuera St.

between Nipomo and Osos, which is more of a raging block party than a produce market. Consult the free weekly *New Times* for info on other local happenings.

Linnaea's Cafe, 1110 Garden St. (541-5888). A popular evening hangout, especially with the artsy set. Displays local artists' works on the wall and features live folk and blues nightly at 8pm, jazz Fri.-Sun. No cover, but a hat is passed around after each performance. Open Sun.-Thurs. 7am-midnight, Fri.-Sat. 7am-12:15am. All ages.

Mother's Tavern, 725 Higuera St. (541-8733). Yukon decor draws mostly Cal Poly kids who pile in for the Wed. night disco party ($1 after 10pm). Happy Hour Mon.-Fri. 3-6pm. Live music Fri.-Sat. (cover $3-4). Open Mon-Fri. 10am-1:30am, Sat.-Sun. 9am-2am. Food served until 9pm. Must be 21 after 9pm.

SLO Brewing Company, 1119 Garden St. (543-1843). SLO's first brewery since Prohibition, and it's about time. Some food, but mostly drink. Live funk, reggae, and rock Thurs.-Sat. (usually free). Amazingly good porter (pints $2.75). Happy Hour (Mon.-Fri. 4-5:30pm) featuring half-price pitchers. Open Mon.-Wed. 11:30am-10pm, Thurs.-Sat. 11:30am-1:30am, Sun. 11:30am-6pm. Must be 21.

Frog and Peach Pub, 728 Higuera St. (595-3764). Big British pub with a laid-back leafy patio along the creek. Mellow sounds like jazz, R&B, or acoustic pop Thurs.-Sat. nights. Celtic jam sessions on the first and third Wed. of the month. Pints $3. Open Mon.-Fri. 11am-2am, Sat.-Sun. 10am-2am. No cover. Must be 21.

SEASONAL EVENTS

Believe it or not, SLO hosts the most rollicking **Mardi Gras** this side of the Mississippi. Celebrated the Saturday before Ash Wednesday (usually) in February. Call 542-2183 for more info. Over Father's Day weekend (June), catch the three-day acoustic showdown at the **Live Oak Music Festival,** in Lake Cachuma Park. Most revelers camp at the park for the mini-Woodstock ($30 per day, 3-day ticket $75; call 781-3030 for info). A favorite wingding is the **Mozart Festival,** in the end of July and early August. Concerts play at Cal Poly, the mission, local wineries, and local churches. Tickets cost around $15, student rush tickets (½hr. early) $7.50. Call 756-2787 for tickets, 546-4195 for info, or write P.O. Box 311, San Luis Obispo 93406. The acclaimed **Shakespeare Festival** (546-4224), runs from mid-July to mid-August at the Learning Pine Arboretum on Cal Poly's campus (tickets $12, students $10, seniors $10). The four-day **International Film Festival** (543-0855), in November, features independent films, documentaries, and seminars ($5 per screening).

■ South of San Luis Obispo

Two beaches just southwest of San Luis Obispo enjoy anonymity; no signs announce their existence to the masses. Well-frequented **Pirate's Cove** has unusually warm water, which is fortunate because most bathers go **nude.** Take U.S. 101 south from San Luis Obispo, exit at the Avila Rd. off-ramp, head west 2 mi. and turn left on Cave Landing Dr., just before the oil tanks. Park in the dirt lot and take a path to the cove. The shores of **Shell Beach,** one mile down U.S. 101 south of Avila and Pirate's Cove, are lined with semi-precious stones (onyx, agate, quartz, and the like) instead of sand. Take the Shell Beach Exit and turn left onto Shell Beach Rd., then drive until you see little brown Coastal Access signs. Park at the gazebo, and climb down to the ocean.

Avila and **Pismo Beaches** are both more developed and crowded. Avila has the typical California beach scene, with a steady stream of cars cruising the bar-lined boardwalk. It also has the warmest air and water of the entire coastline. Drive as if you're going to Pirate's Cove; Avila Beach is on your left after you pass Cave Landing Dr. Pismo Beach, 1½ mi. south of Shell Beach, is even more developed and congested than Avila. This raging spring break party spot is accessible by **Central Coast Area Transit** (I-10) as well as **Greyhound.** Rent all kinds of beach equipment at **Beach Cycle Rentals,** 150 Hinds Ave. (773-5518), next to the pier (open daily 9am-dusk). At the day's end, when sun sets behind the hills that jut into the sea, Pismo beach lights up with a gorgeous sand-on-fire effect.

Pismo Dunes, actually south of Pismo Beach in Grover City, is a State Vehicular Recreation Area, where for a $4 day-use fee, you can take your car or ATV down onto the dunes and spin-out to your heart's content. Call 549-3433 for information. Rent ATV equipment ($30-50 per hr.) from **BJ's ATV,** 197 Grand (481-5411; open daily 9am-5pm). At the south end of the park is **Oso Flaco Lake,** where Cecil B. DeMille left the set of *The Ten Commandments* as is. It is currently being "excavated" (leave it to California to excavate a movie set). **Camping** here is an option for the serious budget traveler (473-7223; sites $6, walk-ins $1). On the weekends, though, the sounds of squealing tires and revving engines can drown out the surf.

■ North of San Luis Obispo

The **Nine Sisters,** a chain of volcanic gnomes, are remnants of a time when SLO county was a hotbed of volcanic activity. Today the lava which once flowed here makes for dramatic shorelines along PCH from Morro Rock to SLO. The northernmost sistah, **Morro Rock,** shadows the tiny burg of **Morro Bay,** just to the north of its namesake park. CCAT bus #7 serves Morro Bay from SLO (5 per day; fare $1.25; for more info call 541-2228). Lodgings here are cheaper than in SLO. Get info from the **Morro Bay Chamber of Commerce,** 880 Main St. (772-4467), which has maps and a rolodex of accommodations (open Mon.-Fri. 8:30am-5pm, Sat. 10am-3pm). For Morro Bay campground info, see **San Luis Obispo: Camping** (p. 221). The town's namesake, **Morro Bay State Park,** is home to coastal cypresses which are a favorite of Monarch butterflies from November to early February. Its **Museum of Natural History** (772-2694), trains its curatorial might on the aquatic environment and the wildlife of the coastal headlands. A bulletin board at the entrance lists a variety of free nature walks led by park rangers in summer (open daily 10am-5pm; admission $2, ages 6-12 $1). South Bay Blvd., which links the town and the park, winds through the new **Morro Bay National Estuary** (528-8126), a sanctuary for great blue herons, egrets, and **sea otters.** Park in the deserted end of the Marina lot and either take the trail or rent a rowboat ($6 per hr.) to roam through the estuary.

The **Embarcadero,** which runs along the beach, is the locus of Morro Bay activity and fish and chips bargains. The **Morro Bay Aquarium,** 595 Embarcadero (772-2694), has over 100 live ocean critters and a seal feeding station (open daily 9am-6pm; admission $1, ages 5-11 50¢). Morro Bay's pride and joy is the **Giant Chessboard,** in Centennial Park on Embarcadero. The board is 256 square feet, and the 18 to 20 pound pieces are carved from redwood.

Gray whales, gaggles of seals, and even more otters frequent **Montana de Oro State Park** (528-0513), 20 minutes west of SLO on Los Osos Valley Rd. The 8000 acres and 7 mi. of shoreline remain relatively secluded. **Spooner's Cove,** across from tidepools and a campground, offers sea cave spelunking (at low tide) and free whale-watching from the bluffs above, at the **Bluff's Trail** trailhead. You can get more info about hikes at the visitors center (772-7434; open daily noon-4pm).

The **wineries** around SLO are well-respected. **Paso Robles,** 25 mi. north of SLO on U.S. 101, is vintner central. The Paso Robles Chamber of Commerce, 1225 Park St. (238-0506), has a list of wineries, including visiting hours, tours, and tastings (open Mon.-Fri. 8:30am-5pm, Sat. 10am-4pm). The SLO Chamber of Commerce has similar info on the wineries (see **Practical Information,** p. 219). Wild Horse, Justin Winery, and Steven Ross are some of the best labels. In August, more than 25 local wineries come together for the **Central Coast Wine Festival** (tickets $15; call 238-0506).

Mission San Miguel Archangel (467-3256), is 43 mi. north of San Luis Obispo in San Miguel, a few blocks from U.S. 101; take the Mission exit. The 1818 complex has colorful frescoes, painted in 1821 by Monterey's Esteban Munras and his crack team of Native American artists (open daily 9:30am-4:30pm; $1 donation requested). For more info, see **A Man with a Mission** (p. 54).

▨ Cambria and San Simeon

The original settlers of the southern end of the Big Sur coast were awestruck by the stunning pastoral vistas and rugged shoreline, reminiscent of the eastern coast of England. In homage to the area's natural beauty, they named it Cambria, the ancient name for Wales. The minuscule San Simeon, six miles north on Hwy. 1, later brought ranch hands and household staff to the foot of newspaper tycoon William Randolph Hearst's "enchanted hill," like vassals beneath the feudal lord's castle. Cambria and San Simeon now house yuppies on weekend getaways and scores of minions on a pilgrimage to William Randolf's towering abode, Hearst Castle.

PRACTICAL INFORMATION

Visitor Information: Cambria Chamber of Commerce, 767 Main St. (927-3624). Maps of the area. Open daily 9am-5pm. **San Simeon Chamber of Commerce,** 9255 Hearst Dr. (927-3500 or 800-342-5613), on the west side of Hwy. 1, look for the blue tourist info signs. Open Mon.-Sat. 9am-5pm; winter Mon.-Fri. 10am-2pm. Both offices sell tickets for Hearst Castle tours.

ATM: Bank of America, 2258 Main St., in Cambria. Also at the castle.

Public Transportation: Central Coast Area Transit (CCAT). Bus #7 runs from SLO to Morro Bay (fare $1.25). Connect to #12 for Cambria (fare $1.25) and San Simeon (fare $1.50). You may have to flag buses to get them to stop. There is no public transportation to Hearst Castle.

Laundromat: Main Street Laundromat, 1601 Main St. Wash $1.50, 48min. dry 50¢. Open daily 7am-10pm.

Emergency: 911.

Police: Morro Bay, 850 Morro Bay Blvd. (772-6225).

Post Office: Cambria, 4100 Bridge St. (927-3654). Open Mon.-Fri. 9am-5pm. **ZIP Code:** 93428. **San Simeon** (927-4156), Hwy. 1, in the back of Sebastian's General Store (and gas pumps). To get there, take the road opposite the entrance to Hearst Castle. Open Mon.-Fri. 8:30am-noon and 1-5pm. **ZIP Code:** 93452.

Area Code: 805.

ACCOMMODATIONS AND CAMPING

Cambria has charming but pricey B&B's. Budget travelers will have better luck in San Simeon. Beware of skyrocketing summer prices when tourists storm the castle.

Creekside Inn, 2618 Main St. (927-4021 or 800-269-5212), in Cambria. Sunny, yellow country cottage. Some rooms have balconies over the creek, and some have color TVs and VCRs (you can rent *Citizen Kane* in town). All have nosegays, gingham, and pink walls. Singles and doubles start at $50, off-season $45.

Sands Motel, 9355 Hearst Dr. (927-3243 or 800-444-0779), west of Hwy. 1 in San Simeon, near the beach. Indoor heated pool. All rooms have cable TV and coffeemakers, some have VCRs and fridges. Doubles start at $50, off-season $39.

Motel 6, 9070 Castillo Dr. (927-8691; fax 927-5341), at the Vista del Mar Exit in San Simeon. Clean, comfy, and classy. Big rooms with 2 queen beds, color TV, and cable TV. Doubles $55, off-season $39.

San Simeon State Beach Campground, just north of Cambria on Hwy. 1. **San Simeon Creek** has 133 sites near the beach and showers. **Washburn** sits on a hill overlooking the ocean. Portable toilets and cold running water only. San Simeon sites $17, winter $14. Washburn sites $10, winter $7. Weekends $1 more, senior discount $2 less. For reservations, call DESTINET (800-444-7275).

FOOD

Food is far more plentiful in Cambria than San Simeon. You'll have to eat by their schedule—most places close between lunch and dinner. Otherwise, you can gather supplies at **Soto's Market,** 2244 Main St. (927-4411; open Mon.-Thurs. 7am-8pm, Fri.-Sat. 7am-9pm, Sun. 8am-6pm), in Cambria. Buy fresh local produce on Main St. at the Cambria **farmer's market,** next to the Veteran's Hall (Fri. 2:30-5:30pm).

CENTRAL COAST

Robin's, 4095 Burton Dr. (927-5007), in Cambria. SLO residents call this the only reason to go to Cambria. Eclectic international cuisine inside a craftsman-style bungalow with gorgeous gardens. Entrees $5-9. Sandwiches $5-7. Lots of veggie options and an extensive wine list. Open daily 11am-9pm, later in the summer.

El Chorlito Mexican Eatery, 9155 Hearst Dr. (927-3872), in San Simeon. Fresh, lard-free, and zippy Cali-Mex food with ocean views. Try the specialty—an unusually spiced green *chile* and cheese soup ($2.75 a cup). Enchiladas $3-6. Open daily noon-10pm in the summer, noon-8pm in the winter.

The Harmony Pasta Factory, 1316 Tamson Dr. (927-5882), in Cambria Village Square. A romantic retreat with amazing views, it feels more expensive than it really is. Good lunch deals (Mon.-Sat. 11am-2:30pm) and early-bird dinners (Mon.-Fri. 5-6pm; entrees $6-9). Open Mon.-Sat. 11:30am-9:30pm, Sun. 9:30am-2pm.

Creekside Gardens Cafe, 2114 Main St. (927-8646), in the Redwood Shopping Center in Cambria. Locals frequent this petite restaurant for the solid, homemade food. Indoor or patio dining. Pancakes with eggs and bacon $4. Desserts ($2-3) made fresh every day. Open Mon.-Sat. 7am-2pm, Sun. 7am-1pm.

SIGHTS AND ACTIVITIES

Big Sur's dramatic coastline begins here and extends north along Hwy. 1. Sea otters, once near extinction, now prosper in the kelp beds of **Moonstone Beach** (on Moonstone Dr. off Hwy. 1 toward San Simeon). Along this stretch of coast surfers are occasionally nudged off their boards by playful seals (and, more rarely, by killer whales and not-so-playful great white sharks, who thrive in these cold waters). The best spot for **whale watching** (Dec.-April) is the scenic **Leffingwell's Landing. San Simeon** and **Hearst State Beaches,** just across from Hearst Castle, are ideal for cliff-climbing and beachcombing and offer the best swimming for miles. A single parking permit ($4) is good for one day at all state parks, but many people avoid the fee by parking on the road outside Hearst Beach's entrance. Look for turn-outs on Hwy. 1 between San Simeon and the lighthouse at Piedras Blancas; these and the nearby wooden stairs over Hearst Corporation fences provide the only legal access.

Hearst Castle

Hearst San Simeon Historic Monument (927-2010), is located 3 mi. north of San Simeon, and about 9 mi. north of Cambria. Casually referred to by founder and funder William Randolph Hearst as "the ranch," it is an indescribably decadent conglomeration of castle, cottages, pools, gardens, and Mediterranean *esprit* perched high above the Pacific. It stands as a testament to Hearst's unfathomable wealth and Julia Morgan's architectural genius. Little Hearst caught a bad case of art collecting at age 10, and spent the rest of his life gathering Renaissance sculpture, tapestries, and ceilings. Yes, ceilings. Ms. Morgan, California's first female architect, orchestrated all of this into a veritable Mediterranean *oeuvre.* Scores of Hollywood celebs flocked (by invitation only) to the castle to bask in Hearst's hospitality. But while countless memorable cast parties were held on these grounds, the only things ever filmed here were 30 seconds of *Spartacus* and a Kodak Funsaver commercial. Its real glamour lay behind the scenes.

Tours are run by the State Parks Department (staff in anachronistic ranger garb roam around the estate) and are a strictly hands-off experience. Fondle the hand rails or stair cases because they're the only things you can touch. **Tour One** covers the photogenic Neptune Pool, the opulent Casa del Sol guest house, fragrant gardens, and the main rooms of the house; this is the best bet for first-time visitors. **Tours Two, Three,** and **Four** cover the living quarters and gardens in greater depth—these tours are recommended for those already familiar with Tour One.

The four daytime tours cost $14 each (ages 6-12 $8, under 6 free), and last about 1¾ hr. The evening tours feature costumed docents acting out the Castle's legendary Hollywood history in new outdoor lighting, and cost $25 (ages 6-12 $13). Be warned that each of the tours involves between 150 and 370 stairs. Call DESTINET 800-444-4445 for reservations, 619-452-8787 for international reservations, or 805-927-2020 for wheelchair accessible tour reservations. You can also reserve tours from the Morro Bay, Cambria, and San Simeon Chambers of Commerce. Tours often sell out, so call weeks in advance, particularly during the summer. Before going to see the castle, your experience may be enhanced by stopping by the **visitors center** at the base of the hill, which features a surprisingly frank portrait of Hearst's failed Harvard days, yellow journalism, and scandalous life. Hearst may be renowned for his business acumen, but in reality, his mistress had to sell her jewels so that construction of her indebted lover's mansion could continue. The **National Geographic Theater** (927-6811), shows the 40-minute film *Enchanted Castle,* which details how the architectural dream became reality, on a 5-story screen (daily 9:30am-5:30pm, on the half-hour; tickets $6, children $4). Or, you can view scenes of perhaps the greatest American film of all time, based on Hearst's life—Orson Welles's *Citizen Kane.*

▓ Big Sur

Upon beholding the startling scope of the Big Sur panorama, you might wish to say, "Golly, that *is* big, sir." Everyone will laugh. Your traveling companion may wish to interject, "It's big, sure." Everyone will laugh again. French friends may add, "Bien sûr!" They will not be nearly as funny. God will then smite you for your insolence. The locals will laugh their arses off and enjoy their little bit o' paradise alone.

PRACTICAL INFORMATION

Visitor Information: Big Sur Chamber of Commerce, P.O. Box 87, Big Sur 93920 (667-2100). Send a self-addressed stamped envelope for a guide to Big Sur. **Big Sur Station** (667-2315), ½mi. south of Pfeiffer Big Sur entrance on Hwy. 1. This multi-agency station includes the **State Park Office,** the **U.S. Forest Service Office,** and the **CalTrans Office,** provides permits and maps, and sponsors ranger-led hikes and campfires. Open daily 8am-6pm.

Public Transportation: Monterey-Salinas Transit (MST) (899-2555). Bus #22 runs through Big Sur daily (May-Oct. only). It leaves from the Monterey Conference Center and runs as far south as Nepenthe, 29mi. below Carmel, stopping at points of interest in between (every 3hr. 7am-4pm). Fare $3, seniors $1.50, under 19 $1.50. Limited space for bikes; call ahead.

Auto Repair: AAA Emergency Road Service (800-400-4222).

Road Conditions: (800-427-7623). **Highway Patrol** (805-549-3261).

Emergency: 911. **Ranger Dispatch** (649-2810).

Post Office: (667-2305). On Hwy. 1, next to the Center Deli in Big Sur Center. Open Mon.-Fri. 8:30am-5pm. **ZIP Code:** 93920.

Area Code: 408.

ORIENTATION

Monterey's Spanish settlers simply called the entire region below their town *El Sur Grande*—the Large South. Today, "Big Sur" is a more explicitly defined coastal region bordered on the south by San Simeon and on the north by Carmel. The coast is thinly inhabited, dotted with a few gas stations and exorbitant "getaway" hotels. Almost everything—fuel, food, beer, toiletries—costs more in Big Sur than anywhere outside it. Last-chance stops for the budget-minded are the supermarket complex on Rio Rd. in Carmel to the north, and the market in Morro Bay to the south.

Despite its isolation, Big Sur can be reached by public transit (see above for details). The drive from Carmel to Big Sur on **Hwy. 1** is simply breathtaking, but everyone knows it, so find a time (early mornings recommended) when traffic won't interfere with your enjoyment of the splendor. Hitching can be difficult, especially near the state parks, where competition is fierce. When the road is crowded with lurching RVs, frustrated speedsters, and oblivious Sunday drivers, walking and bicycling become treacherous, and traffic slows to a crawl.

Spring, when wildflowers bloom and the hills glow with color, is the optimal time to visit Big Sur. No matter what the season, warm and cold weather clothing is necessary for this stretch of coast, where mornings are typically cool and foggy, afternoons sunny, and evenings chilly.

CAMPING

Camping in Big Sur is heavenly. If you neglect to bring equipment, you've made a big mistake. Even if you did, be warned—site prices and availability reflect high demand. Reserve in advance by calling MISTIX (800-444-PARK/7275). If all sites below are booked, check with the U.S. Forest Service (see **Practical Information,** above). Camping is free in the Ventana Wilderness, a backpack-only site at the northern end of Los Padres National Forest (permits at Big Sur Station).

Andrew Molera State Park (667-2315), 5mi. north of Pfeiffer Big Sur. A level ¾mi. trail leads to tent-only campgrounds. No numbered sites and never full. Beach, ornithology center, pit toilets, no showers. 3-night max. stay. Sites $4, seniors and hike-in $3, $1 extra for man's best friend.

Kirk Creek and **Plaskett Creek** (385-5434). Kirk lacks shelter, and Plaskett a view, but both are within walking distance of a beach. Kirk (32 sites) sits 9mi. south of the Big Creek Bridge; Plaskett (43 sites) is 5½mi. farther, near Jade Cove. No showers. Sites $16; hike-ins and bike-ins $4 per person.

Ventana Big Sur (667-2688), 30mi. south of Carmel on Hwy. 1, has 75 sites in a gorgeous redwood canyon, bathhouses with hot showers, picnic tables, fire rings, and water faucets. Sites for up to 2 people $25, leashed dogs $5. Reservations accepted at least 2 weeks in advance.

Pfeiffer Big Sur State Park (667-2315), 26mi. south of Carmel, just south of Fernwood Park campgrounds. The diverse wildlife and terrain, the beautiful Big Sur River, and several hiking trails ensure that all 218 campsites fill up in advance. No hookups. Hot showers, firepits, picnic tables. Sites $17, seniors $15; day use $6 per car, seniors $5, dogs $1. Reservations essential in the summer.

Limekiln State Park (667-2403), 2mi. south of Lucia, off the highway along Limekiln Creek. Pleasant, formerly private campground has 42 sites, direct beach access, and hot showers. Sites for up to 8 people $22, Fri.-Sat. $23. Nov.-March: $20, $21. Each additional car $6. Reserve early.

Big Sur (667-2322), 26mi. south of Carmel, near the Big Sur River. In addition to 82 campsites, there are 4 tent cabins ($44; Oct.-May only). Overseen by a terrific staff. Small store, laundry, playground, volleyball courts, and hot showers. Sites for up to 2 people $24, with RV hookup $27; each additional person (up to 3) and leashed dogs $3. Reservations recommended. Neighboring **Riverside Camp** (667-2414), has similar sites and prices, plus 5 rooms in cabins ($45 per night).

Fernwood (667-2422), 2mi. north of the post office on Hwy. 1, downhill from the burger bar and store (see **Food,** below). Located on the Big Sur River in a redwood forest, the 66 campsites and 2 swimming holes are beautifully situated. Sites for up to 6 people $24, with hookup $27. Fernwood also has a **motel** (doubles $70; quads $103; check-out noon; registration open 8am-midnight).

FOOD

Grocery stores are located at Big Sur Lodge (in Pfeiffer Big Sur State Park), Pacific Valley, and Gorda, and some packaged food is sold in Lucia and at Ragged Point, but it's better to arrive prepared; prices are high.

Center Deli (667-2225), beside the post office, 1mi. south of Big Sur Station. The most reasonably priced goods in the area. Sandwiches ($4-5) include veggie options like avocado and egg salad. Open daily 8am-8:30pm; winter 8am-7:30pm.

Cafe Kevah (667-2344), 3mi. south of Big Sur Station next to its hoity-toity sister, the Nepenthe Restaurant, and ritzy-schmitzy brother, the Phoenix Gift Shop. The outdoor patio stretches to the edge of a strategically scenic cliff. Homemade granola with yogurt $5.75, omelettes $9-10. Stick with water, as drink prices are in the stratosphere (smoothies $4.75, cappuccino $3.75). Open daily 9am-3pm.

Loma Vista Cafe (667-2450), just south of the post office. Recently re-opened restaurant occupies a wide spot on the road with lovely gardens. Fresh food and affordable options. Pancakes $4, sandwiches from $7. Open daily 7am-9:30pm.

Fernwood Bar and Grill (667-2422), 2mi. north of post office on Hwy. 1. Chicken breast $3, hamburgers from $4, veggie burrito $6.50. Full bar and grocery store. Restaurant open daily 10am-10pm, bar noon-midnight, grocery 8am-10pm.

SIGHTS AND ACTIVITIES

Big Sur's state parks and **Los Padres National Forest** beckon outdoor activists of all types. Their **hiking** trails penetrate redwood forests and cross low chaparral, offering even grander views of Big Sur than those available from Hwy. 1. The northern end of Los Padres National Forest has been designated the **Ventana Wilderness** and contains the popular **Pine Ridge Trail.** The Forest Service ranger station supplies maps and permits for the wilderness area (see **Practical Information,** p. 227).

Within **Pfeiffer Big Sur State Park** are eight trails of varying lengths (50¢ map available at park entrance). The **Valley View Trail** is a short, steep path overlooking the valley below. **Buzzard's Roost Trail** is a rugged two-hour hike up tortuous switchbacks, but at its terminus are rewarding panoramic views of the Santa Lucia Mountains, the Big Sur Valley, and the Pacific Ocean.

Roughly at the midway point of the Big Sur coast lies **Julia Pfeiffer Burns State Park** (entrance fee $6), where picnickers find refuge in redwood forest and sea otters in McWay Cove. At the point where the Big Sur River flows into the ocean is a spectacular waterfall, which may be viewed from a path 300 ft. from the park entrance. All of the state parks are local faves, but workday visitors can avoid the throng. Turn-offs along the highway lead to charming secluded inlets. Just to the north of Pfeiffer Burns is one such turn-off, marked with a Fire Road Only barrier. Hoof it down all the way to the water to eyeball terrific rock formations and crashing waves. Big Sur's most jealously guarded treasure is USFS-operated **Pfeiffer Beach,** one mile south of Pfeiffer Burns. Turn off Hwy. 1 at the stop sign and the Narrow Road Not Suitable For Trailers sign, then follow the road 2 mi. to the parking area, where a path leads to the beach. An offshore rock formation protects sea caves and sea gulls from the pounding ocean waves. There are no lifeguards; riptides make swimming dangerous.

Big Sur is not *all* nature and no civilization, however. The **Henry Miller Memorial Library,** just south of Nepenthe and Cafe Kevah, displays books and artwork by the former Big Sur resident. Miller's casual reminiscences and prophetic ecstasies made hundreds of readers aware of Big Sur. His more explicit and rather misogynistic works, like *Tropic of Cancer,* drew many to Big Sur seeking the fictional sex cult he purportedly led (open daily 11am-5pm).

■ Carmel

Genteel Californians migrate to Carmel to live out their fantasies of small-town life, and the town responds remarkably well to their wishes. Carmel possesses pristine beaches, a main street lined with boutiques and art galleries, and a vigorously maintained aura of quaintness. Local ordinances forbid address numbers, parking meters (though police chalk tires to keep careful track of how long you have parked), franchise stores, live music in bars, billboards, and, at one time, eating ice-cream cones outside—all considered undesirable symbols of urbanization. All this effort to make Carmel (pop. 4500) absolutely *precious* ends up imparting a saccharin mall-ish feeling that seems to cast a spell on wealthy, older tourists. But aside from white sand beaches, a lovely mission, and the thrill of potentially seeing resident and former mayor Clint Eastwood walking the streets, there is little to attract the budget traveler. In fact, budget travelers may find Carmel downright unwelcoming.

CENTRAL COAST

PRACTICAL INFORMATION

Visitor Information: Carmel-by-the-Sea Business Association, San Carlos St. (624-2522), on the 2nd fl. of the Eastwood Building between 5th and 6th. Free city maps available here and all over town. Open Mon.-Fri. 9am-5:30pm, Sat. 11am-3pm; July-Aug. Sun. also 11am-3pm.

Public Transportation: Monterey-Salinas Transit (MST) (899-2555, TDD 393-8111). Buses #4, 5, and 24 go through Carmel. Bus #22 runs to Big Sur (2 per day). Schedules available at the Monterey info and transit centers. Fare per zone $1.50, seniors and disabled 75¢, ages 5-18 75¢; same-zone transfers free up to 2hr.

Bike Rental: Bay Bikes (625-BIKE/2453), based in Monterey, will deliver anywhere in Carmel free of charge. Bikes $22 per day (includes helmet and bike lock). Open daily 8:30am-5:30pm.

Post Office: 5th St. (624-1525), between San Carlos and Dolores. Open Mon.-Fri. 9am-4:30pm. **ZIP Code:** 93921.

Area Code: 408.

ORIENTATION

Carmel lies at the southern end of the Monterey Peninsula off **Hwy. 1,** 125 mi. south of San Francisco. The town's main street, **Ocean Ave.,** cuts west from the freeway to (surprise) the ocean. All other east-west avenues are numbered, ascending towards the south. **Junípero Ave.** crosses Ocean Ave. downtown and leads south to the mission at Rio Rd. Free maps of the town are available at most hotels. A public lot on the corner of Junípero Ave. and 3rd St. offers free all-day parking.

ACCOMMODATIONS AND CAMPING

Most **motels** in Carmel offer only double-occupancy rooms (never below $70), and the rates at Carmel's B&Bs and inns are equally high, but usually include full breakfasts. A 15-minute bus ride to Monterey will bring more reasonable prices. Camping is illegal within city limits, and there are no state parks within the vicinity. There is, however, an RV-heavy private campground 4½ mi. east at **Saddle Mountain Ranch,** 27625 Schulte Rd. (624-1617). The 50 sites with showers ($22 per night) are popular; reserve in advance.

FOOD

Jack London's, San Carlos St. (624-2336), between 5th and 6th. "Jack London was a friendly and forthright presence in Carmel and America's foremost adventure writer. Like Jack, our food is fresh and forthright." Believe the hype: fish or fowl $7-8, burgers $6.25 and up. Plant yourself where the action is—at or near the bar. Open daily noon-2am (food served until 1am).

Don Chano's Taquería, Ocean Ave. (624-2105), between Mission and San Carlos. Tasty, filling plates of authentic *mexicana* won't wear out your credit card. Enchilada plate $4.65, tacos $2-4. Mexican beers $2.75. Open daily 10am-10pm.

China Gourmet, 5th St. (624-3941), between San Carlos and Dolores, across from the post office. Delicious Cantonese and Szechuan food (entrees $6-10). Vegetarian options available. Lunch specials ($4.50-5.50) include almond chicken or BBQ pork with snow peas. Open Tues.-Sun. 11am-9:30pm.

Hog's Breath Inn, San Carlos (625-1044), between 5th and 6th. Clint Eastwood's faux British pub-style restaurant serves truly succulent food. Dinner is a bit out of range for budget travelers, but lunch is affordable. Dirty Harry Burger $7. Complimentary hors d'oeuvres Mon.-Fri. 4-6pm. Open Mon.-Sat. 11:30am-3pm and 5-10pm, Sun. 11am-3pm.

Em Le's, Dolores Ave. (625-6780), between 5th and 6th. The *Coast Weekly's* Best Breakfast pick. Omelettes with potatoes or cottage cheese (how Carmel) and toast $6, unique french toast $5.50. Open daily 6:30am-3pm.

SIGHTS AND ENTERTAINMENT

Carmel City Beach, at the end of Ocean Ave., is where the northern Big Sur coast truly begins. No signs mark the exact spot, but it's unmistakable: a crescent of white sand frames a cove of clear, chilly, azure waters. The beach ends abruptly at the base of distant red cliffs, making a fine grandstand for sunsets. The **Carmel River State Beach** lies just to the south of City Beach. This beach is windier and colder, but blessed with a better surf and fewer crowds. Walk about one mile along Scenic Rd. or drive to the end of Carmelo St. off Santa Lucía. The parking lot closes at dusk.

Mission Basilica San Carlos Borromeo del Río Carmelo, 3080 Rio Rd. (624-3600), off Hwy. 1, is a mouthful to say but a marvel to see. Established at its present site in 1771 by Father Junípero Serra, "the Great Conquistador of the Cross," the mission "converted" 4000 Native Americans before it was abandoned in 1836. Lovingly and fastidiously restored in 1931, the mission comes complete with stone courtyard, Mudéjar bell tower, luscious gardens, and a daily mass. Buried here are Father Serra and over 2300 Native Americans. The three museums display the original silver altar furnishings, handsome vestments, and a library (open Mon.-Sat. 9:30am-4:30pm, Sun. 10:30am-4:30pm; June-Aug. daily 9:30am-7:30pm; donation requested). For more info, see **A Man with a Mission** (p. 54).

The **Center for Photographic Art,** San Carlos St. (625-5181; http://www.photography.org), between 8th and 9th, is housed in the Sunset Center offices once occupied by Ansel Adams. Exhibits include work by local and international artists (open Tues.-Sun. 1-5pm; free).

The extraordinary, 550-acre **Point Lobos Reserve,** on Hwy. 1 (624-4909), 3 mi. south of Carmel, is a state-run wildlife sanctuary popular with skindivers and day hikers. Otters, sea lions, seals, brown pelicans, and gulls are visible from footpaths along the cliffs (bring binoculars). Point Lobos has tide pools and marvelous vantage points for watching the winter whale migration, which peaks in winter but continues throughout spring. Free tours are offered daily (call for times). Park on Hwy. 1 before the toll booth and walk or bike in for free (accessible from MST bus #22). Eager divers frequently back up the entrance line by 8am on weekends. (Open daily 9am-6:30pm; in winter 9am-4:30pm. Admission $7 per car, seniors $6. Map 50¢.)

■ Monterey

Monterey was sighted by the Spanish as early as 1542, but the native Ohlone people were largely left in peace until 1770, when Father Serra targeted the area on his journey up the coast. After being claimed by the U.S. in 1846, the city lost its missionary prestige and was eclipsed by San Francisco as a port. The growth of the whaling industry kept Monterey alive until 1880, when sardine fishing and packaging stepped up to take its place. The wharfside flourished as the fisherman's world immortalized by John Steinbeck in the 1940s. Before long, the sardines petered out and Monterey started fishing in the pockets of wealthy tourists. Today, few traces of the Monterey described in *Cannery Row* remain—packing plants have been converted to multiplex souvenir malls, and the old bars where sailors used to drink and fight now feature wax recreations. However, scattered public buildings, adobe houses, and a resilient, if more responsible, fishing community recall bygone days. Along with the beauty of the coastline, the seafood, and a world-class aquarium, these remnants of an earlier era justify a journey to Monterey.

PRACTICAL INFORMATION

Visitor Information: Monterey Peninsula Visitor and Convention Bureau, 380 Alvarado St. (649-1770). Free pamphlets and the 120-page *Visitor's Guide* ($6), which has restaurant, accommodation, and tourist info. Open Mon.-Fri. 8:30am-5pm. A smaller **visitors center** is located at 401 Camino El Estero (649-1770; open June-Sept. Mon.-Sat. 9am-6pm, Sun. 9am-5pm, and Oct.-May Mon.-Fri. 9am-5pm, Sat.-Sun. 9am-4pm).

Public Transportation: Monterey-Salinas Transit (MST), 1 Ryan Ranch Rd. (899-2555, TDD 393-8111). The free *Rider's Guide* contains complete schedules and route info (available on buses, at motels, and at the visitors center). MST serves the region from Watsonville in the north (where it connects to SCMTD; see **Santa Cruz,** p. 239) to Carmel in the south, as well as inland to Salinas. Many buses stop at **Transit Plaza** downtown, where Munras, Tyler, Pearl, Alvarado, and Polk St. converge. MST has 4 zones, each encompassing 1-2 towns. Fare per zone $1.50, seniors and disabled 75¢, ages 5-18 75¢; same-zone transfers free up to 2hr.; exact change. Between Memorial Day and Labor Day, MST offers 2 special services. The **Waterfront Area Visitors Express (WAVE)** follows Monterey sights from the Del Monte shopping center to Pacific Grove. Day pass $1, seniors and disabled 50¢, ages 5-18 50¢; free with MST bus receipt. **Bus #22** runs twice daily between Monterey and Big Sur. Fare $3, seniors and disabled $1.50, ages 5-18 $1.50. MST phone lines open Mon.-Fri. 7:45am-5:15pm, Sat. 10am-2:30pm.

Road Conditions: (800-427-7623).

Taxi: Yellow Cab (646-1234). Initial charge $1.50; each additional mi. $1.75.

Bike Rental: Bay Bikes, 640 Wave St. (646-9090), on Cannery Row. Bikes or in-line skates $10 first 2hr., $4 each additional hr., $22 per day, $10 each additional day. Includes lock and helmet. Open daily 9am-7pm.

Equipment Rental: On The Beach Surf Shop, 693 Lighthouse Ave. (646-9283). Surf store rents surfboards (½ day $10), boogieboards (½ day $5), and wetsuits (½ day $6); full day (8hr.) rentals are twice the price. Open Mon.-Fri. 10am-7pm, Sat. 9am-7pm, Sun. 10am-6pm. **Monterey Bay Kayaks,** 693 Del Monte Ave. (373-KELP/5357 or 800-649-5357), rents kayaks for $25 per day (includes gear and wetsuit). Open daily 9am-6pm.

Library: 625 Pacific St. (646-3930), kitty-corner from City Hall. Pleasant courtyard. Open Mon.-Thurs. 9am-9pm, Fri. 9am-6pm, Sat. 9am-5pm, Sun. 1-5pm.

Laundromat: Surf and Suds, 1101 Del Monte Ave. (375-0874). Wash $1.25, 10min. dry 75¢. Open daily 7am-9pm.

Crisis Lines: Rape Crisis (375-4357). 24hr. **Suicide Prevention** (649-8008). **SPCA Wildlife Rescue** (373-2631). Report unauthorized otter fondling.

Emergency: 911.

Police: 351 Madison St. (646-3830), at Pacific.

Post Office: 565 Hartnell St. (372-5803). Open Mon.-Fri. 8:45am-5:10pm. **ZIP Code:** 93940.

Area Code: 408.

ORIENTATION

The Monterey Peninsula, 116 mi. south of San Francisco, consists of Monterey, Pacific Grove (a largely residential community), and Pebble Beach (an exclusive nest of mansions and golf courses). Motorists can approach Monterey from **U.S. 101** via Rte. 68 west through Salinas, or directly from coastal **Hwy. 1.** Monterey's busiest road, **Alvarado,** runs north-south. At its north end stand luxury hotels and the magnitudinous Conference Center; beyond the brick plaza are a large parking lot, the marina, and Fisherman's Wharf. Perpendicular to Alvarado, **Del Monte Ave.** runs east and north to the coast; on the other side, **Lighthouse Ave.** leads west and north out through Pacific Grove, terminating at the Point Pines Lighthouse. Monterey's primary attractions lie within walking distance or a WAVE ride from Alvarado.

The relative isolation of Monterey does little to insulate the city from prodigious summer **traffic** jams. The Monterey Traffic Department's earnest attempts to correct the congestion with abundant one-way signs and complicated traffic signals haven't helped matters much. A simpler option is to park ($3 per day) in the municipal lot at Del Monte and Washington and explore the city by foot and shuttle. **Bicycling** is a splendid way to see the peninsula, provided you exercise caution on the narrow, twisting roads. There are few designated bike paths, but the Monterey Peninsula Recreation Trail follows the coast from Fisherman's Wharf in Monterey through Pacific Grove, Pebble Beach, and Carmel, then back up Hwy. 1, where a bike lane begins. The circuit takes four leisurely hours, and is popular with rollerbladers.

ACCOMMODATIONS AND CAMPING

Prices often vary by day, month, and proximity to seasonal events. The visitors center (see p. 230) offers free phone connections to selected area hotels and motels; at that price, it's worth calling around. Reasonably priced hotels are found on Lighthouse Ave. in Pacific Grove (bus #2 and some #1 buses) and in the 2000 block of Fremont St. in Monterey (bus #9 or 10). Others cluster along Munras Ave. between downtown and Hwy. 1. The cheapest hotels in the area, however, are in the less appealing towns of Seaside and Marina, just north of Monterey. Call the Monterey Parks line (755-4895 or 888-588-CAMP/2267) for camping info and MISTIX (800-444-7275) for reservations.

Del Monte Beach Inn, 1110 Del Monte Blvd. (649-4410), near downtown and across from the beach. This Victorian-style inn offers pleasant rooms (shared bath) and treats its guests to a free hearty breakfast in a sunny room. TV room, hall phone only. Check-in 2-6pm. Rooms $50-70. Mention you're a grizzled Let's Go budget traveler and save 10% on weekdays. Reservations recommended.

Sunset Motel, 133 Asilomar Blvd. (375-3936), by Lovers' Point in Pacific Grove. Quiet neighborhood, complete breakfast, cable TV. Beautiful rooms start at $50.

Pacific Grove Motel, 1101 Lighthouse Ave. (372-3218 or 800-858-8997), at Grove Acre. Very helpful manager. Hot tub, pool, diver rinse areas, fridges, patios, and cable TV. Singles $54, weekends $69; doubles $69, $79. Prices lower Oct.-March.

Veterans Memorial Park campground, Via Del Rey (646-3865), 1½mi. from downtown (bus #3). Take Skyline Dr. off Rte. 68. From downtown, go south on Pacific, right on Jefferson, and follow the signs. Perched on a hill with a view of the bay. Hot showers. No hookups. Forty sites available on first-come, first-camped basis; arrive before 3pm in summer and on weekends. 3-night max. stay. Sites $15.

Laguna Seca Recreational Area campground (755-4899 or 888-588-2267), on Rte. 68 near the racetrack 10mi. east of Monterey. This hilly, oak-strewn hill camp overlooks verdant valleys and the racetrack. Of the 177 campsites, 103 are equipped with hookups. Push-button showers, restrooms, barbecue pits, tables, and dump station. Sites $15, with hookup $20. Reservations accepted 5 or more days in advance.

FOOD

The sardines may be gone, but the unpolluted Monterey Bay teems with squid, crab, rock cod, sand dab, red snapper, and salmon. Although seafood is bountiful, it is often expensive—try eating an early bird special (usually 4-6:30pm). Head to **Fisherman's Wharf** for smoked salmon sandwiches ($6) and free samples of chowder. Don't despair if you loathe seafare—this is also the land of artichokes and strawberries. Generous free samples of fruit, cheese, and seafood are at the **Monterey farmer's market** (655-8070), which takes over Alvarado St. (Tues. 4-8pm).

Downtown and Cannery Row

Epsilon Restaurant, 422 Tyler (655-8108), at Bonifacio. Stupendous Greek food in a lush setting. The lunch menu has the best deals, but there are even affordable dinner choices like excellent *pastitsio* (pasta layered with meat) with salad ($9). The combo plate ($7) has enough appetizers for two. Open Tues.-Fri. 11am-2:30pm and 5-9:30pm, Sat.-Sun. 5-9:30pm.

Old Monkey Cafe, 489 Alvarado St. (646-1021). Hot, hefty portions favored by locals. Hawaiian omelette has pineapple, ham, and banana ($6.75). Lunch specials $5.50-7.50. Open daily 6:45am-2:30pm.

Amarin Thai Cuisine, 807 Cannery Row (373-8811), near the Aquarium. In a complex of cheesy shops, but don't be fooled—the food is authentic and well-prepared, and the service is prompt and friendly. Many vegetarian dishes ($6-10) such as tofu with vegetables and peanut sauce ($10). Open daily 11am-9:30pm.

Lighthouse Avenue Area

International Market and Deli, 580 Lighthouse Ave. (375-9451), in New Monterey. Not long on ambience, but cheap robust food carries the day. Falafel $3, vegetarian-stuffed grape leaves 35¢. Take-out available. Open Mon.-Sat. 10am-7pm, Sun. 11am-6pm. No credit cards.

Thai Bistro II, 15a Central Ave. (372-8700), Pacific Grove. Graced with good service and a patio ringed with flowers, this Bistro still manages to have budget offerings. Lunch combos ($6) come with delicious soup. Open daily 11:30am-10pm.

Inaka Japanese Cuisine, 125 Ocean View (375-0441), in the American Tin Cannery outlet mall. Fresh, authentic Japanese food. Big bowl of *tempura soba* $7. Open Tues.-Sun. 11:30am-3pm and 5-10pm.

SIGHTS

The biggest of Monterey's attractions is the **Monterey Bay Aquarium,** 886 Cannery Row (648-4888; http://www.mbayaq.org), which feeds on the committed community interest in marine ecology. The facility allows visitors a window (literally) into the most curious creatures of the Pacific. Gaze through the **world's largest window** at an enormous marine habitat containing green sea turtles, 7 ft. ocean sunfish, large sharks, and the oozingly graceful Portuguese Man-o'-War. A million-gallon indoor ocean will leave even the most nonchalant visitor gasping for more—so check out the slithering frenzy of **sea otters** at feeding time, a living kelp forest housed in a two-story-tall glass case, and a petting zoo of damp bay denizens (ever think you'd pet a stingray?). The matter-of-fact impact awareness theme running throughout will open your eyes—don't miss a sobering 45-minute "wasted catch" video on the upper level. The aquarium is jam-packed in the mornings, but things usually calm down after 3pm. (Admission $13.75; seniors, ages 13-17, and students $11.75; disabled and ages 3-12 $6. Open daily 10am-6pm; mid-June to early-Sept. 9:30am-6pm.)

Cannery Row lies along the waterfront south of the aquarium. Once a depressed street of languishing sardine packing plants, this ¾ mi. row has been converted into glitzy mini-malls, bars, and a pint-sized carnival complex. All that remains of the earthiness and gruff camaraderie celebrated by John Steinbeck in *Cannery Row* and *Sweet Thursday* are a few building facades: 835 Cannery Row was the Wing Chong Market, the bright yellow building next door is where *Sweet Thursday* took place, and Doc Rickett's lab at 800 Cannery Row is now owned by a private men's club. For a stylized look at Steinbeck's Cannery Row, take a peek at the **Great Cannery Row Mural,** which depicts Monterey in the 30s and stretches 400 ft. along the "700" blocks of Cannery Row. The lavish **Wine and Produce Visitors Center,** 700 Cannery Row (888-646-5446), gives a taste of Monterey in the 90s—the county has a burgeoning wine industry (6 taste-tests for $3). Well-priced bottles, fresh produce, and free winery maps are all available (open daily 11am-6pm).

Otter-lovers can get their fuzzy-mammal fix from several nearby spots, including **Otter Point,** a few minutes' walk south of the aquarium along the shore. Call the **Friends of the Sea Otter** (625-3290) for info on their otter-spotting program. Touching an otter is illegal, and "harassing" or fondling one in Monterey Bay may lead to a $10,000 fine. Several companies on the wharf offer critter-spotting **boat trips** around Monterey Bay for $6-10, but you can gawk from the dock for free. Located at the base of the wharf in the Historic Customs House Plaza is the new **Maritime Museum of Monterey** (375-2553). Ship models, photos, navigation tools, logs, and other paraphernalia sketch the history of Monterey. The museum's centerpiece is the original Fresnel Lens of Point Sur Lighthouse, a two-story structure of gear-works and cut glass that was later replaced by the electric lighthouse. You need not pay admission to see the 14-minute film on Monterey (open Tues.-Sun. 10am-5pm, and July-Aug. also Mon.; admission $5, seniors and disabled $4, ages 13-18 $3, ages 6-12 $2).

Monterey's early days spawned a unique architectural trend that incorporates Southern details, including wrap-around porches, with Mexican adobe characteristics, such as yard-thick walls and exterior staircases. A $5 pass allows you to enter and tour all **Monterey State Historic Park** buildings. Tickets are available at the visitors center (649-7118), inside the park headquarters in the Customs House Plaza (open daily 10am-5pm, in winter 10am-4pm).

The **Monterey Peninsula Museum of Art** occupies two separate locations. The Civic Center branch, 559 Pacific St. (372-5477), holds changing shows, mostly of California artists. The branch at 720 Via La Mirada (372-3689), near Lake El Estero, houses exhibits on California history, as well as collections of regional Asian and Pacific Rim art (open Wed.-Sat. 11am-5pm, Sun. 1-4pm).

NIGHTLIFE

Monterey knows how to cut loose at night, although some areas of the peninsula quiet down early. Most of the action is along Alvarado St. downtown, with a few Lighthouse Ave. exceptions. Pickings are slim for those under 21, but covers remain reasonable or nonexistent.

- **Plumes Coffee,** 400 Alvarado St. (373-4526), plumes gourmet coffee (latte $2.25) and a hip crowd. Open Sun.-Thurs. 7am-11pm, Fri.-Sat. 7am-midnight.
- **Viva Monterey,** 414 Alvarado St. (646-1415), rarely charges a cover for their smokin' live music offerings. An intense crowd lives it up amid great wall art. Liquid creations like Holy Water and Swedish Passion start at $5. Two pool tables. Open daily 4pm-2am; shows Mon.-Sat. 9:30pm, Sun. 8pm.
- **Mucky Ducky British Pub,** 479 Alvarado St. (655-3031). Don't let the empty front window booths fool you—it's happening in the Beer Garden. Sit around two open hearths or in cozy booths with leather chairs. Open daily 11:30am-2am.
- **McGarrett's,** 321 Alvarado St. (646-9244), at Del Monte, dwarfs the club competition with 2 sprawling levels, a live music stage, 2 dance floors, plush bathrooms, and a greenhoused balcony. Live bands every weekend and adult dancers (both sexes) every Mon. Open Wed.-Mon. 8pm-1:30am.
- **After Dark,** 214 Lighthouse Ave. (373-7828), is the cozy local gay bar. The very dark front room leads to a garden and "Back Lot" bar with open-hearth fire. Live DJs. Cover $3. Open Mon.-Sat. 4:30pm-2am.

SEASONAL EVENTS

Monterey's seasonal offerings are plentiful. Zoom to the **Laguna Seca Raceway** (800-327-7322), on Rte. 68 east of Monterey, between late May and early October (office open Mon.-Fri. 8am-5pm). Highlights include the Monterey Sports Car Grand Prix (late July), the Historic Automobile Races (late Aug.), and the Monterey Grand Prix Indy Car World Series (early Oct.). **Pebble Beach** (649-1533), the West's first golf course, hosts world-renowned golf tournaments like the **AT&T National Pro-Am** (800-541-9091), featuring celebrity and PGA tour match-ups in late January. The **Monterey Bay Blues Festival** (394-2652), held in late June, draws big names and crowds. From late June to early August, **Monterey Bay's Theatrefest** (622-0700) takes place between the Customs House and the Pacific House at the head of Fisherman's Wharf. (Free afternoon theater Sat.-Sun. 11am-5pm. Evening shows $15, students and seniors $8.) In mid-August, a variety of exhibits and performers light up the **Monterey County Fair,** at the Monterey County Fairgrounds and Exhibition Park. In the third week of September, the **Monterey Jazz Festival** (800-307-3378) welcomes the great names of jazz.

■ Near Monterey

Monterey's beach lacks the drama and surf of its neighbors to the west and north. Around the northern end of the peninsula, the beach runs uninterrupted for 3 to 4 mi., first as **Pacific Grove Municipal Beach,** then as **Asilomar State Beach.** Bus #2 stops within 4 blocks of the ocean in Pacific Grove. The numerous tidepools along the rocky shore are curious places to explore.

Many area attractions lie west of Monterey. **Sunset Drive** is, appropriately, the best place for watching the sun go down. People arrive a full two hours before sunset in order to secure front row seats along the road (also known as Ocean Blvd.). At the western tip stands **Point Pinos Lighthouse** (648-3116), the oldest continuously running Pacific Coast lighthouse, which now houses exhibits on Coast Guard history (open Thurs.-Sun. 1-4pm; free).

Pacific Grove took root as a Methodist enclave over a 100 years ago, and many of the Victorian houses are still ship shape. This unpretentious town (which falls eerily quiet at night) has a beautiful coastline, numerous lunch counters, and lots of funky boutiques. Browse in second-hand clothing, book, and music stores along Lighthouse Ave., or outlet-shop-till-you-stop at the **American Tin Cannery** near the border with New Monterey. In addition, Pacific Grove houses thousands of **monarch butterflies,** fleeing from October to March. Look, but don't touch—harming butterflies is a $1000 offense. The **Pacific Grove Museum of Natural History** (648-3116 or 648-3119), Forest Ave. at Central one block north of Lighthouse Ave., has year-round exhibits of the monarchs and other local wildlife. Changing displays and a *cetacean* (whale) room are top-notch (open Tues.-Sun. 10am-5pm; free).

The **17-Mile Drive** meanders along the coast from Pacific Grove through **Pebble Beach** and the forests around Carmel. Once owned by Del Monte, Pebble Beach has become the playground of the fabulously well-to-do. Its enormous, manicured golf courses creep up almost to the shore's edge, in strange contrast to the dramatically jagged cliffs and turbulent surf. The drive is rolling, looping, and often spectacular, though plagued by heavy tourist traffic and an outrageous $7 entrance fee. Save your money and bike it; bicyclists and pedestrians are allowed in at no cost. To drive in and out as you please in one day, present your receipt to the guard and make sure he or she records your license plate number. Along the drive is the **Lone Cypress**—an old, gnarled tree growing on a rock promontory. When viewed in the forgiving dimness of twilight, the tree is a silent testimony to perseverance and solitary strength. Try to forget it's been copyrighted by the Pebble Beach community.

■ Salinas and Salinas Valley

The heart of John Steinbeck Country beats in Salinas, two hours south of San Francisco and 25 mi. inland from Monterey. The renowned author (the only American to win both the Pulitzer and Nobel Prizes) lived here until he was 17. This is where *East of Eden* and *The Red Pony* are set, where many of Steinbeck's characters come from, and where his ashes are buried. Beyond the echoes of Steinbeck's writing and a highly acclaimed rodeo, Salinas has little to offer travelers. It can, however, be a convenient way station for those without camping equipment.

South of Salinas, Hwy. 1 stretches out toward far-away San Luis Obispo, running through the wide, green Salinas Valley, where the towns of **Gonzales, Soledad, Greenfield,** and **King City** serve mainly as farming communities and truck stops. Acre upon acre of tomatoes, artichokes, lettuce, grapes, and garlic thrive here in the self-proclaimed "salad bowl of the nation." But if the Salinas Valley is a bowl of greens, then the mysterious peaks of Pinnacles National Monument are the cherry tomatoes. They make passing through this land of produce worth your while.

PRACTICAL INFORMATION

Visitor Information: Salinas Chamber of Commerce, 119 E. Alisal St. (424-7611), has city maps ($2). Open Mon.-Fri. 8:30am-noon and 1-5pm. **King City Chamber of Commerce and Agriculture,** 203 Broadway (385-3814), King City. Open Mon.-Fri. 10am-noon and 1-4pm.

Trains: Amtrak, 11 Station Pl. (422-7458 or 800-827-7245), Salinas. To: San Francisco ($21), L.A. ($67), and all points between. Open daily 9am-1pm and 3-7pm.

Buses: Greyhound, 19 W. Gabilan St. (424-4418 or 800-231-2222), Salinas, 1 block from the MST center. Several buses per day to San Francisco ($17), L.A. ($36), and Santa Cruz ($11). Open daily 4:15am-midnight.

Public Transportation: Monterey-Salinas Transit (MST), 110 Salinas St. (424-7695), at Central in Salinas. Fare per zone $1.50, seniors and disabled 75¢, ages 5-18 75¢; same-zone transfers free up to 2hr. Bus #20 or 21 will take you to Monterey. See listing for MST in **Monterey: Practical Information,** p. 231.
Road Conditions: (800-427-7623). 24hr.
Emergency: 911
Police: King City (385-8311); other areas of Salinas Valley (755-5111).
Medical Services: Salinas Valley Memorial Hospital, 450 E. Romie Ln. (757-4333), Salinas.
Post Office: Salinas, 100 W. Alisal (758-3823). Open Mon.-Fri. 8:30am-5pm. General delivery at 1011 Post Dr. **ZIP Code:** 93907. **King City,** 123 S. 3rd St. (385-3339), at Bassett. Open Mon.-Fri. 8:30am-4:30pm. **ZIP Code:** 93930.
Area Code: 408.

ACCOMMODATIONS AND CAMPING

As a general rule, the farther south from Salinas you go, the lower prices will be. Salinas is home to several expensive hotels, but the standard chain motels cluster at the airport area off U.S. 101. Other hotels run along N. Main St., including the **El Dorado Motel,** 1351 N. Main St. (449-2442 or 800-523-6506), which offers comfortable and clean rooms with cable TV (doubles $35). Two options in Greenfield are the **Motel Budget Inn,** 452 El Camino (674-5828; doubles $25-32), and the **Greenfield Inn,** 22 4th St. (674-5995; singles $27-32). In King City, try the **Fireside Inn,** 640 Broadway (386-1010). A gargantuan tree grows through the office (doubles $35).

   Camping is only found at **Pinnacles National Monument** (389-4485). The campground is walk-in, but some late-arrivals may land sites bordering the parking lot. The campground has 23 sites, fire pits, restrooms, and picnic tables, so during the spring wildflower season you'll have to fight off daytripping picnickers. (Sites $10 for up to 6 people. Parking fee $5.) East of Pinnacles is **Pinnacles Campground Inc.** (389-4462), a privately owned campground that has 78 tent sites (6-person max.), 15 group sites, 36 RV sites, a pool, flush toilets, and hot showers ($7 per person, 4-night max. stay; electrical hookups $2 extra). All sites are first-come, first-camped. Be warned—there is no road access from the east side of the park to the west side, although it is possible to hike through.

FOOD

Drive in past the fast-food joints lining the freeway and you'll find the greens are always fresh. You'll also find many Mexican joints, which is not surprising given the demographics of the area. **Mi Tierra,** 18 E. Gabilan St. (422-4631), in Salinas, doles out huge portions at low prices—a bean burrito is $2, while a huge combo plate with *chiles rellenos*, an enchilada, rice and beans, salad, and tortillas is $5.25 (open daily 8am-8:30pm). **La Fuente Restaurant,** 101 Oak St. (678-3130), in Soledad, serves up *chiles rellenos* with enchilada ($5.75), well worth your attention (open Mon.-Sat. 11am-9pm, Sun. 9am-9pm). **Fiesta City Cafe,** 246 El Camino Real (647-2837), in Greenfield, is sunny and welcoming with both Mexican- and American-style breakfasts ($5-7; open Mon.-Sat. 6am-8:30pm).

SIGHTS AND ENTERTAINMENT

The town of Salinas salivates over Steinbeck. Photographs, manuscripts, and personal letters are on display at the **Steinbeck Center Foundation,** 371 Main St. (753-6411). The center also offers tours and extensive information on Steinbeck Country (open Mon.-Fri. 10am-4pm, Sat. 10am-2pm). The massive **National Steinbeck Center** (http://www.steinbeck.org) will open in June 1998, bringing 37,000 more square feet of Steinbeck tribute to the world.

   Salinas's biggest non-literary tourist pull is the **California Rodeo Salinas and Intertribal Indian Village.** This rodeo is the fourth-largest in the world, attracting wrestlers, riders, cows, and bulls from across the West in late July. The Indian village showcases the cultures of several tribes. While the rodeo officially lasts for only one weekend, related events—including **cowboy poetry readings**—take place throughout the last three weeks of July. (Tickets are $8-12, season tickets $60-68. Call 757-2951 or 800-549-4989 or write P.O. Box 1648, Salinas, CA 93902 for more info.)

■ Near Salinas: Pinnacles National Monument

Towering dramatically over the chaparral east of Soledad, **Pinnacles National Monument** contains the spectacular remnants of an ancient volcano. Set aside as a national park in 1908, the park preserves the erratic and unique spires and crags that millions of years of weathering carved out of prehistoric lava flows. Thirty miles of hiking trails wind through the park's low chaparral, boulder-strewn caves, and pinnacles of rock; flashlights are required on cave trails. The **High Peaks Trail** runs a strenuous 5¼ mi. across the park between the east and west entrances, and offers amazing views of the surrounding rock formations. For a less exhausting trek, try the **Balconies Trail,** a 1½ mi. promenade from the park's west entrance up to the Balconies Caves. A magnificent array of **wildflowers** bloom in the spring, and the park offers excellent **bird-watching** all year long. Pinnacles has the widest range of wildlife of any park in California, including a number of rare predators: mountain lions, bobcats, coyotes, rattlesnakes, golden eagles, and peregrine falcons. Far from city light sources, with very few clouds, the **night sky** over Pinnacles puts on quite a show. The park entrance (i.e. parking) fee is $5. The park headquarters (389-4485) is at the east side entrance (Rte. 25 to Rte. 146), but friendly rangers also staff a station on the west side (U.S. 101 to Rte. 146).

The **Mission Nuestra Señora de la Soledad,** 36641 Ft. Romie Rd. (678-2586), rests in Soledad, just west of Pinnacles. Constructed in 1791 and aptly named "Our Lady of Solitude," the mission is in the middle of a quiet valley. Floods destroyed the building several times, but it was restored in the 1950s, and today a small museum exhibits various artifacts. An annual fiesta is held the last Sunday in October, and the annual barbecue takes place on the last Sunday in June (mission open Wed.-Mon. 9am-4pm). For more info, see **A Man with a Mission** (p. 54).

■ Santa Cruz

Santa Cruz sports the kind of uncalculated hipness that other coastal towns dream about. The city was born as one of Father Serra's missions in 1791 (the name means "holy cross"), but today, Santa Cruz is nothing if not liberal. One of the few places where the old 60s catch-phrase "do your own thing" still applies, it simultaneously embraces macho surfers, a large lesbian community, and Neil Young, who lives in the hills surrounding the town. Santa Cruz's prime location is crucial to its identity: without a beach, it would be Berkeley; with a better one, it would be Ft. Lauderdale.

If you find yourself thinking Santa Cruz is the land of milk and honey, you're not alone. The atmosphere here is fun-loving but far from hedonistic, intellectual but not even close to stuffy. This small city has enough Northern California cool and Southern California fun for everyone, whether you want to pig out on cotton candy while riding the ferris wheel or sip soy milk while attending a poetry reading. Along the beach and the boardwalk, tourism and surf culture reign supreme. On the other side of Front St., UC Santa Cruz takes over. Restaurants offer avocado sandwiches and industrial coffee; merchants hawk UCSC paraphernalia alongside flyers for courses which query "Should you kill your superego?" Whatever your fancy, check out the comprehensive listings in *Good Times* or *Metro Santa Cruz.*

PRACTICAL INFORMATION

Visitor Information:
Santa Cruz County Conference and Visitor Council, 701 Front St. (425-1234 or 800-833-3494; http://www.infopoint.com/sc/cvc). Extremely helpful staff. Publishes the free *Traveler's, Dining,* and *Accommodations Guides.* Open Mon.-

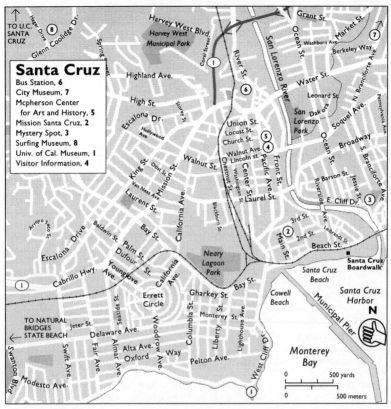

Santa Cruz

Bus Station, 6
City Museum, 7
Mcpherson Center
  for Art and History, 5
Mission Santa Cruz, 2
Mystery Spot, 3
Surfing Museum, 8
Univ. of Cal. Museum, 1
Visitor Information, 4

Sat. 9am-5pm, Sun. 10am-4pm. An **information kiosk** sits at the top of Rte. 17 next to the Summit Inn Restaurant (open daily 10am-4pm).

  California Parks and Recreation Department, 600 Ocean St. (429-2850), across from Holiday Inn. Camping and beach info for state-maintained area facilities in Santa Cruz district. Open Mon.-Fri. 8am-5pm

Trains: Santa Cruz Train Connector (800-872-7245).

Buses: Greyhound/Peerless Stages, 425 Front St. (423-1800 or 800-231-2222). Three buses per day to San Francisco ($13), and L.A. via Salinas ($51). Open daily 7-11am and 1-7pm.

Public Transportation: Santa Cruz Metropolitan Transit District (SCMTD), 920 Pacific Ave. (425-8600, TDD 425-8993; http://www.scmtd.com), at the Metro Center in the middle of the Pacific Garden Mall. The free *Headways* has route info. Fare $1, seniors and disabled 40¢, under 46in. free; day pass $3, $1.10, free. Info line open Mon.-Fri. 8am-5pm. Buses run daily 7am-10pm.

Taxis: Yellow Cab, 423-1234. Initial fee $2.25, each additional mi. $2. Open 24hr.

Bike Rental: The Bicycle Rental Center, 131 Center St. (426-8687), at Laurel. Rents 21-speed mountain/road hybrids, tandems, children's bikes. Bikes $7 for first hr., $2 each additional ½hr.; $25 per day; $50 for 3 days; $75 per week. Helmets and locks provided. Open daily 10am-6pm; winter 10am-5pm.

Library: 224 Church St. (429-3526). Has a lot of books and stuff. Open Tues.-Thurs. 10am-8pm, Fri.-Sat. 10am-5pm.

Laundromat: Washrock, 135 Laurel St. (471-0555), next to Kinko's. Laundry with lattes ($2.20) and a loft lounge for lingering. Has some washing machine things. Wash $1.25, 10min. dry 25¢. 24hr.

Bi-Gay-Lesbian Organizations: Lesbian, Gay, Bisexual, and Transgender Community Center, 1328 Commerce Ln. (425-5422), ½ block north of Pacific Garden Mall. Publishes *Manifesto* and distributes the *Lavender Reader,* an excellent quarterly journal. Supplies info about events, outings, and general concerns. Usually open daily noon-8pm (call before visiting).

Weather Conditions: (429-3460). Operated by County Beach lifeguards Memorial Day through Labor Day, plus weekends in spring and fall.

Crisis Lines: Women's Crisis Line (429-1478). 24hr.

Medical Services: Santa Cruz Dominican Hospital, 1555 Soquel Dr. (462-7700). Take bus #71 on Soquel Ave. from the Metro Center. 24hr.

Emergency: 911.

Police: 809 Center St. (429-3911). 24hr.

Post Office: 850 Front St. (426-5200). Open Mon.-Fri. 8:30am-5pm. Sat. 9am-4pm. **ZIP Code:** 95060.

Area Code: 408.

ORIENTATION

Santa Cruz is on the northern lip of Monterey Bay, two hours south of San Francisco on **U.S. 101** or the more scenic **Hwy. 1.** In town, **Beach Street** runs roughly east-west. The narrow San Lorenzo River runs mainly north-south, dividing the boardwalk scene from quiet, affluent residences. Along the beach and the boardwalk, tourism and surf culture reign supreme. On the other side of Front St., UC Santa Cruz takes over. One-way and resident-traffic-only zones, closed-off ends, and streets that curve, merge, and converge every which way make Santa Cruz highly frustrating to navigate by car, and even by foot. Park at a motel or in free two-hour public lots off Pacific Ave. to avoid the cash-guzzling, beach-vicinity lots and meters.

ACCOMMODATIONS

Like many beach towns, Santa Cruz gets packed solid during the summer, especially on weekends. Room rates skyrocket and availability plummets. Reservations are always recommended. Shop around—price fluctuation can be outrageous. Sleeping on the beach is strictly forbidden and can result in hefty fines.

Carmelita Cottage Santa Cruz Hostel (HI-AYH), 321 Main St. (423-8304), 4 blocks from the Greyhound stop and 2 blocks from the beach. Centrally located, but in a quiet neighborhood, this 32-bed Victorian hostel is run by a friendly staff. Two kitchens, common room, cyclery for bike storage and repair; parking available. In July-Aug., 3-night max. stay and members only (memberships available for purchase). Strict curfew 11pm. Reception open daily 8-10am and 5-10pm. Chore required. Dorms $13-15. Send reservation requests, first night's deposit, and SASE to P.O. Box 1241, Santa Cruz 95061 at least 2 weeks in advance.

Harbor Inn, 645 7th Ave. (479-9731), near the harbor and a few blocks north of Eaton. A beautiful 22-bed hotel well off the main drag. Rooms have queen beds, microwaves, and fridges. Check-out 11am. Check-in until 11pm; call to arrange late check-in. Rooms $45, with private bath $65. Weekends: $65, $85. Summer prices are $10 more. Reservations recommended.

Sunny Cove Beach Motel, 2-1610 E. Cliff Dr. (475-1741), near Schwan Lagoon. Far from downtown, but charming, well-kept suites have kitchens. Rooms $40, weekends $70-80. Summer: $50-90. Weekly rates available.

Villager Lodge, 510 Leibrant Ave. (423-6020), 2 blocks from the beach. Heated pool, TVs, and kitchens. Rooms from $39, weekends $70 and up. AAA discounts.

CAMPING

Reservations for all state campgrounds can be made through DESTINET (800-444-7275) and should be made early. Sites below are listed geographically, moving north toward Santa Cruz. New Brighton State Beach and Big Basin Redwoods State Park, the most scenic spots, are both accessible by public transportation. Campground fees are not cheap (June-Sept. Sun.-Thurs. $17, Fri.-Sat. $18; Oct.-May $16).

Sunset State Beach (763-7063), 12mi. south of Santa Cruz on Hwy. 1. Take San Andreas Rd. and exit right to Sunset Beach Rd. Ninety sites near the beach. Not as nice as New Brighton, but far superior to RV-choked Seacliff State Beach. No hookups. Reservations highly recommended in summer.

Manresa Uplands State Beach Park (761-1795), 10mi. south of Santa Cruz. Take Hwy. 1 and exit at Larkin Valley. Veer right and follow San Andreas for 4mi., then turn right on Sand Dollar. 64 tent sites overlook the ocean. Sheltered beach sometimes guarded. Wheelchair accessible. Seniors $1 off. Day use $6 per car.

New Brighton State Beach (464-6329), 4mi. south of Santa Cruz off Hwy. 1. Take SCMDT bus #54 "Aptos." Located on a coastal bluff, wave breakers murmur to 112 sites (4 bike sites, 2 wheelchair-accessible sites), and the best-looking rangers on the coast. RV sites available (check-out 9am). Showers get crowded 7-9am. 7-night max. stay, off-season 15-night max. stay. No hookups. Check-out noon. Seniors $2 off. Reservations required mid-March to Nov.

Henry Cowell Redwoods State Park, 101 N. Big Trees Park Rd. (438-2396), 2½mi. southeast of Felton. Take Graham Hill Rd. or SCMDT bus #34, 35, or 30. Quiet campgrounds have 113 sites in summer, 50 in winter. Visit the observation deck (½mi. hike) for a good look at the redwoods. Watch out for the rampant poison oak! Hot showers (25¢ for 2min.), fire pits, picnic tables, food lockers. No hookups. One-week max. stay, off-season 15 days.

Big Basin Redwoods State Park (338-8860 or 800-874-8688), 10mi. north of Boulder Creek. Go north on Rte. 9 to Rte. 236. This spectacular park was the first in the California State Park system. Today it offers the best camping between Point Reyes and Big Sur. Mountain air and dark red trees, some over 2000 years old. In addition to 147 campsites with showers, there are 35 tent cabins, and 80mi. of trails, including the 2-day Skyline-to-the-Sea Trail. Backcountry camping $7 per person. Parking $5 per night. Reservations required in summer.

FOOD

Santa Cruz offers an astounding number of budget eateries in various locations, especially by the beach at Capitola. Fresh local produce sells at the **farmer's market** at Cedar and Lincoln in downtown (Wed. 2:30-6:30pm).

Saturn Cafe, 1230 Mission St. (429-8505). A trek from downtown, but you'll be rewarded with vegetarian meals at their Santa Cruz best (most under $6). Every dish is a winner, every smoothie a joy. Wear a wig on Wed. and get 2-for-1 meals. Open Sun.-Thurs. noon-midnight, Fri.-Sat. noon-1am.

Royal Taj, 270 Soquel Ave. (427-2400), at Roberts. You'll be crying *namaste* (I bow to you) after being treated like a king (with food to match) at this Indian restaurant. Daily lunch buffet $6.50. Meat dishes $6-9. Veggie specialties $6. Stellar *lassi* $2. Open daily 11:30am-2:30pm and 5:30-10pm.

Taquería Vallarta I, 608 Soquel Ave. (457-8226). Outstanding Mexican manna. Order at the counter, and the food might beat you back to your chair. Vegetarian plate $4; mind-blowing *aguas fresca* $1.20. Open daily 10am-midnight.

Zoccoli's, the Italian Delicatessen, 1534 Pacific (423-1711), across from the post office. Their made-to-order "special sandwiches" ($4-5) really and truly are special. Daily pasta specials (about $5) come with salad, garlic bread, cheese, and a cookie. Only the freshest ingredients. Open Mon.-Sat. 9am-6pm, Sun. 11am-5pm.

Walnut Ave. Cafe, 106 Walnut Ave. (457-2804; fax 457-9689), at Pacific. All-day breakfasts; try the *chilauiles,* which has 3 eggs scrambled with tortilla chips, chiles, olives, tomatoes, onions, and cheese ($5.25). Anchor Steam $2.50. Vegan friendly. Open Mon.-Fri. 7am-4pm, Sat.-Sun. 8am-4pm.

SIGHTS AND ACTIVITIES

Santa Cruz averages 300 sunshine-filled days per year, but the water remains very cold, and without wetsuits for warmth many casual beachgoers catch their thrills on the **Santa Cruz Boardwalk.** The three-block-long strip of over 25 amusement park rides, guess-your-weight booths, shooting galleries, and caramel apple vendors provides a loud and lively diversion—one that seems to attract every sun-drenched family, couple, and roving pack of teenagers in California. The arcade stocks over 200 old and new video games. Highly recommended is the Big Dipper, a 1924 wooden tower roller coaster ($3). Built more recently is the New Venturer, a "virtual" coaster set on an alien landscape. (Open daily Memorial Day-Labor Day, plus a few weekends and holidays. Rides $1.50-3; all-day $19; some height restrictions.)

The **Santa Cruz Beach** (officially named Cowell Beach) itself is broad, fairly dirty, and generally packed with volleyball players. Jutting off Beach St. is the **Santa Cruz Wharf,** the **longest car-accessible pier on the West Coast** (parking $1 per hr., under 30min. free; disabled patrons free). If you're seeking solitude, try the chillier banks of the San Lorenzo River immediately east of the boardwalk. Folks wanting to exercise their right to bare everything should head north on Hwy. 1 to the **Red White and Blue Beach,** just south of Davenport (look for the line of cars to your right; parking $7), but do not venture here alone. If averse to paying for the privilege of an all-over tan, try the **Bonny Doon Beach,** off Hwy. 1 at Bonny Doon Rd., 11 mi. north of Santa Cruz. Magnificent cliffs and rocks surround this windy and frequently deserted spot. Eighteen other local beaches are listed in the Santa Cruz *Traveler's Guide,* available at the visitors center (see **Practical Information, p. 238**). To try your hand at riding the waves, contact the **Richard Schmidt Surf School** (423-0928). Schmidt is much-respected by the locals, who say (in hushed tones) that he can get anyone surfing (1hr. private lesson $50, 2hr. lesson $75; includes equipment). The best vantage points for watching surfers learn the trade are along W. Cliff Dr., which runs north-south along the shore all the way down to the **Santa Cruz Surfing Museum** (429-3429), at the end of the point. Opened in 1986, the museum was the first of its kind. The main room of the lighthouse displays vintage artifacts, photos, and videos, while the tower contains the ashes of Mark Abbott, a local surfer who drowned in 1965; his parents donated the museum to the city (open Mon. and Wed.-Fri. noon-4pm, Sat.-Sun. noon-5pm; free). **Steamer Lane** is the popular name for the deep off the point, where surfers have flocked since Hawaiian "Duke" Nakahuraka kick-started California's surf culture here 100 years ago. The **Surfer Statue,** a monument "dedicated to all surfers, past, present, and future," is just southwest of the museum. The neck of this inspirational figure, erected in 1992, is often graced with a *lei.*

Around the point at the end of W. Cliff Dr. is **Natural Bridges State Park** (423-4609). While its lone natural bridge has collapsed, the park nevertheless offers a beach, awesome tidepools, and tours during Monarch butterfly season (Oct.-March). During November and December thousands of the stunning *lepidoptera* swarm along the beach (open daily 8am-sunset; parking $6, seniors $5).

Alternatives to the shoreside scene include two museums. The downtown **Museum of Art and History (MAH),** 705 Front St. (429-1964), near the visitors center, features local artists (open Tues.-Thurs. and Sat.-Sun. noon-5pm, Fri. noon-7pm; free). The **Santa Cruz City Museum of Natural History,** 1305 E. Cliff Dr. (429-3773), across the San Lorenzo River from the boardwalk at Pilkington, has exhibits on local geology and biology (open Tues.-Sun. 10am-5pm; free). **Misión de Exaltación de la Santa Cruz,** 126 High St. (turn north onto Emmet off Mission), was a later Christian outpost in California. The peaceful, fragrant church allows some contemplative quiet (open Tues.-Sat. 10am-4pm, Sun. 10am-2pm; donation requested).

Five miles northwest of downtown sprawls the 2000-acre **University of California at Santa Cruz (UCSC)** campus. The campus is accessible by bus #1, auto, and bicycle. Then-governor Ronald Reagan's plan to make UCSC a "riot-proof campus" (i.e. without a central point where radicals could inflame a crowd) when it was built in the late 60s, had a happy effect on its appearance. University buildings sit uncrowded amid spectacular rolling hills and redwood groves, but Santa Cruz is still famous (or infamous) for leftist politics. The curriculum offers such unique programs as "The History of Consciousness." Once the "safety school" of the UC system, UCSC now regularly turns away scores of aspiring Slugs (the school mascot is the banana slug). Student-led tours of the campus are available by reservation only (429-2231; open Mon.-Fri. 8am-5pm). If you drive on weekdays, make sure you have a parking permit. Trails behind the campus are perfect for day hikes, but it is not safe to go alone (parking permits and maps available at the police station). The UCSC arboretum is one of the finest in the state (open daily 9am-5pm; free).

Outdoor sports enthusiasts will find ample activities in Santa Cruz—parasailing and other pricey pastimes are popular on the wharf. Rent ocean-going **kayaks** at the **Kayak Connection,** 413 Lake Ave. (479-1121). An open deck single rents for $33 per day, a closed deck single for $48. Rentals include paddle, life jacket, and a skirt or wetsuit (open Mon.-Fri. 10am-6pm, Sat.-Sun. 8:30am-6pm; 4½hr. lessons $40). You can try **rock climbing** at North America's largest climbing gym, **Pacific Edge,** 104 Bronson St. (454-9254; open Mon. 5am-10pm, Tues. and Thurs. 9am-10pm, Wed. and Fri. 11am-10pm, Sat.-Sun. 10am-7pm; day pass $12).

ENTERTAINMENT AND NIGHTLIFE

Dodge the underage hipsters parked on the sidewalks of Pacific in order to cruise into the Santa Cruzian nightlife. The free weekly *Good Times* has a reputation for very thorough listings. The Boardwalk bandstand offers free Friday night concerts. The Santa Cruz Parks and Recreation Department (see **Practical Information,** p. 238) publishes a free *Summer Activity Guide.*

Kuumbwa Jazz Center, 320-322 Cedar St. (427-2227; http://www.jazznet.com/kuumbwa). Known throughout the region for great jazz and innovative off-night programs. Under 21derlings are welcome in this small and low-key setting. The big names play here on Mon.; the locals have their turn on Fri. Tickets (about $5) sell through Logos Books and Music, 1117 Pacific (427-5100; open daily 10am-10pm), as well as BASS outlets (998-BASS/2277). Most shows around 8pm.

Blue Lagoon, 923 Pacific Ave. (423-7117). Mega-popular gay-straight club has won all awards from "best bartender" to "best place you can't take your parents" from the local press. Bar in front, 3 pool tables in back, and people dancing everywhere. Cover $1-3, Mon. and Wed free. Happy Hour daily 8-10pm. Stronger-than-the-bouncer drinks $1.75-3. Open daily 4pm-2am.

The Poet and Patriot, 320 E. Cedar St. (426-8620), next to Kuumbwa. Low-key Irish pub hosts a cheerful young crowd. Hoist a Black-and-Tan in the amicable front room or play darts in the back. Open daily noon-2am.

The Silver Bullet, 603 Front St. (426-5726), at Soquel. Eclectic jukebox tunes. Specials are really something: $1 pints every Wed., $2 Bloody Marys every Sun. Happy Hour daily 5-7pm. Open daily 10am-2am.

The Catalyst, 1011 Pacific Ave. (423-1336). Boisterous beach bar and dance club draws national, college, and local bands. Pool and darts upstairs, deli and bar downstairs. Sandwiches $2-5. Shows Wed.-Sat. Must be 21. Cover for local bands $1, for bigger acts $5-20. Open Mon.-Sat. 9am-2am, Sun. 9am-5pm; food served Sun.-Tues. until 3pm, Wed.-Sat. until 10pm.

SEASONAL EVENTS

Whale-watching season (425-1234), Dec.-March. Boats depart from the Santa Cruz Municipal Wharf. Trips range from $5-30, and some guarantee sightings.

Monarch Migration Festival (423-4609), early Feb. The largest monarch colony in the West checks out of Natural Bridges State Beach. Catch their return mid-Oct.

Clam Chowder Cook-Off and Great Chowder Chase (429-3477), late Feb.

Santa Cruz Blues Festival (479-9814), 2 days in late May. Big-name blues.

Surf City Classic (429-3477), late June. 50s and 60s theme music and food as well as "woodies on the wharf." Lots of classic wood-paneled cars.

Lesbian, Gay, Bisexual, Transgender Pride Day (425-5422), first Sun. in June. Now in its 24th year. Parade, music, speakers.

Shakespeare Santa Cruz (459-2121), July and Aug., UCSC. Nationally acclaimed, innovative outdoor festival. All-show passes available.

Santa Cruz Hot and Cool Jazz Fest (728-8760), 3 days at the end of July. Jazz artists from the West play in 4 venues along the beach.

CENTRAL COAST

National Nude Weekend (353-2250), mid-July. Celebrated at the Lupin Naturalist Club in the Santa Cruz Mountains. Enjoy bands (playing in the buff) or come paint the posing models (on canvas). Free, but reservations are required.

Cabrillo Music Festival (426-6966), first 2 weeks in Aug. Held in the civic auditorium, the festival brings contemporary and classical music to the Central Coast. It's hard to get tickets ($16-25), so reserve well in advance.

■ Near Santa Cruz

Santa Cruz is surrounded by gently sloping hills that make hiking a delight; the paths are only mildly strenuous and the scenery is magnificent. To the north, **Big Basin Redwoods State Park,** the first and some say the best of California state parks, offers trails novices can enjoy. Farther to the south, the gorgeous **Henry Cowell Redwoods State Park** (see **Santa Cruz Camping,** p. 240) has trails suitable for daytrips.

The **Roaring Camp and Big Trees Narrow Gauge Railroad** (335-4484), Graham Hill Rd., in Felton, runs an old steam-powered passenger train on a spectacularly scenic route from Felton through the redwoods to Bear Mountain (round-trip fare $13, ages 3-13 $9), and holds seasonal historic celebrations. To reach Felton, take Rte. 9, which passes through Henry Cowell Redwoods State Park. In Felton, take Graham Hill Rd. southeast and bear south to Roaring Camp as indicated by road signs.

The **Mystery Spot,** 1953 Branciforte Dr. (423-8897), 3 mi. northeast of Santa Cruz, draws in hordes of international tourists and deliberately and joyously messes with their heads. Its owners play up the effects of the spot's magnetic disturbance with gambits like a tilted house and golf ball tricks. Photography and video encouraged. To get there, take Ocean to Water and turn onto Market, which becomes Branciforte. (Open daily 9am-8:30pm, in winter 9am-4:30pm. Tours leave about every ½hr. Admission $4, ages 5-11 $2.)

San Francisco

San Francisco has an iconic charm. The images are familiar: fog, cable cars, seagulls, Victorian homes, narrow hillside streets, and, of course, that gem in the city's crown, the Golden Gate Bridge. San Fran is somewhat of an American museum piece—not an industrial center, but instead a preserved landscape, physically dating from the early part of this century but spiritually centered around the mid-century, when the hippie revolution rocked the coast. This photogenic landscape does not need to be air-brushed for postcards—it has an aesthetic all its own, an image of "the old days" that has captured the American imagination.

The old days were important here. As the last stop in the colossal Westward Expansion, San Francisco has always been a place where Americans realized their dreams or gave them up forever. Gold miners came through here on their way inland, and almost a century later dreamers continued to follow in their footsteps, forging a modern voice for the "City by the Bay."

The first shouts came in the 50s from the Beat Generation, whose poetic musings combined be-bop rhythms and Buddhist philosophy. The more publicized hippie generation took over a decade later and their liberal, feel-good mantras echoed throughout the country during 1967's "Summer of Love." Today, the city's inhabitants, from cyber-junkies to eco-scenesters, are recycling versions of soul-seeking earlier days. Anti-establishment politics have become almost establishment here, and the spiritual beat has in many ways died, choked by its own trappings.

The challenge now is to keep San Francisco's soul alive. It is the diversity of San Francisco's inhabitants who pump energy into the heart of the city. Community here is defined by heterogeneity—influxes of Central American refugees and Asian immigrants have made San Francisco one of the most racially diverse cities in the U.S. The gay community, now one-sixth of the city's population, emerged in the 70s as one of the city's most visible groups and is still a powerful influence. A persistent pulse can be felt in this cosmopolitan conglomeration of neighborhoods, where a fascinating street culture unfolds. The flowers may be gone, but the power lives on.

■ Practical Information

Visitor Information:

Visitor Information Center, Hallidie Plaza, 900 Market St. (391-2000), at Powell beneath street level in Benjamin Swig Pavilion at the exit of the Powell St. BART stop. Wide range of informational brochures covering area tours, services, and attractions. MUNI passports and maps for sale. Informational recordings in French (391-2003), German (391-2004), Japanese (391-2101), and Spanish (391-2122). Open Mon.-Fri. 9am-5:30pm, Sat. 9am-3pm, Sun. 10am-2pm (off-season 10am-3pm); telephone inquiries accepted Mon.-Fri. 8:30am-5pm.

Redwood Empire Association, 2801 Leavenworth St. (394-5991, outside California 888-678-8509; http://www.redwoodempire.com), Fisherman's Wharf. Selection of maps and brochures, including a free, 48-page guide to the area between San Francisco and Oregon. Open Tues.-Sat. 10am-6pm.

California Welcome Center, Pier 39 (956-3493), in the lobby of the Citibank Cinemax Theater. This state-of-the-art facility carries the mother lode of glossy area guides and brochures. Commercially oriented, the center welcomes advertisements more than curious tourists, but it's a great place to stock up on cheesy postcards (15¢) and free state-wide promotional materials.

Budget Travel: American Youth Hostels Travel Center, 308 Mason St. (788-2525; fax 788-2558), between Geary and O'Farrell St., next door to the Hostel at Union Square. Books and maps available for purchase. HI-AYH members receive 10% discount. Hostel reservations made. Open Tues.-Sat. noon-6pm.

Consulates: Australia, 1 Bush St. #700 (362-6160), at Market. Open Mon.-Fri. 8:45am-5pm. **France,** 540 Bush St. (397-4330), at Stockton. Open Mon.-Fri. 9am-

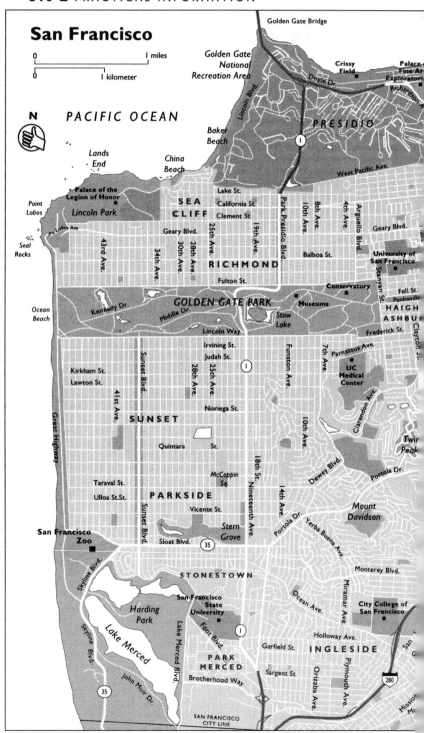

San Francisco

0 ————————————— 1 miles
0 ————————————— 1 kilometer

N

PACIFIC OCEAN

Golden Gate Bridge

Golden Gate
National
Recreation Area

Doyle Dr.

Crissy
Field

Palace
Fine Ar
Exploratori.

Richardson A

Lincoln Blvd.

Baker
Beach

PRESIDIO

West Pacific Ave.

Lands
End

China
Beach

Palace of the
Legion of Honor

Lincoln Park

Point
Lobos

Seal
Rocks

Ocean
Beach

Pt. Lobos Ave.

43rd Ave.

34th Ave.

30th Ave.

28th Ave.

25th Ave.

19th Ave.

Lake St.

California St.

Clement St.

Geary Blvd.

Fulton St.

SEA
CLIFF

RICHMOND

Park Presidio Blvd.

10th Ave.

8th Ave.

4th Ave.

Arguello Blvd.

Balboa St.

Geary Blvd.

University of
San Francisco

Stanyan St.

Conservatory

Fell St.

Panhandle

HAIGH
ASHBU

Clayton St.

GOLDEN GATE PARK

Kennedy Dr.

Middle Dr.

Lincoln Way

Stow
Lake

Museums

Frederick St.

Great Highway

Sunset Blvd.

Kirkham St.

Lawton St.

41st Ave.

28th Ave.

25th Ave.

Irving St.

Judah St.

Noriega St.

Funston Ave.

7th Ave.

Parnassus Ave.

UC
Medical
Center

Clarendon Ave.

SUNSET

Quintara   St.

Taraval St.

Ulloa St.St.

PARKSIDE

Sunset Blvd.

McCoppin
Sq.

Vicente St.

Stern
Grove

Sloat Blvd.

18th St.
Nineteenth Ave.

14th Ave.

10th Ave.

Dewey Blvd.

Twir
Peak

Mount
Davidson

Portola Dr.

Portola Dr.

Yerba Buena Ave.

35

San Francisco
Zoo

Skyline Blvd.

Harding
Park

Lake Merced

Skyline Blvd.

Lake Merced Blvd.

San Francisco
State
University

Font Blvd.

1

STONESTOWN

Monterey Blvd.

Ocean Ave.

Miramar Ave.

City College of
San Francisco

280

San

INGLESIDE

Holloway Ave.

Garfield St.

Orizaba Ave.

Plymouth Ave.

PARK
MERCED

Brotherhood Way

Sargent St.

35

John Muir Dr.

SAN FRANCISCO
CITY LINE

Mission

TO ALCATRAZ
Pier 39

Marina Park

San Francisco Bay

Fisherman's Wharf

Marina Blvd.
Beach St.
Columbus Ave.
Powell St.
Taylor St.
MARINA
Fort Mason
Bay St.
TELEGRAPH HILL
Coit Tower
Chestnut St.
Lombard St.
Van Ness Ave.
Franklin St.
Kearny St.
Montgomery St.
The Embarcadero
San Francisco - Oakland Bay Bridge
101
PACIFIC HEIGHTS
Union St.
Broadway
RUSSIAN HILL
NORTH BEACH
CHINATOWN
Jackson Square
Ferry Building
Pacific Ave.
Washington St.
Transamerica Pyramid
80
Lafayette Park
California St.
Alta Park
JAPAN-TOWN
NOB HILL
Transbay Terminal
Main St.
California St.
Hyde St.
Union Square
Pine St.
Bush St.
Gough St.
101
Larkin
Geary St.
Visitor's Information
2nd St.
Divisadero St.
Geary Expressway
Turk St.
Mission St.
Market St.
Howard St.
3rd St.
Turk St.
Golden Gate Ave.
Steiner St.
Laguna St.
SOMA
8th St.
6th St.
4th St.
5th St.
WESTERN ADDITION
Alamo Square
9th St.
Folsom St.
Brannan St.
Townsend
Berry
China Basin
Oak St.
Haight St.
10th St.
Harrison St.
7th St.
King St.
Buena Vista Park
Duboce Ave.
Central Freeway
CHINA BASIN
Central Basin
101
16th St.
280
Castro St.
Market St.
Treat Ave.
Potrero St.
3rd St.
Mission Dolores
Mariposa St.
Indiana St.
Mission Dolores Park
MISSION
20th St.
20th St.
CASTRO
Diamond St.
Noe St.
S. Van Ness Ave.
Harrison St.
101
Clipper St.
Dolores St.
Guerrero St.
Valencia St.
25th St.
SF General Hospital
POTRERO
NOE VALLEY
Army St.
Army St.
30th St.
Mission St.
San Jose Ave.
Bernal Heights Park
Jerrold St.
Toland St.
BAY VIEW
Cortland Ave.
Quint St.
3rd St.
Mendell St.
Evans Ave.
Bosworth St.
Park St.
280
Oakdale Ave.
India Basin
Fwy.
Alemany Blvd.
Industrial
Innes Ave.
Southern
Silver Ave.
Thornton Ave.
Revere Ave.
Alemany Blvd.
GLEN PARK
Felton Ave.
Hamilton St.
Bayshore Fwy.
3rd St.
HUNTERS POINT
Mission St.
Excelsior Ave.
University St.
Ingalls
Carroll Ave.
Persia Ave.
John McLaren Park
Mansell St.
Jennings
Gilman Ave.
South Basin
France Ave.
Moscow Ave.
101
VISITACION VALLEY
Jamestown Ave.
Fitch St.
Cordova
Visitacion Ave.
Sunnydale Ave.
TO AIRPORT
Candlestick Park
Candlestick Point Recreation Area

1pm. **Germany,** 1960 Jackson St. (775-1061). Open Mon.-Fri. 9am-12:30pm. **Ireland,** 44 Montgomery St. #3830 (392-4214). Open Mon.-Fri. 9am-noon and 2-4pm. **Japan,** 50 Fremont St., 23rd fl. (777-3533), at Mission. Open Mon.-Fri. 9:30am-noon and 1:30-4:30pm. **UK,** 1 Sansome St. #850 (981-3030), at Market. Open Mon.-Fri. 9am-1pm and 2-4pm. For all visas, arrive at the consulate before opening time or else face a long line.

Currency Exchange: Bank of America (BOA), 345 Montgomery St. (622-2451), between California and Pine. These are a dime a dozen. Commission varies. Cash advanced against major credit cards. Open Mon.-Fri. 9am-6pm. **BOA airport branch** (742-8079), in the International Terminal. Open daily 7am-11pm. **Pacific Foreign Exchange Inc.,** 527 Sutter St. (391-2548), near Powell. No commission. Open Mon.-Fri. 9am-6pm, Sat. 10am-3pm. **Foreign Exchange Ltd.,** 415 Stockton St. (397-4700), near Sutter. No commission. Open Mon.-Fri. 9am-5:30pm, April-Sept. also Sat. 10am-4pm.

Taxis: Yellow Cab (626-2345). **Luxor Cab** (282-4141). **DeSoto Cab** (673-1414). Initial charge $1.70, each additional mi. $1.80. You can call for pickup, but it's usually just as easy to hail a cab on the street. 24hr. service.

Car Rental: Ace, 415 Taylor St. (771-7711), near Geary Blvd. Compacts from $29 per day (150 free mi.), $149 per week (1050 free mi.). Must be 21; drivers under 25 pay $5 per day surcharge. **Enterprise** (800-RENT-A-CAR/736-8222 in San Francisco, 800-325-8007 outside city) has city-wide branches and will do pick-ups. Must be 21; drivers under 25 pay $10 per day surcharge. Compacts $36 per day, $189 per week. Unlimited free mi. within California. Weekend specials.

Bike Rental: American Rentals, 2715 Hyde St. (931-0234; http://www.americanrental.com), at Beach St. by Fisherman's Wharf. Bikes $5 per hr., tandem bikes $8 per hr., scooters from $45 per day, motorcycles from $150 per day. Open daily 9am-9pm. **Golden Gate Rentals,** 990 Columbus Ave. (351-1188), at Chestnut St., rents bikes ($4 per hr.) and in-line skates.

Library: Civic Center Public Library, Larkin St. (557-4400), between Grove and Fulton St. Take MUNI #5, 21, or 67. This hyper-modern, earthquake-proof structure has attracted much attention since its 1996 opening, and is just now beginning to show signs of wear. Architecture junkies will delight in the shiny elevators and dizzying steps to the 6th floor. Visitors can browse the shelves for books and the basement cafe for baked goods. California residents can sign out books for free; visitors pay $25 for 3-month privileges (you can avoid the charge by showing mail addressed to you at a local street address). Open Mon. 10am-6pm, Tues.-Thurs. 9am-8pm, Fri. 11am-5pm, Sat. 9am-5pm, Sun. noon-5pm.

Cultural and Community Centers:

Booker T. Washington Community Center (African-American), 800 Presidio Blvd. (928-1430), at Geary. Educational, cultural, and recreational programs. Open daily 11am-7pm.

Chinese Culture Center, 750 Kearny St., 3rd fl. of Holiday Inn (986-1822), at Washington. Info on Chinese community events, cultural programs, and Chinatown walking tours (see **Chinatown,** p. 280). Open Tues.-Sat. 10am-4pm.

Japanese Cultural & Community Center of Northern California, 1840 Sutter St. (567-5505), between Buchanan and Webster. Open Mon.-Fri. 9am-10pm.

Jewish Community Information and Referral, 121 Steuart St. (777-4545). Information on religious services, kosher restaurants, and community events. Open Mon.-Fri. 9am-5pm. In case of emergency, call the Jewish Family and Children Service (567-8860) until 5pm, and the Board of Rabbis (788-3630) after 5pm.

Mission Cultural Center (Latino), 2868 Mission St. (821-1155), between 24th and 25th. Take MUNI #14. Art, info, and cultural exhibits (see **The Mission,** p. 263). Open Tues. 10am-4pm, Wed.-Fri. 10am-6pm, Sat.-Sun. 11am-4pm.

San Francisco Senior Center, 481 O'Farrell St. (771-7950), between Jones and Taylor St. Special events, lunches, dances, art workshops, and films for the over-60 crowd. Open Mon.-Thurs. 9am-4pm, Fri. 9am-3:30pm, Sat.-Sun. 10am-2pm.

Women's Building of the Bay Area, 3543 18th St. (431-1180). Neighborhood and women's center. Tours, info, and referral service. Open daily 9am-5pm.

Bi-Gay-Lesbian Organization: Gay Switchboard & Counseling Services, 2712 Telegraph Ave. (510-548-8283), at Derby in Berkeley. Surprisingly, there is not yet a counterpart in San Francisco. Counseling and info on gay community events, housing, local clubs, etc. *Very* helpful staff. Open Mon.-Fri. 10am-10pm, Sat. noon-4pm, Sun. 6-9pm.

Ticket Agencies: TIX Bay Area, 251 Stockton St. (433-7827), at Union Square Tickets to concerts, clubs, plays, and sports. Half-price tickets often available on day of show (cash only; inquire in person) and on Sat. for Sun.-Mon. events. Carries travel passes and tourist info. Open Tues.-Thurs. 11am-6pm, Fri.-Sat. 11am-7pm. TIX is the full-service downtown outlet of **BASS Tickets** (510-762-2277, 776-1999, or 800-225-2277). Other outlets include **Tower Records,** at Bay St. and Columbus Ave., and **Giants Dugout,** 4 Embarcadero Center. Phones open 24hr.

Laundromats: Brainwash, 1122 Folsom St. (861-3663 or 431-3663), between 7th and 8th, in SoMa. Painfully self-aware combo of restaurant, coffeehouse, live music venue, and laundromat. Sure, work yourself into a lather over the marketing genius here, but your just-washed clothes might smell more like stale beer than fabric softener. Cappuccino $1.50, "Wash-Day Blues" blueberry pancakes $4.75. Live bands Wed., Fri., and Sat. Oh yeah, wash ($1.50) and dry (25¢ for 8min.) services. Open Sun.-Thurs. 7:30am-11pm (last wash 10:30pm), Fri.-Sat. 7:30am-1am (last wash 11pm). **Doo Wash,** 817 Columbus Ave. (885-1222), near Lombard. The happy medium for soaping up and chilling out. Video games, pinball machines, pool table, and TV. Sandwiches and espresso drinks ($3-4) in the foyer. Doo your wash ($1.25) and dry ($1 for 1hr.). Discounts when you buy multiple tokens. Open daily 7am-11pm (last load 9:30pm).

Road Conditions: CalTrans Highway Information Network (557-3755; 916-445-1534 for cave-dwelling rotary callers). 24hr. driving info for the state.

Weather Conditions: National Weather Service (364-7974 in San Francisco; http://www.nws.mbay.net.). Phone recording 24hr.

Crisis Lines: Poison Control (800-523-2222). **Drug Crisis Line** (362-3400). **Rape Crisis Center** (647-RAPE/647-7273), San Francisco Women Against Rape. **Suicide Prevention** (781-0500). **United Helpline** (772-HELP/772-4357 or 800-237-6222). All are open 24hr. **AIDS/HIV Nightline** (434-2437). Open daily 5pm-5am.

24-Hour Pharmacy: Walgreen's, 498 Castro St. (861-3136); 3201 Divisadero St. (931-6417).

Medical Services: San Francisco General Hospital, 1001 Potrero Ave. (206-8000), at 23rd. Take MUNI #48 Quintara from 24th. Emergency room with walk-in service open 24hr. **Haight-Ashbury Free Medical Clinic,** 558 Clayton St. (487-5632). Open for appointments only. Call Mon.-Thurs. 1-9pm, Fri. 1-4:30pm. **Lyon-Martin Women's Clinic,** 1748 Market St. (565-7667), at Valencia. Primary medical care, female-specific, HIV, and lesbian/gay services. Fees on sliding scale. English- and Spanish-speaking staff. Open Mon.-Tues. and Thurs.-Fri. 8:30am-5pm, Wed. 8:30am-7pm. **Health Center,** 1490 Mason St. (705-8500), near Broadway. Contraceptives and counseling. Fees on a sliding scale. Open Mon.-Tues. and Thurs.-Fri. 8:30-11am and 1-4pm, Wed. by appointment only. No walk-ins. Open Mon.-Fri. 8-10:30am and 1-3:30pm. **University of California Dental Clinic,** UCSF Medical Center, 707 Parnassus Ave. (476-1891, emergencies 476-5814). Oral exam $35. No walk-ins. Open Mon.-Fri. 8:30am-5pm.

Internet Access: SF NET (695-9824; http://www.sfnet.com), places coin-op computer terminals in cafes, clubs, and hostels all over the city. Net access costs 25¢ for 5min. and 2 outgoing calls.

Post Office: Civic Center Station, 101 Hyde St. (800-275-8777), at Golden Gate. Open Mon., Wed., and Fri. 6am-5:30pm, Tues. and Thurs. 6am-8:30pm, Sat. 6am-3pm. **ZIP Code:** 94142. **Chinatown Station,** 867 Stockton St. at Clay. Open Mon.-Fri. 9am-5:30pm, Sat. 9am-4:30pm. **ZIP Code:** 94108. **Geary Station,** 5654 Geary Blvd., at 21st. Open Mon.-Fri. 9am-5:30pm, Sat. 9am-4:30pm. **ZIP Code:** 94121.

Area Code: 415.

SAN FRANCISCO

■ Orientation

San Francisco, the fourth-largest city in California (pop. 775,000), is 403 mi. north of
Los Angeles and 390 mi. south of Oregon. The city proper lies at the northern tip of
the peninsula that separates San Francisco Bay from the Pacific Ocean. For information on the other cities surrounding the bay, see **The Bay Area,** p. 291.

GETTING THERE

By Airplane
Busy **San Francisco International Airport (SFO)** (general info 761-0800), is located
on a small peninsula in San Francisco Bay 15 mi. south of downtown via U.S. 101.
Plan your arrival by calling the SFO transportation info line for shuttle schedules
(800-SFO-2008/736-2008).

    San Mateo County Transit (SamTrans) (800-660-4287), runs two buses from
SFO to downtown San Francisco. The express bus #7F takes 35 minutes to reach
downtown and allows only whatever luggage can be held in your lap (runs 5:30am-
12:50am; fare $2.50, seniors $1.25, under 18 50¢). Bus #7B takes nearly an hour to
reach downtown, makes frequent stops, and allows any amount of luggage (runs
4:50am-12:30am; fare $2, seniors $1, under 18 50¢). An **Airporter** bus (495-8404),
runs a shuttle route between all three airport terminals, a downtown terminal at 301
Ellis St., and major downtown hotels (to the airport 5am-11:05pm, to the hotels
6am-midnight; fare $10).

    Lorrie's Travel and Tour (334-9000), provides door-to-door van service to and
from the airport. Reserve a day in advance for service *to* the airport only (vans run
5:30am-11:30pm; fare $10, seniors $9, ages 2-12 $6). **Francisco's** (821-0903), oper-
ates a van between San Francisco and SFO (fare $9, seniors $8, ages 5-11 $6). Call
one day ahead between 4:30am-11pm to arrange a time. Check free area guides (see
Publications, p. 253) for coupons. **Taxi rides** downtown from SFO cost about $30
(for more info, see p. 248).

    Alternatively, flights in and out of Oakland can be cheaper than their counterparts
at SFO, though the Oakland airport is considerably farther from the city. For more
information, see **Oakland: Getting There and Around,** p. 303.

By Bus or Train
Transbay Terminal, 425 Mission St. (495-1575), between Fremont and 1st St. in
downtown, is a regional transportation hub (open 5am-12:35am). Buses from
Golden Gate Transit (Marin County), **AC Transit** (East Bay), and **SamTrans** (San
Mateo County) all stop here. An information center on the second floor has maps,
displays, and free phone lines for each of these systems. **Greyhound** (800-231-
2222), serves the terminal and runs buses to L.A. ($32, with 14-day advance ticket-
ing $29) and Portland (Mon.-Thurs. $45, Fri.-Sun. $48). More in keeping with the
spirit of California is **Green Tortoise** (956-7500 or 800-TORTOIS/867-8647; email
info@greentortoise.com). This "adventure travel" bus line offers overnight service
complete with meals, beds, and a mellow attitude from various destinations along
the coast including L.A. ($35 summer; $30 off-season), Seattle ($59; $49), Portland
($49; $39), Baja, Alaska, Yosemite, and more. Affiliated with the hostel of the same
name, the company will guarantee you a bed there if you ride a Tortoise into town.
Green Tortoise cultivates familial budget travel love, but for expediency and basic
amenities, Greyhound is the way to go. The Transbay Terminal has an **Amtrak** desk
(800-USA-RAIL/872-7245; open daily 6:45am-10:45pm), and on the lower floor, free
buses shuttle passengers to the three Amtrak stations in the city, and its larger hubs
in Oakland and Emeryville (open daily 6:45am-10:45pm; to L.A. $42). **CalTrain**
(800-660-4287 in San Francisco only) is a regional commuter train that runs south to
Palo Alto (fare $3.75, seniors and under 12 $1.75) and San Jose (fare $5, seniors and
under 12 $2.50), with service to Santa Cruz. The depot at 4th and Townsend St. is
served by **MUNI** buses #15, 30, 32 weekdays; buses # 42, 45, and 76 Sundays only.

By Car

The drive from L.A. takes six hours on I-5 if you hustle, eight hours on U.S. 101, or a leisurely nine and a half hours via Hwy. 1, the legendary Pacific Coast Highway. U.S. 101 might offer the best marriage of vistas and velocity, but the stunning coastal scenery that unfolds along Hwy. 1 makes getting there much more fun.

From the south, the city can be reached directly from **U.S. 101, I-280,** and **Hwy. 1.** From inland California, **I-5** approaches the city from the north and south via **I-580** and **I-80,** which runs across the **Bay Bridge** (westbound only toll $2). From the north, U.S. 101 and Hwy. 1 will bring you over the **Golden Gate Bridge** (southbound only toll $3). From the east, all roads converge on the Bay Bridge.

If you're a driver who needs a passenger or a passenger who needs a driver, call **KALX Radio** (510-642-5259), on the Berkeley campus, to put your name and number on the air for free. Or just tune in when they broadcast their ride list, daily at 10am and 10pm. **San Francisco State University** has ride boards in the SFSU Student Union (info desk 338-1111; open Mon.-Thurs. 7:30am-7pm, Fri. 7:30am-6pm), as do lots of coffee shops and student hangouts.

SAN FRANCISCO COMMUNITIES

San Francisco's diverse neighborhoods are loosely organized along a few central arteries. Each neighborhood is compact enough to explore comfortably on foot. Make a mental note of the steep hills in each district—a two-block detour can save you a strenuous and unnecessary hike.

San Francisco radiates outward from its docks, which lie on the northeast edge of the 30 mi. long peninsula, just inside the lip of the bay. Many of the city's most visitor-friendly attractions are found within a wedge formed by **Van Ness Ave.,** running north-south, the **Embarcadero** (Spanish for "dock" but actually a road) curving along the coast, and **Market St.,** running northeast-southwest and interrupting the regular grid of streets.

At the top of this wedge lies the touristy **Fisherman's Wharf** and **Pier 39.** From here, ferries service **Alcatraz Island,** the prison-*cum*-top tourist attraction. **Columbus Ave.** extends southeast from the docks to **North Beach,** a district shared by Italian-Americans, artists, and professional-types. **Telegraph Hill,** which is topped by Coit Tower, emerges as the focal point of North Beach amid a terrific mass of eateries. To the west of Columbus Ave. and North Beach are **Russian Hill** and **Nob Hill,** residential areas with some of the oldest money in California. South of North Beach, the largest **Chinatown** in North America covers around 24 square blocks between Broadway in the north, Bush St. in the south, and Kearny St. in the east. On the other side of the Bush St. gateway of Chinatown lies the heavily developed **Financial District,** where skyscrapers fill the blocks above the northeast portion of Market St. Wander a few blocks west, however, and the economic picture flips menacingly. The core downtown area centered on **Union Square** gives way to the malignant **Tenderloin,** where, despite some urban renewal, drugs, prostitution, and homelessness prevail both night and day. The area is roughly bounded by Larkin St. to the west, Taylor St. to the east, and Post St. to the north, and bleeds down Market St. for a few blocks. The **Civic Center** occupies the acute angle formed by Market St. and Van Ness Ave. at the southern point of the wedge. City Hall, the Civic Center Public Library, and Symphony Hall crown an impressive and ever-growing collection of municipal buildings.

South of the wedge, directly below Market St. lies the **South-of-Market-Area (SoMa),** which teems with young professionals by day and club mavens by night. Here, the best of San Francisco's nightclubs are scattered among darkened office buildings and warehouses. SoMa extends inland from the bay to 10th St., at which point the largely Latino **Mission District** begins and spreads south. The **Castro,** which is the center of the gay community, abuts the Mission District on its west side, roughly along Church St. The Mission and Castro are typically the city's sunniest areas. Nevertheless, travelers should be attentive at night, especially near the housing projects of the Mission. From the landmark **Castro Theater** on the corner of Castro and Market St., the neighborhood stretches to the less flamboyant **Noe Valley** in the south and the undeveloped oasis of the **Twin Peaks** in the southeast.

On the north end of the peninsula, west across Van Ness Ave. from the Wharf area sits the **Marina,** which includes Fort Mason and small yacht harbors. Along with the expansive **Presidio** and the **Golden Gate Bridge** to the west, and the **Marin Headlands** on the other side of the bay, the shoreline comprises the Golden Gate National Recreation Area. Inland from the Marina rise the wealthy hills of **Pacific Heights.** South of Pacific Heights is the **Western Addition,** extending west to Masonic Ave. This district is the site of many of the city's public housing projects and can be dangerous, especially near Hayes St. Other than the shops and restaurants of **Japantown,** the Western Addition has little to interest visitors. Farther west is the rectangular **Golden Gate Park,** which extends west to the Pacific Ocean. The park is bounded by Fulton St. and the residential Richmond neighborhood to the north, and by Lincoln St. and the Sunset District to the south. At its east end juts a skinny panhandle bordered by hippie-trippie **Haight-Ashbury** to the south. A youthful new set of enviro-conscious, politically liberal, and liberally political residents coexist here in relative harmony with the aging beatnik population for which the area is widely known.

GETTING AROUND

Public Transit: BART and MUNI

Street cars and an ever-improving public transit system make San Francisco somewhat of an anomaly in a state of auto-eroticizers; the Bay Area is the easiest place on the West Coast to explore without a car. Connections to neighboring cities are well-coordinated and speedy via **Bay Area Rapid Transit,** or **BART** (992-2278). Though it does not serve the *entire* Bay Area, BART does operate modern, carpeted trains along four lines connecting San Francisco with the **East Bay,** including **Oakland, Berkeley, Concord,** and **Fremont.** All stations provide free maps and schedules. There are seven BART stops in San Francisco proper, but BART is not a local transportation system. All are wheelchair accessible. (BART trains run Mon.-Fri. 4am-midnight, Sat. 6am-midnight, Sun. 8am-midnight. Inter-city transport $1.10, to the East Bay $4.) For regional transportation information, see **The Bay Area,** p. 291.

Most transport within the city falls under the aegis of the San Francisco Municipal Railway (673-MUNI/6864)—somewhat of a misnomer since the **MUNI system** includes buses, cable cars, subways, and streetcars. It is the cheapest and most efficient way to get around the city, especially with MUNI passports, which are valid on all MUNI vehicles, including cable cars (1 day $6; 3 days $10; 7 days $15). The weekly FastPass ($9) are dated, must be bought for each work week by the previous Thursday, and do not entitle their bearers to cable car access (call MUNI for outlet locations). Official MUNI maps ($2, available where passports are sold) cover all regional bus and subway services, and double as excellent street maps. Although all public transit facilities have their own info lines, you can connect to any one of them or get traffic updates free from TravInfo at 817-1717 (TDD 817-1718).

MUNI buses, many of which are clean, quiet, electrical models, run promptly and frequently throughout the city. In addition, **MUNI Metro** runs streetcars through subway tunnels along Market St. and above ground along five lines serving points south and west of downtown. Despite a core series of all-night routes on the Owl Service, coverage decreases considerably after dark. Wheelchair accessibility varies among bus routes, and while all subway stations are accessible, the Metro is not accessible at all above-ground sites. (MUNI bus and streetcar fares $1, seniors and ages 5-17 35¢. Ask for free transfer, valid in any direction for up to 2hr.)

Cable cars are a classic San Franciscan image. Declared a national historic landmark in 1964, San Francisco's cable cars have since made their way into the domain of pop culture—the third series of MTV's *The Real World* captured many artistic shots of the clattering cars audaciously mounting steep slopes. Indeed, the colorful cable cars are much more about image than practicality. The cars are noisy, slow (9.5 mph, to be precise), and usually crammed full, making them an unreliable method of getting around. You won't be the first person to think of taking one to Fisherman's Wharf. In fact, the Union Square stop, en route to the wharf, is nick-named "Fantasy Island" both because it is haunted by the irate ghost of Herve Villacheze and because the car is almost always full by the time it arrives—you're dreaming if you think you'll be able to board. Still, there is something charming about these relics, and you'll probably want to try them, especially if you have a MUNI passport. To avoid the mobs, the best strategy is to get up early and climb the hills with the sunrise. Of the three lines, the **California (C)** line, which runs from the Financial District up through Nob Hill, is the least crowded. The **Powell-Hyde (PH)** line might be the most fun, because it has the steepest hills and the sharpest turns. **Powell-Mason (PM)** runs to the wharf. (All lines run daily 6:30am-12:45am. Fare $2, seniors and disabled $1 before 7am and after 9pm. No free transfers.)

Cars, Bicycles, and Feet

A **car** is not the necessity it is in Los Angeles. **Parking** in San Francisco is rare and expensive even where legal, and a zealous network of traffic cops doles out copious tickets, despite local protests against the city's outrageous regulations. The large number of broken parking meters might indicate an irate citizenry, but the time limit still applies to such spaces, and you may be ticketed up to three times for one such offense. Whatever you do, don't block a sidewalk disabled-access ramp—the ticket is a whopping $250. If you have a car that you'd like to stow while exploring the city, you can leave it parked all day in the Richmond or Sunset districts—just make certain you check for signs indicating weekly street-cleaning times. The street signs admonishing you to "Prevent Runaways" refer not to wayward youths but to cars poorly parked on hills. When parking facing uphill, turn the wheels toward the center of the street and leave the car in first gear (if you're driving a standard). If your car starts to roll, it will stop (hopefully) when the tires hit the curb. When facing downhill, turn the wheels toward the curb and leave the car in reverse. *Always* set the emergency brake. In case you haven't noticed yet, **driving** in San Francisco demands a certain conscientiousness. Contending with the treacherous hills is the first task; if you've arrived in a standard transmission vehicle, you'll need to develop a fast clutch foot, since all hills have stop signs at the crests. If you're renting, get an automatic. Make sure to stop for cable cars because they won't stop for you.

Think twice about attempting to use a **bike** to climb up and down the hills of San Francisco. Even the proudest year-round bike couriers have been spotted walking their bikes up the especially steep grades. Narrow roads and frequent traffic are additional hazards, but descents can be thrilling, and many rental shops supply free maps of area bike routes. Motorcycles and scooters make things a little easier on the quadriceps and are popular in the area. For information on **bike rentals,** see p. 248.

Walking in this city is tame by comparison, though it too is an exciting exertion—there are some sidewalks that are so steep they have steps cut into them. Nevertheless, walking is worthwhile and unavoidable, and it's by far the best way to get to know the neighborhoods. There are many **walking tours** of the city. Some even promise "no steep hills." **In-Room City Guide** (332-9601) has information on free summer tours, and the **Visitor Information Center** (see p. 245) supplies brochures on the many commercial tours.

■ Publications

Free publications flood San Francisco cafes, tourist bureaus, and sidewalk boxes, and offer a **local** spin on upcoming events and activities. The best of the bunch is the *Bay Guardian,* which comes out on Wednesdays. The *San Francisco Weekly,* its major competitor, proudly limits itself to the city proper for its listings and distribution. Harder to find, but worth the effort, are two special-interest rags: *Poetry Flash,* available at discerning bookstores, has the skinny on literary happenings, while the *Bay Area Music Magazine (BAM)* is available at the more rockin' cafes and restaurants in town. The monthly *Source* is comprehensive, but not terribly user-friendly with its endless, undiscriminating list of venues.

Various **tourist**-targeting, coupon-filled free glossies are available from sidewalk boxes in the heavily trafficked Fisherman's Wharf and Union Square areas as well as at visitors centers. Among them are the *Bay City Guide,* the *San Francisco Guide,* and the *San Francisco Quick Guide.* The annual *Chaperon* introduces San Francisco in German, French, Spanish, and Italian. The city administrators print a *Lodging Guide* and *The San Francisco Book,* excellent compilations of tourist info.

With its plethora of direct reprints and uninspired style, the *San Francisco Chronicle* (50¢), the largest Bay Area **daily,** is a pretty shoddy example of a big-city newspaper. Recently the "Chron" lost its biggest asset, with the death of immensely popular society columnist Herb Caen. Nevertheless some find the pink *Datebook* section of the Sunday edition ($1.50) to be a worthwhile entertainment resource. The *San Francisco Examiner,* started by yellow journalist William Randolph Hearst (of *Citizen Kane* fame) has lunchtime and evening editions. (For more on William Randolph, see **Hearst Castle,** p. 226.)

San Francisco has several **gay and lesbian publications.** The *Bay Times* appears monthly with a thorough entertainment section and the work of talented cartoonists. The *Bay Area Reporter* contains articles on gay pride as well as a highly varied "Arts & Entertainment" section. *The Sentinel* offers information on gay community events. The free monthly *Oblivion* is the best guide for gay bars, clubs, and stores, although *ODYSSEY Magazine* is also a smart choice. These publications can be found easily in the neighborhoods around Castro and Polk St.

■ Accommodations

There are a tremendous number of reasonably priced and conveniently located places to stay in San Francisco, but they tend to fill up in peak season, so plan ahead. Unfortunately, many budget accommodations are in the less safe areas—the Tenderloin and parts of North Beach and the Mission can be particularly unsafe. Never hesitate to go elsewhere if you feel uncomfortable about a neighborhood or establishment, even if prices are steeper.

HOSTELS

For those who don't mind sharing a room with strangers, San Francisco's better hostels are homier, cheaper, and safer than most budget hotels. It is advisable to book in advance, but vacancies can usually be found if you arrive early in the day.

San Francisco International Student Center, 1188 Folsom St. (255-8800 or 487-1463), at 8th in **SoMa.** From the airport, take SamTrans #7B bus to 9th and Folsom; from the Greyhound station, take MUNI #14 to 8th and Mission. With bay windows, brick walls, and a big comfy couch, this hostel prides itself on coziness. Guests fill 55 beds and share hall bathrooms with massage showerheads. Free coffee, tea, and Internet access. Reception open 9am-11pm. Check-out 11am. No curfew. Dorms $13, weekly $85 (in winter only). No credit cards.

Pacific Tradewinds Guest House, 680 Sacramento St. (433-7970; fax 291-8801), between Montgomery and Kearny in the **Financial District.** From Transbay Terminal, take MUNI bus #38 to 15, and get off at Kearny and Sacramento. This 30-bed facility has a kitchen, guest phone, showers, and not quite enough bathrooms. Friendly and well-worn common room. Bike storage. 14-night max. stay. No curfew. Office open 8am-midnight. Dorms $16, off-season $14 (double beds available). Discounts for VIP Backpacker and FIYTO cardholders. Key deposit $20. Laundry $6. No wheelchair access. Must be 18.

Easy Goin' Guest House, 555 Haight St. (552-8452; fax 552-8459; email diego@easygo.com), at Fillmore in the **Fillmore.** Take MUNI buses #6, 7, 66, or 71. Has a finger in every piece of the travel pie: travel agency, car and bike rentals, and ride-board. Common room, 2 kitchens with storage space, and clean rooms with 35 beds. Centrally located area can be dangerous at night. German, Spanish, French spoken. No curfew. No max. stay. Dorms $14.

San Francisco International Guest House, 2976 23rd St. (641-1411), at Harrison in the **Mission.** From the Transbay Terminal, take MUNI bus #12, 9, or 14 to 23rd St. No sign marks this beautiful Victorian house with hardwood floors, wall tapestries, and houseplants. Convenient to Mission and Castro. Free sheets, coffee, and foreign magazines. TV area, 2 kitchens, and guest phones. Neighborhood parking. No curfew. 5-night min. stay, 3-month max. Dorms $13, over 28 days $11; private double $26. **Passport with international stamps required.**

Fort Mason Hostel (HI-AYH), Bldg. #240, Fort Mason (771-7277), in the **Marina.** Entrance at Bay and Franklin, 1 block west of Van Ness. Take MUNI bus #42. Wooden buildings give family-oriented campground feel with 160 beds (4-22 per room). Movies, walking tours, kitchens, dining room, laundry, bike storage. Cafe serves free breakfast daily 7:30-11:30am (open Mon.-Fri. 7-11pm). Reception open daily 7am-2pm and 3pm-midnight. Limited access 11am-3pm. Lights out midnight. No alcohol or smoking. Lockers (bring a lock). Free parking. Chore expected. Dorms $16 per night. IBN reservations available. Photo ID required.

Globetrotter's Inn, 225 Ellis St. (346-5786), at Mason **downtown.** Take MUNI bus #14 to Mission and 5th, then #27 to Mason and Ellis or #38 to Mason and Geary. Near the **Tenderloin**—use caution. Intimate hostel has large kitchen, common room with piano, and TV. Check-in 8am-1pm and 5-11pm; check-out 11am. No curfew. No max. stay. Dorms $12; private single $24. Weekly: $75, $150. No credit cards. Laundry and linen provided.

Green Tortoise Guest House, 494 Broadway (834-1000; http://greentortoise.com/hostel), at Kearny between **North Beach** and **Chinatown.** Majestic Victorian holds single-occupancy bathrooms (and some in-room sinks) and 120 wooden bunks. Ballroom-*cum*-common room sports huge TV, couches, pool table. Lockers under each bed; bring a lock. Sauna, Internet access ($2), kitchens, bike storage, and free continental breakfast. 21-night max. stay. Reception open 24hr. Dorms (co-ed and single-sex) $15-18; private doubles $39 (Nov.-May $35). Credit cards accepted if reserving in advance. Linen deposit. Laundry room (wash $1.25, dry 75¢).

Interclub Globe Hostel, 10 Hallam Place (431-0540), off Folsom between 7th and 8th in **SoMa.** Take MUNI bus #14 or 14L to 7th and Mission. Lots of club-hopping Euro-types. Common room has pool table, TV, wild parties, and Globe Cafe (serves breakfast and dinner). Check-out noon. Dorms $16. Linens free. Reservation deposit $10. No credit cards or personal checks. **Passport required.**

SoMa Inn, 1080 Folsom (863-7522), at 8th in **SoMa.** Basic rooms, co-ed showers, 2 kitchens, common room with TV, pool table, and pay phone. Free linens, deli/cafe with dinner specials, bike storage. No curfew. Office open 7am-11pm. Dorms $13; private singles $25; doubles $36. Weekly: dorms $77.

Hostel at Union Square (HI-AYH), 312 Mason St. (788-5604; fax 788-3023), 1 block from **Union Square** near the **Tenderloin.** Take bus #38 or 38L to Mason and Geary. With 230 beds (2-5 per room), this is the 3rd largest hostel in the country. Common room has TV (movies nightly), Internet access, and visitor info. Kitchens have toasters, microwaves, and storage, but no stoves. Reception open 24hr. Quiet hours midnight-7am. Dorms $14, nonmembers $17; under 18 half-price with parent. Key deposit $5. Wheelchair access. Reserve by phone with credit card, or show up at noon. IBN reservations available. No credit cards.

European Guest House, 761 Minna St. (861-6634), off 9th St. between Mission and Howard. Take MUNI bus #14 to 9th. Worn but adequate facilities, including kitchen, roof space, cable TV, laundry, lockers. Desk open 24hr. Dorms $14-16; private doubles $32.

HOTELS

Hostels generally offer a better package, but travelers who put a premium on privacy might prefer to pop for one of the city's hotels. The free *Lodging Guide,* available at the visitors center, can give an idea of rate schemes. Keep in mind that many budget-range hotels in San Francisco are in unsavory areas—in terms of cleanliness and helpfulness, you often get what you pay for. All hotels are busy during the summer months, so it's best to reserve several weeks in advance.

Downtown

Adelaide Inn, 5 Isadora Duncan (441-2261), at the end of a little alley off Taylor near Post, 2 blocks west of Union Square. Warm hosts, lovely furnishings, and low prices make this quiet 18-room oasis the most charming of San Francisco's many "European-style" hotels. Steep stairs, no elevator. All rooms have large windows, TV, and sink. Continental breakfast included. Kitchen with guest fridge available; shared hallway bathrooms. Office closes at 9pm. Singles $45-55; doubles $52-62.

Nob Hill Pensione, 835 Hyde St. (885-2987; fax 921-1648), between Bush and Sutter. Built in 1907 and recently renovated, this snazzy hotel has immaculate rooms with cable TV and phone. Continental breakfast and free nightly wine tasting. Rooms from $50 in summer, with private bath from $80.

Pensione International, 875 Post St. (775-3344 or 800-358-8123), east of Hyde, near Union Square. Artsy building has clean and funky rooms. Continental breakfast included. Single $50-70, winter $45-60; double $60-75, $50-75.

Temple Hotel, 469 Pine St. (781-2565), between Montgomery and Kearny, in the Financial District. Well-maintained hotel has 60s decor and rickety elevator. Rooms have TVs. Checkout 11am. Singles $35-45, with private bath $40-50.

Golden Gate Hotel, 775 Bush St. (392-3702 or 800-835-1118; fax 392-6202), between Powell and Mason near Union Square. Charming hotel, built in 1913, has tasteful antiques and bay windows; treat yourself without going broke. Comfy rooms with TV. Spotless hall bathrooms. Continental breakfast and tea (4-7pm) included. Rooms $65, with bath $99. Garage parking $12 (24hr.).

Hotel Essex, 684 Ellis St. (474-4664, or 800-44-ESSEX/443-7739, out-of-state 800-45-ESSEX/453-7739), at Larkin, north of the Civic Center. Charming rooms with color TVs and phones. Elegant lobby, complimentary coffee and tea. Staff speaks French and German. Desk open 24hr. Check-out noon. Singles $59; doubles $69.

Ansonia Hotel, 711 Post St. (673-2670, 673-7232, or 800-221-6470; fax 673-9217), between Jones and Leavenworth, several blocks from Union Square. All 125 rooms have TV. Breakfast (served 7-8:30am) and dinner (except Sunday) included. Laundry available. Singles $46, with bath $56; doubles $54, $69. Weekly rates available.

Aida Hotel, 1087 Market St. (863-4141 or 800-863-0-AIDA/0243; fax 863-5151). Italian-run *albergo* offers simple rooms and continental breakfast at prices that won't make you cry *"Mamma mia!"* Sinatra serenades the lobby (of course). Singles with shared bath $43.

The Biltmore, 735 Taylor St. (673-4277 or 888-290-5508; fax 673-0453), and **The Amsterdam,** 749 Taylor St. (673-3277 or 800-637-3444; fax 673-0453), between Bush and Sutter, are run by the same owner. The older Amsterdam (built 1909) is more upscale, with a kitchen and outdoor patio; some of its lovely rooms even have jacuzzi and private deck. Continental breakfast included. Singles with shared bath $69; doubles $79. The simpler, newer Biltmore will soon have parking and restaurant. Rooms $59; weekly and monthly rates available. ISIC discount 10%.

The Phoenix, 601 Eddy St. (776-1380 or 800-CITY-INN/248-9466; fax 885-3109), at Larkin, north of the Civic Center in the Tenderloin. Well-secured, but located in a rough area, the Phoenix's main draw is the big-name rock stars who *always* stay here. Gorgeous mural-bottomed pool, *very* comfortably outfitted rooms, parking, and free cable or closed-circuit movies. Backflip cocktail lounge downstairs. Doubles start at a pricey $109—but hey, it's less than 2 tickets to see U2.

Chinatown

Gum Moon Womens Residence, 940 Washington St. (421-8827), at Stockton. *Women over 18 only.* Bright, spacious rooms with shared bath in a large, clean house. Living room has piano, TV, and VCR. Fabulous kitchen. Very secure. Curfew midnight. Reception open 8am-midnight. Singles $26; doubles $21. Weekly: $86. Reserve 2 months in advance. Laundry facilities (wash 50¢, dry 35¢).

YMCA Chinatown, 855 Sacramento St. (982-4412; fax 982-0117), between Stockton and Grant. *Men over 18 only.* Nothing fancy here: 29 rooms are standard YMCA fare. Pool and gym. No visitors allowed. Reception open Mon.-Fri. 6:30am-10pm, Sat. 9am-5pm, Sun. 9am-4pm. Check-out 1pm. No curfew. Singles $29-31; doubles $38. Stay 6 nights, and the 7th is free.

Haight-Ashbury

The Red Victorian Bed and Breakfast Inn, 1665 Haight St. (864-1978), Haight-Ashbury. The Red Vic is more a cosmic understanding than a hotel. All 18 rooms are individually decorated to honor forces of nature, the nearby Golden Gate Park, and the 60s. Even the hall baths have their own names and motifs. Get in touch with your aura under the tie-dyed canopy of the Summer of Love room. Downstairs, peruse artistic affirmations or retreat to the Meditation room. Staff speaks Korean, Portuguese, Spanish, German, Italian, and French. Weekend 2-night min. stay. Check-in 3-6pm or by appointment. Check-out 11am. Breakfast, tea, coffee, and afternoon popcorn and cheese included. Doubles $86-200; 7-14 days $60-120 per night. Discounts on stays longer than 3 days. Reserve well in advance.

LONGER STAYS

Establishments specializing in weekly or monthly accommodations can provide great deals for long-term city visitors. Seasonal apartment shares can sometimes be found through on-line sources like SFNet/Rents (http://www.sfnet.com; see **Practical Information,** p. 245), or the smaller but free UCSF housing office (http://www.ucsf.edu). Be prepared to pay in advance.

Harcourt Residence Club, 1105 Larkin St. (673-7720; fax 474-6729), at Sutter, north of the Civic Center. Popular with the younger set, rentals offered weekly or monthly only. Includes 5-day maid service, 2 meals per day 6 days a week plus Sunday brunch, mailbox, and message service. TV room, laundry room, and sundeck. Reception open 9am-5pm. Weekly $140-225 per person. Reservations deposit $50.

Brady Acres, 649 Jones (929-8033 or 800-6-BRADY-6/627-2396; fax 441-8033), between Geary and Post, north of Tenderloin. Be cautious in the neighborhood. Small rooms with bath are nicely furnished and well-stocked with perks including fridges, microwaves, coffee makers, in-room safes, cable TV, private phone line, and answering machine. Singles from $300 per week ($360 May-Oct.); doubles $360 ($420). Daily rate from $60; doubles $75 (avail. May-Oct. only).

Emperor Norton Inn, 615 Post St. (673-6718 or 922-8998; fax 922-3037), at Taylor, near Union Square. Small but clean 12 rooms have cable TV, fridges, and microwaves. Rooms and linens cleaned weekly. Steep stairs and skinny halls. Singles from $35, with bath $50. Weekly: $175, $250. Each additional person $5 per day.

Park Hotel, 325 Sutter (956-9596), near Stockton, 1 block north of Union Square. Small, dark rooms have shared bath, color TV, and fridge. Security guard on duty 10pm-5am. Reception open 8am-6pm. French spoken. Rooms $41, weekly $131.

■ Food and Sights

San Francisco, like no other American city, is a galaxy of distinct universes. Sampling food in each neighborhood is an excellent way to get a taste for the city's diversity. To get an up-to-date take on the best restaurants, try consulting newspaper reviews—everyone has their own strident opinions, but the *Examiner* and the *Bay Guardian* are reliable. The glossy *Bay Area Vegetarian* can also direct your grazing patterns. Any resident will tell you that San Francisco, like its neighborhoods, is not made of landmarks or "sights," but of neighborhoods. If you blindly rush from the Golden Gate Bridge to Coit Tower to Mission Dolores, you'll be missing the city itself. So when the party in your mouth breaks up, take your time to amble off the calories. The Haight-Ashbury Be-Ins of the 60s may be over, but there's still no better U.S. city to just *be* in. As Frank Lloyd Wright remarked, "What I like best about San Francisco is San Francisco."

DOWNTOWN AND UNION SQUARE

Now an established shopping area, **Union Square** has a dynamic and checkered past. During the Civil War, Unionists made the square their rallying ground. Their placards, reading "The Union, the whole Union, and nothing but the Union," gave the area its name. When the Barbary Coast (now the Financial District) was down and dirty, Union Square's Morton Alley was dirtier. At the turn of the century, murders on the alley averaged one per week, and prostitutes waved to their favorite customers from second-story windows. After the 1906 earthquake and fires destroyed most of the flophouses, a group of merchants moved in and renamed the area **Maiden Lane** in hopes of changing the street's image. Surprisingly enough, the switch worked. Today, Maiden Lane—extending two blocks from Union Square's eastern side—is an enclave of ritzy boutiques and galleries amid the clanging of cable cars and the cooing of fat pigeons. Palm trees and bushes enclose the center square, creating a calm refuge from the storm of shoppers, tourists, and business people. **Public transport** collects at the nearby Powell St. BART station at Market St. MUNI Metro and bus lines (#5, 6, 7, 8, 9, 21, 31, and 71) run along Market before branching into the rest of the city.

Food

Union Square restaurants are often crowded and consistently overpriced. There is a legion of coffee shops, but very little in the way of inexpensive hot food. Corner markets offer fresh fruit (usually 50¢) or baked goods to tide you over until you get a chance to explore the better restaurants of nearby North Beach (see p. 276) or Chinatown (see p. 280). The establishments listed below are a select set of oases.

Indonesia Restaurant, 678-680 Post St. (474-4026). The straightforward name tells it like it is: this humble space serves food so deliciously authentic it might as well be an outpost of the archipelago. Superb *nasi rendang* (beef and coconut), *satay*s ($6-7), and many veggie dishes ($5-7). Open daily 11:30am-10pm.

Puccini and Pinetti, 129 Ellis (392-5500), in the Monticello Hotel. The art may be nouveau, but the formula is old-school: fresh ingredients heaped into generous, affordable portions of pizza, pasta, or *panini* (portobello version, with chips and greens, $7). Open Mon.-Sat. 11:30am-11pm and Sun. 4:30-11pm.

Brother Juniper's, 1065 Sutter St. (771-8929), between Larkin and Hyde. A little out of the way, but the grub is well worth it. Mammoth tofu hash ($5.35) is greasy and delicious. Proceeds go to the adjacent Raphael House homeless shelter. Open Mon.-Fri. 7am-2pm, Sat. 7am-12:30pm.

Yakety Yak, 679 Sutter St. (885-6908), between Mason and Taylor. Relaxed coffee joint serves real food (veggie burrito $3.25) in addition to drinks (Thai iced tea $1.25). Couch and Internet access. Don't talk back. Open daily 7am-10pm.

The Bonaparte of the Bay

Though by nature California is a populist constituency—after all, it puts more questions to voter referendum than any other state—San Franciscans have made at least one notable exception. From 1853 to 1880, locals recognized the self-proclaimed rule of **Joshua Norton the First, Emperor of the United States and Defender of Mexico.** Norton assumed the grandiose title after tough luck in rice speculation wiped out all his money...and perhaps his sanity as well. He donned faux-military attire and an ostrich feather hat and roamed San Francisco's streets with his dogs, Bummer and Lazarus. Locals didn't mind his eccentricities; good-natured merchants accepted the money he printed, and the Central Pacific Railroad allowed him to travel for free. The city even footed the bill for his new clothes. Norton's decrees included starting the tradition of a Christmas tree in Union Square, when he wasn't busy sending suggestions to Abraham Lincoln, Queen Victoria, and the Czar of Russia. When he died, 20,000 people came to wave him on to the next world.

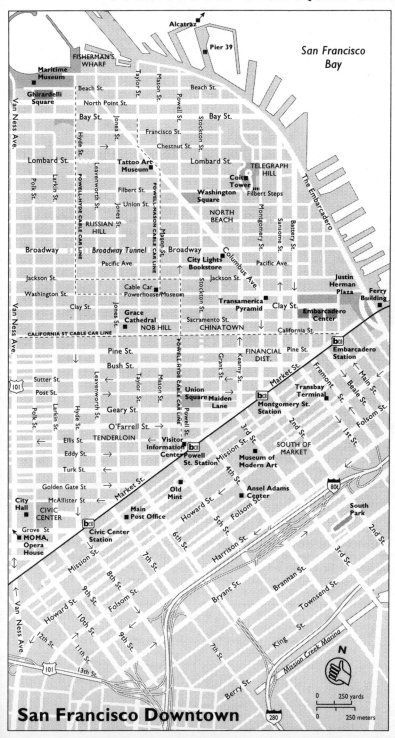

San Francisco Downtown

San Francisco
Bay

Alcatraz

Pier 39

FISHERMAN'S
WHARF

Maritime
Museum

Ghirardelli
Square

Van Ness Ave.

Beach St.
North Point St.
Bay St.

Taylor St.

Mason St.

Powell St.

Stockton St.

Beach St.

Bay St.

Francisco St.
Chestnut St.

Lombard St.

Lombard St.

TELEGRAPH
HILL

Coit
Tower

Tattoo Art
Museum

Filbert Steps

Filbert St.

Washington
Square

Union St.

NORTH
BEACH

Polk St.

Larkin St.

Hyde St.

Leavenworth St.

Jones St.

POWELL-HYDE CABLE CAR LINE

RUSSIAN
HILL

Jones St.

POWELL-MASON CABLE CAR LINE

Mason St.

Montgomery St.

Sansome St.

Battery St.

The Embarcadero

Broadway

Broadway Tunnel

Pacific Ave.

Broadway

Pacific Ave.

City Lights
Bookstore

Columbus Ave.

Jackson St.

Jackson St.

Justin
Herman
Plaza

Ferry
Building

Washington St.

Cable Car
Powerhouse/Museum

Jones St.

Stockton St.

Transamerica
Pyramid

Clay St.

Embarcadero
Center

Clay St.

Grace
Cathedral

NOB HILL

Sacramento St.

CHINATOWN

California St.

CALIFORNIA ST CABLE CAR LINE

Pine St.

FINANCIAL
DIST.

Pine St.

Grant St.

Kearny St.

Embarcadero
Station

Van Ness Ave.

101

Bush St.

Sutter St.

Post St.

Leavenworth St.

Taylor St.

Mason St.

POWELL-HYDE CABLE CAR LINE

Union
Square

Maiden
Lane

Market St.

Transbay
Terminal

Montgomery St.
Station

Fremont St.

Main St.

Beale St.

1st St.

Folsom St.

Geary St.

O'Farrell St.

Polk St.

Hyde St.

Larkin St.

Ellis St.

Eddy St.

Turk St.

TENDERLOIN

Powell St.

Visitor
Information
Center

Powell
St. Station

Mission St.

3rd St.

4th St.

Museum of
Modern Art

SOUTH OF
MARKET

2nd St.

1st St.

Golden Gate St.

McAllister St.

City
Hall

CIVIC
CENTER

Old
Mint

Market St.

Ansel Adams
Center

Howard St.

5th St.

Folsom St.

80

South
Park

2nd St.

Grove St

MOMA,
Opera
House

Civic Center
Station

Main
Post Office

Mission St.

7th St.

6th St.

Harrison St.

3rd St.

Van Ness Ave.

Howard St.

9th St.

8th St.

Folsom St.

10th St.

9th St.

Bryant St.

Branson St.

Townsend St.

King St.

South
Park

12th St.

11th St.

13th St.

101

Berry St.

Mission Creek Marina

N

0 250 yards
0 250 meters

280

SAN FRANCISCO

Sights

Maiden Lane is a pleasant place to stroll for a little while, at least until the boutiques start looking too hob-nobby for comfort. The lane's main architectural attraction is the city's only **Frank Lloyd Wright** building, at 140 Maiden Lane. Shenene don't work at the **Martin Lawrence Gallery,** 465 Powell St. (956-0345), which displays works by pop artists like Andy Warhol and former AIDS activist Keith Haring. Though Haring once distributed his work for free to New York commuters in the form of graffiti, his art now commands upwards of $13,000 even in print form (open Mon.-Sat. 9am-9pm, Sun. 10am-6pm; free). Five floors of galleries (788-4141) are stacked at **49 Geary St.,** including Scott Nichols photography.

Rise to the occasion by taking a free jaunt on the outside elevators of the **Westin St. Francis Hotel,** on Powell St. at Geary. The swift ascent summons the entire eastern Bay Area into view. Ride to the occasion instead on the **Powell St. cable cars** ($2), and take in the busy Chinatown streets on the way to the waterfront. Enjoy a potable on the 30th floor of the **Holiday Inn,** 480 Sutter St. (398-8900; take MUNI bus #2, 3, or 4), where the **Sherlock Holmes Esquire Public House** boasts mysterious artifacts and a glass-enclosed room meticulously decorated to the specifications of 221B Baker St. (libations served Mon.-Thurs. 4pm-midnight, Fri.-Sat. 4pm-2am).

TENDERLOIN

A man in a wheelchair, the veteran of a real or made-up war, coughs up a dozen colors of mucus along with loud, unintelligible epithets. The sign in his lap reads Jesus Says I Am the Way. Across the street, an octogenarian whips her cane around like a young girl practicing her newest yo-yo trick. A man with a grin and a mirror shaped like Zaire sprints past. Welcome to the Tenderloin, an area economically opposed to Union Square but nonetheless geographically adjacent. The uncouth area is north of Market St. (disconcerting activity spills over it as the business day ends) and south of Geary, between Taylor and Larkin. Come in a group or take a drive-through tour during the day and stay away at night. See **Shopping,** p. 282, for a few places worth an assertive, brisk walk.

FINANCIAL DISTRICT

Power suits muscle down boulevards bordered by the Bay Area's biggest buildings. Unless corporate America or steel stamina get you going, there's not much here to attract the casual visitor. The food is standard lunch fare, the whole area shuts down when the workday ends (around 7:30pm), and parking is next to impossible during business hours. If you must drive, park your car in SoMa and walk from there. Otherwise, take MUNI Metro (J, K, L, M, or N) or BART to the Montgomery or Embarcadero station, or MUNI bus (#1, 2, 3, 4, 6, 7, 9, 12, 15, 30, 41, 42, or 45). Slower ways to the district are the California St. cable car and business school.

Food

You may need an MBA to find cheap eats in the Financial District, especially for dinner. Expense-account establishments may look better than they taste—you're probably better off in Chinatown (see p. 280) or North Beach (see p. 276).

Specialty's, 22 Battery St. (896-BAKE/2243), at Bush and Market. Specialty's bakes their own bread and makes fab, filling sandwiches for an entry-level budget. The hearty peanut butter sandwich is a treat—2½ in. slices of bread stuffed with wheat germ, P.B., and generous banana slices ($3.25). The nearby pier and public fountains provide ample space to sit. Open Mon.-Fri. 6am-6pm.

Franciscan Croissant, 301 Sutter St. (398-8276), at Grant, is a tiny food bar with huge croissants (cinnamon raisin $1.65), and delicious sandwiches like hot mushroom florentine ($3.75). Nurse a large coffee (90¢) while ogling passersby from the window counters. Open daily 7:30am-6:30pm.

Krivaar Cafe, 475 Pine St. (781-0894), at Kearny. Middle Eastern and Greek specialties are a notable exception to the district's bland offerings. *Baba ganoush* with pita bread $2.25, *moussaka* with salad $4. Squeeze in at the counter or take grub and grins to go. Open Mon.-Fri. 6am-5pm.

Metropol, 168 Sutter St. (732-7777), between Kearny and Montgomery. Smart players know when to exercise their options. Liberal portions of ambience and table space help make the prices (sandwiches and salads $7-9) seem very competitive. Buy! Open Mon.-Fri. 7am-9pm, Sat. 11am-5pm.

Sights

Modern buildings, architectural history, and the art of fountain-making conjoin in this glass-box wonderland. Those with a zest for contemplating the structural integrity of skyscrapers will find plenty of retrofitted relics with commemorative plates neatly affixed. **Justin Herman Plaza** and its formidable **Vallaincourt Fountain,** at the foot of Market St., invite total visitor immersion. Bands and rallyists often rent out the area during lunch. One such free concert, performed by U2 in the fall of 1987, resulted in the arrest of lead singer and madcap non-conformist Bono for spray painting "Stop the Traffic—Rock and Roll" on the fountain.

The **Hyatt Regency** Hotel, 5 Embarcadero Center (788-1234), adjoins the space. Its 17-story atrium, dominated by a four-story geometric sculpture, is worth a peek. The glass elevator up the building's side leads to the 20th floor and the **Equinox Revolving Rooftop Restaurant and Lounge** (open Mon.-Thurs. 4-10pm, Fri. 4pm-1:15am, Sat. noon-1:15am, and Sun. 11am-midnight). Buy a drink and dawdling time for $3 and up. The newly opened **Skydeck,** also in the Embarcadero Center, commands views from 41 floors up but also demands five hard-earned dollars. Buck the fee at the **Bank of America** building, 555 California St., where the lookout point is a cocktail bar with a one-drink minimum—look fast or fake a rendezvous. The **Transamerica Pyramid,** 600 Montgomery St., between Clay and Washington, may be the leading lady of the city's skyline, but unless you're an employee, you'll have to make do with the virtual viewscapes in the lobby. Though now a show of architectural virtuosity, it was once a show of revolutionary disgruntlement. Around the turn of the century, such scruffy literati as Mark Twain, Robert Louis Stevenson, Bret Harte, and Jack London flooded the bar of the pyramid's predecessor, the Montgomery Block, and Sun Yat-Sen scripted a dynastic overthrow in one of its apartments. History is more immediately evident at the **Wells Fargo History Museum,** 420 Montgomery (396-2619), where two Pony Express-era stagecoaches are on display (open Mon.-Fri. 9am-5pm; free).

SOUTH-OF-MARKET (SOMA)

San Francisco's most nocturnal district, SoMa is the place where hip young professionals dine at chic restaurants before hitting San Francisco's club scene (see **Entertainment,** p. 281). Parking is relatively plentiful, but lock your car securely, don't leave valuables inside, and watch for street cleaning prohibitions which kick in at midnight a few times each week. To reach the area via public transportation, take SamTrans bus #1A or 1L (weekends and holidays) or #1C, 22D, 10L, or 10T (8-10am and 4-6pm only), or take MUNI bus #9x, 12, 14, 15, 26, 27, 30, 45, or 71.

Food

Savvy chefs concoct creative cuisines here, but elevated prices require serious splurging. Consider wandering to the Mission (see p. 263) for more affordable fare.

Vino e Cucina Trattoria, 489 3rd St. (543-6962), at Bryant. Meals cooked by the affable Italian chef are as *autentico* as they are *magnifico*. The *lasagne arrotolate* ($8.50) is a truly transcendent experience. Pastas and pizzas ($7-8) available without meat on request. Open Mon.-Fri. 11am-3pm and 5:30-10:30pm, Sat. 5:30-10:30pm ("Sundays, you rest," says the chef).

The Chat House, 139 8th St. (255-8783), at Minna. One of the few SoMa establishments that opens its doors weekend mornings, this woman-owned cafe well deserves the appreciation of its cool customers. Buttermilk pancakes with bananas and walnuts $5.75, sandwiches and "house plates" like sauteed red trout with pecan sauce $8. Vegetarian friendly. Open Mon.-Tues. 8am-9pm, Wed.-Fri. 8am-1am (food from 11am), Sat. 10am-1am, Sun. 10am-3pm.

LuLu, 816 Folsom St. (495-5775), at 4th. Enticing aromas and atmosphere up to the elevated ceiling work to complement the delicious food. Unique pizzas ($9 and up) and huge family-style plates of fire-roasted veggies fill out an ever-changing menu. Sandwiches and lunch specials (until 3pm) offer good value, but evening brings a better-heeled crowd to the chic bar. Open Sun.-Thurs. 11:30am-10:30pm, Fri.-Sat. 11:30am-11:30pm (limited menu 3-5:30pm). Reservations essential.

Cadillac Bar and Restaurant, 1 Holland Ct. (543-TACO/8226), off Howard between 4th and 5th. This festive converted warehouse serves north-of-the-border sandwiches ($7 and up) as well as mesquite-grilled fajitas ($10). Margaritas cost a little more ($5.75 and up), but they go down easy. Open Mon.-Thurs. 11am-11pm, Fri.-Sat. noon-midnight, Sun. noon-10pm.

Sights

The **San Francisco Museum of Modern Art (SFMOMA),** 151 3rd St. (357-4000; http://www.sfmoma.org), between Mission and Howard, displays an impressive collection of contemporary European and American works. Opened in 1995, the striking, still-pristine, modern complex houses the largest selection of 20th-century work this side of New York. Though some might argue that the museum has been too closely wedded to commercialism, with its slick presentation and its emphasis on design arts (an exhibition of opening spreads from *Wired* magazine is scheduled for early 1998), the five spacious floors are sure to provide something for everyone. The audio tour ($3), a self-paced guide, immerses visitors in the permanent collection. (Open Mon.-Tues. and Fri.-Sun. 11am-6pm, Thurs. 11am-9pm. Admission $8, seniors $5, students $4, under 12 free; Thurs. 6-9pm half-price, 1st Tues. of each month free.) The neighboring **Center for the Arts,** 701 Mission (978-2700; http://www.Yerbabuenaarts.org), in the Yerba Buena Gardens, runs an excellent gallery space and many vibrant programs, emphasizing performance, viewer involvement, and local multicultural work. (Center open Tues.-Sun. 11am-6pm; gardens open daily sunrise-sunset. Admission $5, seniors and students $3, free Thurs. 11am-3pm; free 1st Thurs. of each month, when the center stays open until 8pm.) The **Ansel Adams Center,** 250 4th St. (495-7000), at Howard and Folsom, houses a permanent collection of the master's photographs, as well as temporary shows by other photographers (open Tues.-Sun. 11am-5pm, and until 8pm on 1st Thurs. of each month; admission $5, students $3, seniors $2, ages 13-17 $2, under 13 free).

CIVIC CENTER

The Civic Center is a collection of mammoth buildings arranged around two vast plazas. Street people and itinerant travelers occupy the plaza lawns, despite the city's efforts to relocate them. Parking is easy on streets around the Civic Center. To get there by public transportation, take MUNI Metro (J, K, L, M, or N) to the Civic Center/City Hall stop or to Van Ness Station, MUNI bus (#5, 16x, 19, 21, 26, 42, 47, or 49), or Golden Gate Transit bus (#10, 20, 50, or 70).

Food

Opera- and theater-goers frequent the petite restaurants that dot the outer Civic Center area, while **Hayes St.** offers an extensive selection of cafes. In the summer, produce can be found at the **farmer's market** every Wednesday and Friday in the U.N. Plaza. Use caution in this area at night.

Nyala Ethiopian Restaurant, 39A Grove St. (861-0788), east of Larkin, fuses Ethiopian and Italian cuisine. The *doro wot,* a traditional Ethiopian dish of chicken in a rich garlic and ginger sauce ($6 lunch, $8 dinner) is fabulous. The all-you-can-eat vegetarian buffet ($5 lunch, $7 dinner) features two types of lentils, spicy mushrooms, and other saucy vegetables to ladle onto rice or to scoop up with spongy *injera* bread. Open Mon.-Thurs. 11am-9pm, Fri.-Sat. 11am-11pm.

Ananda Fuara, 1298 Market St. (621-1994), at 9th. Vegetarian menu with vegan tendencies offers creative combinations of super-fresh ingredients. Great sandwiches like the BBQ tofu burger ($5.50) and terrific smoothies ($3). Open Mon.-Tues. and Thurs.-Sat. 8am-8pm, Wed. 8am-3pm. Cash only.

Millennium, 246 McAllister St. (487-9800), between Larkin and Hyde in the Abigail Hotel. All vegan, all the time. Who knew an eye towards health could taste so good? The food astounds, though quality does cost a bit more (entrees $12-16). Impeccable service. Open daily 5-9:30pm.

Tommy's Joynt, 1101 Geary Blvd. (775-4216), at Van Ness. This garishly decorated San Francisco landmark offers beers brewed everywhere from Finland to Peru. A flesh-eater's delight—try the famous buffalo sandwich ($4.75) or the oxtail sautee with buttered noodles ($4.65). With two types of mustard and horseradish on every table, Tommy's knows its target audience. Open daily 11am-2am.

Sights

The palatial **San Francisco City Hall,** 401 Van Ness Ave. (554-4000), modeled after St. Peter's Cathedral, is the centerpiece of the largest gathering of Beaux Arts architecture in the U.S. (Beaux Arts is a style of Neoclassical architecture taught in Paris in the 19th century.) The city hall was the site of the 1978 murder of Mayor George Moscone and City Supervisor Harvey Milk, the first openly gay politician elected to public office in the U.S. To the east across Polk lies the U.N. Plaza and the new main library. Across Van Ness Ave. to the west sit (from north to south) the State House, Veteran's Building, Opera House, and Symphony Hall.

In the evenings, the **Louise M. Davies Symphony Hall,** 201 Van Ness Ave. (864-6000), glittering at Grove, rings with the sounds of the **San Francisco Symphony.** The seating in this glass-and-brass $33-million hall was intended to appeal not only aurally but visually, giving most audience members a close-up view of performers. But while the building may be a visual success, its acoustics are poor, and 11 years after its opening, baffled engineers still tinker with seating arrangements. On the other hand, the orchestra itself has improved greatly, perhaps to compensate for its new hall (open Mon.-Fri. 10am-6pm). Next door, the recently renovated **War Memorial Opera House,** 301 Van Ness Ave. (621-6600), between Grove and McAllister, hosts the well-regarded **San Francisco Opera Company** (864-3330) and the **San Francisco Ballet** (865-2000). For more information on tickets for the opera, ballet, or symphony, see **Entertainment,** p. 281. Also in the block of Van Ness Ave. between Grove and McAllister is the **Veteran's Building** (552-4904), where **Herbst Theatre** (392-4400), hosts string quartets, solo singers, ensembles, and lecturers. (Tours of Davies Symphony Hall, War Memorial Opera House, and Herbst Theatre leave from the Grove St. entrance to Davies Hall every hour. Mon. 10am-2pm. Tours of Davies Hall only by request. Tickets $3, seniors and students $2. For more info, call 552-8338.)

On a smaller scale, the Civic Center area has a number of one- or two-room **galleries.** The **San Francisco Women Artists Gallery,** 370 Hayes St. (552-7392), between Franklin and Gough, began in the 1880s as the Young Ladies Sketch Club. It exhibits women's photographs, paintings, and prints (open Tues.-Sat. 11am-6pm, Thurs. 11am-8pm; 1:30-4pm on the 2nd and 3rd Sun. of each month). Some excellent **bookstores** burrow in and around the Civic Center (see **Shopping,** p. 282).

THE MISSION DISTRICT

Founded by Spanish settlers in 1776, the Mission district is home to some of the city's oldest structures, as well as some of the hottest young people and places around. Colorful murals celebrate the prominent Latino presence which has long defined the Mission, although it grows ever more multicultural. The area is also home to a significant lesbian community. The Mission is relatively safe for daytime walks, but exercise caution at night, especially around housing projects between Valencia and Guerrero close to Market. The district, which lies south of the Civic Center area, is roughly bordered by 16th St. to the north, U.S. 101 to the east, Army St. (renamed Cesar Chavez in some areas) to the south, and the Castro in the West. MUNI bus routes (#9, 12, 22, 26, 27, 33, and 53) lace the area.

Food

The Mission is one of the best places in the city to find excellent, satisfying, cheap food. Inexpensive *taquerías* and other international eateries line the *avenidas*. It also boasts the city's best and cheapest produce. Even the most substantial appetites will be satisfied by the Mexican, Salvadoran, and South American restaurants on 24th St. (east of Mission St.) or the host of other cuisines available along Valencia St. Much of the best Mexican food is served in small restaurants slightly out of the way; try **Chava's**, 3248 18th St. (552-9387; open daily 6am-8pm), **Taco Loco**, 3306 Mission (695-0621), or **El Zocalo**, 2230 Mission (282-2572; open until 4am).

Country Station Sushi Cafe, 2140 Mission (861-0972), between 17th and 18th. Open your mouth if you don't believe your eyes—you'll find this place a fantastic surprise. Japanophiles will find the big-hearted kitsch here as genuine as more classic decor. The friendly proprietress will explain the freshest specials (two-piece *Nigiri* $3-4), speaking only as much English as you need. Traditional sushi combos start at $10. Open Mon.-Thurs. 5-10pm, Fri.-Sat. 5-11pm.

La Taqueria, 2889 Mission (285-7117), at 24th, has a prime location. Claims the "best tacos and burritos in the whole world," and you'd be hard put to contradict them. Tacos $2.25, burritos $3.75. Open Mon.-Sat. 11am-9pm, Sun. 11am-8pm.

• **New Dawn Cafe,** 3174 16th St., at Guerrero. Wake up to a Brobdingnagian breakfast amid the artful dolls' body parts and eggbeaters that adorn this über-hip restaurant. Winner of the Best of San Francisco award for "cheap gluttony," the New Dawn is not too cool to cook with care. Veggie home fries $7 (serves 3-4), sandwiches or burgers $4.25. Long waits on weekend mornings, but the troopers in line are often served coffee. Open Mon.-Thurs. 8:30am-2:30pm, Wed.-Sun. 8:30am-8:30pm.

Ti Couz, 3108 16th St. (252-7373), at Valencia. All about crepes. The salmon and scallion ($5) is a winner, but if that sounds fishy, you can design your own. Delicious dessert crepes ($2.50-5.25) and waitstaff prove equally tantalizing. Often crowded. Open Mon.-Fri. 11am-11pm, Sat. 10am-11pm, Sun. 10am-10pm.

Herbivore, 983 Valencia (826-5657), at 21st. Fresh-off-the-vine produce for vegan dishes doubles as decor. The usual suspects (*seitan* $6.50, charbroiled veggies $5.75), with a range of ethnic influences. Open daily 11am-10pm. Cash only.

Cafe Macondo, 3159 16th, between Guerrero and Valencia. Lengthy shelves of books for patrons accent this appetizing shop, which takes its name from the books of Gabriel García Márquez. The $5 veggie lasagna is the most expensive item on the menu. Dense fruit shakes are a specialty. Open daily 10:30am-10pm.

Sights

The Mission is best seen on foot and in daylight. A walk east or north along Mission St. from the 24th St. BART stop leads to the **murals,** which mark the neighborhood as an ideological and artistic center of the Chicano movement of the late 60s and early 70s. A few blocks down colorful 24th St. from Mission leads to La Galeria de la Raza, 2857 24th St. (826-8009), at Bryant, which celebrates local and international Latino artists with exhibitions and parties (gallery open Tues.-Sat. noon-6pm; free). Most of the area's new cafes, clubs, and bookstores line Valencia south of the 16th St. BART stop. This area has an active nightlife which focuses on local funk and jazz groups, while Latin music flourishes closer to 27th.

Extant for over two centuries, **Mission Dolores** (621-8203), at 16th and Dolores in the old heart of San Francisco, is thought to be the oldest building in the city. The mission was founded in 1776 by Father Junípero Serra and named in honor of St. Francis of Assisi, as was San Francisco itself. But because of its proximity to *Laguna de Nuestra Señora de los Dolores* (Lagoon of Our Lady of Sorrows), the mission became universally known as *Misión de los Dolores*. Bougainvillea, poppies, and birds-of-paradise bloom in the cemetery, which was featured in Hitchcock's *Vertigo*. (Open daily 9am-4:30pm; Nov.-April 9am-4pm. Admission $2, ages 5-12 $1. Masses Mon.-Sat. 7:30 and 9am, Sat. 7:30, 9am, and 5pm, Sun. 8 and 10am; mass in Spanish Sun. noon.) For more info, see **A Man with a Mission** (p. 54).

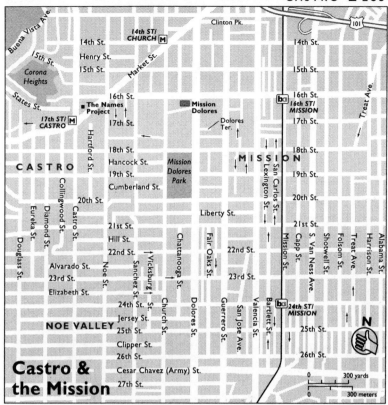

Castro &
the Mission

Osento, 955 Valencia St. (282-6333), between 20th and 21st St., is a bathhouse with that double-X chromosome touch, providing beautiful, clean, and very safe facilities to all (and only) women over 15. Osento has a wet and dry sauna, jacuzzi, and pool (door fee $9-13; cash only). There are several excellent bookstores and thrift stores on Valencia (see **Shopping,** p. 282).

CASTRO

Forget Newt Gingrich—*this* is boys' town. Much of San Francisco's gay community, along with a much smaller number of hip young lesbians, gleefully make the Castro home. The community has felt the impact of AIDS, and the wild days of the 70s have clearly come and gone, but Castro St. remains a proud and assertive emblem of gay liberation with motorcycles and bare chests. Most of the action takes place along Castro St. to the south of Market St., although the neighborhood itself extends south from Market to Noe Valley and west from the Mission to Portola Dr. and Twin Peaks.

Food

Inexpensive cuisine can be elusive in this trendy area. The nearby Mission is a great spot for eating; consider experiencing the Castro by sipping a latte at one of the local cafes. Same-sex cruising is almost inevitably the side dish. Bon appetit!

Josie's Cabaret and Juice Joint Cafe, 3583 16th St. (861-7933), at Market. With a strictly vegetarian menu, Josie's is quintessentially Californian. Filling tofu or tempeh burgers ($5) are even better out on the deck, surrounded by wildflowers. Excellent smoothies in many a flavor. Josie's also hosts live comedy acts at night (see **Entertainment,** p. 281). Open daily 9am-7:15pm. Cash only.

A Case of Spilt Milk

San Francisco's gay community comprises a powerful voting bloc, and in 1977, members rallied behind one of their own. **Harvey Milk** won the race for City Supervisor of District 5, becoming one of the first openly homosexual public official in the United States. He spoke out for civil rights initiatives on both a municipal and a national level, and his charismatic speeches won him powerful allies such as then-mayor George Moscone. But progressive politics make enemies too. Milk advised Moscone against the re-appointment of fellow supervisor Dan White in 1978. In retaliation, White brutally gunned down both Milk and Moscone in their City Hall offices. At his trial, White pleaded the infamous **"Twinkie defense"**—insanity by sugar-high—resulting in a greatly diminished scale of punishment. Outrage over the incident still rankles today, and Milk remains without a clear successor in San Francisco's gay political arena.

Bagdad Cafe, 2295 Market St. (621-4434), at Noe, takes up a whole city block—no small feat in the jam-packed Castro. Giant windows allow plenty of people-watching. The hot turkey sandwich with mashed potatoes ($6.75) is popular. Extensive all-day breakfast menu. When busy, there's a $3.50 minimum. Open 24hr.

Cafe Pozole, 2337 Market St. (626-2666), between Castro and Noe. Known in the neighborhood for its sexy waiters, this colorful restaurant is done up as if for the Day of the Dead. You don't need fluency to get hip with *tacos del mucho macho* or *mi buenos aires querido* (both $7). Wash it down with an icy *negra modela* ($3.25) or sangria ($3). Open Mon.-Thurs. 4-11pm, Fri.-Sun. noon-midnight.

Orphan Andy's, 3991 17th St. (864-9795), near the corner of Market and Castro, has been accommodating appreciative diners for years. Burgers $6, huge milkshakes $4.35. Hodge-podge of vintage posters on the wall. Open 24hr. Cash only.

Hot 'n' Hunky, 4039 18th St. (621-6365), near Castro. Swathed in pink, this joint sports trendy 50s decor with many winks to Marilyn Monroe. The Macho Man (¾lb. beef), or I Wanna Hold Your Ham ($4-5), are some of the hunkiest burgers. Open Sun.-Thurs. 11am-midnight, Fri.-Sat. 11am-1am. No credit cards.

Sights

Most people here seem quite sure of their orientation, but if you need a little help getting started, **Cruisin' Castro** guide Trevor Hailey, a resident since 1972, is consistently recognized as one of San Francisco's top tour leaders. (Daily walking tours leave at 10am and cost $30, including brunch at the famed Elephant Walk Restaurant, at the "gayest four corners on earth." Call Trevor at 550-8110 for reservations.) MUNI bus #24 runs along Castro St. from 14th to 26th. Down the street, **The Names Project,** 2362A Market St. (863-1966), sounds a more somber note. This is the headquarters of an organization that has accumulated over 33,000 three-by-six-foot panels, from 34 countries (and counting) for the **AIDS Memorial Quilt.** Each panel is a memorial to a person who has died of AIDS-related conditions. The Names Project building contains a workshop where victims' friends and families create panels and several panels destined for the ever-enlarging quilt are always on display (open daily noon-5pm; public quilting bees Wed. 8pm).

Where else but in San Francisco's Castro neighborhood would you find a shrine to her fabulousness, Barbra Streisand? **Hello Gorgeous!,** 549A Castro St. (864-2678), at 18th and 19th, is a store/art gallery/museum that *will* convert you to the cult, if you're not already in it. This is kitsch at an all-time high. A Streisand mannequin moves along a truck, her voice is omnipresent in every room, and glassed-in exhibits like a 1960s aquamarine living room, complete (of course) with Barbra on the period TV set. Ogle snapshots of celebrity visitors—Barbra has yet to make an appearance, though she has sent a note—and sign the fan letter on your way out (open Mon.-Thurs. 11am-7pm, Fri.-Sat. 11am-8pm, Sun. 11am-6pm; admission $3).

West of Castro, the peninsula swells with several large hills. On rare fogless nights, the spectacular views of the city from **Twin Peaks,** between Portola, Market, and Clarendon, rise above all others. Just drive toward the hulking three-masted radio tower, known by some as the Great Satan, where a pair of red warning lights blink menacingly from beneath a Mephisthophelean crown. The Spanish called Twin Peaks "Mission Peaks" or *"Los Pechos de la Choca"* (the Breasts of the Indian Maiden). South of the peaks off Portola Dr., also accessible via MUNI bus #36, is **Mount Davidson,** the highest spot in San Francisco (938ft.). The 103 ft. concrete cross is the resilient replacement of two earlier versions that were destroyed in fires.

HAIGHT-ASHBURY

Walking around Haight-Ashbury today is kind of like seeing a film adaptation of a Jane Austen novel—the costumes seem right and the actors are fairly convincing, but you can't shake the fact that it's 1998. You might even say there's a major Gap in your thinking, and it's mixing and matching right at the once-famous "crossroads of counterculture." Located to the east of Golden Gate Park, smack dab in the center of the city, the Haight has aged with uneven grace since the 60s, reenacting an era that many seek to experience, others forget, and some still can't remember. The Grateful Dead blare out of car windows, bars shelter zoned-out regulars who may not have moved since the Nixon administration, and the shady character on the corner will gladly provide you with the very substances that made the decade magical.

Originally a quiet residential neighborhood, the Haight's large Victorian houses—perfect for communal living—drew a massive hippie population in the 60s, and LSD (possession of which was not then a felony) pervaded the neighborhood. The hippie voyage reached its apogee in 1966-67 when Janis Joplin, the Dead, and the Jefferson Airplane all made music and love here within a few blocks of one another. During 1967's "Summer of Love," young people from across the country converged on the grassy panhandle for the celebrated "be-ins." To would-be free-thinkers, the Haight seemed the very confluence of spiritual power. To critics, it was just a scummy street of runaways and bad drugs. Bad karma got the upper hand as the glow wore off in the 70s and into the 80s, though the past decade has seen a slow but steady resurgence.

Though the Haight's deathgrip on its past can be downright pathetic, free-wheeling attitudes still set a diverting scene. Inexpensive cafes, action-packed street life, anarchist literature, vintage clothing stores, and shops selling pipes for, um, tobacco, all contribute to groovy browsing possibilities—for suggestions, see **Shopping,** p. 282. MUNI buses #6, 7, 16, 43, 66, 71, and 33 all serve the area, while Metro line N runs along Carl St., four blocks to the south. The area can get quite dangerous at night—exercise caution.

Food

The Haight has several good bakeries and ethnic restaurants with reasonable prices, but select carefully—quality varies greatly between establishments. Walking a little farther west towards Haight-Fillmore, or south along Cole to the blocks between Frederick and Parnassus can increase your chances of a satisfying meal.

- **Crepes on Cole,** 100 Carl St. (664-1800), at Cole. From strawberries and chocolate ($3.75) to Mexican cheddar cheese ($5.74), this flat fare displays a mastery of the medium. Open Sun.-Thurs. 7am-11pm, Fri.-Sat. 7am-midnight.
- **Ya Halla,** 494 Haight St. (522-1509), at Fillmore. The name means "heartily welcome" in Arabic, and the service backs it up. Flavor pervades both meat and vegetarian sandwiches (chicken shawerma $5.25). Sit on cushions in the restaurant's cool interior or take it to go on your way to the park. Open daily 11am-10:30pm.
- **The Horseshoe Cafe,** 566 Haight St. (626-8852), 1 block west of Ya Halla, houses the SFNet/Rents office (see **Practical Information,** p. 249) in its back room, and (naturally) offers Internet access. Bright neo-Inca murals enliven the disorderly space, creating a welcoming setting for slugging a latte ($2) or pounding a knish ($2.75). Open daily 6:30am-1:30am.
- **Blue Front Cafe** (252-5917), between Ashbury and Masonic. Whether you're drinking beer (pint $2) or ginseng chai ($2), you'll find comfortable company at this

neighborhood nook. Omelettes ($4-5) and light dinner (tabouli plate $5) every night of the week. Open Mon.-Fri. 8am-10pm, Sat.-Sun. 8am-11pm.

Cha Cha Cha, 1801 Haight St. (386-5758), at Stanyan. The wait can be endless, but it's worth it. Tip-top tapas, like fried plantains with black beans and sour cream ($4.50), take up over half the menu. Open Mon.-Fri. 11:30am-4pm and 5-11pm, Sat.-Sun. 5-11:30pm. No reservations.

Sights

See the Haight on foot—scrounging for parking with the hordes who flock here every evening is a real hassle, though unmetered neighborhood spots start just a block off the main drag. Walking down Haight St. from the Golden Gate Park (or up from Fillmore, where the trendiness isn't so in-your-face) and exploring the stores and cafes along the way will acquaint you with the neighborhood. Acquiring funky stuff is the Haight's stock in trade, so get out there and patronize those eclectic stores and, uh, independent vendors. Music and clothing top the list of legal merchandise (see **Shopping,** p. 282). You're sure to run into some characters who are wandering the streets in various shades of purple haze. The former homes of several counterculture legends still survive: check out **Janis Joplin's** old abode at 112 Lyon St., between Page and Oak; the **Grateful Dead's** house at 710 Ashbury St., at Waller; or the **Charles Manson** mansion at 2400 Fulton St., at Willard. If pounding the pavement is just too slow, **Skates on Haight,** 1818 Haight St. (SKATE-85/752-8385), will help you glide (in-line skates, helmet, and pads $7 per hr.; open daily 10am-6pm).

The **Red Vic Movie House,** 1727 Haight St. (668-3994), between Cole and Shrader, is a collectively owned theater that shows foreign, student, and Hollywood films. The movie house (see **Movies,** p. 282) is not affiliated with the B&B, the **Red Vic Bed and Breakfast Inn** (see **Accommodations,** p. 257), which is itself worth a peek. Resembling a dense green mountain in the middle of the Haight, **Buena Vista Park** has a reputation for free-wheeling lawlessness. Enter at your own risk, and once inside, be prepared for those "doing their own thing" and doing enough of it to kill a small animal. However, Buena Vista Park is generally safer (and is rumored to have better reefer) than **Alamo Square,** northeast of the Haight at Hayes and Steiner. The vantage point of a thousand postcards, its gentle, grassy slope is a favorite with photographers—a string of lovely Victorian homes (the "Painted Ladies") glow against the backdrop of the metropolitan skyline. Far out.

LSD: From the Man to the People

Basel, Switzerland, 1943: Albert Hoffman synthesizes a compound called **lysergic acid diethylamide (LSD).** Almost immediately, the medical community touts the effects of the new wonder drug, which is said to have a near-miraculous ability to cure psychoses and alcoholism with a minimum of therapeutic intervention. The U.S. government soon gets into the act. In the early 50s, the CIA attempts to use the hallucinogen as part of **"Operation MK-ULTRA,"** a series of Cold War mind control experiments. By the end of the next decade, LSD has been tested on some 1500 military personnel in a series of ethically shady operations conducted by the U.S. Army Corps of Engineers on many unknowing subjects. However, by the early 60s, the effects of the drug are discovered by the burgeoning hippie population in San Francisco's Haight-Ashbury district. Soon, college students and prominent intellectuals advocate its use as a means of expanding consciousness.

October 6, 1966: The drug is made illegal in California, but it is too late. Once a pet tool of the military-industrial complex, **acid** has become a key part of the massive counterculture of the late 60s, juicing up anti-war protests and orgiastic love-ins across the Bay Area and the rest of America.

GOLDEN GATE PARK AND THE SUNSET DISTRICT

This is where native San Franciscans spend Sundays. In-line skaters, neo-flower children, and sunbathers come together in this wilderness within the city. Frederick Law Olmsted, designer of New York's Central Park, said it couldn't be done when San Francisco's 19th-century elders asked him to build a park to rival Paris's Bois de Boulogne on their city's western side. Engineer William Hammond Hall and Scottish gardener John "Willy" McLaren proved him wrong. Hall designed the 1000-acre park, gardens and all, when the land was still just shifting sand dunes, and then constructed a mammoth breakwater along the oceanfront to protect the seedling trees and bushes from the sea's burning spray. McLaren planted more than one million trees in the park during his 55 years as the Golden Gate's godfather, transforming the sand into soil with sea-bent grass, humus, and truckloads of manure. When the early groundskeepers wanted to preserve the pristine lawns by enforcing a "keep off the grass" rule, McLaren was outraged and threatened to pave over the park if the rule were enforced. A strong-minded character, McLaren disliked statues in "his" park and tried to hide them in bushes, but despite his explicit orders, a statue of him was erected after his death at age 93. The park itself is McLaren's best memorial.

To get to the park from downtown, hop on bus #5, 21, 16, or 71. Bus #44 passes right by the major attractions and serves 6th Ave. to California Ave. to the north and the MUNI Metro to the south. The park is bounded by Fulton St. to the north, Stanyan St. to the east, Lincoln Way to the south, and the Pacific Ocean to the west, except for a strip called the **Panhandle,** jutting east between Fell St. and Oak. (Originally the "carriage entrance," it contains the oldest trees and extends into the realm of Haight-Ashbury.) A heavily trafficked north-south route through the park is named **Park Presidio By-Pass Drive** in the north and **Cross-Over Drive** in the south, and continues all the way up to the Golden Gate Bridge.

South of the park, young San Franciscans sleep (but don't party) in the **Sunset District.** Crawl Irving St. for a surprising cache of inviting bookstores and eateries, including groceries for the perfect picnic lunch.

Food

The park contains two conveniently located **snack bars.** One sits behind the bandstand between the Academy of Sciences and the Asian Art Museum, and the other is located in the Stow Lake boathouse. Nonetheless, bringing your own food is a cheaper (and usually tastier and healthier) option. Neighboring districts offer good food within walking distance. Four blocks north, Geary Blvd. runs parallel to the park, and the stretch between 5th Ave. and 28th is filled with grocery stores, pizzerias, and other fairly inexpensive restaurants. One block south of the park, Irving St. bustles with digestibles around 9th Ave., as well as west in the mid-20s.

Marnee Thai, 2225 Irving St. (665-9500), between 23rd and 24th south of the park. Critics and your tastebuds will agree—this one's a winner. Roasted duck curry is a rare delight ($8). Veggie dishes $6. Open Wed.-Mon. 11:30am-10pm.

Ganges, 775 Frederick St. (661-7290). Innovative, all-vegetarian Indian cuisine and attentive service draws health-conscious locals to this intimate restaurant. Curry dishes ($6) and stuffed bananas ($7) will blow you away. Live music Fri.-Sat. from 7:15pm. Open Tues.-Sat. 5-10pm. Reservations recommended.

Sights

Golden Gate Park (http://www.ci.sf.ca.us/recpark/) should not be rushed through; San Franciscans bask there all weekend long. Intriguing museums and cultural events pick up where the extensive flora and fauna finally leave off, and athletic opportunities abound. In addition to cycling and blading paths, the park also has a municipal golf course, an equestrian center, sports fields, and a stadium. Info and maps can be found at **Park Headquarters** (831-2700), in McLaren Lodge, at Fell St. and Stanyan on the park's eastern edge (open Mon.-Fri. 8am-5pm).

There are three well-regarded **museums** in the park: the California Academy of Sciences, the M.H. de Young Memorial Museum, and the Asian Art Museum—all in one large complex on the east side, where 9th Ave. meets the park. The **California Academy of Sciences** (221-5100), one of the nation's largest institutions of its kind, houses several smaller museums specializing in different fields of science. The **Steinhart Aquarium,** home to members of over 14,000 aquatic species, is more lively than the natural history exhibits (shark feedings every 2hr. Fri.-Wed. 10:30am-4:30pm). At the **Space and Earth Hall,** one exhibit shakes visitors up as they might have been in the great tremor of 1906. More zaniness resides down the corridor, where the **Far Side of Science** gallery pays tribute to Gary Larson. The **Morrison Planetarium** (750-7141), recreates the heavens above with an impressive show (tickets $2.50, students $1.25, seniors $1.25). The **Laserium** (750-7138; http://www.laserium.com), plays its laser show to rockin' themes by bands like Pink Floyd, Morrissey, and Jane's Addiction (tickets $7, seniors $5, ages 6-12 $5; 5pm matinee $6; under 6 not admitted). The Academy is open daily from 9am to 6pm (admission $8.50, seniors $5.50, ages 12-17 $5.50, ages 4-11 $2; free 1st Wed. of each month).

The **M. H. de Young Memorial Museum** (750-3600), takes visitors through a 21-room survey of American art, from the colonial period to the early 20th century, including noteworthy pieces by John Singer Sargent and a Tiffany glass collection. The **Asian Art Museum** (379-8801), in the west wing of the building, is the largest museum outside Asia dedicated entirely to Asian artwork. The beautiful collection includes rare pieces of jade and porcelain, in addition to 3000-year-old bronzes. Both museums offer a variety of free tours—call for details. (Both museums open Wed.-Sun. 9:30am-5pm. Admission $7, seniors $5, ages 12-17 $4; free and open until 8:45 1st Wed. of each month.)

Despite its sandy past, the soil of Golden Gate Park is rich enough today to support a wealth of flowers, particularly in spring and summer. Though closed indefinitely for repairs, the **Conservatory of Flowers** (752-8080), erected in 1879, is a delicate structure and the oldest building in the park (built 1879). The **Strybing Arboretum** (661-1316), on Lincoln Way at 9th, is home to 5000 varieties of plants. The **Garden of Fragrance** is designed especially for the visually impaired; all labels are in Braille and the plants are chosen specifically for their texture and scent (open Mon.-Fri. 8am-4:30pm, Sat.-Sun. 10am-5pm; tours daily 1:30pm, also Thurs.-Sun. 10:30am; free). Near the Music Concourse off of South Dr., the **Shakespeare Garden** contains almost every flower and plant ever mentioned by the herbalist of Stratford-upon-Avon. Plaques with the relevant quotations are hung on the back wall, and there's a map to help you find your favorite hyacinths and cowslips (open daily dawn-dusk, in winter closed Mon.; free). **Rhododendron Dell,** between the Academy of Sciences and John F. Kennedy Dr., honors John McLaren with a splendid profusion of his favorite flower. In the middle of Stow Lake, wreak fruity havoc by getting your thrill on **Strawberry Hill.** At the intersection of Lincoln Way and South Dr., the **Japanese Cherry Orchard** blooms intoxicatingly the first week in April.

Created for the 1894 Mid-Winter Exposition, the elegant **Japanese Tea Garden** is a serene collection of dark wooden buildings, small pools, graceful footbridges, carefully pruned trees, and lush plants. Buy tea and cookies for $2.50 and watch the giant carp circle the central pond. (Open daily 9am-6pm; winter 10am-3pm. Admission $2.50, seniors and ages 6-12 $1, under 6 free. Free 1st Wed of each month.)

In the extreme northwest of the park, the **Dutch Windmill** has done its last good turn. Once the muscle behind the park's irrigation system, the outdated old powerhouse (114ft. from sail to sail) is now the purely ornamental centerpiece of the cheery Queen Wilhelmina garden. Rounding out the days of yore is the **carousel** (c. 1912), which is accompanied by a $50,000 Gebruder band organ. (Open daily 10am-5pm; Oct.-May Tues.-Wed. and Fri.-Sun. 9am-4pm. Admission $1, ages 6-12 25¢.) Brimming **Spreckels Lake,** located on John F. Kennedy Dr., is populated with crowds of turtles who pile onto a turtle-shaped rock to sun themselves—as Geertz said, it's turtles all the way down. The multinational collection of gardens and museums in Golden Gate Park would not be complete without something distinctly American, and what could be more American than a herd of **bison?** A dozen of the shaggy beasts loll about a spacious paddock just west of Spreckels. The just-completed **AIDS Memorial Grove,** covering 15 acres, sounds a sobering note off Middle East Dr. north of the 3rd Ave. entrance.

On Sundays, traffic is banned from park roads, and bicycles and in-line skates come out in full force. Bikes are available for rent at the **Lincoln Cyclery,** 772 Stanyan St. (221-2415), on the east edge of Golden Gate Park. (Mountain bikes $5 per hr., $25 per day. Driver's license or major credit card and $20 deposit required. Open Mon. and Wed.-Sat. 9am-5pm, Sun. 11:30am-5pm.) **Stow Lake** rents tandems ($10 per hr.) and covered multi-rider pedal cars called surreys ($12 per hr.).

South of the park along Irving, another kind of leaf proliferates: some of the city's most outstanding used **booksellers** have set up shop here (see **Shopping,** p. 282).

RICHMOND

Historically a neighborhood of first- and second-generation immigrants, Richmond has been the traditional home to Irish-, Russian-, and now Chinese-American communities. "Inner Richmond," the area east of Park Presidio Blvd., has such a large Chinese population that it has been dubbed "New Chinatown." Extending east from Point Lobos to the Financial District, this mostly residential area is fairly safe. Geary Blvd. is a main thoroughfare through the area. Clement St. and California St. run parallel to Geary. The region, enclosed by these streets, as well as 28th and 5th Ave., sprawls through the numbered avenues to the wealthy area along the Pacific shore.

Food

Some locals claim that the Chinese restaurants in Richmond are better than the ones in Chinatown. The jury's still deliberating, so venture out and decide for yourself. The area also has Thai, Burmese, Cambodian, Japanese, Italian, Russian, Korean, and Vietnamese restaurants. **Clement Street** has the widest variety of options.

New Golden Turtle, 308 5th Ave. (221-5285), at Clement. Vietnamese dishes like *bahn xeo,* or savory crepe ($6.50), are irresistible. Tastes like the food in heaven, only with more ginger. Vegetarian options abound. Dinner entrees $8-9. Open Mon. 5-11pm, Tues.-Sun. 11am-11pm.

The Red Crane, 1115 Clement St. (751-7226), between Funston and 12th St. Chinese veggie-and-seafood restaurant regularly racks up good reviews. Locals wax ecstatic over the spicy Szechuan eggplant ($5), but with over 50 entree items, you can choose your own adventure. Open daily 11:30am-10pm.

The Blue Danube, 306 Clement St. (221-9041). Laid-back cafe caters to its regulars with super service. Besides the usual espresso drinks, there are 4 beers on tap ($3) and amazing gardenburgers ($4). Open Mon.-Thurs. 7am-11:30pm, Fri.-Sat. 7am-12:30am, Sun. 7am-10:30pm.

Toy Boat Dessert Cafe, 401 Clement St. (751-7505), at 5th. Sells San Francisco's famous Double Rainbow ice cream ($1.85) and delicious baked goods as well as trucks, trains, and kitschy trinkets. Open Mon.-Thurs. 7:30am-11:30pm, Fri. 7:30am-midnight, Sat. 8:30am-midnight, Sun. 8:30am-11:30pm.

Ella's, 500 Presidio (441-5669), at California. Busy for breakfast, and with good reason. Chipper staff serves food fit for the first lady of song. Fresh-squeezed O.J. is an eye-opener. House omelettes $7. Long lines for weekend brunch. Open Mon.-Fri 7am-9pm, Sat.-Sun.9am-2pm. Reservations for party of 8 or more only.

Sights

Lincoln Park, at the northwest end of San Francisco, is the bulkiest and best attraction in Richmond. To get there, follow Clement St. west to 34th Ave., or Geary Blvd. to Point Lobos Ave. (MUNI bus #1 or 38). The grounds around the park, which include the **Land's End Path,** offer a romantic view of the Golden Gate Bridge. The **California Palace of the Legion of Honor** (863-3330; http://www.thinker.org), on Legion of Honor Dr. in the park, houses an impressive fine art collection. A thorough catalogue of great masters from medieval to Matisse hangs in the recently renovated marble-accented museum. Temporary exhibits display recent acquisitions and more contemporary work. (Open Tues.-Sun. 9:30am-5pm. Admission $7, seniors $5, ages 12-17 $4. With MUNI passport or transfer, $2 off. 2nd Wed. of each month free.)

Southwest of Lincoln Park at the end of Pt. Lobos/Geary Blvd. sits the precarious **Cliff House,** the third of that name to occupy this spot (the previous two burned down before the present structure was erected in 1909). Next door, the **National Park Service Visitors Center** (556-8642), dispenses info on the wildlife of the cliffs and the wild life of the house (open daily 10am-5pm). Don't feed the coin-operated binoculars which look out over **Seal Rocks**—head into the visitors center instead and have a free look through its telescope. **Ocean Beach,** the largest and most popular of San Francisco's beaches, begins south of Point Lobos and extends down the northwestern edge of the city's coastline. The strong undertow along the point is very dangerous, but die-hard surfers brave the treacherous currents and the ice-cold water to ride the best waves in San Francisco. Swimming is allowed at **China Beach** at the end of Seacliff Ave. on the eastern edge of Lincoln Park. The water is cold here too, but the views are stunning (lifeguards on duty April-Oct.).

To the east of the Cliff House are the ruins of Adolph Sutro's 1896 bath house. Cooled by ocean water, the **Sutro Baths** were capable of squashing in 25,000 occupants at a time, but after an enthusiastic opening surge very rarely did. Various combinations of pools and skating rinks failed to make the operation fly, and the buildings were finally abandoned after a fire gutted them in 1966. Paths lead there from Point Lobos Ave. Be careful when exploring the ruins and nearby cliffs.

South of Ocean Beach, the **San Francisco Zoo** (753-7061), on Sloat Blvd., is distant and unremarkable, but die-hard primate fans may enjoy it (open daily 10am-5pm; admission $7, seniors $3.50, ages 12-15 $3.50, ages 3-11 $1.50). **Temple Emmanuel,** 2 Lake St. (751-2535), at Arguello, is an intriguing specimen of Moorish architecture, designed by the same architect who crafted the Civic Center (free docent tours available Mon.-Fri. 1-3pm; call ahead). The **Presidio Bicycle Shop,** 5335 Geary Blvd. (752-2453), between 17th and 18th, rents bikes for $7 per hour, $25 per day (open Mon.-Fri. 10am-6pm, Sat.-Sun. 10am-5pm).

THE PRESIDIO AND THE GOLDEN GATE BRIDGE

The **Presidio,** a sprawling preserve that extends all the way from the Marina in the east to the wealthy Sea Cliff area in the west, was occupied by the U.S. Army for nearly a century between the Mexican and Second World Wars. Now administered by the National Park Service, the Presidio's otherwise fairly dull expanses are ideal for biking, jogging, and hiking. The preserve also supports the southern end of San Francisco's world-famous Golden Gate Bridge (take MUNI bus #28, 29, or Golden Gate transit buses into the preserve).

Food

Restaurant options in the Presidio begin and end with an isolated mid-park **Burger King.** Pack a picnic, or head to nearby Richmond for real food (see p. 271).

Sights

At the northern tip of the Presidio (and the peninsula), under the tower of the Golden Gate Bridge, **Fort Point** (556-1693), keeps watch over the entrance to San Francisco Bay. Though the spot was recognized as strategically pivotal in the face of diverse historical threats, no battle ever occurred here. There is a museum dedicated to past military occupants, but the fort's thrilling view of the sea-savaged surfers below is much more interesting. Film buffs will recognize the spot where Kim Novak dove into the Bay in Hitchcock's *Vertigo*. Guided tours are given by National Park Rangers. (Museum open Wed.-Sun. 10am-5pm. Programs include cannon-loading demos and short films on Fort Point history and the Golden Gate Bridge construction. Grounds open sunrise-sunset.)

All but synonymous with the city itself, the majestic **Golden Gate Bridge** spans the mouth of San Francisco Bay, a rust-colored symbol of the West's boundless confidence. Countless photographic renderings can't pack the punch of a personal encounter with the suspended colossus itself. The bridge's overall length is 8981 ft.; the main span is 4200 ft. long and the stolid towers are 746 ft. high. Though carefully disaster-proofed against seismic threat, the bridge still claims victims through its suicide appeal (it is the most popular site for suicides in the world) and lack of a traffic divider. If they make it across, southbound cars pay $3; both directions are free for bikes and pedestrians. Just across the bridge, **Vista Point** is just that—an incredible view of the city. **Baker Beach,** in Golden Gate National Recreation Area, is a chilly place to tan and swim. Excellent wind shelter helps keep the **nudist** tradition of the north part alive and kicking, if a trifle pallid.

MARINA AND PACIFIC HEIGHTS

The **Marina** is home to more young, moneyed professionals than any other part of San Francisco. Few signs of the '89 earthquake, which hit this area hard, still mar the elegant finish. Today—thank heaven for tax shelters—there's more waterfront window glass and aerobics studios than ever. **Union** and **Chestnut Streets** bustle with the click of Gucci heels in the evenings, when the neighborhood resembles your average Muffy and Buffy frat party. Come for the daytime panorama of the Golden Gate Bridge, or to inhale the well-manicured bouquet of garden roses and greenbacks in this self-proclaimed "Five-Star Neighborhood." Honey, bring the flip-phone.

A stiff climb into **Pacific Heights** breaks up the blinding whiteness slightly. Snazzy village clothing vendors and tasty eateries line **Fillmore Street,** and are concentrated between Bush and California.

Food

A few cheap eats nestle here among the fancy-schmancy hairdressers. The **Marina Safeway,** 15 Marina Blvd. (563-4946), between Laguna and Buchanan, is legendary as a spot to pick up more than just gourmet groceries. Despite its racier handle, **Wild Oats Community Market,** 2324 Chestnut (921-2992), can't match Safeway's cruise factor, but it does have good chemistry—much of the produce is organic.

Marina

Bepples Pies, 1934 Union (931-6225), at Laguna, would stir up Yankee pride in Robert E. Lee. Munch on comfort food on 2 cozy levels. Dinner pies $5-7, pancakes $4. Open Sun.-Thurs. 8am-midnight, Fri.-Sat. 8am-2am (kitchen closes at 3pm). A second location at 2124 Chestnut (at Steiner) goes to bed an hour earlier.

Sweet Heat, 3324 Steiner St. (474-9191), by Lombard. How sweet it is! T-shirt clad "Tequila Gods" serve big portions beneath a mural of the *danse macabre.* Fire-roasted corn on the cob (brushed with cilantro pesto or hot *chipotle,* $1.75) is heart-warming. Open Sun.-Thurs. 11am-11pm, Fri.-Sat. 11am-midnight.

Soku's Teriyaki and Sushi, 2280 Chestnut (563-0162). Great service, and a $4 lunchtime *obento* box special (2-item combo, with miso soup and rice; served 11:30am-3:30pm). Take out and wander down to the water for a stunning view to go with your stunning meal. Open daily 11:30am-10:30pm.

Pacific Heights

Leon's Bar*B*Q, 1911 Fillmore St. (922-2436), between Pine and Bush. At the southern end of yuppified Fillmore, Leon's serves up great Cajun jambalaya (with 2 corn muffins, $6) and sweet potato pie ($3). Open daily 11am-9pm.

La Méditerranée, 2210 Fillmore St. (921-2956), by Sacramento. Hearty portions at reasonable prices—a rarity around here. Try the Lule Kebab (lean ground lamb with spices, onions, and tomatoes, $7.75), or the Grecian Spinach and Feta Fillo Dough Specialty ($7.25). Open Mon.-Thurs. 11am-10pm, Fri.-Sat. 11am-11pm.

Pizza Inferno, 1800 Fillmore St. (775-1800), at Sutter on the border of Pacific Heights and Japantown. Trippy decor features dancing mermaids made modest by very happy fishies. Pizza lunch specials (from $5) include salad and soda. Open Sun.-Thurs. 11:30am-11pm, Fri.-Sat. 11:30am-midnight.

Sights

Scientific American calls the **Exploratorium,** 3601 Lyon St. (563-7337 or recorded message 561-0360), "the best science museum in the world," and it deserves this heady moniker. Located next to the Palace of Fine Arts along Marina Blvd., this warehouse is a mad scientist's dream. The Exploratorium holds up to 4284 people, and on the first Wednesday of each month, when admission is free, it sometimes does. All sorts flock here, from schoolkids to punks on dates. Displays include interactive tornadoes, computer planet-managing, and giant bubble-makers. (Open Sun.-Tues. and Thurs.-Sat. 10am-6pm, Wed. 10am-9:30pm. Labor Day-Memorial Day, open Tues.-Sun.10am-5pm, Wed. 10am-9:30pm. Admission $9, students $7, seniors $7, ages 6-17 $5. Free 1st Wed. of each month.) Within the Exploratorium dwells the **Tactile Dome** (561-0362), a pitch-dark maze of tunnels, slides, nooks, and crannies designed to help refine your sense of touch. Claustrophobes and darkaphobes beware (open during museum hours; admission $12; reservations required).

Next door to the Exploratorium sits the **Palace of Fine Arts** (Baker St., between Jefferson and Bay). The imposing domed structure and curving colonnades are reconstructed remnants of the 1915 Panama Pacific Exposition, which commemorated the opening of the Panama Canal and signalled San Francisco's recovery from the 1906 earthquake. The palace grounds, complete with swans and a pond, is one of the best picnic spots in the city. Shakespeare is sometimes performed in the summer, and the nighttime illumination is glorious (always open and free). The **Wave Organ** is also a short walk from the Exploratorium's main entrance. The gentle caress of the seaside waves stimulates the organ, designed by local artists Peter Richards and George Gonzales. Listen to the natural *ohm* of the water.

Centered about Union and Sacramento St., **Pacific Heights** boasts the greatest number of **Victorian buildings** in the city, as well as the best view of the Golden Gate. The Heights area was mostly unscathed by the 1906 earthquake, but sustained serious damage in 1989, and Victorian restoration has become a full-fledged enterprise. History takes on a different fabric in the **vintage** clothing stores along Fillmore (see **Shopping,** p. 282). The **Octagon House,** 2645 Gough St. (441-7512), at Union, was built in 1861 with the belief that the architecture would bring good luck to its inhabitants. Its survival of San Francisco's many earthquakes and fires is proof of fortune's favor. (Open Feb.-Dec. 2nd Sun. and 2nd and 4th Thurs. of the month noon-3pm; group tours by arrangement on any weekday.)

Along the water, **Marina Green** seethes with joggers and walkers and is famous for heavy-duty gay cruising. Play pick-up soccer on weekends, or just play pick-up. Biking along the Embarcadero will help you prime those quads. To rent the wheels, contact **Holiday Adventures Sale and Rental,** 1937 Lombard St. (567-1192), between Buchanan and Webster ($19 for 24hr. includes helmet and lock), or **Marina Cyclery,** 3330 Steiner St. (929-0863; mountain bikes $10 per hr. including helmet and lock).

To the east of Marina Green at Laguna and Marina lies **Fort Mason.** Non-profit organizations lease space cheaply in the army's old departure facility. The multicultural-friendly **Craft and Folk Art Museum,** Bldg. A (775-0990), is excellent (open Tues.-Fri. and Sun. 11am-5pm, Sat. 10am-5pm; admission $1-3). The **African-American Historical and Cultural Society Museum,** Bldg. C, #165 (441-0640), focuses on contemporary African arts and crafts (open Wed.-Sun. noon-5pm; admission $1-2). **Museo Italo Americano,** Bldg. C #100 (673-2200), displays works by artists of Italian heritage (open Wed.-Sun. noon-5pm; admission $3, students $1, seniors $1). The **Mexican Museum,** Bldg. D (441-0404), offers free tours, exhibits, and educational workshops; it has excellent photography collections (open Wed.-Sun. noon-5pm; admission $4, students $2, seniors $2, under 10 free). Sam Shepard served as the playwright-in-residence at the **Magic Theater,** Bldg. D, 3rd floor (441-8822), from 1975 to 1985. Today, the theatre stages both world and American premieres. (Shows Wed.-Sat. 8:30, Sun. 3pm. Tickets $15-21. Student rush tickets available ½hr. before show Wed.-Thurs. and Sun. $7, Fri. and Sun. $10.)

FISHERMAN'S WHARF & GHIRARDELLI SQUARE

East along the waterfront is San Francisco's most popular tourist destination. Stretching from Pier 39 in the east to Ghirardelli Square in the west is Fisherman's Wharf, home to ¾ mi. of porcelain figurines, enough t-shirts to have kept Washington's army snug at Valley Forge, and enough salt-water taffy to have made them all violently ill. No wonder the tour buses pile in. Conventional attractions aside, the best way to appreciate the wharf is to wake up at 4am, put on a warm sweater, and go down to the piers to see why it's called Fisherman's Wharf. You can see the loading and outfitting of small ships, the animated conversation, the blanket of the morning mist, and the incredible view—without the rapacious crowds. Go to say you've been there, but one hour is probably plenty. Next!

Food

At most Wharf restaurants, you can go broke eating remarkably unremarkable food. An exception is **Trish's Mini Donuts,** which taste terrific but won't fulfill any portion of the food pyramid (6-on-a-stick $1.75). Those looking for real food might try one of the following alternatives:

Caffe Freddy's, 901 Columbus Ave. (922-0151). Half-orders of flavorful pastas are big enough to serve as lunch ($4.50). Finish off with a sangria and citrus ($3). Open Tues. 11:30am-9:30pm, Wed.-Fri. 11:30am-10pm, Sat. 10am-10pm, Sun. 10am-9pm.

Rico's, 943 Columbus Ave. (928-5404), near Lombard, between Fisherman's Wharf and North Beach. Well worth the 10min. walk, Rico's serves enormous burritos ($3-5) and bottled Mexican beers ($2.50) for a fraction of the price of a Wharf-side snack. Free chips and salsa. Open daily 10am-10pm.

Crab Cake Lounge, 900 North Point St. (929-1730), at Beach and Larkin in Ghirardelli Square. Decadent 6-oyster sampler $9. Calzones and brick oven pizzas of all sorts $5-10. Open daily 11:30am-11pm.

Sights

Easily visible from boats and the waterfront is **Alcatraz Island.** Named in 1775 for its *alcatraces* (pelicans), this former federal prison looms over San Francisco Bay, 1½ mi. from Fisherman's Wharf. During World War I, conscientious objectors were held on the island along with men convicted of violent crimes while in the service. In the 30s, the federal government used it to hold those who had wreaked too much havoc in other prisons, including infamous prisoners like Al Capone and "Machine Gun" Kelly. Of the 23 men who attempted to escape, all were recaptured or killed, except for five who were "presumed drowned" although their bodies were never found. Robert "The Birdman" Stroud, one of the most infamous prisoners, spent 17 years in solitary confinement—no escape for him. Although sentenced to death for killing a prison guard, Stroud was spared by President Wilson and went on to write two books on bird diseases. In 1962, Attorney General Robert Kennedy closed the prison, and the island's existence was uneventful until 1969, when about 80 Native Americans occupied it as a symbolic gesture, claiming "the rock" as their property under the terms of a broken 19th-century treaty. Alcatraz is currently a part of the **Golden Gate National Recreation Area** (561-4345). The **Blue and Gold Fleet** (705-5444 or 705-5555; call daily 7am-8pm), runs boats to Alcatraz from **Pier 41** (call far in advance). Once on Alcatraz, you can wander by yourself or take the audiotape-guided tour, full of clanging chains and the ghosts of prisoners past. (Boats depart every ½hr. from Pier 41, summer 9:15am-4:15pm, winter 9:45am-2:45pm. Tickets $7.75, seniors $6, ages 5-11 $4.50. Tours $3.25, ages 5-11 50¢. Arrive 20min. before departure.) **Red and White Fleet** (447-0597 or 800-BAY-CRUISE/229-2784), operates a 45-minute cruise tour called Round the Rock, which travels "round the rock," but not on it (boats depart from Pier 43½; tickets $11, seniors $9, ages 9-11 $7).

Back on the mainland, **Pier 39** (981-7437), built on pilings that extend several hundred yards into the harbor, juts toward Alcatraz. Its creators designed it to recall old San Francisco, but it ended up looking more like a backdrop from a Ronald Reagan Western (shops open daily 10:30am-8:30pm). Toward the end of the pier is **Center Stage,** where mimes, jugglers, and magicians wow the crowds. You can gawk at the harbor on any of the expensive **tour boats** and **ferries** docked west of Pier 39. Similar opportunities lie aboard the Blue and Gold Fleet or the Red and White Fleet, which were named for the colors of Bay Area rivals Berkeley and Stanford, respectively. Tours cruise under the Golden Gate Bridge past Angel Island and Alcatraz, providing sweeping views of the San Francisco skyline.

Even if you don't know the fo'c'sle from the mizzen, you'll be able to get your sea legs aboard the **Maritime Museum** (929-0202), five vessels docked along the Hyde St. pier and at Pier 45 past the ferries. (Hyde St. open daily 10am-6pm; admission $4, ages 12-17 $2, seniors and under 12 free. Pier 45 open daily 9am-8pm; admission $5, seniors $3, and ages 6-12 $3, under 6 free.)

Aquatic Park is the area of the Bay enclosed by the Hyde St. Pier and the curving Municipal Pier. Unbelievably, members of the **Dolphin Swimming and Boating Club,** 502 Jefferson St. (441-9329), and the neighboring **South End Club,** swim laps in the chilly 57°F water. For $6.50, you too can take a dip in the bay and, perhaps more importantly, thaw out in the club's showers and sauna afterwards (open Tues., Thurs., and Sat. 11am-6pm). Along Aquatic Park is **Municipal Pier,** said to be the inspiration for Otis Redding's "Sittin' On The Dock of the Bay."

Ghirardelli (GEAR-ah-deh-lee) **Square,** 900 N. Point St. (info 775-5500), is the most famous of the shopping malls in the area around Fisherman's Wharf, and rightfully so—it houses some of the best chocolate in the world. Today, the only remains of the machinery from Ghirardelli's original chocolate factory display the chocolate-making process in the rear of the **Ghirardelli Chocolate Manufactory,** an old-fashioned ice-cream parlor. Suddenly got a craving? The nearby Soda Fountain serves up loads of its world-famous hot fudge sauce on huge sundaes ($6). For a dessert extravaganza, try the Earthquake Sundae (with several ravenous friends)—eight flavors of ice cream, eight toppings, bananas, whipped cream, nuts, and cherries for a symbolic $19.06. (Get it?) If your appetite outpaces your financial resources, look for the free chocolate samples inside the Ghirardelli store (771-4903; open daily 10am-midnight). Pricey boutiques fill the old factory's brick buildings, and local performers entertain the masses (stores open Mon.-Sat. 10am-9pm, Sun. 10am-6pm).

NORTH BEACH

Along Columbus Ave. and Stockton St., there is a gradual transition from shops selling ginseng and roast duck to those selling provolone and biscotti. Lying north of Chinatown is the Italian community of North Beach. In the 50s the bohemian Beats (Allen Ginsberg, Jack Kerouac, and local Lawrence Ferlinghetti, among others), raised a ruckus and a few eyebrows here. The Beat Generation is now a 3-CD set, but the Italians remain. North Beach maintains a sense of serene continuity while feeding and entertaining the rest of the Bay.

Food

Excellent cafes, bakeries, and delis butt up against an abundance of great Italian restaurants in North Beach. Not all are in the budget range, but big carbohydrate loads can be worth a few extra dollars after hiking area hills. Many eateries also double as swingin' jazz venues (see **Nightlife,** p. 285).

Sodini's Green Valley Restaurant, 510 Green St. (291-0499), at Grant. In the true heart of North Beach, this is one of the area's oldest family restaurants, established in 1906. The *Ravioli alla Casa* rocks the house ($8.25). Open Mon.-Fri. 5pm-10pm, Sat.-Sun. 5pm-midnight.

Mario's Bohemian Cigar Store Cage, 566 Columbus Ave. (362-0536). A hip, laid-back cafe right at the corner of Washington Square Park. Usually crowded, this is a great place to hang out and grab some first-rate grub. Hot hot sandwiches $6. Open Mon.-Sat. 10am-midnight, Sun. 10am-11pm.

Caffe Greco, 423 Columbus Ave. (397-6261). The code word is casual, though the culinary thrill is not. Focaccia sandwiches $5-6, tiramisu $3.75. You know it's Italian when decaf costs more (Caffe Freddo Sambuca $3). Open Mon.-Thurs. 7am-11pm, Fri.-Sun. 7am-midnight.

The Stinking Rose, 325 Columbus Ave. (PU-1-ROSE/781-7673; fax 781-2833). "We season our garlic with food" is their mantra, and excellent, *very* aromatic cuisine is their masterpiece (pasta $8-13). For the dating crowd, "vampire fare" (i.e. garlic free) is also available. Open Sun.-Thurs. 11am-11pm, Fri.-Sat. 11am-midnight.

L'Osteria del Forno, 519 Columbus Ave. (982-1124), at Green. Prospective patrons pack the patio outside this petite pizza, pasta, and salad joint, so make reservations or go before you're really hungry. Entrees $8. Open Mon. and Wed.-Thurs. 11:30am-10pm, Fri.-Sat. 11:30am-10:30pm, Sun. 1-10pm. Cash only.

Sights

Bordered by Union, Filbert, Stockton, and Powell is **Washington Square,** North Beach's *piazza,* a pretty lawn edged by trees and watched over by a statue of Benjamin Franklin. The wedding site of Marilyn Monroe and Joe DiMaggio, every morning the park fills with men and women practicing *tai chi.* Across Filbert, to the north of the square, the **Church of St. Peter and St. Paul** (421-0809), beckons tired sight-seers to take refuge in its dark, wooden nave (mass in Italian, English, and Cantonese). Mrs. Lillie Hitchcock Coit donated the **Volunteer Firemen Memorial,** in the middle of the square. Rescued from a fire as a girl, Coit seemed hell-bent on thanking the city the rest of her life; she also put up the money to build **Coit Tower** (362-0808), which stands a few blocks to the east of the memorial. The tower sits on **Telegraph Hill,** the steep mount from which a semaphore signalled the arrival of ships in Gold Rush days. (Rumor has it that the tower was built to resemble a fire nozzle, but its other nickname. "coitus tower," gives a cruder approximation.) The view from the hill, or from atop the elevator-accessible tower itself, is spectacular. During the Great Depression, the government's Works Progress Administration employed artists to paint the fantastic and surprisingly subversive murals on the inside of the dome. (Open daily 10am-7pm; Oct.-May 9am-4pm. Elevator fare $3, over 64 $2, ages 6-12 $1, under 6 free.) Take MUNI bus #39, or walk up the **Filbert Steps** which rise from the Embarcadero to the eastern base of the tower. The walk is short, allows excellent views, and passes attractive Art Deco buildings.

North Beach bohemianism exploded when the Beats first moved in. Drawn to the area by low rents and cheap bars, the group came to national attention when Ferlinghetti's **City Lights Bookstore,** 261 Columbus Ave. (362-8193), published Allen Ginsberg's dream poem *Howl.* Banned in 1956, a judge found the book "not obscene" after an extended trial, but the resulting publicity turned North Beach into a must-see for curious visitors. Rambling and well-stocked, City Lights has expanded since its Beat days, and still publishes the works of poets and other writers under its own imprint. Radical political writings line the basement while upstairs a comfortable poetry/reading room contains self-published works, including lots of Beats. Says a clerk, "We're more than a bookstore—we're on to something." (Open daily 10am-midnight.)

The **Tattoo Art Museum,** 841 Columbus Ave. (775-4991), displays a fantastic collection of tattoo memorabilia, including hundreds of designs and exhibits on different tattoo techniques (the largest collection of its kind). In the same room, a modern, clean tattoo studio is run by the eminent professional Lyle Tuttle, himself covered in tattoos from head to foot. The minimum $50 will buy a quick rose on the hip; larger tattoos are $100 an hour. (Open Mon.-Thurs. noon-9pm, Fri.-Sat. noon-10pm.) At the nearby **Goldfield's Tattoo Studio,** 404 Broadway (433-0558), the body *is* art, and patron photos serve as wallpaper (open daily noon-8pm).

The **North Beach Museum,** 1435 Stockton St. (391-6210), at Columbus, accessible through Eureka Bank, depicts the North Beach of yesteryear in a series of vintage photographs (open Mon.-Thurs. 9am-4pm, Fri. 9am-6pm). Venture uphill to the **San Francisco Art Institute,** 800 Chestnut St. (771-7020), a converted mission with a courtyard housing parrots and every imaginable kind of angst-ridden student art project. The view from the school's balcony (with adjoining cafe) was said to have inspired alumnus Stanley Brakhage.

NOB HILL AND RUSSIAN HILL

Beware, O Traveler, for this is the land of the rich and their foofy dogs. In the late 19th century, Nob Hill attracted the great railroad magnates. Today, their ostentatious mansions make it one of the nation's most prestigious addresses. Largely residential, Nob and Russian Hills merit only a brief diversion. There's just not much to *do* here, and the hike up will wear you out—they don't call them "hills" for nothing.

Food

It can be a challenge to find inexpensive restaurants at the tops of Nob and Russian Hills (actually, it can be a challenge just to *get* to the tops of Nob and Russian Hills). However, a short walk east (**Chinatown,** see p. 280) or west (Polk St.) will bring you out of the realm of $5 martinis and into the world of $2 pork buns and $3 chowder.

The Golden Turtle, 2211 Van Ness St. (441-4419). Mind-blowing Vietnamese restaurant serves fabulous entrees ($8-11) amongst intricately carved wooden walls. The spicy lemon grass chicken ($10) and vegetarian exotic lava pot ($9.50) are standouts. Open Tues.-Sun. 5-11pm. Reservations recommended on weekends.

Jona's on Hyde, 1800 Hyde St. (775-2517), at Vallejo, is a darling corner store serving distinctive sandwiches ($4.25) and other edibles, like the stuffed avocado on a bed of greens ($5). Open Mon.-Fri. 8am-7:30pm, Sat. 8am-6pm, Sun. 9am-3pm.

U-Lee, 1468 Hyde St. (771-9774). Scores of written tributes to U-Lee from grateful patrons adorn the walls in this tiny but wildly popular mainstay. The potstickers (6 for $3.85) are legendary. "They were as big as my hand!" says one enthusiast. Many fresh vegetable dishes. Entrees $3-7. Open Tues.-Sun. 11am-9pm.

Nob Hill Noshery Cafe Deli and Catering Co., 1400 Pacific Ave. (928-6674), at Hyde, manages its identity crisis with indomitable charm. Sit on window-side cushions and eat hot entrees ($6-8), or just munch a sandwich ($4-7) with milk ($1). Open Sun.-Thurs. 7am-10pm, Fri.-Sat. 7am-11pm.

Bob's Broiler Restaurant, 1601 Polk St. (474-8161), at Sacramento. Not one of the Chinese owners is named Bob, but they all bob with hospitality—the bulk of their customers return *every single day* to consume diner fare like banana pancakes ($4), or Chinese rice plates ($4). Open Mon.-Tues. and Thurs. 7am-9pm, Wed. 7am-3pm, Fri.-Sun. 7am-10pm.

Sights

After the steep journey up Nob Hill, you will understand what inspired the development of the vehicles celebrated at the **Cable Car Powerhouse and Museum,** 1201 Mason St. (474-1887), at Washington. The building is the working center of the cable-car system—look down on the operation from a gallery or view displays to learn more about the picturesque cars, some of which date back to 1873 (open daily 10am-6pm; Nov.-March 10am-5pm; free).

Grace Cathedral, 1051 Taylor St. (776-6611), the most immense Gothic edifice west of the Mississippi, crowns Nob Hill. The castings for its portals are such exact imitations of Ghiberti's on the Baptistery in Florence that they were used to restore the originals. Inside, modern murals mix San Franciscan and national historical events with scenes from saints' lives (open Sun.-Fri. 7am-6pm, Sat. 8am-6pm; Sun. services at 7:30, 8:30, 11am, and 3:30pm).

Once the site of the enormous mansions of the four mining and railroad magnates who "settled" Nob (Charles Crocker, Mark Hopkins, Leland Stanford, and Collis Huntington), the hilltop is now home to upscale hotels and bars. The competition for the title of Bar with the Best View is fought by two bars: the **Top of the Mark,** One Nob Hill (392-3434), in the Mark Hopkins Hotel at Mason and California, and the **Fairmont Crown,** 950 Mason St. (772-5131), at the Fairmont Hotel. Both views are superb, but unless you consider paying $5.50 per beer or up to $80 for a glass of Remy-Martin to be a privilege, you might want to souse yourself elsewhere. (Cocktails served at the Crown Sun.-Thurs. 11am-12:30am, Fri.-Sat. 11am-1:30am; at the Mark Sun.-Thurs. 4pm-12:30am, Fri.-Sat. 4pm-1:30am. The Mark also has live music Wed.-Sat. and exuberant swing dancing Fri.-Sat. Cover $6-10.)

Nearby **Russian Hill** is named after Russian sailors who died during an expedition in the early 1800s and were buried on the southeast crest. At the top, the famous curves of **Lombard Street** (between Hyde and Leavenworth) afford a fantastic view of the city and harbor. The switchbacks were installed in the 1920s to allow horse-drawn carriages to negotiate the extremely steep hill. After all that climbing, indulge yourself at the **original Swensen's,** 1999 Hyde St. (775-6818), at Union, the store that gave rise to the national chain. Fresh batches made in the window Monday, Wednesday, and Friday (open daily 11:30am-10pm; ice cream $1.45 per scoop).

NIHONMACHI (JAPANTOWN)

Partially prodded by discrimination, Japanese immigrants moved here *en masse* after the 1906 quake, which destroyed this part of town. Today, 12,000 residents make up one of the largest Japanese enclaves outside of Japan (the largest is in São Paulo, Brazil). Nevertheless, this community encompasses an area of only about nine square blocks, and attracts far less tourist traffic than North Beach or China-town. Located one-mile west of downtown, Nihonmachi is bordered to the north by Bush, to the east by Fillmore, to the west by Laguna, and to the south by the Geary Expressway. Take MUNI buses #2, 3, and 4 to Buchanan or #38 to Geary.

Food

Like Japan itself, Nihonmachi can be an expensive place to eat. The best bets are lunch specials and filling bowls of noodle soup. Indulging in sushi is a budget-bending treat. Restaurants cluster in the **Japan Center's** three connected buildings and across the way on pedestrian-only **Buchanan Mall.** As in Japan, plastic models of the food are usually displayed in the window for pre-dining perusal.

Isobune Sushi Restaurant, 1737 Post St. (563-1030), in the Japan Center's Kintetsu Bldg. Cheesy floating sushi boats circle an immense counter, but if you put up with the gimmick and the crowds, you'll be rewarded by outstanding fish (2 pieces $1.20-3). Open daily 11:30am-10pm.

Mifune, 1737 Post St. (922-0337), across the hall from Isobune. Hearty hot soups with choice of *udon* (thick, white noodles) or *soba* (flat, gray noodles) for $4-6. *Sake* $2.25-4.25. Open daily 11am-10pm, in winter Sun.-Thurs. 11am-9:30pm.

Akasaka, 1723 Buchanan Mall (921-5360), between Sutter and Post, next to Fuji Shiatsu. Japanese cuisine "with a touch of Hawaii." Nightly special includes main course, rice, *miso* soup, salad, *tsu kemono* (pickled veggies), *edamane* (bean paste), dessert, and tea for $11. Open Tues.-Thurs. 8am-2:30pm and 5-9:30pm, Fri.-Sat. 8am-2:30pm and 5-10pm, Sun. 8am-2:30pm.

Sapporo-Ya, 1581 Webster St. (563-7400). Ramen noodles made almost every day right in the window. Mountainous bowls $4-7. Not vegetarian-friendly. Open Mon.-Sat. 11am-1:30am.

Sights

Walking from one end of Nihonmachi to the other takes just minutes, and it's the only way to go. Stores hawk the latest Hello Kitty gadgets and karaoke bars emanate cheesy Japan-pop all along Polk around the **Japanese Cultural and Trade Center.** Stretching from Laguna to Fillmore, the five-acre center includes Japanese *udon* houses, sushi bars, and a massage center and bathhouse. The five-tiered **Peace Pagoda,** a gift to the community from the Japanese government, grows fungus in one of the center's courtyards. Brighter examples of Japanese architecture include the **Sokoji Buddhist temple,** outside at the corner of Laguna and Sutter (346-7540; *zazen* services open Sun. 8:30am, Wed. and Fri. 6:30pm; arrive ½hr. early). The **Kabuki 8 Complex,** 1881 Post St. (931-9800), at Fillmore, shows current films, and during early May is the main site of the San Francisco Film Festival (see **Movies,** p. 282). **Japantown Bowl** offers great deals and 24hr. service on the weekends, plus

SAN FRANCISCO

glow-in-the-dark bowling two to three times per week (see **Entertainment,** p. 281).

The weary traveler might want to invest in a rejuvenating massage at **Fuji Shiatsu** (346-4484), upstairs at 1721 Buchanan Mall, between Sutter and Post (open Mon.-Fri. 9am-8pm, Sat. 9am-7pm, Sun. 10am-6pm; morning $33 per hr., afternoon $36).

CHINATOWN

The largest Chinese community outside of Asia (over 100,000 people), Chinatown is also the most densely populated of San Francisco's neighborhoods. The area was founded in the 1880s when, after the gold had been dug and the tracks laid, racism exploded and many deemed Chinese-Americans a "Yellow Peril." In response, the ethnic community banded together to protect themselves in this small section of downtown. As the city grew, speculators tried to take over the increasingly valuable land, but the neighborhood refused to be expelled, and Chinatown, which has gradually expanded, remains almost exclusively Chinese.

Exotic ingestibles line these busy streets, and the fish markets carry some of the freshest and most unusual produce around, from living (though doomed) turtles and frogs to the dried delicacy of shark fin ($149 per lb.). Treat yourself to a bag of fresh *lichee* fruit, and wander to your heart's (or your stomach's) content.

Food

Chinatown is filled with downright cheap restaurants; in fact, their multitude and surface similarity can make a choice nearly impossible. Luckily, it's hard to make a bad choice—many feel that San Francisco's Chinese cuisine is unsurpassed outside of Asia. The poverty of the menu translation often serves as a good measure of a restaurant's authenticity, but if you can't tell the difference, don't sweat it—chances are good you'll like what you get. Gentlemen, let the bingeing begin.

Kowloon Vegetarian Restaurant, 909 Grant Ave. (362-9888), at Jackson. If kitchen-bound Chinese livestock had a patron saint, Kowloon's chef would be it, serving outstanding vegetarian food for ridiculously low prices. Copious lunch specials $3.50 with rice, $4.50 with noodles. Open daily 10am-9:30pm.

House of Nanking, 919 Kearny St. (421-1429), at Pacific and Columbus. Nank and the world nanks with you—if you have no issue with waiting and don't mind a loose interpretation of "service," the famous House cuisine will satisfy. Entrees $5-6, onion cakes $1.75. Open daily 11am-10pm. No credit cards.

Brandy Ho's, 217 Columbus Ave. (788-7527), at Pacific. The paintings of hot peppers are a warning to the unsuspecting: this food is SPICY. Order from the thoughtful "not hot with pepper" category to maintain your cool. Lunch specials $4-5. Open Sun.-Thurs. 11:30am-11pm, Fri.-Sat. 11:30am-midnight.

My Canh, 626 Broadway (397-8888). Fantastic aromas abound in this clean Vietnamese/Chinese restaurant. Rice plates $4, pho noodle soup $3.75, jellyfish, shrimp and pork $5. Open daily 10am-2am.

King Tin, 826 Washington St. (982-7855). A casual joint among casual joints. Patrons laud the simple, well-made fare (most dishes $3.50-8)—the special chicken-swallow-sharkfin soup ($18) is the fancy exception that proves the rule. Open Sun.-Thurs. 8am-midnight, Fri.-Sat 8am-3am.

Sights

Grant Avenue is a sea of Chinese banners, signs, and architecture. The avenue is lined with shops doing brisk business selling Asian-made tourist wares. But once you step off Grant Ave., Chinatown is a real community, not a hokey fabrication. The less famous streets, such as Jackson, Stockton, and Pacific, are a more accurate representation of the neighborhood and the stores there are often less expensive. Pharmacies stock both Western and Eastern remedies for common ailments, produce markets are stacked with inexpensive vegetables, and Chinese newspapers are sold by vendors eating their breakfast ramen out of thermoses.

Squeeze into a tiny doorway to watch fortune cookies being shaped by hand in the **Golden Gate Cookie Company,** 56 Ross Alley (781-3956; bag of cookies $2, with hilarious sexy fortunes $4), between Washington and Jackson, just west of Grant. The famous **Ross Alley** has preserved the atmosphere of old Chinatown, and made many movie memories. You might recognize it from including *Big Trouble in Little China, Karate Kid II,* or *Indiana Jones and the Temple of Doom.* **Portsmouth Square,** at Kearny and Washington St., made history in 1848 when Sam Brennan first announced the discovery of gold at Sutter's Mill there. Today, the square is considerably calmer, filled with Chinese men playing card games. A stone bridge leads from this square to the **Chinese Culture Center,** 750 Kearny St. (986-1822), in the Holiday Inn, which houses exhibits of Chinese-American art and sponsors two **walking tours** of Chinatown (gallery open Tues.-Sat. 10am-4pm, Sun. noon-4pm). The **Heritage Walk** surveys the history of Chinatown (Sat. 2pm; admission $15, under 19 $5), and the **Culinary Walk** teaches the preparation of Chinese food (by arrangement; admission $30, under 19 $15; price includes *dim sum* at Four Seas on Grant Ave.). Both walks require advance reservations. The **Chinese Historical Society,** 650 Commercial St. (391-1188), between Kearny and Montgomery, relates the tale of the Chinese who came to California through books and remarkable artifacts, including a 1909 parade dragon head (open Tues.-Sat. noon-4pm; free).

At Grant and Bush stands the ornate, dragon-crested **Gateway to Chinatown,** given as a gift by the Republic of China in 1969. Some of Chinatown's noteworthy buildings include **Buddha's Universal Church** (720 Washington St.), the **Kong Chow Temple** (855 Stockton St.), and **Old St. Mary's,** (660 California St. at Grant), built in 1854 from Chinese granite, and San Francisco's only cathedral for almost four decades.

■ Entertainment

San Francisco entertainment is the freshmaker. Relaxed bars, wild clubs, serious cinema houses, decent sports teams, lively theater, world-class opera, and provocative bookstores assertively satisfy the wide range of San Franciscans' pleasure needs.

Sports enthusiasts should check out baseball's **San Francisco Giants** (467-8000 or 800-SF-GIANT/734-4268), and five-time Superbowl champions **49ers** (468-2249), both of whom play home games at the notoriously windy **Candlestick Park** (467-1994), officially called 3COM Park, located 8 mi. south of the city via U.S. 101. If you're too lazy or too sick of the NHL to see the Sharks in San Jose, you might want to catch the IHL **San Francisco Spiders** (656-3000), at the **Cow Palace** (469-6065) between October and April. **Bowling** may not be officially recognized, but it's still fun, and **Japantown Bowl** (921-6200), at Post and Webster in Japantown, lifts the art out of the gutter and into the alley with 24-hour weekends and spectacular glitz. Four nights a week are cyberbowl parties under black light—call for reservations (games midnight-9am $1.70 per person, 6pm-midnight $3.25; shoe rental $1.50).

If your ears are ringing with the sound of falling bowling pins, get tickets to the **San Francisco Symphony** through the box office at **Davies Symphony Hall,** 201 Van Ness (431-5400). The **Opera House** box office sells tickets for the **San Francisco Opera** (864-3330) and the **San Francisco Ballet** (703-9400). Tickets can be charged by phone (762-2277), or obtained directly from the box office (open Mon.-Sat. noon-6pm). Standing-room-only tickets on sale two hours before performances.

The **Sights** sections above discuss many entertainment opportunities, but more entertainment listings can be found in local magazines and newspapers (see **Publications,** p. 253), or by calling the **Entertainment Hotline** (391-2001 or 391-2002). The *Bay Guardian* and *SF Weekly* have thorough listings of dance clubs and live music, and the free monthly *Oblivion* has info on San Francisco's **gay** scene.

MOVIES

For a complete listing of features and locations, call MoviePhone (777-FILM/3456).

Landmark (352-0810), has 17 theaters throughout the Bay Area. Shows independent, overlooked, and foreign films. At all branches, general admission is $7.50, seniors and under 13 are $4.50, and a 5-pack of tix goes for $27. **Gateway Landmark,** 215 Jackson St., at Battery and Front, in **North Beach. Clay Landmark,** 2261 Fillmore St., at Clay, in **Pacific Heights. Bridge Landmark,** 3010 Geary Blvd., at Blake, 3 blocks west of **Masonic.**

The Lumière, 1572 California St. (885-3201), at Polk and Larkin. Indie and art films. Occasional double features. Tickets $7, seniors $4, children $4, and first show of the day $4.

Red Victorian Movie House, 1727 Haight St. (668-3994), in the **Haight.** Munch on organic popcorn while watching art films and revivals from couch-like benches. Tickets $6; Wed. and Sat.-Sun. 2pm $5, seniors $3, under 12 $3.

Roxie, 3117 16th St. (863-1087), off Valencia in the **Mission.** Razor-sharp and fashionably foolish retro-punk and New Wave movies. Frisco's trendiest movie house; partly responsible for *Eraserhead* cult. Tickets $6, seniors $3, and under 12 $3.

Castro Theatre, 429 Castro St. (621-6120), near Market in the **Castro.** Landmark 1920s movie palace has live organ music between showings. Eclectic films, festivals, and double-features. Tickets $7, seniors $5, under 12 $5; matinees $5.

Cinemateque, 480 Portrero Ave. (558-8129), between Jones and Leavenworth in **Russian Hill.** Avant-garde movies in the auditorium of the San Francisco Art Institute. Summer screenings at Yerba Buena Gardens, 701 Mission St. (750-3624). Tickets $6, seniors $3, students $3, and disabled $3.

LONG-RUNNING THEATER

The Club Fugazi, 678 Beach Blanket Babylon Blvd. (421-4222), between Powell and Columbus in **North Beach.** *Beach Blanket Babylon,* a cabaret-style revue, is a San Francisco cult classic. Shows Wed.-Thurs. 8pm, Fri.-Sat. 7 and 10pm, Sun. 3 and 7pm. Box office open Mon.-Sat. 10am-6pm, Sun. noon-6pm. Tickets $18-45, Sun. matinee $18-40. Under 21 admitted to matinee only.

Shear Madness, 340 Mason Street (982-5463; http://www.shearmadness.com), at the Mason Street Theater, near Geary. Zany whodunit has a particularly San Franciscan flavor. Shows Tues.-Fri. 8pm, Sat. 6:30 and 9:30pm, Sun. 3 and 7:30pm. Tickets Sun.-Thurs. $28, Fri.-Sat. $32.

■ Shopping

San Francisco is very much about street culture. While L.A. is the land of the strip mall and the chain store, San Francisco is the land of the hole-in-the-wall shop and the serendipitous find. Visitors ramble through the neighborhoods taking in sights, sounds, and smells—often stopping in the stores which, like restaurants, make up the neighborhood's sights. Outlet stores abound in SoMa.

BOOKSTORES

Bountiful crops of literature are a San Francisco staple. The bibliophilic bent to the city can be traced to the Beats and Lawrence Ferlinghetti's publishing house, the **City Lights Bookstore,** which is still in operation (see **North Beach,** p. 276). Used books are a more luscious commodity—strike some of the "news that stays news" at the shops on Irving St. in the **Sunset District.**

A Different Light Bookstore, 489 Castro St. (431-0891; http://www.adlbooks.com), in the **Castro** (with cousins in New York and West Hollywood). This is the biggest **queer** bookseller in America. Copious special-interest subdivisions include several shelves devoted to camp. They claim to stock it all, and that's, well, straight talk. Open daily 10am-midnight.

A Clean Well-Lighted Place for Books, 601 Van Ness St. (441-6670), at **Golden Gate.** A name that goes on may be a name that lasts, but this store lives up to its appellation with wide, well-kept shelves and a full calendar of readers. Open Sun.-Thurs. 10am-11pm, Fri.-Sat. 10am-midnight.

Bound Together Anarchist Collective Bookstore, 1369 Haight St. (431-8355), at Masonic in the **Haight.** Surprisingly orderly stacks of new and used books of a typically Haightian selection, including subjects like "kulture" and "wimmin's studies." Open daily whenever they bind together.

Modern Times Bookstore, 888 Valencia (282-9246), in the **Mission.** Recalls Charlie Chaplin in name, but focuses on academic counterculture and world books in its game. Sexuality/gender and Spanish language sections are big, and the graphic novels are radically cool. Open Mon.-Sat. 11am-9pm, Sun. 11am-6pm.

Sunset Bookstore, 2161 Irving (664-3644), at 22nd in the **Sunset District.** This used bookstore has been a fixture of the neighborhood since the 70s, shining in many categories, especially literature and poetry. Military history section is strong on Civil War books. Stools scattered throughout the store encourage browsing. Open Mon.-Sat. 9am-9pm, Sun. 10am-9pm.

Russian Hill Bookstore, 2234 Polk St. (929-0997), at Vallejo in **Russian Hill.** The younger, snazzier sister of Sunset Bookstore, owned by the same couple. Used books of all types, many of the coffee table sort—art, photography, oversized history, etc. Separate alcove for antique and first edition books and a connected shop for journals, cards, photo boxes, and miscellanea. Open daily 10am-10pm.

McDonald's Bookstore, 48 Turk St. (673-2235), just off Market in the **Tenderloin.** A self-described "dirty, poorly lit place for books" (a stab at the City Center institution), this place stocks enough outdated magazines alone to smother a smaller store. Sorry, no fries with that. Open Mon.-Tues. and Thurs. 10am-6pm, Wed. and Fri.-Sat. 10am-6:30pm.

Chelsea Bookshop, 637 Irving (566-0507), at 8th in the **Sunset District.** Browse and brood over the delightfully broad collection of used and rare books, and relax in the comfy chairs. Open Sun.-Thurs. 11am-10pm, Fri.-Sat. 11am-11pm.

MUSIC STORES

San Francisco marches to the beat of its own drummer, and that beat is often matched by the jungle of clubs around the city. Whether searching for the perfect LP to complete your spinnin' session, or just trying to find the latest radio single, this city has it all. The **Haight** is a great hide-out for second-hand music, and there are even more audio goodies in the **Mission.**

Reckless Records, 1401 Haight St. (431-3434), in the **Haight.** Extensive collection of new and used LPs priced according to the number of scratches and the rarity of the album. Also sells CDs, videos, and tapes. Groove to a private beat at their indie listening station. Open Mon.-Sat. 10am-10pm, Sun. 10am-8pm.

Aquarius Records, (647-2272), in the **Mission.** Tiny store is known worldwide for their obscure selection of music of all genres, and they have a wise staff to fill you in. Only sells music that they love, so it's gotta be good. Indie, black metal, and kraut rock, but their real specialties are jungle, drum'n' bass, and imports from Japan and New Zealand. Open Mon.-Wed. 10am-9pm, Thurs.-Sun. 10am-10pm.

Recycled Records, 1377 Haight St. (626-4075; fax 626-0563), in the **Haight.** Outstanding selection of LPs and a few well-chosen CDs. Indie releases and imports. Open Mon.-Sat. 10am-10pm, Sun. 10am-8pm.

Open Mind Music, 342 Divisidero (621-2244), in the **Lower Haight.** Insane quanitity of used vinyl, and a fair amount of collectibles, but they sell it new, too. Dance, drum 'n' bass, trip-hop, experimental, lounge music, and yes, Zeppelin—now that's an open mind. Open Mon.-Sat. 11am-8pm, Sun. noon-7pm.

Streetlight Records, 3979 24th (282-3550), in **Noe Valley.** More than ½ used. Vinyl, 7"s, CDs, and tapes. They take pride in the condition of their wares—guaranteed quality and generous exchange policy, all for good prices. Open Mon.-Sat. 10am-10pm, Sun. 10:30am-8:30pm; trade-ins until 8pm only.

---

501 Blue Blood

Prague's not the only place where an old pair of 501s is worth more than a used car. Vintage Levis collectors spend hours sifting through the endless racks of dungarees in San Francisco's thrift shops, in hot pursuit of those finer details that turn denim into diamonds. A few telltale signs mark the precious Levis produced before a major 1960s design overhaul. Look for red stitching on the inside legs (known as **"red lines"** in collector lingo), and the **number "2"** underneath the top button snap. Check out the little red tag on the back pocket for the most revealing sign of a valuable pair of jeans. Before 1961, a **capital E** was used in the spelling of the brand name (rather than "LeVI'S," as it appears today). These pre-60s rarities can cost $100-1800, depending on their condition and the shade of denim (dark indigo is worth more). If you're set on being one of the vintage-collecting elite, hunt for a pair of 1940s Levis, when in a show of wartime patriotism, the company skimped on materials by painting on the trademark outside stitches. The **Levi Strauss Museum** (544-0655) showcases samples of these fashion relics. If you don't have any luck in your search, you can always fake it—Levis is putting out a new "Vintage Revival" line, complete with the red lines, "2," and big E. But be warned, you won't fool the members of Frisco's underground leather 'n' Levis community for a minute.

CLOTHING STORES

Not surprisingly, vintage clothes crop up in the same areas as reading matter and revisited rhythms. Spend more than you want to, and have more to show for it, along **Fillmore St.** in Pacific Heights, and the reliable **Haight St.** in Haight Ashbury.

Community Thrift Store, 623 Valencia St. (861-4910), in the **Mission.** This store is more about community than thrift—proceeds go to some 200 Bay area charities. Donations from wealthy patrons looking for a tax break ensure that this is designer thrift, not vintage. Full floor of clothes, bric-a-brac area, collectibles, appliances. High quality everything—even art. Open daily 10am-6:30pm.

Crossroads Trading Co., 1901 Fillmore (775-8885), in **Pacific Heights.** Score the perfect midriff top at this shop for the young and trendy. *Guardian's* Best of the Bay Award for used clothing. Clothes, shoes, and accessories of decades past, as well as the discards from the designer stores down the street. Open Mon.-Sat. 11am-7pm.

Departures from the Past, 2028 Fillmore (885-3377), in **Pacific Heights.** Vintage wares of a more upscale sort. All their clothes are repaired and dry-cleaned, giving them a "fresh" look. Casual sundresses from the 40s are as casual as the clothes get. Vintage blouses $5-18. Open Mon.-Sat. 11am-7pm, Sun. noon-6pm.

Wasteland, 1660 Haight St. (863-3150), in the **Haight.** This store is deserving of notice if only for its fab facade and window displays. Biggest selection of used and vintage on Haight St. New sunglasses and jewelry. Open daily 11am-7pm.

Goodwill, 1700 Haight St. (387-1192), in the **Haight.** A sharp eye and a little luck could net you an amazing find at the mongo Goodwill store. Racks and racks of the ever-popular Levis ($14). Shelves and shelves of everything else: shoes, housewares, books, linens, and some trash. The cars don't fit on the shelves—they are in the lot out back. Open Mon.-Sat. 9am-8pm, Sun. 11am-7pm.

Thrift Town, 2101 Mission St. (861-1132), in the **Mission.** A "yesteryear" section features mens' and womens' clothing of 60s and 70s ilk, while a "better" section features today's thrift. Upstairs are the house and electric wares. They don't buy from the public. Open Mon.-Fri. 9am-8pm, Sat. 10am-7pm, Sun. 11am-7pm.

NOVELTY STORES

Good Vibrations, 1210 Valencia St. (974-8980), in the **Mission.** Get a buzz on at the nationally famous do-it-yourself autoerotica superstore. The tasteful display of antique vibrators includes some from the 19th century that were used to treat hysteria—slogans like "Makes you fairly tingle with the joy of living!" may have lost their popularity, but the feeling lives on. Open daily 11am-7pm. Must be 18.

- **Quantity Postcards,** 1441 Grant (986-8866), at Union St. in **North Beach.** The quantity is over 10,000, and at this store quantity *is* quality. Lose yourself in the antique, art, and tourist postcards. It takes just one dime to reconnect with a long-lost friend. Open Sun.-Mon. 11am-11pm, Fri.-Sat. 11am-12:30pm.
- **Stormy Leather,** 1158 Howard (626-1672), in **SoMa.** One of the country's biggest women's fetish wear boutiques, making waves with its selection of leather, latex, and more. Leather corsets $120-330. Open Mon-Sat. noon-7pm, Sun. 2-6pm.
- **TT Globetrotter USA,** 418 Sutter St. (434-1120), at Stockton in **Union Square.** Schmaltzy Tintin merchandise may be out of economic range, but the books are reasonably priced and the Captain Haddock luggage is a blast. Also on parade are the good-hearted menhir-toters of the *Asterix* series, as well as claymates Wallace and Grommit. Open Mon.-Sat. 10am-6pm, Sun. 11am-5pm.

ARTS AND CRAFTS

Quirky artistic items are sold all over this bohemian city. Find that piece-de-resistance at artists' collectives on **Hayes St.** in the Civic Center or in the **Haight.**

- **Center for the Arts at Yerba Buena Gardens Gift Shop,** 701 Mission St. (978-2700). Sells choice items like Elvis devotional candles ($20). Good selection of jewelry, handcrafted objects, art publications, and cards. Open Tues.-Sun. 11am-6pm.
- **Studio 24,** 2857 24th St. (826-8009), in the **Mission.** Next to the Galeria de la Raza, this gift shop specializes in Mexican-influenced art pieces and jewelry. Folk art from Latin America. Open Tues.-Sat. noon-6pm.

MALLS

If being whisked around by escalator strikes you as being integral to the shopping experience, follow the smell of perfume samples and the tinkle of Muzak to one of San Francisco's ritzy megamalls.

- **San Francisco Shopping Center** (495-5656), on Market at 5th in the **Tenderloin.** This mall is decidedly upscale, with an elegant Nordstrom's and six hypnotic curving escalators (the only ones of their kind in the world) sweeping shoppers through the 9-story atrium. Open Mon.-Sat. 9:30am-8pm, Sun. 11am-6pm.
- **Stonestown Galleria,** on 19th Ave. (Hwy. 1), at Winston Dr. just north of SFSU. Ah, the symphony of a thousand credit cards humming in unison. The car-less can access it via the MUNI M-line from downtown. Parking available.

■ Nightlife

Nightlife in San Francisco is as varied as the city's personal ads. Everyone from "dominant duo looking for a third" to "shy first-timer" to "pre-op transsexual top" can find places to go on a Saturday (or even a Tuesday) night. For weekly listings, check the *Bay Guardian*. Daily, try the Be-At Line (626-4087). Cafes offer non-alcoholic alternatives for the under-21 crowd. More casual bars often don't card until you buy drinks. Primarily queer bars tend to check less stringently, and bouncers keep to the New York rules: the better you look, the less likely they are to ask for ID.

BARS AND CAFES

In San Francisco, as elsewhere, bars tend to absorb the flavors of the neighborhoods they inhabit. Without a central college campus around which to barnacle, cafes insinuate themselves amongst their alcoholic brethren. Swanky hotels are a safe but terribly expensive bet for a slow, mellow burn (see **Nob Hill,** p. 278; **Union Square,** p. 258; and the **Financial District,** p. 260). The chi-chi Marina charges high and peaks fast, while the upper Haight stays doggedly jovial a bit later. For the buzz that lasts, try the Lower Haight or North Beach, but use your street smarts. All of these areas are served every half-hour by Night Owl bus service; know the routes.

Lower Haight

The Mad Dog in the Fog, 530 Haight St. (626-7270), near Fillmore. Irish owners brew a feel-good atmosphere where Guinness is the drink of choice. Pints $2.50 daily until 7pm, $2 Fri. 5-7pm, and free with meal Mon.-Fri. 11:30am-2:30pm. Bangers and mash $5. Open Mon.-Fri. 11:30am-2am, Sat.-Sun. 10am-2am.

Tornado, 547 Haight St. (863-2276), keeps it all above-board: they'll sell you any of a comprehensive list of beers at a good price, and you won't ask for the decor to go beyond signs for those beers. Special bonuses are the steaming spiced mead ($3) and the sociable patrons. Open daily 11:30am-2am.

The Horse Shoe Cafe, 566 Haight St. (626-8852). Offers much goodness: cute staff, chess boards, video games, Internet access, Thai iced tea ($1.75), and big ol' cookies ($1.25). Open daily 7am-1am.

An Bodhran, 668 Haight St. (431-4274), at Pierce. Though they're in "the other Irish bar" on the block, the tough customers here seem quite comfortably dug in for the night. Nurse a stout with them ($3.75), and think wistfully of St. Patrick's Day. Happy Hour daily 4-7pm. Open nightly until 2am.

Upper Haight

Deluxe Club, 1511 Haight St. (552-6949), at Ashbury. As attitudinal as it sounds, the shiny metal and bluish lights really do give you that film-noir tingle. Femmes fatales banter with mysterious strangers, and that's just the bar staff. Smoky live jazz Wed.-Sat.; cover Fri.-Sat. $5. Open Mon.-Sat. 3pm-2am, Sun. 2pm-2am.

Kan Zaman, 1793 Haight St. (751-9656), at Cole. A restaurant claiming "fantasy dining" by day, the joint turns into a sultan's paradise by night—belly dancers, spice wine ($3.25), and fruit-flavored hookahs ($7). Kitchen open Mon. 5-11pm, Tues., Thurs., and Sun. noon-11pm, Fri.-Sat. noon-midnight. Bar stays open until 2am.

North Beach/Chinatown

Caffe Trieste, 601 Vallejo St. (392-6739), at Grant. Seasoned staff harks back to the mellow Beat Era, though historical patrons whose photos line the walls range from Pavarotti to Cosby. Jukebox plays everything from opera to the Carpenters. Coffee drinks $1-3. Live music Sat. 2pm. Open daily 6:30am-midnight.

The Gathering Caffe, 1336 Grant Ave. (433-4247). Small jazz ensembles play in this intimate setting. Coffee and Italian sodas as well as beer and wine. Music Sun.-Thurs. 8:30pm, Fri.-Sat. 9pm. Cover Fri.-Sat. $2. Open nightly 7pm-2am.

Vesuvio Cafe, 255 Columbus Ave. (362-3370), across from the City Lights Bookstore. Vesuvios are again lighting up both city and cigars. Watch poets and chess players from a balcony in this quintessential Beat bar, or hide from them in some dark corner. Drinks $3-6. Open daily 6am-2am.

The Saloon, 1232 Grant Ave. (989-7666), at Columbus and Vallejo. Busts at the seams with regulars. Live nightly blues hurt so good, the crush feels like a warm squeeze. No cover. Weekend shows at 4pm. Open daily 9am-2am.

Tosca, 242 Columbus Ave. (391-1244). Have an illicit rendezvous among red vinyl booths and an old-school Wurlitzer jukebox with old-school prices (3 plays for 25¢). The house special, brandy with steamed milk and chocolate ($3.50), is a holdover from Prohibition days. Open Mon.-Fri. 5pm-1am, Sat.-Sun. 5pm-2am.

Specs, 250 Columbus Ave. (no phone). Old-time photos adorn the walls, but Tosca's unassuming neighbor draws the young and young-at-heart. Anchor Steam ($3) is the drink of choice. Open daily 5pm-2am.

Danny's, 684 Commercial St. (392-5331). More than unassuming, it's downright self-effacing. If you like a mellow bar scene in a nearly empty bar, look no further. Pool table (50¢ per game) and rarely functional Ms. Pac Man machine (kind of) lighten up the endearingly bland decor. Open Mon.-Sat. 2pm-2am.

Elsewhere

Café du Nord, 2170 Market St. (861-5016), between Church and Sanchez in the **Castro.** Painfully hip. Huge bar and pool tables (75¢). Excellent live music nightly. Beer $3.50. Cover after 9pm $3-5. Happy Hour 5-7pm with swank $2 martinis. Open Sun.-Tues. 6pm-2am, Wed.-Sat. 4pm-2am. Must be 21.

Holy Cow, 1535 Folsom (621-6087), near 11th in **SoMa.** Happy collegiate crowd drinks lots of flavored beer and dances (badly) to lots of 80s music. Play pool and watch Seinfeld in—where else?—the back room. Happy Hour Mon.-Thurs. 8-9:30pm. Open Sat.-Thurs. 8pm-2am, Fri. 6pm-2am.

Dragonfly Lounge, 2030 Union (929-8855), in Betelnut Pejiu-Wu Restaurant in the **Marina.** What it lacks in Oriental authenticity it makes up for in James Bond appeal. Only a secret agent could resist drinks like the Taiwan On (Stolichnaya orange with pickled ginger, $5) or Roundai Martini. Open Sun.-Thurs. 11:30am-11pm, Fri.-Sat. 11:30am-midnight.

CLUBS

More powerful than a locomotive...able to fill tall buildings with a swingin' sound...the San Francisco club scene is "mo' superfly" than Superman. It also changes faster than a speeding bullet or a man in a phone booth, so read the *Bay Guardian,* pick up flyers in hip coffee shops and stores, and ask around. The Be-At line (626-4087; 24hr.), is the source for jazz, hip-hop, and funk events, including weekly parties and other hard-to-find-out-about local happenings.

V/SF, 278 11th (621-1530), at Folsom in **SoMa,** is a space for a number of unconnected weekly events. Hot music keeps the good-looking crowd coming back for more in this inviting space of 2 dance floors and an ultra-mellow rooftop patio. Sun. is Spundae (techno/house); Sat. is Pablo's Sugar Shack (techno/disco).

Cat's Grill and Alley Club, 1190 Folsom St. (431-3332), at 8th in **SoMa.** Deftly balancing mellow and happening, this nooked-and-crannied club yowls the night away with a casual international set. Live music or DJ. Call to find out the night's orientation. Happy Hour daily 4-10pm. Cover $5-7.

The Elbo Room, 647 Valencia St. (552-7788; http://www.elbo.com), at 17th in the **Mission.** Various theme nights have a Latin flavor with a funk backbeat. Cool it in the bar downstairs or head up to the mid-sized dance floor with pool, pinball, TV, and $3 pints. Cover $3-6. Open nightly 10pm-2am. Must be 21.

Liquid, 2925 16th St. (431-8889), between **SoMa** and the **Mission.** Simple space is casually attired in hanging wire sculpture and old car seats. Nightly mix usually includes trip-hop or heavy beats. Young crowd fills it up every night—it's the swinginest party in town on Tues. Open until 2am. Must be 21.

Nickie's Barbeque, 460 Haight St. (621-6508), in the **Haight.** This dive is one of the chillest, friendliest small clubs in the whole damn city. Live DJ every night with different themes ranging from "world music" to hip-hop to funk. Great dancing, diverse crowd. Cover around $5. Open daily 9pm-2am.

Cesar's Latin Palace, 3140 Mission St. (648-6611), the **Mission.** Over 1000 people show up at this *huge* Latin dance hall on weekends. If you don't know what salsa is, this is the place to learn. Parking available. Open Thurs. 8pm-2am, Fri.-Sat. 9pm-5am, Sun. noon-5pm and 8pm-2am. All ages.

DNA Lounge, 375 11th St. (626-1409), at Harrison in **SoMa.** Soulful live music and funkilicious spinnin'. Cover around $12. Open daily 10pm-4am. Must be 21.

Covered Wagon Saloon, 917 Folsom St. (974-1585), at 5th in **SoMa.** The 70s are back, and the theme nights in this dive show it, with names like "Power Lounge" and "Stinky's Peep Show." Happy Hour Mon.-Fri. 4-9:30pm features the Shot-'n'-Beer ($3.25). Dancing or karaoke on weekends. Open daily 4pm-2am. Must be 21.

GAY AND LESBIAN CLUBS

Politics aside, nightlife alone is enough to make San Francisco a queer mecca. From the buff gym boys in nipple-tight Ts to tattooed dykes grinding to NIN, there's something for everybody. The boys hang in the **Castro** (around the intersection of Castro and Market), while the grrrls prefer the **Mission** (on and off Valencia); both genders frolic along **Polk St.** (several blocks north of Geary), and in **SoMa.** Polk St. can be a little seedy and SoMa a little barren, so keep a watchful eye for trouble. The best guide to all things queer is the tri-weekly free *Oblivion,* but the straight dope (so to speak) also appears in the bi-weekly *Odyssey.* The annual *Betty and Pansy's Severe Queer Review* is also a definitive source.

Litterbox, 683 Clementina Alley (431-3332), at the Cat's Grill and Alley Club, between Howard and Folsom at 8th in **SoMa.** Mixed alterno-queer crowd of hip lesbians and gay men dancing to anything from "Vogue" and "9-to-5" to the theme music from "I Dream of Jeannie." Beer $3-4. Cover $5. Open Fri. 9pm-2am.

The Cafe, 2367 Market St. (861-3846), the **Castro.** A classic. Queer crowd chills casually during the week, then jacks it up on weekends (come early to beat lines). Pool, pinball, and dancing every night. Repeat *Guardian* reader awards for "Best Gay Bar" and "Best Lesbian Bar." No cover. Open daily 11:30am-2am.

The Box, 715 Harrison St. (206-1652), between 3rd and 4th in **SoMa.** Described by some as "*the* best place to be on Thursdays," The Box pumps funk and soul for a young queer crowd once a week. Extremely diverse—and mixed. Beer $3. Cover $7. Open Thurs. 10pm-4am. Must be 21.

The End Up, 401 6th St. (357-0827), at Harrison in **SoMa.** A friendly San Francisco institution. Theme nights run the gamut from Fag Fridays to Girl Spot Saturdays to mostly straight KitKat Thursdays. Outdoor garden and indoor fireplace contribute to the homey feel. Cover $5. Open Thurs.-Mon. 9pm-3am.

The Stud, 399 9th St. (252-STUD/7883), **SoMa.** This legendary bar/club recreates itself every night of the week—sometimes funk, sometimes the wacky 'n' wild drag and transgender party "Trannyshack." Crowd is mostly gay male, but rough and tumble dykes do "Junk" here Sat. Open daily 5pm-2am.

Club Red (339-8310), at **Blondie's,** 540 Valencia St. between 16th and 17th in the **Mission,** on Sundays; at **Jelly's,** 295 China Basin Way on the **waterfront** 3rd Fri. each month. Hip hop, dance party, and house. Kiss My Black Ass productions throws a fierce party with some fascinating women. Full up in both locations—tiny Blondie's, half consumed by the bar anyway, bursts at the seams. Party starts at 9pm—be prepared to sweat.

Harvey's, 500 Castro St. (431-HARV/4278), 18th in the **Castro,** named for adored former city manager Harvey Milk, is a cruisey and hot newcomer to the scene. Boys pack the drag show Wed. Happy Hour 4-7pm. Open nightly until 2am.

Twin Peaks, 401 Castro St. (864-9470), at Market. Location, location, location: at the gayest intersection on earth in the **Castro,** and only $1.75 for domestic draft. No wonder everyone stops by here on their way home from work. A different kind of view than its namesake, but equally spectacular. Open daily noon-2am.

The Lexington Club, 3464 19th St. (863-2052), at Lexington in the **Mission.** Ladies bellyache louder than laddies about the bar scene, but they can rest happy now: more than a few career dykes relax at the counter any night of the week. Jukebox careens from the Clash to Johnny Cash, hitting all the tuff muff favorites (TLC, Liz Phair, et al) along the way. Happy Hour Mon.-Fri. 4-7pm.Open daily 3pm-2am.

SUPER-SIZING

Mega-clubs, big enough for their own zip codes, are the ultimate in escapism if you enjoy losing yourself in a mass of sweating humanity. Finagle your way into VIP lounges for faster bar service and moments of personal space between crowd-plunges if you can. Clubs this size often reward you with discounted covers for showing up early, and watch for special events with open bars.

Sound Factory, 525 Harrison (club line 979-8686), in **SoMa.** Tight clothing abounds in this huge mixed crowd. Indifferent tracks on the turntable. You'll have plenty of time waiting in line to decide whether fellow patrons are worth the cover charge (around $10). Open Sat. 9:30pm-4am. Must be 21.

Club Townsend, 177 Townsend, in **SoMa.** Sat. "Universe" is populated by folks of all intentions, but Sun. "Pleasure Dome" is a gay male thang. **Club Q** 1st Fri. of each month, one of a very few lesbian nights with any longevity. In a group this size, you're sure to find someone to ogle. Cover $7, last hr. $5.

Trocadero, 520 4th St. (437-4446), at Bryant, in **SoMa.** Known for slick leather fest "Bondage A Go Go" held every Wed. Free drinks for "ladies and trannies hand-cuffed to the bar" before 10pm. Cover $5, after 11pm $7. Must be 18.

SAN FRANCISCO

MUSIC VENUES

If you want the music without the dancing, head to one of these live and loud venues. Audiophiles looking to get an ear to the ground should snag a copy of *BAM* (see **Publications**, p. 253); the *Bay Guardian* also keeps a sharp and trustworthy eye on the scene. The **Transmission Theater**, 314 11th St. at Folsom, and the **Paradise Lounge** share management, a phone number (861-6906), and a beatnut scene in the heart of **SoMa.** Alternarock venues include the legendary **Fillmore**, 1805 Geary (346-6000; http://www.thefillmore.com), at Fillmore in **Japantown** (all ages; wheelchair accessible). **Bimbo's 365 Club**, 1025 Columbus (474-0365; http://www.bimbos365club.com), at Chestnut in **North Beach,** also snags a piece of the musical pie (tickets from $10).

Purple Onion, 140 Columbus Ave. (398-8415), **North Beach.** Hardcore punk, surf rock, and the ilk gets the crowd mighty rowdy. Doors open Fri.-Sat. at 9pm, bands start 10pm. Must be 21.

Bottom of the Hill, 1233 17th St. (621-4455), at Texas, in **Portrero Hill** (south of SoMa). Local punk gods Social Unrest are among those who have blessed this joint with their presence. Cover $3-7. Age limits vary.

The Chameleon, 853 Valencia St. (821-1891), between 19th and 20th in the **Mission.** Diversity is king here: live punk and experimental trip-hop to DJ funk and open mike/spoken word. Ping-pong, pool, pinball, free popcorn, and a pyromaniacal paint job. Open daily 10am-2am. Cover $5. Must be 21.

Slims, 333 11th St. (621-3330), between Folsom and Harrison in **SoMa.** Legendary indie rock hotspot, though world music, ska, and zydeco aren't unprecedented. Gets expensive for bigger names ($15-20). Get tickets in advance through BASS or at the box office (open Mon.-Fri. 10:30am-6:30pm). All ages.

COMEDY CLUBS

Cobb's Comedy Club, 2801 Leavenworth St. (928-4320), at Beach and Hyde in the **Cannery.** Big and small names take on this San Francisco standard. 2-drink min. Must be 18. Purchase tickets (around $10) through BASS or at the club after 7pm.

Josie's Cabaret and Juice Joint, 3583 16th St., (861-7933), at Market in the **Castro.** Shows about "the queer scene," male and female. Mon. is gay comedy open mic ($5). Cover $3-15. By day, it's a funky cafe (see **Castro**, p. 265).

The Punchline, 444 Battery St. (397-4337), between Clay and Washington in the **Financial District.** Local comedy Sun. Cover $5-15. 2-drink min.

■ Seasonal Events

San Francisco hosts an astounding array of seasonal events no matter what time of year you visit. Events below are listed chronologically. The visitors center has a recording of current events (391-2001).

Chinese New Year Celebration (982-3000), Feb. 7-22, Chinatown. North America's largest Chinese community celebrates the Year of the Tiger (4696 on the lunar calendar) with the largest festival in San Francisco. Cultural festivities, parade, fireworks, and the crowning of Miss Chinatown.

Russian Festival (921-7631), early Feb., in the Russian Center. Folk singing and dancing, Russian food, and best of all, flavored vodka tastings.

Tulipmania (705-5512), early March, Pier 39. Your chance to dress up like a little Dutch girl and tiptoe among 40,000 tulips from around the world.

Asian American International Film Showcase (863-0814), mid-March, AMC Kabuki 8 Theater, Japantown. Over 100 Asian and Asian-American feature and short films.

Union/Fillmore St. Easter Celebration (441-7055), features a petting zoo and other fuzzy diversions, plus a parade.

Cherry Blossom Festival (563-2313), April, Japantown. Big parade.

Spike and Mike's Festival of Animation (957-1205), April-May at the Palace of Fine Arts. Animated films from claymation to sick and twisted.

San Francisco International Film Festival (929-5000), April-May. The oldest film festival in North America shows more than 100 international films of all genres.

Bay to Breakers (777-7770), mid-May, starting at the Embarcadero. The *San Francisco Examiner* sponsors this largest road race in the U.S., which covers 7½ mi. in inimitable San Francisco style. Runners win not only on their times but on their costumes as well. Special centipede category. Up to 100,000 participants.

Carnaval and **Cinco de Mayo** (824-8999), May, Mission. Cultural festivities and costume contestation galore.

Stern Grove San Francisco Midsummer Music Festival (252-6252), June-Aug., Stern Grove. Free opera, ballet, jazz, and *a capella* for 10 Sun. Arrive early for best seating. Performances 2pm, pre-performance talks 11am.

San Francisco International Lesbian & Gay Film Festival (703-8663), June, Roxie Cinema (16th St. at Valencia) and Castro Theatre (Castro St. at Market). California's second largest film festival and the world's largest lesbian and gay media presentation shows the flicks.

Fourth of July Celebration (777-8498), July 4, Crissy Field in the Presidio. Free fireworks and live entertainment.

Jazz and All that Art on Fillmore (346-4446), early July, on Fillmore. Food, wine, art, and jazz: the pinnacle of human evolution.

Jewish Film Festival (510-548-0556), July. The world's longest is based in Berkeley but shows also at the Castro.

Cable Car Bell-Ringing Championship (923-6202), July 17, Union Square. Where people who have spent years perfecting their clang go to get recognition.

Blues and Art on Polk (346-4446), late July, on Polk.

Comedy Celebration Day (777-8498), late July, Polo Fields in Golden Gate Park. Local and national comics do 5min. acts.

Nihonmachi Street Fair (771-9861), early Aug., Japantown. Lion dancers, *taiko* drummers, arts and crafts, and karaoke wars.

San Francisco Fair (434-3247), early Sept., Civic Center Plaza at Polk St. and McAllister. Multiculturalism applied to food and multiweirdism applied to entertainment. Competitions include the Impossible Parking Space Race, Fog Calling, and the National Skateboard Championships. Sorta like Xtreme-ly local games.

San Francisco Fringe Festival (931-1094), early Sept., downtown. Experimental theater at its finest.

Festival de Las Americas (826-1401), mid-Sept., Mission. Food, art, and the *cha-cha*. A time to remember the plural nature of the word "America."

San Francisco Blues Festival (826-6837), 3rd weekend in Sept., Fort Mason. The oldest blues festival in America attracts the biggest names in blues every year.

Chinatown Autumn Moon Festival (982-6306), Oct., Grant Ave. Martial arts, lion dancing, and tons of bean-cake satiated spectators.

World Pumpkin Weigh-Off (346-4561), early Oct., City Hall. Overweight pumpkins' support group. Some of them can't be lifted alone!

Castro Street Fair (467-3354), Oct., Castro. Food, live music, and art. A bit more bridled than the end of the month—see **Halloween,** below.

San Francisco Jazz Festival (864-5449), early Nov. Includes Jazz Film Fest.

Halloween Celebration in the Castro, Oct. 31. Some people say the Castro has become less wild with age. Those people have not been there on Oct. 31.

Film Arts Festival (552-FILM/3456), late Oct.-early Nov., Roxie Cinema. Low-budget features, documentaries, and short films made in the Bay Area. Also special events throughout the year.

Sing-It-Yourself-Messiah (564-8086), Dec., Symphony Hall. Some say San Franciscans can't keep their mouths shut—now they don't have to. One of a slew of Christmas events, this one presented by the San Francisco Conservatory of Music.

The Bay Area

San Francisco is known as the City by the Bay, but this distinction deserves to be shared. Sittin' on the dock of the bay and watching the tide roll away may be romantic enough, but beyond the docks are a number of dynamic communities which amply reward exploration. Though San Fran may be its lifeblood, the bay would run dry without the nutrients of the cities and towns around it. Urbanity flows into the bay from Berkeley and Oakland to the east, good taste from Marin and Wine Country to the north, and RAM and relaxation from the Silicon Valley and the San Mateo coast to the south.

EAST BAY

The Bay Bridge is the most-traveled bridge in the country, carrying the weight of San Francisco traffic east to Oakland, from where freeways fan out in all directions. The urbanized port of Oakland sprawls north to the assertively hippie college town of Berkeley. Bonded by the bay and freeway geography, the two towns have long shared an interest in political activism. Berkeley, now more quietly bookish, offers more boutiques and cafes than most college towns, while its sister city Oakland echoes with the sounds of a progressive blues and jazz scene.

■ Berkeley

Berkeley's fame as an intellectual center and haven for iconoclasts is well-founded. Although the peak of its political activism occurred in the 60s and 70s—when students attended more riots than classes—U.C. Berkeley continues to cultivate consciousness and brainy brawn. The vitality of the population infuses the streets, which are strewn with hip cafes and top-notch bookstores. Telegraph Ave.—the Champs-Elysées of the 60s—remains Berkeley's spiritual heart, home to street-corner soothsayers, hirsute hippies, and itinerant street-musicians who never left.

Some of the best food around the Bay can be found in Berkeley, thanks to the presence of a sizeable professional population willing to pay for the freshest and tastiest seasonal ingredients. Alice Waters' Chez Panisse is the landmark home of California Cuisine. Around it, north of campus, the specialty stores and restaurants of the "Gourmet Ghetto" run the gamut of gustatory gumption. As befits Berkeley, however, this pricey cluster has no monopoly on good eats: you can eat well for more moderate cash outlays all around town.

Cheap places to stay, unfortunately, are harder to come by in Berkeley and throughout the East Bay. Relatively convenient access via public transportation makes day-tripping from San Francisco a sensible solution.

PRACTICAL INFORMATION

Visitor Information: Berkeley Convention and Visitor Bureau, 2015 Center St. (549-7040), at Milvia. Helpful street, park, and area maps as well as free pocket-sized local phone books; however, info may not be entirely up-to-date. Usually open Mon.-Fri. 9am-5pm. **24hr. visitor hotline** (549-8710). **U.C. Berkeley Visitor Center,** 101 University Hall, 2200 University Ave. (642-5215). Clear, detailed maps (10¢ suggested donation) and campus info. Guided campus tours leave from the center Mon.-Fri. at 10am, from Sather Tower (see p. 298), Sat. at 10am, and Sun. at 1pm. Open Mon.-Fri. 9am-5pm.
Trains: Amtrak (800-USA-RAIL/872-7245). Closest station is in Oakland, but travelers can board in Berkeley at 2nd St. and University and purchase tickets from the conductor. Call for schedules and fares. **Bay Area Rapid Transit (BART)** (465-2278). For more info, see **Public Transit,** p. 252. **Berkeley station,** 2160 Shattuck

Ave., at Center, close to the western edge of campus. Fare to San Francisco $2.70. **North Berkeley station,** Sacramento St. at Delaware St., just a few blocks north of University Ave. Fare to San Francisco $2.75.

Buses: Greyhound (800-231-2222). Closest station is in Oakland.

Public Transportation: Alameda County (AC) Transit (817-1717 or 800-559-INFO/4636). Buses #15, 40, 43, and 51 run from the Berkeley BART station to downtown Oakland via Martin Luther King, Jr., Telegraph, Shattuck, and College Ave., respectively. Fare $1.25; seniors, ages 5-12, and disabled patrons 60¢; under 5 free. Transfers (25¢) valid 1hr. For more info on taking bus F to San Francisco, see **Getting There and Around,** p. 294.

Transportation Information: Berkeley TRiP, 2033 Center St. (644-POOL/7665). Commuter-oriented information on public transportation, biking, and carpooling. Sells extended-use transit passes and assorted maps. Open Mon.-Wed. and Fri. 8:30am-5:30pm, Thurs. 9am-6pm.

Ride Share: Berkeley Ride Board, 1st level of student store in Student Union. **KALX radio, 90.7 FM** (642-KALX/5259). Ride list broadcasted daily at 10am and 10pm; call to put your request on the air for free.

Taxis: Yellow A l Cab (843-1111). Operates 24hr. **Berkeley Yellow Cab** (841-2265). Operates 24hr.

Car Rental: Budget, 600 Gilman St. (486-0806), at 2nd. Compact $32 per day with unlimited mi. Minimum age 21; drivers under 25 pay $15 per day surcharge. Open Mon.-Fri. 7:30am-6pm, Sat. 8:30am-2:30pm, Sun. 9am-1pm. (Cheaper options in San Francisco.)

Bi-Gay-Lesbian Organizations: U.C. Berkeley Multicultural Bisexual, Lesbian, and Gay Alliance/Queer Resource Center, 305 Eshleman Hall (642-6942) at Bancroft and Telegraph. Open Mon.-Fri. 10am-5pm during the academic year, by appointment only in the summer. **Gay Switchboard & Counseling Services,** 2712 Telegraph Ave. (548-8283), at Derby. Counseling and info on gay community events, housing, local clubs, etc. *Very* friendly and helpful staff. Open Mon.-Fri. 10am-10pm, Sat. noon-4pm, Sun. 6-9pm.

Ticket Agencies: BASS Tix, 762-2277. Calendar of events and show info. Open 8:30am-9pm. **Tower Records,** 2510 Durant St. (841-0101). Open 9am-midnight. **CAL Athletics,** 2233 Fulton #4422 (800-GO-BEARS/462-3277). Lines open Mon.-Fri. 8:30am-4:30pm.

Laundromat: University Coin-Op, 2051 University, at Shattuck. Wash $1; dry 25¢. Public parking lot out back, on Berkeley. Dry cleaning also available. Open 7:30am-10pm daily (last wash 9pm).

Crisis Lines: U.C. Berkeley Switchboard (642-6000). Info on everything from community events to drug counseling. Open Mon.-Fri. 8am-5pm. **Rape Hotline** (845-RAPE/7273). 24hr. **Suicide Prevention and Crisis Intervention** (849-2212). 24hr. **Poison Control Center** (800-523-2222). 24hr.

Medical Services: Berkeley Free Clinic, 2339 Durant Ave. (548-2570), at Dana St. 2 blocks west of Telegraph Ave. Served by AC Transit buses #7, 40, and 51. Medical help and referrals to homeless shelter resources in the area. Open Mon.-Fpi. 9:30-11:30am. If you're calling, the best times to talk to a "real person" are Mon.-Fri. 3:30-8:30pm, Sat. 6-9pm, Sun. 5-8pm. **Men's STD Clinic** and **HIV/AIDS testing** (644-0425). **Peer Counseling** (548-2744). **Berkeley Department of Health & Human Services,** 830 University Ave. (644-8571), at 6th. Medical help on a sliding payment scale. Specialty clinics vary from day to day, so call ahead. Open Mon.-Fri. 9am-5pm. **Berkeley Women's Health Center,** 2908 Ellsworth St. (843-6194), 1 block west of Telegraph. Open Mon. and Fri. 8am-noon and 1-5pm, Tues.-Thurs. 9am-1pm and 2-6pm.

Emergency: 911 or 644-6161. **Campus Emergency** (9-911 from campus phone, 642-3333 otherwise). 24hr.

Police: Berkeley Police (644-6743). **Campus Police,** Sproul Hall Basement (642-6760). 24hr.

Post Office: 2000 Allston Way (649-3174). Open Mon.-Fri. 8:30am-5pm, Sat. 10am-2pm. **ZIP Code:** 94704.

Area Code: 510.

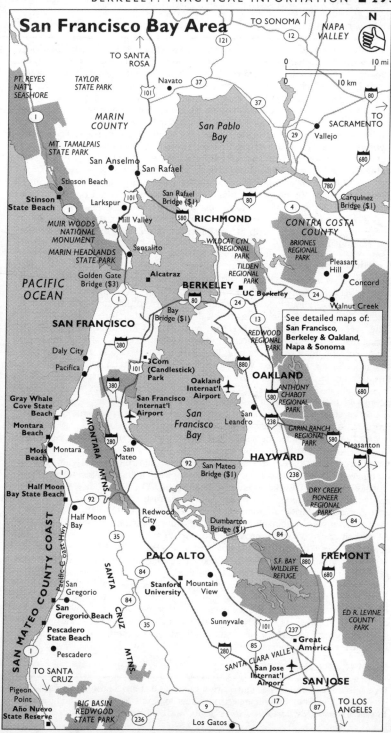

San Francisco Bay Area

N

TO SONOMA

NAPA VALLEY

121

12

0   10 mi

0   10 km

TO SANTA ROSA

Navato

37

37

San Pablo Bay

TO SACRAMENTO

PT. REYES NAT'L SEASHORE

TAYLOR STATE PARK

1

MARIN COUNTY

29

Vallejo

680

80

MT. TAMALPAIS STATE PARK

San Anselmo

San Rafael

CONTRA COSTA COUNTY

780

Stinson Beach

Larkspur

San Rafael Bridge ($1)

80

RICHMOND

4

Carquinez Bridge ($1)

Stinson State Beach

1

101

Mill Valley

580

WILDCAT CYN. REGIONAL PARK

BRIONES REGIONAL PARK

Pleasant Hill

MUIR WOODS NATIONAL MONUMENT

Sausalito

TILDEN REGIONAL PARK

Concord

MARIN HEADLANDS STATE PARK

PACIFIC OCEAN

Golden Gate Bridge ($3)

Alcatraz

BERKELEY

UC Berkeley

24

Walnut Creek

1

SAN FRANCISCO

Bay Bridge ($1)

80

24

13

See detailed maps of:
San Francisco,
Berkeley & Oakland,
Napa & Sonoma

280

Daly City

REDWOOD REGIONAL PARK

Pacifica

101

3Com (Candlestick) Park

880

OAKLAND

680

380

Oakland Internat'l Airport

580

ANTHONY CHABOT REGIONAL PARK

Gray Whale Cove State Beach

San Francisco Internat'l Airport

San Leandro

238

Montara Beach

San Francisco Bay

GARIN RANCH REGIONAL PARK

580

Pleasanton

Moss Beach

Montara

San Mateo

HAYWARD

5

Half Moon Bay State Beach

92

San Mateo Bridge ($1)

238

MONTARA MTNS.

280

1

Half Moon Bay

92

Redwood City

Dumbarton Bridge ($1)

DRY CREEK PIONEER REGIONAL PARK

84

35

84

SANTA CRUZ MTNS.

PALO ALTO

84

880

FREMONT

San Gregorio

Stanford University

Mountain View

S.F. BAY WILDLIFE REFUGE

680

SAN MATEO COUNTY COAST

San Gregorio Beach

84

Pacific Coast Hwy.

35

Sunnyvale

101

237

ED R. LEVINE COUNTY PARK

Pescadero State Beach

Pescadero

280

85

Great America

SANTA CLARA VALLEY

San Jose Internat'l Airport

TO SANTA CRUZ

Pigeon Point

Año Nuevo State Reserve

BIG BASIN REDWOOD STATE PARK

236

9

Los Gatos

17

87

SAN JOSE

TO LOS ANGELES

ORIENTATION

Across the Bay Bridge northeast of San Francisco and just north of Oakland, Berkeley is sandwiched between a series of rolling hills to the east and the docks of the bay to the west. The **University of California** campus and **Tilden Regional Park** climb up the sharp grades (technically into Oakland), but most of the university's buildings are in the westernmost section of campus, near the BART station. Lined with bookstores, cafes, and street vendors, **Telegraph Avenue,** which runs south from the Student Union, is the magnetic heart of town. Undergraduates tend to hang out on the south side of campus, while graduate students occupy the north side. The **downtown** area, around the BART station, contains businesses as well as the public library and central post office. The **Gourmet Ghetto** covers the area along Shattuck Ave. and Walnut St. between Virginia and Rose St. The **Waterfront** district, west of campus and around 4th St., is home to yummy eats and yuppie shops. Quality cafes, music stores, and specialty shops grace the **Rockridge** district on the border between Berkeley and Oakland. Northwest of campus, **Solano Avenue** offers countless ethnic restaurants (the best Chinese food in Berkeley), bookstores, shops, and a discerning movie theater. With increasing crime in the area, lone visitors should take caution at night.

Getting There and Around

There are three Berkeley Exits off I-80, which can be approached directly from the north or via I-580 from the south or west. To drive from San Francisco, cross the Bay Bridge on I-80. Though longer, older, and more traveled than its golden neighbor, the Bay Bridge's steel suspensions block the view and therefore any possibility of fame. Freeway congestion can make driving in the Bay Area frustrating, especially during rush hours. Most commuters head *into* San Francisco to work, meaning that the presentable traveler can often find a free ride between 8 and 9am on weekday mornings. Solitary commuters wishing to take 10-15 minutes off their trip time (and save themselves the bridge toll) by using the carpool lane will pick up two passengers at the Berkeley **Safeway,** at College and Clairmont. Generally, only businesspeople act as passengers, but any safe-looking person has a chance of being picked up. Be careful—ride givers *are* strangers. If you get a ride, you can expect to be dropped off around the Financial District.

BART trains run under the bay for quick and easy transit (fare $2.70). The university **Perimeter Shuttle** (642-5149) connects the BART station, near Telegraph Ave., with the campus (shuttles run Sept.-June Mon.-Fri. 7am-7pm every 10min., except on university holidays; fare 25¢). BART also stops at Virginia and Sacramento St. in North Berkeley. The **Berkeley Electric Shuttle (BEST)** (841-BEST/2378), connects the two BART stations via the Bayview area during rush hours. Buses reach Berkeley even faster than BART. **Alameda County (AC) Transit** (817-1717) bus F leaves from the Transbay Terminal for Berkeley (5:50am-midnight every 30min.). In town, AC Transit **city buses** run approximately every 20 minutes (fare $2.20, seniors, disabled, and ages 5-12 $1.10). Ask a driver for schedules.

Drivers fortunate enough to reach Berkeley despite Bay Area traffic will face congestion, numerous one-way streets, and vexing concrete planters. Reasonably priced public lots allow you to ditch your car and explore on foot—the best way to take in the vibrant Berkeley streets. However, a car can be particularly useful for trips up to North Berkeley and for navigating steep foothills. Berkeley is conscientious about making street facilities accessible to the disabled: wheelchair ramps are at every corner (blocking them results in a three-figure ticket!), and chirping crossing signals aid the visually impaired.

PUBLICATIONS

Free publications can be found in corner boxes and at any of the area's numerous cafes. For up-to-date news on area happenings, look in bookstores and bins around town for the weekly *East Bay Express* (540-7400), which spills over with entertain-

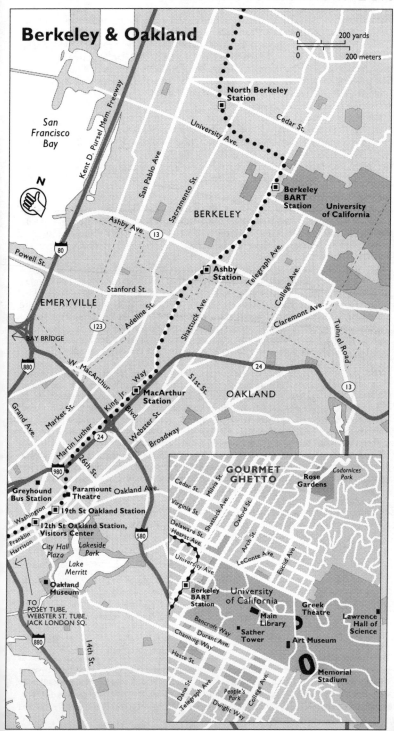

Berkeley & Oakland

San Francisco Bay

N

Kent D. Pursel Mem. Freeway

North Berkeley Station

University Ave.

Cedar St.

San Pablo Ave

Sacramento St.

BERKELEY

Berkeley BART Station

University of California

Ashby Ave.

13

Powell St.

80

Stanford St.

Ashby Station

Telegraph Ave.

College Ave.

EMERYVILLE

Adeline St.

Claremont Ave.

123

Tunnel Road

BAY BRIDGE

880

W. MacArthur

King Jr. Way

Shattuck Ave.

24

13

Grand Ave.

Market St.

Martin Luther

MacArthur Station

51st St.

OAKLAND

Webster St.

Broadway

24

26th St.

980

Greyhound Bus Station

Paramount Theatre

Oakland Ave.

19th St Oakland Station

Washington

12th St Oakland Station, Visitors Center

580

Franklin

Harrison

City Hall Plaza

Lakeside Park

Lake Merritt

Oakland Museum

TO POSEY TUBE, WEBSTER ST. TUBE, JACK LONDON SQ.

880

14th St.

GOURMET GHETTO

Cedar St.

Milvia St.

Shattuck Ave.

Oxford St.

Rose Gardens

Codornices Park

Virginia St.

Arch St.

Delaware St.

Hearst Ave.

University Ave.

LeConte Ave.

Euclid Ave.

Berkeley BART Station

University of California

Main Library

Greek Theatre

Lawrence Hall of Science

Bancroft Way

Sather Tower

Art Museum

Durant Ave.

Channing Way

Haste St.

Memorial Stadium

Dana St.

Telegraph Ave.

People's Park

College Ave.

Dwight Way

0   200 yards
0   200 meters

ment listings, particularly for theater in Berkeley and jazz in Oakland. Many San Francisco newspapers (see **San Francisco: Publications,** p.253), most notably the *Chronicle's Datebook* (the Sunday pink pages), include listings for Berkeley. The *San Francisco Bay Guardian,* which has the most complete Bay Area listings, is also available in Berkeley. *Summer in Berkeley,* available at the end of June, features in-depth write-ups about Berkeley's cafes, pubs, and outlet shops. *Resource* is the guide given to students new to Berkeley. If you can find a recent edition (try the visitor center at 101 University Hall), grab it.

The vast array of UC Berkeley publications vary in content and style. The *Daily Californian* (548-8080; http://www.dailycal.org), is published on Tuesdays and Fridays in the summer and daily during the school year, and carries university news and student interest features. It is easily confused with the weekly *Berkleyan,* the faculty and staff newspaper. Other student efforts come and go—keep an eye out around the campus buildings and nearby cafes.

ACCOMMODATIONS

There are surprisingly few cheap accommodations in Berkeley. The **Bed and Breakfast Network** (547-6380), coordinates 20 East Bay B&Bs with a range of rates. A popular option is to stay in San Francisco and make daytrips to Berkeley.

> **U.C. Berkeley Summer Visitor Housing** (642-5925). For advance info or reservations, contact **University Conference Services,** 2601 Warring St. (624-4444; fax 642-4888; http://www.housing.berkeley.edu). Residence halls are open to visitors from the beginning of June to mid-Aug. Visitors in 1998 will be housed in the spacious, clean rooms of **Stern Hall,** 2700 Hearst Ave., at Highland. Free use of local and campus phone service, ping-pong and pool tables, and TV room. Parking permits, meals, laundry, and photocopying all available for reasonable prices. Shared single-sex bathrooms are in less-than-perfect condition. Singles $38; doubles $50. Linens provided. Personal checks not accepted.
>
> **YMCA,** 2001 Allston Way (848-6800), at Milvia. Adequate, if a bit worn, co-ed rooms are available in this hotel-portion of the YMCA. Registration daily 8am-9:30pm. No curfew. Free use of pool, linens, and newly renovated fitness facilities. In-room phones are for incoming calls only; pay phones are in the hallway. Shared bathrooms. 14-night max. stay; special applications are available for longer stays. Singles $25; doubles $33. Weekly: singles $96; doubles $106. Reservations require 14-day notice and a $25 deposit. Must be 18 or older with ID.
>
> **The Berkeley Budget Inn,** 1720 San Pablo Ave. (524-8778; fax 524-4235), at Delaware. Located outside the campus area, the inn is a sensible alternative for drivers, though AC Transit buses #52 and 72 pass nearby. Clean rooms with queen-sized beds, private baths, and TVs. Free parking. Check-out 11am. Rooms $34, weekends $39.
>
> **Golden Bear Motel,** 1620 San Pablo Ave. (525-6770 or 800-525-6770), at Cedar St. 8 blocks from the North Berkeley BART station. The Shawn and Renee duo took over this beautiful Spanish-style motel three years ago and the place just gets better and better. Check-out noon. Singles $49; doubles $59; up to 2 additional people $5 each. Two-bedroom cottages with kitchen $99. Reservations recommended.
>
> **Travel Inn,** 1461 University Ave. (848-3840; fax 848-3846), 2 blocks from the North Berkeley BART station, 7 blocks west of campus. Perky pink building looks like it belongs in Palm Springs. Rooms are clean and comfortable. All have TV and phone. Free parking and coffee. Singles $45; doubles $65. Laundry. Discounts on stays longer than 5 days.

FOOD

Berkeley's eclecticism does not stop where nourishment begins—given the diverse student population, the variety of dining, munching, and sipping options is hardly surprising. The north end of **Telegraph Avenue** caters to student appetites and wallet sizes—hence the high concentration of pizza joints and trendy cafes. When you've maxed out on caffeine, head away from campus on Shattuck Ave. to the treasure trove of culinary delights in the **Gourmet Ghetto**. Head to Solano Ave. for ethnic cuisine or meander down to San Pablo along the bay for hearty American fare.

Breakfast

Ann Kong's World Famous Bleach Bottle Pig Farm, 2072 San Pablo Ave. (848-7376), between University and Addison. Porky paraphernalia adorns the walls and other surfaces of this roomy space, but somehow the perkiness has no irritating edge. Couches in the back are just for coffee and tea drinkers. Breakfast special 2 eggs, toast, and homefries $3. Ann also serves lunch and dinner, with occasional live acts. Open Tues.-Fri. 7:30am-9pm, Sat. 8am-9pm, Sun. 8am-2pm.

Ann's Soup Kitchen, 2498 Telegraph Ave. (548-8885), at Dwight. A perennial student favorite. Towering portions compensate for crowded dining. Weekday special includes 2 pancakes with bacon and eggs or homefries ($3.55), and you may find an extra cake or egg smiling up at you. Fresh-squeezed juice tastes like a million bucks, but costs only $1.50. Open Mon.-Fri. 8am-7pm, Sat.-Sun. 8am-5pm.

Bette's Oceanview Diner, 1807A 4th St. (644-3230; fax 644-3209), in the Waterfront District. A popular choice for weekend brunch—the earlier you get there the less time you'll have to wait for a silky mimosa ($4). Apple Brandy Soufflé Pancakes ($9) are divine. Sandwiches $5-8. If you don't want to wait, stop in at **Bette's To Go** (548-9494), next door. Diner open Mon.-Thurs. 6:30am-2:30pm, Fri.-Sun. 6:30am-4pm. To Go open Mon.-Sat. 6:30am-5pm, Sun. 8am-4pm.

Cafe Fanny, 1603 San Pablo Ave. (524-5447). Alice Waters' most recent venture, this tiny cafe offers limited seating, standing room, and benches in the shade of the pleasant outdoor trellis. Poached eggs with quality toast ($4.75) rivals buckwheat crepes with fruit and yogurt ($4.75) for your favor. Drink your bowl (yes, bowl) of cappuccino ($2.50) and don't distract the charming cook, even if she is less than a foot away. Open Mon.-Fri. 7am-3pm, Sat. 8am-4pm, Sun. 9am-3pm.

Eat With Your Hands

Cafe Intermezzo, 2442 Telegraph Ave. (849-4592), at Haste. It's doubtful you've ever had a salad as big as the ones here—it's a Berkeley thing. The fresh produce in the tossed green salad ($3.23) and Veggie Delight ($4.57) will fuel you for the rest of the day. Local punks and Cal law students compose the Intermezzo crowd, if not an intermezzo opera. Cheap beer (Anchor Steam $1.75). Sandwiches $4.15. Open Mon.-Fri. 10:30am-9pm.

The Blue Nile, 2525 Telegraph Ave. (540-6777). Huge portions of authentic Ethiopian food in a lavish setting. Waitresses in traditional gowns slip in and out of the beaded curtains that separate the different booths. Wide variety of vegetarian dishes. Lunch entrees $5, dinner entrees $6-8. The *Gomen Wat* (mustard greens steamed in special sauce, served with *injera,* Ethiopian baked bread, and three side dishes for $6.25) will steam your mustard greens! Eat with your fingers, and get blotto on *Tej* (honey wine, $2 a glass). Weekend reservations recommended. Open Tues.-Sat. 11:30am-10pm, Sun. 5-10pm.

Crepes A Go Go, 2125 University Ave. (841-7722). Crepes are on the thick side for hands-on convenience. Cheese and turkey crepes $3.50, honey and kiwi crepes $3.75. Pleasant staff also vends sandwiches and salad to Berkeleyans on the, well, the go go. Open Sun.-Thurs. 9am-10pm, Fri.-Sat. 9am-10:30pm.

Blondie's Pizza, 2340 Telegraph Ave. (548-1129). You should visit this Berkeley landmark if only to read hot-button articles pinned up behind glass along the walls. Dagwood-size slices of greasy 'za $1.75-3; pizza and coke special $2.25. Open Mon.-Thurs. 11:30am-1am, Fri.-Sat. 10:30am-2am, Sun. noon-midnight.

Cafe Del Sol, 1742 Solano Ave. (525-4927; fax 525-4242), at Santa Fe. Pleasant staff and patio setting. Sandwich special with fruit and soup, salad, or fries for $7. Heavy-hitting espresso drinks, plus Happy Hours (Mon.-Fri. 3:30-6:30pm) of mixed and frozen drinks ($2-3). Open Mon.-Fri. 10am-10pm, Sat.-Sun. 9am-10pm.

Eastern and Middle Eastern

La Mediterranée, 2936 College Ave. (540-7773). An open, airy, cafe-style establishment specializing in Greek and Armenian food. Try the cornucopia of treats on the Middle Eastern plate while people-watching on the sunny patio—come early for dinner, though, or you'll be watching them eat. Entrees $7-8. Open Mon.-Thurs. 10am-10pm, Fri.-Sat. 10am-11pm.

Long Life Vegi House, 2129 University Ave. (845-6072). Vast menu full of countless vegetable and "vegetarian meat" options. Most entrees $5-7; portions are huge. Friendly, prompt service. Eat in or take out. Daily lunch special 11:30am-3pm features entree, egg roll, and soup ($3.65). Open daily 11:30am-9:30pm.

Plearn Thai Cuisine, 2050 University Ave. (841-2148), at Shattuck, 1 block west of campus. The *Ma-Kuer-Yud-Sai* (stuffed eggplant) is a winner ($7.75). Curries $7. Plentiful vegetarian options. Have a *Thai Song Kran,* the tea to temper the titillating tang of Thai food. Lunch specials daily 11:30am-3:30pm for $4.75. Open daily 11:30am-10pm.

O Chame, 1830 4th St. (841-8783), Waterfront district. Delicious and innovative California-Japanese fusion cooking. Gobble up a bowl of *soba* or *udon* with tofu skins and spinach ($7.50) and chase it with *sake* ($5 per glass). Open Mon.-Thurs. 11:30am-3pm and 5:30-9pm, Fri.-Sat. 11:30am-3pm, Sun. 5:30-9:30pm.

Berkeley's Best Cafe, 2566B Telegraph Ave. (883-0828). While this tiny restaurant might not live up to its bold moniker, it has earned a small, devoted following. The owners want to make you happy with the individually prepared Chinese dishes. Gotta love the combo deal: entree, egg roll, and rice for $3.50. Eat in or take out. No alcohol. Open Mon.-Sat. 11:30am-9pm. No credit cards.

Create-Your-Own Gourmet Picnic

Monterey Market, 1550 Hopkins St. (526-6042). This bustling grocery features local produce (starfruit anyone?), some of it organic. Add their affordable wines and crusty bread to your satchel and head for the hills. Open Mon.-Sat. 9am-6pm.

Eclair Pastries, 2567 Telegraph (848-4221), off Dwight. Top off with sweets and mouth-watering chocolate-chip meringues, or terrific sticky florentines ($1). Open Mon.-Fri. 6:30am-7pm, Sat. 6:30am-6:30pm, Sun. 7:30am-5:30pm.

SIGHTS

UC Berkeley

In 1868, the private College of California and the public Agricultural, Mining, and Mechanical Arts College coupled to give birth to the **University of California.** Berkeley was the first of the nine University of California campuses, so by seniority it has sole rights to the nickname "Cal." The school has a diverse enrollment of over 30,000 students and 1350 full professors, creating a lively academic community.

Pass through **Sather Gate** into **Sproul Plaza,** both sites of celebrated student sit-ins, and enter the 160-acre Berkeley campus, bounded on the south by Bancroft Way, on the west by Oxford St., on the north by Hearst Ave., and on the east by a vast parkland. Remodeling often occurs during academic down time (June -Aug.), so watch for closings due to structural changes or "seismic corrections." A map from the Visitor Center (see p. 291) will help you navigate the area.The most dramatic campus attraction is **Sather Tower,** much better known as the **Campanile** (Italian for "bell tower"), a 1914 monument to Berkeley benefactor Jane Krom Sather. At 307 ft., the tower is the tallest building on campus, and you can ride to its observation level for a great view (50¢). The tower's 61-bell carillon plays weekdays during the term at 7:50am, noon, and 6pm.

The **Berkeley Art Museum (BAM),** 2626 Bancroft Way (642-0808; http://www.bampfa.berkeley.edu), at College, captures the best of Berkeleyan counterculture tendencies—the rotating exhibitions are mostly experimental. The founding 1963 donation of 47 paintings is today a growing collection of 9,000 pieces of art, including notable collections of 20th-century and Asian art. The museum bookstore is not as gimmicky as most, and the sale racks hold bargain prices. (Museum open Wed. and Fri.-Sun. 11am-5pm, Thurs. 11am-9pm. Admission $6; students, seniors, and ages 12-17 $4; free Thurs. 11am-noon and 5-9pm.) Within the museum, the

Pacific Film Archives (PFA) (642-1412), is home to one of the nation's largest film libraries. PFA shows films in the evening (see **Entertainment: Cinema,** p.300).

The **Lawrence Hall of Science** (642-5132; http://www.lhs.berkeley.edu), a concrete octagonal building in the northeast corner of campus, is one of the finest science museums in the Bay Area. Exhibits stress hands-on science activities. The courtyard offers a stunning view of the bay, a DNA molecule, a whale (you know, for the kids), and stargazing workshops on clear Saturday evenings. Take bus #8 or 65 from the Berkeley BART station (and keep your transfer for $1 off admission); otherwise it's a one-hour walk from the center of campus. (Open daily 10am-5pm. Admission $6; seniors, students, and ages 7-18 $4; ages 3-6 $2.)

Back in the campus center, the **Phoebe Hearst Museum of Anthropology** (643-7648; http://www.gal.berkeley.edu/~hearst), displays selections from its 500,000 catalogued items in Kroeber Hall, though the bulk of the impressive collection is rarely, if ever, seen. (Open Wed. and Fri.-Sun. 10am-4:30pm, Thurs. 10am-9pm. Admission $2, seniors $1, under 16 50¢; free on Thurs.) The **Valley Life Sciences Building** (642-1821; http://www.ucmp.berkeley.edu) displays changing exhibits and life-size Tyrannosaurus Rex and Pterosaur skeletal models in the lobby (open Mon.-Fri. 8am-9pm, Sat.-Sun. 1-5pm). The collection, however, is not open to the public.

During the school year, **Berkeley's Department of Music,** 104 Morrison Hall, presents a number of concert series. Hertz Hall (642-2678), is the music chamber for both **Noon Concerts,** with music by Berkeley's best student and faculty performers, and **Evening Concerts,** featuring such groups as the African Music Ensemble, the Berkeley Contemporary Chamber Players, the Javanese Gamelan, and the 1991 Grammy nominee University Chamber Chorus. **Friday Afternoon Concerts,** 125 Morrison Hall, are undergraduate performances and the most informal of the three series. Specific dates and times are available from the Department of Music.

In the north-central part of campus is the **Greek Theatre** (642-5550), an impressive marble structure donated by William and Phoebe Hearst and modeled after the classical amphitheater in Epidaurus, Greece. The site is used for university ceremonies and rock concerts. The locally grown and internationally known Grateful Dead used to play here every year, but things have gotten quieter in a post-Jerry world.

The **Botanical Gardens,** Centennial Dr. (642-3343), in Strawberry Canyon, contain over 10,000 varieties of plant life. Berkeley's mediterranean climate, moderated by coastal fog, provides a fertile setting for 33 acres of growing things. Agatha Christie is said to have come here to examine a rare poisonous plant whose deadly powers she described in one of her mystery novels (open daily 10am-4pm; free; parking permit $1 for 2hr.). North of campus, the **Berkeley Rose Garden,** Euclid Ave. at Bayview, contains a collection of blooms which will assure you that a rose is a rose is not just a rose. Built by the WPA during the Depression, the garden spills from one terrace to another in a vast semicircular amphitheater. Peep through the trees for a piece-meal view of the bay (open May-Sept. dawn-dusk).

Berkeley is home to many of the country's most esteemed professors, including author Maxine Hong Kingston. If you want to sit in on **classes,** some that come highly recommended are: Ethnic Studies 41: Comparative Survey of Protest Movements, taught by Professor Muñoz, and Art History 10A: History of Western Art, taught by Professors Stahl and Stewart.

Not UC Berkeley

Though Berkeley is dominated by the university, there are noteworthy sights outside of the campus. **Tilden Regional Park** (635-0135), is part of the extensive East Bay park system. Hiking, biking, running, and riding trails crisscross the park and provide impressive views of the Bay Area. A 19th-century carousel delights juvenile thrill-seekers. **Lake Anza** is a popular swimming spot during the hottest days of summer, but the small sandy beach is overrun with screaming kids (lake open 10am-dusk during summer; admission $2). The park also contains a botanical garden and information on California's flora. At the north end of the park, the **Environmental**

Education Center (525-2233), offers exhibits and naturalist-led programs (open Tues.-Sun. 10am-5pm; free). To reach the park by car or bicycle, take Spruce St. to Grizzly Peak Blvd. to Canon. AC Transit buses #7 and 8 run from the Berkeley BART station to Golf Course Dr. at Grizzly Peak Blvd. At **Indian Rock Park,** along Shattuck and Indian Rock Rd., watch rock climbers scale the impossible or ascend the easy side steps yourself for an impressive view of the Headlands.

People's Park, Haste St., one block off Telegraph, is an unofficial testimonial landmark to Berkeley's days of frenzied resistance. A mural depicts the 60s struggle between city officials and local activists over whether to leave the park alone or develop it commercially. During the conflict, then-governor Ronald Reagan sent in the National Guard, an action which led to the death of a Berkeley student. Four years ago, despite heated protests, the city and the university bulldozed part of the park to build beach volleyball courts, basketball courts, and restrooms. The park is patrolled by police officers 24 hours in an attempt to deter vagrants.

Just east of People's Park, on Dwight Way at Bowditch, is the masterpiece of architect Bernard Maybeck, the **First Church of Christ Scientist,** 2526 Dwight St. (845-7199). Built in 1910, the church is a conglomeration of Gothic, Renaissance, Classical, Japanese, Mediterranean, and Industrial architectural styles. The church is closed except for during services (Wed. at 8pm and Sun. at 11am); tours are given at noon on the first Sunday of every month.

ENTERTAINMENT

The university offers a number of quality entertainment options. Hang out with procrastinating students in or around the **Student Union** (643-0693). **The Underground** (642-3825), contains a ticket office, an arcade, bowling alleys, foosball tables, and pool tables, all run from a central blue desk (open Mon.-Fri. noon-8pm, Sat. 10am-6pm). Next door is the **Bear's Lair,** 2475 Bancroft St. (843-0373), a student pub with occasional live music. It's *the* popular campus hangout on sunny Friday afternoons, when quarts of beer are $3 (open Mon.-Fri. 8am-8pm). The **CAL Performances Ticket Office** (642-9988), at the north corner of Zellerbach Hall, has information and tickets for concerts, plays, and movies (open Mon.-Fri. 10am-5:30pm, Sat. 10am-2pm). Big concerts are in the **Greek Theatre** (see p.299) and **Zellerbach Hall.**

Cinema

In Berkeley, the unofficial law of the landscape is that where there is a cluster of cafes, there is a movie house. The result is the screening of a wide selection of offbeat films. In addition to those listed below, there are a number of cinemas lining Shattuck Ave. Most show current releases.

> **U.C. Theater,** 2036 University Ave. (843-6267), between Milvia and Shattuck. Reruns, *film noir,* classics, clever double features, and of course, *Rocky Horror Picture Show* (Sat. midnight). Hong Kong film festivals on Thurs. Schedules available throughout Berkeley. Admission $6.50; seniors, disabled, and under 13 $4.50; first show of the day $4.50.

> **Pacific Film Archives,** 2621 Durant Ave. (642-1412; http://www.bampfa.berkeley.edu), below College in the Berkeley Art Museum. From premieres to classics, the archives are immense. Elements of its filmacopia include alternative visions of the 60s and Greek cinema. Films and videos shown in a state-of-the-art, 234-seat theater. Admission $5.50, seniors, disabled, and under 12 $3.50. Second feature $1.50 if you go to the first. Reservations sometimes necessary. Charge tickets by phone (642-5249; open 11am-5pm; surcharge 50¢).

> **Act I Act 2,** 2128 Center St. (548-7200), between Oxford and Shattuck next to Berkeley BART station. Art films culled from the Palme d'Or nominee list. Only Act 1 theater is wheelchair accessible. Admission $7.50, seniors and under 12 $4.50; matinees 3:30pm or earlier $4.50.

THE BAY AREA

Northside Theatre, 1828 Euclid Ave. (841-6000), at Hearst, ½ block north of campus. Second-run foreign films. Admission $6, seniors and under 12 $3.50; matinees 6pm or earlier $4.

Theater Arts

Dozens of troupes perform in Berkeley, many with progressive messages and political agendas. The **Julia Morgan Theater,** 2640 College Ave. (box office 845-8542), shares space with a pre-school and yoga center in a beautiful building that was once a church. Its namesake and designer was the first female architect in California. Noted for its graceful mix of materials, this building was her first commission; she later built Hearst Castle (see p. 226). The theater hosts diverse performances including classical music recitals. The **Zellerbach Playhouse** is operated by Berkeley's Department of Dramatic Art and hosts student performances in dance, theater, and music during the academic year (tickets $6-10). Summertime shows consist mostly of musicals and romantic comedies (tickets $5-7, students and seniors $3-4). Call CAL Performances (642-9988), for more information. The **Berkeley Repertory Theater,** 2025 Addison St. (845-4700), is the best-known and arguably the finest theater in the area, with an eclectic repertoire of classics and unknowns. (Box office open daily noon-7pm. Half-price tickets may be available Tues.-Thurs. on the day of the show—line up at the box office at noon.)

Bookstores

From a bibliophilic standpoint, Berkeley's book trade just might be the eighth wonder of the world. Leave yourself more time than you think you'll need to browse.

Moe's, 2476 Telegraph Ave. (849-2087), between Haste and Dwight. Featured in *The Graduate.* Four well-arranged floors of second-hand knowledge, from Artaud to Zukofsky. New books at 10% discount. Open Sun.-Thurs. 10am-11pm, Fri.-Sat. 10am-midnight. Art and antiquarian section (849-2133) open daily noon-6pm.

Black Oak Books, 1491 Shattuck Ave. (486-0698 or 486-0699), in the Gourmet Ghetto. Selective stock of used, new, and out-of-print literature, art classics, and other scholarly works. They invite you to "sit down and read"—*and* supply a chair. Regular author readings; call for schedule. Open daily 10am-10pm.

Serendipity Books, 1201 University Ave. (841-7455), at Chestnut. If you know what you want, you might well find it here—but not without a little help from the owner. An awe-inspiring, if cryptically organized, collection has earned Serendipity Bay-wide industry respect. Open Mon.-Sat. 9am-5pm.

Cody's Books, 2454 Telegraph Ave. (845-7852), next to Moe's. The scale of a chain bookstore, but twice the quality and personality to boot. Check out the unbeatable magazine collection. Open daily 10am-10pm.

NIGHTLIFE

Coffeehouses

Catering to the under-21 undergraduate set, cafes have become surrogate bars, libraries, and living rooms. Any hour is ideal for studying or people-watching.

Cafe Milano, 2522 Bancroft Way (644-3100). With its high wood-beam ceilings, 10ft. windows, and brick walls, Milano makes a strong bid for the hippest contender in the Telegraph area cafe-a-thon. Lively discussions about everything from O'Neal (Shaquille) to O'Neill (Eugene). Latte $1.60. Open Mon.-Fri. 7am-10pm, Sat. 7am-midnight, Sun. 8am-10pm.

Cafe Strada, 2300 College Ave. (843-5282), at Bancroft. A glittering jewel of the culinary-intellectual scene. Go to be seen, discuss philosophy, or just enjoy the beautiful outdoor terrace (and the beautiful staff). Cocoa made with white chocolate, pastries, latte $1.60. Open daily 7am-midnight.

Au Coquelet, 2000 University Ave. (845-0433), at Milvia. King of late night—the crowds grow larger as the night gets shorter. The alcohol (Anchor Steam $2.50) may be the draw, but cafe fare is also available in the form of an impressive selection of fresh pastries, sandwiches, and coffee drinks (latte $2.10). Open Mon.-Thurs. 6am-1:30am, Fri. 6am-2am, Sat. 8am-2am, Sun. 8am-1am.

Mediterraneum Cafe, 2475 Telegraph Ave. (549-1128), near Dwight. For a taste of "old Berkeley," visit this landmark cafe—it's laid-back for the locale. Popular with long-time residents, who know they're free to bring a book. The upper level is drabber but quiet with great murals. Latte $1.85. Open daily 7am-11pm.

Wall Berlin Kaffee Haus, 2517 Duran Ave. (540-8449), at Shattuck. This cozy little nook of 2 levels plays great vocal jazz late into the night. Latte $2, croissants $1.50. Open Mon.-Fri. 8am-1am, Sat.-Sun. 9am-1am, but patrons often linger.

Bars and a Punk Club

Spats, 1974 Shattuck Ave. (841-7225), between University and Berkeley. Locals and students flock here for the warmth of the staff, the original drinks (like the Danko Bar Screamer $4.50), and the quirky surroundings. Off-beat decorations include stuffed deer, a Roman soldier, an autographed poster of Walt Disney, and velvet furniture. As one patron enthuses, "you can't beat the armchairs." Hors d'oeuvres served 2pm-1am. Eight-page alcohol menu (Anchor Steam $2.50, mixed drinks $3-5). Entrees $6-10. Open Mon.-Fri. 11:30am-2am, Sat.-Sun. 4pm-2am.

924 Gilman, 924 Gilman St. (525-9926), at 8th. Legendary all-ages club, a staple of the East Bay that has spawned punk bands from Green Day to Operation Ivy and Crimpshrine. Local, national, and international acts rock this joint, though major-label acts are strictly taboo. Most shows start at 8pm. Call for upcoming concerts. Cover $3-5 with purchase of $2 membership card, good for one year.

Jupiter, 2181 Shattuck Ave. (843-8277), across the street from the BART station. The faux-gothic gilt has a warm red glow. Beer garden and terrific pizza ($6 for a loaded 8in. pie). Beers on tap include Anchor Steam ($3 per pint). Particularly vigilant bouncers. Live music Wed.-Sat., no cover. Open Mon.-Thurs. 11:30am-1am, Fri.-Sat. noon-2am, Sun. noon-11pm.

Triple Rock Brewery, 1920 Shattuck Ave. (843-2739). The triple "rock" foundation: ale, stout, and porter ($2.75 per pint). They also brew India Pale Ale and at least one original creation ($3.25 per pint). Cable sports. The shuffleboard court in back awaits those sober enough to stand. Open Sun.-Wed. 11:30am-midnight, Thurs.-Sat. 11:30am-1am. Kitchen closes at midnight; roof garden closes at 9pm.

Blakes, 2367 Telegraph Ave. (848-0886), at Durant. Jam-packed joint is a total meat market, and unashamedly so, but at least the cuts are premium. Blake's bills itself as "the best three bars in Berkeley." The pint-sized upstairs has a loud sports bar feel, while the middle floor is mellow with quite a bit more seating. In the basement, kick it under blacklight to the seriously loud beats of often very cool local bands. Appetizers $1.75-4, meals $4-8. Beverages start at $2.50. Cover $2-5. Must be 21. Happy Hour daily 4-6pm and 8-10pm. Open daily 11:30am-2am.

Berkeley Billiards, 2367 Shattuck Ave. (848-1766), at Durant. Expansive facility with good music and local artists' work. Foosball and pinball for the eight-ball shy. "Berkeley's Best" beer $7 per pitcher, Cider Jack $15.50 per pitcher. Table rates before 7pm: $5 per hr. Table rates after 7pm: Mon.-Thurs. $10 per hr., Fri.-Sat. $12 per hr., Sun. $5 per hr. Open daily noon-2am.

SEASONAL EVENTS

Berkeley's **farmer's market** takes place on Haste between Telegraph and Bowditch (Sun. 11am-3pm). The **Farmer's Market Grand Opening and Parade,** on the second Sunday of July, starts the season, which runs through November. Authors and jazz musicians come together for the **Telegraph Avenue Book Fair** in late July. Call 649-9500 for information about the market or the book fair.

■ Oakland

Oakland strives to refute Gertrude Stein's withering observation: "There is no there there." The city's tourist literature wages a veritable war of attrition against her, assuring visitors that City Square is "always *there* for you," and "there is shopping *there*." Roslyn Mazzilli's sculpture in the square's upper plaza is defiantly entitled *"There!"* One is tempted to pat Oakland on the shoulder and say, "There, there."

Many locals will admit that Stein's statement is apt—the city lacks a sense of place. The City Square's emphatic "there"-ing attempts to restore a center that the city has never had. Oakland residents look instead to San Francisco for excitement and to their individual neighborhoods for identity. These different neighborhoods jumble together in a patchwork or ghettos, wealthy developments, and parks. Despite the geographic segmentation, "Oaktown" characterizes itself through intense political awareness. Oaklanders unite for events of all sorts, from the positive-minded *Festival at the Lake* to the politically charged *Fuck the Police Day.*

Oakland's African-American plurality maintains a progressive jazz and blues scene, but despite being one of the most multicultural cities in the United States, the city does not have the sights to match its ethnic vitality. This sixth biggest city in California only merits a daytrip from the rest of the Bay.

PRACTICAL INFORMATION

Visitor Information: Oakland Convention and Visitors Bureau, 550 10th St., #214 (839-9000). You will find that conventions (and not budget travelers) are this city's main business, but don't hesitate to pick up a free map and visitor's guide. Open Mon.-Fri. 8:30am-5pm.

Public Transportation: Alameda County (AC) Transit (800-559-INFO/4636). City-wide. Fare $1.25, seniors and disabled 60¢, ages 5-12 $1.10; transfers 25¢.

Crisis Lines: Rape Crisis Center (845-RAPE/7273). 24hr.

Medical Services: Central Public Health Center, 470 27th St. (271-4263), at Telegraph. Usually open Mon.-Fri. 8am-5pm; make appointments far in advance. **Highland Hospital,** 1411 E. 31st St. (534-8055), 14th Ave. Emergency care 24hr.

Emergency: 911.

Post Office: Main branch, 1675 7th St. (251-3300), at Peralta. Open Mon.-Fri. 8:30am-5pm. **General delivery,** at 201 13th St. at Harrison. **ZIP Code:** 94617. **Area Code:** 510.

GETTING THERE AND AROUND

The **Oakland International Airport,** 1 Airport Dr. (577-4000; http://www.oaklandairport.com), lands a significant number of Bay Area-bound flights, including all Southwest Air flights. Though more remote from hotels than San Francisco International Airport, the Oakland airport is more cheaply reached by public transport, and an on-site BART station is in the works. The **Coliseum BART station** can be reached from the airport via the Air-BART shuttle bus (every 10min.; fare $2) or the **AC Transit** bus #58 ($1.25). The **Greyhound** station, 2103 San Pablo Ave. (800-231-2222), is in a dangerous part of downtown—be careful after dark. Buses leave daily for Santa Cruz ($14) and Los Angeles ($31). The **Amtrak** station (800-USA-RAIL/872-7245) is across from Jack London Square on the Embarcadero, at Alice St.

Oakland's scarcity of cheap and safe accommodations and noteworthy sites make it a better daytrip than vacation destination. Drivers can take I-80 from San Francisco across the **Bay Bridge** to I-580 and connect with Oakland I-980 South, which has downtown exits at 12th St. or 19th St. **BART** provides another option, running from downtown San Francisco to Oakland's stations at Lake Merritt (Dublin/Pleasanton or Fremont trains), 12th St. (Oakland City Center trains), or 19th St. (Richmond or Pittsburg/Bay Point trains). The Rockridge stop (Pittsburg/Bay Point train) is within easy walking distance of Berkeley. (Fares from downtown San Francisco under $3.) Although all public transit facilities have their own info lines, you can connect to any one of them or get traffic updates free from TravInfo at 817-1717 (TDD 817-1718).

ORIENTATION

Oakland's main artery is **Broadway.** From the waterfront area at **Jack London Square,** Broadway runs northeast past the **Produce Market** on its east side at 3rd St., and separates **Old Oakland** (to the west) from **Chinatown** (to the east). The city center is at 13th St. NE, but the greater downtown area occupies all of **Lake Merritt,** including **Lakeside Park,** on the north side, and the Lake Merritt Channel, on the south side.

To the north of downtown Oakland are Berkeley-esque neighborhoods laced with boutiques, grocers, and restaurants. **Rockridge** lies between Oakland and Berkeley and is accessible from downtown Oakland via AC Transit bus #51 or BART.

ACCOMODATIONS AND FOOD

Although Oakland is full of motels, few are safe, clean, and economical compared to those in San Francisco and Berkeley. If you really want to stay in Oakland, the **Bed and Breakfast Network** (415-696-1690), includes some Oakland addresses. Motels clustered along W. MacArthur Blvd. near the MacArthur BART station range around $30 per night for a room with a private bath. Ask to see a room before checking in.

Oakland's tourist guides boast a variety of international treats, but many of the restaurant choices are upscale and expensive. Nevertheless, careful culinary selections make it possible to sample the cuisine without sapping your budget. Every Friday from 8am to 2pm, the **Old Oakland certified farmer's market** takes over 9th St., between Broadway and Clay. The largest of its kind in Alameda County, the market offers fresh fruits, vegetables, and the wares of some of the best bakers in the Golden State. Nearby is **Ratto's International Market,** 821 Washington St. (832-6503), an Oakland institution frequented by the Frugal Gourmet, among other connoisseurs (open Mon.-Fri. 9:30am-6pm, Sat. 9:30am-5pm, Sun. 10:30am-4pm).

Downtown Oakland

Villa Jardin, 719 Washington St. (835-5505), between 7th and 8th. This friendly Mexican place serves up the usual suspects (tacos, burritos, etc.), but unusually big 'n' tasty versions of them. Lunch buffet of enchiladas, fajitas, tacos, dessert, and more $5.95. Open Mon.-Fri. 8am-3pm, Sat. 10am-3pm. No credit cards.

Caffé 817, 817 Washington St. (271-7965). Acclaimed by the *S.F. Chronicle,* they deploy Italian predilections better than most trendy eateries. Excellent fresh ingredients make up delicious sandwiches ($5). Open Mon.-Fri. 7:30am-5pm, Sat. 10am-4pm. No credit cards.

In Rockridge

The Rockridge Market Hall, 5655 College Ave. (655-7748), is a gastronomic variety house. **Paul Marcus Wines** (420-1005), is Neiman Marcus quality with a staff of connoisseurs. **Grace Baking** (428-2662), bakes breads with amazing grace. Organic sour walnut (small loaf $1.65, large $3.25) and artichoke-mushroom foccaccia. Open Mon.-Fri. 7am-8pm, Sat.-Sun. 7am-7pm.

The Red Tractor Cafe, 5634 College Ave. (595-3500), across from the Market Hall. Most of their country-style dishes are made from scratch. The Farmer's Platter includes an entree, 2 side dishes, and a biscuit ($6.25). Great t-shirts and mini-tractors for sale. Open Mon.-Thurs. 11:30am-9pm, Fri. 11:30am-9:30pm, Sat. 9am-9:30pm, Sun. 9am-9pm.

The Edible Complex, 5600 College Ave. (658-2172). Cafe-style restaurant gets very crowded in the evenings. Tofu burger with chips ($5.25) and ginger snap cookies ($1) are so good you'll gouge your eyes out (too bad, since it's a great spot for ogling passersby). Cappuccino $1.75. Open Mon.-Thurs. 7:30am-midnight, Fri. 7:30am-1am, Sat. 8:30an-1am, Sun. 8:30am-midnight.

SIGHTS

Lagging behind other Bay Area towns in terms of attractions, Oakland has backed various ventures to bolster interest. **Lake Merritt,** situated east of downtown, was dammed off from the San Francisco Bay in 1869, and now provides a place for sailing, biking, and jogging. Activity revolves around **Lakeside Park,** which encompasses a band shell, bird sanctuary, and **Children's Fairyland** park. At night, however, you may want to avoid the lake entirely, lest a would-be mugger give you a real run for your money. Thrift shops, bookstores, and boutiques line the nearby streets of **Lakeshore, Grand,** and **Piedmont.**

The **Oakland Museum of California,** 1000 Oak St. (238-2200), at 10th, on the southwest side of the lake and accessible from the Lake Merritt BART station, is a complex of three museums devoted to California's history, art, and ecology. Though less immediately glamorous than the SFMOMA, the Oakland Museum houses some real gems, including photography by Edward Weston and Dorothea Lange, panoramic shots of San Francisco by Quick-Snap pioneer Edward Muybridge, and cross-cultural modern works. The museum is accessible from the Lake Merritt BART station. (Museum open Wed.-Sat. 10am-5pm, Sun. noon-7pm. Admission $4, students and seniors $2; Sun. 4-7pm free.) Oakland's large African-American population preserves its history in the **Ebony Museum of Art,** 30 Jack London Village, #208/209 (763-0745). Call 2-3 days in advance to arrange a tour ($1 per person). (Open Tues.-Sat. 11am-6pm, Sun. noon-5pm; free.)

Jack London Square, named after the author who lived in and wrote about this area, is now an eight-block commercial district on the waterfront. **Jack London Village,** on Alice St. along the Oakland Estuary, was modeled after a turn-of-the-century wharf, but the *Call of the Wild* has since been tamed by the tourist trap. Half of **Jack London's Cabin,** at Jack London Square near Webster St., was transported from Alaska, where the author prospected for gold in the 1890s. (The cabin has a duplicate in Ottawa, which also claims London as its own.) From here you can ride the **AC Ferry** (522-3300), across the bay to the Financial District or Pier 39 in San Francisco (every 1¼hr; fare $4, seniors and disabled $2.50, ages 5-12 $1.50.)

ENTERTAINMENT AND SEASONAL EVENTS

Baseball's **Oakland Athletics (A's)** and the (re-)transplanted **Oakland Raiders** football team both play in the **Oakland Coliseum** (639-7700), at the intersection of the Nimitz Fwy. (I-880) and Hegenberger Rd. The Coliseum has its own BART station and is a much cozier place than frigid 3Com/Candlestick Park in San Francisco. The NBA's **Golden State Warriors** play in the adjacent **Coliseum Arena** (569-2121).

The **Paramount Theater,** 2025 Broadway (465-6400), at 21st, is an exquisite Art Deco movie palace. The circa 1931 theater shows weekly foreign or classic films, and houses both the **Oakland East Bay Symphony** and the renowned **Oakland Ballet.** The mighty Wurlitzer organ accompanies concerts and movies. Tours of the theater depart from the box office on the first and third Saturdays of the month (no reservations). Throughout the year, the Symphony (446-1992) performs five Friday concerts (tickets $11-35) with open rehearsals the preceding Thursday afternoons (tickets $5). The Symphony also sponsors free noontime ensemble concerts. The Ballet (452-9288) performs several programs, including a not-so-traditional *Nutcracker Suite.* (Box office open Mon.-Thurs. 10am-3pm.)

Free **blues** and **jazz** summer concerts pop up in Jack London Square every Thursday evening. For a more intimate blues setting, try **The Serenader,** 504 Lake Park Ave. (832-2644), or the nearby **5th Amendment,** 3255 Lakeshore Dr. (832-3242). **Yoshi's Japanese Restaurant and Jazz Bar,** 510 Embarcadero W (238-9200; http://www.yoshis.com), draws big names like Branford Marsalis. In mid-June, the **Festival at the Lake** takes over Oakland with a long weekend of food and music. For more info, check local papers.

SOUTH BAY

The San Francisco peninsula extends southward to what was once the netherland of the Bay Area and is now the nexus of the digital world. From Palo Alto to San Jose and beyond, the Silicon Valley makes more chips than a *taqueria*, inedible though they may be. More of an information super-hideaway than superhighway, the computer technology firms would rather remain anonymous. The cities that they support, however, are more colorful. Palo Alto has an active student community and San Jose has a burgeoning nightlife. The San Mateo County Coast shares the peninsula, but not the high-tech fever of the southern cities, remaining a refuge for wildlife and Luddites.

■ Palo Alto

Palo Alto is almost pedestrian-friendly enough to be a real college town, but the profusion of imported cars and fine tapestries tell another story. Much of the city's wealth is due to its position as a corporate adjunct of Silicon Valley, home of Hewlett-Packard and many other prominent high-tech firms. However, it is Stanford University that really puts Palo Alto on the map. (In fact, Hewlett-Packard started in the garage of two young Stanford graduates who wanted to settle near their alma mater.) This private, internationally-acclaimed university, known as "The Farm" for its vast acreage, has acquired a second flora-related alias: "the other Ivy." Stanford is graced with a superb faculty, active and bright students, perfectly groomed grounds, a picturesque lake, and a bulging endowment. Nonetheless, Stanford falls just short of its biggest eastern rivals in the court of public opinion, and seems eternally doomed to the title "the Harvard of the West."

Palo Alto itself is a well-manicured burg with a nightlife that caters to both students and young suburbanites—the median age of permanent residents has yet to break 40. It's easy to forget that neighboring East Palo Alto has at various times been the drug and murder capital of the U.S. Though crime statistics appear to be improving, the sad contrast of this needy community with one of the nation's wealthiest is a textbook example of America's rich-poor gap.

PRACTICAL INFORMATION

Visitor Information: Palo Alto Chamber of Commerce, 325A Forest Ave. (324-3121). Open Mon.-Fri. 9am-5pm. **Stanford University Information Booth** (723-2560), across from Hoover Tower. Free student-led tours leave every day at 11am and 3:15pm; times vary on holidays and during exams. Open daily 9am-5pm.

Trains: CalTrain, 95 University Ave. (323-6105, info 800-660-4287), at Alma in Palo Alto. Street-side stop at Stanford Stadium on Embarcadero Rd. To: San Francisco ($3.75) and San Jose ($2.50). Half-price for seniors and disabled. Operates Mon.-Fri. 5am-10pm, Sat. 6:30am-10pm, Sun. 7am-10pm.

Buses: SamTrans (800-660-4BUS/4287). To: San Francisco downtown ($2.50) and San Francisco International Airport ($1).

Public Transportation: Santa Clara County Transit (408-321-2300 or 800-894-9908; http://www.vta.org). Local and county-wide transit. Fare $1.10, Mon.-Fri. 9am-2:30pm 55¢, seniors and disabled 35¢, ages 5-17 60¢. Express service $1.75. Day passes $2.50, seniors and disabled $1.40, ages 5-17 80¢. **Marguerite University Shuttle** (723-9362). Free bus service around Stanford University. Operates Mon.-Fri. 6am-8pm. Services Palo Alto CalTrain during commute hours.

Car Rental: Budget, 4230 El Camino Real (424-0684, out-of-town reservations 800-527-0770). Economy cars $33 per day, $165 per week with unlimited mi. Credit card required. Open Mon.-Fri. 8am-6pm, Sat.-Sun. 8am-5pm.

Car Repair: AAA Emergency Road Service (595-3411). Members only. 24hr.

Taxis: Yellow Cab (325-1234). 24hr.

Bike Rental: Campus Bike Shop, 551 Salvatierra Ln. (325-2945), across from the Law School in Stanford. Three-speeds $8 with same-day return, $12 overnight. Mountain bikes $10, $15. Helmets $3 per day. Major credit card or $150-300 cash deposit. Open Mon.-Fri. 9am-5pm, Sat. 9am-3pm.

Ticket Agencies: For Stanford University events, call Tressider Memorial Union (725-ARTS/2787), or for athletic events, call the Stanford Department of Athletics (723-1021). Office staffed 10am-4pm. For local and Bay Area events, call **BASS Ticketmaster** (408-998-2277).

Laundromat: Launderland, 405 Waverley (949-3506). Wash $1.25; dry 25¢ per 10min. Open daily 7am-11pm.

Emergency: 911 (9-911 from Stanford University telephones) or 723-9663.

Police: 275 Forest Ave. (329-2406).

Internet Access: Cybersmith, 353 University (325-2005; http://www.cybersmith.com). Access the Internet and email while slurping coffee. Half-hour trial card $5. Open Mon.-Thurs. 10am-11pm, Fri.- Sat. 10am-midnight, Sun 11am-9pm.

Post Office: Main branch, 2085 E. Bayshore Rd. (321-4310). Open Mon.-Fri. 8:30am-5pm. **Stanford branch,** White Plaza (322-0059). Open Mon.-Fri. 9am-5pm. **ZIP Code:** 94303.

Area Code: 415.

ORIENTATION

The pristine lawns of residential Palo Alto are not so distinguishable from the 8200-acre campus grounds of Stanford University. Despite being called **University Ave.,** the main thoroughfare off U.S. 101 belongs much more to the town than to the college, as it is strewn with upscale shops and cafes. **Stanford University** spreads out from the west end of University Ave. Abutting University Ave. and running northwest-southeast through town is **El Camino Real** (part of Rte. 82). From there, **Palm Drive** accesses the heart of Stanford's campus, the **Main Quad.**

Getting There and Around

Palo Alto is 35 mi. southeast of San Francisco, near the southern shore of the bay. From the north take **U.S. 101** to the University Ave. Exit or the Embarcadero Rd. Exit directly to the Stanford campus. Alternatively, motorists from San Francisco can split off onto the **Junípero Serra Hwy. (I-280)** for a slightly longer but more scenic route. From I-280, get off at Sand Hill Rd. and follow it to Willow Rd. and the northwest corner of Stanford University.

To get to Palo Alto by public transportation, take **SamTrans** bus #7F from San Francisco to the Stanford Shopping Center or any later point (runs daily 5am-7pm; fare $1.75, seniors and ages 7-17 85¢). Palo Alto-bound trains also leave from San Francisco's **CalTrain station,** at 4th and Townsend, every one or two hours. The **Palo Alto Transit Center** (323-6105), on University Ave., serves local and regional buses and trains (open daily 5am-12:30am); there is a train-only depot (326-3392), on California Ave. 1¼ mi. south of the Transit Center (open 5:30am-12:30am). The Transit Center is connected to points south by **San Mateo County buses** and to the Stanford campus by the free **Marguerite University Shuttle** (see p. 306).

ACCOMMODATIONS

Motels are plentiful along El Camino Real, but their rates are a bit steep. Generally, the prices vary inversely with distance from Stanford. More reasonably priced accommodations can be found farther north, on El Camino Real towards Redwood City. **University housing** provides a cheaper alternative in the summer, when the hostel outside town is closed. Residence halls are available from late June to early September (singles $33; doubles $48; those under 18 must be accompanied by an adult). For info, call the **Conference Office** (723-3126; open Mon.-Fri. 9am-5pm).

Hidden Villa Ranch Hostel (HI-AYH), 26870 Moody Rd. (949-8648), about 10mi. southwest of Palo Alto in Los Altos Hills. The first hostel on the Pacific Coast is now a working ranch and farm in a wilderness preserve. Heated cabins and 35 beds. Registration open daily 7:30-9:30am and 4:30-9pm. Dorms $10. Reservations required for weekends and groups. Open Sept.-May.

Imperial Inn, 3945 El Camino Real (493-3141 or 800-900-0524), at Los Robles. Clean rooms come with VCR, cable TV, and kitchenettes with microwave and fridge. Free continental breakfast served daily 6-9:30am. Singles $46; doubles $52.

Coronet Motel, 2455 El Camino Real (326-1081), at California. Clean, recently refinished rooms are spacious with big windows and cable TV. Swimming pool. Check-out 11am. Singles $50; doubles $60.

Glass Slipper Inn, 3941 El Camino Real (493-6611 or 800-541-0199), next to the Imperial Inn. Smaller rooms, fewer perks, lower prices. Free coffee; rent a fridge/microwave for $2 per day. Check-out 11am. Singles $42; doubles $44.

FOOD

Mango Cafe, 435 Hamilton Ave. (325-3229). Caribbean cuisine with veggie options available. *Very* spicy Jamaican "jerked joints" ($6), ordered alone or with curried joints, will be at your table quicker than you can smack your lips. Delicious sweet potato pudding $2.75. Open daily 11am-3pm and 6-10pm.

Saint Michael's Alley, 806 Emerson St. (326-2630). During the day, hearty food is served in a relaxed, artsy atmosphere. At night, "St. Mike's" rocks with live music or poetry readings for a diverse crowd (gay friendly). Fresh muffins, scones, bread. Sandwich and salad $5-6. Pizza $7.25. Open Tues.-Thurs. 7am-3pm and 5-10:30pm, Fri.-Sat. 7am-3pm and 5pm-midnight, Sun. 7am-3pm and 5-9:30pm.

The Coffee House, Tressider Union (723-3592), at Stanford. Recent renovations have brightened this student hangout and study haven. Students flock to the "co-ho" for some fro-yo. Sandwiches, burritos, and salad $3-5. Live music select nights at 9:30pm (no cover). Happy Hour Mon.-Fri. 4-6pm with $1.75 pints. Open term-time Mon.-Fri. 11am-2pm, Sat.-Sun. 10am-midnight; hours vary in summer. Tressider Union also houses counters selling salads and Chinese and Mexican food.

The Peppermill Restaurant and Lounge, 10690 N. DeAnza Blvd. (408-996-7750), in Cupertino. If you've got wheels, this refugee-from-Reno style restaurant is well worth giving them a spin; you don't have to be a high roller to feel like one under the beveled glass and artificial flora that flourish here. Sandwiches with sides $7-9. Tequila Sunset $4.50. Open Sun.-Thurs. 6:30am-12:30am, Fri.-Sat. 6:30am-2:30am.

Miyake, 261 University Ave. (323-9449). Fight your way to a table and enjoy 6-piece veggie rolls ($1.20) or fresh local abalone ($2). The pleasure of perfect soft-shell crab concoctions ($4) will quell any anxiety over the chaos, and *obento* box lunches are a steal at $5.25. Open daily 11:30am-10pm.

SIGHTS

Stanford University is undoubtedly Palo Alto's main tourist attraction. Jane and Leland Stanford founded the secular, co-educational school in 1885, to honor their 16-year-old son Leland Jr. who had died of typhoid on a family trip to Italy. The Stanfords loved Spanish architecture and collaborated with Frederick Law Olmsted, designer of New York City's Central Park, to create a red-tiled campus of uncompromising beauty. (Bitter Berkeley students sometimes refer to Stanford as "the World's Largest Taco Time.") Classes began at "The Farm" in 1891.

A few years ago, the undergraduates successfully lobbied the administration to abandon the "Eurocentric" core curriculum. In spite of the change, Stanford's Hoover Institution remains a bastion of right-wing thought and Stanford Law School has produced such eminent conservatives as Chief Justice William Rehnquist. The university has also been an important high-tech center, ever since alumni Hewlett and Packard set up shop near their alma mater in the 30s.

The oldest part of the campus is the colonnaded **Main Quadrangle,** the site of most undergraduate classes. The walkways are dotted with diamond-shaped, gold-numbered stone tiles that mark the locations of time capsules put together by each year's graduating class. Chipper student tour guides will point to other quirky Stanford tidbits on twice-daily tours (see **Practical Information,** p. 306).

Driving and parking (2hr. free in downtown public lots) can be a drag on the mostly permit-only campus, so if you want to see more than the walkable central portions, hop on the free **Marguerite Shuttle** to traverse the far-flung university (see p. 306). Look for the ubiquitous red and white shuttle stop signs. Biking the flat boulevards and path-filled rolling hills on campus can be far more pleasant. For info on bike rental, see p. 307. The vast majority of students own bikes, leading to term-time bicycle traffic jams and accidents, especially at the notorious "corner of death" near the center of campus. Bike theft is a persistent problem—lock it or lose it.

Memorial Church (723-1762), in the Main Quad, is a non-denominational gold shrine with stained glass windows and glittering mosaic walls like those of an Eastern Orthodox church. East of the Main Quad, the observation deck in **Hoover Tower** (723-2053 or 723-2560), has views of campus, the East Bay, and San Francisco (open daily 10am-4:30pm; admission $2, seniors and under 13 $1). Next door is the **Art Gallery** (723-2842), which is temporarily showing works from the Stanford Museum's permanent collection while that facility is being repaired (call for updated info). The **Stanford University Museum of Art** (723-3469), Museum Way off Palm halfway between the Main Quad and El Camino Real, has been closed indefinitely for earthquake-related repairs, but is scheduled to reopen sometime in 1998. In the meantime, the lawn-sprawling **Rodin Sculpture Garden** can still be enjoyed. The museum collection contains a stunning bronze cast of the *Gates of Hell,* among other larger figures (open year-round; free tours Sat. and Sun. 2pm).

Off-campus, the kitschy **Barbie Doll Hall of Fame,** 433 Waverley St. (326-5841), off University, has over 16,000 perky plastic dolls. Hippie Barbie, Disco Barbie, and Benetton Barbie prove that girlhood may be fleeting, but fashion mistakes are forever. Ask about having yourself cloned into a doll. (Open Tues.-Fri. 1:30-4:30pm, Sat. 10am-noon and 1:30-4:30pm. Admission $6, under 12 $4.)

ENTERTAINMENT

The *Stanford Weekly,* put out by the *Stanford Daily,* contains listings of what's going on all over campus. Pick up a free copy of the *Palo Alto Daily News* from downtown sidewalk boxes for the local lowdown.

Dinkelspiel Auditorium (723-4317), at El Camino and Embarcadero. Silly name, great concerts. Snag tix at the ticket office in Tressider Union (723-4317). Open Mon.-Fri. 10am-4pm.

Memorial Auditorium (723-5758), on campus. Flicks shown Sun. during the term (admission $3, students $1). Mostly mainstream films, though the occasional older classic makes the slate.

The Stanford Theatre, 221 University Ave. (324-3700). Dedicated to Hollywood's "Golden Age." Hitchcock and the Marx Brothers are regulars. Double features $6, seniors $4, children $3. Wurlitzer organ plays before and after the 7:30pm show.

The Edge, 260 California Ave. (324-3343), 2 blocks east of El Camino Real. Teens flock here like vultures to a rotting corpse. Cover charges and age restrictions vary. Shows usually begin at 9:15pm.

The Oasis Beer Garden, 241 El Camino Real (326-8896), Menlo Park. Once there were fraternities at Stanford; now there's the Oasis. Let's get rocked, dude! Burgers the way they were meant to be ($4.70), plus a huge selection of brew (pints start at $1.80, pitchers at $5). Open daily 11am-1:15am.

SHOPPING

Chimaera Books and Records, 165 University Ave. (327-1122). Superb array of new and used poetry books. Used CDs $10, or $2.50 with an exchange. Open Mon. 10am-11pm, Tues.-Sat. 10am-midnight, Sun. 11am-10pm.

Kepler's Books, 1010 El Camino Real, Menlo Center (324-4321), Menlo Park. Vast selection of books and magazines from around the world. Open Sun.-Thurs. 9am-11pm, Fri.-Sat. 9am-midnight.

The Stanford Shopping Center (617-8585 or 800-772-9332; http://www.stanford-shop.com), between campus and El Camino Real. Doesn't cater to the budget traveler, but its cool avenues are great for window-shopping and über-commercial reveries. Polo erected its own Hellenic facade; Nordstrom and Neiman Marcus up the ante with free-standing buildings. Coveting is still free. Open Mon.-Fri. 10am-7pm, Sat. 10am-6pm, Sun. 11am-6pm.

■ San Jose

In 1851, San Jose was deemed too small to serve as California's capital and Sacramento assumed the honors. Today, San Jose (pop. 855,000) is the fastest-growing city in California, owing largely to its status as the heart of the computer chip factory known as the Silicon Valley. But therein lies the rub; the economic boom that quadrupled the city's population in a mere 10 years has yet to be matched by cultural and aesthetic refinements. Compared to Berkeley and San Francisco, San Jose is an upstart adolescent. Despite progressive art galleries and a burgeoning night life, the city's reputation for dullness remains fixed in the minds of Bay Area hipsters. The third-safest city in the U.S. (according to the FBI), San Jose is clean, warm, peaceful, and easy to park in. Coolness, though, remains a thing of the future.

PRACTICAL INFORMATION

Visitor Information: Convention and Visitor Bureau, 333 W. San Carlos St., #1000 (977-0900, events line 295-2265; http://www.sanjose.org), just south of Almaden. Superb free maps. Open Mon.-Fri. 8am-5pm. **San Jose State Student Union** (924-1000). Open Mon.-Thurs. 7am-10pm, Fri. 7am-5pm, Sat. 10am-5pm; summer Mon.-Fri. 8:30am-4:30pm.

Airport: San Jose International, 1661 Airport Blvd. (277-4759). Turn right onto Airport Blvd. from Coleman Ave. off I-80 or Guadalupe off U.S. 101. Accessible also by Santa Clara County Transit light-rail. Free shuttles connect the terminals.

Trains: Amtrak, 65 Cahill St. (287-7462 or 800-USA-RAIL/872-7245). To Los Angeles ($77) and San Francisco ($9). **CalTrain,** 65 Cahill St. (291-5651 or 800-660-4287), at W. San Fernando. To San Francisco (1½hr.) with stops at peninsula cities. Fare $4.50, round-trip $9; seniors, under 12, and disabled half-price. Operates hourly Mon.-Fri. 5am-10pm, Sat. 6:30am-10pm, Sun. 7:30am-10pm.

Buses: Greyhound, 70 S. Almaden. (800-231-2222), at Santa Clara. The station feels reasonably safe, even at night. To L.A. ($32) and San Francisco ($7). Luggage lockers for ticketed passengers only. Open daily 5am-midnight.

Public Transportation: Santa Clara County Transit, 4 N. 2nd St. (321-2300), offers ultra-modern buses as well as a light-rail system. Fare $1.10, seniors and disabled 35¢, ages 5-17 55¢; day passes $2.20, 70¢, $1.10; exact change. **BART** (510-441-2278), bus #180 serves the Fremont station from 1st and San Carlos in downtown San Jose (fare $1.75). To San Francisco (fare $3.65; 1¼hr.).

Road Conditions: (800-427-7623).

Crisis Lines: Rape Crisis (287-3000). **Poison Control** (299-5112 or 800-662-9886). **Suicide Prevention/Crisis Intervention** (279-3312). All 24hr.

Medical Services: San Jose Medical Center, 675 E. Santa Clara St. (998-3212), at 14th. Emergency room (977-4444) open 24hr.

Emergency: 911.

Post Office: 105 N. 1st St. Open Mon.-Fri. 9am-5:30pm. **ZIP Code:** 95113.

Area Code: 408.

ORIENTATION

The third-largest city in California and the 11th largest in the U.S., San Jose lies at the southern end of San Francisco Bay, about 50 mi. from San Francisco (via U.S. 101 or I-280) and 40 mi. from Oakland (via I-880). From San Francisco, take I-280 rather than U.S.101, which is full of traffic snarls at all hours. For info on reaching San Jose from San Francisco via public transit, see the listing for CalTrain on p.250.

San Jose is centered around the convention-hosting malls and plazas near east-west **San Carlos St.** and north-south **Market St.** Bars, restaurants, and clubs cluster around **1st St.** The **Transit Mall,** the center of San Jose's transit system, runs north-south along 1st and 2nd St. in the downtown area. The grassy grounds of the **San Jose State University** campus run several blocks between S. 4th and S. 10th St.

ACCOMMODATIONS AND CAMPING

County parks with campgrounds surround the city. It doesn't resemble a cone-shaped bra, but **Mt. Madonna County Park** has 117 campsites in a beautiful setting, occupied on a first-come, first-camped basis. (*Let's Go* does not recommend that you mount Madonna.) **Joseph D. Grant County Park** (348-3741, reservations 358-3751), offers 20 campsites and 40 mi. of horse and hiking trails (open Mon.-Fri. 9am-4pm). The scandalously idyllic hamlet of **Saratoga**, 20 minutes southwest of San Jose on Rte. 85, offers a number of sites ($8, April to mid.-Oct.) and trails in wooded **Sanborn County Park,** on Sanborn Rd. From Rte. 17 (south), take Rte. 9 to Big Basin Way. Along the way sits **Saratoga Springs,** a private campground with 32 sites ($20 for 2 people), hot showers, and a general store.

Sanborn Park Hostel (HI-AYH), 15808 Sanborn Rd. (741-0166), in Saratoga, 13mi. west of San Jose. This utterly beautiful facility is strict about its ground rules; those looking for peace and quiet with indoor plumbing need look no further. No parking, but if you take a bus or train into town between 5-11pm, the hostel will pick you up. This lovely old log building has clean rooms and 39 beds. Piano, kitchen, and fireplaces inside and redwoods outside. Usually has vacancies. Registration open daily 7-9am and 5-11pm. Check-out 9am. Curfew 11pm. Dorms $8.50, nonmembers $10.50, under 18 half-price; doubles $14.50 per person. Limited wheelchair accessibility; call ahead.

San Jose State University, 375 S. 9th St. (924-6180; call before noon), at San Salvador. Singles $22, students $20. Extra for linens and parking.

Park View Motel, 1140 S. 2nd St. (297-8455). This centrally located, but generally quiet, motel has over 40 comfortable rooms with king beds. Kitchenettes and a pool. Check-in after 11am. Singles $40; doubles $55. No wheelchair access.

FOOD

Most of San Jose's cheap eats lie along San Pedro and S. 1st, near San Pedro Square. Asian and Mexican restaurants are less bland and more budget. A **farmer's market** takes place at the Pavilion, at S. 1st and San Fernando (every Thurs. 10am-2pm from late May to mid-Nov.). The places listed below are all in downtown San Jose.

Lan's Garden, 155 E. San Fernando St. (289-8553), at 4th. Whether you want adventurous cuisine (calamari steaks with pineapple $7.50) or tamer fare (*pho* noodle soup $4.50), this Vietnamese restaurant won't disappoint. Lunch specials $4.25, dinner entrees $6-7.50. Open Sun.-Thurs. 10am-11pm, Fri.-Sat. 10am-2am.

La Guadalajara, 45 Post St. (292-7352). This lunch counter has been serving delicious Mexican food and cheap, yummy pastries since 1955. Jumbo burritos $3, combo plates $4. Open daily 8:30am-6:30pm.

White Lotus, 80 N. Market St. (977-0540), between Santa Clara and St. John. One of the few vegetarian restaurants in the area, but omnivores will enjoy *Metro*'s pick for the area's best Vietnamese food, too. *Lotus vermicelli* "salad" and imperial roll $5.75. Steamed plantain with coconut milk ($2) makes a great dessert. Open Tues.-Fri. 11am-2:30pm and 5:30-9pm, Sat. 11am-10pm, Sun. 11am-9pm.

Bagel Basket, 505 E. San Carlos (294-6615), across from the SJSU campus. Narrow scope, but they go to town with their namesake: varieties from apple to wheat sesame are everything bagels should be. Sandwiches (on guess what?) $2.20-4.30. Small coffee 75¢. Open Mon.-Sat. 6am-7:30pm, Sun. 7am-2pm.

House of Siam, 55 Market St. (279-5668). Cozy, elegant Thai eatery serving super-spicy dishes of both the flesh and fleshless varieties. Entrees $7-10. Open Mon.-Fri. 11am-3pm and 5-10pm, Sat.-Sun. 11:30am-10pm.

THE BAY AREA

SIGHTS

San Jose's few main attractions are bizarrely intriguing. If you're looking for a grand tour of the Silicon Valley, forget it—**the Silicon Valley doesn't exist.** The computer companies are scattered throughout the Santa Clara Valley northwest of San Jose and are *very* wary of visitors (industrial sabotage, maybe?). The farmland from the 70s has become the computerland of the 90s, where anonymous-looking buildings, often shielded behind black glass, hint at the companies' attitude towards tourists. Head to the Tech Museum in San Jose for a technological grasp of this region, but if you want to say you've "been there," head to the birthplace of **Hewlett-Packard**— the garage where David Packard and Bill Hewlett chipped away to success is located at 367 Addison Ave., 5 blocks south of University Ave. in Palo Alto.

Nearer San Jose is the **Winchester Mystery House,** 1525 S. Winchester Blvd. (247-2101), piled near the intersection of I-880 and I-280, west of town. Once the home of Sarah Winchester, heir to the Winchester rifle fortune, the Victorian estate is filled with oddities: stairs leading to ceilings, doors opening to walls, and tourist traps. Discover the mysterious motive behind Winchester's order that construction continue on her home without cease. The hours, like the architecture itself, are subject to change (usually open 9am-8pm, with 1hr. tours every 10-25min.; admission $13, seniors $10, ages 6-12 $7).The San Jose city planners love their museums, and growth and expansion have been well-funded. A notable beneficiary is the mushrooming **Tech Museum of Innovation,** 145 W. San Carlos St. (279-7150), which will grow sevenfold in size with the expected 1998 completion of a new building and IMAX theater. Originally called "The Garage" in honor of the humble beginnings of such technological powerhouses as Hewlett-Packard and Apple, the museum features excellent hands-on exhibits on robotics, DNA engineering, and space exploration (open Tues.-Sun. 10am-5pm; July-Sept. Mon.-Sat. 10am-6pm, Sun. noon-6pm; students $6, seniors $4, ages 6-18 $4). Leaping across town and millennia, **Rosicrucian Egyptian Museum and Planetarium,** 1342 Naglee Ave. (947-3636; http:// www.rosicrucian.org), at Park, houses the West's largest collection of Egyptian artifacts, including a walk-in tomb and spooky animal mummies. The collection belongs to the mystical order of the Rosy Cross whose private offices share the grounds and carefully tended gardens with the museum. (Open Wed.-Mon. 9am-5pm. Admission $6, students and seniors $4, ages 7-15 $3.50. Under 18 must be accompanied by an adult. Planetarium show on Egyptian astrology daily at 2pm. 40min. Tickets $4, under 15 $3.)

Other bastions of art stick closer to each other and the contemporary era downtown: the **San Jose Museum of Art,** 110 S. Market (271-6840; http://www.sjliving.com/sjma), at San Fernando, presents mass-appeal modern shows (open Tues.-Wed. and Fri.-Sun. 9am-5pm, Thurs. 9am-8pm; admission $6, students $3, seniors $3). Area galleries are free and open to the public until 8pm on the third Thursday of every month. Don't miss the **San Jose Institute of Contemporary Art (SJICA),** 451 S. 1st St. (283-8155; open Tues.-Sat. noon-5pm) or the **Center for Latino Arts (MACLA),** 510 S. 1st St. (998-ARTE/2783; open Wed.-Sat. noon-5pm).

The little ones go wild over the **Children's Discovery Museum,** 180 Woz Way (298-5437; http://www.cdm.org), behind the Technology Center light-rail station, but even the big ones let the inner child loose when they get their hands on a kazillion science-based toys. Especially popular among people of all stages of development are the bubble room, strobe lights, and free painting (open Tues.-Sat. 10am-5pm, Sun. noon-5pm; admission $6, seniors $5, under 18 $4).

Founded in 1857, **San Jose State University (SJSU),** 1 Washington Sq. (924-5000), is the oldest public college in California, though there's not much to tip you off. The campus is centered around San Carlos and 7th, east of downtown. For info on campus events, call the 24-hour events line (924-6350), or in summer, look in the *Summer Times,* a weekly publication of the *Spartan Daily,* the campus newspaper.

NIGHTLIFE

Copious cops keep the streets quiet and very safe. Off the streets and inside San Jose's music and dance venues, racially and generationally mixed crowds take a while to warm up, but go beyond San Jose's typically tepid tendencies. Young tykes (under 21) can stay on the good side of the law at **Cafe Kismet,** 424 S. 1st St. (538-3205; http://www.kismetart.com), a coffee spot and gallery that hops till the wee hours.

The Flying Pig Pub, 78 S. 1st St. (298-6710). A happily wacky jukebox suits the fly clientele of this mega-chill bistro, which serves both food (3-way chili $3.25) and drinks (full bar). Open Tues.-Fri. 11am-2am, Sat. 4pm-2am, Mon. 3pm-2am.

The B-Hive Bar and Lounge, 372 S. 1st St. (298-2529), buzzes with a relatively youthful crowd. DJs pump different theme selections nightly into tight, smoky rooms. No cover charge Wed.-Sat. Open Tues.-Sun. 9pm-2am.

Katie Bloom's Irish Pub and Restaurant, 150 S. 1st St. (294-4408). It's clear why "pub" comes before "restaurant" in the name and why "Irish" comes before both. Drink imported beers ($2.50) while Oscar Wilde and James Joyce watch from the walls. Extensive space includes many private leather booths as well as rowdier counter spots. Open Mon.-Fri. 11am-2am.

The Agenda, 399 S. 1st St. (287-4087), has a basement DJ sector, but only the upstairs lounge, with its live music features, really merits the visit. Highly assorted listeners (mostly late 20s and up) groove to highly assorted acts for $3 a head. Open Mon.-Fri. 5pm-2am, Sat. 8pm-2am, Sun. 7pm-2am.

ENTERTAINMENT AND SEASONAL EVENTS

For information on any mighty sights and poundin' sounds in San Jose, look for *Metro Weekly,* a periodical hip enough to make San Jose seem interesting (available free on street corners downtown). The Student Union (924-6350), at SJSU, has an amphitheater that often hosts concerts and other performances. Hockey fans may want to check out the **San Jose Sharks,** the city's NHL team, at the San Jose Arena. For tickets, call the Sharks at 287-7070 (Mon.-Fri. 8am-6pm); to avoid the service charge, visit the SJSU ticket office in the campus convention center (open Mon.-Fri. 9:30am-5:30pm, Sun. 9:30am-1pm). Soccer aficionados can kick it with Eric Wynalda and the **San Jose Clash,** the city's new MLS representative, at Spartan Stadium, on 7th off I-280. (Call 985-4625 Mon.-Fri. 8:30am-5pm for tickets.)

City Lights, 529 S. 2nd St. (295-4200; http://www.cltc.org), is a hip local theater company with student discounts. Check *Metro* (a partial sponsor) for details.

Camera Cinemas (998-3300), with 3 locations, definitely helps the "big city soul" San Jose's tourist literature so ardently touts. Art house, classic, and foreign flicks, film festivals, and midnight specials are held at **Camera 1,** 366 S. 1st St., **Camera 3,** S. 2nd St. and San Carlos, or **Towne 3,** 1433 The Alameda (287-1433). Even the cafe at Camera 1 is fly, with sandwiches like "My Dinner with Andre" (roast beef and gouda on sourdough $5.75). Detailed schedules at Camera I.

Topping the list of **annual highlights** is the May **Blues Festival** (924-6261). It's the biggest, baddest, largest free blues concert in Northern California. In early September, head to the **SoFA Street Fair** (295-2265), south of 1st, between San Carlos and Reco. Cool vendors and bands attract more than just your average San Jose crowd (noon-9pm). On the last weekend in September, buzz downtown to the **San Pedro Square Brew-Ha-Ha** (279-1775), which has beer tasting and fun for all (noon-7pm).

■ Santa Clara

One might say Santa Clara stretches from San Jose in the southeast to Great America in the north; originally known as the site of one of the largest California missions, the small town has since both expanded and devolved into a suburb of the gargantuan Great America, a Paramount-owned theme park. To reach Santa Clara, take U.S. 101 to the De La Cruz Exit and follow the signs to the Santa Clara University.

Mission Santa Clara, 500 El Camino Real, was the first California mission to honor a woman—Clare of Assisi—as its patron saint. Located on the Guadalupe River at its 1777 founding, the mission moved to its present site in 1825. The mission church houses a magnificent organ and decorative light fixtures. Masses are held at the mission church during the summer (Mon.-Fri. noon, Sun. 10am; open to the public). For more info, see **A Man with a Mission** (p. 54). In 1851, **Santa Clara University** was established in the old mission. Subsequent restorations have beautified the structures to match the beauty and bliss of the surrounding rose gardens and 200-year-old olive trees.

Paramount's Great America theme park (988-1776), squats on its own parkway north of the city, and teems with impatient children eager to get on one of the gimmicky rides. (Open daily June-Aug., weekends only March-May and Sept.-Oct. Admission $29, seniors and disabled $19, ages 3-6 $16. Parking $5. Special rates for evenings only; coupons in San Jose area stores.) Paramount recently bought **Raging Waters** (654-5450), 1½ mi. east at the Tully Rd. Exit, the area's best collection of waterslides. Great on a hot day, but expect huge crowds to think the same (open daily May-Sept. 10am-7pm; admission $20, seniors $10, under 42in. $16).

■ San Mateo County

The rocky bluffs of San Mateo County Coast quickly obscure the hectic urban pace of the city to the north. Most of the energy here is generated by the coastal winds and waves. The Pacific Coast Highway (Hwy. 1) maneuvers its way through a rocky shoreline, colorful beach vistas, and generations-old ranches. Although it's possible to drive quickly down the coast from San Francisco to Santa Cruz, haste is waste—only the patient explorer will be able to get a full taste of the area.

PRACTICAL INFORMATION AND ORIENTATION

Visitor Information: San Mateo County Coast Convention and Visitors Center, Seabreeze Plaza, 111 Anza Blvd., #410 (800-28-VISIT/288-4748), in Burlingame by the San Francisco International Airport. Panopoly of pamphlets. Open Mon.-Fri. 8:30am-5pm. **San Mateo County Parks and Recreation Department,** James V. Fitzgerald Marine Life Reserve, P.O. Box 451 (728-3584), Moss Beach, off Hwy. 1, 7mi. north of Half Moon Beach. Open daily sunrise to sunset.
Buses: San Mateo County Transit (SamTrans), 945 California Dr. (800-660-4BUS/4287, outside county 508-6455). Service from Burlingame (adjacent to San Francisco) to Half Moon. Fare $1, seniors and disabled 50¢, ages 5-17 50¢. Monthly pass $36, seniors and disabled $18, ages 5-17 $18. Runs daily 6am-7pm.
Auto Repair: AAA Emergency Road Service (595-3411). 24hr. Members only.
Bike Rental: The Bicyclery, 432 Main St. (726-6000), Half Moon Bay. Bikes $6 per hr. with 2hr. min., $24 per day. Helmets $5. Bike accessories for sale. Bike repairs. Open Mon.-Fri. 9:30am-6:30pm, Sat. 10am-5pm, Sun. 11am-5pm.
Crisis Line: San Mateo County Crisis Intervention and Suicide Prevention Hotline (368-6655). 24hr.
Hospital: San Mateo County General Hospital, 222 W. 39th Ave. (573-2222).
Emergency: 911.
Police: 401 Marshall St. (363-4000), Redwood City.
Post Office: Half Moon Bay Post Office, 500 Stone Pine Rd. (726-5517), at Main St. Open Mon.-Fri. 8:30am-5pm, Sat. 8:30am-noon. **ZIP Code:** 94019.
Area Code: 650 (recently changed from 415).

On this stretch of the Pacific coast, a car is the best way to go. Stunning ocean views compete with **Hwy. 1** for drivers' attentions. If you're traveling by sneaker, you'll have a tougher time; **SamTrans** services the area only somewhat successfully (see above for fare info). Bus route maps are available at CalTrain and BART stations. The shore from Pacifica to Half Moon Bay is serviced by buses #1C, 1L, and 90H.

ACCOMMODATIONS AND CAMPING

Pigeon Point Lighthouse Hostel (HI-AYH) (879-0633), on Hwy. 1, 6mi. south of Pescadero and 20mi. south of Half Moon Bay. Accessible by weekday SamTrans service or by Bikecentennial Trail. Four houses, each with a big, homey common room accommodate 52 beds. The old lightkeeper's quarters has a hot tub. Registration open 7:30-9:30am and 5:30-9:30pm. Check-in 4:30pm. Check-out 9:30am. Curfew and quiet time at 11pm. Dorms $12, nonmembers $15; extra $10 for couples' rooms. Chores required. Reservations must be made 48hr. in advance.

Point Montara Lighthouse Hostel (HI-AYH) (728-7177), on Lighthouse Point 25mi. south of San Francisco and 4mi. north of Half Moon Bay. SamTrans stop 1 block north at 14th and Hwy. 1. Wholesome 45-bed facility with 2 kitchens and a hot tub ($5 per hr., 2-person min.). Bike rentals $5 per hr. Registration open 7:30-9:30am and 5-9:30pm. Curfew and quiet time 11pm-7am. Dorms $12, nonmembers $15; extra $10 for couples' rooms. Laundry (wash $1, dry 25¢). Reservations recommended for weekends, groups, and private rooms; request by phone 48hr. in advance with credit card, or by mail with deposit.

Francis Beach campground, 95 Kelly Ave. (726-8820), at Half Moon Bay State Beach, has 56 beachside sites. Most have fire pit and picnic table. Campfires held Sat. in peak season. 7-night max. stay, off-season 14-night max. stay. Check-out noon. Tent sites $16, seniors $15. Hiker/biker sites $3 per person. Pets $1. Free cold outdoor showers. No reservations. Open 24hr; day use 8am-sunset.

Butano State Park campground (879-2040), 5mi. south of Pescadero. From the north, take Pescadero east from Hwy. 1 to Cloverdale. From the south, take Gazos Creek from Hwy. 1 to Cloverdale. Extensive paths lace through the tall, lush redwood forests of the Santa Cruz Mountains. There are 21 drive-in and 18 walk-in campsites. Check-out noon. Vehicles $5; sites Sun.-Thurs. $15, Fri.-Sat. $16. Seniors $1 discount. No showers. Reservations recommended from Memorial Day-Labor Day; call DESTINET (800-444-7275).

FOOD

Despite the area's remote feel, there are a surprising number of restaurants catering to hungry travelers. Those looking for a late night snack or planning to picnic along the coast can find a 24 hr. **Safeway** at the junction of Hwy. 1 and Rte. 92.

Half Moon Bay

The Flying Fish Grill (712-1125), at the corner of Main St. and Rte. 92. Inexpensive seafood straight from the coast. The Salmon Taco Grande ($4) or the pint of clam chowder ($5) will satisfy a seafarer's appetite. Open Tues.-Sun. 11am-8pm.

2 Fools Cafe and Market, 408 Main St. (712-1222), at Mill St. Cool and urbane eatery and drinkery serves many veggie options. Sandwiches $5-8. Open Mon. 7am-2pm, Tues.-Fri. 7am-9pm, Sat.-Sun. 8am-9pm.

Around Half Moon Bay

Arcangeli Grocery Co. and **Norm's Market,** 287 Stage Rd. (879-0147), Pescadero. Established in 1929 by the present owner's grandfather, this extremely popular grocery store has a full meat and deli department, wine, and bakery. Loaves ($1.50-4) including ones that are partially baked for fresh-from-the-oven goodness in your own kitchen. Open Mon.-Sat. 10am-7pm, Sun. 10am-6pm.

San Gregorio General Store, 7615 Stage Rd. (726-0565), 1mi. east of Hwy. 1 on Rte. 84, 8mi. south of Half Moon Bay. The store has served San Gregorio since 1889 with an eclectic selection of hardware, cold drinks, candy, groceries, gourmet coffee, cast iron pots, books, candles—you name it. Have a frothy beer ($2-4) at the bar or stop in for a fresh sandwich ($3). Open Mon.-Thurs. 9am-6pm, Fri.-Sun. 9am-7pm.

Inside the Peninsula

Taquería La Cumbre, 28 North B St. (344-8989; http://www.hotchiles.com), San Mateo. This restaurant, which also has a branch in San Francisco, has won "best burrito" award in every major Bay Area magazine reader poll. Filling, tasty, authentic Mexican meals for under $5. Be prepared for long lines during lunch. Open Sun.-Thurs. 11am-9pm, Fri.-Sat. 11am-10pm.

The Merry Prankster Cafe, 8865 La Honda Rd. (747-0660), in La Honda, keeps Ken Kesey's memory alive. Eat inexpensively all day long: leek and red potato egg scramble $4, fresh vegetable sandwich $5, and 6in. single pizza $4.50. Open Mon. 5-9pm, Tues.-Fri. 7am-9:30pm, Sat.-Sun. 7am-10pm.

Shirin Bakery and Cafe, 5 S. Ellsworth Ave. (343-6722), at Baldwin in San Mateo. A haven for knish-lovers everywhere, conveniently located on the West Coast (knishes $2). Sandwich lunch special $3, iced coffee $1.25. Lots of gorgeous pastry. Open Sun.-Fri. 7am-6pm, Sat. 8am-5pm.

SIGHTS AND ACTIVITIES

Highway I: The Pacific Coast Highway

Highway 1 winds along the San Mateo County Coast from San Francisco to Big Basin Redwoods State Park. This expanse of shore is scattered with isolated and sandy beaches, most of which are too cold for swimming. State beaches charge $5, with admission valid for the entire day at all state parks—keep your receipt. At some beaches the payment for using the beach works on the honor system, but police occasionally make sweeps looking for unpaid cars and gleefully distribute tickets. Keep your eyes peeled for the unmarked beaches along the coast; often they are stunning, crowdless spots and the parking is free. A few miles south of Pacifica (take SamTrans bus #1L) is **Gray Whale Cove Beach,** a privately owned **nude** beach off Hwy. 1. You must be 18 and pay $5.

Not much farther south is the Point Montara Lighthouse Hostel (see p. 315), flanked by quiet **Montara State Beach** and the variegated tide pool life at **Fitzgerald Marine Reserve.** At **Pillar Point Harbor,** 4 mi. north of Half Moon Bay, you can sample smoked salmon, chat with fishermen, or try your hand at reeling in the big ones with the harborside **Captain John's Fishing Trips** (726-2913 or 728-3377). Trips leave daily at 7:30am and return at 3pm (tickets $32, seniors and under 13 $27, weekends $34; check-in 6:30am). Special trips go to the desolate **Farallon Islands Wildlife Refuge.** There are also seasonal salmon fishing trips (1-day fishing license $5.50, rod and reel rental $5, tackle and bait $5.75). For kids over five, the **Sea Horse Ranch** and the **Friendly Acres Ranch** (726-9903), one mile north of Half Moon Bay on Hwy. 1, have horses and ponies for beachside trail rides (1hr. $22; open daily 8am-6pm).

Half Moon Bay is an old coastal community 29 mi. south of San Francisco. Despite local frowning, recent commercialization has not infringed much on the small, easy-going beach town it still is. The fishing and farming hamlet of **San Gregorio** rests 10 mi. south of Half Moon Bay. **San Gregorio Beach** is a delightful destination; you can walk to its southern end to find little caves in the shore rocks. A stream runs into the sea, and may prove a comfortable alternative to dipping in the chillier ocean (open 8am-sunset; day use $4, seniors $3). To find a less-frequented beach, visit the **Unsigned Turnout** at **Marker 27.35.** It's difficult to find without aid; keep an eye out for mysteriously vacant cars parked along the highway. State-owned but undeveloped, this gorgeous stretch of beach is between San Gregorio and Pomponio State Beaches, off Hwy. 1.

The historic little burg of **Pescadero** was established by white settlers in 1856, and was named Pescadero ("fisherman's town") due to the abundance of fish in both the oceans and creeks. Wander through the old town or participate in the local sport of **olallieberry gathering.** This popular pastime originated a couple decades ago when the olallieberry (oh-LA-la-behr-ee) was created by crossing a blackberry, a loganberry, and a youngberry. Get a-pickin' at **Phipp's Ranch,** 2700 Pescadero Rd. (879-0787 or 800-279-0889), in Pescadero, and pay 95¢ per lb. for your stash of strawberries, blackberries, olallieberries, and boysenberries (open daily 10am-7pm).

Pigeon Point (879-0852), takes its name from a hapless schooner that crashed into the rocky shore on its inaugural voyage in 1853. The point turns heads with its tide-pools, wave-washed rocks at Pebble Beach, and 30 ft. plumes of surf. In the late afternoon, the West Coast's second tallest **lighthouse** (879-0633), offers a magnificent view of the **sunset.** Tours of the lighthouse and its 1008 glass prisms are available Sunday 11am-4pm for a small donation. The **Pescadero Marsh** shelters such migratory birds as the elegant blue heron, often seen poised on its spindly legs searching for unlucky fish.

Año Nuevo State Reserve (879-0227), on Hwy. 1 in Pescadero, 7 mi. south of Pigeon Point and 27 mi. south of Half Moon Bay, is the mating place of the 15 ft. long **elephant seal.** Early spring is breeding season, when thousands of seals crowd on the beach. To see this unforgettable show (prime viewing times Dec. 15-Mar. 31), you must make reservations (8 weeks in advance recommended) by calling DESTINET (800-444-7275), since park access is limited. Tickets go on sale November 15 and are generally sold out by the end of the month (2½hr., guided tours $4 per person). SamTrans runs Saturday, Sunday, and holiday round-trip bus service to the reserve from San Mateo that includes a walking tour ($12); call 508-6441 for info. From April to November the reserve is free (parking $5), but you *will* need a free **hiking permit** from the entrance station (open April-Aug. daily 8am-4pm, Sept.-Nov. 8:30am-3pm). Trail lengths in the Wildlife Protection Area ranges between one half and 1½ mi. Arrive before mid-August to catch the last of the "molters" and the young who've yet to find their sea-legs. Don't get too close—they may be fat but they're fast, and mothers are intolerant of strangers who appear to threaten their young. The beach is cold and windy regardless of season, so dress warmly (park open daily 8am-sunset).

Inland

Nestled further inside the peninsula south of the San Francisco International Airport is the **Burlingame Museum of Pez Memorabilia,** 214 California Dr. (347-2301), which has a comprehensive display of dispensers and paraphernalia dating back to 1949. Be sure to see the short Pez factory video. Like all the best things in life, the museum is free (open Tues.-Sat. 10am-6pm).

A winding cross-peninsular trip down Rte. 84 will take you into **La Honda,** the little logging town in the Redwoods where author Ken Kesey lived with his merry pranksters in the 60s, before it got too small and they took off across the U.S. in a psychedelic bus. The breathtaking drive makes this detour worthwhile, even if you aren't familiar with Kesey's gang—but for enhanced understanding, pick up a copy of Tom Wolfe's *The Electric Kool-Aid Acid Test* before you make the journey.

SEASONAL EVENTS

Brew-Ha-Ha (726-7416), first Sun. in May, Half Moon Bay. Slurp over 50 beers.
Coastside County Fair (726-5202), mid-June to mid-July. Crafts, livestock, and a junior rodeo. (Let's Go does not recommend that children ride broncos.)
Chili Cook-Off/Chowder Challenge (726-9275), late June, Half Moon Bay.
Half Moon Bay Bluegrass Festival (726-8380), late Sept. Draws a variety of locally and nationally known outfits.
Half Moon Bay Art and Pumpkin Festival (726-9652), mid-Oct. Locals tout it as the fête of the year. Arts, food, a parade, a masquerade ball, and carving contests.

NORTH BAY AND WINE COUNTRY

Across the Golden Gate from San Francisco, Marin County is the jacuzzi of the bay. Bubbling with money-making and mantra-mouthing residents, Marin stretches north from harborside Marin Headlands. A pristine beach stretches up the coast, and the inland woods crowd green fields of gnarled grape vines. Robert Louis Stevenson described Wine Country (the collective term for the Napa, Sonoma, and Russian River Valleys) as a place where "the stirring sunlight and the growing vines make a pleasant music for the mind, and the wine is poetry." Though only about 5% of California's *vino* is made in this area, that 5% is the state's best. The vineyards here are

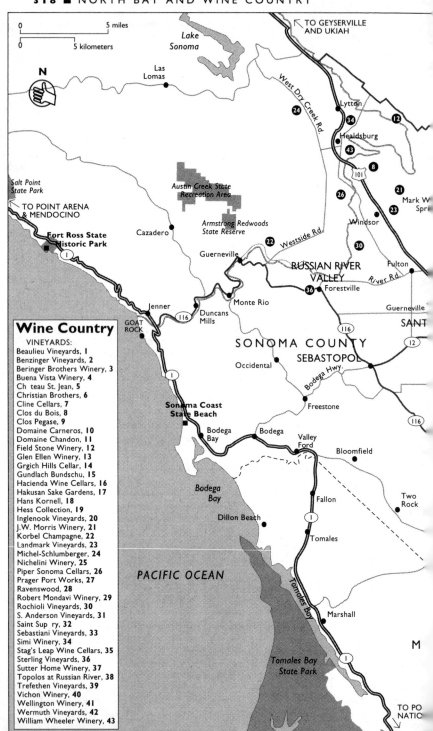

0   5 miles
0   5 kilometers

N

Lake Sonoma

TO GEYSERVILLE
AND UKIAH

Las Lomas

West Dry Creek Rd.

24

34

Lytton

12

Healdsburg

43

101

8

Salt Point
State Park

Austin Creek State
Recreation Area

26

21

23

Mark W
Spri

TO POINT ARENA
& MENDOCINO

Armstrong Redwoods
State Reserve

Cazadero

Windsor

**Fort Ross State
Historic Park**

1

22

Westside Rd.

30

Fulton

Guerneville

RUSSIAN RIVER
VALLEY

River Rd.

Jenner

116

Duncans
Mills

36

Forestville

Guerneville

GOAT
ROCK

Monte Rio

SANT

1

SONOMA COUNTY

116

12

SEBASTOPOL

Wine Country

VINEYARDS:
Beaulieu Vineyards, 1
Benzinger Vineyards, 2
Beringer Brothers Winery, 3
Buena Vista Winery, 4
Ch teau St. Jean, 5
Christian Brothers, 6
Cline Cellars, 7
Clos du Bois, 8
Clos Pegase, 9
Domaine Carneros, 10
Domaine Chandon, 11
Field Stone Winery, 12
Glen Ellen Winery, 13
Grgich Hills Cellar, 14
Gundlach Bundschu, 15
Hacienda Wine Cellars, 16
Hakusan Sake Gardens, 17
Hans Kornell, 18
Hess Collection, 19
Inglenook Vineyards, 20
J.W. Morris Winery, 21
Korbel Champagne, 22
Landmark Vineyards, 23
Michel-Schlumberger, 24
Nichelini Winery, 25
Piper Sonoma Cellars, 26
Prager Port Works, 27
Ravenswood, 28
Robert Mondavi Winery, 29
Rochioli Vineyards, 30
S. Anderson Vineyards, 31
Saint Sup ry, 32
Sebastiani Vineyards, 33
Simi Winery, 34
Stag's Leap Wine Cellars, 35
Sterling Vineyards, 36
Sutter Home Winery, 37
Topolos at Russian River, 38
Trefethen Vineyards, 39
Vichon Winery, 40
Wellington Winery, 41
Wermuth Vineyards, 42
William Wheeler Winery, 43

Occidental

Bodega Hwy.

Freestone

116

**Sonoma Coast
State Beach**

1

Bodega
Bay

Bodega

Valley
Ford

Bloomfield

Two
Rock

Fallon

*Bodega
Bay*

Dillon Beach

1

Tomales

Marshall

PACIFIC OCEAN

Tomales Bay

M

*Tomales Bay
State Park*

1

TO PO
NATIO

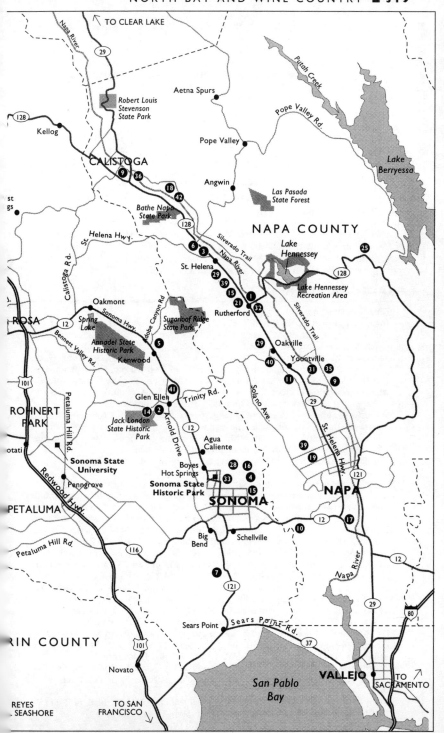

highly regarded by connoisseurs both in the U.S. and abroad, which accounts for the area's high prices and heavy tourism.

Both Marin County and Wine Country are within two hours of San Francisco; it might be wiser to make it a daytrip than to stay here and endure the steep hotel prices. For those in shape, Wine Country's flat, scenic terrain makes it easy to get around via bike; rental shops abound throughout the valleys.

■ Marin County

Home of Dana Carvey, 560 acres of spectacular redwood forest, and Jerry Garcia's memory, Marin (muh-RIN) County boasts a bizarre blend of natural beauty, trendy liberalism, and wealth. Marinites love their real estate values as much as their land-scapes and organic food. Neighboring communities grumble about Marin's excesses—most notably the $350 million oil stock fund left to the county by the late Mrs. Beryl Buck, for which many say Marin has little use. Residents, on the other hand, will tell you there's no hypocrisy in their indulgent and eco-conscious habits. Life is just *better* in Marin.

Marin's pleasure spots lend themselves to daytrips from San Francisco via car, bus, or ferry. Muir Woods National Monument, Marin Headlands, Mt. Tamalpais State Park, and Point Reyes National Seashore offer trails for mountain bikers and hikers looking for anything from a day's adventure to a two-week trek.

PRACTICAL INFORMATION

Visitor Information:
Marin County Visitors Bureau (472-7470; http://www.visitmarin.org), at the end of the Avenue of the Flags off Hwy. 101 in San Rafael. The glossy brochures may be more informative than the staff. Usually open Mon.-Fri. 9am-5pm.
Sausalito Visitors Center, 777 Bridgeway, 4th fl. (332-0505), Sausalito. Open Tue.-Sun. 11:30am-4pm. **Sausalito Chamber of Commerce,** 333 Caledonia St. (331-7262; http://www.sausalito.org). Open Mon.-Fri. 9am-noon and 1-5pm.
Marin Headlands Visitors Center, Field St. (331-1540), at Bunker in Fort Barry. Camping info and park maps. Open daily 9:30am-4:30pm.
Point Reyes National Seashore Headquarters, Bear Valley Rd. (663-1092), ½mi. west of Olema. Provides wilderness permits, maps, and campsite reservations. Museum of cultural and natural history presents an orientation film. Ranger-guided hikes. Open Mon.-Fri. 9am-5pm, Sat.-Sun. 8am-5pm.
San Rafael Chamber of Commerce, 817 Mission Ave. (800-454-4163). Open Mon.-Fri. 9am-noon and 1-5pm.
Public Transportation: Golden Gate Transit (455-2000, in San Francisco 923-2000; http://www.goldengate.org), provides transit between San Francisco and Marin County via the Golden Gate Bridge, as well as local service in Marin. Buses #10, 20, 28, 30, and 50 service Marin from San Francisco's Transbay Terminal. Buses #65 and 24 service Point Reyes and Samuel P. Taylor State Park (fare to Sausalito $2, to West Marin $4). Seniors and disabled 50% off; ages 6-12 25% off.
Ferries: Golden Gate Ferry (455-2000), runs boats from San Francisco to the Sausalito ferry terminal at the end of Market St. (25min., $4.25), and the Larkspur ferry terminal (50min.; Mon.-Fri. $2.50, Sat.-Sun. $4.25). Seniors and disabled 50% off; ages 6-12 25% off. Offices open Mon.-Fri. 6am-8pm, Sat.-Sun. 6:30am-8pm.
Taxis: Radio Cab (485-1234 or 800-464-7234), serves all of Marin County.
Car Rental: Budget, 20 Bellam Blvd. (457-4282), San Rafael. Economy cars $27 per day, with 150 free mi. Must be 21. Under 25 pay $10 per day surcharge.
Bike Rental: For more info, see **Mt. Tamalpais** (p. 323) and **Point Reyes** (p. 324).
Library: Sausalito Library, 420 Litho St. (289-4121). Shares a building with Sausalito City Hall. Open Mon.-Thurs. 10am-9pm, Fri.-Sat. 10am-5pm.
Community Services: Marin Senior Coordinating Council, 930 Tamalpais (456-9062), San Rafael. Health, legal, and counseling services. Open Mon.-Fri. 9am-5pm.
Bi-Gay-Lesbian Organization: Spectrum, 1000 Sir Francis Drake Blvd. (457-1115), San Anselmo. Info and social services. Open Mon.-Thurs. 9am-5pm.

Laundromat: Water Works, 105 2nd St (332-2632), Sausalito. Wash $1.50; dry 75¢. Open Mon.-Fri. 7am-9pm, Sat.-Sun. 8am-9pm.

Weather Conditions: National Weather Service (364-79740).

Crisis Lines: Rape Crisis (924-2100). **Poison Control** (800-876-4766). **Suicide Prevention** (499-1100). All 24hr.

Medical Services: Marin General Hospital, 250 Bon Air Rd. (925-7000), Greenbrae. **Marin Community Clinic,** 250 Bon Air Rd. (461-7400). Open Mon. and Fri. 8:30am-5pm, Wed. 9:30am-5pm, Tues. and Thurs. 8:30am-8:30pm.

Emergency: 911.

Police: San Rafael (485-3000); Marin County (479-2311).

Post Office: San Rafael, 40 Bellam Blvd. (459-0944), at Francisco. Open Mon.-Fri. 8:30am-5pm, Sat. 10am-1pm. **ZIP Code:** 94915.

Area Code: 415 and 650.

ORIENTATION

The Marin peninsula lies at the north end of San Francisco Bay, and is connected to the city by **U.S. 101** via the **Golden Gate Bridge.** U.S. 101 extends north to Santa Rosa and Sonoma County, while **Hwy. 1** creeps north along the Pacific to Sonoma Coast. The **Richmond-San Rafael Bridge** connects Marin to the East Bay via **I-580.**

The eastern side of the county cradles the settlements of **Sausalito, Mill Valley, Larkspur, San Rafael, Terra Linda, Ignacio,** and **Novato.** These towns line U.S. 101, which runs north-south through Marin, creating the inland corridor where most of the population is concentrated. Most of West Marin comprises national seashore and parkland. **Hwy. 1** runs south to north through **Stinson Beach, Olema, Inverness,** and **Point Reyes National Seashore. Sir Francis Drake Blvd.** runs from U.S. 101 in Larkspur west through the San Geronimo Valley. It passes through the towns of **Greenbrae, Kentfield, San Anselmo, San Geronimo,** and **Olema** on the way to Point Reyes and its rendezvous with Hwy. 1.

Gas is scarce and expensive in West Marin, so fill up in town before you head out for the coast. Drivers should take caution in West Marin, where roads are narrow, sharply curved, and perched on the edge of vertiginous bluffs. Hiking alone in Marin's woods alone can be unsafe, particularly after sunset as many signs have been uprooted and it's easy to get lost in the dark.

ACCOMMODATIONS AND CAMPING

Hostels

Marin Headlands (HI-AYH) (331-2777), in old Fort Barry, west of Sausalito and 10mi. from downtown San Francisco. The hostel is a 4½mi. uphill hike from the Golden Gate Transit bus (#2, 10, 50) stop at Alexander Ave., and a 1½mi. walk from the Sausalito ferry terminal. Accessible by car: take the Sausalito Exit from the north or the Alexander Ave. Exit from San Francisco, and then follow the signs into the Golden Gate Recreation Area. These former soldiers' quarters now contain 109 beds, game room, kitchen, and common room. Closed (except for check-in) 9:30am-3:30pm. Check-in 7:30am-11:30pm. Check-out 8:45am. Dorms $12. Under 17 (with adult) half-price. Private doubles $35; each additional child (up to 2) $6. Lockers available. Linen $1; towels 50¢. Laundry (wash/dry 75¢). Key deposit $10.

Point Reyes Hostel (HI-AYH) (663-8811), in the Point Reyes National Seashore. By car, exit west from Hwy. 1 at Olema, then take Bear Valley Rd. to Limantour Rd. and drive 6mi. into the park. Two cabins occupy a spectacular site, near Limantour Beach, wildlife areas, and hiking trails. Kitchen and cozy common room. Registration open 7:30-9:30am and 4:30-9:30pm. Check-out 9am. Quiet time (no showering or kitchen use) after 10pm. Dorms $10-12. Chores expected. Linen $1; towels $1. Weekend reservations recommended; mail request with a deposit (Box 247, Point Reyes Station, CA 94956) or call with credit card. Some wheelchair access.

Campgrounds

Marin Headlands, northwest of the Golden Gate Bridge at Field and Bunker Rd. Most of the 15 sites are primitive, though 2 have running water and one has a cooking area. Permits required. Free. Showers and kitchen ($2 each) at Headlands Hostel (see above). Free outdoor cold showers available at Rodeo Beach (in the Headlands). Reserve up to 90 days in advance by calling the **visitors center** (331-1540; open daily 9:30am-noon).

Mt. Tamalpais State Park, 801 Hwy. 1 (388-2070), offers a number of campground facilities, including 16 walk-in sites. First-come, first-served. Sites $15, weekends $16. **Steep Ravine** has cabins by a coastal bluff overlooking the ocean ($30 for up to 5 people). Stoves, but no running water or electricity. Tent sites $10, weekends $11. Fire pits, but no showers. Make cabin reservations up to 7 months in advance by calling DESTINET (800-444-7275). Reservation fee $6.75.

Samuel P. Taylor State Park, Sir Francis Drake Blvd. (488-9897), 15mi. west of San Rafael. A family campground in a lush setting. 7-night max. stay. Sites $15, weekends $16. Hiker/biker sites $3 per person (no reservations). Pets $1. Hot showers (50¢ for 5min.). Reserve for April-Oct.; call DESTINET (800-444-7275).

Point Reyes National Seashore, in the southern, inner cape portion of Point Reyes, has 4 walk-in campgrounds. Two camps are coastal and two are inland, but all command exquisite views of the ocean and surrounding hills. Pit toilets, fire pits, and tap water. 4-night max. stay. Free. Obtain permits at the Point Reyes National Seashore Headquarters (see **Practical Information,** p. 320). Reservations accepted up to 2 months in advance Mon.-Fri. 9am-noon. For backcountry camping reservations, call 663-8054 (Mon.-Fri. 9am-2pm).

FOOD

Health-conscious Marinites take their fruit juices, tofu, and non-fat double-shot cappuccinos very seriously; restauranteurs know this, and raise both the alfalfa sprouts and the prices. Groceries provide cheap loot for a picnic in one of Marin's countless parks. **Woodland Market,** 735 College St. (457-8160), Kentfield, vends organic sausages and fresh pasta (open daily 8am-8pm). San Rafael's **farmer's markets** take place in the **Marin Civic Center,** off U.S. 101 (open Thurs. and Sun. 8am-1pm), and **downtown** on 4th St. (open Thurs. 6-9pm).

West Marin and Sausalito

Arawan, 47 Caledonia St. (332-0882), 1 block up from Bridgeway in Sausalito. Phenomenal Thai food is locally applauded. Specializing in seafood, more affordable dishes like the red curry chicken ($7) are winners too. Open daily noon-midnight.

Caffe Trieste, 1000 Bridgeway (332-7770), Sausalito. Still serving tasty morsels in the post-beatnik 90s, this solidly Italian spot a few blocks down from the crowded city center sells lattes ($2) and lunches (quiche and salad $6). Sip wine and select from the opera on their jukebox. Open Sun.-Thurs. 7am-11pm, Fri.-Sat. 7am-1am.

Cafe Reyes, (663-9493), on Hwy. 1 in Point Reyes Station. Way hip restaurant serving burgers ($7), Mexican food, quality coffee ($1), beer, and wine. Open daily 11am-9pm. No credit cards.

Old Western Saloon, 11201 Shoreline (663-1661), Point Reyes. Friendly and casual atmosphere for live music and pool tournaments (call for schedule). DJs swing the dance tunes on Fri. and Sat. nights. Open daily 10am-2am.

East Marin

My Thai Restaurant, 1230 4th St. (456-4455), San Rafael. Smiling servers want to make it "your Thai too!" Tasty basil prawns $8, Thai iced tea or coffee $1.50, veggie dishes $6-7. Credit card minimum $15. Open Sun.-Thurs. 11:30am-9:30pm, Fri.-Sat. 11:30am-10pm.

Mama's Royal Cafe, 387 Miller Ave. (388-3261), Mill Valley. Self-aware slackers serve up unusual but very good dishes from a menu as packed as the restaurant. Enchilada El Syd $6.50, Groove Burger $6. Brunch with live music Sat. and Sun. 11am-2pm. Open Mon.-Fri. 7:30am-2:30pm, Sat.-Sun. 8am-3pm.

Cactus Cafe and Taquería, 393 Miller Ave. (388-TACO/8226), behind Mama's, Mill Valley. Cool retreat with many eggplant-based veggie options amidst the cornucopia of burritos ($4-6) and wraps ($6-7). Local brews available in 650mL supersize ($6.25). Take-out available. Open daily 11:30am-9:30pm.

SIGHTS

Marin's proximity to San Francisco makes it a viable daytrip destination. The efficient visitor can hop from park to park and enjoy several short hikes along the coast and through the redwood forests in the same day, and top it off with a pleasant dinner in one of the small cities. Those without cars, however, may find it more worthwhile to linger at one of the two appealing hostel areas.

Sausalito and the Marin Headlands

Sausalito lies at Marin's extreme southeastern tip. Originally a fishing center, it traded its sea-dog days for retail boutiques and big-ticket residences. A block away from the harbor and Bridgeway's posh shops, Caledonia St. is lined with more affordable stores. For beautiful views of San Francisco, take the ferry (see **Practical Information,** p. 320) or bike across the Golden Gate Bridge.

Fog-shrouded hills just to the west of the Golden Gate Bridge comprise the **Marin Headlands.** Abandoned machine gun nests, missile sites, and soldiers' quarters mark the never-used military encampment set up here after the WWII attack on Pearl Harbor; the National Park Service took over the area in the 70s and has since parceled out land to non-profit tenants. The **Headlands Center for the Arts** (331-2787), is an artists' residency program which holds open studios twice a year (permanent collection open Mon.-Fri. 9am-5pm; free). The **Marine Mammal Center** (289-7325), details the rehabilitation of beached marine mammals (open daily 10am-4pm; donation requested). Nearly all the headlands are open to hikers—**berry picking** is permitted but beware of poison oak. For info on camping here, see **Campgrounds,** p. 322. The ¾ mi. hike from the Headlands Visitors Center (see p. 320) parking area down to the sheltered (and usually deserted) beach at **Kirby Cove** is beautiful. In the cooler months, migrating hawks and whales can be seen from hill 129.

Another remnant of the military presence is the massive tidal hydraulic model of the San Francisco Bay at the **Bay Model Visitor Center,** 2100 Bridgeway (332-3871), Sausalito (open Tues.-Sat. 9am-4pm, in summer also Sat.-Sun. 10am-6pm; free).

Muir Woods and Mount Tamalpais

Muir Woods National Monument, a 560-acre strand of primeval coastal redwoods, is located about 5 mi. west of U.S. 101 along Hwy. 1. These centuries-old redwoods are massive and shrouded in silence. The wildlife is scarce in the foothills, but a hike uphill will lead to the action-filled canopy. Rangers at the **visitors center** (388-2595), near the entrance, dispense hiking advice (monument and center open 8am-8pm). Nearby are **Muir Beach** and **Muir Beach Lookout** (open sunrise-9pm). The crowds at Muir Beach thin out significantly after a five-minute climb on the shore rocks to the left; farther along the beach you may stumble upon **nude** sunbathers.

Adjacent to Muir Woods is the isolated, largely undiscovered, and utterly beautiful **Mount Tamalpais State Park** (tam-ull-PIE-us), preferred by locals. The heavily forested park has a number of challenging trails leading to **Mount Tam,** the highest peak in the county, and its stone amphitheater. **Cataract Trail** leads to a bubbling waterfall. Though the invention of the mountain bike was inspired by the park's trails, bikers that go off the fire roads risk incurring the wrath of eco-conscious Marin hikers. Though **Stinson Beach** is often cold and windy, valiant sunbathers and windsurfers attempt to create a Bay Area version of Malibu. **Red Rock Beach,** ½ mi. north, is clothing-optional **(nude).** The park opens a half-hour before sunrise and closes a half-hour after sunset. On weekends, bus #63 runs between Mt. Tam Ranger Station and Stinson Beach.

Point Reyes

Encompassing 100 mi. of coastline along western Marin, the **Point Reyes National Seashore** juts into the Pacific from the eastern end of the submerged Pacific Plate. Sir Francis Drake Blvd. runs from San Rafael through Olema, where it crosses Hwy. 1, to Point Reyes. The infamous **San Andreas Fault** line runs north through Point Reyes towards Eureka, where it shifts west and ends 300 mi. off the coast. Point Reyes's remote position brings heavy fog and strong winds in winter. In summer an explosion of colorful wildflowers attracts crowds of gawking tourists, but with hundreds of miles of amazing trails it's also possible to gawk in solitude. The visitors center (see p. 320) has a map describing where to see various wildflowers.

Lovely **Limantour Beach** sits at the end of Limantour Rd., west of the National Seashore Headquarters, which runs a free shuttle bus to the beach in summer. Both Limantour and Point Reyes boast high, grassy dunes and long stretches of sand, but strong ocean currents along the point make swimming very dangerous. To reach the dramatic **Point Reyes Lighthouse** at the very tip of the point, follow Sir Francis Drake Blvd. to its end and head right along the stairway to Sea Lion Overlook. From December through February, migrating **gray whales** can be spotted from the overlook. The town of **Point Reyes Station** is a welcoming dinner destination. The rocky trails make navigating the seashore by bicycle a thrilling challenge. **Trail Head Rentals** (663-1958), at Hwy. 1 and Bear Valley Rd. in Olema, is near the National Seashore Headquarters. (Rental Mon.-Fri. $17 for 4hr., $20 per day; weekends $20 for 4hr., $24 per day. Open daily 10am-6pm, Wed. by reservation only.)

San Rafael, the largest city in Marin County, lies along U.S. 101 on the bay. Architecture buffs can check out Frank Lloyd Wright's **Marin Civic Center,** 3501 Civic Center Dr. (499-7407), off U.S. 101. An information kiosk in the lobby supplies brochures and pamphlets; phone ahead for a tour (open Mon.-Fri. 7:30am-6pm).

ENTERTAINMENT

Marin closes early, but does offer a variety of (early) evening diversions. The *Independent Journal,* Marin's daily newspaper, lists garage sales by city, and the bargains are often unbelievable. Collectors and bargain-hunters from all over the world flock to **Village Music,** 9 E. Blithedale Ave. (388-7400), close to Mill Valley's downtown square. The store's biggest customers include B.B. King and Mick Jagger. If it's on vinyl, it's here (albums 25¢-$200; open Mon.-Sat. 10am-6pm, Sun. noon-5pm). Unfortunately Marin's bars and clubs do not attract the same big names.

Sweetwater, 153 Throckmorton Ave. (388-2820; http://www.globerecords.com/ sweetwater), downtown Mill Valley. A dark photo-lined bar with live music every night, with an occasional big name like Elvis Costello. Cover $5-15. Two-drink minimum during shows (open daily 12:30pm-1am).

New George's, 842 4th St. (457-8424, show info 457-1515), under a movie-style marquee at Lootens in San Rafael. Frequent winner of the "best live music and nightlife in Marin" award. Cafe becomes jumping club by night. Live music Wed.-Sun. at 9pm (cover $5-15). Pints $4. Open Mon.-Sat. 3pm-1am.

Classic Billiards, 1300 4th St. (455-8511), 1 block from New George's. Offers great student rates and other specials. Too slick for its own good, but the jukebox keeps it rockin' until the wee hours. Weekend nights 2 players $10 per hr. Open Mon.-Thurs. noon-2am, Fri. noon-4am, Sat. 1pm-4am, Sun. 1pm-2am.

Smitty's Bar, 214 Caledonia (332-2637), is the last of the Sausalito fishing community waterholes. Bowling team, pool league, and 2 softball teams. Shuffleboard tourney Wed. 7-11pm. Pints $2.50, Schooners $3.50. Open daily 10am-2am.

■ Napa Valley

While not the oldest, the Napa Valley is certainly the best-known of America's wine-growing regions. The gentle hills, fertile soil, ample moisture, and year-round sunshine are ideal for viticulture. European vines were first planted here as early as the late 1850s, but early producers were crippled by Prohibition, when the grapes were supplanted with figs. The region did not begin to reestablish itself until the 1960s. During the 70s Napa's rapidly improving offerings won the attention of those in the know, and word-of-mouth cemented the California bottle as a respectable choice. In 1976, a bottle of red from Napa's Stag's Leap Vineyard (see p. 326) beat a bottle of Château Lafitte-Rothschild in a blind taste test in Paris, and American wine was suddenly *très cool.* Today, local vineyards continue to reap awards, and the everyday tasting carnival dominates life in the valley's small towns.

PRACTICAL INFORMATION

Visitor Information: Napa Visitors Center, 1310 Town Center (226-7459; fax 255-2066; http://www.napavalley.com/nvcvb.html), on 1st St. Wide brochure collection and free copies of *Inside Napa Valley,* which has maps, winery listings, and a weekly events guide. Open daily 9am-5pm, phones closed Sat.-Sun. The **St. Helena Chamber of Commerce,** 1010A Main St. (963-4456), is open Mon.-Fri. 10am-4:30pm. The **Calistoga Chamber of Commerce,** 1458 Lincoln Ave. (942-6333), is open Mon.-Fri. 9am-5pm, Sat. 10am-4pm, Sun. 10am-3pm.

Buses: The nearest **Greyhound** station is in Vallejo (800-231-2222), but 2 buses per day pass through the valley. Stops in Napa (9:45am and 6pm, Napa State Hospital, 2100 Napa-Vallejo Hwy.), Yountville, St. Helena, and Calistoga.

Public Transportation: Napa City Bus, or Valley Intercity Neighborhood Express (VINE), 1151 Pearl St. (800-696-6443 or 255-7631; TDD 226-9722), covers the valley and Vallejo. Fare $1, seniors and disabled 50¢, ages 13-18 75¢; free transfer. Buses run Mon.-Fri. 6:30am-6pm, Sat. 7:45am-5:30pm. **Winery tours** include the **Napa Valley Wine Shuttle,** 3031 California Blvd. (800-258-8226; day pass $30, children free) and **Napa Valley Holidays** (255-1050; 3hr.; $30).

Car Rental: Budget, 407 Soscol Ave. (224-7845), Napa. Cars $35 per day; ages 21-25 $45. Unlimited mileage. Must be 21 with credit card.

Bike Rental: St. Helena Cyclery, 1156 Main St. (963-7736), Napa. Bikes $25 per day, including maps, helmet, lock, and picnic bag. Open Mon.-Sat. 9:30am-5:30pm, Sun. 10am-5pm.

Crisis Lines: Red Cross (257-2900). **Emergency Women's Service** (255-6397). **Disabled Crisis** (800-426-4263). **Sexual Assault Crisis Line** (258-8000).

Hospital: Queen of the Valley, 1000 Trancas St. (252-4411), Napa.

Emergency: 911.

Police: 1539 1st St. (253-4451), Napa.

Post Office: 1625 Trancas St. (255-1621), Napa. Open Mon.-Fri. 8:30am-5pm. **ZIP Code:** 94558.

Area Code: 707.

ORIENTATION

Rte. 29 (St. Helena Hwy.) runs through the Napa Valley from **Napa** through **Yountville** and **St. Helena,** to **Calistoga.** The **Silverado Trail,** parallel to Rte. 29, is a more scenic and less crowded route. Napa is 14 mi. east of Sonoma on **Rte. 12.** If you're planning a weekend trip from San Francisco, avoid Saturday mornings and Sunday afternoons; the roads are packed with like-minded people. From the city, take U.S. 101 over the Golden Gate, then Rte. 37 east to Rte. 121 north, which will cross Rte. 12 north (to Sonoma) and Rte. 29 (to Napa).

Napa's gentle terrain makes for an excellent **bike** tour. Although the area is fairly flat, small bike lanes, speeding cars, and blistering heat can make routes more challenging, especially after several samples of wine. The 26 mi. Silverado Trail has a wider bike trail than Rte. 29. The luxurious spas of **Calistoga** (north of Napa) will relax any strained muscles. Neighboring towns include **Yountville** and **St. Helena.**

ACCOMMODATIONS AND CAMPING

Rooms in Napa are scarce and go fast despite their high prices (B&Bs and most hotels are a budget-breaking $60-225 per night). Budget options are more plentiful in Santa Rosa and Petaluma, within easy driving distance of the valley. For those without cars, camping is the best option, though the heat is intense in summer.

Calistoga Ranch Club, 580 Lommel Rd. (800-847-6272), off the Silverado Trail near Calistoga. Beautiful setting in the mountains above the valley. Hiking trails lace 167 wooded acres, which include a fishing lake and volleyball. Tent sites $19; RV sites $23; 4-person cabins with shared bath $49; 5-person trailers with kitchen $89.

Silverado Motel, 500 Silverado Trail (253-0892), near Soscol in Napa. Clean, newly remodeled rooms have kitchenettes, cable TV, and a tad more personality than a chain-motel. Check-in noon-6pm. Rooms $40, weekends $80.

Bothe-Napa Valley State Park, 3801 Rte. 29 (942-4575; reservations through DES-TINET, 800-444-7275), north of St. Helena. 49 sites often full. Hot showers. Pool $3, under 18 $2. Sites $16, seniors $14; vehicles $5. Park open 8am-sunset.

Napa County Fairgrounds, 1435 Oak St. (942-5111), Calistoga. First-come, first-camped. Dry grass in a parking lot with showers and electricity. Overrun with RVs. Check-out noon. Sites $18. Closed late June-early July.

FOOD

Eating in Wine Country ain't cheap, but the food is usually worth it. Picnics are a cheap and romantic option—supplies can be picked up at the numerous delis or **Safeway** stores in the area. The Napa **farmer's market** (252-7142), corner of Pearl and West, offers a sampling of the valley's *other* produce (open daily 7:30am-noon).

Curb Side Cafe, 1245 1st St. (253-2307), at Randolph in Napa. Sublime sandwiches $5-6. Tasty breakfasts include the pancake special: 4 buttermilk pancakes, 2 eggs, and ham or sausage ($6). Open Mon.-Sat. 8am-3pm, Sun. 9:30am-3pm.

Calistoga Natural Foods and Juice Bar, 1426 Lincoln (942-5822), Calistoga. One of few natural foods stores around. Organic juice and sandwich bar, with vegetarian specialties like the Garlic Goddess ($4.50) or Tofu Supreme ($5). Open Mon.-Thurs. and Sun. 9am-6pm, Fri.-Sat. 9am-7pm.

Ana's Cantina, 1205 Main St. (963-4921), St. Helena. A small glimmer of nightlife on the otherwise quiet Napa front. Bar has nightly music or karaoke, great Mexican food, and pool tables. Combo platters $7. No cover. Open daily 10am-2am.

Taylor's Refresher, 933 Main St. (963-3486), on Rte. 29 across from the Merryvale Winery. A roadside burger stand with vegetarian and beef burgers ($2.75) and ice-cream. Outdoor picnic area. Open Sun.-Thurs. 11am-7pm, Fri.-Sat. 11am-8pm.

DRINKING

There are more than 250 wineries in Napa County, nearly two-thirds of which line Rte. 29 and the Silverado Trail in the Napa Valley. Wine country's heavyweights call this valley home; vineyards include national names such as Inglenook, Fetzer, and Mondavi. Most wineries have free tastings, and some include special samples of reserve wines in a more private setting for a small fee ($3-6). The wineries listed below (from south to north) are among the valley's larger and more touristy operations. Visitors must be 21 or older to purchase or drink alcohol (yes, they do card).

Clos Du Val Wine Company, Ltd., 5330 Silverado Trail (259-2200), Napa. Take Oak Knoll Rd. to Silverado Trail. Small and stylish grounds attract *lots* of tourists. Admission $3. Open daily 10am-5pm. Tours by appointment only.

Domaine Chandon, 1 California Dr. (944-2280), Yountville. Owned by Moët Chandon of France (the people who make Dom Perignon), this winery produces 5 million bottles of sparkling wine annually—enough for one hell of a New Year's Eve party. Tours (hourly 11am-5pm) and tastings ($3-5). Open daily 11am-6pm; Nov.-April closed Mon.-Tues.

Stag's Leap Wine Cellars, 5766 Silverado Trail (944-2020), Napa. The tiny vineyard that beat Europe's best by leaps and bounds. Landscaped terraces and

Vin Friends and Influence People

For starters, most wines are recognized by the grape-stock from which they're grown—**white** grapes produce Chardonnay, Riesling, and Sauvignon; **reds** are responsible for Beaujolais, Pinot Noir, Merlot, and Zinfandel. **Blush** or **rosé** wines issue from red grapes which have had their skins removed during fermentation in order to leave just a kiss of pink. White Zinfandel, for example, comes from a red grape often made skinless, and is therefore rose in color. Of course, blush is not the wine of choice among wine connoisseurs; it's for plebes and picnics. **Dessert** wines, such as Muscat, are made with grapes that have acquired the "noble rot" *(botrytis)* at the end of picking season, giving them an extrasweet flavor.

When tasting, be sure to follow proper procedures. Always start with a white, moving from **dry** to **sweet** (dry wines have had a higher percentage of their sugar content fermented into alcohol). Proceed through the reds, which go from **lighter** to **fuller bodied,** depending on tannin content. **Tannin** is the pigment red wine gets from the grape skin—it preserves and ages the wine, which is why reds can be young and sharp, but grow more mellow with age. It's best to end with dessert wines. One should cleanse one's palate between each wine, with a biscuit, some *fromage,* or fruit. Don't hesitate to ask for advice from the tastingroom pourer. Tasting proceeds thusly: stare, sniff, swirl, swallow (first three steps are optional). You will probably encounter fellow tasters who slurp their wine and make concerned faces, as though they're trying to cram the stuff up their noses with the back of their tongues. These chaps consider themselves serious tasters, and are aerating the wine in their mouths to better bring out the flavor. Key words to help you seem more astute during tasting sessions are: dry, sweet, buttery, light, crisp, fruity, balanced, rounded, subtle, rich, woody, and complex. Feel free to banter these terms about indiscriminately. *Sally forth, young naifs!*

superb tasting ($3 for 5-6 sips, and you even get to keep the glass). Open daily 10am-4pm. Call a week in advance to arrange a tour.

Hakusan Sake Gardens, 1 Executive Way (258-6160 or 800-HAKUSAN/425-8726), Napa. Take Rte. 12 off Rte. 29, turn left on North Kelly, then left onto Executive. Japanese gardens are a welcome change from the other wineries. *Sake* is a strong Japanese wine with a fruity taste, and it can be served warm or cold. Test your mettle with these generous pourings. Open Thurs.-Tues. 10am-5pm.

Goosecross Cellars, 1119 State Ln. (944-1986), off Yountville Cross Rd. north of Yountville. Small and friendly winery is still in its natural state, nestled among the vineyards. Free wine basics class (Sat. 11am). Tastings daily 10am-5pm ($3).

Robert Mondavi Winery, 7801 Rte. 29 (963-9611), 8mi. north of Napa in Oakville. Originally a viticulture education center, this beautiful winery offers some of the best tours in the valley, covering subjects from tasting to soil conditions. Open daily 10am-4pm; Nov.-April 9:30am-4:30pm.

Vichon Winery, 1595 Oakville Grade (944-2811 or 800-VICHON-1/842-4661), off Rte. 29. Gorgeous views of the valley, but no tour. Picnic tables available for wine-purchasers. Free tasting; reserve tasting $5. Open daily 10am-4:30pm.

Domaine Carneros, 1240 Duhig Rd. (257-0101), off Rte. 121 from Rte. 29. Picturesque estate modeled after a French chateau. Free tour and film, no free tastings (sparkling wine $4 per glass). Open daily 10am-6pm; Nov.-April 10:30am-6pm.

Beringer Vineyards, 2000 Main St. (963-4812 or 963-7115), off Rte. 29 in St. Helena. Huge estate is so mobbed with tourists that it has its own visitors center. Free tours every half hour include tasting. To avoid the crowds and taste Beringer's better wines, try the reserve room on the second floor of the Rhine House mansion (samples $2-6). Open daily 9:30am-4pm.

Sterling Vineyards, 1111 Dunaweal Lane (942-3344), 7mi. north of St. Helena in Calistoga. Aerial tram to vineyard and self-guided tour (admission $6, under 18 $3). Terrace for picnicking. Open daily 10:30am-4:30pm.

NOT DRINKING

Napa does have non-alcoholic attractions. Chief among them is 160-acre **Marine World Africa USA** (643-6722), an enormous zoo-oceanarium-theme park 10 mi. south of Napa, off Rte. 37 in Vallejo. The park has animal shows and special attractions like the Lorikeet Aviary, the Butterfly Walk, and Shark Experience, which provide patron-pet interaction. All proceeds benefit wildlife research and protection programs. The park is accessible by BART (415-788-2278), and the Blue and Gold fleet (415-705-5444), from San Francisco. (Open daily 9:30am-6pm. Admission $27, seniors $23, ages 4-12 $19, under 3 free. Parking $5. Wheelchair accessible.)

Robert Louis Stevenson State Park (942-4575), 4 mi. north of St. Helena on Rte. 29, has a plaque where the Scottish writer, sick and penniless, spent a rejuvenating honeymoon in 1880. The hike up **Mt. St. Helena** (open daily 8am-sunset) is a moderate three-hour climb culminating in dizzying views of the valley (no ranger station; bring water). The **Silverado Museum,** 1490 Library Ln. (963-3757), off Adams in St. Helena, is a labor of love by a devoted collector of Stevensoniana. Manuscript notes from *Dr. Jekyll and Mr. Hyde* are displayed (open Tues.-Sun. noon-4pm; free).

The **Old Faithful Geyser of California** (942-6463), is farther north, 2 mi. outside Calistoga on Tubbs Ln. off Rte. 128. It should not be confused with its more famous namesake in Wyoming, though it performs similarly. About every 40 minutes, the geyser spews a jet of boiling water 60 ft. into the air; the ticket vendor will tell you the estimated time of the next spurt. (Open daily 9am-6pm; winter 9am-5pm. Admission $6, seniors $4, disabled free, ages 6-12 $2. Bathrooms not wheelchair accessible.) **Calistoga** is also known as the "Hot Springs of the West." Sam Brannan, who first developed the area, promised to make the hot springs the "Saratoga of California," but he misspoke and promised instead to make them "The Calistoga of Saratina." His former cottage is now home to the **Sharpsteen Museum,** 1311 Washington St. (942-5911), which traces the town's development (open daily 10am-4pm; in winter noon-4pm; free).

Brannan's dream has come true, and Calistoga is now a center for luxurious spas and resorts. After a hard day of wine tasting, the rich and relaxed converge on Calistoga to luxuriate in mud baths, massages, and mineral showers. Unfortunately, prices are as hot as the mineral water, hitting $80 for a one-hour massage (10% discount coupons available at the chamber of commerce). Massage your wallet by sticking to the less-extravagant **Golden Haven** (942-6793) or **Harbin Hot Springs** (987-2477), where you can plunge into natural springs and explore hiking trails for less. Cooler water can be found at **Lake Berryessa** (966-2111), 20 mi. north of Napa off Rte. 128. Swimming, sailing, and sunbathing on 169 mi. of shoreline are all popular activities.

The annual **Napa Valley Wine Festival** (252-0872) takes place in November. **Napa Valley Fairgrounds** hosts a month-long summer fair in August, with wine-tasting, music, juggling, rides, and a rodeo. In the summer, there are free jazz concerts at **Music-in-the-Park,** downtown at the riverfront. Contact Napa Parks and Recreation Office (257-9529) for more information.

■ Sonoma Valley

The sprawling Sonoma Valley is a quieter alternative to Napa. **Sonoma,** the largest town in the valley, takes pride in its beautiful, expansive eight-acre town plaza. It is surrounded by art galleries, novelty shops, vintage clothing stores, and Italian restaurants, yet—with a playground, plum trees, and a pond—it's the perfect place for a "rural" picnic. **Petaluma,** west of Sonoma, is distinguished by its odd mix of architecture, juxtaposing nearly every 20th-century genre. Oh, and there's wine here too.

PRACTICAL INFORMATION

Visitor Information: Sonoma Valley Visitors Bureau, 453 E. 1st St. (996-1090), in Sonoma Plaza. Open daily 9am-7pm, Nov.-May 9am-5pm. Maps $2. **Petaluma Visitors Center,** 799 Baywood Dr. (769-0429), at Lakeville. Open June-Sept. Mon.-Fri. 9am-5:30pm, Sat.-Sun. 10am-6pm; shorter hours off-season. Look around town for *The Review,* a free weekly with extensive winery listings.

ATM: In Sonoma, 35 Napa St. at 1st. In Petaluma, 101 Western Ave.

Public Transportation: Sonoma County Transit (800-345-7433) serves the entire county, from Petaluma to Cloverdale and the Russian River. Bus #30 runs to Santa Rosa Mon.-Sat. (fare $1.95, students $1.60, seniors and disabled 95¢, under 6 free). Bus #40 goes to Petaluma (fare $1.60). A "Cruisin' Pass" allows unlimited summer rides for the under-18 set ($15). Within Sonoma, bus fare 85¢, students 65¢, seniors and disabled 40¢. County buses stop when flagged down. Buses operate Mon.-Fri. 7am-6pm. **Golden Gate Transportation** (541-2000 from Sonoma County or 415-923-2000 from San Francisco, TDD 257-4554) runs 2 buses per day between San Francisco and Santa Rosa. **Volunteer Wheels** (800-992-1006), offers door-to-door service for people with disabilities.

Taxis: Sonoma Valley Cab (996-6733). 24hr. service.

Bike Rental: Sonoma Valley Cyclery (935-3377), on Broadway in Sonoma. Bikes $6 per hr., $28 per day. Open Mon.-Sat. 10am-6pm, Sun. 10am-4pm. **Bicycle Factory,** 110 Kentucky St. (763-7515), downtown Petaluma. Mountain bikes $8 per hr., $22 per day. Helmet included. Must leave major ID or credit card as deposit.

Laundromat: Launder Land, 122 Petaluma Rd. (763-3042).

Road Conditions: (800-424-9393).

Crisis Lines: Sonoma Valley Crisis Line (938-HELP/4357). 24hr. referrals. **Rape Crisis Hotline** (545-7273). 24hr. **Poison Control** (800-523-2222). **Disabled Crisis** (800-426-4263). **Red Cross** (577-7600).

Hospital: Sonoma Valley, 347 Andrieux St. (935-5000), Sonoma. **Petaluma Valley,** 400 N. McDowell Blvd. (778-1111), Petaluma.

Emergency: 911.

Police: Sonoma (996-3602). **Petaluma** (778-4372).

Post Office: Sonoma, 617 Broadway (996-2459), at Patten. Open Mon.-Fri. 8:30am-5pm. **ZIP Code:** 95476. **Petaluma,** 120 4th St. (769-5350). Open Mon.-Fri. 8:30am-5:30pm, Sat. 10am-2pm. **ZIP Code:** 95476.

Area Code: 707.

ORIENTATION

Rte. 12 traverses the length of Sonoma Valley from **Sonoma,** through **Glen Ellen,** to **Kenwood** in the north. The center of downtown Sonoma is **Sonoma Plaza,** a park which contains City Hall and the visitors center. **Broadway** dead-ends in front of City Hall at Napa St. The numbered streets run north-south. **Petaluma** lies to the west and is connected to Sonoma by **Rte. 116,** which becomes **Lakeville St.** in Petaluma. Lakeville St. intersects **Washington St.,** the central downtown road.

ACCOMMODATIONS AND CAMPING

Pickings are pretty slim for lodging; rooms are scarce even on the weekdays and generally start at $75. Cheaper motels cluster along U.S. 101 in Santa Rosa and Petaluma. Campers with cars should try the Russian River Valley (see p. 334).

Motel 6, 1368 N. McDowell Blvd. (765-0333; fax 765-4577), off U.S. 101 in Petaluma. Cable TV and pool. Quiet, spacious, and almost tastefully decorated. Check-out noon. Singles $41; second adult $6, each additional adult $3.

Sugarloaf Ridge State Park, 2605 Adobe Canyon Rd. (833-5712), north of Kenwood off Rte. 12. Decent campground offers 50 sites, flush toilets, running water, no showers. Sites $16. Call DESTINET (800-444-7275) to reserve.

San Francisco North/Petaluma KOA, 20 Rainsville Rd. (763-1492 or 800-992-2267), off the Penngrove Exit in Petaluma. Activities bring all 300 sites together. Recreation hall has activities, petting zoo, pool, hot showers, store, and jacuzzi.

Overrun by families with screaming kids. Two-person tent sites $27, each additional adult $5, each additional child $2; RV sites $39.

FOOD

Fresh produce is seasonally available directly from the area farms or through roadside stands and farmer's markets. *Farm Trails* maps are free at the Sonoma Valley Visitors Bureau. Those in the area toward the end of the summer should ask about the ambrosial **crane melon**, grown nowhere else in the world but on the Crane Farm north of Petaluma. The **Sonoma Market,** 520 W. Napa St. (996-0563), in the Sonoma Valley Center, is an old-fashioned grocery store with deli sandwiches ($4-6) and *very* fresh produce. For inexpensive fruit, head to the **Fruit Basket,** 18474 Sonoma Hwy. (996-7433). **Safeway,** 477 W. Napa (996-0633), is open 24 hours.

Fay's Garden Court Cafe and Bakery, 13875 Rte. 12 (935-1565). Quite possibly the best restaurant in the valley for the price. Delicious sandwiches and pasta meals ($7-8). Open daily 7am-2pm.

Ford's Cafe, 22900 Broadway (938-9811), near Rte. 12 and Rte. 121 intersection in Sonoma. Where the locals go for huge breakfasts (served until 11:30am). Cheese omelette $5. Open Mon.-Fri. 5am-2pm, Sat.-Sun. 6am-2pm.

Quinley's, 310 D St. (778-6000), at Petaluma. Standard food at great prices. Hugely popular burger counter first opened its doors in 1952, and the tunes of that decade play on.Outdoor bar and picnic tables. Burgers $3, four-scoop shake or malt $1.75. Open Mon.-Thurs. and Sun. 11am-9pm, Fri.-Sat. 11am-10pm. No credit cards.

Sonoma Cheese Factory, 2 Spain St. (996-1931). Forget the *vino* for now—take out a toothpick and start enjoying the billions of free samples at this deli run wonderfully wild. You can even watch the cheese making process in the back room. Sandwiches $3.50-6.50. Open Mon.-Fri. 8:30am-6pm, Sat.-Sun. 8:30am-6:30pm.

The Chocolate Cow, 452 1st St. (935-3564), across from the visitors center. The air is thick with chocolate, the walls are crammed with bovinalia, and the ice cream is Ben and Jerry's. If the chocolate truffles and smoothies aren't enough, go for the chocolate pasta. Open daily 10am-9:30pm.

WINERIES

Sonoma Valley's wineries, located near Sonoma and Kenwood, are less touristed, less tasted, but just as tasty as Napa's—and more of them offer free tastings. Near Sonoma, signs mark the wineries, but in Kenwood they are harder to find.

Benziger, 1833 London Ranch Rd. (936-4046), in Glen Ellen. Tourists flock here for the free tram ride through the vineyards (great views). Self-guided tours lead through the ranch and peacock aviary. Open daily 10am-4:30pm.

Ravenswood, 18701 Gehricke Rd. (938-1960), Sonoma. Poe himself would have approved of their red Zinfandels, appropriately described as "gothic" by those in the know. Quoth the raven, "Pour me more!" Summer weekend BBQs ($5-9). Free tasting; tours by appointment. Open daily 10am-4:30pm.

Château St. Jean, 8555 Rte. 12 (833-4134), Kenwood. Brief self-guided tour. Mediterranean setting includes lookout tower with balcony. Those under 21 can satisfy themselves with *Verjus* (a fancy name for grape juice). Tasting daily 10am-4:30pm.

Buena Vista, 18000 Old Winery Rd. (800-926-1266), off E. Napa. The oldest winery in the valley. Famous old stone buildings are preserved as Mr. Haraszthy built them in 1857, when he founded the California wine industry. Hosts Shakespearian plays July-Sept. Free tastings downstairs, vintage wine and champagne upstairs for a small fee. Tours daily 2pm; also 11am in summer. Tastings daily 10:30am-5pm.

Glen Ellen Winery, 14301 Arnold Dr. (939-6277), 1mi. from Glen Ellen in Jack London Village. Chic cafe has *tres cher* food to enjoy at the picnic tables outside. Also an olive press with oil tasting. Open daily 10am-5pm.

Sebastiani, 389 E. 4th St. (800-888-5532), a few blocks from Sonoma Plaza. This giant mass producer draws 250,000 visitors per year, and is a good place to get an introduction to the noble drink. Tours of the sepulchral aging rooms (20min.) are best during summer harvest, when visitors can watch grapes being crushed (daily 10am-4pm). Free tasting daily 10am-5pm.

SIGHTS AND SEASONAL EVENTS

Local historical artifacts are preserved in the **Sonoma State Historic Park,** at E. Spain and 1st, in the northeast corner of town. Within the park, an adobe church stands on the site of the **Sonoma Mission** (938-9560), the northernmost and last of the Spanish missions. Built in 1826 when Mexico was already a republic, the mission houses a remnant of theoriginal California Republic flag, the rest of which was burned in the 1906 post-earthquake fires (open daily 10am-5pm; admission $2, seniors $1, ages 6-12 $1; includes Vallejo's Home, barracks next door, and Petaluma Adobe). For more info, see **A Man with a Mission** (p. 54).

General Vallejo's Home (938-1519), ¾ mi. northwest of Sonoma Plaza on Spain, is the Gothic-style home of the famed Mexican leader who also served as mayor of Sonoma and as senator for California. Tours include the museum, pond, pavilions, and gardens. The grounds are garnished by a serene picnic area designed in part by Vallejo and his *esposa* (open daily 10am-5pm; admission $2, children $1).

To find the **Jack London State Park** (938-5216), take Rte. 12 north about 4 mi. to Arnold Lane and follow the signs. At the turn of the century, hard-drinkin' and hard-livin' Jack London (author of *Call of the Wild* and *White Fang*) bought 1400 acres here, determined to create his dream home. Today, the land he purchased belongs to the state park bearing his name. London's hopes for the property were never realized—the estate's main building, the Wolf House, was destroyed by arsonists in 1913. London died three years after the fire and is buried in the park, his grave marked by a volcanic boulder intended for the construction of his house. The nearby **House of Happy Walls,** built by his widow, is now a two-story museum devoted to the writer. The park's scenic ½ mi. **Beauty Ranch Trail** passes the lake, winery ruins, and quaint cottages (park open daily 9:30am-sunset; museum open daily 10am-5pm; admission $6 per car). The fragrant forests can also be experienced via a **Sonoma Cattle and Napa Valley Trail Rides** (996-8566; 2hr. ride $45; sunset and night rides available).

Just one mile south of the city center on Broadway, **Traintown** (938-3912), the self-proclaimed "best-developed scale railroad in the U.S.," offers a 20-minute steam engine tour through a 10-acre park (every 30 minutes). Young 'uns will love the petting zoo and merry-go-round. (Open June-Sept. daily 10am-5pm, Oct.-May Fri.-Sun. 10am-5pm. Admission $3.50, children $2.50, seniors $2.50.) Farther south, just past the junction of Rte. 37 and 121, lies **Sears Point Raceway** (800-870-7223). The track revs up for auto and motorcycle racing year-round. Events include the "Festival of Fire," where smoking cars give the word "Zippo" new meaning (tickets $8-45).

Just past Glen Ellen on Rte. 12 lies the village of **Kenwood.** The town hosts a surprising number of excellent, reasonably priced restaurants, including **The Vineyards Inn,** at Rte. 12 and Adobe Canyon Rd. Kenwood heats up July 4, when runners gather for the **Kenwood Footrace,** a tough 10k course through hills and vineyards. A chili cook-off and the **World Pillowfighting Championships** help to pass the rest of the day. There's nothing like straddling a metal pipe over a mud pit and beating the hell out of each other with wet pillows to get the blood racing. Nearby **Petaluma** also merits a visit for its cheap accommodations and magnificent old buildings. Virtually untouched by the 1906 earthquake, the area is home to Spanish churches, Art Deco banks, and hotels with manual elevators.

■ Santa Rosa

Luther Burbank once said, "I firmly believe, from what I have seen, that this is the chosen spot of all the earth, as far as nature is concerned." Little did he know that developers would choose shopping malls and rows of suburban homes as the best way to make use of such beautiful countryside. Sonoma County's commercial hub, this city's pace (pop. 130,000) is more in tune with the surrounding countryside than the hustle associated with a city.

PRACTICAL INFORMATION AND ORIENTATION

Visitor Information: Greater Santa Rosa Conference and Visitor Bureau, 9 4th St. and Wilson (577-8674 or 800-404-ROSE/7673), in an old train depot. Brochures and maps ($1). Open Mon. 9am-5pm, Tues.-Fri. 8:30am-5pm, Sat.-Sun.10am-3pm. **Sonoma County Wine and Visitors Center,** 5000 Roberts Lake Rd. (586-3795), east of U.S. 101 at the Luther Burbank Center for the Arts. Maps of most area wineries, and a tasting directory. Open daily 9am-5pm.
Buses: Greyhound, 421 Santa Rosa Ave. (546-6495), 3 blocks from 2nd St. To San Francisco (3 per day, $12).
Bike Rental: Rincon Cyclery, 4927 Rte. 12, Room H (538-0868), Santa Rosa. Mountain bikes only—shop is near off-road trails. Rental $7 per hr. (2hr. min.), $25 for first day, $20 per additional day, $100 per week. Free maps. Open Mon.-Fri. 10am-6pm, Sat. 9am-6pm, Sun. 10am-5pm.
Crisis Lines: Poison Control (800-523-2222). **Disabled Crisis** (800-426-4263).
Hospital: Santa Rosa Memorial, 1165 Montgomery Dr. (546-3210).
Emergency: 911.
Police: (543-3600).
Post Office: 730 2nd St. (528-8763), between D and E. Open Mon.-Fri. 8am-6pm, Sat. 10am-2pm. **ZIP Code:** 95402.
Area Code: 707.

Santa Rosa rests at the intersection of **U.S. 101** and **Rte. 12,** 57 mi. from downtown San Francisco. **Cleveland Ave.,** which marks the city's western edge, is lined with cheap motels. The town center is occupied by a mall, which interrupts A St. and 2nd through 5th St. **Mendocino Ave.** and **4th St.** define the bustling downtown area, which can be scary after dark. The Railroad Square area, bounded by 4th, 5th, and Wilson, houses Santa Rosa's trendiest shops and cafes.

ACCOMMODATIONS

Santa Rosa offers average lodgings at above-average prices, but that doesn't make them any less popular. Make reservations far in advance for summer.

Astro Motel, 323 N. Santa Rosa Ave. (545-8555), near Sonoma Ave. Conveniently located downtown in an area that can also be a bit unsafe after dark. A haven for late arrivals—they often have vacant rooms. Eclectic clientele and decoration scheme (pink, orange, and red). Singles $45; doubles $48.
Motel 6 has 2 locations: 2760 Cleveland Ave. (546-1500), 5mi. north of downtown off Steele Lane Exit from U.S. 101. Singles $43; each additional person $6. Also at 3145 Cleveland Ave. (525-9010). Singles $36; each additional person $6. Reservations necessary during summer.

FOOD

Although Santa Rosa is not exactly the gourmet capital of California, it offers an assortment of palatable restaurants. Fresh produce can be found at the Thursday night **farmer's market** (5-8:30pm in the summer).

Copperfield's Bookstore and Cafe, 650 4th St. (576-7681), downtown. Central location makes for a grungily hip clientele. Sandwiches are named after authors in this veggie-friendly hangout: try the Alice Walker (hummus, tomato, and avocado, $4.50), or the Dr. Seuss (peanut butter and banana on wheat bread, $3). Also sells books and CDs. Open Mon.-Fri. 7:30am-9pm, Sat. 8:30am-10pm, Sun. 8:30am-6pm.

East-West Cafe, 2323 Sonoma Ave. (546-6142), 10min. from downtown in Montgomery Village. All-organic restaurant has heavenly baked goods. A sort of homemade, hippie Denny's. Eggplant casserole $8.50, Thai chicken salad $7.50. Open Sun.-Mon. 8am-8:30pm (until 8pm in winter), Tues.-Sat. 8am-9pm.

Organic Groceries, 2481 Guerneville Rd. (528-3663), near Fulton. Every organic food you've ever heard of and then some—all in bulk quantities. Open Mon.-Fri. 7am-9pm, Sat.-Sun. 9am-7pm.

SIGHTS, SEASONAL EVENTS, AND ENTERTAINMENT

The **Redwood Empire Ice Arena,** 1667 W. Steele Ln. (546-7144), is decorated with original Snoopy artwork so patrons can glide and giggle at the same time. (Admission $5.50, ages 12-18 $4.50. Skate rental $2.) If you're tired of working for peanuts, get some sympathy next door at **Snoopy's Gallery,** which continues the ice rink's artistic theme. Every souvenir imaginable is sold here. If Peanuts is your religion, then this is your shrine. Good grief! (Open daily 10am-6pm.)

The **Luther Burbank Home and Gardens** (524-5445), at Santa Rosa and Sonoma Ave., is a great place to stop and smell the roses—1.6 acres of them. At the age of 26, the horticulturist fled to California from Massachusetts to carry out his maniacal plant-breeding experiments, and the gardens display several of his hybrids, including the evil white *Agapanthus* (a short, frondy plant popular with California's gas station landscapers). It's alive!!! (Gardens open daily 8am-7pm; free. House open April-Oct. Wed.-Sun. 10am-3:30pm. Admission $2, under 13 free. Free tours on Memorial Day.)

Nearby, homage is paid to Santa Rosa native **Robert Ripley,** of *Ripley's Believe It or Not,* at the memorial museum housed in the famed **"church built from one tree,"** 492 Sonoma Ave. (524-5233). Don't follow the videotaped example of the man smoking cigarettes through his eyes, or you won't be able to see it to believe it (open Wed.-Sun. 10:30am-3:30pm; admission $1.50, children 75¢).

If you are biking or driving, Sonoma County's backroads offer scenery that surpasses even that on Rte. 12. **Bennett Valley Road,** between Kenwood and Santa Rosa, **Petaluma Hill Road,** between Petaluma and Santa Rosa, and **Grange/Crane Canyon Road,** connecting the two, afford particularly good views of the countryside. If you are on a bike, remain conscious of drivers; the surroundings can distract you from the blind turns and hills. Drivers should also lookout for bicyclists.

Annual events include the **Dixieland Jazz Festival** (539-3494; late Aug.), with nonstop music and dancing. The **Sonoma County Fair** is at the end of July. Tartan enthusiasts will enjoy the **Scottish Gathering and Games,** a two-day athletically genealogical frenzy over Labor Day weekend. This event, the largest gathering of Scots outside of the British Isles, features the caber toss, in which kilt-sporting brawny types throw massive logs. In the autumn, Santa Rosa nourishes the countryside at the **October Harvest Fair** and the **World Championship Grape Stomp Contest** (call the Sonoma County Fairgrounds at 545-4200 for info).

If it's hoppin' **nightlife** you're after, you might stop by the **Santa Rosa Brewing Company,** 458 B St. (544-4677), at 7th. Yet another trendy microbrewery, it has wood furniture, sports monitors in every corner, and a CD jukebox. Brenga kelt and get doon to live Celtic music Thursday through Sunday. Standard sandwiches and salads are $6-7, and nothing is over $10. (Happy Hour Mon.-Fri. 5-7pm; open daily 11:30am-2am. All ages.) **A'Roma Roasters and Coffee House,** 95 5th St. (576-7765), in Railroad Sq., is Santa Rosa's alterna-GenX-queer-hipster hangout. Roll a Drum with a green-haired friend and solve the world's problems over espresso ($1). Call for the live jazz and folk music schedule (open Mon.-Thurs. 7am-11pm, Fri. 7am-midnight, Sat. 7:30am-midnight, Sun. 7:30am-10pm).

■ Russian River Valley

The Russian River Valley is a well-kept secret. Although many of the wineries here have been operating nearly as long as their counterparts to the southeast, they are neither as well-known nor as frequently visited. The area encompasses a beautiful coastline, towering redwoods, and a scenic river. If you've had your fill of wine and wineries, the valley is also ideal for hiking and biking, as well as small town browsing. Healdsburg is more upscale, Sebastopol cheaper, and Guerneville hip and gay.

PRACTICAL INFORMATION AND ORIENTATION

Visitor Information: Russian River Visitors Center, 14034 Armstrong Woods Rd. (869-9212 or 800-253-8800), offers comprehensive brochures. Open Mon.-Wed. 9:30am-5pm, Thurs.-Sat. 9:30am-6pm, Sun. 10am-3pm. **Sebastopol Area Chamber of Commerce,** 265 S. Main St. (823-3032; open Mon.-Fri. 9am-5pm). **Healdsburg Chamber of Commerce,** 217 Healdsburg Ave. (433-6935; open Mon.-Fri. 9:30am-12:30pm and 1:30-5pm, Sat.-Sun. 10am-2pm). **Guerneville Chamber of Commerce,** 16200 1st St. (24hr. info line 869-9000; fax 869-9009). Open Mon.-Fri. 10am-4pm.

Public Transportation: Golden Gate Transit (541-2000 from Sonoma, 923-2000 from San Francisco). Connects Russian River and the Bay Area. Bus #78 heads north from 1st and Mission to Guerneville (Mon.-Fri. 4 per day; 2hr.; fare $4.50). **Sonoma County Transit** (576-RIDE/7433 or 800-345-RIDE/7433), has a countywide route (#20) from Santa Rosa to the Russian River area. Leaves from 2nd and Santa Rosa (Mon.-Fri. 4 per day, Sat.-Sun. 3 per day; fare $1.95).

Bike Rental: Bicycle Factory, 6940 McKinley St. (829-1880), downtown Sebastopol. Mountain bikes $8 per hr., $22 per day (includes helmet, lock, and souvenir water bottle). Open Mon.-Fri. 10am-6:30pm, Sat. 9am-5pm, Sun. 10am-4pm. **Mike's Bike Rental,** 16442 Rte. 116 (869-1106), Guerneville, across from the Safeway. Bikes $6 per hr., $28 first day, each additional day $20. Open summer Mon.-Sat. 9am-5pm, Sun. 10am-4pm. Call for winter hours.

Emergency: 911.

Post Office: Sebastopol, 290 S. Main St. Open Mon.-Fri. 8:30am-5pm. **ZIP Code:** 95473. **Healdsburg,** 409 Center St. (433-2267). Open Mon.-Fri. 8:30am-5pm. **ZIP Code:** 95446.

Area Code: 707.

The **Russian River** winds through western Sonoma County before emptying into the Pacific Ocean at Jenner. The river flows south, roughly following **U.S. 101** until **Healdsburg,** where it begins to veer west. A number of small towns, including **Guerneville, Monte Rio,** and **Forestville,** line this latter stretch of the river. **Sebastopol,** while not a river town itself, claims kinship to those towns to its north because of its location on **Rte. 116,** "the road to the Russian River." Traveling west on **Rte. 12** from Santa Rosa will bring you to Sebastopol.

ACCOMMODATIONS AND CAMPING

Although the relative seclusion of the Russian River Valley is one of its most appealing characteristics, one consequence is a decided lack of budget motels. The tourist industry in Russian River caters to a well-heeled, elegant, B&B-staying crowd. Options for the budget traveler, however, include area campgrounds and affordable lodge-resorts. Those with cars should bear in mind that this area is quite compact by California standards; none of the towns are more than a 40-minute drive apart.

Armstrong Woods State Reserve (869-2015), on Armstrong Woods Rd. off Rte. 116 3mi. north of Guerneville. **Bullfrog Pond** campground has 24 secluded tent sites along trails in a redwood grove ($12) and 4 primitive backpacker sites ($7). Self-registration after 4pm. No reservations; the site is popular so arrive early, especially on summer weekends.

Faerie Ring, 16747 Armstrong Woods Rd. (869-2746), just south of Armstrong Woods State Reserve, 1½mi. north of Guerneville. Privately operated gay-friendly campground offers site with tables and fire rings. Hot showers. Tent sites $15, weekends $20; RV sites $20, $25. Reservations recommended, especially on weekends. No children.

Johnson's Beach Resort, 1st St. (869-2022), center of Guerneville. Looks like an overcrowded parking lot, but the campsites and cabins are cheap and centrally located. Sites $7, each additional person $2; cabins (with fridges and TV) $30.

Isis Oasis, 20889 Geyserville Ave. (857-3524 or 800-679-7387), Healdsburg. The Egyptian goddess is still worshiped at this oasis. Populated by unusual people (witches and warlocks) and animals (ocelots, llamas, pygmy goats, and peacocks). Still, the beautiful pool and jacuzzi, and stellar dinner menus (e.g. shrimp jambalaya and pineapple cheesecake), are enough to cast a spell over anyone. Dorms available for groups ($20 per person); teepee $30; *yurt* (a tent with floors) $45.

Schoolhouse Canyon Park, 12600 River Rd. (869-2311). Redwoods tower over these beautiful sites (2 people $20, each additional person $5).

FOOD

While **Sebastopol** is lacking in convenient budget accommodations, this health-conscious community has contributed to the proliferation of good and good-for-you restaurants. For excellent baked goods, head north to **Healdsburg.**

East-West Cafe, 128 N. Main St. (829-2822), Sebastopol. Mediterranean platters make this the best vegetarian restaurant in the county. Free-range chicken or tofu fajitas $8. Cool off with a Thai iced tea or a *lassi* (sweet yogurt drink with rose water). Open Mon.-Fri. 7am-9pm, Sat. 8am-9pm, Sun. 8am-8pm.

Village Bakery, 7225 Healdsburg Ave. (829-8101), Sebastopol. Perhaps your only chance to taste Sebastopol sourdough bread (leavened with a culture from Gravenstein apples and Chardonnay grapes, $2.50). Divine apricot torte $2. Open Mon.-Sat. 7am-5:30pm, Sun. 8:30am-2:30pm.

Food for Thought, 6910 McKinley St. (829-9801), Sebastopol. Large health food store has local organic produce, a large selection of breads, and a deli dispensing sandwiches ($4-4.50) and salads. Open Mon.-Sat. 9am-9pm, Sun. 10am-8pm.

Sweet River Grill, 16251 Main St. (869-3383), in Guerneville. Beautiful outdoor seating for good people-watching. Not so cheap, but you'll know it's worth it when you taste the Navels of Venus (ricotta-filled tortellini; $11.50). Burgers and sandwiches $6-8. Open Mon.-Fri. 10:30am-10pm, Sat.-Sun. 10am-10pm.

Cousteaux French Bakery and Cafe, 417 Healdsburg Ave. (433-1913), Healdsburg. Quite possibly the finest sourdough bread in the universe ($2). Come for "coffee, talk, and tunes" by local artists. Open Mon.-Sat. 6am-6pm, Sun. 7am-4pm.

SIGHTS

Most travelers approach the Russian River Valley from the south, often driving from San Francisco. On the way up, you will pass **Sebastopol, Guerneville,** and **Healdsburg.** In quiet Sebastopol, hippies and farmers co-exist peacefully. This is no surprise, since the locals make a good life for themselves and for the visitors who eat there. Extremely unpretentious Guerneville, with its bustling gay community, is hipper than the surrounding towns. Farther north and east, Healdsburg is a burg of beauty and bucks, and a good base for exploring the wineries.

The **wineries** in the Russian River Valley are not mobbed like those in Napa and Sonoma. The *Wine Country Map of the Russian River Wine Road,* free at every visitors center and chamber of commerce in Wine Country, has an excellent map and lists every winery in the area, complete with their hours, services, and products. Here is the lowdown on some of the larger ones, but keep in mind that Keeping in mind that some of the smaller ones can also be the best. Traveling a few miles northwest along Rte. 116 from Sebastopol brings visitors to **Forestville,** the site of the **Topolos at Russian River Winery,** 5700 Rte. 116 (887-1575 or 800-TOPOLOS/867-6567), which offers free tasting and a posh restaurant. (Open Feb.-Dec. Wed.-Mon.

336 ■ NORTH BAY AND WINE COUNTRY

Restaurant open 11:30am-2:30pm and 5:30-9:30pm. Tasting room open 10:30am-5:30pm. Winter hours vary.) Just outside town are the **Korbel Champagne Cellars,** 13250 River Rd. (887-2294; tours daily 10am-3:45pm; tastings 9am-5pm, in winter until 4pm). **Trentadue Winery,** 19170 Geyserville Ave. (433-3104), one mile north of **Geyserville,** makes delicious wines on a gorgeous estate. Also in Geyserville is the award-winning **Château Souverain,** 400 Souverain Rd. (433-3141), at the Independence Lane Exit. Their chic cafe has stupendous views (tastings daily 10am-5pm).

The river is the reason people originally moved to the area, and it's still just as peaceful as ever. **W.C. "Bob" Trowbridge Canoe Trips** (433-7247 or 800-640-1386), runs daytrips down the river from April to October (4-5hr.; $39 per 2-3 person canoe). **Burke's Canoe Trips** (887-1222), offers similar daytrips ($30), as well as multi-day trips (no credit cards; call ahead for return service to your car). The **Armstrong Woods State Park** (869-2015), has trails in a redwood forest among Napa's golden hills, just 10 minutes north of Guerneville. The easiest hike is one-mile Pioneer Trail, which starts at the visitors center parking lot and skirts Fife Creek.

ENTERTAINMENT AND SEASONAL EVENTS

Guerneville is *the* nightspot in the Russian River Valley. Although it is predominantly a **gay** scene, the crowds are friendly and no one is made to feel unwelcome. The **Rainbow Cattle Co.,** 16220 Main St. (869-0206), is a rowdy gay bar straight outta Texas cow country (open daily 6am-2am). **Stumptown Brewery,** 15145 River Rd. (869-0705), one mile east of Guerneville, has a straighter crowd, live music, and a burger-heavy snack bar (open Mon.-Fri. 10am-2am, Sat.-Sun. 7am-2am). In Healdsburg, **Molly Malone's Irish Pub and Grille,** 245 Healdsburg Ave. (431-1856), is the local hangout, with dancing, darts, pool, and—of course—karaoke (live music Thurs.-Sat.; open daily 11am-2am).

Sebastopol's **Apple Blossom Festival,** in late April, says "this bud's for you" with entertainment, crafts, and food. The **Sebastopol Music Festival** also occurs at this time. There are free concerts each Sunday from May through August in Healdsburg on the Plaza (800-648-9922). The **Russian River Rodeo,** mid-June, is the big event of the season. The **Gravenstein Apple Fair** takes place in mid-August. The **Russian River Jazz Festival** (869-9000), blasts trombone, trumpet, and piano melodies down the river the first weekend after Labor Day (tickets from $26).

The North Coast

The North Coast is a paradise of rugged ocean coastline, rolling farmland, unspoiled black sand beaches, and towering redwoods. Wild rivers roam through peaceful valleys, and inhabitants tend to be nature-loving, artsy, and down-to-earth. The region's powerful beauty sends out a call of the wild, appealing to travelers weary of the more urban sights and sounds of the lower state.

The North Coast begins in the San Francisco Bay Area and continues to the Oregon border. Roadtrippers in the North Coast can take their pick of two scenic highway routes. Hwy. 1 (see below) offers craggy coastal vistas on the shores of Marin, Sonoma, and Mendocino Counties. One hour north of Fort Bragg, Hwy. 1 turns sharply inland and travels away from the coast for miles, merging with U.S. 101 for the journey north. Prior to this union, U.S. 101 meanders through the heart of California's wine country before hitting sleepy farm country and stopover town Ukiah.

The shore the highways leave behind, which is now known as the Lost Coast, offers some of the most rugged scenery in the state. Lost Coast marijuana farmers are (in)famous for cultivating what smokers consider to be some of the finest grass in the world. The inland leg of U.S. 101 brings travelers to the Avenue of the Giants, home of the enormous redwoods that make the region famous. Past Eureka and Arcata, U.S. 101 winds along the coast again while stately redwoods, protected by the long, thin strips of Redwood National Park, tower alongside. Ocean mists, tall trees, and cool air characterize this memorable expanse of the coast.

HIGHWAY 1: THE PACIFIC COAST HIGHWAY

Easy driving it is not, but Rte. 1 (the Pacific Coast Highway, usually called Hwy. 1), north of San Francisco, is one of the most breathtaking stretches of road in California. This famous highway snakes along rugged cliffs, pounding surf, and magnificent trees. Drivers and their passengers will appreciate the opportunities to recover from the heart-stopping journey in the quaint, not-*too*-touristy coastal hamlets. Be prepared, however, for sky-high prices for food and accommodations and slow trailers on the road. A budget traveler's best options are outdoors, camping and hiking. For more on Hwy. 1, see the **Central Coast** (p. 208) and the **Bay Area** (p. 291).

The highway winds its way out of the Bay Area via San Rafael, almost immediately hitting breathtaking Point Reyes National Seashore (see **Marin,** p. 320). A bit farther north, Hwy. 1 takes a brief inland turn before making an ocean rendezvous at Bodega Bay and the Sonoma Coast. The small town of **Bodega Bay** keeps its seafaring roots alive in the form of incredibly fresh salmon and crab at oceanside restaurants. For browsers, Bodega Bay is an antique maven's haven. The **visitors center,** 850 Hwy. 1 (875-3422), has info on the North Coast (open Mon.-Sat. 9:30am-8pm, Sun. 10am-4:30pm). Both Bodega Bay and **Bodega,** 7 mi. inland, were featured in Alfred Hitchcock's *The Birds.*

Just north of Bodega Bay begins the **Sonoma Coast State Park.** The park extends 10 mi. north to Jenner and includes several incredible beaches. Hiking trails along the beaches abound, but don't be tempted to venture too far into the ocean—unpredictable currents make these beaches dangerous for swimming and surfing. Within the state park are two more campgrounds. Off Hwy. 1, there are plenty of trails in the **Sonoma Coast State Park.** Campers can choose from 98 grassy, tree-studded sites at the **Bodega Dunes campground** (875-3483; tent sites $16; hot showers included). **Wright's Beach campground,** 2 mi. north, offers 30 sites ($20; no showers or hot water, but Bodega Dunes facilities are nearby). Call DESTINET (800-444-7275), for reservations at either.

Continuing north on Hwy. 1, you'll find **Jenner,** which sits on the Pacific at the mouth of the Russian River. Jenner's **Goat Rock Beach** is popular with harbor seals in the summer. Eleven miles up the coast from Jenner, **Fort Ross State Historic Park** (847-3286) features the only reconstructed Russian buildings in the continental U.S., relics of the czar's tenuous 19th-century presence. The park has 6 mi. of coastal access and sandy beaches, but bring a jacket to protect yourself from the wind. Those without the wheels (or stomach) to handle Hwy. 1 can reach the park by bus; take the **MTA's** daily coast run from Point Arena on the way to Santa Rosa (see **Sonoma Valley: Practical Information,** p. 329). A lonely wooden stockade perched on the edge of the Pacific cliffs above a small harbor, **Fort Ross** occupies a narrow strip of land hacked from the forest—the eastern limit of imperial Russia's grasp. Siberian Russians migrated here to hunt otters and find farmland for their Alaskan settlers, but the Spanish squeezed the Russians out in 1842, and John Sutter (of mill fame) bought the fort for a song, primarily to acquire the redwood threshing table inside. The fort now houses a limited **Russian Museum** (open daily 10am-4:30pm; admission $6). The park at **The Reef,** 1½ mi. south, offers 20 campsites with flush toilets (sites $12). Campgrounds also seem to appear around each of the many bends of the road north of the fort. **Salt Point State Park** (847-3221; reserve through DESTINET, 800-444-7275), 4 mi. up Hwy. 1, has 109 sites with toilets, showers, and fire pits ($16).

Farther north in Mendocino County (on Hwy. 1), the fog-shrouded **lighthouse** and **museum** (882-2777), of **Point Arena** deserve a stop. The original building dates from 1869, but the 115 ft. lighthouse is of 1906 vintage, constructed after the famed San Francisco earthquake demolished the first (open daily 10am-3:30pm; admission $2.50, children 50¢). The **MTA Coast Bus** (800-696-4MTA/4682), runs one loop daily from Point Arena to Santa Rosa (fare $2.50-6.25, students $1.75-4.50, seniors $1.25-3.25). Point Arena has 46 tent sites as well as hike/bike sites at **Manchester State Beach** (937-5804), where driftwood dots the sand (sites $9, seniors $7). To the east over 27 mi. of Mountain View Rd. is **Boonville,** where the main attraction is **Boontling,** a strange local language developed in the 1880s and still used by many.

■ Mendocino

Perched on bluffs overlooking the ocean, tiny Mendocino is a stylized but beautiful coastal tourist trap of art galleries, craft shops, bakeries, and B&Bs. The town's weathered wood shingles, sloping roofs, and clustered homes seem out of place on the West Coast; perhaps that's why Mendocino masqueraded for years as the fictional Maine village of Cabot Cove in the TV series *Murder, She Wrote.*

PRACTICAL INFORMATION AND ORIENTATION

Visitor Information: Ford House, 735 Main St. (961-6300), is in the former home of the town's founder, Jerome Bursely Ford. Town maps and info on area camping and hiking. Open summers daily 9:30am-4:30pm. **Parks General Information** (937-5804), Russian Gulch Park, east side of Hwy. 1. Open Mon.-Fri. 8am-5pm.

Buses: The nearest **Greyhound** is in Ukiah, 2hr. away. 2 buses per day to Ft. Bragg.

Public Transportation: Mendocino Stage (964-0167), routes 2 buses per day between Ft. Bragg and Navarro. **Mendocino Transit Authority,** 241 Plant Rd. (800-696-4682), in Ukiah, goes to Gualala with connecting service to Ukiah and Santa Rosa (Mon.-Fri.).

Taxis: Fort Bragg Door-to-Door (964-8294). On-call passenger van service available daily 10am-2am.

Equipment Rental: Catcha Canoe and Bicycles, Too! (937-0273), intersection of Hwy. 1 and Comptche-Ukiah Rd. Pricey, but top-quality. Open daily 9:30am-5:30pm. **Lost Coast Adventures Kayak Rental,** 19275 S. Harbor Dr. (961-1143), in Ft. Bragg. 2hr. guided tour $45 (open daily 9am-5pm).

Laundromat: Lucy's Laundry, 124 S. Main St., Ft. Bragg. Open daily 6am-10pm.

Crisis Lines: Rape (964-HELP/4357). **Disabled Crisis** (800-426-4263).

Hospital: Mendocino Coast District, 700 River Dr. (961-1234), Ft. Bragg.

Emergency: 911.

Police: (961-0200). Station in Ft. Bragg. **Sheriff:** (964-6308).

Post Office: 10500 Ford St. (937-5282), 2 blocks west of Main. Open Mon.-Fri. 7:30am-4:30pm. **ZIP Code:** 95460.

Area Code: 707.

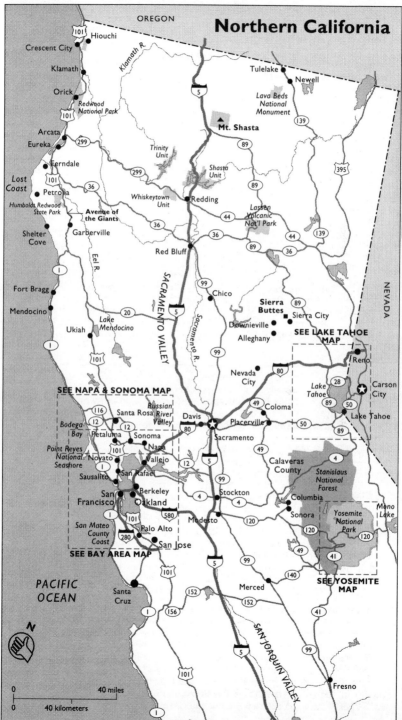

Northern California

THE NORTH COAST

Mendocino sits on **Hwy. I** right on the Pacific Coast, 30 mi. west of U.S. 101 and 12 mi. south of Fort Bragg. The town is tiny, and best explored on foot (parking available in plentiful lots). Weather in the Mendocino area varies from 40-70°F. Travelers should come prepared for chilliness caused by occasional fog.

ACCOMMODATIONS AND CAMPING

It's impossible to find a hotel room in Mendocino for under $60. Fortunately, there are hundreds of campsites nearby; make reservations through DESTINET (800-444-7275). Otherwise, look to Ukiah or Fort Bragg for budget motels.

Jug Handle Creek Farm, (964-4630), 5mi. north of Mendocino at the Caspar Exit off Hwy. 1. A beautiful 120-year-old house with 30 beds sits on 40 acres of overgrown gardens along with campsites and small rustic cabins. Access to the beach and trails in Jug Handle State Park (see **Sights,** below). Dorms $18, students $12; sites $6, children $3; cabins $25 per person. One hour of chores (or $5) required per night. Reserve in advance. No linens.

The Coast Motel, 18661 Hwy. 1 (964-2852), ¼mi. south of the intersection with Rte. 20 in Ft. Bragg. Simple budget motel is woodsy and rustic, with a pool. Shared phone. Singles $46-56; doubles $56-66.

MacKerricher State Park campground (937-5804), 3½mi. north of Ft. Bragg. Excellent views of tidepool life, passing seals, sea lions, and migratory whales, as well as 9mi. of beaches and a murky lake for trout fishing. Drinkable water, showers, and bathrooms. Sites $16; day use free. Reservations advised.

Russian Gulch State Park campground (937-5804), 1mi. north of town on Hwy. 1. Foggy woods shelter 30 sites. Access to a beach, redwoods, hiking trails, and a waterfall. Showers and flush toilets. No hookups. Sites $16, seniors $14; day use $5. Book through DESTINET up to 8 weeks in advance. Open April-Oct.

FOOD

All of Mendocino's breads are freshly baked, all vegetables locally grown, all wheat unmilled, all coffee cappuccino, and almost everything expensive. Most restaurants close at 9pm. Picnicking is the cheapest option; stock up at **Mendosa's Market,** 1909 Lansing St. (937-5879), the closest thing in Mendocino to a real supermarket. Pricey (of course), but all items fresh and delicious (open daily 8am-9pm).

Tote Fête, 10450 Lansing St. (937-3383), has delicious tote-out food, and the crowds know it. Asiago, pesto, and artichoke heart sandwich ($4.25) hits the spot. **Tote Fête Bakery** is in the back with a flowery garden and a small serene pool. Open Mon.-Sat. 10:30am-7pm, Sun. 10:30am-4pm.

Mendocino Bakery and Cafe, 10485 Lansing St. (937-0836), gives a lot but takes so little—big servings, small prices. Variety of items, including the breakfast burrito ($4), fresh pizza and quiche ($3.75), or oatmeal raisin cookie ($1). If you want coffee with that, bring your own mug or ask for one of theirs (just don't take one off the wall, those belong to regulars). Deck outside catches the ocean breeze. Open Mon.-Fri. 7:30am-8pm, Sat.-Sun. 8am-8pm.

Mendocino Cookie Co. (a.k.a. **Cookies**), 10450 Lansing St. (937-4843). Get your caffeine fix and sugar high at once. Double potency super large latte ($3). Tasty fresh-baked cookies like amaretto crisp. Open daily 6:15am-5:15pm.

SIGHTS AND SEASONAL EVENTS

The greatest attribute of the town lies 900 ft. to its west, where the land screeches to a halt and falls off into the Pacific, forming the impressive fog-shrouded coastline of the **Mendocino Headlands.** Beneath wildflower-laden meadows, fingers of eroded rock claw through the pounding ocean surf and seals frolic in secluded alcoves. **Kites** perform stupendously here, catching the sea breeze and soaring over the ocean. Grab one at the **Village Toy Store,** 10450 Lansing St. (937-4633). Rentals are $3 per hour with a $30 deposit, but you can buy one instead for $33.

Poor drainage, thin soil, and ocean winds have created an unusual *bonsai* garden just south of town at the **Pygmy Forest** in **Van Damme State Park** (admission $5). The trees are visible for free from Little Airport Rd. (off of Hwy. 1 past the park; after turning left, drive 3½mi. to a parking lot and a sign for the pygmy forest). The **ecological staircase** at **Jug Handle State Park** is a terrace of five different ecosystems, each roughly 100,000 years older than the one below it and formed by a combination of erosion and tectonic uplift. **Russian Gulch State Park,** north of Mendocino, is the perfect place to watch the fog roll in (trail maps available at park entrance).

Though the area is made of fog and flora to its core, Mendocino County flaunts many a fancy version of *au naturel*—hotspring resorts abound. **Orr Hot Springs,** 13201 Orr Springs Rd. (462-6277), is just south of Mendocino off Comptche Ukian Rd. (1hr. drive over dirt roads). From U.S. 101 take the North State St. Exit. Mineral water baths (both hot and cold) and riotous gardens make the world disappear at this relaxed resort. Clothing optional—bare skin is prevalent. (Open daily 10am-10pm. Day use $19.) Visitors to Mendocino in July can enjoy the **Mendocino Music Festival** (937-2044), a two-week orgy of classical music and opera (tickets $12-20).

▓ Avenue of the Giants

About six miles north of **Garberville** off U.S. 101, the **Avenue of the Giants** winds its way through 31 mi. of the largest living creatures this side of sea level. The tops of the redwoods cannot be seen from inside a car—pull over and get out to avoid straining your neck, wrecking your vehicle, and looking ridiculous. Hiking, swimming, fishing, biking, and rafting abound in this rugged area.

Practical Information The **Humboldt Redwoods State Park Visitors Center** (946-2263), just south of Weott on the Avenue, has a free brochure highlighting the Avenue's groves, facilities, trails, and bike routes. The center also has an exhibit on the 1964 flood, which caused the river to rise to 22 ft.; mud marks can still be seen on the trees. (Open March-Oct. daily 9am-5pm; Nov.-March Thurs.-Sun. 10am-4pm.) Webmeisters can find detailed info on the area by accessing http://redwoods.com/~ebarnett/leggett.ca.html. **Greyhound** (923-3388), runs four buses out of Garberville (2 north and 2 south daily) to Eureka ($14), Portland ($59), and San Francisco ($34). Meet the bus at Singing Salmon Music, 432 Church St., one block east of Redwood Dr. In an **emergency** call 911. The **post office** is at 368 Sprowl Creek Rd. (open Mon.-Fri. 8:30am-5:30pm). The **ZIP code** is 95542.

Accommodations and Camping The **Redway Motel,** 3223 Redwood Dr. (923-2660), in Redway, may have cinderblock walls, but the rooms are bright and clean (some have A/C). Cable and coffee (singles $35; doubles $40).

Along the road in **Humboldt State Park** (946-2409), camping options are plentiful. **Albee Creek,** 5 mi. west of U.S. 101 on Mattpole Rd., is under the wildlife-filled redwood canopy and convenient to biking and hiking trails. **Burlington** is right on the Avenue near the visitors center. **Richardson Grove State Park** (247-3318), 8 mi. south of Garberville off U.S. 101, also offers breathtaking campsites, showers, and bathrooms. Call DESTINET (800-444-7275) to make reservations.

Food Nearby Garberville offers a number of civilized eating options. The **Sentry Market,** on Redwood Dr., is the largest supermarket for miles (open daily 7am-10pm). Locals highly recommend **Calico's Cafe** (923-2253), on Redwood Dr. next to Sherwood Forest Motel. Fresh pasta with the garlicky fettucine gorgonzola ($7) made from scratch (open daily 11am-9pm). **Nacho Mama's,** at Redwood Dr. and Sprowel Creek Rd., is a take-out stand serving Mexican food and refreshing frosties.

Sights and Seasonal Events Scattered throughout the area are several commercialized attractions such as the World Famous Tree House, Confusion Hill, and the **Drive-Thru Tree.** Travelers looking for a more authentic taste of the redwood forests may want to bypass these hokey attractions in favor of more rugged and natural tours. There are a number of great **hiking** trails in the area, marked on maps available at the visitors center ($1). The **Canoe Creek Loop Trail,** across the street from the visitors center, is an easy start. Uncrowded trails snake through the park's northern section around **Rockefeller Forest,** which contains the largest grove of old-growth redwoods (200+ years) in the world. The **Dyerville Giant,** in the redwood graveyard at Founder's Grove about midway through the Avenue, deserves a respectful visit. The ½ mi. loop rail includes the **Founder's Tree** and the **Fallen Giant,** whose massive trunk stretches 60 human body-lengths long and whose three-story rootball looks like a massive vortex. The **Standish Hickey Recreation Area** (925-6482), north of Leggett on U.S. 101, offers fishing, camping, swimming, and hiking (parking $5).

With its sizable artist population, Garberville's **art festivals** are a big draw. **Jazz on the Lake** and the **Summer Arts Fair** begin in late June, followed by **Shakespeare at Benbow Lake** (800-923-2613), in late July. Early August brings **Reggae on the River** (923-4583), a 12-hour music fest on the banks of the Eel River. For more info on events, call the Chamber of Commerce (see **Practical Information,** p. 341).

■ Lost Coast

Lacking paved roads, guard rails, and signs announcing its presence, the Lost Coast can elude even the most observant visitor. The region is so named because when Hwy. 1 was built, the rugged coastline between Usal and Ferndale had to be bypassed and the highway moved inland. Thus, this part of the coast was "lost" to modernization, leaving the craggy cliffs, rocky shores, and black sand beaches comparatively untouched. Bring a map and a 4WD because it is easy to get *lost.* (Oh, the irony.) Be careful when exploring—you *don't* want to wander into someone's marijuana farm. The anti-pot laws of the 1980s have made the proprietors of Humboldt County's #1 cash crop nervous enough to suspect everyone. **Emergency** services for the area include the Garberville **sheriff** (923-2761), **ambulance** (923-3962), **fire and rescue** department (923-3475), and **911.** The **area code** is 707.

SINKYONE WILDERNESS STATE PARK

The area between Usal and Needle Rock is the least accessible part of the Lost Coast, and though it was once part of an active logging community, only ruined buildings and dirt roads remain. To get to **Sinkyone** from the south, take Hwy. 1 to Road 431 (where Hwy. 1 starts to turn towards Leggett). Coming from the north, take U.S. 101 to Redway and follow the signs to **Shelter Cove,** a secluded community located over an extremely steep hill on Point Delgada; despite the short distance, this trip takes over an hour. The **Shelter Cove Information Bureau** is at 21 Sea Crest (986-7069). The **Shelter Cove Deli,** 492 Machi Rd. (986-7474), offers fish 'n' chips and over 100 campsites near the beach (tents $15, RVs $25). A great place to camp on the beach for free is **Black Sands Beach,** reached by turning north on Beach Rd. before Shelter Cove. The gorgeous 25 mi. stretch of black sand is popular for overnight hikes and surfing. The strange town of **Whitethorn** can be reached by turning left onto Briceland Rd. about 10 mi. after Shelter Cove. Ten miles farther is a four-way intersection: to the left is **Road 431,** a very bad road through the park (4WD required); straight ahead is **Road 435** leading to the visitors center, Needle Rock, and Jones Beach; and to the right is the 6 mi. dirt road back to **Shelter Cove** and, eventually, Usal Beach.

At the northern end of the park, Road 431 intersects with Road 435, a treacherous drive for the fearless and/or insane. It is so narrow that it only fits one car at a time, so make a mental note of the last turnoff. As you crawl down the mountain, you will come across **Jones Beach, Needle Rock,** and the **Needle Rock Visitors Center** (986-7711), offering maps ($1), camping permits, and firewood. Eventually this road leads to **Bear Harbor.** The blocked-off road to Jones Beach is about 2 mi. down

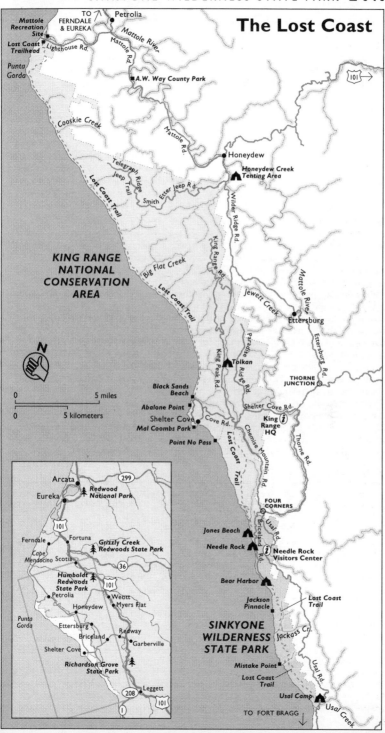

The Lost Coast

THE NORTH COAST

TO FERNDALE & EUREKA
Petrolia
Mattole River
Mattole Recreation Site
Lost Coast Trailhead
Lighthouse Rd.
Mattole Rd.
Punta Gorda
A.W. Way County Park
Cooskie Creek
Mattole Rd.
Honeydew
Honeydew Creek Tenting Area
Telegraph Ridge
Jeep Trail
Etter Jeep Rd.
Smith
Lost Coast Trail
Wilder Ridge Rd.
King Range Rd.
Big Flat Creek
Lost Coast Trail
Jewett Creek
Mattole River
Ettersburg
Ettersburg Rd.

KING RANGE NATIONAL CONSERVATION AREA

N

0   5 miles
0   5 kilometers

Paradise Ridge Rd.
King Peak Rd.
Tolkan
THORNE JUNCTION

Black Sands Beach
Abalone Point
Shelter Cove
Mal Coombs Park
Cove Rd.
Point No Pass
Shelter Cove Rd.
King Range HQ (i)
Lost Coast Trail
Chemise Mountain Rd.
Thorne Rd.

Arcata
299
Redwood National Park
Eureka
101
Ferndale
Fortuna
Grizzly Creek Redwoods State Park
Cape Mendocino
Scotia
36
Humboldt Redwoods State Park
101
Petrolia
Weott
Honeydew
Myers Flat
Punta Gorda
Ettersburg
Briceland
Redway
Garberville
Shelter Cove
Richardson Grove State Park
208
Leggett
101
1

FOUR CORNERS
Briceland Rd.
Usal Rd.
Jones Beach
Needle Rock
Needle Rock Visitors Center (i)
Bear Harbor
Jackson Pinnacle
Lost Coast Trail
Jackass Cr.
SINKYONE WILDERNESS STATE PARK
Mistake Point
Lost Coast Trail
Usal Rd.
Usal Camp
Usal Creek
TO FORT BRAGG

101

Road 435, and a 10 min. hike leads to three primitive campsites and another trail to the beautiful black sand beach. No reservations accepted (sites $11; 14-night max. stay). Usually full in the summer (center hours vary; always closes at 5pm). The road gets worse on the way to Bear Harbor, but there are primitive campsites at each of the three neighboring campgrounds (Orchard, Railroad, and Bear Harbor), which are surrounded by lush ferns and black sand (only accessible by ½mi. hike; no water, pit toilets). Be prepared to share your space with the **Roosevelt elk** who graze here.

One of the more popular Lost Coast beaches, **Usal Beach** has a self-registration kiosk and camping areas (state-maintained sites are unmarked and cost $11, trail camps $3). About 300 ft. farther up its dirt road is a short bridge and another road leading to a parking area and some windy beachside sites (no water). The southern trailhead of the difficult **Lost Coast Trail** begins at Usal and leads 50 mi. up the coast to **Mattole River.** Both Usal Beach and the Lost Coast trail are accessible via an unmarked dirt road from the south. Trail maps are essential for exploring this wilderness and can be found at state parks or the Needle Rock Visitors Center.

HONEYDEW AND PETROLIA

These blink-and-you'll-miss-'em Lost Coast towns are accessible from the north and east; head south from Ferndale or west from Fountain Grove (follow the signs). In **Honeydew,** at the intersection of Wilder Ridge and Mattole, the main attraction is the **general store** (open daily 9am-5pm; cash only for gas).

Mattole Campground, at the end of **Lighthouse Rd.,** is located 45 minutes north of Honeydew off Mattole Rd. (a dirt road marked by a sign right before the bridge for northbound traffic). No permit is required, but there is no water and only pit toilets. Part of the **Kings Range Conservation Area,** the windy, flat beach is framed by high cliffs and a parking lot. A dirt road leads up to the top of the hills 300 ft. before the campground, offering dizzying views of the beach. Beware: some of the area is well-marked private property, where camping is prohibited. Much of the beach can be hiked, but buy tide tables in Garberville or at the nearby Petrolia General Store (see below) to keep your hike dry.

Past Lighthouse Rd. on Mattole is **Petrolia,** which contains a **general store** (open Mon.-Sat. 9am-6pm, Sun. 9am-5:30pm; cash only for gas) and a **post office** (open Mon.-Fri. 8am-4pm). Ten miles north of Petrolia, the road hugs the beach for a spectacular stretch of road framed by cattle on one side and rocky shore on the other. The beach here is private, but public hikes and camping are usually tolerated.

FERNDALE

The northernmost Lost Coast town of **Ferndale** is Disneyesque small town perfection. **Ross Park** makes for perfect picnicking (bring a blanket and bug repellent), and the amphitheater-like **cemeteries** on Ocean Ave. give a great view of the quaint Victorian town and the grazing dairy cattle. Except for exorbitantly priced B&Bs, accommodations here are sparse. The **Eureka Baking Company,** 543 Main St. (786-4741), makes fresh bread, scrumptious chocolate macaroons ($1), a variety of sandwiches, and coffee (70¢) for reasonable prices (open Mon.-Fri. 6:30am-5:30pm, Sat. 7am-4pm, Sun. 9am-4pm). The **Ferndale Meat Co.,** 376 Main St. (786-4501), layers generous slabs of cheese and meat on choice breads ($2.75). Just ignore the deer-head decor (open Mon.-Sat. 8am-5pm). Down the block, the **Kinetic Sculpture Museum,** on Main St., has inherited some of the entries from past Arcata Kinetic Sculpture Races (see **Arcata: Sights,** p. 347). Examples constructed entirely from license plates and fashioned in the shape of an enchanted slipper will make you wonder how they ever managed to move at all, let alone travel 38 racing miles (open daily 10am-5pm; free).

▩ Eureka

Eureka tends to be overlooked by most travelers in favor of its more attractive neighbors. Redwoods tower to the north, the younger, hipper town of Arcata lies just to the northeast, and to the south shines the isolated beauty of the Lost Coast. Eureka just doesn't offer the same caliber of attractions, but the town's efforts at revival have paid off to some degree in the attractive Victorianesque shop fronts and numerous bookstores and bakeries. Totally rebuilt following a devastating earthquake in 1991, the town revolves around a number of art galleries displaying the works of the approximately 4000 local artists; in fact, Eureka has more artists per capita than any other city of its size in the U.S. (quantity, of course, does not equal quality). Despite its small size, Eureka has big-city problems, so don't walk alone at night. A large homeless population congregates around the Victorian mansions.

Practical Information and Orientation Free maps and historical info are available at the **Eureka/Humboldt Visitors Bureau,** 1034 2nd St. (443-5097 or 800-338-7352 in CA, 800-346-3482 out of state; open Mon.-Fri. 9am-noon and 1-5pm). The **Eureka Chamber of Commerce,** 2112 Broadway (442-3738 or 800-356-6381), has helpful info on restaurants and hotels (open June-Sept. Mon. 9am-5pm, Tues.-Fri. 9am-7pm, Sat. 10am-4pm; off-season Mon.-Fri. 9am-5pm). There is an **ATM** at **Bank of America,** at the corner of E and 4th St. **Greyhound,** 1603 4th St. (442-0370 or 800-231-2222), at Q St., provides frequent service between Eureka and Arcata and goes to San Francisco ($32-35) twice per day (open Mon.-Fri. 9am-1:30pm and 2:30-5pm, Sat. 9am-noon and 8-10:20pm). The **Humboldt Transport Authority,** 133 V St. (443-0826), runs regional buses between Scotia and Trinidad, stopping in Arcata. Most buses pick up passengers along 5th or Broadway (open Mon.-Fri. 6am-9:45pm; fare $1.35-1.60). **Adventure's Edge,** 408 F St. (822-4673), rents equipment including tents ($16 per day for the first 3 days, $2 per additional day), sleeping bags ($14, $2), and kayaks ($25 per day). Cross-country ski packages cost $17. (Open Mon.-Fri. 9am-7pm, Sat. 9am-6pm, Sun. 11am-5pm.) The **Summer St. Laundromat** is located at 111 Summer St. (443-7463; open daily 7am-8:30pm). Medical services can be obtained at **Eureka General Hospital,** 2200 Harrison Ave. (445-5111). In an **emergency** call 911 or contact the **police** (441-4044), the **sheriff** (445-7505), or the **fire department** (441-4000). The **post office** is at 337 W. Clark St. (442-1768; open Mon.-Fri. 8:30am-5pm, Sat. noon-3pm). The **ZIP code** is 95501. The **area code** is 707.

Eureka straddles **U.S. 101** 12 mi. south of Arcata and 280 mi. north of San Francisco. In town, U.S. 101 becomes 4th St. (heading towards the south) and 5th St. (heading towards the north).

Accommodations and Camping Travelers will find many budget motels off U.S. 101, which bisects Eureka, but many are unappealing; be selective and *avoid walking alone at night.* **National 9 Inn**, 2846 Broadway (443-9381 or 800-524-9999), is south of town off U.S. 101, in an area much safer than Eureka's downtown. Rooms are cozy and come with cable TV, coffee, and continental breakfast (singles $28-38; doubles $34-48). **Motel 6,** 1934 Broadway (445-9631), also south of town off U.S. 101, offers cable TV (singles $42; doubles $47; each additional person $6). Most of the area's camping is nearer Arcata than Eureka, but **Big Lagoon County Park** (445-7652), 20 mi. north of Eureka on U.S. 101, is a local favorite. The park has 32 sites (no hookups) with pit toilets, drinking water, and a lagoon for swimming, canoeing, or kayaking (sites $10; arrive early).

Food **Eureka Co-op,** 1036 5th St. (443-6027), at L St., sells bulk grains, organic produce, and deli foods (open Mon.-Sat. 10am-7pm, Sun. noon-5pm). There are also two **farmer's markets** that run from July to October (Tues. 10am-1pm at the Old Town Gazebo; Thurs. 10am-1pm at the Eureka Mall). **Ramone's Bakery and Cafe,** 209 E St. (445-2923), between 2nd and 3rd, specializes in devilish desserts like the ever-popular Chocolate Sin, a chocolate and liqueur torte, and local art (open Mon.-Sat. 7am-6pm, Sun. 8am-4pm). **Tomaso's Tomato Pies,** 216 E St. (445-0100), in Old Town Eureka, serves up generous slices of pizza with garlic bread and salad ($4) that can feed two. Salads and sandwiches (both $6) are excellent (open Mon.-Sat. 11:30am-9pm, Sun. 5-8:30pm). **Cafe Marina,** 601 Startare Dr. (443-2233), is located north of town off Woodley Island Exit from U.S. 101. Outdoor dining on the marina is the perfect way to enjoy fresh seafood like the spicy blackened snapper (lunch $8-13, dinner $10-14). The polished bar is the local fishermen's night spot. (Open summers daily 7am-10pm; off-season Sun.-Thurs. 7am-9pm, Fri.-Sat. 7am-10pm.)

Sights Eureka is very proud of its bevy of restored **Victorian homes,** a few of which are actually worth driving past. Most of the really good ones have been turned into expensive B&Bs, including the oft-photographed **Carson Mansion,** which belonged to a prominent logger in the 1850's.

Art galleries are Eureka's main claim to fame, and most of them are located downtown; ask locals about current exhibits. Two of the best are **C.U. Kensugih,** 426 1st St. (443-9225), which has an Indonesian collection, and **308 Showcase,** 308 2nd St. (444-3080), offering all the seascapes a tourist's heart could desire. The **Many Hands Gallery,** 438 2nd St. (445-0455), collects art from around the world into an educational gift shop; replicas available for those who don't carry $3000 in cash. (Open summers Sun.-Thurs. 9:30am-7pm, Fri.-Sat. 9:30am-8pm; off-season daily 10am-6pm.)

The **dunes recreation area** is located in Samoa off Rte. 255 (pass the cookhouse and go left at Samoa Bridge). Once a thriving dune ecosystem, this peninsula now offers beach access and dune hiking.

■ Arcata

Arcata is like Berkeley without San Francisco. Lying at the intersection of U.S. 101 and Rte. 299, Arcata (ar-KAY-ta) typifies the laid-back, stress-free existence that characterizes the North Coast. Arcata's neighbor **Humboldt State University** (Earth First! was founded here) might seem overly liberal and directionless to some, but others (particularly the students) appreciate this chillin' attitude.

Practical Information The **Arcata Chamber of Commerce,** 1062 G St. (822-3619), offers visitor information (open Mon.-Fri. 10am-4pm, Sat. 9am-3pm). Sundry items are available at the **Barnes Arcata Drug Store,** 1080 G St. (822-2496). The most convenient **laundromat** is **M.O.M.'s,** 5000 Valley West Blvd. (822-1181; open daily 7am-10pm). For medical services, go to the **Mad River Hospital,** 3800 Janes Rd. (822-3621). In an **emergency,** call 911. The **post office** is at 799 H St. (open Mon.-Fri. 8:30am-5pm). The **ZIP code** is 95521. The **area code** is 707.

Accommodations and Camping For those with a car, camping is easy near Arcata, and a cluster of budget motels line the Giuntoli Exit off U.S. 101 north of the city. **Clam Beach County Park** (445-7491), 7½ mi. north of Arcata on U.S. 101, provides water, pit toilets, dunes, and a huge sand beach with seasonal clam digging. The park is very popular, so call ahead (sites $8). **Patrick's Point State Park** (677-3570), 15 mi. north of Arcata, has 123 sites with showers and flush toilets, terrific ocean views, lush vegetation, and treasure-hunting in the rocky beach's tidepools and agates (sites $16 per vehicle, no hookups, day use $5, hikers and cyclists $3). Reservations can be made through DESTINET (800-436-7275) and are required at least two weeks in advance in summer. The point is also an excellent spot for watching whales and dolphins. Camping is also available at **Big Lagoon County Park,** near Eureka.

There is, of course, always **Motel 6,** 4755 Valley West Blvd. (822-7061), at the Giuntoli Exit off U.S. 101. The motel is clean and quiet, and offers cable TV, pool, and A/C (singles $38; doubles $44; $7 more in summer). **Arcata Hostel,** 1390 I St. (822-9995), at 14th St., about ½ mi. from the Greyhound station, is a term-time college residence. Facilities are small, but clean and adequate. (Dorms $15 per night. Lock-out 9am-5pm. Check-in 5-11pm. Hostel open from late June to late August.)

Food and Entertainment **Los Bageles,** 1061 I St. (822-3150), between 10th and 11th St., has a wide assortment of pastries, specialty coffees, and fruit drinks. Outdoor seating is comfortable and laid-back. (Open Mon. and Wed.-Fri. 7am-6pm, Sat. 7am-5pm, Sun. 8am-3pm. Most items under $1.) **Hey Juan!,** 1642½ G St. (822-8433), serves up tasty and dirt-cheap Mexi-Cali fare; entree with beans and rice about $4. Tastes and smells better than it looks (open daily 11am-11pm). **Crosswinds,** 860 10th St. (826-2133), in a restored Victorian home, offers a frightening number of breakfast variations. Vegan substitutes are available for all meat used in the Mexican, Italian, and Californian specialties ($3-4), and servings are large (open Tues.-Sun. 7:30am-2pm). The **Arcata Co-op** (822-5947), on 8th St. at I St., feeds its laid-back patrons tofu, tempeh, ginseng cola, and soy milk. Useful ride board (open Mon.-Sat. 8am-9pm, Sun. 8am-8pm). A **farmer's market** offering tie-dyed dresses, candles, and the usual fresh produce invades the Arcata Plaza from June to November (Sat. 9am-1pm).

Arcata is a college town with its fair share of **bars,** most of which are clustered on 9th St. in the town square. **Humboldt Brewery,** 856 10th St. (826-BREW/2739), at I St., is a popular local microbrewery with a cavernous imported beer garden. Unusual beers (like the Red Nectar Ale) go well with the live music on weekends (open Sun.-Thurs. 11:30am-10pm, Fri.-Sat. 11:30am-1am). **Jambalaya** (822-4766), at 9th and H St., is "as cool as it gets" for live jazz and blues.

Sights and Seasonal Events You can fully experience Arcata by taking a **walking tour** or just wandering around the **Arcata Plaza,** in the center of town near the intersection of H and 8th St., which offers folk music on the weekends and an annual **Summer Solstice Festival.** Those who wish to tour the **Humboldt campus** should be sure to see the **whale skulls** by the biological labs and **Redwood Park,** which contains lots of nooks for picnicking among the giants. Five minutes east of the city is the **Arcata Community Forest,** which has picnic spaces, lush meadows, redwoods, and hiking trails (free). A former "sanitary" landfill, the 75-acre **Arcata Marsh and Wildlife Sanctuary** (826-2359), lies at the foot of I St. Wander the trails around the lake or take a tour to see how this saltwater marsh/converted sewer system works with treated waste (tours meet Sat. 8:30am and 2pm at the info center).

The 15-year-old **Kinetic Sculpture Race,** held annually over Memorial Day weekend, may be Humboldt County's oddest festival. A few dozen insane and/or intoxicated adventurers attempt to pilot unwieldy but endearingly artistic homemade vehicles on a grueling three-day 35 mi. trek from Arcata to Ferndale via road, sand, and water. Past vehicles have resembled crabs, eggs, and humans, and are on display at a museum in Ferndale (see **Ferndale,** p. 344).

■ Redwood National Park

With ferns that grow to the height of humans and redwood trees the size of skyscrapers, Redwood National Park, as John Steinbeck said, "will leave a mark or create a vision that stays with you always." Fog rolls between the creaking redwood boughs in a prehistoric atmosphere where you half expect a dinosaur to tromp by at any moment. The redwoods in the park are the last remaining stretch of the old-growth forest which used to blanket 2 million acres of Northern California and Oregon. Wildlife runs rampant here, with black bears and mountain lions in the backwoods and Roosevelt elk grazing in the meadows. While a short tour of the big sights and the drive-thru tree will certainly give visitors ample photo ops, too many of those photos will include fellow tourists. A less exhaustive but more memorable way to experience the redwoods is to head down a hiking path into the quiet of the forest, where you can see the trees as they have been for thousands of years. For the few who tire of the trees, the rocky coast also provides chilly surfing, sunbathing, and swimming.

PRACTICAL INFORMATION

Visitor Information:

Redwood Information Center (488-3461), 1mi. south of Orick on U.S. 101. Shows free films on redwoods, gray whales, and black bears. Maps of the park free; trail maps $1.50. Info on trails and campsites. Enthusiastic and helpful rangers. Entrance is free, but there's a **$6 per car** fee for use of park facilities such as beaches and picnic tables. Open daily 9am-5pm.

Redwood National Park Headquarters and Information Center, 1111 2nd St. (464-6101), Crescent City. Headquarters of the entire national park, but the ranger stations are just as well-informed. Open daily 9am-5pm.

Crescent City Chamber of Commerce, 1001 Front St. (464-3174), Crescent City. Open Mon.-Fri. 8am-7pm, Sat.-Sun. 9am-5pm; Labor Day-Memorial Day Mon.-Fri. 9am-5pm.

Prairie Creek Ranger Station (464-6101, ext. 5301), on U.S. 101 in Prairie Creek Redwood State Park. Open summers only daily 8am-8pm.

Hiouchi Ranger Station (464-6101, ext. 5067), on I-199 across from Jedediah Smith Redwoods State Park. Open May-Oct. daily 9am-5pm.

Jedediah Smith State Park Information Center (464-6101, ext. 5113), on U.S. 199 across from the Hiouchi Ranger Station. Open daily 9am-5pm.

ATM: Wells Fargo Bank, 936 3rd St., Crescent City.

Buses: Greyhound, 500 E. Harding St. (464-2807), in Crescent City. 2 buses per day going north and 2 going south, to San Francisco ($51) and Portland ($53). Open Mon.-Fri. 7-10am and 5-7:30pm, Sat. 7-9am and 7-7:30pm. No credit cards.

Auto Repairs: AAA Emergency Road Service (464-5626). 24hr.

Laundromat: Econ-o-wash, 601 H St. (464-9935), Crescent City. Wash $1, dry 50¢. Open daily 7am-11pm.

Road Conditions: (800-427-7623). **Highway Patrol:** (464-3117).

Crisis Lines: Rape Crisis (465-2851). 24hr.

Medical Services: Sutter Coast Hospital, 800 E. Washington Blvd. (464-8511), Crescent City.

Emergency: 911.

Post Office: 751 2nd St. (464-2151), **Crescent City.** Open Mon.-Fri. 8:30am-5pm, Sat. noon-3pm. **ZIP Code:** 95531. Other post offices at 121147 U.S. 101 in **Orick** (open Mon.-Fri. 8:30am-noon and 1-5pm), and at 141 Klamath Blvd. in **Klamath** (open Mon.-Fri. 8am-4:30pm). **ZIP Code:** 95555.

Area Code: 707.

ORIENTATION

Redwood National Park is only one of four redwood parks between Klamath and Orick, the others being **Jedediah Smith State Park, Del Norte Coast Redwoods State Park,** and **Prairie Creek Redwoods State Park.** The name "Redwood National Park" is an umbrella term for all four parks. **Crescent City,** with park headquarters and a few basic services, stands at the park's northern end. The town of **Orick** is situated at the southern limit, and just south of town is an extremely helpful ranger station. **U.S. 101** connects the two, traversing most of the park. The slower but more scenic **Newton Drury Pkwy.** runs parallel to U.S. 101 for 31 mi. from Klamath to Prairie Creek (watch out for bikers).

ACCOMMODATIONS

Redwood Youth Hostel (HI-AYH), 14480 U.S. 101 (482-8265), 7mi. north of Klamath at Wilson Creek Rd. Overlooking the crashing Pacific surf and housed in the historic DeMartin House, this 30-bed hostel embodies hominess and simplicity. Kitchen, laundry facilities ($1.50 per load), and 2 ocean-view sundecks. The chores and rules (no shoes inside) are a bit oppressive. Check-in 4:30-9:30pm. Check-out 9:30am. Lockout 9:30am-4:30pm. No-frills curfew 11pm. Dorms $12. One private double available. Linens $1. Reservations recommended for the summer; advance payment required. No wheelchair access.

Redwood Logging Town

Rising hundreds of feet above the ground, the trees in Redwood National Park have towered in lush profusion for 150 million years. Native Americans called these lofty giants "the eternal spirit" because of their 2000-year lifespan, ability to adapt to climactic changes, and resistance to insects, fire, and even lightning. The redwoods were indeed almost invincible, until the era of logging began. Unfortunately the trees never evolved to be chainsaw resistant. With money on their minds (one tree builds 22 houses) and saws in their hands, loggers chopped 96% of the virgin coast redwoods in one century. Despite the economic boom that the logging industry brought to the area's small towns, conservationists realized that killing millions of trees was hurting the ecology. Money from private donations slowly bought redwood plots from loggers in the 1920s, and in 1968 the Redwood National Park was formed, preserving these quiet giants for the next few hundred generations.

Camp Marigold, 16101 U.S. 101 (482-3585 or 800-621-8513), 3mi. north of Klamath Bridge, is a pleasantly woodsy alternative to mundane motels. Cute cabins have full kitchens and cable TV. Doubles $38.

Park Woods Motel, 121440 U.S. 101 (488-5175), in Orick, has clean, bare-bones rooms for the lowest prices in town. Cable TV. Singles $30; doubles $32-50.

El Patio, 655 H St. (464-5114), in Crescent City, offers decent rooms with a wood-paneled early-70s look for a modest price. Some rooms have kitchenettes ($5 extra); all have TVs. Singles $30; doubles $37. Key deposit $2.

CAMPING

Redwood National Park offers several backcountry campsites; all are free and accessible only by hiking a short distance from roads or parking lots. **Freshwater Spit Beach,** just south of Orick, the only oceanside campground in the area, has pit toilets and no water. The 14-night max. stay is strictly enforced. Tent area is complete with evening bonfires and drum circles; RV sites also available (free, but $5 donations appreciated). **Nickel Creek campground,** at the end of Enderts Beach Rd. outside of Crescent City, has five sites overlooking the ocean with toilets but no showers or water. **Demartin campsite** is on a redwood prairie and can be reached by parking at U.S. 101 mile marker 14.42 and hiking ½ mi. **Flint Ridge,** off the end of Klamath Beach Rd., has water and toilets but no showers. Exit U.S. 101 and head towards the ocean—no signs posted.

State Park Campsites (464-9533), are all fully developed and easily accessible. The fee is $16 and reservations (necessary in summer) can be made by calling DESTINET (800-436-7275). North of Crescent City on I-199 is the **Jedediah Smith State Park.** Amenities include showers, water, restrooms, picnic tables, and grills. Campfire programs and nature walks also offered. In the **Del Norte Coast State Park,** camping is at **Mill Creek Campground,** where the ocean views are magnificent. Amenities are the same as above, and the ocean view is magnificent. There is usually space available. Camping in **Prairie Creek State Park** is possible at **Elk Prairie** and **Gold Bluffs Beach,** where meadows of elk serenely graze (hot showers). There are also several campgrounds in **Six Rivers National Park** (457-3131). **Big Flat Campground** is 14 mi. up South Fork Rd. off I-199. There are no hookups, but it's near the Smith River and free. **Grass Flat** is 4 mi. east on I-199 and has vault toilets and water.

FOOD

There are more picnic table sites than restaurants in the area, so the best option for food is probably **Orick Market** (488-3225), which has reasonably priced groceries (open Mon.-Sat. 8am-7pm, Sun. 9am-7pm). In Crescent City, head to the 24-hour **Safeway** in the shopping center on U.S. 101 (M St.) between 2nd and 5th. **Alias Jones,** 983 3rd St. (465-6987), is known for serving hearty portions, bizarre tofu smoothies ($3.50), sweet treats, and unusual sandwiches with salad ($5-7; open

Mon.-Fri. 7am-4pm). **Beachcomber Diner** (464-2205), on U.S. 101 just south of
Crescent City, serves fresh seafood with panoramic coastal views. Decor includes
plastic seagulls and harpoons. Red snapper ($9.50) and razor clams ($11.50) are
killer (open mid-Feb.-Oct. Thurs.-Tues. 5-9pm). The **Palm Cafe** (488-3381), on U.S.
101 in Orick, dishes out basic diner food to local boys in rattlesnake cowboy hats
(head and tail still attached), but visitors are also welcome. Old Maid Plate with 2
eggs and a stack of pancakes ($5). Homemade fruit, coconut, and chocolate pies are
positively delicious (open daily 4:45am-8pm).

SIGHTS AND ACTIVITIES

In the park, fruits and berries can be gathered for personal consumption, but all
other plants and animals are protected—even feathers dropped by birds of prey are
off limits. **Fishing licenses** are required for fresh and saltwater fishing, and there are
minimum-weight and maximum-catch requirements specific to both. One-day
licenses $23. Call the ranger station or License and Revenue Office (707-464-2523).

You can see Redwood National Park in just over an hour by car, but the redwoods
are best experienced by foot. The park is divided into several regions, each of which
have information centers and unique attractions. The National Park Service con-
ducts a symphony of organized activities for all ages; a detailed list of junior ranger
programs and nature walks is available at all park ranger stations (see **Practical
Information,** p. 348) or from the **Redwood Information Center** (488-3461). Hikers
should take particular care to wear protective clothing—**ticks** and **poison oak** thrive
in these deep, dark places. After hiking, inspect your body, particularly your lower
legs, scalp, and any area covered by tightly-fitting garments (like socks) for ticks,
which can cause Lyme disease (see **Animal- and Insect-Borne Diseases,** p. 13). If
you suspect you have exposed yourself to poison oak, remove and wash your
clothes and wash your skin immediately with Fels Naphtha Soap (call TeleNurse at
445-3121), and God have mercy! **Roosevelt elk** roam the woods, and are interesting
to watch but dangerous to approach since invaders of their territory are promptly
circled and trampled. Also be on the lookout for the **black bears** and **mountain lions**
that inhabit many areas of the park. Before setting out, get advice and trail maps at
the visitors center.

Orick Area

The Orick Area covers the southernmost section of Redwood National Park. Its **visitors center** lies about one mile south of Orick on U.S. 101 and ½ mi. south of the
Shoreline Deli (the Greyhound bus stop). The main attraction is the **Tall Trees
Grove,** which, if the road is open, is accessible by car to those with a permit (available at the visitors center; free). A minimum of three to four hours should be
allowed for the trip. From the trailhead at the end of Tall Trees Access Rd. (off Bald
Hills Rd. from U.S. 101 north of Orick), it's a 1.3 mi. hike (about 30min.) to the tallest redwoods in the park and, in fact, to the **tallest known tree in the world** (367.8
ft., one-third the height of the World Trade Center). If the road is closed, the hardy
can hike the 16 mi. round-trip **Emerald Ridge Trail** to see these giants.

Orick itself (pop. 650) is a friendly town, overrun with souvenir stores selling
"burl sculptures," wood carvings pleasing to neither eye nor wallet, but also has a
post office and some motels.

Patrick's Point State Park, 15 mi. south of Orick along U.S. 101, offers one of the
most spectacular views on the California coast, and merits a day or two from campers, boaters, and nature enthusiasts heading north to the redwoods (sites $16). Dur-
ing **whale-watching** season (Oct.-Dec. and March-May), the towering cliffs and
rocky geography of the point provide the best seats in the house for observing the
migration of gray whales. Bikers might enjoy the **Newton Drury Scenic Pkwy.,** a 31
mi. jaunt through old growth redwoods, or the magnificent **Coastal Trail,** a 15 mi.
paved ride along the ocean off Davison Rd. from the Prairie Creek Visitors Center.

Prairie Creek Area

The Prairie Creek Area, equipped with a **ranger station** and **state park campgrounds,** is perfect for hikers, who can explore 75 mi. of trails in the park's 14,000 acres. Starting at the Prairie Creek Visitors Center, the **James Irvine Trail** (4½mi. one way) winds through a prehistoric garden of towering old growth redwoods whose height is humbling to humans. Winding through **Fern Canyon,** where small waterfalls trickle down 50 ft. fern-covered walls, it ends at **Gold Bluffs Beach,** whose sands stretch for miles and elk-scattered miles. (The less ambitious can elk-watch on the meadow in front of the ranger station.)

The **Elk Prairie Trail** (1.4mi. one way) skirts the prairie and loops around to join the nature trail. **Revelation** and **Redwood Access Trails** were designed to accommodate people with disabilities. **Big Tree Trail** is an easy walk, and its 306 ft. behemoth is a satisfying substitute for those who don't want to make the long trek to the tallest tree in the world (see **Orick Area,** above).

Klamath Area

The Klamath Area to the north consists of a thin stretch of park land connecting Prairie Creek with Del Norte State Park. The town itself consists of a few stores stretched over 4 mi., so the main attraction here is the ruggedly spectacular coastline. The **Klamath Overlook,** where Requa Rd. meets the Coastal Trail, is an excellent **whale-watching site,** and offers a spectacular view.

The mouth of the **Klamath River** is a popular fishing spot (permit required; see **Sights and Activities,** p. 350) during the fall and spring, when salmon spawn, and during the winter, when steelhead trout do the same. **Coastal Drive** passes by the remains of the **Douglas Memorial Bridge,** where sea lions and harbor seals congregate in the spring and summer, and then continues along the ocean for 8 mi. of incredible views. Just north of Klamath is the **Trees of Mystery,** 5500 U.S. 101 (482-2251 or 800-638-3389), a one-mile walk through spectacular old growth and chainsaw sculpture. Just look for the 200 ft. Paul Bunyan next to the road. Kids may enjoy this spot but naturalists will wince at the noise (did we forget to mention that Paul speaks?) and the price. (Admission $6.50, children $3.50. Open daily 8am-6:45pm.)

Crescent City Area

Crescent City calls itself the city "where the redwoods meet the sea." In 1964, a wrathful Mother Nature took this literally, when a *tsunami* caused by oceanic quakes and leveled the city. Today the rebuilt town offers an outstanding location from which to explore the national park.

The **Battery Point Lighthouse** (464-3089), on a causeway jutting out of Front St., houses a **museum** open only during low tide. Ask guides about the resident **ghost,** and avoid becoming one yourself by keeping an eye out for the incoming tide (open Wed.-Sun. 10am-4pm, tide permitting; admission $2, children 50¢). From June through August, the National Park offers **tidepool walks** which leave from the Endert Beach parking lot (turn-off 4mi. south of Crescent City). Call 464-6101 for details. The **Coastal Trail** runs from Endert in the north to Tall Tree Grove in the south, passing cliffs, beaches, forests, and prairie along the way. Much of the trail is difficult, but the section near Endert Beach (part of the **Crescent Beach Trail**) is relatively easy. The trailhead is at the **Crescent Beach Information Center** on Endert Beach Rd., just off U.S. 101. A scenic drive from Crescent City along **Pebble Beach Drive** to **Point St. George** snakes past coastline that looks transplanted from New England. Craggy cliffs, lush prairies, and an old lighthouse add to the atmosphere.

Annual highlights include the **World Championship Crab Races** (800-343-8300), featuring races and crab feasts on the third Sunday in February. During **Easter in July** (487-8400), the lily completes its biennial bloom with a celebration. The **Weekend in Bear Country** (464-7441), is a mid-August beachfront festival.

Hiouchi Area

This inland region, known for its rugged beauty, sits in the northern part of the park along I-199 and contains some excellent hiking trails, most of which are in Jedediah Smith State Park. Several trails lie off Howland Hill Rd., a dirt road easily accessible from both U.S. 101 and I-199. From I-199, turn onto South Fork Rd. in Hiouchi and right onto Douglas Park Rd., which then turns into Howland Hill Rd. From Crescent City, go south on U.S. 101, turn left onto Elk Valley Rd., and right onto Howland Hill. The wheelchair-accessible **Stout Grove Trail** is a short (½mi.) and tourist-packed jaunt through lush redwoods. The trailhead is near the Hiouchi end of Howland Hill Rd. The **Mill Creek Trail** is a moderate 2½ mi. hike with excellent swimming and fishing, accessible from the Mill Creek Bridge on Howland Hill and from the Jedediah Smith campground. The more strenuous (but wimpy-sounding) **Boy Scout Trail** splits after 3 mi.; the right path goes to the monstrous Boy Scout Tree and the left ends at Fern Falls. Two miles west of Jedediah State Park on I-199 lie the **Simpson-Reed** and **Peterson Trails,** both of which are wheelchair-accessible. A tour map (25¢ at the ranger station) will guide you.

Six Rivers National Forest (457-3131), lies directly east of Hiouchi. The Smith River, the state's last major undammed river, rushes through rocky gorges as it winds its way from the mountains to the coast. The salmon, trout, and steelhead fishing is heavenly, and excellent camping is available on the banks. There are also numerous hiking trails throughout the forest. Call the ranger station for more info.

■ Brookings

Just north of the California-Oregon border on U.S. 101, the rugged Redwoods revisit the civilization that they left behind in Arcata. Brookings, however, is one of the few coastal towns that remains relatively tourist-free. Here, trinket shops do not elbow out hardware stores and warehouses, which makes Brookings more of a stopover on the way to its surrounding beaches and parks than a destination in itself. The beaches lie in a region often called Oregon's "banana belt" due to its mild climate: warm weather is not rare in January, and Brookings' beautiful blossoms bloom early. Strictly speaking, there are two towns here, separated by the Chetco River—Brooking on the north side and **Harbor** on the south. They share everything, including a chamber of commerce, and are referred to collectively as Brookings. Go figure. In town, U.S. 101 is called Chetco Avenue.

Practical Information The **Brookings Welcome Center,** 1650 U.S. 101 (469-4117), maintains an office just north of Brookings (open May-Sept. Mon.-Sat. 8am-6pm, Sun. 9am-5pm; April and Oct. Mon.-Sat. 8am-5pm). The town's **Chamber of Commerce,** 16330 Lower Harbor Rd. (469-3181 or 800-535-9469), is across the bridge to the south, a short distance off the highway. City **maps** are $1, but the Seaside Real Estate map is free (open Mon.-Fri. 9am-5pm and Feb.-Nov. Sat. 9am-1pm). The **Chetco Ranger Station,** 555 5th St. (469-2196), distributes information on the neighboring part of the **Siskiyou National Forest** (open Mon.-Fri. 8am-4:30pm).

The **Greyhound** station, 601 Railroad Ave. (469-3326), at Tanburk, sends two buses daily to Portland, $37; San Francisco, $46. (Open Mon.-Fri. 8:45am-noon and 4-6:30pm, Sat. 8:45am-noon.) The **Maytag Laundry** (469-3975), is known to locals as "The Old Wash House"; you'll find it in the Brookings Harbor Shopping Center (open daily 7am-11pm; wash $1, 10min. dry 25¢). The **post office,** 711 Spruce St. (800-ASK-USPS/275-8777), is open Monday to Friday 9am-4:30pm. The **ZIP Code** is 97415. The **area code** is 541.

Accommodations and Camping Motel rooms and campsites alike are costly in Brookings except in winter, when motel rates tend to drop about $10. The **Bonn Motel,** 1216 U.S. 101 (469-2161), is basic budget bedding. Its three low buildings have a row of hydrangeas lurking behind each room and a somewhat distant view of the ocean out front (singles $38; doubles $48; less in winter). Down the road, the **Beaver State Motel,** 437 U.S. 101 (469-5361), provides spiffier accommodations for a few dollars more. The bedspreads here actually match the curtains (one person $42, two people $49; two people, two beds $59; less in winter).

Harris Beach State Park (469-2021), at the north edge of Brookings, has 68 tent sites amid a grand natural setting. The beach looks across a narrow waterway toward a 21-acre hunk of uninhabited rock and pines known as **Goat Island.** The campground, set back in the trees behind the beach, is equipped with showers, hiker/biker sites ($4), and wheelchair facilities (sites $16, with full hookup $19; open year-round). Make reservations (800-452-5687) for stays between Memorial Day and Labor Day. For campsites off the beaten path, travel 15 mi. east of Brookings on North Bank Rd. to the charming **Little Redwood Campground.** In a forest alongside a burbling, scurrying-salamander-filled creek and the road, the campground has 15 sites ($6) with drinking water and pit toilet. Several other campgrounds along that road are free but have no water. For information, contact the Chetco Ranger District (see **Practical Information,** above).

Food A fishing town at heart, Brookings can batter up a good piece of flounder with the best of them. A number of salty seafood spots can be found near the harbor, among them the local favorite **Marty's Pelican Bay Seafoods,** 16403 Lower Harbor Rd. (469-7971), near the chamber of commerce. Join loggers and fisherfolk for pancakes that truly fill the whole pan ($3.75). All servings are more than generous; for a delicious, if morbid-sounding treat, try the $2 bowl of "graveyard stew" (open Mon.-Thurs. 4am-8pm, Fri.-Sat. 4am-9pm, Sun. 5am-3pm). For serious Mexican food, stick to the highway and head for **Los Amigos,** 541 U.S. 101 (469-4102). The plain, baby-blue exterior may not catch your eye immediately, but the $4.25 super burrito, $5.75 pork tamale, and 30¢ corn tortillas will startle your stomach, and domestic bottles are only $1.50 (open Mon.-Sat. 11am-8pm, Sun. noon-8pm).

Sights, Activities, and Events Brookings is known for its beautiful flowers. Downtown, in **Azalea Park,** large native and non-native azaleas, some more than 300 years old, encircle lawns with flowers from April and June. Two rare weeping spruce trees also grace the park's grounds. The pride of Brookings is its annual **Azalea Festival** (469-3181), held in Azalea Park during Memorial Day weekend. The **Chetco Valley Historical Society Museum,** 15461 Museum Rd. (469-6651), 2½ mi. south of the Chetco River, occupies the oldest building in Brookings and has exhibits on the patchwork quilts of settlers and Native American basketwork. The museum is hard to miss; just look for the **nation's largest cypress tree** in front (open March-Oct. Wed.-Sun. noon-5pm, Nov.-Feb. only Fri.-Sun.; admission $1, children 50¢).

If you're heading north from Brookings by bicycle, take scenic **Carpenterville Road,** the only highway out of town before U.S. 101 was built. The twisty 13½ mi. road features beautiful ocean views. **Boardman State Park** enfolds U.S. 101 for 8 mi. north of Brookings; overlooks and picnic sites provide great views of the coast. Thirty miles north of Brookings in **Gold Beach,** you can ride a mail boat up the **Rogue River. Mail Boat Hydro-Jets** (247-7033 or 800-458-3511) offers 64, 80, and 104 mi. daytrips. Whitewater trips last six to seven and a half hours and start at $30.

Northern Interior

Sleepy Gold Country, nestled east of Sacramento, is set in the heart of even sleepier farm country that extends northward for hundreds of miles. Life here is vastly different than along the fast-paced coast, and such a middle-America atmosphere comes as a welcome break to many who tire of the rigors of urban life. Much of Gold Country, especially the southern area, lives mesmerized by its own bygone days of lively prospecting. The small towns in the northern part of Gold Country are far removed from the less authentic "Main Street" scenes of the south, and the natural beauty of this region handsomely rewards exploration.

The Cascade Mountains interrupt this expanse of farmland to the northeast, where both ancient and recent volcanic activity has left behind a surreal landscape of lava beds, mountains, lakes, waterfalls, caves, and recovering forest areas. The calm serenity of the mountains matches that of the nearby farm country, but its haunting beauty draws visitors in a way the Central Valley cannot.

GOLD COUNTRY

In 1848, California was a rural backwater of only 15,000 people. The same year, sawmill operator James Marshall wrote in his diary: "This day some kind of mettle...found in the tailrace...looks like goald." In the next four years some 90,000 '49ers from around the world headed for California and the 120 mi. of gold-rich seams called the Mother Lode. Despite the hype, few of the prospectors struck it rich. Miners, sustained by dreams of instant wealth, worked long and hard, yet most could barely squeeze sustenance out of their fiercely guarded claims.

Many miners died of malnutrition. Mark Twain described the diet: "Beans and dishwater for breakfast, dishwater and beans for dinner. And both articles warmed over for supper." Poorly constructed mines and risky techniques killed many more eager prospectors. Still, the search continued with almost manic desperation. In Coloma, during one miner's funeral, a mourner spotted "color" (goald) in the open grave. In true California style, the coffin was quickly removed and all in attendance, including the preacher, took to the ground with pick and shovel.

Ultimately, California's gilded terrain proved most profitable to the greedy merchants who outfitted the miners. Prices were astronomical; bread sold for $1 a slice ($2 buttered). Five years after the big discovery, the panning gold was gone, and miners could survive only by digging deeper and deeper into the rock. In some instances, whole towns were destroyed in hopes of finding "color" underneath. All but a few mines were abandoned by the 1870s, along with most of the towns that had sprouted around them. Some of the towns were repopulated years later when new industries arose, or when it became possible to commute from homes in the hills to nearby cities with stronger economic foundations. A few of the old mines have since reopened; sophisticated chemical processing techniques reclaim gold from the discarded ore of previous decades.

Although gold remains in them thar hills, today the towns of Gold Country make their money mining the tourist traffic. Gussied up as "Gold Rush Towns," they solicit tourists traveling along the appropriately numbered Rte. 49, which runs through the foothills, connecting dozens of small Gold Country settlements. Prepare for a stomach-dropping (road) and jaw-dropping (vista) experience when traveling along this vein; travelers without an off-road vehicle should be careful of straying too far from the highway. Traffic from the coast connects with Rte. 49 via I-80 through Sacramento, which today serves as a supply post for tourists instead of the miners of the gold rush. If you tire of Gold Country lore, you're not alone, but don't despair. Vineyard touring, river rafting, and cave exploring are popular and don't involve the g-word. Most of Gold Country is about two hours from Sacramento, three hours from San Francisco.

■ Sacramento

Sacramento is the indistinctive capital of a highly distinctive state. In 1848, Swiss emigré John Sutter, fleeing a debtor's prison back home, purchased 48,000 dusty acres for a few trinkets from the Miwok tribe. His trading fort became the central pavilion for the influx of gold miners to the Valley in the 1850s. Gradually over the next century, mansions and suburban bungalows changed the landscape, paving the way for future residents Ronald Reagan and the Brady Bunch. Although still full of politicians and housewives, Sacramento is also home to a large queer community and a lively coffeehouse scene, centered around the city's youthful midtown. With an area population of 1.6 million and a well-developed downtown, the underdog city of California is still in the running for the trophy status of bustling metropolis. For now, however, Sacramento perches delicately between the quintessentially Californian excitement of the city to the west and the mountains to the east, and yet remains as cozy and slow as any midwestern town (especially in the summer, when temperatures can soar to 115 degrees, even in the shade of the tree-lined streets and parks). Don't let this slow pace fool you, though; Sacramento is plagued by big-city crime problems, so beware of wandering alone at night.

PRACTICAL INFORMATION AND ORIENTATION

Visitor Information: Sacramento Convention and Visitor Bureau, 1421 K St. (264-7777), at 15th. Small and congenial. Open Mon.-Fri. 8am-5pm. The **Beeline** (552-5252) gives recorded events information.

Airport: Sacramento International (929-5411), 12 mi. north on I-5. Cabs are expensive ($22-25 to downtown). Vans are cheaper ($9-10); find out more at the info desks.

Trains: Amtrak, 401 I St. (800-USA-RAIL/872-7245), at 5th. To: San Francisco ($11), Reno ($14), L.A. ($31-70), and Seattle ($84-156). Prices depend on availability. Terminal open daily 4:45am-11:30pm. Travelers should be careful in this area at night.

Buses: Greyhound, 715 L St. (800-231-2222), between 7th and 8th. Be careful at night. Luggage lockers. To: San Francisco ($12), Reno ($20), and L.A. ($35). Open daily 24hr.

Public Transportation: Sacramento Regional Transit Bus and Light Rail, 818 K St. (321-2877), near corner of 9th and K St. Provides transportation around town, although it is notoriously underused. Fare in center of city 25¢, outside destinations $1.25 (free transfer), over 61, 5-12, and disabled 50¢. Day passes $3.

Taxis: Old Checker Cab Company (457-2222). Checkered cab tops. 24hr. service.

Car Rental: Rent-A-Wreck, 500 12th St. (454-0912), at E St. $25 per day. First 100 mi. free. Need driver's license, credit card, and proof of insurance if under 21.

Bike Rental: American River Bike Shop, 9203 Folsom Blvd. (363-6271). Bikes $4 per hr., $20 per day. Grab a friend for a tandem ride—pedal less but pay more ($6 per hr., $30 per day). Open Mon.-Fri. 9am-7pm, Sat.-Sun. 9am-5pm.

Medical Services: U.C. Davis Medical Center, 2315 Stockton Blvd. (734-2011), at Broadway.

Emergency: 911.

Police: 813 6th St. (264-5471), at H St.

Post Office: 900 Sacramento Ave. (556-3410). Open Mon.-Fri. 8:30am-5pm. **ZIP Code:** 95605.

Area Code: 916.

Sacramento is located at the center of the Sacramento Valley. Five major highways converge on the city: **I-5** and **Rte. 99** run north-south, **I-80** runs east-west between San Francisco and Reno, and **U.S. 50** and **Rte. 16** bring traffic in from Gold Country. Numbered streets run north-south and lettered streets run east-west. The capitol building and its auxiliaries, a park, and endless cafes and restaurants occupy the **downtown** area.

ACCOMMODATIONS

Though Sacramento is saddled with motels, large conventions often take them over, making it difficult to find a room; for guaranteed lodging, reserve a month in advance. The cheap hotels that line **West Capitol Ave.** in nearby West Sacramento may be a bit seedy, so be choosy.

Sacramento Hostel (HI-AYH), 900 H St. (443-1691; fax 443-4763), at 9th. A fantastic place to stay in the city, whether or not you're on a tight budget. This newly opened facility looks more like an upscale, elegant B&B than a hostel, with its high sloping ceilings, grand mahogany staircase, stained glass atrium, frescoes, and lace curtains. The restored 4-story Victorian mansion (c. 1885) also boasts a huge modern kitchen and laundry room. Dorm-style rooms are unusually spacious, clean, and beautifully decorated. Check-in 7-9:30am and 5-10pm. Check-out 9:30am. Curfew 11pm, but it's no hassle to sign out a key and stay out later. Members $13 per night, nonmembers $16. Family and couple rooms available. Ask about group rates. Wheelchair accessible.

Sacramento Econo Lodge, 711 16th St. (443-6631 or 800-55-ECONO/553-2266), between G and H St. Recent remodeling puts it a cut above the standard fare; most rooms have hairdryers, refrigerators, free HBO, CNN, and ESPN. Check-in 24hr. Room with queen bed $40, with 2 single beds $47. Breakfast included.

Quality Inn, 818 15th St. (444-3980 or 800-645-7318). Recently renovated rooms are of a much higher quality than the exterior might suggest. Has a small pool that won't be used in a beer commercial any time soon, an airport shuttle, A/C, and TVs with HBO. Singles $49; doubles $59.

FOOD

Most cafes and restaurants are located on J St.or Capitol Ave. between 19th and 29th; the younger set go here for their cappuccino dates. For those who dare to venture into tourist territory, Old Sacramento is home to countless gimmicky restaurants, which tend to be more expensive.

Bernardo's, 2726 Capitol Ave. (443-1180), at 28th St. Small, artsy cafe is the ultimate in California hip. Both waitstaff and food are good-looking, and outdoor seating allows full appreciation of summer evenings. The interior doubles as gallery space, displaying the work of a different local artist each month. Delectable sandwiches, salads ($3.50), and soups ($2-3) change according to the chef's whim, but quality is always high. Open Sun.-Thurs. 7am-10pm, Fri.-Sat. 7am-11pm.

Paesano's Pizzeria, 1806 Capitol Ave. (447-8646), at 18th St. The smell makes you go "mmhhh." Their creative combination of sophisticated toppings (roasted almonds, garlic, pesto, fontina cheese, kalamata olives, among others) make Paesano's the best pizzeria in the competitive Sacramento market. Try their Caribbean pizza with rock shrimp and papaya (small $6.95). Similarly varied selection of salads and pasta. Open Mon.-Tues. 11:30am-9:30pm, Wed.-Thurs. 11:30am-10pm, Fri. 11:30am-10:30pm, Sat. 5-10:30pm, Sun. 4-9pm.

Pescado's, 2610 Fair Oaks Blvd. (483-3474). Decor is a funky mixture of Californian and Mexican surf culture; tin palm trees surround a wall-mounted VW bus, and the menu is written on a hanging surfboard. The casual student crowd looks as relaxed as if they were chillin' on a beach, and no wonder—the food is enough to send anyone to a blissful mental Baja. Try their trademark fish burrito ($3.15), or fresh chips with mind-blowing guacamole ($2.75). Open Mon.-Thurs. 11am-10pm, Fri.-Sat. 11am-11pm. No credit cards.

Lemon Grass Cafe, 900 9th St. (442-7991), between I and J St. Good, cheap, convenient Thai/Vietnamese-influenced chow. Hot dishes $5-6, cold salads $3, Thai iced tea $1. Hot dishes served from 11:30am, the same time the yuppie deluge arrives. Open Mon.-Fri. 7:30am-4pm.

SIGHTS

The **state government** rules over the sights in Sacramento. Stormy debates about immigration, welfare, water shortages, secession, and more rage daily amidst a public audience in the elegant **State Capitol** (324-0333), at 10th and Capitol. You can also take one-hour tours of the stately building; free tickets are distributed in room B27 on a first-come, first-served basis starting 30 minutes before tour time (tours daily 9am-4pm, on the hr.). Colonnades of towering palm trees and grassy lawns make **Capitol Park** a welcome oasis in the middle of downtown's busy bureaucracy and a popular place for youthful gatherings. The **Old Governor's Mansion** (324-0539), at 16th and H St., was built in 1877 and served as the residence of California's governor and his family until Governor Ronald Reagan requested more spacious accommodations (open daily 10am-4pm, tours on the hr.; admission $2, ages 6-12 $1, under 6 free).

Old Sacramento, the city's biggest tourist attraction, has been refurbished to resemble the way it looked in the late 19th century, but suspension of disbelief is definitely put to the test here. Wooden sidewalks and horse-driven carriages are not enough to mask the roaring freeway overhead, the skyscrapers in the background, or the shrieks emanating from the pricey boutiques. If you feel trapped in this tourist miasma, you may want to check out the two area museums. The **California State Railroad Museum** (552-5252, ext. 7245), at 2nd and I St., exhibits 23 historic locomotives (open daily 10am-5pm; admission $6, ages 6-12 $3, under 5 free). The same ticket grants admission to the **Central Pacific Passenger & Depot Station,** at 1st and J St., a reconstruction of a Golden Age station.

Art lovers should stop by the **Crocker Art Museum,** 216 O St. (264-5423), at 3rd St., which exhibits 19th-century European and American oil paintings, Asian art, and contemporary California art. (Open Tues.-Sun. 10am-5pm, Thurs. 10am-9pm. Admission $4.50, ages 7-17 $2, under 7 free. Tours available.)

The original **Tower Records** (444-3000), looms at the corner of 16th and Broadway (open daily 9am-midnight). One of the world's largest music chains, Tower began in 1941 when Russ Solomon sold records in the back of his dad's drugstore. Today, the Tower complex includes a movie theater, a cafe, a bookstore, and a video store (see **Entertainment,** p. 357).

If you'd rather be outdoors, rent a raft from **American River Raft Rentals,** 11257 S. Bridge St. (635-6400), Rancho Cordova, 10 mi. east of downtown on U.S. 50 (open daily 9am-6pm; 4-person raft $30). Exit on Sunrise Blvd. and take it north 1½ mi. to the American River, where the water isn't white, but where there's fun in the sun. Beware of rafters armed with water guns who ruthlessly spray sunbathers.

The **American River Bike Trail and Parkway,** spanning 31 mi. from Discovery Park to Folsom Lake, is a nature preserve where the valley oaks mask cemented suburbia without obscuring the downtown skyline. Four million people a year visit to cycle, jog, swim, fish, hike, and ride horseback on the secluded banks. Picnic areas and emergency phones are scattered along the way. As in any big city public park, it is wise to stay in populated areas and to visit during daylight.

ENTERTAINMENT AND SEASONAL EVENTS

Tower Theater (443-1982), at 16th and Broadway St., across from Tower Records. Though it shows more foreign and art flicks than Hollywood blockbusters, the neon spire is trademark Californian glitz. Tickets $7, matinees $4. For an after-movie drink, stop into the **Tower Cafe,** 1518 Broadway St. (441-0222), where young alterna-types flock to sip wine or guzzle beer. Open Sun.-Thurs. 8am-midnight, Fri.-Sat. 8am-1am. Kitchen closes earlier.

The Original Java City, 1800 Capitol Ave. (444-5282), is one of several neo-Bohemian coffee shops that grace downtown. Caters to anyone with a java joint in their body; punks and aesthetes sip cappuccino ($1.75) on the same street corner. Open Mon.-Thurs. 6am-10pm, Fri.-Sat. 6am-11pm, Sun. 6:30am-10pm.

Old Ironsides (443-9751), at 10th and S St., is a popular club with both the gay and straight communities. Half of the space is devoted to live music (cover free-$5); the other half is a lively bar with cheap beer (drafts $1.50). Open daily 8am-2am.

Faces, 2000 K St. (448-7798). The slickest of the many gay establishments in the area, this high-stylin' club offers 3 bar areas, a capacious dance floor, an ice cream stand, and the occasional wet jockey short contest. Open daily 3pm-1:45am.

Rubicon Brewing Company, 2004 Capitol Ave. (448-7032). Home of India Pale Ale, the winning brew at the 1989 and 1990 American Beer Festivals (pint $2.75). Cool, laid-back microbrewery with top-quality food. The brewing process can be watched from the dining area. Sandwiches $4-7. Open Mon.-Thurs. 11am-11:30pm, Sat. 8:30am-12:30am, Sun. 8:30am-10pm. Kitchen closes earlier.

Summer is the season when sleepy Sacramento wakes up with free afternoon concerts and cheap food. The Friday edition of the *Sacramento Bee* contains a supplement called *Ticket,* which gives a run-down of events, restaurants, and night spots. For weekend music and events, sift through the free weeklies, such as *Sacramento News and Review* and the *Suttertown News.*

Every Thursday night from late May to October, the **Thursday Night Market** takes over the K St. Mall, between 7th and 13th, with fresh produce stands and craft booths. This multi-block party entertains 15,000 people with live music and local color, forcing young and old to throw their shoes off and twist the night away.

Sacramento also hosts one of the world's largest Dixieland Jazz festivals, the **Dixieland Jazz Jubilee** (372-5277), held every Memorial Day weekend, with over 100 bands from around the world luring in the crowds. Local groups perform **Shakespeare in the Park** (277-6060) during summer evenings (June-Aug.) at William Land Park. Picnics are popular, but so are mosquitoes so bring repellent. The agriculturally oriented **California State Fair** (263-3000) takes place from mid-August to early September. If the combination of spinning rides and fairway food gets you down, watch amusements like pig races, where you can bet on your fave slab of bacon.

■ Davis

Davis digs its eco-passions into the dirt 13 mi. west of Sacramento off I-80. Leading the way for the area in energy conservation (they even have energy-saving traffic signals), veganism, flute-playing, and tie-dye wearing, Davis folk come out in full force at events such as the Whole Earth Festival (late May). And they come out on bicycles—there are more bicycles per capita (1 per person) than any other city in the U.S. Town activity is centered around the University of California at Davis. In the summer, students head home and the pace of life slows, although the remaining summer students and bicycling Sacramentans don't let it die away entirely.

Practical Information Visitor information is at the **Chamber of Commerce,** 228 B St. (756-5160; open Mon.-Fri. 9am-noon and 1-5pm), as well as at the **UC Davis Information Center,** in the Griffin Lounge on campus (752-2222, campus events 752-2813; open Mon.-Fri. 9am-4pm). **Amtrak,** 840 2nd St. (800-USA-RAIL/872-7245 or 758-4220), offers one-way tickets to Sacramento ($5) and San Francisco ($12). **Unitrans** (752-2877) connects downtown and the UCD campus (50¢). **Yolo Bus** (371-2877) services Davis and Sacramento ($1, disabled 50¢, kids 25¢; daily and monthly passes available). You can **rent a bike** at **Wheelworks,** 247 F St. (753-3118), $8 per day, $4 each extra day. Open Mon.-Sat. 10am-6pm, Sun. 10am-5pm. The **post office,** 2020 5th St. (753-3496), is open Mon.-Fri. 8:30am-5:30pm, Sat. 10am-1pm. The **ZIP code** is 95817. The **area code** is 916.

Accommodations and Food Motels in Davis do not come cheap, and during university events you'll be lucky to get a room. **Davis Inn,** 1111 Richards Blvd. (756-0910), at the I-80 and Richards Exit, is located six blocks from campus, has recently remodeled rooms, and a fairly large pool. (Doubles with queen bed $70, with king bed $75.)

Those looking to stock a picnic basket should check out the **Davis Food Co-op,** 620 G St. (758-2667), which has a colossal selection of organic produce, raw pasta, hummus, and veggie burgers (open daily 8:30am-10pm). **Caffé Italia,** 1121 Richards Blvd. (758-7200), draws crowds for large portions of pasta ($7-10), pizza ($5 and up), and salads ($5.50 and up). Hanging garlic decorations (vampires beware) and cool wooden interior lend to the Italian atmosphere (open Mon.-Thurs. 6am-10pm, Fri.-Sat. 6am-11pm, Sun. 7-10pm.) **Murder Burger,** 720 Olive Dr. (756-2142), serves massive hamburgers ($2.95)—they're to die for. The thick milkshakes ($2.56) are also popular (open Mon.-Tues. and Thurs.-Sat. 10am-8pm, Fri. and Sun.10am-9pm).

Sights and Activities The **University of California at Davis** is the largest campus (area-wise) in the UC network, and also one of the nation's finest agricultural universities. When they aren't in class, students hang out at **The Graduate,** 805 Russell Blvd. (758-4723), in the University Mall. The Grad's cavernous dining area has eight large-screen TVs, video games, a pool table, outdoor tables, and thematic dance party at night (open daily 10:30am-2am).

The town is laced with more than 40 mi. of bike trails. Rock-climbing is also popular. **Rocknasium,** 720 Olive Dr. (757-2902), next to Murder Burger, offers climbing for all levels. The 70 routes include a bouldering cave and extensive lead climbing. (Open Mon.-Fri. 11am-11pm, Sat.-Sun. 10am-9pm. Admission $10, students $8. Equipment rental $8, students $6.)

■ Sonora

The ravines and hillsides now known as Sonora were once the domain of the Miwok Indians, but the arrival of the '49ers transformed these Sierra foothills into a bustling mining camp. In its Gold Rush heyday, Sonora was a large and prosperous city that vied fiercely with nearby Columbia for the honor of being the richest city of the southern Mother Lode. The drive to Sonora takes about two hours from Sacramento and three and a half hours from San Francisco.

Practical Information and Orientation The **visitors center,** 55 W. Stockton Rd. (533-4420 or 800-446-1333; fax 533-0956), offers several local publications (open Mon.-Sat. 10am-5pm). **Tuolomne General Hospital,** 101 Hospital Rd. (533-7100), offers 24hr. emergency service. In an **emergency,** call 911 or the Sonora **police** (532-8141). The **post office** is at 781 S. Washington St. (532-4304; open Mon.-Fri. 8:30am-5pm, Sat. 10am-2pm). The **ZIP Code** is 95370. The **area code** is 209.

Sonora's layout is complicated by the fact that two highways enter the town from three directions. **Washington St.** runs north-south through town, and at the north end becomes **Rte. 49** North. At the south end, it branches, and the east fork (Mono Way) becomes **Rte. 108.** Midtown, Washington St. intersects **Stockton St.,** which becomes Rte. 49 South.

Pannin' fer Goald I: Theory

It's easy and fun to pan for gold. Let's Go offers a quick, two-part course which will provide all the mental equipment you'll need. Once you're in Gold Country, find one of many public stretches of river. You'll need a 12- or 18-inch gold pan, which will be easily found at local stores. Dig in old mine tailings, at turns in the river, around tree roots, and at the upstream ends of gravel bars, where heavy gold may settle. Swirl water, sand, and gravel in a tilted gold pan, slowly washing materials over the edge. Be patient, and keep at it until you are down to black sand, and—hopefully—gold. Gold has a unique color. It's shinier than brassy-looking pyrite (Fool's Gold), and it doesn't break down upon touch, like mica, a similarly glittery substance. Later, we'll practice this technique (see p. 361).

Accommodations The **Sonora Hostel (HI-AYH),** 11800 Columbia College Dr. (533-2339), on the Columbia College campus 5 min. from Sonora, provides clean, comfortable quads with large bathrooms and kitchenettes, in addition to a recreation room, an on-site mini-mart, and laundry facilities (dorms $12, nonmembers $15). The **Rail Fence Motel,** 19950 Rte. 108 (532-9191), 5 mi. east of Sonora, has 8 rooms with kitschy 70s decor, a pool, and 10 acres of hiking trails (singles $35, weekends $43; doubles $49). The **Sonora Inn and Motel,** 160 S. Washington St. (532-2400), was built in 1896 in a Spanish stucco style. Rooms in the inn are considerably larger and somewhat more modern than those in the motel, and the inn has a saloon, tea room, restaurant, hidden passageways, and balconies (motel singles $59, weekends $69; inn singles $69, weekends $79.)

Food The **Diamondback Grill,** 110 S. Washington St. (532-6661), in the center of Sonora's old-town district, is a tiny, hiply-decorated restaurant that offers big portions and tasty specialty burgers ($5-6), like the pepper jack (open Mon.-Sat. 6am-9pm, Sun. 8am-3pm). A curious but excellent place is **Wilma's Cafe,** 275 S. Washington St. (532-9957), named for the wooden pig perched atop the pie case. Pig out on Wilma's hearty and delicious pies, hickory-smoked barbecue burgers ($5-8), and pancakes (open Sun.-Thurs. 6am-10pm, Fri.-Sat. 6am-midnight).

Sights **Columbia State Park** (532-4301), once the "Gem of the Southern Mines," is on Parrott's Ferry Rd. Rich in placer gold (loose gold found in rivers and dirt), Columbia once supported 5000 people and 150 saloons, shops, and other businesses. Entirely preserved as an 1850s mining town, Columbia now prospects for tourist dollars. In the spirit of authenticity, automobiles are banned, routed instead to large parking lots on the southern and western sides of town. Dedicated to the practice of thinly veiled artifice, the "miners" peel off their beards after work, the outhouse is nailed shut, and the horse and buggy carriages spend the nights in a nearby parking lot. Park visitors can pan for gold and peer into the town's numerous historical buildings as part of the "living history" environment. Entrance to the park and its **mining museum** is free.

■ Southern Mines

Unsuspecting Calaveras County turned out to be literally sitting on a gold mine—the richest, southern part of the Mother Lode—when the big rush hit. Over 550,000 pounds of gold were extracted from the county's earth. A journalist from Missouri by the name of Samuel Clemens, a hapless miner but a gifted spinner of yarns later known as **Mark Twain,** allegedly based *The Celebrated Jumping Frog of Calaveras County*—his first hit—on a tale he heard in a local bar. Life has since imitated (or in this case, capitalized on) art—Calaveras has held annual frog-jumping contests since 1928. Thousands of people gather on the third weekend of May for the festive affair.

Not much is left of the towns that were haphazardly erected by gold-seekers. What remains, however, are not the picturesque ghost towns that Hollywood has made famous, but scattered rural communities whose crumbling buildings are just barely held up by the many commemorative plaques. Calaveras County hops with small towns. **San Andreas,** at the juncture of Rte. 49 and Rte. 26, is the county hub and population center, but it isn't very big. Scattered throughout the rest of the county are **Jackson, Sonora, Columbia, Murphy's, Angels Camp,** and other small towns. Just south of Angels Camp on Rte. 49 is **Tuttletown,** Mark Twain's one-time home, now little more than a historic marker and a grocery store. **Mokelumne Hill,** 7 mi. north of San Andreas, is not a ghost town but rather a ghost story town—its modern claim to fame is an affinity for spooky tales.

The real attractions of Calaveras County are the natural wonders, not the abandoned towns. About 20 mi. due east of Angels Camp on Rte. 4 lies **Calaveras Big Trees State Park** (795-2334; open dawn-dusk; day use $5). Here the *Sequoiadendron giganteum* (Giant Sequoia) reigns not so much with height (like the Redwoods on the coast) but with might; the *giganteum* is the largest living creature to

NORTHERN INTERIOR

ever inhabit the earth. Phat. The North Grove Trail (1mi.) is wheelchair accessible and heavily trafficked. Though all of the fenced-off sequoia are impressive, the giantism seems magnified from inside one tree's buggy-sized, walk-through entrance. The less traveled, more challenging South Grove Trail (4mi.) better captures the forest's beauty and timelessness. The park also offers swimming in Beaver Creek and camping (sites $14 with hot showers); reserve through DESTINET (800-365-2267). The snow comes early (sometimes Sept.) and leaves late (mid-April) at Big Trees, so plan to visit in the summer or bring a hefty pair of snowshoes. Summertime visitors should prepare for gnats and mosquitoes.

Calaveras County boasts gargantuan natural wonders below ground as well as above. **Moaning Cavern** (736-2708), 10 mi. southeast of Angels Camp, is a vertical cave, which can be viewed by descending the 236 steps or by rappelling 180 ft. down into the cave (they used to just use a bucket, so be thankful for modern equipment). Either way, the steep stairs are the only way up at the end and it's a rigorous climb. The hour-long tour of the caves includes morbid interpretations of the moaning cavern formations, like the "screaming skull" (stairs $6.75, ages 3-13 $3.50; rappelling $35 first time, half-price each additional time; open daily 9am-5pm). **Mercer Caverns** (728-2101), 9 mi. north of Angels Camp off of Rte. 4 on Sheep Rd., offers hour-long walking tours of 10 internal rooms. Though not as dramatic as Moaning Cavern, the caves are nearly a million-years-old. (Open daily 10am-8:30pm. Tours every 15min. until 7:30pm. Admission $6, ages 5-11 $3, under 5 free.) **California Caverns** (736-2708), at Cave City, served as a naturally air-conditioned bar and dance floor during the Gold Rush—a shot of whiskey could be had for a pinch of gold dust. The caverns sobered up on Sundays for church services when one stalagmite served as an altar. The caverns are open for walking tours (admission $7.50, ages 3-13 $4) and "wild cavern expedition trips," which explore cramped tunnels, waist-high mud, and underground lakes for two to three hours (admission $75).

Calaveras County has been a producer of fine wines for nearly 150 years. Vineyards stretch along Rte. 49, and wineries abound near Plymouth. Most family-owned wineries offer (the best kind) free **wine tasting.** The **Stevenot Winery** (728-3436), 2 mi. north of Murphy's Main St. on Sheep Ranch Rd., is the county's largest facility (free tastings daily 10am-5pm). **Kautz Ironstone Vineyards** (728-1251), on Six Mile Rd. 1½ mi. south of Murphy's, stores wine in caverns hewn from solid rock (tours daily 11am-5pm).

■ Placerville

Back in 1849, Placerville was known as "Hangtown" because of the town's reputation for handing out justice speedily at the end of a rope. Now small and friendly, the town preserves rowdier times in its well-restored historic district, full of little cafes, diners, bakeries, and antique shops.

About one-third of the way from Sacramento to Lake Tahoe on **U.S. 50,** Placerville is strategically positioned to snare campers, boaters, and skiers. Most streets, including Main St., run parallel to U.S. 50. **Rte. 49** also bisects the town, running north to Coloma (10mi.) and Auburn, and south toward Calaveras County.

Practical Information The Chamber of Commerce, 542 Main St. (621-5885), offers county maps and info (open Mon.-Fri. 8am-5pm). An **ATM** is at River City Bank, 348 Main St. **Greyhound,** 150 Placerville Dr. (800-622-7200), is in a Shell station (open daily 8am-8pm). Buses head to Tahoe (4 per day, $18), Reno (4 per day, $20), and Sacramento (3 per day, $11). Rent a car at **Enterprise,** 583 Placerville (621-0866). Cars from $16 per day; ages 18-21 need proof of insurance, and under

25 pay a $7 per day surcharge. In an **emergency,** call 911. The **police** are at 730 Main St. (642-5210). The **post office** is at 3045 Sacramento St. (622-6443; open Mon.-Fri. 8:30am-5pm), south of U.S. 50. The **ZIP Code** is 95667. The **area code** is 916.

Accommodations, Food, and Sights While the motels in Placerville are of equivalent quality, the prices vary significantly. One of the best deals in this consistently overpriced town is the **National 9 Inn,** 1500 Broadway (622-3884). Comfy beds, spotless new rooms, and a friendly manager who allows guests to use the patio barbecue make this motel irresistible. (Singles $36; doubles $43-48.)

Forage for fresh food at the **Farmer's Market** in the Ivy House parking lot (Thurs. 5-8pm and Sat. 8am-noon). The historic **Placerville Coffee House,** 594 Main St. (295-1481), dates from 1858. High stone walls and numerous nooks and crannies (including a 150ft. walk-in mine shaft) make this a great place to grab a fresh fruit smoothie ($3.50) or espresso. Small stage upstairs hosts live rock, ska, and acoustic bands Thursday through Saturday. (Open Sun.-Wed. 7am-10pm, Thurs.-Sat. 7am-midnight.) **Sweetie Pies,** 577 Main St. (642-0128), is a cheery place known for its huge cinnamon buns, full espresso bar, and light lunches (sandwiches $6). Delicious homemade pie (slice $2.50) is as American as their picket fence (open Mon.-Fri. 6:30am-4pm, Sat. 7am-3pm, Sun. 7am-noon). For a true Dukes of Hazard experience, saunter into **Poor Red's** (622-2901), on El Dorado's Main St. 5 mi. south of Placerville on Rte. 49. Quite the Boss Hogg scene, this dusty place is always packed. Bartenders claim that over 52 tons of ribs ($9.50) were served here in only one year. Watch out for the two-glass "Golden Cadillac" ($3.25), supposedly the strongest drink in the country. (Open Mon.-Fri. 11:30am-2pm and 5-11pm, Sat. 5-11pm, Sun. 2-11pm.)

The hills around Placerville are filled with fruit; travelers with bicycle or car can tour the **apple orchards** and **wineries** off U.S. 50 on Carson Rd., North Canyon Rd., and Carson Dr. in the area known as **Apple Hill.** This association of farms is geared toward family recreation, offering apple picking and eating galore. Fishing, craft fairs, and **pumpkin hunts** also available; a complete listing and map of orchards is available from the Chamber of Commerce (see above). Locals claim that **Denver Dan's,** 4344 Bumblebee Ln. (644-6881), has the best prices, while **Kid's,** 3245 N. Canyon Rd. (622-0084), makes the best apple pie in the area. Most of the orchards are open only September to December, but **Boa Vista Orchards,** 2952 Carson Rd. (622-5522), is open year-round to sell fresh pears, cherries, and other fruits. For free wine tasting, try **Lava Cap Winery,** 2221 Fruitridge Rd. (621-0175; open daily 11am-5pm), or **Boeger Winery,** 1709 Carson Rd. (622-8094; open daily 10am-5pm). The best times to visit Apple Hill are spring (for flowers) and autumn (for apple harvest). **Gold Hill,** an area similar to Apple Hill, features peaches, plums, and citrus fruits.

■ Coloma

The 1848 Gold Rush began in Coloma at John Sutter's water-powered lumber mill, operated by James Marshall. Today, the town tries its darndest to hype this claim to fame, but the effort just makes tiny Coloma feel like Disneyland without the fun. **Accommodations** are sparse, so visitors will probably want to stay in Placerville.

The town basically revolves around the **James Marshall Gold Discovery State Historic Park.** (622-1116. Day-use fee $5 per car, seniors $4. Display your pass prominently in your car window or you will be ticketed.) Near the site where Marshall struck gold is a replica of the original mill. Picnic grounds across the street surround the **Gold Discovery Museum,** 310 Back St. (622-3470), which presents the events of the Gold Rush through dioramas and film. (Open daily 10am-5pm.)

The real reason to come to Coloma may be for the **whitewater rafting** opportunities. The American River's class III currents, among the most accessible rapids in the West, attract thousands of rafters and kayakers every weekend. Many of the rafting outfitters in Coloma and Placerville offer tours. Contact **Three Forks White Water Tours** (800-257-7238), **Ahwahnee** (800-359-9790), **Motherlode River Trips** (800-427-2387), **Oars Inc.** (800-346-6277), or **Whitewater Connection** (800-336-7238) for more info (half-day $69-79, full-day $89-99). Farther north along Rte. 49, the river flows into Folsom Lake and a deep gorge perfect for hiking and swimming.

■ Nevada City

New Age meets past ages in Nevada City, a town full of aging hippies and gaping tourists. Though the area's tourist board seems hell-bent on creating the illusion of yesteryear, the eccentricity of current residents belies the mining-town image, making the tiny burg feel like an old postcard buried in someone's crystal collection. Draped across several hills, Nevada City's winding streets contribute to its charm.

Many buildings in the town are of historical interest, including the dozens of **Victorian homes,** the **National Hotel,** and the **Firehouse** (interior open daily 11am-4pm). A free walking tour map is available from the **Chamber of Commerce** (265-2692 or 800-655-6569; open Mon.-Fri. 9am-5pm, Sat. 11am-4pm), at the end of Commercial St. The vast majority of historical buildings in Nevada City have not been preserved as museums but have been transformed into cappuccino bars, New Age bookstores, and vegetarian eateries.

Nevada City's health-conscious congregate to refuel at **Earth Song,** 135 Argall St. (265-9392), a natural foods market and cafe where vegetarians stock up on egg rolls, soy burgers, and organic produce (market open daily 8am-9pm; cafe open Mon.-Fri. 11am-9pm, Sat.-Sun. 10am-9pm). Another popular hangout is the **Mekka Cafe,** 237 Commercial St. (478-1517). Stop by to admire its leopard-skin decoration, browse among the books and chaises, sip coffee with the hip evening crowd, or munch on a damn fine artichoke heart, pesto, and brie sandwich ($5.75). (Open Mon.-Thurs. 7am-11pm, Fri. 7am-1:30am, Sat. 8am-1:30am, Sun. 8am-11pm.)

A dose of history awaits you at the **Empire Mine State Historic Park** (273-8522), on the Empire St. Exit off Rte. 20 west of town. Peering down into the cool, dark air of the mine shaft, you may wonder whether you'd go 11,000 ft. down for a chance at the big money—$120,000,000 of gold was obtained from the mine. The well-groomed estate and the woods surrounding it make peaceful hikes, but beware of poison oak, rattlesnakes, mountain lions, and horse poo. Living history tours are offered on summer weekends. (Park open in summer daily 9am-6pm; call for winter hours. Admission $3, children $1.)

The Nevada City area has trails for hikers and walkers of every taste and ability. The **Bridgeport State Park,** in Penn Valley off Rte. 20, features an easy 1¼ mi. hike over the largest covered bridge in the West, and around the river canyon. Search for a free souvenir during the park's gold-panning demonstration (for tips, see **Pannin' fer Goald I,** p. 359, and **II,** p. 361). Swimming holes are found along the Yuba River, which has been immortalized in song by countless folk artists, including the under-recognized Richard Ellers. Enjoy them to the fullest by hiking the Independence Trail, sunbathing, and watching nude hippies "drop acid and go whooping around."

The time to visit Nevada City is in the summer, when denizens beat the heat by celebrating in true small-town fashion. The 4th of July parade (held here on even years, and in neighboring Grass Valley on odd) is a classic, as is Constitution Day, when city legislature permits open alcohol containers in the streets. (Strange but true: Nevada City used to have more bars per capita than any other city in California.) The careful observer might even recognize a has-been or two: **resident celebrities** of note include Supertramp singer Roger Hodgeson and seminal Beatnik poet Gary Sneider.

■ The Butte Mountains

Six miles north of **Sierra City,** north of I-80, lie the Butte Mountains, one of the most beautiful, least traveled spots in California, offering amazing camping, hiking, and fishing possibilities. Five miles east of Sierra City, on the corner of Rte. 49 and Gold Lake Rd., sits the **Bassetts Station** (862-1297), an all-purpose establishment that has dispensed lodging, dining, gas, and supplies for over 125 years. Stop in for the low-down on camping, hiking, and fishing. (Open daily 7am-9pm.)

The Bassetts turnoff also leads to **Gold Lake,** 6 mi. from Rte. 49 at the four-way intersection. The adjacent **Gold Lake Pack Station** (836-0940), offers guided horseback rides around the area (from $22 per hr.). **Frasier Falls,** a noisy, 176 ft. cascade, can be reached via a dirt road that starts across from Gold Lake and leads to a parking lot, or by taking the paved drive 6 mi. past Gold Lake and 4 mi. to the parking lot. The falls are a half-hour walk from the parking lot. There are six campgrounds along the route from the Bassetts turnoff to Frasier Falls, all marked by signs. Sites are $10, lack showers, and are available on a first-come, first-camped basis.

The **Butte Mountains** themselves rise farther up Gold Lake Rd. amid a series of small alpine lakes. For trail access, take the Sardine Lake turn-off one mile north of Rte. 49, bear right past Sardine Lake and continue 1½ mi. past Packer Lake.

THE CASCADES

The Cascade Mountains interrupt an expanse of farmland to the northeast of Gold Country. In these ranges, recent volcanic activity has left behind a surreal landscape of lava beds, mountains, lakes, waterfalls, caves, and recovering forest areas. The calm serenity and haunting beauty of the Cascades draw visitors in a way that the Central Valley and Gold Country cannot.

■ Chico

Chico is small-town America; don't go out of your way to come, but if you happen to stumble upon it, you may enjoy the pervasive sense of tranquility. All is not calm, however: beneath the quiet surface lurks Chico State, one of the nation's foremost party schools. To many a gleeful visitor, the best thing about Chico is the cheap beer. Grab another one and rock out, hard core.

Practical Information Get tourist info at the **Chamber of Commerce,** 500 Main St. (891-5556), which has wall-to-wall brochures and a friendly staff. (Open Mon.-Fri. 9am-5:30pm, and also Sat. 10am-3pm in summer.) The **University Information Center** is at 898-4636. (Open Mon.-Thurs. 8am-4:30pm, Fri. 8-11am.) The **Amtrak** station (800-USA-RAIL/872-7245), is just a platform on Orange St. at 5th. Trains go to Sacramento (1 per day, $24) and San Francisco ($39; Amtrak bus $17.50). **Greyhound,** 450 Orange St. (343-8266), at the Amtrak station, sends buses 5 times per day to Sacramento ($13), Red Bluff ($10), and San Francisco ($32). Open Mon.-Fri. 8:30am-1:30pm and 3-5:30pm, Sat. 8:30am-2:30pm. **Enloe Hospital** (891-7300), is at W. 5th and Esplanade. **Emergency:** 911. **Police:** 1460 Humboldt Rd. (895-4911). The **post office** is at 550 Vallombrosa Ave. (343-5531; open Mon.-Fri. 8am-5:30pm, Sat. 9:30am-12:30pm). The **ZIP code** is 95927. The **area code** is 916.

Accommodations and Camping Thunderbird Lodge, 715 Main St. (343-7911), has large clean rooms and a great location in the heart of downtown next to Golden Waffle, which serves cheap, massive breakfasts. (Singles $35-$40; doubles $40-$45.) For outdoor sleeping, pick up a copy of the useful camping brochure at the Chamber of Commerce. It will doubtless direct you up to **Lake Oroville,** 30 mi. from Chico on Rte. 99 south (9mi. from Oroville Dam Exit), and its fishing, swimming, boating, and 35 mi. bike trail. **Bidwell Canyon** is very close to the water and camps mostly RVs (full hookup $20). **Loafer Creek** is more forested than Bidwell, with a beach and swimming area (sites $14; call 534-2409 for reservations).

Food and Cheap Beer There's a 24-hour **Safeway** at 1016 W. Sacramento Ave., and a **farmer's market** is held every Saturday in the parking lot at 2nd and Wall St. (7:30am-1pm). **Oy-Vey's,** 146 W. 2nd. St. (891-6710), at Broadway, is mobbed during the academic year. The "Hungry Man" breakfast (3 eggs, 4 sausages,

5 pancakes, ½ lb. home fries, and a bagel) was meant to be shared with a friend ($6.25; open daily 7am-3pm). **Woodstock Pizza,** 221 Nosmal Ave. (893-1500), has excellent pizzas and lunch specials ($4), and cheap beer galore. (Coors $2.95 per pitcher, Sierra $3.95. Bar open 9pm-midnight; restaurant open daily 11am-1am.) **Madison Bear Garden** (891-1639), at 2nd and Salem, houses a restaurant, bar, and dance hall within its bizarrely decorated walls. Charades as a burger joint during the day, but turns jumpin' at night, with pool tables, dancing (Thurs.-Sat. 9pm-1:30am; free), and occasional live bands. (Open Sun.-Wed. 11am-midnight, Thurs.-Sat. 11am-2am; kitchen closes at 10pm.)

Sights and Cheap Beer Check out the weekly *News and Review* for goings-on. Chico is lean on sights but keen on charm: the pedestrian-friendly streets welcome visitors with parks and shops. **Bidwell Park** (895-4972), is the nation's third-largest municipal park (2400 acres). Extending 10 mi. from downtown, it has been the set for several movies, including *Gone With the Wind* and Errol Flynn's *Robin Hood.* **Swimming holes** can ease the pain of a hot Chico summer: take Manzanita Ave. to Wildwood Ave. and follow a dirt road to Alligator or Bear Hole. Nearby, the historical Bidwell Mansion offers tours (daily from 10am-4pm; $2, children $1). A picnic next to the three-tiered **Honey Covered Bridge,** 5 mi. east on Humbug/Honey Run Rd., will fulfill any Robert-Kincaid-inspired fantasies. Inner tubing is popular among students. **Ray's Liquor,** 207 Walnut St. (343-3249), rents tubes ($2) and sells **cheap beer** to make the ride more thrilling. Cheap beer also flows at the **Sierra Nevada Brewing Co.,** 1075 E. 20th St., which offers tours of the brewery where California's favorite beer is made. (Tours Tues.-Fri. and Sun. 2:30pm, Sat. noon-3pm. Pub open Mon.-Thurs. 11am-9pm, Fri.-Sun. 11am-10pm.)

Although **Cal State Chico** isn't the most architecturally interesting of campuses, it has distinguished itself as a perennial favorite in *Playboy*'s list of the "Top Ten Party Schools." Raucous bashes rage during the term, but a party school of this caliber doesn't completely shut down in the summer. **University Information Center** (898-4636), offers more sedate campus tours Mon., Wed., Fri., and Sat. at 11:30am.

■ Red Bluff

Midway between Chico and Redding, Red Bluff perches on a brick-colored bank of the Sacramento River. This is a good place to fuel up for a jaunt into **Lassen Volcanic National Park** (40mi. away) or points north, but there's nothing to see in town. I-5 skirts Red Bluff's eastern edge, while Rte. 36 (running east to Lassen Park) and Rte. 99 (leading south into the Sacramento Valley) merge with the main streets of town.

Practical Information Get information at the **Chamber of Commerce,** 100 N. Main St. (527-6220; open Mon.-Thurs. 8:30am-5pm, Fri. 8:30am-4:30pm). There is an **ATM** at **Bank of America,** 1060 Main St. (800-346-7693). **Greyhound,** 1425 Montgomery Rd. (527-0434), has service to Redding ($8), Chico ($10), Sacramento ($22), and San Francisco ($32). (Station open Mon., Wed., and Fri. 8:30am-4:30pm, Tues. and Thurs. 8:30am-6:30pm, Sat. 8:30am-3pm.) For **road conditions,** call 800-427-7623. **St. Elizabeth Hospital** is on Sister Mary Columbia Dr. (529-8000). In an **emergency,** call 911. The **police** are at 555 Washington St. (527-3131). The **post office** is at 447 Walnut St. (527-2012), at Jefferson (open Mon.-Fri. 8:30am-5pm). The **ZIP code** is 96080. The **area code** is 916.

Accommodations **Sky Terrace Motel,** 99 Main St. (527-4145), looks like a well-kept ski lodge and offers TV, A/C, petite pool, non-smoking rooms, and coffee makers (singles $26; doubles $32). **Crystal Motel,** 333 S. Main St. (527-1021), has small rooms with soft beds, TV, and A/C. (Singles $22; doubles $24.) If you—like Wayne and Garth—fear change, you can go to Red Bluff's very own **Motel 6,** 20 Williams Ave. (527-9200; singles $33, weekends $35; doubles $36, $50). Nearby Lassen offers superior **campsites** (see p. 367), so it's unnecessary to camp in Red Bluff.

Food Rte. 99 blossoms with **orchards** and **roadside stands** selling fresh produce: peaches, apricots, kiwi, cantaloupe, and plums in summer; pistachios, almonds, walnuts, and apples in fall. Fresh produce also blooms at the **farmer's market** in the Wal-Mart parking lot on S. Main. (Open June-Sept. Wed. and Sat. 8am-noon.) Red Bluff restaurants are generally disappointing; stock up on groceries instead. For that budget-travel staple, the big American breakfast, try **The Feedbag**, 200 S. Main St. (527-3777). Looks and tastes like a Denny's, and their Ranch Hand Breakfast (2 eggs, hash browns, 4 sausages, and 4 slices of toast for $4.75) with bottomless cup o' Joe (70¢) won't let you down. (Open Mon.-Sat. 6:30am-8:30pm, Sun. 7am-2pm.)

Sights and Seasonal Events A few miles north of Red Bluff on Adobe Rd., off Rte. 99, the **William B. Ide Adobe State Historic Park** honors the man who led the 1846 Bear Flag Rebellion. In a drunken fit, California's first and only president "seized" the town of Sonoma from equally inebriated Mexican officials and declared California's independence (open daily 8am-dusk; free). In April, Red Bluff makes it into the record books with the **Red Bluff Roundup**, "the world's largest two-day rodeo." The **Sun Country Fair** in mid-July includes live music, horseshoe tournaments, and a fiery chili cook-off. Call 527-6220 for more info.

■ Lassen Volcanic National Park

Tremors, streams of lava, black dust, and a series of enormous eruptions ravaged the land here in 1914, climaxing a year later when Mt. Lassen belched a 7 mi. high cloud of smoke and ashes into the sky. Even now, the destructive power of this still-active volcano is evident in Lassen's strange, unearthly pools of boiling water, the stretches of barren moonscape, and the occasional sulfur stench. But the eruptions also brought about a flourish of new growth in the form of natural flower beds and rampant animalia (fishing is fantastic in the lakes formed by the land's violent contortions). The park itself is open year-round (rangers ski in to work when the roads close), and is usually quiet until July, when hordes of families descend. The **park entrance fee** is $5 per vehicle or $3 per hiker. Admission is good for seven days.

PRACTICAL INFORMATION

Visitor Information: Lassen Volcanic National Park Headquarters (595-4444), in Mineral. Wilderness permits, knowledgeable rangers, and free newsletter listing trails, campgrounds, conditions, and history. While you're here, check snow conditions (a good idea even in July). Open daily 8am-4:30pm. **Loomis Museum** (595-4444 ext. 5180), by the northwest entrance, has maps, brochures, and exhibits. Open July-early Sept. daily 9am-5pm. **Hat Creek Ranger Station** (336-5521), is off Rte. 299 in Fall River Mills. **Almanor County Ranger Station** (258-2141), is off Rte. 36 in Chester.

Public Transportation: Lassen Motor Transit, (529-2722). Transportation from Red Bluff to Mineral on a mail truck (Mon.-Sat. at 8am). Return trip leaves at 3:30pm (one-way $10).

Emergency: 911.

Post Office: Mineral branch on Rte. 36 (open Mon.-Fri. 8am-12:30pm and 1-4:30pm); Shingletown branch on Rte. 44 (open Mon.-Fri. 8am-4:30pm). **ZIP Codes:** 96063 in Mineral and 96088 in Shingletown.

Area Code: 916.

ORIENTATION

Lassen Volcanic National Park is accessible by **Rte. 36** from Red Bluff to the southwest and **Rte. 44** from Redding to the northwest. Both drives are about 50 mi. **Rte. 89,** running north-south, intersects both roads before they reach the park and carries travelers through the scenic park area. It's the park's only through-road. **Mineral,** along Rte. 36, and **Shingletown,** along Rte. 44, are the "gateway" towns and good places to buy supplies. From the southeast (Susanville and the Lake Almanor area), take Rte. 36 west to the intersection with Rte. 89. **Chester,** the nearest spot for gas and supplies on the north shore of Lake Almanor, is on the way to Warney Valley and Juniper Lake, located in the park's southeastern corner. To the northeast, the Butte Lake region is accessible by a dirt road (marked by a sign) off Rte. 44.

Weather in Lassen is **unpredictable.** Some years, 20 ft. snowdrifts clog the main road until July; in other years, an early melt clears the road by April. Crazy as it may sound, it can snow any day of the year. Savvy travelers will call ahead and be prepared for a variety of temperatures. In the winter, there is decent skiing, but because roads are closed you may have to ski into the park itself.

CAMPING

Because of the chance of rockslides and lava flows, there are few permanent structures in the park. The nearest indoor accommodations are 12 mi. north in **Old Station.** Less costly motels are in **Redding** 370 and **Red Bluff** 365 to the west, and in **Chester** to the east. Fortunately, camping in the park is beautiful and abundant. Unfortunately, you may experience near-freezing night temperatures, even in August. Check the snow situation before you leave; campgrounds often remain closed well into the summer. The maximum stay is 14 days, except at Summit Lake, which limits visitors to one week. All sites are doled out on a first-come, first-camped basis; register on-site. The last two campgrounds listed are not accessible from Rte. 89.

North Summit Lake, 12mi. south of the Manzanita Lake entrance. Summit Lake's deep blue glitters through the sparse strands of pine trees surrounding 46 popular sites. Drinking water, flush toilets, no showers. Sites $12.

South Summit Lake, in the middle of the park, 12mi. south of the Manzanita Lake entrance. All 48 sites have the same views and facilities as North Summit, but no flush toilets. Lots of trails begin here. Be sure to bring a sleeping pad; the soil is rocky. Drinking water, pit toilets, no showers. Sites $10.

Manzanita Lake, just inside the park border, near the northwest entrance. All 179 sites have impressive views of Lassen Peak reflected in the lake. Always the first to fill. Drinking water, toilets, and showers. Sites $12.

Crags, used for overflow from Manzanita Lake (5mi. away), but all 45 sites are much nicer. Piped water and chemical toilets. Sites $8.

Southwest, near the entrance. A walk-in, hilly campground for those weary of waking to the sweet strains of their neighbor's car. Potable water and 21 sites near the visitors center and chalet. Trailhead to several hikes. Sites $10.

Juniper Lake, 13mi. north up a rough dirt road from Chester on the eastern shore of Juniper Lake. 18 sites. Pit toilets, fireplaces, lake water only. Sites $8.

Warner Valley, 17mi. up another dirt road from Chester (consult a ranger). 18 sites with pit toilets, piped water, and fireplaces. Very, very remote. Sites $10.

Backcountry camping is allowed one mile or more from developed areas and roads, with a free wilderness permit available at any park ranger station (see **Practical Information,** p. 366). Fires (including lighters and lanterns) are prohibited, as is the use of all soaps (including biodegradable ones) in the lakes. Avoid camping near Bumpass Hell, Devil's Kitchen, and other areas that suddenly spew boiling lava or hot steam. A list of restricted areas is available at ranger's stations (see p. 366).

Lassen National Forest surrounds the park, encompassing several developed campgrounds. A half-dozen, all with water and toilets but no showers, line Rte. 89 to the north for the first 10 mi. out of the park. **Big Pine** is the closest (19 sites). **Bridge** and **Cave** campgrounds have only trailer sites (but tents may be used if you don't mind bumpy ground). **Rocky** has eight dull tent sites with limited parking. All sites range from $6-11. For more info, call the Hat Creek Ranger Station (336-5521). Two campgrounds sit on Rte. 36 near the southwest park entrance, in the Almanor Ranger District (258-2141). To the west is **Battle Creek** (sites $12), and to the east **Gurnsey Creek** (sites $9). A number of campgrounds dot the southwestern shore of **Eagle Lake,** in eastern part Lassen National Forest. **Christie, Merrill,** and **Aspen Grove** have piped water and are in the Eagle Lake Ranger District (257-4188).

If you long for the creature comforts, try **Rim Rock Ranch** (335-7114), in Old Station on Rte. 44, 14 mi. off Rte. 89. Rustic cabins dating from the 1930s come with linens, utensils, and pots. (2-person cabin $40; 4-person $55; each additional person $5, up to a total of 6 people. Open April-Nov.)

FOOD

The budget Lassen meal consists of groceries bought in one of the outlying towns. For prepared fare, try the **Lassen Chalet** (595-3376), an inexpensive cafeteria-style restaurant and gift shop just inside the Mineral entrance to the park. Their large burgers ($5) are filling fuel. (Open daily 9am-6pm.) There is often a park volunteer at the chalet to answer questions. At the park's other end, the **Manzanita Camper Service Store** (335-2943), at the Manzanita Lake Campground, sells pricey groceries, plywood postcards, fishing licenses, guides, and maps (open daily 8am-8pm). There are hot **showers** next door (open 24hr.; 3min. 25¢). A **laundromat** is in the same building (open daily 8am-9pm; wash $1.50, 10min. dry 50¢).

SIGHTS AND HIKES

Lassen is very drivable: roadside sights are clearly numbered for tourists, and most are accessible from Rte. 89. Drivers can pick up the *Lassen Road Guide,* a booklet keyed to roadside markers, at any park entrance ranger station ($3.25). A comfortable drive through the park (including a few stops) should take about two hours, but allow a full day to accommodate short hikes.

Along Route 89 from South to North

From the south along Rte. 89, the first sight is **Sulfur Works,** where the earth hisses its grievances. The guard rails may prevent you from getting burned, but if the wind changes direction, you're likely to get a faceful of pungent mist. The boardwalk is easily accessible for handicapped visitors. A bit farther north, **Emerald Lake,** when partially thawed by summer sun, shimmers for a bright green, icy-cold 300 ft. around a snowy center. Swimming is fine for fish, but too cold (40°F) for the warm-blooded humans who may want to frolic with the fishies.

Things heat up again about ½ mi. past Emerald Lake. The 1½ mi. hike to **Bumpass Hell** wanders through the park's largest hydrothermal area. Pick up a guide (35¢) at the trailhead. Bumpass Hell is a massive cauldron of muddy, boiling, steaming water in which its discoverer lost his leg; to avoid any danger to your own life and limb, stay on the trail. In spite of year-round snow, the water appears to ever-boil at **Cold Boiling Lake** (4mi. farther north, closer to the King's Creek trailhead also known as marker #32) due to its placement above a flatulent fissure.

Mt. Lassen is the world's largest plug-dome volcano. From marker #22, it's a steep 2½ mi. trek to the 10,457 ft. summit (allow 4-5 hr.). Even if it's sunny and 90°F at the trailhead, take along extra clothes (especially a windbreaker) for the windy crest, as well as sunblock and water. Solid shoes are important too; 18 inches of snow can clog the upper 2 mi. of trail even in summer. **Brokeoff Mountain,** nearby, has a trailhead at marker #2 (allow 5hr.).

A less imposing hike starts at marker #32 and follows **King's Creek,** which either babbles or roars depending on the month and the previous year's snow. It's an easy two- to four-hour hike with great views of Lassen and the mountains.

The **Upper Meadow** by King's Creek and **Dersch Meadow** north of Summit Lake are good locations to spot grazing deer and circling birds of prey. The vast, ravaged area (markers #41, 44, and 50) on the northeast face was formed the last time Mt. Lassen erupted. The mountain is slowly healing, and scientists conduct research here in the hope of aiding the recovery of the Mt. Saint Helens area.

As you near the northwestern entrance, **Manzanita Lake** will be on your left. The trail around the lake is a simple and pleasurable day hike.

Overnight Hikes

Given the heavy year-round snow cover, much of Lassen is not suitable terrain for backpackers. Of the 150 mi. of trails (including a stretch of the **Pacific Crest Trail;** for more info, see **From Crest to Crest: the Trail of the West** on p. 409), only the **Manzanita Creek Trail,** near Manzanita Lake campground, and the **Horseshoe Lake** area, east of Summit Lake, are customarily dry by mid-June. Both make enjoyable overnight trips. Manzanita Creek Trail parallels a lovely creek which runs through rolling woodlands, bearing scant resemblance to the boiling cauldrons to the south. To the east, the Horseshoe Lake area is rich in ice-cold lakes and pine forests filled with deer. A number of challenging day hikes cut through the eastern area, with parking available near most trailheads.

By mid-summer, the shallow waters of Lakes Manzanita and Summit usually warm to swimming temperatures. Several lakes in the park have native **rainbow trout,** and Hat Creek is a renowned trout stream. A state license is required, and some areas may have additional rules (Manzanita, for example, has a "catch and release" policy). Be sure to check with the park rangers (see **Practical Information,** p. 366).

■ Near Lassen: Wilderness Areas

The following three wilderness areas are even less traveled than their neighboring Lassen. Pick up a free **wilderness permit** from the National Forest Service. Be sure to buy a topographic map of the area ($4) at one of the ranger stations—they are invaluable for finding trails or for figuring out what the heck you're staring at.

Caribou Wilderness borders the park to the east—for the easiest border access, take Rte. 44 or Rte. 36 to the A-21 road for 14 mi., then take Silver Lake Rd. to the **Caribou Lake Trailhead.** Its many quiet, clean lakes support water lilies and wildflowers in early summer, as well as hikers hungry for solitude. The more desolate **Cone Lake Trailhead** can be reached by turning onto F.S. 10, on Rte. 44 north of the A-21 intersection. For the ultimate in isolated beauty, make the trek to the **Hay Meadows Trailhead.** Take F.S. 10 from Rte. 36 (near Chester) and head north, then turn left after 14 mi. F.S. 10 can be very rough—you'll need a 4WD.

Thousand Lakes Wilderness (and all the trout in those lakes) can be accessed from F.S. 16 off Rte. 89. Seven miles from Rte. 89 the road forks; F.S. 16 continues to the left to **Magee Trailhead,** a strenuous trail which leads to Magee Peak (8594ft.) and deserted Magee Lake. Insect repellent is a must. An easier trail begins at the **Tamarack Trailhead** and travels to Lake Eiler via Eiler Butte. Going north, take F.S. 33 N25 and hook a left just after Wilcox Rd. When the road forks, turn left onto F.S. 33 N23Y. These 7 mi. of road require a 4WD. **Subway Cave,** off Rte. 89 about ¼ mi. north of its junction with Rte. 44, invites exploration of its 1800 ft. long lava tubes. The cave is pitch black and cool, and the footing is uneven, so bring a friend, sturdy shoes, a sweater, and a lantern or a strong flashlight (with extra batteries).

The spectacular **Ishi Wilderness,** named for the last survivor of a Yahi Yana tribe, is comprised of rugged terrain at a lower altitude, making it friendly to off-season exploration. Take Rte. 36 from Red Bluff 15 mi. to Plum Creek Rd. and turn right on Ponderosa Way. This rough road skirts the eastern edge of the wilderness, where most trailheads lie. Ishi is a series of river canyons with dense islands of Ponderosa pine and sunburnt grasslands in the south (very hot in the summer). **Mill Creek Trailhead** runs along the 1000 ft. canyon, where gentle waters await swimmers. Keep an eye out for red-tailed hawks and golden eagles. The Tehana Deer Herd, the largest migratory herd in California, spends its winters in Ishi (no hunting allowed). The **Deer Creek Trail** is another scenic and popular hike, with a trailhead at the southern end of the Ishi Wilderness on Ponderosa Way.

■ Redding

Woody Guthrie wrote "This Land Is Your Land" while in Redding in the 1930s. Anyone who spends any time in this sunbaked town will understand why Guthrie was so anxious to share the land—or even give it away. However, Redding's position at the crossroads of I-5, Rte. 299, and Rte. 44 and its plenitude of hotels and restaurants makes it a convenient supply stop for **Shasta Lake** 15 mi. north, **Lassen National Park** 48 mi. east, and the sublime **Trinity Wilderness** to the west.

Practical Information Plop down on the comfy couches and get informed at the **Visitors Center,** 777 Auditorium Dr. (225-4100), up Butte and over the freeway at the Convention Center interchange. (Open Mon.-Fri. 8am-5pm, Sat.-Sun. 9am-5pm.) Call the **Shasta Lake Ranger District,** 6543 Holiday Rd. (275-1589), for local conditions or camping info (open Mon.-Fri. 8:30am-4pm). There is an unstaffed **Amtrak** station at 1620 Yuba St. (800-USA-RAIL/872-7245). Buy your ticket on the train or through a travel agent. Trains leave once daily for Sacramento ($35), San Francisco (train and bus $50), and Portland ($99). **Greyhound,** 1321 Butte St. (241-2531), at Pine, has a 24 hr. terminal. Buses go to Sacramento (9 per day, $20); San Francisco (4 per day, $36), and Portland (9 per day, $50). **Enterprise,** 361 E. Cypress St. (223-0700), rents cars for $36 per day with unlimited mileage. (Must be 21 with major credit card; under 25 pay $7 per day surcharge.) A 24-hour **rape hotline** is at 244-0117. **Redding Medical Center,** 1100 Butte St. (244-5400), downtown, offers 24-hour care. In an **emergency,** call 911. The **police** are at 1313 California St. (225-4200). The **post office** is at 2323 Churn Creek Rd. (223-7502; open Mon.-Fri. 7:30am-5:30pm, Sat. 9am-2pm). The **ZIP Code** is 96049. The **area code** is 916.

Accommodations and Camping Pick up a free vacation planner in the visitors center before you head to a motel: it has a coupon for $5 off. The comfy **Colony Inn,** 2731 Bechelli Ln. (221-0562), adjacent to I-5, has big rooms and offers cable TV, free local calls, coffee and donuts, a pool, and a convenient location in a good section of town. (Singles $35; doubles $43; $5 discount for AAA members.) **Motel Orleans,** 2240 Hilltop Dr. (221-5432 or 800-626-1900), has spotless, large rooms, cable, A/C, and pool. (Singles $40; doubles $53.) **Oak Bottom campground,** Rte. 299 (241-6584), is 13 mi. west of Redding on beautiful Whiskeytown Lake, which has beaches and swimming areas. The camp has 105 sites, cold showers, and no hookups. (May-Sept. tents $16, RVs $14; Oct.-April $10, $8.) Make reservations through DESTINET (800-365-2267). If it's too late to go on to a park, try **Salt Creek campground,** just off I-5 on Salt Creek Rd. (238-8500), near houseboat-infested Shasta Lake and up a steep dirt road 20 mi. north of Redding. This commercial campground has laundry, pool, volleyball and basketball courts, showers, general store, and full hookups. (Tents $16; RVs $19; each additional person $3. 20% discount Sept. 15-May 1.)

Food The **Safeway Market,** 1191 W. Cypress St. (241-4545), at Pine, is a logical place to pick up fruits and cold cuts (open 24hr.). Buy your seafood at **Buz's Crab,** 2159 East St. (243-2120), next to Safeway. When local police officers eat there you know it's gotta be good or cheap, and Buz's is both, with fish and chips ($2-5), charbroiled snapper and swordfish ($6-9), and yummy salmon burgers ($4; open daily 11am-9pm). For breakfast, head on down to the **Wild Heifer Restaurant,** 1177 Shasta St. (241-2575), where the orange juice is squeezed fresh every day ($1) and the pancakes are always tasty ($5; open Tues.-Sat. 6:30am-2pm and 5-9pm, Sun.-Mon. 6:30am-2pm). For Mexican food, try **Tortilla Flats,** 2800 Park Marina Dr. (244-3343). You probably won't walk out saying "Olé," but the prices are decent considering the huge serving size. In addition to combination plates and great *chilis rellenos* (both $6), there are several vegetarian options. (Open daily 11am-10pm.)

■ Mount Shasta

You can see the rugged snow-capped top of Mt. Shasta from 100 mi. away. It's *that* big: 14,161 ft. to be exact (it used to be 14,162 ft. before some guy swiped the top rock). Maybe its gravity attracts people closer, because every summer thousands come to Mt. Shasta to gawk, climb, and commune.

Shasta Indians believed that a great spirit dwelled within the giant volcano, and modern day spiritualists are drawn to the mountain by its mystical energy. In 1987, thousands of New Age believers converged here to witness the great clerical event of Harmonic Convergence, which climaxed when a resident turned on her TV set and saw an angelic vision displayed on the screen. Others are drawn to the mountain for different reasons. Climbers come to challenge the ice-covered slopes, while overstressed yuppies are attracted by the region's fragrant air and peaceful atmosphere. The town of Mt. Shasta is moderately touristy in a New Age sort of way: vegetarian restaurants, spiritual bookstores, and Shasta pilgrims crowd the streets.

PRACTICAL INFORMATION

Visitor Information: Mount Shasta Visitors Center, 300 Pine St. (800-926-4865), has lots of brochures and info about the area. Open Mon.-Sat. 9am-5pm, Sun. 9am-3pm. **Shasta-Trinity National Forest Service,** 204 W. Alma St. (926-4511 or 926-4596, TDD 926-4512), is across the railroad tracks from the intersection of Alma St. and Mt. Shasta Blvd. Find out which campgrounds and trails are open, and grab maps, info, fire permits, and pamphlets. Climbers challenging Mt. Shasta must pick up **wilderness permits** (free) and **summit passes** ($15) here. Outside is a trail register that climbers and solitary hikers must sign. Open Mon.-Sat. 8am-4:30pm; closed Sat. Labor Day-Memorial Day.

ATM: American Savings Bank, 168 Morgan Way (800-788-7000).

Trains: Amtrak's nearest connection is at the unattended station in **Dunsmuir** (about 10mi. from Mt. Shasta), 5750 Sacramento Ave. (800-872-7245). Trains leave once daily for Portland ($91), Redding ($14), and San Francisco ($66).

Buses: Greyhound doesn't have a depot in town, but drivers may pick up and drop off passengers here if notified in advance. Depot in **Redding,** 1321 Butte St. (241-2531 or 800-231-2222), at Pine, about 60mi. away.

Public Transportation: The Stage (842-3531), offers minibus transit between Weed, Mt. Shasta (next to the Black Bean Diner in the Mt. Shasta Shopping Center), and Dunsmuir. Fare 90¢. Operates daily; call for times.

Car Rental: California Compacts (926-2519), at Mott-Dunsmuir Airport; take Mott Ave. from I-80. Compacts $30 per day, $170 per week. First 100mi. free, 24¢ per additional mi. Must be 21 with major credit card.

Equipment Rental: 5th Season, 300 Mt. Shasta Blvd. (926-3606). Very friendly and knowledgeable staff. Sleeping bags $18 per 3 days, each additional day $5; 2-person tent $28 per 3 days. Cross-country ski rental in winter. Bike rentals $5.50 per hr., $25 first day, each additional day $20 (helmet and pump included). Also rents mountain-climbing gear: crampons and ice axe $13 per day, $16 for 2-3 days, each additional day $4. Open Mon.-Fri. 9am-6pm, Sat. 8am-6pm, Sun. 10am-5pm.

Weather and Climbing Conditions: 926-5555 (5th Season's recording). 24hr. The Ranger Station offers a live report (926-4511).

Crisis Lines: Poison Control (800-342-9293). **Missing Climber Notification,** County Sheriff's office (841-2911).

Hospital: Mercy Medical Center, 914 Pine St. (926-6111).

Emergency: 911.

Police: 303 N. Mt. Shasta Blvd. (926-2344), at Lake.

Post Office: 301 S. Mt. Shasta Blvd. (926-3801). Open Mon.-Fri. 8:30am-5pm. **ZIP Code:** 96067.

Area Code: 916.

ORIENTATION

Mt. Shasta is located 60 mi. north of Redding on **I-5**, 50 mi. west of Lassen Volcanic National Park, and 292 mi. north of San Francisco (5hr. drive). If you're traveling by car, you can use the town of Shasta as a base for exploring Lava Beds, Lassen, Burney Falls, and the Shasta Recreation Area. The town is easy to find from any direction— just look toward the giant mountain.

ACCOMMODATIONS AND CAMPING

Alpenrose Cottage Hostel, 204 Hinckley St. (926-6724), next to the KOA drive-way. Roses arching over the sidewalk, gentle windchimes, and a sundeck with a view of Mt. Shasta give this Swiss-style chalet a homey appeal that the in-town motels lack. Wood-burning stove, open kitchen, laundry, TV room, and library. Closed noon-5pm, curfew 11pm. Limited availability with only 13 beds. Adults $15, children $7.50; rent the entire hostel for $150. Showers $2. Reservations recommended, especially in the summer.

Shasta Lodge Motel, 724 Mt. Shasta Blvd. (926-2815 or 800-SHASTA1/742-8721), is close to the center of town and noisy trains. Simple, clean rooms in a friendly atmosphere. Cable TV, A/C, phones. Singles $29; doubles $36.

Travel Inn, 504 S. Mt. Shasta Blvd. (926-4617). Recently renovated rooms are small with TV and phones. Singles $39; doubles $42.

Lake Siskiyou Campground (926-2618), 3mi. southwest of town. Flee I-5 via Lake St. Exit, follow Hatchery Lane ¼mi., then go south on Old Stage Rd. and W.A. Barr Rd. This family-oriented campground has access to a beach, encourages swimming, and rents paddleboats, motorboats, and canoes. Sites $13; day use $1. Coin-operated laundry. Reservations recommended.

McBride Springs Campground, on Everitt Memorial Hwy. Nine sites with water and hiking access. No showers or sinks. 7-night max. stay. Sites $10.

Gumboot Lake Campground, 20mi. west on South Fork Rd., is the most isolated camping area. The drive is long and the 10 sites are primitive, but the lake is utterly serene. Bug repellent is essential. Free.

Castle Lake Campground, 9mi. southwest of town, is primitive (pit toilets, no water, and only 6 sites). Freestyle camping is permitted more than 200ft. from the lake, ½mi. beyond the campground. Free.

The **U.S. Forest Service** runs a few area campgrounds; call 926-4511 for more info.

FOOD

Shasta has many grocery stores, the largest of which is **Ray's Food Place,** 160 Morgan Way (926-3390), in the Mt. Shasta Shopping Center off Lake St. (open daily 7am-11pm). In the summer, a **produce stand** across the street provides cheaper and fresher fruits and veggies. The **Mt. Shasta Supermarket** (926-2212), at the corner of Chestnut and E. Alma, is a pricier specialty store (open Mon.-Sat. 8am-7pm, Sun. 8am-6pm). **Berryvale Natural Foods,** 305 S. Mt. Shasta Blvd. (926-1576), caters to the health-conscious with organic produce, soy products, and enough tie-dye to help you fit in with the natives (open Mon.-Sat. 8:30am-7:30pm, Sun. 10am-6pm).

Avalon Square Heart Rock Cafe, 401 N. Shasta Blvd. (926-4998). Tiny cafe in a tiny building in the center of town has fantastic sandwiches (salmon pesto cheese $6) and interesting smoothies like the Whitney Glacier, made with banana and rice milk ($2.75). Open Mon.-Fri. 7am-6pm, Sat. 8am-2pm. No credit cards.

Black Bear, 401 W. Lake St. (926-4669). Busy all-night diner with friendly waitstaff and monster portions that are "un-bear-ably filling." Hungry Bear's Breakfast (3 eggs, sausage, hash browns, 2 biscuits, and a 1lb. ham steak, all for $8) is enough to feed you, a friend, the guy seated next to you, and the waitress. Open 24hr.

Willy's Bavarian Kitchen, 107 Chestnut St. (926-3636), offers imported beers, vegetarian dishes, and the ever-favorite *gulasch mit nudeln* (goulash with noodles) with soup or salad ($8) out of an honest-to-goodness wood shack. Anyone who's not a fan of German cuisine may want to stick with one of their huge hamburgers, which are considered the best around. Open daily 11am-10pm. No credit cards.

Bagel Cafe and Bakery, 105 E. Alma St. (926-1414). Local hangout serves up espresso ($1.50), fresh bagels (84¢), and New Age theology (free). Check the door for spiritual events, local bands, and the latest in Chinese acupuncture. Open Mon.-Sat. 6:30am-9pm, Sun. 6:30am-3pm. No credit cards.

SIGHTS AND ACTIVITIES

Hiking Mt. Shasta

Climbing Mt. Shasta is possible by car or on foot or using a little of both. Most climbers attempt Mt. Shasta in one or two days (some lug snowboards and skis up too, and come streaming down on the snow which lingers into the summer). Early daybreak starts are highly recommended for safety reasons. All climbers need to stop at the Forest Service (see **Practical Information,** p. 371) for weather updates, climbing conditions, safety registration, wilderness permit (free), summit pass ($15), and the **mandatory human waste pack-out system.** Relatively easy ascents of Shasta, sometimes not requiring ice equipment, are possible during August from trailheads at the **Ski Bowl** or **Bunny Flat,** both off Everitt Memorial Hwy. From Bunny Flat, a short but steep trail leads to Horse Camp, where hikers will find the historic **Sierra Club Cabin.** In the summer, the cabin is occupied by an informed caretaker. There is a $3 fee to camp near the cabin (no accommodations in the cabin itself). Be sure to take along extra clothing and plenty of drinking water.

Other trails on the mountain are less imposing, but don't reach the summit. The **Grey Butte Trail** begins at Panther Meadows campground, crosses the meadow, and heads up the eastern side of **Grey Butte.** The trail is about 1½ mi., but takes a couple of hours. The **Horse Camp Trail** at Horse Camp is another short but interesting hike. It begins at Sand Flat and goes about 2 mi., affording great views of Avalanche Gulch and the Red Banks. Sand Flat and Panther Meadows are both on Everitt Memorial Hwy., though car access past Bunny Flat to Panther Meadows may be restricted. The road ends at **Old Ski Bowl,** where you can take a trail (2mi.) above Grey Butte and then around the north side of Red Butte.

You can enjoy Mt. Shasta without breaking a sweat if you let your car do the work. The **Everitt Memorial Highway** provides excellent views of the mountain as it winds its way 13 mi. from Mt. Shasta to the Ski Bowl trailhead. Avalanches from Avalanche Gulch destroyed many areas of the slope. (Parking at Bunny Flats $5.)

Things that Make You Go Ohm

The mystic and psychic energies that concentrate in the Mt. Shasta area have not allayed **fears of The Big One,** the quake that will dim the California Light and spread an oozing black aura across the coast. From a Mt. Shasta newspaper, here are some precautions you can take to cleanse and purify the One's Nature:

1) Refer to the map of California. Note the missions, because they were each built upon an energy vortex and they are the foci for the Lord Mary and her son Lord Jesus The Cosmic Christ of Divine Love.

2) Point to each mission, tune in, and ask your Higher Self to go there, taking some level of you along for the ride.

3) State aloud: *"As an embassy of the Most High Light, I call forth Absolute God Protection for this location. I invoke the* **raspberry sherbet Son of Divine Mother** *to secure this mission area for 1000 mi. in all directions. I call the California Earthquake Patrol (inner plane angels and masters) to take command of the area and install earthquake release devices to vent the tremendous interior pressures of Mother Earth."*

4) Repeat: *"I call for all beings in California and all the world to now awaken and realize their divinity and Oneness with all that is. All violence, negative karma, despair, and abuse is now dissolved by the tryptic power of* **Lord Melatron, Lord Michael, and Melchizidek.** *It is so done!"* (3x)

Hiking Beyond Mt. Shasta

Hiking is plentiful. Nearby **Black Butte Mountain** is a far easier climb than Shasta, though still steep and rocky (2½mi. to the top). To get to the trailhead, go north on the Everitt Memorial Hwy. for 2 mi., turn left at the Penny Pines sign and follow the dirt road to the right 2½ mi. The road will cross an overhead powerline and split—take the road to the left for ½ mi. to the trailhead. The trail is steep, dry, and hot, so bring plenty of water and watch out for rattlesnakes.

The Forest Service has information on many other hiking trails in the area. The 9 mi. **Sisson-Callahan National Recreation Trail** offers great scenery and follows a route taken by 19th-century trappers and prospectors. For great views of the mountain, try the trail that runs between Castle Lake and Bradley Lookout. The Pacific Crest Trail (for more info, see **From Crest to Crest: the Trail of the West** on p. 409) also passes through the area, offering access to several serene alpine lakes. Access the trail at South Fork Rd. Maps and permits available at the Forest Service.

Other Outdoor Activities

Almost as popular as the mountains in the area are the **numerous lakes.** Around Mt. Shasta are several alpine lakes that are great for secluded swimming and fishing, including **Deadfall Lake, Castle Lake, Toad Lake,** and **Heart Lake.** The artificially controlled **Lake Siskiyou** is less remote and, not surprisingly, more crowded. Day use of the beach at Lake Siskiyou campground is $1. Thirty minutes south on I-5 is the enormous **Lake Shasta,** where houseboats explore the 450 mi. of shoreline.

Although **mountain bikes** are not allowed on hiking trails, logging roads in the national forests make excellent backcountry biking trails. Experienced bikers wishing to issue a challenge to the mountain can take a chairlift from **Mt. Shasta Ski Park** (926-8600), and bike or co-o-o-ast down (passes $10, seniors $8, under 12 $6).

Although volcanic rock is not the best for climbing, **rock climbers** will find many opportunities to challenge gravity in the Mt. Shasta region. Those in search of a wilderness climb should check out **Castle Crag State Park,** south of Dunsmuir on I-5, where the excellent granite climbing on glacier-polished cliffs is sure to leave climbers exhausted but smiling. Nearby **Cantara Cave** has good beginners' rock faces and **Pluto Caves** is excellent for bouldering. Call 5th Season (926-3606), for more info. The Mt. Shasta Ski Park (926-8600), has an artificial wall, which is popular with enthusiasts of all skill levels. (One climb $3, 3 climbs $5, ½ day $8.)

In Town

The **Mt. Shasta State Fish Hatchery,** 3 Old State Rd. (926-2215), ½ mi. west of I-5, monitors the production of more than five million baby trout every year in the state's oldest facility. Throw food in the ponds, watch the frenzy, and pet the fish when they calm down (open daily 8am-sunset; free). Next door, the **Sisson Museum** (926-5508), has exhibits on the area's geology and history (open April-Oct. daily 10am-4pm).

If you prefer a more spiritual experience, start at the **Village Books Bookstore,** 320 Mt. Shasta Blvd. (926-3228). Information about the latest New Age activities in the area is posted on the bulletin board out front. Step inside to peruse the spiritual book collection or enjoy the small coffee shop. The store's friendly owner can fill you in on local happenings. (Open Mon.-Sat. 10am-6pm, Sun. 11am-2pm.)

Another popular New Age destination is **Stewart Mineral Springs,** 4617 Stewart Springs Rd. (938-2222), in Weed. Mr. Stewart was brought here on the brink of death, and attributed his subsequent recovery to the healing energy of the water; many claim Mt. Shasta's spiritual energy penetrates the spring and passes into those who soak. Whether or not there's any truth to this, an afternoon spent relaxing in the saunas and hot tubs is an affordable luxury ($15).

The Sacramento River's headwaters are in the **Mt. Shasta City Park,** just north of town on Mt. Shasta Blvd. The tiny bubbling pool is a funny little novelty considering how big this river gets farther down. The water flows into Cold Creek, the northernmost of the Sacramento's feeder streams.

NORTHERN INTERIOR

Skiing

In winter, skiing opportunities abound. **Downhill** enthusiasts can tackle **Mt. Shasta Ski Park** (926-8600), 10 mi. east of I-5. Most of the ski trails are intermediate. (Ski rental $17 per day, seniors and children $14. Snowboard rental $25 per day. Lift tickets $29, Super Tuesday $17. Night skiing Wed.-Sat. $18, Wed.-Thurs. 2 tickets for the price of 1.) **Cross-country** skiers can try the **Ski Parks Nordic Center** (trail passes $11, rentals $12), or go on their own for challenging backcountry skiing.

■ Lava Beds National Monument

Lava Beds National Monument consists of acres of flat, dry, and seemingly barren land broken only by clumps of sagebrush, but beneath this unpromising surface lies a complex web of 350 **lava-formed caves** and otherworldly tunnels. Cool, quiet, and often eerie, caves created by the lava range from 18-inch crawl spaces to 80 ft. cathedrals. Lava tubes are formed from a slow lava flow: as the outer lava is exposed to air it cools faster and insulates the molten lava inside, which eventually drains away and leaves hollow conduits under the earth.

Since the beds are located a significant distance from any major towns and are not accessible by public transportation, the almost-deserted trails, caves, and campsites afford plenty of space. However, those not into cave-crawling may find themselves itching to leave Lava Beds quickly.

Some were not so eager to leave the fertile regions around the monument: in 1872, the lava beds became the site of the **Modoc War** between U.S. troops and the Native Americans when the Modoc resisted relocation efforts. Modoc chief "Captain Jack" and 52 of his warriors held their ground against 2500 U.S. soldiers for over five months by making use of the natural fortifications of the lava beds.

Today the Lava Beds monument offers wildlife as well as natural cave formations. In spring and fall, nearby Tulelake provides a stopover for thousands of migratory birds, some of which come from as far away as Siberia. The fall migration is particularly spectacular, when a million ducks and half a million geese literally darken the sky. In winter, this is the best place in the continental U.S. to see a **bald eagle.**

ORIENTATION AND PRACTICAL INFORMATION

Lava Beds is situated southwest of Tulelake and northeast of Mt. Shasta. The visitors center is in the southeast corner. There are three **northern** entrances near Tulelake. The north entrance is on Rte. 139. The road to the northeast entrance leaves Rte. 139 about 5 mi. south of Tulelake, and winds through the wilder northern areas of the monument for 25 mi., eventually reaching the visitors center. Visitors coming from the south on I-5 need to take a circuitous route, following U.S. 97 north, then Rte. 161 east past Tulelake, and Hill Rd. south. The **southeast** entrance (25mi. south of town) is closest to the visitors center. The two **east** entrances are closer to Klamath Basin Wildlife Refuge and the Oregon border.

Pick up free maps from the well-informed staff at **Lava Beds Visitors Center** (667-2282), 30 mi. south of Tulelake on Rte. 139. (Open daily 9am-6pm, Labor Day-June 15 8am-5pm. $4 per vehicle.) The center has exhibits on Modoc culture, slide presentations on the caves and the Modoc tribes, and is near a cluster of caves accessible by foot. The park staff also lends out heavy-duty flashlights to cave explorers (free; must be returned by 5:30pm, 4:30pm in winter).

Although the high altitude makes cold weather possible at any time of the year, summer weather tends to be quite moderate with minimal precipitation. It takes about a day to really appreciate the park (perhaps more, depending on your subterranean nerve), and you'll need a car or bike to see the northern areas. The nearest spot to catch a bus, rent a car, or find a hospital is across the Oregon border in **Klamath Falls,** 50 mi. north of Lava Beds. Redding, CA and Medford, OR also offer these services but are a few hours away. There is no public transportation to the area; hitching is difficult and not recommended. The **area code** for the region is 916.

ACCOMMODATIONS AND FOOD

The only developed campground in Lava Beds is **Indian Wells** (667-2282; no reservations accepted), opposite the visitors center. From the entrance sites, there's nothing to see but sagebrush, but farther along a view emerges of the mountains and small lakes of the nearby wildlife refuge. Drinking water and flush toilets are available from May to October (40 sites; $10). The monument has two **wilderness areas**, one on each side of the main north-south road. A wilderness permit is not required within the park. Cooking is limited to stoves, and camps must be at least ¼ mi. from trails and 150 ft. from cave entrances (check visitors center for other rules). **Modoc National Forest** borders the monument on three sides, and offers free off-road camping. Nearby are **Medicine Camp** and **Hemlock** campgrounds, both of which have water, flush toilets, and opportunities for fishing, swimming, and boating ($5 each). More info is available at the **Modoc National Forest Doublehead Ranger Station** (667-2248), one-mile south of Tulelake on Rte. 139 (open Mon.-Fri. 8:30am-4:30pm).

Tulelake's **Ellis Motel** (667-5242), one mile north of Tulelake on Rte. 139, sits serenely behind a large, manicured lawn, and has clean and attractive rooms (singles $30; doubles $35-40). Just south of town, also on Rte. 139, is the **Park Motel** (667-2913). Don't be misled by the garish exterior's cracking paint: the rooms are small, cozy, and decorated in light pastels (singles $33; doubles $39). **Jock's** (667-2612), at Modoc and Main, is a decently sized grocery store (open Mon.-Sat. 8am-8pm, Sun. 9am-6pm). **Captain Jack's Stronghold Restaurant** (664-5566), 6 mi. south of Tulelake, one-mile south past the turn-off to the Lava Beds, serves homemade soups and breads and has a sizable salad bar, making it one of the best options in this sparsely populated area. (Open Tues.-Sat. 6:30am-8pm, Sun. 9am-8pm. Off-season Tues.-Thurs. 7am-8pm, Fri.-Sat 7am-9pm, Sun. 9am-8pm.)

SIGHTS AND ACTIVITIES

Spelunking

If your subterranean experience has been limited to subways and parking garages, you should be warned that the footing in these lava caves is uneven and the ceilings may take a toll on your head. Sturdy shoes and helmets ($3.25 at the visitors center) are essential. No matter how hot it is outside, the underground caves are always cool and damp—take a sweatshirt or jacket. Exploring the caves alone is generally not a good idea and it is strongly discouraged by the rangers; if you decide to do it anyway, check in at the ranger station and take three light sources (lights must be battery operated; fumes or gases damage the caves). Solo travelers can take advantage of the group tours that leave from the visitors center daily at 2pm. Check at the center to see which caves are open, as they close depending on where the bats are.

The **Mushpot Cave,** located in the middle of the visitors center's parking lot, has a short, well-lit, self-guided trail which will acquaint visitors with cave formations (open summers only). On the 2¼ mi. **Cave Loop Rd.,** which starts and finishes at the visitors center, there are 13 caves with little more to guide you than an entrance stairway; parking is available at each entrance. Lava caves are usually single rocky tubes, so tricky side passages are rare, though **Catacombs Cave** has many interconnected passageways and requires a good deal of crawling. **Golden Dome,** which sparkles like gold due to the yellow bacteria growing on the walls, is less confusing. A few miles north is **Skull Ice Cave,** where one explorer found two human skeletons alongside the bones of several animals. The floor of this cave is covered with ice year-round. To the south is **Valentine Cave,** which is known for its frozen pools and waterfalls of lava, and its unusually smooth floor. Experienced spelunkers may want to consider checking out one of the many undeveloped caves in the park.

Two miles north of the visitor center is **Schonchin Butte.** The steep ¾ mi. ascent takes about 30 minutes and leads you to a working fire lookout that gives a broad view of the area, which includes Mt. Shasta. Farther toward Lava Bed's northern entrance is **Captain Jack's Stronghold,** the natural lava fortress where Modoc warriors held back Colonel Wheaton's troops during the Modoc War. There's an excellent self-guided trail through the area (guides 25¢). Just outside the northern entrance is **Petroglyph Point,** site of one of the largest collections of carvings in California, some of which date back to the first century AD.

Hiking

A few trails, of varying difficulty, provide hikes around the park. The **Whitney-Butte Trail** goes through rocky brush and around the mountain to the black Callahan Lava Flow, a 3½ mi. one-way route from the trailhead at Merrill Cave. The short, easy hike to the **Thomas-Wright Battlefield** leads to the site of a Modoc ambush that killed 50 U.S. soldiers, now a small meadow. The field is rather dull unless you consider the rattlesnakes. For an overnight hike, the **Lyons Trail** traverses 9½ mi. from Skull Cave to Hospital Rock over the rocky, hot plain in the park's eastern reaches. Be sure to consult a ranger before you go.

■ Beyond Lava Beds

Tulelake National Wildlife Refuge, visible on the drive from Tulelake to Lava Beds, is a bird-watcher's paradise and teems with waterfowl. An even better way to see it is from Rte. 161, just north of Tulelake. Each season brings a different set of animals to this refuge, the first area so designated by the U.S. government (in 1905 by Teddy Roosevelt). The migration period begins in early September, and over a million birds come through the refuge each year, including bald eagles, pelicans, and Canadian geese. Car tours are available in the Tulelake and Lower Klamath Refuges—just drive around and read the signs, making sure to stay in your car so that you don't disturb the habitat. A 10 mi. trail open to hiking, biking, and cross-country skiing meanders through the **Klamath Marsh Refuge.** The still waters and low mountains make perfect photographic frames for images of the active wildlife. For more info, contact the refuge manager in Tulelake (667-2231). The Lava Beds Visitors Center also sells books about local flora and fauna.

For a taste of the dark side of American history, you can visit the remains of a **Japanese Internment Camp,** where more than 18,000 Japanese-Americans were held by the U.S. government during World War II. The camp is located in Newell, 4 mi. south of the northern entrance to Lava Beds. However, due to the government's embarrassment over the incident, there is not much left to see of the camp, except a plaque and a couple of ruined buildings.

▓ Ashland

With a casual, rural setting just north of the California-Oregon border on I-5, Ashland mixes hippies and "Globe-al" history, making it the perfect stage for the world-famous **Shakespeare Festival.** From mid-February to October, drama devotees choose from a repertoire of 11 plays performed in Ashland's three elegant theaters. Over the festival's 60-year history, the town has evolved with it, giving rise to businesses like "All's Well Herbs and Vitamins" and a vibrant population of artists, actors, and Bard-buffs. Extravagant Shakespearean and contemporary productions draw both connoisseurs and casual observers. Ashland has its tourists and its tourist industry, but the town has not yet sold its soul. Culture comes with a price, but low-cost accommodations and tickets reward those who investigate. And though all the world may know Ashland as only a stage, Oregonians also recognize Ashland's fabulous restaurants, art galleries, and concerts.

PRACTICAL INFORMATION AND ORIENTATION

Visitors Information: Chamber of Commerce, 110 E. Main St. (482-3486). A busy (but friendly) staff frenetically answers phones and dishes out free play schedules and brochures, several of which contain small but adequate **maps.**

(Oddly, the best maps of Ashland are in the to-go menu at **Omar's,** 1380 Siskiyou Blvd., 482-1281.) The chamber *does not sell tickets to performances.* Open Mon.-Fri. 9am-5pm. The chamber also staffs an **info booth** in the center of the plaza. Open in summer daily 9am-5pm. **Ashland District Ranger Station,** 645 Washington St. (482-3333), off Rte. 66 by Exit 14 on I-5. Hiking, mountain biking, and other outdoor info, including words of wisdom on the Pacific Crest Trail (for more info, see **From Crest to Crest: the Trail of the West** on p. 409) and area camping. Open Mon.-Fri. 8am-4:30pm.

Tickets: Oregon Shakespeare Festival Box Office, 15 S. Pioneer St., P.O. Box 158, Ashland 97520 (482-4331; fax 482-8045), next to the Elizabethan Theater. Rush tickets (½ price) occasionally available 30min. before performances not already sold out. Ask at the box office for more options; the staff is full of tips for desperate theatergoers. The best bet, though, is to write for tickets in advance.

Buses: Greyhound (482-8803 or 800-231-2222). No depot in Ashland. Pick-up and drop-off at the BP station, 2073 Rte. 99 N., at the north end of town. Three buses run daily to Sacramento ($40) and San Francisco ($47). **Green Tortoise** (800-867-8647), stops at I-5 Exit 14 outside the Copper Skillet Cafe on the east side of Rte. 66. Buses to San Francisco (Sun. and Thurs. 11:45pm; $39).

Public Transportation: Rogue Valley Transportation (779-2877), in Medford. Schedules at the chamber of commerce. Base fare $1, seniors 50¢, ages 10-17 50¢, under 10 free. Bus #10 serving Ashland runs daily every 30min. 5am-6pm between the transfer station at 200 S. Front St. in Medford and the Ashland Plaza.

Taxi: Yellow Cab, 482-3065. 24hr.

Library: Ashland Branch Library, 410 Siskiyou Blvd. (482-1197), at Gresham St. Open Mon.-Tues. 10am-8pm, Wed.-Thurs. 10am-6pm, Fri.-Sat. 10am-5pm.

Laundromat: Main St. Laundromat, 370 E. Main St. (482-8042). Wash $1, 9min. dry 25¢. Ms. PacMan 25¢. Open daily 9am-9pm.

Equipment Rental: Ashland Mountain Supply, 31 N. Main St. (488-2749). Internal frame backpacks $7.50 per day ($100 deposit or credit card). External frame backpacks $5 per day ($50 deposit). Mountain bikes $10 per 2hr., $25 per day. Discounts for longer rentals. Open Mon.-Sat. 10am-6pm, Sun. 11am-5pm. **The Adventure Center,** 40 N. Main St. (488-2819 or 800-444-2819). Mountain bikes $20 per 4hr., $25 per 8hr. Guided bike tours ($59 for 4hr. with lunch) and raft trips ($59 per 4hr., $110 per day) also offered.

Crisis Line: Intervention Services (779-4357 or 888-609-HELP/4357). 24hr.

Emergency: 911.

Police: 1155 E. Main St. (482-5211).

Post Office: 120 N. 1st St. (482-3986), at Lithia Way. Open Mon.-Fri. 9am-5pm. **ZIP Code:** 97520.

Area Code: 541.

Ashland is located in the foothills of the Siskiyou and Cascade Ranges, 15 mi. north of the California border, near the junction of I-5 and Rte. 66. Cutting through the middle of town and creating a northwest-southeast access is Rte. 99. Its local name changes from N. Main St. to E. Main at the triangular plaza, where a medley of shops and restaurants form Ashland's downtown. Farther south, Main St. changes name again to Siskiyou St. **Southern Oregon State College (SOSC),** another few blocks down Siskiyou, is flanked by affordable motels and so-so restaurants.

ACCOMMODATIONS AND CAMPING

> *"Now spurs the lated traveler apace to gain the timely inn."*
> Macbeth, III.iii.6.

In winter, Ashland is a budget traveler's paradise of vacancy and low rates; in summer, hotel and B&B rates double, and the hostel overflows with travelers. Only rogues and strumpets arrive without reservations. Travelers should be aware that part of Ashland's water supply contains dissolved sulfurous compounds. It is perfectly safe to drink and bathe in, but it lends some bathrooms a repugnant and permanent odor.

Ashland Hostel, 150 N. Main St. (482-9217). Well-kept and cheery, this hostel has an air of elegance worthy of the Bard himself. The Victorian parlor, sturdy bunks, and front-porch swing play host to a mixed crowd of budget travelers and theater-bound families wise to money-saving ways. Laundry facilities and kitchen. Check-in 5-11pm. Curfew midnight. Lockout 10am-5pm. Dorms $14 with any hosteling card, $15 without; private rooms (sleep 4) $37-40; private women's rooms$22 for 1, $30 for 2. $3 discounts and free laundry for Pacific Crest Trail hikers or touring cyclists. Reservations advised March-Oct.

Columbia Hotel, 262½ E. Main St. (482-3726 or 800-718-2530). A European-style home, 1½ blocks from the theaters. Spacious rooms with wood panelling, sepia-toned photos, and muted colors. No TVs. Bathroom and pay phone down the hall. Singles $49; doubles $59. Nov.-Feb.: $30; $34. March-May: $42; $46. 10% off-season discount for HI-AYH members; under 12 free. Call ahead.

Vista Motel, 535 Clover Lane (482-4423), just off I-5 at Exit 14, behind a BP station. Small rooms in a low red, white, and blue building resembling a Lego building. Not center-stage, but there is cable, A/C, a small pool, and an amiable staff. Singles $37; doubles $45. Winter and spring discounts of about $10.

Ashland Motel, 1145 Siskiyou Blvd. (482-2561), across from the college. Fresh and tidy with a pale pink facade and an interior that puts little to no unique spin on the ubiquitous "motel brown" motif. Coin laundry, phones, cable, A/C, and a good-sized pool. Singles $43; doubles $63. Off-season rates $5-12 lower.

Mt. Ashland Campground, 9mi. west of I-5 south at Exit 6. Follow signs to Mt. Ashland Ski Area and take the high road from the far west end of the lot (sign for Grouse Gap Snowpeak). Exquisitely placed on the side of a mountaintop, looking south across the valley to Mt. Shasta. Seven primitive sites set in the high grass. Fire pits and vault toilets, but no drinking water. Free and seasonal.

Jackson Hot Springs, 2253 Rte. 99 N. (482-3776), 2mi. north of Ashland on Rte. 99; from I-5 go west ½mi. from Exit 19 and turn right on Rte. 99. The nearest campground to downtown. Separate tent area in a grassy, open field encircled by RV sites. Laundry facilities, hot showers, and overpriced indoor mineral baths ($20 per person, $25 per couple). Tent and RV sites $10, with full hookup $15.

FOOD

> *"Give them great meals of beef and iron and steel, they will eat like wolves and fight like devils."*
>
> Henry V, III.vii.166.

The incredible selection of eats 'n' mead available on North and East Main St. has earned the plaza a reputation independent of the festival. Even the ticketless come from miles around to dine in Ashland's fine restaurants. Beware the pre-show rush—a downtown dinner planned for 6:30pm can easily become a late-night affair. Many businesses close at 8:30 or 9pm, when the rush has receded into the theaters. **Ashland Community Food Store CO-OP,** 237 N. 1st St. (482-2237), at A St., has a lively spirit and a great selection of organic produce and natural foods (open Mon.-Sat. 8am-9pm, Sun. 9am-9pm; 5% senior discount). Less expensive groceries are available at **Safeway,** 585 Siskiyou Blvd. (482-4495; open daily 6am-midnight).

Geppetto's, 345 E. Main St. (482-1138). The local favorite for a late-night bite. The staff is fun, the walls covered in baskets, and the menu conversational, offering 6 feta and spinach wontons for $3.50. Dinner specials ($15) are enticing, but there are smaller ticket options, too, like a pile of sauteed vegetables ($3) or a marinated cucumber sandwich ($4.25). Lunches $4-6, breakfasts slightly more. Try the pesto omelette ($7.50). Open daily 8am-midnight.

Greenleaf Restaurant, 49 N. Main St. (482-2808). Healthy, delicious food, right on the plaza with creekside seating out back. Omelettes and fritattas are a bargain in the morning for $5-6.50. Tremendous array of salads ($1.50-9.50), pastas ($5-9), and spuds that are meals in themselves ($2.25-6.50). Chomp inside or take it down the block for a picnic in nearby Lithia Park. Open daily 8am-9pm; off-season Tues.-Sun. 8am-8pm. Closed Jan.

Thai Pepper, 84 N. Main St. (482-8058), one level below the street. A hotspot in the coolest area of town, with decks in the leafy green shade over Ashland Creek. Delicious entrees, exotic and reasonably priced for Ashland ($10-14). The best deal is lunch, when you don't have to wait for a seat outside, and your choice of 3 small dishes (including curry, spring rolls, and satay) is a steal at $6.50. Open Mon.-Thurs. 5-9:30pm, Fri.-Sat. 5-10pm, Sun. 5-8:30pm.

Brothers Restaurant and Delicatessen, 95 N. Main St. (482-9671). A block off the trampled tourist track, this New York-style deli and cafe feeds the locals. Some offbeat selections like the zucchini burger ($4.25) join the more traditional deli fare. Sandwiches ($7); bagel and cream cheese ($2.25). Open Mon. and Wed.-Fri. 7am-2pm, Tues. 7am-8pm, Sat. and Sun. 7am-3pm.

Five Rivers, 139 E. Main St. (488-1883), one flight up from street level. Slip upstairs to the warm smells of eastern spices and delicious Indian cuisine. Elegant Indian artwork and music set an intimate tone. Entrees $5.50-11.50; vegetarian options all below $7. Daily lunch buffet $5.50. Open daily 11am-2:30pm and 5-10pm.

Evo's Java House, 376 E. Main St. (482-2261). Chill out away from the crowds with a bowl of coffee ($1) or a Zaffiro Smoothie (blackberries, blueberries, and OJ, $2.50). College students and cool cats hang here. Live jazz every Sun. night attracts a crowd (open daily 7am-10pm).

THE SHAKESPEARE FESTIVAL

"This is very midsummer madness."

Twelfth Night, III.iv.62.

The **Shakespeare Festival,** the brainchild of local college teacher Angus Bowmer, began in 1935 with two plays performed in the Chautauqua Theater by schoolchildren as an evening complement to daytime boxing matches. Today, professional actors perform 11 plays in repertory. As the selections have become more modern, Shakespeare's share has shrunk to four plays; the other seven are classical and contemporary dramas. Performances run on the three Ashland stages from mid-February through October, and any boxing now is over the extremely scarce tickets ("Lay on, Macduff! And damned be him that first cries, 'Hold, enough!'" *Macbeth,* V.vii.62). On the side of the Chautauqua theater stands the 1200-seat **Elizabethan Stage,** an outdoor theater modeled after one in 18th-century London. Open only from mid-June through early October, the Elizabethan hosts three Shakespeare plays per season. The **Angus Bowmer** is a 600-seat indoor theater that stages one Shakespeare play and several classical dramas. The newest of the theaters is the intimate **Black Swan,** home to one Shakespeare play and other small, offbeat productions.

Due to the tremendous popularity of the festival, the box office recommends that you purchase tickets six months in advance. General mail-order ticket sales begin in January, but phone orders are not taken until February ($15-40 spring and fall, $18.75-45 in summer, plus a $3.50 handling fee per order for phone, fax, or mail orders; children under 5 not admitted to any of the shows). For complete ticket information, write Oregon Shakespeare Festival, P.O. Box 158, Ashland 97520 (482-4331; fax 482-8045; www.mind.net/osf). Spontaneous theatergoers should not abandon hope. The **box office** at 15 S. Pioneer St. opens at 9:30am on theater days; prudence demands arriving a few hours early. Local patrons have been known to leave their shoes to hold their places in line, and you should respect this tradition. At 9:30am, the box office releases any unsold tickets for the day's performances. If no tickets are available, limited priority numbers will be given out. These entitle their holders to a designated place in line when the precious few tickets that festival members have returned are released (1pm for matinees, 6pm for evening performances). At these times, the box office also sells twenty clear-view standing room tickets for sold-out shows on the Elizabethan Stage ($10, obtained on the day of the show).

Unofficial ticket transactions also take place just outside the box office, "on the bricks," though scalping is illegal. ("Off with his head!"—*Richard III,* III.iv.75.) Ticket officials advise those buying on the bricks to check the date and time on the ticket carefully, to pay only the face value, and to check with the box office before purchasing any tickets that have been altered. From March to May, half-price rush tickets are often available an hour before every performance that is not sold out. Additionally, in the spring and in October, some half-price student-senior matinees are offered. Spring and summer previews (pre-critic, full-performance shows) are offered at the Black Swan and Elizabethan Stage for a discounted price ($16-36).

Backstage tours provide a wonderful glimpse of the festival from behind the curtain. Tour guides (usually actors or technicians) divulge all kinds of anecdotes—from bird songs during an outdoor *Hamlet* to the ghastly events that take place every time they do "that Scottish play." Tours last almost two hours and usually leave from the Black Swan (Tues.-Sun. 10am; tickets $8.50-9.50, ages 5-17 $6.30-7, children under 5 not admitted). Admission includes a trip to the **Exhibit Center** for a close-up look at sets and costumes (open Tues.-Sun. 10am-4pm, fall and spring 10:30am-1:30pm; without tour $2, ages 5-17 $1.50). Further Shakespearean immersion can be had at two-hour discussion **seminars** offered every Friday between Memorial and Labor Day (9:30-11:30am) by Southern Oregon State College (tickets $5). Call 552-6331 for more information. The Shakespeare festival also includes special events, such as the **Feast of Will** in mid-June, a celebration honoring the annual opening of the Elizabethan Theater. Dinner and merry madness in Lithia Park start at 6pm (tickets $16; call 482-4331 for exact date).

SIGHTS AND ACTIVITIES

> "Mischief, thou art afoot, Take though what course thou wilt!"
> Julius Caesar, III.ii.259.

Before it imported Shakespeare, Ashland was naturally blessed with lithia water—water containing dissolved lithium salts, reputed to have miraculous healing powers. (It is said that only one other spring in the world has a higher lithium concentration—depression, be gone!) The mineral springs have given their name to the well-tended **Lithia Park,** west of the plaza off Main St. To quaff the vaunted water itself, hold your nose (the water contains dissolved sulfur salts) and head for the circle of fountains in the center of the plaza. Free concerts, readings, and educational nature walks happen early every day, in and around the park's hiking trails, Japanese garden, and the swan ponds by Ashland Creek. Events are listed in brochures at the chamber of commerce (see **Practical Information,** above).

If you have not yet perished from cultural overload, hang around Ashland even after the festival ends. ("Give me excess of it, that, surfeiting, the appetite may sicken and so die," *Twelfth Night,* I.i.2-3.) Artists love to play to the town's characteristically enthused audiences, so there is always something to attend. The **Oregon Cabaret Theater,** P.O. Box 1149 (488-2902), at 1st and Hagardine St., stages light musicals in a pink former church with drinks, dinners, and optional Sunday brunch (tickets $11-18; box office open Mon. and Wed.-Sat. 11am-6:30pm, Sun. 11am-4pm). Small groups, such as **Actor's Theater of Ashland** (535-5250), **Ashland Community Theatre** (482-7532), and the theater department at Southern Oregon State (552-6346) also raise the curtains sporadically year-round. The travelling **Rogue Valley Symphony** and the **State Ballet of Oregon** perform at the Music Recital Hall at SOSC and in Lithia Park when they are in town. In July and August, the ballet strike the stage on Mondays at 7:30pm; the Ashland City Band (488-5340) fires itself up at the same time on Thursdays in Lithia Park. The **Palo Alto Chamber Orchestra** (482-4331) performances in late June (tickets $13) in the Elizabethan Theater, weather permitting, are also a hit. Contact the chamber of commerce for a current schedule of events.

If your muscles demand a little abuse after all this theater-seat R&R, hop on the **Pacific Crest Trail** (for more info, see **From Crest to Crest: the Trail of the West** on p. 409) at Grouse Gap. Take Exit 6 off I-5 and follow the signs along the Mt. Ashland Access Rd. At the top of the 9 mi. road is **Mount Ashland,** a small community-owned ski area on the north face of the mountain, with 23 runs. (Open Thanksgiving Day-April, daily 9am-4pm; night skiing Thurs.-Sat. 4-10pm. Day ticket weekdays $20, seniors $14, ages 9-12 $14; weekends $25, $18, $18; full rental $15; snowboard and boots $25.) Contact **Ski Ashland,** P.O. Box 220 (482-2897). For **snow conditions,** call 482-2754. Over 100 mi. of free cross-country trails surround Mt. Ashland. **Bull Gap Trail,** which starts from the ski area's parking lot, is also good for skiing (and for biking after the snow has melted). It winds 2½ mi. down 1100 ft. to paved Tollman Creek Rd., 15½ mi. south of Siskiyou Blvd.

Join flocks of kids on the double-flumed, 280 ft. **waterslide** at **Emigrant Lake Park** (776-7001; 10 slides for $4 plus a $3 entry fee). The park is also a popular place for boating, hiking, swimming, and fishing. Although only 6 mi. east of town on Rte. 66, the lake is in a different geological region from Ashland. The parched hills that surround it are part of the Great Basin, where cows graze freely and render the lake water unsuitable to drink (open 10am-sunset, waterslide noon-6:30pm).

BARS AND CLUBS

"Come, come; good wine is a good familiar, if it be well us'd."
Othello, II.iii.308.

Catwork, 66 E. Main St. (482-0787). This nascent club and restaurant adds style and eccentricity to Ashland's post-show scene. Caters to the less traditional with DJs, live music, and assorted other entertainment (fashion shows!). Pacific Rim cuisine stars alongside a full bar and micropints. Open daily 11:30am-2am.
The Black Sheep, 51 N. Main St. (482-6414), upstairs on the Plaza. This English pub serves its brew in bulk: all pints are imperial (20oz.) and cost $4. Food is fabulous. Freshly baked scones and jam ($3.50), salt and vinegar "chips" ($3), and herbs grown in the British owner's bonny backyard. Open daily 11am-1am; minors welcome ("to dine") until 11pm.
Mark Antony Hotel, 212 E. Main St. (482-1721). Small and spare, with booths and a prominent stage. Live acts Mon.-Sat. have a $3-6 cover and include blues jams Mon. and comedy Tues. Weekend dancing. Et tu, wet blankets? Daily Happy Hour brings microbrews and imports down from $3 to $2.25 and domestics from $2.25 to $1.50. Open Mon.-Thurs. 3pm-1am, Fri.-Sat. 11am-2am, Sun. 3-9pm.
Siskiyou Micro Pub, 31B Water St. (488-5061). Replacing the Rouge Brewery and Public House a mere 6 months after a severe creek flood destroyed it, this spacious "Hell or Highwater Pub" promises a bawdy time. Wooden tables inside, patio seating outside. Live music every Fri. and Sat. at 9pm is usually free. 14 micros on tap (pints $3-3.50), bottled beers ($3), and full restaurant fare. Open Sun.-Thurs. 11am-midnight, Sat.-Sun. 11am-1am.

The Sierra Nevada

The Sierra Nevada is the highest, steepest, and most physically stunning mountain range in the contiguous United States. Thrust skyward 400 million years ago by plate tectonics, and shaped by erosion, glaciers, and volcanoes, this enormous hunk of granite stretches 450 mi. north from the Mojave Desert to Lake Almanor near Lassen Volcanic National Park. The glistening clarity of Lake Tahoe, the heart-stopping sheerness of Yosemite's rock walls, the craggy alpine scenery of Kings Canyon and Sequoia National Parks, and the abrupt drop of the Eastern Sierra into Owens Valley are unparalleled sights.

Temperatures in the Sierra Nevada are as diverse as the terrain. Even in the summer, overnight lows can dip into the 20s (check local weather reports). Normally, only U.S. 50 and I-80 are kept open during the snow season. Exact dates vary from year to year, so check with a ranger station for local road conditions, especially from October through June. Come summer, protection from the high elevations' ultraviolet rays is necessary; always bring sunscreen and a hat. For additional outdoors advice, see **Essentials: Camping and the Outdoors,** p. 43.

LAKE TAHOE AND VICINITY

The area surrounding Lake Tahoe is a rare find in the High Sierra: a pristine mountain setting with nearby outposts of urbanity, offering the best of both worlds. Lake Tahoe and Donner Lake glitter in both sun and snow. The innumerable outdoor recreation opportunities reel in visitors from all over the state, and after the sun goes down they all head to South Lake Tahoe and Reno, just across the Nevada border. Both cities offer glitzy gambling and all the accompanying nightlife—enough to keep even the staunchest of outdoorsmen up all night.

■ Lake Tahoe

In the winter of 1844, fearless explorer John C. Fremont led his expedition over the Sierra—a fool's errand, as anyone in the Donner Party would have told you. Luckily for him, the sight of the beautiful alpine lake was enough to boost the morale of his 36 starved and weary companions. Fremont left it unnamed, and it passed through several identities, from Bigler to Lake of Beer, before the state of California officially named it Tahoe in 1945.

As soon as settlers rolled into California in the late 18th century, Tahoe became a playground for the wealthy. One hundred years ago, staid shrines to old money peppered the shores. After roads were cut into the forested mountain terrain, new money arrived in the form of casinos, summer homes, and motels. Today, members of all tax brackets can enjoy Tahoe's pure blue waters, tall pines, and high-rises silhouetted by the deep auburn glow of the setting sun. Tahoe is an outdoor adventurist's dream in any season, with miles of biking, hiking, and skiing trails, long stretches of golden beaches, lakes stocked with fish, and many hair-raising whitewater activities.

PRACTICAL INFORMATION

Visitor Information:
   U.S. Forest Service and Lake Tahoe Visitors Center, 870 Emerald Bay Rd. (573-2600), 3mi. north of South Lake Tahoe on Rte. 89. Supervises campgrounds and publishes *Lake of the Sky Journal* (loaded with recreational coupons). Info on summer and winter recreation. Mandatory (but free) **wilderness permits** for backcountry hiking available. Open Mon.-Fri. 8am-4:30pm.

South Lake Tahoe Chamber of Commerce, 3066 Lake Tahoe Blvd. (541-5255). Energetic staff supplies useful brochures, info, and advice. Open Mon.-Fri. 8:30am-5pm, Sat. 9am-4pm.

Lake Tahoe/Douglas Chamber of Commerce, 195 U.S. 50 (702-588-4591), in Zephyr Cove, NV. Open Mon.-Fri. 9am-6pm, Sat.-Sun. 9am-5pm.

Tahoe North Visitor and Convention Bureau, 245 N. Lake Blvd. (583-3494; fax 581-4081). Pamphlets on outdoor recreation, camping, and lodging. Helpful staff makes lodging reservations. Hours vary by season, so call ahead. Open Mon.-Fri. 7am-7pm, Sat.-Sun. 9am-2pm. A **visitors center** near Taylor Creek on Emerald Bay Rd. is staffed mid-June to Oct. daily 8am-5:30pm; off-season weekends only.

ATM: U.S. Bank, 2850 Lake Tahoe Blvd. (542-1221), in S. Lake Tahoe, and at 705 N. Lake Blvd. (800-872-2657), in Tahoe City. Open Mon.-Thurs. 9am-5pm, Fri. 9am-6pm, Sat. 9am-1pm.

Buses: Greyhound (702-588-4645 or 800-231-2222), in Harrah's Casino on U.S. 50 in Stateline, NV. To San Francisco (3 per day, $21) and Sacramento (3 per day, $19). No lockers. Open daily 8am-1pm and 2:30-6pm.

Public Transportation: Tahoe Casino Express (800-446-6128), provides shuttle service between the Reno airport and Tahoe casinos (6:15am-12:30am). Fare $17, round-trip $30, under 12 free. **Tahoe Area Regional Transport (TART)** (581-6365), connects the western and northern shores from Tahoma (Meeks Bay in the summer), Truckee, and Incline Village (12 buses daily 6:10am-6:23pm). Fare $1.25, day pass $3. **South Tahoe Area Ground Express (STAGE)** (542-6077), operates buses around South Tahoe and to the beach (every hr.). Connects Stateline and Emerald Bay Rd. Fare $1.25, day pass $2, 10-ride pass $10. Most **casinos** operate free shuttle service along Rte. 50 to California ski resorts and motels. A summer **beach bus** program connects STAGE and TART at Meeks Bay to service the entire lake area.

Taxis: Sierra Taxi (577-8888). 24hr.

Car Rental: Enterprise (702-586-1077), in the Horizon in Stateline, NV. Must be 21 with credit card. Economy cars $32 per day, $160 per week with unlimited mi.

Library: South Lake Tahoe Library, 233 Warrior Way (573-3185). Open Tues.-Wed. 10am-8pm, Thurs.-Sat. 10am-5pm.

Laundromat: La Washmatique, 950 N. Lake Blvd. in Tahoe City. Open daily 7am-10pm. **Tahoe Keys Laundromat,** 2301 Lake Tahoe Blvd. (541-1848), in South Lake Tahoe. Open daily 7am-11pm.

Road Conditions: Nevada (702-793-1313).

Crisis Hotlines: General (800-992-5757). **Compulsive Gambling Center Hotline** (800-LOST-BET/567-8238). **Poison Control Center** (800-342-9293). **Lake Tahoe AIDS Task Force** (542-0131).

Medical Services: Stateline Medical Center, 176 U.S. 50 (702-588-3561), at Kahle in Stateline, NV. Open daily 8am-8pm.

Emergency: 911.

Post Office: Tahoe City, 950 N. Lake Blvd., #12 (583-3936), in the Lighthouse Shopping Center. Open Mon.-Fri. 8:30am-5pm. **ZIP Code:** 96145. **South Lake Tahoe,** 1046 Tahoe Blvd. (544-2208). Open Mon.-Fri. 8:30am-5pm, Sat. 10am-2pm. **ZIP Code:** 96151.

Area Code: 916 in CA, 702 in NV.

ORIENTATION

Situated in the northern Sierra on the border between California and Nevada, Lake Tahoe is a three and a half hour drive from San Francisco. The two main trans-Sierra highways **I-80** and **U.S. 50 (Lake Tahoe Blvd.)** run east-west through Tahoe, skimming the northern and southern shores of the lake, respectively. Lake Tahoe is 118 mi. northeast of Sacramento and 35 mi. southwest of Reno on I-80. From the Carson City and Owens Valley area, **U.S. 395** runs north along Tahoe's eastern shores.

The lake is roughly divided into two main regions known as North Shore and South Shore. The North Shore includes **King's Beach, Tahoe City,** and **Incline Village,** while **Emerald Bay** and **South Lake Tahoe City** are the hubs of the South

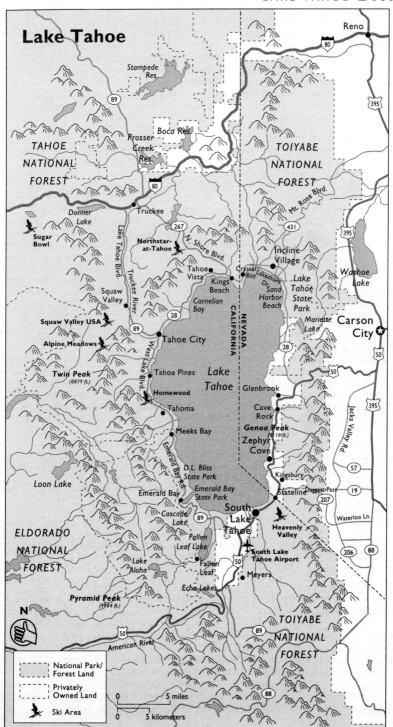

Lake Tahoe

THE SIERRA NEVADA

Shore. **Rte. 89** and **Rte. 28** form a 75 mi. ring of asphalt around the lake; the complete loop takes nearly three hours. Rte. 89 is also known as **West Lake Blvd.** and **Emerald Bay Rd.** while Rte. 28 masquerades as **North Lake Blvd.** and **Lakeshore Dr.** in Tahoe City and the western shore.

Road conditions in Tahoe can be treacherous from September through May, when **tire chains** may be required and a **4WD** is highly recommended. As Tahoe is a popular weekend destination, traffic is fierce on Friday afternoons and Sunday evenings. During winter, cars on the way to or from Tahoe City ski resorts pack the roads around 9am and 5pm.

ACCOMMODATIONS

The strip off U.S. 50 on the California side of the border supports the bulk of Tahoe's motels. Particularly glitzy and cheap in South Lake Tahoe, motels also line the quieter area along Park Ave. and Pioneer Trail. The North Shore offers more woodsy accommodations along Rte. 28, but rates are especially high in Tahoe City. Lodgings are booked solid and well in advance for weekends and holidays, when rates skyrocket. Fall and spring are the most economical times of the year to visit Tahoe because of the off-season bargains. Look for discount coupons (as much as $10 off weekday rates) in newspapers. The cheapest deals are clustered near Stateline on U.S. 50. Nearby campgrounds are a good option in the warmer months.

North Shore

Cedar Glen Lodge, 6589 N. Lake Blvd. (546-4281 or 800-341-8000), in Tahoe Vista. Family-operated motel is nestled in pine trees near the lake, with a private beach, pool, and indoor hot tub and sauna. Rustic rooms have wooden walls. Outdoor grounds include barbecue pits, playground, hammock, and rabbit hutch. Free continental breakfast and morning newspaper. Check-in 2pm. Check-out 11am. Doubles $55-75. Cottages with kitchens also available.

Tahoe City Inn, 790 N. Lake Blvd. (581-3333 or 800-800-8246; fax 583-5030), in Tahoe City next to Safeway supermarket. Clean, comfortable rooms come with two queen beds and cable TV. Check-in 3pm. Check-out 11am. Doubles $50, weekends $63. Off-season: $42, $53. Extra bed $10.

Hostel at Squaw Valley, 1900 Squaw Valley Rd. (581-3246), is a 100-bed hostel at the base of Squaw Valley. Roll out of bed and stroll out to the ski lifts. Social common area. Dorms $22, weekends and holidays $27. Open mid-Nov. to mid-April.

South Shore

Roadway Inn, 3520 Lake Tahoe Blvd. (544-1177, 544-1268, or 800-556-2500), in South Lake Tahoe. Recently remodeled rooms are large and clean with firm beds. Coffee and donuts in the morning. Heated pool and cable TV. Singles $39, weekends $69; doubles $49, $79.

Motel 6, 2375 Lake Tahoe Blvd. (542-1400; fax 542-1400), in South Lake Tahoe. Reliably sterile rooms with firm beds. Singles $50; each additional person $5. AARP discount. Reservations recommended.

Lake Shore Lodge, 3496 Lake Tahoe Blvd. (544-2834), in South Lake Tahoe. Standard rooms with TVs. Pool and free continental breakfast. Smoking rooms available. Singles $20, weekends $35; doubles $28, $48.

CAMPING

The U.S. Forest Service at the visitors center provides up-to-date information on camping (see **Practical Information,** p. 383), and rangers supply detailed leaflets on surrounding trails and wilderness areas. Rte. 89 is scattered with state campgrounds from Tahoe City to South Lake Tahoe. **Bayview** (544-5994), is the only free campground for miles (open June-Sept.; 2-night max. stay; no reservations). Campgrounds are often booked for the entire summer, so reserve well in advance; call DESTINET (800-365-2267), for state campgrounds. Backcountry camping is allowed (with a permit from the Forest Service) in Desolation Wilderness, but areas anywhere near the lake are off-limits due to environmental concerns.

LAKE TAHOE ■ 387

South Shore
D.L. Bliss State Park (525-7277), on Rte. 89 a few mi. north of Emerald Bay. Camp by the beach near emerald waters and granite boulders, or in secluded forest sites. Popular day-use beach, but entrance restricted by the number of parking spaces. The 9mi. **Rubicon Trail** (see **Hiking,** p. 389), leads to Emerald Bay, Vikingsholm, and Eagle Falls. 168 sites. 14-night max. stay. Sites $16; near-beach sites $20. Day parking $5. Pets $1. Open June to Labor Day.

Eagle Point at Emerald Bay State Park (525-7277), 10mi. west of South Lake Tahoe on Rte. 89. Less shade and more rocks than D.L. Bliss, but also more intimate. 14-night max. stay. Sites $15, seniors $14. 5min. hot showers 50¢. Open June-Labor Day.

Nevada Beach (544-5944), 1mi. north of Stateline on U.S. 50. Popular with families. Sites are 300ft. from the shore and afford views of the lake and snow-capped mountains. Flush toilets and drinking water. No showers. Sites $16. Call (800-280-2267) for reservations. Open June-Labor Day.

West and North Shores
General Creek at **Sugar Pine Point State Park** (525-7982), on the west shore south of Tahoma and across Rte. 89. Nestled in the pines, the grounds include tennis courts, cross-country ski trails, bike trials, nature center, historic mansion, and lakeside dock. BBQ pits and flush toilets. Sites $16, seniors $14; day use $5, seniors $4. Hot showers 50¢. Open year-round.

Sandy Beach (546-7682), off Rte. 28 in King's Beach. Hookups, showers, and flush toilets. Tent sites $15; RV sites $20. Open June-Labor Day.

Tahoe State Recreation Area (583-3074), at the north edge of Tahoe City on Rte. 28. One acre of land along the lake, but also along the road, has a long pier. 39 sites. Showers. Single sites $16, seniors $14. Open Memorial Day-Labor Day.

FOOD

The casinos offer perpetually low-priced buffets, but there are restaurants along the lakeshore with reasonable prices, similarly large portions, and much better food. Groceries are cheaper on the California side. Try a **Safeway,** in South Lake Tahoe, on the corner of Lake Tahoe Blvd. and Johnson, or in Tahoe City at 850 N. Lake Blvd. (both open 24hr.). Alternatively, you could go *au naturel* at **Grass Roots Natural Foods,** 2040 Dunlap (541-7788), one block east of the Rte. 89 and U.S. 50 intersection (open Mon.-Sat. 9:30am-7pm, Sun. 10am-6pm).

South Shore
Margarita's Mexican Cafe, 2495 Lake Tahoe Blvd. (544-6907), in South Lake Tahoe. Amazingly good Mexican cuisine served up by a friendly waitstaff. Combination plates ($6.95), enchiladas, *chimichangas,* and cilantro salsa. Open Wed.-Mon. 11:30am-9pm. No credit cards.

Killer Chicken, 2660 Lake Tahoe Blvd. (542-9977), in South Lake Tahoe. The "antichain" restaurant serves BBQ chicken sandwiches ($6-7) that aren't as deadly as the name implies—everything is "fresh and healthy." Whole chickens done Jamaican Jerk, Cuban Roast, Caribbean, or mild herb style ($13 with cornbread and side order). Veggie and low-fat items available. Open daily 11:30am-9:30pm.

Red Hut Waffles, 2749 Lake Tahoe Blvd. (541-9024). Good home-style cooking, a homey atmosphere, and a familial staff—altogether more like a home than a hut. Plate-size waffle piled with fruit and whipped cream $4.50, 4-egg monster omelette $6, bottomless cup of coffee 70¢. Open daily 7am-3pm.

North Shore
The Bridgetender, 30 W. Lake Blvd. (583-3342), in Tahoe City off Rte. 89. The specialty is a ½lb. burger ($4-6)—try a Cajun bacon cheeseburger ($5.45). Supersized salads ($4.25) and sandwiches. Diners can eat on the outdoor patio and watch the Truckee River roll by. Wide range of beers on tap, pool table, and festive nighttime crowd. Open Mon.-Fri. 11am-11pm, Sat.-Sun. 11am-midnight; bar open until 2am.

Bluewater Brewing Company, 850 N. Lake Blvd. (581-2583), behind the Safeway in Tahoe City. Swimming with homemade brews—Misty Mountain Oatmeal Stout is a favorite (pitcher $10). Fish and chips in beer batter $7.50. Two pool tables and occasional live bands make this a happening night spot for the college crowd. Open Tues.-Sun. 11:30am-10pm; brewery open Tues.-Sun. 11:30am-midnight.

Steamers, 8290 N. Lake Blvd. (546-2218), at King's Beach. The photo-covered walls tell the story of the restaurant's namesake, the old steamer "Tahoe," whose captain sunk it in the lake so that it would not serve in WWII. Delicious pizzas in a casual but lively setting. Outdoor patio bar with lakeside view. Open daily 11am-11pm.

SUMMER SIGHTS AND RECREATION

Beaches

Lake Tahoe supports many beaches perfect for a day of sunning and people-watching. Parking generally costs $3-5.

On the South Shore, **Pope Beach,** off Rte. 89, is a wide, pine-shaded expanse of shoreline, which becomes less trafficked on its east side. **Nevada Beach** is close to the casinos off U.S. 50, offering a quiet place to reflect on gambling losses while gazing upon the mountains. **Zephyr Cove Beach** is a favorite spot for the younger college crowd. Beach volleyball, beer, bikinis, and boogie beats make it the closest thing to Southern California in Lake Tahoe. On the western shore of the lake, **Chambers Beach,** between Homewood and Tahoma, also draws in a younger crowd, who happily occupy the public volleyball nets, but eagerly eye the private pool and bar. **Meeks Bay,** 10 mi. south of Tahoe City, is family oriented. In the summer, the Tahoe City and South Tahoe Buses connect here.

On the North Shore, **Sand Harbor Beach,** south of Incline Village, has gorgeous granite boulders and clear waters that attract swimmers, sunners, and scuba divers in droves. The beach is a bit of a trek from the parking lot ($6; usually full by11:30am). **Hidden Beach,** also south of Incline Village, and **Kings Beach,** just across the California border on Rte. 28, come complete with wave boards. Kings has volleyball nets, a basketball court, and a playground for kids. Jet skis, windsurfs, and kayaks can be rented at both beaches.

Biking

Lake Tahoe is a biking paradise. The excellent paved trails, logging roads, and dirt paths have not gone unnoticed, so be prepared for company if you plan to pedal around the area. The Forest Service and bike rental stores can provide advice, publications like *Bike West Magazine,* maps, and info about trails. No cycling is allowed in the Desolation Wilderness, or on the Pacific Crest or Tahoe Rim Trails (except from Tahoe City to Mt. Rose, and from Heavenly to Desolation Wilderness). Bike rental shops abound, especially near the trails; rentals are usually $6-7 per hour and $20-25 per day. **Anderson's Bicycle Rental,** 645 Emerald Bay Rd. (541-0500), is convenient to the well-maintained bike trails along the western shore. (Mountain bikes ½ day $20, full-day $25; helmets and maps available; deposit of ID required. Open daily 9am-6pm.) **Tahoe Cyclery,** 3552 Lake Tahoe Blvd. (541-2726), South Lake Tahoe, is a grungy but friendly shop offering a wide range of rentals. (Mountain bikes $6 per hr., ½ day $18, full day $24; in-line skates $5 per hr.; snowboards $18 per day; skis or snowshoes $10 per day. Open daily 9am-7pm).

South Shore boasts a variety of scenic trails for all abilities. For less strenuous adventures, several paved trails circle the lake. The **Pope-Baldwin Bike Path** (3.4mi.) runs parallel to Rte. 89, while the **South Lake Tahoe Bike Path** runs from El Dorado Beach over the Upper Truckee River. The smooth and easy ride and the lake views make these trails quite popular. Parking is available at the Truckee River trailhead (Rte. 89, south of Tahoe City), Kaspian campground (Skyland), and General Creek campground at Sugar Pine Point State Park (south of Homewood). **Fallen Leaf Lake,** just west of South Lake Tahoe, is a spectacular destination (by bike or by car), but watch out for the swerving tourists in boat- and trailer-towing vehicles, especially on the narrow mountain roads. The steep mountain peaks that surround the lake are breathtaking when viewed from beside Fallen Leaf's icy blue waters. Bikers looking for a real challenge can try the 7 mi. ring around the lake, but beware—it's more difficult than it looks. U.S. 50, Rte. 89, and Rte. 28 are all bicycle-friendly but the drivers aren't, especially in heavy traffic areas like South Lake Tahoe. **Angora Ridge** (4mi.), accessible from Rte. 89, meanders past Fallen Leaf Lake to the Angora Lakes for a moderate challenge. For serious mountain bikers, **Mr. Toad's Wild Ride** (3mi.), reached from U.S. 50 or Rte. 89, is a *very* difficult, winding trail that climbs to 9000 ft. The **Flume Trail** is touted as the best in Tahoe for its magnificent views of the lake 1500 ft. below. This advanced 23 mi. loop begins at Spooner Lake campground with the **Marlette Lake Trail**, a 5 mi. sandy road.

The North Shore, known more for its ski trails, offers bikers steeper rides. The **Tahoe Rim Trail**, from Kings Beach to Tahoe City, offers intermediate-level, hilly biking. The trail can be accessed from Tahoe City or Brockway Summit (see below for more info). **Squaw Valley**, northwest of the lake on Rte. 89, opens its slope to hikers and mountain bikers during the summer. The cable car (full-day pass $24) transports bikers and their wheels 2000 vertical feet. You find your own way down—the slopes are steep, but fairly easy. The **West Shore Bike Path**, a 10 mi. stretch from Tahoe City to Sugar Pine Point, is a flat, scenic way to tour the lake.

Hiking

Hiking is one of the best ways to explore the beautiful Tahoe Basin. The visitors center and ranger stations provide detailed info and maps for all types of hikes. Back-country users must obtain a free **wilderness permit** from the Forest Service (see **Practical Information**, p. 383) for any hike into the Desolation Wilderness, which is the most visited natural wilderness area in the U.S. Only 700 hikers are allowed in this area on any given day. Due to erratic weather conditions in the Sierra, hikers should always bring a jacket and drinking water. Buy a topographical map before you go and ask where the snow has (or has not) melted—it's not usually gone until July and finding a trail under a foot of hard snow is next to impossible. **Alpenglow Sport Shop**, 415 N. Lake Blvd. (583-6917), Tahoe City, sells great trail maps ($7).

The (still) partially completed **Tahoe Rim Trail** circles the entire lake, following the ridge tops of the Lake Tahoe Basin. Hiking is moderate to difficult, with an average grade of 10%. On the western shore, it is part of the Pacific Crest Trail (for more info, see **From Crest to Crest: the Trail of the West**, p. 409). Current trailheads are at Spooner Summit on U.S. 50, Tahoe City off of Rte. 89 on Fairway Drive, Brockway on Rte. 267, Grass Lake on the north side of Rte. 89, and Big Meadows on Rte. 89, 5½ mi. south of the junction of U.S. 50 and Rte. 89. Hiking enthusiasts can donate their time to help build the trail (702-588-0686).

The South Shore offers many moderate to strenuous hiking trails. The picturesque **Emerald Bay,** in the lake's southwest corner, embraces Lake Tahoe's only island and most photographed sight—tiny, rocky **Fannette.** The alpine lakes and dramatic waterfalls make this a mini-paradise. Emerald Bay State Park, which connects to the Desolation Wilderness, offers hiking and **biking** trails of varying difficulty, camping, and terrain for **rock climbing.** The **Vikingsholm** (541-3030) tour and exhibit may deepen your appreciation of the area with fun historical Tahoe tidbits, including the story behind tea room nestled on top of Fannette's rocky exterior. (Open mid-June to Labor Day daily 10am-4pm. Tours every ½hr. Admission $3, under 18 $2.) One of the best hikes in Tahoe is the **Rubicon Trail**, which runs 7¼ mi., wrapping around the beach and granite cliffs of Emerald Bay. The trailheads are at D.L. Bliss Park and Vikingsholm. The **Eagle Falls Trail** is accessible from the Vikingsholm's parking lot by hiking to Eagle Lake (1½mi.) and the Desolation Wilderness.

Those looking for a more leisurely excursion will enjoy the **nature trails** around the area around the visitors center at Taylor Creek, west of South Lake Tahoe. The **Lake of the Sky Trail** (½mi. round-trip) is dotted with informative signs about the origins of the lake, its early inhabitants, and its current non-human inhabitants. The trail leads to the **Tallac Historic Site**, which features a look at turn-of-the-century

Tahoe life (read: casino life). Also at Taylor Creek is the underground **Stream Profile Chamber,** which allows face-to-window interaction with fish, including the bright red salmon that fill the chamber in a fall spawning spree (temporarily closed due to flood damage; call the visitors center at 573-2600 for updated info).

Lower and **Upper Echo Lakes,** off U.S. 50 south of Tahoe, are a smaller, but wilder version of Tahoe; gray stone and pine trees tower around the lakes, providing an unmatched feeling of seclusion. **Echo Chalet** (659-7207), located 2 mi. off U.S. 50 near the top of Echo Summit, operates boat service to the other side of the lake (8am-6:30pm; one-way $6.50). A well-maintained trail (part of the Pacific Crest Trail; for more info, see **From Crest to Crest: the Trail of the West,** p. 409) skirts the north side of the lakes to the Upper Lake boat landing and into the Desolation Wilderness. Day hiking permits for the wilderness are available at the Chalet. Another 2 mi. along U.S. 50, just before **Twin Bridges,** is the **Horsetail Falls** trailhead. The waterfalls here make those at Eagle Lake look like a leaky faucet. To access them, you'll have to make the short (1¼mi.) but tough hike through the slippery canyon. Inexperienced hikers should beware—each year, some people need to be helicopter-rescued by the Forest Service.

There is plenty of great hiking on the northern and eastern shores of the lake. The **Stateline Lookout,** near Kings Beach, has free telescopes, a short self-guided nature trail, and spectacular views. To get there, take Rte. 28, turn north onto Reservoir Dr., right onto Lakeshore Ave., and left onto Forest Service Rd. 1601. The **Marlette Lake Trail** begins at Spooner Lake, at the junction of U.S. 50 and Rte. 28, and leads through moderately difficult terrain of the **North Canyon.** The **Granite Chief Wilderness,** behind Squaw Valley, is another good option; its rugged hiking trails wind through secluded forests and fields of wildflowers. At 10,778 ft., **Mt. Rose** is one of the tallest mountains in the Tahoe region as well as one of the best climbs. It starts out as an easy dirt road hike, but becomes a rocky scramble after mile three. Take Rte. 431 from Incline Village to the trailhead, which is a deceptive mile south of the summit (the hike itself is 6mi.).

Rock Climbing

Invaluable climbing information is available from **Alpine Skills International (ASI)** (see **Truckee and Donner Lake: Accommodations,** p. 393). The **Alpenglow Sport Shop,** 415 North Lake Blvd. (583-6917), Tahoe City, provides free rock- and ice-climbing literature. **The Sports Exchange,** 10095 W. River St. (582-4510), Truckee, rents climbing shoes (indoor $3 per day, outdoor $7 per day) and also houses Gym Works, a challenging indoor climbing gym with over 2500 square ft. of bouldering and climbing space ($8 per day). **Headwall Climbing Wall** (583-6985), at Squaw Valley, offers several challenging routes in the Cable Car Building.

There are many popular climbs in Lake Tahoe, but climbing should never be undertaken without knowing the ropes—proper safety precautions and equipment are a must. Those unprepared for dangerous climbs can try bouldering at **D.L. Bliss State Park** and at Split Rock in **Donner Memorial State Park.** The climbing at Donner Summit is world-renowned. Along Old Hwy. 40 by Donner Pass, climbers ascend **School Rock** (beginner) or the precarious **Snow Shed** (advanced). A host of popular climbing spots are scattered through South Shore and the Donner Summit area. The **90 ft. Wall** at Emerald Bay, **Twin Crags** at Tahoe City, and **Big Chief** near Squaw Valley are some of the more famous area climbs. **Lover's Leap,** in South Lake Tahoe, is a rad climb of two giant cliffs. On the east of South Lake Tahoe off of U.S. 50, **Phantom Spires** has amazing ridge views, while **Pie Shop** has great exposure.

Water Activities

River rafting can be a refreshing way to appreciate the Tahoe scenery, but depending on the water levels of the American and Truckee Rivers, rafting can range from a thrilling whitewater challenge to a boring bake in the sun. If water levels are high, check out raft rental places along the Truckee River and at Tahoe City. For more info, call **Truckee River Rafting** (583-RAFT/7238), or **Tahoe Whitewater Tours**

(581-2441). When droughts make conventional rafting scarce, many would-be rafters turn to **inner tubes.** Make sure inner tubes are permitted in the waters you select, use the buddy system, and know what lies ahead before you shove off. In the summer (July-Oct.), **Windsurf North Tahoe,** 7276 N. Lake Blvd. (546-2369), in Tahoe Vista, rents windsurfs ($15) and provides lessons for even the most timorous first-timers. **Tahoe Paddle and Oar** (581-3029), in Kings Beach, rents kayaks (singles $10 per hr., doubles $20 per hr.). From Kings Beach, paddle past natural hot springs and through boulder fields until you reach the spectacular Crystal Bay. Local lore maintains that these frigid temperatures (average 39°F) prevent the decomposition that would ordinarily make corpses float to the surface. Changes in water temperature and current movements have on occasion brought perfectly preserved bodies to the surface.

Several marinas rent motorboats, jet skis, paddle boats, canoes, and fishing boats. On the North Shore, try **North Tahoe Marina,** 7360 N. Lake Blvd. (546-4889), on Rte. 28 in Tahoe Vista, or **Lighthouse Watersports Center,** 950 N. Lake Blvd. (583-6000), Tahoe City. On the South Shore, try **Zephyr Cove Marina** (702-588-3833), on U.S. 50. The visitors center will have current info on **fishing** regulations. Licenses are available at local sporting good stores. Because of its depth (1600ft. in places) and strange formation, Tahoe is a notoriously difficult lake to fish; bring a good book (may we suggest the one you are currently reading) and be prepared to walk away empty-handed.

Horseback Riding

Horseback riding is both popular and plentiful around Tahoe. Trails are often accessible to horses as well as hikers—ask the Forest Service for specifics. **Camp Richardson Corral** (541-3113), on Rte. 89 between Tahoma and South Lake Tahoe, provides one-hour trail rides for $20. **Alpine Meadows Stables,** Alpine Meadow (583-3905), in Tahoe City, has the area's lowest-priced ride at $15 per hour.

WINTER SIGHTS AND RECREATION

Downhill Skiing

With its world-class alpine slopes, knee-deep powder, and notorious California sun, Tahoe is a skier's mecca. There are approximately 20 ski resorts in the Tahoe area. The visitors center provides info, maps, publications like *Ski Tahoe* (free), and coupons (see **Practical Information,** p. 383). All the major resorts offer lessons and rent equipment. Look for multi-day packages that offer significant discounts over single-day rates. Lifts at most resorts operate daily from 9am to 4pm. (Arrive early for the best skiing and the shortest lines.) Prices do not include ski rental, which generally costs $15-20 for a full day. Skiers on a tight budget should consider night skiing or half-day passes. Skiing conditions range from bikini days to frost-bitten finger days, and snow (artificial or otherwise) might cover the slopes into early summer. Off-season skiing may not compete with winter skiing in terms of snow quality, but it's generally much cheaper. Rates listed below are for winter.

Squaw Valley (583-6985 or 800-543-4350; fax 581-7114), off Rte. 89 just north of Alpine Meadows, was the site of the 1960 Olympic Winter Games, and with good reason—the groomed bowls and tree runs make for some of the best skiing in the West. Squaw boasts 4200 acres of terrain across 6 Sierra peaks. The 31 ski lifts access high elevation runs for all levels. The resort also offers night and cross-country skiing, bungee jumping, swimming, rock climbing, and ice skating in Olympic Ice Pavilion. Full-day ticket $46, ½ day $31, seniors and under 13 $5.

Alpine Meadows (583-4232 or 800-441-4423), 6mi. northwest of Tahoe City on Rte. 89. An excellent, accessible family vacation spot with more than 2000 skiable acres. Not as commercial as Squaw, it has long expert bowls with good powder skiing, but few runs for beginners. Alpine is also notorious for avalanches, so be careful if skiing out of boundaries. Full-day lift ticket $46, ages 65-69 $29, over 70 $6, ages 7-12 $18, under 6 $6. Basic ski rental $22, ages 7-12 $15, under 6 $9.

Heavenly (702-586-7000 or 800-2-HEAVEN/243-2826), on Ski Run Blvd. off U.S. 50, is one of the largest and most popular resorts in the area, with well-groomed freeway-width runs and enough moguls to make skiing feel like jump aerobics. Reaching over 10,000ft., it is also Tahoe's highest ski resort. Few shoots or ridges. With 23 lifts and 4800 skiable acres, it spreads across the California and Nevada boundary and has dizzying views of both. Full-day lift ticket $47, over 65 and under 13 $20; ½ day $30, over 65 and under 13 $15.

Mt. Rose (702-849-0747 or 800-SKI-ROSE/754-7673), 11mi. from Incline Village on Rte. 431, is a local favorite because of its long season, short lines, intermediate focus, and less expensive lift tickets. Full-day lift ticket $38, seniors $19, ages 6-12 $14, under 6 free.

Ski Homewood (525-2992), on the western shore between Tahoe City and Tahoma, is a relatively inexpensive ski area. Catering primarily to locals, it offers decent skiing at affordable prices by avoiding expensive frills. Terrain for all levels, but season is short since the resort is at lake level. Full-day lift ticket $35, ages 14-18 $25, ages 9-13 $11, under 9 free.

Northstar (562-1330 or 562-1010), on Rte. 267 between Truckee and Kings Beach. Well-groomed and tame slopes are great for intermediates and several kids' skiing programs. Full-day lift ticket $45, ages 13-22 $37, ages 5-12 $10.

Boreal Ridge (426-3663), 10mi. west of Truckee on I-80, opens earlier than most resorts and saves skiers the drive to Tahoe. Mostly beginner and intermediate slopes are good for snowboarding. Full-day lift ticket $34, ages 5-12 $5, under 5 free. Call about mid-week discounts and night skiing; both vary seasonally.

Numerous smaller ski resorts offer cheaper tickets and shorter lines but less acreage. **Diamond Peak Ski Resort** (832-1177), off Country Club Dr. in Incline Village, has some hair-raising tree skiing and is right on the beach, while **Sugarbowl** (426-3847), 3 mi. off I-80 at Soda Springs Exit, just doubled in size and has decent terrain.

Cross-Country Skiing and Snowshoeing

One of the best ways to enjoy the solitude of Tahoe's pristine snow-covered forests is to cross-country ski at one of the resorts. Alternatively, rent skis at an independent outlet and venture onto the thick braid of trails around the lake. **Porters,** located at the Lucky-Longs Center (587-1500), in Truckee, and at 501 N. Lake Blvd. (583-2314), in Tahoe City, rents skis for $6-9.

Royal Gorge (426-3871), on Old Hwy. 40 below Donner Summit, is the nation's largest cross-country ski resort, with 80 trails covering 300km of beginner and expert terrain. **Spooner Lake** (749-5349), at the intersection of U.S. 50 and Rte. 28, offers 21 trails and incredible views (adult trail fee $15, children $3; mid-week special $11). **Hope Valley** (694-2266), has 11 trails of varying difficulty (free). Take Rte. 89 south from South Lake Tahoe and turn left on Rte. 88.

Some might prefer the less strenuous activity of **snowshoeing,** which allows one to traverse more varied terrain. Follow hiking or cross-country trails or trudge off into the woods (make sure to bring a map). Rentals are available at many sporting goods stores for about $15 per day.

▓ Truckee and Donner Lake

Truckee got its name from a classic tale of miscommunication. When a Paiute Indian greeted the Stephen-Townsend-Murphy party in 1844 with the word "Trokay" ("peace"), they thought it was his name and gave it to a local river, and in turn, to a lumber camp at the foot of the Sierra. Truckee remained a rugged mining and railroad town until the outdoor recreation industry took hold and transformed it into a cutesy tourist stop for skiiers and hikers en route to Tahoe. Restaurants and shops on the well-preserved "Old West" Commercial Row accommodate visitors from the much more spectacular Lake Tahoe just 15 mi. away.

Two miles west of Truckee and encircled by gray granite cliffs lies Donner Lake, the site where the ill-fated Donner Party got snowed in for the winter. Travelers will notice numerous memorials to the gruesome event (see **Bad Trip: The Donner Party,** below). Travelers will likely find Donner Lake much more fun than the pioneers did—now warmer than Tahoe, the lake is a popular place for swimming, boating, camping, and hiking.

PRACTICAL INFORMATION

Visitor Information:
   Truckee-Donner Chamber of Commerce, 12036 Donner Pass Rd. (587-2757 or 800-548-8388), across the street from the factory outlet mall. Brochures, maps, and handouts. Open Mon.-Fri. 9am-5pm.
   U.S. Forest Service Truckee Ranger District, 10342 Rte. 89 (587-3558), just off I-80. Info on camping and recreation in the Tahoe National Forest. Open Mon.-Fri. 8am-4:30pm.
Trains: Amtrak, 10065 Donner Pass Rd. (800-USA-RAIL/872-7245), in Truckee. Trains leave once daily for Reno ($13), Salt Lake City ($115), Sacramento ($45), and San Francisco ($53). Station is not staffed; order tickets in advance.
Buses: Greyhound, 10065 Donner Pass Rd. (587-3822 or 800-231-2222). To: Reno (5 per day, $8), San Francisco (7 per day, $31), Sacramento (7 per day, $20). Open Mon.-Sat. 6:30am-8pm, and Sun. for bus arrivals only.
Auto Repairs: AAA Emergency Road Service (800-222-4357).
Equipment Rental: Sierra Mountaineer (587-2025), at the corner of Bridge and Jibbom, 1 block off Donner Pass Rd. in downtown Truckee. Get the lowdown on the area's outdoors. Backpacks $8 per day, sleeping bags $7.50 per day, 3-person tent $21.50 per day, camping stoves $6 per day. Prices lower for multi-day rentals. Open Mon.-Sat. 10am-6pm, Sun. 10am-5pm.
Weather Conditions: (546-525). **Road Conditions:** (800-427-7623 or 587-3158).
Medical Services: Tahoe Forest (587-6011), at Pine Ave. and Donner Pass Rd.
Emergency: 911.
Post Office: Truckee (587-3442), 1 block north of Commercial Row on Rte. 267. Open Mon.-Fri. 8:30am-5pm, Sat. 11am-2pm. **ZIP Code:** 96160.
Area Code: 916.

ORIENTATION

Truckee lies just off **I-80** in the Sierra Nevada, 100 mi. northeast of Sacramento, 33 mi. west of Reno, and 15 mi. north of Lake Tahoe. The town is a three-hour drive from San Francisco, depending on road conditions. **Donner Pass Rd.** (part of Rte. 89), the main drag, leads east into downtown, where it becomes **Commercial Row,** and west to Donner Summit and Donner Lake, where it is known as "Old Hwy. 40." *Be extremely cautious along Donner Pass—there are not always barriers along the cliffside edge of the road.* In summer, potholes make for a hair-raising drive; in winter it is usually closed due to snow and ice; stick to I-80.

CAMPING, ACCOMMODATIONS, AND FOOD

Truckee and Donner Lake have few finds for the budget hostel-seeker. Many more budget accommodation options can be found in Tahoe, especially in South Lake. **Donner Spitz Hütte ASI Lodge** (426-9108; fax 426-3063), on Old Hwy. 40 between Norden and Donner Memorial State Park, and near Royal Gorge and Sugar Bowl on the top of Donner Pass. Accessible by car only. This charming Swiss-style ski lodge provides a great base for skiiers, hikers, and climbers, and popular outdoor programs. Sleeping bag bunks and breakfast for $24. Call ahead for reservations since the owner sometimes takes off to guide groups.

Twelve **campgrounds** lie within 12 mi. of Truckee. The **U.S. Forest Service** (587-3558), operates sites clustered northward along Rte. 89 and Stampede Meadows Rd., which is at the Hirshdale Exit off I-80. Sites around Boca and Prosser Res-

> ### Bad Trip: The Donner Party
>
> It's hard to pass through Donner Lake without seeing numerous memorials to the Donner Party. "What's it all about?" you may wonder. Well, it began when 90 midwesterners (led by the Donner family), headed for the comfort of California in April 1846. The ill-fated group took a "short-cut" advocated by daring but guileless adventurer, Lansford Hastings. The party hacked through the wilderness, losing cattle and abandoning wagons as they went. Though the area was brushed with barely a foot of snow the year before, the onset of an early winter at Truckee (later Donner) Lake in December devastated the group. Trapped by 22 ft. of snow (and without powder skis), many turned to cannibalism before they were rescued. Grody. Only 40 survived. The Donner Party is remembered in the **Donner Memorial State Park** (582-7892), 3 mi. west of Truckee, and on countless t-shirts. To get to the park, take I-80 to the Donner Lake Exit, then go west on old U.S. 40 until you reach the park entrance. The park includes the **Emigrant Trail Museum,** which documents the infamous incident with dramatic multi-media flair c. 1975. Yum. (Museum open daily 10am-5pm. Admission $2, under 12 $1.)

ervoirs on Rte. 89 charge $8-10; sites at Stampede Meadows Dr. are either free or cost $12 per night. Stop at the ranger station on Rte. 89 just off I-80 for more maps and info (open Mon.-Fri. 8am-4:30pm). The **Donner Memorial Park,** 12593 Donner Pass Rd., is an expansive campground with fully equipped sites. Scenic views of Donner Lake and Summit make this site especially popular (sites $14). All campgrounds recommend reservations, especially on weekends (call MISTIX at 800-444-7275).

Take your pick of touristy restaurants and coffee shops in Truckee, or else forage for yourself at the **Safeway** supermarket on Rte. 89, about one mile west of downtown (open 24hr.). **Squeeze-In,** 10060 Commercial Row (587-9814), across from the Fire Station, offers 57 varieties of omelettes and sandwiches ($6-8) named after colorful locals like Luscious Lucy or Captain Avalanche, all squeezed into one little restaurant (open daily 7am-2pm; cash only).

SIGHTS AND SEASONAL EVENTS

The local historical society (582-0893) oversees a short town trail (maps at the Chamber of Commerce), as well as a small museum in the **Old Truckee Jail,** on Jibbom St. Though many Old West criminals were tarred and feathered, the lucky bad guys and girls were spared and locked up in this wood and stone prison until it closed in 1964 (open May-Oct. 11am-4pm; free).

While the Old Truckee Jail has its charms, most visitors come to Truckee for the outdoor recreation opportunities in Tahoe National Forest and Donner Memorial State Park. Check the *Truckee Activity Guide and Visitor Information,* available at the visitors center, for current info. The Truckee Ranger District of **Tahoe National Forest** has three lake-sized reservoirs, a number of streams, as well as small trout-trafficked lakes, which are excellent for fishing and boating. Some areas are easily accessible by car, but some require a short hike. Hiking at this popular weekend spot is more low-impact than around the rocky mountains surrounding Lake Tahoe. In winter, these snow-packed roads are good for cross-country skiing. The Sierra Mountaineer (see p. 393) sells a good area map ($8.95). The popular **Donner Memorial State Park** is the local playground, despite its morbid namesake. There are about 2½ mi. of hiking trails, the scenic Donner Lake, and picnic tables (parking $5 per day).

March brings the **Snowfest** winter carnival (583-7625). Celebrations color the sky with the **Truckee-Tahoe Air Show** (582-9068), at the end of June. And the second week in August brings a **Rodeo** (582-9852). The **Annual Donner Party Hike** (587-8808) reenacting the fateful journey takes place every October.

░ Reno

If a Hollywood exec ever got the great idea to cross the Elizabeth Berkley opus *Showgirls* with *The Golden Girls*, the result would be Reno. Hoping to strike it rich at the card tables, busloads of the nation's elderly flock to Reno for all its hedonistic splendor. The kaleidoscope of casinos, 24-hour bars, seedy motels, mountain vistas, strip clubs full of aspiring dancers, and neon-lit pawnshops make Reno a strange and memorable place. The fascination with Reno began in the early 1920s when several renowned public figures, including "America's Sweetheart" Mary Pickford, chose this Nevada city for expedient divorce settlements. Reno's nouveau fame attracted wealthy people and one-armed bandits alike, making it the so-called "biggest little city in the world."

As this oxymoronic slogan might suggest, Reno verges on schizophrenia. On one side is the California wilderness where verdant trees and azure lakes beckon with tranquility. On the other side the neon tubes and fog machines of casinos produce a technicolor haze of lights. Some say it lacks the frenzied fervor of its southern twin, but Reno's prime location amidst the awe-inspiring vistas of the Sierra is a jackpot that Vegas can only covet.

PRACTICAL INFORMATION

Visitor Information: Reno-Sparks Convention and Visitors Center, 300 N. Center St. (800-FOR-RENO/367-7366; http://www.playreno.com.), on the first floor of the National Bowling Stadium. Full of pamphlets, booklets, and the sound of falling bowling pins. Open Mon.-Sat. 7am-8pm, Sun. 9am-6pm.

Drinkin' an' Gamblin' Age: 21.

Compulsive Gamblers Hotline: 800-LOST-BET/567-8238. 24hr.

Kwik Cash: ATMs in most casinos. Most charge $1.50 for out-of-state withdrawals.

Bank: There are a number of banks in the city center—almost as many as there are casinos. **U.S. Bank,** 300 S. Virginia St. (688-3555), has good exchange rates.

Airport: Cannon International, 2001 E. Plumb Lane (328-6400), at Terminal Way on U.S. 395, 3 mi. southeast of downtown. Serves major airlines such as Southwest Airlines, a no-frills, discount West Coast carrier. Most major hotels have free shuttles for their guests; otherwise, take bus #24 from the city center. Taxis between downtown and the airport run around $9-10.

Trains: Amtrak, 135 E. Commercial Row (329-8638 or 800-USA-RAIL/872-7245). Ticket office open daily 8am-4:45pm. Arrive 30min. in advance to purchase ticket. To: San Francisco (1 per day, $36-66); Sacramento (1 per day, $32-60); Salt Lake City (1 per day at 5:45pm, $109); Chicago (1 per day at 5:45pm, $214).

Buses: Greyhound, 155 Stevenson St. (322-2970 or 800-231-2222), ½ block from W. 2nd St. Open 24hr. Prices are lower when traveling Mon.-Thurs., slightly higher Fri.-Sun. To: San Francisco (17 per day, $30/32); Salt Lake City (4 per day, $45/47); L.A. (11 per day, $40/42); Las Vegas (1 per day, $61). The station has lockers (up to 6hr. $2; 6-24hr. $4), a minimart, and a restaurant. **Arrow Trans** (786-2376) offers a van service to S. Lake Tahoe ($18 per person, 4-person min., or $72 base fare).

Public Transportation: Reno Citifare (348-7433) serves the Reno-Sparks area. Main terminal at 4th and Center St. Most buses operate 5am-7pm, though city center buses operate 24hr. Buses stop every 2 blocks. Fare $1.25, seniors and disabled 60¢, ages 6-18 90¢.

Taxis: Yellow Cab (355-5555). **Whittlesea Taxi** (322-2222). $1.50 initial fee, $1.40 per mi. 24hr. service.

Car Rental: Lloyd's International Rent-a-Car, 1201 Kietzke (348-4777 or 800-654-7037). Driver's license required. Minimum age 25, with full insurance 21. Credit card or cash deposit required. Prices depend on season and availability—usually around $30 per day, $130 per week; 150 free mi. per day.

Auto Repair: AAA Emergency Road Service, 826-5322 or 800-222-4357. 24hr.

Marriage: Men and women over 18 can pick up a marriage license (as an estimated 80% of Reno's visitors do) at the **Courthouse,** 117 S. Virginia St. (328-3274), for $35—all you need is a partner and an ID (open daily 8am-midnight). There are numerous chapels in Reno eager to help you tie the knot. **Adventure Inn,** 3575 S. Virginia St. (828-9000 or 800-937-1436), offers deluxe wedding packages that include a ceremony in the romantic Waterfall Chapel, music, photographs, flowers, stretch limo service, and 2 nights in one of their theme suites. Choose from such exotic rooms as the Amazon Suite, the Adam and Eve suite, or the Super Space Suite, which features an 18ft. pool, strobe lights, fog machine, and an 8-ft. heart-shaped bed. Call and hear the breathy, dramatic descriptions of different packages. Rooms "insure true adventure!" while supersuites "take you beyond imagination." For those on a strict budget, the bare-bones service is available at the **Starlite Chapel,** 80 Court St. (786-4949), for $77. Free parking during ceremony is an added bonus.

Divorce: To obtain a divorce permit, you must be a resident of Nevada for at least 6 weeks and pay a $140 service fee. Permits are available at the courthouse divorce office Mon.-Fri. 8am-5pm. Call 328-3535 for info. **Divorce Made Easy,** 790 S. Virginia St. (323-3359), offers "While-U-Wait" service for those who want to leave the paperwork to the pros. Fees ($230-400) depend on age of children and amount of property in dispute. Office open Mon.-Thurs. 8am-5pm.

Laundromat: Launderland & Coin-op Laundry, 680 E. 2nd St. (329-3733). Wash $1.25-2.75, depending on the size of the load; dry free. Open daily 7am-9:30 pm.

Road Conditions: Nevada (793-1313).

Crisis Lines: Rape Crisis, 800-992-5757; **Poison Control,** 328-4129; **Red Cross,** 856-1000; **Northern Nevada Language Bank,** 323-0500. Help in 15 languages. Open 24hr. **National HIV & AIDS Information Services,** 800-342-2437.

Pharmacy: Cerveri Drug Store, 190 E. 1st St. (322-6122), at 1st and Lake St. Open Mon.-Fri. 7:30am-6pm, Sat. 9am-5pm.

Medical Services: St. Mary's Hospital, 235 W. 6th St. (323-2041, emergency 789-3188), near Arlington Ave. Open 24hr. **Health Care Plus,** 6580 S. Virginia St. (853-3333). St. Mary's clinic. Open Mon.-Fri. 8am-5pm, Sat.-Sun. 9am-4pm.

Emergency: 911.

Post Office: 50 S. Virginia St. (800-275-8777), at Mill St., 2 blocks south of city center. Open Mon.-Fri. 7:30am-5pm, Sat. 10am-2pm. **ZIP Code:** 89501.

Area Code: 702.

ORIENTATION

Only 14 mi. from the California border and 443 mi. north of Las Vegas, Reno sits at the intersection of **I-80** and **U.S. 395,** which runs along the eastern slope of the Sierra Mountains and the scenic Truckee River. Scan West Coast papers for gambler's specials on bus and plane fare excursion tickets. Some include casino credits.

Although the city sprawls for miles, most of the major casinos are clustered **downtown** along Virginia and Sierra St., between 2nd and 4th. The wide and night-bright streets in downtown Reno are heavily patrolled in the summer, but be streetwise and avoid walking alone near the northeast corner at night. In the adjacent city of **Sparks** several casinos line I-80. Many of the buses conveniently stop at the major casinos in Reno and Sparks. The *Reno/Tahoe Travel Planner,* available at the visitors center, contains a local map and is an excellent guide to the city.

ACCOMMODATIONS AND CAMPING

There are a number of ways to go about getting accommodations in Reno. To truly experience the decadent splendor that is Reno, try staying at one of the many hotel-casinos. Although prices are usually on the high side, gamblers' specials, weekday rates, and winter discounts can make some great rooms affordable to budget travelers. Prices fluctuate unpredictably, so be sure to call ahead. **Fitzgerald's,** 225 N. Virginia St. (786-3663); **Atlantis,** 3800 S. Virginia St. (825-4700); **Circus Circus,** 500 N. Sierra St. (329-0711); and **Sundowner,** 450 N. Arlington Ave. (786-7050), have been known to offer some good deals to go along with their central locations and massive casino facilities.

Reno is packed with inexpensive hotels, though the many inner-city hotels can be unsavory. Southwestern downtown has the cheapest lodging. The prices below don't include Reno's 9% hotel tax, but your bill will. Also, public displays of affection by homosexual couples are illegal in Nevada. Members of the same sex sharing a hotel room may be required to book a room containing two twin beds.

El Cortez Hotel, 239 W. 2nd St. (322-9161). Decent hotel has A/C and a few long-time visitors. Singles $29, weekends $34; doubles $32, weekends $37.

Motel 6 has four locations in Reno, all of which live up to the chain's promise of clean, comfortable, and cheap rooms. Locations at 866 N. Wells Ave. (786-9852), north on I-80 Exit 14; 1901 S. Virginia St. (827-0255), 1½ mi. down Virginia St. at Plumb Ln.; and 1400 Stardust St. (747-7390), north on I-80 Keystone Exit and west onto Stardust. All supplement their rooms with pools and HBO. The motel at 666 N. Wells Ave. (329-8681), south on Wells off of I-80 Exit 14, has no pool, but is more centrally located. Summer rates: singles and doubles $30, weekends $38. Cheaper Oct.-May. Make summer reservations 2 weeks in advance.

To escape Reno's constant hum of slot machines, those equipped to camp can make the drive to the woodland sites of **Davis Creek Park** (849-0684), 17 mi. south on U.S. 395, then ½ mi. west (follow the signs). Wrap yourself in a rustic blanket of pines and sage at the base of the Sierra Nevada's Mt. Rose and camp at one of the 63 sites. You'll find full service, including showers, and a small pond stocked with fish, but no hookups. Sites available on first-come first-serve basis ($10 per site per vehicle, $1 per pet). Picnic area open 8am-9pm. The nearby 14 mi. Offer Creek Trail leads to Rock and Price Lakes and interlocks with the Tahoe Rim Trail. Camping and fishing on the trail are free but require permits (available at grocery and sporting goods stores). You can also camp along the shore at **Pyramid Lake** (see p. 398). To stay closer to Reno, park and plug in your RV overnight at the **Reno Hilton,** 2500 E. 2nd St. (789-2000), for a full hookup of $16.34.

FOOD

Eating in Reno is cheap. To entice gamblers and to prevent them from wandering out in search of food, casinos offer a range of all-you-can-eat cuisine. Bargain cuts of prime rib, massive buffets, and 99¢ breakfasts offer huge quantities of food at low prices. However, buffet fare can be greasy, overcooked, and tasteless, and rumors of food poisoning abound. Reno's other inexpensive eateries offer better food. The large Basque population, which immigrated from the Pyrenees to herd sheep in Nevada, have brought with them a spicy and hearty cuisine locals enthusiastically recommend.

The Blue Heron, 1091 S. Virginia St. (786-4110), 9 blocks from downtown. Without slot machines or video poker, the Blue Heron is a rare bird in Reno, appealing to a younger crowd in search of a respite from the rampant casino culture. This youthful energy is captured in the Fountain of Youth and other delicious smoothies ($2.85). The Heron offers hearty and healthy vegetarian cuisine (well-stuffed avocado sandwich $5.50). Dinner entrees ($9) include freshly baked bread and soup or salad. Open Mon.-Sat. 11am-9pm, Sun. noon-9pm.

Louis' Basque Corner, 301 E. 4th St. (323-7203), at Evans St., 3 blocks east of Virginia, is a local institution. The family-style dining, friendly waitstaff, spicy cuisine, and hearty portions will make you want to join up with the Basque separatists. Succulent tripe, savory rabbit. Lunch $7-8. Full-course dinners $15. Open Tues.-Sat. 11:30am-2:30pm and 5-9:30pm, Sun. 5-9:30pm.

Santa Fe Hotel, 235 Lake St. (323-1891), offers Basque cuisine. Wood bar, ancient slots, and jukebox take you back to the 50s. Hefty portions, served family-style. Local favorite for good food and friendly atmosphere. Bar is full of cowboy-hatted big men and bigger women. Lunch $7. Dinner includes soup, salad, stew, side dishes, meat entree, wine, and Basque cheese (all for $12). Open Mon.-Fri. noon-2pm and 6:15-9pm, Sat.-Sun. 6:15-9pm.

Miguel's Fine Mexican Food, 1415 S. Virginia St. (322-2722), a short drive from downtown. Peppy Mexican music sets this place apart from Reno's glitz. Voted best Mexican food in Nevada by *Nevada Weekly*'s readers, the tacos, enchiladas, and fajitas are indeed scrumptious. Entrees $6-9. Open Sun.-Thurs. 11am-9pm, Fri.-Sat. 11am-10pm.

The Nugget, 233 N. Virginia St. (323-0716), is a legendary 24-hr. bar-and-stool coffee shop. Signs that say things like "9 out of 10 vegetarians don't eat here" define the diner's gestalt. Breakfast special (99¢) includes two frisbee-sized pancakes and an egg. The "Awful Awful" burger is awfully big and comes with an equally huge portion of fries ($3.50).

SIGHTS AND ENTERTAINMENT

Reno is one big amusement park. The **casinos,** of course, are the main attraction. Many casinos offer free gaming lessons and minimum bets vary between establishments. Drinks are either free or incredibly cheap if you're gambling, but be wary of a casino's generous gift of highly alcoholic, risk-inducing, inhibition-dropping wallet-looseners. Don't forget that gambling is illegal for persons under 21; if you win the jackpot at age 20, it'll be the casino's lucky day and not yours.

Almost all casinos offer live night-time entertainment, but unless you like schmaltzy Wayne Newton standards or delight at the thought of Tom Jones autographing your underwear, these shows are generally not worth the steep admission prices. **Harrah's,** 219 N. Center St. (786-3232), is the self-consciously hip complex where Planet Hollywood capitalizes on the movie lust, magically transforming Hollywood knick-knacks into precious relics. Though the stars do make occasional appearances, the encased dummies and star-glitzed paraphernalia are as close as most visitors will come to fulfilling their fame-hungry fantasies. Harrah's also features a Playboy revue, where that wild west dancing hits on those nerves of American nostalgia. Call for ticket prices and showtimes. At **Circus Circus,** 500 N. Sierra (329-0711), a small circus above the casino performs "big-top" shows every half hour. Not exactly the Shriners, but just as much kitsch value. These shows and others are listed in the weekly *Showtime* publication which also offers prime selection of gambling coupons. *Best Bets* provides listings of discounted local events and shows. *Encore* lists upcoming arts events in northern Nevada. *Nevada Events & Shows,* a section of *Nevada* visitors' guide, lists sights, museums, seasonal events, and other goodies. These free papers are available in most hotels and casinos. More info is in the local *Reno-Gazette Journal.*

Though it may come as a surprise, Reno is not yet one big casino. Special events in the area can make for a distinct experience. The local Basque influence breaks through the seams of the blanketing casino culture at Reno's annual **Basque Festival** (329-1476), held in August. This weekend of frenetic bacchanalia features traditional contests, dancing, live music, and more food than the Circus Circus buffet. The first week in August roars into chrome-covered, hot-rod splendor with **Hot August Nights** (356-1956), a celebration of America's love affair with the cars and the rock and roll of the 50s and 60s, with shows, auctions, and a parade. The annual **Reno Rodeo** (329-3877), one of the biggest in the West, gallops over eight days in late June. In September, the **Great Reno Balloon Race** (325-7159), in Rancho San Rafael, and the **National Championship Air Races** (972-6663), at the Stead Airport, draw an international group of contestants and spectators. Also in September, nearby **Virginia City** hosts **Camel Races** (847-0311), where camels and ostriches race through town, at about the same time. To get to the site of this crazy festival, take U.S. 395 south, then Rte. 341 about 25 mi. Reno hits the big-time in road racing with the **Reno Hilton Grand Prix** (789-2000 or 800-FOR-RENO/367-7366), also in September. Vroom! Reserve hotel rooms in advance for any of the special events.

■ Near Reno: Pyramid Lake

Thirty miles north of Reno on Rte. 445, on the Paiute Indian Reservation, lies emerald green Pyramid Lake, one of the most stunningly beautiful bodies of water in the U.S. The pristine waters of Pyramid Lake are set against the backdrop of a barren desert, making it a soothing respite from neon Reno. It is the remnant of Ice-Age-era-Lake Lahontam, which once covered 8450 sq. mi. John Fremont renamed the lake for the white man when he came across it and the pyramid-shaped island off the eastern shore in 1844. Now the 26 mi. lake is frequented by sun-soakers, swimmers, and water-skiers.

Camping is allowed anywhere on the lake shore, but only designated areas have toilet facilities. A $5 **permit** is required for use of the park and the area is carefully patrolled by the Paiute tribe. Permits are available at the **Ranger Station** 3 mi. left from Rte. 445 at Sutcliffe (476-1155; open Mon.-Sat. 9am-5pm). The Lake is an angler's paradise from October through June, when trophy-size cutthroat trout are reeled in with great frequency. Heat resistant hikers can climb the bizarre tufa formations that saddle the lake on the north shore and visit the hot springs at Needles. Those looking for solitude should try the south and east shores; the areas north of the ranger station are clogged with RVs.

NATIONAL PARKS AND FORESTS

Lost in the heart of the central Sierra, a traveler would hardly know that this was still California. Far from the urban centers and industry of the coastal areas, the central Sierra is nature as it was meant to be. Clear streams splash over stones and trout, and the snowy peaks are populated only by endless pine trees. No need to fear an end to this wilderness—almost all of it is protected by the government. The two main park areas are Yosemite National Park (near Stanislaus National Forest and Mono Lake), and Sequoia and Kings Canyon National Parks (framed by the Sierra National Forest to the north and the Sequoia National Forest to the south). National parks may conserve the natural surroundings, but they also attract adventure-hungry tourists from around the world. Those seeking solitude might want to listen to the call of the wild and stick to the backcountry in less popular national forests.

■ Yosemite National Park

In 1868 a young Scotsman named John Muir arrived by boat in San Francisco and asked for directions to "anywhere that's wild." Anxious to run this crazy youngster out of town, Bay Area folk directed him toward the heralded lands of Yosemite. The wonders that Muir beheld there not only sated his wanderlust but also spawned a lifetime of conservationism. His efforts won Yosemite national park status by 1880.

If Muir's 19th century desire to flee the concrete confines of civilization was considered crazy, then today we live in a world gone mad. In 1996, almost four million visitors poured into the park; while Yosemite's granite cliffs, thunderous waterfalls, lush meadows, and thick pine forests are awe-inspiring, they are often marred by a tourist throng. A swarm of snack shops, souvenir stands, and gas stations has sunk the valley into commercial chaos, and automobile traffic in the park's most popular areas often rivals that of an L.A. freeway at rush hour. Nevertheless, Yosemite remains a paradise for outdoor enthusiasts: visitors congregate in only 6% of the park (Yosemite Valley), leaving thousands of beautiful backcountry miles in relative peace and quiet.

PRACTICAL INFORMATION AND ORIENTATION

Visitor Information:
General Park Information (372-0265, 24hr. recording 372-0200, TTY 372-4726). Info on accommodations, activities, and weather. Open Mon.-Fri. 9am-5pm. All visitors centers have free maps, copies of *Yosemite Guide,* and wilderness permits (reserve in advance; for more info see **Backcountry,** p. 407). All hours listed are valid May-Sept. unless otherwise noted.

THE SIERRA NEVADA

Yosemite Valley Visitors Center (372-0299), Yosemite Village. Sign language interpreter. Open mid-June-Labor Day daily 8am-9pm; winter 9am-5pm.

Wilderness Center, P.O. Box 545, Yosemite National Park 95839 (372-0308), Yosemite Village. **Backcountry** info. Open daily 8:30am-4:30pm.

Tuolumne Meadows Visitors Center (372-0263), on Tioga Rd. 55mi. from Yosemite Village. The headquarters of **high-country** activity, with trail info, maps, and special programs. Open summers only 8am-7pm.

Big Oak Flat Info Station (379-1899), Rte. 120 west in Crane Flat/Tuolumne Sequoia Grove. Open daily 8am-6pm. Wilderness permits daily 7:30am-6pm.

Wawona Info Station (375-9501), Rte. 141 at the southern entrance near the Mariposa Grove. Open daily 8:30am-5pm.

Yosemite Area Travel Info: General info (http://www.nps.gov/yose). **Visitor info** (http://www.yosemite.org). **Project updates and photographs** (http://www.connect.net/yosemite).

ATM: Bank of America, next to the Art Activity Center in Yosemite Village. Also a check-cashing service. Open daily 8am-4pm.

Gas Stations: Chevron stations in Yosemite Valley (open daily 7am-9pm), Crane Flat (open daily 8am-8pm), and El Portal (open Mon.-Sat. 7am-7pm, Sun. 8am-7pm). Tank up before driving into the High Sierra—prices rise with the elevation.

Auto Repairs: Village Garage (372-8320), tows cars 24hr. Open daily 8am-5pm. **AAA Emergency Road Service** (372-1221).

Bike Rental: Yosemite Lodge (372-1208) and **Curry Village** (372-8319) for $5.25 per hr., $20 per day. Both open daily 8am-7pm.

Equipment Rental: Yosemite Mountaineering School (372-8344 or 372-1244), Rte. 120 at Tuolumne Meadows. Sleeping bags and backpacks both $4 per day, snowshoes $11 per day. Climbing shoes rented to YMS students only. Driver's license or credit card required. Open daily 8:30am-5pm. **Stables** at Yosemite Valley (372-8348), Wawona (375-6502), and Tuolumne Meadows (372-8477). Guided rides start at $35 for 2hr. For info on **ski** and **snowshoe** rental, see **Wintertime in Yosemite,** p. 408.

Laundromat: In summer, laundry facilities open at **Housekeeping Camp.** Wash $1.25, 10min. dry 25¢. Open daily 7:30am-7pm. In winter, laundry facilities available at **Camp 6,** across the street from the Village Store. Open daily 8am-11pm.

Showers: Facilities available in summer at **Housekeeping Camp** ($2 includes towel and soap; open daily 7am-8pm) and **Curry Village** (open 24hr.). Also at **Tuolumne Meadows** and **White Wolf Lodges** ($2).

Weather and Road Conditions (372-0200). 24hr.

Medical Services: Yosemite Medical Clinic (372-4637), in Yosemite Village near Ahwanee Hotel. Open Mon.-Fri. 8am-9pm, Sat. 9am-noon. Emergency room 24hr. **Emergency:** 911.

Internet Access: Yosemite Bug Hostel (966-6666), 30mi. west of Yosemite on Rte. 140 in Midpines. Internet access $2 for 15min.

Post Office: Yosemite Village, next to the visitors center. Open Mon.-Fri. 8:30am-5pm, Sat. 10am-noon. **Curry Village,** near the registration office. Open June-Sept. Mon.-Fri. 11:30am-3pm. **Yosemite Lodge,** open Mon.-Fri. 9am-1pm and 2-4:30pm. **Wawona,** open Mon.-Fri. 9am-5pm. **Tuolumne Meadows,** open Mon.-Fri. 9am-4:30pm, Sat. 9am-noon. **ZIP Code:** 95389.

Area Code: 209.

In all, Yosemite covers 1189 square mi. of mountainous terrain. The park's most enduring monuments—El Capitan, Half Dome, and Yosemite Falls, among others—lie in Yosemite Valley, and were carved out by glaciers over thousands of years. Much is to be seen away from the valley and its gaggle of gawkers, however. Little Yosemite Valley, easily accessible by hiking trails, is home to the spectacular Vernal and Nevada Falls. Tuolumne Meadows (pronounced ta-WALL-um-ee), in the park's northeastern corner, is an Elysian expanse of alpine meadow surrounded by cliffs and swift-running streams. Mariposa Grove is a forest of giant sequoia trees at the park's southern end. The **park entrance fee** is $10 per hiker, biker, or bus rider, or $20 per car (pass valid for seven days). A **one-year pass** is $40.

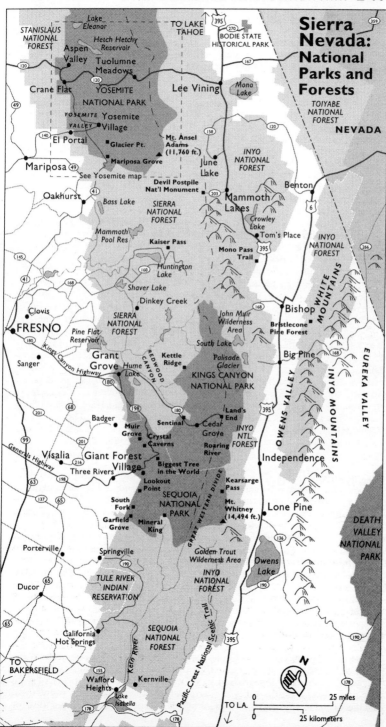

Sierra Nevada: National Parks and Forests

STANISLAUS NATIONAL FOREST

Lake Eleanor

TO LAKE TAHOE

BODIE STATE HISTORICAL PARK

Hetch Hetchy Reservoir

Aspen Valley

Tuolumne Meadows

Crane Flat

YOSEMITE NATIONAL PARK

Lee Vining

Mono Lake

TOIYABE NATIONAL FOREST

YOSEMITE VALLEY

Yosemite Village

NEVADA

El Portal

Glacier Pt.

Mt. Ansel Adams (11,760 ft.)

INYO NATIONAL FOREST

Mariposa

Mariposa Grove

June Lake

See Yosemite map

Oakhurst

Devil Postpile Nat'l Monument

Benton

Bass Lake

SIERRA NATIONAL FOREST

Mammoth Lakes

Mammoth Pool Res

Kaiser Pass

Crowley Lake

Tom's Place

INYO NATIONAL FOREST

Mono Pass Trail

Huntington Lake

Shaver Lake

Dinkey Creek

Clovis

John Muir Wilderness Area

Bishop

WHITE MOUNTAINS

Bristlecone Pine Forest

FRESNO

SIERRA NATIONAL FOREST

Pine Flat Reservoir

South Lake

Sanger

Kings Canyon Highway

Grant Grove

Hume Lake

REDWOOD CANYON

Kettle Ridge

Palisade Glacier

KINGS CANYON NATIONAL PARK

Big Pine

EUREKA VALLEY

INYO MOUNTAINS

OWENS VALLEY

Badger

Muir Grove

Sentinel

Land's End

Cedar Grove

INYO NTL. FOREST

Crystal Caverns

Roaring River

Visalia

Giant Forest Village

Generals Highway

Three Rivers

Biggest Tree in the World

Independence

Lookout Point

SEQUOIA NATIONAL PARK

Kearsarge Pass

South Fork

Garfield Grove

Mineral King

Mt. Whitney (14,494 ft.)

Lone Pine

GREAT WESTERN DIVIDE

Porterville

Springville

Golden Trout Wilderness Area

Owens Lake

DEATH VALLEY NATIONAL PARK

Ducor

TULE RIVER INDIAN RESERVATION

INYO NATIONAL FOREST

California Hot Springs

SEQUOIA NATIONAL FOREST

Kern River

Pacific-Crest National Scenic Trail

TO BAKERSFIELD

Wafford Heights

Kernville

Lake Isabella

TO L.A.

N

0 25 miles

0 25 kilometers

THE SIERRA NEVADA

GETTING THERE AND GETTING AROUND

Yosemite lies 200 mi. east of San Francisco (a 3½hr. drive) and 320 mi. northeast of Los Angeles (a 6-9hr. drive, depending on the season). It can be reached by taking **Rte. 140** from Merced, **Rte. 41** north from Fresno, and **Rte. 120** east from Manteca or west from Lee Vining.

By Bus or Train

Yosemite runs public **buses** that connect the park with **Merced** and **Fresno**. **Yosemite VIA,** 300 Grogan Ave., Merced 95340 (742-5211 or 800-VIA-LINE/842-5463), runs three buses per day from the Merced Amtrak station to Yosemite (7am, 10:40am, and 3:30pm; $20, round-trip $38). VIA also runs **Yosemite Gray Line (YGL)** (722-0366), which meets trains arriving in Merced from San Francisco and takes passengers to Yosemite. YGL also runs to and from Fresno ($20). **Amtrak** (800-USA-RAIL/872-7245), runs from San Francisco to Merced (one-way $20) and connects with the waiting YGL bus. Amtrak also provides transport via shuttle bus and train from L.A. to Fresno ($25) and Merced ($29).

The best bargain in Yosemite is the free **shuttle bus system.** Comfortable but often crowded, the buses have knowledgeable drivers and wide viewing windows. (Shuttles run daily every 10min. 7am-10pm, every 20min. before 7am and after 10pm.) **Hikers' buses** run daily to Glacier Point (spring-autumn) and to Tuolumne Meadows/Lee Vining (late June-Labor Day; for info call 372-1240).

Tour tickets are available at any lodging facility or at the tour desk in front of the Village Store. The basic **Valley Floor Tour** lasts two hours and points out Half Dome, El Capitan, Bridalveil Falls, and Happy Isles. The tour is conducted on an open-air tram (fare $17, ages 5-12 $8). The **Glacier Point Tour** lasts four hours and climbs to the point for a 3200 ft. high view of the valley (June-Oct.; fare $20, ages 5-12 $10.25). The two-hour **Moonlight Tour,** given on nights with a full (or near-full) moon, offers unique nighttime views of the cliffs ($16). Call (372-1240) for reservations, departure times, and locations. An excellent way to see both the "essentials" and the off-the-beaten-path spots is to take an **Incredible Adventures** tour (800-777-8464; info@incadventures.com; http://www.incadventures.com). Catering to an international backpacker clientele, the informative guides lead 4-day, 3-night hiking tours leaving from San Francisco on Wednesdays and Sundays. The incredible adventure is an incredible bargain; the $169 fee covers meals, entrance fee, equipment, transportation, and tax. Daytrips run throughout the year ($75).

By Car

Although the inner valley is often congested with traffic, the best way to gain a rapid overview of Yosemite is by **car.** Drivers should keep in mind that the devastating floods of January 1997 have damaged many valley roads; delays can be expected at all times of day. A more relaxing (and environmentally friendly) option is to park at one of the lodging areas and ride the shuttle to see the valley sights, then hop back into your car to explore other places. Drivers intending to visit the high country in spring and fall should have **snow tires** (sometimes required even in summer). Of the five major approaches to the park, Rte. 120 to the Big Oak Flat entrance is the curviest. A less nauseating alternative is to take Rte. 140 from Merced into Yosemite Valley. The eastern entrance, Tioga Pass, is closed during snow season but makes for a breathtaking summer drive. (For more info on winter driving, see **Wintertime in Yosemite,** p. 408.) Driving is convenient and fast, but be sure to leave motorized transport behind for some wilderness exploration or you'll miss the park's spirit.

Not by Car

Cycling is also an excellent way to see Yosemite Valley; there are bike paths everywhere and most sights are within a 4 mi. diameter across the Valley center (for rental info, see **Practical Information,** p. 399). A particularly popular bike trial is the wide paved road from the valley campgrounds to Mirror Lake (3mi. round-trip), which is closed to motorized vehicles. Although Yosemite's bike paths are ideal for

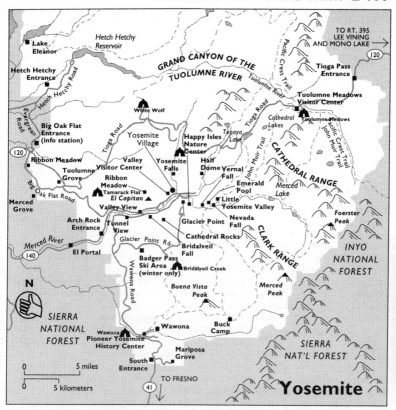

leisurely rides and for circumventing automobile traffic, serious cyclists should not expect a workout, and off-road mountain biking isn't permitted in the park.

Guided **horseback trips** into Yosemite's backcountry are available by reservation only. The park has three stables (see **Practical Information,** p. 399).

ACCOMMODATIONS

When American transcendentalist Ralph Waldo Emerson visited Yosemite in 1884, the park's accommodations were so simple that the group was awakened in the morning by the clucking of a hen climbing over their beds. These days, Yosemite's accommodations have become much more comfortable. At times, however, you may feel as if you need to be a dignitary of Emerson's stature to get a room in the valley—spring and summer rates are high (suites at the luxurious Ahwahnee Hotel start at $227 in season), and space is tight. Reservations are necessary and can be made up to one year in advance by calling 209-252-4848. All park lodgings provide access to dining and laundry facilities, showers, and supplies. Rates are in constant flux, but tend to be higher on weekends and during the summer (those given below are for summer weekends). Check-in hovers around 11am.

Yosemite Lodge, in Yosemite Valley west of Yosemite Village and directly across from Yosemite Falls. Tiny cabins are as close to motel accommodations as the valley gets. Singles and doubles $87, with bath $101.

Curry Village, southeast of Yosemite Village. Swimming pool, nightly shows at the amphitheater, snack stands, cafeteria, and ice rink in winter. Noisy back-to-back cabins $56, with bath $73. Canvas-sided cabins $41.

Housekeeping Camp, west of Curry Village. Canvas-capped concrete "cottages" ($48) accommodate up to 4 people and include double beds, chairs, and stoves.

Tuolumne Meadows Lodge, on Tioga Rd. in northeast corner of park. Canvas-sided cabin $43 for 2, each additional adult $6.50, child $3.25.

White Wolf Lodge, west of Tuolumne Meadows on Tioga Rd. Cabins with bath $65. Tent cabins $41.25 for 2, each additional adult $6.50, child $3.50.

The Redwoods (325-6666), 23mi. south of the valley in Wawone. These 11 homes have 6 bedrooms; some a satellite dish and barbecue. Check-in 3pm. From $82.

Yosemite Bug Hostel (966-6666; fax 966-6667; http://yosemitebug.com), 30mi. west of Yosemite on Rte. 140 in Midpines. Beer on tap, pool table, dart board, and library. Offers outdoor expeditions and tremendous food ($3.50-$7). Dorms and tent sites $12; private rooms $18. Linens $1. Laundry $2. Internet access $2.50.

CAMPGROUNDS

To most visitors, Yosemite is camping country. Hence most of the valley's campgrounds are choked with tents, trailers, and RVs. Reservations can be made through DESTINET (800-436-7275; from outside the U.S. 619-452-8787), up to five months in advance. Visitors to the park this year should bear in mind that the **winter floods** ravaged many valley campsites—the Upper and Lower River campgrounds are closed indefinitely for repair. **Cancellation lotteries** are held at the campground reservations office in Curry Village, but the odds are against you (daily 8am and 3pm). In summer, there is a 14-night maximum stay for campers outside the valley, except Wawona (7-night max. stay) and a seven-night maximum stay for those in the valley. At all campgrounds served by natural stream water (Tamarack Flat, Yosemite Creek, and Porcupine Flat), the **water must be boiled, filtered, or treated** to prevent *giardia,* a nasty intestinal disease. Iodine water treatments can be purchased at any supply store. Backcountry camping is prohibited in the valley, but not outside it (see **Beyond Yosemite Valley: Backcountry,** p. 408).

Inside Yosemite Valley

Sunnyside, at the west end of Yosemite Valley past the Yosemite Lodge Chevron station. A walk to the climber's camp will immerse you in the climbing subculture, in which seasoned adventurers swap stories of exploits on vertical rock faces. Be prepared to meet new friends, since every site is filled with 6 people, regardless of the size of your group. Water, toilets, and tables. $3 per person. Often fills up early with reservation-less visitors. Open year-round.

Backpacker's Camp, 1½mi. east of Yosemite Village across the river, behind North Pine Campground. Must have a wilderness permit and be a backpacker without a vehicle to camp here. Low on facilities, high on camaraderie. Fishing is popular. Running water and toilets nearby. 2-night max. stay. $3 per person. Open May-Oct.

Lower Pines, in the busy eastern end of Yosemite Valley. Commercial and crowded. Toilets, water, showers, and tables. Sites $15. This is the designated **winter camping** spot and the only one in the valley which allows pets.

Beyond Yosemite Valley

Hodgdon Meadow, on Rte. 120 near Big Oak Flat entrance. Warm enough for winter camping. Thickly-wooded sites provide some seclusion even when the campground is full. Water, tables, and toilets. Sites $15.

Tuolumne Meadows, 55mi. east on Rte. 120. Half of the 314 sites can be reserved through DESTINET; other sites are for same-day reservations. Drive into the sprawling campground or escape the RVs by ambling to the 25 walk-in sites. Great scenery and nearby trailheads. Pets allowed in the western section only. Water, toilets, and tables. Drive-in sites $15, backpacker sites $3 per person. Open Aug.-Sept., depending on snowpack.

Wawona, 27mi. south of the valley off Rte. 41. Characterless and somewhat cramped, these 100 sites are near the Merced River. Tables, toilets, and water. No showers. Pets allowed. Sites $15.

Tamarack Flat, 23mi. northeast of Yosemite Valley. Take Rte. 120 east and follow the rough road for 3mi. (if your car can take it) to 52 rustic drive-in sites. Pit toilets and waterless facilities mean that Tamarack fills up later than other campgrounds, but hardy campers are rewarded by the awe-inspiring views from nearby hillsides. Pets allowed. Sites $6. Open July-Oct.

Bridalveil Creek, 25mi. south of the valley on Glacier Point Rd. Peaceful grounds have 110 first-come, first-camped sites. Convenient to Glacier and Taft Points; 2min. walk to beautiful McGurk Meadow. Sites $10. Open June-Sept.

Porcupine Flat, off Rte. 120 east. RV access to front section only. Pit toilets, potable stream water. 52 sites. Sites $6. Open late June-Sept.

White Wolf, off Rte. 120 east. Water, toilets, tables, fire pits. Pets allowed. 87 sites. Sites $10. Open late June-Sept., depending on snowpack.

FOOD

Since the Delaware North Company monopolizes Yosemite's only industry, that of tourism, restaurants are expensive and dreary. Cooking a campfire feast is a much more interesting option. Overpriced groceries can be found at **Yosemite Lodge, Wawona,** or the **Village Stores** (open daily 8am-10pm; Oct.-May 8am-9pm). A better idea is to buy supplies in Merced or Fresno before coming to the park.

Pasta Place (372-8381), above Degnan's Deli in the Yosemite Village complex. It's, well, a pasta place. Pasta and caesar salad $5.35. Open daily 11:30am-9pm.

Village Grill, in Yosemite Village. A low-priced snack bar—filling but certainly not gourmet. Hamburgers $3, breakfast (2 eggs, sausage, biscuit, hash browns) $2.20. Open daily 7:30am-8pm.

Degnan's Delicatessen, in Yosemite Village. Inside a convenience store and adjacent to an ice cream parlor. Sandwiches $4. Open daily 7am-10:30pm.

SIGHTS AND THE OUTDOORS

By Car

Although the view is better if you get out of the car, you can see a large part of Yosemite from the bucket seat. The *Yosemite Road Guide* ($3.95 at every visitors center) is keyed to roadside markers and outlines a superb tour of the park—it's almost like having a ranger tied to the hood. Spectacular panoramas are omnipresent during the drive east along **Tioga Road** (Rte. 120). This stretch of road is the highest highway strip in the country; as it winds down from Tioga Pass through the park's eastern exit it plunges over a mile to reach the lunar landscapes of Mono Lake. The drive west from the pass brings you to **Tuolumne Meadows** and its open, alpine spaces, to shimmering **Tenaya Lake,** and innumerable scenic views of granite slopes and canyons. No less incredible are the views afforded by the southern approach (Rte. 41) to Yosemite. Chief among these is the **Wawona Tunnel** turnout, which even fledgling visitors will immediately recognize as the subject of many Ansel Adams photographs. If you can squirm your way through the crowds, you will be treated to the sight of 7569 ft. **El Capitan** (the largest granite monolith in the world), misty Bridalveil Falls, and the **Three Brothers** (three adjacent granite peaks). A drive into the heart of the valley leads to **Yosemite Falls** (the highest in North America at 2425ft.), **Sentinel Rock,** and **Half Dome.**

For a different perspective on the valley, drive to **Glacier Point,** off Glacier Point Rd. Hovering 3214 ft. above the valley floor, this gripping overlook is guaranteed to impress the most jaded traveler. Half Dome rests majestically across the valley, and the sounds of **Vernal** and **Nevada Falls** provide enough white noise to drown out the roar of the tour buses and their ceaselessly chattering passengers.

To investigate Yosemite's most famous flora, take the short hiking trail through the giant sequoia of **Mariposa Grove.** This interpretive walk begins off Rte. 241 at the **Fallen Monarch,** a massive trunk lying on its side, and continues to both the 209 ft., 2700-year-old **Grizzly Giant** and the fallen **Wawona Tunnel Tree.** Ancient Athens was in its glory when many of these trees were saplings.

Day Hiking in the Valley

To have the full Yosemite experience, visitors must travel the outer trails on foot. A wealth of opportunities reward anyone willing to lace up a pair of boots, even if only for a daytrip. Day-use trails are usually busy, sometimes positively (or rather, negatively) packed, and occasionally (i.e. July 4th weekend) the site of human traffic jams. Hiking early—just after sunrise—is the best (and sometimes only) way to beat the crowds. A colorful trail map with difficulty ratings and average hiking times is available at the visitors center (50¢; see **Practical Information,** p. 399). **Bridalveil Falls,** another Ansel Adams favorite, is an easy ¼ mi. stroll from the nearby shuttle bus stop, and its cool spray is as close to a shower as many Yosemite campers ever get. The **Mirror Lake Loop** is a level 3 mi. walk. These two trails, as well as **Lower Yosemite Falls Trail,** are wheelchair-accessible.

Upper Yosemite Falls Trail, a back-breaking 3½ mi. trek to the windy summit, rewards the intrepid hiker with an overview of the 2425 ft. drop. Those with energy to spare can trudge on to Inspiration Point, where views of the valley below rival those from more-heralded Glacier Point. The trail begins its extremely steep, unshaded ascent behind the village gas station. Leaving the marked trail is not a wise idea—as one sign reads, "If you go over the waterfall, you will die."

From the Happy Isles trailhead, the **John Muir Trail** leads 211 mi. to **Mt. Whitney,** but most visitors prefer to take the slightly less strenuous 1½ mi. **Mist Trail** past **Vernal Falls** (only visible from this trail) to the top of **Nevada Falls.** This is perhaps the most popular day-use trail in the park, and for good reason—views of the falls from the trails are outstanding, and the indefatigable drizzle that issues from the nearby water-assaulted rocks is more than welcome during the hot summer months (although it can be slippery). There is a **free shuttle** from the valley campgrounds to Happy Isles; no parking is available. The Mist Trail continues past Nevada Falls to the base of **Half Dome,** Yosemite's most recognizable monument and a powerful testament to the power of glaciation. Look closely from below—the profile of an Ahwahnee princess is supposedly stained into the rock. For those who aren't up to the rigor of rock climbing, there is a challenging hike up the back side which requires the aid of climbing cables (open in summer only). You'll need all day to make it here and back in time for the last shuttle—this 17 mi. round-trip is considered the most difficult hike in the valley. Skip the climb if it looks stormy; lightning has been known to strike the wet summit of Half Dome and run down along the metal cables.

Fire Follies

Yosemite is widely known for its falling water (dozens of whitewater cascades), for its falling earth (Happy Isles' 1996 rockslide incident), and for its falling temperatures in winter. But few visitors know that fire once fell within park boundaries as well. Staged **"Fire Falls"** were once a major tourist draw in Yosemite. From 1822 to 1868, park officials would occasionally build a substantial fire at the edge of Glacier Point and scrape its coals over the cliffs at 9pm sharp. The resulting effect matched the daytime grandeur of the valley's waterfalls and attracted big-spending gawkers from far and wide.

As park objectives progressed from capitalism to conservationism, however, Fire Falls were scaled back and eventually eliminated altogether. Fortunately, Hollywood has preserved this historic phenomenon for posterity. To see a Fire Fall today, simply make it a Blockbuster night: pop Bogie's *The Caine Mutiny* (1954) into the VCR and relax. Forty-five minutes after the opening credits, you will be treated to a fabulous seven-second Fire Fall in stunning Technicolor.

The wildflower-laden **Pohon Trail** starts from Glacier Point, crossing Sentinel River (spectacular **Sentinel Falls,** the park's second-largest cascade, lies to the north) on its way to Taft Point and other secluded lookouts. A hikers' bus leaves from the valley in the morning for the **Four Mile Trail** (4¾mi. one way) and the **Panorama Trail** (8mi. one way), both of which also start at Glacier Point.

Activities

Park rangers lead a variety of informative hikes and other activities for visitors of all ages. **Junior ranger** (ages 8-10) and **senior ranger** (ages 11-12) activities allow children to hike, raft, and investigate aquatic and terrestrial life. These three-hour summer programs, usually held mid-week, require reservations at least a day in advance through the Yosemite Valley Visitors Center and cost $2 (see **Practical Information,** p. 399). Rangers also guide a number of free walks. **Explore Yosemite!** tours (60-90 min.) address a variety of historical and geological topics. All leave daily at 9am, and most are wheelchair-accessible. Rangers also lead strenuous, four-to-eight-hour **Destination Hikes** into the high country from Tuolumne Meadows. Other free, park-sponsored adventures include morning photographic hikes, art classes in the **Art Activity Center** (372-1442; open daily 9am-5pm; art instruction 10am-2pm; bring your own supplies), Native American cultural events in the Miwok-Paiute Village, and spectacular stargazing from Glacier Point. Further interpretive information can be garnered at the **Yosemite Village Museum** next to the visitors center. Inside is a modest art gallery and a reconstruction of an Ahwahnee village (open daily 8am-5:30pm). Events are listed in the *Yosemite Guide* (available at all visitors centers).

In 1903, John Muir gave Teddy Roosevelt a now-famous tour of Yosemite. The renowned **thespian** Lee Stetson has assumed Muir's role, leading free, one-hour hikes along the same route. Stetson also hosts *The Spirit of John Muir,* a 90-minute one-man show, and *Conversation with a Tramp* (Tues.-Fri. 8pm; tickets $5, under 12 $2; buy tickets at the door or from the visitors center).

The world's best climbers come to Yosemite to test themselves at angles past vertical. If you've got the courage (and the cash), you can join the stellar Yosemite rock climbers by taking a lesson with the **Yosemite Mountaineering School.** Basic **rock climbing classes,** offered daily in summer (mid-April to Oct.), teach basic skills on the ground before ascending an 80 ft. cliff and introducing bouldering and rappelling ($60 for 3 or more classes; $120 for individual courses; intermediate lessons on weekends and alternating weekdays $50-60; advanced classes also offered). Reservations are useful and require advance payment, though drop-ins are accepted if space allows. For more info contact Yosemite Mountaineering School, Yosemite 95389 (372-8344; open daily 8:30am-5pm).

Fishing is allowed April through November in any of Yosemite's lakes, streams, or rivers, but don't expect to catch anything. Each year a few of the lakes are selected to be stocked with trout, but the names of these lakes are not made public. Anglers may obtain a **fishing license** from grocery or sporting goods stores in Yosemite Valley, Wawona, Tuolumne, and White Wolf (resident license $26.50, one-day $10; non-resident $72; 16 and under fish free). There are also two free fishing days each season. Consult the *Fishing in Yosemite National Park* handout for specific guidelines. Tackle is available at the **Village Sport Shop** (372-1286; open daily 8:30am-7pm).

Rafting is permitted on the Merced River from 10am to 6pm, but no motorized crafts are allowed. **Swimming** is allowed throughout the park except where posted. Those who prefer their water chlorinated can swim in the **public pools** at Curry Village and Yosemite Lodge (open daily 10am-5pm; admission $1.50 for non-guests). **Bird watchers** should pick up a field checklist at the visitors center. Those inspired by Muir's conservationism can join a group of **ecotourists** who restore damaged park assets and work to maintain natural habitats (call 372-0265 for info).

THE SIERRA NEVADA

BEYOND YOSEMITE VALLEY: BACKCOUNTRY

Most folks never leave the valley, but a wilder, lonelier Yosemite awaits those who do. The **Wilderness Center** in Yosemite Valley offers maps and personalized assistance in selecting an appropriate backcountry route. (For advice on keeping yourself and the wilderness intact, see **Essentials: Wilderness Concerns,** p. 46.) Topographical **maps** and hiking guides are especially helpful in navigating Yosemite's nether regions. Equipment can be rented or purchased through the Mountaineering School at Tuolomne Meadows (see **Practical Information,** p. 399) or through the **Mountain Shop** at Curry Village, but backpacking stores in major cities are more economical.

Backcountry **camping** is prohibited in the valley (you'll get slapped with a stiff fine if caught), but it's generally permitted along the high country trails with a free **wilderness permit** (call 372-0310 for general info; you must have a planned itinerary and ranger approval to obtain a permit). Each trailhead limits the number of permits available, so reserve by mail between March to May (write Wilderness Center, P.O. Box 577, Yosemite National Park 95389), or take your chances with the 50% quota held on 24-hour notice at the Yosemite Valley Visitors Center, the Wawona Ranger Station, and Big Oak Flat Station (see **Practical Information,** p. 399). Popular trails like Little Yosemite Valley, Clouds Rest, and Half Dome fill quotas quickly.

In the high country, many hikers stay at the undeveloped mountain campgrounds, which offer both company (to feed the soul) and bear lockers (to seal the food). Hikers can also store food in hanging bear bags (see **Essentials: Bear in Mind,** p. 47) or in rentable plastic **canisters** from the Yosemite Valley Sports Shop ($3 per day). Canisters may be mandatory on more popular hiking routes.

Several **high country hikes** provide access to seldom-seen, out-of-the-way areas of the park. Some trailheads are accessible via a free shuttle bus to **Tuolumne Meadows.** For a taste of "real" rock climbing without requisite equipment and training, Yosemite day hikers scramble up **Lembert Dome** above Tuolumne Meadows. This gentle (by rock climbing standards) incline riddled with foot and hand holds is nonetheless a solid granite face. The 4 mi. approach to **Cathedral Lakes** from the west end of the meadows is another worthwhile hike, winding its way through dense forest to the Cathedral Lakes basin. For those hikers with something more rigorous in mind, a tough scramble past **May Lake** leads to the peak of **Mt. Hoffman** (10,850ft.). Visitors should always be willing to experiment with new or unfamiliar trails—scarcely a hike exists in Yosemite that won't reward hikers with jaw-dropping vistas and quiet moments of harmony with the elements.

WINTERTIME IN YOSEMITE

Icy waterfalls and meadows masked with soft snow dramatically transform Yosemite's landscape in its quietest season. The Sierra are known for heavy winter snowfall, and Yosemite is no exception, but unlike the rest of the range Yosemite remains accessible year-round. **Rte. 140** from Merced is a designated "all-weather" entrance, so it is usually open and clear. Although Tioga Rd. and Glacier Point Rd. invariably close at the first sign of snowfall, Rte. 41 from the south typically remains traversable. Verify road conditions before traveling (372-0200), and carry chains.

Many valley facilities remain open even during the harshest winters. **Camping** is generally permitted in Lower Pines, Sunnyside (Camp 4), Hodgden Meadows, and Wawona, and most indoor accommodations offer reduced off-season rates. Park tours move "indoors" to heated buses, and even the Merced and Fresno **buses** (see **Getting There and Getting Around,** p. 402) operate when road conditions permit.

Cross-country skiing is free, and several well-marked trails cut into the backcountry of the valley's South Rim at **Badger Pass** and **Crane Flat.** Both areas have blazes on the trees so that the trails can be followed even when there's several feet of fresh snow. The same snow also transforms many summer hiking trails into increasingly popular **snowshoe** trails. Rangers host several snowshoe walks, but the peaceful winter forests are perhaps best explored *sans* guidance. Both nordic skis and snowshoes can be rented from the **Yosemite Mountaineering School** (372-1000; rentals start at $11) or from **Yosemite Concession Services** (372-1338; rentals $14.50 and up).

The state's oldest ski resort, **Badger Pass Ski Area,** south of Yosemite Valley on Glacier Point Rd. (372-1000), is the only downhill ski area in the park. Its family-fun atmosphere encourages learning and restraint (no snowboards). Free shuttles connect Badger Pass with the Yosemite Valley lodges. (Ski lessons $22 for 2hr., private lessons from $40. Rental packages $18 per day. Lift tickets Sat.-Sun. $28 per day, Mon.-Fri. $22. Over 60 and exactly 40 free. Lifts open 9am-4:30pm. Discount ski packages for weekdays available through Yosemite Lodge.)

Ice Skating at Curry Village costs $5 (children $4.50) for a day's admission and $2 for skate rental (open in winter Mon.-Fri. noon-9:30pm, Sat.-Sun. 8:30am-9:30pm). **Sledding** and **tobogganing** are permitted at Crane Flat off Rte. 120.

From Crest to Crest: the Trail of the West

As the longest hiking path in America, the **Pacific Crest Trail (PCT)** snakes, swerves, and scales up 2638 mountainous miles from Mexico to Canada. One of eight official National Scenic Trails, it traverses seven National Parks, 23 National Forests, and 37 Wilderness Areas, going through climates from desert to sub-Arctic along the way. True to its name, the PCT always keeps to the crests—the trail maintains an average elevation of over 5000 ft. But the trail is just as much about vistas as it is about volume; there's one hell of a view from the summit of **Mt. Whitney** (14,494 ft.), the highest peak in the contiguous U.S. (see p. 431). From the border near Campo, CA, the PCT climbs the San Jacinto Mountains and winds north along the spine of the Sierra, passing through several national parks (see p. 399), Lake Tahoe (see p. 383), and the volcanic summits of the Cascades (see p. 366) before moving into Oregon. Though the PCT was begun in 1968, the trail-blazing task was so immense that it was not officially completed until 1993.

Most people just trek small portions of the trail, but every year a few die-hard mountaineers rise to the challenge and hike the entire length, a four- to six-month endeavor. No matter how much you choose to take on, proper supplies, conditioning, and acclimatization are vital. The Pacific Crest Trail Association, the trail's maintenance organization, gives tips on how to prepare for the journey. Contact them at 5325 Elkhorn Blvd., Box 256, Sacramento, CA 95842 (916-349-2109 or 888-PC-TRAIL/728-7245; http://www.gorp.com/pcta).

■ Stanislaus National Forest

Well-maintained roads and campsites, craggy peaks, dozens of cool topaz lakes, forests of Ponderosa pines, and wildflower meadows make up the 900,000 acres of the Stanislaus National Forest. Here, peregrine falcons, bald eagles, mountain lions, and bears sometimes surprise the (un)lucky traveler. In addition to great hiking trails, fishing, and campsites, Stanislaus offers a chance for a bit of solitude—something its better-known neighbor, Yosemite, doesn't have.

Park headquarters are located at 19777 Greenly Rd., Sonora (532-3671; open summer 8am-5pm; call for winter hours). Camping permits are required for Carson-Iceberg, Mokelumne, and Emigrant Wilderness; permits are also needed for building fires in wilderness areas. Only Pinecrest accepts reservations; all other sites are available on a first-come, first-camped basis.

Along Routes 4 and 108

For a quick, scenic tour of the forest, the curvy and narrow drives along **Rte. 4** or **108** are local favorites. Drivers are rewarded by the views from over Ebbett's Pass and Pacific Grade Summit. Be aware, however, that roads are often closed during the winter months and occasionally through much of the fall and spring.

THE SIERRA NEVADA

The **Summit District** is the most popular spot in the Emigrant Wilderness because of its well-maintained trails and pristine lakes. The **ranger station** is off Rte. 108 at **Pinecrest Lake** (965-3434; open Mon.-Sat. 8am-5:30pm, Sun. and holidays 8am-4:30pm). **Campsites** abound to the east along Rte. 108. **Cascade Creek,** 11 mi. from the ranger station, and **Niagara,** 16 mi. from the station on Eagle Meadow Rd., are both free. **Pinecrest** (800-280-CAMP/2267 for reservations), ½ mi. from the ranger station, has 200 campsites, drinking water, flush toilets, and proximity to the lake (open May-Oct.; sites $12).

Pinecrest Lake, about 30 mi. east of Sonora on Rte. 108, is popular with the gosh-darn-what-am-I-gonna-do-with-the-kids-this-weekend set. The alpine lake is set amidst granite mountains and several thousand pine trees; the hike (4mi.) that encircles the lake goes through both. Kayaks and paddle boats are popular, though water-skis and jet skis are not permitted. With a restaurant, boat rental, and summer outdoor movies, Pinecrest is a bit like a day-use resort.

Along Rte. 108 in the Summit District are a number of **self-guided trails.** Pick up a brochure at the ranger station before you head out—the numbered stakes that dot the trails are confusing. The trail names are generally more exciting than the events they describe. The **Trail of the Gargoyles,** east of the station off Rte. 108 on Herring Creek Rd., is lined with shapely geological formations, documenting nature's labor in lava flows, *lahar* (hardened mud), and ash. The **Trail of the Ancient Dwarves,** 15 mi. east of Pinecrest on Rte. 108, provides great views of the mountain range as it follows a line of *bonsai* trees. For stunning views of the Stanislaus River and its dammed reservoir, take Rte. 108 18 mi. east of Pinecrest to **Donnell Vista.**

The **Carson-Iceberg Wilderness,** in the northeast section of the forest just off Rte. 4, is steeped in Stanislaus's solitude. The absence of lakes and the steep terrain in this region eliminate it from most itineraries, but high mountain peaks, meadows, and wildflowers reward the adventurous traveler. Stanislaus Peak and Sonora Peak are accessible from the **Pacific Crest Trail** (for more info, see **From Crest to Crest: the Trail of the West,** p. 409) and reward persevering climbers with a humbling panorama of the Sierra. The Pacific Coast Trail includes a 5 mi. round-trip cross-country scramble from Saint Mary's Pass, one mile before Sonora Pass on Rte. 108. It has one of the best views of the valley, but the 3000 ft. climb will leave you winded.

The adjacent **Calaveras District,** with a **ranger station** (795-1381; open Mon.-Sat. 8am-5pm), on Rte. 4 at Hathaway Pines, contains the **Dardanelles,** a series of volcanic by-products. There is a campground at the reservoir (8mi. southwest of Rte. 4) with piped water, pit toilets, and wheelchair access (open June-Oct.; sites $10).

The Groveland District

The **Groveland District** covers the area south of Sonora and west of Yosemite, and serves as the overflow destination for Yosemite campers. The **ranger station** (962-7825), is 9 mi. past Groveland on Rte. 120 (open Mon.-Fri. 7am-4:30pm, Sat. 7am-3:30pm, Sun. 7am-noon). **Carlon** is the closest campsite to the entrance (pit toilets and potable water; free). **Little Nellio Falls** lies in the district's deserted southeast corner. The Groveland District is logged and littered with pockets of private property, as is the **Miwok District**—the more interesting districts lie to the north.

Cherry Creek Canyon, which is a bit scarred from a recent fire, is north of Cherry Lake just west of Yosemite. The canyon, carved by glaciers, has just enough walking space at its floor for hikers. A trailhead at **Eagle Meadow** leads down to **Coopers Meadow** and **Three Chimneys,** a brick-red volcanic formation.

■ Sequoia and Kings Canyon National Parks

These twin parks may not attract the thunderous hordes of visitors that the "Big Three" (Yellowstone, Yosemite, and the Grand Canyon) do each summer, but Sequoia and Kings Canyon can match any park in the U.S. sight-for-sight, or at least tree-for-giant tree. The parks are home to a host of beneedled bohemoths, including the General Sherman Sequoia Tree—47,450 cubic feet of raw, unadulterated lumber and the largest living organism in the world (unless you get picky and count a giant underground fungus recently discovered in Michigan).

Though the sequoia tower over the landscape upon which they grow, the landscape itself is sprinkled with emerald meadows, roaring waterfalls, and hidden lakes, and beneath it all lie miles of pristine underground caverns. Most of these sights can be accessed by motor vehicle or by short walking expeditions, but two-thirds of the parks are completely undeveloped, providing hardy hikers with 800 mi. of beautiful backcountry trails. The park **entrance fee** is $5 for bicycles and pedestrians, $10 for cars, and $20 for a **year-long pass.** All passes are valid in both parks for seven days.

PRACTICAL INFORMATION AND ORIENTATION

There are no banks or ATMs in either park. Camping supplies, gas, and groceries in the parks are of low quality and high price. The San Joaquin Valley (see p. 432), Reedley (45mi. west off Rte. 180), and Three Rivers (8mi. southwest on Rte. 198), are better places to stock up.

Visitor Information:
  Kings Canyon and Sequoia Main Line (565-3341; http://www.nps.gov/seki). Offers 24hr. direct contact with a park ranger in addition to dispatch service to any office within the parks.
  National Park Service Headquarters (565-3341), 1mi. beyond the Three Rivers entrance to Sequoia on Rte. 198 out of Visalia. For info by mail, write Superintendent, Ash Mountain, Three Rivers, CA 93271. Provides info on both parks, maps, wilderness permits, and free brochures about the sequoia in German, French, Spanish, and Japanese. Open daily 8am-5pm; Nov.-May 8am-4:30pm.
  Backcountry Information (565-3708; fax 565-3797). Backcountry **permits** are free. Reserve 15 days in advance. One-third of the permits for any given trail are held on a first-come, first-served basis at the trailhead or at the nearest ranger station. Open Mon.-Fri. 8am-4:30pm.
Public Transportation: Shuttle buses operate out of Giant Forest in Sequoia National Park and service Lodgepole, Moro Rock, Sherman Tree, and Crescent Meadow (every 40min. daily 8am-6pm). Fare $1 per person, $3 per family; day pass $4 per person, $6 per family.
Horse Rental: Stables located at **Wolverton Pack Station** (565-3445), Grant Grove (565-3464), **Cedar Grove,** and **Mineral King** (561-4142) are open in the summer for horse rentals and guided tours. Rates vary; call for info. **Bicycles** are not permitted on hiking trails or in the backcountry.
Road Conditions: Park Road and Weather Conditions (565-3341). Provides info on campgrounds as well. 24hr. recording, updated daily around 9am. **California Highway Patrol** (488-4321 or 734-6767).
Hospitals: Fresno Community Hospital (442-6000), at Tulare and R St., in Fresno; **Kaweah Delta Hospital** (625-2211), off Rte. 198, in Visalia.
Emergency: 911.
Police: Fresno County Sheriff (488-3111). **Tulare County Sheriff** (733-6218).
Area Code: 209.

Sequoia

  Visitor Information: Foothills Visitors Center (565-3341), at the park headquarters (see above). Open daily 8am-5pm; Nov.-April 8am-4pm. **Lodgepole Visitors Center** (565-3782, ext. 782), on Generals Hwy. 4mi. east of Giant Forest. Open daily 8am-6pm; Oct.-April 9am-5pm. Campground reservations daily 9am-5pm; wilderness permits daily 7am-4pm (for permits, call 565-3775). **Giant Forest Village Information Booth** is open in summer daily noon-4pm. **Mineral King Ranger Station** (565-3768), 1mi. before the end of Mineral King Rd., is the headquarters for this remote southern region of the park. Maps, hiking info, books, first aid, and wilderness permits. Open in summer daily 7am-5pm.

THE SIERRA NEVADA

Ski Rental: Sequoia Ski Touring Center, Sequoia 93262 (565-3435 or 565-3381). Cross-country ski and snowshoe rentals. Open daily 10am-5pm.

Gas: Gasoline is not available in the park. The nearest option is in **Three Rivers.**

Auto Repair: AAA Emergency Road Service (565-3381 or 800-400-4AAA/ 4222).

Market: Lodgepole's Market is well stocked. Open daily 8am-8pm. The smaller **Giant Forest Market** keeps the same hours. Two stores in Three Rivers: **Village Market** (open Mon.-Fri. 8am-7pm, Sat.-Sun. 9am-5pm) and **Three Rivers Market** (open daily 7:45am-7pm), offer better selections and prices.

Showers and Laundromat: Across from Lodgepole Visitors Center. 2min. shower 25¢. Wash $1, 10min. dry 75¢. Showers open 8am-1pm and 3-8pm; laundry open 7am-8:45pm.

Post Office: At Lodgepole. Open Mon.-Fri. 8:30am-1pm and 1:30-4pm. A stamp machine is located in the lobby (open 24hr.). **ZIP Code**: 93262.

Kings Canyon

Visitor Information: Grant Grove Visitors Center (335-2856), Grant Grove Village, 2mi. east of the Big Stump entrance by Rte. 180. Books, maps, and exhibits. Nightly campfire programs and daily hikes. Open daily 8am-6pm, winter 9am-5pm. **Cedar Grove Ranger Station** (565-3793), 30mi. farther down Rte. 180 by Kings River. Near trailheads into Kings Canyon high country. Books, maps, first aid, and wilderness permits. Open in summer daily 9am-5pm; closed in winter. **Road's End Kiosk,** located 6mi. east of Cedar Grove Village, issues wilderness permits. Open summer daily 7am-2:45pm.

Gas: Gasoline is not available inside the park. The nearest options are at **Hume Lake Christian Camp** (335-2881), 10mi. from Grant Grove, and **Kings Canyon Lodge** (335-2405), 15mi. from Grant Grove.

Auto Repair: Attendants at **Grant Grove** (335-9071 or 335-2314 after 5pm) can handle minor repairs and lockouts. For major repairs or service outside the Grant Grove area, call **Michael's** (638-4101), in Reedley. **AAA Emergency Road Service** (800-400-4AAA/4222).

Market: Grant Grove Market and **Cedar Grove Market** carry a selection of camping basics and groceries. Both open summer daily 8am-9pm.

Laundromat: Cedar Grove Chevron station (open in summer 8am-8pm). Wash 75¢, 10min. dry 25¢. Last load 6:30pm.

Showers: Grant Grove Lodge (open summer daily 11am-3pm). **Cedar Grove Chevron station** (open summer daily 8am-8pm). Adults $2.50, children $1.

Post Office: Grant Grove Village, across from the visitors center. Open June-Sept. Mon.-Sat. 9am-3pm. A stamp machine and mailbox are located next to the visitors center year-round. **ZIP Code: 93633.**

The parks' most popular sights are concentrated in four developed areas: **Giant Forest** and **Mineral King** in Sequoia and **Grant Grove** and **Cedar Grove** in Kings Canyon. Beautiful backcountry comprises the northern two-thirds of Kings Canyon and the eastern two-thirds of Sequoia. **Seasonal changes** are dramatic in this area of the Sierra. Summer season (Memorial Day through Labor Day) is the high season here (Aug. is the busiest month)—the days are warm and attract flocks of visitors, many of whom are unprepared for plunging nighttime temperatures. Dogwood, aspen, and oak provide brilliant color in October and November. Snow season is from November to March, although some trails may have snow as late as mid-June. Spring here is unpredictable, bringing late storms, low fogs, and run-off flooding.

GETTING THERE AND AROUND

Cars can access the two parks only from the west. From Fresno, **Rte. 180** runs west 60 mi. to Kings Canyon's **Grant Grove** entrance and terminates 30 mi. later in Cedar Grove at the mouth of the Canyon itself. The road to Cedar Grove was badly damaged in the floods of 1997 (repairs could cause intermittent delays) and is typically closed from November to May due to the threat of winter storms and falling rocks. From Visalia, **Rte. 198** winds its way past Lake Kaweah to Sequoia's **Ash**

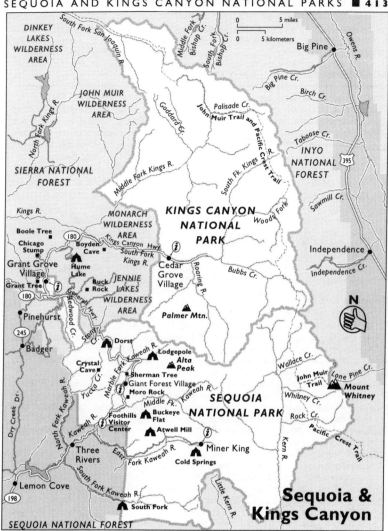

Sequoia & Kings Canyon

THE SIERRA NEVADA

Mountain entrance, where it becomes known as the **Generals Highway,** a deliciously serpentine speedway which snakes through 130 spine-tingling turns and 12 major switchbacks as it ascends 2000 ft. Barring construction delays, the drive from Ash Mountain through Sequoia's Giant Forest to **Grant Grove** takes about two hours. In winter, the Generals Highway is usually covered by over 15 ft. of snow, barring even plows and monster trucks from accessing the area. Rte. 198, which despite these heavy snows usually opens from mid-May to October, branches into the **Mineral King** turn-off. This road is punctuated by high-country panoramas, but drivers beware—those who lose themselves in the views may end up wishing they had never tackled this treacherous two-hour drive. The only park access from east is by trail—hikers can enter either park from the **John Muir Wilderness** and the **Inyo National Forest,** both of which are accessible from spur roads off **U.S. 395.**

Public transportation to the parks is **nonexistent,** but the limited **shuttle** service can free you from your car once you are inside Sequoia (see **Practical Information,**

p. 411). **Sequoia-Kings Canyon Guest Services** (565-3381) operates a daily bus tour through Kings Canyon, but it is pricey and leaves little time to explore (8hr. tour $25, seniors $20, children $13). Inquire at visitors centers.

ACCOMMODATIONS AND CAMPING

Sequoia Guest Services, Inc. (SGS), P.O. Box 789, Three Rivers, CA 93271 (561-3314), has a monopoly on lodging (and food) in the parks, meaning that budget accommodations are scarce—motel-style rooms inside the parks start at $70 per night. Those determined to sleep indoors will find more reasonable options in **Three Rivers,** 6 mi. west of the park on Rte. 198. This typical "gateway" town hosts, appropriately enough, **The Gateway Lodge** (561-4133; singles $50) and the **Sequoia Motel** (561-4453; singles $45).

Although **campgrounds** sometimes fill to the brim, you should be able to drive up late and snatch a spot on most non-holiday weekends. Only Lodgepole, in Sequoia, fills regularly, partly because of its proximity to Giant Forest Village and partly because it's the only campground in either park that accepts summer reservations. Most campgrounds are open from mid-May to October, with a 14-night maximum stay in summer (one month otherwise). There are **no RV hookups** in the parks, but dump stations are available at campsites where noted. Contact a ranger station for more info, or call 565-3351 for a 24hr. recording. **Backcountry camping** is free with the requisite permit (see **Practical Information,** p. 411).

Sequoia Campgrounds

Lodgepole, 4mi. northeast of Giant Forest Village by the Kaweah River at the center of the park's ranger-led activities. RV-dominated clientele. Nearby Wolverton has phones, a store, and stables. Aside from its reservation policy, there's no good reason to pay the extra $2 to stay here—sites are crowded and offer little shade. Sites $14, off-season $10 (free after major snowstorms). Reserve through DESTINET (800-436-7275) mid-May to mid-Sept.

Buckeye Flat, past park headquarters, a few mi. from the Ash Mountain entrance on Rte. 198. Buckeye's shady sites are closed to RVs; the drone of Winnebago generators is pleasantly supplanted by the roar of a nearby waterfall. RVs *are* welcome at **Potishwa,** a full-service campground nearby with 44 well-spaced sites. Both campgrounds provide restrooms and drinking water, and both are good choices for cold nights because of their lower elevation. Sites $12.

Atwell Mill and **Cold Springs,** 20mi. along Mineral King Rd., in the Mineral King area. Secluded and primitive (pit toilets), but offering piped water and picnic tables for the 50 tent sites. Steep, winding roads and a ban on trailers keep the RVs away. Store, restaurant, phone, and gas (from an antique pump, not always available) are 3mi. away in Silver City. Sites $6; free in winter when the water is turned off.

South Fork, on South Fork Rd., 13mi. from Rte. 198. Near ranger station and some backcountry roads. Pit toilets. Not recommended for trailers or RVs. Sites $6.

Dorst, 12mi. north of Giant Forest. Huge campground (218 sites) convenient to Sequoia attractions. Flush toilets. Zero privacy and a sea of RVs. Sites $12.

Kings Canyon Campgrounds

Sunset, Azalea, and **Crystal Springs** are within a stone's throw of Grant Grove Village but remain quiet nonetheless. Azalea has a trailer dump station and Sunset features flat tenting spots, brilliant views of the San Joaquin Valley, and an amphitheater with daily programs. Crystal Springs is the smallest and most remote. All offer restrooms, water, and plenty of privacy. Sites $12; free in winter.

Hume Lake, 10mi. northeast of Grant Grove off Rte. 180 in Sequoia National Forest. Prime location beside the fish-heavy lake. Flush toilets. 75 sites.

Sheep Creek, Sentinel, Canyon View, and **Moraine,** at the Kings River near Cedar Grove 32mi. east of Grant Grove on Rte. 180. Store, food, laundry, and showers nearby. Within a few mi. of Road's End and Kings Canyon trailheads. Sheep Creek has a dump station. Sentinel is near Cedar Grove Amphitheater. By far the nicest tent sites at Sheep Creek and the flatter Sentinel are in the back.

Moraine, with its canyon vistas, serves primarily as overflow and opens only on the busiest weekends. All have restrooms and water. Access roads and campgrounds typically closed Oct.-May. Sites $12. Canyon View accepts reservations from groups only.

FOOD

National parks are not playgrounds for capitalism—Sequoia Guest Services is the only competitor in the food market. Though the food isn't as bad as you might expect, you can keep costs down by doing your own cooking. A camping stove is always a useful culinary device, but old-fashioned campfires or newfangled kitchen-equipped cabins provide other cook-it-yourself venues. Supplies purchased at the park-operated **Village Market** (561-4441), in Three Rivers, may produce an affordable meal, *if* you're cooking for a group (open Mon.-Sat. 8am-7pm, Sun. 9am-5pm). Outside the parks' culinary vacuum lie a few tempting alternatives, particularly in Three Rivers.

Grant Grove Restaurant (335-2314), Grant Grove Village. Coffee-shop atmosphere. If the residents eat here (and they do), it must be good. Breakfast $4-6, lunch $5-7, dinner $8-12. Open daily 7am-9pm.

Noisy Water Cafe, 41775 Sierra Dr. (561-4517), in Three Rivers. "The Home of the Hummingbirds," named for the frequent visitors to the feeders that hang outside the back window, is the overwhelming favorite among townfolk and men in cowboy hats. Great omelettes ($6) and lunches ($5). Open daily 6:30am-10pm.

Anne Lang's Emporium, 41651 Sierra Dr. (561-4937), in Three Rivers. The lingering scent of potpourri and coffee permeate the air in this country store where the employees are genuinely happy to see you. Sandwiches ($4) and soups (a steal at $1-2). Open Mon.-Fri. 10am-4pm, Sat.-Sun. 11am-4pm.

SEQUOIA SIGHTS AND ACTIVITIES

Giant Forest is the center of activity in Sequoia and hosts one of the world's greatest concentrations of giant sequoia trees. The grove was named by John Muir, who explored the area at length, counting tree rings, taking trunk measurements, and preaching preservation. The tallest of Muir's marvels is the **General Sherman Tree,** discovered in 1879 and believed to be the world's largest living thing (other than the aforementioned Michigan fungus). Standing 275 ft. tall and measuring 102 ft. around at its base, its trunk weighs in at 1385 tons. Despite this height and might, sequoia have shallow root systems and compaction of the soil can be deadly—hence, the protective fences. The 2 mi. **Congress Trail,** the park's most popular trail, boomerangs around General Sherman. Other trails wind through Giant Forest, past dozens of giants and younger trees. Trail guides to Giant Forest are available at the Lodgepole Visitors Center (see **Practical Information,** p. 411).

The granite monoliths and meadows of the Giant Forest area are perhaps more impressive than the trees that have made it famous. The region's most spectacular view can be found atop **Moro Rock,** 1½ mi. from the village, where a granite staircase leads to a stunning 360° view of the southern Sierra. If the arduous climb up the stairs doesn't leave you breathless, the vista certainly will—the Great Western Divide lies to the east and pine-covered foothills recline into the San Joaquin Valley to the south and west. Beware—the dizzying height of the rock and the vertiginous abyss below can be very scary, especially for young children and paranoid parents. Near Moro Rock is the fabulous **Crescent Meadow,** called by Muir "the gem of the Sierra." Its emerald grasses are dotted with ruby and amethyst wildflowers which gleam against the cedars and sequoia that line it. Though human voices often shatter the serenity, a quick hike to **Tharp's Log,** a hollowed-out sequoia and former living space, guarantees a more peaceful view of the meadow. The road to Moro Rock and Crescent Meadow also offers access to many other wonders, including two testaments to the long and storied relationship between trees and automobiles: the **Tunnel Log,** a fallen sequoia with a trunk big enough for cars to drive through, and the **Auto Log,** a fallen sequoia with a trunk big enough for cars to drive on.

THE SIERRA NEVADA

Hikes

Sequoia harbors many treasures easily reached via simple day hikes. **Redwood Mountain Grove,** the world's largest grove of redwood trees, lies near Quail Flat, 6 mi. south of Grant Grove and 4 mi. from Giant Forest Village. A 7 mi. trail forms two loops through the grove along Redwood Creek, a tributary of the Kaweah River's North Fork which is surrounded by blooming azaleas in May and June. The redwoods are dense but not as imposing as in other groves. Another pleasant day hike goes through **Garfield Grove,** 5 mi. up the Kaweah River from the South Fork campground at the extreme southern boundary of the park. The **Muir Grove,** just west of the Dorst campground, is less pristine but more accessible.

Hundreds of miles of curvy **backwoods trails** afford even more spectacular views. The 7 mi. **Marble Falls Trail** begins by the Potwisha campground and twists through hills to a 2000ft. peak at Marble Falls. Moderately strenuous hikes from the Lodgepole Visitors Center to the glistening **Twin Lakes** (6mi. round-trip) and **Pear Lake** (10mi. round-trip) pass marvelous meadows. When in the backcountry, keep an eye out for **bears,** which might be adorable and fuzzy, but are also dangerous. Group tours led by the park's pack stations (563-3445) provide safety in numbers. The essential guide to backcountry safety, *Backcountry Basics,* is available at the ranger station.

Nine miles from Giant Forest Village on Rte. 198 is **Crystal Cave,** discovered by two fishermen in 1918 and one of the few caves on Sequoia's western side open to the public. Reached by a ½ mi. hike, the cave is lined with smooth limestone stalagmites and stalactites, moistened by a dark underground stream, and inhabited by hordes of Mexican free-tailed bats. **Marble Hall,** the cave's largest chamber, is 141 ft. long and over 40 ft. high. The temperature inside is a constant 50°F, so wear warm clothing. (Cave open daily 10am-3pm. Naturalist tours late June to Labor Day every ½hr., May-June and Sept. Fri.-Mon. every hr. Admission $5, ages 6-12 $2.50. Purchase tickets in advance at the Lodgepole or Foothills Visitors Centers 8am-4pm.)

The **Mineral King** area was acquired by the park system in 1978 after lawsuits prevented the Walt Disney Corporation from building a ski resort on the site. Disney probably would have built a better road, but some of the best scenery in the park has been preserved for those willing to brave the winding drive, complete with blind-corners and steep drop-offs, to get to it. The valley is 7500 ft. deep, with steep trails leading up to mountain lakes and meadows. Some of the surrounding peaks stand over 12,000 ft. tall. A bonanza mining area in the 1800s, the region now offers magnificent day and backcountry hiking and climbing. The walk to **Aspen Flat** from Mineral King Pack Station is an easy, rewarding day hike. The trail is flanked by soda springs and wildflowers. Longer hikes, such as the **Atwell-Hackett, Eagle Lake,** and **Farewell Gap Trails,** are more strenuous but offer amazing views in quiet country.

KINGS CANYON SIGHTS AND ACTIVITIES

The most developed portion of the park is **Grant Grove,** named for its most commanding attraction, **General Grant Tree.** The 3500-year-old general is the third-largest sequoia in the world (267.4ft.), and also an aesthetic wonder with its display of "classic" sequoia form. It has been designated the "Nation's Christmas Tree" and serves as a living shrine for the American war dead (especially from the Civil War). Just north of the park entrance on Rte. 180 lies the **Big Stump Basin Trail,** a self-guided walk through an old logging camp. Here remain scars left by early loggers who erroneously viewed the enormous sequoia as a timber gold mine. They abandoned their efforts after assailing the unyielding trees with dynamite and hatchets.

The **Grant Tree Trail** just past the Sunset campground consists of a quick 0.6 mi. loop and a glance at the mammoth sequoia. The trail is the best way to see the huge **Fallen Monarch** (another toppled sequoia), which used to house a saloon and a stable, and the 24 ft. wide **Centennial Stump,** which stubbornly resisted nine days of hacking. When the tree arrived at the 1876 Centennial Exposition in Philadelphia, Easterners refused to display it, dismissing it as "another California hoax."

Hidden in the visitors center parking lot behind the post office is the steep, switchback-ridden road to **Panoramic Point** (RVs prohibited). In addition to affording awesome mountain views, the point serves as the trailhead for **Park Ridge Trail,** one of the most scenic and fly-riddled treks in the park. The 1½ mi. round-trip hike along the **Dead Giant Loop,** borders national park and national forest lands, and provides interpretive information on land-management differences between them.

Cedar Grove

The most incredible sights in Kings Canyon lie east of Grant Grove. **South Fork Kings River** has carved the park's eponymous canyon and made it the deepest in the U.S., deeper even than the Grand Canyon. The canyon's towering granite walls can be experienced from **Cedar Grove.** Though accessible via U.S. 180, Cedar Grove is nevertheless one of the parks' most secluded areas. The drive to Cedar Grove is scenic and mountainous, but expect some delays due to recent flood damage. Sheer rock walls dominate the views, and at the bottom of the canyon, the Kings River glistens with crystalline splendor—be sure to stop at roadside turnoffs for a peek.

Once within the budding grove, you can explore the Kings River's banks and marvel at the depth of the canyon (8200ft. in spots). This region becomes virtually in the hours just before dusk, when the setting sun dances brilliantly off the gilded promontories. **Zumwalt Meadows,** accessible via a 1½ mi. trail loop, has a rocky overlook from which bears and white-tailed deer can be seen foraging in the flora below. **Roaring River Falls** and **Mist Falls** are at their best in late spring and early summer, when the streams that feed them are swift and swollen. Roaring River Falls is easily reached by road; Mist Falls requires a mellow four-hour hike.

Road's End is exactly that, a naturally U-shaped glacial valley at the end of Rte. 180 with parking for those entering the backcountry. The most popular backcountry foray from Road's End is the **Rae Lakes Loop,** which traverses a sampling of the Sierra's best: glaciated canyons, gentle meadows, violent rapids, and inspiring lake vistas. Most hikers take a clockwise route to avoid a daunting uphill grade. Well-spaced campgrounds pace the four- or five-day trek at 7 mi. intervals. Obtain permits at Cedar Grove or the Road's End Kiosk (see **Practical Information,** p. 411).

In the summer, rangers organize a variety of activities including nature walks, children's campfires, day hikes, and films. Contact a ranger station or look in the *Sequoia Bark,* the free park newspaper, for a calendar of events.

▒ Sierra National Forest

Covering 1.3 million acres, the Sierra National Forest fills the gap between Yosemite National Park and Sequoia and Kings Canyon National Parks. Its terrain is diverse, encompassing both the alpine peaks of the Sierra Nevada and the oak-covered foothills on the edge of the San Joaquin Valley. The region's rivers and lakes serve as recreational centers for the national forest activities. Information on these centers and other popular destinations can be obtained in spades at the **Sierra National Forest Supervisor's Office,** 1600 Tollhouse Rd., Clovis 93611 (297-0706), along Rte. 168 just outside the gateway town of Clovis (open Mon.-Fri. 8am-4:30pm).

A **backcountry permit** is required for designated wilderness areas, which comprise 46% of the forest—obtain one at any ranger station. Trailhead quotas are in effect from July to Labor Day in the Ansel Adams, John Muir, Dinkey Lakes, and Kaiser Wilderness areas. Despite the fact that there are over 60 campsites, reservations are essential ($3 per person; call MISTIX at 800-280-CAMP/2267). .

Information on the northwestern **Mariposa District** can be obtained by calling or writing the **Batterson Office,** 43060 Rte. 41, Oakhurst 93644 (683-4665; open Mon.-Fri. 8am-4:30pm). **Bass Lake** is thronged in summer by parched San Joaquin Valley residents, who take advantage of fishing, boating, and water-skiing opportunities. Some of the best hikes in the Sierra are also nearby. **Nelder Grove** contains a campground and a mile-long trail through 106 seldom-visited sequoia. A separate trail affords the rare opportunity to see a 246 ft. giant—**Bull Buck Tree**—without the gaping crowds. The lonely **Willow Creek Trail,** which passes both **Angel Falls** and the aptly-named **Devil's Slide Waterfall** en route to McLeod Flat Rd., is another option, as is the meandering **Way of the Mono Trail.** (Take Rte. 41 to the Bass Lake turn-off and follow Rd. 222 about 4mi. to the parking lot at the trailhead.)

The far reaches of the **Kings River District** rise as high as 13,000 ft. at the Sierra Crest. Most of the region's activity centers around the not-so-diminutive **Dinkey Creek** area and the **Pine Flat Reservoir,** where there is a paved road. **Whitewater rafting** on the Kings River is popular, especially in spring. **Kings River Expeditions** (233-4881), and **Spirit White Water** (408-373-3275), offer a variety of guided trips; get a group together to reduce costs. Trailbikes and 4WD vehicles raise dust on the five off-highway routes which provide access to camping and fishing.

Easily accessible from Rte. 168, the **Pineridge District** is the forest's most popular region. The **Pineridge Ranger District Office,** 29688 Auberry Rd., P.O. Box 559, Prather, 93651 (855-5355), is one of the forest's busiest centers (open daily 8am-4:30pm). The **Shaver Lake Chamber of Commerce,** P.O. Box 58, Shaver Lake 93664 (841-3350), also provides info (open Mon.-Tues. and Fri. 9am-5pm). **Huntington Lake** lies farther east along Rte. 168 and its shimmering waters see a lot of use. Sailboat regattas occur all summer. In winter, **cross-country ski** trails, snowmobile routes, and rollicking "snowplay" areas are maintained along Rte. 168. Beyond Kaiser Pass, the road becomes narrow and slightly treacherous—honk your horn on the sharp blind turns. The terrain at the upper end of this road is definitively High Sierra—alpine lakes, flowers, and craggy summits. **Mountain bikers** can enjoy dozens of trails ranging from the leisurely **Tamarack Trail** to the **Dusy/Ershin Rd.**

■ Sequoia National Forest

Sequoia National Park is not the last word on the southern Sierra. Under the moniker of the **Sequoia National Forest,** the majestic mountain range continues its southward march 60 mi. below the park boundary before petering out in the low ranges of the Mojave Desert. The forest is bounded on the north by the Kings River and on the west and east by the San Joaquin Valley and the Owens Valley. The **Kern River** slices through its middle.

The **forest headquarters,** 900 W. Grand Ave. (784-1500), in Porterville 15 mi. east of Rte. 99 on Rte. 65, offers informative handouts and detailed maps of the forest ($3.25; open Mon.-Fri. 8am-4:30pm). Prominently featured on this map are the national forest's six designated **wilderness areas.** All backcountry excursions require wilderness permits, available at any district ranger's office.

Mountain biking is a popular activity on the Kern Plateau. The Porterville headquarters offers a handout detailing almost 20 national forest biking trails of varying difficulty, most of which include steep descents where bikers plummet to glory (or to doom). The terrain of the **Sherman Pass Trail** and the **Boonie Meadow Trail** challenges even experienced hikers, and the 2.3 mi. **Packsaddle Cave Trail** (trailhead is 16mi. north of Kernville on State Mtn. 99) takes you to its namesake.

The northern section of Sequoia National Forest surrounds Kings Canyon Hwy., the road connecting to Kings Canyon National Park's Grant Grove area. The **Hume Lake District** offers ample recreation opportunities and contains the impressively ugly **Boole Sequoia** and most of the **Monarch Wilderness Area.** The **Trail of 100 Giants** is a beautiful 45-minute walk through a giant sequoia grove (across from Redwood Meadow campground along the Western Divide Hwy.). Experienced hikers can take the **Deer Cove Creek Trail** to Grand Dike's remarkable rock outcropping and wildflowers (trailhead is 1mi. before Rte. 180 re-enters Kings Canyon National Park near Cedar Grove). The **Hume Lake Ranger District Office,** 35860 E. Kings Canyon Rd. (338-2251), in Dunlap on Rte. 180 east of Fresno near the forest entrance, provides camping info (open Mon.-Sat. 8am-4:30pm; winter closed Sat.).

THE EASTERN SIERRA

While the western side of the Sierra descends slowly over a number of miles, the eastern side drops off precipitously, its jagged rock faces forming a startling silhouette against the porcelain skies above. Although barely visible from the San Joaquin Valley to the west, the peaks of the High Sierra tower fearsomely over Owens Valley to the east and contrast strangely with the desert to the south.

The sharp dropoff is a result of the lifting and faulting processes that shaped the Sierra ridge some 10 million years ago. The Sierra's eastern slope traces the fault line where the Owens Valley collapsed to expose 14,000 ft. tall slabs of rock to glaciation. The western slope, watered by cooling ocean air rising to its crest, is carpeted by dense forests at middle elevations. The clouds dissipate before they can cross the entirety of the mountains, however, leaving the eastern side remarkably arid.

The tiny towns that stretch from Mount Whitney to Yosemite National Park are linked by U.S. 395, the access route to the eastern face of Sierra. Small as they are, these towns eagerly support the crowds of campers, climbers, and camera-carriers who congregate in the Owens Valley each summer.

■ Mono Lake

As fresh water from streams and springs drains into the "inland sea" of Mono Lake, it evaporates, leaving behind a mineral-rich, 13-mile-wide expanse Mark Twain once called "the Dead Sea of the West." Unlike its Middle Eastern counterpart, however, Mono is teeming with life: brine flies and shrimp provide a buffet for thousands of waterfowl. The lake derives its lunar appearance from towers of calcium carbonate called *tufa*, which form when calcium-rich springs well up in the carbonate-filled salt water. At one-million-years-old, this is the Western Hemisphere's oldest enclosed body of water—truly the old man of the seas.

Today, Mono is asked to support not only its own ecosystem, but also that of greater metropolitan Los Angeles. The steady diversion of water to the dry south has lowered the lake's level nearly 50 ft. since 1941, endangering the delicate *tufa* and the California's shore gulls who nest here. Increased salinity has devastated the trout stock of adjacent streams, and newly exposed dust is polluting local air. In the past 10 years, however, locals and lake lovers have rejoiced to see the combined efforts of Congress, the Forest Service, and the Audubon Society succeed in reducing the flow south. The lake's level is expected to rise 17 ft. in the next 20 years.

PRACTICAL INFORMATION AND ORIENTATION

Addresses in Lee Vining consist of P.O. Box numbers, which are of little use to the traveler, so general directions or cross streets are provided instead.

Visitor Information:
  Mono Lake Visitors Center and Lee Vining Chamber of Commerce (647-6595 or 647-6629), in the large orange and blue building on Main St. at 3rd, in Lee Vining. Feels like an eco-gift shop, with exhibits, articles, books, and a free slide show. Walking and canoe tours available (see **Sights and Activities,** p. 420). Open late June-Labor Day daily 9am-10pm; off-season 9am-5pm.
  Mono Basin National Forest Scenic Area Visitors Center (647-3044; email info@monolake.org), ½mi. north of Lee Vining off U.S. 395. Interpretive tours (free) and info on Mono County's wilderness areas. Topographic maps and **wilderness permits** available. Tour of the center's exhibits and the lake's South Tufa Grove $2. Open in summer Mon.-Fri. 9am-7pm, Sat.-Sun. 9am-8pm.
  Lee Vining Ranger Station (647-6525), 2mi. west of U.S. 395 on Rte. 120. Camping info and **backcountry permits** (free), distributed daily on a first-come, first-served basis, unless reserved March-May. Open in summer daily 8am-4:30pm; in winter Mon.-Fri. only.

Buses: Greyhound (647-6301 or 800-231-2222), in the Lee Vining Market. To L.A. ($42) and Reno ($30). Buy your ticket at the next stop, because they don't sell them here. Open daily 8am-9pm.
Emergency: 911.
Post Office (647-6371), behind the blue house on 4th St. in Lee Vining. Open Mon.-Fri. 8:45am-2pm and 3-5:15pm. **ZIP Code:** 93541.
Area Code: 619.

The town of **Lee Vining** provides the best access to Mono Lake and the ghost town of **Bodie,** once "a sea of sin, lashed by the tempests of lust and passion." Lee Vining is located 70 mi. north of **Bishop** on U.S. 395 and 10 mi. west of the Tioga Pass entrance to **Yosemite.** Bodie is 28 mi. northwest of Lee Vining off U.S. 395.

ACCOMMODATIONS, CAMPING, AND FOOD

Lee Vining's location makes it an ideal stopover on the way from Reno or Death Valley to Yosemite. As a result, hotel accommodations are often scarce on Friday afternoons and holidays. Even if you are fortunate enough to get a room, lodging and meals are always expensive; camping and picnics are cheaper alternatives. Many hotels and campgrounds are closed in winter, so call ahead. Most of the affordable options are on Main St. **El Mono Motel** (647-6310), on Main St. at 3rd St., offers slice of modern Californiana complete with faux Spanish name, hip espresso bar, and alternative rock in the lobby (open April-Oct.; singles $45). **Gateway Motel** (647-6467), on Main St. at 4th St., has rooms with TVs and great views of the lake (singles $69-89, off-season $32-39). **The King's Inn** (647-6300), Main St. at 2nd St., offers TVs, private baths, and continental breakfasts (singles $55, off-season $30).

None of the area's campgrounds take reservations, but they are ubiquitous, so a pre-noon arrival time will almost always guarantee a spot. Most sites are clustered west of Lee Vining along Rte. 120. The six **Inyo National Forest campgrounds** (free-$8), lying within 15 minutes of town, are the best locations for travelers headed for Mono Lake. The **June Lake** area south of town on U.S. 395 also has numerous sites ($10). June Lake itself has the **Oh! Ridge campground,** which features flush toilets, a swimming beach, and, for aspiring NRA members, a nearby gun range (sites $10, open April-Nov.). **Ellery Lake campground** (647-6525), has sites ($8) next to a burbling brook with drinking water and chemical toilets.

The **Lee Vining Market** (647-6301), on the south end of town on U.S. 395, is the closest thing to a grocery store (open daily 8am-9pm). **Nicely's** (647-6477), north of the visitors center on U.S. 395, lives up to its name. Salads are $7, and hot sandwiches are $4-5 (open daily 6am-10pm; closed Wed. during winter). **Mono Cone,** on the north end of town on U.S. 395, is a local institution whose opening signals the beginning of summer. Their corn dogs ($1.65), floats ($2.25), and frosty cones ($1) are the best in town (open in summer daily 11am-8pm).

SIGHTS AND ACTIVITIES

In 1984, Congress set aside the 57,000 acres of land surrounding Mono Lake and called it the **Mono Basin National Forest Scenic Area** (647-3044). For a $2 fee, you can investigate the **South Tufa Grove,** which harbors an awe-inspiring collection of calcium carbonate formations. (Take U.S. 395 south to Rte. 120, then go 4mi. east and take the Mono Lake Tufa Reserve turn-off 1mi. south of Tufa Grove.) The *tufa* towers, which resemble giant drip sandcastles, poke through the smooth surface of this solemn sea. Four miles north of Lee Vining on U.S. 395 is **Mono Lake County Park,** a public playground with bathrooms, picnic tables, swings, wheelchair access to the lake, and a smaller *tufa* grove.

On weekends, the **Mono Lake Committee** offers guided canoe tours of the lake that include a crash course on Mono's natural history and conservation. Tours leave from the visitors center at 8, 9:30, and 11am on Saturday and Sunday from mid-June to September; earlier is better for birdwatching. Arrange tours at the visitors center (tickets $12, ages 4-12 $6).

The unique terrain of this geological playground makes it a great place for **hikers** of all levels. Easy trails include the ¼ mi. **Old Marina Area Trail,** east of U.S. 395 one mile north of Lee Vining, the **Lee Vining Creek Nature Trail,** which begins behind the Mono Basin Visitors Center, and the **Panum Crater Trail** 5 mi. south on U.S. 395. Gluttons for punishment should head 10 mi. east of U.S. 395 on Rte. 120, where an exceptionally steep trail leads to the glistening **Gardisky Lake.** The Mono Basin Visitors Center offers tours of sights including Panum Volcano and June Lake.

June Lake, a canyon carved by glaciers and now filled with water, is 10 mi. south of Lee Vining on U.S. 395 (but the loop along Rte. 158 is more scenic). The sparkling lake and its surrounding ring of mountains seem almost like a wayward slice of the Alps. During the summer, June Lake is stocked with trout. Swimming, boating, and fishing are within easy distance of the **June Lake Loop.** The simple **Parker Lake** trail begins 2 mi. west of the loop on Parker Lake Rd., and the difficult 7 mi. trek to the inviting **Bloody Canyon** begins just off the loop beside Grant Lake.

Bodie

One of the best preserved ghost towns this side of the Mississippi, Bodie was "the most lawless, wildest, and toughest mining camp the West has ever known," though it doesn't look that way now. Named after Waterman S. Bodie, who discovered gold here in 1859, the town's heyday was 1878-82, when it was home to 10,000 people, 65 saloons, and one homicide per day. Bodie survived until the 1940s, when the toughest town in the West was destroyed by the now-infamous Bodie Bill, a 2½-year-old child who leveled 90% of the town with one match. The remaining 10%, however, is a ghost-town: absolutely genuine and brimming with romantic appeal. Today the streets and buildings are strewn with abandoned furniture, automobiles, and train engines, well-preserved by the dry climate and the state government. Bodie is accessible by a paved road off U.S. 395, 15 mi. north of Lee Vining (the last 3mi. are a dusty delight) or by a dirt road all the way from Rte. 167 out of Mono Inn. (Bodie open daily 8am-7pm; Labor Day to Memorial Day 8am-4pm. Admission $2, dogs $1. Self-guide booklet $1. For more info, contact Bodie State Historic Park at 647-6445 or P.O. Box 515, Bridgeport, CA 93517.)

■ Mammoth Lakes

Home to one of the most popular ski resorts in the United States, the town of Mammoth Lakes has transformed itself into a giant, year-round playground. Mammoth Mountain makes a summer metamorphosis from ski park to bike park, and fishing, rock climbing, and hiking complement the area's more popular wintertime pursuits. Every establishment in town seems to exist solely for the excursionist's benefit; even the McDonald's looks like a ski lodge. The weekend nightlife is lively and entirely full of athletic types who come to this alpine paradise to get vertical and have mammoth fun.

PRACTICAL INFORMATION AND ORIENTATION

Visitor Information: Inyo National Forest Visitors Center and Chamber of Commerce (934-2712, 888-GO-MAMMOTH/466-2666, or 800-367-6572), east off U.S. 395 north of town. Discounts on hotels, food, and info on campgrounds, roads, sights, and public transportation. Also offers the *Mammoth Times* (free), the *Mammoth Trails Hiking Guide* ($2), and nature exhibits and walks. Open July-Sept. daily 6am-5pm; Oct.-June Mon.-Sat. 8am-5pm.

Bank: Bank of America, 3069 Main St. (934-6839). Open Mon.-Thurs. 9am-5pm, Fri. 9am-6pm, Sat. 9am-2pm.

Buses: Greyhound (213-620-1200), stops in the parking lot behind McDonald's on Main St. One bus daily to Reno ($32) and L.A. ($40). Tickets at the next station.

Public Transportation: Inyo-Mono Dial-A-Ride (872-1901), provides service to Bishop, Bridgeport, Lee Vining, June Lake, and Crowley Lake from Mammoth McDonald's and Bishop K-Mart. Fare $2.50. Call 1 day ahead for door-to-door pickup. **Mammoth Area Shuttle (MAS)** (934-0687), offers a red line shuttle to town and the main lodge. During ski season, shuttles connect to chairlifts (every 15min. 7:30am-5:30pm; free). **Mammoth Shuttle Service** (934-3030), provides year-round on-call service (daily 7am-11pm). Fare within town $3, to lodge $8.

Car Rental: U-SAVE (934-4999 or 800-207-2681). Compacts from $200 per week with 700 free mi. 4WD vehicles from $275 per week. Rentals also available at the **Chevron** (934-8111), next to the post office. Compacts from $30 per day; 150 free mi., each additional mi. 18¢.

Auto Repairs: AAA Emergency Road Service (934-3385 or 800-400-4222).

Equipment Rental: Sandy's Ski Sport (934-7518), Main St. Mountain bikes $7 per hr., $21 per ½ day, $28 per day. Tents $9 for 1 night, $5 each additional night. Ski packages from $16 per day. Backpacks, fishing poles, and sleeping bags available. Open daily 8am-8pm. **Rick's Sport Center** (760-934-3416), corner of Rte. 203 and Center St. Tackle ($10), daily rod rental ($8), and licenses ($9 per day, $25 per year). Open daily 6am-8pm, in winter 7am-7pm.

Laundromat: Mammoth Lakes Laundromat (934-2237), on Laurel Mountain Rd., ½ block off Main St. Wash $1.25, 10min. dry 25¢. Open Mon.-Sat. 8:30am-6:30pm, Sun. 8:30am-5pm.

Weather Conditions: (934-7669). **Ski Conditions: Mammoth Mountain Snow Conditions** (934-6166). **Mammoth Mountain Ski Area** (934-2571). **June Mountain Ski Area** (648-7733).

Medical Services: Mammoth Hospital, 185 Sierra Park Rd. (934-3311). 24hr.

Emergency: 911.

Post Office: 3330 Main St. Open Mon.-Fri. 8:30am-5pm. **ZIP Code:** 93546.

Area Code: 619.

Mammoth Lakes is on **U.S. 395** about 160 mi. south of Reno and 40 mi. southeast of the eastern entrance to Yosemite. **Rte. 203** runs through the town as **Main St.** and then veers off to the right as **Minaret Summit Rd.** In the winter, the roads from L.A. are jammed with weekend skiers making the six-hour journey up to the slopes.

ACCOMMODATIONS AND CAMPING

As with most ski resorts, lodging is much more expensive in the winter, but prices tend to be cheaper on weekdays. Condo rentals are a comfortable choice for groups of three or more, and start at $55 per night in summer. **Mammoth Reservation Bureau** (800-462-5571), can make rental arrangements. For lone travelers, dorm-style motels are the cheapest lodging option. Reservations should be made far in advance.

There are nearly 20 Inyo Forest public **campgrounds** (sites $8-11) in the area, at **Mammoth Lakes, Mammoth Village, Convict Lake,** and **Red's Meadow.** All sites have piped water and most of them are near fishing and hiking. For more info, contact the Mammoth Ranger District (924-5500). Reservations can be made for all sites, as well at nearby Sherwin Creek, through MISTIX (800-280-CAMP/2267; reservation fee $7.85 for individual sites, $15.75 for group sites).

Davison St. Guest House, 19 Davison St. (924-2188; fax 544-9107). Perched on the hill, Davison houses one of the best views in town. Kitchens and fireplaces. Dorms $13; singles $30. Winter: $17, $55.

Twin Lakes campground, ½mi. off Lake Mary Rd. about 2mi. outside town. The 94 magnificent sites are mere feet from fishing and swimming at Twin Lakes. One of the most popular campsites around despite its relatively remote location. Piped water and restrooms. 7-night max. stay. Sites $11. Open June-Nov.

New Shady Rest campground, on Rte. 203 across from McDonald's. Camping isn't the same when you can see the Golden Arches through the trees, but the site is densely wooded and manages to seem a world away from civilization. 14-night max. stay. Sites $10. Half of the 95 sites available year-round for walk-in tenting.

FOOD AND NIGHTLIFE

Fast-food franchises seem to exert hegemonic control over cheap meals, but adventurous palates need not despair. True, some places have prices as high as the neighboring peaks, but others are more down to earth.

Angel's (934-7427), at Main and Sierra, is unanimously recommended by locals. A tad expensive (dinner entrees $6-13) but, after a day on the slopes, you'll feel you've earned it. Angel's specializes in BBQ, which accounts for the delicious aroma, but huge, tasty beef burritos ($7) are also available. The bar features over 70 beers. Open Mon.-Fri. 11:30am-10pm, Sat.-Sun. 5-10pm.

The Stove (934-2821), on Old Mammoth Rd. 4 blocks from Main St. In the minds of most locals, The Stove equals big breakfasts. Visitors will flip at the sight of the huge stack of pancakes ($3.75). Down-home cookin' even for dinner—try the crabmeat sandwiches ($8-10). Open daily 6:30am-9pm.

Good Life Cafe, 126 Old Mammoth Rd. (934-1734), behind the Chart House. The pictures of buffed skiers and mountain bikers on the walls remind visitors to stay healthy, and the food makes it easy to oblige. Hearty meals like chicken stir-fry ($6.50) and fresh fruit bowls ($4) make for a good lunch, if not a good life. Open Sun.-Thurs. 6:30am-3pm, Fri.-Sat. 6:30am-3:30pm.

Grumpy's on 37 Old Main St. (760-934-8587). Get your order of food and fuel up for some tough competition on the pool tables. Many come to Grumpy's to shoot pool. Hamburgers with fries $6. Pasta of the day $9. Open daily 11:30am-1:30am.

Whiskey Creek (934-2555), at Main and Minaret, is more than a creek; it's a ravenous river with live entertainment Thurs.-Sat. Wraps are the new item on the bar menu. Microbrews $3 per pint. Happy Hour (Mon.-Fri. 5-7pm) drafts $1. Open nightly until 1:30am.

SIGHTS

There's plenty to see in Mammoth Lakes but, unfortunately, most of it is accessible only by car. The **MAS,** however, does offer service to some areas (see p. 421). **Devil's Postpile National Monument,** an intriguing geological formation of basalt columns 40 to 60 ft. high, was formed when lava flows oozed through Mammoth Pass thousands of years ago. After the lava cooled, ancient glaciers exposed and polished the posts, whose cross-sections are geometrically precise.

A pleasant three mile walk from the center of the monument is **Rainbow Falls,** where the middle fork of the San Joaquin River drops 101 ft. into a glistening green pool. From U.S. 395, the Devil's Postpile/Rainbow Falls trailhead can be reached by a 15 mi. drive past Minaret Summit on paved Rte. 203. The road and nearby campground (sites $9) are operational only in summer and may open as late as July in years with heavy snows. In an effort to keep the area from being completely trampled, rangers have introduced a **shuttle service** between the parking area at the Mammoth Mountain Inn and the monument center, which all visitors—drivers and hikers alike—must use between 7:30am and 5:30pm (round-trip $8, ages 13-18 $6, ages 5-12 $4, under 4 free). Visitors with wheels can save themselves a load of cash by driving to the monument during nightly free access hours (5:30pm-7:30am).

Hiking and Fishing

Although there are over 100 lakes near town (60 of them within a 5mi. radius), not one actually goes by the name of "Mammoth Lake." The biggest, hairiest lake in the basin, the one-mile-long **Lake Mary,** is popular for boating, sailing, and fishing. **Twin Lakes** is the closest lake to the village, only 3 mi. down Rte. 203. A quick ½ mi. hike from the Twin Lakes turn-off culminates in spectacular views from **Panorama Dome. Lake Mamie** has a picturesque picnic area and many short hikes lead out to **Lake George,** where exposed granite sheets attract climbers. For short but stunning hikes through wildflowers and amazing scenery, trek the **Crystal Lake Trail** (2mi.) or the **Barrett Lake Trail,** both of which leave from the Lake George entrance parking lot. **Horseshoe Lake** is a popular swimming spot and is also the trailhead for the impressive **Mammoth Pass Trail**. The fork in the trail leads to **McLeod Lake** on the left or **Red's Meadow** on the right.

It's an easy ¼ mi. jaunt to the **Inyo Craters,** the spectacular water-filled volcanic blast holes that are a favorite spot for area waterfowl. The trailhead can be reached from **Mammoth Scenic Loop Rd.,** a gently winding thoroughfare that provides access to sights located between Rte. 203 and U.S. 395. **Obsidian Dome** lies 14 mi. north of Mammoth Junction and one mile west of U.S. 395 on Glass Flow Rd. (follow the sign to Lava Flow). The dark, glassy volcanic rock is a wobbly climb, so sturdy shoes and long pants are necessary. **Mammoth Sporting Goods** (934-3239), can equip more experienced hikers with gear and info on more challenging climbs.

Anglers converge on the Mammoth area each summer to test their skills on some of the best trout lakes in the country. Permits are required (the visitors center has info on other regulations). Fanatics will find the frequent **fishing derbies** well worth the price of entry, but less competitive types might prefer to try their luck at the area's serene and well-stocked backcountry waters. In Owens Valley is **Lake Crowley** (935-4301), 12 mi. south of town, which yields over 80 tons of rainbow trout each summer. (Motorboat rental $48 per day; parking free with rental, otherwise $6 per day. Campsites with full hookup $25.)

Even the **Hot Creek Geothermal Area,** 5 mi. south of town off U.S. 395 (exit on Hot Creek Rd.), allows some catch-and-release fishing. The waters here are warmed by hot springs formed by a volcanic blast 700,000 years ago. Several trails lead to the springs, but be careful—a close look may result in a severe burn. Tours of the springs and neighboring fish hatchery are available.

Visitors can ride the **Mammoth Mountain Gondola** (934-2571) to get a view that's miles above the rest (open in summer daily 9:30am-5:30pm; round-trip $10, children $5; day pass $20 for gondola and trail use). Exit the gondola at the top for a mountain biking extravaganza over the twisted trails of **Mammoth Mountain Bike Park,** where the ride starts at 11,053 ft. and heads straight down on rocky ski trails. Yes, helmets are required. Get tickets and info at the **Mammoth Adventure Connection** (934-0606), in the Mammoth Mountain Inn at the base of the mountain (bike rental including helmet $25 for 4hr., $35 for 8hr.; open daily 9:30am-6pm). The park has more than 50 mi. of trails, most easier than the famed **Kamikaze run,** as well as an obstacle arena and slalom race course. Free orientation rides offered.

Other Sports and Seasonal Events

Mammoth is like a Mountain Dew commercial come to life—"extreme" activities abound, from wall-climbing to dogsledding. The **Mammoth Adventure Connection** (934-0606 or 924-5683 for reservations), in the Mammoth Mountain Inn, offers a **ropes course** ($40 adults, $10 youth program) and **climbing wall** ($5 per climb or $15 per hr.; open July-Labor Day).

Summers in Mammoth are packed with small festivals celebrating everything from chili cooking to motorcross racing. A new event, the **Mammoth Lakes Jazz Jubilee** (934-2478), in mid-July has already become a local favorite. The **Mammoth Motorcross Race** (934-0642), at the end of June, is one of the most popular of the area's many athletic competitions, and the **National Mountain Biking Championships** (934-0651), in early July, attracts nearly 50,000 people.

SKIING AND WINTER RECREATION

With 132 downhill runs, over 26 lifts, and miles of nordic **skiing** trails, Mammoth is one of the country's premier winter resorts. The season extends from mid-November to June; in a good year, alpine skiing can last through July. Visiting during a slow time can keep costs low (avoid weekends and especially any time near or on a major holiday). Economical multi-day lift tickets are available (regular price $45 per day, seniors $23, ages 13-18 $34, under 13 $23; 5-day pass $191). Rent skis in town; resort-run shops usually charge 10-20% more. **Mammoth Mountain** lift tickets can be purchased at the **Main Lodge** (934-2571), at the base of the mountain on Minaret Rd. (open Mon.-Fri. 8am-3pm, Sat.-Sun. 7:30am-3pm), at **Stormriders,** at Minaret

Rd. and Canyon Blvd. (open daily 8am-9pm), or at **Warming Hut II** (934-0787), at the end of Canyon Blvd. and Lakeview (open Mon.-Fri. 8am-3pm, Sat.-Sun. 7:30am-3pm). A free shuttle bus (MAS) transports skiers between lifts, town, and the Main Lodge (see p. 421). The Forest Service provides information and tips on the area's cross-country trails.

Mammoth has miles of trails and open areas for snowmobiles. The **Mammoth Lake Snowmobile Association** (934-6157), maps out open and restricted areas. Visitors over 16 can rent snowmobiles at **Center Street Polaris** (934-4020; from $32 per hr.). For those seeking a new winter adventure, the Mammoth area is pioneering **bobsledding.** Though runs are slow enough for non-Olympians, they are still plenty exhilarating, especially at night.

June Mountain Ski Area (648-7733), located 20 mi. north of Mammoth Lakes at Lake U.S. 395 north and Rte. 158 west, has less stellar skiing than Mammoth. Lift tickets ($37 per day, seniors $20, ages 13-18 $27, ages 7-12 $20), are available in the Tram Haus next to the parking lot.

■ Bishop and Owens Valley

In 1861, Samuel Bishop brought 600 cattle and a pair of boots from Fort Tejon to settle at what is now Bishop Creek. The herds have diminished somewhat, but they still graze along U.S. 395 on the way into town. Once a haven for highwaymen and thieves, Bishop now serves as a rancher's rendezvous and a rest stop for travelers en route to trout fishing in the surrounding wilderness areas of Owens Valley.

PRACTICAL INFORMATION

Visitor Information:
  Bishop Chamber of Commerce, 690 N. Main St. (873-8405), at the City Park. Maps and info on the area. Get a free copy of the *Bishop Visitors' Guide* for up-to-date listings of special events. Open Mon.-Fri. 9am-5pm, Sat.-Sun. 10am-4pm.
  White Mountain Ranger Station: 798 N. Main St. (873-2500). Excellent lists of campgrounds and nearby trails. Weather report and a message board. Backcountry campers must obtain one of the limited **wilderness permits** by writing to the White Mountain Ranger District March-May. Ranger Station programs include Sat. evening campfire talks. Open late June-Sept. 15 daily 7am-5pm; winter Mon.-Fri. 8am-4:30pm.
  Fishing Licenses: Permits and regulations available at K-mart and sporting goods stores. Maps at the ranger station.
Bank: Bank of America, 536 N. Main St. (800-338-6430). Open Mon.-Thurs. 9am-5pm, Fri. 9am-7pm, Sat. 9am-2pm.
Greyhound: 201 S. Warren St. (872-2721), behind the J.C. Penney. One bus per day to L.A. ($40) and Reno ($40). Open daily 1-2pm *only.*
Public Transportation: Dial-A-Ride, 872-1901. Round-trip within Bishop city limits 50¢, to areas just outside of the city $1. Will drop you at a trailhead for $30 per hr. Shuttles to Mammoth Lakes ($2.50) and Crowley Lake ($1.75). Call the day before for schedules and reservations (limited number of seats). Open Mon.-Thurs. 8am-5pm, Fri.-Sat. 8am-1am.
Car Rental: Luther Motors, 380 S. Main St. (873-4234). Compacts $25 per day; first 150 mi. free, each additional mi. 20¢. Must be 23.
AAA Emergency Road Service: (800-400-4222).
Bike Rental: Bikes of Bishop, 651 N. Main St. (872-3829). Maps of area tours. Mountain bikes $20 per day.
Laundromat: Wash-Tub, 263 N. Warren St. (873-6627). Wash $1.25, 10min. dry 25¢. Pool tables and video games galore. Open daily 7am-10pm, last load 8pm.
Showers: Sierra Bodies Gym, 192 E. Pine St. (872-2445), behind the Whiskey Creek restaurant. Fee of $3 includes soap, shampoo, and a towel. Open Mon.-Fri. 6am-9pm, Sat.-Sun. 8am-6pm.
Road Conditions: 800-427-ROAD/7623.

Hospital: Northern Inyo Hospital, 150 Pioneer Lane (873-5811), North Inyo. Emergency service 24hr.
Emergency: 911.
Police: 207 W. Line St. (873-5866 or 873-5823).
Post Office: 595 W. Line St. (873-3526). Open Mon.-Fri. 8:15am-4:45pm, Sat. 10am-2pm. **ZIP Code:** 93514.
Area Code: 619.

ACCOMMODATIONS

Hotels are plentiful in Bishop, but *cheap* hotels aren't; the best are listed below. If you want to save money, you may be better off camping in or near Bishop.

El Rancho Motel, 274 Lagoon St. (872-9251), 1 block west of Main. Quintessential motel: you can drive right to your door. Rooms include A/C, TV, coffee makers, refrigerators and, for $8 extra, a kitchen. Singles $43; doubles $54.

Chalfont House, 213 Academy St. (872-1790). This charming bed and breakfast is worth the few extra bucks. Built in 1898, it has creaking hardwood floors, patchwork quilts, and a potbelly stove in the parlor. Rooms for 1-2 people from $60.

Elms Motel, 233 E. Elm St. (873-8118 or 800-848-9226). A dutchman's attention to detail (a sign out front reads "Dutch Clean") keeps these two-room cottages dirt-free. A/C, cable TV, and City Park access. Singles $34; off-season $30.

If you're traveling in a group, and especially if you are looking to fish, a cabin may be your best option. Bishop Creek's **Cardinal Village Resort** (760-873-4789), is nestled in a magnificent mountain glen 16 mi. west of Bishop on Rte. 168. This former mining village now consists of nine cabins (from $80) which sleep 4-16 people each. Recreational activities abound, but those in the know head for the area's incomparable lakes and fishing streams; the general store sells tackle and the creek is routinely stocked with trout and alpers. The lodge serves yummy meals, including buckwheat pancakes ($3), homemade chili ($5), and the Saturday Night Steak BBQ ($9). **Bishop Creek Lodge** (873-4484), on South Lake Rd., is another option. Take Rte. 168 14 mi. west from Bishop, then follow the signs toward South Lake Recreation Area. The complex includes a general store, lodge, restaurant, and cocktail bar ($75 per night for 2; $165 per night for 8; 2-night min. stay; prices go up $10 for 1-night stays).

CAMPING

Most campgrounds around Bishop are well-kept and conveniently located minutes from major roads. Sites have a consistent flow of campers throughout summer but are especially crowded during the **Mule Days** celebration in late May and **rodeo** season in late August and early September, for which you should book a year in advance.

Brown's Town Campground (873-8522). Turn west on Schober Lane, 1mi. south of town on U.S. 395, to reach this family-run place. From the friendly help at the small cafe and general store to the Old West picnic, everything is clean and well-kept. Many of the 160 sites are shaded, 44 have electric and water hookups, and 10 have cable TV. Picnic area available for day use. Tent sites $12; R/V sites with full hookups $15; 7min. showers 50¢ (for campers only).

Mill Pond Campground (873-5342), 6½mi. northwest of Bishop on U.S. 395, ¼mi. south on Ed Powers Rd., 1mi. west on Sawmill Rd. Next to Mill Pond Riding Stables. Like a resort hotel without the walls. Piped and stream water, pond for swimming and sailing, tennis courts, softball diamond, archery, horseshoe pits, and flush toilets. Sites $10; hookups $13.

There are over 25 **Inyo National Forest** campgrounds in the Bishop Ranger District. **First Falls** at Big Pine, **Grandview** in the Bristlecone Forest, and **Mosquito Flat** (Rock Creek Drainage) are all **free.** Grandview has no water; the other three have only stream water, which you must treat before drinking. The creatively named

Intake 2 is the closest site to town ($8). **Bishop Creek Canyon** is a trout fishing hotspot which rests alongside the road to North Lake (restrooms, water; $12 per night). There are 11 sites along the north and south forks which provide comfortable, tree-lined camping, restrooms, water, and easy access to streams and lakes for fishing. For the most current campsite information, visit the locale or call the **Bishop Creek Entrance Station** (873-2527), 9 mi. west of Bishop on Rte. 168 (open summers daily 7am-3:30pm).

FOOD

Fast food chains abound, but more interesting fare can be found at one of the following options. Stock up on groceries at **Vons Supermarket,** 174 S. Main St. (873-4396; open daily 6am-midnight).

Whiskey Creek, 524 N. Main St. (873-7174). Not the cheapest place in the world, but locals swear it's worth every penny. Particularly popular for breakfast, when prices are more manageable. Their dinner "favorites" (which include burritos and a rib basket) require a shorter stack of cents ($6-9) than most of their specialties, which climb as high as $20. Open Sun.-Thurs. 7am-9pm, Fri.-Sat. 7am-10pm.

Erick Schat's Bakkery, 763 N. Main St. (873-7156). While Erick's speling may be a little lakking, his bakking prowess is not to be denied. Pick up a loaf of sheepherder's bread ($2.25), admire Erick's clog collection, or follow him into the 90s and purchase a whole wheat "energy bar" ($1). Open Mon.-Thurs. 6:30am-6pm, Fri.-Sat. 6:30am-8pm.

Pyrenees Soup and Sandwiches, 150 N. Main St. (873-7275). Half a world away from its namesake, but well-frequented by locals for the homemade soups, hearty sandwiches, and peaceful atmosphere. A real mom 'n' pop operation; Dick cooks and Suzanne serves. Light lunches $4-5. Open Mon.-Sat. 10am-3pm.

SIGHTS AND ACTIVITIES

East of Bishop

The Owens Valley is a backpacker's Eden. East of Bishop in the other half of Inyo National Forest (which is split by U.S. 395), the yellow sands of the aptly-named **White Mountains** rise to heights rivaling the Sierra. If you want to tackle the strenuous one mile climb to the top of White Mountain itself (14,246ft.), park your car (preferably 4WD) on White Mountain Rd., 22 mi. from Rte. 168. Free camping is available at **Grandview Campground,** 4 mi. south of Schulman at Barcroft Lab's gate on White Mountain Rd. Pit toilets, tables, and grills available, but no water.

Scattered across the face of the White Mountains are California's **bristlecone pines, the oldest living things on the planet.** Gnarled, twisted, and warped into fantastic shapes, the trees may grow only one inch every 100 years. The slow growth at extreme altitudes (up to 12,000ft.) has allowed the "Methuselah" specimen in Schulman Group to survive 4700 years to date (to preserve the tree, they don't tell you which one it is). To get to the **Ancient Bristlecone Pine Forest,** follow Rte. 168 off

Tomorrow, and Tomorrow, and Tomorrow...

Nestled among the trees in the Ancient Bristlecone Pine Forest, a plaque proclaims "Sweet are the uses of adversity." The quote is from Shakespeare, and refers to the fact that the ancient trees have thrived for millennia in conditions which thwart the growth of other plants. When the Bard wrote this, many of these trees were already over 4000 years old.

Bristlecone pines are so old that tree ring readings taken from samples have been used to recalibrate carbon-dating procedures. With this new information, historians have determined, among other things, that Balkan/European cultures predate those of Mesopotamia. Bristlecones may yet be responsible for disproving that world history we've all worked so hard to learn.

THE SIERRA NEVADA

U.S. 395 at Big Pine for 12 mi. Turn left at the sign to the Bristlecone Pine Forest and the White Mountains Research Station. The 11 mi. paved road takes you to Schulman Grove, where there are two short hikes as well as a **visitors center** (873-2500; open the last Fri. in June through Sept. 15 daily 7am-4:30pm, the rest of the year hours vary). The 12 mi. drive on unpaved roads to **Patriarch Grove** is beautiful but treacherous; 4WD is recommended.

Beyond the Inyos from Deep Springs, southeast of Inyo and northwest of Death Valley lies the uninhabited **Eureka Valley.** The valley's magnificent and haunting **sand dunes** are the **largest landlocked dunes in the world.** If the sand is cool, flip off your shoes, climb to the top of the dunes, and roll down. The friction between the sand you disturb and the nearly 700 ft. of grain beneath makes a bizarre, unfathomably deep sound. Local Native Americans called it "the singing of the sands." Roads lead into the valley from the Owens Valley near Big Pine and various points on the Nevada side, but none are reliable and not even the proverbial wild horses could drag you through when the road is washed out or snowed in. Check with the visitors center for specifics, and see **Desert Survival,** p. 175, for tips on desert travel.

Seven miles south of Big Pine on U.S. 395 is a wildlife viewpoint where you can get a great view of the valley and sometimes (early morning or evening) **elk herds.** Elk also congregate on the mowed alfalfa fields just south of Big Pine on U.S. 395.

West of Bishop

The Owens Valley cradles enough wilderness areas to sate any explorer or adventurer. Head west on Cracker St. for 10 mi. to get to the glaciers of **Big Pine Canyon,** which guide Big Pine Creek through the thick groves of Jeffery Pines. The North Fork Trail is a popular destination for hikers as well as rock- and ice-climbers. The trail passes Lakes 1, 2, and 3 and the stone cabin of Hollywood legend Lon Chaney before getting to the Palisade Glacier, the Sierra's largest ice block. **Fishing** enthusiasts favor Big Pine's seldom-traveled **South Fork Trail,** which leads to lakes laden with fun-to-fish trout.

Follow Line St. 14 mi. west of Bishop to the lakes and campgrounds of **Bishop Creek Canyon.** Here hikers can fork onto the **South Lake Trailhead,** where leisurely trails lead to **Green, Treasure,** and **Chocolate Lakes** and mountain meadows filled with wildflowers. Continue west four mile to **Sabrina Basin** for secluded hiking and fishing opportunities. Steeper switchbacks off the main trail lead to less populated **George Lake.** Sabrina, North, and South Lakes provide spectacular **trout fishing.** The official angling season spans May-October. Contact the chamber of commerce (873-8405), for tournament and general fishing info. **Tackle** and **taxidermy** are available at Parcher's Resort, Bishop Creek Lodge, and Cardinal Village on North Fork Trailhead. (Camping sites with piped water near Sabrina and South Lakes $12.) Serious **hikers** may want to connect here with the Inyo Segment (11,000ft.) of the **Pacific Crest Trail** (for more info, see **From Crest to Crest: the Trail of the West,** p. 409), which is 8 mi. west of the **White Mountain Visitors Center,** 873 N. Main St. (873-2500), in Bishop, which offers permits.

The recreation areas along **Rock Creek Canyon** are frequented year-round. Hairraising precipices, plunging canyons, and velvet wildflowers mesmerize earnest photographers and casual gawkers alike. To get there, take U.S. 395 24 mi. north of Bishop, turn west on Rock Creek Rd., and continue up Rock Creek Canyon to the end of the road (park at Mosquito Flat). **Little Lakes Valley** is surrounded by 13,000 ft. peaks and lakes full of trout. **Mono Pass Trail** leads to beautiful **Ruby Lake** and its staggering sheer granite walls. There are numerous campgrounds on the way to **Mosquito Flat** and plenty of day-parking at each of the five trailheads. (Sites with toilets $11.) **Mosquito Flat Trailhead** is a free walk-in site with stream water only. The campgrounds are closed during the winter months, though the trails remain open for phenomenal cross-country skiing.

For those who tire of outdoor adventure, the exhibits at the **Paiute Shoshone Indian Cultural Center,** 2300 W. Line St. (873-4478), illustrate the history and culture of some of the seven local tribes. Don't miss the poster Tobacco: Use it in a sacred way (open Mon.-Fri. 9am-5pm, Sat.-Sun. 10am-4pm). The **Laws Railroad Museum** (873-5950), on Silver Canyon Rd. off Rte. 6 is a monument to the Carson & Colorado railroad that belched through the Owens Valley for 80 years. Authentic 1880s rusty barbed wire at the store is $1. (Open daily 10am-4pm. Free.)

In **winter,** the evergreen forests, lake basins, and peaceful "range of light" (as Muir described the Eastern Sierra), make for spectacular **cross-country skiing.** Bishop Creek and Rock Creek drainages are the best areas. **Rock Creek Lodge** (935-4170), has groomed trails and a ski school. The ranger station has details (see p. 425).

SEASONAL EVENTS

Though raging activity and unbridled excitement permeate everyday life in Bishop, several annual events add even more spice to this swinging metropolis. Haul your ass to town in late May for the largest mule event in the world, **Mule Days** (872-4263). View 110 mule sporting events, 40,000 mule-obsessed fans, and the famous Mule Days Parade, which is long enough to be listed in the Guinness Book of World Records (there may even be a display at the Guinness World Records Museum, p. 200). The **50s and 60s Dance and Classic Car Show** happens every February, and the Bishop **Fly-In** airshow is in September. The City Park (behind the visitors center) has hosted free Monday **evening concerts** in the gazebo for 40 consecutive summers (June-Aug. 8-9pm). A massive **rodeo** and **fair** happens in town every Labor Day weekend and you can park your RV at the fairgrounds for $7 per night (873-8405). Each night during the rodeo and fair, after the cowfolk finish taming the wyld stallynz, they settle down with some herbal tea and clove cigarettes and recite some of their favorite verse at the **Cowboy Poetry Festival,** imported from Elko, NV, the "cowboy capital of the world."

■ Lone Pine

Lone Pine has stereotypical small-town America down to a science. Doo-wop tunes blare from diner jukeboxes, chrome covers the tops of coffee shop tables, and locals eye the hyperkinetic throngs of visitors with laid-back smiles. Nestled between searing Death Valley to the east and the snow-capped Sierra Nevada mountains to the west, Lone Pine was founded in the 1870s as a mining supply hub. Much has changed since—the lone pine is long gone, the mines are closed, and a devastating earthquake has created nearby **Diaz Lake**—but the town still clings tightly to its Old Western feel.

Movie producers have certainly thought this to be the case. The nearby Alabama Hills have provided the setting for Western classics from the *Lone Ranger* to *Maverick.* The town attracts more than just Hollywood folk; Lone Pine serves as a base for the stunning Inyo National Forest and its crown jewel, 14,484 ft. tall Mount Whitney, the highest peak in the contiguous U.S.

PRACTICAL INFORMATION AND ORIENTATION

Visitor Information:
Interagency Visitors Center (876-6222), at U.S. 395 and Rte. 136 about 1 mi. south of town. Excellent selection of maps and guidebooks, plus small exhibits. Informative handouts about hiking in the area. Open daily July-Sept. 7:30am-7pm, Oct.-June 8am-4:50pm.
Chamber of Commerce, 126 S. Main St. (876-4444; fax 826-4533; http://www.cris/lpc), in Lone Pine. Same services as the visitors center, but at a more convenient location. Somewhat lacking in brochures but the delightful employees (make that 'employee') are knowledgeable. Open Mon.-Fri. 7:30am-4pm.
Mt. Whitney/Inyo National Forest Ranger Station, 640 S. Main St. (876-6200), in "downtown" Lone Pine. Naturalists sponsor programs on the region's wildlife and history. Topographical and trail maps for backcountry camping. Pick up **wilderness permits** (required in the backcountry) here. There are 15-person quotas for some popular trails within the forest, and slightly larger ones

for Mt. Whitney. Half of permits available daily on a first-come, first-served basis; the other half can be obtained by mail March-May. Open mid May-mid Oct. daily 8am-4:30pm; in winter Mon.-Fri. 8am-4:30pm (may vary). **Wilderness Reservations,** P.O. Box 430, Big Pine, CA 93545 (888-374-3773; fax 938-1137).

Fishing Licenses: Slater's Sporting Goods, 130 S. Main St. (876-5020). Local fishing information, license ($9 per day, $26 annually, more for non-CA residents), and supplies. Open daily 7am-6pm.

ATM: Bank of America, 400 N. Main St. (876-5513), in Lone Pine Center.

Greyhound: 1452 S. Main St. (876-5300), at the airport. One bus per day to Reno ($48) and L.A. ($32). Open Mon.-Fri. 7am-7pm, Sat. 7am-3:25pm and 6-7pm.

Car Rental: Lindsay Automotive, 316 S. Washington St. (876-4789). Rates from $59 per day. 150 free mi. Must be 21 with credit card. Open daily 8am-5pm.

Auto Repairs: Don's Texaco, 840 S. Main St. (876-5902). Gasoline and free public restrooms, as well as car repair services. Open daily 8am-8pm. **AAA Emergency Road Service:** (876-4600).

Showers: Cleansing available at **Kirk's Barber Shop,** 104 N. Main St. (876-5700; 876-4354 if Kirk's gone), and on the mountain at **Whitney Portal** store ($3).

Hospital: Southern Inyo, 501 E. Locust (876-5501).

Emergency: 911.

Police: Inyo County Sheriff, Lone Pine Substation (876-5606); Headquarters (878-2441).

Post Office: 121 Bush St. (876-5681), between Main and Jackson. Open Mon.-Fri. 9am-5pm. **ZIP Code:** 93545.

Area Code: 619.

Lone Pine straddles **U.S. 395** and is the first Sierra town you hit when traveling northeast on **Rte. 136** from Death Valley. **Independence,** the county seat, lies 14 mi. to the north. L.A. is a four-hour drive away, 212 mi. south along U.S. 395 and southwest along Rte. 14. Yosemite is a four-hour, 142 mi. long drive north on U.S. 395.

ACCOMMODATIONS AND CAMPING

Motels abound here but prices can be high. Weekday prices are cheapest, but rates fluctuate; call ahead. Camping is cheap, scenic, and conveniently located. For info on showers and camping supplies, see **Practical Information,** p. 429. For both motels and campsites, be sure to make reservations or arrive early.

Dow Villa Motel, 310 S. Main St. (876-5521). Lone Pine's historic hotel comes complete with a John Wayne plate display. Pool and jacuzzi open 24hr. Singles $35, with bath and phone $45.

Alabama Hills Inn, 1920 S. Main St. (876-8700; fax 876-8704; http://www.touringusa.com), 1mi. south of Lone Pine. Named for the frequently filmed hills nearby, this new motel is close to Peter's Pumpkin, Wounded Knight, and other rock sculptures. Cable, refrigerator, hair dryer, and microwave. Heated pool and jacuzzi open 24hr. Weekday singles $53; doubles $63.

Whitney Portal Campground, 13mi. west of town on Whitney Portal Rd. Surrounding evergreens and phenomenal views make this an exceptional campground. Contact the Mt. Whitney Ranger (876-6200 or 800-280-2267), for reservations. Sites $12; group sites $25. 7-night max. stay. Open March-Oct.

Diaz Lake Campground (876-5656), on U.S. 395 2mi. south of Lone Pine. Overlooking Diaz Lake are 200 quiet, tree-lined sites. Watersports fanatics will love the grassy sites on the lake's far shore; their plushiness makes for sound sleeps and smooth watercraft launches. Flush toilets, showers, grills, and well water. Sites $7, 2-week max. stay. Open year-round.

Tuttle Creek Campground, follow Whitney Portal Rd. 4mi. west of Lone Pine, turn south onto Horseshoe Meadows Rd. This base camp for day hikers has 85 sites, restrooms, a creek, and a clear view of the Sierra. No drinkable water. No charge, but donations accepted. Open March-Oct.

FOOD

Lone Pine has its share of coffee shops and 24 hr. mini-marts, but not much else. Grab groceries in town at **Joseph's Bi-Rite Market,** 119 S. Main St. (876-4378; open Mon.-Sat. 8:30am-8pm, Sun. 8:30am-7pm). Most eateries in town are nondescript, but cheap, decent fare is available.

PJ's Bake and Broil, 446 Main St. (876-5796). Down-to-earth food and prices. Their mammoth chicken-fried steak ($7) is an excellent post-climb treat. If you have room left, the pie à la mode (freshly made every day; $2.50) is fabulous. A favorite of the locals, it's the only restaurant open and serving breakfast 24hr.

Sierra Cantina, 123 N. Main St. (876-5740). The lunch ($7) and dinner ($10) buffets offer a scrumptious variety of original Mexican recipes. The warm decor sets you up for that afternoon siesta. Open Thurs.-Mon. 11:30am-8pm.

Totem Cafe, 131 S. Main St. (876-5204). Enjoy stacked meat sandwiches ($5) or dripping char-broiled burgers ($5-6) between a giant fish tank and a poster of John Wayne. Not a Native American object in sight. Open June-Sept. daily 7am-9pm, Oct.-May Wed.-Sun. 7am-9pm.

SIGHTS AND ACTIVITIES

With the craggy edges of **Mount Whitney** as the star of the show, the parts of **Inyo National Forest** bordering Kings Canyon and Sequoia National Parks make up a suitable supporting cast. All of the Sierra's tallest peaks are here (many over 14,000ft.), generally within 10 to 15 minutes of U.S. 395. Cheap national forest campgrounds provide a good base for day hikes or overnight trips. All campsites have water and are about $6 per site. Beware of altitude sickness and allow extra time for hikes. The Inyo National Forest is comprised of scattered land parcels, many of which don't contain a single tree. The definition of "forest" was evidently stretched by the water-hungry in order to protect this important Sierra watershed from development.

Hiking

The **Whitney Trailhead** (876-6200), is 13 mi. west of Lone Pine on Whitney Portal Rd. The canyon entrance at **Whitney Portal** provides fantastic camping with piped water and supplies (sites $12). The 11 mi. trek to the top of Mt. Whitney usually takes two to three days. While more of a strenuous hike than a climb, you may still need an ice axe and crampons in the spring and early summer. For rock-climbers, Mt. Whitney's **East Face** is a year-round challenge. **Pack trips** are available through **Mt. Whitney Pack Trams** on Whitney Portal Rd. (935-4493, 872-8331 winter).

Many less strenuous **day hikes** penetrate the Eastern Sierra. The **Cottonwood Lakes Trail** (10,000ft. at the trailhead) squeezes between the forests that abut the John Muir Wilderness and Sequoia National Park. Follow Whitney Portal Rd. for 4 mi. from Lone Pine and take Horseshoe Meadow Rd. 20 mi. to the trailhead. The hour-long hike along **Horseshoe Meadow Trail** to **Golden Trout Wilderness** passes several dozen high mountain lakes that mirror the Inyo Mountains. Horseshoe Meadow has camping and **equestrian facilities** (horses $10, camping $5). The **Whitney Portal Trail** offers a more challenging six-hour hike from the Lone Pine campground to Whitney Portal campground. The trail follows Lone Pine creek to the densely forested higher altitudes and offers incredible views of Mt. Whitney and Owens Valley.

If you enjoy pain and cycling, the annual **Death Valley to Mt. Whitney Bicycle Road Race** (over Mother's Day weekend) was designed with you in mind. Perennially ranked as one of the most masochistic organized activities in the United States, the two-day race starts at Stovepipe Wells (elevation 5ft.) and ends at the Mt. Whitney trailhead some 100 mi. and 8355 ft. later. In spite of its status as an official United States Cycling Federation event, nonmembers are welcome to join in the torture...er, fun. Call the Chamber of Commerce (see **Practical Information,** p. 429) for an entry form. If running's more your style, Lone Pine hosts a **marathon** the previous weekend. The course climbs 6200 ft. and is among the nation's hardest.

THE SIERRA NEVADA

Historical Sights

Well before Whitney Portal, along Whitney Portal Rd., is **Movie Road,** which leads to the scenic **Alabama Hills.** The hills, named for the Union ship Alabama, were scarred by many 1860s Native American skirmishes. Later the hills became the stage set for fictionalized Hollywood cowboy 'n' Indian tales like the 1920s *How the West Was Won.* In all, over 250 Westerns were filmed here, including such television shoot-'em-ups as *Bonanza* and *Rawhide.* Lone Piners celebrate the Hill's glamorous career with the annual **Lone Pine Film Festival** (876-4314), each Columbus Day.

The **Eastern California Museum,** 155 N. Grant St. (878-2411, weekends 878-2010), in Independence, has a highly specialized collection featuring local Paiute and Shoshone handicrafts, exhibits on miners and ranchers, and a display on Manzanar (see below; open Wed.-Mon. 10am-4pm; donation $1).

North of Lone Pine along U.S. 395 lies **Manzanar Relocation Camp,** site of one of the most shameful chapters in American history. Recently named a national historic site, the camp was the first of ten **internment centers** established after Japan's 1941 attack on Pearl Harbor to contain Japanese-Americans, who were seen as enemy sympathizers by the U.S. government. From March 1942 through 1945, 11,000 people were held here. All visitors can walk through the remaining structures and grounds for no charge; a large delegation makes an annual pilgrimage here on the last Saturday of each April. Aggressively and conspicuously ignored by the government, little remains to be seen of the camp except a few building foundations and some barbed wire.

THE SAN JOAQUIN VALLEY

The San Joaquin Valley quietly minds its own agribusiness. Lifestyles here are conservative, unadorned, and far from the spotlight that scrutinizes the Valley's western neighbors. Known as the "middle-of-nowhere" that separates Los Angeles and San Francisco, the San Joaquin is one of the most vital agricultural regions in the country, stretching from the Tehachapi Range south of Bakersfield to just north of Stockton. The valley is the only route to the national parks and forests of the Sierra, but it is practically cut off from the coast. The land is flat, the air is oven-hot, and the endless onion fields and rows of fruit trees are broken only by the razor-straight slashes of I-5 and Rte. 99. Nowhere else in the state does one feel so far from California.

■ Stockton

Stockton lies in the fertile farmland surrounding the Sacramento River Delta, but its agrarian roots have been overshadowed by inner-city ills. The city's location makes it a convenient rest stop, but be warned; it is at best uninteresting and at worst unsafe. Our advice: keep right on driving or make it a quick stop.

The **Stockton/San Joaquin Convention and Visitor Bureau,** 46 W. Fremont St. (943-1987 or 800-350-1987), provides info, maps, and brochures (open Mon.-Fri. 8am-5pm). **Amtrak** is at 735 S. San Joaquin Dr. (946-0517). Four trains per day go to San Francisco ($16) and Los Angeles ($62). **Greyhound,** 121 S. Center St. (466-3568), sends buses to San Francisco (6 per day, $11), Sacramento (13 per day, $11), and L.A. (11 per day, $32). The local bus system is **Stockton Metropolitan Transit District** (given the acronym SMART for reasons lost in the mists of some dyslexic past; 943-1111), which runs on the half-hour daily 5:30am-10pm (fare $1.10, seniors 55¢, ages 6-17 85¢). **Dameron Hospital** is at 525 W. Acacia St. (944-5550). In an **emergency,** call 911. Call the **police** at 937-8377. The **post office** is at 4245 West Ln. The **ZIP Code** is 95208. The **area code** is 209.

Motels north of town on I-5, at the March Lane Exit, are nicer and feel safer than places downtown. **Sixpence Inn** (931-9511), off Rte. 99, north of Stockton at Waterloo Exit, offers A/C and cable TV (singles $26; doubles $32). Stockton is in the Land

Greetings from Let's Go Publications

The book in your hand is the work of hundreds of student researcher-writers, editors, cartographers, and designers. Each summer we brave monsoons, revolutions, and marriage proposals to bring you a fully updated, completely revised travel guide series, as we've done every year for the past 38 years.

This is a collection of our best finds, our cheapest deals, our most evocative description, and, as always, our wit, humor, and irreverence. Let's Go is filled with all the information on anything you could possibly need to know to have a successful trip, and we try to make it as much a companion as a guide.

We believe that budget travel is not the last recourse of the destitute, but rather the only way to travel; living simply and cheaply brings you closer to the people and places you've been saving up to visit. We also believe that the best adventures and discoveries are the ones you find yourself. So put us down every once in while and head out on your own. And when you find something to share, drop us a line. We're **Let's Go Publications,** 67 Mount Auburn St., Cambridge, MA 02138, USA (email: fanmail@letsgo.com; http://www.letsgo.com). And let us know if you want a free subscription to **The Yellowjacket,** the new Let's Go Newsletter.

When in 172-1011,
do as the 172-1011's do.

**All you need for the
clearest connections home.**

Every country has its own AT&T Access Number which makes calling from overseas really easy. Just dial the AT&T Access Number for the country you're calling from and we'll take it from there. And be sure to charge your calls on your AT&T Calling Card. It'll help you avoid outrageous phone charges on your hotel bill and save you up to 60%.* For a free wallet card listing AT&T Access Numbers, call 1 800 446-8399.

I t ' s   a l l   w i t h i n   y o u r   r e a c h .

http://www.att.com/traveler

of Fast Food, but there are some decent eateries nonetheless. The **Cancun Restaurant,** 248 N. El Dorado St. (465-6810), serves up lunch specials ($3) that include burritos, enchiladas, or quesadillas (open Sun.-Thurs. 11am-10:30pm, Fri.-Sat. 11am-3am). **Le Kim's,** 631 N. Center St. (943-0308), dishes out Vietnamese cuisine like coconut-curry chicken ($5; open Mon.-Sat. 10am-10pm).

▓ Fresno

Fresno (pop. 406,000) offers all the amenities and disadvantages of a big city *sans* the attractions and charm. Fresno is dusty, hot, and in many places crime-ridden. Even so, what California's eighth-largest city lacks in exuberance it makes up for in efficiency—it is, after all, the banking center of the San Joaquin Valley. The trains run on time, the streets are freshly paved, and there are no lines at the post office. Residents take pride not only in this practicality, but also in the city's artistic heritage (William Saroyan and Ansel Adams survived here for years despite the lack of scenery) and its agricultural prowess—half the country's nectarines are grown here. But nectarines do not a nightlife make; Fresno's after-hours scene is slow, and the city's chief allure is its convenience en route to or from the Sierra Nevada.

PRACTICAL INFORMATION AND ORIENTATION

Visitor Information: Convention and Visitor Bureau, 808 M St. 93721 (233-0836 or 800-788-0836). Info on city businesses, events, and attractions. Not used to budget travelers looking for a place to crash, but they'll try their best. Open Mon.-Fri. 8am-5pm. **Fresno County and City Chamber of Commerce,** 2331 Fresno St. (233-4651; email tourfresno@aol.com). Open Mon.-Fri. 9am-5pm.

Airport: Fresno Air Terminal, 1575 E. Clinton Way (498-4095), northeast of downtown (bus #26).

Trains: Amtrak, 2650 Tulare Ave. (486-7651 or 800-872-7245), at Santa Fe. Four trains per day to San Francisco ($27) and Los Angeles ($25).

Buses: Greyhound, 1033 Broadway (800-231-2222). To San Francisco (4 per day, $21) and Los Angeles (9 per day, $19). Lockers for ticketed passengers only.

Public Transportation: Fresno Area Express (FAX) (488-1122), has 15 routes; most leave from the courthouse, at Fresno and Van Ness, or 2 blocks west at Fresno and Broadway. Fare 75¢, seniors and disabled 35¢; exact change. The city's commuter transportation system is the **Fresno Area Regional Transport,** but no one calls it by its acronym. Most routes run every ½hr. Mon.-Sat. 6am-6:30pm, Sun. 10:30am-5:45pm. Route maps at the office in Manchester Shopping Center.

Car Rental: Action, 2100 Willow Ave. (291-1982), offers the cheapest wheels in town. Compacts $16 per day with 50 free mi. per day, each additional mi. 15¢. Must be 21 with a credit card.

Equipment Rental: Herb Bauer's Sporting Goods, 6264 N. Blackstone (435-8600). Good selection of camping supplies—stock up here before heading into the Sierra. Open Mon.-Fri. 9am-9pm, Sat. 9am-6pm, Sun. 10am-5pm.

Laundromat: Plaza, 3097 Tulare Ave. (266-1107), at U St. Wash 75¢. Open 24hr.

Road Conditions: CalTrans (800-427-ROAD/7623). 24hr. recording.

Weather Conditions: (442-1212). **Ski Report:** (233-3330).

Events: Beeline (443-2400, ext. 1516).

Emergency: 911.

Post Office: 1900 E St. (233-0170), at El Dorado. Open Mon.-Fri. 8:30am-5pm. **ZIP Code:** 93706.

Area Code: 209.

Fresno is an ideal base for entry into the cool peaks of the Sierra Nevada. **Rte. 41** heads due north, bound for Yosemite National Park, **Rte. 168** winds northeast past Huntington Lake through Sierra National Forest, and **Rte. 180** traverses the eastern valley before climbing into Sequoia National Forest and Kings Canyon National

Park. **Rte. 99** cuts northwest-southeast, **Rte. 180** runs east-west, and **Rte. 41** north-south. Before entering the city, arm yourself with a detailed map. The irregular road layout and one-way streets make downtown navigation bewildering.

Fresno has a high rate of violent crime, even for California; as always, exercise **caution,** especially in the area around Broadway.

ACCOMMODATIONS

There are plenty run-of-the-mill motels in Fresno, but the town of **Merced** (mur-SED), an hour north of Fresno, serves as an alternative base for northward excursions. **Merced Home Hostel (HI-AYH)** and the **Yosemite Gateway Home Hostel** (both at 725-0407; singles $12, nonmembers $15), also provide info about bus service from Merced to Yosemite. **Campgrounds** in the area around both Fresno and Merced serve the purpose—but it's not far to Yosemite, Kings Canyon, or Sequoia National Park, so why stick around?

> **Economy Inns of America,** 5021 N. Barcus Ave. (276-1910; fax 276-2974). Economical comfort in a soothing blue decor. Singles with queen bed $30.
>
> **Brooks Ranch Inn,** 4278 W. Ashlan (275-2727 or 800-241-2727; fax 275-9103), at the Ashlan Exit off Rte. 99. The architecture looks fascist, but the inside is surprisingly pleasant. Singles with double bed $40.
>
> **Motel 6 Best Western,** 949 N. Parkway Dr. (233-3913; fax 498-8526), right beside the highway. Clean, small rooms with cable TV and A/C. Singles $27.

FOOD AND ENTERTAINMENT

Thanks to the county's rich harvests (and to its Armenian, Mexican, and Southeast Asian communities), good food abounds in Fresno. The old **Chinatown,** west of the railroad tracks at Kern, has many Asian and Mexican restaurants and stores, while the **Tower District,** bordered by Olive and Wish, is the center of Fresno's mediocre nightlife. Caution should be exercised in both places after dark. At the **outdoor produce market,** at Merced and N St., vendors drive pick-ups into a parking lot, hang scales from their awnings, and sell, sell, sell (open Tues., Thurs., and Sat. 7am-3pm).

> **Café Moná,** 2011 Tuolumne Ave. (497-8535). Pronounced like the name of the French Impressionist. A cool, relaxed lunch parlor which serves delicious sandwiches ($5, including salad) that will melt in your mouth, not in your hand. Gourmet coffees and teas are a steal at $1-2. Open Mon.-Fri. 8am-2pm.
>
> **Central Fish Market,** 1535 Kern Ave. (237-2049), at G St., doubles as a full grocery store and a Japanese restaurant. Fresh fish and produce. Entree of shrimp or chicken, veggies, rice, and salad all for $3-4. Market open Mon.-Sat. 8am-8pm, Sun. 8am-7pm; restaurant open Mon.-Sat. 11am-6:30pm, Sun. 11am-5:30pm.
>
> **Santa Fe Hotel,** 935 Santa Fe Ave. (266-2170), at Tulare. Family-style Basque food served at long tables. The decor isn't much, but they make up for it in both quality and quantity of food. Enormous lunches $7, dinner $8-12, under 12 half-price. Open Tues.-Sat. 11:30am-2pm and 5-9pm, Sun. 11:30am-2pm and 4:30-8pm.

SIGHTS AND SEASONAL EVENTS

The **Baldasare Forestiere Underground Gardens** (271-8734), one block east of Rte. 99 on Shaw northwest of town, houses a subterranean farm. Forestiere migrated from Sicily with high hopes for agricultural success in California, but found his land had poor topsoil. After digging a basement and toying with skylights, he discovered he could grow crops underground. Forestiere's subterranean success led to a year-round growing season and a 20-crop rotation. The farm is an historic landmark (admission $4; weekend tours hourly noon-3pm).

The **Fresno Metropolitan Museum of Art, History, and Science,** 1559 Van Ness Ave. (441-1444), at Calaveras, features a permanent exhibit on the life of Fresno native and Pulitzer Prize-winning novelist and playwright William Saroyan, but also shows regional and traveling exhibits. (Open daily 11am-5pm. Admission $4, seniors $3, students $3, under 12 $3; first Wed. of each month $1. Take bus #28.)

Fresno goes out of its way to please Saroyan fans. At the end of April, the **Saroyan Festival** includes writing contests and Armenian folk music. The convention center is named after him, as are the symposium and bicycle race. And if you find your Saroyan obsession not yet sated, try the bus ($24) or agricultural ($13) tours (800-788-0836). If you're here in March, ask the visitor bureau about the **Blossom Trail,** a 62 mi. long self-guided driving tour that highlights the wonders of Fresno's agriculture. The **Clovis Rodeo** (299-8838), also in late April, is the largest two-day rodeo held anywhere in California.

■ Bakersfield

What it lacks in cultural verve, Bakersfield makes up in commercial completeness. Every major restaurant and motel chain is represented here. As the population of 213,000 attests, not everyone you see is just stopping over—there is a large L.A. commuter population—but it's mostly an enclave of humanity amid lots of cows.

The **Greater Bakersfield Chamber of Commerce,** 1033 Truxtun Ave. (327-4421), has helpful info (open Mon. 9am-5pm, Tues.-Fri. 8am-5pm). Cars are available from **Rent-A-Wreck,** 1130 24th St. (322-6100), at M St. Cheap deals ($25 per day) are only for the 21-and-up set. **Bakersfield Memorial Hospital,** 420 34th St. (327-1792), at Q St., provides 24-hour care. The **police** are at 1601 Truxtun Ave. (327-7111). The **post office** is at 1730 18th St. (861-4346). The **ZIP Code** is 93302. The **area code** is 805.

Motel 6, 5241 Olive Tree Court (392-9700), has four locations in Bakersfield, but the Olive Tree Ct. site has the cheapest rates (singles $27; doubles $31). The **Economy Inn of America,** 6100 Knudsen (392-1800), offers TV and pool for a mere $26.

Gatsby's Cafe, 1300 Coffee Rd. (588-3088), is one of the few places where Popeye, the Beatles, and country music coexist in peace (sandwiches $6; open daily 7am-2pm). **Maitia's Basque Restaurant,** 3535 N. Union Ave. (324-4711), offers a $6 all-you-can-eat lunch (open Mon.-Fri. 10:30am-2pm and 4:30-10pm, Sat. 4:30-10pm, Sun. 4-9pm). Mexican food fans should salsa to **El Adobe Mexican Restaurant,** 2620 Ming Ave. (397-1932), where four-item combos go for $5 (open daily 11am-9pm).

HAWAII

Hawaii is paradise. Milton was wrong—the human race never lost Eden. We just misplaced it for a while, and it's not too surprising. Hawaii, 2400 mi. off mainland America, is the most geographically isolated place in the world. The location of the islands have set them apart in both landscape and lifestyle. Lush vegetation encroaches on endless beaches while sultry breezes stir the surf and keep the weather wonderful year-round. Acres of untainted tropical forest grow up the slopes of active volcanoes and border luxurious resort areas and bustling urban enclaves. Sound Elysian? It is.

Unfortunately, while you can still wander along luxurious white sand beaches, hundreds of sunburned Minnesotans are likely to be doing so with you. Tourism has penetrated almost every aspect of Hawaiian culture, from the t-shirt stands in the streets of Honolulu to the bastardized hula performances touted as "native."

Still, the state is one of the most ethnically diverse regions in the world, which makes for a fascinating, albeit hidden, native culture. The state serves as a bridge between East and West, a nexus of Asian, Western, and Polynesian influences.

The Hawaiian chain is comprised of 132 islands, though only seven are inhabited. Honolulu, the cosmopolitan capital, is on the island of Oahu, as are most of the state's residents and tourists. The Big Island of Hawaii is famed for its Kona coffee, macadamia nuts, and black sand beaches. Maui boasts the historic whaling village of Lahaina, fantastic windsurfing, and the dormant volcanic crater of Haleakala. The garden isle of Kauai, at the northwestern end of the inhabited islands, ranks first for sheer beauty. Molokai, once stigmatized because of its leper colony, is the friendliest spot in the islands. On tiny Lanai, exclusive resorts have replaced pineapples as the primary commodity. The seventh populated isle, Niihau, is closed to most visitors, supporting just a few hundred plantation families who still converse in the Hawaiian language. In the words of Twain, together these present "the loveliest fleet of islands that lies anchored in any ocean."

▓ Practical Information

Visitor Information: Hawaii Visitors Bureau, 2270 Kalakaua Ave., #801, Honolulu 96815 (923-1811). Open Mon.-Fri. 8am-4:30pm. The ultimate source. Other islands staff offices in major towns, as listed in the appropriate sections. **Department of Land and Natural Resources,** 1151 Punchbowl St. (587-0300; P.O. Box 621, Honolulu 96809). Info and trail maps. Open Mon.-Fri. 8am-4:30pm; state park permits issued until 3:30pm. **National Park Service,** Prince Kuhio Federal Bldg., 300 Ala Moana Blvd., #6305 (541-2693). Permits issued at individual park headquarters. Open Mon.-Fri. 8am-4pm.

Consulates: The only consulates in Hawaii are in Honolulu. **Australian Consulate,** 1000 Bishop St. (524-5050). Open Mon.-Fri. 8am-4pm. **German Consulate,** 2003 Kalia Rd., #11 (946-3819). Open Mon.-Fri. 9am-1pm. **Japanese Consulate,** 1742 Nuuanu Ave. (536-2226). Open Mon.-Fri. 8-11:30am and 1-3pm.

Telephones: Calls within each island 25¢. Inter-island calls must be preceded by 808; prices vary depending on time of day. Most hostels, and some shops, in Honolulu carry Phone Line USA vending machines, which dispense cards with enough money on them to make international phone calls at reduced charges.

Postal Abbreviation: HI.

Area Code: 808.

Capital: Honolulu.

Time Zone: Hawaii (3hr. behind Pacific in spring and summer; 2hr. otherwise). 11-13hr. of daylight year-round.

Drinking Age: 21.

Sales Tax: 4%. **Road Tax:** $2 per day for rented cars.

Major Newspapers: On Oahu, the *Advertiser* and the *Honolulu Star-Bulletin*. On Maui, *The Maui News*.

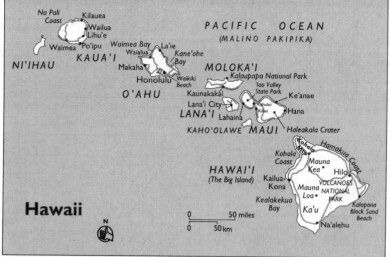

Hawaii

IMPRACTICAL INFORMATION

Motto: *Ua mau keea o kaaina i ka pono.* (The life of the land is perpetuated in righteousness.)

State Bird: *Nene,* an evolved form of the Canadian goose.

State Fish: *Humuhumunukunukuapuaa,* a colorful reef triggerfish.

State Flower: Hibiscus.

State Tree: *Kukui.* In addition to its use as light source and fashion accessory, the kukui nut is a powerful laxative. As the Hawaiians say, "One nut, you walk to the bathroom. Two nuts, you run to the bathroom. Three nuts, it's all over." Literally.

■ Getting There

Reaching paradise isn't as expensive as you might think. While prices increase in winter (Dec.-April), reasonable fares can be found even then. Investigate the *L.A. Times* or the *New York Times* "Sunday Travel" section for discount packages, which usually include airfare from major mainland cities, accommodations, and a bevy of fringe benefits such as car rental. Be sure to learn the nitty-gritty details; tour packages often list sights without including admission fees, and rates listed are almost always a per person rate based on double occupancy. Solo travelers usually wind up paying more.

If all you want is a plane ticket, look for special advance purchase fares or bulk rates from cut-rate travel agencies. From Los Angeles and San Francisco, tickets on many major carriers start at $300 round-trip and go up from there. **Cheap Tickets** (947-3717 in Hawaii; 310-645-5054 in California), in Honolulu, for instance, offers fares substantially below APEX rates. (See also **Essentials: Getting There and Getting Around,** p. 24.) If you're traveling to the mainland from Hawaii, cut-rate tickets can sometimes be found in the classified section of major island newspapers.

■ Island Hopping

The major **inter-island** carriers (Hawaiian, Aloha, Island, and Mahalo) can **fly** you quickly (about 30min.) from Honolulu to any of the islands. There are few direct flights between the smaller islands; most inter-island flights pass through Honolulu. **Mahalo Airlines** is the cheapest, but they fly slower turboprop planes and have been known to have scheduling screwups in the past. **Hawaiian** and **Aloha** fly faster jets and have many more flights per day. **Island** has the most extensive service to the smaller airports on Lanai and Molokai.

Savvy budget travelers should buy tickets from local travel agencies (found on every island except Lanai), which should sell inter-island coupons for $35 to $45 (buying directly from the airlines costs much more—$60-80). Destination does not need to be specified upon purchase. When buying a ticket, be sure it is not one of the "restricted" tickets, which are reserved for locals. Inter-island flights are often extremely scenic, particularly in the early morning or late afternoon. For the best views, sit on the right side heading north and on the left flying south. Surfboards and bikes cost an extra $20 each way (call the airline for size limits).

Mahalo Air (833-5555 on Oahu, 800-4-MAHALO/462-4256 from the mainland), is the cheapest airline. Flies to every island but Lanai and Molokai. Inter-island coupons $60. Open daily 5am-9:30pm.
Hawaiian Airlines (838-1555 on Oahu, 800-367-5320 from the mainland). Inter-island coupons $80. Open daily 5am-9:30pm.
Aloha Airlines (484-1111 on Oahu, 800-367-5250 from the mainland). Inter-island coupons $66, with AAA discount $57. Open daily 5:30am-9:30pm.
Island Air (484-2222 on Oahu, 800-323-3345 from the mainland). Smaller planes fly to resorts and rural airports. Inter-island coupons $66. Open daily 5:30am-9:30pm.

The only **ferry, Expeditions** (661-3756), runs between Lahaina, Maui and Manele, Lanai. (For more info, see **Maui: Practical Information,** p. 462.)

ON THE ISLANDS

To get around in Hawaii, do as the Hawaiians do: drive. While the **bus** system is fairly reliable and extensive on Oahu, on the other islands it is at best patchy and at worst nonexistent (for more info, see individual island listings). One option is staying at hostels that offer daytrips to their island's better sights. For flexibility's sake, however, you'll probably want to **rent** a car on any island other than Oahu. If you're under 21, you may find it's a real pain trying to get your hands on a steering wheel. Since most chains won't rent to younger travelers, the best option is to ask at hostels and check local publications. Most rental companies offer a **collision damage waiver (CDW),** which limits the renter's liability. However, CDWs tend to be a scam—most companies already have insurance. Many insurance plans from back home will cover rental cars, and several credit card companies (including AmEx) cover collision damages in rental vehicles if you decline the CDW. Written proof of this additional insurance may get you out of a required CDW.

Bicycle and **moped rentals,** available in most tourist centers, are an enjoyable and economical way to see Hawaii. Most companies require only a driver's license and a credit card. Tourist publications at the airport often offer discounts for moped rentals. Bringing a bike on a flight costs around $20 inter-island, $50 from the mainland.

■ Accommodations and Camping

Despite rumors to the contrary, reasonable room rates do exist on the islands. Hotels closer to major attractions and beaches charge more, and rates at larger resorts vary frequently with special events and with the season (rates higher Dec.-April). Look for special deals that include rental car and air transportation.

Hostels are one of the best bets for budget accommodations, providing cheap beds and a network of travelers and info to help you structure your trip. Many also run airport shuttles and sightseeing trips and offer discounts on car rentals, inter-island flights, and activities. **YMCAs** also provide affordable lodgings, but offer fewer amenities than hostels. **B&Bs** are a quieter option, offering rooms in private homes. Prices generally start at $55, but most B&Bs give better rates to those who call from the islands. **All Islands B&B** (263-2342 or 800-542-0344; open Mon.-Fri. 8am-5pm), and **B&B Hawaiian Islands** (261-7895 or 800-258-7895; open Mon.-Fri. 8am-5pm), can make reservations.

Camping is probably Hawaii's best deal. It's a great way to experience the islands' natural beauty, and it's cheap too—never more than $3 per night. Not all sites have drinkable water; heed posted warnings, as drinking untreated water can cause serious intestinal problems. Parks on the islands are regulated through the national, state, and county park systems. **National** campgrounds on Maui and the Big Island require no permit, but they do enforce three- or five-day maximum stays. The popular **state** parks require free camping permits (applicants must be at least 18 years old; permits available from the Dept. of State Parks in Honolulu and from state park offices on individual islands). Camping is limited to five nights per 30 days. Sites are open Friday through Wednesday on Oahu, daily on the other islands. **County** parks make up the bulk of Hawaiian camping options; they are numerous and the permits are cheap (free on Oahu, $3 for all other islands; available from the Parks and Recreation offices on each island), but they are not as well-maintained as the state parks. County parks also tend to be popular with occasionally unwelcoming locals, so be wary of any semi-permanent encampments. Though illegal, camping in nondesignated areas is a common occurrence, and the low-profile camper usually runs into few, if any, problems. Permit checking does not seem to be common, but of course, *Let's Go* does not recommend camping without a permit. For a good overview of the outdoor scene on the islands, check out *Camping Hawaii*, by Robert McMahon.

■ Protecting Yourself

Outside of Honolulu, the major crime threat is robbery. Car break-ins are common, in beach parking lots in particular. Never leave valuables in your car, and if you must do so, shift things into the trunk *before* you arrive at the beach. If there is nothing valuable in your vehicle, police advise leaving the car unlocked so that thieves won't be tempted to break a window or lock.

Although Hawaiians are generally a friendly bunch, they react strongly to the **stink eye,** or angry glare, commonly used on American highways to indicate frustration with a particularly slow or erratic driver. Especially in Honolulu, this is considered extremely offensive, so just curse quietly to yourself and keep driving.

■ Life and Times

HISTORY

Between 25 and 40 million years ago, molten rock welled up from the depths of the earth and burst through the ocean floor at the bottom of the Pacific Ocean. Over millennia, as the Pacific Plate shifted to the northeast, the 1600 mi. archipelago known as the Hawaiian Islands was formed. The oldest islands in the northwest have been worn away to tiny coral atolls by the erosion of the sea, while at the other end of the chain you can feel the earth move under your feet as the fiery eruptions continue to expand the islands.

Long before plate tectonics had gained wide scientific currency, the ancient Hawaiians had grasped the idea of how the volcanic mechanism worked. Their legends told of the fire goddess Pele, who fled from island to island, moving southeast down the chain to escape the watery intrusions of her older brother, Kanaloa, the ocean. Their journey to the islands was no less remarkable—traveling across thousands of miles of ocean as early as the 6th century AD, the first inhabitants carried with them roots, seeds, dogs, chickens, and a pig or two in their double-hulled canoes. From these meager beginnings, the Polynesian settlers founded a culture. They formed several skirmishing kingdoms, worshiped a host of gods, and considered themselves *kamaaina* (children of the land). By the time Captain Cook "dis-

HAWAII

A Sovereign Idea

Native Hawaiians have sought a greater voice in state government since the U.S.-backed overthrow of Queen Liliuokalani in 1893, but a strong pro-Hawaiian movement has only surfaced in the last ten years, fueled by ancient property disputes with resort developers and the U.S. Navy. More recently, *kanaka maoli* (ethnic Hawaiians) have broadened the cause to include social problems, since they suffer higher amounts of poverty, infant mortality, and unemployment than other racial groups in the state. However, the movement has been plagued by uncertain leadership and a divided platform—some *kanaka maoli* merely advocate greater recognition of Hawaiian culture, while more radical wings endorse complete secession. In August, 1996, *kanaka maoli* passed a resolution to elect delegates to the state government who would work toward creating a native Hawaiian government, but what this means remains unclear. *Kanaka maoli* only constitute 13% of Hawaii's population, and while some of their causes are backed by Hawaii's Asian and Caucasian pluralities, the more extreme demands, like reintroduction of the Hawaiian language, will probably stay unfulfilled.

covered" the islands in 1778, a rigidly hierarchical society and advanced irrigation techniques supported a population estimated to be 800,000. The *kapu* system of laws and customs maintained religious, political, and social order, while allowing the ancient Hawaiians to develop skills in agriculture, medicine, the arts, dance, and of course, surfing.

But the imperial story played out in other colonized nations took its course in Hawaii; Cook's inadvertent stop propelled Hawaii into the modern world. King Kamehameha I of the Big Island—today revered as the leader who united the islands and created modern Hawaii—exploited the introduction of Western arms and conquered all of the other islands except Kauai within 20 years of Cook's arrival. However, the European trade ships brought more than just weapons. Western diseases, primarily syphilis and tuberculosis, decimated the Hawaiian population. One hundred years after Cook's arrival, only 50,000 native Hawaiians remained.

Following the arrival of Calvinist missionaries from Boston in 1820, the *haole* (HOW-lee, referring to Caucasians) presence in island life became entrenched. By 1853, over 30% of Hawaiians belonged to Christian churches. An expanding sugar (and later pineapple) industry supplanted the original whaling and sandalwood trade. American plantation owners brought in Chinese, Japanese, and Filipino workers to supplement the Hawaiian work pool. American sugar magnates, leery of a strong monarchy and seeking to ensure a market for their product, overthrew Queen Liliuokalani in 1893 and asked that the U.S. annex the islands. In 1898, in the midst of swatting Spain in the "splendid little war," the U.S. heeded their request.

Hawaiian commerce developed uneventfully until the Japanese attack on Pearl Harbor dramatically summoned the U.S. into World War II. In the heat of the panic, *nisei* (first generation Japanese-Americans) were denied, at first, the right to serve in the U.S. armed forces. The government's eventual relaxation of their unjust ruling and the valiant service of the *nisei* in combat were factors in mitigating racial prejudice. In 1959, denied the right to become independent and not wishing to remain a colony, Hawaii became the 50th star on the spangled banner.

Today, Hawaiian culture is a mixture of the old and new. In the face of ever-increasing Westernization, traditional Polynesian culture has gotten lost among many disinterested youth. There is a growing campaign, however, to preserve Hawaiian traditions, a movement backed by the older generations and the legions of college-educated graduates who realize that negligence will write the final chapter of their culture's 2000-year history.

LITERATURE

Many foreign and indigenous writers have chronicled the Hawaiian spirit in their novels, stories, and poems. Mary K. Pukui's anthologies translate selected Hawaiian verses spanning ancient through missionary times. Three renowned authors, Mark Twain, James Michener, and Jack London, captured their impressions of the islands in stories or essays; Michener's mammoth text *Hawaii* takes the reader all the way from the island's volcanic formation through statehood.

For an overview of the Hawaiian literati, page through one of these books: Martha Beckwith, *Hawaiian Mythology;* Jack London, *Stories from Hawaii;* James A. Michener, *Hawaii;* Mary Kawena Pukui and Alfons L. Korn, *The Echo of Our Song: Chants and Poems of the Hawaiians;* Gordon Morse, *My Owhyhee* and *My Molokai;* Mary Kawena Pukui, *Olelo Noeau: Hawaiian Proverbs and Poetical Sayings;* Marjorie Sinclair, *Kona;* Liliuokalani, *Hawaii's Story;* Mark Twain, *Letters from Hawaii;* W.D. Westervelt, *Myths and Legends of Hawaii.*

ART

Visitors of an artistic bent will find a rich heritage of native crafts, and a smattering of coveted Western import in Hawaii. Perhaps the islanders' most celebrated handicraft is the production of *leis.* Although commercial vendors have bastardized the original craft with synthetic materials, you can still find the traditional garlands of leaves, flowers, nuts, and shells in local shops. **Niihau shell leis,** perhaps the ultimate status symbols of the islands, are still painstakingly made by hand from seashells found on that tiny island. Ornate **woodcarvings** and baskets, hats, and table mats woven out of *lauhala* (the leaf of the pandanus tree) are crafted by native artisans throughout the islands. **Scrimshaw** first came to Hawaii when mainland sailors idled away their free time by carving images onto whales' bones and teeth; the craft was later refined and practiced by residents. Today, because so many species of whales are endangered, most of the "scrimshaw" you will see is synthetic.

The ethnographic **Bishop Museum** in Honolulu houses the world's best collection of Polynesiana and Hawaiiana, with extensive galleries, archives, and demonstrations of Hawaiian crafts. The Honolulu Academy of Art has a wide collection of Western works, while the Contemporary Museum of Art hosts exhibitions on present-day artistic themes. Hawaii's most impressive collection of Asian art is housed at the East-West Center Learning Institute at the University of Hawaii. **Art marts** throughout the islands display the work of contemporary Hawaiian artists.

Hawaii's cities are an amalgamation of contrasting architectural styles. Oriental temples, Hawaiian huts, and Western structures coexist, but there has been no recognizable cohesive architectural style particular to the islands (although the State Capital, built in 1969, is a remarkable—and remarkably ugly—attempt). Landscape design, rather than architecture, is the forte of Hawaiian designers, as a stroll through the islands' sculpted parks and gardens will attest.

FOOD AND DRINK

Hawaiian food is unlike the fare in any other part of America. The groceries are largely imported, bringing the costs way up. Traditional Hawaiian dishes and local favorites can be found all over the islands, but each island also has its own specialties. The Big Island is the macadamia nut capital of the world and also provides the slopes for Kona coffee. Maui has sweet onions and potato chips, Kauai produces fantastic cookies, Molokai has watermelon and bread, and Oahu offers scrumptous international cuisine.

For a taste of Hawaii as pleasing to the wallet as the palate, go to one of the local take-out establishments. Plate lunches, a long-standing island tradition, are served at lunchwagons and take-out stands everywhere for about $5. A typical plate includes two scoops of rice, one scoop of macaroni salad, and an entree such as chicken *katsu* (a breaded cutlet) or teriyaki beef. Wash it all down with a tropical fruit juice. Many plate lunch specials feature such Hawaiian staples as *kalua* pig, *lau lau* (pork or chicken wrapped in *ti* and *taro* leaves), *lomi* salmon (a mixture of tomatoes, onions, and salmon), *haupia* (coconut pudding), and two-finger *poi* (a taro root pudding thick enough to be eaten with two fingers). Construct an interesting meal

HAWAII

out of a potpourri of island *pupus* (appetizers). Hawaiian chefs like the TV icon Sam Choy take great pride in using only the freshest ingredients, which results in top-notch chow.

Tourists are bombarded with attempts to lure you to a *luau*. These commercial feasts are usually pricey ($30-50) and a far cry from real native celebrations. Festooned with cameras of all types and sizes, wide-eyed tourists pay through the nose to watch performers cook a *kailua* (pig) in an underground oven before dancing to the tunes of "Hawaiian" music (the hokey kind). Opt for Hawaiian fare in plate lunches at much lower fares instead.

One of the great perks about Hawaii is the abundance of tropical produce. Fresh pineapple, mango, and papaya are all cheap and plentiful in the islands. More exotic are lychee, guava, and the round breadfruit. Pomegranates and star fruit are also worth trying, as is the *lilikoi* (passion fruit). These fruits can be had for mere fractions of the mainland cost. Instead of $6 per lb., papayas are six for $1.

WEATHER

Being a weather forecaster in Hawaii is a lot like working as a bank security guard—long stretches of the same old thing interspersed with moments of sheer panic. With the exception of the occasional hurricane, most of the state's general forecasts could be made from a cave—mostly sunny, in the 80s, chance of showers. Despite the overall consistency, however, the eight major islands and the more than 100 smaller islands that comprise Hawaii exhibit 21 of the earth's 22 climatic zones. Within each island one finds incredible diversity; Kauai contains the wettest spot on earth, but it is only 15 mi. from sunny, dry Poipu. Seasons are virtually nonexistent, although local weather around any given island fluctuates constantly. Coastal areas *(makai)* are usually drier; the leeward (sheltered) side of a mountain is usually drier as well as hotter than the windward side. From April to October, temperatures range 73-88°F; November to March, it's slightly cooler (65-83°F) and wetter. The Big Island's Hilo is a tropical rain forest—over a hundred inches of precipitation fall each year—while the land to the south at Kau is a sun-scorched desert. The mountain areas *(mauka)* catch a cool breeze, especially at night and early morning, so pack a sweater. On any island, be prepared for mountain showers and "liquid sunshine," a cool mixture of rain sprinkles, sunshine, and rainbows.

Oahu

Banzai Pipeline, 2
Bellows Field State Park, 11
Haiku Gardens, 8
Kailua Beach Park, 10
Keaiwa Heiau State Park, 9
Malaekahana State Park, 5
Sacred Healing Stones, 6
Sandy Beach, 12
Sunset Beach, 3
Toilet Bowl, 13
Valley of the Temples, 7
Waimea Beach Park, 1
Waemea Valley, 4

PACIFIC OCEAN

Oahu

Oahu bears the mixed blessing of being the cultural, economic, and tourist center of Hawaii. Honolulu Harbor has played host over the years to Chinese traders and military seafarers, and, consequently, has acted as the catalyst for Oahu's rise to prominence. The harbor continues to be a major Pacific seaport, and most of Hawaii's industry is found here. Several decades ago, a major international airport was added to the island's transportation resources, and the high-rise jungle of Waikiki is a testament to the island's superior accessibility. Beachgoing crowds have turned Waikiki into a non-stop tourist buffet which can be exciting, but quickly wears on many. The Windward Coast and North Shore of the island remain distant from this pandemonium, sanctuaries from the commercial storm. For the budget traveler, Oahu is about as good as it gets, offering superior public transportation and a gaggle of cheap places to stay.

ORIENTATION

Oahu can be roughly divided into four sections. **Honolulu** and its suburbs constitute the metropolitan heart of the island. The **North Shore,** from Kahuku to Kaena Point, is the most rural part of the island and home to some mighty big waves. The **Windward Coast** (on the east), lies between sculpted mountains and colorful reefs, and the **Leeward Coast** (on the west) is raw and rocky.

The slopes of two now-extinct volcanic mountain ridges, **Waianae** in the west and **Koolau** in the east, make up the bulk of Oahu's 600 square miles. The narrow inlets of **Pearl Harbor** push in at the southern end of the valley between the two ridges. Honolulu spreads along 6 mi. of oceanfront southeast of Pearl Harbor, hemmed in by the Koolau Range. Three miles east of downtown, **Waikiki Beach** extends outward toward the volcanic crater of **Diamond Head,** the island's southernmost extremity. Honolulu continues around Diamond Head to Koko Head in **Hawaii-kai.**

■ Honolulu

Honolulu is City Lite. It's got all the trappings of a major city: industry, transportation centers, towering skyscrapers, and horrible traffic. There are all-night restaurants, housing developments, and lots of sleaze. But Honolulu isn't hopelessly citified: tropical fish swim in the harbor, a beautiful beach runs the length of the city, and the local news anchors wear Aloha shirts on Friday. The tourist mecca of Waikiki crowds 70,000 hotel rooms along its sands, and the result, aside from crowded beaches, is a high-powered nightlife and more t-shirt shops than seems physically possible.

Honolulu, and especially Waikiki, is considered by many to be too busy and fast-paced. A traveler who does not leave this section of Oahu will see only a small segment of what Hawaii has to offer. Other areas are less crowded, less developed, and more peaceful. If the cars and convenience stores begin to wear you down, quieter locales slumber serenely to the north and east.

PRACTICAL INFORMATION

Visitor Information: Hawaii Visitors Bureau, 2270 Kalakaua Ave., 8th fl. (923-1811), in the Waikki Business Plaza. Not especially budget-traveler-friendly. Offers the *Accommodation Guide, Restaurant Guide,* a map of points of interest, and a walking tour of downtown Honolulu (all free). Most brochures contain info for disabled travelers. Open Mon.-Fri. 8am-4:30pm. Info centers at the airport and the Ala Moana Shopping Center. **Hawaiian Main Chamber of Commerce,** 1132 Bishop St., #200 (522-8800). Open Mon.-Fri. 8am-4:30pm. **Department of State Parks,** 1151 Punchbowl St., #310 (587-0300), at S. Beretania. Info, trail maps, and free permits for state park campgrounds (available up to 30 days in advance for Oahu state parks, 1 year for all other islands). Open Mon.-Fri. 8am-4pm. **Department of Parks and Recreation,** 650 S. King St. (523-4525). Info and free permits for Oahu's county parks (available up to 2 weeks in advance). Open Mon.-Fri. 7:45am-4pm. **TDD Info** (643-8TDD/8833 or 1-511 from any payphone for the hearing-impaired, 1-711 for the deaf).

American Express: 2424 Kalakaua Ave. (926-5441), in the Hyatt Regency, Waikiki. The only Oahu office that accepts client mail. Open daily 8am-8pm.

Public Transportation: The Bus (848-5555 or off-hours 296-1818, ext. 8287), is the best public transportation in Hawaii and covers all of Oahu. Free Honolulu/Waikiki route maps available at tourist kiosks throughout Waikiki. All buses wheelchair accessible. Fare $1. Month ($25) and 4-day passes ($10) available at grocery stores and 7-11s. Special rates available with a medicare card: 1 year pass $10, 2yr. pass $20 (requires application and doctor approval). These passes are available at 711 Kapiolani Blvd., #275, Honolulu 96813 (523-4083). The **Handi-van** (454-5050), transports handicapped travelers throughout the city (runs daily 6:30am-midnight). **Handicabs** are wheelchair-accessible taxis (airport to Waikiki $35). Give 1-day advance notice (runs Mon.-Fri. 8am-5pm, Sat. 8:30am-4:30pm).

Taxis: Sida, 439 Kalewa St. (836-0011), charges 50¢ per ¼mi. Flag rate $2. Airport to Waikiki $20. **The Cab** (422-2222), has 24hr. service.

Car Rental: Major companies are at the airport and in Waikiki. **Adventure,** 1705 Kalakaua Blvd. (944-3131), rents jeeps ($90 per day) to those over 18. Open daily 8am-6pm. **Paradise Isle,** 151 Ulunin Ave. (922-2224), at Kuhio Ave., rents for $40 per day. Under 21 pay $20 surcharge. Open daily 8am-6pm.

Moped and Bicycle Rental: Mopeds, though not as safe as cars, are a great way to get around, especially on Kalanianaole Hwy. They can cover 40mi. on $1 worth of gas. **Adventure Rentals,** 1705 Kalalaua Blvd. (944-3131), rents mopeds (12hr. $15, $20 per day), bikes, and in-line skates ($15 for 24hr.). Credit card or $50 deposit required. Must be 18. Open daily 8am-6pm. **Moped Connection,** 750A Kapahulu Ave. (732-3366), rents mopeds for $20 per day, $85 per week. Must be 18. Credit card deposit required. Open Mon.-Fri. 9am-6pm, Sat.-Sun. 9am-3pm. Check tourist publications for coupons.

Camping Equipment: The Bike Shop, 1149 S. King St. (596-0588). Camping advice and equipment to buy or rent. Weekend-long tent or pack rental $35. Credit card or $200 deposit required. Open Mon.-Fri. 9am-8pm, Sat. 9am-5pm, Sun.10am-5pm.

Water Equipment: Rental stands populate area beaches. Quality boards, along with helpful lessons, are at **Star Beachboys,** Kuhio Beach, to the left of the Kuhio Beach pavilion. Canoe rides $10, private surfing lessons $25 per hr., longboards $8 per hr., and boogieboards $5 per hr. Ubiquitous **Snorkel Bob's,** 700 Kapahulu Ave. (735-7944), rents snorkel sets for $3.50 per day (or $7 per day for higher quality equipment), $9 per week. Inter-island returns free. If going to Hanauma Bay, consider renting there. Open daily 8am-5pm.

Library: Hawaii State Library, 478 S. King St. (586-3500), next to Iolani Palace. Extensive Pacific collection. Open Tues. and Thurs. 9am-8pm, Wed. 10am-5pm, Fri.-Sat. and Mon. 9am-5pm. **Waikiki Public Library,** 400 Kapahulu Ave. (733-8488). Open Mon. and Thurs.-Sat. 10am-5pm, Tues.-Wed. 10am-8pm.

Bi-Gay-Lesbian Organization: Gay and Lesbian Community Center, 1566 Wilder Ave. (951-7000), in the YWCA. Open Mon.-Fri. 10am-2pm.

Laundromat: Waikiki Laundromats (923-2057), has several locations, including one across from the International Market Place (open daily 7am-10pm), and one in Outrigger East, 150 Kaiulani Ave. (open daily 6:30am-11pm). Wash $1, dry $1.

Swimming Pool: Manoa Recreation Center, 2721 Kaaipu Ave. (988-6868). Bus #5 from Ala Moana Center to stop after Waioli Tea Room. Open Mon.-Sat. 10:30am-12:30pm for laps, Mon.-Fri. 3:15-5pm, and Sun. 1-5pm for recreation. Free.

Weather Conditions: Normally sunny and 70-85°F. If in doubt, call the National Weather Service (836-2102), for confirmation. Surf Report (973-4383). 24hr.

Crisis Lines: Info and Referral Service (ASK-2000/275-2000). Info on government human services. Open Mon.-Fri. 8am-6pm. **Coast Guard Search/Rescue** (800-552-6458). Open 24hr. **AIDS Hotline** (922-1313).

Late-Night Pharmacy: The Pillbox, 1133 11th Ave. (737-1777), Kaimuki. Open Mon.-Sat. 9am-11pm, Sun. 7-11pm. **Kuhio Pharmacy,** 2330 Kuhio Ave. (538-9011). Open Mon.-Tues. and Thurs.-Fri. 9am-4:30pm, Wed. and Sat. 9am-1:30pm.

Medical Services: Queen's Medical Center, 1301 Punchbowl St. Emergency room (547-4311), 24hr. **Waikiki Health Center,** 277 Ohua Ave. (922-4787), Waikiki. Open Mon.-Thurs. 9am-8pm, Fri. 9am-4:30pm, Sat. 9am-4pm.

Emergency: 911.

Internet Access: Internet Cafe, 559 Kapahulu Ave. $7.50 per hr. (735-JAVA/5285; open 24hr.). **Coffee Haven,** 1026 Kapahulu Ave. (732-2090), near the overpass. $4 per hr. (open Mon.-Fri. 7am-midnight, Sat. 8am-midnight, Sun. 8am-9pm). **Coffee Cove,** 2690 S. King St. (955-COVE/2683), Puck's Alley. $6 per hr. (open Mon.-Wed. 7am-midnight, Thurs.-Fri. 7am-2am, Sat. 10am-2am, Sun. 10am-midnight).

Post Office: General delivery should be sent to the main office, 3600 Aolele Ave. (423-3990), near the airport. Open Mon.-Fri. 7:30am-8:30pm, Sat. 8am-2:30pm. **ZIP Code:** 96820. **Waikiki Branch,** 330 Saratoga Rd. (800-275-8777). Open Mon.-Fri. 8am-4:30pm, Sat. 9am-noon. **ZIP Code:** 96815.

Area Code: 808.

ORIENTATION

Honolulu International Airport is 20 minutes west of downtown, off the **Lunalilo Freeway** (H-1). If Waikiki is your destination, take the Honolulu Exit, then move immediately into the left lane to get the interchange into town. Although slightly longer, the **Nimitz Hwy.** (Rte. 92) will also take you to Waikiki, as will buses #19

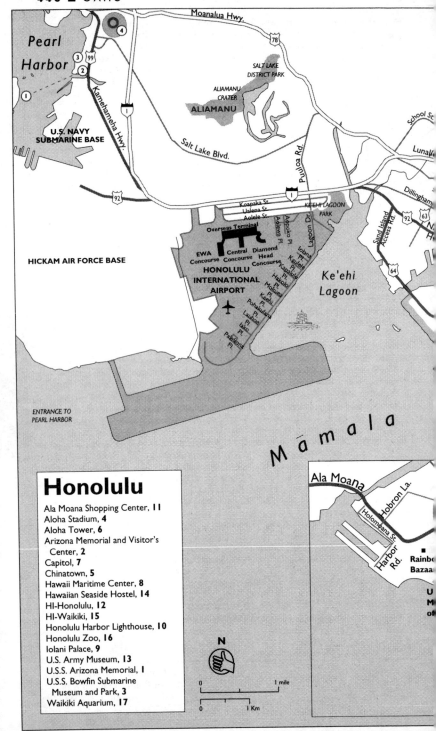

Moanalua Hwy.

78

Pearl
Harbor

SALT LAKE
DISTRICT PARK

ALIAMANU
CRATER

ALIAMANU

99

3

2

1

School St.

Kamehameha Hwy.

1

Salt Lake Blvd.

Puuloa Rd.

Lunale

U.S. NAVY
SUBMARINE BASE

92

1

Koapaka St.
Ualena St.
Aolele St.

KE'EHI LAGOON
PARK

Lagoon Dr.

Dillingham

Sand Island
Access Rd.

92 63

N
H

Overseas Terminal

Aolele Pl.
Iolani Pl.
Kailele Pl.
Kapalulu Pl.
Hanolei Pl.
Mokuea Pl.
Kieli Pl.
Pohaulaua Pl.
Laulae Pl.
Iaka Pl.
Puuhonu Pl.

64

HICKAM AIR FORCE BASE

EWA
Concourse

Central
Concourse

Diamond
Head
Concourse

HONOLULU
INTERNATIONAL
AIRPORT

Ke'ehi
Lagoon

ENTRANCE TO
PEARL HARBOR

Māmala

Ala Moana

Hobron La.

Holomoana St.

Honolulu

Ala Moana Shopping Center, 11
Aloha Stadium, 4
Aloha Tower, 6
Arizona Memorial and Visitor's
  Center, 2
Capitol, 7
Chinatown, 5
Hawaii Maritime Center, 8
Hawaiian Seaside Hostel, 14
HI-Honolulu, 12
HI-Waikiki, 15
Honolulu Harbor Lighthouse, 10
Honolulu Zoo, 16
Iolani Palace, 9
U.S. Army Museum, 13
U.S.S. Arizona Memorial, 1
U.S.S. Bowfin Submarine
  Museum and Park, 3
Waikiki Aquarium, 17

Harbor Rd.

■
Rainb
Bazaa

U
M
of

N

0   1 mile

0   1 Km

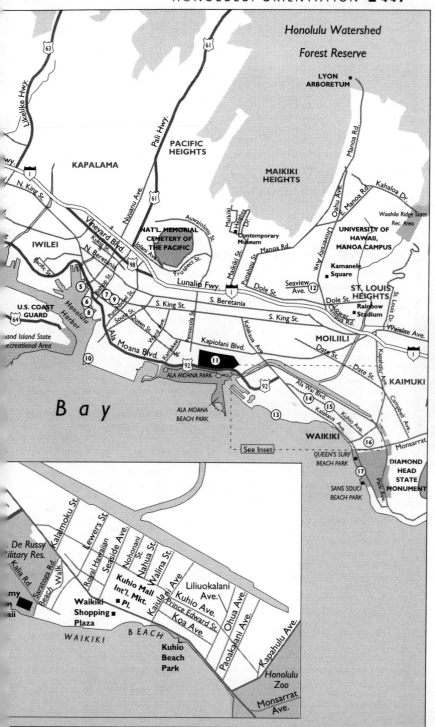

and 20, but they may not allow luggage on board. The **Airport Waikiki Express** (566-733), travels to any hotel or hostel in Waikiki ($8, round-trip $13).

Driving in Honolulu is hellish; traffic is heavy and there are numerous one-way streets. If all else fails, locals are generally helpful with directions, but they may use unfamiliar words like *mauka* (inland), *makai* (seaward), *ewa* (west; pronounced EHVA), and Diamond Head (east). Downtown is about six blocks long and four blocks wide; its main drags are **Kapiolani Blvd., King St.** (running east only), and **Beretania St.** (running west only). In Waikiki, the main streets are **Ala Wai Blvd., Kuhio Ave.,** and **Kalakaua Ave.,** all parallel to the ocean. Most streets have metered parking or other restrictions, so read signs carefully. Many streets have free parking on Sundays. **Hitchhiking** is illegal and extremely ill-advised in Honolulu.

ACCOMMODATIONS

Honolulu would not be the tourist trap that it is without its thriving accommodations industry. Amidst the bevy of hotels adorned in price-jacking Hawaiian kitsch are a number of affordable options. Check for housing specials in the *Honolulu Advertiser*, available on street corners (50¢). The ever-expanding bed and breakfast scene offers convenient and affordable lodging (see **Hawaii: Accommodations,** p. 438, for B&B agencies). Reserve in advance when possible.

Near Waikiki

Interclub Waikiki, 2413 Kuhio Ave. (924-2636). Take any Waikiki bus to the intersection of Kuhio and Kaiulani St. and look for the five flags flying fearlessly. Enjoy the company of a youthful, spirited crowd and a gaggle of resident housepets. Perks include a pool table (50¢ per game), cable TV, free use of longboards and boogieboards, and an excellent location. 24hr. reception. Check-out 10am. No curfew. Single-sex rooms available. 6-bunk dorms $15; singles and doubles $45. Kids under 12 free. Lockers $1. Safe-deposit boxes $3. Key and linen deposit $10. Picture ID required.

Polynesian Hostel, 2584 Lemon Rd. (922-1340). Take any Waikiki bus to the corner of Kuhio and Kapahulu St. and walk 2 blocks towards the beach. Comfortable, clean rooms connected by colorfully decorated stairways. Enthusiastic staff hosts pizza parties and free movies daily at 9pm. Well-furnished lounge, TV/VCR room, board games, laundry, and hot breakfast served. 24hr. reception. No curfew. No single-sex rooms. 6-bunk dorms $14; 4-bunk dorms $17.25; singles $32; doubles $39-52. Free security boxes. Linens provided.

Hale Aloha (HI-AYH), 2417 Prince Edward St. (926-8313). Take any Waikiki bus to the intersection of Kuhio and Uluhiu St., trek beachward 1 block, and turn right. Unbeatable location just 2 blocks from the beach, but surprisingly subdued for the area. Ideal for curling up with a book as you nurse your sunburned shoulders. Full kitchen, lounge, and TV room. No curfew, but lights out 11pm. Reception open daily 7am-3am. 5-bunk dorms (single-sex) $16, nonmembers $19; doubles $40, nonmembers $46. Sheets $2. Key deposit $10. Reservations strongly recommended.

Hawaiian Seaside Hostel, 419-E Seaside Ave. (924-3306). Take any Waikiki bus to the corner of Seaside Ave. and Kuhio St., then head away from the beach for 2min. The hostel is tucked behind the Cooper apartments on the right side. Hipsters lounge on the open patio furnished with cable TV and pool table. Newly renovated rooms might make you claustrophobic. Free use of surfing gear, Sega Genesis, email, and Internet services. 24hr. reception. No curfew. Single-sex and co-ed dorms. 6-bunk dorms $12; 2-bed dorms $15; singles $32. Discount coupons available at the airport. Free lockers and safes. Laundry. Key and linen deposit $10. Airline ticket required.

Hale Pua Nui Hotel, 228 Beachwalk Ave. (923-9693). Take any Waikiki bus to the Kuhio-Kalaimoku crossing, walk beachward 1 block, turn left, and make the 2nd right. Well-equipped green kitchenettes and sparkling peach bathrooms. All rooms come with A/C and cable TV. Reception open 8am-6pm. Prices are higher during Dec.-March and July-Sept. Singles and doubles $57. Off-season: $45. Weekly: $349, off-season $269. Key deposit $20.

Elsewhere in Honolulu

YMCA, 401 Atkinson Dr. (941-3344), across from Ala Moana Shopping Center. Reminiscent of a college dorm, the facility offers clean, spartan rooms and use of pool, sauna, athletic facilities, and TV lounge. Ideal for families with children. Daily activities include *tai chi, tae kwan do,* and jazz lessons. Check-in and check-out at noon. Rooms with shared bath available for men only: singles $29; doubles $40. Rooms with private showers and toilets available for men and women: singles $36.50; doubles $51.50. Key deposit $10. Must be 18. Valid photo ID required for stay.

HI-Honolulu (HI-AYH), 2323A Seaview Ave. (946-0591; fax 946-5904). 1½mi. north of Waikiki near University of Hawaii at Manoa. Take University Ave. Exit #24B off H-1 or ride bus #6 from Ala Moana Shopping Center to this quiet, outdoorsy hostel. An inviting outdoor courtyard is flanked by a kitchen, TV room, and single-sex dorms. Beds guaranteed 3 nights for members; space allowing, you can stay for up to a week. Reception open 8am-noon and 4pm-midnight. Lights out 11pm. 8-bed dorms $12.50, nonmembers $15.50. Rooms not locked. Linen $2. Key deposit $10. Reservations recommended.

Island Hostel, 1946 Ala Moana Blvd., Ste. 130 (942-8748). Take bus #19 or #20 to the Hilton Hawaiian Village, turn right on Ala Moana. Converted motel now houses hostel rooms, each with 4-6 beds, A/C, bathroom, fridge, and TV. Cooking facilities available. Dim lighting is eerie. Check-in 24hr. Check-out 10am. Dorms $10 first night, $15 each additional night; singles $55. Off-season: singles $45. Weekly: dorms $105; singles $350, off-season $275. Significantly reduced rates if you pay in advance. Key and linen deposit $20.

CAMPING

Four **state parks** (Sand Island, Keaiwa Heiau, Kahana Bay, and Malaekahana) allow camping. Numerous **county parks** do too, but the safety of these parks is dubious. If semi-permanent locals give stink eyes to you and your shiny rental car, take the hostile greeting as a hint and leave. State and county parks enforce a five-day limit and are closed Wednesday and Thursday. Free camping **permits** available at the Dept. of State Parks and Dept. of Parks and Recreation (see **Practical Information,** p. 444).

Malaekahana State Park, off the Kamehameha Hwy. north of Laie. Popular campground near a peaceful beach. Showers, toilets, picnic tables, and BBQ pits. The **Friends of Malaekahana** (293-1736), also run a pair of cabins here (6-person cabin $40, 10-person cabin $50). Reserve 6 months in advance for cabins.

Bellows Field County Park (523-4525), just north of Waimanalo Bay. Take Tinker Rd. at the sign for Bellows Air Force Station. Facilities are a little rough-hewn, but the beach is beautiful and good for swimming or windsurfing. Showers, restrooms, picnic area. Open weekends only.

Keaiwa Heiau State Park, 5mi. west of Kaneohe. From Waikiki, follow H-1 to Moanalua Hwy. (Rte. 78) and take Aiea turn-off. Remains of a *heiau* (temple), an herb garden, and cargo plane wreckage. Area #4 is grassy and sheltered from winds. Trail (4½mi.) around park. Restrooms, cold showers, tables, and BBQ pits.

Kahana Beach State Park, north of Kaneohe Bay off Kamehameha Hwy. Take bus #55 (Kaneohe/Circle Island). Sheltered swath of grass at the head of a calm bay offers hiking and excellent swimming, but highway traffic can be loud. Restrooms, picnic tables, outdoor showers, and BBQ pits.

FOOD

Though Honolulu swims in an endless stream of homogeneous buffets and fast food, the neighborhoods surrounding Waikiki are full of inexpensive local restaurants. **Kapahulu, Kaimuki, Moiliili,** and **downtown** are accessible by bus or on foot from Waikiki. Small Chinese food counters serve affordable lunches and *dim sum* all over **Chinatown,** especially off **Hotel St.** A variety of ethnic restaurants are located between the 500 and 1000 blocks of **Kapahulu Ave.**

HAWAII

Stock up on groceries at the **Food Pantry,** 2370 Kuhio Ave. (923-9831; open 24hr.), or **Star Market,** 2470 S. King St. (973-1666; take University Ave. from Waikiki and turn left on S. King; open daily 6am-midnight). Bargain for **local specialties** at the Ward **farmer's market** in the Kewalo Basin on Auahi St. They have fresh seafood and reasonably priced Hawaiian favorites like *lau lau*—a *ti* leaf stuffed with spinach and pork (open Mon.-Sat. 7am-6pm, Sun. 7am-1pm).

Ono Hawaiian Foods, 726 Kapahulu Ave. (737-2275). Locals line up on outdoor benches to get this authentic Hawaiian fare. Combo plates ($7-10) include an entree and all the fixins, including *poi* and *haupia* (sweet coconut gelatin). Fortunately, Yoko has yet to show up. Open Mon.-Sat. 11am-7:30pm.

Auntie Pasto's, 1099 S. Beretania St. (523-8855), at Pensacola. Crowded and lively red-brick *ristorante* believes in feeding people well, starting with the complimentary fresh baked bread and antipasto. Stuffed calamari $7.50, pasta $5.50 and up. Open Mon.-Thurs. 11am-10:30pm, Fri. 11am-11pm, Sat. 4-11pm, Sun. 4-10:30pm.

KC Drive-in, 1029 Kapahulu Ave. (737-5581), near the H-1 overpass. Hefty portions, mini prices, and unusual fare belie the typical drive-in exterior. Waffle hot dogs are $1.80—how'd they get the meat in there? Oxtail soup with ginger $6.70. Open Sun.-Thurs. 6am-11:30pm, Fri.-Sat. 6am-1:30am. No credit cards.

Irifune, 750 Kapahulu Ave. (737-1141). Fusion of European and Asian influences. Dinners, such as the garlic chicken and vegetable stir fry ($8.50), come with *miso* soup and rice. The walls have info on upcoming events. Open Tues.-Sun. 5-9pm.

Rainbow Drive-In, 3308 Kanaina Ave. (737-0177), at Kapahulu. Locals and savvy tourists alike are drawn to the end of the Rainbow for its rock-bottom prices and tasty cuisine. Sandwiches under $2, and hearty plate lunches, such as *mahi mahi,* around $5. Open daily 7:30am-9pm.

Leonard's Bakery, 933 Kapahulu Ave. (737-5591). Diet-whipping menu tempts diners with fresh bread, baked goods, and hot *malasadas* (super-delectable sugared fried dough, 46¢). Open Sun.-Thurs. 6am-9pm, Fri. and Sat. 6am-10pm.

Perry's Smorgy, 2380 Kuhio Ave. (922-1907), at Kaiulani Ave. in Waikiki. Perry's secret: volume, plain and simple. He packs people in, and they all eat until they're fit to bust. One price gets you all the buffet fare you can handle. Open daily for breakfast (7-11am, $5), lunch (11:30am-2:30pm, $6), and dinner (5-9pm, $9.)

SIGHTS AND ACTIVITIES

Honolulu's sights fall into two general categories. On one hand, there are those attractions that illuminate the city's history, culture, and ethnic heritage. On the other hand there are those that come with the city's remarkable natural environment. Common to most of these sights is commercialism.

There are several strategies for getting out to see the sights. Cars are convenient, but finding parking is a pain. Mopeds are only a little slower and a lot more hassle-free. Buses go to all the attractions cheaply, but they can be time-consuming. Bus #14 makes a one-hour loop through a sampling of Honolulu's varied neighborhoods. Waikiki is, of course, centered around Waikiki Beach; Kaimuki and Kahala are small, close-knit communities; Moiliili's lifeblood is the university; downtown and Chinatown are the shipping and business districts. The **Waikiki Trolley** (591-2561) stops at major sites and museums in Waikiki and downtown, allowing tourists to stay on the 2½-hour narrated tour or get on and off at their leisure. Stops include Chinatown, the Capitol, Bishop Museum, the Aquarium, the Academy of Arts, and Iolani Palace. Trolleys leave from the Royal Hawaiian Shopping Center every 15 minutes from 8am to 4:30pm (day pass $18, under 11 $5, 5-day pass $30, under 11 $10).

Waikiki

Originally a marshy swampland and hideaway for Hawaiian royalty, Waikiki's wetlands were drained into the Ala Wai Canal to launch the island's tourist industry. In the 1950s, the image of a ¾ mi. crescent of white sand set against the profile of **Diamond Head** lured legions of vacationers and honeymooners to Waikiki. The low-rise tangle, known as the Waikiki jungle, began to give way to the high-rises that now dominate the Honolulu skyline. Today, visitors of all ages flock to Waikiki for rest, relaxation, sun, surf, nightlife, tacky souvenirs, random sex, and romance.

Waikiki Beach, actually composed of several smaller stretches of sand, is Waikiki's main attraction. Farthest to the east is the **Sans Souci Beach,** in front of the Kaimona Otani Hotel. Site of an old natatorium (an outdoor swimming pool with impressive stone bleachers) built as a war memorial, Sans Souci has shower facilities but no public restrooms. Hippies and hip yuppies share the sand, all without any cares in the world. The **Queen's Surf Beach,** closer to downtown and known as "Walls" to locals, attracts boogieboarders, surfers, and rollerbladers. The beach area to the left of the snack bar is a popular **gay** tanning spot. Between the Hawaiian Regent and the Hyatt Regency, breakers shelter **Kuhio Beach County Park** from the heavy surf. Soft sand and gentle waves nurture beginning surfers.

Next to the Waikiki Beach Center (across from the Hyatt Regency) are four *kahuna* stones, which are said to possess healing powers. Stop by after a day at the beach to help the sunburn. A statue of **Duke Kahanamoku,** world-championship surfer and Olympic swimmer, welcomes hordes to the ever-shrinking beach space. For a taste of an earlier age in Hawaiian tourism, wander through the lobbies of the newly renovated turn-of-the-century **Moana Surfrider Hotel,** which surrounds a phenomenal banyan tree on Waikiki Beach, or the **Royal Hawaiian Hotel,** whose pink grandeur was unveiled in 1927. At the far west end of the beach, **Fort de Russy Beach County Park** hosts the liveliest games of beach volleyball this side of L.A.

Leaving behind Waikiki Beach and its minions, you will come across more peaceful shores at **Kahala Beach,** which is blocked by houses and private property but accessible by public paths (all Hawaiian beaches are public). Snorkeling here, away from the crowds, affords a peek at calmer creatures. To get to the beach, go east on Diamond Head Rd. until you hit Kahala Ave.

Three museums in Waikiki are devoted to different aspects of Hawaiian history. The **Lucoral Museum,** 2414 Ave., (922-1999), at Kaiulani Ave., has dazzling rocks and exhibits, including a dinosaur egg from China and a fossilized fish from the Middle East (open Mon.-Sat. 9am-5:30pm). The **Damien Museum,** 130 Ohua Ave. (923-2690), behind the St. Augustine Church, details Father Damien de Veuster's contributions to the leper colony on Molokai (open Mon.-Fri. 9am-3pm; free). The **U.S. Army Museum of Hawaii** (438-2821), at Kalia and Saratoga, covers the military history of Hawaii and the Pacific, with comprehensive exhibits of tanks, military paraphernalia, and some *really* big guns (open Tues.-Sun. 10am-4:30pm; free).

If you thought the Waikiki Beach crowd was a wild bunch, check out the residents of the **Honolulu Zoo,** 151 Kapahulu Ave. (971-7175), across from Kapiolani Park on the east end of Waikiki. Daily activities for children include shows and animal demonstrations. The new Africa Savannah section covers nine acres and hosts such wildlife as cheetahs, giraffes, and white and black rhinos. The zoo also sponsors a free summer concert series (see **Entertainment,** p. 454; open daily 9am-4:30pm; admission $6, ages 6-12 $1). Wetter wildlife populates the **Waikiki Aquarium,** 2777 Kalakaua Ave. (923-9741). Stars of this aquarium include a *mahi mahi* (yellowfin tuna) hatchery and Hawaiian monk seals (open daily 9am-5pm; admission $6, students $4, ages 13-17 $2.50, under 12 free). Outside the zoo, local painters exhibit their work in the **Art Mart** (Sun. 10am-4pm). The **Kahala Mandarin Hotel** (739-8888), has free dolphin feedings daily at 11am, 2, and 4pm. The **Pacific Beach Hotel** (922-1233), boasts the world's largest indoor oceanarium (3 stories high), complete with manta rays and the state fish, *humuhumunukunukuapuaa* (open daily 6am-10pm; free).

Those who want to see Waikiki at its photogenic best will delight in a **Kodak Hula Show,** at the **Waikiki Shell** off Monsarrat Ave. near the zoo. This production packages hula dancing and palm tree climbing into a series of *those* moments. It is touristy, but nonetheless entertaining. Watch your fellow tourists interact with the game-show-style host, or say you're on your honeymoon and get "leid" in front of everyone (1hr. shows Tues.-Thurs. at 10am; free). The **Hawaii Visitor Bureau** (923-1811), can give info about upcoming performances or competitions among the **hula** halau (schools). Major competitions are usually held in the spring. The **Queen Kapiolani Rose Garden,** at Monsarrat and Paki, is a welcoming and fragrant retreat. Look, but don't touch; the roses are protected by magic *kahuna* stones (open 24hr.; free).

Dominating Waikiki's eastern skyline is the dormant volcano of **Diamond Head.** The one-mile hike into the **crater** can offer a welcome respite from endless sun and surf. To get there, take bus #58 from Waikiki. Bring a flashlight for the short tunnel. The view of Waikiki is spectacular, and if you go on the right day, you might catch a rainbow. The stately mansions on the slopes of Diamond Head belong to scions of Hawaii's original missionary families.

Downtown

Considerable cultural and historical attractions are located downtown. **Chinatown,** radiating from the intersection of Nuuanu and Hotel, is a sensory delight and a great place to pick up chickens' feet and pigs' ears. It's also a rather tough area, so be careful. The **Chinese Chamber of Commerce,** 42 N. King St. (533-3181), has info on the Chinese community and sponsors walking tours of Chinatown (open Mon.-Fri. 8am-4:30pm; tours run Tues. 9:30am-noon; $5). Luxurious *leis* ($3 each) dangle in the kiosks lining Mauna Kea St. These *leis* were once bestowed upon tourists arriving by boat, but the modern jet traveler must treat him or herself to a garland (see **Getting Leid in Hawaii,** p. 453).

The waterfront offers more attractions, nautical and otherwise. The **Maritime Museum,** Pier 7, Honolulu Harbor, is a fascinating collection of all things briny, ranging from one of only two existing humpback whale skeletons to an exhibit on the history of surfing. The museum includes a tour of the **Falls of Clyde** (536-6373), a 19th-century ship so well-preserved that you may wish to sign up for the merchant marines and get a tattoo (open daily 8:30am-5pm; admission $7.50, ages 6-17 $4.50). The observation deck of the **Aloha Tower** affords excellent views of downtown and the harbor (open Sun. 9am-6pm, Mon.-Fri. 9am-4pm, Sat. 9am-10pm; free). The expanded center is also home to restaurants and boutiques galore.

If you've ever seen *Hawaii Five-O,* you'll recognize the **Iolani Palace** (522-0832), at King and Richard; it was the backdrop for many scenes. The palace is the only royal residence in America, built by King Kalakaua, the "Merry Monarch," when Hawaii was still independent. The furnishings reflect European influence and the buildings had electricity even before the White House did. (Tours begin every 15min. Tues.-Sat. 9am-2:15pm. Admission $8, ages 5-12 $3, under 5 not admitted. No credit cards. Call 522-0832 for reservations, or go to the palace grounds a half hour beforehand.) The palace grounds include the **Coronation Pavilion,** where the Royal Hawaiian Band gives free concerts on Fridays at noon.

Across King St. stands the **Kamehameha I statue,** erected in 1883 in honor of the Hawaiian ruler who unified the islands in 1791. On King Kamehameha Day (June 11), parading horseback riders drape the statue with *leis*. At the corner of Beretania and Richard stands Hawaii's postmodern **State Capitol,** an architectural mosaic of Hawaii's landscape. The pillars represent palm trees, the inverted dome of the house chambers rises like a volcano, and reflecting pools call to mind the blue Pacific (open Mon.-Fri. 9am-4pm; free). The **Kawaiahao Church** stands tall south of the State Capitol, at Punchbowl and King. The church, built from bits of coral, was completed in 1842. Services are held in Hawaiian at 8 and 10:30am on Sundays. The church is sometimes called "the Westminster Abbey of Hawaii" because it was used for coronations and funerals of Hawaiian kings and queens. The *Capitol District Walking Tour,* from the Hawaii Visitor Bureau, has a complete guide to Honolulu's historic district.

The **Honolulu Academy of Arts,** 900 S. Beretania St. (532-8701), displays Asian art and temporary exhibits around a series of gardens and open-air exhibition halls (open Tues.-Sat. 10am-4:30pm, Sun. 1-5pm; admission $5, students $3, seniors $3; free 1hr. tours Tues.-Sat. 11am, Sun. 1pm). Accessible via bus #2 from Waikiki, the **Bishop Museum,** 1525 Bernice St. (847-3511), in Kalihi, houses a disorganized collection of artifacts from the Indo-Pacific region. The museum's planetarium features a show on the history of Polynesian celestial navigation (shows daily at 11:30am, 1:30, and 3:30pm; museum open daily 9am-5pm; admission $15, ages 6-17 $12).

Wake up early on Saturday or Sunday morning and pop over to the immense **swap meet** held from 7am to 3pm in Aloha Stadium. Rows of vendors encircle the entire stadium, selling everything from bootleg Nike apparel to juicy local fruits (admission 50¢).

Pearl Harbor

On December 7, 1941, a stunned nation listened to the reports of the Japanese bombing of the U.S. Pacific Fleet in Pearl Harbor. Today, the **U.S.S. Arizona National Memorial** (422-2771), commemorates the event. The simple monument rests over the rusting hulk of the battleship *Arizona,* which was destroyed in a massive internal explosion and remains the tomb of over 1000 sailors. Veterans often throw *leis* into the viewing well over the hull. This trip has the air of a pilgrimage and is affecting even for those not directly connected to the tragedy. The Navy offers free tours of the memorial from 8am to 3pm, including a 30 minute film, and sends launches out to the hull every 15 minutes (no children under age 6 or under 45in. admitted; no swimsuits or flip-flops). The **visitors center** is open daily from 7:30am to 5pm, with the last program starting at 3pm. Take bus #20 from Waikiki, #50, 51, or 52 from Ala Moana, or the $3 shuttle (839-0911) from the major Waikiki hotels. Tickets to the memorial are free, but plan ahead; two-hour-plus waits are not unusual, and first-come, first-serve tickets often run out by noon. While waiting for your number to be called, you can visit the **U.S.S. Bowfin Submarine Museum and Park** (423-1341), next door. The museum features World War II submarine memorabilia, pictures, exhibits, and a movie, but the real attraction is a hands-on tour of a 62-year-old retired attack sub. Climbing through the tiny hatches and looking at the minuscule bathrooms and sardine-can bunks makes any hostel seem luxurious (open daily 8am-5pm; admission $8, military $6, ages 4-12 $3). If you're at Pearl Harbor on the first Saturday of the month, stop by the Nimitz Gate at noon for a free four-hour tour of the **Navy Visit Ship** at the Pearl Harbor Navy Base (471-0281).

Inland Honolulu

For those who can tear themselves away from the coastal attractions, the less-touristy *mauka* (inland) areas, especially the verdant **Nuuanu** and **Manoa Valleys,** hold hidden delights. At the mouth of the Manoa Valley lies the **University of Hawaii,** where lecture attendance drops as the surf rises. Campus bulletin boards have loads of information on apartments for rent, tickets for sale, and upcoming film, theater, and music events.

"Getting Leid in Hawaii"

It's not really hard at all—even if you're from MIT or CalTech. And if you're not feeling lucky, it's surprisingly easy to just do it yourself! *Leis,* beautiful strands of flowers, nuts, seeds, and even shells, are, as Hawaiians say, made with love and given with love. The tradition of adorning that special someone began with the Polynesian explorers who were draped with *leis* upon their departure to distant lands. Today, Hawaiians wear leis for any occasion—weddings, birthdays, Fridays, paydays, good-hair days (to draw attention to themselves), and even bad-hair days (to draw attention away from that errant snip at the barber shop). You can buy leis at any flower shop, starting at about $8 for plumeria. More exotic materials can cost up to $500, but the cheapest and most rewarding leis are the kind you make yourself. All you need is a *lei* sewing needle (about $3), some heavyweight string, and about 50 flowers. Hook the string on the needle and "load" on six flowers, with each stem fitting into the seat of the next. Grasping the entire bunch with your hand, slide the "load" onto the string; eight loads are sufficient for a neck *lei.* Lastly, don't forget to tie the ends together—the circular shape represents continous love.

HAWAII

The **Lyon Arboretum,** 3860 Manoa Rd. (988-3177), at the end of Manoa Valley past Paradise Park, is a rambling garden with a superb collection of tropical foliage (open Mon.-Sat. 9am-3pm; $1 suggested donation; free tours 1st Fri., 3rd Wed., and 3rd Sat. of each month). The visitors center has a map of short hikes.

A more somber sight is the **National Memorial Cemetery of the Pacific,** 2177 Puowaina Dr. (566-1430). This memorial, also known as the **Punchbowl Cemetery** (946-6383), because of its location in the amphitheater-like Puowaina Crater, contains the graves of 38,000 soldiers. (Guided 2hr. tours leave daily at 11am. Tickets $15, including hotel pick-up. Park gates open March-Sept. 8am-6:30pm, Oct.-Feb. 8am-5:30pm.) The **Contemporary Museum,** 2411 Makiki Heights Dr. (526-1322), is on the outside slope of Punchbowl (open Tues.-Sat. 10am-4pm, Sun. noon-4pm; admission $5, 3rd Thurs. of each month free).

Parallel to the Manoa Valley, the **Pali Hwy.** (Rte. 61) winds its way through Nuuanu Valley and over into Kailua, on the windward side of the island. On the way resides **Hanaiakamalama (Queen Emma's Summer Palace),** 2913 Pali Hwy. (595-3167), former posh summer retreat of Kamehameha IV and Queen Emma. Self-guided tours are facilitated by a free pamphlet (open daily 9am-4pm; admission $5, seniors $4, under 18 $1). Take bus #4 (Waikiki) or any bus that begins with "Kailua"or "Kaneohe" from **Ala Moana Shopping Center;** the ride is about 30 minutes. Drivers should pull into the **Pali Lookout** as they near the top of Pali. Although this observation point is always packed, the view over the windward side is undoubtedly worth putting on the brakes for. Hold on to your hat—there's some serious wind. According to legend, Kamehameha the Great consolidated his kingdom when the wind blew Oahu's soldiers over this dramatic cliff.

ENTERTAINMENT AND NIGHTLIFE

Honolulu parties hard at night. Bars, restaurants, and theaters abound in the downtown and Waikiki areas, making nightlife as wild as your feet and liver will allow. The heart of Waikiki throbs along **Kuhio Ave.** and **Lewers St.,** attracting throngs of tourists. The locals do their bumping and grinding downtown around the **Aloha Tower** and **Restaurant Row;** reports tell of heavenly beer in these areas. For a little relaxation in the dark, the University of Hawaii's **Hemenway Theatre** (956-6468), in the Physical Sciences Building, shows second-run films ($3.50). The **Honolulu Academy of Arts,** 900 S. Beretania St. (532-8768), features foreign films and classics. The **Kam Drive-In,** 98-850 Mauna Loa Rd. (483-5533), lets you maximize your rental car use under the stars. There is a full season of symphony and opera at the **Niel Blaisdell Center** (591-2211; box office open Mon.-Fri. 10am-6pm, Sat. 9am-5pm). Year-round theater is staged at the **Manoa Valley Theater** (988-6131). The **Honolulu Zoo's** "wildest show in town" is a summer series of Wednesday night concerts, sporting events, and concerts (971-7171; free; concerts start at 6pm). The free alterna-paper *Honolulu Weekly,* distributed on Tuesdays, has excellent entertainment information.

Bars and Clubs

Mixx, 1210 Queen St. (593-8744), at Ala Moana in downtown, boasts the biggest stereo setup in Hawaii: 25,000 watts pump up a *huge* local crowd. Eye-popping $200 bootie-shaking contest Sun. at 2:30am. Cover $5. Open Mon. 9pm-midnight, Tues.-Sun. 9pm-4am. Must be 18 Thurs. and Sun.; must be 21 Fri.-Sat.

The Wave, 1877 Kalakaua Ave. (941-0424), on the edge of Waikiki. A sea of people dances to live alternative music Wed.-Sun. 10pm-1:30am. Afterwards, the DJ spins hot tracks to keep 'em moving. Every other Mon., a $20 dance contest starts at midnight. Cover $5. Open daily 9pm-4am. Must be 21.

Pier Bar (536-2166), in the Aloha Tower, features live Hawaiian or jazz nightly, and throngs pack the outdoor patio to drink and groove. Bikini contest Sat. night at 11pm. Happy Hour 4-7pm. No cover. Open daily 11am-2am.

World Cafe, 500 Ala Moana Blvd. (599-4450), Restaurant Row at Punchbowl Ave. Drop in for Happy Hour (5-9pm, $2 drinks) and to shoot pool ($5 per hr.) til the party rages. Cover Fri.-Sat. $3. Open Mon.-Thurs. 5pm-2am, Fri. 5pm-4am, Sat. 7pm-4am, Sun. 7pm-midnight. Must be 21.

Fusions, 2260 Kuhio Ave. (924-2422), Waikiki. One of the newest and hottest gay and lesbian clubs. Heart-thumping alternative and house draws a large crowd. Cover $5. Open daily 10pm-4am. Tues., Thurs., and Sun. are Kid Klub (18 and over); must be 21 other nights.

Scruples, 2310 Kuhio Ave. (923-9350), Waikiki. Boisterous beach club gets surfers and tourists jamming to top-40 and house. Bikini night every Thurs. Ages 18-21 $15, over 21 $5. Open daily 8pm-4am.

Moose McGillycuddy's, 310 Lewers St. (923-0751), Waikiki. This professional frat party has a lively pick-up scene, popular with tourists and military. Sun. is Ladies Night—guys get in free after midnight, in time to catch the bikini contest. Live bands Mon.-Sat. Cover Tues. $5, Fri.-Sun. $3. Open daily 9pm-3:30am.

▓ Seasonal Events

The Hawaii Visitor Bureau publishes a *Calendar of Events* which gives complete listings of seasonal events. Also check the "What's-On" listings in the Friday paper and the calendar in *Honolulu Weekly*.

Narcissus Festival (533-3181), early Feb., Chinatown. Celebrates the Chinese New Year with fireworks and a raucous lion dance.

Buffalo's Annual Big Board Surfing Classic, late Feb., Makaha Beach, leeward Oahu. A surfing competition with entertainment and food.

Cherry Blossom Festival (949-2255), late Feb.-March, all over the island. The Japanese community puts on tea ceremonies, cooking lessons, and fashion shows.

Hawaiian Challenge International Sportkite Championships (735-9059), Feb.-March. The longest-running sportkite competition in the world.

Hawaii State Fair (595-4606), mid-May. Entertainment, booths, and rides.

King Kamehameha Day (536-6540), early June. A parade through downtown and Waikiki follows *lei*-draping ceremony at the Kamehameha statue on King St. Many stores and offices close down.

King Kamehameha Annual Hula and Chant Competition (536-6540), late June, Neil Blaisdell Center, Honolulu. Modern and ancient hula and chant competition. *Halaus* (schools) compete amid cheers from a boisterous crowd.

Prince Lot Hula Fest (839-5334), mid-July, at Moanalua Gardens. Ancient Hawaiian games, arts and crafts, and food.

Aloha Week Festivities (545-1771), Oct., all over the island. Week-long events finish with an elaborate parade.

Triple Crown of Surfing (377-5850), late Nov.-early Dec. The finals are held at Banzai Pipeline and aired on national TV.

▓ Windward and Southeast Oahu

Oahu's Windward (East) Coast is as refreshing as a long, cool drink after a hot Honolulu afternoon. This 40 mi. string of sleepy towns is colored in vibrant shades of green and blue by the dramatic Koolau Mountains on one side and the Pacific Ocean on the other. The tradewind swells create year-round conditions ideal for boogieboarding and windsurfing, the sports for which Windward Oahu is best known. Fast highways and expedient public transportation make it a good daytrip option from Honolulu.

ACCOMMODATIONS AND CAMPING

While the Windward Coast is postcard-perfect, the accommodations picture is not as pretty. This part of the island seems tourism-resistant—the dearth of hotels and the four-person limit on B&B accommodations leaves the budget traveler with few affordable options. Check the Yellow Pages covering Windward Oahu under "Camping" and "Bed and Breakfast" for rookie enterprises. For more information, see **Accommodations and Camping,** p.438.

One budget option is the **YWCA Camp Kokokahi,** 45-035 Kaneohe Bay Dr. (247-2124; fax 247-2125; email Kokokahi@gte.net), Kaneohe. Take bus #56 from downtown Honolulu. The camp offers two-bunk cottages ($12 per person), campsites for tents ($8 per person), a great view of the bay, and up-close encounters with audacious salamanders and lascivious toads. (Reception open daily 8am-8pm.)

Another possibility is camping in one of the county parks along the coast such as **Malaekahana State Recreation Area, Bellows Field State Park,** and **Kahana Beach State Park** (see **Honolulu: Camping,** p. 449). Be wary when putting up your tent, however, as police warn that campground crime is on the rise. Also make sure that you secure the necessary permits from the state and county offices in Honolulu before setting up camp (see **Honolulu: Practical Information,** p. 444).

FOOD

Frankie's Drive-Inn, 41-1610 Kalanianaole Hwy. (259-7819), Waimanalo, just before Rte. 72 intersects with Rte. 61. Locals have stayed loyal to this late-lunch paradise since 1953. Plates $4, burgers a cheap 80¢. Outdoor seating only. Open Mon.-Sat. 9:30am-4:30pm.

Bueno Nalo, 41-865 Kalanianaole Hwy. (259-7186), Waimanalo, next to the beach county park. Piñatas, chile lights, and a black velvet painting of a matador—what else could you want in a Mexican restaurant? How about excellent south-of-the-border cuisine (entrees $5-10). Bring your own beer. Open daily 11:30am-9pm.

Waimanalo Fish Market, 41-1537 Kalanianaole Hwy. (259-8008), Waimanalo Shopping Center. As fresh snapper and tuna are laid out before your eyes, feast on sandwich combos for under $4. The "Sushi Express" plates (starting at $1.79) hit the market on Fri. and Sat. evenings. Open Sat.-Tues. 8am-5pm, Wed.-Fri. 8am-7:30pm, Sun. 9am-4pm.

Kaaawa Country Kitchen and Grocery, 51-480 Kamehameha Hwy. (237-8484), Kaaawa. Take your chow across the street to Swanzy Beach County Park. This mom-and-pop country drive-in has kept the locals satisfied for more than 30 years. Teri-beef $4.50, "Hawaiian Nutrition" alternatives $5.50. Open Mon.-Sat. 5:30am-2:30pm, Sun. 6am-2:30pm. No credit cards.

SIGHTS AND ACTIVITIES

Hanauma Bay to Sealife Park

To explore this section of the southeast coast, take **Kalanianaole Highway** (Rte. 72) east or ride bus #22 (popularly dubbed the Beach Bus) from Waikiki. Some of the most colorful fish in the Pacific reside in **Hanauma Bay,** formed where the ocean has washed away the crater's eastern wall. Its federally protected waters are the best spot for **snorkeling** in Oahu. For the clearest underwater trip, come early in the morning. On display are such alluring creatures as octopi, spiny lobster, convict tangs, damselfish, Moorish idols, and large schools of sunburned vacationers. Snorkel rentals are available at the beach (complete set $6, prescriptive lens set $10, plus a deposit of rental car keys, major credit card, or $30; rentals open 8am-4:30pm). One tube of fish food ($2) will make gaggles of 5 lb. fish frolic to your feet. The fury of the Pacific stirs up at **Witch's Brew,** a 20-minute walk to the right of the beach. Stand on the cliff where monstrous waves crash and send 60 ft. towers of water into the air. A 20-minute walk (wear shoes—it's rocky) to the left of the beach brings you to the **Toilet Bowl.** Locals climb into the large volcanic tube when it's full and get flushed up and down as waves fill and empty the chamber through natural lava plumbing. Swimmers should be cautious of the slippery sides, especially when the surf is high (admission to the park $3; parking $1). One mile farther on Kalanianaole Hwy. is the **Halona Blowhole,** which erupts with a weak squirt or a full-blown Old Faithful spout, depending on tidal conditions. The island of Molokai, 20 mi. away, is easily visible, and on a clear day you might be able to observe as many as three of the neighboring islands.

Sandy Beach, just beyond Halona (a 50-min. ride on bus #22), is a primo spot for bodysurfing, boogieboarding, and people-watching. This expansive beach is the center of the Hawaiian summer surf circuit—ground swells burst onto the shore with spine-crushing force, making swimming a hazard for all but the most expert beachgoer. The grassy field behind the beach is a landing spot for hang-gliders.

The landscape undergoes a dramatic change at **Makapuu Point,** where one twist of the highway takes you from the semi-arid hills around Hanauma Bay to the vertical shades of green provided by the **Koolau Mountains.** Along with Sandy Beach, **Makapuu Beach,** 41-095 Kalanianaole Hwy., boasts boogieboarding and bodysurfing bliss. Lifeguards hoist colored flags to indicate surf conditions (red signals danger). Across from Makapuu lies **Sea Life Park** (259-7933), a minor-league Sea World, with performing penguins and the world's only "wholphin," a whale-dolphin hybrid (open daily 9:30am-5pm; admission $20, seniors $16, ages 4-12 $10). Look in *Oahu This Week* for coupons that will make the price less painful.

Waimanalo Bay to Kailua Bay

The Kalanianaole Hwy. (Rte. 72) continues along the coastal area from Waimanalo Bay and Kailua Bay (take bus #57 from Ala Moana). **Waimanalo Beach** is a long, graceful white crescent of coastline that embraces the offshore islands of **Manana** and **Kaohikaipu.** Its gentle waves nurture beginning surfers. Turn down Aloilo St. by the McDonald's for a more secluded section of beach. The best novice bodysurfing and boogieboarding is found at **Sherwoods** and at **Bellows Air Force Base,** on Kalanianaole Hwy. off the road to Kailua, but both are without lifeguards. If you thought the only polo in Hawaii was in the outlet stores, think again. The **Waimanalo Polo Club,** across from the Waimanalo McDonald's on Kalanianaole Hwy., fires up chuckers every Sunday at 2pm ($5).

Kailua Town and nearby **Kailua Beach County Park,** 450 Kawailoa Rd., are *the* places to go for prime beach area unadulterated by large hotels. Take Kailua Rd. from where Kalanianaole Hwy. terminates. This is excellent **windsurfing** territory, as enthusiastic beach locals will attest. In fact, the sport was invented here 20 years ago by the Naish family. Nonexistent waves and strong, steady onshore winds make for excellent windsurfing, kayaking, and canoeing conditions. Paddle out to **Popoia Island,** whose beach is one of the most photographed in Oahu, but tread carefully once you get there—it's a seabird sanctuary and our winged friends built their nests in the ground. To rent top-quality gear, head to **Kailua Sailboard Company,** 130 Kailua Rd. (262-2555), two blocks from the park. Half- and full-day rentals available (windsurfs $25-30, single kayaks $22-28, double kayaks $29-38), as well as three-hour windsurfing lessons (daily at 10:30am and 2pm; $39).

White sand, emerald green waters, and mild waves make nearby **Lanikai Beach,** Mokulua Dr. east of Kailua, a popular family beach. Grab your snorkel gear and swim out into the bay—better yet, use an inner tube and float around effortlessly. Flora enthusiasts should visit the **Haiku Gardens,** 46-316 Haiku Rd. (247-6671), where many weddings are held (open daily sunrise to sunset; free).

Kaneohe Bay to Laie

A few miles north of Kaneohe, **Kahekili Highway,** the inland road through the town, merges with the coastal **Kamehameha Highway** (Rte. 83), which goes up to the northern tip of Oahu and down to the North Shore. The following sights (except the Valley of the Temples) are accessible on the #55 bus route from Ala Moana.

Near Kaneohe Bay is the **Valley of the Temples,** 47-200 Kahekili Hwy. Take bus #19, 20, or 47 to the King and Kalakea St. intersection and catch bus #65 to the entrance of the burial ground. The **Byodo-In Temple** was built in 1968 as a replica of a temple in Uji, Japan to commemorate the 100th anniversary of Japanese immigrants' first arrival in Hawaii. Stroll through the tropical gardens and by the running stream filled with 10,000 brightly colored Japanese carp. Ring the three-ton brass bell to bring happiness and the blessings of the Buddha (open daily 8am-4:30pm; admission $2, children and seniors $1).

HAWAII

Approaching the North Shore on the Kamehameha Hwy. are **Kualoa Regional Park** and **Chinaman's Hat,** an island named for its conical shape. Much of *Karate Kid II* was filmed on the island, which must have made local favorite Pat Morita pretty giddy. North of here, **Swanzy Beach State Park, Kaaawa Beach County Park, Kahana Bay Park,** and **Punaluu Beach** possess secluded stretches of sand shared only with the wind and the waves. When Hurricane Iniki hit Kauai in 1992, the film crews for *Jurassic Park* completed the film in the **Kaaawa Valley.** Right around the bend from **Punaluu** is the entrance to **Sacred Falls Park,** a scenic 50 ft. waterfall in a dramatic, narrow canyon. The 2 mi. trail from the parking lot to the falls takes about an hour each way, but the dramatic falls and refreshing pool underneath make the hike worthwhile. Stick to the trail, though—hikers have gotten lost in past months, possibly lured away by those sneaky velociraptors.

Past **Laie,** the land gives way to abandoned sugar plantations. Shrimp and corn are now the crops of choice and can be sampled fresh at a number of roadside stands. Rounding the island's northern tip at Kahuku, you will also see strange two-armed windmills gyrating on the hillside—it's nothing extraterrestrial or dinosaurian, just another experimental energy project. The **Polynesian Cultural Center,** 55-370 Kamehameha Hwy. (293-3333), staffed by Mormon students from adjacent Brigham Young University, is the home of an overpriced "living museum" that seeks to capture the flavor of seven Polynesian cultures. You can see authentic natives here as well as the same tourists you left in Waikiki (open Mon.-Sat. 12:30-9:30pm; admission $47, children $30).

■ North Shore and Central Oahu

As the stunningly verdant home to cane fields and surfers, it is hard to believe that the North Shore is on the same island as Honolulu. Many Oahu residents working in hectic Honolulu come home to the "country" of the North Shore at night. The pace is slow and peaceful in the summer, but between October and March, furious storms create the shore-pounding ground swells at the world-famous breaks of **Sunset, Waimea,** and the **Banzai Pipeline.** As *the* surfing mecca, the North Shore becomes a wild spectacle of board-toting, tattoo-sporting tanned bodies. The professional world tour closes here with the nationally televised **Triple Crown of Surfing.** If you want to be a part of it, put the book down now and make your reservations. The North Shore can be easily reached by bus #52 from Ala Moana.

ACCOMMODATIONS

North Shore accommodations are few and far between. If you're coming in the winter, book early or you'll be squeezed out by the zealous hordes arriving to challenge the surf. Although early summer is pretty slow, the penultimate waves still draw hefty crowds in July and August.

Backpackers, 59-788 Kamehameha Hwy. (638-7838; fax 638-7515; http://backpackers-hawaii.com), opposite Sunset Beach. Bus #52 from Ala Moana stops at the front door. Nine restored plantation cottages have clean, well-kept rooms and kitchenettes. Resident roosters provide a free wake-up service for early risers. Discounts on local attractions including scuba diving as well as free use of the lodging's surfing gear. Reception open daily 7am-7pm. Check-out 10am. 8-bed dorms $15; doubles $45-$55; 4-person studios $80-95. Key and linen deposit $20.

Camp Mokuleia, 68-729 Farrington Hwy. (637-6241), Waialua. A 5min. drive from Honolulu, near Dillingham Air Force Base. This Episcopal church conference center, sitting on Mokuleia Beach, offers immaculate, well-furnished rooms with stunning views of Waialua Bay. Canoe and kayak tours available for $30 per hr. Doubles with shared bath $50-55, with private bath $60-65. Tenting sites $8 per person. Meals available $5-7. Advance reservations required.

FOOD

Rosie's Cantina, 66-165 Kamehameha Hwy. (637-3538), in the Haleiwa Shopping Center. This hip Tex-Mex joint draws a lively crowd every night with hefty entrees ($6-10). The real secret to Rosie's success: $1.75 margaritas until 5pm. Popular with both college kids and families. Open daily 7am-9pm.

Kua Aina Sandwich, 66-214 Kamehameha Hwy. (637-6067), across from the Haleiwa Shopping Center. Crowds line up at lunchtime for giant burgers on kaiser rolls ($4.60). The mahi and ortega sandwich ($5.40) is a taste extravaganza. Open daily 11am-8pm. No credit cards.

Coffee Gallery, 66-250 Kamehameha Hwy. (637-5571), in the North Shore Marketplace. Relaxed atmosphere and jazzy patio assures that lunch can, and often does, turn into an afternoon's affair. Humongous pastries, rich slabs of pie, great vegetarian fare, and deservedly popular yogurt fruit cup (any of these from $1.50-6). Fresh ground coffee $12-16 per lb. Open Mon.-Fri. 6am-9pm, Sat.-Sun. 7am-9pm.

SIGHTS AND ACTIVITIES

Surfing is king on the North Shore, but there's still plenty to do here even if you don't know the difference between Mr. Zog's Sex Wax and K-Y jelly. The action on the North Shore centers around **Haleiwa,** once a plantation town, but now the enlivened community of surf shops and art galleries. **Surf-n-Sea,** 62-595 Kamehameha Hwy. (638-0074), is world famous for quality gear and instruction. (Snorkeling gear $9.50 per day; windsurfing gear $12 first hr., $8.50 per additional hr.; surfboards $5 first hr., $3.50 per additional hr. Two-hr. beginning surf lessons $65. Open daily 9am-7pm.) For a boating experience of any kind, head to the **Haleiwa Boat Harbor.** Take Kamehameha Hwy. into Haleiwa, cross the narrow bridge, and take the first right. The **Watercraft Connection** (637-8006) provides a number of rental options for the harbor. Make sure to protect your eyes from the salty spray. (Waverunners and jet skis $35 per ½hr., $60 per hr.; kayaks $10 per hr. Open daily 10:30am-5pm).

To the north of Haleiwa is **Waimea Beach County Park,** where locals and Budweiser-emboldened tourists jump off a high rock formation ilto the sea. The beach shares its name with **Waimea Valley** (638-8511), an 1800-acre nature preserve with tropical gardens and a 45 ft. waterfall extravaganza. Performers dive off the cliffs daily at 11:15am, 1:15, 2:45, and 4:15pm (also 5pm in the summer). Admission to the park is almost as steep as the falls ($20, people in wheelchairs and one companion $10, ages 6-12 $5, under 6 free; open daily 10am-5:30pm). Prices are reduced on the day before and the day of the full mooh. Call for free round-trip shuttle service from Waikiki. About ¼ mi. north of Waimea lies **Puu O Mahuka Heiau.** Don't get too close—it was used for human sacrifices until 1794. The serene setting and spectacular panorama of Waimea Bay and surrounding countryside make the winding trip over camouflaged speed bumps worth the sacrifice. Turn right off Kamehameha onto Pupukea Rd. at Foodland and follow the signs for State Monument.

Back on Kamehameha Hwy., another few minutes drive will bring you to breathtaking **Sunset Beach** and the **Banzai Pipeline,** infamous winter wavelands of the world. During the summer, the surf disappears and these big beaches are excellent for swimming. For some outstanding snorkeling, head to **Shark's Cove.** Not to fear—it's named not for man-devouring beasts, but for shark-shaped rocks. Not far past Sunset, on Kamehameha Hwy., sits a 25 ft. wooden **statue** of the god Maui rising out of the earth. Next to the sculpture is the **Hawaiian Trading Post,** operated by a guy whose name also happens to be Maui. Even if you don't have anything to trade, stop in and check out the shrine in the garage and the merchandise ranging from old typewriters and foreign coins to Polynesian idols and woven hats (open daily 1-4:30pm). For a bird's eye view, you can fly (or fall 10,000 ft.) with **Skydive Hawaii,** Rte. 930, Dillingham Airfield. (Tandem jumping $275. Call 637-9700 for reservations and free pickup from Waikiki.) A cheaper and lower-altitude option for the aerial perspective is **The Original Glider Rides** (677-3404), at the other end of the airfield. The 20-minute ride skirts you across the North Shore, and if the winds

HAWAII

are good, you can get up high and see Honolulu. Check in with the original Mr. Bill (single $100, 2-passenger $120; extra 10 min. of flight $20). For a grounded perspective of the North Shore, head to secluded, beautiful, and windy **Makuleia Beach.**

Rte. 82 winds through **Wahiawa,** another plantation town and home to tattoo parlors and the **Sacred Healing Stones,** which became so popular in the first part of this century they had to be enclosed in a concrete, cubical "temple" for their protection. On the way, take a poke around the unapologetically commercial **Dole Pineapple Pavilion,** 64-1550 Kamehameha Hwy. (621-8408). Displays offer the visitor a crash course on the ins and outs of the pineapple business and the legacy of Jim Dole, the "Pineapple King," who arrived in Hawaii in 1887 with a horticulture degree from Harvard. Check out pineapples from around the world in the garden (open daily 9am-6:30pm).

You've Seen These Islands Before

Most likely, a visit to the Hawaiian islands will give you a strong sense of deja vu. Even if you weren't King Kamehameha in a past life, you'll recognize the landscape from the many productions filmed in Hawaii. *Hawaii Five-O* owes many of its shots to the Iolani Palace in Oahu (p. 443). Who can forget the wacky exploits of Rick, Higgins, and TC on *Magnum, P.I.* (Waikiki, p. 450), the stunning waterfall at the beginning of *Fantasy Island* (Kauai, p. 494), or the *Brady Bunch Goes to Hawaii* episode? (For more Brady Bunch nostalgia, see p. 202.)

However, some of the most popular visions of Hawaii have been those shown on the Big Screen. Kauai especially has served as a lush backdrop in a number of famous movies. In the 40s, producers were drawn to the beautiful sands of Lumahai Beach (p. 495) for the epic musical *South Pacific*. The Na Pali Coast (p. 495) was featured in *King Kong* (1976). The Okinawa scenes in *Karate Kid II* (starring Noriyuki "Pat" Morita) were filmed in Lihue. More recently, the blockbuster thrillers *Jurassic Park I* and *II* were filmed in the lush Kauai outback of the Olokele and Hanapepe valleys (which are only accessible by helicopter tour, p. 493), and the Wailua River (p. 494) was seen in the Dustin Hoffman flick *Outbreak*. The Coco Palms resort was the site of Elvis' film *Blue Hawaii*. If the King approved of it, it's got to be good.

Off the Big Island's Kona coast (p. 473), the mega-costly debacle *Waterworld* was filmed. This movie brought $25 million to the economy, so you can be sure locals will continue to embrace the film crews.

HAWAII

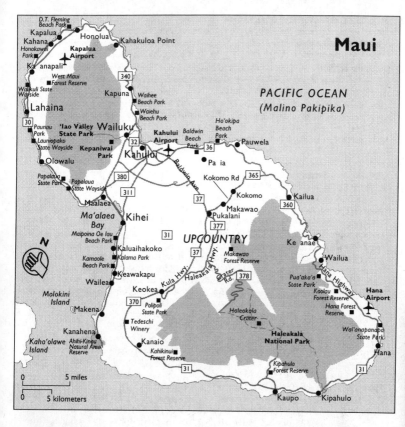

Maui

The image shows a map of Maui with the following labels:

D.T. Fleming Beach Park, Kapalua, Kahana, Honokowai Park, Honolua, Kahakuloa Point, Kapalua Airport, **Maui**, Ka'anapali, West Maui Forest Reserve, *PACIFIC OCEAN (Malino Pakipika)*, 340, Kapuna, Waihee Beach Park, Waiuli State Wayside, Lahaina, Waiehu Beach Park, Ho'okipa Beach Park, 30, Paunau Park, 'Iao Valley State Park, Wailuku, Baldwin Beach Park, Kahului Airport, 36, Pauwela, Launiopoko State Wayside, Kepaniwai Park, 32, Kahului, Pa'ia, Olowalu, 380, Kokomo Rd, 365, Papalaua State Park, Papalaua State Wayside, 311, Kokomo, 37, Kailua, Maalaea, Kihei, Makawao, 360, Ma'alaea Bay, Pukalani, Ke'anae, Maipoina Oe Iau Beach Park, 31, UPCOUNTRY, 377, Kaluaihakoko, Kamaole Beach Park, Kalama Park, 37, Makawao Forest Reserve, Wailua, Keawakapu, Pua'aka'a State Park, Hana Airport, Wailea, Keokea, 378, Koolau Forest Reserve, Hana Forest Reserve, Molokini Island, 370, Polipoli State Park, Haleakala Crater, Makena, Tedeschi Winery, Wai'anapanapa State Park, Kanahena, Kanaio, Haleakala National Park, Hana, Kaho'olawe Island, Ahihi-Kinau Natural Area Reserve, Kahikinui Forest Reserve, Kipahulu Forest Reserve, 31, 31, 0 5 miles, 0 5 kilometers, Kaupo, Kipahulu, N

Maui

Fun-loving Maui is appropriately named after the demigod renowned for mischief. According to legend, the sun once moved too quickly across the sky, leaving behind unripened fruits, too little daylight for farmers and fishermen to do their work, and too little warmth for women to dry their clothes. Hoping to save the day, Maui ran to the top of Haleakala (House of the Sun) and captured the sun with 16 ropes. The sun begged to be freed, promising to move more slowly. Today, the sun holds up its end of the bargain with a more laid-back pace, and island life follows suit.

With some of Oahu's bustle and plenty of the pristine beauty of the sleepier isles, Maui strikes a good balance for the traveler who wants quiet beaches during the day but lively entertainment at night. Two's company, three's a crowd, and two million will drown you in a sea of tourists; venture off the beaten path, however, and you may discover why Maui is known as "the Valley Isle." Consisting of two mountains joined by an isthmus, the island's acres of sugarcane nod in the breeze and lush jungles spill over sheer seaside cliffs. Just about everyone can find the Hawaii they seek here, so eat, drink, and be *Maui*.

PRACTICAL INFORMATION

Visitor Information:
  Visitor Information Kiosk (872-3893), at the Kahului Airport. Free maps. Open daily 6:30am-9pm.
  Maui Visitors Bureau, 1727 Wili Pa Loop (244-3530), has brochures and advice on activities and accommodations.
  Haleakala National Park, P.O. Box 369, Makawao 96768 (572-9306), provides info on weather, ranger-guided hikes, camping, cabins, and special activities. Open daily 7:30am-4pm.
  Department of Parks and Recreation, War Memorial Gym, 1580C Kaahumanu Ave. (243-7389), between Kahului and Wailuku. Info on county parks and permits ($3). Open Mon.-Fri. 8am-4pm.
  Division of State Parks, 54 S. High St., #101 (984-8109), by the parking lot, at Main St. in Wailuku. Offices are in the basement. Info for Maui and Molokai. Open Mon.-Fri. 8am-noon and 1-4pm.
Budget Travel: Regal Travel, 250 Alamaha St., #NIIA (871-8141), sells inter-island coupons. Mahalo $36, Hawaiian $44; resident discounts for Aloha and Island. Open Mon.-Fri. 8am-5:30pm, Sat. 9am-3pm.
Public Transportation: Trans Hawaiian (877-7308), has a booth at Kahului Airport's baggage claim. Runs from the airport to Lahaina-Kaanapali (every ½hr. 9am-4pm; fare $13). Reserve 1 day in advance for transit to the airport. **Speedi Shuttle** (875-8070), will pick up and drop off virtually anywhere. Airport to Lahaina $26. Operates 5am-10:30pm. **West Main Shopping Express** connects Lahaina and Kaanapali. Schedules available at shopping centers in Lahaina (fare $1; operates 8:45am-10:15pm). **Hawaii Care Van** (669-2300), provides shuttle and tour service for disabled travelers. Airport to Lahaina $65.
Ferries: Ferries are a fun and cheap mode of transport between Maui and Lanai. **Expeditions** (661-3756), runs 6 trips per day between Lahaina and Manele, Lanai (fare $25; 1hr.). Check-in 15min. before departure at the dock in front of the Pioneer Inn. Reservations recommended.
Taxis: Resort Taxi (661-5285). Airport to Wailuku $10.
Car Rental: National chains have desks or courtesy phones at the airport. Hostels can occasionally get you better rates. **Regency** (871-6147), at the airport, rents economy cars $25 per day, ages 18-25 $30. Discounts for weekly rentals. Open daily 8am-8pm. **Word of Mouth,** 150A Hana Hwy. (877-2436 or 800-533-5929), rents used cars for $115 per week. Must be 25. The free *Maui Bulletin* (available at airport car rental desks and all over town) lists cars to rent or buy.
Bike Rental: Cycling is easy on West Maui, with its flat roads and fat shoulders, but only experienced riders should tackle the twisting Hana Hwy. **The Island Biker,** 415 Dairy Rd. (877-7744), off Hana Hwy. across from K-Mart, rents mountain bikes for $25 per day, $85 per week. Open Mon.-Sat. 9am-5pm. Reservations recommended. **A&B Rentals,** 3481 Lower Honoapiilani Rd. (669-0027), near Kaanapali, rents bikes for $15 per day, $60 per week. Open daily 8:30am-5:30pm.
Moped and Scooter Rental: A&B Moped and Scooter Rentals, 3481 Lower Honoapiilani Rd. (669-0027). Scooters $13 for 2hr., $18 for 4hr., $22 for 6hr., $24 for 8hr. Open daily 8:30am-5:30pm. **Wheels R Us,** 150 Lahainaluna Rd. (667-7751), Lahaina. Mopeds $20 for 4hr., $26 for 8hr. Credit card deposit ($100) required; under 25, cash deposit ($200). Must be 18 with credit card and driver's license. Open daily 8am-5pm.
Water Equipment: Rental Warehouse, in Lahaina (661-1970), and in Kihei (875-4050), rents used equipment at rock-bottom prices. Snorkel sets $2 per day, boogieboards $2, bikes $10, surfboards $5. Open daily 7am-6pm. The **Maui Windsurf Company,** 520 Keolani Pl. (877-4816 or 800-872-0999), near Kahului Airport, rents sailboards for $45 per day, $295 per week. Roof rack and harness included. Beginner lessons $60 (2½hr.; equipment included). Reserve in advance for a 10% discount. Unlimited exchange of equipment. Open daily 8:30am-6pm. **Maui Dive Shop** is at Azeka Pl. in Kihei (879-3388; open daily 7:30am-9pm) and 626 Front St. in Lahaina (667-0722; open daily 6am-9pm). Snorkel sets $7.50 per

day, $15 per week; wetsuits $5 per day; scuba sets $25 per day, extra tank $7. Intro dives $70.

Outdoor Equipment: Maui Sporting Goods, 92 N. Market St. (244-0011), in Wailuku, sells tents, backpacks, and more. Open Mon.-Thurs. 9am-6pm, Fri. 9am-8pm, Sat. 8am-5pm.

Library: Wailuku Library, 251 High St. (243-5566). Open Mon. and Thurs. 10am-8pm, Tues.-Wed. and Fri. 10am-5pm. Non-residents $10 for 3 months.

Laundromat: W&I Washerette, 125 S. Wakea Ave. (877-0353), next to Kaahumanu Shopping Center in Kahului. Wash $1.50, 5min. dry 25¢. Suck down a Maui Waki Rainbow shave ice ($1.25) while your underwear dries! Open daily 6am-9pm. **Koin-Op Laundromat** (669-1587), in Kahana Gateway Shopping Center. Wash $1.50, 7min. dry 25¢. Open daily 6am-10pm.

Weather Conditions: Land (877-5111); **marine** (877-3477).

Crisis Lines: Sexual Assault Crisis Center (242-4357). 24hr.

Hospital: Maui Memorial, 221 Mahalani St. (244-9056, emergency 242-2343), Wailuku. 24hr.

Emergency: 911. **Coast Guard Rescue** (800-331-6176).

Internet Access: Whaler's Way B&B, 521-541 Kupulau Dr. (879-1420), off Rte. 31, lets you surf the web.

Post Office: Lahaina, 1760 Honoapiilani Hwy. (667-6611). Open Mon.-Fri. 8:30am-5pm, Sat. 10am-noon. **ZIP Code:** 96761. **Paia,** 39 Baldwin Ave. (579-9205). Open Mon.-Fri. 8am-4:30pm, Sat. 10:30am-12:30pm. **ZIP Code:** 96779. **Wailuku,** 250 Imi Kala St. (244-4815), by The Mill Yard. Open Mon.-Fri. 8:30am-5pm, Sat. 8am-noon. **ZIP code:** 96793. **Kihei,** 1254 S. Kihei Rd. (879-2403), in Azeka Market Place. Open Mon.-Fri. 9am-4:30pm, Sat. 9-11am. **ZIP Code:** 96753.

Area Code: 808.

ORIENTATION

Maui's highways follow the shape of the island in a broken figure-eight pattern. The **Kahului Airport** sits on the northern coast of the isthmus. To the west lie Kahului and Wailuku. **Rte. 30 (Honoapiilani Hwy.)** leads to the resort areas of Lahaina and Kaanapali. **Rte. 34/340** leads counter-clockwise around the same loop from the isthmus through remote West Maui. Circling the slopes of Haleakala, **Rte. 31** passes Kihei and Wailea. **Rte. 36/360 (Hana Hwy.)** meanders around hairpin curves to Hana. **Rte. 37** leads to **Rte. 377** and **Rte. 378** before heading up 10,023 ft. Mt. Haleakala. Heed 4WD warnings—most rental car contracts stipulate that drivers tackle dirt roads at their own risk. **Hitchhiking is illegal** but popular. The usual method is to stand by the road with arms crossed. Despite our sympathy for the car-less, *Let's Go* does not recommend hitching or picking up hitchers.

The cool **Upcountry** includes the area along the west slope of Haleakala and is home to *paniolos* (cowboys) and painters. The **Hana Coast** is the island's wet and wonderful southeast shore, covered with rainforests and waterfalls. **Central Maui,** wedged between two of the wettest spots on earth, averages only 30 inches of rain per year, yet through a miracle of engineering supports acres upon acres of sugar cane (each pound of refined sugar requires one ton of water to grow). The **north shore** still maintains its rural charm, despite the more recent influx of international surfers and windsurfers, and the subsequent invasion of shopping malls and gas stations in the towns of Wailuku and Kahului. Finally, **West Maui,** home of the resort centers of Kaanapali and Lahaina, provides dazzling valleys and seascapes. Along the southwest coast, long beaches collect most of Maui's tourists around **Kihei** resorts.

ACCOMMODATIONS AND CAMPING

Staying in Maui can be surprisingly inexpensive. During the winter, though, and especially around windsurfing events, hostels are packed—book as early as possible. Wailuku makes an excellent base for exploring the island, and the resort areas of Lahaina and Kaanapali also offer relatively inexpensive options. Vacation rentals can be another affordable lodging option; check the Maui Visitors Bureau and the classified section of the *Maui News* for info. **Maui International Connection,** 520 Keolani Pl. (877-4999 or 800-963-6284), Kahului, offers package deals including the $850 hotel-car-windsurfing combo (open Mon.-Sat. 9am-2pm).

Camping on the beach is not allowed outside of designated campgrounds. Three **national park sites** on Maui **(Oheo, Haleakala,** and **Hosmer Grove)** allow free walk-in camping (3-night max. stay). Two state parks, **Waianapanapa** and **Polipoli,** also allow camping, though the latter is accessible only by 4WD (5-night max. stay; free). Tenters can also set up camp at the county park at **Kanaha Beach** (sites $3). Permits are officially required at both state and county parks, but monitoring is infrequent at best (for more info, see **Practical Information,** p.444).

Central Maui

Northshore Inn, 2080 Vineyard St. (242-8999), Wailuku. Clean and relaxed hostel hosts international windsurfers and tourists. Kitchen, TV, and fridge in every room. Bulletin board offers inter-island tickets, bike rental, and suggestions for small-wave days. Free movie nightly 9pm. Reception open 7:30am-9pm. Dorms $15; singles $30; doubles $41. Linens $1. Laundry ($1 wash, 75¢ dry).

Banana Bungalow Hotel and International Hostel, 310 N. Market St. (244-5090 or 800-846-7835; fax 244-3678), at Kapoai St., Wailuku. Frequented by an eclectic crowd. TV room, hot tub, hammocks, volleyball court, and basic kitchen. Free beach shuttle. Dorms $14; singles $32; doubles $39. Key deposit $5.

Maui Palms Hotel, 150 Kaahumanu Ave. (877-0071; fax 871-5797), at Lono Ave., Kahului. Sleepy hotel by the ocean is decorated with a 60s Polynesian twist. Free airport shuttle. Pool and TV. Some rooms have A/C. Check-in at the lobby of Maui Beach, next door. Rooms for 1-3 people $52. Front desk open 24hr.

West Maui and Kihei Resort Area

Whaler's Way and **Sunset B&B,** 521-541 Kupulan Dr. (879-1420 or 879-7984), Rte. 31. Both B&Bs offer 8 units in the beautiful Maui Meadows. Immaculate rooms with refrigerators, TVs, microwaves, and phones. Whaler's Way also has a jacuzzi and Internet access. Doubles $55; cottages $80.

Old Lahaina House, 407 Ilikahi St. (667-4663 or 800-847-0761; fax 667-5615), at Rte. 30 and Shaw St. Luxurious rooms pamper the weary tourist. A/C, TV, pool, and breakfast. Flexible 3-night min. stay. Rooms $60-95. Reservations required.

Aloha Lani Inn, 13 Kauaula Rd. (661-8040), at Rte. 30 and Shaw St., offers 3 small rooms. Shared bath, kitchen, and coffee. Rooms $55-65. Call ahead.

Windmills Park campground, between Honolua and Honokohau. Located on a stunning white sand beach near Honolua Bay, it's a prime snorkeling spot. No facilities. Campground operated by the Maui Land and Pineapple Company (669-6201). Permit required ($5); available at their Honolua office, 4900 Honoapiilani Hwy., opposite the Napili Plaza (open Mon.-Fri. 6:30am-3pm).

Pecusa campground, 800 Olowalu Village (661-4303), on Rte. 30 ½mi. north of mi. marker 14. Limited cabin sites; tent sites on loose dirt and large mats. Snorkeling and kayaking beach nearby. Outdoor shower, wash basin, portable toilets, and tables. Check-in 8am-5pm. Walk-in sites $5 per person.

Hana Coast

YMCA Camp Keanae (242-9007), Hana Hwy. in Keanae, halfway between Paia and Hana. Located on a point commanding a long view of the coast and the Keanae peninsula. Large cabins have small, tightly packed bunks. Insect repellent essential for when the mosqitoes come out to wine and dine. Hot showers in rustic bathrooms. Dorms $10. Telephone reservations required (phones open Mon.-Fri. 6am-9pm, Sat. 8am-4pm, Sun. 10am-4pm).

Joe's Place, 4850 Uakea Rd. (248-7033), Hana. On the right after taking the left fork of Hana Hwy. south. Clean, pink, comfortable rooms in the center of town. TV, dining room, and kitchen. Check-in after 3pm, check-out 10am; reservations held until 6pm. Rooms $45, with private bath $55.

Waianapanapa State Wayside campground, just north of Hana off Hana Hwy. Perched above a black sand beach and flanked by dramatic lava formations. Near a *heiau,* hiking trails, and the Waianapanapa Caves, these grassy sites are the island's premier state camping facilities. Six-person cabins equipped with linen, towels, kitchen, refrigerator, and stove. Restrooms, picnic tables, barbecue grills, and outdoor showers. Cabins $10 for 1 person, $14 for 2, $30 for 6. Camping free with required permit. Cabin reservations required (up to 1 year in advance).

Oheo campground, at mi. marker 42 on Rte. 31, next to Kipahulu Ranger Station. Flat, grassy campground sports 2 portable toilets but no drinking water. Nearby hikes include a trek to the pools of Oheo Gulch and another through a bamboo forest to Waimoku Falls. 3-night max. stay. Free.

Upcountry

Hosmer Grove campground, off Rte. 378 up Haleakala. Small campground has drinking water, toilet, grills, firewood, and covered tables. Excellent self-guided nature trail through a grove of fragrant pines. At this elevation (6700ft.), it gets a bit chilly and wet, so bring a sleeping bag and rain gear. Part of Haleakala National Park; no permit required. 3-night max. stay. Camping free.

Haleakala Crater campground, P.O. Box 369, Makawao 96768 (572-9306), 4mi. from Halemauu parking lot. Camping and cabins inside the crater itself. The cabins at **Holua, Kapalua,** and **Paliku** are each equipped with 12 bunks, wood-burning stove, and cooking utensils. They lie 4, 6, and 10mi. from the parking lot. Holua and Paliku also have campsites. Free camping permits issued at park headquarters (1mi. up from guard booth). Cabins, 2-night max. stay; camp sites 3-night max. Cabins allocated by lottery; apply at least 3 months in advance.

Honokalani Naturalist Resort (248-7220), on 19 acres next to Waianapanapa State Park's black sand beach. **Clothing-optional** facility features hot tub, grill, volleyball, kayaking, and airplane tours. Two-person apartments $10; bungalows $50; sites $23. Day use $13.

Polipoli State Park campground, off Rte. 377 on Waipoli Rd. Near hiking. Great view from 6200ft. Cold at night. Switchback dirt road makes 4WD necessary after rain. No showers or electricity. The single cabin has gas lanterns ($45 for 1-4 people; each additional person $5). Camping free. Reserve up to 1yr. in advance.

FOOD

Maui is the land of plenty. Surfcasters and spear fishermen wade ashore with the daily catch, ripe fruit falls into unsuspecting convertibles, and tropical delights such as pineapples, sugar cane, and the sweet kula onion sprout in vast fields. On Wednesdays, these goodies come in from the fields and head for the **farmer's market** (573-1934), at the Kahului Shopping Center, near the intersection of Rte. 32 and Puunene Ave. (open 8:30am-noon).

The cheapest places to eat are away from the resorts. **Wailuku** supports the largest concentration of inexpensive restaurants. **Down to Earth Natural Foods,** 1169 Makawao Ave. (572-1488), in Makawao, is a health food store that offers a small salad bar (open daily 8am-8pm). When in Kahului, stop by the **Maui Swap Meet,** on S. Puunene Ave. next to the post office. Unearth bargain prices on everything from fresh island produce to t-shirts with slogans like "My fourth-cousin went to Maui and all I got was this lousy t-shirt" (Sat. 7am-noon; 50¢).

Central Maui

Sam Satos, 1750 Wili Pa Loop (244-7124), up the street from the visitors center in Wailuku. Sit-down service at drive-in prices. Don't be daunted by the size of the noodle bowls ($3). The *manju* (a sweet bean pastry) is worth the extra calories (45¢). Open Mon.-Sat. 7am-2pm. No credit cards.

Tasty Crust, 1770 Mill St. (244-0845), Wailuku. Locals happily pile into this divine diner to eat the state's best hotcakes ($2.40). Burgers ($2.50) and pies ($2.40) make the perfect luncheon treat, and there is even a scale to assess the post-meal damage. Open Mon.-Tues. 5:30am-1pm, Wed.-Sun. 5:30am-1pm and 5-9pm.

Chum's, 1900 Main St. (244-1000), just past Ooka's market in Wailuku. Hefty portions may make you wish you had an elastic waistband. Omelette combos $5-6, plate lunches $6-7. Open Sun.-Thurs. 6:30am-10pm, Fri.-Sat. 6:30am-10:30pm.

The Vegan, 115 Baldwin Ave. (579-9144), Paia. Only vegetarian restaurant on Maui. Feel the New Age spirit while you munch on tofu tacos ($3.25) and Thai tapioca ($3). Great place for Kosher diners. Open daily 4-8:30pm.

Pic-Nics, 30 Baldwin Ave. (579-8021), Paia. Creative sandwiches ($4-6) and picnic lunches complete down to the cookie ($8), all in a relaxed atmosphere. The Spinach Nut Burger ($5.75) and mango shakes ($3.25) are fantastic. Menu doubles as a guide to Hana. Open daily 7am-7pm. No credit cards.

West Maui and the Kihei Resort Areas

Aloha Mixed Plate, 1285 Front St. (661-3322), just north of the Mala Wharf in Lahaina, is the best option in this well-oiled tourist trap of a town. Filling dinner combos ($5-7) are served on an outdoor patio as the ocean waves gently lap against the backyard. Small sports bar is packed at night, especially when Hawaiian bands play (Fri.-Sat.). Open Sun.-Thurs. 7:30am-10pm, Fri.-Sat. 7:30am-midnight.

Old Lahaina Cafe, 505 Front St., (667-1998), between Prison and Shaw St., is perfect for a reunion dinner with the tourists you left at the hotel. Fish and vegetable *pupus* (appetizers) $4-8. Traditional dinner plates $8. Open daily 7:30am-9pm.

Hana Coast

The culinary options in this sparsely settled area are slim—in fact, there are only six places to eat in all of Hana—so your best bet is to bring groceries from Kahului. Numerous fruit stands line Hana Hwy. (Rte. 36/360).

Hana Ranch Restaurant, Mill Rd. (248-8255), off Hana Hwy. Pizzas from $8.50, huge helpings of pasta $9. Call before 11am for take-out. Open Sun.-Tues. and Thurs. 6:30am-7pm, Wed., and Fri.-Sat. 6:30am-4pm. No credit cards.

Tutu's (248-8224), on Hana Bay next to the pier. Basic take-out cafe serves chow to fishermen and beachgoers. Haul your stash to the picnic tables and enjoy lunch on the black sand beach. Sandwiches $3-4, plates $6. Open daily 8:30am-3:30pm.

Upcountry

Komoda Store and Bakery, 3674 Baldwin Ave. (572-7261), at Makawao Ave. The Komodas live behind their shop and rise before dawn to prepare their famous baked goods. Locals arrive soon after for the tasty, tasty donuts (45¢). Open Mon.-Tues. and Thurs.-Fri. 7am-5pm, Sat. 7am-2pm. No credit cards.

Casanova's Italian Restaurant and Deli, 1188 Makawao Ave. (572-0220). Winner of "Best Italian Place" and "Best Late Nite in Maui" awards. Sandwiches and entrees ($5-9) save you the money you need to be a *real* Casanova. Equally seductive deli next door. Open Mon.-Sat. 7am-1am, Sun. 8:30am-1am.

Grandma's Coffee House (878-2140), Rte. 37 in Keokea. Grandma has been cultivating a special strain of coffee on the slopes of Haleakala for decades and her delicious brew shows it. For a few beans more you can indulge in delicious baked goods ($1-2) and sandwiches ($3-5). Open Mon.-Sat. 7am-5pm, Sun. 7am-3pm.

SIGHTS AND ACTIVITIES

Maui's cultural and historical sights focus on the missionaries, the diverse ethnic background of the sugar workers, and the natural history of Maui itself. The Thursday "Scene" section of the *Maui News* has comprehensive listings of local events.

Central Maui

The geographical highlight of this "saddle" area of the island is the lush **Iao Valley,** parts of which average over an inch of rain per day. West on Rte. 32, just before the valley, lies the deceptively calm **Kepaniwai Park.** In 1790, Kamehameha I slaughtered the Maui army here, filling the brook with the dead in what is called the *kepaniwai* (the damming of the waters). Their blood reputedly ran all the way down to what is now called the Wailuku (bloody) River. Today, the park is home to pavilions dedicated to some of the peoples who have populated Maui: Japanese, Filipino, Chinese, Hawaiian, and Portuguese. The **Iao Valley State Park** (open daily 7am-7pm), at the end of Rte. 32, blooms with wild orchids and includes the **Iao Needle**, a 1200 ft. basalt spire. Some say the name is onomatopoeic—the cry of an unfortunate god who sat on this pointed peak. A more likely legend names the valley after Iao, Maui's daughter. When one of Iao's suitors was untrue, Maui petrified the offending part of his anatomy. Nearby is the **John F. Kennedy Profile,** a cliff that bears a dubious basalt likeness of the former president. Conspiracy, anyone?

In the 19th century, the Baileys, a New England missionary family, sailed around Cape Horn to reach Maui's pagan paradise. Mr. Bailey eventually bailed out of the missionary business, founded the Wailuku Sugar Mill, and began raising cane. Decked in period decor, the Baileys' home serves as the **Maui Historical Society Museum,** 2375A Main St. (244-3326), between Wailuku and the Iao Valley (open Mon.-Sat. 10am-4pm; admission $4, seniors $3.50, under 11 $1). On a nearby hill, you can visit a relic of the ancient religion that the Baileys attempted to stifle. The **Halekii** (House of Images) served as a place of worship throughout the 18th century until it was destroyed by natural erosion in 1819. Reconstructed in 1958, the *heiau* (temple) is now a temple of love, as local high school sweethearts will confirm. Follow Rte. 32 to the traffic light at Rte. 330. Make a left, pass the macadamia grove, and turn right on Rte. 340. Continue to Kuhio Place, and follow route to the right.

The **Maui Tropical Plantation,** on Rte. 30 in Waikupu, between Wailuku and Lahaina, displays produce fun-facts (open daily 9am-5pm; grove tours daily 10am-4pm; admission $8.50, ages 5-12 $3.50). Swimmers should head east from Wailuku on Rte. 36 to **Baldwin Beach Park,** which has lifeguards, showers, and restrooms. To the left (west) of the beach is **Baby Beach,** a cove cradled by a high reef which prevents big waves from forming and is safe for young children. The beach is also convenient to West Maui hostels, and less crowded than Kihei or Kaanapali.

Surfers and **windsurfers** flock to **Kanaha Beach, Spreckelsville Beach,** and world-famous **Hookipa Beach Park** for wind and waves. Kanaha, just northeast of Kahului on Amala St. off Rte. 380, is popular with beginners. Spreckelsville, between Kahului Airport and Paia, has showers, restrooms, and some of the best wind on the north coast. World-famous **Hookipa Beach Park,** off Rte. 36, is true bliss for expert windsurfers. North shore swells in the winter can average six- to eight-feet in the bay. Farther along Rte. 36, **Paia** is an old plantation town-*cum*-windsurfer haven. Most windsurfers are eager to get a good start on the next day's waves—nightlife is limited.

West Maui and the Lahaina-Kaanapali Resort Area

Rte. 30 winds around the West Maui Mountains to **Lahaina** and **Kaanapali.** The road follows the breathtaking *pali* (cliffs)—designated scenic stops are great for whale watching, especially in the winter. Mile marker 14 indicates one of the most spectacular swimming spots in Hawaii—for hungry sharks, that is (enter *Jaws* theme music). Snorkeling fanatics should head a few miles farther, near Olowalu, where there are several beaches ideal for snorkeling, small-wave surfing, and picnicking. **Launiupoko State Wayside Park,** between Lahaina and Kaanapali, is one such beach with picnic tables, restrooms, outdoor showers, and barbecue grills.

Lahaina rose to prominence in 1810 when it was chosen by Kamehameha the Great as the capital for his pan-Hawaiian empire and by whaling ships as their preferred port-of-call. In 1845, Hawaii's capital moved to Honolulu, leaving behind a rough, dusty town where brothels stood next door to churches and grog was the drink of choice. Today, Lahaina has regained prominence as Maui's tourist center and as the capital of a robust whale-watching—rather than whale-killing—trade.

Evening fun is still important here, as Lahaina provides most of the nightlife on this otherwise early-to-bed island. The town revolves around the oceanside **Front St.**

The center of town is shaded by an East Indian **banyan tree,** rivaling Kauai's for the title of Hawaii's largest. The tree was already 8 ft. tall when it was brought from India in 1873, and today, with 12 main trunks, it shades two-thirds of an acre. In the harbor rests the **Carthaginian** (661-8527), a restored brig which now houses a whaling museum (open daily 10am-4pm; admission $3, seniors $2, family $5). Across Front St. from the library sits the **Baldwin Home** (661-3262). The Baldwins were New England missionaries who came to the islands to stamp out what they thought was debauchery and idolatry, but weren't above getting ship carpenters to build them a house for petty wages. Today, they remain one of the richest families on Maui. The house is furnished in period design (open daily 10am-4pm; admission $3, seniors $2, families $5).

Lahaina is home to many art galleries, some of which are good. Friday night is so-called **art night,** and the galleries stay open late; mingle with the local intelligentsia while taking advantage of the free wine and hors d'oeuvres. An **OMNI theater,** 824 Front St. (661-8314), in Lahaina, presents Hawaii's history on the big, BIG screen, with the breathtaking *Hawaii: Island of the Gods!* (Shown daily 10am-10pm on the hr. Admission $7, ages 3-12 $4. Coupons available at timeshare desks nearby.)

Offshore at the Pioneer Inn boat docks, surfers and boogieboarders battle the waves while tourists soar 900 ft. above. It's a bird, it's a plane…it's **Parasail Kaanapali** (669-6555; $36, 6:30-7am early-bird special $21). **Atlantis Submarines** (800-548-6262) goes 120 ft. below the surface to show you a glimpse of the ocean floor (tours $70, children $40). The "Sugarcane Train," the **Lahaina-Kaanapali and Pacific Rail Road** (669-0089), makes three lick smackin' stops in West Maui ($9.50, round-trip $13).

Those seeking nirvana should seek out the largest **Buddha** outside Japan at the **Jodo Mission,** 12 Ala Moana St., on the north end of Front St., built to commemorate the arrival of Japanese immigrants in 1868. The **Wo Hing Temple,** 858 Front St. (661-3262), also preserves Maui's historical legacy. Built by Chinese sugar cane workers as a dining hall, it now screens Thomas Edison's turn-of-the-century films of Hawaiian life (open daily 10am-4pm). Native Hawaiian culture is as evident in the free **hula shows** at the Hale Kahiko, in Lahaina Center off Front St. (Wed. and Fri. at 2 and 6pm). Hip tourists can wiggle theirs every Tuesday and Wednesday (5-6pm).

Just past Lahaina stretches the 4 mi. long **Kaanapali Beach,** a resort area from which you can see the neighboring islands of Lanai (to your left), Molokai (to the right), and Oahu (center). The golden sand and calm waves are Hawaii at its best. The bordering **Whaler's Village** shopping center has a **food court.** Past Kaanapali lie several gorgeous beaches with fewer crowds. **Napili Beach,** 5 mi. north on Rte. 30, has excellent snorkeling and swimming conditions when it's calm, but strong rip currents when the large waves come rolling in. **Kapalua Beach** is a magnificent white sand beach shielded by rocky outcroppings. Snorkelers can see sea urchins, butterfly fish, and wrasses in the rocks along the right side of the beach. A couple of miles past Kapalua, **Fleming Beach Park** is another favorite for snorkeling and bodysurfing. **Slaughterhouse Beach,** named for the abattoir which used to overlook the beach, is popular with snorkelers and **nudists** alike, despite the sharp coral.

For a truly remarkable experience, continue north on Rte. 34 around the west end of the island. This winding passage reveals deep, cloud-shrouded valleys populated only by wandering cows and weathered fence posts, sheer seaside cliffs sheltering secluded bays, and small coastal villages nestled amid the shoulders of windswept mountains. It is well worth the two-hour trip back to Kahului.

East Maui and the Kihei Resort Area

Kihei, in East Maui, is the island's other resort area, keeping tourists sequestered in condominiums and hotels. The three **Kamaole Beach parks** are perennial favorites

Eye of the Tiger

In November 1991, Marty Morrell was out for her morning swim on a Maui beach when she was attacked and killed by a **shark.** There were four more attacks in the next four months and the state of Hawaii, deciding there were simply too many sharks in the water, set up a Shark Task Force whose job it was to kill as many sharks as possible. Despite this controversial and short-lived effort, the tiger shark population skyrocketed as did their attacks on humans. The 1991 attack was not, as claimed, the first one in 33 years, but rather the 32nd one since 1980. Equally shocking is the fact that there have been more than 50 great white attacks off the Northern Californian coast in the past three years. Nonetheless, sharks are not the merciless marauders that Hollywood makes them out to be. More often than not, attacks on humans are simple misunderstandings, as surfers look similar to tasty seals from a fish-eye view. Sharks usually realize their mistake after the first bite, and most victims live to tell about their brush with death. Survivors say the best way to repel a shark is to hit it squarely on its nose, the center of its sensitive nervous system.

for families and sun worshipers, with facilities including showers, toilets, and BBQ grills. Past Kihei, **Makena's** beaches are quiet and quite **swimsuit-free,** the most popular beach being **Little Beach** at the far right end of **Big Beach.** Oneloa (Long Sand), stretches 3000 ft. long and 100 ft. wide. Next to it, on the other side of a cinder cone, is the more secluded **Puuolai** (Earthquake Hill), a great site for spotting giant humpback whales. These beaches are ideal for sunbathing, but strong currents make swimming dangerous.

Farther south, **Ahihi Bay** and **La Perouse,** two of Maui's marine reserves, are excellent **snorkeling** spots (no facilities). Off Kihei lies the half-crater "island" of **Molokini.** It is a designated bird sanctuary, but boat trips carry visitors to its bay, resplendent with aquatic flora and fauna. Check *This Week in Maui* for half- or full-day snorkeling tours—$39 for an afternoon tour is the going rate. The underwater experience may be disappointing, as snorkelers seem to outnumber the fish.

Hana Coast

During the 70s, the Hana Coast's hypnotic beauty and unique ecosystem prompted calls for the establishment of a national park in the area. The native Hawaiians living there resisted and opted to preserve their cultural heritage and land rights instead. Maui residents, wanting to "keep Hawaii Hawaiian," have similarly countered developers's attempts to construct a golf course here. The area still remains largely untouched and retains its charm.

The **Hana Highway** provides auto-touring at its finest. Carved from cliff faces and valley floors, its alternate vistas of smooth sea and lush terrain are concealed behind the bends of hundreds of tight turns and tiny bridges. The road to Hana is not a means to an end; most sights lie along the way, not in the small and simple town of Hana itself. A leisurely trip takes a full day—pulling over is an essential way to savor the sights along the way and loosen your grip on the steering wheel. Wild ginger plants and fruit trees dripping with mangos, guavas, and bananas perfume the air. Numerous companies put out audio cassette tours of the drive for a steep $20, but unless you are an obsessed fact-fanatic the money could be better spent elsewhere.

At mile marker 2, a short walk leads to **Twin Falls,** two 35 ft. waterfalls separated by a small patch of forest. These shady spots are popular for refreshing swims and exhilarating jumps. Ten miles farther is **Haipuaena Falls** (mi. marker 11½), a gentle waterfall that empties into a pool deep enough for swimming. Surrounded by wild ginger and dense ferns, Haipuaena can be reached by following the path from the bridge. Down the road, at mi. marker 17, the **Keanae Botanical Gardens** bring the casual stroller through amazing Hawaiian vegetation, both native and imported (keep an eye out for the rainbow-barked tree). **Keanae,** situated on a small peninsula, is worth the five-minute detour for its coastal panoramas and lava formations.

The two-mile-long **Hana-Waianapanapa Coastal Trail,** the ancient Hawaiian "King's Highway," leads from the campground on Pailoa Bay to Kainalimu Bay. A few of the stepping stones placed long ago along the jagged lava remain, though most have eroded. Between Kuaiwa Point and Paina Point, the trail passes an ancient Hawaiian *heiau* (temple), about ½ mi. from the Waianapanapa campground. At the entrance to Hana, the campground is a good place to stop for picnicking and sunbathing. Near the campground are the **Waianapanapa** (Glistening Water) and **Waiomao** (Green Water) **Caves.** Hardy locals bring a flashlight and swim in the underground lava tubes, now filled with fresh water. According to legend, a Hawaiian princess once hid from her cruel husband in these caves. Unfortunately, her hiding place did not deceive him, and when the prince found his wife he murdered her. Every spring, red shrimp turn the cave waters crimson, a living reminder of the slain woman.

The wee burg of **Hana,** on the eastern slope of Haleakala, is a one-horse town operating on "Hawaiian time" (at least 15min. slower than a mainland watch). According to the hummable local song, "you can find everything you need at the **Hasegawa General Store"** (248-8231; open Mon.-Sat. 8am-5:30pm, Sun. 9am-4:30pm). Hana Bay, with its silky black shore, is calm enough for *keiki* (children), while *makua* (parents) can check out **Kayak Hana Bay** for a snorkeling/sea-kayaking eco-cruise in the sheltered waters of the bay. Look for the rack of colorful kayaks next to the water ($28 per hr.). **Red Sand Beach** (or Kaihalulu Beach) is a small cove favored by **nude** suntanners. To reach the beach, follow the path at the end of Uakea Rd. for 10 minutes. The sand is coarse, but the beach is beautiful and surrounded by cliffs. Two miles past Hana on Haneoo Rd. is scenic **Koki Beach,** where fishermen and bodysurfers share the surf with magma monuments. The dark sand of **Hamoa Beach** is nearby; facilities include the Hotel Hana-Maui, restrooms, and (you gotta love it) showers.

Farther south from Hana along Rte. 31 is the **Kipahulu District,** part of Haleakala National Park. Over 20 pools exist in the one mile of the **Oheo** stream immediately above the ocean. Oheo (the gathering of pools) is also known as "the Seven Sacred Pools." According to an imaginative hotel guide, swimmers can gain seven of the most sacred virtues in life by paddling in each pool. From Oheo, a lovely path (2mi.) leads up Oheo Gulch to Waimoku Falls. The trail climbs along the river, granting views of rushing falls and deep pools, and also passes through a tasty guava grove and a bamboo forest which would be tasty if you were a panda. The canyon wall at the end of the trail is bathed by dual 400 ft. falls. **Charles Lindbergh's grave** lies in the Kipahulu Hawaiian Church's idyllic graveyard, about 2 mi. down the road from the pools. The aviator spent his last years here and helped to restore the church.

Continuing along this route brings you to a dirt and gravel road and the spectacular scenery of the Hawaiian outback. The rocky path traverses the wilderness of **Kaupo** and eventually leads around the mountain to the Upcountry district through **Ulupalakua** and **Keokea.** Despite the scenic draw, this route is difficult without a 4WD, and some car rental companies may prohibit it.

Upcountry and Haleakala

The "up" in Upcountry is provided by the massive slopes of **Haleakala Volcano,** the largest dormant volcano in the world (10,023ft. above sea level). This testament to volcanic might is crowned by the **Haleakala crater,** which is not actually the result of an eruption, but rather the erosion of the mountain's slopes. The crater's surreal landscape of cinder cones and lava flows resembles the surface of the moon so much that NASA astronauts trained here for their lunar landing in the late 60s.

Haleakala National Park is open 24 hours; daily admission is $10 per car for a seven-day pass (though a late-night arrival may get you in free). The **Park Headquarters** (572-9306), about one mile from the guard booth, provides camping **permits,** displays on Haleakala wildlife, and wacky postcards (open daily 7:30am-4pm). **Haleakala Visitors Center,** near the summit, has a few exhibits on the region's geology, archaeology, and ecology, as well as a great view of the crater (open daily sunrise-3pm). The **Puuulaula** (Red Hill) **Summit Building** is where you'll end up if you forget a sweater or jacket (open 24hr.). Free natural history talks are given at 9:30, 10:30, and 11:30am. Other free events include three-hour guided hikes (meet at Hosmer Grove Shelter, Mon. and Thurs. at 9am), two-hour crater hikes (meet at Sliding Sands Trailhead, Tues. and Fri. at 10am), and summer star-gazing. (See **Camping**, p. 463, for info on **campgrounds** in Haleakala National Park.)

Sliding Sands Trailhead is located at the visitors center and steeply descends four miles to the bottom of the crater. If you can spare the time for an 11½ mi. hike, **Halemanu** (Birdhouse) **Trailhead** takes about seven hours and leads out of the crater. Park Headquarters can arrange a ride to the summit for visitors who leave their cars at the Halemanu parking lot. The Sliding Sands Trail connects with the trail to **Kaluuokaoo** (the plunge of the digging stick) **Pit,** the closest major cinder cone. Early Hawaiians buried the umbilical cords and placentas of their newborns in private shrines near this cinder cone to protect the spirit of the child. Lower elevations afford a chance to glimpse the rare **silversword** plant (which can only grow in red cinder soil) and Hawaiian *nene* geese.

Sunrise over Haleakala (House of the Sun) is a deservedly popular event that attracts hundreds to the chilly summit each morning. The best way to enjoy the dawn in solitude is by viewing it from the **Leleiwi overlook** before the summit. Those with flashlights can also head down the Sliding Sands Trail for about five minutes to get a view of the greater crater. Morning temperatures are generally in the low 40s; coffee and blankets are a very good idea, as is arriving at least half an hour before sunrise.

Farther south on Rte. 37 is the **Tedeschi Winery** (878-6058), which offers tiny but free tastes of their "Maui Blanc" pineapple wine (free tours every ½hr. 9:30am-2:30pm; open daily 9am-5pm). **Makawao**, on Rte. 365 off of Rte. 37, is a tiny town straight out of the Old West. New Age holistic shops are the only misplaced element among these dusty avenues, big-hatted *paniolos,* and Western storefronts.

ENTERTAINMENT

Despite all of its daytime activity, Maui reserves some energy for its nightlife. Most of the folks are found in the Lahainan-Kaanapali area, particularly around Front St., which buzzes with buzzed tourists and equally tanked locals. The groovier hotspots are Paia and Makawno. **Hamburger Mary's,** 2020 Main St. (244-7776), in Wailuku, attracts a **gay** clientele at night (open Wed.-Thurs. to midnight, Fri.-Sat. to 2am).

Tsunami, 3850 Wailea Alanui Dr. (875-1234), in Grand Wailea Hotel, Kihei. A tidal wave of locals and travelers flood the "hottest 10,000 square feet in town." Thurs. (Ladies' Night) and Wed. nights are free; cover Fri.-Sat. $5. Open Wed. 9pm-1am, Thurs.-Sat. 9pm-3am. Must be 21.

Moose McGillicuddy's, 844 Front St. (667-7758), Lahaina. Drafts ($1) and margaritas ($2) attract a young tourist crowd with beer goggles strapped on tight and libido revvin' like a barnyard beast. Happy Hour daily 3-6pm. Tues. and Thurs.-Sat. $3 cover with live band. Steeper cover ($5) on Wed., but cheaper cocktails ($1) all night. Absolut Monday with $2 drinks. Dancing nightly (except Wed.) 9:30pm.

World Cafe, 900 Front St. (661-1515), Lahaina. International beers bring the world to you at this boisterous bar and pool hall. Pool daily ($5 per hr., $10 per hr. after 9pm), live bands nightly, and more drink specials than you can remember (that's the point). Late night *poohana* (Happy Hour) with $2.25 beers, margaritas, and lava flows. Wed. and Fri.-Sat. nights the disco upstairs is opened for some heavy bootie-shaking with the local crowd. Cover $5. Open daily noon-2am. Must be 21.

Casanova's, 1188 Makawao Ave. (572-0220), Makawao. Beautiful people and Don Juans love this Upcountry hangout. Cover $5 for live bands (Thurs. and Fri.

HAWAII

nights benefit the Maui AIDS Foundation). Wed. disco is a fave with surfers. Special performances (e.g. Persian bellydancing) every 2 weeks. Cover $7-10. Open Mon.-Sat. until 1:30am.

SEASONAL EVENTS

O'Neill Invitational, first week in April, Hookipa Beach Park, Paia. International windsurfing tournament. Hostels and hotels are booked.

Seabury Hall Crafts Fair, mid-May, Makawao. Largest crafts fair on the island held at this pastorally picturesque school. Admission $4.

King Kamehameha Canoe Regatta, mid-June, Kahului Harbor. Free viewing from nearby beaches. The canoe season's inaugural event.

Makawao Parade and Rodeo (572-2076), early June, Makawao. *Paniolo*-style celebration of the 4th, complete with country music.

Quiksilver Cup (877-2111), mid-July, Kanaha Beach Park. Pro and amateur windsurfing competition.

Hi-Tech Pro Am, early Sept., Hookipa Beach Park, Paia. International windsurfing tournament. Speed competition at the Molokai Channel Crossing.

Maui County Fair (874-1000), War Memorial Complex, Wailuku. Local foods, entertainment, rides, and crafts.

Maui Grand Prix, mid-Oct., Hookipa Beach Park, Paia. No, not a car race, but a major surfing event. Surfers from 12 countries compete.

Aloha Classic (575-9151), late Oct., Hookipa Beach, Paia. One of the biggest windsurfing events at Hookipa and the final event of the pro World Tour.

Halloween (667-9175), Oct. 31. This is a big event in Lahaina. One of your few chances to dress like a clawed Hawaiian goose and get drunk in public.

The Run to the Sun, late Sept., a 36mi. jog from the beach to Haleakala's summit. Call the Valley Isle Road Runners (871-6441) for details.

Ice Cream Festival (244-5508), early Aug., War Memorial Complex, Wailuku. All-you-can-eat ice cream ($5) and games.

HAWAII

Hawaii (Big Island)

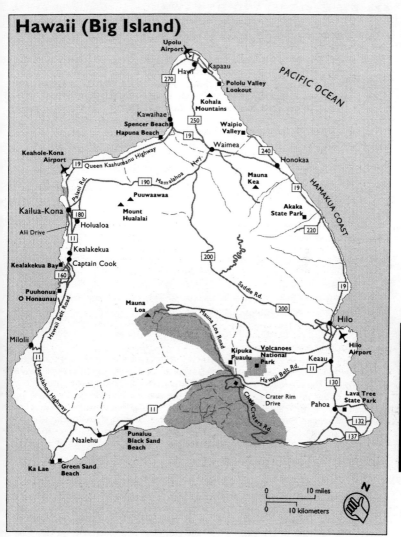

The Big Island of Hawaii

Tahitians, the first immigrants to the Hawaiian islands, named this vast isle *Hawaii* after the mythical homeland they sought to attain. Ever since, this island—called simply the "Big Island"—has attracted millions of beauty-seeking immigrants. The most notable of these immigrants has been Pele, the Polynesian goddess of the volcanoes, who chose it as her final residence after exploring all the volcanoes in the Pacific. According to legend, Pele generates the dry weather of the Kona (leeward) side, while her lover, Kamapuaa (an eight-eyed hog who can turn into a Romeo at will), is responsible for the drenching rains of the Hilo (windward) side. Their frequent meetings mix things up, creating the 14 climatic zones of the Big Island, including the desert-like Kohala Coast, the snow-covered peaks of Mauna Kea, the savannah of the South Coast, and the rainforests, valleys, and waterfalls of the Hamakua Coast.

Hawaii ain't called the Big Island fer nothin'. In fact, it is twice as large as all the other islands combined. Its dominant feature, the volcano Mauna Loa, is large enough (when measured from the sea floor) to contain the entirety of California's Sierra Nevada mountain range. Despite its large area, the island is home to only 130,000 residents—one-tenth of the state's population. This low population density results in long stretches of undisturbed wilderness rare on the other islands.

The volcanic forces which forged the island chain are still showcased on the Big Island. Kilauea and Mauna Loa are active volcanoes which pipe molten rock from the hotspot in the Pacific plate, miles below the southern coast. For a magical magma moment, trek down to Kilauea, which erupts about once a year. The volcano landscape is often only a few years (or even weeks) old, and provides an awe-inspiring glimpse into the power of Mama Earth.

ORIENTATION

You'll need a car to enjoy the countryside, but keep a careful eye on the fuel gauge, as distances between gas stations can be great. If you decide to rent a car in Kailua and drop it off in Hilo (or vice versa), ask about the drop-off charge—it can be steep (about $60). The Big Island has a rudimentary bus system, but don't count on it for access to sights. The trip from Hilo to Kailua-Kona via **Rte. 19** (called **Kamehameha Hwy.** in Hilo) takes just over two hours; via **Rte. 11** (called **Kanoelehua Hwy.** in Hilo, **Mamalohoa Hwy.** around the south tip of the island, and **Kuakini Hwy.** in Kona), just over three hours. Despite its deceivingly short appearance on a map, **Saddle Road** (also called **Rte. 200**) is no faster than Rte. 19. **Rte. 132** is called **Pahoa-Pohoiki Rd.** where it passes near Pahoa.

Hawaiian Airlines fly between the two city airports for three months of the year (one-way $25). Keep in mind that there is no public transportation from the airports to the towns. The coastal towns of **Hilo** and **Kailua-Kona,** on opposite sides of the island, are the main tourist gates. The rest of the island is considered "country" by residents. The northwest corner is the **Kohala Peninsula,** former sugar land and the northern border of the island's gigantic cattle range. The southern portion of the island is **Kau,** where the first Polynesian immigrants settled.

■ Hilo

After Honolulu, Hilo is the largest city in the state—yet it is devoid of high-rises and tourist crowds. Only 14 years ago, a Mauna Lea eruption came within 8 mi. of frying the city, but the locals here are still as laid-back as they come. Downtown is a walkable collection of five-and-dime stores, cheap restaurants, and a bi-weekly farmer's market. The outlying areas are residential and hide such unexpected delights as boiling waterfalls and winding caves. Hilo (pop. 33,000) is a good base from which to visit the island's main attractions: the rugged **Hamakua Coast** (½hr. north), the green **Waipio Valley** north of Hamakua, and **Volcanoes National Park** (¾hr. southwest). Hilo gets over 100 in. of rain per year, so it *will* rain; the important question you should ask is when.

PRACTICAL INFORMATION AND ORIENTATION

Visitor Information:
Big Island Visitor Bureau, 250 Keawe St. (961-5797), next to the hair salon. Convenient location and amiable help. Open Mon.-Fri. 8am-4:30pm.
Visitor Information Kiosk, 300 Kamehameha Ave. (935-4356), across the parking lot, is a good source for bus schedules, maps, brochures, and a self-guided walking tour of historic downtown Hilo. Hours vary.
Big Island Center for Independent Living, 400 Hualanai #16D (935-3777), assists visitors with disabilities. Open Mon.-Fri. 8am-4:30pm.

Wailoa Center, 200 Piopio St. (933-4360), next to the State Building. Extensive cultural info, maps, and displays. Open Mon.-Fri. 8am-4:30pm. **Local Attractions and Cultural Events Information** (935-4360), is also located in the building. Open Mon.-Tues. and Thurs.-Fri. 8am-4:30pm, Wed. noon-4:30pm, Sat. 9am-3pm.

Outdoors Information:

County Parks and Recreation Office, 25 Aupuni St., #210 (961-8311). From the Kamehameha Hwy. turn left onto Pauahi, pass Wailua Park, and turn left on Aupuni. County park info and permits ($1 per person per night). Open Mon.-Fri. 7:45am-4:30pm.

Department of Land and Natural Resources, 75 Aupuni St., #204 (974-6200), in the State Building. State park info. Free camping permits valid 5 days; cabin permits from $30. Permits available Mon.-Fri. 8am-noon; office open Mon.-Fri. 7:45am-4pm.

Volcanoes National Park Visitors Center (967-7311), 13mi. from Hilo on Rte. 11. Trail maps and free guided hikes. Call for eruption updates; after hours, try the 24hr. hotline (985-6000). Open daily 8am-5pm.

Division of Forestry and Wildlife, 1643 Kilauea Ave. (974-4221). Info on hunting, fishing, hiking, and forest regulations. Open Mon.-Fri. 7:45am-4:30pm.

Airport: Hilo Airport (934-5801), 3 mi. from downtown. Serves inter-island and mainland flights. Visitor info booths have maps and coupon booklets. No public transportation.

Public Transportation: Hele-on-Bus, 630 E. Lanikaula St. (961-8744), offers bus schedules and tickets. Office open Mon.-Fri. 7:45am-4:30pm. Bus operates Mon.-Sat. between Kona and Hilo once per day (fare $5.45). Makes stops in Kau, Waimea, and Honokaa (Mon.-Fri. only; fare $1-5). Travelers with disabilities can get door-to-door service: call one day in advance (961-8777 in Hilo; 323-2085 in Kona). Vintage 1940s **Sampans** (959-7864) operate in cheesy style around Hilo Mon.-Fri. 9am-5pm. Fare $2 one-way, $7 all day. Nine stops include some hotels.

Taxis: Ace Taxi (935-8303). Airport to downtown $9. Open 24hr.

Car Rental: National and state chains are located at Hilo airport. Make reservations several days in advance or take advantage of fly/drive deals for cheaper rates. Rental cars are not permitted on Saddle Rd. (Rte. 200). **Budget** (800-527-0707), rents economy cars for $40 per day. **Harper,** 1690 Kamehameha Ave. (969-1478), offers fluctuating rates of $35-60 per day. Drivers must be 25 with a major credit card. Open Mon.-Thurs. 6:30am-5pm, Fri.-Sun. 6:30am-6pm.

Equipment Rental: Nautilus Dive Center, 382 Kamehameha Ave. (935-6939). Snorkel set $5 per day. Beginner ($65) and certified ($55) dive charters. Certification $125. Open Mon.-Sat. 8:30am-5pm.

Bookstore: Basically Books, 46 Waianuenue Ave. (961-0144), has maps and Hawaii-specific titles and collectibles. Open Mon.-Fri. 9am-5pm, Sat. 10am-4pm.

Library: Hilo Public Library, 300 Waianuenue Ave. (933-4650). Open Mon.-Tues. 10am-5pm, Wed.-Thurs. 9am-8pm, Fri.-Sat. 9am-5pm.

Laundromat: Tyke's, 1454 Kilauea Ave. Open daily 6am-10pm.

Weather Conditions: Hilo (935-8555) or whole island (961-5582).

Crisis Line: (969-9111).

Medical Services: Hilo Medical Center, 1190 Waianuenue St. (974-4700), by Rainbow Falls. Emergency service 24hr.

Emergency: 911.

Police: (961-2211).

Post Office: Convenient downtown location at 154 Waianuenue Ave. (933-7095). Open Mon.-Fri. 8am-4pm, Sat. noon-4pm. **ZIP Code:** 96721. Other location on Kekuanaou St. (935-6685), by the airport. Open Mon.-Thurs. 8:15am-5pm, Fri. 8:15am-5:30pm, Sat. 8:30am-12:30pm. **ZIP Code:** 96720.

Area Code: 808.

Hilo rests at the mouth of the Wailuku River. In the city, **Rte. 19** is called **Kamehameha Hwy.** and **Rte. 11** is called **Kanoelehua Hwy.**

ACCOMMODATIONS AND CAMPING

Hilo's lack of tourists is a two-edged sword: sights and attractions are uncrowded but budget accommodations are hard to find. Hilo makes a good base for exploring Volcanoes National Park or the Hamakua Coast. Campers should frequent rain.

Arnott's Lodge, 98 Apapane Rd. (969-7097; fax 961-9638), near Onekahakaha Beach Park in Keokea. Off Keokea Loop Dr. from the Kalanianaole Ave. Exit off Rte. 19 or 11. One of the state's best hostels. Uncrowded dorm rooms have their own kitchens. Deck, laundry, TV/VCR, BBQ grills, and nearby lava-rock beach. Daytrips available ($35, non-guests $40-75). Check-in 8am-noon and 4-10pm. Free airport pickup and drop off. Tents $9; dorms $17; singles $31; doubles $42.

Wild Ginger Inn, 100 Puueo St. (800-882-1887 or 800-935-5556), over the Keawe-Wailuku Bridge. Hammock, tropical garden, and wicker chairs encourage heavy relaxation. Small non-smoking rooms come with fridges and breakfast. Reception open 9am-9pm. Singles $39; doubles $44; deluxe rooms with cable TV $59.

Hale Lamalani, 27-703A Kaieie Rd. (964-5401), in Papaikoi. Heading north on Rte. 19 from Hilo, go left onto Kaieie Rd. near the 7mi. marker and continue for 1½mi. before turning left at the green barn and stopping at the last house on the right. Scenic country-house B&B and hostel offers kitchen use and breakfast on the garden-side *lanai*. Hostel-style singles $21, 3 or more nights $18 per night; doubles $28-31. B&B singles $40-45; doubles $50-55.

Kolekole Beach County Park, 12mi. north of Hilo, is the only legal camping site near the city. Pavilions and restrooms, but no showers or drinking water. Permit required (for more info on permits, see **Practical Information,** p. 474).

FOOD

Downtown Hilo is loaded with small, inexpensive ethnic restaurants that have excellent lunch plates and sushi counters. The only downtown supermarket is **KTA,** 321 Keawe St. (935-3751; open Mon.-Sat. 7am-9pm, Sun. 7am-6pm). A 24-hour **Safeway,** located behind Prince Kuhio Plaza on Kanoelehua Hwy., has a better selection and more palatable prices. A **farmer's market** is held in front of the bus stop at Mamo and Kamehameha (Wed. and Sat. sunrise- 3pm).

Cafe 100, 969 Kilauea Ave. (935-8683), offers delicious, cheap, and simple cuisine. The Loco Moco (hamburger patties on rice topped with egg) is a Hilo tradition ($1.75). Most sandwiches under $3, beverages under $1. Open Mon.-Thurs. 6:45am-8:30pm, Fri.-Sat. 6:45am-9:30pm.

Dotty's, 2100 Kanoelehua Ave. (959-6477), in the Puainako Town Center. Great bargains for sit-down service. Steak combo dinners $8.25, chicken $7. Open Mon.-Sat. 7am-2pm and 5-8pm, Sun. 7am-11am.

Broke the Mouth, 55 Mamo St. (934-7670), across from the farmer's market. When the locals say, "Ho! Broke da mouth!" it means something is good—and this sure is. Organic food made with farm-fresh ingredients. The *Bomboola* ($5.50) is a lunch as big as it sounds. *Manapua* (75¢ stuffed rolls) include your choice of *kulolo, taro* (potato salad), coconut, or banana filling. Open Tues. and Thurs.-Fri. 9am-2pm, Wed. and Sat. 7am-2pm.

Bears' Coffee, 106 Keawe St. (935-0708), downtown. Friendly waitstaff serves excellent sandwiches ($4-5) and enormous Belgian waffles ($3.35) to the soft sounds of Billie Holliday. Good coffee selection. Covered outdoor patio. Open Mon.-Thurs. 6:30am-5pm, Fri.-Sat. 6:30am-10:30pm.

Ken's Pancake House, 1730 Kamehameha Ave. (935-8711). A Hawaiian house of pancakes complete with orange vinyl. Ken dishes out breakfast all day, as well as burgers and sandwiches ($3.50-5). Macadamia nut, coconut, or fresh banana pancakes $4.85. Variety of syrups (coconut and passion fruit). Open 24hr.

Suisan's Retail Fish Market (935-9349), Lihiwai Ave. at Banyan, lets you look your dinner in the eye before eating it. A good place to get those hard-to-find ingredients like octopus tentacle; the daily fish auction is worth an early morning (7:45am) visit. Open Mon.-Sat. 8am-3:45pm.

SIGHTS AND ACTIVITIES

The pace in Hilo is slower than that in Kona (see p. 473), and visitors will be hard-pressed for entertainment. One of the few nightclubs in town is **Shooters,** 121 Banyan Dr. (969-7069). The blue neon sign welcomes a mellow twenty-something crowd to dance and shoot darts. (Open daily 11am-2am. Cover Fri.-Sat. $5-8. Must be 21.) Next door is **Breakwater,** 97 Banyan Dr. (969-3333), in the Naniloa Hotel. Where else can you find a wheel of fortune at a disco? (Open Fri.-Sat. 10pm-2am. Cover $5. Must be 21. Collars required, and no open-toed shoes allowed.)

While Hilo's heavy rainfall means you'll probably get wet, it also results in amazing tropical splendor. The lush mountainsides around Hilo are draped in a tangle of greenery and the city's roads are framed by blossoming hedges and world-famous orchids. The elaborate **Liliuokalani Garden** is constructed Japanese-style, and is linked by a little footbridge to palm-covered **Coconut Island,** which gives a great view of Mauna Kea on clear days.

Hilo is the **orchid capital of the world,** where enough botanical gardens and nurseries have sprung up to supply every senior prom in the U.S. Many nurseries charge a tour fee or request donations, so the cheapest option is to view the spectacular front-yard flora along beautiful residential streets or the 4 mi. Pepeekeo Dr. off Rte. 19 north of Hilo.

The best sights in Hilo lie on the outskirts of town. **Rainbow Falls** is worth an early wake-up call—at sunrise, rainbows appear everywhere in the mist of the falls. To get there, take Waianuenue Ave. inland, head right at the fork in the road, and watch for the sign. The pools above Rainbow Falls are the **Boiling Pots,** where bowl-shaped depressions "boil" with high tide (no swimming). If you've ever wanted to go underground, the **Kaumana Caves,** on Rte. 200 up Waianuenue, is the place to do it. These fascinating lava tubes require a flashlight for exploration, but the undulating interiors are worth the trouble of obtaining the requisite equipment.

The **Panaewa Zoo Rainforest** (959-7224), south of Hilo on Rte. 11, in the Panaewa Forest Reserve halfway to Volcanoes National Park, is a small but entertaining zoo with a wide variety of inhabitants including a pygmy hippo, tropical birds, and performing tigers. (Open Mon.-Fri. 9am-4pm, Sat. 11am-2pm. Feedings at 9:15am and 3pm. Free.) The **Mauna Loa Macadamia Nut Visitors Center** (966-8618), is another 1½ mi. south on Rte. 11. A left turn will take you through an immense macadamia grove posted with nutty trivia. Visitors can watch macadamia brittle being made or peruse the massive array of products crafted from the mac daddy of nuts (open daily 8:30am-5pm; free tours every hr. 10am-4pm).

Historic Hilo is quaint but dull. The walking tour pamphlets distributed at the visitors center lead past older Hilo buildings, now either empty or occupied by shops. The **Lyman House Museum,** 276 Haili St. (935-5021), has two separate buildings. One contains exhibits detailing the island's ethnic heritage, geology, and native wildlife, and the other is a restored mission house offering a guided tour. (Both buildings open Mon.-Sat. 9am-5pm, Sun. 1-4pm. Tours on the ½hr. in the morning, on hr. in afternoon. Admission $4.50, children and seniors $2.50.)

■ Southeast of Hilo

Between Hilo and Volcanoes National Park lies the **Puna** district, an area of rugged coast, small towns, and black sand beaches. The red road passes under *lauhala* trees (the ones with the teepee roots), through lava fields, and along coastal tidepools. To get to the laid-back town of **Pahoa,** which has the highest concentration of hippies in the state, take Rte. 11 south from Hilo to Rte. 130. The **Bamboo House** (965-8322), an attractive two-room unit, is in the middle of this flower power. Rooms come with bathroom, cable TV, and fridge (singles $45, 3 or more nights $35 per night; doubles $50). Inquire about rooms at **Pahoa Natural Health Food Store,** on Main St. across from the Bank of Hawaii (open Mon.-Sat. 9am-9pm, Sun. 9am-6pm). South of Pahoa on Rte. 132 is **Lava Tree State Park,** featuring eerie lava casts of trees petrified since the 1790 eruption. Continuing around the loop on Rte.

132 will take visitors past the **Kapoho Lighthouse** and its gardens, the only remnants of Kapoho Village after a 1960 lava flow. One mile north of **Isaac Hale Beach Park** is the huge lava-lined pool heated by volcanic steam at **Pualaa Thermal Springs Park.** Along the coast, **Kehena Beach,** accessible via a trail from Rte. 137, is a small black sand beach popular with dolphins and nudists. A gate marks the spot where lava flows have ended Rte. 137. In 1990, the entire town of Kalapana was buried by Pele's wrath, but, miraculously, the tour bus parking lot was spared. Visitors can trek over the lava field to view the remains of **Kaimu Beach.** Kaimu used to be the most famous black sand beach in the state, but it'll be 100,000 years or so before it again claims this distinction.

■ Hawaii Volcanoes National Park

Resting above the geological hot spot that fashioned each of the Hawaiian islands in turn, the two mountains in Volcanoes National Park continue to erupt and change, adding acres of new land each year. **Kilauea Caldera,** with its steaming vents, sulfur fumes, and periodic eruptions, is the park's star, though the less active **Mauna Loa** and its dormant northern neighbor, **Mauna Kea,** are in some respects more amazing. Each towers nearly 14,000 ft. above sea level and plummets some 16,000 ft. to the ocean floor. Mauna Loa is the **largest volcano in the world,** while Mauna Kea, when measured from its ocean floor base, is the **tallest mountain on earth** (33,000ft.+). The **park entrance fee** is $10 per car, valid for seven days.

ACCOMMODATIONS AND CAMPING

Holo Holo In, 19-4036 Kalani-Honua Rd. (967-7950; fax 967-8025), Volcano Village. From Hilo, take Rte. 11 almost to the national park, turn right at Haunani Rd. in Volcano Village, then left on Kalani-Honua. This uncrowded home-hostel is a quiet delight in a perfect locale, just 2mi. from the visitors center. Large, wood-floored rooms come with blankets and slippers for the cool nights. Dorms $17. Call after 4:30pm. Reservations recommended.

My Island Volcano Inn, 17-3896 Old Volcano Rd. (967-7216; email myisland@ilhawaii.net), Volcano Village. Beautiful rooms in a historic mission-style home amid 5 acres of flower gardens. All-you-can-eat breakfast served daily 7-8:30am. Check out the square redwood tub. Singles $40, with bath $50; doubles $65, $70. The owners rent other apartments and houses on the island. Call or write P.O. Box 100, Volcano 96785 for additional info. No credit cards.

Al's Volcano Ranch Guesthouse and Hostel, 13-3775 Kalapana Hwy. (965-8800), 3mi. south of Pahoa on Rte. 130. Gay and lesbian friendly. Clothing optional. Overlooking a field of sheep, the ranch also has a sauna built over a steam vent. Trailer bunks $20 each; luxurious doubles $50-70.

Volcano House (967-7321), P.O. Box 53, Hawaii Volcanoes National Park 96718. The opportunity to eat and sleep on the rim of an active volcano is expensive. Rooms without a crater view start at $79. The hotel also runs the Namakani Paio cabins, located 3mi. behind the Volcano House in an *ohia* forest. Check-in 3pm, at the Volcano House. Picnic tables and outdoor grills. Rooms $32, each additional person $6. Linens and blankets provided. Key deposit $15.

Volcanoes National Park (967-7311). Excellent campsites at **Kipuka Nene** and **Namakani Paio** (near Kilauea Crater). No registration required. Free. Other well-maintained campsites at **Kamoamoa** and **Napau Crater** can be reached by easy hikes. Campers must register at the visitors center by 4:30pm. All sites free. 7-night max. stay. Two patrol cabins on the Mauna Loa Summit Trail may be used for free by hikers en route to the summit. One is at **Red Hill,** bordering Puuulaula Caldera, 7½mi. from the end of Mauna Loa Strip Rd. (10,000ft.). The other is 9½mi. farther, at **Mauna Loa Summit,** next to Mokuaweoweo Caldera (13,250ft.). Bunks, mattresses, and blankets sometimes provided; bring your own sleeping bag, stove, and fuel. The ascent takes 3 days. No reservations necessary, but hikers should register at the Kilauea Visitors Center (see below).

Mauna Kea State Park, off Rte. 200 on the slopes of Mauna Kea (off-limits to rental cars). Views of both Mauna Kea and Mauna Loa. Permit is required for 7 available cabins. Prices start at $45 for 4 people. Camping *officially* prohibited. Cool nights at high elevations (6500ft.).

FOOD

Since the best time to view the lava is after dark, you may want to pack a dinner and spend the late hours in the park. The **Kilauea General Store** (967-7555), on Old Volcano Rd. in Volcano Village, sells groceries, homemade banana bread, and sandwiches ($3.50; open Mon.-Sat. 7am-7:30pm, Sun. 7am-7pm; no credit cards). The island's best-kept secret sustenance source is the cafeteria at the **Kilauea Military Camp** (967-8356), on Crater Rim Dr. behind the main lobby. The KMC likes to keep its officers healthy; nutritious but delicious dinner buffets $8.50, under 11 $5.50. Wednesdays and Fridays are Western and Luau nights, respectively, when dinner comes with a free show (admission $10.95, children $5.50; dinner served nightly 5:30-8pm). The **Volcano Winery** (967-7479), at the end of Volcano Golf Course Rd. (Piiamauna Rd.), is worth a trip (and a sip) if only to taste wine from the southernmost winery in the U.S. Exotic wines are made from passion fruit, yellow guava, and honey ($8-11 per bottle; free tasting; open daily 10am-5pm).

SIGHTS

Since volcanic activity is so unpredictable, the sights of the park are constantly changing. Don't come expecting to take photos of dramatically surging lava; eruptions are infrequent. The **Puu Oo spatter cone** has been for the past 15 years the only consistent source of flowing lava in the park. Rangers try to monitor visitor activity for safety, but there are no rangers in the park after dark, so use your head. Be wary not only of the 2192°F lava (the hottest possible temperature of lava), but also of more subtle dangers such as unstable new lava beds, sulfur fumes, and the steam plume by the ocean, which contains ingredients like hydrochloric acid and gaseous glass.

Over 70 million years of volcanic activity deserve more than a moment's glance. Tourists usually spend just a day, hoping to witness an eruption in action, but they miss out on the park's many other worthwhile sights. Over 150 trails criss-cross the lava flows. Ranging in length from 0.3 to 11.6 mi., these trails have spectacular panoramas and few travelers. The **Kilauea Visitors Center,** just inside the park gates (967-7311), is a good first stop. There are exhibits and films on the geology, history, and mythology of the area as well as several excellent ranger-led walks (check the bulletin board; notices posted by 9am). A free movie detailing eruptions shows daily

The Pele's the Thing

The volcano area is the home of Pele, the powerful Hawaiian volcano goddess. Cognizance of superstitions will keep you safe from vexing evil omens and such.

1) When driving, if you see an old woman by the side of the road, pick her up; it may be Pele. (*Let's Go* does not recommend hitchhiking.)
2) If there is a black dog by the side of the road, do not ignore it; superstitious Hawaiians carry a raw piece of meat with them in the car to feed the dog if they see it. Failure to comply results in nausea, illness, and a slow death.
3) If you notice there is an old woman in the back of your car, ignore her; this is just Pele. She is benign if left alone.
4) Avoid Saddle Rd.; many Hawaiians believe it is haunted.
5) Offerings to Pele in the volcanoes (and at trailheads) include *leis,* fruit or sweets, rocks wrapped in *ti* leaves, and the occasional virgin. You will see stacks of rocks a few feet high dotting the strange landscape of the lava flows.
6) If you truly want to appease Pele, take a bottle of gin with you and pour it into one of the lava lakes; Pele will then smile on your adventure.

on the hour (9am-4pm). You can also get the latest reports on the park's ever-changing volcanic activity (open daily 7:45am-5pm). Arnott's Lodge (see **Accommodations,** p. 476) has excellent weekly trips to the park for both guests and non-guests.

When exploring, you will notice that drops and strands of lava often bear names such as "Pele's Tears" and "Pele's Hair." Heed the rangers' advice, however, and leave these excretions with Pele lest she bring you bad luck. Many tourists spirit them away, only to regret the thievery and mail the rocks back. The park keeps a collection of these returned fragments, along with the apologetic letters accompanying them, in the lobby of the Kilauea Military Camp (open daily 7:30am-6pm).

Hiking, Driving, and Flying

The 11 mi. scenic drive around the Kilauea Caldera on **Crater Rim Drive** is a good way to see the volcano by car. The road is accessible via Rte. 11 from the east and west. Well-marked trails and lookouts dot the way. The best view of **Puu Oo** is from the **Napau Crater,** a 7 mi. hike from the **Chain of Craters Rd.** A more convenient and accessible glimpse can be had from **Puu Huluhulu,** an easy 3 mi. hike from the same road. The vista-filled **Crater Rim Trail** is an easy hike, traversing *ohia* and giant fern forests, and *aa* (rough) and *pahoehoe* (smooth) lava flows covering a wide spectrum of volcanic phenomena, from sulphur vents and steam clouds to cinder cones, lava beds, and dormant craters. The five-minute hike to the dormant **Halemaumau Crater** leads to Pele's official residence. A complete caldera circumnavigation is 11.6 mi. The **Thurston Lava Tube** (0.3mi., 15min. hike) was formed by lava that cooled around a hot core, which then continued to move, leaving the inside hollow. The prehistoric tunnel is guarded by immense ferns, in a landscape that brings to mind *Jurassic Park*. **Devastation Trail** is a one-mile trip though landscape blasted out of Dalí's imagination. The cinder cones and dead *ohia* trees were scorched by Kilauea Iki ("little Kilauea," west of "big" Kilauea Crater) in 1959.

The 4 mi. **Kilauea Iki Trail** is Hawaii's version of the Yellow Brick Road—the Black Lava Path, starting at the Kilauea Iki overlook on Crater Rim Rd. This excellent two-hour hike is an absolute must for those who want to explore the park in more detail; it's also the one the visitors center recommends most. It leads around the north rim of Kilauea Iki, through a forest of tree ferns, down the wall of the little crater, past the vent of the 1959 eruption, over steaming lava, and back to Crater Rim Rd. On the way are several *ohelo* bushes laden with red berries; legend has it that you must offer some berries to Pele before eating any, or you'll incur her wrath. The trail through the crater can be difficult to discern, especially if it's raining, so keep an eye out for the stone pilings guiding the path. **Jaggar Museum** (967-7643), explains the myth, mechanics, and measurement of the volcanoes and their outbursts. Other displays focus on Hawaiian legends (open daily 8:30am-5pm; free). The 3½ mi. **Mauna Iki Trail** begins 9 mi. southwest of park headquarters on Rte. 11 and passes footprints left in the ash in 1790 by a passing army of Kamehameha the Great. From here the coastal area is accessible by hike.

Kipuka Puaulu (Bird Park), north off Mauna Loa Rd., is a patch of green land that eons of lava flows have miraculously missed. An easy one-mile loop trail leads through Kipuka Puaulu from the parking lot. Keep an eye out for native Hawaiian birds such as the bright red *apapane.*

The best views of any flows, without a doubt, is from the air. **Island Hoppers** (969-2000; http://planet_hawaii.com/above), flies four-person planes at speeds slow enough to allow a good view. Not only do they have a 100% safety record, they will also match any published competitive price (¾hr. flights from $69).

Mauna Kea

Moving from the terrestrial to the celestial, **Mauna Kea,** to the north, has long served as an international center for visual astronomy. Meaning "White Mountain," Mauna Kea is home to Pele's archrival Poliahu, goddess of snow and ice. The **Keck Observatory** houses the world's largest mirror telescope, attracting many a vain scientist (open daily 10am-4:30pm). A short walk from the side of the road near the summit to **Lake Waiwai** brings you to one of the highest bodies of water in the world. A winding drive, navigable by 4WD only, leads to the summit from Rte. 200. Due to the sensitivity of the observatory, cars are prohibited from going up in the night without a special red headlight filter. The terrain is stark, the views unearthly, and the high elevation (13,796 ft., 40% above the earth's atmosphere) may cause queasiness. Arnott's Lodge (see **Accommodations,** p. 476) offers a great daytrip to this otherwise difficult-to-access locale (if you make the trip, bring lots of water and aspirin). **Onizuka Visitor Information Station** (961-2180), at 9300 ft., is accessible to those without 4WD. During the day, the visitors station offers informative talks and a film, and at night the public can stargaze through the telescopes on site (open Thurs. 5:30-10pm, Fri. 9am-noon, 1-4:30pm, and 6:30-10pm, Sat.-Sun. 9am-noon, 1-2pm, and 6:30-10pm).

■ Kau and South Kona

The Hawaii Belt Rd. (Rte. 11) curves around the southern coast of the island between Volcanoes National Park and Kona, passing sandy beaches, desolate fields, and the southernmost point in the U.S. along the way. The journey offers a glimpse of a rural Hawaii that most visitors never see. Swimmers and campers will love the **Punaluu Black Sand Beach,** about 20 mi. from Volcanoes. A county park, windy Punaluu has wheelchair-accessible bathrooms, pavilions, outdoor showers, fire pits, public phones, and an unsurpassed view of the rising sun. It's a favorite haunt of frisky **Hawksbill turtles,** and you're likely to see one either cruising in the shallows or pulled up for some sun on the beach. Consumption of these creatures makes for big trouble with protective authorities.

Naalehu, 7 mi. past Punaluu, is the halfway point between Hilo and Kona and the southernmost town in the U.S. Don't blink—you might miss it. For a lunch stop, head to the **Kaalaiki Lunch Shop** (929-7147), at the booth behind home plate at the baseball field, where the specialty fish plates ($7.50) are huge (open daily 6am-5pm). The charming burg of **Waiohinu,** 58 mi. southeast of Kailua-Kona, houses the southernmost hotel in the U.S., **Shirikawa's Motel,** 95-6040 Kuakini Hwy. (929-7462). Its clean rooms have private baths (singles $30; doubles $35).

From Waiohinu, it's a 12 mi. drive down a rough, one-lane road to **Ka Lae,** or **South Point** (off-limits to most rental cars), where windswept fields and massive windmills mark the landscape. Follow the road to the left to reach the seasonal seaside cliffs rising out of water as blue as a swimming pool. Some bold folks have taken thrilling leaps off the 50 ft. cliffs, but Let's Go never recommends cliff-diving. Farther down the coast is a 2½ mi. trail to **Green Sands,** where a cinder cone has partially washed away to carve out a spectacular natural green beach. Back on the Hawaii Belt Rd. towards Kona, drivers can take a brief detour to the camping-friendly county park in **Milolii,** a traditional fishing village (i.e. no electricity).

The **Puuhonua O Honaunau,** often referred to as the "Place of Refuge" is a must-see (take Rte. 160 off Rte. 11). About 25 mi. south of Kailua-Kona, it served as a sanctuary for ancient Hawaiians fleeing battle or escaping punishment for breaking the *kapu* (the sacred laws that ruled Hawaiian life). Having reached the *puuhonua* and received absolution at the hands of the *kahuna pule* (priest), the ritually purified offender could safely resume life at home. King Kamehameha II destroyed all other such sanctuaries when he abolished the *kapu* in 1819, but saved this one because it contained the bones of his ancestors. Maps are available at the **visitors center** (328-2288; open daily 7:30am-5:30pm; free orientation talks 10am-3:30pm). Picnicking and sunbathing are forbidden, and swimming in solemn Keoneeleele Cove is highly inappropriate—despite the hordes of tourists, this unique site maintains a sense of sanctity that other attractions have lost. The area is particularly striking around sunset, when the crowds fade and the sun sinks behind the grimacing idols. A picnic area nearby has restrooms, tidepools, BBQ pits, coconut trees, and coastal trails (open Mon.-Thurs. sunrise-8pm, Fri.-Sun. sunrise-11pm; $2 park entrance fee).

HAWAII

> ### The Strange Death of Captain Cook
> A few miles north of Puuhonua O Honaunau is **Kealakekua Bay,** a marine reserve with superb snorkeling. From Rte. 11 turn onto Napoopoo Dr.; this winding road leads to the historic bay (about 15min.) and the town of Captain Cook. In 1779, Captain Cook anchored in this bay to restock his ship and was wined and dined by the Hawaiians. Though the prevailing myth is that Cook was mistaken for a god, the captain was probably treated so hospitably because he arrived during a a time of political tension between the islands of Hawaii and Maui, and the Big Island's leaders were probably trying to secure Cook as an ally. Relations turned less than peachy a month later, when a storm forced Cook to return to the island. During a skirmish over the alleged theft of a cutter, Cook was fatally stabbed. A white monument marks the site of his death. Rumors about the treatment of Cook's body live on. Was part of the body eaten? Stories of emasculation and bizarre rituals are unsubstantiated, but the corpse *was* cremated and some bones preserved as prescribed by Polynesian rites.

A detour on the road to Puuhonua O Honaunau worth investigating is **St. Benedict's Catholic Church.** This small Gothic building has been dubbed "Painted Church" because of the murals and frescoes on its side panels and ceiling. Built by a Belgian priest, the 19th-century church was painted to look like the Cathedral of Burgos in Spain (open daily sunrise-sunset).

■ Kailua-Kona

The Big Island's sun floods the white sand beaches of this resort center, and a phalanx of hotels marches along the sea. Kona's dry and hot leeward coastline is backed by mountains which amount to a hill of beans—coffee grows on the volcanic slopes above and produce world-renowned gourmet java. Kailua-Kona is the island's tourist center, but remains more relaxed than the outposts of Waikiki and Lahaina. The oceanfront boulevard Alii Dr. is home to a wide collection of restaurants, shops, and historic sites. To the south of Kailua, Puuhonua O Honaunau National Historical Park and Kealakekua Bay are worth a visit. To the north are graceful stretches of sand such as Hapuna Beach.

PRACTICAL INFORMATION AND ORIENTATION

Visitor Information: Hawaii Visitors Bureau, 75-5719 W. Alii Dr. (329-7787), across from the Kona Inn Shopping Center. Bus schedules, maps, and accommodations info. Open Mon.-Fri. 8am-noon and 1-4pm. **Department of Parks and Recreation** (327-3560), by the police station on Alii Dr. in Hale Halawai Park. Info on county parks, camping, and permits ($1). Open Mon.-Fri. 7:45am-noon and 1-4:30pm. See also **Hilo Practical Information,** p. 474.

Budget Travel: Regal Travel, 75-5751 Kanoelehua Hwy., #103 (329-0536), next to 7-11. Inter-island flight coupons: Mahalo $34; Hawaiian $44; Aloha $42. Open Mon.-Fri. 8:30am-5pm.

Public Transportation: Hele-on-Bus (961-8744). Traverses the west coast Mon.-Sat. once a day. Leaves for Hilo 6:45am from Waldenbooks in Lanihau Center. Arrives 9:45am in Old Hilo Town ($5.45). **Alii Shuttle** (775-7121) travels Alii Dr. from the Kona Surf to the Lanihau Center 8:30am-10pm. Each way $2, all day $5.

Taxis: Sprint Taxi (329-6974). To Kailua-Kona from Keahole Airport $15.

Car Rental: Major car rentals at Kona airport.

Bike and Moped Rental: All moped rentals require valid driver's license. **DJ's,** 75-5663A Palani Rd. (329-1700), across from King Kamehameha Hotel. Mopeds $8 per hr., $30 for 24hr. $250 cash or credit card deposit. Open daily 7:30am-6pm. **Hawaiian Pedals** (329-2294), Kona Inn Shopping Village. Mountain bikes $20 per day, $70 per week. Open daily 9am-6pm.

Equipment Rental: Snorkel Bob's, 75-5831 Kahakai Rd. (329-0770), off Alii Dr. Friendly service and free snorkel map with rental. Snorkel set $2.50 per day, $14 per week. Boogieboards $6.50 for 24hr. Open daily 8am-5pm.

Library: Kailua-Kona, 75-138 Hualalai Rd. (327-4327). Open Tues. 10am-8pm, Wed.-Thurs. 9am-6pm, Fri. 11am-5pm, Sat. 9am-5pm.

Laundromat: Hele Mai, 75-5629 Kuakini Hwy. (329-3494), at the Palani intersection. Wash $1, 10min. dry 25¢. Open daily 6am-10pm.

Medical Services: Kona-Kohala Medical Associates, 75-137 Hualalai Rd. (329-1346). Open Mon.-Fri. 8:30am-5pm, Sat.-Sun. 8:30am-noon. All medical insurance accepted. **Kona Hospital** (322-9311), off Rte. 11 south of Kailua-Kona. Follow well-marked signs on road. Emergency room open 24hr.

Emergency: 911.

Police: 74-5221 Kaahumanu Hwy. (326-4646).

Post Office: 74-5577 Palani Rd. (329-1927), behind First Hawaiian Bank in Lanihau Center. Open Mon.-Fri. 8:30am-4:30pm, Sat. 9:30am-1:30pm. **ZIP Code**: 96745.

Area Code: 808.

Kailua-Kona is served by **Keahole Airport,** 9 mi. north of town. The city is split by two streets running parallel to the ocean: Alii Dr. nearest the ocean, and Kuakini Hwy. (Rte. 11) one block *mauka* (inland). Kealakekua Bay and the town of Captain Cook are 9 mi. south on Rte. 11 (Mamalahoa Hwy.).

ACCOMMODATIONS

Kailua-Kona has more rooms than anywhere else on the island, but most are of the pricey resort variety. Most budget accommodations are some distance from the beach. In general, Kailua-Kona is great for the Kohala Coast beach cruisers, but it makes more sense for the volcano-bound traveler to stay in Hilo.

Manago Hotel (323-2642), on Kuakini Hwy. between mi. markers 109 and 110 in Captain Cook. This hotel offers a taste of the past, from the long-time owners and the classic sign out front to the well-worn interior. Generally older clientele fits the ambiance. Office open 5am-7:30pm. Musty and noisy singles $23; doubles $26. Spacious and elegant rooms with bath from $36; doubles $39.

Teshima's Inn, 79-7251 Kuakini Hwy. (322-9140), behind Teshima's Restaurant 2 blocks south of the Rte. 180 junction in Kealakekua. Small rooms have new beds and shiny bathrooms. Reception (in the restaurant) open daily 6:30am-2pm and 5-9:30pm. Singles $20. Reservations recommended.

Kona Hotel, 76-5908 Kuakini Hwy. (324-1155), at Rte. 180 in Holualoa between mi. markers 4 and 5. Small but clean rooms show their age (70 years). Communal bathroom. Bedroom doors do not lock. Reception open 8am-9pm. Singles $20; doubles $26-30. No credit cards.

Patey's Place, 75-195 Ala Ona Ona St. (326-7018), in Kailua-Kona off Kuakini Hwy. A fun and happy crowd gathers in this conveniently located hostel decorated with sea life murals. Newly renovated exterior, but rooms retain a much older feel. Island excursions ($40-55) and free use of snorkeling equipment. Airport shuttle $5. Reception open 8am-10pm. Dorms $18; singles $32; doubles $42.

Hale Maluhia (House of Peace) Inn, 76-770 Hualalai Rd. (329-5773 or 800-559-6627), ¼mi. west of the Rte. 11 junction. Nestled among banyan trees, this delightful inn offers buffet breakfast, library, game room, pool table, and a jacuzzi overlooking a Japanese garden and waterfall. Doubles start at $75; 10% discount on 3-6 night stays, 15% for 7 or more nights. Reserve early.

FOOD

Kailua-Kona's restaurants tend toward the touristy, but local favorites do exist. **Sack 'n' Save** (326-2729), in Lanihau Center, has a bakery, deli, and large selection of value-priced groceries (open daily 5am-midnight). **Kona Healthways,** 74-5588 Palani Rd. (329-2296), in the Kona Coast Shopping Center, sells health foods, vitamins, and sprout-filled sandwiches (open Mon.-Sat. 9am-8pm, Sun. 9am-7pm).

HAWAII

484 ■ THE BIG ISLAND OF HAWAII

Kona coffee is available at the **Royal Aloha Coffee Mill,** 160 Napoopoo Rd. (328-9852), in Napoopoo. Informative displays describe the history and mechanics of Kona coffee making (open daily 9am-6pm). For a special roast (such as espresso), swagger down to the **Bad Ass Coffee Company,** 75-5699D Alii Dr., on Rte. 11 in Keauhou—but prepare to pay more for its bad-assedness. The donkey-decorated bathrooms are a must-see (for more bad-assed coffee, see the Bad Ass Coffee Plant, p. 487). Check the *Coffee Times* (available free at most supermarkets) for coupons and info on cafes and performances. Wherever you go, avoid "Kona-blended" coffee—foreign beans dilute the power of Kona.

Sam Choy's, 73-5576 Kauhola St. (326-1545). From Rte. 19 turn inland onto Hini Lani St. into Kalako Industrial Park, then take the first right and the second left. The world-famous chef whips up *great* local food that has earned this restaurant the name "original home of Kona cuisine." Huge portions and low prices. Breakfast all day. Locals stampede in for lunch at 11:30am. Open Sun. 8am-2pm, Mon.-Sat. 6am-2pm, Tues.-Sat. also 5-9pm. No credit cards.

Holuakoa Cafe (322-2233), on Rte. 11 across from the Kona Hotel in Holualoa. Soothing cafe serves Kona coffee and light food in a marvelous terraced garden. Pastries, desserts, and salads $1-4. Open Mon.-Sat. 6:30am-5pm.

Aloha Cafe Theater (322-3383), on Rte. 11 after the 113mi. marker, across from the 76 gas station in Kealakekua. Delicious organic cuisine served in a building dating from the 1930s. Balcony overlooks a park and the ocean. Healthy meals ($7) and fresh-baked muffins ($1.50). Open Mon.-Sat. 8am-8pm, Sun. 8am-2pm.

Ocean View Inn, 75-5683 Alii Dr. (329-9998), across from the boat dock. Comfortably faded oceanside joint serves crowd-pleasing Chinese and Hawaiian fare while carousing locals crowd the bar. The *laulau* and *poi* is a good choice ($3). Breakfast $4.50, lunch $3-7, dinner $7-10. Vegetarian dishes around $4. No smoke-free sections. Open Tues.-Sun. 6:30am-2:45pm and 5:15-9pm. No credit cards.

Cassandra's Greek Taverna, 75-5719 Alii Dr. (334-1066), across from the Kona Inn Shopping Village. Classy restaurant's pleasingly blue interior makes for an enjoyable evening out. Salads start at $5, kebabs at $14. Greek bellydancing Fri. and Sat. nights. Open Mon.-Sat. 11am-10pm, Sun. 4:30-9pm.

SIGHTS AND ACTIVITIES

Although most sun-worshiping tourists make daytrips to the outstanding beaches north of Kailua-Kona (see **Kohala and Hamakua Coasts,** p. 485), those who stick around can still find sand to fill up their suits. **Magic Sands,** 77-6452 Alii Dr. at mi. marker 3, is also called "Disappearing Sands" because the sands get washed away for a few weeks every winter and then mysteriously return. It's a very popular place for wading, snorkeling, bodysurfing, and boogieboarding. **Honokohau Beach** is 1500 ft. north of Honokohau Small Boat Harbor off Rte. 19. This is Kailua's only **nude beach.** Surfing is popular here, and the **snorkeling** is the best on the island.

Kuhuluu Beach Park, at mi. marker 5, is a sheltered cove that's commonly overrun by sea turtles. Local youth love to paddle canoes, sandboard, and jump off the pier into this beach's cool waters. A long but rewarding drive down to Napoopoo brings fish fans to **Kealakekua Bay,** waters chock full of marine animals of every sort. The bay sparkles with friendly **dolphins** in the early morning (6-10am). **Sportfishing** is offered by a gaggle of companies operating out of **Honokohau Bay.** The budget traveler's best option is the **Sea Wife II** (329-1806 or 888-329-1806), which takes mariners out for an exciting four-hour battle with the sea's mightiest fish (anglers $60, spectators $37). For those prone to seasickness, the daily **weigh-ins** at 11:30am and 4:30pm may be a close enough encounter with the marine kind. The **Kona Surf Hotel** off Alii Dr. near Keauhou Bay, offers an eerie creature feature. At sundown, they illuminate the water with spotlights while stealth-bomber-like **manta rays** come out to feed on plankton. Brave souls can snorkel among the harmless (but u-u-u-gly!) animals.

Hulihee Palace, 75-5718 Alii Dr. (329-1877), was built in 1838 for King Kalakaua. The palace is situated in a prime oceanside spot and filled with beautiful furniture (open daily 9am-4pm; admission $5, seniors $4, under 18 $1). Across from the palace is **Mokuaikaua,** the first Christian church in Hawaii. The building was completely constructed from native Hawaiian wood in 1837, and is still used for sermons. The church is also called the Church of the Chimes because (surprise!) of the chimes that sound daily at 4pm (open daily sunrise-sunset). The **Hilton Hotel's** mammoth complex, on Wikola Beach Dr., offers theme park entertainment for both kiddies (rides on boats and electric trains) and parents (the 1mi. museum walkway displays hundreds of pieces from around the world). The hotel's **Dolphin Quest** allows visitors to swim with the aquatic mammals ($80 per person). Drop a card in the Dolphin Quest booth to enter the lottery and win a spot.

Up Hualalai Rd. on Rte. 180, **Holualoa** moves to a slower tempo than the resort coast below. The quiet coffee town has several art galleries along its main street, including the **Kona Arts Center** in an abandoned coffee mill. The center offers craft workshops and exhibits the work of local artists (open Tues.-Sat. 10am-4pm).

ENTERTAINMENT AND NIGHTLIFE

Kailua-Kona is the center of Big Island nightlife. Resort activities attract tourists, while more local crowds can be found at bars along **Alii Dr.,** the beachfront boulevard. The more culturally (and sober) minded visitor should head to the Kona Surf Hotel, 78-128 Ehukai St. (322-3411), at Keauhou Bay, for a quality 1½ hr. **Polynesian Culture and Hula Show** (Tues. and Fri. 5:30-7pm; free). This convention center is also the place to catch big musical acts.

Eclipse, 75-5711 Kuakini Hwy. Kona's hottest (read: only) disco is the place to be Fri. or Sat. night. A young crowd rages to top-40 music and plays at pool tables and dartboards. Cover $3. Must be 21.

Merry Wahine Bar (885-8805), in the **Big Island Steak House** at the King's Shops, Waikoloa Beach. Popular spot for young surfers and vacationers hearkens back to the day when sailors came to Kona lookin' for some "R&R." DJ spins music under a hula-dancing gorilla Fri.-Sun. nights from 10pm. No cover. Must be 21.

Michelangelo's, 75-5770 Alii Dr. (329-4436), in Waterfront Row. Huge and rowdy local crowd gathers to dance, drink, ogle, and laugh at *haoles* (light-skinned folks). Wed. is Ladies' Night, and the place is hopping. No cover, sandals, or shorts. Must be 21. Open daily 11am-10pm; bar open Fri.-Sat. till 2am.

Mask Bar (329-8558), in Kopiko Pl. under Lanihau Shopping Plaza. Wall-to-wall mirrors flank this lively gay and lesbian bar while a thumping stereo system keeps things upbeat. Karaoke nightly. Disco Fri.-Sun. nights. Open daily 6pm-2am.

■ The Kohala and Hamakua Coasts

The drive along the northwestern coast takes you into the rural heartland of Hawaii. The Kona side of Kohala is an area of white sand beaches and rolling green meadows that run to the sea. The center (or North Kohala) contains rolling cattle lands where *paniolos* (cowboys) ride beneath pine trees and open sky. The Hilo side, known as the Hamakua Coast, is a land of forested valleys and roaring waterfalls, with the emerald Waipio Valley as its crown jewel. These strikingly beautiful regions are largely devoid of visitors, and their jaw-dropping natural sights should not be missed, but they are only accessible by car or moped. It's a stretch for cyclists: 55 mi. from Hilo to Kamuela/Waimea, 39 mi. from Kona.

ACCOMMODATIONS AND CAMPING

Out here, quality budget hotels and hostels are like honest lawyers: you just can't seem to find them. Instead, camping is your best bet. All parks require a $1 **permit,** available at the county parks office (see **Hilo Practical Information,** p. 474), except for Hapuna Beach State Park, where the permit is free. Mahukona and Kapaa Beach Parks have restroom facilities and allow camping, but both are perched on rocky coastlines rather than beaches.

HAWAII

Kohala Coast

Hapuna Beach State Park (974-6200), 3mi. south of Kawaihae off Rte. 19. Not very scenic, but near Hapuna Beach. Caretaker lives next door and keeps an eye on the cabins. A-frame shelters and wooden sleeping benches available; no tent camping. 5-night max. stay. Sites $20 (4-person max.). Reserve in advance.

Spencer Beach County Park, off Rte. 27 near Kawaihae. Rocky but shaded area crowds tents. Beach is great for sunbathing and swimming. BBQ pit, basketball court, restrooms, outdoor showers, covered pavilion. Wheelchair accessible.

Keokea Beach County Park, off Rte. 27; turn left 6mi. past Hawi and continue to the end of the winding country lane. Grassy oceanside camping area is at the head of a bay framed by tall red cliffs. Restrooms, outdoor showers, lighted pavilion. Space usually available.

Don's Tropical Valley Hostel (889-0369), off Rte. 270 in a very sleepy part of Makapala. Freshly painted house offers 3 hostel beds ($16), a private single ($36), and a private double ($36). Linens provided.

Hamakua Coast

Campers can stay in the beautiful, isolated **Waimanu Valley** (see p. 487), one ridge from Waipio Valley. Contact the State Division of Foresty and Wildlife in Hilo (974-4221) for the necessary, free permits.

Hotel Honokaa Club, 45-3480 Mamane St. (Rte. 240; 775-0678 or 800-808-0678), across from the Honokaa Park entrance ¼mi. east of the post office. Hostel beds downstairs sag a bit, but rooms are tidy. Dorms $15; singles $20; doubles $30. Hotel upstairs is nice enough to make you jump, jump! Spacious rooms have cable TV. Doubles from $45. Reception open 7:30am-9pm.

Waipio Motel (775-0368 in Waipio, 935-7466 in Hilo—call often, and wait a while), in Waipio Valley. Accessible only by 4WD or 1hr. hike from Waipio Lookout. An enchanting place with an enchanting owner—Tom here's 'bout 85 years old, and his memory of the valley goes back a long way. No electricity, but gas lamps, cold showers, and communal kitchens (bring your own food). $15 per person. Reservations required. No credit cards.

Kalopa State Park Campground, at the end of Kalopa Rd. 3mi. inland from Rte. 19 between Honokaa and Hilo. Picnicking and nature trails in the surrounding *obia* forest. Free permit required for camping. 8-person cabins $55.

SIGHTS

Kohala Coast

White, sandy beaches line the coast through Kailua and up Rte. 19 to the very beautiful and very crowded **Hapuna Beach** and **Spencer Beach Parks,** 35 mi. north. These palm-lined swaths of sand are exactly the sort of beaches that come to mind when you think of tropical shores: in fact, Hapuna Beach is consistently rated one of the world's best in annual competitions. Both parks are wheelchair accessible and have shade, snack bars, restrooms, and excellent snorkeling. **Hapuna Harry's** is a necessary chow stop. Luckily, Harry has class—prices remain low even though he owns the only snack bar around. (Sandwiches $2-3. Snorkel sets and boogieboards $5 for 4hr. Open daily 10am-4:30pm.)

Going north up Rte. 19, the tropical paradise gives way to desolate lava fields adorned with environmentally friendly "graffiti" (white stones set against the black rock spell out the affections of local sweethearts). **Puukohola Heiau,** at the intersection of Rte. 19 and 270, is the last major religious structure of ancient Hawaiian culture. Kamehameha the Great built this *heiau* (temple) about 200 years ago in honor of his war god Ku Kailimoku. The shrine was used until King Kamehameha's death in 1819 and the abandonment of the *kapu* (taboo) system.

Rte. 270 leads out of the desert and around the Kohala Mountains to the plantation town of **Hawi.** The birthplace of King Kamehameha is marked by a cast of the statue of him in Honolulu. The route ends at the **Pololu Valley Lookout,** where a half-hour hike leads down to a broad black sand beach.

From the Kona Coast beyond Hapuna Beach, Rte. 250 heads up the mountain. The climb through rolling pasture offers superior vistas of Mauna Kea, and Mauna Loa farther in the distance. Rte. 250 ends in **Waimea,** also known as **Kamuela,** in the heart of ranch country. The **Parker Ranch,** a.k.a. the "Texas of the Tropics," is the largest privately owned cattle ranch in the United States. It spans 225,000 acres, an area about three-quarters the size of Oahu. Its visitors center and museum (885-7655), at the junction of Rte. 19 and 190, offer audio-visual presentations on the history, operations, and lifestyles of Parker Ranch and its *paniolos* (cowboys; open daily 9am-5pm, last ticket sold at 4pm; admission $5, ages 4-11 $3.75).

The **Kamuela Museum** (885-4724), on Rte. 19 just south of the Rte. 250 junction, has a collection of artifacts ranging from stuffed bears to royal Hawaiian shark hooks, formerly baited with human flesh. The Chinese roses are marvelous (open daily 8am-5pm; admission $5, under 12 $2).

Hamakua Coast

The town of **Honokaa,** 15 mi. east of Kamuela, marks the beginning of the Hamakua Coast, essentially one long botanical garden stretching south to Hilo. The drive from Kamuela passes cattle country strewn with misty, rolling hills. Honokaa, like many Hamakua towns, was once a sugar plantation. Sugar no longer fuels the coast's dwindling economy, but Honokaa proudly basks in its title of "Macadamia Nut Capital of the World." You can watch the mac nut at work and/or pay tourist prices at the **Bad Ass Coffee Plant,** on Lehua St. downhill from the post office (store open daily 9am-5pm; factory in operation Aug.-March). **Simply Natural,** 3625 Mamane St. (775-0119), is the only vegetarian restaurant in town. Sandwiches $4-6 (open Mon.-Sat. 9am-5pm, Sun. 11am-5pm).

A great way to experience the valley is on **horseback.** Unless Tonto was able to fit in your luggage, contact **Waipio Naalapa,** P.O. Box 992, Honokaa 96727 (775-0419). Knowledgeable guides make a visit to the Waipio Valley feel like a trip to the salad bar, as they point out edible rose apples and guava. Without a guide, this can be a trip to a less-than-royal throne: the tempting kukio nut is a potent alternative to Ex-Lax (2½hr. tour departs Mon.-Sat. 9:30am and 1pm; $75).

Waipio Valley

The lush **Waipio Valley,** 8 mi. down Rte. 240 from Honokaa, is one of the most beautiful and sacred places in Hawaii. This 2000 ft. gorge is the crowning point of a series of breathtaking canyons between Waipio and Pololu. The vertical green walls of the valley glitter with silver cascades and the flat valley floor is organized by taro fields. As the breadbasket of the Big Island, the Waipio Valley was the residence of Hawaiian royalty. Home to 10,000 people in the 19th century, the valley today has only 50 or so residents, all of whom live without electricity or water (it must be brought in from Hilo). Resident families live much like their ancestors did, cultivating their gardens and fishing in the Waipio River.

The **Waipio Lookout,** at the end of Rte. 240 on the edge of the valley, offers one of the most striking panoramas in the islands. For those with the legs and the lungs, a 25-minute hike down into the valley and a grueling 40-minute hike back up offers a better glimpse of the amazing beauty. Hiking on the valley floor is flat and easy, with trails leading both through the valley and along the beach. Heading along the main road towards the back of the valley is the best bet for daytrippers, but the friendly residents will gladly point the way to other trails. The best paths lead to **Hiilawe Falls** and the amazing black sand **Waipio Beach** at **Waimanu Bay.** All paths are wet, muddy, and mosquito-infested—bring appropriate shoes and bug repellent. Gurgling mountain springs, aromatic *awapuhi* trees, edible *hoio* ferns, and guava and avocado trees abound.

Waipio Beach is a 10-minute walk from the road. This is a prime sunbathing and boogieboarding location, but the rough waves have forced swimmers to congregate farther down the coast, near the mouth of the Waipio River. Once cast as "Dry Land" in the box-office *Waterworld,* the beach is perfect for camping and picnicking—on weekends, locals eat, drink, and party here. The 9 mi. **Waimanu Valley** hike, which passes ancient Hawaiian ruins and sublime scenery, is best done as an overnight trip. The steep **Switchback** or **Zig-Zag Trail** begins at the far end of Waimanu Bay, beyond the river. For extended periods of exploration, hikers may wish to contact the **Waipio Valley Tree House and Environmental Center** (775-7160). The friendly staff offers great advice.

The valley can also be seen through the windows of the **Waipio Valley Shuttle** (775-7121), which provides a nonstop, narrated, and air-conditioned 1½ hr. tour. Purchase tickets and check in at the **Waipio Woodworks Art Gallery** (775-0958), ½ mi. from the Waipio Lookout on Rte. 240. Reservations are highly recommended. (Open Mon.-Sat. 8am-4pm. Fare $35, under 11 $15. Buses take off whenever a small crowd has gathered.)

Between Honokaa and Hilo

Kalopa State Park, just past Honokaa, hides several rewarding trails. Few people know of the **Native Forest Trail** (0.7mi.), which leads through *ohia* and *kopiko* groves. *Kalij* pheasants, imported from India 100 years ago, scurry in the undergrowth. **Kolekole Beach Park** is halfway between Hilo and Honokaa; to get there, turn right after Kolekole Bridge, ¾ mi. after mi. marker 15. The beach is a popular weekend hangout for Hiloites, but the surf sometimes makes it hard to swim. On the way to Hilo lies **Hawaii's tallest waterfall, Akaka Falls.** Accessible by a turn-off at mi. marker 13½ on Rte. 220, the 442-foot-tall waterfall is surrounded by ginger plants, bamboo groves, and wild orchids—truly an awe-inspiring sight.

■ Seasonal Events

Merrie Monarch Festival (935-9168), the week after Easter Sun., Hilo. Hula contests, local music, and festivities.

Parker Ranch Rodeo and Horse Races (885-7311), July 4, Waimea (Parker Ranch Arena). Wild West entertainment. Yee-haw!

Queen Liliuokalani Outrigger Canoe Races (329-0833), end of August. The world's largest long distance canoe race.

Hawaiian International Bluefish Tournament (329-6155), early August. The Olympics of big game fishing.

Gatorade Ironman World Triathlon (942-4767, ask for Rob Perry), Oct., Kailua-Kona. The original and ultimate endurance test: a 2.4mi. swim, 112mi. cycle, and 26.2mi. run. If you're not up to the challenge, pick up a t-shirt and pretend.

Kona Coffee Festival, weekend after Veteran's Day, Kona. High-strung morning people converge to pay homage to the caffeine god.

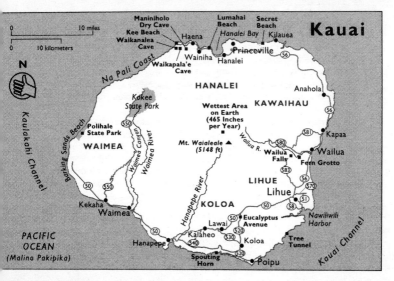

Kauai

Anything nature does, Kauai can do better. Formed over six million years ago by the now-extinct Mt. Kawaikini volcano, Kauai, the oldest island in the Hawaiian archipelago, has had a lot of time to nurture its nature. As a result, the splendor of the Garden Isle is unsurpassed anywhere in Hawaii. The beaches are more graceful, the mountains more outrageous, and the waterfalls have, well, more water and more fall. When producers of the films *South Pacific, Raiders of the Lost Ark, Jurassic Park,* and *Outbreak* sought out a primeval paradise, they ended up here.

Kauai's Mt. Waialeale is the wettest spot on earth, with over 450 inches of rain per year and a spectacular profusion of tropical lushness. Flowers crowd the roadsides and violently verdant flora bathes the mountain slopes. The island also boasts long stretches of sunny and dry beachfront, sheltered bays, and the amazing Waimea Canyon, a 3000-foot gorge straight out of a Western movie.

Though the number of tourists on the island is increasing faster than a population of bunny rabbits, Kauai has escaped the fate of noisy, bustling Oahu. Locals maintain a leisurely pace and a familial attitude. And don't worry about towering hotels popping up all over the place: the building code stipulates that construction cannot exceed the height of the island's coconut palm trees. Let the aloha spirit move you, and, like the locals say, "No worries!"

PRACTICAL INFORMATION

Visitor Information:
Hawaii Visitors Bureau, Lihue Plaza Bldg., 3016 Umi St. #207 (245-3971), at Rice in Lihue. Stop by to pick up the fun and informative *Kauai Illustrated Pocket Map.* Write or call the hotline (246-1400) for their vacation planner, directory of services, events, and coupons. Open Mon.-Fri. 8am-4:30pm.
Kauai Chamber of Commerce, P.O. Box 1969, 4272B Rice St. (245-7363), Lihue. Open Mon.-Fri. 8am-4:30pm.
Kauai County Parks Office, Moikeha Bldg., 4444 Rice St. #150 (241-6670), Lihue. Permits for camping in county parks ($3 per person per night, also available on-site for $5). Open Mon.-Fri. 7:45am-4:30pm.
Division of State Parks, State Office Bldg., 3060 Eiwa St. #306 (274-3444), at Hardy in Lihue. Camping info for state parks. Permits issued Mon.-Fri. 8am-4pm.

Airport: Lihue Airport, 2 mi. east of Lihue and 8 mi. south of Kapaa towns, is Kauai's major airfield. It serves Hawaiian, Aloha, and Mahalo airlines. **Princeville Airport** on the North Shore and **Port Allena Airport** on the South Shore are serviced by helicopter adventure companies. Kauai is a 26-minute jet flight or 40-minute turboprop ride from Honolulu.

Budget Travel: Mokihana Travel Service, Lihue Plaza Bldg. (245-5338), below the visitors center. Offers the best deals on inter-island flights. Open Mon-Fri. 8am-5pm, Sat. 8am-noon.

Public Transportation: Kauai Bus (241-6410), is based in Lihue and runs as far as Hanalei to the north and Kekaha to the west. No big packs, luggage, or boogieboards. Fare $1, seniors 50¢. Buses run very roughly Mon.-Fri. 5:30am-6pm, Sat. 7:30am-3pm. Less than reliable. Schedules available at some gas stations and the visitor information booths located at shopping centers throughout the island.

Taxis: An expensive and difficult-to-find last resort. **AAA Island Style Taxi** (245-5999 or 821-7774), the only 24hr. service on the island, also offers tours. **North Shore Cab** (826-6189), offers specials for hikers. Open daily 6am-10pm.

Car Rental: The best deals come as part of hotel-car or air-car packages. Make reservations. **Alamo,** Lihue Airport (800-327-9633 or 246-0646). **Budget,** Lihue Airport (800-527-0700 or 245-9031). Cars $25 per day, depending on season and package. Open daily 5:45am-9:15pm. Also ask around at your **hostel;** cheap cars can be had for as low as $20 per day.

Bike Rental: Kauai's main roads leave little room for slow 2-wheelers, so think twice before renting and plan your journey carefully. On the North Shore, try **Pedal 'n' Paddle,** P.O. Box 1413, Ching Young Village (826-9069), Hanalei. Mountain bikes $15 per day, $80 per week. Open daily 9am-6pm. On the South Shore, head to **Outfitters Kauai,** 2827A Poipu Rd. (742-9667). Mountain bikes $20 per day, $100 per week. Open Mon.-Sat. 9am-5pm.

Camping and Water Equipment Rental: Scuba diving and kayaking are big here and many stores offer rental services. On the North Shore, try **Pedal 'n' Paddle** (see Bike Rental listing above). Snorkeling equipment and bodyboards $5 per day, $20 per week, kayaks $25 per day. Dome tent $10 per day, $30 per week. Backpacks and trail stoves also available. **Kauai Scuba** (826-7711), is part of Pedal 'n' Paddle. Scuba set $40 per day; certification $250. Divemaster Sean gives one of the cheapest and most personal intro dives around. Open daily 9am-6pm. **Activity Warehouse,** 4788 Kuhio Hwy. (822-4000), Kapaa, across from McDonald's. Snorkel gear $2, golf clubs $10-15, boogieboards $6, surfboards $15-20, kayaks $20. (All prices are for 24hr., except for kayaks, which are due at 4:30pm.) Open daily 7:30am-9pm. **Kayak Wailua,** 159 Wailua Rd. (822-3388 or 822-4274), is conveniently located on the river. Kayaks $5 per hr., $25 per day. Open daily 9am-5pm. On the South Shore, **Sea Sport,** 2827 Poipu Rd. (742-9303 or 800-685-5889), in Koloa, rents snorkeling gear and boogieboards for $4-8 per day, $15-25 per week. Full scuba gear $40 per day. Open daily 8am-5pm.

Library: Lihue Public Library, 4344 Hardy St. (241-3222), Lihue. Open Mon. and Wed. 10am-8pm, Tues. and Thurs.-Fri. 9am-5pm, Sat. 9am-1pm.

Laundromat: Kapaa Laundry Center (822-3113), in Kapaa Shopping Center off Kuhio Hwy. Drop off Mon.-Fri. 7:30am-1pm, self-service daily 7:30am-9:30pm.

Weather Conditions: (245-600). **Marine Conditions:** (245-3564).

Rape Crisis Line: (245-4144). 24hr.

Medical Services: Wilcox, O.N. Memorial Hospital and Health Center, 3420 Rte. 56, Lihue (245-1100). **Kauai Veterans,** 4643 Waimea Canyon Rd. (338-0431), Waimea. Both open 24hr.

Emergency: 911.

Police: 3060 Umi St. (241-6711), Lihue.

Post Office: 4441 Rice St. (246-0793), Lihue. Open Mon.-Fri. 8am-4:30pm, Sat. 9am-1pm. **ZIP Code:** 96766.

Area Code: 808.

ORIENTATION

Kauai is the farthest northwest of the main islands in the Hawaiian chain. Roughly circular, the island falls away from **Mt. Waialeale** at its center to a coastline ringed by the two-lane Rte. 50/56 (also called Kuhio Hwy.). The island is divided into five districts: the commercial center of **Lihue** to the east; the resort area of **Koloa** to the south; **Kawaihau** to the north of Lihue, centered at Kapaa; **Hanalei,** on the North Shore; and rugged **Waimea** ("reddish water") to the west. The north experiences frequent showers, but the south and the west are fairly dry.

The public transportation in Kauai is unreliable, so driving is a must. Kauai's roads are efficient, but tend to get crowded between Lihue and Kapaa around 8am and 5pm. **Hitchhiking** is illegal on Kauai, but hitchers say prospects are nonetheless good, and report getting the best results by extending their index finger rather than the traditional thumb. From Lihue, **Wailua** is 7 mi., **Kapaa** 10 mi., **Hanalei** 35 mi., and **Haena** 41 mi. counterclockwise on **Rte. 56.** Clockwise on **Rte. 50, Poipu** ("crashing waves") lies 14 mi. and **Waimea** 36 mi. from Lihue. The Rte. 50/56 circuit leaves a wide, roadless gap on the remote northwestern **Na Pali Coast** of Kauai. Thirty miles from Lihue, **Waimea Canyon Rd.** branches off Rte. 50 and heads up Waimea Canyon to Kokee. There is a $25 fine for not wearing a seatbelt.

ACCOMMODATIONS

When deciding where to stay on Kauai, consider each region's different appeal. The Lihue-Kapaa area (where the majority of accommodations are found) is centrally located, the North Shore offers a quiet setting and the lion's share of activities, the South Shore hosts many resorts, and the West Side is the most rugged area. For groups, vacation rentals can be an excellent deal: beachfront locations start at about $50. Check airports, supermarkets, and bulletin boards for the latest info.

Kauai International Hostel, 4532 Lehua St. (823-6142 or 800-858-2295 from the islands), Kapaa. From Rte. 56 turn left after the bell statue at Niu St. Airport pickup available ($6). Across from the beach and several restaurants. Full kitchen, cable TV, pool table, laundry facilities, co-ed and single-sex dorms. Daytrips to many of Kauai's hidden spots ($20). Reception open daily 8am-10pm. Check-out 10am. Dorms $15, nonmembers $16; private room $40. Key deposit $10.

Garden Island Inn, 3445 Wilcox Rd. (245-7227 or 800-648-0154; email garden@aloha.net), across Nawiliwili Harbor in Kalapaki. Next to the island's best swimming beaches and 2mi. from Lihue Airport. Tropical and tranquil with fruit trees that guests can pick, *koi* pond, and fresh flowers for every room. Free use of beach gear. Traffic off Rte. 50 can be noisy. Reception open daily 7am-9pm. Check-out 11am. Singles and doubles from $59; 1-night advance deposit required.

YMCA-Camp Naue (246-9090), on the North Shore, between mi. markers 7 and 8, in Haena. Basic bunkhouses in a drop-dead gorgeous location, feet from the beach with mountains and waterfalls behind. Individual shower stalls. No reservations—call first, especially in the summer. Dorms $12 (bring your own linen). Tent sites $10; each additional person $7. No credit cards.

YWCA-Camp Slogett (335-6060 for camping or hosteling; 245-5959 to reserve the lodge), off Rte. 550. Upon reaching Kokee State Park, stay on the main road, and take the first right after the museum and lodge. Follow the extremely bumpy dirt road, and signs will lead you from there. Bunkhouse is tightly packed; campground has big open plots. Reception open daily 9am-8pm. Dorms $20. Tent sites $10. Spacious, comfortable 5-person lodge $100. No linens.

Kahili Mountain Park, P.O. Box 298, Koloa 96756 (742-9921), off Rte. 50. From Waimea, it's on the right after mi. marker 7. Peaceful grounds offer a small lake and hiking trails at bottom of mountains. Run by the Adventist Church. Check-in noon. Check-out 10am. Cabinette for 5 with small kitchen and shared bath $37.

HAWAII

Cabins for 4 with private bath, shower, and kitchen $50. Laundry. Linen, dishes, and detergent provided. Reserve in advance; balance due before arrival.

Tip Top Motel, 3173 Akahi St. (245-2333; fax 246-8988), Lihue, near the intersection of Rte. 56 and 570. Newly renovated building offers clean but windowless rooms with A/C and cable TV. Cafe and bar downstairs. Reception open daily 6:30am-2pm and 5:30-9:30pm. Singles and doubles $44. Key deposit $10.

Mahina's, 4433 Panihi Rd. (823-9364), Kapaa. Women's guest house on Keike Beach offers hostel style accommodations in a 3-bedroom house. Outdoor shower. Straight, bisexual, and lesbian friendly. Dorms $20; doubles $30. Linens provided for guests.

Mokihana Timeshare, 796 Kuhio Hwy. (822-3971, for reservations 360-676-1434), across from McDonald's in Kapaa. TV room, pool, tennis court, putting range, and view of Wailua Beach. Spiffy rooms with ranges, fridges, and coffeepots. Reception open daily 7am-9pm. Check-out noon. Studio with kitchenette and beach view $65. Two-bedroom unit (big enough for four) with full kitchen $75. Non-refundable 25% deposit required. Call in advance.

Kokee Lodge Cabins, P.O. Box 819, Waimea 96796 (335-6061), at the end of Rte. 550, offers cabins for 2 to 6 people with fridges, stoves, showers, utensils, and linens. Fabulous location near Waimea Canyon and Kalalau Lookout. 5-night max. stay. Reception open daily 9am-4pm. Simple cabin $35, fragrant cedar cabin $45. Full payment required, refundable on 1-week notice. Book early for summer.

Motel Lani, 4240 Rice St. (245-2965), Lihue, at the intersection of Hardy and Rice St. Older motel offers small, moderately furnished rooms. Officially quiet after 10pm, but peace prevails long before then. Reception open daily 6:30am-9:30pm. Singles and doubles $34 per night, $32 per night for two or more. No credit cards.

CAMPING

Three state parks and five county parks officially allow camping, though people put up tents on many of the island's beaches. Of the state parks, Kokee is inland, Polihale is on a beach, and the Na Pali Coast is only accessible by boat or hike. **State permits** are available free from the Division of State Parks (see **Practical Information,** p. 489), with a five-night maximum stay. County parks allowing camping are Haena, Hanalei, Anini, Anahola, and Lucy Wright. **County permits** are available for $3 per day for a maximum of seven days per park and 60 total days per year from the County Parks Office (on-site $5). Both the state and county offices offer free maps of the parks.

Heed posted warnings about local swimming conditions—some apparently calm areas may have deadly currents. Also remember to treat any water from mountain streams before drinking it. The higher elevations can be cool and you may actually need something warmer than a t-shirt.

Na Pali Coast State Park, at the end of Rte. 560. Park in the Kee Beach lot. Three campgrounds lie along the steep but beautiful Kalalau Trail. **Hanakapiai** lies 2mi. out, **Hana Koa** at 6mi., and the awe-inspiring **Kalalau Valley** at the end of the 11mi. trail. Novices should stick to Hanakapiai. No water.

Anini Beach County Park, off Rte. 56 on the North Shore. Coming from Lihue, take the second right turn onto Kalihiwai Rd. and follow the left fork past the boat ramp and polo field. The most popular of the county parks, families and friendly locals crowd the beach. Pavilion, outdoor sink, and toilet.

Polihale State Park, Rte. 50, about 37mi. northwest of Lihue at the end of a 5mi. dirt road. The haul cane road (right turn at the yellow "road narrows" sign) gets you into the park proper, but it is rough and sandy. The splendor of the Na Pali coast looms over this gorgeous beach park, one of the sunniest spots on the island and great for bodysurfing. Take bug spray for the flies. Picnicking and tent facilities. Restrooms, showers, BBQ pits.

Kokee State Park, at the end of Rte. 550, 16mi. north of Kekaha. Quiet tent and RV camping near extensive trails, picnic facilities, scenic forests, and canyon. Prime plum picking, pig hunting, and trout fishing in season. Gets cool at night. Restrooms, showers, BBQ pits.

Haena Beach County Park, near the end of Rte. 560 on the North Shore. Grassy and adjacent to an awesome beach, this campground is scenic, if crowded. Near hiking, beaches, and water-filled caves. Bathrooms, showers, BBQ.

FOOD

Kauai has as many tasty, inexpensive eateries as it does amazing beaches, but with so much natural splendor around, you'll probably want to picnic as much as possible. For the supplies to do so, check out the **Big Saves:** in Kapaa on Kuhio Hwy. (open daily 7am-11pm); in Lihue at Hardy and Rte. 56; in Waimea at 9861 Rte. 56 (7am-10pm); in Ching Young Village in Hanalei (7am-9pm); and in Old Koloa at 5510 Rte. 530 (6am-11pm). The 24 hr. **Safeway,** 831 Kuhio Hwy. (822-0706), in Kapaa has a **pharmacy** (open Mon.-Fri. 8:30am-7:30pm, Sat.-Sun. 8:30am-5pm). **Papaya's Natural Foods** (823-0910), Kauai Village in Kapaa, offers natural foods, a cafe, and, not surprisingly, papayas (open Mon.-Sat. 9am-8pm).

Each island has its special cuisine, and Kauai is no different—this island is sweet on sweets. *Lilikoi* (passion fruit) pie is a fave found in most bakeries. **Omoide's** (335-5291), in Hanapepe, sells a particularly fine example for $1.30 a slice (open Tues.-Sun. 7am-9pm). Lap up the finest ice cream on the island at one of the three branches of tourist-trapping **Lappert's.** The founders of the company, Walter and Mary Lappert, are local celebrities. The *Kauai Pie* flavor, a tantalizing combo of Kona coffee, mac nuts, coconut, and fudge, is a favorite.

Hamura's Saimin Stand, 2956 Kress St. (245-3271), off Rice in Lihue. Cheap, good food served with local flair. Huge portions of *saimin* (Japanese) noodles under $4.50. Open Mon.-Fri. 10am-11:30pm, Fri.-Sat. 10am-12:30am, Sun. 10am-9:30pm.

Bubba's, 1384 Kuhio Hwy. (823-0069); http://planet-hawaii.com/bubba), Kapaa; also in Hanalei Center (826-7839), Hanalei. Bill Clinton is neither part owner nor paid endorser of Bubba's, though he would appreciate the burgers ($2.50). In Kapaa, open Mon.-Sat. 10:30am-8pm; in Hanalei, open daily 10:30am-6pm.

Beezer's, 1380 Kuhio Hwy. (822-4411), Kapaa, near the hostel. Old-fashioned ice cream in a 50s-style soda bar. Only use premium ingredients, and the malts and milkshakes (both $4.95) will have you back for more. Open daily 11am-10pm.

Sueoka's Snack Shop, 5392 Koloa Rd. (742-1112), Old Koloa. Natives come en masse to take out plate lunches (from $4) and fabulous cheeseburgers ($1.35). Open Sun.-Fri. 10am-3pm, Sat. 10am-4pm.

Taco Dude's, 484 Kuhio Hwy. (822-1919), Coconut Marketplace. Nothing on this Mexican menu goes north of the $6 border. The big portions are, like, tubular. Open Mon.-Sat. 11am-8pm, Sun. 10am-4pm. No credit cards.

SIGHTS AND ACTIVITIES

Kauai's shore holds some of the most secluded and spectacular beaches in Hawaii as well as great surfing, snorkeling, and diving. The interior is a land of lush mountains, secret valleys, and countless cascades, much of which can be viewed only by **helicopter.** Though expensive, an aerial tour of Kauai ranks with life's most exhilarating experiences—if you're going to ride one in Hawaii, do it here. Make sure your tour includes the Kalalau Valley and Na Pali Coast, and bring a camera. **Bali Hai,** 1-3547 Rte. 50 (335-3166 or 800-325-TOUR/8687 from mainland), in Hanapepe, has a perfect safety record. Their location close to the sights means less wasted ferry time. Tours run $115-140 per person (cheaper if booked in advance) but specials can knock up to $50 off, so call ahead (open daily 8am-7pm). If you want the adrenaline rush without the height, consider the cheaper, and somewhat less frightening, adventure of zooming down the 12 mi. of road winding from the rim of the Waimea Canyon. **Bicycle Downhill** (742-7421), puts a motorcycle helmet on your head and a bike (fitted with power brakes) under your rear. On the way down, your knowledgeable guides will tell you interesting bits of Hawaiiana ($65 per person).

HAWAII

Fortunately for the budget traveler, most of Kauai's points of interest are free. Picturesque views exist around every bend both above and below the water; many visitors are satisfied just watching the expert surfers tackle the waves.

East Shore: Lihue

The **Kauai Museum,** 4428 Rice St. (245-6931), is a small museum featuring well organized exhibits on local history and culture. Native Hawaiian crafts, *paniolo* ranch life, and natural history receive particular attention. The museum annex through the patio cafe houses half of the exhibits (open Mon.-Fri. 9am-4pm, Sat. 10am-4pm; admission $5, seniors $4, ages 13-17 $1).

Kilohana Plantation, 3-2087 Rte. 50 (245-5608), 1.7 mi. south of Lihue, was the plantation estate of Gaylord Park Wilcox. Those who wish to see what life was like on an old Hawaiian plantation can take a carriage ride throughout the grounds (20min. ride; daily 11am-6:30pm; fare $8, under 12 $4). There is no charge for roaming around the house itself, although you may find yourself charmed out after 20 minutes by the shops which now occupy most of the rooms (open daily 9am-9:30pm; free).

Kalapaki Beach lies next to Nawiliwili Harbor and is considered one of the best swimming beaches on Kauai. Wilcox Rd. next to Nawiliwili Harbor leads to the **Alekoko Fishpond.** This artificial lagoon is nicknamed the Menehune Fishpond after the mythical mischief-makers *(menehune)* who supposedly built it in a single night.

Heading north on Rte. 56, turn inland on Rte. 583 to reach **Wailua Falls,** which was pictured in the opening of the TV series *Fantasy Island.* If you listen very, very closely, you may be able to hear the whispering ghost of Herve Villacheze. Steep and primitive trails lead down to the falls from the end of the road. To get to **Lydgate State Park,** turn right after the Wailua Golf Course on Rte. 56 north and park at the far end of the lot. The path along the shore will lead you to the "city of Refuge," part of an ancient *heiau* (temple) located just past the white sand beach and wading pool.

Kauai is the only inhabited Hawaiian island with navigable rivers, so pick up a kayak and paddle away. Heading up the Wailua River, veer right at the fork and hike 30 min. to the **Secret Falls,** a beautiful and secluded spot. **Wailua Marina State Park,** 7 mi. north of Lihue before the Wailua River Bridge, is the starting point for boats heading up the Wailua River to the **Fern Grotto. Smith's Motor Boats** (821-6892 or 821-6893), runs boats that leave every half hour daily from 9am to 4pm (round-trip 80min.; fare $15, under 12 $7.50). The cheesy island music and mandatory hula dancing on the boat ride may steer you to rent a kayak instead (see **Practical Information,** p. 490), but be prepared to compete with the tour boats and water-skiers for space. In spite of the crowds, **Smith's Tropical Paradise,** 174 Wailua Rd. (821-6895 or 822-6896), in Kapaa is a verdant 30 acres of gardens and lagoons (open daily 8:30am-4pm; admission $5, under 12 $2.50). The **Sleeping Giant** (Mt. Nounou) slumbers along the Coconut Coast, just before Kapaa.

North Shore: Hanalei, Haena, and the Na Pali Coast

A drive along Rte. 56 opens up the wonders of Kauai's North Shore. The **Kilauea Point National Wildlife Refuge** (828-1413), rests 709 ft. above sea level on a bluff near Kilauea Bay; signs from the highway clearly lead the way. The expanse of wilderness offers amazing views of thousands of seabirds and an occasional dolphin or seal (open daily 10am-4pm; admission $2). A bit farther down Rte. 56, take a right onto Kalihiwai Rd., another right onto the first dirt road, and park at the end to take the steep public access path to the crystalline water of **Secret Beach,** one of the most breathtaking beaches on the island. Some sunbathers go **nude** here—apparently, they're not too concerned about keeping secrets. The far right of the beach shelters a waterfall watched over by **Kilauea Lighthouse.** Around the left sit explorable caves, and to the back of the valley, guava and mango trees bear ample fruit. Don't come to this beach in the winter—the surf shrinks it considerably.

Off Anini Rd. from Rte. 56 is **Anini Beach,** a narrow spot sheltered by cliffs on either side. In August, celebrities play at the polo club across the street. The **Hanalei Valley Lookout,** off the left side of the road, spans a valley of *taro* patches and rice paddies. The town of **Princeville** is essentially one big golf course, but cars parked by the sign saying Queen's Bath Closed Until Further Notice indicate the way to Queen's Bath, a legally protected turquoise pool at the end of a coastal trail. Swimming may be unsafe during high surf.

The land of **Hanalei** was made famous by Peter, Paul, and Mary in their song "Puff the Magic Dragon." Some locals have their own interpretation of the title, "Little Jackie Paper," which they interpret as referring to the *pakalolo,* some of the best marijuana in the world (also called *wowy maui*), which is grown in the middle of various cane fields. Their version of the song goes, "When you see / ooh, ooh / Hanalei by moonlight / You will be in the heavens / by the sea…" If you squint, you may be able to make out the shape of a dragon from gorgeous **Hanalei Bay.** His snout, so say fattie-fueled imaginers, rests on the far left of the bay. Hanalei is an excellent destination for surfers of different levels, but beginners should stay inside the reef near the Hanalei Pier on the east side of the bay. To reach the pier, turn on Aku St. just before Ching Young Village and right on Weke Rd. The postcard pictures of **Lumahai Beach** don't do it justice. For the best view of the beach, park off Rte. 56 and walk down the trail next to the Danger: No Lifeguard sign. Parking is also available next to the beach itself.

Terrific **snorkeling** and **scuba diving** abound at **Tunnels,** a protected reef area with lots of fish that was named for the lava rock tubes forming the underwater reef. Tunnels is somewhat distant, but legal parking is available at nearby Haena Beach Park. Many people, shall we say, *avoid* the law and park on the side of the road, but *Let's Go* does not advocate law-bustin'.

On the drive to **Haena** lurks the huge **Maniniholo Dry Cave,** named after the head fisherman of the legendary *menehunes.* Farther along is **Haena State Beach Park.** Parking is available in the visitor lot. **Waikapalae Cave** is spelunkable, and the murky lagoon of **Waikanaloa Cave** hosts a giant beast, according to legend. Between the two caves and to your left, there is an old path leading to the entrance of the secluded **Blue Room** cave, so called because a strange lighting phenomenon results in water that is a bright fluorescent blue even though it's over 50 ft. deep. Swim through the small passageway on the right side of the main cavern to reach the Blue Room itself.

At the end of Rte. 56 are **Haena Bay** and **Kee Beach,** popular among swimmers and novice snorkelers. Kee is noted particularly for its sunsets, and was the site of passionate beach love scenes in *The Thorn Birds.* The trailhead for the **Kalalau Valley Trail,** which follows an ancient Hawaiian path 11½ mi. down spectacular Na Pali Coast, begins at the Kee Beach parking lot.

The world-famous **Na Pali Coast** is a must-see. Na Pali, literally "the cliffs," is a bland name for this breathtaking spectacle where sheer cliffs fall to empty white sand beaches washed by the vibrant blue seas. **Hanakapiai Beach** lies 2 mi. in and a marvelous waterfall lies another 2 mi. up Hanakapiai Valley. The mind-blowing **Kalalau Valley** lies at the end of 11 steep, challenging miles, but the trek is worth it: Kalalau is said by many to be **the most beautiful place on earth** (see **Kauai Camping,** p. 492 for accommodations options). The vistas in the valley are divine; travelers throw the adjective "edenic" around a lot when here, but they do not exaggerate. When it rains—and boy, does it rain—the mist pulls across the ridges like a shower curtain.

The wilderness coastal areas beyond Haena are accessible only by hiking or kayaking. Hikers planning on going all the way to Kalalau may want to have **Captain Zodiac** (826-9371 or 800-422-7824), in Hanalei, drop off their extra gear on Kalalau Beach ($30). The Cap'n may take people to the beach too (one-way $70; May-Sept. only; reserve in advance; office open daily 6am-9pm). If you're hiking all the way in, pack light and go the full distance in one day. Riptides from September through April make swimming at Kalalau perilous.

HAWAII

West End: Poipu and the Waimea Canyon

The west end of the island can be reached by Rte. 520 from Rte. 50 west of Lihue. You'll pass through the arching **Tree Tunnel** of eucalyptus trees to the restored **Old Koloa Town,** Hawaii's first sugar mill town, now full of boutiques with historical plaques detailing former generations of owners. At the end of Rte. 520 is a fork at the Welcome to Poipu Beach sign. A right turn takes you along a rugged coast to **Spouting Horn,** a series of lava-tube blow holes. There are several **secluded beaches** beyond Spouting Horn (at the end of the road and past the cliffs) or along the left fork at **Mahaulepu Beach,** a favorite spot of rare Hawaiian **monk seals** (take the dirt road at the end of Poipu Beach Rd. for about 10 minutes, make a right at the stop sign and register at the guard booth; open daily 7:30am-7pm). Around the corner to the left of the parking lot is the main beach; the trail along the stream at the right side leads to red rock caves. Two other nearby beaches are more accessible: **Brennecke's** (known for bodysurfing) and **Acid Drops** (for surfing).

Resting west of Lihue is **Hanapepe,** the "biggest little town in Kauai." The delightful combination of bakeries and art galleries in this quiet hamlet challenges passersby to eat or not to eat. Just west of Hanapepe along Lolokai Rd. is **Salt Pond Beach Park,** and an immaculate and protected swimming beach. (It has lit pavilions, showers, and restrooms, but no camping.) The red flats to the side of the beach continue to produce salt.

Thirty miles west of Lihue, Rte. 50 meets Rte. 550 at tiny **Waimea,** site of Captain Cook's first landing on Kauai in 1778. One mile east of Waimea is **Infinities,** Hawaii's best "left" (a beach where the waves break left instead of right). You can park by the road, but you'll have to put up with some bull to reach the beach, which is only accessible through a cow pasture. Try not to intrude upon the locals or the regular surfers; they can be hostile to outsiders. Off the highway, 1½ mi. down Menehune Rd., a marker points to the interlocking stones of **Kikiaola** (or *Menehune*) **Ditch.** Little remains of this ancient aqueduct.

Turning inland, Rte. 550 winds up the rim of the dramatic **Waimea Canyon,** known as the **"Grand Canyon of the Pacific."** Thrill-seeking drivers will enjoy the twisted majesty of **Waimea Canyon Drive,** surrounded by the crimson-streaked walls of this three-foot-gorge. You may spot feral goats clinging to the canyon walls; they were brought here by Captain Cook, but have become an environmental hazard. Avoid the busloads of tourists by coming in the early morning or late afternoon.

Continue up Rte. 550 to enter **Kokee State Park.** Pick up food and drink before you head up the canyon, because the overpriced restaurant at Kokee Lodge is the only source of food past Waimea (open daily 9am-3:30pm). The lodge's small but free museum gives the lowdown on Kauai's wildlife and weather (open daily 10am-4pm). Outside, you can find detailed information about the park's network of trails.

Near the end of Rte. 550 is the gorgeous **Kalalau Valley Lookout.** Still farther up the road rests the entrance to the muddy **Pihea Trail.** Take some time to hike the ridge overlooking the lush Kalalau Valley before turning into the Alakai swamp.

The far **west end** harbors two beaches with more sun, fewer tourists, and more meager facilities than the beaches farther east. Rte. 50 west will take you to **Barking Sands Beach.** Walking across the sand supposedly causes the particles to make a "woofing" sound: throngs of visitors delight in the futile attempt to produce the effect. **Polihale Beach Park,** a great spot for bodysurfing and the sunniest place on Kauai, abuts the Na Pali Cliffs. Get there by driving to the end of Rte. 50 and then along 5 mi. of rough dirt road. The sunset seen from the west end can be particularly dramatic when light refraction makes the sky flash green.

ENTERTAINMENT

Kauai residents garner their chief entertainment from nature, not nightlife—evening activities are scarce. However, the Garden Isle has several groovin' clubs and bars which liven up the night scene. The island is so small that any native can keep you abreast of local happenings. And, of course, there's always the **Elvis impersonation,** every Wednesday at 5 pm at Coconut Marketplace. The young man is entertaining, but so are the women swooning in the audience.

The **Lizard Lounge** (821-2205), off Kuhio Hwy. in the Foodland Plaza, is a relaxing place to scratch your stomach before you fill it with sandwiches ($4) and the island's best piña colada ($5.50). The live Hawaiian music can only be topped by the fabulous motto "time is fun when you're having flies" ($2 beers during Happy Hour, 2pm-6pm; open daily 10am-2am). Merry musicmakers party at **Tahiti Nui,** 5134 Kuhio Hwy. (826-6277), in Hanalei. Hawaiian music performed (almost) nightly 9pm-1am; occasional reggae on weekends (Fri. and Sat. cover $3). The **Side-Out Bar and Grill,** 41-1330 Kuhio Hwy. (822-0082), in Kapaa, isn't just for volleyball enthusiasts. Nightly local entertainment spikes the mixed gay and straight crowd (open daily noon-2am). If dancing is more yo' thang, head to Dance Party Kauai, on Fridays at **Kuhio's Nightclub** (742-1234), in the Hyatt Regency on Poipu Rd. near the 1500 block. (No open-toed shoes permitted. Non-hotel guest cover $5 on Fri. and Sat. Open daily 9pm-2am.) On Saturday nights, the place to shake it is **Gilligan's** (245-1955), at the **Outrigger Hotel** off Kuhio Hwy. in Kapaa. The music may be thumping, but half the crowd plays the wallflower (open Fri. and Sat. 9:30pm-2am; non-hotel guest cover $5).

SEASONAL EVENTS

Waimea Town Festival (338-9957), late Feb., Waimea. Canoe races and festivities.
Prince Kuhio Festival (822-5521), last week in March, Lihue. Pageantry, song, and dance from the era of Prince Kuhio.
Anini Beach Polo (826-6177), each Sun. May-Sept.
Prince Albert Music Festival (826-9644), in May in the Princeville Hotel. Song and *hula* in honor of the only child of Queen Emma and King Kamehameha IV.
King Kamehameha Day, June 11, Lihue. *Hoolaulea* (a festive gathering).
Kauai County Fair (828-2120), mid-Aug., the Kauai Memorial Convention Hall, Lihue. Exhibits, entertainment, games, and food booths.
Mokihana Festival (822-2166), late Sept. Spotlights the local cultural and artistic community. *Lei*-making contest, local crafts, food, live entertainment, and more.

HAWAII

Molokai

Once upon a time (a few years ago), a would-be developer called a town meeting to propose a high-rise resort on Molokai. Of the island's 6800 residents, 6000 were on hand to hear the plan. As the developer began to speak, a woman in the audience stood and said, "You haven't yet called this meeting to order with prayer." After the prayer, the residents sat through the proposal and then voted it down almost unanimously. Though the developer couldn't be convinced, this island is known as the "friendly isle," and few places live up to their nickname so well. Essentially one big small town, this island's locals welcome you to their community with a true spirit of *aloha*. It shouldn't be a surprise that the Molokai's residents stick together and share a friendly, easy-going lifestyle—it's in their blood. Almost half of the residents are full or part Hawaiian, making it the most Hawaiian isle aside from tiny Niihau.

Molokai's modern history began in the 16th century with its designation as a place of training for *kahuna* (high priests). These powerful sorcerers relied on their poisonwood idol carvings and mysterious reputations to frighten away potential invaders from Oahu and Maui. Molokai amplified its forbidden reputation in 1865, when King Kamehameha V established a colony here for people afflicted with leprosy. Honolulu businessmen bought most of the island in the 1890s and converted it into a major agricultural center. In the 1920s, Molokai was the world's leading honey exporter and produced 50% of Dole's pineapple crop.

Visitors have traditionally shied away from Molokai, leaving it pleasantly free of the high-rise resorts and hokey t-shirt stands that clog the other islands. Those who make the trip will discover a place where the pace is slower, the smiles are warmer, and the livin' is fine. As cheerful residents proclaim, "Molokai Mo' Bettah."

PRACTICAL INFORMATION

Visitor Information: Molokai Visitor Association (553-3876 or 800-553-0404 inter-island, 800-800-6367 from the mainland), at mi. marker 0 on Kamehameha Hwy. Maps of Kaunakakai and the sights of the island. Open Mon.-Fri. 8am-4:30pm. The two **free local newspapers,** *Dispatch* and the *Molokai Advertiser-News,* list weekly events and news along with occasional classified ads. **Molokai Division of Parks** (553-3204), behind the baseball field and fire station in the Mitchell Pauole Center at the east end of Kaunakakai. Info on camping and county parks. Issues permits for Papohaku and One Alii ($3, children 50¢). Open Mon.-Fri. 8am-4pm. **Division of State Parks** (567-6083), Kalae. Free permits for Palaau State Park.

Budget Travel: Friendly Isle Travel, 64 Ala Malama Ave. (555-5357), sells inter-island coupons (Mahalo $34, Island $45). Open Mon.-Fri. 8am-5pm.

ATM: Two machines on Ala Malama across from Chevron.

Airport: Hawaiian Air (553-3644 or 800-367-5320), runs frequent flights from Maui to Molokai ($80), as does **Island Air** (800-652-6541 inter-island, 800-323-3345 from mainland; $80, with AAA discount $61). Cheaper alternatives include the **Molokai Air Shuttle** (567-6847 from Molokai, 545-4988 from Oahu), and **Mahalo Air** (800-277-8333 inter-island, 800-462-4256 from mainland), which flies to or from any island for $42. **Paragon Air** shuttles to and from all Maui, Molokai, and Lanai airports for $80 round-trip.

Taxis: Kukui Tours (553-5133), has 24hr. service. Prices are steep: airport to west end $16, airport to Kaunakakai $16. **Molokai Style Services** (553-9090).

Car Rental: Budget (567-6877 on Molokai, 800-451-3600 inter-island, 800-527-0700 from the mainland), at the airport. Cars $50 per day in summer, different in winter. Credit card required. Must be 25. Open daily 6:30am-7pm. **Molokai Style Services** (553-9090), Kaunakakai. Used cars $38. Must be over 18. Owner Thadd is *the* man when it comes arranging hiking, fishing, and boat tours. Call 24hr.

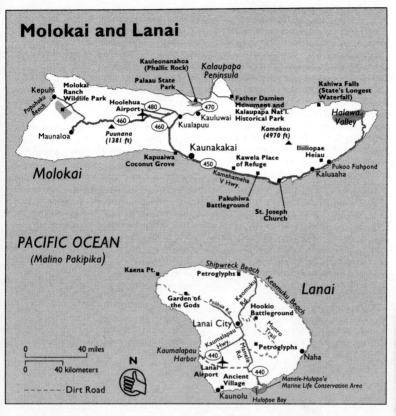

Molokai and Lanai

PACIFIC OCEAN
(Malino Pakipika)

0 ___ 40 miles
0 ___ 40 kilometers
N
– – – – Dirt Road

HAWAII

Equipment Rental: Molokai Fish and Dive Shop (553-3926), Ala Malama Blvd., Kaunakakai. Complete snorkel set $9. Boogieboards $7, ice chest and ice $4, friendly info free. Open Mon.-Sat. 9am-6pm, Sun. 8am-2pm.

Library: 15 Ala Malama St. (553-5483), Kaunakakai. Open Mon.-Tues. and Thurs.-Fri. 9am-5pm, Wed. noon-8pm.

Laundromat: Kaunakakai Launderette, Makaena Pl. behind the Outpost Store. Wash $1, dry $1. Open daily 7am-9pm. **Kualapuu Launderette,** behind Kualapuu Cookhouse. Wash $1, dry $1. Open daily 5am-6pm.

Crisis Lines: Sexual Assault Crisis Center (242-4357). Call collect to Maui.

Medical Services: Molokai General Hospital (553-5331), Kaunakakai. **Molokai Family Health Center** (553-5353), Ala Malama Blvd., Kaunakakai.

Emergency: 911.

Police: (553-5355), Ainoa St., Kaunakakai.

Post Office: Kaunakakai, Ala Malama St., (553-5845). Open Mon.-Fri. 9am-4:30pm, Sat. 9-11am. **ZIP Code:** 96748. To send an edible memento to the folks back home, visit the **Hoolehua** office, Puupeelue Ave. (567-6144); send a coconut to the mainland for $3-5. Open Mon.-Fri. 7:30-11:30am and 12:30-4:30pm. **ZIP Code:** 96729.

Area Code: 808.

ORIENTATION

Molokai, situated between Maui and Oahu in the middle of the Hawaiian chain, is 10 mi. wide and 38 mi. long. The island is divided into two regions: the **east end** and **west end.** Molokai's principal town, **Kaunakakai,** is between the east and west ends, 8 mi. south of the airport on the southern shore. **Kamehameha V Hwy.** (Rte. 450) leads to the east end, winding through the remote **Halawa Valley.** The **Maunaloa Hwy.** (Rte. 460), leads to the dry west end and terminates in **Maunaloa. Kalae Hwy.** (Rte. 470), goes north toward **Kalaupapa. Farrington Ave.** (Rte. 480) branches left off Rte. 470 and heads east through **Kualapuu. Hoolehua Airport,** a 55 mi. (22min.) flight from Honolulu, is in Molokai's center, accessible by all major roads.

ACCOMMODATIONS AND CAMPING

Molokai doesn't have enough visitors to support the extensive hotel development of most other islands, but cheap rooms still exist. Write to the **Hawaiian Island Bed and Breakfast Association,** P.O. Box 726, Volcano, HI 96788 for a list of B&Bs.

Campsites on Molokai are easily accessible, uncrowded, and beautiful. There are three sites scattered across the island: **Papohaku Beach County Park** (west end), **Palaau State Park** (North Shore), and **One Alii Beach County Park** (South Shore). Permits are officially required for all three, but enforcement is lax. Because of the dearth of visitors, you will probably have the parks to yourself (women may not feel safe). The squeamish should pack a can of Raid—Molokai raises big **roaches.**

Pau Hana Inn (553-5342 or 800-423-6656 from the mainland), on Oki Rd. off Kamehameha V Hwy. in Kaunakakai. One of the best deals on the island, and popular with locals from other islands. Swimming pool and an oceanfront garden with a 100-year-old banyan tree out front. Rooms from $45. Office open 6am-6pm.

Ka Hale Mala, 7 Kamakana Pl. (553-9009), in Kaunakakai. The hospitable owners of this home rent out the ground floor and its bedroom, bathroom, kitchen, and living room with a TV, VCR, and stereo. Free use of bikes, beach gear, and laundry. Rent their 4WD for $70 per day. Doubles $60, each additional person $10. Breakfast $5.

Hotel Molokai (553-5347 or 800-423-6656 from the mainland), off Kamehameha V Hwy. in Kuanakakai. Rooms in this aging Polynesian-style hotel on the beach have carved wooden walls, bath, fans, and *lanai* (porch). Pool and breadfruit tree outside. Rooms from $59. 6-person family unit $125. Office open 6am-2pm.

Papohaku Beach County Park, near Kaluakoi resort on the distant west end. Beautifully maintained and secluded beach spot make this one of the best campgrounds in Hawaii. Shaded, grassy sites have restrooms, water, BBQ pits, and showers. 3-night max. stay. County permit ($3) required.

Palaau State Park, about 9mi. northwest of the airport on Rte. 470; follow the signs to Kalaupapa. Sites in the wet central uplands have restrooms (no showers), picnic tables, and BBQ pits. Near the Kalaupapa Overlook and hiking trails. Purify water before drinking. 5-night max. stay. Free state permit required.

FOOD

Without a single fast-food outlet on the island, Molokai fare remains local, and the island's watermelon and bread are delicacies. Kaunakakai has most of the island's restaurants as well as the best grocery store, **Friendly Market,** Ala Malama St. (open Mon.-Fri. 8:30am-8:30pm, Sat. 8:30am-6:30pm). Most stores are closed on Sundays.

Molokai Drive-Inn (553-5655), on Kamoi Ave. at Kamehameha V Hwy. in Kaunakakai. Closest thing to fast food on the island; these healthy-sized portions fit even the most parsimonious wallet. Cheeseburgers, shave ice, and mounds of fries (eat til you burst for $6). Open Sun.-Thurs. 5:30am-10pm, Fri.-Sat. 5:30am-10:30pm.

Kanemitsu Bakery, 79 Ala Malama St. (553-5855), Kaunakakai. Bakes scrumptious exotic bread flavors like pineapple-papaya ($2.45 per loaf), and serves real food too—breakfast of coffee, sausage, 2 eggs, and toast $4.25. Bakery open Wed.-Mon. 5:30am-6:30pm; restaurant open daily 5:30am-1pm.

Kualapuu Cook House (567-6185), Farrington Ave. (Rte. 480), off Rte. 470 in Kualapuu; look for the old wagon out front. Proudly proclaims itself a "slow food chain." Lunch plates and 9 types of burgers ($3-4). Open daily 7am-9pm.

Banyan Tree (553-5342), at the Pau Hana Inn, serves up simple fare at reasonable prices. Best values are the $7 dinner plates; lunches $6-7. Open Mon.-Sat. 6-10:30am, 11am-2pm, and 6-9pm; Sun. 6am-2pm and 6-9pm.

SIGHTS AND ACTIVITIES

Aside from the historic sights and a handful of tours, there are few structured activities for Molokai's tourists. Spearfishing, bone-carving, *lei*-sewing, and hula dancing can be found here, but only with a little effort. Ask **Molokai Style Services** (see **Practical Information,** above), or B&B owners about craft lessons.

Central Molokai and Kalaupapa

Amid the fields and forests of the central Molokai highlands lies **Palaau State Park,** off Rte. 460 from Rte. 470. From the parking lot past the park, a short trail leads to the **Kalaupapa Overlook,** where you can view the site where lepers had to settle, as well as the spectacular Makanalua Peninsula, 1500 ft. below. Another short trail, well-marked and well-trodden, leads to **petroglyphs** carved on the bottom face of a suspended stone and to the 5 ft. **Kauleonanahoa,** nicknamed the **Phallic Rock.** The stone is purported to be the petrified member of a man who killed his wife as the result of a tragic love triangle. According to legend, a childless woman will become pregnant after spending the night under its shadow (presumably alone).

Just before Palaau Park, a dirt footpath leads down to the original **Kalaupapa Lookout** and the beginning of the 3 mi. trail that leads down into the **Kalaupapa National Historical Park.** In 1865, King Kamehameha banished all lepers to this isolated peninsula. Since the development of sulfone drugs in the 1940s led to a leprosy vaccine, the patients may come and go as they please, but many remain. The population (average age 73 years old) has dwindled from an original 6,000 to a current 58. The only way to see the park is with **Father Damien Tours** (567-6171). The guides are themselves former patients (4hr. tours $30; leave Mon.-Sat. 10:30am). There are three ways to travel the 3 mi. down to the peninsula. The free way is to walk the *pali* trail, which is liberally sprinkled with mule dung; be sure to call Damien Tours (7-9am or 5-7pm) to let them know you are coming. If you don't want to hoof it yourself, call **Molokai Mule Rides** (567-6088 or 800-567-7550), which costs $120 (includes $30 permit and lunch). A third option is to **fly** from Molokai's Hoolehua Airport to the Kalaupapa Airport. **Molokai Air Shuttle** (567-6847; $25), and **Island Air** (800-652-6541; $45) both service the area. An informa-

HAWAII

Leprosy and the Martyr of Molokai

Leprosy is caused by a bacterium which 96% of people are naturally immune to, and contrary to popular opinion, the disease does not cause fingers to fall off. Rather, it attacks the nerves and skin of its sufferers so the victim is more prone to cuts, infections, and gangrene. Though it is difficult to contract, ignorance about leprosy's nature caused victims by the hundreds (many of whom were not even afflicted) to be shipped off to the coast of Molokai, where they were thrown from the boats and left to sink or swim to their crude settlement. They lived a life of misery until Father Damien de Veuster, the "Martyr of Molokai," arrived from Belgium to help ease the suffering. The unlucky Father Damien actually contracted leprosy himself and died in 1889 from the disease after serving the colony intermittently for 15 years. Father Damien is buried in Belgium, but his right hand was sent to the island in 1994; everyone was very excited. Recent efforts to canonize the good father were stymied by the Vatican's skepticism that he performed a legitimate miracle and rumors that he succumbed to the easy sexual mores of the Hawaiians. Gossip not withstanding, the priest was beatified in July 1995 and is now honored as the Blessed Father Damien.

tive and caloric stop down the hill from the Kalaupapa Lookout is **Purdie's Nut Farm,** Lihipali Ave. (567-6601), off Farrington. Tuddie Purdie himself gives tours of his grove, detailing the finer points of mac-nut harvesting. You can sample the wares for free (open Mon.-Fri. 9:30am-3:30pm, Sat. 10am-2pm).

Smack in the middle of Molokai, the **Kamakou Preserve rainforest** covers 2,774 acres. Unfortunately, the area is inaccessible without a 4WD. The Nature Conservancy requires all visitors to sign in at the gate. About 3 mi. after the gate is the **Sandalwood Pit,** now just a grassy concave pit, but formerly a very important grassy concave pit; Hawaiian kings used it to measure sandalwood trees to fit ships' holds when trading with American tradesmen. The **Waikolu Lookout,** 3600 ft. up, offers a panoramic view of the waterfalls and native Hawaiian flora in the Pelekunu Valley to the north.

Kaunakakai, East End, and Halawa Valley

From the airport, Rte. 460 eventually becomes the Kamehameha V Hwy. (Rte. 450), leading to tiny **Kaunakakai.** The island's biggest town, Kaunakakai has the majority of Molokai's restaurants and supermarkets, a ½ mi. ferry wharf, and not one traffic light. Before reaching town, glance at the century-old **Kapuaiwa Coconut Grove.** Planted in 1864 at the request of Kamehameha V (who was also known as Kapuaiwa or "mysterious taboo"), about 2000 trees remain of the original 3200. Near the canoe shack on Ala Malama is a stone foundation—all that remains of the king's summer home.

Along the scenic route east on Kamehameha V Hwy. past Kaunakakai to Halawa, are the first in a series of **Hawaiian fishponds** built by hand between 1300 and 1700 and used to raise saltwater fish. The two picturesque churches, **St. Joseph's** and **Our Lady of Sorrows,** between mi. markers 10 and 15, were built by Father Damien in the 1870s. Mile marker 20 is the island's best spot for **snorkeling.** The shallow reefs and calm waters along the east end of the beach are ideal for beginners.

Molokai Wagon & Horse Ride (558-8380), offers tours of the 13th-century **Iliiliopae Heiau,** a mango grove, and a chance to see Hawaiian crafts in a refreshingly non-commercial atmosphere (wagon rides $35, horse rides $40; both tours leave Mon.-Sat. at 10:30am; reservations recommended). The road to **Halawa Valley** winds east from Kaunakakai for 32 mi. Alongside it are the ruins of the **Moanui** (big chicken) **Sugar Mill,** which operated from 1870 to 1900. The overlook at mi. marker 28 offers the first glimpse of the spectacular ravine and the **Moaula** (red chicken) **Falls,** which is no longer accessible to visitors. The way into the valley to the beach is a winding, one-lane series of ruts and the beach's surf is dangerous.

The best way to explore the North Shore is by **boat. Maa Hawaii Action Adventures** (558-8184), can take you on a thrilling cruise across huge waves to see the tallest seacliffs in the world (2-5hr. tours $75 per person, $250 for 4 people). The company also does an all-day rifle hunt ($250 per person) and a fantastic spear fishing tour ($50 per person). Call for details.

West End

The Mauna Loa Hwy. (Rte. 460) heads west from Kaunakakai to Molokai's arid west end, where Molokai's most **scenic beaches** lie. For lots of sand and serious surf, take a right off Rte. 460 at the Kaluakoi turn-off. **Kepuhi** is a long white sand cove, where the **Kaluakoi Resort** now stands. The resort consumes much of the island's limited water supply, causing resentment among the local farmers. Beyond the hotel's golf course to the right, dirt tracks lead to several secluded coves, but deep water and offshore currents make this area suitable only for experienced snorkelers. Continuing past the resort leads to remote **Papohaku,** Hawaii's longest white sand beach (2mi.), and the site of excellent camping facilities (see **Accommodations and Camping,** p. 500). **Dixie Maru Beach,** just beyond Papohaku, is popular with local surfers and boogieboarders. As with other west-end beaches, sunbathing is hot, but recreational swimming is not—the undertow is lethal.

Rte. 460 continues through dry hills to the dusty plantation town of **Maunaloa.** This hamlet was pineapple central until Dole pulled up roots in 1976, and today cattle graze in the fields where fruit once grew. Those cattle belong to the owners of **Molokai Ranch,** the second largest in the state. Zebra, several types of antelope, and African rams roam the Serengeti-esque landscape of the **Molokai Wildlife Conservation Park** (552-2791 or 800-254-8871). You can take a Jurassic Park-style guided tour of the park in a safari van—rest assured, there are no T-rexes en route. (Open Tues.-Sat. 8am-5pm. Admission $35, ages 13-17 $18, ages 3-10 $10. 1½hr. tours at 9am and 1pm. Reservations required.) Take advantage of the trade winds at the **Big Wind Kite Factory** (552-2364), on Rte. 460 in Maunaloa. Free factory tours show kites in progress and free flying lessons demonstrate the final product (open Mon.-Sat. 8:30am-5pm, Sun. 10am-2pm).

SEASONAL EVENTS

Molokai Makahiki (553-3673), in January, is a traditional Hawaiian "time of peace" celebrated with sporting events, ancient games, and food. **Molokai Ka Hula Piko** (553-3876), the third Saturday in May, commemorates the birth of the *hula* on Molokai with cultural demonstrations and visits to sacred sites. On July 4, the **Hoolaulea** is a seafest of eating, ocean activities, and entertainment off the Kuanakakai Wharf. In September, women-powered canoes race from Molokai to Oahu (22mi.) in the **Bankoh Na Wahine O Ke Kai.** October brings **Aloha Festivals,** with street dances, *luaus,* athletic events, and parades. Later in the month, there's the **Bankoh Molokai Hoe,** the male version of the Na Wahine O Ke Kai.

HAWAII

Lanai

More than 1000 years after the Polynesians had inhabited the other Hawaiian islands, Lanai remained empty—empty of people, that is. Hawaiians believed that evil spirits dwelled on the island until it was purged by Kaululaau, the 12-year-old son of a Maui king. Banished for uprooting breadfruit trees, this troublemaker was left for dead off Lanai's shores. His cunning outwitted the evil *akua* (spirits), who fled the island to take up residence in the goatfish swimming offshore, leaving it free for humans.

The more recent history of Lanai (la-NAH-ee—say la-NYE, and you'll have booked a trip out to the "porch" instead), is recorded in the annals of corporate mythology. In the mid-19th century, Walter Gibson came to the island in order to start a Mormon colony. He was excommunicated and his colony failed, but Gibson answered his true calling as a rancher and landowner, amassing 90% of the island by his death. In 1922, the young entrepreneur James Dole bought 98% of the island to grow pineapples, which did so well in Lanai's volcanic soil that the island was dubbed "Pineapple Isle." Castle and Cooke Company, of which Dole is a subsidiary, still owns 98% of Lanai, but the pineapple, undersold by foreign competition, was phased out in the early 90s. Now most of the island's 2400 residents work for the luxury resorts.

In the past few years, Lanai has started to resemble an episode of *Lifestyles of the Rich and Famous,* hosting cameo appearances by NBA, NFL, and *90210* stars. Microsoft mogul Bill Gates rented out the whole island in 1993 for his wedding on the Manele Bay Hotel golf course. Though most visitors are paying out the nose, the resourceful budget traveler need not avoid the isle. Camping on Hulopoe Beach is an almost-free way to experience Lanai, and vaguely affordable B&Bs have also cropped up. Because car rental prices seem to have misplaced decimal points, rent only for one or two days dedicated exclusively for cross-country exploration.

Those who do venture here will be amply rewarded. Lanai is a paradise for scuba divers, boasting some of the best dive sites in Hawaii. For those who bask in backroad solitude, the gaggle of unused hiking trails are heaven itself. Only 30 mi. of paved roads touch the island; the rest must be explored by foot or jarring Jeep rides. The June 1994 opening of a modern airport has made Lanai much more accessible—don't let the opportunity to see the old and rugged Hawaii pass you by.

PRACTICAL INFORMATION AND ORIENTATION

Visitor Information: Destination Lanai, 730 Lanai Ave. (565-7600 or 800-947-4774), in the yellow building across from the Lanai City post office. Maps and copies of the *Jeep Safari Drive Guide.* Open Mon.-Fri. 10am-noon and 1-3pm. **Lanai Company,** 730 Lanai Ave. (565-3982), in the same yellow building. Camping permits for 7-night max. stay. Open Mon.-Fri. 8am-4pm.

ATM: First Hawaiian Bank, Lanai Ave., just past Dole Park on the right.

Airport: Hawaiian Airlines and **Island Air** fly to **Lanai Airport,** near the southern end of the island.

Local Transportation: Although there is no mass transit on the island, the resort hotels provide a shuttle service which may occasionally provide the polite traveler with a ride. **Hitching** on this small island is rather safe, though not common (and not recommended by *Let's Go*).

Ferries: Expeditions (661-3756), runs 6 times daily between Manele Harbor, Molokai and Lahaina, Maui (fare $25). **Tom Barefoot's Cashback Tours,** 834 Front St. (661-8889), in Lahaina, Maui sails tourists to Lanai ($80). The tour spends the day at **Club Lanai** (871-1144).

Taxis: Lanai City Services, 1036 Lanai Ave. (565-7227). Airport to Lanai City $5. Open daily 7am-7pm.

Car Rental: Lanai City Services, 1036 Lanai Ave. (565-7227, from Oahu 944-1544), at 11th St. Cars $60 per day; 4WD vehicles $119. Must be 21 with credit card. Open daily 7am-7pm. A jeep is absolutely necessary on this island of unpaved roads. **Dreams Come True** (565-6961), also rents jeeps ($104 per day). Must be 18 with credit card.

Water Equipment: No rental equipment available, but **Trilogy Excursions** (800-874-2666), runs expensive scuba diving expeditions (intro dive $140).

Library: Fraser Ave. (565-6996). Open Mon. 1-8pm, Tues.-Fri. 8am-5pm.

Laundromat: Launderette Lanai, on 7th St. near Blue Ginger Cafe. Wash $1.25, 5min. dry 25¢, detergent 75¢. Open 6am-9pm.

Hospital: 628 7th St. (565-6411). Emergency room open 24hr.

Emergency: 911.

Police: On the corner of 8th and Fraser St. (565-6428). Check out the outdoor "jail."

Post Office: On Lanai Ave. (565-6517), on the north end of Dole Park in Lanai City. Open Mon.-Fri. 9am-4:30pm, Sat. 10am-noon. **ZIP Code**: 96763.

Area Code: 808.

The few paved roads on Lanai all converge in **Lanai City,** where all but a handful of the island's residents dwell. **Lanai Ave.** is the backbone of the burg. **Rte. 440** starts in the southwest **Kaumalapau Harbor,** passes Lanai Airport, and bends back to the southeast, ending at **Manele Bay** and **Hulopoe Beach.** The stunning natural rock formations of the **Garden of the Gods** are perched on the northern tip, accessible via Polihua Rd. Outside Lanai City, most roads are unpaved dirt paths leading through pineapple fields—maps don't even bother labeling street names.

ACCOMMODATIONS AND CAMPING

Rooms fill up well ahead of time on weekends, and between January and May you'll be fighting for spaces with gun-toting men (hunting season for quail, deer, and turkey). **B&Bs** provide reasonable lodging choices, and are all conveniently located in town. **Dreams Come True,** 547 12th St. (565-6961 or 800-566-6961; http://www.go-nature.com/inns/0117.html), off Lanai Ave., has three small but well-appointed rooms, all with private bath. Cable TV, organic fruits, and breakfast are included (singles $61; doubles $83). The owners also rent a fully furnished house with three bedrooms; surrounded by a papaya garden, this house really *is* a dream come true ($165, weekends $209). Reservations strongly recommended. **Hale Moe,** 502 Akolu St. (565-9520), reposes at the end of Lanai Ave. Japanese art collector Moni Suzuki rents two rooms in her brand-new home and allows full use of kitchen, washer/dryer, and an outdoor patio (smaller room $65; larger room $75; whole house $200). Reservations are recommended. **Dolores Fabrao,** 538 Akahi Pl. (565-6134), also rents out two extra beds in her house, with private bath (double $60, with children $75).

Hulopoe Beach, 20 minutes from the city, is the only campground on the island. A marine preserve, Hulopoe is the island's best swimming and snorkeling beach. Pay the Lanai Company (565-3982), $5 per person per day plus $5 registration to sleep on one of six grassy sites, but locals just camp on the beach for free. Wherever you pitch your tent, you'll have access to tables, BBQ grills, restrooms, and showers.

FOOD

Variety is not one of the spices of life on Lanai, and the food is no exception. There are a whopping four restaurants on the island, and few places accept plastic or checks, so it's best to deal in green. Procure provisions at **Richard's Shopping Center,** 434 8th St. (565-6047; open Mon.-Sat. 8:30am-6:30pm), or at **Pine Isle Market,** 356 8th St. (565-6488; open Mon.-Sat. 8am-7pm), next to the police station.

HAWAII

Blue Ginger Cafe, 7th St. (565-6363), in Dole Park. Nothing sophisticated or fancy here, just local favorites served out by nice waitresses for good prices (ok, the parrots are a little something extra). Mixed plates $5-7, baked goods under $1. Open daily 6am-2pm and 3-9pm.

Tanigawa's, 7th St. (565-6537), in Dole Park. Small eat-and-run diner serving breakfast, lunch, and dinner. Deluxe burger $2.50, mixed plates $5-7. Open Thurs.-Sun. 6:30am-1pm and 4:30-8pm, Mon.-Tues. 6:30am-1pm.

Pele's Garden, 811 Houston St. (565-9628), in Dole Park. Pele smiles on these nutritious sandwiches ($5) and fresh pizzas ($13). There's even a juice bar ($3.25 and up). The nutrition store in the back has everything from organic vitamins to carob cookies. Open Mon.-Thurs. 11am-7pm, Fri.-Sat. 11am-11pm.

Nani's Corner (565-6915), on Lanai Ave. next to Lanai City Service gas station. As fast as food gets here on Lanai. Burgers ($2) and dogs ($1.30) zip from the kitchen to your plate. Open Mon.-Thurs. 6am-3pm, Fri. 6am-9pm.

SIGHTS

A Jeep and patience will get you around the island—new dirt roads are forged by farmers and tourists every year. The *Jeep Safari* from Destination Lanai (see **Practical Information,** p. 504) has excellent instructions. Maps are useless because so few roads are included, but don't worry about losing your way on Lanai; the island's routes are either short and circular or dead ends. If exploring, get tanked first—the only gas is in Lanai City. Leave the wild turkey costume at home and wear something bright, as men with guns frequent this island to test their wits against the fowl.

South of Lanai City

Lanai's most celebrated sights lie along the **Munro Trail,** a loop through the rainforest where naturalist George C. Munro planted specimens of plant life from his native New Zealand about 80 years ago. Take Rte. 440 north out of Lanai City, and turn right onto Cemetery Rd. Hiking the 9 mi. trail will take nearly a full day; driving is an option for those with 4WD, but beware of pot holes the size of kitchen appliances.

Along the trail, Lanai pines, ferns, ginger, and *lilikoi* (passion fruit) scent the air deliciously. After two steep miles, you'll see **Hookio Ridge,** where Lanai warriors unsuccessfully defended their home against Big Island invaders in 1778. The route continues along the **Lanaihale Ridge,** overlooking pineapple plants on one side and a bottomless valley on the other. On a clear day, head all the way up to the 3370 ft. overlook for a view of the other islands. The road becomes exceedingly treacherous to vehicles after climbing the Lanaihale Ridge. Eventually, Awehi Rd. descends to Rte. 440, which heads back to Lanai City to the right, or snakes to Manele Bay on the left. The **Luahiwa Petroglyphs** are between Lanai City and Hulopoe Beach; ancient Hawaiians etched petroglyphs of humans and animals on the large black rocks. The area is difficult to find, so ask a local for directions.

The best beach on Lanai is **Hulopoe Beach Park,** at the southern end of Manele Rd. (Rte. 441), 9 mi. south of Lanai City. This wide, sloped beach has well-kept facilities and excellent surf as well as good snorkeling, but fishing is prohibited at this marine preserve. The Manele Bay Hotel up the hill provides beach chairs and sunscreen. Next to Hulopoe Bay is **Manele Bay,** a black sand beach. Both bays are favorite haunts for **spinner dolphins.** Although they frequent these protected coves most often in the winter (Dec.-May), you may catch sight of their acrobatics summers too.

North of Lanai City

You won't find Maui's onions growing at the **Garden of the Gods.** Cool rock formations, however, abound. From Lanai City, take Fraser Ave. north and then follow the dirt Polihua Rd. 7 mi. The 20-minute drive passes through **Kanepuu Preserve,** a dryland forest home to 48 species of native Hawaiian plants. Continuing north along the rocky road will bring you to **Kaena Point,** Lanai's northern-most point. Though it's only 4 mi. from Garden of the Gods, the one-hour drive will leave your jeep pleading for mercy. Turtles nest at **Polihua Beach,** but beware of strong currents.

East of Lanai City

Lanai's east coast harbors historical sights and two worthwhile beaches. Keomuku Hwy. (Rte. 430) runs northeast from the city to **Shipwreck Beach.** When the paved road ends after 6 mi., take the dirt road to the left. The sandy beach is ideal for exploring: littered with wind-blown refuse, it's full of shells and glass balls that float ashore from as far away as Japan. These waters were used as a dumping ground for old ships—a large wreck lies 750 ft. from the beach. It's a favorite spot for divers (and sharks, including "Granddaddy," an 18 ft. tiger shark who lives under the barge). At the end of the road, a short path leads to well-preserved **petroglyphs.**

To the south of Shipwreck Beach, **Keomuku Beach** stretches for 12 mi., sand-wiched between the ocean and *kiawe* trees. A 4WD is necessary. At Keomuku's southern tip, the ancient fishing village of **Naha** is unremarkable except during turtle-mating season, when the critters line the seaside. From this vantage point over the Pacific, it feels as though you can see all the way to California.

HAWAII

APPENDIX

HOLIDAYS AND FESTIVALS

Festivals and holidays are a great time to experience and celebrate the region that you're visiting; even better, these events usually mean free fun. Yeehaaww! But while holidays lead to extended hours at some tourist attractions, banks and offices are often closed, leaving unprepared travelers broke and hungry.

Date	Holiday
National Holidays in 1998	
Thursday, January 1	New Year's Day
Monday, January 19	Martin Luther King Jr.'s Birthday
Monday, February 16	President's Day
Monday, May 25	Memorial Day
Saturday, July 4	Independence Day
Monday, September 7	Labor Day
Monday, October 12	Columbus Day
Wednesday, November 11	Veteran's Day (Armistice Day)
Thursday, November 26	Thanksgiving
Friday, December 25	Christmas Day

Regional Festivals

The following are some especially unique seasonal events. For more comprehensive listings, see **Seasonal Events** listings in individual cities.

Festival	Date	Description
California		
Tournament of Roses Parade and Rose Bowl, Pasadena	January 1	Wild New Year's Eve parties, a kick-ass parade and float display, and the Rose Bowl Game, which is arguably *the* biggest college football game in the country.
Penguin Day Ski Fest; Mission Bay, San Diego	January 1	Participants water-ski in the very cold ocean or lie on a block of ice without a wet suit. Others laugh at them.
Monarch Migration Festival, Santa Cruz	early February	The largest monarch colony in the West checks out of Natural Bridges State Beach. Catch their return mid-Oct.
Chinese New Year Celebration; Chinatown, San Francisco	February 7-22	North America's largest Chinese community celebrates the Year of the Tiger (4696 on the lunar calendar) with the largest festival in San Francisco.
Cinco de Mayo, everywhere in California	May 5	Huge celebrations mark the day the Mexicans kicked the French out of Mexico.
Mule Days, Bishop	late May	The largest mule event in the world. View 110 mule sporting events, 40,000 mule-obsessed fans, and the famous Mule Days Parade.
Gay Pride Weekend, West Hollywood	June 27-28	L.A.'s lesbian and gay communities celebrate in full effect. Art, dances, and a big, gay parade.

The Pageant of the Masters, Laguna Beach	July to August	Life imitates art as residents don makeup and costumes of figures in famous paintings and pose for 90-second tableaux, astonishingly similar to the original artwork.
U.S. Open Sand Castle Competition; Imperial Beach Pier, San Diego	mid-August	Sand-sculpting demigods exercise their craft in this largest and longest-running sand castle event. Parades, fireworks, and children's castle contests.
Halloween in the Castro, San Francisco	October 31	Some people say the Castro has become less wild with age—they have not been there on October 31.

Hawaii

King Kamehama Hula Chant Competition, Honolulu	late June	Modern and ancient hula and chant competition. *Halaus* (schools) compete to boisterous cheers.
Gatorade IronMan World Triatholon, Kailua-Kona	October	Original ultimate endurance contest. Competitors swim 2.4 mi., cycle 112 mi., and run 26.2 mi.
Triple Crown of Surfing, Honolulu	late November	The national surfing finals, held at the Banzi pipeline and aired on national television.

CLIMATE

Temp in °F Rain in inches	January		April		July		October	
	Temp	Rain	Temp	Rain	Temp	Rain	Temp	Rain
Death Valley	66/38	0.1	90/60	0.1	116/87	0.3	91/59	0.0
Honolulu	77/70	4.1	78/69	1.9	82/73	0.7	82/72	1.9
Las Vegas	60/29	0.7	81/45	0.2	103/68	0.5	84/47	0.3
Los Angeles	65/46	3.1	70/50	1.2	81/60	0.0	76/54	0.6
San Diego	63/47	1.9	66/53	0.8	73/63	0.1	71/57	0.3
San Francisco	55/45	4.5	62/49	1.5	65/53	0.0	68/54	1.1

To convert from °C to °F, multiply by 1.8 and add 32. For an approximation, double the Celsius and add 25. To convert from °F to °C, subtract 32 and multiply by 0.55.

°C	-5	0	5	10	15	20	25	30	35	40
°F	23	32	41	50	59	68	77	86	95	104

TIME ZONES

California resides entirely within one time zone, Pacific, which is one hour behind Mountain, two hours behind Central, three hours behind Eastern Standard, and eight hours behind Greenwich Mean Time (GMT). California (and most of the United States) observes daylight savings time from the first Sunday in April (April 5, 1998) to the last Sunday in October (October 25, 1998) by advancing clocks ahead one hour. Hawaii is one of the few U.S. states that doesn't employ daylight savings, so during the summer months when the rest of the country is enjoying their light nights, Hawaii is three hours behind California. During the rest of the year, when much of the U.S. gets dark early, Hawaii is two hours behind California.

AREA CODES

Berkeley	510
Oakland	510
San Francisco	415
Palo Alto	415
Santa Barbara	805
San Luis Obispo	805
Las Vegas	702

North Coast	707
Eureka	707
Crescent City	707
Wine Country	707
Yosemite	209
Sequoia	209
King's Canyon	209

San Diego	619
Death Valley	619
San Jose	408
Santa Cruz	408
Lake Tahoe, CA	916
Lake Tahoe, NV	702
Hawaii	808

Los Angeles Area

Downtown L.A.	213
Hollywood	213
Orange County	714
San Bernardino County	909

Westside	310
Santa Monica and Venice	310
Long Beach	562
Southern L.A. County	310

Pasadena	626
San Fernando Valley	818
Ventura County	805
Eastern L.A. County	310

Country Codes

Australia	61
Canada	1
Germany	49

Ireland	353
Japan	81
New Zealand	64

South Africa	27
UK	44
USA	1

MEASUREMENTS

APPENDIX

Although the metric system has made considerable inroads into American business and science, the British system of weights and measures continues to prevail in the U.S. The following is a list of U.S. units and their metric equivalents:

1 inch (in.) = 25 millimeter (mm)	1 millimeter (mm) = 0.04 inch (in.)
1 foot (ft.) = 0.30 meter (m)	1 meter (m) = 3.33 foot (ft.)
1 yard (yd.) = 0.91 meter (m)	1 meter (m) = 1.1 yard (yd.)
1 mile (mi.) = 1.61 kilometer (km)	1 kilometer (km) = 0.62 mile (mi.)
1 ounce (oz.) = 25 gram (g)	1 gram (g) = 0.04 ounce (oz.)
1 pound (lb.) = 0.45 kilogram (kg)	1 kilogram (kg) = 2.22 pound (lb.)
1 quart (qt.) = 0.94 liter (L)	1 liter (L) = 1.06 quart (qt.)

Comparative Values Of Measurement

1 foot	= 12 inches
1 yard	= 3 feet
1 mile	= 5280 feet
1 pound	= 16 ounces (weight)

1 cup	= 8 ounces (volume)
1 pint	= 2 cups
1 quart	= 2 pints
1 gallon	= 4 quarts

MILEAGE

Town entries are listed both vertically and horizontally. To find the distance from Los Angeles to San Francisco, read down from Los Angeles (column 4) and across from San Francisco (row 8) to find 385 mi. All distances are given in miles (mi.).

	Bishop	Crescent City	Las Vegas, NV	Los Angeles	Monterey	Oakland	Sacramento	San Diego	San Francisco	San Luis Obispo	Santa Barbara	Tahoe
Crescent City	615											
Las Vegas, NV	261	910										
Los Angeles	270	720	274									
Monterey	315	462	517	327								
Oakland	274	344	566	376	117							
Sacramento	260	356	578	388	188	78						
San Diego	366	843	337	124	450	499	511					
San Francisco	283	345	575	385	114	9	87	508				
San Luis Obispo	333	578	406	190	149	234	287	314	234			
Santa Barbara	320	671	369	97	242	327	379	221	327	93		
Tahoe	179	456	440	486	286	176	100	609	185	384	477	
Yosemite	130	518	390	308	201	174	170	431	183	224	180	180

GLOSSARY

In Hawaii, most islanders speak a melange of English and Hawaiian. The following is a list of words that are in this guide and that are commonly used on the islands.

A

aa	rough lava
ahupuaa	basic land division from the ocean to mountains
aikane	friend
aina	land or earth
akua	spirits
aloha	a traditional greeting which also means love
apapane	a bright red native Hawaiian bird
awapuhi	tree

E

elepaio	bird
ewa	west

H

hala	tree
halau	Hula school

	hale	house or building
	haleakala	house of the sun
	halemanu	birdhouse
	haole	referring to Caucasians; light skinned folks
	haupia	coconut pudding
	heiau	temple
	hoio	edible ferns
	honua	land or earth
	hoolaulea	a festive gathering
	Humuhumu-nukunukua-puaa	the Hawaiian State fish; a colorful reef triggerfish
	hula	traditional Hawaiian dance and music
K	**kailua**	pig
	kalij	pheasants, imported from India 100 years ago
	kaluuokaoo	the plunge of the digging stick
	kamaaina	children of the land
	kanaka maoli	ethnic Hawaiians
	kapu	a sacred system of laws and customs that maintained religious, political, and social order
	katsu	a breaded cutlet
	kahuna	priest; someone who is skilled in a field
	kai	sea
	kaukau	food
	keiki	children
	kepaniwai	the damming of the waters
	kiawe	a type of thorny tree
	Kukui	the Hawaiian State tree; in addition to its uses as a light source and fashion accessory, the kukui nut is a powerful laxative
	kulolo	potato salad
L	**lanai**	porch or balcony
	lauhala	the trees that have the teepee roots
	lau lau	a *ti* leaf stuffed with spinach, pork, or chicken
	lei	although commercial vendors have bastardized the original craft with synthetic materials, the traditional garlands were made of leaves, flowers, nuts, and shells
	lilikoi	passion fruit
	lomi	a mixture of tomatoes and onions with salmon
	luau	a traditional Hawaiian feast; now usually a commercial one that is often pricey ($30-50) and a far cry from real native celebrations
M	**mahalo**	thank you
	makai	the coastal areas; seaward
	makua	parents
	malasadas	super-delectable sugared fried dough
	manapua	stuffed rolls
	manju	a sweet bean pastry
	mauka	the mountain areas; inland
	menehune	mythical mischief-makers

moaula	red chicken
nene	the Hawaiian State bird; it's a goose
nisei	first generation Japanese-Americans
ohana	family
pahoehoe	smooth lava
pakalolo	some of the best marijuana in the world
pali	cliff
paniolo	cowboy
poi	a taro root pudding thick enough to be eaten with two fingers
poohana	Happy Hour
puaa	pig
pupus	appetizers.
puuulaula	red hill
taro	edible Hawaiian plant
tsunami	tidal wave
wai	water
waimea	reddish water
wowy maui	another name for some of the best marijuana in the world

N
O
P
T
W

Index

INDEX

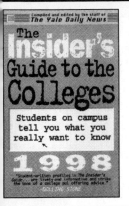

★Let's Go 1998 Reader Questionnaire★

Please fill this out and return it to **Let's Go, St. Martin's Press,** 175 Fifth Ave., New York, NY 10010-7848. All respondents will receive a free subscription to **The Yellowjacket,** the Let's Go Newsletter.

Name: _____

Address: _____

City: _____ **State:** _____ **Zip/Postal Code:** _____

Email: _____ **Which book(s) did you use?** _____

How old are you? under 19   19-24   25-34   35-44   45-54   55 or over

Are you (circle one)   in high school   in college   in graduate school   employed   retired   between jobs

Have you used Let's Go before? yes no **Would you use it again?** yes no

How did you first hear about Let's Go? friend   store clerk   television   bookstore display   advertisement/promotion   review   other

Why did you choose Let's Go (circle up to two)? reputation budget focus   price   writing style   annual updating   other: _____

Which other guides have you used, if any?   Frommer's $-a-day   Fodor's   Rough Guides   Lonely Planet   Berkeley   Rick Steves   other: _____

Is Let's Go the best guidebook? yes no

If not, which do you prefer? _____

Please rank each of the following parts of Let's Go 1 to 5 (1=needs improvement, 5=perfect). packaging/cover   practical information   accommodations   food   cultural introduction   sights   practical introduction ("Essentials")   directions   entertainment   gay/lesbian information   maps   other: _____

How would you like to see the books improved? (continue on separate page, if necessary) _____
_____

How long was your trip? one week   two weeks   three weeks   one month   two months or more

Which countries did you visit? _____

What was your average daily budget, not including flights? _____

Have you traveled extensively before? yes no

Do you buy a separate map when you visit a foreign city? yes no

Have you seen the Let's Go Map Guides? yes no

Have you used a Let's Go Map Guide? yes no

If you have, would you recommend them to others? yes no

Did you use the Internet to plan your trip? yes no

Would you use a Let's Go: recreational (e.g. skiing) guide   gay/lesbian guide   adventure/trekking guide   phrasebook   general travel information guide

Which of the following destinations do you hope to visit in the next three to five years (circle one)? South Africa   China   South America   Russia   Caribbean   Scandinavia   other: _____

Where did you buy your guidebook?   Internet   chain bookstore   independent bookstore   college bookstore   travel store   other: _____